ELECTION LAW
IN THE AMERICAN POLITICAL SYSTEM

ASPEN CASEBOOK SERIES

ELECTION LAW
IN THE AMERICAN POLITICAL SYSTEM

THIRD EDITION

JAMES A. GARDNER
BRIDGET AND THOMAS BLACK SUNY DISTINGUISHED PROFESSOR
UNIVERSITY AT BUFFALO SCHOOL OF LAW,
STATE UNIVERSITY OF NEW YORK

GUY-URIEL CHARLES
CHARLES OGLETREE, JR. PROFESSOR OF LAW
HARVARD LAW SCHOOL

To contact Customer Service, e-mail customer.service@aspenpublishing.com, call 1-800-950-5259, or mail correspondence to:

    Aspen Publishing
    Attn: Order Department
    PO Box 990
    Frederick, MD 21705

Printed in the United States of America.

1 2 3 4 5 6 7 8 9 0

ISBN 978-1-5438-1979-3

Library of Congress Cataloging-in-Publication Data

Names: Gardner, James A., 1959- author. | Charles, Guy-Uriel E., 1970- author.
Title: Election law in the American political system / James A. Gardner,
   Bridget and Thomas Black SUNY Distinguished Professor, University at
   Buffalo School of Law, State University of New York; Guy-Uriel Charles,
   Charles Ogletree, Jr. Professor of LawHarvard Law School.
Description: Third edition. | Frederick : Aspen Publishing, 2023. | Series:
   Aspen casebook series | Includes bibliographical references and index. |
   Summary: "A view of election law through the lenses of theoretical premises,
   accumulated political ideals, and evolving socio-political conventions"—Provided
   by publisher.
Identifiers: LCCN 2022042761 | ISBN 9781543819793 (hardcover) | ISBN
   9781543826838 (ebook)
Subjects: LCSH: Election law—United States. | LCGFT: Casebooks (Law)
Classification: LCC KF4886 .G37 2023 | DDC 342.73/07—dc23/eng/20220924
LC record available at https://lccn.loc.gov/2022042761

About Aspen Publishing

Aspen Publishing is a leading provider of educational content and digital learning solutions to law schools in the U.S. and around the world. Aspen provides best-in-class solutions for legal education through authoritative textbooks, written by renowned authors, and breakthrough products such as Connected eBooks, Connected Quizzing, and PracticePerfect.

The Aspen Casebook Series (famously known among law faculty and students as the "red and black" casebooks) encompasses hundreds of highly regarded textbooks in more than eighty disciplines, from large enrollment courses, such as Torts and Contracts to emerging electives such as Sustainability and the Law of Policing. Study aids such as the *Examples & Explanations* and the *Emanuel Law Outlines* series, both highly popular collections, help law students master complex subject matter.

Major products, programs, and initiatives include:

- **Connected eBooks** are enhanced digital textbooks and study aids that come with a suite of online content and learning tools designed to maximize student success. Designed in collaboration with hundreds of faculty and students, the Connected eBook is a significant leap forward in the legal education learning tools available to students.
- **Connected Quizzing** is an easy-to-use formative assessment tool that tests law students' understanding and provides timely feedback to improve learning outcomes. Delivered through CasebookConnect.com, the learning platform already used by students to access their Aspen casebooks, Connected Quizzing is simple to implement and integrates seamlessly with law school course curricula.
- **PracticePerfect** is a visually engaging, interactive study aid to explain commonly encountered legal doctrines through easy-to-understand animated videos, illustrative examples, and numerous practice questions. Developed by a team of experts, PracticePerfect is the ideal study companion for today's law students.
- The **Aspen Learning Library** enables law schools to provide their students with access to the most popular study aids on the market across all of their courses. Available through an annual subscription, the online library consists of study aids in e-book, audio, and video formats with full text search, note-taking, and highlighting capabilities.
- Aspen's **Digital Bookshelf** is an institutional-level online education bookshelf, consolidating everything students and professors need to ensure success. This program ensures that every student has access to affordable course materials from day one.
- **Leading Edge** is a community centered on thinking differently about legal education and putting those thoughts into actionable strategies. At the core of the program is the Leading Edge Conference, an annual gathering of legal education thought leaders looking to pool ideas and identify promising directions of exploration.

Summary of Contents

Contents		ix
Preface to the Third Edition		xxix
Acknowledgments		xxxiii
Chapter 1	Liberal Democracy	1
Chapter 2	Illiberalism	37
Chapter 3	The Vote	109
Chapter 4	Representation	181
Chapter 5	Racial Discrimination and the Right to Vote	321
Chapter 6	Candidates and the Ideal of Impartial Public Service	481
Chapter 7	The Party System	531
Chapter 8	Free Speech, Political Information, and the Liberal Democratic Order	637
Chapter 9	Money, Politics, and Law	733
Chapter 10	Election Administration and Remedies	933
Appendix: U.S. Constitution		1053
Table of Cases		1071
Table of Authorities		1079
Index		1103

CONTENTS

Preface to the Third Edition   **xxix**

Acknowledgments   **xxxiii**

Chapter 1   Liberal Democracy   **1**

A. Liberal Democracy in Decline: A Global Perspective   3

    Democratic Backsliding   4

    "Competitive Authoritarianism"   5

    The Authoritarian's "Playbook"   5

    Autocratic Legalism   7

    A Case Study of Democratic Backsliding: Hungary   7

B. The Liberal Inheritance   9

    1. Basic Tenets of Liberalism   10

        Robert Kagan, The Strongmen Strike Back (2019)   10

        John Locke, Second Treatise of Government (1690)   12

        The Declaration of Independence (1776)   15

      Modern Liberalism   15

    2. Liberal Conceptions of Democracy   17

      Democratic Minimalism   17

      Aggregative Theories of Democracy   18

        Anthony Downs, An Economic Theory of Democracy (1957)   18

      Modern Theories of Political Pluralism   20

      Pitfalls of Pluralism   21

      Thicker Theories of Democracy   21

        John Rawls, Political Liberalism (1993)   22

      Deliberative Democracy   24

      Elections in Liberal Democracies   25

    3. Majoritarianism in Liberal Elections   26

        John Locke, The Second Treatise of Government (1690)   26

        Jean-Jacques Rousseau, The Social Contract (1762)   27

      Pluralist Justifications for Majority Rule   28

      The Wisdom of the Multitude   28

      a. What Counts as Majority Rule?   29

Scope of the Franchise   29

Majority of What Kinds of Votes?   30

Low Voter Turnout   30

Rational Non-Participation ?   31

A Duty to Vote?   32

Which Majority? Cycling and the Indeterminacy Problem   33

b. Liberal Justifications for Limiting Majority Power   34

Tyranny of the Majority   34

Constitutional Solutions   35

Chapter 2   Illiberalism   **37**

Joseph de Maistre, Considerations on France (1796)   37

A.   Illiberal Alternatives   38

The Populist Challenge   39

Jan-Werner Müller, What Is Populism? (2016)   39

Varieties of Populism   40

History of American Populism   41

Populism and Democracy   42

Is Populism Inherently Illiberal?   43

Why the Turn to Populist Authoritarianism?   43

Lack of Performative Success   44

Alienation   45

Bigotry and Hate   46

B.   Is the United States a Liberal Democracy?   47

The Baseline of Analysis   47

The Story of an Inherently Liberal America   48

1. Accommodating the *Ancien Régime*   49

a. Republicanism   50

Beliefs about Popular Self-Government   50

Michael J. Klarman, The Framers' Coup: The Making of the
United States Constitution (2016)   51

Democratic Optimization?   53

The Influence of Republican Skepticism on
Constitutional Structure   54

The Federalist, No. 10 (Madison) (1787)   54

The Republican Presidency   58

The Federalist, No. 68 (Hamilton) (1788)   58

The Republican Senate   60

	b. Federalism	61
	The Power to Regulate Federal Elections	61
	The Role of Local Governments	62
	Federal Rights Protection	63
	Indirect Federal Power	63
	Uniformity or Diversity?	64
C.	Illiberal Strands of American Social Thought and Practice	65
	Harriet Martineau, Society in America (1837)	65
	Liberalism and Slavery	66
	The Three-Fifths Clause	67
	Garry Wills, The Negro President (2003)	67
	Rogers M. Smith, Civic Ideals 14-17 (1997)	70
D.	The Long, Slow Path Toward Democratization	71
	The Decline of Republican Ideology	72
	The Institutional Evolution of Presidential Elections	73
	Ray v. Blair	*74*
	State Enforcement of Elector Pledges	76
	The National Popular Vote Plan	78
	The Transformation of the Senate	79
	The Fall of Slavery and Its Aftermath	79
	Guinn v. United States	*80*
	Lane v. Wilson	*82*
	The South as an "Authoritarian Enclave"?	84
	Disenfranchisement and the Civil Rights Movement	85
	Taylor Branch, Parting the Waters: America in the King Years, 1954–63 (1988)	85
	The Enduring Political Impact of Slavery	92
E.	Prospects for Liberal Democracy in the United States	93
	1. Fair Party Competition	93
	Jacob S. Hacker and Paul Pierson, Restoring Healthy Party Competition (2020)	93
	Kim Lane Scheppele, The Party's Over (2018)	96
	2. Adherence to Democratic and Constitutional Norms	99
	Steven Levitsky and Daniel Ziblatt, How Democracies Die (2018)	99
	Unwritten Constitutional Norms?	100
	3. An Independent Judiciary	103
	4. How Committed Are Americans to Liberalism?	106
	How Committed Are Americans to Democracy?	107

Chapter 3   The Vote   **109**

    Identifying the Self-Governing *Demos*   109
    The American *Demos*   110
A. Qualifications Based on Membership   112
    1. Citizenship   112
        Minor v. Happersett   *114*
        Alienage and Voting   119
        Voting in the District of Columbia and the Territories   120
        The Equality of Citizens: Multiple Votes?   121
    2. Residency   123
        Carrington v. Rash   *123*
        Durational Residency Requirements   126
        Durational Residency Requirements in Presidential Elections 128
        Students as State Residents   129
        Citizenship and Residency: Better Together?   129
        Multiple Residency and Voting Eligibility   130
        Voting by Nonresidents   131
    3. Defining Geographical Communities   132
        Hunter v. City of Pittsburgh   *132*
        Milliken v. Bradley   *134*
        The Significance of Local Government Boundaries   137
    4. Non-Geographical Sub-Communities   138
        Kramer v. Union Free School District No. 15   *139*
        Eligibility Based on Lineage   143
B. Qualifications Based on Competence   143
    1. Literacy   144
        Lassiter v. Northampton County Board of Elections   *144*
        Discriminatory Administration of Literacy Tests   145
        United States v. Louisiana   *146*
        Katzenbach v. Morgan   *148*
        Congressional Extension of the Literacy Test Ban   152
        The Vitality of *Morgan*   152
        Contemporary Political Behavior in the United States   153
        Angus Campbell et al., The American Voter (1960)   154
        Rehabilitating Voter Competence   156
        Rational Ignorance?   157

    Anthony Downs, An Economic Theory of Democracy (1957)   157

    Rational Irrationality?   158

  2. Age and Mental Disability   159

    "Manner" vs. "Qualifications"   160

    Voting at 16?   161

    Disenfranchisement for Mental Disability   162

  3. Wealth   162

    Property Qualifications   162

    Franklin's Position on Property Qualifications   163

      Harper v. Virginia Board of Elections   *164*

  4. Felony Convictions   167

      Richardson v. Ramirez   *167*

    Justifications for Felon Disenfranchisement   172

    Felon Disenfranchisement Abroad   173

      Hunter v. Underwood   *174*

    Felon Disenfranchisement and Race   176

    Felon Disenfranchisement and Partisan Politics   177

    Disenfranchisement for Election Crimes   178

    Restoration of Voting Rights   178

Chapter 4   Representation   **181**

A. Introduction   181

      Edmund Burke, Speech to the Electors of Bristol (1774)   181

    The Right to Instruct Representatives in America   182

  1. Principles of Representation   184

    Reciprocity of Representation and Interests?   186

    Representation of the Whole or the Parts?   186

    Representation of Minorities   188

    Positive Political Theory: Alignment of Preferences and Policy   188

  2. Non-Elective Forms of Representation   191

    The Problem of Virtual Representation   191

      Bernard Bailyn, The Ideological Origins of the American
        Revolution (1967)   192

      Holt Civic Club v. City of Tuscaloosa   *195*

    Other Forms of Non-Electoral Representation   199

B. Apportionment   201

  1. The "Political Thicket"   202

  2. General Districts   203

Malapportionment of Congress   203
Malapportionment of State Legislatures   206
   Reynolds v. Sims   *206*
What Is the Harm from Malapportionment?   214
How Equal Is Equal?   215
What Justifications for Population Deviation Are Valid?   218
Local Governments   218
Judicial Elections   218
The Relevant Population Base   219
The Strange Case of Counting Incarcerated Non-Voters   221
Counting Relevant "Persons": The Problem of Minority Undercounts   222
The Census and Citizenship   224
The Remedy: Developing a Redistricting Plan   225
The Judicial Role in Redistricting   226
Redistricting and Local Community   226
3. Nationwide Congressional Apportionment   227
4. Special Districts   229
   Salyer Land Co. v. Tulare Lake Basin Water Storage District   *230*
The Variety of Special Districts   237
Voting Equality Abroad   239
C. Discriminatory Manipulation of Representation   240
1. Methods of Election   241
Origins: *Whitcomb v. Chavis*   242
   White v. Regester   *243*
   Disparate Impact vs. Disparate Treatment   246
   City of Mobile v. Bolden   *246*
The Demise of Multimember Districts   257
Alternatives to Pure At-Large Elections and Single-Member Electoral Systems   258
2. Gerrymandering   261
   Gomillion v. Lightfoot   *262*
A Half-Century of Judicial Indecision   264
First Attempt: *Davis v. Bandemer*   264
Partisan Gerrymandering as a "Self-Limiting Enterprise"   266
Back to the Drawing Board   267
   Rucho v. Common Cause   *268*
What Is So Bad About Partisan Gerrymandering?   290

Distortion of Policy	290
Decline in Electoral Competitiveness	292
Lack of Governmental Accountability	292
Lack of Legislator Responsiveness	293
Voter Alienation	294
Legislative Polarization	295
How Bad Is It?	298
Partisan Gerrymandering under State Constitutions	299
League of Women Voters v. Commonwealth	*299*
Partisan Gerrymandering Standards	303
Re-Redistricting	305
The Call for Independent Districting Commissions	307
Arizona State Legislature v. Arizona Independent Redistricting Commission	*310*
Are the People Sovereign?	318
Public Participation and Transparency as a Solution?	319
Discerning the Popular Will: The Aggregation Problem	319
Chapter 5 Racial Discrimination and the Right to Vote	**321**
A. Introduction	321
B. The South as an "Authoritarian Enclave"?	325
C. The VRA and the Power of Congress	327
The Scope and Standard of Section 5	330
Intentional Discrimination and Nonretrogression	332
Judging Retrogression by the Baseline Plan	333
The Three-Judge Court	334
Bail-in	334
The Constitutionality of Sections 4 and 5	335
South Carolina v. Katzenbach	*335*
Congressional Reauthorization of Section 5	338
Constitutionality Redux	340
Shelby County, Alabama v. Holder	*341*
What Does *Shelby County* Mean for Section 5?	354
State Responses to *Shelby County*	356
What Now?	357
D. Section 2	359
Thornburg v. Gingles	*360*
The "*Gingles* Factors"	380

Participation in the Political Process   381
The "Opportunity" to Participate and Elect   382
Maximization of Minority Voting Power   382
Section 2 and Proportional Representation   383
"Safe," "Coalitional," and "Influence" Districts   383
Influence Districts Under Section 2   385
Judicial Elections   387
The Impact of Breaking Up At-Large Systems in the South   387
Can Section 2 Do the Work of Section 5?   387
Section 2 and Felon Disenfranchisement   388
E.   Race, Representation, and the Constitution   389
     1. Section 5: Race as a Redistricting Criterion   391
              United Jewish Organizations of Williamsburgh, Inc. v. Carey   391
         Creating a "Safe" Minority-Controlled Seat   397
         The Problem of "Filler People"   398
         Race and the Problem of "Authentic" Representation   399
         Representation Quotas   404
     2. Section 2: Race, Redistricting, and the *Shaw* Cases   405
         The *Shaw* Decision   405
         What Harm Did the Plaintiffs Suffer in *Shaw*?   407
         Standing to Challenge Racial Gerrymandering   408
              Miller v. Johnson   409
         What Interests Are Compelling?   421
         When Is Race the "Predominant Factor" in Redistricting?   421
         Extending the "Predominant Factor" Test to Partisan Gerrymandering? 423
         The Search for Neutrality in Districting   424
              Compactness and Contiguity   424
              Respect for Political Boundaries and Communities of Interest 426
              Protection of Incumbents   429
         The Indeterminacy Problem, Again   429
         Can Districting Be Eliminated?   431
     3. *Easley*: Détente & Equilibrium   432
              Easley v. Cromartie   433
         Understanding *Cromartie II*   442
         Polarization, Partisanship, and Race   442
         Does the VRA Produce Mere Token Representation?   443
         Black Interests and Black Legislators   444
         Descriptive Representation Revisited   445

4. The New *Shaw* Cases   446
   Cooper v. Harris   447
Effect of the New *Shaw* Cases   458
5. The End of the Section 2?   459
   Brnovich v. Democratic National Committee   461
Evaluating *Brnovich:* Much Ado About Nothing?   476
   Voter Fraud and the Big Lie   477
   Does Section 2 Allow Private Rights of Action?   478
   The Future of the VRA?   478
   Fear of a Multiracial Future; Fear of a Liberal
   Democratic Future?   479
   Hope: Election Law Federalism?   479

Chapter 6 Candidates and the Ideal of Impartial Public Service   481

A. Politics and the Characteristics of Elected Officials   481
   Henry St. John Bolingbroke, The Idea of a Patriot King (1738)   481
   Robert Wiebe, The Search for Order 1877–1920 (1967)   484
B. Qualifications for Office   486
   The Exclusivity of Constitutional Qualifications   487
   U.S. Term Limits, Inc. v. Thornton   488
   Subsequent Efforts to Establish Congressional Term Limits   498
   Term Limits for State Officials   499
   The Effect of Term Limits   500
   District Residency Requirements   501
   Other Candidate Qualifications   502
   Additional Presidential Qualifications   502
   Qualifications for Nonelective Offices   503
C. Conditions of Candidacy   504
  1. Resign-to-Run Requirements   504
   Clements v. Fashing   504
  2. Forgoing Government Employment   511
   *United States Civil Service Commission v. National Association of
   Letter Carriers, AFL-CIO*   512
   Coercion by Private Employers   517
  3. Disclosure of Personal Financial Information   517
   Even More Disclosure?   519
D. Disqualification and Removal   521
   Vote of No Confidence   521

Impeachment   522
  Impeachable Offences   522
  Uses of Impeachment   523
  Procedures   523
Automatic Removal for Misbehavior   524
Removal for Incompetence   524
Recall Elections   526
Expulsion   527
Lustration   527
Techniques of Militant Democracy: Party Bans and Individual
  Disqualification   529

Chapter 7   The Party System   **531**

A. Introduction: What Is a Political Party?   531
      George Washington, Farewell Address   531
    Republicanism and Anti-Party Politics   532
    Jacksonian Democracy and the Rise of the Modern Party   534
    Progressivism and Nonpartisanship   536
      Austin Ranney, The Doctrine of Responsible Party
        Government (1954)   537
    Interest Pluralism, Political Parties, and Factions   540
    Where Are Political Parties?   541
    What Kind of Party System Do We Have?   541
    The Legal Treatment of Parties: The First Amendment Right of
      Association   542
    Party Control over Membership   543
B. Ballot Access and the Two-Party System   544
    1. Access to the Official Ballot   545
    Filing Fees   546
    The Reign of Equal Protection in Ballot Access Cases   548
      Anderson v. Celebrezze   *548*
    The Individual Rights Model   556
    2. Write-In Votes   558
      Burdick v. Takushi   *558*
      The *Anderson-Burdick* Framework   563
    Write-In Votes in the Real World   564
    Other Expressive Ballot Options   564

3. State Institutionalization of the Two-Party System   565
    Timmons v. Twin Cities Area New Party   565
Origins of the Two-Party System   575
Two-Party vs. Multiparty Systems   576
A Two-Party System vs. Two Specific Parties   577
The Two-Party System as One-Party System   578
C. Candidate Selection   579
1. Eligibility to Vote in Primaries: The White Primary Cases   580
    Smith v. Allwright   581
    Terry v. Adams   583
2. Federal and State Power to Regulate Partisan Primaries   587
    Federal Power to Regulate Primaries   587
State Regulatory Power   589
    EU v. San Francisco County Democratic Central Committee 590
Political Parties: Public or Private Entities?   593
The Associational Coherence of Political Parties   594
Parties, Government, and Party Regulation by Government   595
    New York State Board of Elections v. Lopez Torres 596
3. Eligibility to Vote in Primaries: Party Membership   601
    Tashjian v. Republican Party of Connecticut   602
    California Democratic Party v. Jones   607
Party Autonomy in Primary Elections   617
The Consequences of *Jones* for Other Kinds of Primaries   619
Party Control over Candidate "Branding"   619
Post-*Jones* Developments in California   622
Judicial Review of Constitutional Claims by Parties   622
Party Nominations in Presidential Elections   623
D. Political Patronage   624
    Elrod v. Burns   624
Developments Following *Elrod*   631
How Effective is Patronage?   632
E. Final Thoughts on Parties   632
    E.E. Schattschneider, Party Government (1942)   633
The Nature of Contemporary Partisanship   634

Chapter 8   Free Speech, Political Information, and the Liberal Democratic Order   **637**

A. Introduction   637
 1. Free Speech and the Liberal Democratic Equilibrium   637
 2. Short History of Political Campaigns   640
  Eighteenth-Century Campaigns   640
  Nineteenth-Century Campaigns   641
  The Twentieth Century and the Modern Era   642
 3. Restrictions on Speech   643
  First Amendment Doctrine   643
  Underlying Theories   644
B. Restrictions on the Content of Campaign Speech   646
 1. False Statements   646
  Libel Law as a Mechanism for Policing Falsehoods   646
   Monitor Patriot Co. v. Roy   *648*
  The Efficacy of Libel Suits   651
  Fair Campaign Codes   652
   Vanasco v. Schwartz   *652*
  Why Regulate Deceptive Campaign Speech?   656
  Post–*New York Times* Fair Campaign Codes   656
  Campaign Speech by Words or by Money   657
  New Forms of Voter Deception   658
  "Fake News"   659
  Indirect Regulation of Campaign Speech by Treating
   It as Evidence   659
 2. Campaign Promises   660
   Brown v. Hartlage   *660*
  Promises and Bribes   664
 3. Constraints of Office   665
C. Restrictions on the Time, Place, and Manner of Campaign Speech   666
   Burson v. Freeman   *666*
   Minnesota Voters Alliance v. Mansky   *672*
  Campaign-Free Election Days   680
  Speech on the Ballot   680
   Racial Designations   680
   Designation of Substantive Issue Position   680
   Suggestive Wording of Ballot Measures   681
  Agenda-Setting and Framing   682

	Prohibition of Exit Polling	683
	Robocalls	684
	Ballot Selfies	685
D.	Campaign Speech in the Mass Media	686
	Mills v. State of Alabama	*687*
	Red Lion Broadcasting Co. v. Federal Communications Commission	*688*
	The Fairness Doctrine	693
	Miami Herald Publishing Co. v. Tornillo	*694*
	Less Is More?	697
	Regulation of Political Speech Abroad	697
E.	Compelled Speech: Disclosure	698
	1. Disclosure of the Identity of the Speaker	699
	McIntyre v. Ohio Elections Commission	*699*
	Anonymous Statements About Candidates' Character	704
	Disclosure and Deterrence	705
	Effects of Anonymity on Behavior	706
	2. Disclosure of Monetary Contributions	706
	Buckley v. Valeo	*707*
	Developments in Disclosure Since *Buckley*	713
	The Likelihood of Retaliation and Harassment	714
	Identity of Speakers vs. Contributors	716
	How Effective Is Disclosure of Contributions?	716
	The Collateral Consequences of Disclosure	717
	Disclosure of Contributions for Ballot Measures	718
	3. Disclosure of Petition Signing	718
	Doe #1 v. Reed	*719*
	Trump v. Twitter	*726*
Chapter 9	**Money, Politics, and Law**	**733**
A.	Short History of Campaign Finance Reform	736
	1. Limitations on Campaign Contributions	743
	2. Limitations on Expenditures	744
	3. Reporting and Disclosure	745
	4. Public Financing	746
	5. Federal Election Commission	746
	6. Prohibition on Contributions and Expenditures by National Banks, Corporations, and Labor Unions	747

B. PACs   750
    1. Party Committees   750
    2. PACs: Nonconnected Committees and Separate, Segregated Funds   750
    3. Two Special Kinds of PACs: Leadership PACs and Super PACs   751
    4. 527s   753
    5. 501(c)(4) Organizations   754
C. The *Buckley* Settlement   754
    1. FECA in the Court   755
        Buckley v. Valeo   755
    2. Justifications for Campaign-Finance Regulation   768
        a. Anti-Corruption Justifications   768
        What Does the Constitution Say About Corruption?   768
        What Is Corruption?   769
            Dependence Corruption?   769
            Three Conceptions of Corruption   770
            Bribery   770
            Corruption of Politics   771
        The Appearance of Corruption   771
        Extortion   772
        b. Equality Justifications   772
        "Buying" Office   772
        Overrepresentation of the Rich   773
        Disproportionate Influence of Institutional Entities   774
        Equalizing Opportunity to Influence Politics   774
        c. Unintended Harm to Representation and Politics   776
        Excessive Time Spent Raising Funds   776
        Coarsening of Campaign Discourse   777
    3. What Does Political Money Buy?   777
        Observational Data: Winners Spend More   778
        The Aggregate View: The Minimal Effects Thesis   778
        Effects of Spending on Vote Share   779
        Mechanisms: Spending to Persuade   780
        Mechanisms: Agenda-Setting, Framing, and Priming   781
        Mechanisms: Spending to Mobilize   782
        The Ontology of Citizenship   783
    4. Reaction to *Buckley*   783
        "Wholly Foreign to the First Amendment"   784
        Equating Spending and Speech   785

	The "Tank of Gas" Metaphor	786
	The Significance of the Campaign Period	787
	The Balance of Liberties	788
	The Contribution/Expenditure Distinction and Its Consequences	789
	Campaign Finance in Other Countries	790
	Campaign Finance in Judicial Elections	790
D.	BCRA and *McConnell*	791
	1. Soft Money	791
	2. Issue Advocacy	793
	3. The Bipartisan Campaign Reform Act of 2002	794
	4. *McConnell v. FEC*	797
	McConnell v. Federal Election Commission	*797*
	Corruption, Again	814
	Deference to Whom?	815
E.	Expenditure Limitations: PACs, Parties, and Corporations	819
	1. Independent Expenditures by Ideological but Nonpartisan PACs	820
	Federal Election Commission v. National Conservative Political Action Committee	*820*
	The Role of PACs	822
	Why Do PACs Spend?	823
	The PAC Ecosystem	825
	PACs and Access	826
	Where in the Process Do PACs Have Influence?	826
	2. Independent Expenditures by Political Parties	828
	Colorado Republican Federal Campaign Committee v. Federal Election Commission [Colorado Republican I]	*828*
	The Treatment of Political Parties	833
	Colorado Republican II	835
	The Distinctiveness of Parties	837
	3. Independent Expenditures by Nonprofit Issue Advocacy Corporations	838
	Federal Election Commission v. Massachusetts Citizens for Life	*839*
	4. Independent Expenditures by Corporations and Unions	849
	Pipefitters Local Union No. 562 v. United States	*849*
	First National Bank of Boston v. Bellotti	*856*
	Austin v. Michigan xChamber of Commerce	*863*
	"Distorting Effects"	870
	The Source of Corporate Speech Rights	870

F. A New Chapter: *Citizens United*   871

        Citizens United v. Federal Election Commission   *871*

    Reaction to *Citizens United*   890

    The Court's Understanding of "Corruption"   891

    Who Is the Speaker?   891

    Do Corporations Have Free Speech Rights to Engage in Political
        Speech?   893

    How Best to Understand the Court's Decision?   893

    Rightly Decided for the Wrong Reasons?   897

    Can Corporate Spending Be Controlled by Other Means?   898

        Corporate Democracy Controls   898

        Intensified Disclosure   899

        Lobbying Reform   901

    Political Spending by Foreign Nationals   902

    Developments Since *Citizens United*   903

    The Impact of *Citizens United*   903

    Counteracting the Effects of *Citizens United?*   905

        McCutcheon v. Federal Election Commission   *906*

    The End of the *Buckley* Settlement?   910

    Corruption Once More   910

    Right of Political Participation?   910

G. Public Financing of Elections   911

        Buckley v. Valeo   *911*

        Arizona Free Enterprise Club's Freedom Club PAC v. Bennett   *916*

    The Chilling Effect of Public Financing   927

    Justifications for Public Financing   927

    Public Financing of Elections in the United States   927

    Utilization of Public Funds   928

    Effects on Electoral Competitiveness   928

    Other Forms of Public Financing   929

    Final Thoughts: Is Campaign Finance Reform Effective?   930

Chapter 10   Election Administration and Remedies   **933**

A. Introduction: The Consequences of Electoral Procedures   933

        Gould v. Grubb   *933*

    The Ballot Order Effect   935

    Substantive Consequences of Procedural Choices   936

    Procedural Neutrality?   938

		Bush v. Gore	*938*
		Reaction to *Bush v. Gore*	943
		The Politicization of Election Procedure	944
B.		Electoral Integrity	946
	1.	What Counts as a "Good" Election?	946
		The Concept of "Electoral Integrity"	946
		Democratic "Best Practices"	946
		Administrative Challenges of U.S. Elections	948
		Considerations of Cost	949
	2.	Fraud	949
		What Does It Take to Steal an Election?	949
		Nicole Etcheson, Bleeding Kansas: Contested Liberty in the Civil War Era (2005)	950
		Hearing Before a Subcommittee of the Senate Committee on the Judiciary, Statement of Dan K. Webb, U.S. Attorney for the Northern District of Illinois (1983)	952
		The Modern Revival of Charges of Vote Fraud	955
		Vote Fraud and Race	956
		Challenges of Detection	957
	3.	Securing Electoral Integrity: Institutional Options	957
		a. The Administrative Model	958
		Decentralization of U.S. Election Administration	958
		b. Partisanship in Election Administration	960
		Richard L. Hasen, Beyond the Margin of Litigation: Reforming U.S. Election Administration to Avoid Electoral Meltdown (2005)	960
		Elected Election Officials	962
		c. The Judicial Oversight Model	964
		Elected Judges	964
		Republican Party of Minnesota v. White	*966*
		Nonpartisan Elections After *White*	972
		Williams-Yulee v. Florida Bar	*973*
		Should Judicial Elections Be Eliminated?	983
		Appointed Judges and Partisan Capture	984
C.		The Administrative Model in Action: Front-End Enforcement of Eligibility Requirements	987
	1.	Voter Registration	987
		Alexander Keyssar, The Right to Vote (2000)	988
		False Positives and False Negatives	989

The Motor Voter Law   990

Time Lags and Purges   990

2. Voter Identification Requirements   992

   Crawford v. Marion County Election Board   992

   Election Modernization   993

   Voter ID Requirements Following *Crawford*   1004

   Voter ID in the Courts   1005

   Analogies to ID Requirements in Other Contexts   1006

3. HAVA and Election Technology   1007

   Stewart v. Blackwell   1009

   Race and Accurate Voting   1016

   Voting Technology and Security Risks   1016

      Report on the Investigation into Russian Interference in the
      2016 Presidential Election, Office of the Special Counsel
      (March 2019)   1018

      Legal Consequences of Foreign Interference in Elections   1022

D. Post-Canvass Remedies and Judicial Oversight   1023

   1. Recounts   1023

      The Frequency and Result of Recounts   1024

   2. Election Contests   1024

      Georgia Code §§21-2-521 et seq.   1024

      Taint of Process vs. Substantive Change in Outcome   1026

   3. The Availability of Judicial Oversight   1026

      Colegrove v. Green   1026

      Baker v. Carr   1028

      Election Litigation   1030

      Doctrines of Judicial Restraint   1031

   4. Judicial Remedies   1032

      Whitley v. Cranford   1032

      The Role of State Constitutions   1040

      Reluctance to Invalidate   1041

         Disfranchising the Innocent   1041

         Respecting Expressions of the Popular Will   1041

         Adjustment of Vote Totals   1043

         Breach of Ballot Secrecy   1043

E. Congress as Election Administrator: Special Problems of Presidential
   Elections   1044

      The Constitutional Framework   1044

The Electoral Count Act   1046
Resolution of Disputes under the ECA   1046
Congressional Counting prior to 2021   1049
The 2021 Electoral Vote Count   1049
The "Independent State Legislature Doctrine"   1050

Appendix: U.S. Constitution   **1053**
Table of Cases   **1071**
Table of Authorities   **1079**
Index   **1103**

The 2020 election cycle marked a radical departure from any prior regime of American election law. In our view, there is election law before 2020 and election law after 2020, and a new edition is necessary to make sense of, and coherently to present, the new regime.

This edition of *Election Law in the American Political System* is guided by three foundational premises. First, as the title of the book indicates, we believe that election law cannot be meaningfully studied as an isolated body of legal doctrine. On the contrary, because election law is the way by which societies operationalize their commitment to democratic, popular self-rule, it cannot be fully understood unless it is examined in the context of the political system in which it is embedded. This commitment has guided the book since its first edition and is the reason why it contains what is, for a law book, an unusual amount of contextual material drawn from political and democratic theory, history, empirical political science, and sociology.

The other two premises of the edition are new, and respond directly to the radically changed political context in which American election law now finds itself. Our second premise is that liberal democracy — the form of democracy that has guided the United States and most of the free world since the conclusion of the Second World War — is in decline around the globe, and that the United States has recently become an active participant in this trend. In its place, populist authoritarianism has proven itself a vigorous competitor for dominance at home and abroad. This development puts democracy itself — and thus the practice of meaningful elections, conducted under a firm commitment to the rule of law — in severe jeopardy.

Our third premise is that this is a very bad development. Liberal democracy, to be sure, has its warts. Liberal democracies have done an unconscionably poor job of responding to urgent contemporary problems such as growing economic inequality and climate change. In many liberal democracies, unintended connections between capitalism and democracy have over the last half-century transferred a great deal of political power from ordinary citizens to the economically well-off. These are problems that demand solutions, but we do not believe that abandoning liberal democracy altogether — especially in favor of authoritarianism — is a wise or promising approach. Liberal democracy, we believe, is at bottom a good form of government — perhaps the best that human ingenuity has ever devised, or at the very least, in Winston Churchill's famous formulation, the least bad.[1] And it is surely the only form of government that can be relied on to any significant degree to protect fundamental rights of political participation and basic human dignity.

---

1. Churchill is reputed to have remarked: "Democracy is the worst form of government — except for all the others," or words to that effect.

As a result, we do not in this edition follow the traditional practice of legal casebooks of formal neutrality in the evaluation of legal developments (as superficial as this neutrality sometimes actually is). The book, to be sure, is *even-handed* in that we aim to present the current trend of populist authoritarianism in its own best light, but it is not *neutral.* Our position is clear: illiberalism is a profoundly distasteful aspect of the American inheritance that must be overcome, not capitulated to; that the establishment of liberal democracy has long been, and remains, the right aspiration for the United States (and quite possibly for any modern polity); and that any steps taken in that direction, no matter how incomplete or imperfect, represent significant political and human achievements that demand the greatest possible respect.

In taking this position, we follow the evidence wherever it leads. One place it leads is to the conclusion that Donald Trump, though not our first populist president (Andrew Jackson holds that position), was our first authoritarian president, placing him wholly outside more than two centuries of inherited political tradition—a kind of anti–George Washington. A second conclusion to which the evidence inexorably leads is that support for populist and authoritarian alternatives to liberal democracy is not randomly distributed in the American polity. Rather, it is concentrated in the Republican Party, and in states and government institutions controlled by Republicans.

This is by no means to suggest that every rank-and-file member of the Republican Party, or even every member of the party leadership, supports the direction in which the party has moved. Clearly, many Republicans dislike Donald Trump, some abhor him, and some refuse to vote for him under any circumstances. Ten Republican members of the House voted to impeach Trump following the January 6, 2020 insurrection at the Capitol, and Rep. Liz Cheney of Wyoming, a lifelong conservative and former member of the House Republican leadership, called Mr. Trump "a domestic threat that we have never faced before." Nevertheless, it is equally clear that a far-right faction of the Republican Party now controls it, and that faction supports Trump, in many cases with a degree of zealotry that is deeply alarming.

The Democratic Party, in contrast, still appears to adhere to long-standing, inherited principles of liberal democracy. As a result, the United States is no longer a nation characterized by competition for power among two major parties committed to liberal democracy; it is now a polity in which a liberal democratic party competes against an illiberal and authoritarian party. This is an entirely new development in the history of American politics.

To confront these dramatic changes, we have completely reorganized substantial portions of the book to place it firmly in the deeply disorienting new context. New material considers the declining condition of democracy around the world. We focus much more closely than in prior editions on the political inheritance of contemporary Americans, beginning with liberalism and democracy and moving on to consider directly some of the long-standing illiberal strands in American political thought. The book now devotes significant and explicit attention to the contemporary wave of populism, taking it seriously as a competing conception of democracy, albeit, we believe, an illiberal one. Throughout the book, we address several questions that are critical to any meaningful study of election law in the contemporary context: Do the conditions upon which a successful liberal democracy depends presently exist in the United States? Does election law even remain a meaningful field of law, with a legal structure and jurisprudence that can be taken seriously? Or has it become little more than a political football, to be manipulated cynically by those to whom holding power in a superficially democratic regime is the only goal, and thus about which not much more can or need be said?

To put this even more directly, the field of election law requires both meaningful elections and the rule of law. Whether these foundational conditions still exist is precisely what developments since 2020 have called into question. Users of the book will have to decide for themselves. Our goal in this edition is nothing more than to put them in a position to reach their own conclusions.

James A. Gardner
Guy-Uriel Charles

November 2022

No project of this magnitude can be brought off without the contributions and assistance of many people. For able research assistance, we are indebted to Jenn Bandy, Briana Brake, Michele Huang, Lynn King, Laura Pisoni, Scott Ptak, and Nick Proukou. Tim Conti provided valuable administrative support. We profited greatly from research undertaken in Jim Gardner's seminar in Campaign Speech and Finance by Amanda Dermady, Mary Saitta, and Kyle D. Taylor. Lisa Mueller provided outstanding help in designing diagrams. Luis Fuentes-Rohwer, Heather Gerken, and several anonymous reviewers provided valuable feedback on the manuscript. Most of all, we are indebted to Sue Martin for diligent and constant assistance in preparing and updating the manuscript over many years, and especially during the push toward publication, as well as for her management of the process of obtaining copyright permissions.

On the subject of such permissions, we are grateful to the following for permission to reprint excerpts of their work:

Aleinikoff, T. Alexander and Samuel Issacharoff. Race and Redistricting: Drawing Constitutional Lines After Shaw v. Reno, 92 Mich. L. Rev. University of Michigan Law School. Copyright © 1993. Reprinted with the permission of T. Alexander Aleinikoff.

Bailyn, Bernard. The Ideological Origins of the American Revolution. Copyright © 1967, 1992 the President and Fellows of Harvard College.

Bender, Thomas. Community and Social Change in America. Copyright © 1978 Rutgers, the State University of New Jersey. Reprinted with the permission of the publisher.

Branch, Taylor. Parting the Waters: America in the King Years, 1954-1963 (1988, Simon & Schuster). Copyright © 1988 Taylor Branch. All rights reserved.

Cain, Bruce E. Party Autonomy and Two-Party Electoral Competition. 149 U. Pa. L. Rev. (2001). The University of Pennsylvania Carey Law School. Copyright © 2001. Reprinted with the permission of the author.

Campbell, Angus, Philip E. Converse, Warren E. Miller, Donald E. Stokes. The American Voter. University of Chicago Press. Copyright © 1954.

Charles, Guy-Uriel E. & Luis E. Fuentes-Rhower. The Court's Voting Rights Decision Was Worse Than People Think. TheAtlantic.com (July 2021), https://www.theatlantic.com/ideas/archive/
2021/07/brnovich-vra-scotus-decision-arizona-voting-right/619330/. Copyright © 2021 Guy-Uriel E. Charles and Luis E. Fuentes-Rhower.

Cohen, Joshua. "Deliberation and Democratic Legitimacy," in The Good Polity: Normative Analysis of the State (Alan Hamlin and Phillip Petit, editors). Basil Blackwell. Copyright ©1989. Reprinted with the permission of the author.

Etcheson, Nicole. Bleeding Kansas: Contested Liberty in the Civil War Era. University Press of Kansas. Copyright © 2006. Reprinted with the permission of the publisher.

Fishkin, Joseph. The Dignity of the South. 123 Yale L.J. (2013). The Yale Law Journal Company, Inc. Copyright © 2013. Reprinted with the permission of the author.

Hasen, Richard L. Beyond the Margin of Litigation: Reforming U.S. Election Administration to Avoid Electoral Meltdown, 62 Wash. & Lee L. Rev. (2005). Reprinted with the permission of the author.

Kagan, Robert. "The Strongmen Strike Back," The Washington Post (March 14, 2019). Reprinted with the permission of the author.

Keyssar, Alexander. The Right to Vote: The Contested History of Democracy in the United States. Basic Books. Copyright © 2009. Reprinted with the permission of the author.

Klarman, Michael J. The Framers' Coup: The Making of the United States Constitution. Oxford University Press. Copyright © 2016. Reprinted with the permission of the author.

Phillips, Anne. The Politics of Presence. Oxford University Press. Copyright © 1998.

Pildes, Richard H. Foreword: The Constitutionalization of Democratic Politics. 118 Harv. L. Rev. (2004). The Harvard Law Review Association. Copyright © 2004. Reprinted with the permission of the author.

Ranney, Austin. The Doctrine of Responsible Government. University of Illinois. Copyright © 1954.

Rawls, John. Political Liberalism. Columbia University Press. Copyright © 1993.

Scheppele, Kim Lane. "The Party's Over" in Constitutional Democracy in Crisis? (Alan Hamlin and Phillip Petit, editors). Oxford University Press. Copyright © 1989. Reprinted with the permission of the author.

Siegel, Neil. S. "The Trump Presidency, Racial Realignment, and the Future of Constitutional Norms" in Amending America's Unwritten Constitution (Richard Albert, Yaniv Roznai, & Ryan C. Williams, editors). Cambridge University Press. Copyright © 2021. Reprinted with the permission of the author.

Smith, Rogers M. Civic Ideals: Conflicting Visions of Citizenship in U.S. History. Copyright © 1997 Yale University Press.

Wiebe, Robert. The Search for Order, 1877-1920. Excerpt from "Revolution in Values." Copyright © 1967 Robert H. Wiebe.

Wills, Gary. The Negro President. Copyright © 2003 by Gary Wills. Reprinted with the permission of the author.

ELECTION LAW
IN THE AMERICAN POLITICAL SYSTEM

CHAPTER 1
LIBERAL DEMOCRACY

Here is a snapshot of major developments in American election law during two periods:

1960–1974:

- The Supreme Court ruled racial gerrymandering unconstitutional.
- The Court invalidated malapportionment of election districts, holding that the Constitution requires all districts to be of equal population.
- The Court struck down restrictive voter eligibility requirements based on residency, payment of poll taxes, and property ownership.
- It invalidated burdensome ballot access requirements relating to signatures, filing fees, and possession of property.
- The Court struck down bans on election-day campaigning and restrictions on criticism of incumbent public officials.
- Congress enacted the Voting Rights Act (VRA), creating for the first time an effective mechanism for enforcing the Fifteenth Amendment's prohibition on racial discrimination in voting.
- Upon proposing the VRA to Congress, the President of the United States, Lyndon B. Johnson, said:

> Mr. Speaker, Mr. President, members of the Congress. I speak tonight for the dignity of man and the destiny of democracy. . . . At times, history and fate meet at a single time in a single place, to shape a turning point in man's unending search for freedom. So it was at Lexington and Concord. So it was a century ago at Appomattox. So it was last week in Selma, Alabama. There, long-suffering men and women peacefully protested the denial of their rights as Americans. Many were brutally assaulted. One good man, a man of God, was killed. There is no cause for pride in what has happened in Selma. There is no cause for self-satisfaction in the long denial of equal rights of millions of Americans. But there is cause for hope and for faith in our democracy in what is happening here tonight. . . . Our mission is at once the oldest and the most basic of this country: to right wrong, to do justice, to serve man. . . . [T]o deny a man his hopes because of his color or race, his religion or the place of his birth, is not only to do injustice, it is to deny America and to dishonor the dead who gave their lives for American freedom. . . .

1

> A century has passed, more than a hundred years, since the Negro was freed. And he is not fully free tonight. . . . The time of justice has now come. And I tell you that I believe sincerely that no force can hold it back. It is right, in the eyes of man and God, that it should come. And when it does, I think that day will brighten the lives of every American.

- The Supreme Court, by an 8-1 vote, upheld the VRA in its entirety.

2012–2021:

- The Supreme Court invalidated Section 4 of the VRA, crippling the Act's single most effective mechanism for policing racial discrimination in voting by state governments.
- The Court ruled that partisan gerrymandering presents a political question that federal courts lack jurisdiction to address, thereby withdrawing the federal judiciary from enforcing constitutional limits on the practice.
- Several states have adopted programs of aggressive, and often highly inaccurate, purging of voter registration rolls.
- Some states have enacted legislation imposing onerous fines, or even criminal liability, on civic groups conducting voter registration drives. Offenses include failure to turn in new voter registration forms within a very short period of time, and failing to satisfy burdensome record-keeping requirements. Many states have made voting more difficult for registered voters by requiring production of often highly selective kinds of photographic identification at the polling place. For example, in Texas and Tennessee, acceptable forms of identification include gun licenses but not student ID cards.
- Numerous states have made voting less convenient by reducing the number of polling places, repealing early or extended voting hours that make it easier for working people to vote, prohibiting the use of university campuses as polling places, and even in some cases criminalizing the provision of food or water to individuals waiting in line to vote. Many states have limited the availability of voting by mail, even during a pandemic.
- Several states have enacted legislation revoking or undermining the independence of professional election administrators by subjecting their work to review by partisan legislatures. In some cases, election administrators are now subject to criminal penalties for errors of administration.
- The President of the United States, Donald J. Trump, speaking of a federal House bill designed to make voting easier, remarked: "The things they had in there were crazy. They had levels of voting, that if you ever agreed to it you'd never have a Republican elected in this country again."

Clearly, something significant has changed. But what, exactly, and how should we understand it? In this chapter and the next, we put recent developments into perspective. Part A below provides a quick overview of the global political context. Part B introduces foundational concepts of liberalism and liberal democracy, which historically have provided the ideals toward which American election law aspires. Chapter 2 examines various forms of illiberalism, including populist authoritarianism, and traces longstanding illiberal strands of thought and practice woven deeply into American political history.

A.   *LIBERAL DEMOCRACY IN DECLINE: A GLOBAL PERSPECTIVE*

For most of human history, democracy was exceedingly rare. When the Framers of the U.S. Constitution gathered in 1787, they had few examples to study for inspiration, and most of those were from the ancient world. Following the American and French revolutions, however, democracy began to attract a following around the world, and over the course of the nineteenth century, possession of the franchise gradually became more common and widespread. This democratizing trend reversed during the 1930s, when illiberal and authoritarian forms of government enjoyed a robust efflorescence, but reversed again following the Second World War. The defeat of powerful fascist states by an alliance of liberal democracies badly discredited illiberal regimes, initiating a so-called "second wave" of democratic expansion. A third wave of new democracies appeared after 1989, following the collapse of the Soviet Union, when it seemed to much of the world as though liberal democracy had, after a vigorous struggle with communism, proved itself the more successful form of government. By the late 1990s, "most of the countries on Earth were democracies . . . and a third of all states were fairly liberal." LARRY DIAMOND, ILL WINDS 53 (2019).

Today, however, there has been a precipitous turn globally away from liberal democracy and toward authoritarian forms of governance. In Hungary, Poland, Turkey, Venezuela, Brazil, the Philippines, and many other places, young but seemingly stable democracies have turned to authoritarian leaders who have dismantled liberal institutions. Pro-democratic uprisings in the Arab world and Eastern Europe sputtered and resulted mainly in the further consolidation of illiberal autocracy. Even more troubling is the new phenomenon of "democratic backsliding," in which longstanding, stable democracies such as the U.S., the U.K., and Italy, have suffered slow, incremental degradation of previously reliable democratic institutions.

According to Freedom House, an organization that tracks liberty around the world, the last year in which the number of countries becoming more democratic exceeded the number becoming less democratic was 2005. In each year since 2015, the number of countries backsliding on democratic norms has been approximately double the number advancing on democratic metrics, and the number of "highly defective democracies" around the world doubled between 2006 and 2010. In 2016, *The Economist*'s Democracy Index downgraded the United States to a "flawed democracy." Thirty-five percent of the world's population now lives in "autocratizing nations." Seraphine F. Maerz, *et al.*, *State of the World 2019: Autocratization Surges — Resistance Grows*, 27 DEMOCRATIZATION 909 (2020).

That the United States has been caught up in these global trends is indubitable:

> Does President Trump fit the authoritarian-populist classification? We think so. His speeches feature a mélange of xenophobic fear-mongering and Islamophobia, narcissism, misogyny and racism, conspiracy theories ('millions of fraudulent votes'), and isolationist 'America First' policies. It is in his legitimation of authoritarian values that Trump represents the gravest threat to American democracy with his equivocal treatment of neo-Nazi and white supremacist hate groups, his open approval of some of the world's most repressive regimes, attacking the press and using Twitter to

slam 'fake news,' seeking border limits on migrants from Muslim-majority
countries and promising to build a wall to keep out Mexicans, casting
doubts on the integrity of American elections and the independence of
the judiciary, prioritizing military security and American jobs over defending democracy and human rights abroad, weakening multilateral cooperation and international conventions, and disparaging the rule of law. Like
other authoritarian rulers, he shows a casual disregard for the truth and a
willingness to challenge the legal constraints on his powers. Many of the
tensions observed in his administration arise from his rejection of democratic restraints.

PIPPA NORRIS AND RONALD INGLEHART, CULTURAL BACKLASH: TRUMP, BREXIT, AND
AUTHORITARIAN POPULISM 9-12 (2019). And this summary does not even mention
Trump's attacks on the loyalty and integrity of the federal civil service, his interference with law enforcement activities directed against himself and his associates, his
nepotism in political appointments and attempts to profit personally from official
activities, his denial of the authority of Congress to oversee or even to question his
activities, or his attempts to manipulate foreign powers into interfering with American democratic processes for his own advantage — all characteristics of authoritarian rule.

>> *Democratic Backsliding.*   What is democratic backsliding and how does it actu-
ally occur? During earlier periods, and especially during the mid-twentieth century,
regime change from democracy to authoritarianism typically occurred essentially
in open view, through either a military coup or by massive electoral fraud. The
regime's authoritarianism was plainly expressed, and dissent was crushed through
force or terror. During the twenty-first century, however, transitions from democracy to authoritarianism have generally been much less transparent, and have
hidden their goals and methods behind a surface commitment to democratic language and rituals.

In a seminal article on the topic, Nancy Bermeo identified three methods by
which contemporary authoritarians undermine democracy. One is what Bermeo
calls a "promissory coup": "Promissory coups frame the ouster of an elected government as a defense of democratic legality and make a public promise to hold
elections and restore democracy as soon as possible," a promise which is never fulfilled. A second method is "executive aggrandizement," in which "[legitimately]
elected executives weaken checks on executive power one by one, undertaking a
series of institutional changes that hamper the power of opposition forces to challenge executive preferences." The third method, often paired with the second, is
most directly relevant for present purposes:

> Strategic election manipulation is a third form of backsliding. It too
> is on the rise, being often joined with executive aggrandizement. Strate-
> gic manipulation denotes a range of actions aimed at tilting the electoral
> playing field in favor of incumbents. These include hampering media
> access, using government funds for incumbent campaigns, keeping oppo-
> sition candidates off the ballot, hampering voter registration, packing
> electoral commissions, changing electoral rules to favor incumbents, and

harassing opponents—but all done in such a way that the elections themselves do not appear fraudulent. Strategic manipulation differs from blatant election-day vote fraud in that it typically occurs long before polling
day and rarely involves obvious violations of the law. It is "strategic" in that
international (and often domestic) observers are less likely to "catch or
criticize" it.

A number of important studies explain strategic manipulation as an
unintended consequence of the rise of international election monitoring.
They argue that politicians found new ways to ensure victory once better monitoring made straight-up fraud "more costly." Whatever the explanation, scholars agree that much if not most election-related backsliding
now occurs before election day. There is also widespread agreement that
electoral misconduct "is not declining in the aggregate." Blatant election-
day fraud is rarer, but other and subtler forms have filled in.

Nancy Bermeo, *On Democratic Backsliding*, 27 J. DEMOC. 5 (2016).

>> *"Competitive Authoritarianism."*   One of the most common results of the kind
of democratic backsliding described above is a previously unknown kind of hybrid
regime sometimes referred to as "competitive authoritarianism" or "electoral
autocracy." In these regimes, international or domestic pressure on authoritarian leaders to maintain democratic institutions—particularly elections—is sufficiently strong to deter them from completely eliminating democracy, at least in
its outward manifestations. Thus, unlike forms of "full" authoritarianism, in which
"no viable channels exist for the opposition to contest legally for executive power,"
in a competitive authoritarian regime "[e]lections are held regularly and opposition parties are not legally barred from contesting them. Opposition activity is
above ground: Opposition parties can open offices, recruit candidates, and organize campaigns, and politicians are rarely exiled or imprisoned. In short, democratic procedures are sufficiently meaningful for opposition groups to take them
seriously as arenas through which to contest for power." STEVEN LEVITSKY AND
LUCAN A. WAY, COMPETITIVE AUTHORITARIANISM: HYBRID REGIMES AFTER THE
COLD WAR 6-7 (2010). As a result, the opposition can occasionally win elections,
and may even mount a serious challenge for the chief executive position.

On the other hand, competitive authoritarianism remains distinct from
democracy because "incumbent abuse of the state violates at least one of the three
defining attributes of democracy: (1) free elections, (2) broad protection of civil
liberties, and (3) a reasonably level playing field." *Id.* at 7. Elections are held, but
they are "often unfree and almost always unfair." Civil liberties are "nominally
guaranteed and at least partially respected. Independent media exist and civic and
opposition groups operate above ground." But civil rights are frequently violated,
and the political opposition and journalists may be harassed or arrested. Incumbents have better access to resources with which to campaign, better access to
media, and biased access to law. *Id.* at 9-12.

>> *The Authoritarian's "Playbook."*   So common has this pattern of democratic
backsliding become that several comparativists have compiled what they sometimes
call an "authoritarian's playbook" laying out the common set of tactics by which

authoritarian leaders undermine meaningful democracy. Here is a fairly comprehensive list put together by political scientist Larry Diamond.

1. *Begin to demonize the opposition as illegitimate and unpatriotic,* part of the
   discredited or disloyal establishment, hopelessly out of touch with
   the real people.
2. *Undermine the independence of the courts* . . . by purging judges and
   replacing them with political loyalists, or by restructuring the judiciary so it can be packed and placed under partisan control.
3. *Attack the independence of the media,* by denouncing them as partisan
   fabulists, mobilizing public fervor against them, regulating them[,
   and] finally taking over their ownership. . . .
4. *Gain control of any public broadcasting,* politicize it, and make it an
   instrument of ruling party propaganda.
5. *Impose stricter control of the internet,* in the name of morality, security, or
   counterterrorism, thus further chilling free speech and the freedom
   to organize.
6. *Subdue other elements of civil society*—civic associations, universities, and
   especially anticorruption and human rights groups—by painting
   them as part of the arrogant, effete, selfish elite that have betrayed
   the people and the country. Make university professors afraid to criticize the government in their writings and classrooms. Render student groups liable to prosecution for peaceful protest. Create new,
   fake civic organizations that will be faithful to the populist leader
   and party.
7. *Intimidate the business community* into ending its support for political
   opposition. Threaten to unleash tax and regulatory retribution on
   businesses that fund opposition parties and candidates. . . .
8. *Enrich a new class of crony capitalists* by steering state contracts, credit
   flows, licenses, and other lucre to the family, friends, and allies of the
   ruler and his clique.
9. *Assert political control over the civil service and the security apparatus.* Start
   referring to professional civil servants and military officers loyal to
   the democratic constitution as members of a "deep state." Purge
   them. . . .
10. *Gerrymander districts and rig the electoral rules* to make it nearly impos-
    sible for opposition parties to win the next election. Ensure that the
    ruling party can retain its grip on power even if it fails to win most of
    the vote.
11. *Gain control over the body that runs the elections,* to further tilt the elec-
    toral playing field and institutionalize de facto authoritarian rule.
12. *Repeat steps 1 to 11,* ever more vigorously, deepening citizens' fear of
    opposing or criticizing the new political order and silencing all forms
    of resistance.

DIAMOND, *supra,* at 64-65. We will take up items 10 and 11 later in this book.

By the criteria listed above, has the U.S. become authoritarian, or at least more
authoritarian than it had been? What about at the state level? For an application of

these criteria to the behavior of American state governments, see James A. Gardner, *Illiberalism and Authoritarianism in the American States*, 70 Am. U. L. Rev. 829 (2021); and Jacob M. Grumbach, *Laboratories of Democratic Backsliding*, https://csap .yale.edu/sites/default/files/files/grumbach-apppw-4-20-22.pdf. Both conclude that Wisconsin and North Carolina are among the states that have moved furthest down the path toward authoritarianism.

≫ *Autocratic Legalism.*   One of the distinctive characteristics of the approach outlined above to consolidating authoritarian rule is its surface adherence to respect for the rule of law—what Kim Lane Scheppele calls "autocratic legalism":

> [T]he autocrats who hijack constitutions seek to benefit from the superficial appearance of both democracy and legality within their states. They use their democratic mandates to launch legal reforms that remove the checks on executive power, limit the challenges to their rule, and undermine the crucial accountability institutions of a democratic state. Because these autocrats push their illiberal measures with electoral backing and use constitutional or legal methods to accomplish their aims, they can hide their autocratic designs in the pluralism of legitimate legal forms. . . . While democracy, constitutionalism, and liberalism once marched arm in arm through history, we now see liberalism being pushed out of the parade by a new generation of autocrats who know how to game the system. Intolerant majoritarianism and plebiscitary acclamation of charismatic leaders are now masquerading as democracy, led by new autocrats who first came to power through elections and then translated their victories into illiberal constitutionalism.

Kim Lane Scheppele, *Autocratic Legalism*, 85 U. Chi. L. Rev. 545, 547-548 (2018).

≫ *A Case Study of Democratic Backsliding: Hungary.*   At the conclusion of World War II, the victorious nations divided Europe into two spheres of influence based largely on the territories that their military forces happened to occupy when the war ended. Western Europe was allocated to the sphere of influence of the Allies (the U.S, Britain, and France), and Eastern Europe to that of the Soviet Union. The Soviet Union immediately imposed its own system, communism, on those countries within its sphere of influence. Hungary, which was in the Soviet-controlled area, took poorly to the imposition of communism, and in 1956 a popular uprising overthrew the Soviet-sponsored communist government. The Soviet Union responded immediately with a violent military crackdown, suppressing rebellion and installing a puppet government. However, Hungarians chafed under these restrictions, and soon began establishing commercial and tourism contacts with the West.

When the Soviet Union collapsed in 1989, Hungary's leaders declared the country a republic and drastically amended their 1949, Soviet-era constitution to create a western-style liberal democracy. For the next fifteen years, Hungary continued to strengthen and consolidate its democracy, to the point where, in 2004, it obtained membership in the European Union, which requires of all members a strong commitment to democracy, the rule of law, and human rights.

Hungary's pro-democratic parties were badly splintered when democracy arrived in 1989, creating fears that the anticipated democratic parliamentary government would be unstable due to the difficulty of forming a governing coalition. In an effort to ensure stable, majoritarian government, constitutional amendments provided an electoral bonus of parliamentary seats to parties that earned the largest plurality of votes. Unforeseeably, this provision proved to be the weak spot in the constitutional plan through which an authoritarian party eventually seized power and then undermined not only the country's democracy, but its liberalism.

In the 2006 parliamentary election, the Hungarian Socialist Party (MSZP), a post-communist version of the party that had governed the country during the Soviet era and which had since committed itself to liberal, free-market policies, was the top vote-getter, with 43 percent of the popular vote. Due to the electoral bonus, this total gave it about 49 percent of the seats, and it was able to form a government in coalition with other, smaller parties. However, following a major scandal and a poor record of governance, MSZP was trounced in the 2010 election by its main competitor, Fidesz, a party which had run on a platform that was socially and economically conservative, but well within the bounds of democratic liberalism. Fidesz earned 53 percent of the votes cast, but because of the electoral bonus system, earned 68 percent of the seats in parliament. Its leader, Victor Orbán, became prime minister.

Although Fidesz had not run on any policies critical of the existing constitutional order, its two-thirds supermajority allowed it to amend the constitution at will, which it proceeded immediately to do, amending it twelve times during its first year in office. Several of these amendments attacked the Hungarian Constitutional Court (HCC), which had played an active role in checking governmental power and protecting human rights under prior regimes. One amendment altered the method for selecting judges of the Constitutional Court, which had required agreement on a nomination from a majority of parliamentary parties, to allow Fidesz to nominate and seat judges without input from other parties. Another amendment, enacted after the Court invalidated a Fidesz-backed law taxing exit bonuses for government employees, deprived the Court of jurisdiction over fiscal matters. Another amendment increased the size of the Constitutional Court, allowing Fidesz to pack it with party loyalists.

Perhaps the most significant of the early amendments, however, lowered the parliamentary vote threshold for adoption of a new constitution from four-fifths to two-thirds, enabling Fidesz not merely to amend the constitution freely, but to replace it outright. With this provision in place, Fidesz in 2011 enacted a new constitution that further reduced the authority of the Constitutional Court; lowered the judicial retirement age, forcing nearly 300 judges into retirement; established a new body that put all judicial nominations under party control; and undermined the independence of numerous previously independent government bodies, including the State Audit Office and the Central Bank. Once Fidesz gained controlled of the HCC, it enacted additional amendments to the new constitution reinstating provisions that the HCC had previously invalidated under the old constitution.

Fidesz also worked to entrench itself through many legislative measures. In 2011, it reduced the number of parliamentary seats from 386 to 199, eliminated runoff voting in individual districts, and badly gerrymandered the existing districts. It adopted a parliamentary rule of procedure that prevented opposition MPs from speaking on the floor. It adopted a media law that asserted government control over all media, required registration as a condition of publication, and authorized a government oversight agency to suspend media outlets for "unbalanced" or "immoral reporting," or "inciting hatred," including hatred of the government or of the ruling majority. Although these and other measures were unpopular, and its vote share in 2014 fell below 45 percent, Fidesz retained its two-thirds parliamentary majority following that election, and retained it again in 2018 on 49 percent of the vote.

Meanwhile, prime minister Viktor Orbán has been increasingly vocal and transparent about his government's goals, explicitly characterizing Hungary as an "illiberal democracy." In a 2014 speech, Orbán said: "[W]e have to abandon liberal methods and principles of organizing a society, as well as the liberal way to look at the world." "Checks and balances," he remarked a few months later, "is a U.S. invention that for some reason of intellectual mediocrity Europe decided to adopt and use in European politics." And he has frequently suggested, often in the course of defending strongly anti-immigrant policies, that Hungary is properly understood as a Christian nation whose traditions must be secured against immigration by Muslim refugees. In 2015, at the height of Europe's refugee crisis, Hungary erected a fence on its borders with Serbia and Croatia to keep out immigrants, and Orbán has refused to comply with EU refugee resettlement policies. The Orbán government has criminalized the offering of certain kinds of assistance to migrants.

Orbán's government also so severely harassed the Central European University, an internationally well-respected university in the western liberal tradition, that it relocated itself in 2019 from Hungary to Austria. In 2015, the government enacted legislation requiring directors of nonprofit organizations to disclose their personal finances, and in 2017 organizations receiving funding from abroad were required to register as foreign agents. Many of these actions were justified by a conspiracy theory promoted by Orbán and other Fidesz leaders holding that the Hungarian-American billionaire George Soros — not coincidentally, a Jew — is bankrolling an international effort to subvert the Orbán government.

On January 3, 2022, as Orbán campaigned for reelection, former U.S. President Donald Trump formally endorsed him: "Viktor Orbán of Hungary truly loves his Country and wants safety for his people. He has done a powerful and wonderful job in protecting Hungary, stopping illegal immigration, creating jobs, trade, and should be allowed to continue to do so in the upcoming Election. He is a strong leader and respected by all. He has my Complete support and Endorsement for reelection as Prime Minister!"

What is the significance of these developments for democracy in the United States? The next part provides some necessary context.

B.   THE LIBERAL INHERITANCE

A society's body of election law represents its attempt to operationalize and institutionalize an antecedent commitment to democracy. Consequently, before we can usefully examine any particular society's election law, we must understand something about democracy; about that society's understanding of democracy and democratic practice; and about the nature and depth of the society's commitment to democratic principles.

Today, democracy is usually, although not universally, associated with a set of philosophical commitments known as *liberalism*. In this context, the term *liberalism* does not refer to any particular set of policy commitments, or any particular position on the contemporary spectrum of political opinion. Rather, liberalism in its philosophical sense refers to a collection of ideas, first developed by political thinkers of the Enlightenment during the seventeenth and eighteenth centuries, about human nature, social organization, and the sources of political and legal authority. Liberalism raises big and fundamental questions: Who rules whom? How? On what authority?

The United States indisputably was founded on liberal principles, though how fully Americans have been faithful to those commitments is a different question which will be taken up in the next chapter, as well as at many additional points in this book.

We begin our consideration of liberalism with a brief review of its basic principles.

1. *Basic Tenets of Liberalism*

Liberalism is a comprehensive political philosophy. It begins with a theory of human nature, and from that foundational building block ultimately derives a theory of legitimate political authority, including well-supported conceptions of when obedience to constituted authority is required and when it is not. Yet even though liberalism is in this sense an "affirmative" political theory, meaning that it stands fully on its own bottom, without reference to other political theories to which it is opposed, its origins are "negative." That is, liberalism was devised during the Enlightenment to justify opposition to the political order that had prevailed continuously in Europe since the Middle Ages—the so-called *ancien régime*. According to the ideology by which the *ancien régime* justified itself, all political authority was derived from God, who appointed monarchs to exercise His authority on earth. Monarchs consequently ruled by divine right, and dissent was thus transformed from a political offense into a theological one—a profound sin—creating a powerful, natural alliance between monarchs and the Church. This alliance in turn gave rise to a dense, deeply penetrating network of mutually reinforcing political and theological authority with what was, for the time, significant powers of deterrence and enforcement.

Robert Kagan

The Strongmen Strike Back

Washington Post (Mar. 14, 2019)

Today, authoritarianism has emerged as the greatest challenge facing the liberal democratic world. . . . Or, more accurately, it has reemerged, for authoritarianism has always posed the most potent and enduring challenge to liberalism, since the birth of the liberal idea itself. . . . It has returned armed with new and hitherto unimaginable tools of social control and disruption that are shoring up authoritarian rule at home, spreading it abroad and reaching into the very heart of liberal societies to undermine them from within. . . .

We don't remember what life was like before the liberal idea. . . . Traditional society was ruled by powerful and pervasive beliefs about the cosmos, about God and gods, about natural hierarchies and divine authorities, about life and afterlife, that determined every aspect of people's existence.

Average people had little control of their destiny. They were imprisoned by the rigid hierarchies of traditional society—maintained by brute force when necessary—that locked them into the station to which they were born. Generations of peasants were virtual slaves to generations of landowners. People were not free to think or believe as they wished, including about the most vitally important questions in a religious age—the questions of salvation or damnation of themselves and their loved ones. The shifting religious doctrines promulgated in Rome or Wittenberg or London, on such matters as the meaning of the Eucharist, were transmitted down to the smallest parishes. The humblest peasant could be burned at the stake for deviating from orthodoxy. Anyone from the lowest to the highest could be subjected to the most horrific tortures and executions on the order of the king or the pope or their functionaries. People may have been left to the "habitual rhythms" of work and leisure, but their bodies and their souls were at the mercy of their secular and spiritual rulers.

Only with the advent of Enlightenment liberalism did people begin to believe that the individual conscience, as well as the individual's body, should be inviolate and protected from the intrusions of state and church. And from the moment the idea was born, it sparked the most intense opposition. Not only did Enlightenment liberalism challenge traditional hierarchies, but its rationalism also challenged the traditional beliefs and social mores that had united communities over the centuries. Its universalist understanding of human nature and the primacy of the individual cut against traditional ties of race and tribe—and even of family.

The new revolutionary liberalism, therefore, never existed peacefully side by side with traditional autocratic society. Traditional rulers and societies fought back with an anti-liberal worldview—an "ideology"—as potent and comprehensive as liberalism itself. . . .

The autocracies of Russia, Austria and Prussia that crushed the French Revolution during the early 19th century tried afterward to establish an order to keep liberalism at bay. . . . Metternich's Austria and Alexander I's Russia were the early prototypes of the modern police state. They engaged in extensive censorship, closed universities, maintained networks of spies to keep an eye on ordinary people, and jailed, tortured and killed those suspected of fomenting liberal revolution.

Nor did they limit their attacks against liberalism to their own lands. They intervened with force to crush stirrings of liberalism in Spain, Italy, Poland and the German principalities. Alexander I even contemplated extending the anti-liberal campaign across the Atlantic, to Spain's rebellious colonies, prompting President James Monroe to proclaim his famous doctrine.

To 19th-century Americans, European authoritarianism was the great ideological and strategic challenge of the era. The American republic was born into a world dominated by great-power autocracies that viewed its birth with alarm—and with good reason. The American revolutionaries founded their new nation on what, at the time, were regarded as radical liberal principles, set forth most clearly by the 17th-century Enlightenment philosopher John Locke, that all humans were endowed with "natural rights" and that government existed to protect those rights. If it did not, the people had a right to overthrow it and, in the words of the Declaration of Independence, to form a new government "most likely to effect their Safety and Happiness.". . .

We long ago lost sight of what a radical, revolutionary claim this was, how it changed the way the whole world talked about rights and governance, and how it undermined the legitimacy of all existing governments. As David Ramsay, a contemporary 18th-century American historian, put it: "In no age before, and in no other country, did man ever possess an election of the kind of government, under which he would choose to live." Little wonder, as John Quincy Adams later observed, that the governments of Europe, the church, the "privileged orders," the various "establishments" and "votaries of legitimacy" were "deeply hostile" to the United States and earnestly hoped that this new "dangerous nation" would soon collapse into civil war and destroy itself, which it almost did.

The battle between liberalism and traditional authoritarianism was the original ideological confrontation, and it remained the ideological confrontation for another century and a half. The principles of Enlightenment liberalism, as set forth in the Declaration of Independence, were the core issue over which the Civil War was fought. When the United States miraculously survived that war and emerged as a great power in its own right in the late 19th century, the autocratic challenge remained in the form of a Germany still ruled by Hohenzollerns, a Russia still ruled by the czars, an Austria still ruled by Habsburgs, a Turkey still ruled by Ottomans, and a Japan and China still ruled by emperors.

It has been said that liberal ideas were "in the air" during the seventeenth and eighteenth century, and in consequence writers in numerous different places throughout Europe seemed to invent it independently. In the Anglo-American tradition, of which the United States, along with other former members of the British Commonwealth, are heirs, the most important and influential text was, and remains, John Locke's *Second Treatise of Government*.

John Locke

Second Treatise of Government (1690)

4. To understand political power right and derive it from its original, we must consider what state all men are naturally in, and that is a state of perfect freedom to order their actions and dispose of their possessions and persons as they think fit, within the bounds of the law of Nature, without asking leave or depending upon the will of any other man.

A state also of equality, wherein all the power and jurisdiction is reciprocal, no one having more than another, there being nothing more evident than that creatures of the same species and rank, promiscuously born to all the same advantages of Nature and the use of the same faculties, should also be equal one amongst another without subordination or subjection.

14. It is often asked as a mighty objection, where are, or ever were, there any men in such a state of Nature? To which it may suffice as an answer at present, that since all princes and rulers of independent governments all through the world are in a state of Nature, it is plain the world never was, nor ever will be, without numbers of men in that state.

95. Men being, as has been said, by nature all free, equal, and independent, no one can be put out of this estate and subjected to the political power of another without his own consent. The only way whereby any one divests himself of his natural liberty and puts on the bonds of civil society is by agreeing with other men to join and unite into a community for their comfortable, safe, and peaceable living, one amongst another, in a secure enjoyment of their properties and a greater security against any that are not of it. This any number of men may do, because it injures not the freedom of the rest; they are left, as they were in the liberty of the state of Nature. When any number of men have so consented to make one community or government, they are thereby presently incorporated, and make one body politic, wherein the majority have a right to act and conclude the rest.

123. If man in the state of Nature be so free, as has been said, if he be absolute lord of his own person and possessions, equal to the greatest and subject to nobody, why will he part with his freedom, why will he give up his empire and subject himself to the dominion and control of any other power? To which it is obvious to answer, that though in the state of Nature he hath such a right, yet the enjoyment of it is very uncertain, and constantly exposed to the invasion of others; for all being kings as much as he, every man his equal, and the greater part no strict observers of equity and justice, the enjoyment of the property he has in this state is very unsafe, very unsecure. This makes him willing to quit a condition which, however free, is full of fears and continual dangers; and it is not without reason that he seeks out and is willing to join in society with others who are already united, or have a mind to unite, for the mutual preservation of their lives, liberties, and estates, which I call by the general name, property.

127. Thus mankind, notwithstanding all the privileges of the state of nature, being but in an ill condition, while they remain in it, are quickly driven into society. Hence it comes to pass, that we seldom find any number of men live any time together in this state. The inconveniences that they are therein exposed to, by the irregular and uncertain exercise of the power every man has of punishing the transgressions of others, make them take sanctuary under the established laws of government, and therein seek the preservation of their property. It is this makes them so willingly give up every one his single power of punishing, to be exercised by such alone, as shall be appointed to it amongst them; and by such rules as the community, or those authorized by them to that purpose, shall agree on. And in this we have the original right of both the legislative and executive power, as well as of the governments and societies themselves.

131. But though men when they enter into society give up the equality, liberty, and executive power they had in the state of Nature into the hands of the society, to be so far disposed of by the legislative as the good of the society shall require, yet it being only with an intention in every one the better to preserve himself, his liberty and property (for no rational creature can be supposed to change his condition with an intention to be worse), the power of the society, or legislative constituted by them, can never be supposed to extend farther than the common good, but is obliged to secure every one's property by providing against [the] defects . . . that made the state of Nature so unsafe and uneasy. And so, whoever has the legislative or supreme power of any commonwealth, is bound to govern by established standing laws, promulgated and known to the people, and not by extemporary decrees, by indifferent and upright judges who are to decide controversies by those laws; and to employ the force of the community at home only in the execution of such laws, or abroad to prevent or redress foreign injuries, and secure the community from inroads and invasion. And all this to be directed to no other end, but the peace, safety, and public good of the people.

211. He that will, with any clearness, speak of the dissolution of government ought in the first place to distinguish between the dissolution of the society and the dissolution of the government. . . . Whenever the society is dissolved, it is certain the government of that society cannot remain.

220. [W]hen the government [but not the society] is dissolved, the people are at liberty to provide for themselves by erecting a new legislative, differing from the other, by the change of persons or form, or both, as they shall find it most for their safety and good.

221. There is . . . another way whereby governments are dissolved, and that is, when the legislative or the prince, either of them, act contrary to their trust. First, The legislative acts against the trust reposed in them when they endeavor to invade the property of the subject, and to make themselves or any part of the community masters or arbitrary disposers of the lives, liberties, or fortunes of the people.

222. [W]henever the legislators endeavor to take away and destroy the property of the people, or to reduce them to slavery under arbitrary power, they put themselves into a state of war with the people who are thereupon absolved from any further obedience, . . . and it devolves to the people, who have a right to resume their original liberty, and by the establishment of a new legislative (such as they shall think fit), provide for their own safety and security, which is the end for which they are in society.

223. To this perhaps it will be said, that the people being ignorant and always discontented, to lay the foundation of government in the unsteady opinion and uncertain humor of the people is to expose it to certain ruin; and no government will be able long to subsist if the people may set up a new legislative whenever they take offense at the old one. To this I answer, quite the contrary. People are not so easily got out of their old forms as some are apt to suggest. They are hardly to be prevailed with to amend the acknowledged faults in the frame they have been accustomed to. And if there be any original defects, or adventitious ones introduced by time or corruption, it is not an easy thing to get them changed, even when all the world sees there is an opportunity for it.

224. But it will be said this hypothesis lays a ferment for frequent rebellion. To which I answer: . . . such revolutions happen not upon every little mismanagement in public affairs. Great mistakes in the ruling part, many wrong and inconvenient laws, and all the slips of human frailty, will be born by the people without mutiny or murmur. But if a long train of abuses, prevarications, and artifices, all tending the same way, make the design visible to the people, and they cannot but feel what they lie under and see whither they are going, it is not to be wondered that they should then rouse themselves, and endeavor to put the rule into such hands which may secure to them the ends for which government was at first erected, and without which ancient names, and specious forms are so far from being better, that they are much worse than the state of nature or pure anarchy; the inconveniences being all as great and as near, but the remedy farther off and more difficult.

240. Here, it is like, the common question will be made, Who shall be judge whether the prince or legislative act contrary to their trust? This, perhaps, ill-affected and factious men may spread amongst the people, when the prince only makes use of his due prerogative. To this I reply, The people shall be judge; for who shall be judge whether his trustee or deputy acts well and according to the trust reposed in him, but he who deputes him and must, by having deputed him, have still a power to discard him when he fails in his trust? If this be reasonable in particular cases of private men, why should it be otherwise in that of the greatest moment, where the welfare of millions is concerned, and also where the evil, if not prevented, is greater and the redress very difficult, dear, and dangerous?

The Declaration of Independence

Declaration of Independence, ¶2

We hold these truths to be self-evident: that all men are created equal; that they are endowed, by their Creator, with certain unalienable rights; that among these are life, liberty, and the pursuit of happiness. That to secure these rights, governments are instituted among men, deriving their just powers from the consent of the governed; that whenever any form of government becomes destructive of these ends, it is the right of the people to alter or to abolish it, and to institute a new government, laying its foundation on such principles, and organizing its powers in such form, as to them shall seem most likely to effect their safety and happiness. Prudence, indeed, will dictate, that governments long established, should not be changed for light and transient causes; and accordingly all experience hath shown, that mankind are more disposed to suffer, while evils are sufferable, than to right themselves by abolishing the forms to which they are accustomed. But when a long train of abuses and usurpations, pursuing invariably the same object, evinces a design to reduce them under absolute despotism, it is their right, it is their duty, to throw off such government, and to provide new guards for their future security. Such has been the patient sufferance of these colonies; and such is now the necessity which constrains them to alter their former systems of government. The history of the present King of Great Britain is a history of repeated injuries and usurpations, all having in direct object the establishment of an absolute tyranny over these states. To prove this, let facts be submitted to a candid world.

———

Richard Henry Lee, one of the signers of the Declaration, accused Jefferson of lifting the key language and ideas of the Declaration straight from Locke's *Second Treatise. See* CARL BECKER, THE DECLARATION OF INDEPENDENCE 25 (1922).

≫ *Modern Liberalism.* Since the Enlightenment, despite considerable and continuing debate over the content of liberalism, and what a commitment to liberalism requires, a broad consensus has emerged over its core principles. These tend to include:

1. *The basic equality of citizens:* All citizens are equal for political purposes.
2. *Popular sovereignty:* The people rule themselves; they are not ruled by others, except by their own consent, granted via procedures and under terms approved by the people.
3. *The rule of law:* A liberal society lives under laws that it prescribes for itself according to duly established procedures, and the laws apply equally to all. Sometimes the principle of the rule of law is said to include constitutionalism — the idea that a constitution, duly adopted by the people for their own governance, provides the society's most fundamental law, and can be changed only by the people themselves.
4. *Normalization of political opposition:* Oppositional politics is legitimate, free, and a normal, expected feature of any well-functioning regime. Periodic alternation of the party controlling the government is possible, expected, and considered vital to the accountability of office holders to the people.
5. *A free civil society:* Civil society is a domain of private activity in which individuals form their political opinions, free from government influence, and then bring those opinions into the political arena.
6. *A basic package of human rights:* Minimally, such rights guarantee the ability of citizens to participate meaningfully in whatever processes of self-governance the society has created for itself. In many accounts, liberalism also inherently carries the idea of individual rights that protect the dignity of the person, such as rights against torture and cruel punishments, slavery, or compulsory religious beliefs.

Beyond these core principles, some disagreement tends to arise. For example, some view liberalism as requiring, perhaps for pragmatic more than theoretical reasons, limited government and dispersion of power. Others believe liberalism fully compatible with a powerful, highly centralized state. Most controversially, some view liberalism as embodying inherently a commitment to free markets. Obviously, under any conception of liberalism, disagreements will arise over the boundaries of any particular liberal commitment, or over the priority of different liberal commitments when they come into conflict.

The U.S. Constitution institutionalizes in many ways the Framers' commitments to their particular brand of liberalism. It clearly, from its opening words, embraces a theory of popular sovereignty in which the people decide for themselves how they will be ruled: "We the People . . . do ordain and establish this Constitution." The Supreme Court's decision in *Marbury v. Madison,* 5 U.S. 137 (1803), early on established the principle of constitutionalism — that the Constitution is superior to ordinary legislation. Cases like *U.S. v. Nixon,* 418 U.S. 683 (1974), and *Trump v. Vance,* 591 U.S. __ (2020) (both holding the president amenable to subpoenas issued in the ordinary course of legal proceedings), establish a robust rule of law in which no one, including the president, is above the law. A vigorous First Amendment jurisprudence establishes freedom of thought and the freedom publicly to offer dissenting points of view (see Chapter 8). The Equal Protection Clause established the basic equality of persons, and generates, under the one-person, one-vote doctrine (Chapter 4) a jurisprudence of specifically political equality.

Can you think of other ways in which the Constitution embraces principles that sound in classic liberalism? What about ways in which the Constitution falls short of liberal ideals? Slavery, which directly denies the basic equality of persons, is of course the most acute violation of liberal commitments appearing in the Constitution or in the law that has grown up around it (more on slavery in Chapter 2, and on racial discrimination throughout this volume). Are there others? Does your answer depend on how broadly you define the human rights associated with liberalism? If so, what is the basis for your own understanding of inherent human rights? Is your view a majority or minority view, and if you are in the minority, can a society that falls short of your conception of rights properly count as liberal?

2. *Liberal Conceptions of Democracy*

The core commitment of liberalism is popular sovereignty, but so long as basic human rights are observed, nothing in liberalism requires the popular sovereign to exercise its discretion in any particular way. As a result, nothing in liberal philosophy requires adoption of a democratic form of government. Locke, after all, wrote to justify a constitutional monarchy, albeit it one whose monarch operated under a set of significant constraints. So long as the citizenry consents to any particular form of governance, liberalism holds the government in question to exercise legitimate authority, to which obedience may properly be demanded.

Nevertheless, it has often been remarked that as a historical matter, liberalism and democracy seem to go hand in hand. That is, since the late eighteenth century, most states committed to liberalism have in fact chosen a democratic form of government, and virtually all genuine democracies have simultaneously committed themselves to liberal principles. Is there, then, some theoretical reason, or at least some set of pragmatic reasons, why liberalism and democracy are so often found together?

>> ***Democratic Minimalism.*** The thinnest and least demanding liberal conception of democracy is often referred to as "democratic minimalism." As the twentieth-century economist Joseph Schumpeter famously summed up this view, "the democratic method is that institutional arrangement for arriving at political decisions in which individuals acquire the power to decide by means of a competitive struggle for the people's vote." JOSEPH SCHUMPETER, CAPITALISM, SOCIALISM AND DEMOCRACY 269 (1950). In other words, governance is an activity conducted entirely by elites, and what distinguishes democracy from any other form of elite governance, such as monarchy or aristocracy, is that the people have an opportunity periodically to change their rulers by voting them out of office. The role of the people in this system is indeed minimal, and almost entirely passive—to go to the polls periodically to express nothing more than gross approval or disapproval of the performance of the set of elites presently exercising power.

While this definition of democracy is indeed minimal, it does provide a useful, baseline metric for evaluating how democratic a system is: if the people are unable to remove an incumbent regime from office—to "throw the bums out" —then a system, regardless of any other virtues it may possess, cannot be counted as "democratic." As we have seen, the increasingly widespread establishment of competitive authoritarianism, in which elections are held but the electoral rules are severely tilted in favor of incumbent power holders, cannot satisfy even a minimally liberal definition of democracy.

>> *Aggregative Theories of Democracy.* A somewhat thicker, but still relatively thin conception of democracy is "aggregative." The seeds of aggregative democratic theories were sown in the eighteenth century when Adam Smith's theory of economic markets provided a basis for legitimating the pursuit of self-interest. According to Smith, self-interested economic behavior benefits not merely the individuals who pursue it, but society as a whole because it leads to the efficient allocation of resources. As a result, a valuable public good is obtained through the uncoordinated, overtly selfish, and even quite possibly thoughtless, behavior of millions of individuals, each acting fundamentally alone.

In the mid-nineteenth century, the founders of utilitarianism, led by Jeremy Bentham, refined and formalized this idea and generalized it into a full-blown theory of politics. According to utilitarianism, a good society is one that achieves, in Bentham's famous phrase, "the greatest happiness of the greatest number." Consequently, the only proper goal of society is to maximize overall utility. Overall utility, in turn, is understood simply as the sum of the individual utilities of each member of society. Individuals, for their part, maximize their own utility simply by pursuing their personal self-interest however they are able. Utilitarianism provides, then, that political actions are best understood as attempts by individuals to maximize their own personal utility. This means, of course, that all public and political acts are by definition taken in pursuit of private self-interest. Although this leads to a political life of competitive struggle, the overall effect is good: the political process of bargaining and compromise through which citizens maximize their own individual utility also leads to the maximization of overall social utility and, consequently, to the good of the society in a genuinely ethical sense.

An extremely influential formulation of this theory was developed by Anthony Downs. Downs's work provides the foundation for virtually all contemporary rational choice and public choice analysis of politics.

Anthony Downs

An Economic Theory of Democracy (1957)

Our model is based on the assumption that every government seeks to maximize political support. We further assume that the government exists in a democratic society where periodic elections are held, that its primary goal is reelection, and that election is the goal of those parties now out of power. At each election, the party which receives the most votes (though not necessarily a majority) controls the entire government until the next election, with no intermediate votes either by the people as a whole or by a parliament. . . .

In the broadest sense, a political party is a coalition of men seeking to control the governing apparatus by legal means. By *coalition*, we mean a group of individuals who have certain ends in common and cooperate with each other to achieve them. By *governing apparatus*, we mean the physical, legal, and institutional equipment which the government uses to carry out its specialized role in the division of labor. By *legal means*, we mean either duly constituted elections or legitimate influence.

According to this definition, anyone who regularly votes for one party and occasionally contributes money or time to its campaigns is a member of that party, even if he aspires to hold no political office. The party is thus a loosely formed group of men who cooperate chiefly in an effort to get some of their number elected to office. However, they may strongly disagree with each other about the policies which those elected should put into practice. . . .

We assume that every individual, though rational, is also selfish. The import of this *self-interest axiom* was stated by John C. Calhoun as follows:

> That constitution of our nature which makes us feel more intensely what affects us directly than what affects us indirectly through others, necessarily leads to conflict between individuals. Each, in consequence, has a greater regard for his own safety or happiness, than for the safety or happiness of others: and, where these come in opposition, is ready to sacrifice the interests of others to his own.

Throughout our model, we assume that every agent acts in accordance with this view of human nature. Thus, whenever we speak of rational behavior, we always mean rational behavior directed primarily towards selfish ends. . . .

From the self-interest axiom springs our view of what motivates the political actions of party members. We assume that they act solely in order to attain the income, prestige, and power which come from being in office. Thus politicians in our model never seek office as a means of carrying out particular policies; their only goal is to reap the rewards of holding office per se. They treat policies purely as means to the attainment of their private ends, which they can reach only by being elected.

Upon this reasoning rests the fundamental hypothesis of our model: parties formulate policies in order to win elections, rather than win elections in order to formulate policies. . . .

In order to plan its policies so as to gain votes, the government must discover some relationship between what it does and how citizens vote. In our model, the relationship is derived from the axiom that citizens act rationally in politics. This axiom implies that each citizen casts his vote for the party he believes will provide him with more benefits than any other. . . .

The benefits voters consider in making their decisions are streams of utility derived from government activity. . . . Given several mutually exclusive alternatives, a rational man always takes the one which yields him the highest utility . . . , i.e., he acts to his own greatest benefit. . . .

All citizens are constantly receiving streams of benefits from government activities. Their streets are policed, water purified, roads repaired, shores defended, garbage removed, weather forecast, etc. These benefits are exactly like the benefits they receive from private economic activity and are identified as government-caused only by their source. Of course, there are enormous qualitative differences between the benefits received, say, from national defense and from eating mince pie for dessert. But no matter how diverse, all benefits must be reduced to some common denominator for purposes of allocating scarce resources. This is equally true of benefits within the private sector. The common denominator used in this process we call utility. . . .

Each citizen in our model votes for the party he believes will provide him with a higher utility income than any other party during the coming election period. To discover which party this is, he compares the utility incomes he believes he would receive were each party in office. . . .

Thus every election is a signaling device as well as a government selector. However, in a two-party system, it is limited to giving one of two signals. The incumbents always regard reelection as a mandate to continue their former policies. Conversely, the opposition party regards its triumph as a command to alter at least some of the incumbents' policies; otherwise, why would people have voted for it? In short, the outcome calls for either "no change" or "change." Hence it always makes a difference which party is elected, no matter how similar their records. . . . If the opposition wins, it is sure to carry out policies different from those the incumbents would have carried out had they been reelected.

>> *Modern Theories of Political Pluralism.*   A somewhat thicker version of aggregative democracy is founded in more contemporary—and surely more realistic—conceptions of political pluralism. The theory of interest pluralism holds that politics consists of a competitive struggle among the various groups comprising society for control over governmental power. These groups might include, for example, corporations, labor unions, economic classes, or political parties, and might be organized around a virtually limitless variety of shared interests—economic, geographical, social, or otherwise. According to the theory, such groups seek power for the purpose of using it to pursue their own self-interest. Pluralist theories are democratically "thicker" because they understand political success to require coordinated action by groups of people with shared interests, an activity that in turn presupposes meaningful and often deeply intertwined social and political relations among like-minded collections of individuals.

In a pluralistic system of democracy, individuals are not free-floating atoms each of whom makes up his or her mind in isolation from other humans, but rather members of ongoing sociopolitical communities organized around the pursuit and achievement of shared goals. In a famous formulation of pluralist theory, the democratic theorist Robert Dahl argued that what we call "democracy"—rule of the people, conceived as a collectivity—is better described as "polyarchy," a system in which different groups or coalitions of groups essentially take turns controlling the levers of power to pursue their own goals. When power rotates among such groups or coalitions, the result is a relatively wide and roughly fair distribution of benefits among sectors of society that have organized themselves for effective political participation. ROBERT A. DAHL, A PREFACE TO DEMOCRATIC THEORY (1956).

It is commonplace among contemporary political scientists to favor pluralist theories of democracy on the ground that they capture more accurately than competing theories the nature of modern mass democratic politics. Do you agree? Do people pursue their self-interest in political decision making, or do they have other goals? Do they behave rationally in their political decision making?

>> *Pitfalls of Pluralism.*   Like other thin theories of democracy, pluralism does not rely on the virtue of citizens to bring about substantively good governance, so it is not susceptible to criticism on the ground of citizen incapacity—for example, insufficient virtue and selflessness. On the other hand, pluralism does rely for good results on the proper operation of the *institutions* of governance. As political scientist Bruce Cain has observed, "[p]luralism places few demands on citizens beyond voting in periodic elections. Instead, it relies on democratic contestation between interest groups and political parties to foster accountability." Bruce E. Cain, Democracy More or Less: America's Political Reform Quandary 11 (2015). If these institutions are deficient, pluralist methods for securing governance for the common good may be thwarted. In particular: "It is not enough to ensure electoral competition. As policy contestation extends into the legislative, executive, and legal realms, an explicitly pluralist approach would aim to make the competition between intermediaries as fair, inclusive, and transparent as possible and to incentivize aggregation, negotiation, and compromise among them." *Id.* at 21.

Is political contestation among interest groups in the United States conducted on terms that are "fair, inclusive, and transparent"? Do political institutions facilitate negotiation and compromise? If not, in what ways does the system fall short, and which groups or interests might benefit unfairly at the expense of others?

According to some accounts, institutional advantages enjoyed by elites, especially the wealthy, significantly enhance their ability successfully to make use of the levers of political influence compared to less advantaged groups also competing for influence in the same public space. As a result, public policy reflects disproportionately the beliefs and interests of the well-off. *See, e.g.,* Martin Gilens and Benjamin I. Page, *Testing Theories of American Politics: Elites, Interest Groups, and Average Citizens,* 12 Persp. on Pol. 564 (2014); Martin Gilens, Affluence and Influence: Economic Inequality and Political Power in America (2012).

>> *Thicker Theories of Democracy.*   The dominance among political scientists of the pluralist model of democracy eventually generated a backlash among political theorists, who found much to criticize in the pluralist conception of elections as occasions for the mere mechanical aggregation of opinions and desires held individually by voters or groups. These theorists tend to accept the pluralist account of democratic societies as comprised of groups and individuals with fundamentally different views—indeed, often widely divergent and not always fully compatible views—but to reject the single-minded pursuit of self-interest as a legitimate basis for a democratic politics. In these thicker versions of liberal democracy, production of a meaningful democratic will requires much more from citizens than casual reflection on their own self-interest: it requires sincere effort to bridge divides of understanding, and to reach at least a partial consensus that will be sufficiently, even if not fully, acceptable to all citizens. Only in this way can all democratic citizens understand themselves to be contributing meaningfully to the substance of collective decision making, to thus to consider themselves participants in a process of genuine collective self-rule rather than mere recipients and objects of decisions made by others.

John Rawls

Political Liberalism (1993)

_____

A modern democratic society is characterized not simply by a pluralism of comprehensive religious, philosophical, and moral doctrines but by a pluralism of compatible yet reasonable comprehensive doctrines. No one of these doctrines is affirmed by citizens generally. . . . [The] problem of political liberalism [therefore] is: How is it possible that there may exist over time a stable and just society of free and equal citizens profoundly divided by reasonable though incompatible religious, philosophical, and moral doctrines? . . . What must be shown is that a certain arrangement of basic political and social institutions is more appropriate to realizing the values of liberty and equality. . . . The initial focus, then, of a political conception of justice is the framework of basic institutions and the principles, standards, and precepts that apply to it, as well as how those norms are to be expressed in the character and attributes of the members of society who realize its ideals. . . . [Another] feature of a political conception of justice is that its content is expressed in terms of certain fundamental ideas seen as implicit in the public political culture of a democratic society. . . .

[The] political culture of a democracy is characterized (I assume) by three general facts understood as follows. The first is that the diversity of reasonable comprehensive religious, philosophical, and moral doctrines found in modern democratic societies is not a mere historical condition that may soon pass away; it is a permanent feature of the public culture of democracy. . . . They are not simply the upshot of self- and class interests, or of peoples' understandable tendency to view the political world from a limited viewpoint. Instead, they are in part the work of free practical reason within the framework of free institutions.

A second and related general fact is that a continuing shared understanding on one comprehensive religious, philosophical, or moral doctrine can be maintained only by the oppressive use of state power. . . . In the society of the Middle Ages, more or less united in affirming the Catholic faith, the Inquisition was not an accident; its suppression of heresy was needed to preserve the shared religious belief. The same holds, I believe, for any reasonable comprehensive philosophical and moral doctrine, whether religious or nonreligious. . . . Call this "the fact of oppression.". . .

Finally, a third general fact is that an enduring and secure democratic regime, one not divided into contending doctrinal confessions and hostile social classes, must be willingly and freely supported by at least a substantial majority of its politically active citizens. . . . [A] political conception of justice must be one that can be endorsed by widely different and opposing though reasonable comprehensive doctrines.

Since there is no reasonable religious, philosophical, or moral doctrine affirmed by all citizens, the conception of justice affirmed in a well-ordered democratic society must be a conception limited to what I shall call "the domain of the political" and its values. . . .

[A] well-ordered democratic society meets a necessary condition of realism and stability . . . so long as, first, citizens who affirm reasonable but opposing comprehensive doctrines belong to an overlapping consensus: that is, they generally endorse that conception of justice as giving the content of their political judgments on basic institutions; and second, unreasonable comprehensive doctrines . . . do not gain enough currency to undermine society's essential justice. These conditions do not impose the unrealistic—indeed, the utopian—requirement that all citizens affirm the same comprehensive doctrine, but only . . . the same public conception of justice. . . . This enables that shared political conception to serve as the basis of public reason in debates about political questions when constitutional essentials and matters of basic justice are at stake. . . .

Reasonable persons . . . are not moved by the general good as such but desire for its own sake a social world in which they, as free and equal, can cooperate with others on terms all can accept. They insist that reciprocity should hold within that world so that each benefits along with the others.

By contrast, people are unreasonable in the same basic aspect when they plan to engage in cooperative schemes but are unwilling to honor, or even to propose, except as a necessary public pretense, any general principles or standards for specifying fair terms of cooperation. They are ready to violate such terms as suits their interests when circumstances allow. . . .

A political society . . . has a way of formulating its plans . . . and making its decisions. . . . The way a political society does this is its reason. . . . Not all reasons are public reasons. . . . In aristocratic and autocratic regimes, when the good of society is considered, this is done not by the public, . . . but by the rulers. . . . Public reason is characteristic of a democratic people: it is the reason of its citizens, of those sharing the status of equal citizenship. The subject of their reason is the good of the public. . . .

[Why] should citizens in discussing and voting on the most fundamental political questions honor the limits of public reason? . . . [Our] exercise of political power is proper and hence justifiable only when it is exercised in accordance with a constitution the essentials of which all citizens may reasonably be expected to endorse in the light of principles and ideals acceptable to them as reasonable and rational. This is the liberal principle of legitimacy. And since the exercise of political power itself must be legitimate, the ideal of citizenship imposes a moral, not a legal, duty—the duty of civility—to be able to explain to one another on those fundamental questions how the principles and policies they advocate and vote for can be supported by the political values of public reason. The duty also involves a willingness to listen to others and a fairmindedness in deciding when accommodations to their views should reasonably by made. . . .

Understanding how to conduct oneself as a democratic citizen includes understanding an ideal of public reason. . . . Thus, when the political conception is supported by an overlapping consensus of reasonable comprehensive doctrines, the paradox of public reason disappears. The union of the duty of civility with the great values of the political yields the ideal of citizens governing themselves in ways that each thinks the others might reasonably be expected to accept; and this ideal in turn is supported by the comprehensive doctrines reasonable persons affirm. Citizens affirm the ideal of public reason, not as a result of political compromise, as in a modus vivendi, but from within their own reasonable doctrines.

>> *Deliberative Democracy.* A related, and if anything even thicker conception
of liberal democracy is offered by a group of political theorists traveling under the
banner of "deliberative democracy," a theory that places a heavy emphasis on the
formation of a collective democratic will through engaged discussion of and meaningful deliberation on political ideas and actions. An early and influential account
of deliberative democracy appears in Joshua Cohen, *Deliberation and Democratic
Legitimacy, in* THE GOOD POLITY: NORMATIVE ANALYSIS OF THE STATE (Alan Hamlin
and Philip Pettit eds., 1989):

> By a deliberative democracy I shall mean, roughly, an association
> whose affairs are governed by the public deliberation of its members. . . .
> [This idea is justified by three principles.] First, in a well-ordered democ-
> racy, political debate is organized around alternative conceptions of the
> public good. So an ideal pluralist scheme, in which democratic politics
> consists of fair bargaining among groups each of which pursues its par-
> ticular or sectional interest, is unsuited to a just society. . . . Second, the
> ideal of democratic order has egalitarian implications that must be satis-
> fied in ways that are manifest to citizens. The reason is that in a just society
> political opportunities and powers must be independent of economic or
> social position . . . and the fact that they are independent must be more
> or less evident to citizens. Ensuring this manifestly fair value might, for
> example, require public funding of political parties and restrictions on
> private political spending, as well as progressive tax measures that serve to
> limit inequalities of wealth and to ensure that the political agenda is not
> controlled by the interests of economically and socially dominant groups.
>
> Third, democratic politics should be ordered in ways that provide
> a basis for self-respect, that encourage the development of a sense of
> political competence, and that contribute to the formation of a sense of
> justice. . . . In addition, democratic politics should also shape the ways in
> which the members of the society understand themselves and their own
> legitimate interests. . . .
>
> [Under a regime of deliberative democracy], outcomes are demo-
> cratically legitimate if and only if they could be the object of a free and
> reasoned agreement among equals. . . . Ideal deliberation is *free* in that
> it satisfies two conditions. First, the participants regard themselves as
> bound only by the results of their deliberation. . . . Second, the partici-
> pants suppose that they can act from the results, taking the fact that a cer-
> tain decision is arrived at through their deliberation as a sufficient reason
> for complying with it. Deliberation is *reasoned* in that the parties to it are
> required to state their reasons for advancing proposals, supporting them
> or criticizing them. They give reasons with the expectation that those
> reasons (and not, for example, their power) will settle the fate of their
> proposal. . . . In ideal deliberation parties are both formally and substan-
> tive *equal.* . . . Everyone with the deliberative capacities has equal stand-
> ing at each stage of the deliberative process. Each can put issues on the
> agenda, propose solutions, and offer reasons in support of or in criticism
> of proposals. And each has an equal voice in the decision. . . .

Finally, ideal deliberation aims to arrive at a rationally motivated
consensus—to find reasons that are persuasive to all who are committed to
acting on the results of a free and reasoned assessment of alternatives by
equals. Even under ideal conditions there is no promise that consensual
reasons will be forthcoming. If they are not, then deliberation concludes
with voting, subject to some form of majority rule. [But even when things
end in this way, the] commitment [to deliberative democracy] carries with
it a commitment to advance the common good and to respect individual
autonomy.

Do you find this conception of a deliberative democracy attractive? Feasible? Does
it make demands of citizens that they are capable of satisfying? That they will willingly undertake? It has been suggested that deliberative democracy relies too heavily on public speech, and that the ability to speak persuasively in a public forum is
no more equally distributed than are the economic resources central to pluralist
conceptions of democracy. *See, e.g.,* Lynn M. Sanders, *Against Deliberation*, 25 POL.
THEORY 347 (1997). One is put in mind here of a quip by Oscar Wilde explaining
why he is not a socialist: "it takes up too many evenings." Are these serious problems for deliberative democracy?

An enormous amount has been written on deliberative democracy in the last
several decades. For further reading, see, e.g., JÜRGEN HABERMAS, BETWEEN FACTS
AND NORMS: CONTRIBUTIONS TO A DISCOURSE THEORY OF LAW AND DEMOCRACY
(William Rehg, trans.) (1996); IRIS MARION YOUNG, JUSTICE AND THE POLITICS OF
DIFFERENCE (1990); DELIBERATIVE DEMOCRACY: ESSAYS ON REASON AND POLITICS
(James Bohman and William Rehg eds., 1997); RON LEVY AND GRAEME ORR, THE
LAW OF DELIBERATIVE DEMOCRACY (2016).

>> ***Elections in Liberal Democracies.*** Suppose a liberal society chooses, as most
have, to adopt a democratic form of governance. How, then, should we understand
the role of elections in such a system? What functions do they perform? How ought
they to operate? Does liberalism impose constraints on what an election must
accomplish, or the ways in which it must be conducted?

In the social science tradition, rooted in utilitarian, aggregative approaches, a
prominent metric of the extent to which electoral processes count as "democratic"
looks at the degree to which the policies adopted by government actors correspond
to the actual preferences of voters. Proceeding on the theory that democratic popular self-rule means precisely that the government does just what the people wish it
to do, this approach counts a regime as more democratic the more its policy decisions mirror the wishes of the public. *See* ROBERT S. ERICKSON, GERALD C. WRIGHT,
AND JOHN P. MCIVER, STATEHOUSE DEMOCRACY: PUBLIC OPINION AND POLICY IN
THE AMERICAN STATES (1993).

A somewhat less demanding variant of this approach looks instead to the correspondence between the preferences of voters and the preferences of legislators.
This approach recognizes that elected officials sometimes need to exercise independent judgment, or that they may gain access to facts with which their constituents are unacquainted, and that the acquisition of such information or the testing
of opinions in the crucible of legislative debate may cause officials to adopt policies

at variance from the less informed or less tested preferences of their constituents. It also recognizes that institutional structures of government itself—separation of powers, bicameralism, federalism, procedural limitations, and so on—may impede the ability of officials to adopt the policies their constituents desire. *See* Nicolas O. Stephanopoulos, *Elections and Alignment*, 114 COLUM. L. REV. 283 (2014).

Thicker forms of liberal democracy agree that elections, and subsequent legislative outcomes, should reflect the popular will, but they disagree about the nature of the popular will that counts. In these theories, that will is not the aggregated sum of individual policy preferences, but a collective will formed through processes of civic participation and public deliberation. How, in actual practice, could such a will be formed, and how could it be reliably identified, if not through the actual casting of votes? *See* James A. Gardner, *The Incompatible Treatment of Majorities in Election Law and Deliberative Democracy*, 12 ELECTION L.J. 468 (2013).

3.   *Majoritarianism in Liberal Elections*

It is clear that the idea of the "will of the people" plays an important role in liberal conceptions of democracy and elections. But if liberal societies are by definition societies whose members hold a wide variety of views, how is the popular will determined? In particular, when portions of the polity disagree, does liberalism require majoritarianism—rule by a majority?

That the will of a majority should take precedence over the will of a minority sometimes seems so obvious and so natural that it is difficult to articulate any additional justification for the principle. Following are some attempts by prominent political theorists to do so.

John Locke

The Second Treatise of Government (1690)

95. . . . When any number of men have . . . consented to make one community or government, they are thereby presently incorporated, and make one body politic wherein the majority have a right to act and conclude the rest.

96. For when any number of men have, by the consent of every individual, made a community, they have thereby made that community one body, with a power to act as one body, which is only by the will and determination of the majority; for that which [actuates] any community being only the consent of the individuals of it, and it being necessary to that which is one body to move one way, it is necessary the body should move that way whither the greater force carries it, which is the consent of the majority; or else it is impossible it should act or continue one body, one community, which the consent of every individual that united into it agreed that it should; and so every one is bound by that consent to be concluded by the majority. And therefore we see that in assemblies empowered to act by positive laws, where no number is set by that positive law which empowers them, the act of the majority passes for the act of the whole and of course determines, as having by the law of Nature and reason the power of the whole.

97. And thus every man, by consenting with others to make one body politic under one government, puts himself under an obligation to every one of that society to submit to the determination of the majority and to be concluded by it; or else this original compact, whereby he with others incorporates into one society, would signify nothing, and be no compact, if he be left free, and under no other ties than he was in before in the state of nature. . . .

98. For if the consent of the majority shall not, in reason, be received as the act of the whole and conclude every individual, nothing but the consent of every individual can make anything to be the act of the whole; but such a consent is next to impossible ever to be had if we consider the infirmities of health, and avocations of business, which in a number, though much less than that of a commonwealth, will necessarily keep many away from the public assembly. To which [we must] add the variety of opinions and contrariety of interests, which unavoidably happen in all collections of men. . . . Such a constitution as this would make the mighty Leviathan of a shorter duration than the feeblest creatures, and not let it outlast the day it was born in; which cannot be supposed, till we can think that rational creatures should desire and constitute societies only to be dissolved. For where the majority cannot conclude the rest, there they cannot act as one body, and consequently will be immediately dissolved again.

Jean-Jacques Rousseau

The Social Contract (1762)

There is only one law which by its nature requires unanimous assent. This is the social pact: for the civil association is the most voluntary act in the world; every man having been born free and master of himself, no one else may under any pretext whatever subject him without his consent. To assert that the son of a slave is born a slave is to assert that he is not born a man.

If, then, there are opposing voices at the time when the social pact is made, this opposition does not invalidate the contract; it merely excludes the dissentients; they are foreigners among the citizens. After the state is instituted, residence implies consent: to inhabit the territory is to submit to the sovereign.

Apart from this original contract, the votes of the greatest number always bind the rest; and this is a consequence of the contract itself. Yet it may be asked how a man can be at once free and forced to conform to wills which are not his own. How can the opposing minority be both free and subject to laws to which they have not consented?

I answer that the question is badly formulated. The citizen consents to all the laws, even to those that are passed against his will, and even to those which punish him when he dares to break any one of them. The constant will of all the members of the state is the general will; it is through it that they are citizens and free. When a law is proposed in the people's assembly, what is asked of them is not precisely whether they approve of the proposition or reject it, but whether it is in conformity with the general will which is theirs; each by giving his vote gives his opinion on this question, and the counting of votes yields a declaration of the general will. When, therefore, the opinion contrary to my own prevails, this proves only that I have made a mistake, and that what I believed to be the general will was not so. If my particular opinion had prevailed against the general will, I should have done something other than what I had willed, and then I should not have been free.

This presupposes, it is true, that all the characteristics of the general will are still to be found in the majority; when these cease to be there, no matter what position men adopt, there is no longer any freedom.

>> *Pluralist Justifications for Majority Rule.*   At first glance, it seems as though pluralist theories of democracy should have no trouble justifying majority rule. As noted above, such theories rely on utilitarianism, according to which the goal of political organization is the maximization of social utility. To maximize overall social utility, everyone's utility must be taken into account; only then can an accurate aggregation of social interests be undertaken. The majority, it seems, must have its way because the overall utility at stake among members of the majority necessarily exceeds the overall utility at stake among the smaller group constituting the minority.

Yet this syllogism is false, or at least rests on a highly significant but very shaky assumption. The utilitarian justification would work well if elections were tallied according to total utility, but they are not—they are tallied according to total votes cast. When each person gets only one vote, the utility of a majority of voters will exceed the utility of a minority only if all voters have at stake in the election roughly equivalent amounts of utility. But that need not be the case. A minority may care about an issue much more intensely than a majority. Under a system of ordinary vote tallying, a largely indifferent majority has the power to adopt policies that are strongly disfavored by a sizable minority, which can result in an overall loss of utility. For example, although some Southern whites in the Jim Crow South strongly favored segregation, there is evidence that many Southern whites—perhaps a large majority of them—preferred it only slightly. On the other hand, blacks hated segregation passionately. On the numbers alone, however, whites repeatedly retained such policies, resulting in what was very probably an overall negative social utility.

Within utilitarian pluralism, what justifies allocating votes on a per capita basis, rather than on the basis of intensity of preference? For one discussion, see CHARLES R. BEITZ, POLITICAL EQUALITY: AN ESSAY IN DEMOCRATIC THEORY (1989).

>> *The Wisdom of the Multitude.*   One justification for majority rule with a respectable pedigree is what the philosopher Jeremy Waldron has called the "Doctrine of the Wisdom of the Multitude." Jeremy Waldron, *The Wisdom of the Multitude*, 23 POL. THEORY 563 (1995). The idea that the many, collectively, might be wiser than the few found early expression in Aristotle's *Politics*. Aristotle argued that even though each individual may not be good, "when they meet together [the many] may be better than the few . . . , if regarded not individually but collectively, just as a feast to which the many contribute is better than a dinner provided by a single [person]. For each individual among the many has a share of excellence and practical wisdom, and when they meet together, . . . so too with regard to their character and thought" (Bk. 3, ch. 11). It seems to follow that if the many know better than the few, they have a better claim to rule.

Is Aristotle correct? What do the many pool to greater advantage than the few? Their knowledge of facts about the world? Their judgment? Their virtue? *See* Daniela Cammack, *Aristotle on the Virtue of the Multitude*, 41 POL. THEORY 175 (2013).

The doctrine of the wisdom of the multitude was given a modern, more scientific spin by a remarkably foresighted mathematician and philosopher, the Marquis de Condorcet, in the late eighteenth century:

> Two hundred years ago Condorcet recognized that majorities of individuals are likely to be more often correct than individuals. Whether understood by the participants or not, this is one fact that makes democracy "work." The Condorcet jury theorem says that if each individual is somewhat more likely than not to make the "better" choice between some pair of alternatives (along some specified evaluative dimension) and each individual has the same probability of being correct in this choice, then (with each voter voting independently) the probability of the group majority being correct increases as the number of individuals increases, towards a limiting value of 1. Moreover, even if individuals have varying competence—where by *competence* we mean the individual probabilities of making the "correct" (dichotomous) choice (i.e., the choice that has the higher value along the specified evaluative dimension)—then so long as the *average* competence is greater than. 5, the probability of the group majority being correct still increases to 1 as the group gets large.

Bernard Grofman and Scott L. Feld, *Rousseau's General Will: A Condorcetian Perspective*, 82 Am. Pol. Sci. Rev. 567, 569 (1988).

Do you find Condorcet's assumptions plausible? Are people more likely to be right than wrong? How likely is it that individual political judgments will be "independent" of one another in the mathematical sense?

Modern social science has collected many examples of situations in which large numbers of not particularly well-informed people outperform even the most intelligent or expert individuals—information and financial markets, for example. *See* James Surowiecki, The Wisdom of Crowds (2004); Cass R. Sunstein, Infotopia (2006). On the other hand, what if people err not occasionally and randomly, but frequently and systematically? Suppose they suffer from various kinds of shared bias, or systematically fail to attend to certain kinds of facts or arguments. *See* Bryan Caplan, The Myth of the Rational Voter: Why Democracies Choose Bad Policies (2007). And even if larger groups can be shown to have better judgment than smaller groups in some domains, like determining facts or predicting future performance in the stock market, does it follow that the same principles of judgment hold in the realm of politics?

a. What Counts as Majority Rule?

It is easy enough to state a preference for majority rule, but it can be considerably more difficult to pin down exactly what majority rule means. A majority may be required, but a majority of whom? Counted how? Does majority rule require an absolute majority of all votes cast, or merely the highest vote total?

>> *Scope of the Franchise.* When the United States was founded, the scope of the franchise was greatly restricted. Women could not vote. Slaves could not vote. In some cases, free blacks and other non-whites were excluded from the franchise. Some states maintained property qualifications for voting that excluded a significant number of white males. Under these circumstances, election by a majority

of voters inevitably meant election by a rather small minority of persons or citizens. On what grounds could such an election have been understood to satisfy the theoretical justifications for majority rule? Additionally, given Condorcet—the larger the group, the greater probability that the group will arrive at the "right" decision—does it follow that the franchise should be given the broadest scope and that a polity should have a preference for maximum turnout of voters so that the polity might make the "right" legislative choices?

»   *Majority of What Kinds of Votes?*   In the 2016 presidential election, Donald Trump received 62,979,879 votes, about three million fewer votes than Hillary Clinton's total of 65,844,954. However, Mr. Trump was elected President because he received a majority of votes cast in the Electoral College, 306 to 232. In the 2000 election, George W. Bush received 50,456,167 votes, about half a million fewer than Al Gore's total of 50,996,064. Yet Bush was elected President because he obtained a majority of votes cast in the Electoral College, 271 to 266. In American presidential elections, the principle of majority rule applies, but it applies to the Electoral College vote, not to the popular vote. Does this kind of arrangement satisfy the theoretical justifications for majority rule?

»   *Low Voter Turnout.*   Even in a political system of universal suffrage, majority rule typically refers to a majority not of all those eligible to vote, but of those who actually turn out to vote. If voter turnout is low, then the number of eligible voters who support the winning candidate may fall well short of a majority of all potential voters. Over the last century, voter turnout in the United States has been notoriously low. Below are figures for voter turnout in American presidential elections.

Voter Turnout in Presidential Elections as a Percent of Eligible Voters

Year	Percent	Year	Percent	Year	Percent	Year	Percent
1788	11.8	1848	66.5	1908	65.0	1968	60.5
1792	15.7	1852	64.1	1912	56.0	1972	56.4
1796	25.7	1856	74.3	1916	60.5	1976	55.0
1800	28.9	1860	77.8	1920	48.3	1980	54.7
1804	22.5	1864	73.2	1924	48.2	1984	55.9
1808	32.1	1868	76.6	1928	56.4	1988	53.0
1812	40.4	1872	71.9	1932	56.8	1992	58.0
1816	16.8	1876	82.9	1936	60.9	1996	51.4
1820	10.0	1880	80.6	1940	62.0	2000	54.2
1824	26.9	1884	78.6	1944	55.4	2004	60.6
1828	55.4	1888	80.4	1948	52.4	2008	62.7
1832	54.3	1892	75.5	1952	63.2	2012	58.0
1836	54.2	1896	78.9	1956	61.2	2016	60.2
1840	76.7	1900	72.6	1960	64.8	2020	66.8
1844	73.8	1904	64.7	1964	62.0		

Sources: Curtis Gans, Voter Turnout in the United States, 1788–2009 (CQ Press 2011); United States Election Project.

Presidential elections are typically the highest profile and most involving electoral contests in the nation, and thus tend to attract the highest levels of voter turnout. Voter turnout in off-year federal elections and state and local races is often substantially lower. For example, turnout in off-year congressional elections has hovered lately around 37 percent. What justifies treating an election in which fewer than half the voters cast ballots as satisfying the principle of majority rule?

Moreover, low voter turnout is not distributed evenly among the population. According to a recent study, "those who do show up at the polls are disproportionately wealthy: while nearly 80 percent of high-income citizens vote, barely 50 percent of low-income citizens do." JAN E. LEIGHLEY AND JONATHAN NAGLER, WHO VOTES NOW? DEMOGRAPHICS, ISSUES, INEQUALITY, AND TURNOUT IN THE UNITED STATES 1 (2014). This skew in voter characteristics leads to a corresponding skew in the expression and subsequent enactment of policy preferences because "[v]oters and nonvoters do not prefer the same policies," and "policy makers cater more to the wishes of voters than nonvoters." *Id.* at 2. Is low turnout merely a problem of minority rule, or is it a problem of rule by a particular minority?

>> *Rational Non-Participation?* Low voter turnout is assumed by most theories of democracy to indicate a problem—a lack of attention by citizens to their political duties, for example, or some kind of irrational behavior by the electorate. But can non-participation be a rational response by perfectly normal citizens to their political environment? In some pluralist theories of democracy, non-participation can be rational:

> In the real world, uncertainty and lack of information prevent even the most intelligent and well-informed voter from behaving in precisely the fashion [that classical theories of democracy require]. Since he cannot be certain what his present utility income from government is, or what it would be if an opposition party were in power, he can only make estimates of both. He will base them upon those few areas of government activity where the difference between parties is great enough to impress him. When the total difference in utility flows is large enough so that he is no longer indifferent about which party is in office, his *party differential threshold* has been crossed. Until then, he remains indifferent about which party is in power, even if one would give him a higher utility income than the other. The existence of thresholds raises the probability that the expected party differential will be zero, i.e., that abstention will occur.

ANTHONY DOWNS, AN ECONOMIC THEORY OF DEMOCRACY 45-46 (1957).

In economic models of democracy, another factor that can inhibit voting is the voter's knowledge that his or her vote, individually, is unlikely to affect the outcome of the election. Indeed, any voter's chance of actually influencing the election result is often so small that the expected utility from voting may be close to zero, even where the voter's expected party differential is great.

Under these circumstances, why would anyone vote at all? Voter turnout in the United States may be low, to be sure, but approximately half of all voters do vote in presidential elections. Why? Political scientists have struggled with this question, which they sometimes term the "paradox of voting."

➤ *A Duty to Vote?*   Wholly apart from accurate utility maximization, is there an ethical duty to vote? For example, do citizens owe a duty of civic virtue that requires them to participate in the political life of the community? But if civic virtue requires participation, does it require of every citizen the same kind of participation? Might some people discharge their civic responsibility in other, equally beneficial ways, such as by teaching or doing charitable work? What about those who are ignorant of the issues and the candidates: do they owe a duty to vote, or do they better discharge their obligation to their neighbors by abstaining? For discussion of these questions, see JASON BRENNAN, THE ETHICS OF VOTING (2011).

If there is a duty to vote, should it be enforced through law? Only a handful of countries, including Australia, Belgium, and Uruguay, make voting compulsory and enforce the requirement. Compulsory voting laws have been found to increase voter turnout. Do they also thereby improve the quality of electoral decision making? Are they worth the cost of making people do something they would rather avoid? *See* JASON BRENNAN AND LISA HILL, COMPULSORY VOTING: FOR AND AGAINST (2014).

In view of recent attempts in the United States to make voting more difficult, often in ways that are targeted against populations known to exhibit specific voting patterns (see Chapter 10), it has been suggested that a move in the U.S. to compulsory voting would, in addition to any other possible benefits, also help insulate vulnerable communities from tactics designed to suppress their vote. Ekow N. Yankah, *Compulsory Voting and Black Citizenship*, 90 FORDHAM L. REV. 639 (2021); *Lift Every Voice: The Urgency of Universal Civic Duty Voting* (Brookings Institution, July 20, 2020). Experience from abroad suggests, however, that a move to universal, compulsory voting would not necessarily be neutral—it is likely to have partisan consequences. In Australia, the introduction of compulsory voting in 1914 reduced the electoral dominance of wealthier and land-owning Australians, resulting in a 7–10 percent increase in votes for the Labor Party, the more liberal of Australia's two dominant parties. Anthony Fowler, *Electoral and Policy Consequences of Voter Turnout: Evidence from Compulsory Voting in Australia*, 8 Q.J. POL. SCI. 159 (2013).

In the United States, studies that have attempted to estimate the impact of universal voting have shown equivocal results. One early study found that voters are, as a group, somewhat more conservative than the entire adult population, and that universal voting would have brought "modest changes" in presidential elections and in public policy. Benjamin Heighten and Raymond E. Wolfinger, *The Political Implications of Higher Turnout*, 31 BRIT. J. POL. SCI. 179 (2001). Another study concludes that although universal voting would produce slightly higher vote totals for Democrats, the general lack of competitive races, at least for U.S. Senate seats, means that few outcomes would change. Jack Citrin, *et al.*, *What If Everyone Voted? Simulating the Impact of Increased Turnout in Senate Elections*, 47 AM. J. POL. SCI. 75 (2003).

If people have a duty to vote, or otherwise choose to vote, are they under any ethical obligations as to *how* they vote? Does the majority owe the minority some form of duty of care and concern? Does the majority bear a "fiduciary" obligation to the minority? *See* D. Theodore Rave, *Fiduciary Voters?*, 66 DUKE L.J. 331 (2016). Is there an ethical duty to cast votes solely based on the common good, rather than on personal self-interest? If there is, then what if two candidates would serve the common good more or less equally well? Can personal self-interest then be used as a "tie-breaker"? For an affirmative answer, see Annabelle Lever, *Must We Vote for the Common Good?, in* POLITICAL ETHICS (Emily Crookston, *et al.*, eds. 2016).

>> *Which Majority? Cycling and the Indeterminacy Problem.*   Suppose that a democratic jurisdiction has three voters (1, 2, and 3), who must elect a representative. Three potential candidates (X, Y, and Z) are interested in running for office. A pollster comes to town to take the pulse of popular opinion. The pollster finds that if X were to run against Y, X would beat Y by two votes to one. The pollster also determines that if Y were to run against Z, Y would beat Z, also by two votes to one.

What would happen if X were to run against Z? It's obvious, isn't it? If X beats Y, and Y beats Z, then X must beat Z easily, right? The pollster puts this question to the voters and is surprised to find that they answer differently: if X ran against Z, Z would win by two votes to one. The pollster is confused: the data shows that X beats Y, Y beats Z, and Z beats X. How is that possible? These results, known as "cycling," are possible if the voters have the following ranked preferences among the three candidates:

	First Choice	Second Choice	Third Choice
Voter 1	X	Y	Z
Voter 2	Y	Z	X
Voter 3	Z	X	Y

In this situation, two voters (1 and 3) prefer X over Y. Two different voters (1 and 2) prefer Y over Z. And two altogether different voters (2 and 3) prefer Z over X. Consequently, a *different majority* can be found to prefer any of the candidates over any of the others.

This result, first noted by Kenneth Arrow in his groundbreaking work SOCIAL CHOICE AND INDIVIDUAL VALUES (2d ed. 1963), poses a powerful challenge to conventional notions of majority rule because who wins the election depends not upon discovering "the will of the majority," but on which of the three candidates actually end up competing against each other in the election. Arrow's finding is commonly understood to mean that the concept of a majority will is incoherent because the majority wills no single thing; instead, different majorities simultaneously will different and conflicting things. Alternatively, Arrow's Theorem is often understood to show that real power in apparently democratic decision-making systems is held not by a majority of voters, but by whichever individual or group is capable of manipulating the agenda by which choices are brought to and framed for the electorate. Since a majority might be found for many different alternatives, whoever wields the power to set the agenda possesses in functional terms the power to decide the outcome.

Just how far does Arrow's Theorem impugn conventional understandings of majority rule? Does it mean, literally, that majority rule is impossible, and that democracy itself is thus impossible? Or does it undermine only certain relatively narrow conceptions of democratic self-governance? The prominent social choice theorist William Riker argued that Arrow's Theorem destroyed what he called the "populist" theory of democracy. By populism, Riker meant a democratic ideology in which legitimacy derives from the fact that public policy in democratic systems "embod[ies] the will of the people in the action of officials." On this view, which Riker associated with Rousseau, "[t]he way to discover the general will, which is the objectively correct common interest of the incorporated citizens, is to compute it by consulting the citizens." WILLIAM H. RIKER, LIBERALISM AGAINST POPULISM: A CONFRONTATION BETWEEN THE THEORY OF DEMOCRACY AND THE THEORY OF SOCIAL CHOICE 11-12 (1982). By contrast, Riker believed that what he called "liberal" theories of democracy could survive Arrow's Theorem because liberal theories demanded for legitimacy only that law issue from an authorized legislature, not that it conform to the wishes of the majority.

For a good account of the various interpretations of Arrow's Theorem and an argument that we should not understand it to do much damage to our beliefs about democracy, see Richard H. Pildes and Elizabeth Anderson, *Slinging Arrows at Democracy: Social Choice Theory, Value Pluralism, and Democratic Politics*, 90 COLUM. L. REV. 2121, 2128-2143 (1990).

b. Liberal Justifications for Limiting Majority Power

Despite the privileged role accorded by liberalism to majority rule, liberal states tend to place many restrictions on the power of majorities to have their way.

>> *Tyranny of the Majority.*   As we shall see at greater length in Chapter 2, the Framers of the U.S. Constitution were deeply skeptical of the basic political competence, and even virtue, of ordinary people. For this reason, they feared popular majorities. As Hamilton put it at the convention, "[g]ive all power to the many, they will oppress the few." JAMES MADISON, NOTES OF DEBATES IN THE FEDERAL CONVENTION OF 1787 (Norton 1987), at 135. (Granted, Hamilton was an equal opportunity skeptic: "Give all power to the few," he continued, "they will oppress the many.") A tyrannical majority oppressing a minority is an especially daunting problem when the same groups or individuals repeatedly end up in the minority:

> Majority rule, which presents an efficient opportunity for determining the public good, suffers when it is not constrained by the need to bargain with minority interests. When majorities are fixed, the minority lacks any mechanism for holding the majority to account or even to listen. Nor does such majority rule promote deliberation or consensus. The permanent majority simply has its way, without reaching out to or convincing anyone else.
>
> Any form of less-than-unanimous voting introduces the danger that some group will be in the minority and the larger group will exploit the numerically smaller group. This is especially problematic to defeated groups that do not possess a veto over proposals and acts that directly affect them or implicate concerns they value intensely. Thus, the potential for instability exists when any significant group of people ends up as permanent losers.
>
> The fundamentally important question of political stability is how to induce losers to continue to play the game. Political stability depends on the perception that the system is fair to induce losers to continue to work within the system rather than try to overthrow it. . . . As Tocqueville recognized, "[T]he power to do everything, which I should refuse to one of my

equals, I will never grant to any number of them." . . . Politics becomes a battle for total victory rather than a method of governing open to all significant groups. . . .

LANI GUINIER, THE TYRANNY OF THE MAJORITY 10-11 (1994).

>> *Constitutional Solutions.* The American constitutional tradition offers two distinct kinds of solutions to the problem of majority tyranny. One solution, the kind preferred by the Framers and written into the original Constitution, is structural. In this model, minorities are granted formal powers that allow them to influence, or even to veto, decisions of the majority. A leading example is the U.S. Senate, in which smaller states are given a voice and a vote equal to that of larger and far more populous states.

A second kind of solution is based on individual rights. In this model, a constitution distributes rights to individuals, or in some cases to groups, which they can then deploy, usually in a judicial forum, to veto actions of the majority that invade those rights. The difference here is that a rights-based model identifies only a range of fixed interests that minorities might wish to protect. A structural model is not subject to substantive limits — minorities may use their influence to protect whatever interests they deem salient at the moment in which they feel those interests threatened.

Around the globe, the rights model has proved the more popular and ubiquitous. Few modern constitutions disperse power as widely as the U.S. Constitution, mainly because radical dispersion of power is thought to present an unacceptable risk of government ineffectiveness. The consensus view internationally seems to be that minorities are better protected by a generous helping of individual rights which are available to check a fundamentally effective majoritarian government than they are by reducing the likelihood that government will invade minority rights by making it ineffective. And, of course, the U.S. Civil War made it clear that the structural approach was inadequate to redress American problems of majority tyranny. Indeed, it would be fair to say that the post–Civil War amendments (Thirteenth, Fourteenth, and Fifteenth) altered the primary constitutional strategy for protecting against majority tyranny from a predominantly structural to a predominantly rights-based model.

CHAPTER 2

ILLIBERALISM

Joseph de Maistre

Considerations on France (1796)

We are all bound to the throne of the Supreme Being by a flexible chain which restrains without enslaving us. The most wonderful aspect of the universal scheme of things is the action of free beings under divine guidance. . . .

In the political and moral world, as in the physical, there is a usual order and there are exceptions to this order. . . . In the physical order, into which man does not intrude as a cause, he is quite ready to admire what he does not understand; but in the sphere of his own activity, where he feels he acts freely as a cause, his pride easily leads him to see *disorder* wherever his own power is suspended or upset. . . .

Can the French Republic last? It would be better to put a different question: *Can the Republic exist?* . . . What arguments have been put to Frenchmen to persuade them that a republic of twenty-four million people is possible? Only two: (1) There is nothing to prevent something being created that has never been known before; (2) the discovery of the representative system allows us to do things which our predecessors could not do. . . .

If the world had witnessed the successive growth of new forms of government, we would have no right to claim that such and such a form is impossible just because it has never been known; but the contrary is the case. Monarchies have always been known, and republics have sometimes been known. . . .

That is the end of the matter. . . . Let us not confuse the essence of things with their modifications; the first are unalterable and always recur; the second change and alter the picture a little, at least for the multitude; for every practiced eye easily sees through the changing garb in which eternal nature dresses according to time and place. . . .

Thus, there is nothing new, and a great republic is impossible, since there has never been a great republic. . . .

Man can modify everything in his sphere of activity, but he creates nothing: such is the law binding him in the physical as in the moral world.

No doubt a man can plant a seed, raise a tree, perfect it by grafting, and prune it in a hundred ways, but never has he imagined that he can make a tree.

How has he thought that he has the power to make a constitution? . . .

[In all prior constitutions] can be seen the signs by which God warns of our weakness and of the right he has reserved to himself in the formation of governments.

No government results from a deliberation; popular rights are never written, or at least constitutive acts or written fundamental laws are always only declaratory statements of anterior rights, of which nothing can be said other than that they exist because they exist.

God, not having judged it proper to employ supernatural means in this field, has limited himself to human means of action, so that in the formation of constitutions circumstances are all and men are only part of the circumstances. Fairly often, even, in pursuing one object they achieve another. . . .

The rights of the *people*, properly speaking, start fairly often from a concession by sovereigns, and in this case they can be established historically; but the rights of the sovereign and of the aristocracy, at least their essential rights, those that are constitutive and basic, have neither date nor author. . . .

No nation can give itself liberty if it has not it already. . . . [L]iberty has always been a gift of kings, since all free nations have been constituted by kings.

———————

Joseph de Maistre was a lawyer and minor French aristocrat who was deeply opposed to the French Revolution. He is often considered the quintessential "reactionary," that is, someone who seeks to justify the restoration of a prior social or political order following upheaval and change.

A.   ILLIBERAL ALTERNATIVES

In the broad sweep of political thought, liberalism is a relatively recent arrival. For most of human history, governments and politics have been "illiberal." But what exactly is illiberalism?

Because the content of liberalism itself is contested, illiberalism likewise can take many forms. For present purposes, it is useful to think of illiberalism as any body of thought or form of governance that denies any of the basic precepts that make a system of thought liberal. For example, a system of thought is illiberal if it:

- Denies the fundamental political equality of citizens, conceiving of citizens instead as occupying different places in a permanent hierarchy of political status.
- Holds that civil society is not free, but is instead controlled strictly by higher laws of religious or traditional origin that establish unalterable ways of life.
- Rejects the rule of law, as for example by taking the position that leaders establish law for others, but are themselves unconstrained by law.
- Denies popular sovereignty by considering political power not as a contingent delegation of authority from the people to their agents, but as an entitlement held by those properly destined to wield it.
- Considers democracy as unnecessary, and possibly inimical to, societal well-being to the extent that it acts as an impediment to the leader's unrestrained pursuit of the good of society, properly understood.

On any account of illiberalism, however, there is little doubt that illiberal forms of government would include theocracy, in which God rules rather than the people; and autocracy, in which an absolute ruler, such as a monarch or dictator, rules without constraint. Some flavor for the nature of modern illiberalism may be gleaned from some well-known assertions of modern autocrats. For example, Óscar Benavides, a military dictator of Peru in the early twentieth century, is reputed to have remarked: "For my friends everything; for my enemies, the law." Recep Erdoğan, the present ruler of Turkey, has said: "Democracy is like a streetcar. You ride it until you arrive at your destination, then you step off." Hungary's autocratic ruler Viktor Orbán, has asserted: "[W]e have to abandon liberal methods and principles of organizing a society, as well as the liberal way to look at the world." To these well-known capsule summaries of illiberalism we might perhaps add another, a recent assertion of U.S. President Donald J. Trump: "When you are the president, the power is total."

>> **The Populist Challenge.** As we saw in Chapter 1, a robust global trend toward the adoption of liberal democracy has reversed course in the last two decades. What happened? While no two countries display precisely the same conditions, there is a definite pattern, and the element common to the great majority of cases is the rise of populism.

Jan-Werner Müller

What Is Populism? (2016)

Populism, I suggest, is a particular *moralist imagination of politics*, a way of perceiving the political world that sets a morally pure and fully unified—but, I shall argue, ultimately fictional—people against elites who are deemed corrupt or in some other way morally inferior. Otherwise, anyone criticizing the powerful and the status quo in any country would by definition be a populist. In addition to being antielitist, populists are always antipluralist: populists claim that they, *and only they*, represent the people. Other political competitors are just part of the immoral, corrupt elite, or so populists say, while not having power themselves; when in government, they will not recognize anything like legitimate opposition. The populist core claim also implies that whoever does not really support populist parties might not be part of the proper people to begin with. In the words of the French philosopher Claude Lefort, the supposedly real people first has to be "extracted" from the sum total of actual citizens. This ideal people is then presumed to be morally pure and unerring in its will.

Populism arises with the introduction of representative democracy; it is its shadow. Populists hanker after . . . "holism": the notion that the polity should no longer be split and the idea that it's possible for the people to be one and—all of them—to have one true representative. The core claim of populism is thus a moralized form of antipluralism. Political actors not committed to this claim are simply not populists. Populism requires a *pars pro toto* [the part stands for the whole] argument and a claim to exclusive representation, with both understood in a moral, as opposed to empirical, sense. There can be no populism, in other words, without someone speaking in the name of the people as a whole. . . .

This is the core claim of populism: only some of the people are really the people. Think of Nigel Farange [leader of the U.K. Brexit Party] celebrating the Brexit vote by claiming that it had been a "victory for real people". . . . Or consider a remark by Donald Trump . . .: "the only important thing is the unification of the people — because other people don't mean anything." . . .

The [populist] leader does not have to "embody" the people. . . . But a sense of direct connection and identification needs to be there. Populists always want to cut out the middleman, so to speak, and to rely as little as possible on complex party organizations as intermediaries between citizens and politicians. The same is true of wanting to be done with journalists: the media is routinely accused by populists of "mediating." . . .

What distinguishes democratic politicians from populists is that the former make representative claims in the form of something like hypotheses that can be empirically disproven on the basis of the actual results of regular procedures and institutions like elections. . . . [D]emocrats make claims about the people that are self-limiting and are conceived of as fallible. . . . Populists, by contrast, will persist with their representative claim no matter what; because their claim is of a moral and symbolic — not an empirical — nature, it cannot be disproven. When in opposition, populists are bound to cast doubt on the institutions that produce the "morally wrong" outcomes. Hence they can be accurately be described as "enemies of institutions". . . .

⟫ *Varieties of Populism.*   Although all varieties of populism are characterized by a belief in a titanic, Manichean struggle between "the people" and corrupt "elites," populism itself need not carry any particular political valence — it can arise on the political left or the right.

> Left and right populist parties in Western Europe share criticism of political elites and dissatisfaction with vested political parties. Although they also tend to share a hostile attitude to globalization and the EU [European Union], their ideologies and policies only marginally overlap. Left and right populists conceive the people and elites in different ways. Left-wing populist parties define *the people* primarily in economic terms, referring mostly to the divide between elites and the people in terms of economic inequality. They mainly seek to protect the people from exploitation by capitalist elites. In contrast, right-wing populist parties define *the people* on a cultural [basis] and seek to protect the people against cosmopolitan elites and ethnic or cultural minorities that are perceived as dangerous others. . . . At the core of right-wing populist programs is a xenophobic nationalism while the programs of left populist parties are based on a socialist or social-democratic ideology. Both these ideologies could potentially challenge liberal tenets of democracy. Xenophobic nationalists can be exclusivist with regard to ethnic, religious or cultural minorities. A radical left socio-economic ideal of equality can be exclusivist regarding groups that are considered to be "class-enemies."

However, studies that compare these two types of populist parties indicate that left-wing populist parties in Western Europe nowadays tend to embrace an inclusive view of the people, while right-wing populists tend to have an exclusive view of the people. . . . [R]adical right populists like National Front [France] or Lega Nord [Italy] . . . portray immigration as a "threat to national identity" and refer to the menace of "islamicization." Such a cultural and exclusionist view is absent from radical left-wing populist parties. Podemos in Spain has a left-libertarian universalistic profile advocating minority rights. . . . As surveys show, voters of left-wing populist parties are in contrast to those of right-wing populist parties, not inclined to exclusivist attitudes of the people.

Tjitske Akkerman, *Populist Parties under Scrutiny — One Common Vision or a Scattered Agenda?, in* POPULISM AND DEMOCRACY (Sascha Hardt, et al., eds., 2020), pp. 58-59.

Left-wing populism has been especially common in Latin America, where authoritarian strongmen like Juan Perón in Argentina (president 1946–1955 and 1973–1974), or Hugo Chávez in Venezuela (president 1999–2013), enjoyed significant popular support, at least initially, on promises to share economic benefits more widely and improve the lives of ordinary people. Evo Morales, the first indigenous president of Bolivia (2006–2019), obtained office on an inclusive, left-wing populist platform of integrating Bolivia's indigenous peoples more fully into the nation's political life, a program in which he had some success. All these regimes, however, slid eventually from democracy into authoritarianism, a phenomenon discussed further below.

In contrast, European and North American populists have tended to be right-wing. This was clearly true of Donald Trump (2016–2020), but it is also true of other leaders such as former U.K. Prime Minister Boris Johnson; Silvio Berlusconi, the former prime minister of Italy; Jean and Marine Le Pen, leaders of the National Front in France; and numerous populist parties in many European countries. The prime minister of India, Narendra Modi, is also typically associated with right-wing populism, in his case strongly allied with Hindu nationalism.

>> *History of American Populism.*   Donald Trump was not the nation's first populist leader, nor even its first populist president. If populism is, as Müller contends, representative democracy's "shadow," it is to be expected that populist movements will arise periodically in liberal democracies.

America has a long and entrenched tradition of populism. Echoing the 'Right of the People' to rule that was enshrined in the Declaration of Independence . . ., a succession of populist movements have since claimed to speak on behalf of the people against corrupt, self-serving and out-of-touch elites. A key American harbinger was . . . Andrew Jackson. . . . Jackson lauded the virtues of the productive common white man against the idle rich, including bankers, and portrayed America as a unique self-governing republic. Another important early example was the American Party of the 1850s, formerly a secret society whose members were commonly called the "Know Nothings" (because when asked about the movement they would respond 'I know nothing'). They sought to defend

America's Protestant historic stock from new Catholic immigrants, who they feared were part of a papist conspiracy to rule America.

Then came a series of other movements that also helped to mould the populist tradition. The People's Party of the 1890s . . . briefly attracted a significant following. "Radio Priest" Father Coughlin and Senator Huey Long's "Share Our Wealth" movement in the 1930s, and the anti-communist campaigns led by Senator Joseph McCarthy in the 1950s, though very different, also attracted many supporters. Others followed, including the blatantly racist [Alabama] Governor George Wallace. . . . Wallace ran as the American Independent Party candidate for the presidency in 1968, attacking "pointy-headed" intellectuals and "bearded beat-nik bureaucrats" in Washington. In the 1990s, Pat Buchanan ran for the presidency on a mix of hostility to economic elites and sympathy for hard-working ordinary people, combined with an "America First" nationalism which was notably out of keeping with Republican globalism, though his social views were more in line with the conservative right. . . .

ROGER EATWELL AND MATTHEW GOODWIN, NATIONAL POPULISM: THE REVOLT AGAINST LIBERAL DEMOCRACY 49-51 (2018).

≫   *Populism and Democracy.*   If populists, particularly on the right, take an exclusivist view of "the people," and if the claims of populists to be entitled to lead are primarily moral rather than empirical, what is populism's attitude toward democracy and democratic elections?

[P]opulist democracy is the name of a new form of representative government that is based on two phenomena: a direct relation between the leader and those in society whom the leader defines as the "right" or "good" people; and the [supreme] authority of the audience. Its immediate targets are the "obstacles" to the development of those phenomena: intermediary opinion-making bodes, such as parties; established media; and institutionalized systems for monitoring and controlling political power. . . . Populists want to replace *party* democracy with *populist* democracy; when they succeed, they stabilize their rule through unrestrained use of the means and procedures that party democracy offers. Specifically, populists promote a permanent mobilization of the public (the audience) in support of the elected leader in government; or they amend the existing constitution in ways that reduce constraints on the decision-making power of the majority. . . .

[Populism is] a *representative process*, through which a collective subject is constructed so that it can achieve power. . . . [P]opulism is [thus] incompatible with nondemocratic forms of politics. This is because it frames itself as an attempt to build a collective subject through people's voluntary consent, and as an attempt to question a social order in the name of people's interests. . . . Populist movements and leaders compete with other political actors with regard to the representation of the people; and they seek electoral victory in order to prove that "the people" *they* represent are the "right" people and that they deserve to rule for their own good. . . .

Populism in power does not challenge the practice of elections but rather transforms it into the celebration of the majority and its leader, and into a new form of elitist governing strategy, based on a (supposedly) direct representation between the people and the leader. On this framing, elections work as plebiscite or acclamation. They do what they are not supposed to: show what is *ex ante* taken to be the right answer and serve as confirmation of the right winners.

Nadia Urbinati, Me the People: How Populism Transforms Democracy 4-7 (2019). On the populist conception, then, elections are not contests for power staged before the voters, nor ought they to be meaningfully competitive; they are, on the contrary, moments in which the people express, by acclamation, their approval and support of the true leader, one whose identity is discerned antecedently, before the election.

⟫ *Is Populism Inherently Illiberal?* If populism transforms democracy in ways that are inconsistent with some of democracy's foundational justifications, what is its relation to the liberalism on which many of those justifications rest? Hungary's authoritarian leader Victor Orbán has expressly described his regime as one of "illiberal democracy." Is such a thing possible? Can democracy be practiced meaningfully in a society that is illiberal?

Some scholars think so. Fareed Zakaria, for example, has described certain contemporary states as "illiberal democracies" in which elections are more or less free and fair, and thus count as "democratic," but in which "what happens *after* the elections" flouts liberal principles, sometimes egregiously. Fareed Zakaria, *The Rise of Illiberal Democracy*, 76 For. Aff. 22, 23 (1997). Yascha Mounk similarly sees liberalism and democracy as two distinct phenomena, and argues that they are in many places "deconsolidating," producing either "democracy without rights" or "rights without democracy." Yascha Mounk, The People vs. Democracy (2018). Others insist that any kind of meaningful liberalism is impossible without democracy. Gábor Halmai, for example, argues "not only that democracy presupposes liberalism, but [that] there is no liberalism without democracy." Gábor Halmai, *Illiberalism in East-Central Europe* (European University Institute Working Paper Law 2019/05). Jan-Werner Müller claims that "illiberal governments are inherently undemocratic: 'if opposition parties have been hindered in making their case to the electorate, and journalists do not dare to report on the government's failures, the ballot boxes have already been stuffed.'" Jan-Werner Müller, *The Problem with Illiberal Democracy*, Social Europe (Jan. 27, 2016).

What do you think? Is populism inherently inconsistent with the presuppositions and commitments of liberalism? Is any tension simply a matter of some contingent tendency of populist regimes to disrespect human rights? Or, if there is a tension, does it run deeper? And if populism and liberalism are not inherently opposed, how might they co-exist as a practical matter?

⟫ *Why the Turn to Populist Authoritarianism?* If liberal democracy was riding high at the turn of the twenty-first century, what explains the precipitous decline, around the globe and at home, of popular support for liberal democratic forms of governance, and the associated turn to populist strongmen? While there is no widespread consensus on this question, several influential explanations have been advanced.

Lack of performative success. One widely offered explanation is economic — that liberal democracy has failed to produce prosperity and economic well-being where it is practiced; or more specifically, that the prosperity that liberal democracy has produced has been captured overwhelmingly by a tiny fraction of the populace, leading to unprecedented economic inequality and generally poor prospects for the masses. Large-scale processes of globalization, on this account, have produced "the gradual disappearance of low-skilled decent jobs," along with the "growth of a knowledge economy" and a shift of "the best jobs into a few large urban centres." Noam Gidron and Peter A. Hall, *The Politics of Social Status: Economic and Cultural Roots of the Populist Right*, 68 BRIT. J. SOC. 57, 63-64 (2017).

Thus, although liberal democracy produced great successes in the twentieth century when the priorities of democratic nations were winning world wars and protecting liberty from tyranny, the argument goes, when the main problems are economic, liberal democracy has had less success. Some point to the global economic crisis of 2008 as a turning point, although data on voting in countries where populist parties exist seems to show a trend of increasing support for populism dating back to the 1980s. PIPPA NORRIS AND RONALD INGLEHART, CULTURAL BACKLASH: TRUMP, BREXIT, AND AUTHORITARIAN POPULISM 9 (2019). These economic trends, on this account, tend to align economic winners and losers along a cleavage that also divides the educated from the uneducated, urban from suburban and rural populations, and globally oriented cosmopolites from locally rooted traditionalists, lending itself to the standard populist interpretation of a virtuous, "true" people aligned against a corrupt elite out only for itself.

In any case, the nub of the explanation is that governments, no matter how appealing their basic commitments, must eventually demonstrate their ability to perform successfully. Initially, people may feel a strong commitment to working within a democratic system, voting out politicians who don't get the job done on the theory that what is wrong isn't the system, but the inadequacies of those selected to run it. Eventually, however, when enough people begin to feel that their legitimate expectations are not being met no matter how many times they replace leadership, they become open to the possibility that the problem lies not with the leaders, but with the system itself, in turn opening them to the idea that replacing liberal democracy with a different system might yield better results.

Interestingly, feelings of economic threat and deprivation sufficient to activate support for populist authoritarianism need not be rooted in any objectively accurate self-assessment of economic condition. Those who support populist parties and leaders are generally not themselves poor, and their support for populists typically is not affected by the fact that even Americans living below the official poverty line, much less working class Americans, are far better off than the poor in most of the world. More often, support for populist authoritarianism is found among those who either harbor deep-seated fear of a deterioration in their economic condition (i.e., downward economic mobility); or resentment that a disproportionate slice of today's economic prosperity is seemingly captured by those who are already economically very comfortable — it is a function, that is, of "a growing sense of *relative* deprivation." EATWELL AND GOODWIN, *supra*, at 181 (emphasis added).

There is, incidentally, no evidence that populist governments provide better economic performance than liberal democratic ones, and much evidence suggesting the opposite. An early and seminal study of the relationship between populism and economic performance in Latin America identified a typical pattern: "After a short period of economic growth and recovery, bottlenecks develop provoking unsustainable macroeconomic pressures that, at the end, result in the plummeting of real wages and severe balance of payment difficulties. The final outcome . . . has generally been galloping inflation, crisis, and the collapse of the economic system." Rudiger Dornbusch and Sebastian Edwards, *The Macroeconomics of Populism, in* THE MACROECONOMICS OF POPULISM IN LATIN AMERICA (Rudiger Dornbusch and Sebastian Edwards, eds., 1991), at 1. One of the reasons, especially in cases of left-wing populism, is "the populist's emphasis on short-term growth and a disregard for long-term sustainability." Manuel Funke, *et al., Populist Leaders and the Economy* 37 (Kiel Working Paper No. 2169, Oct. 2020). That is, populists come to power denouncing inequality and promising to address it, and do so in a way that delivers some immediate results, but in a way that is not sustainable.

Moreover, according to a recent wide-ranging analysis, populists who come to power promising a reduction in economic inequality do not in fact deliver. *Id.* Another analysis by the same authors concludes that countries "underperformed [economically] by approximately one percent per year after a populist came to power." Manuel Funke, *et al., The Cost of Populism: Evidence from History*, VOX EU (Feb. 16, 2021). In some cases, the results have been catastrophic. Argentina, for example, has lurched from one economic crisis to another as a series of populist leaders have repeatedly undermined the country's long-term economic health in favor of short-term measures designed to provide immediate relief to their electoral base. As a result, Argentina has frequently defaulted on its debt, experienced repeated cycles of hyperinflation—at one point reportedly reaching an annualized rate of 20,000 percent—and has devalued its currency several times, producing significant losses of domestic wealth. Similarly, Venezuela's populist leader Hugo Chávez presided over the almost complete destruction of one of Latin America's strongest economies.

There is also mounting evidence that populist leaders perform worse in other domains as well. For example, a recent study concludes that populist governments have done considerably worse than liberal democratic ones in responding to the Covid-19 pandemic. The authors attribute this poor performance to the populist tendency to rely on "'quick-fixes,' characterized by simple solutions for the short term," and their tendency "to advocate anti-scientific attitudes, which are rooted in an 'anti-elite' populist discourse." Michael Bayerlein, *et al., Populism and COVID-19: How Populist Governments (Mis)Handle the Pandemic* (V-Dem Institute, Working Paper 121, 2021).

Alienation. A second explanation for the rise of populism focuses on social and political feelings of alienation, and claims that popular support for liberalism is wavering because it is unable to fulfill certain kinds of basic human needs. On this account, "Authoritarianism may be a stable condition of human existence, more stable than liberalism and democracy. It appeals to core elements of human nature that liberalism does not always satisfy—the desire for order, for strong leadership, and perhaps above all, the yearning for the security of family, tribe, and nation."

Robert Kagan, The Jungle Grows Back: America and Our Imperiled World 147 (2018).

Another critique of liberal democracy from this perspective focuses on the loss of feelings of connectedness to government, and the associated beliefs that the government is responsive to and serves the people rather than imposing itself upon them. On this view, government has become enormous and so complex that ordinary citizens cannot comprehend it. Legislators represent so many people that they cannot possibly know, or even listen to, more than a tiny fraction of them. Complaints to government are routed not to accountable and democratically responsive legislators, but to impersonal and unaccountable bureaucracies. Government is run not by ordinary people, but by trained, unelected, and democratically unaccountable technocrats who have become in essence a governing class to which ordinary people have little access. Eatwell and Goodwin, *supra,* at 85. As a result, when a demagogic populist appears promising to pay attention to ordinary people and to do their bidding, a thin and formalistic commitment to democracy can be eclipsed by hopeful feelings of renewed meaning and connection.

Bigotry and hate. A third explanation sometimes offered to explain the rise of populist authoritarianism is that recent events, especially global patterns of migration, have activated latent racial and religious prejudices among people who were never that committed to liberalism in the first place, and that their feelings of fear and threat drive their attraction to authoritarianism. This account begins with a rejection of the economic explanation: "The tendency to portray Trump as a refuge for poverty-stricken whites . . . is deeply problematic. During the US primaries, the median household income of a Trump voter was $72,000, compared to $61,000 for supporters of Hillary Clinton and Bernie Sanders, and $56,000 for the average person." In some states, including Texas and Florida, the annual income of Trump voters exceeded the state average by as much as twenty thousand dollars. Eatwell and Goodwin, *supra,* at 4-5.

Similarly, according to a recent study documenting the fragility of Americans' support for democratic values, "in every case the factor most strongly associated with support for antidemocratic sentiments is ethnic antagonism." These results, the author cautions, do not imply that

> ethnic antagonism is a necessary basis for antidemocratic sentiment, or that ethnic antagonism always and everywhere erodes public commitment to democracy. One of the most politically salient features of the contemporary United States is the looming demographic transition from a majority-White to a "majority-minority" country. . . . For those who view demographic change as a significant threat to "the traditional American way of life," the political stakes could hardly be higher. . . . Analysts of the 2016 presidential election have emphasized the activation of long-standing racial resentment and concerns about immigration as important factors contributing to President Trump's support.

Larry M. Bartels, *Ethnic Antagonism Erodes Republicans' Commitment to Democracy,* PNAS (Jan. 2020). Another study argues that "the anti-immigrant, racially tinged and anti-Muslim appeals that are at the centre of most populist right platforms today are well configured to speak directly to people who feel that their social status is threatened. Overt or covert appeals that evoke threats to the status of white men potentially posed by moves toward greater gender or racial equality may have parallel power." GIDRON AND HALL, *supra*, at 63.

B.   IS THE UNITED STATES A LIBERAL DEMOCRACY?

We have seen that the most urgent conflict in contemporary American politics is one that pits supporters of liberal democracy against supporters of populist authoritarianism. Internal political struggles, however, do not occur in the abstract; they occur in specific, ongoing societies with particular histories, established institutions, and inherited conventions of conflict-resolution. These factors can exert a profound influence on the forms in which political conflict emerges, the strategies pursued by the combatants, and the ultimate outcome of the conflict.

The balance of this chapter contextualizes the contemporary struggle among American liberals and populists by examining the playing field—the major constitutional, institutional, and social structures—upon which that conflict is presently waged. As we shall see, much of the contemporary conflict has played out in the form of a bitter struggle over the rules by which elections are conducted—in the domain, that is, of election law itself—and we will examine that struggle in later chapters. The terms of the struggle, however, and the ways in which it is conducted, are influenced significantly by larger institutional factors.

≫   *The Baseline of Analysis.*   Before going any further, we must confront a preliminary question about how to understand recent developments in U.S. politics, one that concerns the starting point, or baseline, of analysis. That is, do recent developments represent a *departure* from previous practices, or a *continuation* of them? If they represent a departure, from what, exactly? The answer to these questions has important ramifications for how we diagnose current problems.

More specifically, if the United States simply *is* a liberal democracy, and has always been one, and its people simply *are* and always have been committed, as a matter of fundamental political identity, to liberalism and its associated ideals of equality, popular sovereignty, and the rule of law, then illiberalism, authoritarianism, and right-wing populism can be readily dismissed as nothing more than foreign invaders—cancers that have inexplicably infected the body politic and must be fought off. The current situation, on this view, is merely an unfortunate political illness of no particular significance, to be survived like any disease, and promptly forgotten as soon as health is restored.

But *is* the United States in fact a liberal democracy? Are Americans in fact committed to liberal democracy, and, if so, how strongly? If the United States is *not* simply, from top to bottom, a pure liberal democracy—or, even after 230 years, not yet one—then we might need to explore a different diagnosis. In particular, we might need to ask whether the American body politic might possibly be some kind of "carrier" of illiberalism, and whether the current difficulties thus result from a flare-up of an innate predisposition to a particular kind of political pathology.

That is, might some degree of acceptance of, or tolerance for, illiberal ideals such as permanent social inequality or even authoritarianism be in some sense intrinsic to American political life—baked into our political DNA, so to speak? If so, then is illiberalism better thought of as a chronic American condition that erupts periodically, one that must be addressed not through a one-time treatment but through potentially burdensome protocols of chronic management?

>> *The Story of an Inherently Liberal America.*   The idea that the U.S. simply *is* and has always been a liberal democracy through and through, and that Americans share a profound, longstanding, and universal commitment to liberalism, is traceable in large part to one of the most important intellectual works of the twentieth century, Louis Hartz's 1955 classic, *The Liberal Tradition in America.* Exerting immense influence on late twentieth-century thought, the book argued that the liberal philosophy of John Locke had not merely influenced the founding generation, but had provided the template for an enduring national consensus on political first principles—in Hartz's words, "a Lockian creed." This creed, Hartz argued, follows Locke in taking as its centerpiece a "basic social norm, the concept of free individuals in a state of nature."

In this respect, according to Hartz, the U.S. differed significantly from Europe. In Europe, a history stretching back beyond human memory of monarchy, aristocracy, feudalism, and class distinctions meant that liberal, Enlightenment ideals of human political equality and popular sovereignty based on the voluntary consent of free individuals were deeply threatening to those who, by long tradition, had enjoyed a previously unquestioned entitlement to rule—the so-called *ancien régime.* As a result, in Europe liberal ideals had to be fought for, bitterly, at great length, and often through deeply disruptive revolutionary means, of which the French Revolution, with its attendant brutal violence and internal social upheaval, was the paradigm.

In America, Hartz claimed, things were different. Europeans settling in America perceived themselves to be arriving in a world without any established society whatsoever, and thus one without inherited social hierarchies, and indeed life in the North American colonies was considerably more egalitarian than the one the settlers had left behind. Americans, on this view, had simply "skip[ped] the feudal stage of history," and instead had "inherited the freest society in the world," which appeared natural to them rather than an achievement to be struggled for. "Because," Hartz argued, "the basic feudal oppressions of Europe had not taken root [in America], the fundamental social norm of Locke ceased in large part to look like a norm and began . . . to look like a sober description of fact." In consequence, the idea of the state of nature and its inherent equality became, under North American conditions, "the master assumption of American political thought . . .: the reality of atomistic social freedom." And this freedom, Hartz claimed, was to Americans so obvious and natural as to be, in the words of the Declaration of Independence, "self-evident."

Hartz wrote, however, at the height of post-World War II liberal euphoria, a period during which liberal democracy's defeat of fascism in 1945 was understood in the West as an affirmation of the superiority of liberal democracy to its ideological competitors. Hartz's critics have long complained, persuasively in our view, that the historical circumstances in which Hartz wrote blinded him—and indeed, most of an entire generation of American intellectuals — to numerous glaring holes in his analysis.

The preceding chapter focused on the liberalism of the American founding. This part, in contrast, focuses on illiberal strands woven into American political thought and practice, and asks whether and how they may have influenced our present legal regime of democratic popular self-rule, and the political struggles to which it is now subject.

1. Accommodating the Ancien Régime

On the eve of the Revolution, few would have described the American colonies as liberal societies in any modern sense. American colonists were British subjects, ruled by a king who claimed authority by divine grant. They were, moreover, residents of distant imperial possessions of the British Crown which, consistent with longstanding European practice, conferred upon them a subordinate status that permitted considerably more intrusive and direct rule from the imperial center than was possible within the mother country itself. In addition to political subordination, colonial society was rife with forms of social subordination:

> [A]t any one moment as much as one-half of colonial society was legally unfree. Most conspicuously, of course, were the half million Afro-Americans reduced to the utterly debased position of lifetime hereditary servitude. . . . Legal unfreedom, however, was not confined to blacks. Tens of thousands of whites, usually young men and women, were indentured as servants or apprentices and bound to masters for periods ranging from a few years to decades. As late as 1759 Benjamin Franklin thought that most of the labor of the middle colonies was being performed by indentured servants brought from Britain, Ireland, and Germany. It has been estimated that one-half to two-thirds of all immigrants to the colonies came as indentured servants. . . .
>
> Servitude was common on both sides of the Atlantic, [but in] the colonies servitude was a much harsher, more brutal, and more humiliating status than it was in England. . . . Colonial bonded servants in fact shared some of the chattel nature of black slaves. Although they were members of their master's household and enjoyed some legal rights, they were a kind of property as well. . . . And as expensive property, most colonial servants could be bought and sold, rented out, seized for the debts of their masters, and conveyed in wills to heirs. . . . They could not marry, buy or sell property, or leave their households without their master's permission. . . .

GORDON S. WOOD, THE RADICALISM OF THE AMERICAN REVOLUTION 51-53 (1991).

When the Americans rose up against the British, from what, exactly, did they free themselves, and with what consequences? As we have seen, liberal theory teaches that a justified revolution reinstates in the revolutionary society the liberty its members enjoyed in the state of nature. In that condition of full, natural liberty they are free to found a new society, "laying its foundation on such principles, and organizing its powers in such form, as to them shall seem most likely to effect their safety and happiness." The Americans did just that: they declared themselves free and wrote a new and imaginative constitution for their society, one that has endured for more than 230 years—more than ten times as long as the average constitution. But in so doing, did they in fact make a clean break with the past? Is such a thing even possible? Consider the following account.

> Social contract theory imagines political societies as resting on a fundamental agreement, adopted at a discrete moment in hypothetical time, that both bound individual persons together into a single polity and set fundamental rules regarding that polity's structure and powers. . . . [But] constitutions do not come into being against the background of a state of nature of isolated individuals. . . . Constitutions are enacted in ongoing societies . . . with preexisting laws and legal systems, political organizations, cultural and linguistic and religious divisions, and norms and mores. Moreover, the practice of constitutionalism is usually, at least in part, a practice of *reconciling* those legacies to a new political order. . . . Most constitutions cannot be well understood by retrospectively characterizing them as the kind of complete and radical break with the past envisioned by social contract theory.
>
> Contractarian blinders lead us to look for greater individualism, greater social unity, and greater coherence of principles than can actually be expected of constitutions or constitutionalism. Real constitutional orders appropriate, incorporate, and channel the histories and divisions of the societies they govern. . . .
>
> More generally, what we might call *positivist contractarian constitutionalism* accords ultimate authority to the will of the enacters of a constitution. . . . "[W]e the people" adopt a complete system at a particular moment in time. Once that system has been adopted there may be considerable deference to the past—but the relevant past goes back *no further in time than the moment of adoption.* . . . [But] there is no non-question-begging reason why constitutions must derive from and ground legitimacy in a national people with pre-constitutional unity, rather than a plurality of pre-constitutional groups or institutions working or evolving together. . . .

Jacob T. Levy, *Not so* Novus *an* Ordo: *Constitutions without Social Contracts,* 37 Pol. Theory 191 (2009).

If Levy is correct, and a constitution founded in an ongoing society necessarily must make some kinds of concessions to inherited, pre-constitutional forms of social and political thought and organization, to what extent does the U.S. Constitution do so, and what is the nature of any such concessions?

a. Republicanism

>> *Beliefs about Popular Self-Government.* The Framers were well-educated gentlemen familiar with history and the political philosophy of their day, including the various forms of government adopted by past societies. During the debates at the constitutional convention, and in their correspondence, many delegates distinguished carefully not only among basic forms of government such as democracy,

oligarchy, and monarchy, but among numerous variations of these archetypes, including hereditary and elective monarchies, and among pure democracies, republics, and compound republics. Positions taken at the constitutional convention often were premised on differing views about which form of government was best given the particular circumstances facing the new nation.

One thing emerges clearly from an examination of the Constitution and Madison's notes of the constitutional convention: the Framers were united in rejecting a purely democratic form of government in which principal responsibility for governing would fall on the people. Instead, the Framers set up a *republic*—a government in which the people's only role was to select the officers of government; these officers would then rule the nation. In defending the proposed new Constitution against its critics, Madison observed, as a point in its favor, that the Constitution's defining feature was its "total exclusion of the people in their collective capacity." *The Federalist*, No. 63 (Madison).

But why not a genuine democracy? One reason, alluded to by Madison, was the sheer size of the contemplated nation; it would be impossible for all the people to play a role in governing because they could not all meet and decide upon a single course of action. The people would have to be represented. Yet even conceding the necessity of representation, there remains the issue of governmental responsiveness to the popular will; a representative form of government can be designed in ways that make it more or less sensitive to the policy preferences of the people. On this question, the Framers largely agreed that the government they were creating should *not* be highly responsive to popular sentiment, and as we shall see, they designed constitutional structures to insulate government officials, in varying degrees, from popular opinion. Why?

One important reason for many convention delegates was a deep suspicion of the people themselves. For example, during the debates Elbridge Gerry of Massachusetts declared himself to be against any kind of popular election for President because "[t]he people are uninformed and would be misled by a few designing men." Roger Sherman of Connecticut argued that "[t]he people . . . should have as little to do as may be about the government. They want information, and are constantly liable to be misled." John Mercer of Maryland warned that voters would make "the worst possible choice" since "[t]he people cannot know and judge of the character of candidates."

Other delegates such as Rufus King, John Dickinson, and Benjamin Franklin defended the abilities of the people. Yet no one at the convention seemed to think that the United States ought to be predominantly democratic in the sense of giving the people "in their collective capacity" the power to determine the course of public policy.

Michael J. Klarman

The Framers' Coup: The Making of the United States
Constitution (2016)

Two months before the Continental Congress in July 1776 declared American independence from Great Britain, it urged the colonies to draft their own constitutions, which most of them did. . . . From the outset, some political leaders feared that these constitutions were too democratic, rendering the governments overly dependent upon the people and providing insufficient protection for property rights. In 1776, Charles Carroll of Maryland predicted that the separation from Great Britain would ruin America, not so much because of the "calamities of war" as because of the bad governments it would produce in the states: "[T]hey will be simple democracies, of all governments the worst, and will end as all other democracies have, in despotism." Robert R. Livingston, one of the drafters of the Declaration of Independence and soon to become New York's first chancellor, warned of the danger of creating new governments at a time when people had such "absurd ideas" on the subject, such as direct popular election of government officials. . . . In the mid-1780s, some of the worst fears of these political leaders were realized.

The United States endured a severe economic depression in the wake of the Revolutionary War—described by many historians as the worst economic climate suffered by the nation until the Great Depression of the 1930s. . . . Amid a depressed economy, most states imposed tax increases to fund their war debt and to satisfy congressional requisitions—which were themselves designed primarily to service the nation's own enormous war debt. . . . Given the scarcity of specie and the falling prices of land and farm produce, large numbers of farmers could not pay the increased taxes. When governments cracked down on enforcement, tens of thousands lost their farms. In the 1780s, 60 to 70 percent of taxpaying farmers in some particular stricken Pennsylvania counties saw their property foreclosed upon. . . .

Seeking political remedies for their woes, financially strapped farmers petitioned state legislatures for fiscal, monetary, and debt relief, and the legislatures were highly responsive. . . . The most widely sought form of relief was state issuance of paper money, which would facilitate trade by increasing the circulating medium and enable the payment of debts and taxes. . . . With several states capitulating to constituent pressure for monetary relief, other states found it increasingly difficult to resist following that path. . . .

From the perspective of more affluent Americans, people's failure to pay taxes was primarily attributable to their indolence and licentiousness. Governor William Livingston of New Jersey . . . complained of the "lazy, lounging, lubberly" fellows who sat around drinking, "working perhaps but two days in the week and receiving for that work double the wages [they] earn. . . ." To most well-to-do Americans, the tax and debtor relief legislation of the mid-1780s [reflected a problem of] excess democracy. State governments had proved too responsive to the public will – to the derogation of property rights. . . .

The delegates [of the 1789 constitutional convention] were disdainful of democracy for a very concrete reason: The populist politics of the mid-1780s, refracted through the relatively democratic state constitutions drafted in the mid-1770s, had pressured most state legislatures to issue paper money and enact tax and debtor relief legislation, which most elite statesmen abhorred. . . . Most of the delegates agreed, as [Pierce] Butler put it, that "the great object of government" was to protect property, and that the states were doing a lousy job of it. . . .

Because the Framers blamed relief legislation on "democratic licentiousness," they designed the federal government to be insulated from the populist politics that had produced such measures in the states. Thus, they opted for huge districts for congressional representatives, and indirect elections and lengthy terms in office for both senators and presidents. They also rejected, for federal legislators, instruction, mandatory rotation, and recall. In addition, they created a powerful executive armed with a veto power that could be used to block any populist economic measures that might somehow sneak through a legislature designed to squelch them. To the extent that the Framers were thinking about judicial review at all, they mostly conceived of it as another potential check on such relief legislation.

Indeed, most of the delegates to the Philadelphia convention would have preferred a constitution that shielded the federal government even more from populist pressures. Yet their choices were constrained by the role that popularly elected state ratifying conventions would play in deciding whether to approve the Constitution. . . . The Antifederalists were not off base when they charged the Framers with seeking to establish an aristocracy of sorts. . . . In fact, the Federalists had little confidence in the ability of ordinary people to participate in government decision-making. . . . [Their] deep distrust of the people was evident . . . in nearly every substantive choice made in the Constitution that bore on the new federal government's susceptibility to popular influence. . . .

>> *Democratic Optimization?*   Does Klarman go too far in charging the Framers with being interested primarily in protecting property against levelling democratic impulses? In evaluating the Framers' work, it must be acknowledged that the constitution they wrote was, in historical terms, remarkable for the degree to which the people played any role at all, whether direct or indirect, in deciding who should rule them and by what means. Before the American Revolution demonstrated the feasibility of another path, people virtually everywhere were simply subjects of some monarch—and often subjects of a long string of monarchs who conquered and reconquered the same territory—and thus merely voiceless recipients of policy decisions made by their rulers and social superiors. From their own point of view, then, might not the Framers have been justified in thinking their handiwork remarkably democratic? Isn't it only when measured by contemporary rather than eighteenth- or nineteenth-century standards that the U.S. Constitution seems undemocratic? Might it be more useful to think of the design problem the Framers confronted not as one of democratization but as one of optimization—to create a government that would be as democratic as possible while still preserving liberty to the greatest practicable degree? Indeed, is this not precisely the dilemma facing every liberal state: to empower majorities to rule while simultaneously protecting minorities from majority tyranny?

Some insight into how the Framers chose to strike this balance can be gleaned from Madison's account in *The Federalist* No. 39. There, Madison argued that a government counts as "republican" if

> it derives all its powers directly or indirectly from the great body of the people, and is administered by persons holding their offices during pleasure for a limited period, or during good behavior. It is *essential* to such a government that it be derived from the great body of the society, not from

an inconsiderable proportion or a favored class of it; otherwise a handful of tyrannical nobles, exercising their oppressions by a delegation of
their powers, might aspire to the rank of republicans and claim for their
government the honorable title of republic. It is *sufficient* for such a government that the persons administering it be appointed, either directly or
indirectly, by the people; and that they hold their appointments by either
of the tenures just specified. . . .

On comparing the Constitution planned by the convention with
the standard here fixed, we perceived at once that it is, in the most rigid
sense, conformable to it. The House of Representatives, like that of one
branch at least of all the State legislatures, is elected immediately by the
great body of the people. The Senate, like the present Congress and the
Senate of Maryland, derives its appointment indirectly from the people.
The President is indirectly derived from the choice of the people, according to the example in most of the States. Even the judges, with all other
officers of the Union, will, as in the several States, be the choice, though a
remote choice, of the people themselves.

⯮ *The Influence of Republican Skepticism on Constitutional Structure.*   If the Framers
decided to strike the balance in favor of insulating the new government from popular political sentiment, how did they do so? Their principal strategy relied on constitutional *structure*. Democratic unresponsiveness is baked into the constitutional
structure in several important respects. Most prominently, power is widely dispersed
under the constitutional plan: the government is divided into three branches, and
the legislative branch is further divided into a House of Representatives and Senate. Of these, the Constitution originally decreed that only the House should be
democratically elected.

The materials immediately following examine in greater depth three constitutional structures that reveal the Framers' presuppositions and design calculations: the decision to create a large republic with what were, for the time,
unprecedentedly large election districts; the process for selecting a president; and
the structure of the Senate.

The Federalist, No. 10 (Madison) (1787)

Among the numerous advantages promised by a well-constructed Union,
none deserves to be more accurately developed than its tendency to break and control the violence of faction. . . . Complaints are everywhere heard from our most
considerate and virtuous citizens, equally the friends of public and private faith
and of public and personal liberty, that our governments are too unstable, that the
public good is disregarded in the conflicts of rival parties, and that measures are
too often decided, not according to the rules of justice and the rights of the minor
party, but by the superior force of an interested and overbearing majority. However
anxiously we may wish that these complaints had no foundation, the evidence of
known facts will not permit us to deny that they are in some degree true. . . . These
must be chiefly, if not wholly, effects of the unsteadiness and injustice with which a
factious spirit has tainted our public administration.

By a faction I understand a number of citizens, whether amounting to a majority or minority of the whole, who are united and actuated by some common impulse of passion, or of interest, adverse to the rights of other citizens, or to the permanent and aggregate interests of the community.

There are two methods of curing the mischiefs of faction: the one, by removing its causes; the other, by controlling its effects.

There are again two methods of removing the causes of faction: the one, by destroying the liberty which is essential to its existence; the other, by giving to every citizen the same opinions, the same passions, and the same interests.

It could never be more truly said than of the first remedy that it was worse than the disease. Liberty is to faction what air is to fire, an aliment without which it instantly expires. But it could not be a less folly to abolish liberty, which is essential to political life, because it nourishes faction than it would be to wish the annihilation of air, which is essential to animal life, because it imparts to fire its destructive agency.

The second expedient is as impracticable as the first would be unwise. As long as the reason of man continues fallible, and he is at liberty to exercise it, different opinions will be formed. As long as the connection subsists between his reason and his self-love, his opinions and his passions will have a reciprocal influence on each other; and the former will be objects to which the latter will attach themselves. The diversity of the faculties of men, from which the rights of property originate, is not less an insuperable obstacle to a uniformity of interests. . . .

The latent causes of faction are thus sown in the nature of man; and we see them everywhere brought into different degrees of activity, according to the different circumstances of civil society. A zeal for different opinions concerning religion, concerning government, and many other points . . . have, in turn, divided mankind into parties, inflamed them with mutual animosity, and rendered them much more disposed to vex and oppress each other than to co-operate for their common good. So strong is this propensity of mankind to fall into mutual animosities that where no substantial occasion presents itself the most frivolous and fanciful distinctions have been sufficient to kindle their unfriendly passions and excite their most violent conflicts. . . .

It is in vain to say that enlightened statesmen will be able to adjust these clashing interests and render them all subservient to the public good. Enlightened statesmen will not always be at the helm. Nor, in many cases, can such an adjustment be made at all without taking into view indirect and remote considerations, which will rarely prevail over the immediate interest which one party may find in disregarding the rights of another or the good of the whole.

The inference to which we are brought is that the causes of faction cannot be removed and that relief is only to be sought in the means of controlling its effects.

If a faction consists of less than a majority, relief is supplied by the republican principle, which enables the majority to defeat its sinister views by regular vote. It may clog the administration, it may convulse the society; but it will be unable to execute and mask its violence under the forms of the Constitution. When a majority is included in a faction, the form of popular government, on the other hand, enables it to sacrifice to its ruling passion or interest both the public good and the rights of other citizens. To secure the public good and private rights against the danger of such a faction, and at the same time to preserve the spirit and the form of popular government, is then the great object to which our inquiries are directed. . . .

By what means is this object attainable? Evidently by one of two only. Either the existence of the same passion or interest in a majority at the same time must be prevented, or the majority, having such coexistent passion or interest, must be rendered, by their number and local situation, unable to concert and carry into effect schemes of oppression. . . .

From this view of the subject it may be concluded that a pure democracy, by which I mean a society consisting of a small number of citizens, who assemble and administer the government in person, can admit of no cure for the mischiefs of faction. A common passion or interest will, in almost every case, be felt by a majority of the whole; a communication and concert results from the form of government itself; and there is nothing to check the inducements to sacrifice the weaker party or an obnoxious individual. Hence it is that such democracies have ever been spectacles of turbulence and contention; have ever been found incompatible with personal security or the rights of property; and have in general been as short in their lives as they have been violent in their deaths. Theoretic politicians, who have patronized this species of government, have erroneously supposed that by reducing mankind to a perfect equality in their political rights, they would at the same time be perfectly equalized and assimilated in their possessions, their opinions, and their passions.

A republic, by which I mean a government in which the scheme of representation takes place, opens a different prospect and promises the cure for which we are seeking. Let us examine the points in which it varies from pure democracy, and we shall comprehend both the nature of the cure and the efficacy which it must derive from the Union.

The two great points of difference between a democracy are: first, the delegation of the government, in the latter, to a small number of citizens elected by the rest; secondly, the greater number of citizens and greater sphere of country over which the latter may be extended.

The effect of the first difference is, on the one hand, to refine and enlarge the public views by passing them through the medium of a chosen body of citizens, whose wisdom may best discern the true interest of their country and whose patriotism and love of justice will be least likely to sacrifice it to temporary or partial considerations. Under such a regulation it may well happen that the public voice, pronounced by the representatives of the people, will be more consonant to the public good than if pronounced by the people themselves, convened for the purpose. On the other hand, the effect may be inverted. Men of factious tempers, of local prejudices, or of sinister designs, may, by intrigue, by corruption, or by other means, first obtain the suffrages, and then betray the interests of the people. The question resulting is, whether small or extensive republics are most favorable to the election of proper guardians of the public weal; and it is clearly decided in favor of the latter by two obvious considerations.

In the first place it is to be remarked that however small the republic may be the representatives must be raised to a certain number in order to guard against the cabals of a few; and that however large it may be they must be limited to a certain number in order to guard against the confusion of a multitude. Hence, the number of representatives in the two cases not being in proportion to that of the constituents, and being proportionally greatest in the small republic, it follows that if the proportion of fit characters be not less in the large than in the small republic, the former will present a greater option and consequently a greater probability of fit choice.

In the next place, as each representative will be chosen by a greater number of citizens in the large than in the small republic, it will be more difficult for unworthy candidates to practice with success the vicious arts by which elections are too often carried; and the suffrages of the people being more free, will be more likely to center on men who possess the most attractive merit and the most diffusive and established characters.

It must be confessed that in this, as in most other cases, there is a mean, on both sides of which inconveniences will be found to lie. By enlarging too much the number of electors, you render the representative too little acquainted with all their local circumstances and lesser interests; as by reducing it too much, you render him unduly attached to these, and too little fit to comprehend and pursue great and national objects. The federal Constitution forms a happy combination in this respect; the great and aggregate interests being referred to the national, the local and particular to the State legislatures.

The other point of difference is the greater number of citizens and extent of territory which may be brought within the compass of republican than of democratic government; and it is this circumstance principally which renders factious combinations less to be dreaded in the former than in the latter. The smaller the society, the fewer probably will be the distinct parties and interests composing it; the fewer the distinct parties and interests, the more frequently will a majority be found of the same party; and the smaller the number of individuals composing a majority, and the smaller the compass within which they are placed, the more easily will they concert and execute their plans of oppression. Extend the sphere and you take in a greater variety of parties and interests; you make it less probable that a majority of the whole will have a common motive to invade the rights of other citizens; or if such a common motive exists, it will be more difficult for all who feel it to discover their own strength and to act in unison with each other. Besides other impediments, it may be remarked that, where there is a consciousness of unjust or dishonorable purposes, communication is always checked by distrust in proportion to the number whose concurrence is necessary.

Hence, it clearly appears that the same advantage which a republic has over a democracy in controlling the effects of faction is enjoyed by a large over a small republic — is enjoyed by the Union over the States composing it. . . . The influence of factious leaders may kindle a flame within their particular States but will be unable to spread a general conflagration through the other States. A religious sect may degenerate into a political faction in a part of the Confederacy; but the variety of sects dispersed over the entire face of it must secure the national councils against any danger from that source. A rage for paper money, for an abolition of debts, for an equal division of property, or for any other improper or wicked project, will be less apt to pervade the whole body of the Union than a particular member of it, in the same proportion as such a malady is more likely to taint a particular county or district than an entire State.

In the extent and proper structure of the Union, therefore, we behold a republican remedy for the diseases most incident to republican government. . . .

Publius

***

As the preceding materials illustrate, republicanism did not hold ordinary people in very high regard. They were thought to possess, at most, the capacity to identify good leaders and to elect them, but not the capacity to make the kinds of decisions leaders must make. Montesquieu put it thusly:

> The people are extremely well qualified for choosing those whom they are to intrust with part of their authority. They have only to be determined by things to which they cannot be strangers, and by facts that are obvious to sense. They can tell when a person has fought many battles, and been crowned with success; they are, therefore, capable of electing a general. They can tell when a judge is assiduous in his office, gives general satisfaction, and has never been charged with bribery: this is sufficient for choosing a praetor. They are struck with the magnificence or riches of a fellow-citizen; no more is requisite for electing an edile [executive]. These are facts of which they can have better information in a public forum than a monarch in his palace. But are they capable of conducting an intricate affair, of seizing and improving the opportunity and critical moment of action? No; this surpasses their abilities.

BARON DE MONTESQUIEU, THE SPIRIT OF THE LAWS (1748) (Franz Neumann ed. and Thomas Nugent trans., 1949), Bk. II, ch. 2, at 9-10. Thus, in the eighteenth century, the citizen "was entrusted with the responsibility of identifying and evaluating his superiors," those with a legitimate claim to leadership. Richard R. Beeman, *Deference, Republicanism, and the Emergence of Popular Politics in Eighteenth-Century America*, 49 WM. & MARY Q. 401, 407 (1992).

>> *The Republican Presidency.*   The influence of republican principles is probably seen most clearly in the structure of the presidency.

The Federalist, No. 68 (Hamilton) (1788)

The mode of appointment of the Chief Magistrate of the United States is almost the only part of the system, of any consequence, which has escaped without severe censure, or which has received the slightest mark of approbation from its opponents. . . . I venture somewhat further, and hesitate not to affirm, that if the manner of it be not perfect, it is at least excellent. It unites in an eminent degree all the advantages, the union of which was to be wished for.

It was desirable that the sense of the people should operate in the choice of the person to whom so important a trust was to be confided. This end will be answered by committing the right of making it, not to any preestablished body, but to men chosen by the people for the special purpose, and at the particular conjuncture.

It was equally desirable, that the immediate election should be made by men most capable of analyzing the qualities adapted to the station, and acting under circumstances favorable to deliberation, and to a judicious combination of all the reasons and inducements which were proper to govern their choice. A small number of persons, selected by their fellow-citizens from the general mass, will be most likely to possess the information and discernment requisite to such complicated investigations.

It was also peculiarly desirable to afford as little opportunity as possible to tumult and disorder. This evil was not least to be dreaded in the election of a magistrate, who was to have so important an agency in the administration of the government as the President of the United States. But the precautions which have been so happily concerted in the system under consideration, promise an effectual security against this mischief. The choice of SEVERAL, to form an intermediate body of electors, will be much less apt to convulse the community with any extraordinary or violent movements, than the choice of ONE who was himself to be the final object of the public wishes. And as the electors, chosen in each State, are to assemble and vote in the State in which they are chosen, this detached and divided situation will expose them much less to heats and ferments, which might be communicated from them to the people, than if they were all to be convened at one time, in one place.

Nothing was more to be desired than that every practicable obstacle should be opposed to cabal, intrigue, and corruption. These most deadly adversaries of republican government might naturally have been expected to make their approaches from more than one quarter, but chiefly from the desire in foreign powers to gain an improper ascendant in our councils. How could they better gratify this, than by raising a creature of their own to the chief magistracy of the Union? But the convention have guarded against all danger of this sort, with the most provident and judicious attention. They have not made the appointment of the President to depend on any preexisting bodies of men, who might be tampered with beforehand to prostitute their votes; but they have referred it in the first instance to an immediate act of the people of America, to be exerted in the choice of persons for the temporary and sole purpose of making the appointment. And they have excluded from eligibility to this trust, all those who from situation might be suspected of too great devotion to the President in office. No senator, representative, or other person holding a place of trust or profit under the United States, can be of the numbers of the electors. Thus without corrupting the body of the people, the immediate agents in the election will at least enter upon the task free from any sinister bias. Their transient existence, and their detached situation, already taken notice of, afford a satisfactory prospect of their continuing so, to the conclusion of it. The business of corruption, when it is to embrace so considerable a number of men, requires time as well as means. Nor would it be found easy suddenly to embark them, dispersed as they would be over thirteen States, in any combinations founded upon motives, which though they could not properly be denominated corrupt, might yet be of a nature to mislead them from their duty.

Another and no less important desideratum was, that the Executive should be independent for his continuance in office on all but the people themselves. He might otherwise be tempted to sacrifice his duty to his complaisance for those whose favor was necessary to the duration of his official consequence. This advantage will also be secured, by making his re-election to depend on a special body of representatives, deputed by the society for the single purpose of making the important choice. . . .

The process of election affords a moral certainty, that the office of President will never fall to the lot of any man who is not in an eminent degree endowed with the requisite qualifications. Talents for low intrigue, and the little arts of popularity, may alone suffice to elevate a man to the first honors in a single State; but it will require other talents, and a different kind of merit, to establish him in the esteem and confidence of the whole Union, or of so considerable a portion of it as would be necessary to make him a successful candidate for the distinguished office of President of the United States. It will not be too strong to say, that there will be a constant probability of seeing the station filled by characters pre-eminent for ability and virtue. And this will be thought no inconsiderable recommendation of the Constitution, by those who are able to estimate the share which the executive in every government must necessarily have in its good or ill administration. . . .

Publius

>> *The Republican Senate.*   The Senate, too, was a highly republican institution. During his presidency, George Washington is said to have analogized the Senate to the saucer of a teacup. Apparently, it was customary at the time to pour excessively hot tea into the saucer to allow it to cool, and then to return it to the cup. Washington likened the teacup to the House, boiling over with the heat of popular passion. The Senate, one step removed from the people, was the place in which these popular passions could be allowed to cool, and where they could be examined more objectively and deliberately, by men selected (by the state legislature rather than by the people) for their wisdom and reason rather than their popular appeal.

It has often been suggested that the constitutional plan for the U.S. Congress was inspired by the design of the British Parliament: a House of Commons whose members are elected by the people, but whose influence is moderated by a House of Lords, a body whose members were appointed for life by the Crown, and whose qualifications were based on social station and lifetime achievement. The ancients often spoke of "mixed government," in which a good form of government was said to be one that combined rule of the one (a monarch or other chief executive), the few (an aristocracy), and the many (the people). Thus conceived, the House of Lords, and by analogy the U.S. Senate, might be understood to reserve a role in government for the few. *See, e.g.,* M.J.C. VILE, CONSTITUTIONALISM AND THE SEPARATION OF POWERS 37 (2d ed. 1998).

Although the U.S. has neither royalty nor formal aristocracy, it is nevertheless true that the Senate has become known as a "Millionaire's Club": the median net worth of senators as of 2020 was just over $1 million. The wealthiest senator, Rick Scott of Florida, listed on his financial disclosure form assets worth more than $250 million. Are the members of the U.S. Senate distinguished by their virtue? Their experience? Their pragmatism? Or merely their wealth? Does wealth correlate with any of these qualities?

b. Federalism

Another set of concessions made by the Framers to pre-constitutional conditions concerned the power and independence of each of the thirteen states comprising the union. In the Declaration of Independence, each former colony declared itself essentially an independent nation, and between 1776 and 1789, each state governed itself fully under its own constitution, a status recognized by the Articles of Confederation, which provided that "[e]ach state retains its sovereignty, freedom and independence." Articles of Confederation, art. 2. Although sentiment was widespread by 1789 that the government created by the Articles needed to be replaced by a more centralized one with greater power, it was by no means entirely clear to the delegates just what degree of power and independence the states would be willing to surrender. Consolidating the states into a single, undivided polity was clearly off the table, as was depriving the states of any very considerable degree of authority over their own self-governance. Consequently, the Framers understood clearly that only some form of federalism, in which power was divided between the national and state levels, could possibly survive ratification. The main question, therefore, was how to strike this power balance in a way that would avoid the mistakes of the Articles without precipitating rejection of the document by the states and their political supporters.

>> *The Power to Regulate Federal Elections.* The consequences of this decision for democratic processes and election law were profound. Although the federal distribution of power can create complexities in many areas of law, in no instance is the entanglement of powers more complex than in the field of electoral regulation.

There are more than 500,000 elected officials in the United States. Since only slightly more than 500 of these officials are elected to positions in the federal government, the overwhelming majority of elections are obviously to state and local positions (in fact, nearly all are at the local level), and such elections are regulated almost entirely by state law.

In a federal system of government, there is nothing at all unusual about states regulating their own elections. What is odd about the U.S. system, however, is that the same principle does not govern elections at the federal level. In a system in which the power to regulate national activities is allocated to Congress, it is one of the great oddities of the U.S. Constitution that it allocates much of the power to regulate federal elections to the states.

The Constitution interweaves state and national regulatory power over elections in numerous ways. For example, Article I, §4 provides:

> The Times, Places and Manner of holding Elections for Senators and Representatives, shall be prescribed in each State by the Legislature thereof; but the Congress may at any time by Law make or alter such Regulations, except as to the Place of Chusing Senators.

This provision thus gives *states* in the first instance the express power to regulate *national* elections for Congress, although Congress is granted ultimate power over the subject. Interestingly, at the time of the founding, distrust of the proposed new central government was so strong at the state ratifying conventions that the only controversy surrounding Article I, §4 concerned not whether the states should have power to regulate congressional elections—that was taken for granted—but whether Congress should be given any power whatsoever to overrule state law on the subject. The question, that is, turned on whether the state or national governments could be more fully trusted to regulate congressional elections, with Federalists inclined to trust the central government more than the states, and vice versa for Antifederalists. See 2 THE FOUNDER'S CONSTITUTION 248-280 (Philip B. Kurland & Ralph Lerner, eds., 1987).

Another provision intertwining state and national authority is Article I, §2, cl. 1, which provides:

> The House of Representatives shall be composed of Members chosen every second Year by the People of the several States, and the Electors in each State shall have the Qualifications requisite for Electors of the most numerous Branch of the State Legislature.

Similarly, the Seventeenth Amendment states in part:

> The electors in each State shall have the qualifications requisite for electors of the most numerous branch of the State legislatures.

Thus, the Constitution not only provides that the states would have the initial responsibility for regulating federal elections, but also provides that the states would set voting qualifications for congressional elections. And unlike Article I, §4, which provides for congressional oversight, the only limitation here is that the same voter qualifications apply to both state and federal electors.

Federalism is likewise deeply woven into the constitutional system for electing presidents. Most obviously, the Electoral College system requires that presidential candidates collect electoral support not by winning votes from individuals regardless of their location, but by winning votes on a state-by-state basis. This generally requires successful candidates to have more than a regional appeal; highly concentrated support in some states, however enthusiastic, will not make up for a lack of support in others. See TARA ROSS, ENLIGHTENED DEMOCRACY: THE CASE FOR THE ELECTORAL COLLEGE (2d ed. 2012). Moreover, Article II, §1, cl. 2 provides: "Each State shall appoint, in such Manner as the Legislature thereof may direct, a Number of Electors, equal to the whole Number of Senators and Representatives to which the State may be entitled in the Congress." This provision seems to give states even greater control over national elections for President than they exert over elections for Congress: the manner of selecting electors appears to be committed to the absolute discretion of the state legislature. See McPherson v. Blacker, 146 U.S. 1 (1892). Yet it seems clear that the national government has at least as much of an interest in exercising supervisory oversight in presidential elections as in congressional elections.

>> *The Role of Local Governments.*   Further complicating the distribution of regulatory powers is the universal practice in the states of further re-delegating authority over elections to the local level. Decentralization of power from the state to the local level can serve many of the same functions as federalism serves on the national level. In practice, then, virtually every election, for every office at every level, is run in the first instance by municipal or county governments. These governments are

typically subject to state oversight in most of their activities. In national elections, states and localities may be subject to additional oversight at the national level.

» ***Federal Rights Protection.*** The picture is complicated yet again by the presence in the federal Constitution of individual rights provisions that constrain the authority of states to regulate not just national elections, but state and local elections as well. As we shall see in greater detail in subsequent chapters, the Equal Protection Clause and the First Amendment have frequently been invoked to invalidate state regulation of the electoral process that treats different classes of voters differently, or that restricts the rights of free speech and association in electoral contests. Thus, a not atypical pattern of election regulatory activity involves an initial state delegation of regulatory authority to the local level; an election administered by a local government within parameters established by state law; the possibility of a federal statute, such as the Voting Rights Act or the National Voter Registration Act, operating in the background; the involvement by federal executive officials, such as the Department of Justice; the involvement of state executive officials, such as the state Attorney General, in defending the state's behavior; and federal and state judicial oversight of the application of national and state constitutional principles to elections run by localities. All three levels of government, in other words, can sometimes be involved simultaneously.

» ***Indirect Federal Power.*** Yet another complication concerns the difference between the theoretical and practical reach of national regulatory power. Under Article I, §4, Congress has the final authority to regulate only elections to Congress. Typically, however, states structure their election calendar so that elections to national and state offices occur on the same day—the usual Election Day in November. (In some states, however, *local* elections are sometimes held on a different day, often in March or April.) In these circumstances, if Congress exercises its authority to regulate congressional elections, it will in practice also be regulating the conditions in which state elections take place.

For example, Section 2 of the National Voter Registration Act (NVRA, or "motor voter" law) provides:

> [N]otwithstanding any other Federal or State law, in addition to any other method of voter registration provided for under State law, each State shall establish procedures to register to vote in elections for Federal office—(1) by application made simultaneously with an application for a motor vehicle driver's license. . . .

52 U.S.C. §20503 (1993). Under this section, then, Congress directs states to take steps to allow voters to register to vote at the same time as they apply for a driver's license. What gives Congress the authority to tell states how to register voters for state and local elections? Nothing. Congress has the authority to regulate only elections to Congress. However, since elections at which voters elect Senators and Representatives are also the elections at which they usually elect governors and state legislators, unless a state wishes to bear the burden of administering separate voter registration systems for state and national elections, it will apply the NVRA to registration for all elections, including state and local ones. Thus, as a practical matter, Congress ends up regulating the voter registration processes of states.

At the same time, Congress is extremely dependent upon the states for administering federal elections. The states both regulate and administer federal elections, as there is no federal apparatus or personnel for administering federal elections. There are no federal poll workers, polling places, voter registrants, and the like. Moreover, because of the variation in state election rules and practices, the regulation and administration of federal elections also differ from state to state.

Finally, Congress can make use of another feature of the federal system—its power to bribe states into compliance through exercise of its spending power—to influence the ways in which states regulate the electoral process. For example, in 2002 Congress enacted the Help America Vote Act (HAVA). Enacted in response to problems that arose during the 2000 election, HAVA provides financial incentives to states to modernize their voting apparatus. Section 102(a)(2) of HAVA provides:

> A State shall use the funds provided under a payment under this section . . . to replace punch card voting systems or lever voting systems (as the case may be) in qualifying precincts within that State with a voting system (by purchase, lease, or such other arrangement as may be appropriate) that—(A) does not use punch cards or levers. . . .

52 U.S.C. §20902 (2002). As a consequence of its power to spend, Congress thus manages as a practical matter to regulate the kinds of voting systems states may use, even in state and local elections.

This stew of regulatory authority is without a doubt complex. But is it appropriate? Should regulatory authority over elections be shared by different levels of government? Should such authority be shared *in the same elections*? If authority is shared, who is to be held accountable if things go wrong? We shall return to this question in Chapter 10.

>> *Uniformity or Diversity?*   The federal structure of electoral regulation allows for state-level diversity in the way elections are conducted. That is of course typical of federal regimes, in which states or provinces may have authority to make law in many fields. But the intertwining of national and state authority over national elections means that this diversity extends not just to the way state elections are run, but to the way national elections also are run. For example, there is at present no uniform, centralized mechanism by which candidates for President may run for office nationwide. Instead, candidates for president must qualify for a place on the ballot in all 50 states, one by one, under 50 different ballot access regimes (see Chapter 7). Similarly, the procedures that apply to candidates running for the U.S. Senate or the U.S. House of Representatives may differ considerably in different states.

Some reformers have called for Congress to step in to create greater uniformity in procedures for election to federal office. Would that be desirable? Is there anything to be said for permitting states to regulate and administer federal elections according to their own views of the best governing principles? Might principled views about democratic self-governance differ from state to state? If so, is it appropriate for such differences of opinion to find expression in regulatory regimes? *See* Anthony Johnstone, *The State of the Republican Form of Government in Montana*, 74 Mont. L. Rev. 1 (2013).

Although states generally have yielded readily to exercises of congressional regulatory authority that have the effect of making federal elections more uniform, states do not always go along graciously. Recently, for example, Arizona pushed back hard against federal laws that prohibit states from demanding documentary proof of citizenship as a prerequisite for voter registration for elections at which federal offices are on the ballot. After legal challenges to federal authority failed, Arizona moved to confine the effect of federal rules by establishing separate electoral systems within the state, one for state and local offices and the other for federal offices. The financial cost to the state and the potential confusion to voters are obvious, but those costs were evidently thought to be worth incurring. Is this an example of principled state resistance to ill-advised and overambitious centralization of government authority? Or is it an example of purely partisan resistance at the state level to policies enacted by the party in control of Congress? *See* Jessica Bulman-Pozen, *Partisan Federalism*, 127 HARV. L. REV. 1077 (2014). Or is it an example of a state tilting toward illiberalism and using its authority to undermine liberal principles of democratic election?

C. ILLIBERAL STRANDS OF AMERICAN SOCIAL THOUGHT AND PRACTICE

Harriet Martineau

Society in America (1837)

[Harriet Martineau, an English writer who was one of the founders of modern sociological research methodology, arrived in America in 1834 and spent two full years traveling around the country, observing its people and their ways of life. Martineau found much to admire about the young republic, but also much to criticize.]

What social virtues are possible in a society of which injustice is the primary characteristic? In a society which is divided into two classes, the servile and the imperious? . . . The inherent injustice of the system extinguishes all [virtues], and nourishes a whole harvest of false morals towards the rest of society.

The personal oppression of the negroes is the grossest vice which strikes a stranger in the country. It can never be otherwise when human beings are wholly subjected to the will of other human beings, who are under no other external control than the law which forbids killing and maiming; — a law which it is difficult to enforce in individual cases. . . .

It is a common boast in the south that there is less vice in their cities than in those of the north. This can never, as a matter of fact, have been ascertained; as the proceedings of slave households are, or may be, a secret; and in the north, what licentiousness there is may be detected. But such comparisons are bad. Let any one look at the positive licentiousness of the south, and declare if, in such a state of society, there can be any security for domestic purity and purpose. . . .

A southern lady, of fair reputation for refinement and cultivation, told the following story in the hearing of a company, among whom were some friends of mine. She spoke with obvious unconsciousness that she was saying anything remarkable: indeed such unconsciousness was proved by her telling the story at all. She had possessed a very pretty mulatto girl, of whom she declared herself fond. A young man came to stay at her house, and fell in love with the girl. "She came to me," said the lady, "for protection; which I gave her." The young man went away, but after some weeks, returned, saying he was so much in love with the girl that he could not live without her. "I pitied the young man," concluded the lady; "so I sold the girl to him for 1,500 dollars."

———————————

» *Liberalism and Slavery.* The idea that the United States was born a liberal society would appear to be refuted most directly by the institution of slavery. Nothing seems more contrary to liberal and democratic ideals than the doctrine of black racial inferiority. How can a society whose members, according to the Declaration of Independence, hold it a "self-evident truth" that "all men are created equal" reconcile that belief to the practice of slavery?

According to one view, Southerners dissolved the paradox of slavery in the only way they could: by declaring blacks to be subhuman, and thus excluded from self-governance on account of lacking the kind of "self" needed to participate in the enterprise of collective self-rule. According to historian Carl Degler, this move only shows "how close in values the South was" to the rest of the nation:

> For only if the South had *not* found it necessary to defend slavery on grounds of [the inferiority of the black] race would it have shown itself to have a different value system from the North. The reason the other slave societies of the New World did not find it necessary to arrive at a racial defense of slavery is that they saw no fundamental contradiction between slavery and the social order. In those slave societies slavery was only one of several forms of subordination, albeit a severe one. In the United States, on the other hand, with its historic emphasis on equality and freedom, slavery was an anomaly.

Because slavery conflicted with American liberal ideals and the historical American commitment to popular sovereignty, Degler argued, slavery could be defended in the American context of equality only on the ground that "some persons were not truly men." As a consequence, America became the only slave society in which race became an important ground of defense of slavery. Carl N. Degler, Place Over Time: The Continuity of Southern Distinctiveness 89-90 (1977).

Another, and in many ways more straightforward view, was articulated in the clearest possible way by the prominent abolitionist William Lloyd Garrison, who condemned the Constitution as a "covenant with death" and "an agreement with hell" for permitting the practice of slavery to continue. On this view, slavery and liberalism are simply incommensurable, and the United States was thus built, from its inception, on an unworkable, and certainly unprincipled, compromise between liberalism and illiberalism. The Founders, on this view, made a terrible deal on purely instrumental grounds: to secure their goal of constructing a unified nation of continental scale, they sacrificed their liberal principles.

Is it possible for a compromise of this magnitude to produce a coherent state? What kind of politics can be produced when any collective action will require the agreement of liberal and illiberal social subgroups?

>> *The Three-Fifths Clause.*   The conceptual difficulties posed by American racial subordination are nowhere more obvious than in the opportunistic way in which Southerners of the early republic freely switched grounds for political advantage. One might think that if slaves were not human, they should not be entitled to representation in Congress. Nevertheless, Southerners of the founding era pressed the claim that slave populations should be taken into account for purposes of congressional representation in the House of Representatives, even though they could not vote, were property, and were not political subjects.

As a result of difficult negotiations at the Constitutional Convention of 1787, a compromise position was reached in which slaves would be counted for purposes of apportioning representation in Congress, but only partially. In consequence, Article I, §2, cl. 3 of the original Constitution provided: "Representatives . . . shall be apportioned among the several States which may be included within this Union, according to their respective Numbers, which shall be determined by adding to the whole Number of free Persons . . . three fifths of all other Persons." Under this clause, representation of each state in the House was proportionate to its population, except that slave states were entitled to add to their population totals three-fifths of all slaves, even though those slaves were of course ineligible to vote. This compromise gave the South considerably greater political weight in national decision making than it would have had if representation in Congress had been based exclusively on the number of people entitled to vote for congressional representatives. The Three-Fifths Clause thus had profound ramifications for the course of American politics before the Civil War.

Garry Wills

The Negro President (2003)

What did Thomas Jefferson's Federalist critics mean, after 1800, when they called him the "Negro President"? . . . [T]hose first calling him the Negro President were not prying into his private life. They were challenging his public boast that the election of 1800 was a "second revolution" based on the votes of a popular majority. It was no such thing, they argued. In number of actual votes cast, John Adams was reelected. The second revolution never occurred.

If real votes alone had been counted, Adams would have been returned to office. But, of course, the "vote" did not depend solely on voters. Though Jefferson, admittedly, received eight more votes than Adams in the Electoral College, at least twelve of his votes were not based on the citizenry that could express its will but on the blacks owned by Southern masters. A bargain had been struck at the Constitutional Convention — one of the famous compromises on which the document was formed, this one intended to secure ratification in the South. The negotiated agreement decreed that each slave held in the United States would count as three fifths of a person — the so-called federal ratio — for establishing the representation of a state in the House of Representatives (and consequently in the Electoral College . . .).

It galled the Federalists that Jefferson hailed his 1800 victory as a triumph of democracy and majority rule when, as the newspaper *Mercury and New-England Palladium* of Boston said (January 20, 1801), he had made his "ride into the TEMPLE OF LIBERTY, on the *shoulders of slaves.*" He was president only because of "somber" or "sable" nonvotes, and the *Columbian Centinel* noted (December 24, 1800) that the half-million slaves affecting the outcome had no more will in the matter than "New England horses, cows, and oxen." . . . Senator William Plumer of New Hampshire wrote that "the negro votes made Mr Jefferson president." He felt that "negro Electors exceed those of four states, and their representative are equal to those of six states." . . .

The Federalists predicted that this Negro "representation" would grow year by year so long as the federal ratio were retained. This prospect is what they meant by "the slave power." They did not mean the power that plantation owners exerted over their black slaves, or the power slaves might someday use in retaliation. They meant the power that slave states wielded over non-slave states. The Federalists said that the plantation men were *their* masters. As William Plumer wrote in a public appeal to his New Hampshire constituents:

> Every five of the Negro slaves are accounted equal to three of you. . . .
> Those slaves have no voice in the elections; they are mere property; yet a
> planter possessing a hundred of them may be considered as having sixty
> votes, while one of you who has equal or greater property is confined to a
> single vote.

. . . [T]he power of the South was not measured solely in terms of an overall majority. On crucial matters, when several factions were contending, the federal ratio gave the South in Congress a voting majority. Without the federal ratio as the deciding factor in House votes, slavery would have been excluded from Missouri; [Andrew] Jackson's Indian removal policy [removing Indians from territories they occupied in several states] would have failed; the 1840 gag rule [protecting slavery in the District of Columbia] would not have been imposed; the Wilmot Proviso would have banned slavery in territories won from Mexico; the Kansas-Nebraska bill [outlawing slavery in Nebraska territory and allowing it in Kansas] would have failed. Other votes were close enough to give opposition to the South a better chance, if the federal ratio had not been counted into the calculations from the outset. Elections to key congressional posts were affected continually by the federal ratio, with the result that Southerners held "the Speaker's office for 79 percent of the time [before 1824], Ways and Means for 92 percent."

Leonard Richards shows another pervasive influence of the three-fifths clause. Even when it did not affect the outcome of congressional votes, it dominated Democratic caucus and convention votes, since the South had a larger majority there than in the total body. The federal ratio guaranteed presidential nominations that would be friendly to the slave interest. . . . It gave the South a permanent head start for all its political activities:

> The slave states always had one-third more seats in Congress than their
> free population warranted — forty-seven seats instead of thirty-three in
> 1793, seventy-six instead of fifty-nine in 1812, and ninety-eight instead of
> seventy-three in 1833. The Deep South also imported more slaves from
> Africa in the twenty years from 1788 to 1808 [the year the international
> slave trade was legally banned] than in any other twenty-year period . . .
> the three fifths rules would also play a decisive role in every political cau-
> cus and every political convention.

The federal ratio, and its ripple of side effects, had a great deal to do with the fact
that for over half a century, right up to the Civil War, the management of government was disproportionately controlled by the South:

> In the sixty-two years between Washington's election and the Compro-
> mise of 1850, for example, slaveholders controlled the presidency for
> fifty years, the Speaker's chair for forty-one years, and the chairmanship
> of House Ways and Means [the most important committee] for forty-two
> years. The only men to be reelected president — Washington, Jefferson,
> Madison, Monroe, and Jackson — were all slaveholders. The men who
> sat in the Speaker's chair the longest — Henry Clay, Andrew Stevenson,
> and Nathaniel Macon — were slaveholders. Eighteen out of thirty-one
> Supreme Court justices were slaveholders.

Seven justices delivered the majority opinion in the Dred Scott decision, and a
majority of them were slaveholders. The lower courts, too, were stocked with pro-
slavery men. . . .

Control of the presidency rested on the slave power's deep roots in the
patronage and court systems of the Jeffersonian party. A survey of the highest federal office holders in this time showed that half of them were southerners, though
the North had almost twice the free population of the South. Southerners held
57 percent of the high civil service posts under Adams, 56 percent under Jefferson,
57 percent under Jackson. And this imbalance was not merely a matter of quantity.
It had to do with quality as well, since the South promoted strong, even extreme,
proponents of slavery to office while keeping critics of slavery, even of the mildest
sort, from among the northerners winning confirmation. In many ways, direct and
indirect, this reflected the advantage given by the federal ratio. In 1843, Adams
told the House of Representatives, "Your country is no longer a democracy, it is not
even a republic — it is a government of two or three thousand holders of slaves, to
the utter exclusion of the remaining part." An abolitionist would point out, in the
1850s, that six slave states, taken together, had a free population with 199 fewer
people than Pennsylvania alone — which meant that the people in those states had
twelve senators to the Pennsylvanians' two. . . .

One of the great achievements of the slave power was to use its political clout
to silence opposition. Freehling calls this its blackmail power over the Northern
Democrats who needed the southern part of their coalition. The price of this bargain was that slavery be ignored as an issue in the North. The Democrats there were
able to brand abolitionists as "extremists," as disturbers of sectional harmony, as
enemies of immigrant laborers (who did not want free black competition). It was in
the name of "law and order," ironically, that prominent men encouraged the mobs

that beat or intimidated abolitionists. The result was that, even after the formal gag rules were defeated in Congress, there was a gentleman's agreement not to push the slavery issue in ways that would embarrass the South. In 1858 Lincoln accurately described the general attitude toward slavery:

> You must not say anything about it in the free States, *because it is not here.* You must not say anything about it in the slave States, *because it is there.* You must not say anything about it in the pulpit, because that is religion and has nothing to do with it. You must not say anything about it in politics, *because that will disturb the security of "my place."* There is no place to talk about it as being a wrong, although you say yourself it *is* a wrong. . . .

The national reticence continued long after the Civil War. It skewed the historiography of Reconstruction for decades. In the early twentieth century, it whitewashed the South in popular culture and at sites like Monticello and Mount Vernon. It entertained the absurd notion that the Civil War was not fought over slavery but over tariffs, or states' rights, or federal usurpation. . . .

Slavery may have been the most prominent strand of illiberalism in American political thought and practice, but was it the only one? Consider the account below.

Rogers M. Smith

Civic Ideals 14-17 (1997)

What does it mean to be an American citizen? A widely quoted passage by historian Philip Gleason expresses the leading answer. Historically, to be an American, "a person did not have to be of any particular national, linguistic, religious, or ethnic background. All he had to do was to commit himself to the political ideology centered on the abstract ideals of liberty, equality, and republicanism. Thus the universalist ideological character of American nationality meant that it was open to anyone who willed to become an American." . . . On this view, then, Americans have always officially defined full membership in the American civic community in terms of readiness to embrace egalitarian, liberal, republican political principles. . . . [T]hese political tenets have no specific religious presuppositions and can be shared by people of widely differing faiths. . . .

The standard view captures important truths. But . . . it fails to give due weight to inegalitarian [movements] that have shaped the participants and the substance of American politics throughout history. . . . [F]or at least two-thirds of American history, the majority of the domestic adult population was . . . ineligible for full citizenship [because of race, national origin, or gender]. For these people, citizenship rules gave no weight to how liberal, republican, or faithful to other American values their beliefs might be.

Nor is it true that these exclusions were all present at the outset of the nation as vestiges or prerevolutionary institutions, but then were steadily eliminated.

American civic history has been far more serpentine, and major liberalizing changes have come more rarely and at far higher costs than many celebratory accounts reveal. . . .

[Many nineteenth-century reports by European visitors to the U.S. viewed American society as remarkably egalitarian] because they center on relationships among a minority of Americans – white men, largely of northern European ancestry—analyzed in terms of categories derived from the hierarchy of political and economic status such men held in Europe. . . . [I]t is understandable that from America's inception they thought that the most striking fact about the new nation was the absence of one specific type of fixed, ascriptive hierarchy. There was no hereditary monarchy or nobility native to British America itself, and the Revolution rejected both the authority of the British king and aristocracy and the creation of any new American substitutes. . . .

But the relative egalitarianism that prevailed among white men . . . was surrounded by an array of fixed, ascriptive hierarchies, all largely unchallenged by the leading American revolutionaries. Men thought themselves naturally suited to rule over women, within both the family and the polity. White northern Europeans thought themselves superior, culturally and probably biologically, to Africans, native American Indians, and all other races and civilizations. . . . [M]any British Americans treated religion as an inherited condition and regarded Protestants (or some subset thereof) as created by God to be morally and politically, as well as theologically, superior to Catholics, Jews, Muslims, and others. . . .

D.   THE LONG, SLOW PATH TOWARD DEMOCRATIZATION

If the United States was not born a liberal democracy in the modern or Hartzian senses, did it eventually become one? Did it purge itself of its illiberal inheritances, and if so, when, how, and to what extent?

History suggests that neither liberalism nor democracy arrives in a place suddenly and spreads uniformly, in linear fashion. Rather, liberalism and democracy tend to gain small initial footholds from which they then gain and lose ground repeatedly, often over the course of lengthy, vigorous, and repeated struggles against beneficiaries and defenders of the illiberal regimes they replace. *See, e.g.,* SHERI BERMAN, DEMOCRACY AND DICTATORSHIP IN EUROPE (2019). Full consolidation of liberal democracy thus often takes a very long time. Even in the United States, a place unusually receptive from the beginning to liberal democracy, democratic consolidation occurred in fits and starts over the space of more than a century-and-a-half, and in the view of many, did not arrive fully until enactment of major national civil rights legislation during the 1960s, or even later. In the opinion of one scholar of the American South, for example, "the United States was not a fully democratic polity until preparations were well under way for the celebration of the bicentennial of the Declaration of Independence." ROBERT MICKEY, PATHS OUT OF DIXIE: THE DEMOCRATIZATION OF AUTHORITARIAN ENCLAVES IN AMERICA'S DEEP SOUTH, 1944-1972 (2015), at 32. This makes American liberal democracy—or even, more modestly, America's closest approach to liberal democracy—a recent, and thus fragile phenomenon.

>> *The Decline of Republican Ideology.*   America's march toward democracy began almost immediately after the founding. The founders' republicanism, as we have seen, held ordinary people in low regard. Yet it was not long before republican ideology gave way to a different, more democratic public philosophy. The arc of this development began in earnest with Jacksonian egalitarianism and the concomitant expansion of the franchise, moved through late-nineteenth-century populism, and found what was perhaps its most advanced expression in the Progressive movement of the early twentieth century. All of these movements not only held the common people in much higher regard than did republicanism, but usually deemed them to be smarter and more virtuous than the government officials who served them.

By the first decade of the nineteenth century, Americans, in the words of historian Gordon Wood, "came to believe that no one in a basic down-to-earth and day-in-and-day-out manner was really better than anyone else. . . . Good republicans had to believe in the common sense of the common people." Gordon S. Wood; The Radicalism of the American Revolution, 234-235 (1992). When combined with a well-established American skepticism of government, this belief in intrinsic equality soon led to an idea even further removed from republican concepts of a natural aristocracy: the idea that the people were actually superior to their representatives. Consequently, as political theorist Elaine Spitz observes, "a belief in the general populace as the repository of natural civic virtue became commonplace," Elaine Spitz, Majority Rule 3 (1984), a belief that was put into practice by the rapid expansion of suffrage and, somewhat later, by the introduction in the states of numerous devices of direct democracy.

By the Jacksonian period of the 1820s and '30s, egalitarianism had become the norm of American political discourse. Politicians of this era professed "an appreciation of the common man, and a desire to serve his needs and aspirations." Glyndon G. Van Deusen, The Jacksonian Era, 1828-1848 (1959), at xi. This faith in the common person rested on a belief in the purity of the popular will and on the people's responsiveness to rational argument, qualities that Jacksonians, following Jefferson, often attributed to the independence and self-sufficiency of what they took to be the typical American yeoman. Jacksonians thus claimed that the people were good, trustworthy, and capable of self-rule.

This formulation—a virtuous and competent citizenry whose will had been obstructed either by corrupt individuals or unsuitable governmental structures and institutions—continued to dominate American public political thought through the nineteenth century and on into the twentieth. While populists like William Jennings Bryan proclaimed in Jacksonian fashion their faith in the common people, it was the Progressives who developed a full-blown theory of popular virtue and capacity for self-rule, along with a package of institutional reforms designed to put these beliefs into action by turning over substantial direct political power to the people themselves at the expense of their representatives. At the center of the Progressive democratic ideology lay the conviction that the average contemporary American citizen is fully competent to exercise extremely close oversight and control over the apparatus of government. According to Benjamin Parke De Witt, an early historian of the Progressive movement,

> With the telephone, the telegraph, the railroad, the newspaper, and the magazine, with the spread of education and the increase in the

intelligence of the average voter, there is every reason why the people should exert more and more influence on government rather than less and less. There is every reason why a majority of the people, expressing their opinions in an open, legal way should control the acts of presidents, judges, and legislators rather than that they should allow corporations and banking interests to control them in a secret and illegal way. To make the federal government more democratic by eliminating the impediments to popular rule is not to make it less representative; it is merely to change the persons represented.

BENJAMIN PARKE DE WITT, THE PROGRESSIVE MOVEMENT 143 (1915) (University of Washington Press ed. 1968).

If leading Progressives believed in the intelligence and intrinsic goodness of the average person, they also believed that these qualities imposed upon citizens an obligation to improve society through their active participation in politics. Unlike earlier admirers of the public, who nevertheless often remained suspicious of democracy and feared popular power, Progressives put their beliefs into practice by a carefully coordinated and extremely successful campaign for political reform. Among their widely adopted innovations are such now-familiar mechanisms of direct democracy as the initiative, referendum, direct primary, and recall election. They also sought to tighten popular control over government through extension of the franchise to women, popular election of Senators, improved voter registration systems, corrupt practices acts, and the short ballot. In introducing these innovations, Progressives took a view of the function of representation that could not have been more different from its republican predecessor: far from exercising independence based on their wisdom and virtue, government officials, on the Progressive view, "served as little more than highly intelligent coordinators who responded to all manner of rational public demands, integrated them, and arranged for their fulfillment." ROBERT H. WIEBE, THE SEARCH FOR ORDER 1877-1920 (1967), at 162. Clearly, behind such a conception of politics lies an extremely robust conception of popular competence, wisdom, and virtue.

>> *The Institutional Evolution of Presidential Elections.* Despite the Framers' attempt to limit the people's role in the structure of American government, the nation from the start displayed a distinct tendency to drift toward ever more democratic practices. The Electoral College, described so proudly by Hamilton, never worked the way the Framers intended; from the outset, electors campaigned for office by pledging to cast their electoral votes for particular individuals. Thus, electors were chosen not on the basis of their wisdom and political judgment, but on the basis of their fidelity to a particular presidential candidate. A custom soon developed binding electors to cast their electoral votes for the presidential candidate whom they had pledged to support. This custom has been formalized by changes in state balloting procedures: rather than cast votes directly for presidential electors pledged to particular candidates, voters now mark their ballots for the presidential candidate they prefer. The state then uses this vote to select a slate of

presidential electors. Since the vast majority of voters do not even know the identity of the individuals whom the state will select as electors (and many may not even realize that they are voting indirectly for electors rather than directly for presidential candidates), the moral and political obligation of electors to abide by the popular vote is greatly strengthened.

In theory, however, electors have always been free to vote for whomever they choose despite their pledges to the voters. Nothing in the language of the Twelfth Amendment binds presidential electors to vote for any particular candidate, yet the Framers seemed to intend that electors exercise independent judgment. On a few occasions, presidential electors have cast votes for candidates other than those whom they pledged to support. For example, in 1820, a Democratic-Republican elector voted for John Quincy Adams instead of James Monroe, his party's nominee. In 1968, a North Carolina elector pledged to Richard Nixon voted for George Wallace. In 1976, a Washington elector pledged to Gerald Ford voted for Ronald Reagan. Elector defections reached a record high in the 2016 election, when seven electors cast votes for candidates other than their party's nominee. Two electors pledged to Donald Trump, the Republican nominee, voted for other Republican candidates. Five electors pledged to Hilary Clinton, the Democratic nominee, voted for other candidates; three crossed party lines to vote for Colin Powell, a retired army general and former Secretary of State, and a Republican.

>>   *Ray v. Blair.*   The Supreme Court had occasion to consider the question of elector defection in connection with the 1948 presidential election when electors from Alabama refused to vote for the Democratic candidate for President. In May 1948, Alabama held its Democratic presidential primary election. The state's Democrats selected a slate of unpledged delegates who at the national convention voted for Georgia Senator Richard B. Russell. The convention, however, nominated the incumbent, Harry Truman. The Alabama delegates, disturbed by Truman's civil rights positions, reconvened in Birmingham and, in defiance of the Democratic Party establishment, nominated their own "Dixiecrat" candidate, Governor J. Strom Thurmond of South Carolina. The Alabama members of the Electoral College then voted for Thurmond following the general election, depriving Truman of the state's electoral votes.

The Democratic-controlled state legislature reacted to this defection by enacting a law that required any candidate for presidential elector at a primary election to sign the following pledge: "By casting this ballot I do pledge myself to abide by the result of this primary election and to aid and support all the nominees thereof in the ensuing general election."

As the 1952 presidential primary election approached, Edmund Blair filed as a candidate for presidential elector, but refused to sign the pledge. As a result, the State Democratic Party refused to certify him as a candidate for presidential elector at the Democratic presidential primary. Blair filed suit seeking a court order directing the State Democratic Party to certify him as an elector. He argued that the pledge violated the Twelfth Amendment to the United States Constitution by restricting the freedom of presidential electors. The Supreme Court rejected this contention in *Ray v. Blair*, 343 U.S. 214 (1952):

It is true that the Amendment says the electors shall vote by ballot. But it is also true that the Amendment does not prohibit an elector's announcing his choice beforehand, pledging himself. The suggestion that in the early elections candidates for electors—contemporaries of the Founders—would have hesitated, because of constitutional limitations, to pledge themselves to support party nominees in the event of their selection as electors is impossible to accept. History teaches that the electors were expected to support the party nominees. . . . Indeed, more than twenty states do not print the names of the candidates for electors on the general election ballot. Instead, in one form or another, they allow a vote for the presidential candidate of the national conventions to be counted as a vote for his party's nominees for the electoral college. This long-continued practical interpretation of the constitutional propriety of an implied or oral pledge of his ballot by a candidate for elector as to his vote in the electoral college weighs heavily in considering the constitutionality of a pledge, such as the one here required, in the primary.

[Moreover, a] candidacy in the primary is a voluntary act of the applicant. He is not barred, discriminatorily, from participating but must comply with the rules of the party. Surely one may voluntarily assume obligations to vote for a certain candidate.

In dissent, Justice Jackson argued that a lengthy customary practice cannot trump the freedom that the constitutional text confers on presidential electors:

No one faithful to our history can deny that the plan originally contemplated, what is implicit in its text, that electors would be free agents, to exercise an independent and nonpartisan judgment as to the men best qualified for the Nation's highest offices. . . . Certainly under that plan no state law could control the elector in performance of his federal duty, any more than it could a United States Senator who also is chosen by, and represents, the State.

This arrangement miscarried. Electors, although often personally eminent, independent, and respectable, officially become voluntary party lackeys and intellectual nonentities. . . . As an institution the Electoral College suffered atrophy almost indistinguishable from *rigor mortis*.

However, in 1948, Alabama's Democratic Party Electors refused to vote for the nominee of the Democratic National Convention. To put an end to such party unreliability the party organization . . . closed the official primary to any candidate for elector unless he would pledge himself, under oath, to support any candidate named by the Democratic National Convention. . . . In effect, before one can become an elector for Alabama, its law requires that he must pawn his ballot to a candidate not yet named, by a convention not yet held, of delegates not yet chosen. Even if the nominee repudiates the platform adopted by the same convention, as Democratic nominees have twice done in my lifetime (1904, 1928), the elector is bound to vote for him. It will be seen that the State has sought to achieve control of the electors' ballots. But the balloting cannot be constitutionally subjected to any such control because it was intended to be free, an act performed after all functions of the electoral process left to the States have been completed. . . .

It may be admitted that this law does no more than to make a legal obligation of what has been a voluntary general practice. If custom were sufficient authority for amendment of the Constitution by Court decree, the decision in this matter would be warranted. Usage may sometimes impart changed content to constitutional generalities, such as "due process of law," "equal protection," or "commerce among the states." But I do not think powers or discretions granted to federal officials by the Federal Constitution can be forfeited by the Court for disuse. A political practice which has its origin in custom must rely upon custom for its sanctions.

>> *State Enforcement of Elector Pledges.*   But even if, following *Blair*, the state may require presidential electors to take a pledge to support the winning nominee, can it actually enforce the pledge, and if so, by what means? Fifteen states have created enforcement schemes that sanction electors who violate their pledges. In most cases, the elector is subject to removal; in some states, the elector must pay a monetary fine. Recently, the Supreme Court considered the case of three presidential electors from Washington State who violated their pledges in 2016 by casting Electoral College votes for Colin Powell rather than for Hillary Clinton, who had won Washington's general election for president. The state fined them $1,000 each. They sued, claiming that they were entitled under Article II and the Twelfth Amendment to use their unfettered discretion in deciding how to cast their votes in the Electoral College. Consistent with its ruling in *Ray v. Blair*, the Court upheld the fines:

Article II, §1's appointments power gives the States far-reaching authority over presidential electors, absent some other constitutional constraint. . . . [E]ach State may appoint electors "in such Manner as the Legislature thereof may direct." Art. II, §1, cl. 2. . . . And the power to appoint an elector (in any manner) includes power to condition his appointment — that is, to say what the elector must do for the appointment to take effect. A State can require, for example, that an elector live in the State or qualify as a regular voter during the relevant time period. Or more substantively, a State can insist (as *Ray* allowed) that the elector pledge to cast his Electoral College ballot for his party's presidential nominee, thus tracking the State's popular vote. Or — so long as nothing else in the Constitution poses an obstacle — a State can add, as Washington did, an associated condition of appointment: It can demand that the elector actually live up to his pledge, on pain of penalty. Which is to say that the State's appointment power, barring some outside constraint, enables the enforcement of a pledge like Washington's.

And nothing in the Constitution expressly prohibits States from taking away presidential electors' voting discretion as Washington does. The Constitution is barebones about electors. Article II includes only the instruction to each State to appoint, in whatever way it likes, as many electors as it has Senators and Representatives (except that the State may not appoint members of the Federal Government). The Twelfth Amendment then tells electors to meet in their States, to vote for President and Vice

President separately, and to transmit lists of all their votes to the President of the United States Senate for counting. Appointments and procedures and . . . that is all.

The Framers could have done it differently; other constitutional drafters of their time did. In the founding era, two States—Maryland and Kentucky—used electoral bodies selected by voters to choose state senators (and in Kentucky's case, the Governor too). The Constitutions of both States, Maryland's drafted just before and Kentucky's just after the U. S. Constitution, incorporated language that would have made this case look quite different. Both state Constitutions required all electors to take an oath "to elect without favour, affection, partiality, or prejudice, such persons for Senators, as they, in their judgment and conscience, believe best qualified for the office." Md. Declaration of Rights, Art. XVIII (1776); see Ky. Const., Art. I, §14 (1792) (using identical language except adding "[and] for Governor"). The emphasis on independent "judgment and conscience" called for the exercise of elector discretion. But although the Framers knew of Maryland's Constitution, no language of that kind made it into the document they drafted. . . .

The Electors and their amici object that the Framers . . . expected the Electors' votes to reflect their own judgments. Hamilton praised the Constitution for entrusting the Presidency to "men most capable of analyzing the qualities" needed for the office, who would make their choices "under circumstances favorable to deliberation." The Federalist No. 68, p. 410 (C. Rossiter ed. 1961). So too, John Jay predicted that the Electoral College would "be composed of the most enlightened and respectable citizens," whose choices would reflect "discretion and discernment." Id., No. 64, at 389.

But even assuming other Framers shared that outlook, it would not be enough. Whether by choice or accident, the Framers did not reduce their thoughts about electors' discretion to the printed page. . . . "Long settled and established practice" may have "great weight in a proper interpretation of constitutional provisions." The Pocket Veto Case, 279 U.S. 655, 689 (1929). As James Madison wrote, "a regular course of practice" can "liquidate & settle the meaning of " disputed or indeterminate "terms & phrases." Letter to S. Roane (Sept. 2, 1819), in 8 Writings of James Madison 450 (G. Hunt ed. 1908); see The Federalist No. 37, at 225. The Electors make an appeal to that kind of practice in asserting their right to independence. But "our whole experience as a Nation" points in the opposite direction. Electors have only rarely exercised discretion in casting their ballots for President. From the first, States sent them to the Electoral College—as today Washington does—to vote for pre-selected candidates, rather than to use their own judgment. And electors (or at any rate, almost all of them) rapidly settled into that non-discretionary role. See Ray, 343 U. S., at 228–229. . . . Washington's law, penalizing a pledge's breach, . . . reflects a tradition more than two centuries old. In that practice, electors are not free agents; they are to vote for the candidate whom the State's voters have chosen. The history going the opposite way is one of anomalies only. . . .

Chiafalo v. Washington, 591 U.S. ___ (2020). What do you make of a decision by an avowedly originalist court holding that longstanding constitutional practice can override the intentions of the framers and ratifiers for purposes of determining constitutional meaning?

>> *The National Popular Vote Plan.* Complaints about the Electoral College began almost as soon as contested elections themselves began, after George Washington announced he would retire after his second term. In earlier times, the Electoral College was criticized mainly because of the possibility that no candidate would earn a majority of electoral votes, throwing the election into the House and thereby subverting the intended operation of the system. In more recent times, the Electoral College has been criticized for its antidemocratic structure, under which a candidate can win the presidency in the College without earning a majority of the popular vote—as has happened in several elections, most recently in 2016. Ironically, of course, the *independence* of the Electoral College from mass, popular opinion was the very characteristic that appealed to the Framers. And, as we have seen, the Electoral College never worked the way the Framers intended, as an independent, deliberative body of wise and virtuous citizens.

A new, clever plan that is making the rounds of state legislatures now raises the prospect of in effect doing away with the Electoral College entirely by replacing it with a plebiscitary presidential election, and without a constitutional amendment. Under the so-called National Popular Vote Plan (NPV), state legislatures would commit themselves to pledge their electoral votes to the candidate who polls a majority of the nationwide popular vote for President. These pledges would become operative only when enough states to make a majority in the Electoral College have signed onto the plan. If the plan were to go into effect, the candidate winning the popular vote would be guaranteed to win the presidency because states with a majority of electoral votes would commit those votes unanimously to the winner of the popular vote tally.

This arrangement is said to have many benefits. First and most obviously, it would make the presidency turn on the outcome of the popular vote rather than the electoral vote. Second, it would eliminate perverse campaigning incentives created by the odd structure of the College. At the moment, candidates have little incentive to campaign in states that reliably support one party or the other. This has led to a drastic shrinkage in the number of "battleground" states that are genuinely in play, from 24 states, accounting for 327 electoral votes, in 1960, to only 13 states, accounting for 159 electoral votes, in 2004. Voters in "safe" states that are not seriously in play are unlikely either to be exposed to presidential campaigning, or to see issues of concern to them be placed on the presidential campaign agenda.

Legislation to effectuate the NPV plan has at this writing been enacted in 15 states and the District of Columbia, accounting for 195 (72 percent) of the 270 electoral votes needed to win the presidency. Similar legislation has been introduced in at least ten other states. *See* www.nationalpopularvote.com.

Meanwhile, opponents of NPV have argued that it may be unconstitutional under the U.S. Constitution's Compact Clause, Art. I, §10, cl. 3 ("No state shall, without the Consent of the Congress, enter into any Agreement or Compact with another state"). *See, e.g.,* Derek T. Muller, *The Compact Clause and the National Popular Vote Interstate Compact,* 6 ELECTION L.J. 372 (2007). For a more wide-ranging critique, see Norman R. Williams, *Reforming the Electoral College: Federalism, Majoritarianism, and the Perils of Subconstitutional Change,* 100 GEO. L.J. 173 (2011).

>> *The Transformation of the Senate.*   Like the presidency, strong currents of increasingly democratic public opinion have transformed the way in which U.S. senators are selected. Unlike the institutional evolution of presidential elections, however, change to the method of senatorial selection has been formal and complete.

Under the original Constitution, each state's senators were selected by its legislature. Art. I, §3. Democratic pressures, however, soon undermined the system contemplated by the Framers and replaced it with one that, though still republican in form, was popular in substance and operation. Here, the vehicle was the "advisory" party primary election, first used as early as the 1860s. In these races, candidates hoping for legislative appointment to a Senate seat competed for votes in primary elections held by their political parties. Although the results were advisory in the sense that state legislators were not bound by the results, in actual practice "the legislators, as a rule, were guided by the results. Otherwise, they incurred the risk of losing the party's backing for [their own] reelection" to the state legislature. C.H. HOEBEKE, THE ROAD TO MASS DEMOCRACY: ORIGINAL INTENT AND THE SEVENTEENTH AMENDMENT 88 (1995).

Eventually, reformers were able to argue persuasively for a constitutional amendment providing for direct, popular election of senators on the ground that such a system already existed. and such an amendment would do little more than ratify an institutional change that had already occurred in practice. The Seventeenth Amendment, providing for popular election of senators, was ratified in 1913.

>> *The Fall of Slavery and Its Aftermath.*   Following the Civil War, the fate of African Americans was addressed in three separate amendments to the U.S. Constitution. The Thirteenth Amendment, ratified in 1865, dealt with the most immediate problem by prohibiting slavery outright. Having accomplished this goal, however, Congress was left to consider much more complex questions concerning the integration of the newly freed slaves into American life. Some of these questions were addressed by the Fourteenth Amendment, ratified in 1868, which made the freed slaves citizens of the states in which they resided; protected their privileges and immunities as American citizens from infringement by the states; and guaranteed them equal protection of the laws:

> Section 1. All persons born or naturalized in the United States, and subject to the jurisdiction thereof, are citizens of the United States and of the State wherein they reside. No State shall make or enforce any law which shall abridge the privileges or immunities of citizens of the United States; nor shall any State deprive any person of life, liberty, or property, without due process of law; nor deny to any person within its jurisdiction the equal protection of the laws.

After ratification of the Fourteenth Amendment, some members of Congress believed that they had adequately addressed the problem of guaranteeing the political rights of African Americans. Experience soon showed this view to be unjustified, resulting in the ratification of the Fifteenth Amendment in 1870:

> Section 1. The right of citizens of the United States to vote shall not be denied or abridged by the United States or by any State on account of race, color, or previous condition of servitude —
> Section 2. The Congress shall have power to enforce this article by appropriate legislation.

How effective were the Reconstruction Amendments in protecting the political rights of black Americans? Consider the following materials.

Guinn v. United States

238 U.S. 347 (1915)

Mr. Chief Justice WHITE delivered the opinion of the court:
This case . . . arose from an indictment and conviction of certain election officers of the state of Oklahoma (the plaintiffs in error) of the crime of having conspired unlawfully, wilfully, and fraudulently to deprive certain negro citizens, on account of their race and color, of a right to vote at a general election held in that state in 1910, they being entitled to vote under the state law, and which right was secured to them by the 15th Amendment to the Constitution of the United States. . . .
Suffrage in Oklahoma was regulated by §4a, article 3, of the Constitution under which the state was admitted into the Union. Shortly after the admission there was submitted an amendment to the Constitution making a radical change in that article, which was adopted prior to November 8, 1910. At an election for members of Congress which followed the adoption of this amendment, certain election officers, in enforcing its provisions, refused to allow certain negro citizens to vote who were clearly entitled to vote under the provision of the Constitution under which the state was admitted; that is, before the amendment; and who, it is equally clear, were not entitled to vote under the provision of the suffrage amendment if that amendment governed. The persons so excluded based their claim of right to vote upon the original Constitution and upon the assertion that the suffrage amendment was void because in conflict with the prohibitions of the 15th Amendment, and therefore afforded no basis for denying them the right guaranteed and protected by that Amendment. And upon the assumption that this claim was justified and that the election officers had violated the 15th Amendment in denying the right to vote, this prosecution, as we have said, was commenced. . . .
The original clause, so far as material, was this:

> The qualified electors of the state shall be male citizens of the United States, male citizens of the state, and male persons of Indian descent native of the United States, who are over the age of twenty-one years, who have resided in the state one year, in the county six months, and in the election precinct thirty days, next preceding the election at which any such elector offers to vote.

And this is the amendment:

No person shall be registered as an elector of this state or be allowed to vote in any election held herein, unless he be able to read and write any section of the Constitution of the state of Oklahoma; but no person who was, on January 1st, 1866, or any time prior thereto, entitled to vote under any form of government, or who at that time resided in some foreign nation, and no lineal descendant of such person, shall be denied the right to register and vote because of his inability to so read and write sections of such Constitution. . . .

The United States insists that the provision of the amendment which fixes a standard based upon January 1, 1866, is repugnant to the prohibitions of the 15th Amendment because in substance and effect that provision, if not an express, is certainly an open, repudiation of the 15th Amendment, and hence the provision in question was stricken with nullity in its inception by the self-operative force of the Amendment, and, as the result of the same power, was at all subsequent times devoid of any vitality whatever.

For the plaintiffs in error, on the other hand, it is said . . . the standard fixed does not in terms make any discrimination on account of race, color, or previous condition of servitude, since all, whether negro or white, who come within its requirements, enjoy the privilege of voting, there is no ground upon which to rest the contention that the provision violates the 15th Amendment. . . . No question is raised by the government concerning the validity of the literacy test provided for in the amendment under consideration as an independent standard since the conclusion is plain that that test rests on the exercise of state judgment, and therefore cannot be here assailed either by disregarding the state's power to judge on the subject, or by testing its motive in enacting the provision. The real question involved, so the argument of the government insists, is the repugnancy of the standard which the amendment makes, based upon the conditions existing on January 1st, 1866, because on its face and inherently considering the substance of things, that standard is a mere denial of the restrictions imposed by the prohibitions of the 15th Amendment, and by necessary result re-creates and perpetuates the very conditions which the Amendment was intended to destroy. . . .

The operation and effect of the 15th Amendment. This is its text:

Section 1. The right of citizens of the United States to vote shall not be denied or abridged by the United States or by any state on account of race, color, or previous condition of servitude.

Section 2. The Congress shall have power to enforce this article by appropriate legislation.

. . . While in the true sense . . . the Amendment gives no right of suffrage, it was long ago recognized that in operation its prohibition might measurably have that effect; that is to say, that as the command of the Amendment was self-executing and reached without legislative action the conditions of discrimination against which it was aimed, the result might arise that, as a consequence of the striking down of a discrimination clause, a right of suffrage would be enjoyed by reason of the generic character of the provision which would remain after the discrimination was stricken out. *Ex parte Yarbrough*, 110 U.S. 651 (1884); *Neal v. Delaware*, 103 U.S. 370 (1880). A familiar illustration of this doctrine resulted from the effect of the adoption of the Amendment on state Constitutions in which, at the time of the adoption of the Amendment, the right of suffrage was conferred on all white male citizens, since by the inherent power of the Amendment the word "white" disappeared and therefore all male citizens, without discrimination on account of race, color, or previous condition of servitude, came under the generic grant of suffrage made by the state.

With these principles before us how can there be room for any serious dispute concerning the repugnancy of the standard based upon January 1, 1866 (a date which preceded the adoption of the 15th Amendment), if the suffrage provision fixing that standard is susceptible of the significance which the government attributes to it? Indeed, there seems no escape from the conclusion that to hold that there was even possibility for dispute on the subject would be but to declare that the 15th Amendment not only had not the self-executing power which it has been recognized to have from the beginning, but that its provisions were wholly inoperative because susceptible of being rendered inapplicable by mere forms of expression embodying no exercise of judgment and resting upon no discernible reason other than the purpose to disregard the prohibitions of the Amendment by creating a standard of voting which, on its face, was in substance but a revitalization of conditions which, when they prevailed in the past, had been destroyed by the self-operative force of the Amendment. . . .

Lane v. Wilson

307 U.S. 268 (1939)

Mr. Justice FRANKFURTER delivered the opinion of the Court.

The case is here on certiorari to review the judgment of the Circuit Court of Appeals for the Tenth Circuit affirming that of the United States District Court for the Eastern District of Oklahoma, entered upon a directed verdict in favor of the defendants. The action was one for $5,000 damages brought under Section 1979 of the Revised Statutes, 8 U.S.C. §43, by a colored citizen claiming discriminatory treatment resulting from electoral legislation of Oklahoma, in violation of the Fifteenth Amendment. . . .

The constitution under which Oklahoma was admitted into the Union regulated the suffrage by Article III, Okl. St. Ann., whereby its "qualified electors" were to be "citizens of the State who are over the age of twenty-one years" with disqualifications in the case of felons, paupers and lunatics. Section 1. Soon after its admission the suffrage provisions of the Oklahoma Constitution were radically amended by the addition of a literacy test from which white voters were in effect relieved through the operation of a "grandfather clause." Okl. St. Ann. Const. art. 3, §4a. The clause was stricken down by this Court as violative of the prohibition against discrimination "on account of race, color, or previous condition of servitude" of the Fifteenth Amendment. This outlawry occurred on June 21, 1915. In the meantime the Oklahoma general election of 1914 had been based on the offending "grandfather clause." After the invalidation of that clause a special session of the Oklahoma legislature enacted a new scheme for registration as a prerequisite to voting.

Oklahoma Laws of 1916, Act of February 26, 1916, c. 24. Section 4 of this statute (now Section 5654, Oklahoma Statutes 1931, 26 Okl. St. Ann. §74) was obviously directed towards the consequences of the decision in *Guinn v. United States, supra.* Those who had voted in the general election of 1914, automatically remained qualified voters. The new registration requirements affected only others. These had to apply for registration between April 30, 1916 and May 11, 1916, if qualified at that time, with an extension to June 30, 1916, given only to those "absent from the county during such period of time, or prevented by sickness or unavoidable misfortune from registering within such time." The crux of the present controversy is the validity of this registration scheme, with its dividing line between white citizens who had voted under the "grandfather clause" immunity prior to *Guinn v. United States, supra,* and citizens who were outside it, and the not more than 12 days as the normal period of registration for the theretofore proscribed class. . . .

The petitioner, a colored citizen of Oklahoma, who was the plaintiff below and will hereafter be referred to as such, sued three county election officials for declining to register him on October 17, 1934. He was qualified for registration in 1916 but did not then get on the registration list. The evidence is in conflict whether he presented himself in that year for registration and, if so, under what circumstances registration was denied him. The fact is that plaintiff did not get on the register in 1916. Under the terms of the statute he thereby permanently lost the right to register and hence the right to vote. The central claim of plaintiff is that of the unconstitutionality of Section 5654. . . .

The reach of the Fifteenth Amendment against contrivances by a state to thwart equality in the enjoyment of the right to vote by citizens of the United States regardless of race or color, has been amply expounded by prior decisions. *Guinn v. United States,* 238 U.S. 347 (1915); *Myers v. Anderson,* 238 U.S. 368 (1915). It hits onerous procedural requirements which effectively handicap exercise of the franchise by the colored race although the abstract right to vote may remain unrestricted as to race. When in *Guinn v. United States, supra,* the Oklahoma "grandfather clause" was found violative of the Fifteenth Amendment, Oklahoma was confronted with the serious task of devising a new registration system consonant with her own political ideas but also consistent with the Federal Constitution. We are compelled to conclude, however reluctantly, that the legislation of 1916 partakes too much of the infirmity of the "grandfather clause" to be able to survive.

Section 5652 of the Oklahoma statutes makes registration a prerequisite to voting. By Sections 5654 and 5659 all citizens who were qualified to vote in 1916 but had not voted in 1914 were required to register, save in the exceptional circumstances, between April 30 and May 11, 1916, and in default of such registration were perpetually disenfranchised. Exemption from this onerous provision was enjoyed by all who had registered in 1914. But this registration was held under the statute which was condemned in the *Guinn* case. Unfair discrimination was thus retained by automatically granting voting privileges for life to the white citizens whom the constitutional "grandfather clause" had sheltered while subjecting colored citizens to a new burden. The practical effect of the 1916 legislation was to accord to the members of the negro race who had been discriminated against in the outlawed registration system of 1914, not more than 12 days within which to reassert constitutional rights which this Court found in the *Guinn* case to have been

improperly taken from them. We believe that the opportunity thus given negro
voters to free themselves from the effects of discrimination to which they should
never have been subjected was too cabined and confined. The restrictions imposed
must be judged with reference to those for whom they were designed. It must be
remembered that we are dealing with a body of citizens lacking the habits and traditions of political independence and otherwise living in circumstances which do
not encourage initiative and enterprise. To be sure, in exceptional cases a supplemental period was available. But the narrow basis of the supplemental registration,
the very brief normal period of relief for the persons and purposes in question, the
practical difficulties, of which the record in this case gives glimpses, inevitable in
the administration of such strict registration provisions, leave no escape from the
conclusion that the means chosen as substitutes for the invalidated "grandfather
clause" were themselves invalid under the Fifteenth Amendment. They operated
unfairly against the very class on whose behalf the protection of the Constitution
was here successfully invoked. . . .

   Reversed and remanded.

———————

   Between 1890 and 1902, South Carolina, Louisiana, Alabama, Mississippi,
and Virginia held constitutional conventions, the express purpose of which
was to preserve white political power by evading the direct command of the Fifteenth Amendment. As one delegate to the 1901 Virginia convention forthrightly
explained: "Discrimination! Why that is precisely what we propose; that, exactly,
is what this convention was elected for." VIRGINIA CONSTITUTIONAL CONVENTION,
PROCEEDINGS 3076-3077 (1901–1902). Among the mechanisms employed by these
conventions to impede or eliminate voting by blacks were grandfather clauses, literacy tests, poll taxes, property qualifications, and mandatory purges of voter registration rolls.

   Not coincidentally, whites from the lower economic classes, who were often
poor and illiterate, were frequently barred from voting by the constitutional restrictions enacted at the disenfranchising conventions. The evidence suggests that many
Southern Democrats were grateful for the occasion to use the disenfranchisement
of blacks as cover for simultaneously disenfranchising the natural political base of
populist and agrarian movements that might have threatened one-party Democratic dominance in the Southern states. So great was the impact of the disenfranchising conventions that in Virginia, "the active electorate was so small that from
1905 to 1948 state employees and office-holders cast approximately one-third of
the votes in state elections." J. MORGAN KOUSSER, THE SHAPING OF SOUTHERN POLI-
TICS: SUFFRAGE RESTRICTION AND THE ESTABLISHMENT OF THE ONE-PARTY SOUTH,
1880-1910 (1974), at 181.

>>   *The South as an "Authoritarian Enclave"?*   Recent scholarship informed by
comparative study of democracy around the world has begun to suggest a different and in some ways even darker understanding of the American South during
the antebellum and Jim Crow eras. This analysis begins with the observation that
the transition from authoritarianism to democracy often does not occur at a uniform pace, and that it is common for democratizing states to contain lingering

enclaves of authoritarian rule long after much or most of the country has become democratic. On this account, the South was "a regional bloc of authoritarian states that was firmly integrated into the structure of national political life. The political regimes of these states were unambiguously undemocratic by any definition of the concept. Political competition was severely restricted, and so was voting." EDWARD L. GIBSON, BOUNDARY CONTROL: SUBNATIONAL AUTHORITARIANISM IN FEDERAL DEMOCRACIES 35 (2012).

The Civil War constituted a massive national intervention to promote local democratization. It was followed by a second phase in which Southern politicians for nearly a century successfully sealed off their enclave from further national interference not by imposing isolation, but by participating with great effectiveness in the national political system. This tactic allowed Southern leaders to maintain local authoritarian rule without fear of national intervention. In short, Southern rulers created "institutions to demobilize white electorates, extrude blacks from electoral politics, and forestall workers' challenges to state institutions and policies. Enclave rulers carefully protected their polity's conditional autonomy and skillfully deployed federal officeholders to block potential interference, especially concerning voting rights and state-sponsored violence." ROBERT MICKEY, PATHS OUT OF DIXIE: THE DEMOCRATIZATION OF AUTHORITARIAN ENCLAVES IN AMERICA'S DEEP SOUTH, 1944-1972 (2015), at 34. On this view, democracy was not consolidated in the U.S. until late in the twentieth century. But was it consolidated even then? When is democracy "fully consolidated" to the point where there is no turning back? Is such a condition even possible?

>> *Disenfranchisement and the Civil Rights Movement.* The following excerpt is from a Pulitzer Prize–winning history of the civil rights movement. It describes some early efforts, undertaken in 1961, to encourage blacks to register to vote (not vote — *register* to vote) in Mississippi. These efforts were initiated by Bob Moses, a leader of the Student Non-Violent Coordinating Committee (SNCC), a civil rights organization founded by black college students and dedicated to the nonviolent principles by which Gandhi and his followers successfully resisted British rule in India. SNCC members challenged segregation through sit-ins, protests, freedom rides and, by 1961, voter registration programs.

Unlike the freedom rides and lunch counter sit-ins, which embarrassed the newly installed Kennedy administration, the voter registration program had the full backing of the U.S. Department of Justice, which had legal authority to enforce the Fifteenth Amendment and several pertinent enforcement statutes.

Taylor Branch

Parting the Waters: America in the King Years, 1954–63 (1988)

C.C. Bryant was a practical, plainspoken leader [of the black community in McComb, Mississippi]. . . . [H]e was a railroad man who drew his paycheck from the faraway mecca of Chicago, which guaranteed him a measure of freedom from the local white economy of McComb. Although Bryant worked as a laborer, operating a loading crane for the Illinois Central, his independent stature rose above the teachers and preachers and the few other local Negroes* from the traditional leadership positions. He was a deacon, a Sunday school teacher, a Boy Scout leader, and president of the Pike County NAACP chapter. He was also a high official of the Freemasons, and in this capacity he gained permission for Bob Moses to use the second floor of the all-Negro Masonic Temple as a voter registration school. The first floor was rented out to a butcher.

Moses knocked on doors through the blistering August days, telling all those who would listen that he was C.C. Bryant's voter registration man. His studies at Amzie Moore's house already had made him an expert in Mississippi's arcane registration laws, which, among other tests, required applicants to interpret a section of the state constitution to the satisfaction of the county registrar. This obstacle alone put voting out in the wild yonder of dreams among Mississippi Negroes, and Moses counted it as an initial victory if he could get someone in a McComb household even to imagine being inside the registrar's office in the county courthouse, where few Negroes dared to venture. Behind that psychological barrier lay fears of being branded a renegade, plus piercing doubts of literacy, self-worth, and entitlement. Moses addressed all these each night in his class at the Masonic Temple. Voter registration, as Amzie Moore and C.C. Bryant had perceived, was a full-time job.

Hollis Watkins, a teenager from the tiny hamlet of Summit, Mississippi, poked his head into Moses' office one day and said he'd heard a rumor that Martin Luther King was in town working on some big mysterious project—was he Martin Luther King? Moses, sensing that there was a hard kernel of grit behind Watkins' youthful naivete, said he didn't know anything about Martin Luther King coming to McComb but that there was a new class in town to teach Negroes how to vote so they could become first-class citizens. Watkins was interested. He had "plans" to go to college but no money or job. Living with his parents, staving off the inevitable plunge into adult worries, he had plenty of time. Very shortly he and a similarly situated teenager named Curtis Hayes became the project's first two volunteers. They distributed leaflets advertising the registration classes.

Luckily for Moses, a few of those attending his first classes on August 7 were people who had been promising Bryant that they would try to register. Four of them pronounced themselves willing after the first night's class. Moses accompanied them to the county courthouse in the nearby town of Magnolia the next day, and three of the four were registered. Three people came forward after the second night's class, of whom two were accepted by the registrar the next day. Their success and another night's class produced nine more volunteers on the third day. By then the registrar was alerted to the possibility that this surge of Negro traffic through his office was not incidental, and he approved only one of the nine applicants.

Pike County's racial barometer was sensitive enough that the appearance of sixteen Negroes in the courthouse on three successive days was a development

---

* "[T]he word 'Negro' is employed here in narrative covering the years when that term prevailed in common usage. Far from intending a political statement, I merely hope to recreate the feeling of the times, the better to capture the sweep of many changes including the extraordinary one in which the entire society shifted from 'Negro' to 'black' almost overnight." [From the author's preface, at xii.]

worthy of a story in the McComb *Enterprise-Journal*. While warning local segregationists, the news generated excitement among the Negroes scattered through the
depressed farm-and-timber country of southern Mississippi. Within days, farmers
from the surrounding countryside made their way into McComb and up to Moses'
corner of the Masonic Temple. After listening to his talks on nonviolence, elementary civics, and the Mississippi constitution, they beseeched him to expand his
fledgling project into two of the adjacent counties, where not a single person from
the Negro majority population had voted within memory. Relative to the rural wil-
derness of Amite and Walthall counties, McComb's 12,000 people and 250 registered Negro voters made it a progressive metropolis.

Moses could not bring himself to tell them that it was too dangerous, or that
it was tactically unwise for him to divert attention from McComb. After discussions with Bryant, he also decided that he could not earn the trust of the unregistered populace if he avoided what he called the "tough areas." Accordingly, Moses
addressed the logistical problems of working without money outside McComb. To
cover large distances in the countryside he would need to borrow a car, and he
needed a place to stay in remote areas. It took time and patience to arrange such
things in a region where spare cars were scarce and an educated Northerner suspect. Sometimes he spent half the day arranging where he would spend the night.
But soon a farmer in Amite County named E. W. Steptoe offered to put him up.
Steptoe and his wife had nine children, all but two of whom were grown. He had
been a leader of the county NAACP chapter until the sheriff had confiscated the
membership rolls two years earlier. The NAACP had been defunct in Amite County
since then.

On the morning of August 15, Moses and the first three Amite County volunteers drove to the county courthouse in the town of Liberty, some twenty-five
miles from McComb. A plaque on the lawn proclaimed that it was the oldest courthouse in Mississippi, built in 1839, and boasted that Cecil Borden's condensed
milk had been invented in Liberty, as had Dr. Tichener's antiseptic powder. The
four Negroes passed the plaque and the Confederate memorial statue, entered the
enormous white brick structure, and made their way to the office of the county registrar, who asked rather sternly what had brought them there.

A very old Negro man waited helplessly for one of the two women volunteers
to reply, but both of them also stood speechless with fear. Moses finally spoke up
from behind. "They would like to try to register to vote," he said. The registrar
questioned Moses about his interest in the matter and then told them all to wait.
While they did, curious officials came by for silent looks at the oddities who were
making themselves the chief topic of the day's conversation. The sheriff stopped in,
followed by deputies, clerks from the tax office, and an examiner from the driver's
license bureau. A Mississippi highway patrolman sauntered in and took a seat.

Six hours later, Moses finally escaped the tension of the courthouse. His three
volunteers knew they would be rejected as voters, but they were elated anyway,
because they had been allowed to fill out the forms. This was a first for them, and
they celebrated until they noticed the highway patrolman from the registrar's office
coming up behind them. He followed them at bicycle speed for ten miles down
Highway 24 toward McComb. Fear grew steadily among the Negroes as they pulled
off the highway, took side roads, and did everything they could think of to salvage

the hope that the tail was a coincidence. The patrolman matched every maneuver. At last he turned on his flashers, pulled them over, and ordered them to follow him. Now there were moans of apprehension and regret in their car, as the Amite County volunteers vowed never again to set foot in the registrar's office.

In McComb, Moses alone was placed under arrest. The Pike County attorney rushed down from Magnolia that same evening. At first he proposed booking Moses for the crime of interfering with an officer in the act of making an arrest, but he changed his mind upon reflecting that Moses was the only one who had been arrested. He substituted the vaguer charge of interfering with an officer in the discharge of his duties. Then he notified the local justice of the peace and asked Moses if he was prepared to stand trial. Moses requested the proverbial one phone call.

When permission was granted, he fished an emergency number from his wallet. He had never spoken to John Doar [Assistant U.S. Attorney General for Civil Rights], and had no idea whether Doar would be in his office so late at night. For effect, he amplified his instructions to the operator: Washington, D.C., he said, the United States Department of Justice. When Doar not only came on the line but also agreed to accept a collect call, Moses felt a surge of relief. Noting the surprised looks on the faces around him, he gave Doar a description of the day's events. It was detailed, clinical, and neutral in all but his conclusion that his arrest was fraudulent of purpose and clearly designed to discourage voter registration by acts under the color of law, as prohibited by the Civil Rights Acts of 1957 and 1960. After conferring with Doar about the prospects for a federal investigation, Moses signed off and pronounced himself ready for trial.

The justice of the peace found Moses guilty that night and fined him $50. Perhaps sensitive to the prisoner's obvious connections with the U.S. Justice Department, he offered to suspend the fine if Moses would pay $5 in court costs—what amounted to a nominal fee for pulling the judge away from his supper. Moses quietly explained that he could not pay the fee, because it was part of an unjust prosecution, whereupon the judge sent him to the Pike County jail. Moses spent his first night behind bars. His was the first SNCC jailing in Mississippi other than the Freedom Riders, who were still landing in prison by way of the Jackson bus station.

Two days later, an NAACP lawyer came down from Jackson to secure Moses' release by paying the full fine. He did so with the grudging approval of NAACP superiors who considered this another case of getting stuck with legal bills for activities that were neither sponsored nor approved by the NAACP. The bruised feelings of NAACP officials were not assuaged any by the fact that Moses was less than totally grateful for their generosity. He was happy to be out of jail, but he had refused on principle to pay the fine himself and was ambivalent about whether others should have done so.

Moses went into McComb and found that the Masonic Temple had been transformed during his brief absence. Nearly a dozen Freedom Riders had come into town from Jackson, where the convictions of Bevel and Lafayette on contributing to the delinquency of minors had halted sit-in recruitments temporarily, and several SNCC leaders had made their way into McComb after the fractious debates at the Highlander Folk School. The news of Moses' arrest had blurred the sharp distinctions drawn at Highlander between "safe" voter registration and "dramatic"

nonviolent demonstrations. Overnight, McComb became the summer's new mag-
net town. Ruby Doris Smith, one of the four SNCC veterans of February's Rock Hill
jail-in, arrived in a Freedom Rider group, and Charles Sherrod came in from his
fledgling registration project in Georgia. Charles Jones was on his way, as was former SNCC chairman Marion Barry. Picking up on Moses' door-to-door registration
work, they added a twist from Jackson by recruiting local high school students to
help them.

Moses missed most of the new excitement in McComb. He returned quickly
to Steptoe's farm out in Amite County, hoping to repair the damage caused by the
harrowing experience of his first three volunteers. Word of his arrest had spread
through the county. Steptoe reported that Negroes working around the courthouse
had overheard whites talking about how the Moses project was being discussed
at meetings of the White Citizens Council. With such fearful news on the Negro
grapevine, it took days for Moses and Steptoe to persuade anyone to go near a registration class. Steptoe himself, though bold enough to give lodging to Moses, was
not quite ready to try registering. Nor did he want too many people to be seen coming and going near his farm, which sat directly across the road from the home of
Mississippi state representative E. H. Hurst. As Steptoe explained it to Moses, Hurst
was a pillar of segregation, but the real threat was his daughter's husband, Billy
Jack Caston, whose name had a fearful ring to the ears of Amite County Negroes.
Caston had a reputation as a wild, violent ruffian.

Steptoe did not rest until he had arranged for Moses to hold his registration
classes in a one-room Baptist church, way out in the woods—the same church into
which the sheriff had burst to confiscate the Amite County NAACP records. (The
sheriff, in another touch of Faulknerian reality, was Billy Jack Caston's cousin.)
A few of the boldest Amite County Negroes appeared at the nightly meetings to
hear Moses talk about registration. He refrained from pressuring them, to the point
of never asking whether anyone wanted to try to register. The unspoken question
was left hanging. Finally, nearly two weeks after the first attempt, a farmer named
Curtis Dawson volunteered to go down, and an old man known only as Preacher
Knox jumped up to join him. Though their offer was applauded heartily in the
meeting, Moses and Steptoe discussed it long into the night. Dawson was solid, they
agreed, but Preacher Knox was flighty, voluble, and sometimes daft—given to random enthusiasms and endorsements of all opinions. Moses worried about whether
it would be correct to refuse Knox's offer, and if he did, whether it would be fair to
let Dawson go alone. Moses decided to take his chances on Knox.

The next morning, August 29, the three of them found the sidewalk near
the courthouse blocked by three young white men. Dawson recognized the one in
front as Billy Jack Caston; the second was another of the sheriff's cousins, and the
third was the sheriff's son. There was very little talk. Caston asked Moses where he
was going. To the registrar's office, Moses replied. Caston said no he wasn't and
struck a quick, swiping blow to Moses' forehead with the handle of his knife.

In a mystical discovery even more vivid than the pains shooting through his
head, Moses felt himself separating from his body as he staggered on the sidewalk.
He floated about ten feet up in the air so that he could watch the attack on himself
comfortably. His fears became as remote as Caston's grunts, and time slowed down
so that he could hear Preacher Knox running away on the sidewalk before he saw

Caston slapping and shaking him. In peaceful surrender, he saw Caston hit him again behind the right temple, saw himself sink to his knees, saw Caston drive his face to the pavement with a crushing blow to the top of the head. Through waves of concussion, he distinctly heard Curtis Dawson pleading with Caston to stop the beating.

His first thoughts, upon hearing the feet of his attackers depart were that he could function in spite of his wounds and that it was urgently important to reach the courthouse. "We've got to go on to the registrar," he said, as Dawson struggled to overcome his horror at the sight of the blood flowing down from the gashes in Moses' head. Preacher Knox returned to help him to his feet. "We can't let something like this stop us," said Moses. "That's the whole point." Dawson replied bravely that he was ready; Preacher Knox agreed. Moses was deeply moved by their decision, and most especially by Preacher Knox's unexpected courage, but as the three of them crossed the street toward the courthouse he wondered whether Knox, with shock compounding his scrambled ways, really knew what he was doing.

The county registrar reserved a practiced, well-what-have-we-got-here look for Negro customers, but it vanished in a gasp at the sight of Moses, whose bloody head and shirt combined with his serene, quiet voice to give him a presence as eerie as Banquo's ghost. The registrar gamely sought refuge in bursts of businesslike indifference, excessive politeness, and put-upon impatience, before all his bureaucratic poses collapsed under the weight of his nerves. He said he was closing the office and asked the three Negroes to leave.

They retraced their steps from the courthouse, watched by scattered clumps of bystanders. Dawson drove out to the Steptoe farm, where Moses' weakening condition caused a great stir of mumbled anguish, and then, as there was no Negro doctor in Amite County, they drove back to McComb to visit one newly arrived from Fisk University in Nashville. The doctor, who had taken no part in the voter registration previously, talked with Moses while putting nine stitches into three head wounds. Before he finished, he offered the registration project the use of his car. Moses arrived at the Masonic Temple just in time to be whisked off to the first mass meeting in McComb's history, following its first sit-in arrests. In his absence, Charles Sherrod and others from the influx of Freedom Riders had been conducting classes in nonviolent discipline, much like James Lawson's Nashville workshops, and the young McComb students—too young to vote, and frustrated by the passivity of the elders they canvassed—had been seized with enthusiasm to do something themselves, like the Freedom Riders. Marion Barry had urged the McComb students to demonstrate against the town library, which did not admit Negroes. During the sit-in, the McComb police had arrested Moses' two volunteers, Hollis Watkins and Curtis Hayes, for breach of the peace.

They were in the Pike County jail when Moses came back to McComb with his head wounds, and the furor among the town's Negroes was such that James Bevel came down from Jackson to address a mass meeting of some two hundred people. With his high-pitched voice and shooting-star images, Bevel preached the fire of nonviolent witness. Moses, in telling of the day's events in Liberty, spoke reluctantly and almost inaudibly, as always, but the core of his message was the same: that the important thing was to keep going. His offhand announcement that he intended to return to the Liberty courthouse the next day swept the crowd no less than Bevel's hot gospel. A white reporter from the local newspaper warned his readers that the Negroes might be serious.

In his reflections later that night, Moses decided that it was imperative for him to act as though he and other Negroes enjoyed the same legal rights as Mississippi white people. Accordingly, he drove back to the Liberty courthouse the next day and told the Amite County attorney that he wanted to swear out a complaint against Billy Jack Caston for criminal assault. This statement unsettled the prosecutor as thoroughly as Moses' appearance had shocked the registrar the day before. As the seriousness of the request registered, the prosecutor said that of course he had heard about the beating, and it was a terrible thing. He seemed to become more troubled as he talked about his legal duties and Moses' theoretical rights, and finally he said that, yes, he would put the case to a jury in the name of Amite County. But he stressed the practical reality that if Moses followed through on his complaint, no one could guarantee Moses' life — or his own legal career — against the wrath of the local white people. He recommended a night's sleep on the decision, and Moses left the office with the impression that the county attorney was a decent man.

At Steptoe's that night, Moses was surprised to learn that although the beating had put a severe fright into nearly all their registration candidates, there was one old farmer named Weathersbee who suddenly was determined to go to the courthouse. Possessed of some choleric defiance that pointed him in the opposite direction from his fearful neighbors, Weathersbee wanted to register the next day if Moses would go with him. Steptoe was less surprised by Weathersbee than by the idea of pressing charges against Caston. With no chance of success, it would enrage every white person in the county and was the sort of notion that did not even occur to sane Negroes.

The county attorney, who seemed to have braced himself for the appearance of Moses and his two witnesses the next day, arranged with the justice of the peace for a country-style prosecution. They summoned Billy Jack Caston by telephone, impaneled a six-man jury, and put out the word in the courthouse. By the time the trial commenced two hours later, white citizens had driven into town from all across the county, many of them in pickups with shotgun racks. Some were amused by the thought of seeing someone so prominent as Billy Jack Caston in the dock on the word of a nigger. Some were angry, and many were a little of both. Their numbers swamped the tiny courtroom, so that they overflowed onto the courthouse lawn outside. When Moses, Dawson, and Preacher Knox finished testifying for the prosecution, they found more than a hundred white men in a surly mood, inflamed partly by a simultaneous affront on the other side of the courthouse.

Weathersbee was trying to register. Travis Britt, a Freedom Rider from New York, had come over from McComb to be with Weathersbee while Moses testified. The registrar had ordered Britt to wait outside, alone and beleaguered under a shower of taunts, and as Moses moved through the crowd to join him the blast of several gunshots sent everyone ducking. No one was hit. It may have been a malicious prank, but it was enough to make the sheriff notify Moses that he and his friends were due for an emergency police escort to the county line. They read in the next day's newspaper that the jury had acquitted Caston.

Back in McComb, there was a fever of commotion on both the white and Negro sides of town. The local students, further inspired by James Bevel's invitations to nonviolent direct action, had staged a sit-in the day before at the Greyhound lunch counter. Police had arrested three of them, and what stirred much of the controversy within both races was the particular fact that one of them, Brenda Travis, was a sixteen-year-old girl. Whites were saying that it was irresponsible of the Negroes to allow a mere child to bear the brunt of such dangerous, illegal business, and Negroes were furious that the white authorities put Travis in the Pike County jail with adult criminals. Unable to make bail, she served thirty days there and missed the first month of school.

Her trial in McComb and Caston's in nearby Liberty occurred on the last day of August. These events marked the end of Moses' first month in Mississippi. There still were no registered Negro voters in Amite County, and only a few new ones in Pike County. . . .

» *The Enduring Political Impact of Slavery.*   Congress banned the slave trade in 1808, at the earliest opportunity permitted by the Constitution. Art. I, §9. The Thirteenth Amendment banned the institution of slavery in 1865. The Civil Rights Act of 1964 and the Voting Rights Act of 1965 secured the civil and political rights of black Americans in the mid-twentieth century. Another half-century has passed since then; surely the influence of slavery on American politics is long dead and over. Or is it? Consider the following:

> Southern slavery has had a lasting effect on Southern political attitudes and therefore on regional and national politics. Whites who live in parts of the South that were heavily reliant on slavery and the inexpensive labor that the institution provided . . . are more conservative today, more cool toward African Americans, and less amenable to policies that many believe could promote black progress. By contrast, whites who live in places without an economic and political tradition rooted in the prevalence of slavery . . . are, by comparison, more progressive politically and on racial issues. These regional patterns have persisted historically, with attitudes being passed down over time and through generations. [This] persistence has been reinforced both by formal institutions, such as Jim Crow laws . . ., and also by informal institutions, such as family socialization and community norms. . . . Present-day regional differences, then, are the direct, downstream consequences of the slaveholding history of these areas, rather than being simply attributable exclusively to contemporary demographics or contemporary political debates. . . .
>
> [I]nstitutions and norms (and also political attitudes . . .) change remarkably slowly over time. Slavery was abolished only around 150 years ago — which represents the lifetime of two seventy-five-year-olds put together. These facts point us to the possibility of a historical persistence in terms of not just ambient culture, but also political attitudes. . . . [W]e argue that ideas, norms, and behaviors can be passed down . . ., and they interact with institutions, reinforcing each other over time. This type of path dependence posits that behaviors, not just institutions, become self-reinforcing; once we start down a path of development in political culture, it becomes harder and harder to extract ourselves from that path. . . . At its core, behavioral path dependence suggests that the political attitudes of a place or a region . . . can persist across generations, nurtured by institutions, laws, families, and communities. . . .

AVIDIT ACHARYA, ET AL., DEEP ROOTS: HOW SLAVERY STILL SHAPES SOUTHERN POLITICS 5, 7 (2018). Among their many findings, the authors note that racial resentment is strong among Southern whites who grew up in the South, but not among those who grew up elsewhere and then moved to the South, "a finding entirely consistent with the literature on childhood socialization." *Id.* at 170.

Suppose these findings, and those of Gibson and Mickey described above, are correct: slavery set the American South on a path-dependent, self-reinforcing course of both racial resentment and a preference for, or at least a capacity to tolerate, authoritarian forms of governance. If so, has the American South ever actually embraced liberalism?

E. PROSPECTS FOR LIBERAL DEMOCRACY IN THE UNITED STATES

In light of the various developments laid out above, where do things now stand in the United States? In particular, do the conditions for liberal democracy remain sufficiently in place to sustain it as the American mode of self-governance? The answer to that question has profound implications for how we think about American election law. Should we think about election law the way we think about other domains of law — as a coherent body of jurisprudence that aims for internal integrity in the pursuit of shared and transparent underlying principles? Or should we think of it as nothing more than one of many arenas of a new kind of bitter political conflict, in which the law governing democratic processes is viewed, at least by some, instrumentally – as simply a route to power?

The most basic condition necessary for liberal democracy is free and fair elections. Is the United States now in a position to conduct free and fair elections? In this Part we examine briefly four conditions necessary for elections to be free, fair, and meaningful: fair party competition; the willingness of political actors to adhere to democratic and constitutional norms; the availability of an independent judiciary to defend liberal and democratic principles when they come under attack; and the extent of popular support for liberal principles and democratic models of governance.

1. Fair Party Competition

Jacob S. Hacker and Paul Pierson

Restoring Healthy Party Competition, in Democracy Unchained: How to Rebuild Government for the People

(David W. Orr, et al., eds., 2020), pp. 41-47

To operate well, [the American party system] requires the major political parties to exhibit a significant capacity for cooperation and tolerance. That the need for this cooperation was rarely noticed reflected the fact that usually the system managed to produce it. The dominant (conservative) coalition of the 1940s and 1950s was bipartisan. So was the liberal coalition of the mid-1960s and early 1970s. . . . [G]overnment rested on fluid majorities that encapsulated elements of both parties and shifted from issue to issue. . . . [C]oalitions were loose and fluid, reflecting not only national partisan battles but also the multiple pulls of geographic, sectoral, and cultural constituencies that divided as well as unified parties.

Thus, even as the American political system *necessitated* compromise, it also *facilitated* it through electoral and governing incentives that cross-cut party lines. Most of the time prior to 1990, major legislation in the United States was bipartisan. As a result, even periods of divided government . . . did not prevent action on pressing public issues.

No more. Over the past few decades, the political fluidity of the Madisonian [pluralist] system has given way to an increasingly entrenched partisan divide. . . . Individual politicians, beholden to national organization, are less free to defect on issues based on local conditions. Most powerful interest groups have also chosen sides. . . . Even voters . . . are increasingly attached to national partisan identities and outlooks. They are also increasingly antagonistic toward politicians, groups, and citizens on the other side of the aisle. Mass and elite polarization generally work in tandem. . . .

Combined, these shifts have created a new kind of partisanship: one that is more cohesive, more consistent, more homogeneous, and much, much more intense. The nationalization of American politics in recent decades has eroded the cross-cutting cleavages that our institutions silently relied upon. The forces pushing for consensus have weakened. The electoral incentives for cooperation have evaporated. Norms supporting compromise and partisan restraint have crumbled. Under the weight of these trends, the federal government's capacity to address collective problems — from climate change to rising health care costs to skyrocketing inequality — has virtually collapsed. That collapse, in turn, has helped [fuel] voter discontent, alienation, and a search for scapegoats. We face a real threat of a downward spiral, in which failed governance undercuts political legitimacy, further diminishing the capacity to govern and throwing open the doors of government to demagogues. . . .

There is a common diagnosis of this problem: "partisan polarization." The two parties, in this view, have moved away from the center, creating a yawning gulf and intensifying mistrust. This polarization makes shared governance impossible. . . .

[W]e see this diagnosis as seriously flawed. . . . [W]ith ever-greater clarity, [the] evidence leads to a basic conclusion: the main challenge we face is not polarization but *asymmetric* polarization. The GOP has not only moved much further to the right than Democrats have moved left; it has embraced positions that undermine longstanding governing institutions and norms, limit or subvert electoral competition, and incite us-versus-them tribalism among both political elites and supporters. In the language of comparative politics, Republican are now an "anti-system" party — one that challenges not just its opponents but the legitimacy of the system itself. . . . This asymmetry can be seen in congressional voting patterns. It can be seen in the relative positions on the issues . . . of the two parties' presidential and vice-presidential candidates. It is evident in the relative positions of each party's judicial nominees. . . .

In addition to moving right, Republicans have become much more confrontational—willing to use aggressive tactics that, while technically legal in most cases, had previously been shunned as un-civil or anti-democratic. Crucial figures in developing these tactics—again, predating Trump—were congressional leaders Newt Gingrich and Mitch McConnell, among others. . . . At the national level, Republicans have led the way and deserve exclusive or primary responsibility for

- routinized use of the filibuster to block virtually all initiatives of the majority party;
- repeated government shutdowns;
- using the periodic raising of the authorized ceiling on federal debt (to finance spending *already appropriated* by Congress) to extract concessions from Democrats – in effect, taking the full faith and credit of the United States hostage so as to ransom it for favored GOP policies;
- refusal to accept *any* Democratic appointment to key positions, most dramatically in the case of Merrick Garland's nomination to the U.S. Supreme Court; and
- the use of congressional oversight as a weapon designed to foster distrust and alienation.

Initiatives at the state level where Republicans have gained control have been equally troublesome:

- Resorting to mid-decade reapportionments . . . in order to gerrymander house seats.
- Post-election efforts to remove political authority from offices when voters have chosen to select Democratic Party candidates.
- Repeated legislative reversals of voter-passed initiatives on issues from expansion of Medicaid to the disenfranchisement of ex-felons.
- Systematic efforts to disenfranchise younger, lower-income, and non-white voters viewed as unlikely to support the GOP.

The list is not short, nor are the items trivial. . . . The Trump presidency has launched attacks on the infrastructure of democracy—the press, the courts, law enforcement, the political opposition—that would have been unthinkable only a few years ago. Yet these norm-exploding stances have faced little to no resistance within the GOP. . . . In short, it is now polarization all the way down. . . .

Some of the episodes referred to in the excerpt above include the following.

- In North Carolina, immediately following the 2016 gubernatorial election in which Democrat Roy Cooper defeated the incumbent Republican Pat McCrory, the legislature enacted and Governor McCrory signed a package of bills that transferred control of the Board of Elections from the governor to the legislature; subjected gubernatorial cabinet appointments to senatorial confirmation; stripped the governor of power to appoint trustees of the University of North Carolina system; and reduced the authority of the governor to hire and fire government employees.

- In 2018 in Wisconsin, following wins by Democratic candidates for governor and attorney general, the outgoing Republican-controlled legislature enacted, and the lame-duck Republican governor signed, legislation that deprived the governor of control over significant public programs and transferred from the attorney general to the legislature authority to withdraw from various kinds of litigation.
- In 2018, following a sweep of statewide offices by Democrats, the Republican-controlled Michigan legislature enacted and the lame-duck Republican governor signed legislation limiting executive authority to oversee campaign finance laws.
- Following passage in 2018 of an initiative amendment to the Florida Constitution eliminating permanent disenfranchisement of convicted felons, the Florida legislature enacted a law that prohibited restoration of voting rights to convicted felons until they had paid off all fees, costs, and other financial obligations associated with their convictions. The state had no reliable way of informing felons of the amounts they owed, and convicts just released from prison of course have few opportunities to pay off prior debts unless they were financially well-off prior to conviction and retained resources throughout the period of incarceration.

Kim Lane Scheppele

The Party's Over, in Constitutional Democracy in Crisis?

(Mark A. Graber, et al., eds. 2018)

[I]f one traces the failing and failed democracies, one will generally find that traditional parties in that country had first fallen victim to insidious infighting, ideological drift, or credibility collapse in a way that disrupted the ability of those mainstream parties to screen out toxic choices put to voters. And the voters, not realizing that the safety checks had disappeared when they were offered up seriously bad options, picked one of the options they were given—which in turn sent their countries down the rabbit hole of autocracy. Collapsing democracies follow on collapsing political parties. . . .

In collapsing democracies around the world, elected leaders have now become the primary agents of democratic destruction. . . . Why do voters vote for leaders who become—either immediately or eventually—autocrats?

Closer looks at collapsing democracies make it clear that voters do not in general intend to give up their rights to make democratic choices in the future by openly electing an autocrat. At times of trouble, voters vote for new policies, for fresh faces, to get politics unstuck. They vote to "throw the bums out" by supporting the opposition after the governing party had been in power long enough to have worn out its welcome. But in altogether too many places, voters vote for what looks like a legitimate party and autocracy is the result. . . .

In general, the new autocrats are not particularly ideological in the twentieth century totalitarian sense. Their parties do not generally announce a political program that threatens the supremacy of democracy or constitutional government as political forms. . . . [T]he face that the populist puts forward in an election is the face of a law-respecting democrat. . . . How can constitutions defend against parties that do not announce their leaders' autocratic ambitions? . . .

Venezuela and Hungary are striking in their similarities. In both countries, an earlier dictatorship was immediately followed by a robust multiparty democratic government, featuring a vibrant array of parties. Observers found each country to be the most impressive and stable democracy in its region. But eventually, multiple parties collapsed into a two-party system and a punishing-vote practice emerged in which the electorate threw out the government at every opportunity. . . . Joint crises involving violence in the streets and extreme austerity measures began a political death spiral in which all those associated with either problem — the violence or the austerity — were driven out of politics. Voters eventually voted for the one party leader left standing in a key election in which all other parties were weakened, discredited, or untried. And that person turned out to be someone who swiftly consolidated power in an autocratic manner under a new constitution while running on a substantively conventional party platform. The paths that led to Chávez and Orbán involved progressively narrowing party choices, ending eventually in an election in which the budding autocrat was the only reasonable-looking option among the available choices. In short, party collapse preceded democratic collapse. . . .

In both cases, their ascents to power were preceded by economic crisis in each country that in turn required foreign-generated radical austerity programs. In both cases, the timing of the economic crises meant that Left governments in power at the time were the ones forced to slash budgets, which meant acting contrary to their political programs. But when voters voted for the other guy — the parties of the Right in what had become two-party systems — voters got more of the same, eventually destroying the ability of Right-leaning parties to carry out their promises as well. As voters in these two countries learned, in the cosmopolitan and interdependent world in which we all now live, the broad outlines of economic policy are largely beyond national control. As a result, when voters alternate between competing parties, they quickly learn that their votes cannot produce enough change to fix the insufficiency and maldistribution of economic resources. Voters then vote for the party or leader that promises to defend the country against foreign influences — the nationalists of either the Left or Right. And that person governs as an autocrat. . . .

If this is the script that leads to the new autocracy, then we can see that the people have not failed democracy by becoming unreasonable populists eager to follow a Pied Piper into unfreedom. Instead, democratic publics are doing what they are supposed to do: voting to rotate power and to shake things up in systems in which the prior leaders have failed to keep their promises. But the people are betrayed by party systems that fail to put forward reasonable alternatives when the time comes to change leaders. . . . Preventing toxic choices from being put before the voters is an important role for parties, a role that is no longer performed when a party system is weakened or fails. . . .

———————————

If Scheppele is right, and the main fault lies with the parties for failing to offer high quality, responsible candidates fully committed to liberal democracy, why is that the case? What allowed Donald Trump to win the Republican nomination twice? Why can't the parties exercise control over the identity of their nominees?

For most of American history, ordinary citizens not only did not participate in the nomination process — they did not *expect* to participate. Of course, the machinations of the various political parties in convention were the stuff of great drama. Ordinary citizens read the newspaper accounts from the convention cities with great interest. When radio became ubiquitous, they huddled around to hear live the speeches coming from the convention. And as the mid-century point passed, they watched the conventions unfold on television. But the only way ordinary citizens could have a say in who they nominated was to participate in party politics at the precinct, county, and state levels and hope to eventually get to participate at their state convention where the national convention delegates were usually chosen.

Thus, from 1796 to 1968, the candidates for president were chosen in a process that was by and large closed to the public. . . .

The . . . McGovern-Fraser Commission . . . was formed in the aftermath of the contentious 1968 Democratic convention when anti-war protesters inside and outside the convention hall complained that they had been shut out of the nomination process. . . . [The convention nominated the mainstream candidate, Vice President Hubert Humphrey, who remained committed to the Johnson Administration's policies in Vietnam, over the anti-war candidate, Sen. Eugene McCarthy. As a result of the protests, the Commission recommended a set of reforms, most prominently that presidential candidates be selected mainly by primary elections, and that party delegates to the nominating convention be required to vote on the first ballot for the winner of their state's primary.]

In the years prior to these reforms, delegates were, more or less, free agents at their conventions, subject only to the wishes of the political power structures in their states. But once the rules required that state delegations fairly reflect the will of the voters, the role of delegates and power brokers diminished and the role of the primary voter increased. As more and more states adopted binding state-run primaries, the Democratic Party's reforms had a second unintended consequence — they reformed the Republican Party's nomination system as well. . . .

The modern nomination system allows anyone to declare themselves a candidate for the nomination. All a person needs to do is pull together the modest amount of money needed to get on primary ballots and be able to afford a coach ticket to cities hosting presidential primary debates. . . . [B]oth political parties have found themselves having to make room on the stage for presidential candidates who have decided (for reasons only they can fathom) that they should be president. But, as we saw in 2008 and again in 2016, the public regards its role in the nomination process as a right. The Bernie Sanders campaign and the Hillary Clinton campaign agreed on a convention resolution and a commission that would reduce the number of unpledged superdelegates at the 2020 convention. . . . [This episode] underscored just how, in an increasingly polarized and paranoid electorate, there is no legitimacy given to leaders of the party even though they are elected by the same people. Given the antipathy — both historic and current — Americans hold towards political parties and politicians, it would be nearly impossible to turn back the clock and return power to the party establishment in each party. There is now an entire generation of voters who have never experienced the old-fashioned method of party-based nominations. . . .

Elaine C. Kamarck, *Returning Peer Review to the American Presidential Nomination Process*, 93 N.Y.U. L. Rev. 709 (2018).

This account argues that one reason why American parties cannot be counted on to put forward high quality candidates is their delegation of the choice of nominees, through the system of primary elections (see Chapter 7.B), to rank-and-file voters, who may from time to time prefer worse quality candidates than party elites would choose to offer. If this is the case — if the voters are ultimately to blame for the selection of bad candidates — then can Scheppele be correct that the danger of a stealth autocratic takeover through democratic means, at least in the U.S., is the fault of the parties rather than of the people? Is responsibility shared? What are the obligations of parties? Does democracy require, paradoxically, *un*democratic internal party processes? Does a successful democracy depend upon the voters functioning as passive recipients of elite choices, in the minimalist mode described by Schumpeter?

2. Adherence to Democratic and Constitutional Norms

Steven Levitsky and Daniel Ziblatt

How Democracies Die 97-112 (2018)

For generations, Americans have retained great faith in their Constitution. . . . But are constitutions, by themselves, enough to secure a democracy? We believe the answer is no. . . . [Careful constitutional drafting in Weimar Germany and postcolonial Latin America] did little to prevent fraudulent elections in the late nineteenth century, military coups in 1930 and 1943, and Perón's populist autocracy. . . .

If the constitution written in Philadelphia in 1787 is not what secured American democracy for so long, then what did? [W]e believe much of the answer . . . lies in the development of strong democratic norms. All successful democracies rely on informal rules that, though not found in the constitution or any laws, are widely known and respected. . . . [T]wo norms stand our as fundamental to a functioning democracy: mutual toleration and institutional forbearance.

Mutual toleration refers to the idea that as long as our rivals play by constitutional rules, we accept that they have an equal right to exist, compete for power, and govern. We may disagree with, and even strongly dislike, our rivals, but we nevertheless accept them as legitimate. This means recognizing that our political rivals are decent, patriotic, law-abiding citizens . . .; we do not view them as an existential threat. Nor do we treat them as treasonous [or] subversive. . . . Put another way, mutual toleration is politicians' collective willingness to agree to disagree. . . . In just about every case of democratic breakdown we have studied, would-be authoritarians—from Franco, Hitler, and Mussolini in interwar Europe to Marcos, Castro, and Pinochet during the Cold War to Putin, Chávez, and Erdoğan most recently—have justified their consolidation of power by labeling their opponents as an existential threat.

A second norm critical to democracy's survival is what we call institutional forbearance. *Forbearance* means "patient self-control; restraint and tolerance," or "the action of restraining from exercising a legal right." For our purposes, institutional forbearance can be thought of as avoiding actions that, while respecting the letter of the law, obviously violate its spirit. Where norms of forbearance are strong, politicians do not use institutional prerogatives to the hilt, even if it is technically legal to do so, for such actions could imperil the existing system. . . .

Think of democracy as a game that we want to keep playing indefinitely. To ensure future rounds of the game, players must refrain from either incapacitating the other team or antagonizing them to such a degree, that they refuse to play again tomorrow. . . . In politics, this often means eschewing dirty tricks or hardball tactics in the name of civility and fair play. . . . Acts of forbearance—for example, a Republican-controlled Senate approving a Democratic president's Supreme Court pick—will reinforce each party's belief that the other side is tolerable, promoting a virtuous circle.

But the opposite can also occur: The erosion of mutual toleration may motivate politicians to deploy their institutional powers as broadly as they can get away with. When parties view each other as mortal enemies, the stakes of political competition heighten dramatically. . . . The result is politics without guardrails[:] a "cycle of escalating constitutional brinksmanship."

––––––––––

>> *Unwritten Constitutional Norms?*   The excerpt from Levitsky and Ziblatt above focuses on norms of *democracy*. But are there other sources of norms of official behavior? More specifically, to what degree does a written constitution provide a complete set of instructions to government officials about how they ought to behave?

In the United Kingdom, which does not have a written constitution, guidance to officials often takes the form of unwritten "constitutional conventions." Adherence to these conventions, or norms of behavior, is thought in the U.K. to be obligatory, though the conventions are considered to be judicially unenforceable. But even countries that have a written constitution sometimes understand the document to be incomplete, and have recognized the existence of constitutional conventions that officials are expected to obey. For example, Section 55 of the Canadian Constitution plainly states that the Governor General—the British Monarch's appointed representative in Canada—has the authority to veto federal legislation, yet by longstanding convention that power is never exercised. The Governor General's assent to federal legislation is still required for its validity, and such consent is routinely given, but it is now given exclusively on the advice of the Prime Minister and cabinet, converting the giving of royal assent from a discretionary function of approval to a ministerial task of ritual signature.

Does the U.S. Constitution include unwritten norms of official behavior? Consider the following:

> Although many understand law enforcement to be a paradigmatic executive function, there is today a set of structural norms that insulate some types of prosecutorial and investigatory decisionmaking from the President. These rules constrain the President's choice of FBI Director and limit the authority of the President to fire the FBI Director without cause. The norm also prohibits presidential direction in individual investigatory matters. These unwritten rules coexist with the President's authority, if not responsibility, to set law enforcement policy and priorities. . . . A second norm type prohibits presidential self-dealing or the corruption of government power. Unwritten rules impose limits beyond the textual provisions on emoluments and the ethics-related statutes, many of which formally exclude the President from coverage. . . . While the principal conflict-of-interest statute excludes the President from its coverage, Presidents have long complied with a structural norm pursuant to which the President conducts himself as if bound by those statutory restrictions.

Daphna Renan, *Presidential Norms and Article II*, 131 HARV. L. REV. 2187, 2201-08, 2215-16 (2018).

What about the behaviors listed below? They are anomalous, but do they constitute violations of norms of constitutional stature? Norms of democracy? Regardless of the source of these norms, does the successful continuing practice of democracy require compliance by leaders with these norms of behavior?

- Trump refused to release his tax returns notwithstanding bipartisan practice over the previous forty years. The public did not know, among other things, whether he had financial connections to Russia and other counties, and whether he profited from the major tax cut bill that he signed into law or from foreign policy decisions that he made.
- Trump sought to politicize federal criminal law enforcement, including by threatening to jail Hillary Clinton, his political opponent in the 2016 presidential election; repeatedly proclaiming that she belonged in jail; calling for criminal investigations into her behavior; firing the FBI Director for refusing to pledge his loyalty to Trump and for overseeing a criminal investigation into his conduct and that of his inner circle; assailing his first Attorney General for properly recusing himself from oversight of that investigation; and using the pardon and commutation powers of the Presidency to benefit political allies. . . .
- Unlike how other Presidents have long conducted themselves, Trump did not just criticize institutions that he viewed as opposing him. He

consistently attacked their legitimacy. Targets included Democratic politicians, the media, the judiciary, the FBI, the DOJ, the national security establishment, federal election security officials, and state election officials of both parties.

- Over time, Trump replaced executive branch officials who were more norm-sensitive (and so inclined to push back against some of what the President wanted to do) with officials who were less norm-sensitive (and so inclined to validate whatever the President wanted to do). Examples include the White House Chief of Staff, the White House Counsel, the National Security Advisor, the Attorney General, the Secretary of State, the Secretary of Defense, and numerous inspectors general.
- More than once (Russia, Ukraine), Trump publicly or privately encouraged foreign meddling in presidential elections to help him win. . . .
- Notwithstanding the norm that voters vote for electors, Trump attempted to steal the 2020 election by alleging repeatedly that he won and massive voter fraud cost him the election; filing numerous meritless lawsuits challenging the results; pressuring Republican state politicians to reject the will of the voters in their states; and preventing the transition from beginning for weeks amidst pressing national security concerns and a worsening pandemic.
- Unlike prior Presidents, Trump refused to disjoin public service from personal and familial financial interests. Examples included his refusals to divest from his business interests; his cultivation of those interests through regular visits to his properties around the United States; the large amount of public money spent on ensuring his security during those visits; his populating the White House with family members; and the frequent use of the Trump Hotel by representatives of foreign governments who sought to curry favor with his administration. . . .
- Trump indulged in or validated racism, Islamophobia, and misogyny to an extent without parallel in modern American political life. Targets included, among others, people of color, Mexicans, Americans of Mexican heritage, Muslims, and female politicians, news anchors, and reporters.
- Trump and his administration were contemptuous of science and expert knowledge—including, but not limited to, in their response to the pandemic—to an extent that is likely unprecedented by a presidential administration.
- Trump encouraged or applauded political violence throughout his Presidency, culminating in loss of life, serious injuries, and desecration of the Capitol after he incited his supporters at a rally to immediately interfere with Congress's affirmation of the election results.
- Most troubling of all, Trump lied (or was disconnected from reality) with a frequency that likely has no parallel in American political history. He appeared to deny the existence or relevance of truth as a category of political life.

Neil S. Siegel, *The Trump Presidency, Racial Realignment, and the Future of Constitutional Norms, in* AMENDING AMERICA'S UNWRITTEN CONSTITUTION (Richard Albert, Yaniv Roznai, & Ryan C. Williams eds., 2021).

3. An Independent Judiciary

A typical feature of liberal democracy is an independent and impartial judiciary that, through the mechanism of judicial review, ensures that elected leaders and other government officials comply with constitutional and legal constraints on the exercise of power. These constitutional courts (as they are known in most nations) have sometimes been willing to protect constitutionally embedded norms by invalidating actions of populist leaders, even in the face of intense political pressure placed on the courts by those leaders. For example, the Constitutional Court of Colombia invalidated an effort by the populist president Álvaro Uribe to run for president in violation of a provision of the Colombia constitution imposing term limits. Uribe, who gained immense popularity after successfully ending a period of violence and anarchy fomented by drug cartels, succeeded in amending the constitution to allow himself a second term, but then sought to do so again. At that point, the court intervened.

> A third term raised the specter that Colombia would succumb to the Latin American tradition of rule by *caudillos*, the strongmen who hold to power indefinitely and become the gravitational center of political life. . . . Under the circumstances, the constitutional court emerged as the sole check on the prospect of increasingly unilateral executive power. . . . [Although the court lacked a democratic pedigree], the court could assert itself as the guardian of a popularly accepted constitutional order that had to restrain the momentary desires of popular majorities. . . .

SAMUEL ISSACHAROFF, FRAGILE DEMOCRACIES 148-149 (2015). As we shall see, the U.S. Supreme Court itself, during the mid- and late twentieth century, often protected democratic values against attempts by state and local governments to rig the system in favor of incumbents.

However, it is precisely the capacity of independent courts to block populist initiatives to consolidate power that makes them one of the first targets when populist authoritarians assume office. In most cases of democratic backsliding, the tactics deployed to undermine judicial independence have been direct, aggressive, and initiated by an authoritarian executive, usually with the cooperation of a legislature controlled by the leader's party. These tactics include court-packing through manipulation of the size of the apex court; seizing control of the appointments process; or the use of credible, coercive threats against sitting judges. For example, in 2004 the Venezuelan National Assembly increased the size of the Venezuelan Supreme Court by more than half, allowing the Chávez regime a large number of new appointments, and enacted legislation making it easier for the Chavista congress to dismiss judges. The Turkish ruling party domesticated its constitutional court in 2010 by ramming through constitutional amendments that increased the number of seats, imposed term limits on judges, and altered the appointment system to the advantage of the regime. A 2010 policy proposal by the government of Ecuadorean populist leader Rafael Correa threatened judges with personal liability for unfavorable rulings. David Landau and Rosalind Dixon, *Abusive Judicial Review: Courts against Democracy*, 53 U.C. Davis L. Rev. 1313 (2020).

The characteristic evidence that such measures have successfully captured constitutional courts is a sudden shift in jurisprudence and legal reasoning—the court's methods and decisions are liberal until, suddenly and suspiciously, they are not. Thus, in Bolivia, for example, a constitutional provision limiting presidential terms was considered by the Bolivian high court, in a 2015 decision, to be a clear and valid restriction on the ability of President Evo Morales to continue in office. *Declaración Constitucional Plurinacional* 0194/2015. Following an aggressive program of court-packing, the court two years later reversed itself and, in an opinion riddled with dubious reasoning, invalidated the constitution's presidential term limits as a violation of international human rights law. Landau and Dixon, *supra*, at 1362-63.

Is the U.S. Supreme Court—and the federal judiciary generally—sufficiently independent of the Republican Party to defend liberal and democratic values against populist authoritarianism?

> The era of strong political polarization has affected the Court in multiple ways, of which two are most direct. The first is a change in the criteria for nomination of Justices. Throughout American history some presidents have emphasized policy considerations in their selection of nominees to the Court, but on the whole policy has been only one of several criteria for choices of Justices. Since the beginning of President Reagan's second term in 1985, ideology has risen in importance.
>
> This is especially true of Republican presidents. Political activists who are associated with the Republican Party have made the selection of conservative Justices a high priority. . . .
>
> Partisan sorting among prospective nominees has had an effect as well. Increasingly, credible candidates for Supreme Court appointments are like other members of political elites: if they are conservative, they are almost certain to be Republicans, and liberals are nearly as likely to be Democrats. . . .
>
> The second effect of higher polarization relates to Justices' social identities. Polarization in its various forms has changed the Supreme Court's environment, splitting that environment along ideological lines to a much greater degree than was true a few decades ago. . . . In a parallel development, the news media have become more bifurcated. . . .
>
> To a considerable degree, Supreme Court Justices have become part of this new polarized world. Justice increasingly come to the Court with strong ties to conservative or liberal elites, ties that they maintain as Justices. . . . As a result, Justices are reinforced in the ideological tendencies they bring to the Court.
>
> In this new world, the ideological content of Justices' votes and opinions is less susceptible to change than it was in the preceding period. Democratic appointees are liberals who interact primarily with other liberals; Republicans are conservatives who are oriented toward other conservatives. This reality reinforces the appointment process in hardening

ideological positions, especially on the Right. Consequently, the days when some Republican appointees drifted toward more liberal positions are behind us. . . .

Neal Devins and Lawrence Baum, The Company They Keep: How Partisan Divisions Came to the Supreme Court 149-151 (2019). See Chapter 10 below for more on the issue of judicial partisanship.

On one highly perceptive account, the methodology of legal analysis that has come to dominate the Court's jurisprudence over the last two decades is not only sympathetic to populist claims, but in fact has already taken on board populist assumptions and predispositions.

> Populist leaders claim to represent the will of a morally pure people against a corrupt, out-of-touch, or unresponsive elite. They present that people as a unified whole, with a single, undifferentiated will to which the populist leader claims exclusive, unmediated access. Populists use this image—one leader, one people, one will—to suggest that political questions have one correct answer: the answer the populist provides. They deny the very possibility of legitimate disagreement and seek to exclude those who diverge from the populist's view, labeling them outsiders or even enemies. . . .
>
> *Judicial populism* draws on political populism's tropes, mirrors its traits, and enables its practices. Like political populists, judicial populists insist that there are clear, correct answers to complex, debatable propositions. They disparage the mediation and negotiation that characterize democratic institutions and reject the messiness inherent in a pluralistic democracy. Instead, they simplify the issues legal institutions address and claim special access to a true, single meaning of the law. . . . [J]udicial populists present good judging as primarily a matter of using the correct method. This presentation imagines away judges' unavoidable participation in the production of law in our system, and relieves them of responsibility for the consequences of their actions. . . .
>
> The rhetoric of judicial populism is replete with instructions regarding what *not* to do. It revels in exposing falsehoods that corrupt legal thinking and declaring various consideration or methods off limits. They present the legal sphere as tainted by these methods and considerations, and position themselves as saviors who will make legal interpretation great again. . . .
>
> Judicial populism, like political populism, presents simplicity as empirically achievable and normatively preferable. . . . The populist alone can authoritatively discern and articulate that understanding. . . .
>
> Like political populists, textualists claim a direct line of contact with the people, an undifferentiated entity that understands the law in some uniform way which, it turns out, only textualists themselves are able to discern. It is judges who are left to speak for the people and the legislature, to say what they must want and how it must work. . . . [Similarly, originalists claim] privileged access to hidden—yet binding—commitments that courts have made ever since the founding. . . .

Anya Bernstein and Glen Staszewski, *Judicial Populism*, 106 MINN. L. REV. 283 (2021).

4. *How Committed Are Americans to Liberalism?*

In 1954, at the height of the Cold War, Samuel Stouffer, a Harvard sociologist, conducted a large and wide-ranging survey aimed at determining the degree to which Americans supported the application of core civil liberties to unpopular groups — socialists, communists, and atheists. In a book published the following year, Stouffer revealed some shocking conclusions. Nearly one-third of respondents thought a socialist advocating nationalization of industry should not be allowed to speak in their community. Sixty percent believed that an atheist should not be permitted to speak, sixty percent believed a book written by an atheist should be removed from public libraries, and eighty-four percent said that an atheist should not be permitted to teach in a college or university. Two-thirds said a book by a communist should be removed from a library, and ninety-one percent that a communist high-school teacher should be fired. Seventy-seven percent thought the citizenship of an admitted communist should be revoked, and more than half thought he should be jailed. Two-thirds thought that the government should be able to eavesdrop on private telephone conversations to gather evidence of communism. SAMUEL A. STOUFFER, COMMUNISM, CONFORMITY, AND CIVIL LIBERTIES: A CROSS-SECTION OF THE NATION SPEAKS ITS MIND (1955).

Similar results were obtained by other researchers in numerous follow-up studies. In a 1984 study, McCloskey and Zaller found that seventy percent still believed a community should not allow its civic auditorium to be used by an atheist group; seventy-nine percent supported prayer and religious observances in public schools; and fifty-four percent believed censorship of book publication an appropriate strategy to protect public morality. Forty-nine percent — half of all respondents — agreed that "[w]hen it comes to the things that count most, all races certainly are not equal." Although ninety-seven percent affirmed their belief in freedom of speech, seventy-six percent said that fascists and communists should not be allowed to hold meetings or to express their views in the community. HERBERT McCLOSKEY AND JOHN ZALLER, THE AMERICAN ETHOS: PUBLIC ATTITUDES TOWARD CAPITALISM AND DEMOCRACY (1984).

Even today, investigators continue to document similar public attitudes. In a 2015 poll, for example, researchers asked the following question: "Thomas Jefferson wrote in the Declaration of Independence that 'All men are created equal.' Do you believe this statement is true or false?" Twenty-two percent of Americans answered "false." In a 2017 survey of college-educated Americans, about half agreed that speakers advancing various kinds of unpopular views — ranging from the contention that whites are racist to the view that Muslims should be barred from immigrating to the United States, and from assertions of the backwardness of Christians to claims about the superiority of men over women at math — should not be allowed to speak on college campuses. In another recent poll, one in three expressed opposition to the separation of church and state. Forty-one percent expressed discomfort with a Muslim teaching elementary school. One-third believe the aim of Muslims in the United States is to establish Sharia law as the governing legal regime for all Americans. 60 Minutes/Vanity Fair Poll (June 2015); Emily Ekins, *The State of Free Speech and Tolerance in America* (Cato Institute, Oct. 31, 2017); Daniel Cox, *et al., What It Means to Be an American: Attitudes in an Increasingly Diverse America Ten Years after 9/11* (Brookings, Sept. 6, 2011).

These studies generally support two kinds of conclusions. One is that Americans by and large support civil liberty in the abstract, but are willing to tolerate the exercise of such liberties only selectively, and in particular, not by groups and ideologies they find objectionable. In other words, Americans are supportive of the exercise of civil liberties except in the only situations in which the protection afforded by such liberties would matter. Civil liberties, evidently, are for me and my group, not for you and yours.

Relatedly, these studies suggest that a latent illiberal intolerance can be readily activated, even in citizens otherwise predisposed to tolerance, by a perception of threat, or by priming associated with some group perceived as an "enemy." Thus, for example, studies of intolerance find American intolerance more or less stable over time, but focused on different groups in different periods—communists in the 1950s, but "Radical Muslims" today (with atheists and communists close behind, even after fifty years).

Second, these studies have consistently shown that elites—community leaders, business leaders, leaders of trade and bar associations, party and elected officials—as a group display greater commitment to civil liberties and greater tolerance for political deviance than ordinary people. This in turn suggests of course that the comparatively strong record of the United States on civil liberties since the late twentieth century results principally from the efforts of governing elites rather than of the citizenry, and that more robust and responsive democracy—of, say, the populist kind now emerging—is likely to produce less rather than more liberal results. Indeed, one factor commonly accepted as contributing to Donald Trump's political rise is the transfer of control over presidential nomination, beginning in the 1970s, from party elites to the party rank and file through primary elections. *See, e.g.,* Elaine C. Kamarck, *Returning Peer Review to the American Presidential Nomination Process,* 93 N.Y.U. L. Rev. 709 (2018).

⯈⯈   How Committed Are Americans to Democracy?   If a substantial minority of the American public hold views on the merits of public policy that are illiberal—or that, if liberal, are readily abandoned under minimal pressure—a similarly substantial minority also demonstrates a declining commitment to democracy. In a recent study, Yascha Mounk found that the percentage of Americans who though it "essential" to live in a democracy declined from 71 percent among those born in the 1930s to only 29 percent among those born in the 1980s. One in four millennials believes that democracy is a "bad" or "very bad" system of government. In 1995, Mounk reports, "34 percent of young Americans aged 18–24 felt that a political system with a strong leader who does not have to bother with Congress or elections was either good or very good. By 2011, 44 percent of young Americans felt the same way." Support in the U.S. for direct military rule rose from 8 percent of 18–24 year olds in 1995 to 24 percent in 2011, and for all ages rose from 7 to 16 percent. Yascha Mounk, The People vs. Democracy: Why Our Freedom Is in Danger and How to Save It (2018).

In a similar study, Larry Diamond obtained less dire results, but concluded that "we still have serious cause for concern." Diamond's study found overall American support for democracy still strong—somewhere between about 75 and 85 percent for most formulations of the question—but found that the proportion of Americans who support "a strong leader who does not have to bother with Congress and elections" was 24 percent, much higher than in Canada, France, and Germany. Support among Americans for military rule in the United States rose from 8 to 18 percent between 1995 and 2017. Only 54 percent, Diamond found, "consistently hold a prodemocracy position," and 28 percent "gave a nondemocratic response" on two of five items on which he surveyed. LARRY DIAMOND, ILL WINDS: SAVING DEMOCRACY FROM RUSSIAN RAGE, CHINESE AMBITION, AND AMERICAN COMPLACENCY (2019).

Are we, then, "living in a postliberal moment"?

> A new conservatism, unlike any in recent memory, is coming into view. Ideas once thought taboo are being reconsidered; authors once banished are being rehabilitated; debates once closed are reopening. . . . Nationalists, populists, identitarians, futurists, and religious traditionalists are vying to define conservatism in ways previously unimaginable. To a remarkable degree, they dissent from an orthodoxy that seemed settled as recently as 2016. They take as a premise, not a possibility, that American conservatism as it has defined itself for generations is intellectually dead. . . . Perhaps more significantly, they see it as an obstacle to the future they already embody: a political right prepared to dismantle liberal institutions, not simply manage their decline.

MATTHEW ROSE, A WORLD AFTER LIBERALISM: PHILOSOPHERS OF THE RADICAL RIGHT 2-3 (2021).

The rest of this book is, in a way, an inquiry into the questions posed at the beginning of this section. Are elections in the United States free and fair? If they are not, do the underlying conditions necessary for free and fair elections exist to a sufficient degree such that legal reforms or routine judicial enforcement of constitutional and statutory provisions can restore or secure those conditions? At the end of the day, is election law a coherent and legitimate body of law, guided by defensible principles of democratic popular self-rule? Or is it something else, and if so, what?

CHAPTER 3
THE VOTE

⟫ *Identifying the Self-Governing* **Demos.** The core tenet of Enlightenment liberalism is popular sovereignty. No people, on this view, is destined for subjection by others who unilaterally impose laws upon them. On the contrary, a people on this view is entitled inherently to rule itself, by the voluntary consent of its members, under rules and practices to which they have collectively agreed. It is such agreement, and, according to classic liberalism, only such agreement, that legitimizes the application of law to a political community because it is only in these circumstances that a people can truly be said to give law to itself, rather than passively receiving it from others.

One of the great shortcomings of liberal thought, however, is that it does not in practice offer any uncontroversial way to determine the identity of "the people" that is entitled to rule itself. In principle, liberal theory does offer an answer to this question: the people, or *demos*, entitled to self-rule is comprised of those who have agreed among themselves to exit the state of nature and to abide by the decisions of the group concerning the form and manner of collective self-governance. But this central story of liberalism is a fable, a hypothetical meant principally to establish and justify a baseline of individual freedom against which the legitimacy of limitations on freedom may be evaluated.

In actual historical practice, however, new societies are nearly always built on the remains of predecessor societies, and the kind of voluntary consent necessary to legitimize a new political order, if it is sought at all, is nearly always conferred retroactively, after a new government is already exercising power over specific individuals residing in a specific territory. These commonplace social facts raise difficult questions of who ought to be counted as a member of the new *demos*. Is everyone residing within the boundaries of the new state at the time of its founding *ipso facto* a member of the new society? Does that include those who opposed creation of the new state, or even took up arms against it, and who are clearly submitting to its authority only under duress? If the former society included social or political hierarchies, are those status distinctions carried forward in the new society or discarded? Are descendants of the founding generation included in the *demos*? Can newcomers join the society, and if so, how and on what terms?

This lacuna in liberal thought provides the opening through which fierce battles may emerge over membership in the self-ruling *demos*. Distinctions might be drawn, for instance, between citizens (full members) and resident aliens (nonmembers, or provisional members). Different classes of membership might be hypothesized, with distinct qualifications and privileges. Excluded groups may argue for inclusion, claiming that their exclusion constitutes an illegitimate form of subordination. And these disputes over membership, complex and unruly as they are, may be further distorted if they are merely parasitic on underlying disputes over policy. After all, if a group cannot achieve its policy goals through persuasion on the merits, it may well divert its efforts toward excluding from the decision making process those who hold opposing views.

≫   *The American* **Demos.**   The United States has a long history of disputes over the identity of the self-governing *demos,* disputes that have frequently taken the form of struggles over eligibility to vote. At the time of the founding, state voting qualifications based on race, gender, and property often excluded a considerable portion of the resident population from full participation in democratic self-governance. According to a leading historian of American democracy, "as the revolution approached, . . . the proportion of adult white males who were eligible to vote was probably less than 60 percent." ALEXANDER KEYSSAR, THE RIGHT TO VOTE: THE CONTESTED HISTORY OF DEMOCRACY IN THE UNITED STATES 7 (2000).

Over time, however, the *demos* came to be understood in ever broader and more inclusive terms, and formal restrictions on the franchise began to drop away. State property qualifications largely disappeared during the 1820s and 1830s. Racial qualifications were outlawed by the Fifteenth Amendment in 1870. Gender qualifications fell with ratification of the Nineteenth Amendment in 1920. The Twenty-Fourth Amendment, adopted in 1964, invalidated payment of poll taxes as a voting qualification in federal elections. The Twenty-Sixth Amendment, ratified in 1971, extended the franchise to those between the ages of eighteen and twenty-one.

As early as 1835, an astute visitor to the United States, the French aristocrat Alexis de Tocqueville, foresaw universal suffrage as the only logical stopping point following the introduction in the U.S. of democratic self-rule:

> When a nation begins to modify the elective qualification, it may easily be foreseen that, sooner or later, that qualification will be entirely abolished. There is no more invariable rule in the history of society: the further electoral rights are extended, the greater is the need of extending them; for after each concession the strength of the democracy increases, and its demands increase with its strength. The ambition of those who are below the appointed rate is irritated in exact proportion of those who are above it. The exception at last becomes the rule, concession follows concession, and no stop can be made short of universal suffrage.

ALEXIS DE TOCQUEVILLE, 1 DEMOCRACY IN AMERICA 59 (Vintage ed. 1945) (1835).

By the late twentieth century, Tocqueville appeared to have been proven largely correct: many Americans—though perhaps not all—seemed to consider it settled that universal suffrage was our destiny as a democratic people. Recently, however, that consensus, if it ever existed, seems to be crumbling, especially on the right. In 2018, political commentator David Frum, who had previously worked in the George W. Bush White House, remarked: "[i]f conservatives [i.e., Republicans] become convinced that they cannot win democratically, they will not abandon conservatism. They will reject democracy." DAVID FRUM, TRUMPOCRACY: THE CORRUPTION OF THE AMERICAN REPUBLIC 206 (2018).

That prediction has been accurate. Leading Republicans have been increasingly vocal and transparent about their wish to restrict the scope of the *demos.*

Nearly twenty years ago, Paul Weyrich, an influential Republican activist and founder of both the Moral Majority and the Heritage Foundation, proclaimed: "I don't want everybody to vote. [The Republican Party's] leverage in the elections quite candidly goes up as the voting populace goes down."[1] More recently, a sitting Republican United States Senator, addressing supporters on the topic of voting by college students, told them: "there's a lot of liberal folks in those other schools who maybe we don't want to vote. Maybe we want to make it just a little more difficult. And I think that's a great idea."[2] A Republican member of Congress openly praised property qualifications for voting—not in 1812, but in 2012.[3] The President of the United States himself, remarking on a federal House bill designed to make voting easier, remarked in 2020: "The things they had in there were crazy. They had levels of voting, that if you ever agreed to it you'd never have a Republican elected in this country again."[4]

In consequence, the United States is currently riven by a bitter fight over the scope of the self-ruling *demos*. This war is being waged on two fronts. The greatest amount of activity has occurred in the area of indirect restrictions on the franchise. These measures do not affect basic qualifications to vote, but instead make voting more or less difficult for those already eligible. Commonplace measures of this type include regulation of the availability of mail voting, the duration of early voting periods, voter identification requirements at polling places, ease of voter registration, the number and accessibility of polling places, and many other aspects of electoral administration. Measures that regulate access on these and similar grounds, although facially neutral, often have disproportionate effects on segments of the population known to support one party or the other. These are taken up in Chapter 10.

A second front in the current voting wars concerns direct restrictions on the franchise in the form of basic qualifications to vote. Most of the recent activity of this type focuses on the voting eligibility of felons, who historically have been excluded from the franchise. This issue is taken up at the end of this chapter.

If there is any good news here, it seems to be that support for universal or near-universal suffrage remains sufficiently strong to render politically unwise direct attacks on the voting eligibility of any but the most socially reviled categories of people. Furthermore, longstanding constitutional doctrines protecting the right to vote may exercise a significant deterrent effect on direct, frontal attacks on the voting eligibility of most of the population.

This chapter explores the gradual emergence in the United States of a constitutional jurisprudence recognizing and protecting the right of Americans to vote.

---

1. Quoted in Carol Anderson, One Person, No Vote: How Voter Suppression Is Destroying Our Democracy 48 (2019).

2. Paul Waldman, "GOP senator: Voting should be 'a little more difficult' . . . if you're a Democrat," Washington Post, Nov. 16, 2018.

3. Jed Handelsman Shugerman, *Hardball vs. Beanball: Identifying Fundamentally Antidemocratic Tactics*, 119 Colum. L. Rev. Online 85, 111 (2019).

4. Philip Bump, Trump Just Said What Republicans Have Been Trying Not to Say for Years, Washington Post (May 29, 2020).

Historically, restrictions on voting eligibility have been imposed for two kinds of reasons: lack of membership in the relevant polity and lack of competence. This chapter takes up each family of restrictions in turn.

A.   QUALIFICATIONS BASED ON MEMBERSHIP

1.   Citizenship

The most basic kind of membership in a political society is what we nowadays think of as "citizenship." Does citizenship in a democratic or republican state necessarily carry with it the right to vote? To answer this question, we must first consider what it means to be a citizen. Broadly speaking, Americans of the founding generation inherited two very different philosophical models of citizenship, one from ancient Greece and the other from the Enlightenment. Aristotle believed that man is a "political animal." Just as the ultimate nature of a lion is to live the life of a hunter and the nature of a rabbit is to live the life of the hunter's prey, so the essence of a person is to live a political life—that is, a life shared with others in a community devoted to deliberating upon the nature of and attempting to achieve "the good life." It followed that the highest activity that a citizen of such a community could undertake was thinking about, discussing, and debating the issues facing the community and, to the extent permitted under the community's form of government, implementing the common good through political action.

On the other hand, Aristotle, and to an even greater extent Plato and Socrates, believed that not all citizens had the same capabilities. One person might have a natural talent for carpentry, another for farming, another for medicine. And just as it was proper to entrust the care of a sick person to someone skilled in medicine—you take the sick to a doctor, not to a farmer—so it was proper to entrust political decisions to those skilled in politics. The citizens deemed to have such skill were generally those who had undergone some sort of proper training and education, which might include instruction in philosophy, gymnastics, and music. Thus, under the Greek model, citizens could have very different roles, and not all citizens could make a legitimate claim to participate directly in the overtly political life of the community.

The Enlightenment notion of citizenship broke sharply with the Greek one. According to John Locke (see Chapter 1), every person is equal in the state of nature, and all individuals possess equally a natural right to self-governance. Upon entering society, people surrender some of their natural rights on terms that they find satisfactory, but the ultimate right to self-determination can never be given away. The members of society then decide among themselves what form of government to create and what powers to give it. Thus, the role of the citizen in such a regime is not determined by some sort of natural endowment, but by the rational choice of the members of society.

Under this model, it is not necessary for a citizenry to establish a democratic form of government; they may rationally choose a limitless variety of forms of governmental organization. Nevertheless, when a people does decide to establish a democratic form of government, one may well ask: why have they done so? Presumably, those who create a democratic form of government wish to retain a significant role in the political decisions of the state. Does this suggest that citizenship in a democratic state presumes an equal ability to participate in politics and, thus, to vote? Consider the following account by a leading political theorist:

> [In a democracy, by definition, the] members believe that no single member, and no minority of members, is so definitely better qualified to rule that the one or the few should be permitted to rule over the entire association. They believe, on the contrary, that all the members of the association are adequately qualified to participate on an equal footing with the others in the process of governing the association.
>
> I am going to call this idea the Strong Principle of Equality. . . .
>
> If we were to deny that the Strong Principle of Equality could properly be applied to all the members of an association, it would be extremely difficult, and perhaps impossible, to make a reasonable argument that all the members of the association ought to be full citizens. . . . Conversely, however, if the Strong Principle does properly apply to all members, then on what grounds could one reasonably deny that all the members should participate, as equals, in governing themselves?
>
> [A foundation for the Strong Principle] can be constructed by joining it with a second assumption that has been a cornerstone of democratic beliefs (as it has also been of liberal thought). This is the assumption that no person is, in general, more likely than yourself to be a better judge of your own good or interest or to act to bring it about. Consequently, you should have the right to judge whether a policy is, or is not, in your best interest. . . . You may choose to delegate the choice of *means* to those you judge to be more qualified than yourself to select the most appropriate means. But you could not . . . yield your right to judge whether the results (intended and actual) were in your interests. I am going to call this the Presumption of Personal Autonomy.

ROBERT A. DAHL, DEMOCRACY AND ITS CRITICS 31, 98, 99 (1989).

On the other hand, Locke's theory does not require a polity to embrace strong principles of equality. In Locke's system, a society is free to choose almost any form of government it desires, including monarchy or oligarchy. There is thus no theoretical impediment to the creation of a state in which the vote is granted to some citizens and not to others. The question, then, in Lockean political theory is usually: what did the people actually do—what kind of government did they create?

From the very beginning, voting in the United States was not universal. Slaves, of course, could not vote, but were not regarded as citizens (even though they counted for three-fifths of a person in the census, Art. I, §2, cl. 3). Among those who were considered citizens, women rarely had the vote, and even free blacks were often denied suffrage. Many states imposed property qualifications on voting as well on the theory that only property ownership gave a person a sufficient stake in the welfare of society to enable him to exercise the franchise responsibly. As you read the following materials, consider whether these approaches to the franchise reflect a plausible theory of citizenship. What does it mean to be a member of the state? Were these restrictions on the voting rights of citizens the legitimate result of rational choices made by the people when they created their state and national governments, or were they a usurpation of power by a minority? What social or political assumptions might account for the limited distribution of the vote in earlier times?

Minor v. Happersett

88 U.S. 162 (1874)

THE CHIEF JUSTICE [WAITE] delivered the opinion of the court.

The question is presented in this case, whether, since the adoption of the fourteenth amendment, a woman, who is a citizen of the United States and of the State of Missouri, is a voter in that State, notwithstanding the provision of the constitution and laws of the State, which confine the right of suffrage to men alone. . . .

The argument is, that as a woman, born or naturalized in the United States and subject to the jurisdiction thereof, is a citizen of the United States and of the State in which she resides, she has the right of suffrage as one of the privileges and immunities of her citizenship, which the State cannot by its laws or constitution abridge.

There is no doubt that women may be citizens. They are persons, and by the fourteenth amendment "all persons born or naturalized in the United States and subject to the jurisdiction thereof" are expressly declared to be "citizens of the United States and of the State wherein they reside." But, in our opinion, it did not need this amendment to give them that position. Before its adoption the Constitution of the United States did not in terms prescribe who should be citizens of the United States or of the several States, yet there were necessarily such citizens without such provision. There cannot be a nation without a people. The very idea of a political community, such as a nation is, implies an association of persons for the promotion of their general welfare. Each one of the persons associated becomes a member of the nation formed by the association. He owes it allegiance and is entitled to its protection. Allegiance and protection are, in this connection, reciprocal obligations. The one is a compensation for the other; allegiance for protection and protection for allegiance.

For convenience it has been found necessary to give a name to this membership. The object is to designate by a title the person and the relation he bears to the nation. For this purpose the words "subject," "inhabitant," and "citizen" have been used, and the choice between them is sometimes made to depend upon the form of the government. Citizen is now more commonly employed, however, and as it has been considered better suited to the description of one living under a republican government, it was adopted by nearly all of the States upon their separation from Great Britain, and was afterwards adopted in the Articles of Confederation and in the Constitution of the United States. When used in this sense it is understood as conveying the idea of membership of a nation, and nothing more.

To determine, then, who were citizens of the United States before the adoption of the amendment it is necessary to ascertain what persons originally associated themselves together to form the nation, and what were afterwards admitted to membership.

Looking at the Constitution itself we find that it was ordained and established by "the people of the United States," and then going further back, we find that these were the people of the several States that had before dissolved the political bands which connected them with Great Britain, and assumed a separate and equal station among the powers of the earth, and that had by Articles of Confederation and Perpetual Union, in which they took the name of "the United States of America," entered into a firm league of friendship with each other for their common defence, the security of their liberties and their mutual and general welfare, binding themselves to assist each other against all force offered to or attack made upon them, or any of them, on account of religion, sovereignty, trade, or any other pretence whatever.

Whoever, then, was one of the people of either of these States when the Constitution of the United States was adopted, became ipso facto a citizen—a member of the nation created by its adoption. He was one of the persons associating together to form the nation, and was, consequently, one of its original citizens. As to this there has never been a doubt. Disputes have arisen as to whether or not certain persons or certain classes of persons were part of the people at the time, but never as to their citizenship if they were.

Additions might always be made to the citizenship of the United States in two ways: first, by birth, and second, by naturalization. This is apparent from the Constitution itself, for it provides that "no person except a natural-born citizen, or a citizen of the United States at the time of the adoption of the Constitution, shall be eligible to the office of President," and that Congress shall have power "to establish a uniform rule of naturalization." Thus new citizens may be born or they may be created by naturalization. . . .

But if more is necessary to show that women have always been considered as citizens the same as men, abundant proof is to be found in the legislative and judicial history of the country. Thus, by the Constitution, the judicial power of the United States is made to extend to controversies between citizens of different States. Under this it has been uniformly held that the citizenship necessary to give the courts of the United States jurisdiction of a cause must be affirmatively shown on the record. Its existence as a fact may be put in issue and tried. If found not to exist the case must be dismissed. Notwithstanding this the records of the courts are full of cases in which the jurisdiction depends upon the citizenship of women, and not one can be found, we think, in which objection was made on that account. Certainly none can be found in which it has been held that women could not sue or be sued in the courts of the United States. . . .

Other proof of like character might be found, but certainly more cannot be necessary to establish the fact that sex has never been made one of the elements of citizenship in the United States. In this respect men have never had an advantage over women. The same laws precisely apply to both. The fourteenth amendment did not affect the citizenship of women any more than it did of men. In this particular, therefore, the rights of Mrs. Minor do not depend upon the amendment. She has always been a citizen from her birth, and entitled to all the privileges and immunities of citizenship. The amendment prohibited the State, of which she is a citizen, from abridging any of her privileges and immunities as a citizen of the United States; but it did not confer citizenship on her. That she had before its adoption.

If the right of suffrage is one of the necessary privileges of a citizen of the United States, then the constitution and laws of Missouri confining it to men are in violation of the Constitution of the United States, as amended, and consequently void. The direct question is, therefore, presented whether all citizens are necessarily voters.

The Constitution does not define the privileges and immunities of citizens. For that definition we must look elsewhere. In this case we need not determine what they are, but only whether suffrage is necessarily one of them.

It certainly is nowhere made so in express terms. The United States has no voters in the States of its own creation. The elective officers of the United States are all elected directly or indirectly by State voters. The members of the House of Representatives are to be chosen by the people of the States, and the electors in each State must have the qualifications requisite for electors of the most numerous branch of the State legislature. Senators are to be chosen by the legislatures of the States, and necessarily the members of the legislature required to make the choice are elected by the voters of the State. Each State must appoint in such manner, as the legislature thereof may direct, the electors to elect the President and Vice-President. The times, places, and manner of holding elections for Senators and Representatives are to be prescribed in each State by the legislature thereof; but Congress may at any time, by law, make or alter such regulations, except as to the place of choosing Senators. It is not necessary to inquire whether this power of supervision thus given to Congress is sufficient to authorize any interference with the State laws prescribing the qualifications of voters, for no such interference has ever been attempted. The power of the State in this particular is certainly supreme until Congress acts.

The amendment did not add to the privileges and immunities of a citizen. It simply furnished an additional guaranty for the protection of such as he already had. No new voters were necessarily made by it. Indirectly it may have had that effect, because it may have increased the number of citizens entitled to suffrage under the constitution and laws of the States, but it operates for this purpose, if at all, through the States and the State laws, and not directly upon the citizen.

It is clear, therefore, we think, that the Constitution has not added the right of suffrage to the privileges and immunities of citizenship as they existed at the time it was adopted. This makes it proper to inquire whether suffrage was coextensive with the citizenship of the States at the time of its adoption. If it was, then it may with force be argued that suffrage was one of the rights which belonged to citizenship, and in the enjoyment of which every citizen must be protected. But if it was not, the contrary may with propriety be assumed.

When the Federal Constitution was adopted, all the States, with the exception of Rhode Island and Connecticut, had constitutions of their own. These two continued to act under their charters from the Crown. Upon an examination of those constitutions we find that in no State were all citizens permitted to vote. Each State determined for itself who should have that power. Thus, in New Hampshire, "every male inhabitant of each town and parish with town privileges, and places unincorporated in the State, of twenty-one years of age and upwards, excepting paupers and persons excused from paying taxes at their own request," were its voters; in Massachusetts "every male inhabitant of twenty-one years of age and upwards, having a freehold estate within the commonwealth of the annual income of three pounds, or any estate of the value of sixty pounds"; in Rhode Island "such as are admitted free of the company and society" of the colony; in Connecticut such persons as had "maturity in years, quiet and peaceable behavior, a civil conversation, and forty shillings freehold or forty pounds personal estate," if so certified by the selectmen; in New York "every male inhabitant of full age who shall have personally resided within one of the counties of the State for six months immediately preceding the day of election . . . if during the time aforesaid he shall have been a freeholder, possessing a freehold of the value of twenty pounds within the county, or have rented a tenement therein of the yearly value of forty shillings, and been rated and actually paid taxes to the State"; in New Jersey "all inhabitants . . . of full age who are worth fifty pounds, proclamation-money, clear estate in the same, and have resided in the county in which they claim a vote for twelve months immediately preceding the election"; in Pennsylvania "every freeman of the age of twenty-one years, having resided in the State two years next before the election, and within that time paid a State or county tax which shall have been assessed at least six months before the election"; in Delaware and Virginia "as exercised by law at present"; in Maryland "all freemen above twenty-one years of age having a freehold of fifty acres of land in the county in which they offer to vote and residing therein, and all freemen having property in the State above the value of thirty pounds current money, and having resided in the county in which they offer to vote one whole year next preceding the election"; in North Carolina, for senators, "all freemen of the age of twenty-one years who have been inhabitants of any one county within the State twelve months immediately preceding the day of election, and possessed of a freehold within the same county of fifty acres of land for six months next before and at the day of election," and for members of the house of commons "all freemen of the age of twenty-one years who have been inhabitants in any one county within the State twelve months immediately preceding the day of any election, and shall have paid public taxes"; in South Carolina "every free white man of the age of twenty-one years, being a citizen of the State and having resided therein two years previous to the day of election, and who hath a freehold of fifty acres of land, or a town lot of which he hath been legally seized and possessed at least six months before such election, or (not having such freehold or town lot), hath been a resident within the election district in which he offers to give his vote six months before said election, and hath paid a tax the preceding year of three shillings sterling towards the support of the government"; and in Georgia such "citizens and inhabitants of the State as shall have attained to the age of twenty-one years, and shall have paid tax for the year next preceding the election, and shall have resided six months within the county."

In this condition of the law in respect to suffrage in the several States it cannot for a moment be doubted that if it had been intended to make all citizens of the United States voters, the framers of the Constitution would not have left it to implication. So important a change in the condition of citizenship as it actually existed, if intended, would have been expressly declared. . . .

And still again, after the adoption of the fourteenth amendment, it was deemed necessary to adopt a fifteenth, as follows: "The right of citizens of the United States to vote shall not be denied or abridged by the United States, or by any State, on account of race, color, or previous condition of servitude." The fourteenth amendment had already provided that no State should make or enforce any law which should abridge the privileges or immunities of citizens of the United States. If suffrage was one of these privileges or immunities, why amend the Constitution to prevent its being denied on account of race, &c.? Nothing is more evident than that the greater must include the less, and if all were already protected why go through with the form of amending the Constitution to protect a part? . . .

But we have already sufficiently considered the proof found upon the inside of the Constitution. That upon the outside is equally effective.

The Constitution was submitted to the States for adoption in 1787, and was ratified by nine States in 1788, and finally by the thirteen original States in 1790. Vermont was the first new State admitted to the Union, and it came in under a constitution which conferred the right of suffrage only upon men of the full age of twenty-one years, having resided in the State for the space of one whole year next before the election, and who were of quiet and peaceable behavior. This was in 1791. The next year, 1792, Kentucky followed with a constitution confining the right of suffrage to free male citizens of the age of twenty-one years who had resided in the State two years or in the county in which they offered to vote one year next before the election. Then followed Tennessee, in 1796, with voters of freemen of the age of twenty-one years and upwards, possessing a freehold in the county wherein they may vote, and being inhabitants of the State or freemen being inhabitants of any one county in the State six months immediately preceding the day of election. But we need not particularize further. No new State has ever been admitted to the Union which has conferred the right of suffrage upon women, and this has never been considered a valid objection to her admission. On the contrary, as is claimed in the argument, the right of suffrage was withdrawn from women as early as 1807 in the State of New Jersey, without any attempt to obtain the interference of the United States to prevent it. Since then the governments of the insurgent States have been reorganized under a requirement that before their representatives could be admitted to seats in Congress they must have adopted new constitutions, republican in form. In no one of these constitutions was suffrage conferred upon women, and yet the States have all been restored to their original position as States in the Union. . . .

Certainly, if the courts can consider any question settled, this is one. For nearly ninety years the people have acted upon the idea that the Constitution, when it conferred citizenship, did not necessarily confer the right of suffrage. If uniform practice long continued can settle the construction of so important an instrument as the Constitution of the United States confessedly is, most certainly it has been done here. Our province is to decide what the law is, not to declare what it should be.

———————————

Many of the original restrictions on suffrage have been overturned by constitutional amendment. The Fifteenth Amendment prohibits abridgement of the right to vote on account of race; the Nineteenth Amendment prohibits such abridgement on account of sex; the Twenty-Fourth Amendment prohibits conditioning the vote in federal elections on payment of a poll tax; and the Twenty-Sixth Amendment requires extension of the vote to 18-year-olds.

>> *Alienage and Voting.* If women, who were citizens, did not thereby gain a constitutional right to vote, it seems clear that noncitizens—aliens—could not have such a right. Although the Supreme Court has never squarely so held, it has strongly suggested that aliens would not have a constitutionally based right to vote. *See, e.g., Sugarman v. Dougall,* 413 U.S. 634, 649 (1973) ("implicit in many of this Court's voting rights decisions is the notion that citizenship is a permissible criterion for limiting such rights"). However, one need not have a constitutionally based right to vote in order to enjoy the franchise: governments are generally understood to be free to grant suffrage more broadly than the minimal constitutional requirements.

At various points in American history, aliens have been the beneficiaries of franchise-extending policies. For example, South Carolina permitted French Huguenots to vote in the seventeenth and eighteenth centuries, and Pennsylvania permitted unnaturalized German immigrants to vote in the mid-eighteenth century. One reason these policies appeared was that each colony, and then each state, was free to develop its own definition of citizenship until the U.S. Constitution centralized the naturalization power in the national government. Another reason was that contemporary understandings of nationalism and national identity did not begin to take shape until the middle or so of the nineteenth century. Before this ideological shift, eligibility to vote tended to be defined more in terms of residency than citizenship. Thus, early statutes and state constitutions spoke more frequently of "inhabitants" than of "citizens." Sometimes, granting the franchise to unnaturalized inhabitants paid other kinds of dividends: for example, the United States permitted noncitizens to vote in the western territories as part of a deliberate policy to encourage settlement.

Should aliens be understood to have a formal right to vote, or at least a moral claim to the franchise? Why isn't residency in itself a sufficient basis to entitle people to vote in the place where they reside?

> The being an inhabitant, and the paying tax, are circumstances which give an interest in the borough. The being an inhabitant, gives an interest in the police or regulations of the borough generally; the paying tax gives an interest in the appropriation of the money levied. A right, therefore, to a voice mediately or immediately in these matters, is founded in natural justice. . . . It is the wise policy of every community to collect support from all on whom it may be reasonable to impose it: and it is but reasonable that all on whom it is imposed would have a voice to some extent in the mode and object of the application.

Stewart v. Foster, 2 Binn. 110, 122 (Pa. 1809) (Brackenridge, J., dissenting). The passage above is a dissent from a ruling involving the construction of a statute that granted the right to vote in Pittsburgh local elections to "inhabitants." A majority of the Pennsylvania Supreme Court construed the term "inhabitant" to imply a requirement of citizenship, and so rejected the suit of a resident alien who was denied the opportunity to vote in municipal elections. How would you have interpreted the statute?

Several U.S. cities have chosen to extend the franchise to noncitizens in local elections. Most notably, in 2021 New York City enacted a law (since invalidated under the state constitution) opening elections for municipal offices to more than 800,000 adult city residents who are not U.S. citizens. Other jurisdictions have extended the franchise to noncitizens only for specific offices; Chicago, for example, permits noncitizens to vote in local school board elections. Should eligibility of noncitizens to vote depend on the office for which votes are cast? Is permitting noncitizens to vote in local elections different from permitting them to vote for Congress or governor? The Supreme Court has ruled that states and local governments may not refuse a free public education to the undocumented children of illegal immigrants. *Plyler v. Doe*, 457 U.S. 202 (1982). If their children cannot be denied a public education, do noncitizen parents of schoolchildren have a better argument for being granted the right to vote for members of the local school board than for other municipal offices?

For reviews of the history of, and arguments supporting, alien suffrage, see Gerald M. Rosberg, *Aliens and the Right to Vote*, 75 MICH. L. REV. 1092 (1977); Jamin B. Raskin, *Legal Aliens, Local Citizens: The Historical, Constitutional and Theoretical Meanings of Alien Suffrage*, 141 U. PA. L. REV. 1391 (1993); RON HAYDUK, DEMOCRACY FOR ALL (2006).

Noncitizen voting is permitted in many countries, especially in local elections. In Chile, Malawi, New Zealand, and Uruguay, permanent legal residents may vote in national elections regardless of citizenship. *See* DAVID C. EARNEST, OLD NATIONS, NEW VOTERS: NATIONALISM, TRANSNATIONALISM, AND DEMOCRACY IN THE ERA OF GLOBAL MIGRATION (2008).

>> *Voting in the District of Columbia and the Territories.*   Article I, §2, cl. 1 of the U.S. Constitution provides that the House of Representatives "shall be composed of Members chosen every second Year by the People of the several *States*" (emphasis added). The Seventeenth Amendment likewise provides that Senators shall be chosen "from each *State*, elected by the people thereof" (emphasis added). Although the District of Columbia has about 690,000 residents—more than Vermont and Wyoming—under the Constitution, it is not a "state," but a "District." Art. I, §8, cl. 17. As a result, D.C. residents are not permitted to vote for members of Congress—even though the overwhelming majority of them are citizens of the United States and citizens of the District itself, and thereby entitled to vote under the federal home rule statute for city offices within the District.

The unfairness of this situation has long been recognized. It was alleviated in part by the Twenty-Third Amendment, ratified in 1961, which gave the District electoral votes in presidential elections on an equal footing with the states. But efforts to grant D.C. residents the right to vote in Congress have routinely stalled due to partisan politics: Republicans in Congress have long resisted admitting the District as a state on the assumption, likely valid, that it would routinely elect two Democratic Senators and a Democratic Representative.

Proponents of D.C. voting have attempted to bypass the congressional impasse by resort to the courts, but without success. A lawsuit that invoked functional arguments based on changed circumstances to challenge this disenfranchisement was dismissed in *Adams v. Clinton*, 90 F. Supp. 2d 35 (D.D.C.) (three-judge court), *summarily aff'd*, 531 U.S. 941 (2000). A similar suit was brought in 2020, but a largely sympathetic court felt itself obliged to dismiss: "We recognize that District residents' lack of the congressional franchise is viewed by many, even most, as deeply unjust, and we have given each aspect of Plaintiffs' claims most serious consideration, but our ruling today is compelled by precedent and by the Constitution itself."

Ultimately, the court ruled, relief may be provided only by Congress, which may admit the District as a state, or by constitutional amendment. *Castañon v. United States,* 444 F.Supp.3d 118 (D.D.C 2020) (three-judge court).

In 2004, the Inter-American Commission on Human Rights (an agency of the Organization of American States) ruled that the United States' refusal to allow D.C. residents to vote in federal elections violates international law, including the American Declaration of the Rights and Duties of Man, to which the United States is a signatory. The ruling had no binding effect.

Like residents of the District of Columbia, residents of Puerto Rico—an American "commonwealth" that lacks the constitutional status of a state—cannot vote in congressional elections, nor, lacking any equivalent to the Twenty-Third Amendment, can they vote in presidential elections. Legal challenges have been repeatedly turned back. In the most recent iteration, the First Circuit held in *Igartua de la Rosa v. United States,* 417 F.3d 145 (1st Cir. 2005) (en banc):

> [T]he make-up of the electoral college is a direct consequence of how the framers of the Constitution chose to structure our government—a choice itself based on political compromise rather than conceptual perfection. . . . That the franchise for choosing electors is confined to "states" cannot be "unconstitutional" because it is what the Constitution itself provides. Hence it does no good to stress how important is "the right to vote" for President. Although we recognize the loyalty, contributions, and sacrifices of those who are in common citizens of Puerto Rico and the United States, . . . [t]he path to changing the Constitution lies not through the courts but through the constitutional amending process, U.S. Const. art. V; and the road to statehood—if that is what Puerto Rico's citizens want—runs through Congress.

Federal courts have reached similar conclusions in cases originating in the Territory of Guam and the U.S. Virgin Islands. *Attorney General of the Territory of Guam v. United States,* 738 F.2d 1017 (9th Cir. 1984); *Ballentine v. United States,* 486 F.3d 806 (3d Cir. 2007)

» *The Equality of Citizens: Multiple Votes?* Does having or not having the vote implicate the equality of citizens? Does denial of the franchise to some citizens accord them lesser status than other citizens? Is there some norm of citizen equality that requires all to have the same status regarding the franchise?

Even if all must have the vote, does it follow that all must have the same *influence?* For example, might some be entitled to more votes than others? Consider the following passage from John Stuart Mill:

> But though every one ought to have a voice—that every one should have an equal voice is a totally different proposition. When two persons who have a joint interest, differ in opinion, does justice require that both opinions should be held of exactly equal value? If with equal virtue, one is superior to the other in knowledge and intelligence—or if with equal intelligence, one excels the other in virtue—the opinion, the judgment, of the higher moral or intellectual being, is worth more than that of the inferior: and if the institutions of the country virtually assert that they are

of the same value, they assert a thing which is not. One of the two, as the wiser or better man, has a claim to superior weight: the difficulty is in ascertaining which of the two it is; a thing impossible as between individuals, but, taking men in bodies and in numbers, it can be done with a certain approach to accuracy. . . .

[In] national affairs . . . no one needs ever be called upon for a complete sacrifice of his own opinion. It can always be taken into the calculation, and counted at a certain figure, a higher figure being assigned to the suffrages of those whose opinion is entitled to greater weight. There is not, in this arrangement, anything necessarily invidious to those to whom it assigns the lower degrees of influence. Entire exclusion from a voice in the common concerns is one thing: the concession to others of a more potential voice, on the ground of greater capacity for the management of the joint interests, is another. The two things are not merely different, they are incommensurable. Every one has a right to feel insulted by being made a nobody, and stamped as of no account at all. No one but a fool, and only a fool of a peculiar description, feels offended by the acknowledgement that there are others whose opinion, and even whose wish, is entitled to a greater amount of consideration than his. To have no voice in what are partly his own concerns, is a thing which nobody willingly submits to; but when what is partly his concern is also partly another's, and he feels the other to understand the subject better than himself, that the other's opinion should be counted for more than his own, accords with his expectations, and with the course of things which in all other affairs of life he is accustomed to acquiesce in. It is only necessary that this superior influence should be assigned on grounds which he can comprehend, and of which he is able to perceive the justice.

I hasten to say, that I consider it entirely inadmissible, unless as a temporary makeshift, that the superiority of influence should be conferred in consideration of property. . . . [That] criterion is [too] imperfect; accident has so much more to do than merit with enabling men to rise in the world. . . . The only thing which can justify reckoning one person's opinion as equivalent to more than one, is individual mental superiority; and what is wanted is some approximate means of ascertaining that. If there existed such a thing as a really national education, or a trustworthy system of general examination, education might be tested directly. In the absence of these, the nature of a person's occupation is some test. An employer of labour is on the average more intelligent than a labourer; for he must labour with his head, and not solely with his hands. A foreman is generally more intelligent than an ordinary labourer, and a labourer in the skilled trades than in the unskilled. A banker, merchant, or manufacturer, is likely to be more intelligent than a tradesman, because he has larger and more complicated interests to manage. . . . [T]wo or more votes might be allowed to every person who exercises any of these superior functions. The liberal professions, when really and not nominally practiced, imply, of course, a still higher degree of instruction; and wherever a sufficient examination, or any serious conditions of education, are required before entering on a profession, its members could be admitted at once to a plurality of votes. The same rule might be applied to graduates of universities; and even to those who bring satisfactory certificates of having passed through the course of study required by any school at which the higher branches of knowledge are taught, under proper securities that the teaching is real, and not a mere pretence. . . .

JOHN STUART MILL, CONSIDERATIONS ON REPRESENTATIVE GOVERNMENT, ch. viii (1861).

It is of course unacceptable in the contemporary United States to suggest that some should get more votes than others on the basis of competence. However, there may be other grounds on which some might be granted more votes than others. Consider the following argument for granting additional votes to parents of children under 18:

> [I]t seems likely that the failure to enfranchise children has substantial effects on public policy outcomes. This is no doubt a good thing, to the extent that children might exert\ influence through immature or unreflective votes. But if there were a mechanism by which the interests of children could be taken into account through more reflective voting—and the votes of others thereby given less proportionate say—then political effects might well follow that could not so easily be dismissed. Public expenditures on schools and playgrounds, on early-intervention public health measures, or on the preservation of endangered species and virgin forests might be higher, for instance, whereas expenditures on benefits for the elderly, or on research to prevent diseases that typically strike later in life, might be lower.
>
> But there is such a mechanism. It is widely assumed that voters who are parents cast the single votes they now receive in part at least in pursuit of the interests of their children. Why then should those parents not be given extra votes on account of their children? There are no doubt substantial arguments that extra votes for parents would be unconstitutional, but the most obvious of those arguments seem a good deal less than decisive. And enacting a constitutional amendment is always possible. That is the way in which the vote was extended to the emancipated slaves, to women, and to eighteen-year-olds. . . .

Robert W. Bennett, *Should Parents Be Given Extra Votes on Account of Their Children?: Toward a Conversational Understanding of American Democracy*, 94 Nw. L. Rev. 503, 504-505 (2000).

2. *Residency*

Carrington v. Rash

380 U.S. 89 (1965)

Mr. Justice STEWART delivered the opinion of the Court.

A provision of the Texas Constitution prohibits "[a]ny member of the Armed Forces of the United States" who moves his home to Texas during the course of his military duty from ever voting in any election in that State "so long as he or she is a member of the Armed Forces." The question presented is whether this provision, as construed by the Supreme Court of Texas in the present case, deprives the petitioner of a right secured by the Equal Protection Clause of the Fourteenth Amendment. . . .

The petitioner, a sergeant in the United States Army, entered the service from Alabama in 1946 at the age of 18. The State concedes that he has been domiciled in Texas since 1962, and that he intends to make his home there permanently. He has purchased a house in El Paso where he lives with his wife and two children. He is also the proprietor of a small business there. The petitioner's post of military duty is not in Texas, but at White Sands, New Mexico. He regularly commutes from his home in El Paso to his Army job at White Sands. He pays property taxes in Texas and has his automobile registered there. But for his uniform, the State concedes that the petitioner would be eligible to vote in El Paso County, Texas.

Texas has unquestioned power to impose reasonable residence restrictions on the availability of the ballot. *Pope v. Williams*, 193 U.S. 621. There can be no doubt either of the historic function of the States to establish, on a nondiscriminatory basis, and in accordance with the Constitution, other qualifications for the exercise of the franchise. Indeed, "the States have long been held to have broad powers to determine the conditions under which the right of suffrage may be exercised." *Lassiter v. Northampton Election Bd.*, 360 U.S. 45, 50. "In other words, the privilege to vote in a State is within the jurisdiction of the State itself, to be exercised as the State may direct, and upon such terms as to it may seem proper, provided, of course, no discrimination is made between individuals in violation of the Federal Constitution." *Pope v. Williams, supra*, at 632.

This Texas constitutional provision, however, is unique. Texas has said that no serviceman may ever acquire a voting residence in the State so long as he remains in service. It is true that the State has treated all members of the military with an equal hand. And mere classification, as this Court has often said, does not of itself deprive a group of equal protection. *Williamson v. Lee Optical Co.*, 348 U.S. 483. But the fact that a State is dealing with a distinct class and treats the members of that class equally does not end the judicial inquiry. "The courts must reach and determine the question whether the classifications drawn in a statute are reasonable in light of its purpose. . . ." *McLaughlin v. Florida*, 379 U.S. 184, 191.

It is argued that this absolute denial of the vote to servicemen like the petitioner fulfills two purposes. First, the State says it has a legitimate interest in immunizing its elections from the concentrated balloting of military personnel, whose collective voice may overwhelm a small local civilian community. Secondly, the State says it has a valid interest in protecting the franchise from infiltration by transients, and it can reasonably assume that those servicemen who fall within the constitutional exclusion will be within the State for only a short period of time.

The theory underlying the State's first contention is that the Texas constitutional provision is necessary to prevent the danger of a "takeover" of the civilian community resulting from concentrated voting by large numbers of military personnel in bases placed near Texas towns and cities. A base commander, Texas suggests, who opposes local police administration or teaching policies in local schools, might influence his men to vote in conformity with his predilections. Local bond issues may fail, and property taxes stagnate at low levels because military personnel are unwilling to invest in the future of the area. We stress—and this is a theme to be reiterated—that Texas has the right to require that all military personnel enrolled to vote be bona fide residents of the community. But if they are in fact residents, with the intention of making Texas their home indefinitely, they, as all other qualified residents, have a right to an equal opportunity for political representation. Cf. *Gray v. Sanders*, 372 U.S. 368. "Fencing out" from the franchise a sector of the population because of the way they may vote is constitutionally impermissible. "The exercise of rights so vital to the maintenance of democratic institutions," *Schneider v. State*, 308 U.S. 147, 161, cannot constitutionally be obliterated because of a fear of the political views of a particular group of bona fide residents. Yet, that is what Texas claims to have done here.

The State's second argument is that its voting ban is justified because of the transient nature of service in the Armed Forces. As the Supreme Court of Texas stated: "Persons in military service are subject at all times to reassignment, and hence to a change in their actual residence . . . they do not elect to be where they are. Their reasons for being where they are . . . cannot be the same as [those of] the permanent residents." 378 S.W.2d, at 306. . . .

But only where military personnel are involved has Texas been unwilling to develop more precise tests to determine the bona fides of an individual claiming to have actually made his home in the State long enough to vote. The State's law reports disclose that there have been many cases where the local election officials have determined the issue of bona fide residence. These officials and the courts reviewing their actions have required a "freely exercised intention" of remaining within the State, *Harrison v. Chesshir*, 316 S.W.2d 909, 915. The declarations of voters concerning their intent to reside in the State and in a particular county is often not conclusive; the election officials may look to the actual facts and circumstances. *Stratton v. Hall*, 90 S.W.2d 865, 866. By statute, Texas deals with particular categories of citizens who, like soldiers, present specialized problems in determining residence. Students at colleges and universities in Texas, patients in hospitals and other institutions within the State, and civilian employees of the United States Government may be as transient as military personnel. But all of them are given at least an opportunity to show the election officials that they are bona fide residents. . . .

We deal here with matters close to the core of our constitutional system. "The right . . . to choose," *United States v. Classic*, 313 U.S. 299, 314, that this Court has been so zealous to protect, means, at the least, that States may not casually deprive a class of individuals of the vote because of some remote administrative benefit to the State. By forbidding a soldier ever to controvert the presumption of nonresidence, the Texas Constitution imposes an invidious discrimination in violation of the Fourteenth Amendment. "There is no indication in the Constitution that . . . occupation affords a permissible basis for distinguishing between qualified voters within the State." *Gray v. Sanders*, 372 U.S. 368, 380.

We recognize that special problems may be involved in determining whether servicemen have actually acquired a new domicile in a State for franchise purposes. We emphasize that Texas is free to take reasonable and adequate steps, as have other States, to see that all applicants for the vote actually fulfill the requirements of bona fide residence. But this constitutional provision goes beyond such rules. "[T]he presumption here created is . . . definitely conclusive—incapable of being overcome by proof of the most positive character." *Heiner v. Donnan*, 285 U.S. 312, 324. All servicemen not residents of Texas before induction come within the provision's sweep. Not one of them can ever vote in Texas, no matter how long Texas may have been his true home. "The uniform of our country . . . [must not] be the badge of disfranchisement for the man or woman who wears it.". . .

≫ ***Durational Residency Requirements.***   *Carrington* says that a state may constitutionally limit the franchise to "bona fide residents." But it is not always so easy to distinguish bona fide residents from transients who are merely residing temporarily in the state and thus ought to vote in their home states by absentee ballot. By what means may a state decide which residents are bona fide? One common strategy was the use of durational residency requirements under which new residents of the state were ineligible to vote until they had resided in the state for some period of time. The Court examined one such durational residency in *Dunn v. Blumstein*, 405 U.S. 330 (1972). *Dunn* concerned a Tennessee statute forbidding state residents to vote until they had resided in the state for one year, and in their present county of residence for three months. In an opinion written by Justice Marshall, the Court invalidated the restriction.

> Durational residence laws penalize those persons who have traveled from one place to another to establish a new residence during the qualifying period. Such laws divide residents into two classes, old residents and new residents, and discriminate against the latter to the extent of totally denying them the opportunity to vote. . . . By denying some citizens the right to vote, such laws deprive them of "'a fundamental political right, . . . preservative of all rights.'" *Reynolds v. Sims*, 377 U.S. 533, 562 (1964). . . . [A]s a general matter, "before that right [to vote] can be restricted, the purpose of the restriction and the assertedly overriding interests served by it must meet close constitutional scrutiny." *Evans v. Cornman*. . . . This exacting test is appropriate for another reason . . . : Tennessee's durational residence laws classify bona fide residents on the basis of recent travel, penalizing those persons, and only those persons, who have gone from one jurisdiction to another during the qualifying period. Thus, the durational residence requirement directly impinges on the exercise of a second fundamental personal right, the right to travel.
>
> Tennessee tenders "two basic purposes" served by its durational residence requirements: [ensuring the "purity of the ballot box" and promoting intelligent exercise of the franchise. With regard to the first interest, t]he main concern is that nonresidents will temporarily invade the State or county, falsely swear that they are residents to become eligible to vote, and, by voting, allow a candidate to win by fraud. Surely the prevention of such fraud is a legitimate and compelling government goal. But it is impossible to view durational residence requirements as necessary to achieve that state interest.
>
> Preventing fraud, the asserted evil that justifies state lawmaking, means keeping nonresidents from voting. But, by definition, a durational residence law bars newly arrived residents from the franchise along with

nonresidents. The State argues that such sweeping laws are necessary to prevent fraud because they are needed to identify bona fide residents. This contention is particularly unconvincing in light of Tennessee's total statutory scheme for regulating the franchise.

Durational residence laws may once have been necessary to prevent a fraudulent evasion of state voter standards, but today in Tennessee, as in most other States, this purpose is served by a system of voter registration. Tenn. Code Ann. §2-301 et seq. (1955 and Supp. 1970). Given this system, the record is totally devoid of any evidence that durational residence requirements are in fact necessary to identify bona fide residents. The qualifications of the would-be voter in Tennessee are determined when he registers to vote, which he may do until 30 days before the election. Tenn. Code Ann. §2-304. His qualifications—including bona fide residence—are established then by oath. Tenn. Code Ann. §2-309. There is no indication in the record that Tennessee routinely goes behind the would-be voter's oath to determine his qualifications. Since false swearing is no obstacle to one intent on fraud, the existence of burdensome voting qualifications like durational residence requirements cannot prevent corrupt nonresidents from fraudulently registering and voting. . . . Indeed, the durational residence requirement becomes an effective voting obstacle only to residents who tell the truth and have no fraudulent purposes. . . .

Our conclusion that the waiting period is not the least restrictive means necessary for preventing fraud is bolstered by the recognition that Tennessee has at its disposal a variety of criminal laws that are more than adequate to detect and deter whatever fraud may be feared. At least six separate sections of the Tennessee Code define offenses to deal with voter fraud.

. . . Finally, the State urges that a longtime resident is "more likely to exercise his right [to vote] more intelligently." . . . We note that the criterion of "intelligent" voting is an elusive one, and susceptible of abuse. But without deciding as a general matter the extent to which a State can bar less knowledgeable or intelligent citizens from the franchise, . . . the durational residence requirements in this case founder because of their crudeness as a device for achieving the articulated state goal of assuring the knowledgeable exercise of the franchise. The classifications created by durational residence requirements obviously permit any longtime resident to vote regardless of his knowledge of the issues—and obviously many longtime residents do not have any. On the other hand, the classifications bar from the franchise many other, admittedly new, residents who have become at least minimally, and often fully, informed about the issues. . . . Given modern communications, and given the clear indication that campaign spending and voter education occur largely during the month before an election, the State cannot seriously maintain that it is "necessary" to reside for a year in the State and three months in the county in order to be knowledgeable about congressional, state, or even purely local elections. . . .

In *Marston v. Lewis*, 410 U.S. 679 (1973), the Court sustained a durational residency requirement of 50 days for state and local elections. In *Burns v. Fortson*, 410 U.S. 686 (1973) (per curiam), the Court upheld a 50-day durational residency requirement for voting in elections for federal Senators and Representatives.

In an era in which transportation technology allows such ease of mobility, and in which people are much more willing than previously to relocate for work, marriage, climate, recreation, and other considerations, are durational residency requirements justifiable at all? *See* Eugene D. Mazo, *Residency and Democracy*, 43 FLA. ST. U. L. REV. 611 (2016).

▶▶ *Durational Residency Requirements in Presidential Elections.*   Under Article I, §4 of the United States Constitution, Congress has extremely broad powers to regulate elections for federal offices; for example, Congress could by law provide that elections for all federal offices be run by federal officials under federal rules. In practice, however, Congress has largely left the running of elections to the states. As a consequence, federal officials are elected at elections run by state officials according to state election codes. This means that a state's durational residency requirement, assuming it is constitutional, must be satisfied before a voter can register to vote for *any* office, including federal offices. The Court concedes in *Dunn* that states have a legitimate interest in confining the franchise to bona fide state residents, but does this interest apply to voting for *federal* offices?

In Section 202 of the Voting Rights Act, Congress concluded that states have no such interest with respect to elections for President and Vice President. Congress feared that the imposition of durational residency requirements would deprive people who move from one state to another shortly before a presidential election of the ability to vote for President in any state. Consequently, Congress barred the application of all durational residency requirements to presidential elections. In a splintered ruling in *Oregon v. Mitchell*, 400 U.S. 112 (1970), the Court upheld this provision against a constitutional challenge. Justice Black reasoned as follows:

> In Title II of the Voting Rights Act Amendments Congress . . . provided that in presidential and vice-presidential elections, no voter could be denied his right to cast a ballot because he had not lived in the jurisdiction long enough to meet its residency requirements. Furthermore, Congress provided uniform national rules for absentee voting in presidential and vice-presidential elections. In enacting these regulations Congress was attempting to insure a fully effective voice to all citizens in national elections. . . . Acting under its broad authority to create and maintain a national government, Congress unquestionably has power under the Constitution to regulate federal elections. The framers of our Constitution were vitally concerned with setting up a national government that could survive. Essential to the survival and to the growth of our national government is its power to fill its elective offices and to insure that the officials who fill those offices are as responsive as possible to the will of the people whom they represent.

Justice Douglas agreed on the ground that voting for national officers is a privilege and immunity of national citizenship under the Fourteenth Amendment, and Congress was empowered by Section 5 of the Fourteenth Amendment to enforce it in this way. Six other Justices concurred on the ground that the application of durational residency requirements to elections for national offices burdened the right of interstate travel.

▶▶ *Students as State Residents.*   In several cases, election boards have taken the position that college students who live in dormitories are not bona fide residents of the state in which they attend college. Federal courts have generally rejected this policy under *Dunn*:

> [I]n these days of an increasingly mobile society, it would be the rare citizen who could swear honestly that he intended to reside at his present address permanently; . . . many citizens [have] "definite" hopes of moving to better job opportunities, more pleasant climates, and the like. If such a test [of residency] were in fact imposed on all citizens, it would go too far in restricting the vote to the more immobile elements of the populace; it would penalize, perhaps irrationally, those who make definite plans, while allowing the drifters who have uncertain plans to vote. And if the test were in fact only applied to students, then it would impermissibly discriminate against them.

Ramey v. Rockefeller, 348 F. Supp. 780, 788 (E.D.N.Y. 1972) (three-judge court). *See also Williams v. Salerno*, 792 F.2d 323 (2d Cir. 1986).

▶▶ *Citizenship and Residency: Better Together?*   Should both citizenship *and* residency be required for voting? Suppose someone resides outside the country of his or her citizenship—i.e., is an "expatriate." Is there any period of time after which an expatriate's connection to his or her country of citizenship becomes too weak to justify continued enjoyment of the franchise? The United States imposes no such limitation. However, other countries do so: the U.K. imposes a fifteen-year limit on voting rights for continuous nonresidents. Australia imposes a six-year limit, which may be extended indefinitely. New Zealand imposes a three-year limit, but it is reset when a nonresident citizen returns for a visit. *See* Richard Lappin, *The Right to Vote for Non-Resident Citizens in Europe*, 65 INT'L & COMP. L.Q. 859 (2016). Are these policies justifiable? On what grounds?

In *Frank v. Canada (Attorney General)*, 2019 SCC 1, the Supreme Court of Canada considered whether Canada's five-year limit on expatriate voting violated the Canadian Charter of Rights and Freedoms, the rights-granting portion of the Canadian Constitution. Unlike the U.S. Constitution, the Canadian Charter expressly provides: "Every citizen of Canada has the right to vote in an election of members of the House of Commons or of a legislative assembly. . . ." The court invalidated the restriction:

> There is little to justify the choice of five years as a threshold or to show how it is tailored to respond to a specific problem. It is also clear that the measure improperly applies to many individuals with deep and abiding connections to Canada and to Canadian laws, and that it does so in a manner that is far broader than necessary to achieve the electoral fairness objective advance by the [government]. The disenfranchisement of these citizens not only denies them a fundamental democratic right, but also comes at the expense of their sense of self-worth and their dignity. These

deleterious effects far outweigh any speculative benefits that the measure
might bring about. . . .

[T]he role of residence in our electoral system must be understood
in its historical context. The requirement emerged at a time when citizens were generally unable to travel as easily and extensively as they do
today and tended to spend their lives in one community. At that time, the
right to vote was linked to the ownership of land. . . . Today, in contrast,
we live in a globalized society. . . . Many Canadians live abroad, and many
do so for five years or more. . . . [I]n 2009, approximately 2.8 million
Canadians—or 8 percent of the population at the time—had been living
abroad for one year or more, and there were well over one million Canadians to whom the non-residence limit in the Act applied. . . . In sum, the
world has changed. . . .

>> *Multiple Residency and Voting Eligibility.* The model of voting eligibility based
on residency seems to presuppose that people reside in a single jurisdiction, and
that this jurisdiction is the place in which they are entitled to vote. While that
may generally be a relatively reasonable assumption, not everyone in these days of
great mobility and widely distributed wealth lives in just one place. Some people —
retirees, for example, or the very rich—may live regularly in two places, spending
equal amounts of time in both and having an equally strong interest in the public
policy of both jurisdictions. Yet the nearly universal rule among American jurisdictions is to make ineligible anyone who legally votes in another jurisdiction. The
result is that nearly everyone who has two residences must choose one residence as
the exclusive locus of citizenship, and thus of voting. Is the practice of putting people to this kind of choice constitutional? Or might it be said that long-term, established residency, even if only part-time, gives people a sufficient interest to require
as a matter of constitutional law that the opportunity to vote be available to them in
each place in which they reside?

The Second Circuit considered this question in *Wit v. Berman*, 306 F.2d 1256
(2d Cir. 2002). The plaintiffs were New York City residents who also owned homes
in the fashionable beach communities of Southampton and East Hampton, at the
eastern end of Long Island. Each had formerly been registered to vote in New York
City, but had switched registration to the Hamptons. They challenged on equal
protection grounds a provision of New York State's election law permitting citizens
to register to vote only in one community within the state, arguing that their ownership of homes and substantial periods of part-time residence in both places made
their treatment under state law arbitrary.

The court sustained the law. Conceding that "in modern times, domicile is
very often a poor proxy for a voter's stake in electoral outcomes," the court nevertheless held that a system of interest-based voter registration would pose insurmountable "administrative problems" for the state, and expressed concern about
the possibility of fraudulent multiple registration. Moreover, the court said, "[t]he
one-or-the-other rule does not in any sensible use of the word 'discriminate' against
appellants. Indeed, the Election Law's permissive approach allows appellants to
align their strongest, personal political interests with the appropriative voting location." This, the court suggested, was actually an "enhancement" of the plaintiffs'
"voting power."

Why is it necessary to restrict citizens to voting in only one jurisdiction? Consider the following proposal:

If . . . people have multiple attachments [throughout a] metropolitan area, including attachments to places where they shop or work, a different system of representation might be better. Consider a plan, for example, in which everyone gets five votes that they can cast in whatever local elections they feel affect their interest ("local" still being defined by traditional city boundaries). They can define their interests differently in different elections, and any form of connection that they think expresses an aspect of themselves at the moment will be treated as adequate. Under such an electoral system, mayors, city council members, and neighborhood representatives . . . would have a constituency made up not only of residents but of workers, shoppers, property-owners, the homeless, and so forth. People are unlikely to vote in a jurisdiction they don't care about, but there are a host of possible motives for voting. . . . There is also no reason to assume that the constituency would be limited solely to those who live in the region. These days . . . , people feel connected to areas far away as well as close to home. Puerto Ricans in New York, therefore, may want to vote not only in New York but in San Juan; of course, if they do, that would leave them one vote fewer for local elections in the New York region. . . .

GERALD FRUG, CITY MAKING: BUILDING COMMUNITIES WITHOUT BUILDING WALLS 106-107 (1999).

» *Voting by Nonresidents.* It is clear from the case law that an American jurisdiction may constitutionally make residence, like citizenship, a condition of the vote. But *must* a jurisdiction make residence a voting qualification? Is residence a constitutionally minimal requirement, or may a jurisdiction choose to extend the vote to nonresidents?

The Tenth Circuit considered this issue in *May v. Town of Mountain Village*, 132 F.3d 576 (10th Cir. 1997). The town of Mountain Village is located near Telluride, Colorado, a popular and well-heeled ski resort area. In 1996, the people of the town voted to adopt a Town Charter that extended the right to vote to any owners of real property located within the Town who are not legal residents of the Town, so long as they (a) have been owners of record for at least 180 consecutive days immediately prior to the date of the election; (b) during that 180 days owned a minimum of 50 percent of the fee title interest in certain real property; (c) are at least 18 years old on the date of the election; and (d) are natural persons. The provision limited the right of nonresidents to vote to matters of exclusively local interest. As of January 2, 1996, a Town census disclosed that in addition to approximately 505 eligible resident voters in the Town, there were approximately 541 nonresident property owners eligible to vote pursuant to the Charter. The court observed:

Nonresidents entitled to vote currently own over 34% of the assessed value of real property in the Town, while residents own only about 5%. About 61% of the assessed value of real property in the Town is owned by nonresident corporations and trusts, which are not entitled to vote in Town elections. Nonresidents pay over eight times more in property taxes than the residents do, and it is fair to state that in the future such nonresident property owners will continue to contribute significant revenues to the Town.

Several permanent residents of the town sued to invalidate the extension of the franchise to nonresidents, arguing that permitting nonresidents to vote unconstitutionally diluted the value of the votes of permanent residents (vote dilution is taken up in Chapter 4). The court analyzed the charter provision using the rational basis standard on the ground that "Section 2.4(b) of the Town Charter does not restrict the right to vote—it expands it to include nonresidents owning real property in the Town." The extension of the franchise was rational, the court concluded, because "the Town . . . is a unique resort community where nonresident landowners own the majority of property and pay more than eight times the amount of property tax. . . . Moreover, the nonresidents continue to bear the weight of the financial burden for the Town. [P]roviding the nonresident landowners the right to vote gives them a voice in the Town's future."

Are you satisfied by the court's reasoning? Has the court taken into account all the interests at stake? Does it matter that this decision was made by the town residents themselves, i.e., was not imposed from above by the state legislature?

In the U.S., eleven states have by law authorized localities to extend the franchise to nonresidents. *See* Joshua A. Douglas, *The Right to Vote under Local Law*, 85 GEO. WASH. L. REV. 1039 (2017).

3.   Defining Geographical Communities

If the vote is to be allocated on the basis of membership in a geographical community, an antecedent question concerns how properly to identify the geographic community in issue. In some cases, identifying the community seems easy or trivial. For example, we tend to presume that the geographical community relevant to electing a President is the entire nation; for U.S. Senators, it is states. On the other hand, defining the relevant community can become considerably more difficult where the community unit in question is smaller than those specifically provided for in the Constitution—that is, smaller than a state. The following cases deal with the nature of these local governments.

Hunter v. City of Pittsburgh

207 U.S. 161 (1907)

Mr. Justice MOODY delivered the opinion of the court.

The plaintiffs in error seek a reversal of the judgment of the Supreme Court of Pennsylvania, which affirmed a decree of a lower court, directing the consolidation of the cities of Pittsburgh and Allegheny. This decree was entered by authority of an act of the General Assembly of that State. . . . The act authorized the consolidation of two cities . . . if upon an election the majority of the votes cast in the territory comprised within the limits of both cities favor the consolidation, even though, as happened in this instance, a majority of the votes cast in one of the cities oppose it. . . . This procedure was followed by the filing of a petition by the City of Pittsburgh; by an election in which the majority of all the votes cast were in the affirmative, although the majority of all the votes cast by the voters of Allegheny were in the negative, and by a decree of the court uniting the two cities. . . .

Briefly stated, the [plaintiffs claim] that the Act of Assembly deprives [them] of their property without due process of law, by subjecting it to the burden of the additional taxation which would result from the consolidation. The manner in which the right of due process of law has been violated, as set forth in the first assignment of error and insisted upon in argument, is that the method of voting on the consolidation prescribed in the act has permitted the voters of the larger city to overpower the voters of the smaller city, and compel the union without their consent and against their protest. The precise question thus presented has not been determined by this court. It is important, and, as we have said, not so devoid of merit as to be denied consideration, although its solution by principles long settled and constantly acted upon is not difficult. . . .

Municipal corporations are political subdivisions of the State, created as convenient agencies for exercising such of the governmental powers of the State as may be entrusted to them. For the purpose of executing these powers properly and efficiently they usually are given the power to acquire, hold, and manage personal and real property. The number, nature and duration of the powers conferred upon these corporations and the territory over which they shall be exercised rests in the absolute discretion of the State. Neither their charters, nor any law conferring governmental powers, or vesting in them property to be used for governmental purposes, or authorizing them to hold or manage such property, or exempting them from taxation upon it, constitutes a contract with the State within the meaning of the Federal Constitution. The State, therefore, at its pleasure may modify or withdraw all such powers, may take without compensation such property, hold it itself, or vest it in other agencies, expand or contract the territorial area, unite the whole or a part of it with another municipality, repeal the charter and destroy the corporation. All this may be done, conditionally or unconditionally, with or without the consent of the citizens, or even against their protest. In all these respects the State is supreme, and its legislative body, conforming its action to the state constitution, may do as it will, unrestrained by any provision of the Constitution of the United States. Although the inhabitants and property owners may by such changes suffer inconvenience, and their property may be lessened in value by the burden of increased taxation, or for any other reason, they have no right by contract or otherwise in the unaltered or continued existence of the corporation or its powers, and there is nothing in the Federal Constitution which protects them from these injurious consequences. The power is in the State and those who legislate for the State are alone responsible for any unjust or oppressive exercise of it.

Applying these principles to the case at bar, it follows irresistibly that this assignment of error, so far as it relates to the citizens who are plaintiffs in error, must be overruled.

Milliken v. Bradley

418 U.S. 717 (1974)

Mr. Chief Justice BURGER delivered the opinion of the Court.

We granted certiorari in these consolidated cases to determine whether a federal court may impose a multidistrict, areawide remedy to a single-district *de jure* segregation problem absent any finding that the other included school districts have failed to operate unitary [i.e., nonsegregated] school systems within their districts. . . . The complaint . . . alleged that the Detroit Public School System was and is segregated on the basis of race as a result of the official policies and actions of the defendants and their predecessors in office, and called for the implementation of a plan that would eliminate "the racial identity of every school in the [Detroit] system and . . . maintain now and hereafter a unitary, nonracial school system." . . . On September 27, 1971, the District Court issued its findings and conclusions on the issue of segregation, finding that "Governmental actions and inaction at all levels, federal, state and local, have combined, with those of private organizations, such as loaning institutions and real estate associations and brokerage firms, to establish and to maintain the pattern of residential segregation throughout the Detroit metropolitan area." 338 F. Supp. 582, 587 (E.D. Mich. 1971). . . . Turning to the question of an appropriate remedy for these several constitutional violations, the District Court [ordered] the state defendants . . . to submit desegregation plans encompassing the three-county metropolitan area despite the fact that the 85 outlying school districts of these three counties were not parties to the action and despite the fact that there had been no claim that these outlying districts had committed constitutional violations. . . . [T]he District Court held that it "must look beyond the limits of the Detroit school district for a solution to the problem," and that "[school] district lines are simply matters of political convenience and may not be used to deny constitutional rights." *Id.*

[T]he court designated 53 of the 85 suburban school districts plus Detroit as the "desegregation area" and appointed a panel to prepare and submit "an effective desegregation plan" for the Detroit schools that would encompass the entire desegregation area. . . . [On appeal,] the Court of Appeals . . . agreed with the District Court that "any less comprehensive a solution than a metropolitan area plan would result in an all black school system immediately surrounded by practically all white suburban school systems, with an overwhelmingly white majority population in the total metropolitan area." The court went on to state that it could "not see how such segregation can be any less harmful to the minority students than if the same result were accomplished within one school district."

Accordingly, the Court of Appeals concluded that "the only feasible desegregation plan involves the crossing of the boundary lines between the Detroit School District and adjacent or nearby school districts for the limited purpose of providing an effective desegregation plan." It reasoned that such a plan would be appropriate because of the State's violations, and could be implemented because of the State's authority to control local school districts. Without further elaboration, and without any discussion of the claims that no constitutional violation by the outlying districts had been shown and that no evidence on that point had been allowed, the Court of Appeals held:

> [The] State has committed de jure acts of segregation and . . . the State controls the instrumentalities whose action is necessary to remedy the harmful effects of the State acts.

An interdistrict remedy was thus held to be "within the equity powers of the District Court." . . .

Ever since *Brown v. Board of Education*, 347 U.S. 483 (1954), judicial consideration of school desegregation cases has begun with the standard:

> [In] the field of public education the doctrine of "separate but equal" has no place. Separate educational facilities are inherently unequal.

This has been reaffirmed time and again as the meaning of the Constitution and the controlling rule of law. . . . In *Brown v. Board of Education*, 349 U.S. 294 (1955) (*Brown II*), the Court's first encounter with the problem of remedies in school desegregation cases, the Court noted:

> In fashioning and effectuating the decrees, the courts will be guided by equitable principles. Traditionally, equity has been characterized by a practical flexibility in shaping its remedies and by a facility for adjusting and reconciling public and private needs.

Id., at 300 (footnotes omitted). . . .

Viewing the record as a whole, it seems clear that the District Court and the Court of Appeals shifted the primary focus from a Detroit remedy to the metropolitan area only because of their conclusion that total desegregation of Detroit would not produce the racial balance which they perceived as desirable. Both courts proceeded on an assumption that the Detroit schools could not be truly desegregated—in their view of what constituted desegregation—unless the racial composition of the student body of each school substantially reflected the racial composition of the population of the metropolitan area as a whole. . . .

Here the District Court's approach to what constituted "actual desegregation" raises the fundamental question, not presented in *Swann*, as to the circumstances in which a federal court may order desegregation relief that embraces more than a single school district. The court's analytical starting point was its conclusion that school district lines are no more than arbitrary lines on a map drawn "for political convenience." Boundary lines may be bridged where there has been a constitutional violation calling for interdistrict relief, but the notion that school district lines may be casually ignored or treated as a mere administrative convenience is contrary to the history of public education in our country. No single tradition in public education is more deeply rooted than local control over the operation of schools; local autonomy has long been thought essential both to the maintenance of community concern and support for public schools and to quality of the educational process. Thus, in *San Antonio School District v. Rodriguez*, 411 U.S. 1, 50 (1973), we observed that local control over the educational process affords citizens an opportunity to participate in decisionmaking, permits the structuring of school programs to fit local needs, and encourages "experimentation, innovation, and a healthy competition for educational excellence."

The Michigan educational structure involved in this case, in common with most States, provides for a large measure of local control, and a review of the scope and character of these local powers indicates the extent to which the interdistrict remedy approved by the two courts could disrupt and alter the structure of public education in Michigan. The metropolitan remedy would require, in effect, consolidation of 54 independent school districts historically administered as separate units into a vast new super school district. . . .

Of course, no state law is above the Constitution. School district lines and the present laws with respect to local control, are not sacrosanct and if they conflict with the Fourteenth Amendment federal courts have a duty to prescribe appropriate remedies. . . . Before the boundaries of separate and autonomous school districts may be set aside by consolidating the separate units for remedial purposes or by imposing a cross-district remedy, it must first be shown that there has been a constitutional violation within one district that produces a significant segregative effect in another district. Specifically, it must be shown that racially discriminatory acts of the state or local school districts, or of a single school district have been a substantial cause of interdistrict segregation. . . . Conversely, without an interdistrict violation and interdistrict effect, there is no constitutional wrong calling for an interdistrict remedy.

The record before us, voluminous as it is, contains evidence of *de jure* segregated conditions only in the Detroit schools. . . . The constitutional right of the Negro respondents residing in Detroit is to attend a unitary school system in that district. Unless petitioners drew the district lines in a discriminatory fashion, or arranged for white students residing in the Detroit District to attend schools in Oakland and Macomb Counties, they were under no constitutional duty to make provisions for Negro students to do so. . . .

In *Lockport v. Citizens for Community Action*, 430 U.S. 259 (1976), the Court considered a New York law providing that a new county charter might take effect only if it was approved in a referendum election by separate majorities of those voters who lived within the county's cities, and of those who lived outside the cities. In 1972, a proposed charter for Niagara County was put to a referendum. The charter created the new offices of County Executive and County Comptroller. City voters approved the charter by a vote of 18,220 to 14,914, but noncity voters disapproved the charter by a vote of 11,594 to 10,665. Despite the fact that a majority of voters voting in the county favored the charter, under state law the charter was deemed rejected. Some voters then challenged the state law on the ground that "all voters in a New York county have identical interests in the adoption or rejection of a new charter, and that any distinction, therefore, between voters drawn on the basis of residence and working to the detriment of an identifiable class is an invidious discrimination."

The Court rejected this argument. It found first that city and noncity voters did not have identical interests in county governance due to the "realities of the distribution of governmental powers in New York," and that the state had "wide discretion . . . in forming and allocating governmental tasks to local subdivisions." The Court then analogized the reorganization of county authority under the proposed charter to the annexation decision at issue in *Hunter.*

If [this were] annexation proceedings, the fact that the residents of the annexing city and the residents of the area to be annexed formed sufficiently different constituencies with sufficiently different interests could be readily perceived. The fact of impending union alone would not so merge them into one community of interest as constitutionally to require that their votes be aggregated in any referendum to approve annexation. Cf. *Hunter v. Pittsburgh*, 207 U.S. 161. Similarly a proposal that several school districts join to form a consolidated unit could surely be subject to voter approval in each constituent school district.

Yet in terms of recognizing constituencies with separate and potentially opposing interests, the structural decision to annex or consolidate is similar in impact to the decision to restructure county government in New York. In each case, separate voter approval requirements are based on the perception that the real and long-term impact of a restructuring of local government is felt quite differently by the different county constituent units that in a sense compete to provide similar governmental services. Voters in these constituent units are directly and differentially affected by the restructuring of county government, which may make the provider of public services more remote and less subject to the voters' individual influence.

Applying a rational basis standard of review, the Court sustained the challenged law.

Is the view expressed in *Lockport* closer to the one expressed in *Hunter* or in *Milliken*?

» ***The Significance of Local Government Boundaries.*** What exactly does a local government boundary signify? Is it merely a line drawn by the state to divide itself into convenient administrative subunits? Or do local boundaries demarcate meaningfully distinct political communities?

Today, we are accustomed to the election of representatives from election districts. But until the Supreme Court's 1964 ruling in *Reynolds v. Sims* (Chapter 4), the dominant method of legislative representation on the state level was representation by local governmental unit, most often by county, though in New England the system of representation centered on the individual town. Under these systems, each county or town was entitled to elect one or more representatives to the state legislature. Why would earlier generations of Americans have preferred to allocate representation by geographically fixed counties or towns rather than by the kind of geographically flexible election district we use today? Consider the following:

The local community [of the colonial period] had a closed quality . . . [and] provided within itself a focus for the economic, political, social, and religious lives of the townspeople. It was not so much a segment of the larger commonwealth as it was a miniature of the commonwealth. . . . There was infrequent resort to outside institutions, and the norm was for endogamous marriages. . . . The tight pattern of informal and intimate social interaction was, for all intents, organically complete.

The economic life of New England drew men to the town as effectively as did the religious and social ideals they shared. . . . One must not, however, imagine a situation of complete economic isolation. Even the smallest village had some trade beyond its immediate neighborhood. . . . Yet the economy was fundamentally local, and trading relationships were generally familial and intimate. . . .

The town, not the individual, was the basic unit of political representation. Political decisions were made through "discussion" and consensus rather than through interest-group conflict. . . . Religious life was similarly bounded by the town. . . . The family and the Christian fellowship provided the basis for local life. Family, church, and town provided overlapping context of life. . . . The town was essentially homogeneous: It had one religious belief, a unified political vision, even a fairly even distribution of wealth and a narrow range of occupations. It was a remarkably undifferentiated society, and it was difficult to draw the line between family and community, private and public. . . .

The politics of the town was embedded in the organic pattern of social relations. The informal and personal relationships that maintained the essential unity of the town also produced a strong impulse toward political consensus. Within the town, this produced a substantial degree of unity, if not always harmony. It also allowed the town to speak to the larger society with one political voice. The votes of Massachusetts towns on matters of provincial or, later, state concern were unanimous or nearly unanimous with extraordinary frequency. . . .

Although Americans continued to act out their lives within the context of the town, the town and the experience of community took on a new quality after about 1820. These changes made the nineteenth-century town, as a locus of community, increasingly different from its eighteenth-century counterpart. . . . Each town had its own pattern of local values independent of national ones, though not in conflict with them. These local values, typically in the custodianship of the local elite, could vary significantly from town to town, and these differences could mean distinctive social experiences. The common denominator of local life was, however, the experience of community. Role performance and status at the local level were differentiated from one's role as a national citizen, and the boundaries of most social roles coincided with the local community. . . .

THOMAS BENDER, COMMUNITY AND SOCIAL CHANGE IN AMERICA (1978). Does this account have any explanatory force as a historical matter? Does it accurately describe communal life today? Is the contingent social character of local life relevant to the treatment of localities in the law?

4.   Non-Geographical Sub-Communities

Just because membership in geographical communities is commonly a prerequisite to voting, does it follow that *all* otherwise qualified residents may vote? May a polity subdivide itself in ways other than geographically, and grant the franchise to certain groups and not others? If so, to what kinds of sub-communities may the vote be restricted?

Kramer v. Union Free School District No. 15

395 U.S. 621 (1969)

Mr. Chief Justice WARREN delivered the opinion of the Court.

In this case we are called on to determine whether §2012 of the New York Education Law is constitutional. The legislation provides that in certain New York school districts residents who are otherwise eligible to vote in state and federal elections may vote in the school district election only if they (1) own (or lease) taxable real property within the district, or (2) are parents (or have custody of) children enrolled in the local public schools. Appellant, a bachelor who neither owns nor leases taxable real property, filed suit in federal court claiming that §2012 denied him equal protection of the laws in violation of the Fourteenth Amendment. [A] three-judge District Court dismissed appellant's complaint. Finding that §2012 does violate the Equal Protection Clause of the Fourteenth Amendment, we reverse. . . .

"In determining whether or not a state law violates the Equal Protection Clause, we must consider the facts and circumstances behind the law, the interests which the State claims to be protecting, and the interests of those who are disadvantaged by the classification." *Williams v. Rhodes*, 393 U.S. 23, 30 (1968). And, in this case, we must give the statute a close and exacting examination. "Since the right to exercise the franchise in a free and unimpaired manner is preservative of other basic civil and political rights, any alleged infringement of the right of citizens to vote must be carefully and meticulously scrutinized." *Reynolds v. Sims*, 377 U.S. 533, 562 (1964). This careful examination is necessary because statutes distributing the franchise constitute the foundation of our representative society. Any unjustified discrimination in determining who may participate in political affairs or in the selection of public officials undermines the legitimacy of representative government. . . .

Therefore, if a challenged state statute grants the right to vote to some bona fide residents of requisite age and citizenship and denies the franchise to others, the Court must determine whether the exclusions are necessary to promote a compelling state interest. See *Carrington v. Rash.*

And, for these reasons, the deference usually given to the judgment of legislators does not extend to decisions concerning which resident citizens may participate in the election of legislators and other public officials. Those decisions must be carefully scrutinized by the Court to determine whether each resident citizen has, as far as is possible, an equal voice in the selections. Accordingly, when we are reviewing statutes which deny some residents the right to vote, the general presumption of constitutionality afforded state statutes and the traditional approval given state classifications if the Court can conceive of a "rational basis" for the distinctions made are not applicable. See *Harper v. Virginia Bd. of Elections*, 383 U.S. 663, 670 (1966). The presumption of constitutionality and the approval given "rational" classifications in other types of enactments are based on an assumption that the institutions of state government are structured so as to represent fairly all the people. However, when the challenge to the statute is in effect a challenge of this basic assumption, the assumption can no longer serve as the basis for presuming constitutionality. And, the assumption is no less under attack because the legislature which decides who may participate at the various levels of political choice is fairly elected. Legislation which delegates decision making to bodies elected by only a portion of those eligible to vote for the legislature can cause unfair representation. Such legislation can exclude a minority of voters from any voice in the decisions just as effectively as if the decisions were made by legislators the minority had no voice in selecting. . . .

Besides appellant and others who similarly live in their parents' homes, the statute also disenfranchises the following persons (unless they are parents or guardians of children enrolled in the district public school): senior citizens and others living with children or relatives; clergy, military personnel, and others who live on tax-exempt property; boarders and lodgers; parents who neither own nor lease qualifying property and whose children are too young to attend school; parents who neither own nor lease qualifying property and whose children attend private schools.

Appellant asserts that excluding him from participation in the district elections denies him equal protection of the laws. He contends that he and others of his class are substantially interested in and significantly affected by the school meeting decisions. All members of the community have an interest in the quality and structure of public education, appellant says, and he urges that "the decisions taken by local boards . . . may have grave consequences to the entire population." Appellant also argues that the level of property taxation affects him, even though he does not own property, as property tax levels affect the price of goods and services in the community.

We turn therefore to question whether the exclusion is necessary to promote a compelling state interest. First, appellees argue that the State has a legitimate interest in limiting the franchise in school district elections to "members of the community of interest"—those "primarily interested in such elections." Second, appellees urge that the State may reasonably and permissibly conclude that "property taxpayers" (including lessees of taxable property who share the tax burden through rent payments) and parents of the children enrolled in the district's schools are those "primarily interested" in school affairs.

We do not understand appellees to argue that the State is attempting to limit the franchise to those "subjectively concerned" about school matters. Rather, they appear to argue that the State's legitimate interest is in restricting a voice in school matters to those "directly affected" by such decisions. The State apparently reasons that since the schools are financed in part by local property taxes, persons whose out-of-pocket expenses are "directly" affected by property tax changes should be allowed to vote. Similarly, parents of children in school are thought to have a "direct" stake in school affairs and are given a vote.

Appellees argue that it is necessary to limit the franchise to those "primarily interested" in school affairs because "the ever increasing complexity of the many interacting phases of the school system and structure make it extremely difficult for the electorate fully to understand the whys and wherefores of the detailed operations of the school system." Appellees say that many communications of school boards and school administrations are sent home to the parents through the district pupils and are "not broadcast to the general public"; thus, nonparents will be less informed than parents. Further, appellees argue, those who are assessed for local property taxes (either directly or indirectly through rent) will have enough of an interest "through the burden on their pocketbooks, to acquire such information as they may need."

We need express no opinion as to whether the State in some circumstances might limit the exercise of the franchise to those "primarily interested" or "primarily affected." Of course, we therefore do not reach the issue of whether these particular elections are of the type in which the franchise may be so limited. For, assuming . . . that New York legitimately might limit the franchise in these school district elections to those "primarily interested in school affairs," close scrutiny of the §2012 classifications demonstrates that they do not accomplish this purpose with sufficient precision to justify denying appellant the franchise.

Whether classifications allegedly limiting the franchise to those resident citizens "primarily interested" deny those excluded equal protection of the laws depends, inter alia, on whether all those excluded are in fact substantially less interested or affected than those the statute includes. In other words, the classifications must be tailored so that the exclusion of appellant and members of his class is necessary to achieve the articulated state goal. Section 2012 does not meet the exacting standard of precision we require of statutes which selectively distribute the franchise. The classifications in §2012 permit inclusion of many persons who have, at best, a remote and indirect interest in school affairs and, on the other hand, exclude others who have a distinct and direct interest in the school meeting decisions.[15]

Nor do appellees offer any justification for the exclusion of seemingly interested and informed residents — other than to argue that the §2012 classifications include those "whom the State could understandably deem to be the most intimately interested in actions taken by the school board," and urge that "the task of . . . balancing the interest of the community in the maintenance of orderly school district elections against the interest of any individual in voting in such elections should clearly remain with the Legislature." But the issue is not whether the legislative judgments are rational. A more exacting standard obtains. The issue is whether the §2012 requirements do in fact sufficiently further a compelling state interest to justify denying the franchise to appellant and members of his class.

Justice STEWART, dissenting:

Although at times variously phrased, the traditional test of a statute's validity under the Equal Protection Clause is a familiar one: a legislative classification is invalid only "if it rest[s] on grounds wholly irrelevant to achievement of the regulation's objectives." It was under just such a test that the literacy requirement involved in *Lassiter* was upheld. The premise of our decision in that case was that a State may constitutionally impose upon its citizens voting requirements reasonably "designed to promote intelligent use of the ballot." 360 U.S. at 51. A similar premise underlies the proposition, consistently endorsed by this Court, that a State may exclude nonresidents from participation in its elections. Such residence requirements, designed to help ensure that voters have a substantial stake in the outcome of elections and an opportunity to become familiar with the candidates

---

15. For example, appellant resides with his parents in the school district, pays state and federal taxes and is interested in and affected by school board decisions; however, he has no vote. On the other hand, an uninterested unemployed young man who pays no state or federal taxes, but who rents an apartment in the district, can participate in the election.

and issues voted upon, are entirely permissible exercises of state authority. Indeed, the appellant explicitly concedes, as he must, the validity of voting requirements relating to residence, literacy, and age. Yet he argues—and the Court accepts the argument—that the voting qualifications involved here somehow have a different constitutional status. I am unable to see the distinction.

Clearly a State may reasonably assume that its residents have a greater stake in the outcome of elections held within its boundaries than do other persons. Likewise, it is entirely rational for a state legislature to suppose that residents, being generally better informed regarding state affairs than are nonresidents, will be more likely than nonresidents to vote responsibly. And the same may be said of legislative assumptions regarding the electoral competence of adults and literate persons on the one hand, and of minors and illiterates on the other. It is clear, of course, that lines thus drawn cannot infallibly perform their intended legislative function. Just as "illiterate people may be intelligent voters," nonresidents or minors might also in some instances be interested, informed, and intelligent participants in the electoral process. Persons who commute across a state line to work may well have a great stake in the affairs of the State in which they are employed; some college students under 21 may be both better informed and more passionately interested in political affairs than many adults. But such discrepancies are the inevitable concomitant of the line drawing that is essential to law making. So long as the classification is rationally related to a permissible legislative end, therefore—as are residence, literacy, and age requirements imposed with respect to voting—there is no denial of equal protection.

Thus judged, the statutory classification involved here seems to me clearly to be valid. New York has made the judgment that local educational policy is best left to those persons who have certain direct and definable interests in that policy: those who are either immediately involved as parents of school children or who, as owners or lessees of taxable property, are burdened with the local cost of funding school district operations. True, persons outside those classes may be genuinely interested in the conduct of a school district's business—just as commuters from New Jersey may be genuinely interested in the outcome of a New York City election. But unless this Court is to claim a monopoly of wisdom regarding the sound operation of school systems in the 50 States, I see no way to justify the conclusion that the legislative classification involved here is not rationally related to a legitimate legislative purpose. . . .

The Court is quite explicit in explaining why it believes this statute should be given "close scrutiny":

> The presumption of constitutionality and the approval given "rational" classifications in other types of enactments are based on an assumption that the institutions of state government are structured so as to represent fairly all the people. However, when the challenge to the statute is in effect a challenge of this basic assumption, the assumption can no longer serve as the basis for presuming constitutionality.

I am at a loss to understand how such reasoning is at all relevant to the present case. The voting qualifications at issue have been promulgated, not by Union Free

School District No. 15, but by the New York State Legislature, and the appellant is of course fully able to participate in the election of representatives in that body. There is simply no claim whatever here that the state government is not "structured so as to represent fairly all the people," including the appellant. . . . The appellant is eligible to vote in all state, local, and federal elections in which general governmental policy is determined. He is fully able, therefore, to participate not only in the processes by which the requirements for school district voting may be changed, but also in those by which the levels of state and federal financial assistance to the District are determined. He clearly is not locked into any self-perpetuating status of exclusion from the electoral process. . . .

Today's decision can only be viewed as irreconcilable with the established principle that "the States have . . . broad powers to determine the conditions under which the right of suffrage may be exercised. . . ." Since I think that principle is entirely sound, I respectfully dissent from the Court's judgment and opinion.

≫ *Eligibility Based on Lineage.* In *Rice v. Cayetano*, 528 U.S. 495 (2000), the Court considered a Hawaiian law that restricted voting in elections for trustees of the Office of Hawaiian Affairs (OHA). OHA is a government agency charged with administering a trust holding funds that by law are to be expended only for the benefit of native Hawaiians, defined principally as those descended from Hawaiians inhabiting the islands in 1778, the year in which Captain James Cook's expedition arrived. The statute limited eligibility to vote in elections for trustee to the population for whose benefit the trust existed: descendants of the native Hawaiian population that preceded European colonization.

The Court invalidated this lineage eligibility requirement on the ground that it was a racial qualification that violated the Fifteenth Amendment. The majority found that "[a]ncestry can be a proxy for race. It is that proxy here." In dissent, Justice Stevens argued that "[t]he OHA voter qualification speaks in terms of ancestry and current residence, not of race or color. . . . The ability to vote is a function of the lineal descent of a modern-day resident of Hawaii, not the blood-based characteristics of that resident, or of the blood-based proximity of that resident to the 'peoples' from whom that descendant arises." *See also Davis v. Commonwealth Election Commission*, 844 F.3d 1087 (9th Cir. 2016) (invalidating a provision limiting voting on amendments to the Northern Mariana Islands Constitution to "persons of Northern Marianas descent").

If the Court's decision rests on the racial distinctiveness of native Hawaiians, does that mean that lineage restrictions on voting eligibility are permissible when they occur among people of the same race?

B. QUALIFICATIONS BASED ON COMPETENCE

Many limitations on eligibility to vote have roots in conceptions of the competences that are necessary to enable individuals to participate appropriately in democratic processes. This section considers restrictions based on literacy, age, mental disability, wealth, and felony convictions.

1. *Literacy*

Lassiter v. Northampton County Board of Elections
360 U.S. 45 (1959)

Mr. Justice DOUGLAS delivered the opinion of the Court.

This controversy started in a Federal District Court. Appellant, a Negro citizen of North Carolina, sued to have the literacy test for voters prescribed by that State declared unconstitutional and void. . . . The literacy test is a part of §4 of Art. VI of the North Carolina Constitution. . . .

We come then to the question whether a State may consistently with the Fourteenth and Seventeenth Amendments apply a literacy test to all voters irrespective of race or color. . . .

The States have long been held to have broad powers to determine the conditions under which the right of suffrage may be exercised, absent of course the discrimination which the Constitution condemns. Article I, §2 of the Constitution in its provision for the election of members of the House of Representatives and the Seventeenth Amendment in its provision for the election of Senators provide that officials will be chosen "by the People." Each provision goes on to state that "the Electors in each State shall have the Qualifications requisite for Electors of the most numerous Branch of the State Legislature." So while the right of suffrage is established and guaranteed by the Constitution (*Ex parte Yarbrough*, 110 U.S. 651, 663-665; *Smith v. Allwright*, 321 U.S. 649, 661-662) it is subject to the imposition of state standards which are not discriminatory and which do not contravene any restriction that Congress, acting pursuant to its constitutional powers, has imposed. See *United States v. Classic*, 313 U.S. 299, 315. While §2 of the Fourteenth Amendment, which provides for apportionment of Representatives among the States according to their respective numbers counting the whole number of persons in each State (except Indians not taxed), speaks of "the right to vote," the right protected "refers to the right to vote as established by the laws and constitution of the State." *McPherson v. Blacker*, 146 U.S. 1, 39.

We do not suggest that any standards which a State desires to adopt may be required of voters. But there is wide scope for exercise of its jurisdiction. Residence requirements, age, previous criminal record are obvious examples indicating factors which a State may take into consideration in determining the qualifications of voters. The ability to read and write likewise has some relation to standards designed to promote intelligent use of the ballot. Literacy and illiteracy are neutral on race, creed, color, and sex, as reports around the world show. Literacy and intelligence are obviously not synonymous. Illiterate people may be intelligent voters. Yet in our society where newspapers, periodicals, books, and other printed matter canvass and debate campaign issues, a State might conclude that only those who are literate should exercise the franchise. It was said last century in Massachusetts that a literacy test was designed to insure an "independent and intelligent" exercise of the right of suffrage.[7] In Mississippi the applicant must be able to read and write

---

7. Nineteen States, including North Carolina, have some sort of literacy requirement as a prerequisite to eligibility for voting. Five require that the voter be able to read a section

a section of the State Constitution and give a reasonable interpretation of it. He must also demonstrate to the registrar a reasonable understanding of the duties and obligations of citizenship under a constitutional form of government. Miss. Code Ann. §3213. *Stone v. Smith,* 159 Mass. 413-414, 34 N.E. 521. North Carolina agrees. We do not sit in judgment on the wisdom of that policy. We cannot say, however, that it is not an allowable one measured by constitutional standards.

Of course a literacy test, fair on its face, may be employed to perpetuate that discrimination which the Fifteenth Amendment was designed to uproot. No such influence is charged here. On the other hand, a literacy test may be unconstitutional on its face. In *Davis v. Schnell,* 81 F. Supp. 872, *aff'd,* 336 U.S. 933, the test was the citizen's ability to "understand and explain" an article of the Federal Constitution. The legislative setting of that provision and the great discretion it vested in the registrar made clear that a literacy requirement was merely a device to make racial discrimination easy. We cannot make the same inference here. The present requirement, applicable to members of all races, is that the prospective voter "be able to read and write any section of the Constitution of North Carolina in the English language." That seems to us to be one fair way of determining whether a person is literate, not a calculated scheme to lay springes for the citizen. Certainly we cannot condemn it on its face as a device unrelated to the desire of North Carolina to raise the standards for people of all races who cast the ballot.

▶▶ *Discriminatory Administration of Literacy Tests.*   Did the Court fully grasp the motivations behind the literacy test and the problems with its administration? Consider the following account of the administration of the literacy test in Louisiana,

---

of the State or Federal Constitution and write his own name. Five require that the elector be able to read and write a section of the Federal or State Constitution. Alabama also requires that the voter be of "good character" and "embrace the duties and obligations of citizenship" under the Federal and State Constitutions. Ala. Code, Tit. 17, §32 (1955 Supp.).

Two States require that the voter be able to read and write English. Wyoming and Connecticut require that the voter read a constitutional provision in English, while Virginia requires that the voting application be written in the applicant's hand before the registrar and without aid, suggestion or memoranda. Washington has the requirement that the voter be able to read and speak the English language.

Georgia requires that the voter read intelligibly and write legibly a section of the State or Federal Constitution. If he is physically unable to do so, he may qualify if he can give a reasonable interpretation of a section read to him. An alternative means of qualifying is provided: if one has good character and understands the duties and obligations of citizenship under a republican government, and he can answer correctly 20 of 30 questions listed in the statute (e.g., How does the Constitution of Georgia provide that a county site may be changed?, what is treason against the State of Georgia?, who are the solicitor general and the judge of the State Judicial Circuit in which you live?) he is eligible to vote. Geo. Code Ann. §§34-117, 34-120.

In Louisiana one qualifies if he can read and write English or his mother tongue, is of good character, and understands the duties and obligations of citizenship under a republican form of government. If he cannot read and write, he can qualify if he can give a reasonable interpretation of a section of the State or Federal Constitution when read to him, and if he is attached to the principles of the Federal and State Constitutions. La. Rev. Stat., Tit. 18, §31.

taken from a civil rights prosecution brought by the United States. The literacy test in Louisiana required a voter to demonstrate his or her ability to understand any section of the state constitution.

United States v. Louisiana, 225 F. Supp. 353 (E.D. La. 1963): First of all, a Louisiana registrar has the power to use or not to use the interpretation test. . . . In the twenty-one parishes where it has been shown that the interpretation test has been used, as of December 31, 1962, only 8.6 per cent of the adult Negroes were registered as against 66.1 per cent of the adult white persons registered. Before the interpretation test was put into use, a total of 25,361 Negroes were registered in the twenty-one parishes using the test. By August 31, 1962, total Negro registration in these parishes was 10,351. During the same period, white registration was not discernibly affected. . . .

The registrar's whim alone determines which applicants will be tested. The Constitution merely states that applicants "shall be able to understand and give a reasonable interpretation" of a section of a constitution. Some registrars, for example, those in LaSalle, Lincoln, and Webster parishes, have interpreted this to mean that the applicant need not actually interpret the constitution, only that he have the ability to do so. The State Board of Registration maintained at one time that the correct interpretation was that the applicant must demonstrate his ability in all cases. It has, however, changed its understanding or interpretation of this very section of the Constitution. After the institution of this suit, the Board prescribed another test, instructing registrars to cease requiring an interpretation. The change in the interpretation given the interpretation-test provision of the Constitution by the State agency charged with enforcing it and the wide variety of interpretations adopted by the registrars reaffirm the impossibility of achieving objective standards for an interpretation of the Constitution acceptable to the State. Pity the applicant asked to interpret the interpretation test.

The Louisiana Constitution contains 443 sections, as against 56 sections in the United States Constitution, and is the longest and the most detailed of all state constitutions. The printed copy published by the State, unannotated, contains 600 pages, not counting an index of 140 pages. The evidence clearly demonstrates great abuses in the selection of sections of the constitutions to be interpreted. Some registrars have favorite sections which they apparently use regardless of an applicant's race. Some open a volume containing the United States and Louisiana Constitutions and, like soothsayers seeking divine help from the random flight of birds, require an applicant to interpret the section on the page where the book opens. The Segregation Committee distributed to registrars sets of twenty-four cards, each containing three sections of the Constitution with instructions that they be used in administering the interpretation test. The Registrar of Ouachita Parish used a set of test cards containing sections chosen by the Citizens' Council. The Registrar of Plaquemines used cards and answers prepared by Mr. Leander Perez, District Attorney for the Parish. It is evident from the record that frequently the choice of difficult sections has made it impossible for many Negro applicants to pass. White applicants were more often given easy sections, many of which could be answered by short, stock phrases such as "freedom of speech," "freedom of religion," "States' rights," and so on. Negro applicants, on the other hand, were given [more difficult] parts of the Louisiana Constitution.

As in the selection process, gross abuses of discretion appear in the evaluation of the interpretations. . . . [T]he record shows that interpretations far less responsive to the constitutional text selected have been accepted from whites than from Negroes. Compounding this with the fact that Negroes were often given more difficult sections to interpret, the bias in favor of the whites becomes readily apparent. Some parishes administered written examinations and kept records of the questions asked and the responses accepted. In these examinations the registrar usually employed one or more of several sets of cards containing selected sections of the Constitution and a space for the applicant's interpretation of it. Even the most cursory glance at the records in these parishes underscores the heavy burden under which Negro applicants were laboring. In one set of cards, there is great disparity in the difficulty of the questions asked. This enables the registrar to select cards with simple sections for white applicants and difficult cards for Negroes. There is unmistakable evidence that many white applicants were shown cards with sample answers on them. Some applicants admitted this, and there is even an instance of a white applicant having, by mistake, signed the sample answer card. Negroes were not allowed to see the acceptable answers, let alone copy them. Similarly, the pattern of the answers indicates that the registrars often told white applicants the currently acceptable answers. The phraseology of almost every answer in one parish changed right along with the registrar's change in the wording of the acceptable answer.

Registrars were easily satisfied with answers from white voters. In one instance "FRDUM FOOF SPETGH" was an acceptable response to the request to interpret Article 1, §3 of the Louisiana Constitution. On the other hand, the record shows that Negroes whose application forms and answers indicate that they are highly qualified by literacy standards and have a high degree of intelligence have been turned down although they had given a reasonable interpretation of fairly technical clauses of the constitution. For example the Louisiana Constitution, Article X, §16 provides: "Rolling stock operated in this State, the owners of which have no domicile therein, shall be assessed by the Louisiana Tax Commission, and shall be taxed for State purposes only, at a rate not to exceed forty mills on the dollar assessed value." The rejected interpretation was: "My understanding is that it means if the owner of which does not have residence within the State, his rolling stock shall be taxed not to exceed forty mills on the dollar."

In another instance the registrar rejected the following interpretation of the Search and Seizure provision of the Fourth Amendment: "(N)obody can just go into a person's house and take their belongings without a warrant from the law, and it had to specify in this warrant what they were to search and seize." Another rejected interpretation of the same Amendment by a Negro applicant was: "To search you would have to get an authorized authority to read a warrant." The Louisiana Constitution Article I, §5 provides: "The people have the right peaceably to assemble." A registrar rejected the following interpretation: "That one may assemble or belong to any group, club, or organization he chooses as long as it is within the law."

Each of these incidents could conceivably be an isolated event, indicating personal dereliction by one registrar, regrettable, but basically trivial in the general administration of the interpretation test. However, the great number of these and other examples, illustrative of a conscious decision, show conclusively that the discriminatory acts were not isolated or accidental or peculiar to the individual registrar but were part of a pervasive pattern and practice of disfranchisement by discriminatory use of the interpretation test.

———————————

In 1965, Congress enacted the Voting Rights Act (VRA), which we will consider in detail in Chapter 5. Section 4(e) of the VRA prohibited states from using English language literacy as a basis for denying the franchise to any person who had received a sixth-grade education in a foreign language. The provision was designed primarily to prevent disenfranchisement of citizens of Puerto Rico, a United States commonwealth, when they moved to the U.S. mainland. Section 4(e) was challenged on the ground that Congress could not use its power under Section 5 of the Fourteenth Amendment to enforce the Equal Protection Clause by prohibiting a practice that the Supreme Court had ruled did not violate the Constitution. In the following case, the Supreme Court sustained the challenged provision.

Katzenbach v. Morgan
384 U.S. 641 (1966)

Mr. Justice BRENNAN delivered the opinion of the Court.

These cases concern the constitutionality of §4(e) of the Voting Rights Act of 1965.[1] 79 Stat. 439, 42 U.S.C. §1973(b)(e) (1964 ed., Supp. I). That law, in the respects pertinent in these cases, provides that no person who has successfully completed the sixth primary grade in a public school in, or a private school accredited by, the Commonwealth of Puerto Rico in which the language of instruction was other than English shall be denied the right to vote in any election because of his inability to read or write English. Appellees, registered voters in New York City, brought this suit to challenge the constitutionality of §4(e) insofar as it *pro tanto*

———————————

1. The full text of §4 (e) is as follows:

(1) Congress hereby declares that to secure the rights under the fourteenth amendment of persons educated in American-flag schools in which the predominant classroom language was other than English, it is necessary to prohibit the States from conditioning the right to vote of such persons on ability to read, write, understand, or interpret any matter in the English language.

(2) No person who demonstrates that he has successfully completed the sixth primary grade in a public school in, or a private school accredited by, any State or territory, the District of Columbia, or the Commonwealth of Puerto Rico in which the predominant classroom language was other than English, shall be denied the right to vote in any Federal, State, or local election because of his inability to read, write, understand, or interpret any matter in the English language, except that in States in which State law provides that a different level of education is presumptive of literacy, he shall demonstrate that he has successfully completed an equivalent level of education in a public school in, or a private school accredited by, any State or territory, the District of Columbia, or the Commonwealth of Puerto Rico in which the predominant classroom language was other than English.

prohibits the enforcement of the election laws of New York requiring an ability to read and write English as a condition of voting. . . .

We hold that, in the application challenged in these cases, §4(e) is a proper exercise of the powers granted to Congress by §5 of the Fourteenth Amendment and that by force of the Supremacy Clause, Article VI, the New York English literacy requirement cannot be enforced to the extent that it is inconsistent with §4(e).

Under the distribution of powers effected by the Constitution, the States establish qualifications for voting for state officers, and the qualifications established by the States for voting for members of the most numerous branch of the state legislature also determine who may vote for United States Representatives and Senators, Art. I, §2; Seventeenth Amendment; *Ex parte Yarbrough,* 110 U.S. 651, 663. But, of course, the States have no power to grant or withhold the franchise on conditions that are forbidden by the Fourteenth Amendment. . . .

The Attorney General of the State of New York argues that an exercise of congressional power under §5 of the Fourteenth Amendment that prohibits the enforcement of a state law can only be sustained if the judicial branch determines that the state law is prohibited by the provisions of the Amendment that Congress sought to enforce. More specifically, he urges that §4(e) cannot be sustained as appropriate legislation to enforce the Equal Protection Clause unless the judiciary decides—even with the guidance of a congressional judgment—that the application of the English literacy requirement prohibited by §4(e) is forbidden by the Equal Protection Clause itself. We disagree. Neither the language nor history of §5 supports such a construction. As was said with regard to §5 in *Ex parte Virginia,* 100 U.S. 339, 345, "It is the power of Congress which has been enlarged. Congress is authorized to enforce the prohibitions by appropriate legislation. Some legislation is contemplated to make the amendments fully effective." A construction of §5 that would require a judicial determination that the enforcement of the state law precluded by Congress violated the Amendment, as a condition of sustaining the congressional enactment, would depreciate both congressional resourcefulness and congressional responsibility for implementing the Amendment. It would confine the legislative power in this context to the insignificant role of abrogating only those state laws that the judicial branch was prepared to adjudge unconstitutional, or of merely informing the judgment of the judiciary by particularizing the "majestic generalities" of §1 of the Amendment.

Thus our task in this case is not to determine whether the New York English literacy requirement as applied to deny the right to vote to a person who successfully completed the sixth grade in a Puerto Rican school violates the Equal Protection Clause. [T]he question before us here [is: w]ithout regard to whether the judiciary would find that the Equal Protection Clause itself nullifies New York's English literacy requirement as so applied, could Congress prohibit the enforcement of the state law by legislating under §5 of the Fourteenth Amendment? In answering this question, our task is limited to determining whether such legislation is, as required by §5, appropriate legislation to enforce the Equal Protection Clause.

By including §5 the draftsmen sought to grant to Congress, by a specific provision applicable to the Fourteenth Amendment, the same broad powers expressed in the Necessary and Proper Clause, Art. I, §8, cl. 18. The classic formulation of the reach of those powers was established by Chief Justice Marshall in *McCulloch v. Maryland*, 4 Wheat. 316, 421:

> Let the end be legitimate, let it be within the scope of the constitution, and all means which are appropriate, which are plainly adapted to that end, which are not prohibited, but consist with the letter and spirit of the constitution, are constitutional.

Ex parte Virginia, 100 U.S., at 345-346, decided 12 years after the adoption of the Fourteenth Amendment, held that congressional power under §5 had this same broad scope. . . . Thus the *McCulloch v. Maryland* standard is the measure of what constitutes "appropriate legislation" under §5 of the Fourteenth Amendment. Correctly viewed, §5 is a positive grant of legislative power authorizing Congress to exercise its discretion in determining whether and what legislation is needed to secure the guarantees of the Fourteenth Amendment.

We therefore proceed to the consideration whether §4(e) is "appropriate legislation" to enforce the Equal Protection Clause, that is, under the *McCulloch v. Maryland* standard, whether §4(e) may be regarded as an enactment to enforce the Equal Protection Clause, whether it is "plainly adapted to that end" and whether it is not prohibited by but is consistent with "the letter and spirit of the constitution."[2]

There can be no doubt that §4(e) may be regarded as an enactment to enforce the Equal Protection Clause. Congress explicitly declared that it enacted §4(e) "to secure the rights under the fourteenth amendment of persons educated in American-flag schools in which the predominant classroom language was other than English." . . . More specifically, §4(e) may be viewed as a measure to secure for the Puerto Rican community residing in New York non-discriminatory treatment by government—both in the imposition of voting qualifications and the provision or administration of governmental services, such as public schools, public housing and law enforcement.

Section 4(e) may be readily seen as "plainly adapted" to furthering these aims of the Equal Protection Clause. The practical effect of §4(e) is to prohibit New York from denying the right to vote to large segments of its Puerto Rican community. Congress has thus prohibited the State from denying to that community the right that is "preservative of all rights." *Yick Wo v. Hopkins*, 118 U.S. 356, 370. . . . This enhanced political power will be helpful in gaining nondiscriminatory treatment in public services for the entire Puerto Rican community. . . . It was well within congressional authority to say that this need of the Puerto Rican minority for the vote warranted federal intrusion upon any state interests served by the English literacy requirement. . . .

---

2. Contrary to the suggestion of the dissent, §5 does not grant Congress power to exercise discretion in the other direction and to enact "statutes so as in effect to dilute equal protection and due process decisions of this Court." We emphasize that Congress' power under §5 is limited to adopting measures to enforce the guarantees of the Amendment; §5 grants Congress no power to restrict, abrogate, or dilute these guarantees. Thus, for example, an enactment authorizing the States to establish racially segregated systems of education would not be—as required by §5—a measure "to enforce" the Equal Protection Clause since that clause of its own force prohibits such state laws.

We therefore conclude that §4(e), in the application challenged in this case, is appropriate legislation to enforce the Equal Protection Clause and that the judgment of the District Court must be and hereby is

Reversed.

Justice HARLAN, dissenting:

Worthy as its purposes may be thought by many, I do not see how §4(e) of the Voting Rights Act of 1965, 79 Stat. 439, 42 U.S.C. §1973b(e) (1964 ed. Supp. I), can be sustained except at the sacrifice of fundamentals in the American constitutional system — the separation between the legislative and judicial function and the boundaries between federal and state political authority. . . . Although §5 most certainly does give to the Congress wide powers in the field of devising remedial legislation to effectuate the Amendment's prohibition on arbitrary state action, *Ex parte Virginia,* 100 U.S. 339, I believe the Court has confused the issue of how much enforcement power Congress possesses under §5 with the distinct issue of what questions are appropriate for congressional determination and what questions are essentially judicial in nature.

When recognized state violations of federal constitutional standards have occurred, Congress is of course empowered by §5 to take appropriate remedial measures to redress and prevent the wrongs. See *Strauder v. West Virginia,* 100 U.S. 303, 310. But it is a judicial question whether the condition with which Congress has thus sought to deal is in truth an infringement of the Constitution, something that is the necessary prerequisite to bringing the §5 power into play at all.

. . . The question here is not whether the statute is appropriate remedial legislation to cure an established violation of a constitutional command, but whether there has in fact been an infringement of that constitutional command, that is, whether a particular state practice or, as here, a statute is so arbitrary or irrational as to offend the command of the Equal Protection Clause of the Fourteenth Amendment. That question is one for the judicial branch ultimately to determine. Were the rule otherwise, Congress would be able to qualify this Court's constitutional decisions under the Fourteenth and Fifteenth Amendments, let alone those under other provisions of the Constitution, by resorting to congressional power under the Necessary and Proper Clause. In view of this Court's holding in *Lassiter,* that an English literacy test is a permissible exercise of state supervision over its franchise, I do not think it is open to Congress to limit the effect of that decision as it has undertaken to do by §4(e). In effect the Court reads §5 of the Fourteenth Amendment as giving Congress the power to define the *substantive* scope of the Amendment. If that indeed be the true reach of §5, then I do not see why Congress should not be able as well to exercise its §5 "discretion" by enacting statutes so as in effect to dilute equal protection and due process decisions of this Court. In all such cases there is room for reasonable men to differ as to whether or not a denial of equal protection or due process has occurred, and the final decision is one of judgment. Until today this judgment has always been one for the judiciary to resolve.

I do not mean to suggest in what has been said that a legislative judgment of the type incorporated in §4(e) is without any force whatsoever. . . . [But] we have here not a matter of giving deference to a congressional estimate, based on its determination of legislative facts, bearing upon the validity *vel non* of a statute, but rather what can at most be called a legislative announcement that Congress believes a state law to entail an unconstitutional deprivation of equal protection. Although this kind of declaration is of course entitled to the most respectful consideration, coming as it does from a concurrent branch and one that is knowledgeable in matters of popular political participation, I do not believe it lessens our responsibility to decide the fundamental issue of whether in fact the state enactment violates federal constitutional rights.

––––––––––––

» *Congressional Extension of the Literacy Test Ban.* As *Morgan* relates, in the Voting Rights Act of 1965, Congress initially banned the use of literacy tests only in relation to its use to discriminate against non-English-speaking groups. Congress eventually recognized that the literacy test was also (and perhaps primarily) used to disenfranchise blacks, and so in 1970 amended the VRA to extend the literacy test ban to any jurisdiction in which its use had not already been banned under the 1965 Act. The Court unanimously upheld this provision in *Oregon v. Mitchell*, 400 U.S. 112 (1970).

» *The Vitality of* **Morgan.** *Morgan* has long been a controversial decision because it permits Congress to enact expansive civil rights legislation that takes a more generous view of the content of the Fourteenth and Fifteenth Amendments than does the Supreme Court itself. Some decisions of the Supreme Court under the VRA, however, seem to lay the groundwork for a possible future erosion or reversal of *Morgan*. In a line of cases beginning with *Shaw v. Reno*, 509 U.S. 630 (1993), and *Miller v. Johnson*, 515 U.S. 900 (1995), taken up in detail in Chapter 5, the Court has intimated that certain provisions of the Voting Rights Act, though constitutional under the Fifteenth Amendment, may violate the Fourteenth Amendment. This is significant because the provision of the VRA that the Court has found objectionable in those cases is based on a view of the Fifteenth Amendment that is more expansive than the view taken by the Court. While the actual holding of *Morgan* is not directly threatened by this development, it may reduce *Morgan* functionally to a case of merely academic interest. A more thorough consideration of these issues is deferred until Chapter 5.

An even more direct threat to *Morgan* may come from the Court's decision in *City of Boerne v. Flores*, 521 U.S. 507 (1997). In *Boerne*, the Court struck down the federal Religious Freedom Restoration Act of 1993 (RFRA). Congress enacted RFRA in response to the Court's 1990 decision in *Employment Division v. Smith*, 494 U.S. 872 (1990), which interpreted the Free Exercise Clause of the First Amendment in a way that made it easier for governments to avoid making accommodations to religious practices. In RFRA, a piece of civil rights legislation enacted under Section 5 of the Fourteenth Amendment, Congress decreed that certain kinds of free exercise claims must be evaluated under a balancing test, rather than the less demanding level of analysis the Court utilized in *Smith*. In *Boerne*, the Court invalidated RFRA on the ground that it represented a congressional attempt to overturn a Supreme Court decision interpreting the Constitution. Congressional power under Section 5, the Court held, is "remedial" only. The Court dealt briefly with *Morgan* in the following passage:

There is language in our opinion in *Katzenbach v. Morgan* which could be interpreted as acknowledging a power in Congress to enact legislation that expands the rights contained in §1 of the Fourteenth Amendment. This is not a necessary interpretation, however, or even the best one. . . . The Court provided two related rationales for its conclusion that §4(e) could "be viewed as a measure to secure for the Puerto Rican community residing in New York nondiscriminatory treatment by government." *Id.*, at 652. Under the first rationale, Congress could prohibit New York from denying the right to vote to large segments of its Puerto Rican community, in order to give Puerto Ricans "enhanced political power" that would be "helpful in gaining nondiscriminatory treatment in public services for the entire Puerto Rican community." *Ibid.* Section 4(e) thus could be justified as a remedial measure to deal with "discrimination in governmental services." *Id.*, at 653. The second rationale, an alternative holding, did not address discrimination in the provision of public services but "discrimination in establishing voter qualifications." *Id.*, at 654. The Court perceived a factual basis on which Congress could have concluded that New York's literacy requirement "constituted an invidious discrimination in violation of the Equal Protection Clause." *Id.*, at 656. Both rationales for upholding §4(e) rested on unconstitutional discrimination by New York and Congress' reasonable attempt to combat it. As Justice Stewart explained in *Oregon v. Mitchell, supra*, at 296, interpreting *Morgan* to give Congress the power to interpret the Constitution "would require an enormous extension of that decision's rationale."

If Congress could define its own powers by altering the Fourteenth Amendment's meaning, no longer would the Constitution be "superior paramount law, unchangeable by ordinary means." It would be "on a level with ordinary legislative acts, and, like other acts, . . . alterable when the legislature shall please to alter it." *Marbury v. Madison*, 1 Cranch at 177. Under this approach, it is difficult to conceive of a principle that would limit congressional power. . . .

Does the Court do an adequate job of distinguishing *Morgan?*

▷▷ *Contemporary Political Behavior in the United States.* We saw in Chapter 2 that American thinking about popular self-governance contains a strand of inherited republican thought that is highly skeptical of the competence of ordinary people to understand and evaluate the kind of complex policy issues that government officials often face. Populists and Progressives later took a different view, claiming that ordinary citizens are fully capable of meaningful, substantively good self-government. A literacy requirement for voting seems in some ways to split the difference: it seems to presume the innate capacity of citizens, but to view capacity alone as insufficient. An intellectually able citizenry must also be informed if it is to rule itself well and wisely, and literacy is singled out as the key to information.

Today, virtually all Americans are literate. But are they in consequence sufficiently well informed to govern themselves intelligently? Much contemporary political science research has been devoted to examining this question. The excerpt immediately below is taken from a ground-breaking work that has deeply influenced political scientists' thought about American voting behavior.

Angus Campbell et al.

The American Voter (1960)

Commentaries on democracy often assume two basic facts about the electoral decision: first, that the public is generally in possession of sufficient information regarding the various policy alternatives of the moment to make a rational choice among them (that is, that it has clear goals and is able to assess what the actions of government mean for these goals), and, second, that the election in fact presents the electorate with recognizable partisan alternatives through which it can express its policy preferences. Let us review the evidence as to the policy awareness of the electorate. To what extent does the public have policy goals, either discrete or structured as general ideological dimensions? Does it relate these goals to current policy issues? And does it perceive the position of the parties on current policy issues? The answers to these questions have a good deal to say about the guidance that policy-forming elites receive from the mass electorate.

Our detailed inquiry into public attitudes regarding what we took to be the most prominent political issues of the time revealed a substantial lack of familiarity with these policy questions. Some individuals are sensitive to the full range of contemporary political events; they know what they want their government to do and they use their vote in a very purposive manner to achieve within their power the policy alternatives that they prefer. Such people do not make up a very large proportion of the electorate. The typical voter has only a modest understanding of the specific issues and may be quite ignorant of matters of public policy that more sophisticated individuals might regard as very pressing. Our measures have shown the public's understanding of policy issues to be poorly developed even though these measures usually have referred to a general problem which might be the subject of legislation or (in the area of foreign affairs) executive action, rather than to particular bills or acts.

Neither do we find much evidence of the kind of structured political thinking that we might expect to characterize a well-informed electorate. We have been able to identify a pattern of attitudes regarding certain questions of welfare legislation and a similar cluster of attitudes toward internationalist foreign policies. These express rather gross dimensions of opinion, however; they do not relate to each other or to other political attitudes with which one might expect to find them associated in a larger attitudinal structure. When we examine the attitudes and beliefs of the electorate as a whole over a broad range of policy questions — welfare legislation, foreign policy, federal economic programs, minority rights, civil liberties — we do not find coherent patterns of belief. The common tendency to characterize large blocs of the electorate in such terms as "liberal" or "conservative" greatly exaggerates the actual amount of consistent patterning one finds. Our failure to locate more than a trace of "ideological" thinking in the protocols of our surveys emphasizes the general impoverishment of political thought in a large proportion of the electorate.

It is also apparent from these protocols that there is a great deal of uncertainty and confusion in the public mind as to what specific policies the election of one party over the other would imply. Very few of our respondents have shown a sensitive understanding of the positions of the parties on current policy issues. Even among those people who are relatively familiar with the issues presented in our surveys — and our test of familiarity has been an easy one — there is little agreement as to where the two parties stand. This fact reflects the similarity of party positions on many issues, as well as the range of opinion within parties. But it also reflects how little attention even the relatively informed part of the electorate gives the specifics of public policy formation.

We have, then, the portrait of an electorate almost wholly without detailed information about decision making in government. A substantial portion of the public is able to respond in a discrete manner to issues that *might* be the subject of legislative or administrative action. Yet it knows little about what government has done on these issues or what the parties propose to do. It is almost completely unable to judge the rationality of government actions; knowing little of particular policies and what has led to them, the mass electorate is not able to appraise either its goals or the appropriateness of the means chosen to serve these goals.

It is not altogether surprising that this statement is true. For a large part of the public, political affairs are probably too difficult to comprehend in detail. For example, we may suppose that the people we have described as feeling "politically ineffective" are virtually beyond the reach of political stimulation. An additional part of the electorate is no doubt capable of informing itself about political matters but is unwilling to pay the cost that such information-getting would entail. Very few people seem motivated strongly enough to obtain the information needed to develop a sensitive understanding of decision making in government. It is a rather unusual individual whose deeper personality needs are engaged by politics, and in terms of rational self-interest, the stakes do not seem to be great enough for the ordinary citizen to justify his expending the effort necessary to make himself well informed politically.

———————

Numerous subsequent studies have confirmed the findings of *The American Voter* concerning the extremely limited political knowledge of the average voter. For example, the author of a 1989 study concluded: "[t]he typical American voter . . . knows little about politics, is not interested in politics, does not participate in politics, does not organize his or her political attitudes in a coherent manner, and does not think in structured, ideological terms." ERIC R.A.N. SMITH, THE UNCHANGING AMERICAN VOTER 1-2 (1989). Another study confirmed voters' lack of political knowledge, but reached the perhaps even more troubling conclusion that political knowledge is unevenly distributed throughout the population:

> [subject]-specific differences [in knowledge] are ultimately dwarfed by a larger, more consistent pattern in which the same groups of citizens (whites, men, the more educated, the more generally politically interested and engaged) are relatively better informed about virtually all aspects of politics. . . . [P]olitical ignorance is not randomly distributed but is most likely to be found among those who arguably have the most to gain from effective political participation: women, blacks, the poor, and the young.

MICHAEL X. DELLI CARPINI AND SCOTT KEETER, WHAT AMERICANS KNOW ABOUT POLITICS AND WHY IT MATTERS 176-177 (1996).

>> *Rehabilitating Voter Competence.*   The findings and conclusions of the authors of *The American Voter* and subsequent studies of the electorate's political knowledge shocked many people, and prompted much hand-wringing and morose reflection on the decline of American devotion to the public welfare, and on the reduced willingness of Americans to fulfill the minimal duties of citizenship. Recently, however, some political scientists have begun to challenge the depressing conclusions drawn from studies showing widespread voter ignorance: that voters lack factual information about politics and government performance does not, they argue, necessarily demonstrate that voters are incompetent.

Some have argued, for example, that findings of public fickleness and instability in political opinions say more about the poor state of public opinion polling than about the cognitive abilities of voters. *See* JOHN R. ZALLER, THE NATURE AND ORIGINS OF MASS OPINION (1992). Others argue that the acquisition of detailed knowledge about politics is so costly and time-consuming that few voters have time for it. Instead, voters quite rationally develop "information shortcuts" or "heuristics"—ways of thinking about politics that allow them to reach conclusions in which they are entitled to have confidence, but that do not require a great deal of effort in collecting and thinking through large amounts of information. *See, e.g.,* SAMUEL L. POPKIN, THE REASONING VOTER: COMMUNICATION AND PERSUASION IN PRESIDENTIAL CAMPAIGNS (1991).

Another well-known account argues that the ability to recall great masses of factual information is not only unnecessary for good democratic decision making, but also does not accurately describe the way the human mind uses information. On this account, voters keep a kind of "running tally" on subjects of interest. Using this strategy, voters make initial judgments but then hold those judgments stable without attending to them until some new piece of information forces the voter to reconsider his or her standing opinion. Once voters have a baseline opinion, they can rely on it without any need to recall all the many original judgments and considerations giving rise to the current tally. Thus, the running tally method allows voters, in essence, to know what they think without requiring them to recall why they think it, offering voters the benefit of a well-informed opinion without the burden of remembering every detail that went into formulating it. *See* MORRIS P. FIORINA, RETROSPECTIVE VOTING IN AMERICAN NATIONAL ELECTIONS (1981); Marco R. Steenbergen and Milton Lodge, *Process Matters: Cognitive Models of Candidate Evaluation, in* ELECTORAL DEMOCRACY (Michael B. MacKuen and George Rabinowitz eds., 2003).

Yet another argument for voter rationality does not contest the ignorance or even the irrationality of individual voters so much as it argues that voters *collectively* act in ways that are rational and well informed. On this view, it is not necessary for each individual voter to have extensive information and devote extensive thought to political decision so long as collective processes of democracy lead the public collectively to good results. BENJAMIN I. PAGE AND ROBERT Y. SHAPIRO, THE RATIONAL PUBLIC: FIFTY YEARS OF TRENDS IN AMERICANS' POLICY PREFERENCES (1992). Other recent work finds that, despite their seeming ignorance, voters manage to "vote correctly"—that is, vote in accordance with the way they would vote were they more fully informed and attentive—most of the time, at least in simple, two-candidate races featuring ideologically distinct opponents. In multi-candidate races, however, or in situations such as primary elections where candidates are not obviously distinct ideologically, voters do not perform as well. RICHARD R. LAU AND DAVID P. REDLAWSK, HOW VOTERS DECIDE: INFORMATION PROCESSING DURING ELECTION CAMPAIGNS (2006).

» ***Rational Ignorance?*** An even more direct challenge to dire conclusions about voter ignorance comes from economic theories of democracy. Once again, Downs put the case as directly and succinctly as anyone.

Anthony Downs

An Economic Theory of Democracy (1957)

Traditional economic theory assumes that unlimited amounts of free information are available to decision-makers. In contrast, we seek to discover what political decision-making is like when uncertainty exists and information is obtainable only at a cost. . . .

The main steps of rationally deciding how to vote and then voting are as follows:

1. Gathering information relevant to each issue upon which important political decisions have been (or will be) made.
2. For each issue, selecting from all the information gathered that which will be used in the voting decision.
3. For each issue, analyzing the facts selected to arrive at specific factual conclusions about possible alternative policies and their consequences.
4. For each issue, appraising the consequences of every likely policy in light of relevant goals. This is a value appraisal, not a strictly factual one.
5. Coordinating the appraisals of each issue into a net evaluation of each party running in the election. This is also a value judgment personally tailored to the goals of the voter himself.
6. Making the voting decision by comparing the net evaluations of each party and weighting them for future contingencies.
7. Actually voting or abstaining.

Every one of these steps except the last can be delegated to someone other than the voter himself [as a way of reducing cost]. . . .

Of what does this cost consist? By definition, any cost is a deflection of scarce resources from some utility-producing use; it is a forgone alternative. The main scarce resource consumed in the steps above is the time used for assimilating data and weighing alternatives, but many other resources may also be involved, particularly in the gathering and transmission steps. . . .

Because of the division of labor, most citizens in modern democracies do not gather for themselves the information they need for political decision-making. Thousands of specialized agencies gather, interpret, and transmit such information, making it available to the citizenry in a tremendous variety of forms, from television broadcasts to encyclopedias. But since the resources any citizen can devote to paying for and assimilating data are limited, he finds himself in a situation of economic choice: from among these many sources of information, he must select only a few to tap. . . .

Even when most of his political data are prefocused on areas of general relevance, the rational man in politics must take further steps to increase his efficiency. Therefore he seeks (1) to expend no more time and money obtaining political information than its returns warrant and (2) to receive as many data as possible from whatever sources he does use. . . . For all these reasons, our *a priori* expectation is that rational citizens will seek to obtain their free political information from other persons if they can. . . .

Apparently, men with zero party differentials [i.e., voters who do not expect any difference in personal utility whether one party or the other holds office] are irrational if they invest in any political information to help them make their voting decision. . . .

The result is an enormously diminished incentive for voters to acquire political information before voting.

Although we cannot make *a priori* predictions of just how small this incentive is, it seems probable that for a great many citizens in democracy, rational behavior excludes any investment whatever in political information *per se*. No matter how significant a difference between parties is revealed to the rational citizen by his free information, or how uncertain he is about which party to support, he realizes that his vote has almost no chance of influencing the outcome. Therefore why should he buy political information? . . . [Thus,] we believe that it is rational for a great part of the electorate to minimize investment in political data. For them, rational behavior implies both a refusal to expend resources on political information *per se* and a definite limitation of the amount of free political information absorbed.

▶▶ *Rational Irrationality?* If the thought that it is rational for democratic citizens to remain ignorant is not depressing enough, how about the idea that it is rational for democratic citizens to behave irrationally? On this view, because of the improbability that their own votes will change electoral and policy outcomes, people rarely have to live with the result of seeing their own preferences enacted into policy. "In real-world political settings, the price of ideological loyalty is close to zero. So we should *expect* people to 'satiate' their demand for political delusion, to believe whatever makes them feel best. After all, it's free. The fanatical protectionist who votes to close the borders risks virtually nothing, because the same policy wins no matter how he votes." In other words, because extreme views are unlikely actually to prevail, voters can freely indulge their taste for extreme or even bizarre political positions without fear that their views would ever be enacted into law. BRYAN CAPLAN, THE MYTH OF THE RATIONAL VOTER: WHY DEMOCRACIES CHOOSE BAD POLICIES 18 (2007).

Ever since Downs published his book, political theorists have struggled with the questions he raised. For a wide-ranging examination of these issues, see CITIZEN

Competence and Democratic Institutions (Stephen L. Elkin and Karol Edward Soltan eds., 1999).

2. Age and Mental Disability

As with literacy, the obvious justification for establishing age qualifications for voting has primarily to do with individual competence. The legal question is rarely one of the adequacy of this justification but, typically in the American system, one of power: at what level is the power to regulate the age of voting vested?

In a splintered and complex ruling, the Court in *Oregon v. Mitchell*, 400 U.S. 112 (1970), considered the authority of Congress to regulate the age of voters in elections for both national and state offices. The issue arose following enactment by Congress of the Voting Rights Act Amendments of 1970, which lowered the voting age in all elections, state and national, to 18; in most states it had previously been 21. Congress enacted the law in response to growing public resistance to the Vietnam War. A commonly heard argument that gained traction in Congress was that if men could be drafted and sent to fight at age 18, they surely ought to be able to vote. This was maintained partly on the ground that the competence required to vote is no greater than the competence required for military service, and partly on the ground that men of draft age should have a democratic voice in the formulation of policies that might send them abroad to fight and possibly to die.

Four Justices ruled that Congress may lower the voting age in state and national elections. This group argued principally that such congressional power is granted by Section 5 of the Fourteenth Amendment, and Congress may lower the voting age to prevent a violation of equal protection. Four other Justices ruled that Congress lacked the power to alter the voting age in either state or national elections. This group reasoned primarily that the power to regulate voting age is granted entirely by the Constitution to the states, not Congress, and that only a new constitutional amendment could expand the franchise beyond the limits that states chose to place upon it.

In a swing vote, Justice Black split the baby, holding that Congress had the power to lower the voting age in federal elections, but not in state elections. Justice Black found congressional power to regulate voting qualifications in federal elections to be implied by the constitutional structure, but also found it limited, by structural implication, to the regulation only of national elections.

> I would hold, as have a long line of decisions in this Court, that Congress has ultimate supervisory power over congressional elections. Similarly, it is the prerogative of Congress to oversee the conduct of presidential and vice-presidential elections and to set the qualifications for voters for electors for those offices. It cannot be seriously contended that congress has less power over the conduct of presidential elections than it has over congressional elections.
>
> On the other hand, the Constitution was also intended to preserve to the States the power that even the Colonies had to establish and maintain their own separate and independent governments, except insofar as the Constitution itself commands otherwise. . . . No function is more

essential to the separate and independent existence of the States and
their governments than the power to determine within the limits of the
Constitution the qualifications of their own voters for state, county, and
municipal offices and the nature of their own machinery for filling local
public offices. . . .

Under the split result of *Oregon v. Mitchell,* Congress was constitutionally permitted to lower the voting age to 18 in federal elections, but not in state elections.
This split decision created

> an administrative and logistical nightmare for state election officials.
> Voters under twenty-one would have to be registered and tracked sepa-
> rately; cities and towns would have to either purchase additional voting
> machines (and set them up in age-segregated booths) or utilize special
> machines constructed to permit selective blocking of particular election
> contests. The projected costs ran into the millions of dollars, and some
> states were not sure that the changes could be carried out before the 1972
> elections. Compounding the problem was the fact that many states could
> not possibly alter their constitutions to adopt a lower state voting age by
> 1972: doing so often required votes in successive legislatures followed by
> popular referenda.
>
> Faced with this crisis, Congress moved expeditiously to rectify the
> mess that it had helped to create. A month after the *Oregon* decision,
> [Senator] Jennings Randolph introduced a proposal for a constitutional
> amendment that barred the United States or any state from denying or
> abridging the right to vote of any citizen aged eighteen or over on account
> of age. In March 1971, the Senate, with no dissenting votes, approved the
> amendment. Within a few weeks, the House had done the same. . . . State
> legislatures then rushed to ratify the amendment. By the end of June,
> thirty-eight states had done so, and the Twenty-Sixth Amendment was law.
> The ratification process was by far the most rapid in the history of the
> republic.

ALEXANDER KEYSSAR, THE RIGHT TO VOTE: THE CONTESTED HISTORY OF DEMOC-
RACY IN THE UNITED STATES 281 (2000).

The Twenty-Sixth Amendment provides: "The right of citizens of the United
States, who are eighteen years of age or older, to vote shall not be denied or
abridged by the United States or by any State on account of age." Does the reasoning of *Oregon v. Mitchell* survive its mooting by the Twenty-Sixth Amendment? Could
Congress set or alter other voting qualifications in national elections?

➤➤ *"Manner" vs. "Qualifications."* In *Arizona v. Inter Tribal Council of Arizona, Inc.,*
570 U.S. 1 (2013), the Court in dicta cast doubt on the congressional power to
regulate voting qualifications in federal elections. The case concerned a somewhat
technical question of preemption under the National Voter Registration Act. In the
course of its decision, however, the Court said that the "Elections Clause," Article I,
§4, "empowers Congress to regulate *how* federal elections are held, but not *who* may
vote in them." "Prescribing voting qualifications," the Court went on, "'forms no
part of the power to be conferred upon the national government.'" This appears

to be a rejection of the reasoning employed by Justice Black (for himself alone) in *Oregon v. Mitchell.*

One of the difficulties flagged by the decision in *Intertribal Council* concerns the distinction between regulation of the "manner" of holding elections—expressly granted to Congress by Article I, §4—and regulation of voter qualifications, expressly granted to the states by Article I, §2 and the Seventeenth Amendment. Congress enacted the NVRA to promote and facilitate voter registration. Nothing in the Act prohibited states from establishing citizenship requirements to vote, but the registration form adopted by the federal government policed this requirement by asking voters who sought to register by mail merely to aver under oath that they are citizens. Arizona law, in contrast, required documentary evidence of citizenship from all applicants. The Court held that the federal decision to use the form in question, along with its averment requirement, preempted the conflicting Arizona documentation requirement. The Court expressed concern that Arizona's "power to establish voting requirements is of little value without the power to enforce those requirements," but found that federal administrative procedures offered the state an opportunity to work with the federal government to obtain compliant documentation of citizenship from registrants.

This analysis poses a difficult question. If states have the unquestioned power to set voter qualifications, and that power is meaningless without the power of effective enforcement, at what point does the congressional power to regulate the "manner" of federal elections become relevant? Don't administrative requirements governing registration to vote relate to the manner of holding elections? Is the Court trying to say that Congress has *no* ability to overrule state rules policing voter eligibility qualifications no matter how burdensome and restrictive those rules might be?

≫   *Voting at 16?*   Is the 18-year-old threshold for voting still too high? Numerous countries, including Argentina, Austria, Brazil, Cuba, Ecuador, Malta, and Nicaragua, use age 16 as their cutoff for participation in national elections. Other jurisdictions, such as Scotland and some German states, allow 16-year-olds to vote in regional elections. In the U.S., the Maryland municipality of Takoma Park in 2013 lowered the voting age in city elections to 16. *See* Takoma Park Municipal Charter, art. 6.

The main reason *not* to lower the voting age to 16 is obvious: the lack of knowledge, experience, and maturity demanded of citizens in a modern, complex society. What then is the justification for lowering the voting age? The most commonly advanced justification for doing so is a kind of training justification: early participation in politics provides the foundation for lifelong habits of political participation, engagement, and satisfaction with democratic politics. Empirical evidence on this hypothesis has been conflicting. Studies from Austria suggest no net gain in political knowledge or informed voting as a result of an earlier onset of participation, whereas results from Norway and Sweden suggest long-term improvements in political engagement and efficacy. *See* LOWERING THE VOTING AGE TO 16: LEARNING FROM REAL EXPERIENCES WORLDWIDE (Jan Eichhorn and Johannes Bergh, eds., 2020). If you were a state legislator and a bill were introduced to lower the voting age in your state to 16, how would you vote? Why?

>> *Disenfranchisement for Mental Disability.*   The principal nondiscriminatory purpose of literacy requirements seems to be to prevent ignorant or irrational people from influencing the results of elections by casting votes. Another kind of provision with a similar aim examines the mental health of voters: most states expressly disqualify from voting persons suffering from a serious mental disability. Such provisions seem to reflect a commonplace belief that popular political decisions should be well considered and rational, and that meaningful, rational participation in politics requires some minimal level of mental competence.

Defining the relevant mental disability is a complex task, and states have taken a variety of approaches. Some of the older provisions disqualify "idiots" or the "insane." Many states provide for disqualifications on grounds of "mental incompetence" or "mental incapacity." Nevada disqualifies those who are "non compos mentis." Some disqualify only those who have been formally adjudicated incompetent, who are under formal guardianship, or who have been involuntarily committed to a mental institution. Oregon's unique provision combines disqualification for mental incompetence with an extension of protection against disqualification to the merely disabled: "A person suffering from a mental handicap is entitled to the full rights of an elector, if otherwise qualified, unless the person has been adjudicated incompetent to vote as provided by law." Or. Const. Art. II, §3.

In its treatment of mental disability, the U.S. may be lagging behind evolving international standards. The United Nations Convention on the Rights of Persons with Disabilities largely discards older frameworks of guardianship, in which decisions are made for a mentally disabled person by a fiduciary, in favor of "supported decision-making," in which the mentally disabled participate in making relevant decisions with support of various kinds, as circumstances may require. In the domain of voting, this might mean that instead of being disqualified, a mentally disabled person would still be able to vote with appropriate assistance. In Japan, for example, an eligible voter suffering from mental disability may appoint an adult representative to cast his or her vote subject to instructions, with a second adult witness present to ensure that the instructions are carried out. Trevor Ryan, *et al.*, *Voting with an "Unsound Mind"? A Comparative Study of the Voting Rights of Persons with Mental Disabilities*, 39 UNSW L. J. 1038 (2016).

3.   Wealth

>> *Property Qualifications.*   For about a century, property qualifications for the franchise were common in the American colonies and then the United States. They first appeared in significant numbers during the mid-eighteenth century, until the rise of a repeal movement in the mid-nineteenth century inspired by Jacksonian notions of equality. Property qualifications were typically justified on the ground that

> those without property were not free agents. Those who owned no property were powerless and dependent; they were nearly always subject to the will of those who commanded resources. Because they were not their own men, they lacked political capacity. The political community simply could not trust such men with the important task of selecting magistrates

or legislative representatives because they could never exercise independent judgment. They would always be compelled to do the bidding of the wealthy. . . . [For example, John Adams wrote:] "Such is the frailty of the human heart that very few men who have no property, have any judgment of their own. They talk and vote as they are directed by some man of property, who has attached their minds to his interest. . . . [They are] to all intents and purposes as much dependent upon others, who will please to feed, clothe, and employ them, as women are upon their husbands, or children on their parents."

Robert J. Steinfeld, *Property and Suffrage in the Early American Republic*, 41 STAN. L. REV. 335, 340-341 (1989).

Historical evidence suggests that this view was not entirely inaccurate — not because people lacked inherent capacity, to be sure, but as a matter of custom and convention. American society of the eighteenth century was hierarchical, characterized by strict social ranks and occupational categories. The lower social and economic orders cultivated long-established habits of deference to their social superiors, who dealt with them within a model of patriarchal patronage and dependence. According to one estimate, at least half the population at any given time was in an unfree state of slavery, indentured servitude, or apprenticeship. Intricate networks of personal loyalties and obligations existed within a small, close world of personal relationships and little privacy, making it exceedingly difficult freely to develop or to exercise political independence. Eventually, only changes in social customs and expectations associated with the Revolution were able to break lengthy traditions of political dependence. *See* GORDON S. WOOD, THE RADICALISM OF THE AMERICAN REVOLUTION (1992).

≫ *Franklin's Position on Property Qualifications.* "Today a man owns a jackass worth fifty dollars and he is entitled to vote; but before the next election the jackass dies. The man in the mean time has become more experienced, his knowledge of the principles of government, and his acquaintance with mankind, are more extensive, and he is therefore better qualified to make a proper selection of rulers — but the jackass is dead and the man cannot vote. Now gentlemen, pray inform me, in whom is the right of suffrage? In the man or in the jackass?" Benjamin Franklin (1828).

Poll taxes — fees that must be paid as a prerequisite to voting — were first levied during the mid-nineteenth century. Such taxes serve as a kind of property qualification, yet American attitudes toward the franchise had so altered during the preceding century that no state attempted to justify poll taxes on the political independence grounds that had been invoked during the eighteenth century. Indeed, the rationale for poll taxes was quite different: historically, poll taxes were used primarily to discriminate against blacks.

The Twenty-Fourth Amendment, ratified in 1964, provides:

The right of citizens of the United States to vote in any primary or other election for President or Vice President, for electors for President or Vice President, or for Senator or Representative in Congress, shall not be

denied or abridged by the United States or any State by reason of failure
to pay any poll tax or other tax.

By its terms, the amendment thus forbids the imposition of poll taxes in elections
of *federal* officials. The amendment, however, says nothing about the use of poll
taxes in elections for state and local offices. In the following case, the Supreme
Court confronted a challenge to a state poll tax based on the Equal Protection
Clause.

Harper v. Virginia Board of Elections

383 U.S. 663 (1966)

Mr. Justice DOUGLAS delivered the opinion of the Court.

These are suits by Virginia residents to have declared unconstitutional Virginia's poll tax. . . .

While the right to vote in federal elections is conferred by Art. I, §2, of the
Constitution (*United States v. Classic*, 313 U.S. 299, 314-315), the right to vote in
state elections is nowhere expressly mentioned. It is argued that the right to vote
in state elections is implicit, particularly by reason of the First Amendment and
that it may not constitutionally be conditioned upon the payment of a tax or fee.
We do not stop to canvass the relation between voting and political expression.
For it is enough to say that once the franchise is granted to the electorate, lines
may not be drawn which are inconsistent with the Equal Protection Clause of the
Fourteenth Amendment. That is to say, the right of suffrage "is subject to the imposition of state standards which are not discriminatory and which do not contravene any restriction that Congress, acting pursuant to its constitutional powers, has
imposed." *Lassiter v. Northampton Election Board*, 360 U.S. 45, 51. We were speaking
there of a state literacy test which we sustained, warning that the result would be
different if a literacy test, fair on its face, were used to discriminate against a class.
Id. at 53. But the *Lassiter* case does not govern the result here, because, unlike a poll
tax, the "ability to read and write . . . has some relation to standards designed to
promote intelligent use of the ballot." *Id.* at 51.

We conclude that a State violates the Equal Protection Clause of the Fourteenth Amendment whenever it makes the affluence of the voter or payment of
any fee an electoral standard. Voter qualifications have no relation to wealth nor to
paying or not paying this or any other tax. Our cases demonstrate that the Equal
Protection Clause of the Fourteenth Amendment restrains the States from fixing
voter qualifications which invidiously discriminate.

Long ago in *Yick Wo v. Hopkins*, 118 U.S. 356, 370, the Court referred to "the
political franchise of voting" as a "fundamental political right, because preservative
of all rights." Recently in *Reynolds v. Sims*, 377 U.S. 533, 561-562, we said, . . .

A citizen, a qualified voter, is no more nor no less so because he lives in
the city or on the farm. This is the clear and strong command of our Constitution's Equal Protection Clause. This is an essential part of the concept
of a government of laws and not men. This is at the heart of Lincoln's
vision of "government of the people, by the people, [and] for the people."

> The Equal Protection Clause demands no less than substantially equal state legislative representation for all citizens, of all places as well as of all races.

Id. at 568.

We say the same whether the citizen, otherwise qualified to vote, has $1.50 in his pocket or nothing at all, pays the fee or fails to pay it. The principle that denies the State the right to dilute a citizen's vote on account of his economic status or other such factors by analogy bars a system which excludes those unable to pay a fee to vote or who fail to pay.

It is argued that a State may exact fees from citizens for many different kinds of licenses; that if it can demand from all an equal fee for a driver's license, it can demand from all an equal poll tax for voting. But we must remember that the interest of the State, when it comes to voting, is limited to the power to fix qualifications. Wealth, like race, creed, or color, is not germane to one's ability to participate intelligently in the electoral process. Lines drawn on the basis of wealth or property, like those of race (*Korematsu v. United States*, 323 U.S. 214, 216), are traditionally disfavored. To introduce wealth or payment of a fee as a measure of a voter's qualifications is to introduce a capricious or irrelevant factor. The degree of the discrimination is irrelevant. In this context—that is, as a condition of obtaining a ballot—the requirement of fee paying causes an "invidious" discrimination that runs afoul of the Equal Protection Clause. . . .

We agree, of course, with Mr. Justice Holmes that the Due Process Clause of the Fourteenth Amendment "does not enact Mr. Herbert Spencer's Social Statics" (*Lochner v. New York*, 198 U.S. 45, 75). Likewise, the Equal Protection Clause is not shackled to the political theory of a particular era. In determining what lines are unconstitutionally discriminatory, we have never been confined to historic notions of equality, any more than we have restricted due process to a fixed catalogue of what was at a given time deemed to be the limits of fundamental rights. Notions of what constitutes equal treatment for purposes of the Equal Protection Clause do change. . . .

In a recent searching re-examination of the Equal Protection Clause, we held, as already noted, that "the opportunity for equal participation by all voters in the election of state legislators" is required. *Reynolds v. Sims, supra,* at 566. We decline to qualify that principle by sustaining this poll tax. Our conclusion, like that in *Reynolds v. Sims,* is founded not on what we think governmental policy should be, but on what the Equal Protection Clause requires.

We have long been mindful that where fundamental rights and liberties are asserted under the Equal Protection Clause, classifications which might invade or restrain them must be closely scrutinized and carefully confined. Those principles apply here. For to repeat, wealth or fee paying has, in our view, no relation to voting qualifications; the right to vote is too precious, too fundamental to be so burdened or conditioned. . . .

Mr. Justice HARLAN, whom Mr. Justice STEWART joins, dissenting.

The final demise of state poll taxes, already totally proscribed by the Twenty-Fourth Amendment with respect to federal elections and abolished by the States themselves in all but four States with respect to state elections, is perhaps in itself not of great moment. But the fact that the coup de grace has been administered by this Court instead of being left to the affected States or to the federal political process should be a matter of continuing concern to all interested in maintaining the proper role of this tribunal under our scheme of government.

. . . In substance the Court's analysis of the equal protection issue goes no further than to say that the electoral franchise is "precious" and "fundamental," and to conclude that "to introduce wealth or payment of a fee as a measure of a voter's qualifications is to introduce a capricious or irrelevant factor." These are of course captivating phrases, but they are wholly inadequate to satisfy the standard governing adjudication of the equal protection issue: Is there a rational basis for Virginia's poll tax as a voting qualification? I think the answer to that question is undoubtedly "yes."

Property qualifications and poll taxes have been a traditional part of our political structure. In the Colonies the franchise was generally a restricted one. Over the years these and other restrictions were gradually lifted, primarily because popular theories of political representation had changed. Often restrictions were lifted only after wide public debate. The issue of woman suffrage, for example, raised questions of family relationships, of participation in public affairs, of the very nature of the type of society in which Americans wished to live; eventually a consensus was reached, which culminated in the Nineteenth Amendment no more than 45 years ago.

Similarly with property qualifications, it is only by fiat that it can be said, especially in the context of American history, that there can be no rational debate as to their advisability. Most of the early Colonies had them; many of the States have had them during much of their histories; and, whether one agrees or not, arguments have been and still can be made in favor of them. For example, it is certainly a rational argument that payment of some minimal poll tax promotes civic responsibility, weeding out those who do not care enough about public affairs to pay $1.50 or thereabouts a year for the exercise of the franchise. It is also arguable, indeed it was probably accepted as sound political theory by a large percentage of Americans through most of our history, that people with some property have a deeper stake in community affairs, and are consequently more responsible, more educated, more knowledgeable, more worthy of confidence, than those without means, and that the community and Nation would be better managed if the franchise were restricted to such citizens. Nondiscriminatory and fairly applied literacy tests, upheld by this Court in *Lassiter v. Northampton Election Board*, 360 U.S. 45, find justification on very similar grounds.

These viewpoints, to be sure, ring hollow on most contemporary ears. Their lack of acceptance today is evidenced by the fact that nearly all of the States, left to their own devices, have eliminated property or poll-tax qualifications; by the cognate fact that Congress and three-quarters of the States quickly ratified the Twenty-Fourth Amendment; and by the fact that rules such as the "pauper exclusion" in Virginia law, Va. Const. §23, Va. Code §24-18, have never been enforced.

Property and poll-tax qualifications, very simply, are not in accord with current egalitarian notions of how a modern democracy should be organized. It is of course entirely fitting that legislatures should modify the law to reflect such changes in popular attitudes. However, it is all wrong, in my view, for the Court to adopt the political doctrines popularly accepted at a particular moment of our history and to declare all others to be irrational and invidious, barring them from the range of choice by reasonably minded people acting through the political process. It was not too long ago that Mr. Justice Holmes felt impelled to remind the Court that the Due Process Clause of the Fourteenth Amendment does not enact the laissez-faire theory of society, *Lochner v. New York,* 198 U.S. 45, 75-76. The times have changed, and perhaps it is appropriate to observe that neither does the Equal Protection Clause of that Amendment rigidly impose upon America an ideology of unrestrained egalitarianism.

4. *Felony Convictions*

Forty-eight states (all but Maine and Vermont) deny the right to vote to convicted felons while they are serving their prison terms. Sixteen states disenfranchise felons on parole or probation. Eleven states permanently disenfranchise felons who have fully served their sentences, including probation and parole periods. In three of these states—Alabama, Mississippi, and Tennessee—one of every thirteen people cannot vote on account of a felony conviction. It is estimated that as many as five million American citizens presently cannot vote as a result of felony disqualifications, including more than two million who have completed their sentences. The Sentencing Project, www.sentencingproject.org. In the following case, the Supreme Court addressed the constitutionality of the disenfranchisement of felons.

Richardson v. Ramirez

418 U.S. 24 (1974)

Mr. Justice REHNQUIST delivered the opinion of the Court.

The three individual respondents in this case were convicted of felonies and have completed the service of their respective sentences and paroles. They filed a petition for a writ of mandate in the Supreme Court of California to compel California county election officials to register them as voters. They claimed, on behalf of themselves and others similarly situated, that application to them of the provisions of the California Constitution and implementing statutes which disenfranchised persons convicted of an "infamous crime" denied them the right to equal protection of the laws under the Federal Constitution.

Article XX, §11, of the California Constitution has provided since its adoption in 1879 that "[laws] shall be made" to exclude from voting persons convicted of bribery, perjury, forgery, malfeasance in office, "or other high crimes." At the time respondents were refused registration, former Art. II, §1, of the California Constitution provided in part that "no alien ineligible to citizenship, no idiot, no insane person, no person convicted of any infamous crime, no person hereafter convicted of the embezzlement or misappropriation of public money, and no person who shall not be able to read the Constitution in the English language and write his or her name, shall ever exercise the privileges of an elector in this State.". . .

Each of the individual respondents was convicted of one or more felonies, and served some time in jail or prison followed by a successfully terminated parole. . . . All three respondents were refused registration because of their felony convictions.[9] . . .

Unlike most claims under the Equal Protection Clause, for the decision of which we have only the language of the Clause itself as it is embodied in the Fourteenth Amendment, respondents' claim implicates not merely the language of the Equal Protection Clause of §1 of the Fourteenth Amendment, but also the provisions of the less familiar §2 of the Amendment:

> Representatives shall be apportioned among the several States according to their respective numbers, counting the whole number of persons in each State, excluding Indians not taxed. But when the right to vote at any election for the choice of electors for President and Vice President of the United States, Representatives in Congress, the Executive and Judicial officers of a State, or the members of the Legislature thereof, is denied to any of the male inhabitants of such State, being twenty-one years of age, and citizens of the United States, or in any way abridged, *except for participation in rebellion, or other crime,* the basis of representation therein shall be reduced in the proportion which the number of such male citizens shall bear to the whole number of male citizens twenty-one years of age in such State. (Emphasis supplied.)

Petitioner contends that the italicized language of §2 expressly exempts from the sanction of that section disenfranchisement grounded on prior conviction of a felony. She goes on to argue that those who framed and adopted the Fourteenth Amendment could not have intended to prohibit outright in §1 of that Amendment that which was expressly exempted from the lesser sanction of reduced representation imposed by §2 of the Amendment. This argument seems to us a persuasive one unless it can be shown that the language of §2, "except for participation in rebellion, or other crime," was intended to have a different meaning than would appear from its face.

. . . [W]hat legislative history there is indicates that this language was intended by Congress to mean what it says. . . . Throughout the floor debates in both the House and the Senate, in which numerous changes of language in §2 were proposed, the language "except for participation in rebellion, or other crime" was never altered. The language of §2 attracted a good deal of interest during the debates, but most of the discussion was devoted to its foreseeable consequences

---

9. Respondent Ramirez was convicted in Texas of the felony of "robbery by assault" in 1952. He served three months in jail and successfully terminated his parole in 1962. In February 1972 the San Luis Obispo County Clerk refused to allow Ramirez to register to vote on the ground that he had been convicted of a felony and spent time in incarceration. Respondent Lee was convicted of the felony of heroin possession in California in 1955, served two years in prison, and successfully terminated his parole in 1959. In March 1972 the Monterey County Clerk refused to allow Lee to register to vote on the sole ground that he had been convicted of a felony and had not been pardoned by the Governor. Respondent Gill was convicted in 1952 and 1967 of second-degree burglary in California, and in 1957 of forgery. He served some time in prison on each conviction, followed by a successful parole. In April 1972 the Stanislaus County Registrar of Voters refused to allow Gill to register to vote on the sole ground of his prior felony convictions.

in both the Northern and Southern States, and to arguments as to its necessity or wisdom. What little comment there was on the phrase in question here supports a plain reading of it.

Congressman Bingham of Ohio, who was one of the principal architects of the Fourteenth Amendment and an influential member of the Committee of Fifteen, commented with respect to §2 as follows during the floor debates in the House:

> The second section of the amendment simply provides for the equalization of representation among all the States of the Union, North, South, East, and West. It makes no discrimination. New York has a colored population of fifty thousand. By this section, if that great State discriminates against her colored population as to the elective franchise, (except in cases of crime,) she loses to that extent her representative power in Congress. So also will it be with every other State.

Cong. Globe, 39th Cong., 1st Sess., 2543 (1866). Two other Representatives who spoke to the question made similar comments. Representative Eliot of Massachusetts commented in support of the enactment of §2 as follows:

> Manifestly no State should have its basis of national representation enlarged by reason of a portion of citizens within its borders to which the elective franchise is denied. If political power shall be lost because of such denial, not imposed because of participation in rebellion or other crime, it is to be hoped that political interests may work in the line of justice, and that the end will be the impartial enfranchisement of all citizens not disqualified by crime.

Id. at 2511. Representative Eckley of Ohio made this observation:

> Under a congressional act persons convicted of a crime against the laws of the United States, the penalty for which is imprisonment in the penitentiary, are now and always have been disfranchised, and a pardon did not restore them unless the warrant of pardon so provided.
>
>   . . . But suppose the mass of the people of a State are pirates, counterfeiters, or other criminals, would gentlemen be willing to repeal the laws now in force in order to give them an opportunity to land their piratical crafts and come on shore to assist in the election of a President or members of Congress because they are numerous? And let it be borne in mind that these latter offenses are only crimes committed against property; that of treason is against the nation, against the whole people — the highest known to the law.

Id. at 2535. . . .

Further light is shed on the understanding of those who framed and ratified the Fourteenth Amendment, and thus on the meaning of §2, by the fact that at the time of the adoption of the Amendment, 29 States had provisions in their constitutions which prohibited, or authorized the legislature to prohibit, exercise of the franchise by persons convicted of felonies or infamous crimes. More impressive than the mere existence of the state constitutional provisions disenfranchising felons at the time of the adoption of the Fourteenth Amendment is the congressional treatment of States readmitted to the Union following the Civil War. For every State thus readmitted, affirmative congressional action in the form of an enabling act was taken, and as a part of the readmission process the State seeking readmission was required to submit for the approval of the Congress its proposed state constitution. In March 1867, before any State was readmitted, Congress passed "An act to provide for the more efficient Government of the Rebel States," the so-called Reconstruction Act. Act of Mar. 2, 1867, c. 153, 14 Stat. 428. Section 5 of the Reconstruction Act established conditions on which the former Confederate States would be readmitted to representation in Congress. It provided:

> [T]he people of any one of said rebel States shall have formed a constitution of government in conformity with the Constitution of the United States in all respects, framed by a convention of delegates elected by the male citizens of said State, twenty-one years old and upward, of whatever race, color, or previous condition, who have been resident in said State for one year previous to the day of such election, except such as may be disfranchised for participation in the rebellion or for felony at common law. . . .

A series of enabling acts in 1868 and 1870 admitted those States to representation in Congress. The Act admitting Arkansas, the first State to be so admitted, attached a condition to its admission. Act of June 22, 1868, c. 69, 15 Stat. 72. That Act provided:

> *Be it enacted* . . . That the State of Arkansas is entitled and admitted to representation in Congress as one of the States of the Union upon the following fundamental condition: That the constitution of Arkansas shall never be so amended or changed as to deprive any citizen or class of citizens of the United States of the right to vote who are entitled to vote by the constitution herein recognized, except as a punishment for such crimes as are now felonies at common law, whereof they shall have been duly convicted, under laws equally applicable to all the inhabitants of said State. . . .

Despite this settled historical and judicial understanding of the Fourteenth Amendment's effect on state laws disenfranchising convicted felons, respondents argue that our recent decisions invalidating other state-imposed restrictions on the franchise as violative of the Equal Protection Clause require us to invalidate the disenfranchisement of felons as well. They rely on such cases as *Dunn v. Blumstein*, 405 U.S. 330 (1972), *Bullock v. Carter*, 405 U.S. 134 (1972), *Kramer v. Union Free School District*, 395 U.S. 621 (1969), and *Cipriano v. City of Houma*, 395 U.S. 701 (1969), to support the conclusions of the Supreme Court of California that a State must show a "compelling state interest" to justify exclusion of ex-felons from the franchise and that California has not done so here.

As we have seen, however, the exclusion of felons from the vote has an affirmative sanction in §2 of the Fourteenth Amendment, a sanction which was not present in the case of the other restrictions on the franchise which were invalidated in the cases on which respondents rely. We hold that the understanding of those who adopted the Fourteenth Amendment, as reflected in the express language of §2 and in the historical and judicial interpretation of the Amendment's applicability to state laws disenfranchising felons, is of controlling significance in distinguishing such laws from those other state limitations on the franchise which have been held invalid under the Equal Protection Clause by this Court. . . .

Pressed upon us by the respondents, and by *amici curiae*, are contentions that these notions are outmoded, and that the more modern view is that it is essential to the process of rehabilitating the ex-felon that he be returned to his role in society as a fully participating citizen when he has completed the serving of his term. We would by no means discount these arguments if addressed to the legislative forum which may properly weigh and balance them against those advanced in support of California's present constitutional provisions. But it is not for us to choose one set of values over the other. If respondents are correct, and the view which they advocate is indeed the more enlightened and sensible one, presumably the people of the State of California will ultimately come around to that view. . . .

Mr. Justice MARSHALL, with whom Mr. Justice BRENNAN joins, dissenting.

. . . The Court construes §2 of the Fourteenth Amendment as an express authorization for the States to disenfranchise former felons. Section 2 does except disenfranchisement for "participation in rebellion, or other crime" from the operation of its penalty provision. As the Court notes, however, there is little independent legislative history as to the crucial words "or other crime"; the proposed §2 went to a joint committee containing only the phrase "participation in rebellion" and emerged with "or other crime" inexplicably tacked on. . . .

Disenfranchisement for participation in crime, like durational residence requirements, was common at the time of the adoption of the Fourteenth Amendment. But "constitutional concepts of equal protection are not immutably frozen like insects trapped in Devonian amber." We have repeatedly observed:

> [The] Equal Protection Clause is not shackled to the political theory of a particular era. In determining what lines are unconstitutionally discriminatory, we have never been confined to historic notions of equality, any more than we have restricted due process to a fixed catalogue of what was at a given time deemed to be the limits of fundamental rights.

Harper v. Virginia Board of Elections, 383 U.S. 663, 669 (1966). Accordingly, neither the fact that several States had ex-felon disenfranchisement laws at the time of the adoption of the Fourteenth Amendment, nor that such disenfranchisement was specifically excepted from the special remedy of §2, can serve to insulate such disenfranchisement from equal protection scrutiny.

In my view, the disenfranchisement of ex-felons must be measured against the requirements of the Equal Protection Clause of §1 of the Fourteenth Amendment. . . .

I think it clear that the State has not met its burden of justifying the blanket disenfranchisement of former felons presented by this case. There is certainly no basis for asserting that ex-felons have any less interest in the democratic process than any other citizen. Like everyone else, their daily lives are deeply affected and changed by the decisions of government. . . .

The disenfranchisement of ex-felons had "its origin in the fogs and fictions of feudal jurisprudence and doubtless has been brought forward into modern statutes without fully realizing either the effect of its literal significance or the extent of its infringement upon the spirit of our system of government." *Byers v. Sun Savings Bank*, 41 Okla. 728, 731 (1914). I think it clear that measured against the standards of this Court's modern equal protection jurisprudence, the blanket disenfranchisement of ex-felons cannot stand.

>> *Justifications for Felon Disenfranchisement*   Felon disenfranchisement may be constitutional, but is it good policy? What justifies the disenfranchisement of felons? Why is losing the franchise an apt punishment for commission of a crime? Consider the following explanations:

> The early exclusion of felons from the franchise by many states could well have rested on Locke's concept, so influential at the time, that by entering into society every man "authorizes the society, or which is all one, the legislature thereof, to make laws for him as the public good of the society shall require, to the execution whereof his own assistance (as to his own decrees) is due." . . . A man who breaks the laws he has authorized his agent to make for his own governance could fairly have been thought to have abandoned the right to participate in further administering the compact.

Green v. Board of Elections, 380 F.2d 445, 451 (2d Cir. 1967).

> The manifest purpose is to preserve the purity of the ballot box, which is the sure foundation of republican liberty, and which needs protection against the invasion of corruption, just as much as against that of ignorance, incapacity, or tyranny. The evil infection of the one is not more fatal than that of the other. The presumption is, that one rendered infamous by conviction of felony, or other base offense indicative of great moral turpitude, is unfit to exercise the privilege of suffrage, or to hold office, upon terms of equality with freemen who are clothed by the State with the toga of political citizenship. It is proper, therefore, that this class should be denied a right, the exercise of which might sometimes hazard the welfare of communities, if not that of the State itself, at least in close political contests. The exclusion . . . [is] imposed for protection, and not for punishment. . . .

Washington v. State, 75 Ala. 582, 585 (1884).

Do these explanations justify a *lifetime* disqualification, one that extends beyond the completion of the sentence imposed?

An additional possibility is that disenfranchisement harks back to Roman and medieval concepts of civil death, in which a person, as punishment for some transgression against the community, is deemed civilly not to exist. *See* Alec C. Ewald, *"Civil Death": The Ideological Paradox of Criminal Disenfranchisement Law in the United States*, 2002 Wis. L. Rev. 1045.

A more contemporary justification focuses on the authority of political communities to define their own identities. On this view, felon disenfranchisement is a justifiable choice for a state that wishes "to put the criminal at political arm's length from the community, that is, to deem him as one who has failed to meet minimal standards for remaining a full member of the community." In so doing, a political community is exercising the right of all such communities to "defin[e] the identity of the state in a certain way," that is, to define itself as a community of the law-abiding. Andrew Altman, *Democratic Self-Determination and the Disenfranchisement of Felons*, 22 J. APPLIED PHIL. 263, 265 (2005). However, Altman believes this principle includes a requirement of proportionality: "Revocation of the right to vote for life in the case of crimes that do not receive lifetime imprisonment would arguably be disproportionate and create a kind of internal inconsistency in the system." *Id.* At 269. *See also* Mary Sigler, *Defensible Disenfranchisement*, 99 IOWA L. REV. 1725 (2014).

Is a felony disenfranchisement provision a restriction based on membership or on competence?

>> *Felon Disenfranchisement Abroad.* The United States is evidently the only western nation that permits permanent disenfranchisement of those convicted of crimes. Many nations, including Albania, Azerbaijan, Denmark, Finland, Serbia, Spain, Sweden, and Switzerland, permit all prisoners to vote. Many others, including Israel, France, Germany, and Greece, permit at least some incarcerated inmates to vote. *See* Shai Dothan, *Comparative Views on the Right to Vote in International Law: The Case of Prisoners' Disenfranchisement, in* COMPARATIVE INTERNATIONAL LAW (Anthea Roberts et al. eds., 2016); Ewald, *supra*, at 1046 n.3.

In 2002, the Supreme Court of Canada invalidated a federal law denying the right to vote to all inmates serving sentences of more than two years; the Court held that this provision violated the Canadian Charter of Rights and Freedoms:

> Denying penitentiary inmates the right to vote misrepresents the nature of our rights and obligations under the law and consequently undermines them. In a democracy such as ours, the power of lawmakers flows from the voting citizens, and lawmakers act as the citizens' proxies. This delegation from voters to legislators gives the law its legitimacy or force. Correlatively, the obligation to obey the law flows from the fact that the law is made by and on behalf of the citizens. In sum, the legitimacy of the law and the obligation to obey the law flow directly from the right of every citizen to vote. . . . The government gets this connection exactly backwards when it attempts to argue that depriving people of a voice in government teaches them to obey the law. The "educative message" that the government purports to send by disenfranchising inmates is both anti-democratic and internally self-contradictory. Denying a citizen the right to vote denies the basis of democratic legitimacy. It says that delegates elected by the citizens can then bar those very citizens, or a portion of them, from participating in future elections. But if we accept that governmental power in a democracy flows from the citizens, it is difficult to see how that power can legitimately be used to disenfranchise the very citizens from whom the government's power flows.

Sauve v. Canada, [2002] 218 D.L.R. 4th 577.

In 2004, the European Court of Human Rights invalidated a British law disenfranchising all prisoners serving life sentences on the ground that it violated the European Convention for the Protection of Human Rights and Fundamental Freedoms. *Hirst v. United Kingdom (No. 2)*, No. 74025/01 (Mar. 30, 2004). Endorsing the Canadian court's reasoning, the European court found that the disenfranchisement served no legitimate purpose, and that the punishment of disenfranchisement was disproportionate to the offense. In 2007, the High Court of Australia invalidated a federal law disenfranchising all incarcerated prisoners. *Roach v. Electoral Commissioner*, [2007] HCA 43. In 2015, the New Zealand High Court struck down a similar ban. *Taylor v. Attorney-General*, [2015] NZHC 1706.

Hunter v. Underwood

471 U.S. 222 (1985)

Justice REHNQUIST delivered the opinion of the [unanimous] Court.

We are required in this case to decide the constitutionality of Art. VIII, §182, of the Alabama Constitution of 1901, which provides for the disenfranchisement of persons convicted of, among other offenses, "any crime . . . involving moral turpitude." Appellees Carmen Edwards, a black, and Victor Underwood, a white, have been blocked from the voter rolls pursuant to §182 by the Boards of Registrars for Montgomery and Jefferson Counties, respectively, because they each have been convicted of presenting a worthless check. . . .

In a memorandum opinion, the District Court found that disenfranchisement of blacks was a major purpose for the convention at which the Alabama Constitution of 1901 was adopted. . . .

Various minor nonfelony offenses such as presenting a worthless check and petty larceny fall within the sweep of §182, while more serious nonfelony offenses such as second-degree manslaughter, assault on a police officer, mailing pornography, and aiding the escape of a misdemeanant do not because they are neither enumerated in §182 nor considered crimes involving moral turpitude. It is alleged, and the Court of Appeals found, that the crimes selected for inclusion in §182 were believed by the delegates to be more frequently committed by blacks. . . . [T]he Court of Appeals implicitly found the evidence of discriminatory impact indisputable:

> The registrars' expert estimated that by January 1903 section 182 had disfranchised approximately ten times as many blacks as whites. This disparate effect persists today. In Jefferson and Montgomery Counties blacks are by even the most modest estimates at least 1.7 times as likely as whites to suffer disfranchisement under section 182 for the commission of nonprison offenses. . . .

Presented with a neutral state law that produces disproportionate effects along racial lines, the Court of Appeals was correct in applying the approach of *Arlington Heights* to determine whether the law violates the Equal Protection Clause of the Fourteenth Amendment: "[Official] action will not be held unconstitutional solely because it results in a racially disproportionate impact. . . . Proof of racially discriminatory intent or purpose is required to show a violation of the Equal Protection Clause." . . . Proving the motivation behind official action is often a problematic undertaking. . . . But [such] difficulties . . . do not obtain in this case. Although understandably no "eyewitnesses" to the 1901 proceedings testified, testimony and opinions of historians were offered and received without objection. These showed that the Alabama Constitutional Convention of 1901 was part of a movement that swept the post-Reconstruction South to disenfranchise blacks. The delegates to the all-white convention were not secretive about their purpose. John B. Knox, president of the convention, stated in his opening address: "And what is it that we want to do? Why it is within the limits imposed by the Federal Constitution, to establish white supremacy in this State." 1 Official Proceedings of the Constitutional Convention of the State of Alabama, May 21st, 1901 to September 3rd, 1901, p. 8 (1940). Indeed, neither the District Court nor appellants seriously dispute the claim that this zeal for white supremacy ran rampant at the convention. . . .

The evidence of legislative intent available to the courts below consisted of the proceedings of the convention, several historical studies, and the testimony of two expert historians. Having reviewed this evidence, we are persuaded that the Court of Appeals was correct in its assessment . . . that §182 was enacted with the intent of disenfranchising blacks. . . .

Appellants contend that the State has a legitimate interest in denying the franchise to those convicted of crimes involving moral turpitude, and that §182 should be sustained on that ground. The Court of Appeals convincingly demonstrated that such a purpose simply was not a motivating factor of the 1901 convention. In addition to the general catchall phrase "crimes involving moral turpitude" the suffrage committee selected such crimes as vagrancy, living in adultery, and wife beating that were thought to be more commonly committed by blacks:

> Most of the proposals disqualified persons committing any one of a long list of petty as well as serious crimes which the Negro, and to a lesser extent the poor whites, most often committed. . . . Most of the crimes contained in the report of the suffrage committee came from an ordinance by John Fielding Burns, a Black Belt planter. The crimes he listed were those he had taken cognizance of for years in his justice of the peace court in the Burnsville district, where nearly all his cases involved Negroes.

M. McMillan, Constitutional Development in Alabama, 1798-1901, p. 275 and n. 76 (1955) (quoted in testimony by appellees' expert).

At oral argument in this Court, appellants' counsel suggested that, regardless of the original purpose of §182, events occurring in the succeeding 80 years had legitimated the provision. Some of the more blatantly discriminatory selections, such as assault and battery on the wife and miscegenation, have been struck down by the courts, and appellants contend that the remaining crimes — felonies and moral turpitude misdemeanors — are acceptable bases for denying the franchise. Without deciding whether §182 would be valid if enacted today without any impermissible motivation, we simply observe that its original enactment was motivated by a desire to discriminate against blacks on account of race and the section continues to this day to have that effect. As such, it violates equal protection. . . .

The single remaining question is whether §182 is excepted from the operation of the Equal Protection Clause of §1 of the Fourteenth Amendment by the "other crime" provision of §2 of that Amendment. Without again considering the implicit authorization of §2 to deny the vote to citizens "for participation in rebellion, or other crime," see *Richardson v. Ramirez*, 418 U.S. 24 (1974), we are confident that

§2 was not designed to permit the purposeful racial discrimination attending the enactment and operation of §182 which otherwise violates §1 of the Fourteenth Amendment. Nothing in our opinion in *Richardson v. Ramirez* suggests the contrary.

>> *Felon Disenfranchisement and Race.*   As the Court indicated in *Underwood*, there is significant evidence that modern practices of felon disenfranchisement originated in the desire in Southern states during the late nineteenth century to find a way to legally prevent blacks from voting. *See* Angela Behrens, Christopher Uggen, and Jeff Manza, *Ballot Manipulation and the "Menace of Negro Domination": Racial Threat and Felon Disenfranchisement in the United States, 1850-2000,* 109 Am. J. Soc. 559 (2003). If that is the case, how can contemporary felon disenfranchisement laws survive?

First, not all felon disenfranchisement provisions were enacted in the Jim Crow South: such provisions exist, for example, in Alaska, Hawaii, Massachusetts, and Oregon, among others. Second, not all felon disenfranchisement provisions even in Southern states date to the Jim Crow period. In *Cotton v. Fordice,* 157 F.3d 388 (5th Cir. 1998), the Fifth Circuit rejected an *Underwood*-type challenge to a provision of Mississippi's constitution disenfranchising felons. Despite the undisputed fact that this provision originally was enacted with the intention of preventing blacks from voting, the court held that subsequent good faith amendments to and reenactments of the disputed provision in 1950 and 1968 cleansed it of its original taint. For a critique of *Cotton,* see Gabriel J. Chin, *Rehabilitating Unconstitutional Statutes: An Analysis of* Cotton v. Fordice, 71 U. Cin. L. Rev. 421 (2002).

Even if not all contemporary felon disenfranchisement provisions were motivated by racial discrimination at the time of their adoption, it is indisputable that they have a racially disproportionate impact. While nationwide one out of every 44 adults is disenfranchised due to a current or previous felony conviction, among African Americans the rate is one out of every 13 adults, a group that is overwhelmingly male. In Florida, Kentucky, and Virginia, more than twenty percent of the adult black population is disenfranchised. In *Village of Arlington Heights v. Metropolitan Housing Development Corp.,* 429 U.S. 252 (1977), the Supreme Court said that evidence of discriminatory intent can include the actual "impact of the official action. . . . Sometimes a clear pattern, unexplainable on grounds other than race, emerges from the effect of the state action even when the governing legislation appears neutral on its face." Does the racial impact of felon disenfranchisement furnish such evidence? *Hunter v. Underwood* deals solely with the legislature's motivation at the time of its *adoption* of felon disenfranchisement laws; might the same reasoning apply to the legislature's continued *maintenance* of such laws? Or does a non-discriminatory intent at the time of adoption immunize a law from subsequent challenge on grounds of discrimination even when its originally unintended consequences later become clear?

A further complication, as we will see in Chapter 5, is that in the contemporary United States race often cannot easily be disentangled from partisanship—racial minorities tend to vote Democratic. In those circumstances, exclusion from voting of members of a certain race can be tantamount to exclusion from voting on the basis of political leanings, and thus ideological commitments. If felon disenfranchisement laws are vulnerable to attack on the ground of racial discrimination, might they also be vulnerable to attack on the ground that they discriminate on the basis of viewpoint, and thus on the basis of speech or ideas? *See* Janai S. Nelson, *The First Amendment, Equal Protection, and Felon Disenfranchisement: A New Viewpoint*, 65 FLA. L. REV. 111 (2013).

>> *Felon Disenfranchisement and Partisan Politics.*   As indicated above, the number of people disenfranchised on account of crime has reached a magnitude where policies of felon disenfranchisement have the potential to influence electoral outcomes in close races. One study concluded that observed declines since 1972 in voter turnout in national elections are attributable not to increased abstention from voting by eligible voters, but to dramatic increases during that period in the number of ineligible voters among the voting age population. Ineligible felons constitute a significant proportion of this group. *See* Michael P. McDonald and Samuel L. Popkin, *The Myth of the Vanishing Voter*, 95 AM. POL. SCI. REV. 963 (2001).

This decline in turnout, however, is not necessarily politically neutral. Indeed, felon disenfranchisement has a predictable partisan impact. An influential 2002 study concluded that six Senate elections since 1978 in states with lifetime felon disenfranchisement would have been won by a Democrat instead of a Republican in the absence of the disenfranchisement policy (Virginia and Texas 1978; Kentucky 1984 and 1998; Florida and Wyoming 1988). This difference could have been sufficient to have left the Senate in Democratic hands after the 1994 election, when Republicans took control. Christopher Uggen and Jeff Manza, *The Political Consequences of Felon Disenfranchisement Laws in the United States*, 67 AM. SOC. REV. 777 (2002). Felon disenfranchisement might also have been sufficient to have swung Florida narrowly for Bush in the 2000 presidential election. JEFF MANZA AND CHRISTOPHER UGGEN, LOCKED OUT: FELON DISENFRANCHISEMENT AND AMERICAN DEMOCRACY (2006).

More recently, this conclusion has been disputed on the ground that felons vote at much lower rates than the general population, both before and after committing their crimes, so that re-enfranchisement of felon populations might have only a trivial impact on actual voting outcomes. *See* Michael Haselswerdt, *Con Job: An Estimate of Ex-Felon Voter Turnout Using Document-Based Data*, 90 SOC. SCI. Q. 262 (2009); Randi Hjalmarsson et al., *The Voting Behavior of Young Disenfranchised Felons: Would They Vote If They Could?*, 12 AM. L. & ECON. REV. 356 (2010); Tilman Klumpp, et al., *The Voting Rights of Ex-Felons and Election Outcomes in the United States*, 59 INT'L REV. L & ECON. 40 (2019). However, even given the comparatively low turnout rates of felons as a group, the impact of disenfranchisement may not be racially neutral, and thus have some partisan effect. According to one recent study, jail sentences have little demobilizing effect on white convicts, whereas voting by Latino and black convicts following a jail sentences drops by roughly thirteen percent. Ariel White, *Misdemeanor Disenfranchisement? The Demobilizing Effects of Brief Jail Spells on Potential Voters*, 133 AM. POL. SCI. REV. 311 (2019).

Another troubling partisan aspect of felon disenfranchisement arises from the methods of census-taking that are sometimes used to count incarcerated persons. Typically, incarcerated populations are counted for census purposes in the places where they are incarcerated rather than in the places where they lived prior to incarceration. In urbanized states, a disproportionate number of felons come from urban areas of the state, but are incarcerated overwhelmingly in prisons located in rural districts. This means that population counts of rural, often conservative, and largely Republican areas are artificially inflated by populations of prisoners who are disqualified from voting, creating safer seats for Republican incumbents from those districts. Conversely, population counts of urban areas with large populations of color are reduced, making it slightly harder to create safe Democratic seats in those districts. As a result, there is a slight but measurable shift in political power from urban to rural and from Democratic to Republican areas of the state. *See* Peter Wagner, *Importing Constituents: Prisoners and Political Clout in New York* (Prison Policy Initiative Report 2002), www.prisonpolicy.org.

It has been suggested that the racial impact of felon disenfranchisement, combined with its political effects, may make the policy illegal under the Voting Rights Act (taken up in Chapter 5). Such challenges have long been rejected. *See, e.g., Baker v. Pataki*, 85 F.3d 919 (2d Cir. 1996) (en banc); *Johnson v. Governor of the State of Florida*, 405 F.3d 1214 (11th Cir. 2005) (en banc); *Simmons v. Galvin*, 575 F.3d 24 (1st Cir. 2009); *Hayden v. Pataki*, 449 F.3d 305, 315-316 (2d Cir. 2006) (en banc); *Farrakhan v. Washington*, 623 F.3d 990 (9th Cir. 2010) (en banc).

>> *Disenfranchisement for Election Crimes.*   Apart from disenfranchisement of felons, some states provide specifically for permanent disqualification of individuals who commit crimes against the electoral process itself, most commonly by committing election fraud by bribing voters to register or to vote. Do crimes against the electoral process offer a stronger case for permanent disqualification than commission of ordinary crimes against the person or property of another? Perhaps one who commits election fraud not only has shown a specific disregard for the ground rules of politics established by the social contract, but also presents a threat to the basic processes of self-governance that assure the legitimacy of governmental power. In these circumstances, permanent disenfranchisement may constitute both just desert as well as a prudent precautionary measure for the protection of the electoral process. *See Washington v. State*, 75 Ala. 582, 585 (1884): "It is proper, therefore, that this class should be denied a right, the exercise of which might sometimes hazard the welfare of communities, if not that of the State itself, at least in close political contests. The exclusion . . . [is] imposed for protection, and not for punishment." But does permanent disenfranchisement provide any additional increment of protection against election crime recidivism beyond what is provided by direct criminal penalties?

>> *Restoration of Voting Rights.*   Many states permit felons to vote after they have served their sentences, but this often requires the ex-convict to apply for a restoration of rights, in turn requiring an affirmative response from state government. The process of restoring voting rights can be slow and inefficient, and bureaucratic hurdles can be significant. *See* Jessie Allen, *Documentary Disenfranchisement*, 86 TUL. L. REV. 389 (2011). In some cases, restoration of voting rights is subject to potentially onerous conditions. In some states, for example, voting rights must be restored by an act of executive clemency following an application from the offender. In others, restoration of voting rights is conditional upon the payment of court-ordered fines, costs, fees, and restitution to victims. Often, convicts eligible in theory for restoration of voting rights upon discharge from prison or parole will have no resources with which to pay these debts, and thus will remain ineligible to vote. Beth A. Colgan, *Wealth-Based Penal Disenfranchisement*, 72 VAND. L. REV. 55 (2019).

In Tennessee, restoration of voting rights is also conditional upon being current with child support payments. In a 2010 decision, the Sixth Circuit sustained Tennessee's restitution and child support conditions against an equal protection challenge. The court applied rational basis review on the theory that, "[h]aving lost their voting rights, Plaintiffs lack any fundamental interest to assert." *Johnson v. Bredesen*, 624 F.3d 742 (6th Cir. 2010).

In 2018, Florida voters approved Amendment 4, an amendment to the Florida Constitution that automatically restored voting rights to ex-felons who had completed their sentences. Shortly thereafter, the Florida legislature enacted S.B. 7066, a law that interpreted the language of the amendment to require, as a condition of restoration of voting rights, the full payment of all fines, fees, and restitution associated with the conviction and sentence. Felons released from jail often are destitute. Florida courts often impose various kinds of fees and fines as a pro forma element of sentencing. However, only about twenty percent of these financial obligations are ever repaid, and apparently Florida does not really expect repayment, so before S.B. 7066 there were no real consequences for failing to do so. Several lawsuits were filed challenging the new law as contrary to the language of Amendment 4, the intentions of the voters, and various provisions of the U.S. and Florida constitutions. The Florida Supreme Court upheld S.B. 7066 as a valid interpretation of Amendment 4, but federal courts then invalidated the law as a form of discrimination based on wealth. After further litigation the Eleventh Circuit, sitting *en banc*, upheld the law in full, rejecting arguments under the Equal Protection Clause and the Twenty-Fourth Amendment (prohibiting poll taxes). *Jones v. Governor*, 950 F.3d 795 (11th Cir. 2020). As a result, ex-felons in Florida may not vote unless they pay off all debts, which few will be able to do. *See* Michael Morse, *The Future of Felon Disenfranchisement Reform: Evidence from the Campaign to Restore Voting Rights in Florida*, 109 Cal. L. Rev. 1141 (2021).

An interesting, recent empirical experiment sought to evaluate the impact on ex-felon voting of Florida's new requirement of full fee repayment. The researchers identified recently released convicts who qualified for restoration of voting rights under Amendment 4, but could not make the repayments required by S.B. 7066. Using donated funds, the researchers paid off the debts of roughly 1,500 recently released felons, and compared their subsequent voting behavior to similarly situated felons who did not pay off their debts. The authors found that paying off the state-imposed debt increased turnout in the subject population by about 26 percent, refuting, in their view, the idea that low participation rates by ex-felons reflect primarily a lack of interest in politics. Neel U. Sukhatme, *et al., Felony Financial Disenfranchisement*, 75 Vand. L. Rev. __ (2023).

Not all the recent developments in this area have worked against felons. In Iowa, the governor signed an executive order automatically restoring voting rights for some felons upon completion of their sentences. Maryland and New York recently enacted legislation requiring state prisons to provide voter registration forms to convicts upon their release. Virginia recently replaced its prior system, which required eligible ex-felons affirmatively to apply for restoration of their voting rights, with one of automatic restoration of rights.

CHAPTER 4

REPRESENTATION

A. INTRODUCTION

The last chapter focused on voting, but that is hardly the end of the story of democratic self-governance; indeed, voting is only the beginning of a complex process—but a process of what, exactly? We vote, and in so doing elect representatives, but what do they do? Obviously, representatives "represent," but what is representation? Whom does a representative represent, and in what capacity? What does representation involve and how does it work?

We begin with one of the oldest problems in the theory of democratic representation: What do representatives owe to those they represent? Are representatives obliged ministerially to implement the wishes of their constituents? Or must they exercise their own independent judgment and discretion? The excerpt that follows is from Edmund Burke's famous campaign speech in the 1774 election for the British Parliament. Burke was a prominent politician and intellectual who was running for reelection in the district of Bristol. During the campaign, his opponent raised the issue of constituent "instructions" to members of Parliament. The right of voters to instruct their representatives—that is, to direct them how to vote on particular issues—had been bouncing around English political thought for some time. In the speech below, Burke rejects the idea that a representative owes constituents an obligation to follow their instructions.

Edmund Burke

Speech to the Electors of Bristol (1774)

Certainly, gentlemen, it ought to be the happiness and glory of a representative to live in the strictest union, the closest correspondence, and the most unreserved communication with his constituents. Their wishes ought to have great weight with him; their opinion, high respect; their business, unremitted attention. It is his duty to sacrifice his repose, his pleasures, his satisfactions, to theirs; and above all, ever, and in all cases, to prefer their interest to his own. But his unbiassed opinion, his mature judgment, his enlightened conscience, he ought not to sacrifice to you, to any man, or any set of men living. These he does not derive from your pleasure; no, nor from the law and the constitution. They are a trust from Providence, for the abuse of which he is deeply answerable. Your representative owes you, not his industry only, but his judgment; and he betrays, instead of serving you, if he sacrifices it to your opinion.

My worthy colleague [i.e., his opponent in the election] says, his will ought to be subservient to yours. If that be all, the thing is innocent. If government were a matter of will upon any side, yours without question, ought to be superior. But government and legislation are matters of reason and judgment, and not of inclination; and what sort of reason is that, in which the determination precedes the discussion; in which one set of men deliberate, and another decide; and where those who form the conclusion are perhaps three hundred miles distant from those who hear the arguments?

To deliver an opinion, is the right of all men; that of constituents is a weighty and respectable opinion, which a representative ought always to rejoice to hear; and which he ought always most seriously to consider. But *authoritative* instructions; *mandates* issued, which the member is bound blindly and implicitly to obey, to vote, and to argue for, though contrary to the clearest conviction of his judgment and conscience — these are things utterly unknown to the laws of this land, and which arise from a fundamental mistake of the whole order and tenor of our constitution.

Parliament is not a *congress* of ambassadors from different and hostile interests; which interests each must maintain, as an agent and advocate, against other agents and advocates; but parliament is a *deliberative* assembly of *one* nation, with *one* interest, that of the whole; where, not local purposes, not local prejudices, ought to guide, but the general good, resulting from the general reason of the whole. You choose a member indeed; but when you have chosen him, he is not a member of Bristol, but he is a member of *parliament*. If the local constituent should have an interest, or should form an hasty opinion, evidently opposite to the real good of the rest of the community, the member for that place ought to be as far, as any other, from any endeavour to give it effect. Beg pardon for saying so much on this subject. I have been unwillingly drawn into it; but I shall ever use a respectful frankness of communication with you. Your faithful friend, your devoted servant, I shall be to the end of my life: a flatterer you do not wish for.

Burke was elected to Parliament from Bristol, a large, populous district, in 1774, 1776, and 1778. However, he was turned out of office in 1780 because some of his policy positions, most notably concerning his advocacy for fair treatment of Irish Catholics, were unpopular with voters. He thereafter ran for and won election to Parliament from the "pocket borough" of Malton — so called because the district was a sparsely populated one controlled by (in the pocket of) Burke's patron, the Marquess of Rockingham. How does Burke's actual political career square with his philosophy of democratic representation?

≫ *The Right to Instruct Representatives in America.*   Americans of the Revolutionary period did not typically hold to the Burkean view. For example, the Massachusetts Constitution of 1780, drafted by John Adams and believed to be the oldest continually operating constitution in the world, contained (and still contains) this provision in its Declaration of Rights: "The people have a right, in an orderly and peaceable manner, to assemble to . . . give instructions to their representatives. . . ." Mass. Const., Declaration of Rights, art. XIX. This provision was subsequently copied by constitutional drafters in numerous states, and exists today in the constitutions of California, Idaho, Indiana, Maine, Michigan, Nevada, and several other states.

Does the constitutional right to instruct representatives have any legal bite? Generally not. State courts construing these provisions typically have refused to treat them as authorizing constituents to issue binding instructions to their representatives. At most, the right to instruct under state constitutions has been treated as the right to communicate requests and advice to government officials, who are under no obligation to comply. *See, e.g., Fuller v. Haines*, 112 N.E. 873 (Mass. 1916):

> The purpose of that sentence in general is to enable the voters to have full and free discussion and consultation upon the merits of candidates for public office and of measures proposed in the public interests. [But it] never has been suggested, so far as we are aware, that the vote of such a [town] meeting had a legally binding force upon [elected officials]. . . . Advisory expressions of public opinion participated in by large numbers of people may have been deemed likely to be a sufficiently strong incentive to action by [elected] officers. It is no idle form to secure a definite conception in this form of what the people think on any subject of general interest.

Under the U.S. Constitution, the Supreme Court has made clear that no popular right to instruct congressional representatives exists. In 1996, the people of Missouri by initiative amended their state constitution to instruct members of the state's congressional delegation to introduce into Congress and to vote for a proposal to amend the U.S. Constitution to impose term limits on U.S. Senators and Representatives. The Missouri amendment contained a sly enforcement mechanism: any Missouri Senator or Representative who ran for reelection after failing to follow the state's instructions on voting for federal term limits would receive a notation to that effect on the ballot immediately adjacent to his or her name: "DISREGARDED VOTERS' INSTRUCTION ON TERM LIMITS." In *Cook v. Gralike*, 531 U.S. 510 (2001), the Supreme Court struck down this provision of state law. The Court first reviewed the historical evidence, finding that the Framers did not intend to permit members of Congress to be bound by constituent instructions:

> [T]he First Congress rejected a proposal to insert a right of the people "to instruct their representatives" into what would become the First Amendment. 1 Annals of Cong. 732 (1789). The fact that the proposal was made suggests that its proponents thought it necessary, and the fact that it was rejected by a vote of 41 to 10, id. at 747, suggests that we should give weight to the views of those who opposed the proposal. It was their view that binding instructions would undermine an essential attribute of Congress by eviscerating the deliberative nature of that National Assembly. See, e.g., id. at 735 (remarks of Rep. Sherman) ("When the people have chosen a representative, it is his duty to meet others from the different parts of the Union, and consult, and agree with them to such acts as are for the general benefit of the whole community. If they were to be guided by instructions, there would be no use in deliberation; all that a man would have to do, would be to produce his instructions, and lay them on the table, and let them speak for him"). As a result, James Madison,

then a Representative from Virginia, concluded that a right to issue binding instructions would "run the risk of losing the whole system." Id. at 739;
see also id. at 735 (remarks of Rep. Clymer) (the proposed right to give
binding instructions was "a most dangerous principle, utterly destructive
of all ideas of an independent and deliberative body, which are essential
requisites in the Legislatures of free Governments").

The Court then went on to hold that state power under Article I, §4 to regulate the
"manner" of elections did not extend to the kind of ballot notations at issue.

How should we understand the concept of representation? The materials that
follow explore some of the leading theoretical issues.

1. *Principles of Representation*

Representatives undoubtedly can perform many tasks, but the material on
democratic theory covered in Chapter 1 suggests that one of the most important functions of representatives, perhaps their single most important function, is
to make laws. Representation, then, has something to do with the plausibility of
claims that the people collectively — rather than merely a majority of the people,
or a minority, or a Madisonian faction — are the makers or the "authors" of their
own laws. That is, in a properly representative system, nobody else is making laws
and *imposing* them illegitimately on the people; the people rule themselves, in the
Lockean sense, by making their own laws through their duly chosen and properly
authorized representatives.

That makes a start, but it is far from solving the problem because there are
many different ways in which representatives can go about the lawmaking process,
and many different kinds of relations that representatives can have with those they
represent. A classic taxonomy of the possible relations between representative and
represented can be found in HANNA FENICHEL PITKIN, THE CONCEPT OF REPRESEN-
TATION (1967). According to Pitkin, relationships of representation can be usefully
broken down into several categories.

1. *Authorization.* Representation relates to "the giving and having of authority. [A] representative is someone who has been authorized to act. This
   means that he has been given a right to act which he did not have before,
   while the represented has become responsible for the consequences of
   that action as if he had done it himself."
2. *Descriptive representation.* "True representation . . . requires that the legislature be so selected that its composition corresponds accurately to that
   of the whole nation; only then is it really a representative body. [As John
   Adams wrote, a] representative legislature . . . 'should be an exact portrait,
   in miniature, of the people at large, as it should think, feel, reason and act
   like them.'"
3. *Agency, or delegate representation.* A representative is an "agent," one who
   "acts not merely autonomously but for, instead of, on behalf of, someone
   else. . . . When we call a man someone's agent we are saying that he is the
   tool or instrument by which the other acts."

4. *Trustee.* "Representative government . . . 'by its essential nature . . . is a trusteeship.' A representative parliament is 'the trustee which the nation has authorized to act on its behalf; and it exercises sovereign power, under the terms of its trust, for the nation.'"

5. *Representing general interests.* "[P]olitical representation is the representation of interest." The members of a legislature "are an elite group, discovering and enacting what is best for the nation; that activity is what representation means. . . . Government should rest on wisdom and not on will; [thus] government is not to be conducted according to anyone's wishes," but according to what rational deliberation shows to be in the best interest of the nation as a whole.

6. *Representing particular interests.* Representation means "representation of persons," each of whom "has many interests in respect of various needs and situations at various times. . . . A man's interest is what he thinks it is," not what the legislature takes it to be, and even if those interests change from time to time or differ from person to person, "representatives of the people will seek to further those plural, shifting interests."

Note that some of these kinds of representation can come into conflict. A representative cannot easily serve simultaneously as a trustee and as a delegate unless the people happen to direct their delegates to act consistent with whatever the legislature conceives to be its public trust. Nor can a representative easily pursue simultaneously the interests of his constituents and the abstract good of all unless the particular interests of his constituents happen fortuitously to align with the common good. Thus, at least in Pitkin's typology, a democratic polity generally must make a choice about how it wants its representatives to conduct themselves.

More recently, drawing on modern empirical research examining the ways in which representatives and constituents actually interact, democratic theorists have supplemented Pitkin's baseline account with additional or alternative taxonomies. These accounts often distinguish forms of representation along different dimensions, such as the aims of the representative, the sources of information representatives consult in making judgments, and the responsiveness of representatives to sanctioning methods available to the electorate. *See, e.g.,* Andrew Rehfeld, *Representation Rethought: On Trustees, Delegates, and Gyroscopes in the Study of Political Representation and Democracy,* 103 AM. POL. SCI. REV. 214 (2009). For example, democratic theorist Jane Mansbridge, in *Rethinking Representation,* 97 AM. POL. SCI. REV. 515 (2003), argues that representation as it is actually practiced can be described by four ideal categories, although actual instances of representation, she readily concedes, often mix the ideal types.

7. *"Promissory representation."* This is the classic principal-agent form of representation based on a forward-looking conception of power in which principals (the voters) retain agents (elected officials) to do their bidding following the election.

8. *"Anticipatory representation."* In this form of representation, representatives do not follow instructions from the electorate, but rather look forward to the next available occasion for electoral disciplining—typically their reelection campaign—in order to anticipate what behavior will please

their constituents sufficiently to earn reelection. This account is consistent with the political science concept of "retrospective voting," in which voters base their votes on an assessment of the past performance of their representatives.

9. *"Gyroscopic representation."* Here, "voters select representatives who can be expected to act in ways the voter approves *without* external incentives." Representatives do what voters wish, but because they follow their own internal compasses, which happen to lead them in the direction in which voters would wish them to go if voters bothered to pay attention and impose discipline (things they tend to avoid).

10. *"Surrogate representation."* This is a form of representation in which a citizen is represented by someone despite the absence of an electoral relationship. For example, members of a local Jewish or Muslim community might develop a relationship with a Jew or Muslim representing a different district when the person representing their own district is a Christian. The same might be true of liberals or conservatives, racial groups, animal fanciers, or any other minority within a jurisdiction.

▶▶   *Reciprocity of Representation and Interests?*   Many of the dominant conceptions of representation, especially those that conceive the representative relationship as one between principal and agent, presuppose the existence of a concrete community with static, antecedent interests that seeks representation to advance those interests in the legislative forum. But is this a complete account? Might it be more accurate, at least some of the time, to say not only that the interests of the constituents guide the representative, but that the representative reciprocally influences how the constituency understands its own interests, and perhaps even its own identity? According to another recent critique of Pitkin's ground-breaking approach,

> representation in politics is at least a two-way street: the represented play a role in choosing representatives, and representatives "choose" their constituents in the sense of portraying them or framing them in particular, contestable ways. If I allege that you, a potential constituent of mine, possess key characteristic X, and if I can get you to accept this, I can then present myself as possessing capacity or attribute Y that enables me to represent you.

Representation thus possesses a "performative" aspect in which those who seek to represent make claims to their putative constituency about their own characteristics as a group, give reasons why constituents should accept the proffered self-understanding, and then offer themselves as best suited to represent the community, so understood. Michael Saward, *The Representative Claim*, 5 CONTEMP. POL. THEORY 297 (2006). To put this differently, the act of being represented influences the represented themselves; the institution of representation is thus dynamic, not static.

▶▶   *Representation of the Whole or the Parts?*   The American colonists, like other Englishmen, were deeply attached to the principle of "parliamentary sovereignty"—the idea that the British Parliament is the supreme governmental authority, answerable only to the people. The effort to establish parliamentary sovereignty, which required wresting power violently from the Crown, cost decades of bloody civil strife, culminating in the Glorious Revolution of 1688. The American founders, influenced by this history, generally shared the English Whig theory of the executive, which conceived it as weak, serving primarily as "a kind of agent of the legislative power." JEREMY D. BAILEY, THE IDEA OF PRESIDENTIAL REPRESENTATION 33 (2019). On this view, the American people were represented by Congress, not by the President, who was merely an exalted minister who did the bidding of the people's representatives in Congress.

Andrew Jackson was the first American president to advance a different view. In his first message to Congress, Jackson argued that the President is the only official in the U.S. government who represents the entire people of the nation, and called for replacement of the Electoral College by direct presidential election. *Id.* at 68. The unique status of the presidency, Jackson claimed, gave the holder a special connection with the people, and a corresponding special obligation to see that their will is carried out.

Jackson's view remained controversial for decades, until a subsequent president, Woodrow Wilson, articulated a similar conception of the presidency that laid the foundation for how we think about the chief executive today. In view of the complexity of twentieth-century governance, Wilson de-emphasized the ministerial, "executive" aspects of the presidency and played up instead the idea of presidential leadership:

> As legal executive, his constitutional aspect, the President cannot be thought of alone. He cannot execute laws. Their actual daily execution must be taken care of by the several executive departments and by the now innumerable body of federal officials throughout the country. . . . It is therefore becoming more and more true, as the business of the government becomes more and more complex and extended, that the President is becoming more and more a political and less and less an executive officer. His executive powers are in commission, while his political powers more and more centre and accumulate upon him and are in their very nature personal and inalienable. . . .
>
> [He] is also the political leader of the nation, or has it in his choice to be. The nation as a whole has chosen him, and is conscious that it has no other political spokesman. His is the only national voice in affairs. Let him once win the admiration and confidence of the country, and no other single force can withstand him, no combination of forces will easily overpower him. . . . He is the representative of no constituency, but of the whole people. . . . .

WOODROW WILSON, CONSTITUTIONAL GOVERNMENT IN THE UNITED STATES 67 (1918).

Who "represents" the American people — Congress or the President? Or do they represent in different ways, the Congress representing the parts and the President representing the whole? Or does the President represent only a majority, and the minority must make do with representation in Congress? If Edmund Burke was correct, and members of a legislature represent the entire polity rather than merely their individual districts, what is the point of a legislature containing many individuals? What advantage is gained by multiplicity? Why not adopt the populist view that a single individual is not only good enough, but can do the job better and more efficiently?

▶▶ *Representation of Minorities.*   One of the most pressing problems of contemporary democratic theory and practice concerns the capacity of representative institutions to represent minorities. The problem comes in two principal varieties. In its most basic form, it amounts to this: if you are a member of a *political* minority, you are by definition either not successfully electing representatives at all, or are electing few of them. The problem can also take on a more charged dimension when a political minority is also an ethnic, racial, or religious minority in a plural or divided society. The representation of racial minorities in the United States has of course been an agonizing problem of long standing.

Much of the difficulty turns on how one understands the consequences for representation of losing electoral contests. If the candidate for office you backed loses the contest, are you in consequence "unrepresented" in the legislature?

Note that different theories of representation answer this question differently. For the nineteenth-century British political philosopher John Stuart Mill, losers were *not* represented in government, and any system that permitted such a result was "false democracy." True democracy, he argued, meant government of the whole people by the whole people. The British system of plurality (or first-past-the-post) winners, however, offered instead government of the whole people by "a mere majority of the people, exclusively represented." This makes it, he contended, "a government of privilege, in favour of the numerical majority, who alone possess practically any voice in the State," a circumstance he described as "the complete disenfranchisement of minorities." "In a really equal democracy," Mill argued, "every or any section would be represented, not disproportionately, but proportionately." As a result, Mill strongly favored proportional representation (PR) — a system in which each party wins seats in the legislature in proportion to its share of the popular vote — as the only system capable of actually representing all rather than some. JOHN STUART MILL, CONSIDERATIONS ON REPRESENTATIVE GOVERNMENT (1861).

Do you agree that a legislature elected through plurality or other non-PR methods does not truly represent the people of the jurisdiction? Is representation binary — either on or off? Or can the relationship of representation exist across a spectrum along which representation may be better or worse, or more or less thorough or complete, or more or less effective, or efficient, or legitimate?

What about those who can't or don't vote? Are children "unrepresented" in government? What about resident aliens? Eligible nonvoters? If elected representatives in fact consider the interests and welfare of these groups when making policy, are they not in fact "represented"?

▶▶ *Positive Political Theory: Alignment of Preferences and Policy.*   Much of modern political science is based on the foundational assumption that the purpose of democracy is to establish and maintain "a close correspondence between the laws of a nation and the preferences of citizens who are ruled by them." Rehfeld, *supra*, at 214. The policies adopted by a legislature, in other words, should be those desired by the voters. We will call this the "vector theory of representation."

Vector Theory of Representation

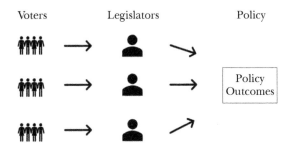

On this view, voters communicate their policy preferences through the act of choosing a representative of similar views. Those representatives then go on in the legislature to negotiate among themselves for laws and policies that reflect the preferences of their own constituents. The benchmark of correspondence between policy and preference in this theory is often said to be the degree to which policies adopted by the legislature correspond to the preferences of the "median voter," a hypothetical individual who sits precisely at the center of popular opinion. *See, e.g.*, MICHAEL D. MCDONALD AND IAN BUDGE, ELECTIONS, PARTIES, DEMOCRACY: CONFERRING THE MEDIAN MANDATE (2005).

Median voter

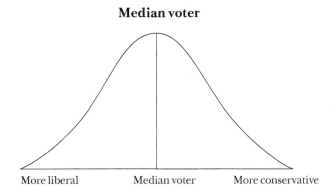

Thus, on this set of assumptions, the purpose of institutions of representation is to create the smoothest and most accurate translation of preferences into policies. The standard mechanics usually involve campaigning, inclusive suffrage, and mechanisms of representative accountability—most commonly simple voting out of office—but sometimes are said to include such disciplining measures as initiative lawmaking, popular referendums, and recall of underperforming officials. On this basis, political scientists sometimes pronounce certain forms of democratic organization better or worse than others because they do a better or worse job of translating the position of the median voter into public policy. *See, e.g.*, G. BINGHAM POWELL, ELECTIONS AS INSTRUMENTS OF DEMOCRACY (2000) (arguing that proportional representation does a better job than majoritarian electoral systems of maintaining congruence between popular preferences and public policy).

Is enactment of the policy preferences of voters a goal that elected officials ought to pursue? There are strong arguments in favor of such a goal. *See* Nicholas O. Stephanopoulos, *Elections and Alignment,* 114 COLUM. L. REV. 283 (2014). Some theories of democracy clearly view such correspondence as an affirmative good. In a Downsian approach, for example, social utility is maximized only when government policy reflects the properly aggregated preferences of voters. Other theories of democracy, however, place a considerably lower value on congruence between popular policy preferences and enacted law. Edmund Burke did not think it important for elected representatives to follow the wishes of constituents, and modern theorists of deliberative democracy place little weight on public opinion that has not been tested in the crucible of deliberation—a function that Burke maintained was performed for the people by their representatives assembled in the legislature.

Furthermore, responsiveness to public opinion is clearly not the only value that democratic societies seek to pursue. Some institutional arrangements, such as federalism, separation of powers, bicameralism, a bill of rights, and judicial review, all deliberately *impair* the capacity of a majority to translate its preferences into policy; that is their point. Consequently, the more interesting question may not be whether policy responsiveness is a good thing, but rather how much of it, if any, is required to deem the quality of political representation democratically adequate. Or, conversely, to what extent does a lack of alignment between public opinion and enacted policy constitute evidence of improperly undemocratic basic institutions, improper functioning of otherwise acceptable institutions, or both? Suppose, for example, that it can be shown that the views of elected legislators on some issues are closer to those of their major campaign donors than they are to the views of their median constituents. Does this lack of congruence, by itself, support a charge that electoral institutions are flawed in their structure or operation? *See* Nicholas O. Stephanopoulos, *Aligning Campaign Finance Law,* 101 VA. L. REV. 1425 (2015).

In a frequently cited article, two political scientists, Jeffrey Lax and Justin Phillips, assessed the responsiveness of state policies on abortion, education, health care, and several other issues to the policy preferences of state electorates on those issues. Jeffrey R. Lax and Justin H. Phillips, *The Democratic Deficit in the States,* 56 AM. J. POL. SCI. 148 (2012). The authors reached the following conclusion: "we have . . . uncovered a clear 'democratic deficit'—states effectively translate majority opinion into policy only about half the time, a clear 'failing' grade on the congruence test." *Id.* at 164. Is that kind of performance a "failure" of political representation? Political theorists have sometimes criticized the tendency of empirical political scientists to compare "the status quo . . . to a simplistic normative model of democracy whereby democratic majorities are to get whatever they want, on every issue, and in short order." Andrew Sabl, *The Two Cultures of Democratic Theory: Responsiveness, Democratic Quality, and the Empirical-Normative Divide,* 13 PERSP. ON POL. 345, 346 (2015).

There is now a growing literature in political science concluding that, where representation is understood as the relationship between policy preferences and public policy outcomes, American democracy does a better job of representing the preferences of rich Americans than the preferences of middle-class and poor Americans. *See, e.g.,* MARTIN GILENS, AFFLUENCE AND INFLUENCE: ECONOMIC INEQUALITY AND POLITICAL POWER IN AMERICA (2012); KAY LEHMAN SCHLOZMAN, SIDNEY VERBA, AND HENRY E. BRADY, THE UNHEAVENLY CHORUS: UNEQUAL POLITICAL VOICE AND THE BROKEN PROMISE OF AMERICAN DEMOCRACY (2012); JACOB HACKER AND PAUL PIERSON, WINNER-TAKE-ALL POLITICS: HOW WASHINGTON MADE THE RICH RICHER—AND TURNED ITS BACK ON THE MIDDLE CLASS (2010); LARRY M. BARTELS, UNEQUAL DEMOCRACY: THE POLITICAL ECONOMY OF THE NEW GILDED AGE (2008); Lawrence R. Jacobs and Benjamin I. Page, *Who Influences U.S. Foreign Policy?*, 99 AM. POL. SCI. REV. 107 (2005). Does a condition of perfect congruence between public preferences and enacted policy furnish the normative ideal?

If some degree of responsiveness is a good thing, does it follow that more responsiveness is necessarily better? If representatives only and always do the bidding of the electorate, does that collapse the difference between direct and representative forms of democracy? Does representation provide some value added compared with direct democracy? If so, what is the nature of that added value, and if not, why can't we simply dispense with representation altogether?

2. Non-Elective Forms of Representation

>> *The Problem of Virtual Representation.* Most contemporary theories of representation place a great deal of emphasis on a formal electoral linkage between the representative and the represented. Historically, however, this was by no means always the case. Disagreement over the proper nature of representation played a crucial role in the American Revolution. As every school child knows, the British government levied taxes on the American colonies at the same time as the colonists were denied the right to elect members of Parliament; this gave rise to the famous slogan "no taxation without representation." The British justified their actions with the doctrine of "virtual representation," according to which the colonists, although not represented literally in the form of elected officials, were nevertheless fully represented in Parliament insofar as Parliament was cognizant of and sensitive to the actual interests of the colonies.

The doctrine of virtual representation was first formulated to justify the unchanging composition of Parliament in the face of drastic changes in the distribution of the English population. The right to send members to Parliament had been doled out in what was probably a roughly proportional way in medieval times. As the population shifted, new towns and cities sprang up and others declined, but representation in Parliament remained fixed. The most dramatic result of this fixed allocation was that by the mid-eighteenth century the cities of Manchester and Birmingham, which had not existed when representatives were first apportioned, could send no representatives to Parliament. In contrast, certain sparsely populated rural districts were entitled to elect several members of Parliament.

The Americans decisively rejected the concept of virtual representation. The following excerpt discusses this key historical conflict between the Americans and the British.

Bernard Bailyn

The Ideological Origins of the American Revolution (1967)

The question of representation was the first serious intellectual problem to come between England and the colonies. The intellectual position worked out by the Americans had deep historical roots; it crystallized, in effect, three generations of political experience.

What had taken place in the earlier years of colonial history was the partial re-creation, as a matter of fact and not of theory, of a kind of representation that had flourished in medieval England but that had faded and been superseded by another during the fifteenth and sixteenth centuries. In its original, medieval, form elective representation to Parliament had been a device by which "local men, locally minded, whose business began and ended with the interests of the constituency," were enabled, as attorneys for their electors, to seek redress from the royal court of Parliament, in return for which they were expected to commit their constituents to grants of financial aid. Attendance at Parliament of representatives of the commons was for the most part an obligation unwillingly performed, and local communities bound their representatives to local interests in every way possible. . . .

By the time the institutions of government were taking firm shape in the American colonies, Parliament in England had been transformed. The restrictions that had been placed upon representatives of the commons to make them attorneys of their constituencies fell away; members came to sit "not merely as parochial representative, but as delegates of all the commons of the land." Symbolically incorporating the state, Parliament in effect had become the nation for purposes of government, and its members virtually if not actually, symbolically if not by sealed orders, spoke for all as well as for the group that had chosen them. . . .

But the colonists, reproducing English institutions in miniature, had been led by force of circumstance to move in the opposite direction. Starting with seventeenth-century assumptions, out of necessity they drifted backward, as it were, toward the medieval forms of attorneyship in representation. Their surroundings had recreated to a significant extent the conditions that had shaped the earlier experiences of the English people. The colonial towns and counties, like their medieval counterparts, were largely autonomous, and they stood to lose more than they were likely to gain from a loose acquiescence in the action of central government. More often than not they felt themselves to be the benefactors rather than the beneficiaries of central government, provincial or imperial; and when they sought favors from higher authorities they sought local and particular — in effect private — favors. Having little reason to identify their interests with those of the central government, they sought to keep the voices of local interests clear and distinct; and where it seemed necessary, they moved — though with little sense of innovating or taking actions of broad significance, and nowhere comprehensively or systematically — to bind representatives to local interests. . . .

All of this, together with the associated experience common to all of the colonies of selecting and controlling agents to speak for them in England, formed the background for the discussion of the first great issue of the Anglo-American controversy. For the principal English argument put forward in defense of Parliament's right to pass laws taxing the colonies was that the colonists, like the "nine tenths of the people of Britain" who do not choose representatives to Parliament, were in fact represented there. The power of actually voting for representatives, it was claimed, was an accidental and not a necessary attribute of representation, "for the right of election is annexed to certain species of property, to peculiar franchises, and to inhabitancy in certain places." In what really counted there was no difference between those who happened to live in England and those in America: "none are actually, all are virtually represented in Parliament," for, the argument concluded,

> every Member of Parliament sits in the House not as representative of his own constituents but as one of that august assembly by which all the commons of *Great Britain* are represented. Their rights and their interests, however his own borough may be affected by general dispositions, ought to be the great objects of his attention and the only rules for his conduct, and to sacrifice these to a partial advantage in favor of the place where he was chosen would be a departure from his duty.

In England the practice of "virtual" representation provided reasonably well for the actual representation of the major interests of the society, and it raised no widespread objection. It was its opposite, the idea of representation as attorneyship, that was seen as "a new sort of political doctrine strenuously enforced by modern malcontents." But in the colonies the situation was reversed. There, where political experience had led to a different expectation of the process of representation and where the workings of virtual representation in the case at hand were seen to be damaging, the English argument was met at once with flat and universal rejection, ultimately with derision. It consists, Daniel Dulany wrote in a comprehensive refutation of the idea, "of facts not true and of conclusions inadmissible." What counts, he said in terms with which almost every writer in America agreed, was the extent to which representation worked to protect the interests of the people against the encroachments of government. From this point of view the analogy between the nonelectors in England and those in America was utterly specious, for the interests of Englishmen who did not vote for members of Parliament were intimately bound up with those who did and with those chosen to sit as representatives. . . . But no such "intimate and inseparable relation" existed between the electors of Great Britain and the inhabitants of the colonies. The two groups were by no means involved in the same consequences of taxation: "not a single actual elector in England might be immediately affected by a taxation in America imposed by a statute which would have a general operation and effect upon the properties of the inhabitants of the colonies."

Once a lack of natural identity of interests between representatives and the populace was conceded, the idea of virtual representation lost any force it might have had; for by such a notion, James Otis wrote, you could "as well prove that the British House of Commons in fact represent all the people of the globe as those in America." . . . It was a notion, Arthur Lee wrote, . . . that "would, in the days of superstition, have been called witchcraft," for what it means is that while "our privileges are all *virtual,* our sufferings are *real.* . . . We might have flattered ourselves that a *virtual obedience* would have exactly corresponded with a *virtual representation.*" But the colonists' discussion of representation did not stop with the regulation of the claims made for virtual representation. The debate broadened into a general consideration of the nature and function of representation — in situations where interests of electors and elected, franchised and disfranchised, coincided as well as where they did not. The virtues of binding representatives by instructions were now explicitly explored. Some approached the question cautiously, arguing that, though the idea "that the constituent can bind his representative by instructions" may in recent years have become "an unfashionable doctrine," nevertheless, "in most cases" the "persuasive influence" if not the "obligatory force" of instructions should be insisted upon: "a representative who should act against the explicit recommendation of his constituents would most deservedly forfeit their regard and all pretension to their future confidence." But the dominant voices were direct and decisive. The right to instruct representatives, Arthur Lee declared in the fourth of his "Monitor" papers, has been denied only "since the system of corruption which is now arrived to so dangerous a height began first to predominate in our constitution. Then it was that arbitrary ministers and their prostituted dependents began to maintain this doctrine dangerous to our liberty, that the representatives were independent of the people. This was necessary to serve their own tyrannical and selfish purposes." Constituents, it was agreed, had nothing less than "an inherent right to give instructions to their representatives." For representatives, James Wilson concluded, were properly to be considered the "creatures" of their constituents, and they were to be held strictly "accountable for the use of that power which is delegated unto them." . . . With the result, it was concluded, that a representative assembly "should be in miniature an exact portrait of the people at large. It should think, feel, reason, and act like them." . . . Where government was such an accurate mirror of the people, sensitively reflecting their desires and feelings, consent was a continuous, everyday process. In effect the people were present through their representatives, and were themselves, step by step and point by point, acting in the conduct of public affairs. No longer merely an ultimate check on government, they *were* in some sense the government. Government had no separate existence apart from them; it was *by* the people as well as *for* the people. . . .

———————

Did the Americans really reject entirely the notion of virtual representation? Recall that at the time of the founding the vote was widely denied to blacks, women, young men, and adult males who did not own sufficient property. Would it be more correct to say that the Americans accepted the concept of virtual representation in principle, but merely rejected the English contention that Britain and all its colonies were a homogeneous people, with a single common interest, capable of being virtually represented in the same body? *See* GORDON WOOD, THE CREATION OF THE AMERICAN REPUBLIC, 1776-1787 (1969), at 178-179. Or is the denial of the franchise in the early United States simply another example of the inability of Americans fully and fairly to live up to the high principles to which they dedicated themselves in the Constitution?

The gradual enfranchisement of the great majority of citizens has left the United States with one highly visible instance of what the colonists would have considered virtual representation: the District of Columbia, which contains nearly 700,000 residents (more than Vermont and Wyoming, and not many fewer than Alaska), elects no U.S. Representatives or Senators. A constitutional amendment, the District of Columbia Voting Rights Amendment, cleared Congress in 1978 but was not ratified by a sufficient number of state legislatures. It was widely assumed at the time that ratification was blocked by Republicans, who feared (with some justice) that the District would elect two Democratic Senators and one Democratic Representative.

Holt Civic Club v. City of Tuscaloosa

439 U.S. 60 (1978)

Mr. Justice REHNQUIST delivered the opinion of the Court.

Holt is a small, largely rural, unincorporated community located on the northeastern outskirts of Tuscaloosa, the fifth largest city in Alabama. Because the community is within the three-mile police jurisdiction circumscribing Tuscaloosa's corporate limits, its residents are subject to the city's "police [and] sanitary regulations." Ala. Code §11-40-10 (1975). Holt residents are also subject to the criminal jurisdiction of the city's court, Ala. Code §12-14-1 (1975), and to the city's power to license businesses, trades, and professions, Ala. Code §11-51-91 (1975). Tuscaloosa, however, may collect from businesses in the police jurisdiction only one-half of the license fee chargeable to similar businesses conducted within the corporate limits. *Ibid.*

In 1973 appellants, an unincorporated civic association and seven individual residents of Holt, brought this statewide class action in the United States District Court for the Northern District of Alabama, challenging the constitutionality of these Alabama statutes. They claimed that the city's extraterritorial exercise of police powers over Holt residents, without a concomitant extension of the franchise on an equal footing with those residing within the corporate limits, denies residents of the police jurisdiction rights secured by the Due Process and Equal Protection Clauses of the Fourteenth Amendment. . . .

Appellants focus their equal protection attack on §11-40-10, the statute fixing the limits of municipal police jurisdiction and giving extraterritorial effect to municipal police and sanitary ordinances. Citing *Kramer v. Union Free School Dist.*, 395 U.S. 621 (1969), and cases following in its wake, appellants argue that the section creates a classification infringing on their right to participate in municipal elections. The State's denial of the franchise to police jurisdiction residents, appellants urge, can stand only if justified by a compelling state interest. . . .

From . . . our . . . voting qualifications cases a common characteristic emerges: The challenged statute in each case denied the franchise to individuals who were physically resident within the geographic boundaries of the governmental entity concerned. No decision of this Court has extended the "one man, one vote" principle to individuals residing beyond the geographic confines of the governmental entity concerned, be it the State or its political subdivisions. On the contrary, our cases have uniformly recognized that a government unit may legitimately restrict the right to participate in its political processes to those who reside within its borders. See, e.g., *Dunn v. Blumstein*, 405 U.S. 330, 343-344 (1972); *Kramer v. Union Free School Dist.*, 395 U.S., at 625; *Carrington v. Rash*, 380 U.S. 89, 91 (1965). . . .

Appellants' argument that extraterritorial extension of municipal powers requires concomitant extraterritorial extension of the franchise proves too much. The imaginary line defining a city's corporate limits cannot corral the influence of municipal actions. A city's decisions inescapably affect individuals living immediately outside its borders. The granting of building permits for high rise apartments, industrial plants, and the like on the city's fringe unavoidably contributes to problems of traffic congestion, school districting, and law enforcement immediately outside the city. A rate change in the city's sales or ad valorem tax could well have a significant impact on retailers and property values in areas bordering the city. The condemnation of real property on the city's edge for construction of a municipal garbage dump or waste treatment plant would have obvious implications for neighboring nonresidents. Indeed, the indirect extraterritorial effects of many purely internal municipal actions could conceivably have a heavier impact on surrounding environs than the direct regulation contemplated by Alabama's police jurisdiction statutes. Yet no one would suggest that nonresidents likely to be affected by this sort of municipal action have a constitutional right to participate in the political processes bringing it about. And unless one adopts the idea that the Austinian notion of sovereignty,* which is presumably embodied to some extent in the authority of a city over a police jurisdiction, distinguishes the direct effects of limited municipal powers over police jurisdiction residents from the indirect though equally dramatic extraterritorial effects of purely internal municipal actions, it makes little sense to say that one requires extension of the franchise while the other does not.

Given this country's tradition of popular sovereignty, appellants' claimed right to vote in Tuscaloosa elections is not without some logical appeal. We are mindful, however, of Mr. Justice Holmes' observation in *Hudson Water Co. v. McCarter*, 209 U.S. 349, 355 (1908):

> All rights tend to declare themselves absolute to their logical extreme. Yet all in fact are limited by the neighborhood of principles of policy which are other than those on which the particular right is founded, and which become strong enough to hold their own when a certain point is reached. . . . The boundary at which the conflicting interests balance cannot be determined by any general formula in advance, but points in the line, or helping to establish it, are fixed by decisions that this or that concrete case falls on the nearer or farther side.

The line heretofore marked by this Court's voting qualifications decisions coincides with the geographical boundary of the governmental unit at issue, and we hold that appellants' case, like their homes, falls on the farther side.

Thus stripped of its voting rights attire, the equal protection issue presented by appellants becomes whether the Alabama statutes giving extraterritorial force to certain municipal ordinances and powers bear some rational relationship to a legitimate state purpose.

Government, observed Mr. Justice Johnson, "is the science of experiment," *Anderson v. Dunn*, 6 Wheat. 204, 226 (1821), and a State is afforded wide leeway

---

* [Justice Rehnquist refers to John Austin, an English philosopher who, in a famous work, defined "law" as the command of a sovereign that must be obeyed. — EDS.]

when experimenting with the appropriate allocation of state legislative power. This Court has often recognized that political subdivisions such as cities and counties are created by the State "as convenient agencies for exercising such of the governmental powers of the State as may be entrusted to them." *Hunter v. Pittsburgh*, 207 U.S. 161, 178 (1907). In *Hunter v. Pittsburgh*, the Court discussed at length the relationship between a State and its political subdivisions, remarking: "The number, nature and duration of the powers conferred upon [municipal] corporations and the territory over which they shall be exercised rests in the absolute discretion of the State." 207 U.S., at 178. While the broad statements as to state control over municipal corporations contained in *Hunter* have undoubtedly been qualified by the holdings of later cases such as *Kramer v. Union Free School Dist.*, *supra*, we think that the case continues to have substantial constitutional significance in emphasizing the extraordinarily wide latitude that States have in creating various types of political subdivisions and conferring authority upon them.

The extraterritorial exercise of municipal powers is a governmental technique neither recent in origin nor unique to the State of Alabama. In this country 35 States authorize their municipal subdivisions to exercise governmental powers beyond their corporate limits. Although the extraterritorial municipal powers granted by these States vary widely, several States grant their cities more extensive or intrusive powers over bordering areas than those granted under the Alabama statutes.

Our inquiry is limited to the question whether "any state of facts reasonably may be conceived to justify" Alabama's system of police jurisdictions, and in this case it takes but momentary reflection to arrive at an affirmative answer.

The Alabama Legislature could have decided that municipal corporations should have some measure of control over activities carried on just beyond their "city limit" signs, particularly since today's police jurisdiction may be tomorrow's annexation to the city proper. Nor need the city's interests have been the only concern of the legislature when it enacted the police jurisdiction statutes. Urbanization of any area brings with it a number of individuals who long both for the quiet of suburban or country living and for the career opportunities offered by the city's working environment. Unincorporated communities like Holt dot the rim of most major population centers in Alabama and elsewhere, and state legislatures have a legitimate interest in seeing that this substantial segment of the population does not go without basic municipal services such as police, fire, and health protection. Established cities are experienced in the delivery of such services, and the incremental cost of extending the city's responsibility in these areas to surrounding environs may be substantially less than the expense of establishing wholly new service organizations in each community.

Nor was it unreasonable for the Alabama Legislature to require police jurisdiction residents to contribute through license fees to the expense of services provided them by the city. The statutory limitation on license fees to half the amount exacted within the city assures that police jurisdiction residents will not be victimized by the city government. . . .

In sum, we conclude that Alabama's police jurisdiction statutes violate neither the Equal Protection Clause nor the Due Process Clause of the Fourteenth Amendment.

Mr. Justice BRENNAN, with whom Mr. Justice WHITE and Mr. Justice MARSHALL join, dissenting.

. . . I would reverse the judgment of the District Court and hold that appellants' equal protection claim should have been sustained.

It is, of course, established that once a "franchise is granted to the electorate, lines may not be drawn which are inconsistent with the Equal Protection Clause of the Fourteenth Amendment." *Harper v. Virginia Bd. of Elections*, 383 U.S. 663, 665 (1966). Because "statutes distributing the franchise constitute the foundation of our representative society," *Kramer v. Union Free School Dist.*, 395 U.S. 621, 626 (1969), we have subjected such statutes to "exacting judicial scrutiny." *Id.* at 628. Indeed, "if a challenged statute grants the right to vote to some citizens and denies the franchise to others, 'the Court must determine whether the exclusions are *necessary* to promote a *compelling* state interest.' [*Kramer v. Union Free School Dist.*, 395 U.S.] at 627 (emphasis added)." *Dunn v. Blumstein*, 405 U.S. 330, 337 (1972). The general rule is that "whenever a state or local government decides to select persons by popular election to perform governmental functions, the Equal Protection Clause of the Fourteenth Amendment requires that each qualified voter must be given an equal opportunity to participate in that election. . . ." *Hadley v. Junior College Dist.*, 397 U.S. 50, 56 (1970). . . .

There is no question but that the residents of Tuscaloosa's police jurisdiction are governed by the city.[10] Under Alabama law, a municipality exercises "governing" and "lawmaking" power over its police jurisdiction. Residents of Tuscaloosa's police jurisdiction are subject to license fees exacted by the city, as well as to the city's police and sanitary regulations, which can be enforced through penal sanctions effective in the city's municipal court. The Court seems to imply, however, that residents of the police jurisdiction are not governed enough to be included within the political community of Tuscaloosa, since they are not subject to Tuscaloosa's powers of eminent domain, zoning, or ad valorem taxation. But this position is sharply contrary to our previous holdings. In *Kramer v. Union Free School Dist.*, 395 U.S. 621 (1969), for example, we held that residents of a school district who neither owned nor leased taxable real property located within the district, or were not married to someone who did, or were not parents or guardians of children enrolled in a local

---

10. Appellants have included in their brief an unchallenged addendum listing the ordinances of the city of Tuscaloosa . . . that have application in its police jurisdiction. [These include ordinances regulating licensing of] ambulances, bottle dealers, junk dealers, general business[es], florists, hotels, motels, industry; [a building code regulating] inspection service, enforces codes, dams, building permits, electrical codes, fire prevention codes, incinerators, discharge of cinders; [regulation of] mobile home parks [with respect to] plumbing, disposal of human waste, and wells; Public Health [regulations concerning] birds, dogs, smoking on buses, gas stations, sale of produce from trucks, food establishments, food inspectors, boardinghouses, milk, mosquito control; Traffic Regulations [concerning] stop and yield signs, mufflers, brakes, vehicle inspection, vehicle operation, hitchhiking, load limit on bridges, driving while intoxicated, reckless driving, medians, emergency vehicles, speed limits, truck routes; and Criminal Ordinances [regulating] misdemeanors, wrecked cars on premises, nuisances, obscene literature, destruction of plants, swimming in nude, trespass to boats, shooting galleries, obscene films; [as well as] cigarette tax, public parks and recreation, [and] taxis.

district school, nevertheless were sufficiently affected by the decisions of the local school board to make the denial of their franchise in local school board elections a violation of the Equal Protection Clause. . . .

The Court today does not explain why being subjected to the authority to exercise such extensive power does not suffice to bring the residents of Tuscaloosa's police jurisdiction within the political community of the city. Nor does the Court in fact provide any standards for determining when those subjected to extraterritorial municipal legislation will have been "governed enough" to trigger the protections of the Equal Protection Clause.

The criterion of geographical residency relied upon by the Court is of no assistance in this analysis. Just as a State may not fracture the integrity of a political community by restricting the franchise to property taxpayers, so it may not use geographical restrictions on the franchise to accomplish the same end. . . .

The criterion of geographical residency is thus entirely arbitrary when applied to this case. It fails to explain why, consistently with the Equal Protection Clause, the "government unit" which may exclude from the franchise those who reside outside of its geographical boundaries should be composed of the city of Tuscaloosa rather than of the city together with its police jurisdiction. It irrationally distinguishes between two classes of citizens, each with equal claim to residency (insofar as that can be determined by domicile or intention or other similar criteria), and each governed by the city of Tuscaloosa in the place of their residency.

The Court argues, however, that if the franchise were extended to residents of the city's police jurisdiction, the franchise must similarly be extended to all those indirectly affected by the city's actions. This is a simple non sequitur. There is a crystal-clear distinction between those who reside in Tuscaloosa's police jurisdiction, and who are therefore subject to that city's police and sanitary ordinances, licensing fees, and the jurisdiction of its municipal court, and those who reside in neither the city nor its police jurisdiction, and who are thus merely affected by the indirect impact of the city's decisions. . . .

Appellants' equal protection claim can be simply expressed: The State cannot extend the franchise to some citizens who are governed by municipal government in the places of their residency, and withhold the franchise from others similarly situated, unless this distinction is necessary to promote a compelling state interest. No such interest has been articulated in this case. . . .

>> *Other Forms of Non-Electoral Representation.* Ancient Athens is often held up as the paradigm of popular democratic self-rule, and many important collective decisions were made by citizens directly, voting by voice in the Assembly. Yet every organized society requires a government to carry out its decisions, and Athenians did not use elections to choose their leaders. Instead, most governmental functions were performed by officials selected by lot, although offices that required specialized skills were filled by appointment. Indeed, the Greeks tended to view mechanisms of representation as inherently oligarchical because of what they viewed as the tendency of representative arrangements to create a professional class of government officials who, it was believed, would inevitably come to dominate the populace. BERNARD MANIN, THE PRINCIPLES OF REPRESENTATIVE GOVERNMENT 27-32 (1997).

Is there any reason why democratic commitments in a modern society cannot be adequately honored if public offices are filled by lot? We select jurors by lot, and they exercise a highly significant public function. Why not legislators? *See* Jorge R. Roig, *A Quantum Congress*, 90 CHI.-KENT L. REV. 431 (2015). Note that if we take seriously the notion that a perfectly representative legislature should be, as John Adams claimed, an "exact portrait in miniature" of the populace, the best way to produce such a legislature would be to eliminate elections altogether and substitute random selection. Robert Weissberg, *Collective vs. Dyadic Representation in Congress*, 72 AM. POL. SCI. REV. 535 (1978). Would not the filling of offices by lot better honor foundational liberal beliefs about the fundamental political equality of citizens? What, if anything, would be lost?

If we have qualms about putting the machinery of government fully into the hands of amateurs, what about revising our practices of bicameralism to make one chamber elected and the other filled by lottery? In one such proposal, a second, randomly selected chamber would have the power to propose legislation to the first chamber, but would play no formal role in approving it, and its functions would be mainly advisory. Pierre-Etienne Vandamme and Antoine Verret-Hamelin, *A Randomly Selected Chamber: Promises and Challenges*, 13 J. PUB. DELIB. 1 (2017). Would such a chamber perform any useful function? As a matter of practical politics, would the elected chamber be able successfully to resist suggestions from its randomly selected counterpart? Does it depend on how well the randomly selected chamber performs?

Another proposal would apply random selection at the other end: the legislature would be elected, but those entitled to vote would be randomly selected from the entire pool of eligible voters. Under this proposal, inspired by principles of deliberative democracy, those randomly selected to vote would be required to undergo a process of education to acquaint them with the salient issues as a way of enhancing their knowledge and competence. CLAUDIO LÓPEZ-GUERRA, DEMOCRACY AND DISENFRANCHISEMENT: THE MORALITY OF ELECTORAL EXCLUSIONS (2014). Would the choices made by such a group be accepted politically by the rest of the populace simply in the knowledge that those who voted were better informed?

Finally, what about forms of representation by individuals or organizations *outside* the formal structure of governance? The Sierra Club, the National Wildlife Federation, and Greenpeace, for example, claim to represent the interests of environmentalists, which they do through lobbying of legislatures and administrative agencies, as well as through litigation and public communication. Nobody elected these groups to perform these functions, yet they sometimes influence the content of legislation and administrative regulations. Does this relationship count nonetheless as "democratic"?

> [T]he case for an actor's credentials as a democratic representative can and should be developed out of a basic normative intuition that lies at the heart of most contemporary democratic theories: those potentially affected by a collective decision should have opportunities and capacities to influence that decision. . . . From this perspective, actors whose claims to represent rely on self-appointment may play an important role in democracy, particularly in a complex and globalizing world, where

electoral constituencies fail to coincide with those affected by collective decisions.

Laura Montanaro, *The Democratic Legitimacy of Self-Appointed Representatives*, 74 J. POLS. 1094, 1094 (2012). On the other hand, is part of what makes a relationship of representation democratic the *accountability* of the representative to the represented? If the Sierra Club is doing a poor job of representing environmentalists before legislatures and administrative bodies, can it be voted out of office and replaced? By what means?

Even non-democratic states occasionally create mechanisms of popular representation. In Singapore, for example, a one-party, authoritarian state in which elections are fully controlled by the ruling party, the government in 1990 created the office of "nominated members of parliament" (NMPs). These officials are appointed by the president, on the recommendation of a parliamentary committee, and after solicitation of nominations from various sectors of society which, in the opinion of the ruling party, have information or views that could be of value in parliamentary decision making. In this capacity, NMPs are conceived as "representing" the views and interests of the social sector from which they are appointed. Recent NMPs have been appointed to represent academia, various professions, business interests, women, ethnic groups, youth, and other, similar kinds of groups. NMPs can speak on any issue, and may vote on all matters except money bills, amendments to the constitution, and votes of no-confidence in the government. GARRY RODAN, PARTICIPATION WITHOUT DEMOCRACY, 70-92 (2018). Does this arrangement count as "representation"? Does it conflate "representation" with "voice"?

B. APPORTIONMENT

Complete deprivation of the ability to vote for a particular office, known as "vote denial," is the clearest form of disenfranchisement—but is it the only form? The question of voting seems binary: either one has the vote or one does not. Nevertheless, in the cases that follow, the Supreme Court recognized a different form of interference with the right to vote, one based not on outright deprivation or vote denial but on the "dilution" of a voter's vote through legislative malapportionment.

Apportionment refers to the number of people represented by the different members of an elected body. The term "malapportionment" is typically invoked to describe a system of election districts in which widely different numbers of people live in different districts. Malapportionment is said to be a kind of vote dilution because the vote of a person in a highly populous district counts less than—does not go as far toward electing a representative as—the vote of a person in a less populous district. Thus, in a district that contains 100 voters, one person's vote amounts to one-fifty-first of the total number of votes necessary to elect a representative, whereas a voter who lives in a district containing 1,000 voters can cast a vote that goes only one-tenth as far toward electing a representative.

This section considers three distinct types of apportionment problems: those arising with respect to voting for general legislatures; those arising with respect to allocating Representatives to Congress among the 50 states; and those arising in connection with elections from special districts to bodies that exercise limited rather than general governmental powers. Before turning to those issues, however, we consider a more basic question: is it appropriate for federal courts to interfere with the way in which a state structures its system of popular representation?

1.   The "Political Thicket"

The Court first heard a constitutional challenge to malapportionment in *Colegrove v. Green*, 328 U.S. 549 (1946). Voters in Illinois challenged the state's apportionment of congressional districts, the smallest of which contained just over 112,000 voters and the largest of which contained some 914,000 voters. The apportionment was made in 1901, using 1900 census data, at which time all districts were approximately equipopulous. No reapportionment had occurred since, and in the intervening half-century, population distributions had changed dramatically. The plaintiffs challenged this situation as a denial of equal protection.

In a plurality opinion, Justice Frankfurter argued that the claim should be dismissed as a nonjusticiable political question. In *Colegrove*, Justice Frankfurter uttered his famous warning that courts "ought not enter [the] political thicket" and should refrain from adjudicating malapportionment claims. Instead, courts should leave it up to state legislatures or Congress to remedy unequally apportioned districts.

Sixteen years later, the Court reversed field in *Baker v. Carr*, 369 U.S. 186 (1962). In a malapportionment case brought from Tennessee, the Court read *Colegrove* narrowly and held that a majority of Justices in that case did not find it presented a nonjusticiable political question. In a lengthy opinion for the Court, Justice Brennan extensively reviewed the Court's political question jurisprudence and concluded that the type of claim brought in a malapportionment case was not the type of case to which the political question doctrine applied:

> The question here is the consistency of state action with the Federal Constitution. We have no question decided, or to be decided, by a political branch of government coequal with this Court. Nor do we risk embarrassment of our government abroad, or grave disturbance at home if we take issue with Tennessee as to the constitutionality of her action here challenged. Nor need the appellants, in order to succeed in this action, ask the Court to enter upon policy determinations for which judicially manageable standards are lacking. Judicial standards under the Equal Protection Clause are well developed and familiar, and it has been open to courts since the enactment of the Fourteenth Amendment to determine, if on the particular facts they must, that a discrimination reflects no policy, but simply arbitrary and capricious action.

Justice Frankfurter wrote a blistering dissent in which he accused the Court of embarking on an enterprise well beyond the bounds of judicial competence:

> What, then, is this question of legislative apportionment? Appellants invoke the right to vote and to have their votes counted. But they are permitted to vote and their votes are counted. They go to the polls, they cast their ballots, they send their representatives to the state councils. Their

complaint is simply that the representatives are not sufficiently numerous or powerful—in short, that Tennessee has adopted a basis of representation with which they are dissatisfied. Talk of "debasement" or "dilution" is circular talk. One cannot speak of "debasement" or "dilution" of the value of a vote until there is first defined a standard of reference as to what a vote should be worth. What is actually asked of the Court in this case is to choose among competing bases of representation—ultimately, really, among competing theories of political philosophy—in order to establish an appropriate frame of government for the State of Tennessee and thereby for all the States of the Union.

Is Frankfurter's objection persuasive? Does judicial enforcement of equality in apportionment require courts to act as political philosophers rather than judges? Is Frankfurter right that all that matters under the Constitution is whether a voter can vote and not how the vote is weighted? As you consider the cases that follow, consider whether Frankfurter's warnings about entering the political thicket were well founded.

2. *General Districts*

The term "general election district" refers to districts that elect members of a general legislative body. Such a body is one that exercises the "general"—primary, principal, or unrestricted—legislative power of the polity. Most forms of political organization provide for one such body at every level of government. In the United States, general legislatures include Congress, state legislatures, and the principal local legislatures such as city councils and town boards. Such bodies are to be distinguished from "special legislatures"—and the "special districts" from which they are elected. These specialized bodies, which include school boards, water districts, and sewerage districts, exercise much narrower and more limited powers than general legislatures.

Following its decision in *Baker v. Carr*, cases soon reached the Court challenging the constitutionality of malapportionment in the composition of the national and state legislatures.

≫ *Malapportionment of Congress.* The first case to reach the Court, *Wesberry v. Sanders*, 376 U.S. 1 (1964), concerned malapportionment of the districts from which members of Georgia's delegation to the U.S. House of Representatives were elected. Under Georgia's congressional districting plan, populations in the ten congressional districts varied widely. Although the average population across all districts was 394,312, the Fifth District had a population of 823,680, whereas the Ninth contained only 272,154 people, less than one-third as many. In an opinion by Justice Black (a Southerner and former U.S. Senator from Alabama), the Court found that this apportionment plan "grossly discriminates against voters in the Fifth Congressional District." Because a member of Congress from the Fifth District represented two or three times as many voters as representatives from other districts, the apportionment plan "contracts the value of some votes and expands that of others."

The Court's analysis focused not on equal protection, but on Article I, §2, which requires that Representatives be chosen "by the People of the several States." This means, the Court said, "that as nearly as is practicable one man's vote in a congressional election is to be worth as much as another's." Comparing districting to at-large election of a state's congressional delegation, the Court said that "[i]t would be extraordinary to suggest that in such statewide elections the votes of inhabitants of some parts of a State, for example, Georgia's thinly populated Ninth District, could be weighted at two or three times the value of the votes of people living in more populous parts of the State, for example, the Fifth District around Atlanta." What could not be done overtly could not be done through the use of malapportioned districts: "To say that a vote is worth more in one district than in another would not only run counter to our fundamental ideas of democratic government, it would cast aside the principle of a House of Representatives elected 'by the People,' a principle tenaciously fought for and established at the Constitutional Convention."

In support of this contention, the Court reviewed the debates of the 1787 Constitutional Convention. "The question of how the legislature should be constituted," the Court observed, "precipitated the most bitter controversy of the Convention." Some wanted representation to be on the basis of equally counted individuals whereas others wanted representation by state, regardless of population. As a result of the Great Compromise, representation in the Senate was to be by state but representation in the House was, under Article I, §2, "apportioned among the several States . . . according to their respective Numbers." This principle, the Court held, embraced "equal representation in the House for equal numbers of people." The Framers were aware of the severe malapportionment (the so-called rotten boroughs) of the British Parliament, in which "one man could send two members to Parliament to represent the borough of Old Sarum while London's million people sent but four." Article I, §2 thus embraced the principle of "one person, one vote."

Justice Harlan wrote a biting dissent, which is worth quoting at some length:

> I had not expected to witness the day when the Supreme Court of the United States would render a decision which casts grave doubt on the constitutionality of the composition of the House of Representatives. . . . [T]he court holds that the provision in Art. I, §2, for election of Representatives "by the People" *means* that congressional districts are to be "as nearly as is practicable" equal in population. . . . The fact is, however, that Georgia's 10 Representatives *are* elected "by the People" of Georgia, just as Representatives from other states are elected "by the People of the several States." This is all that the Constitution requires. . . .
>
> [T]he very sentence of Art. I, §2, on which the Court exclusively relies confers the right to vote for Representatives only on those whom *the State* has found qualified to vote for members of "the most numerous Branch of the State Legislature." So far as Article I is concerned, it is within the State's power to confer that right only on persons of wealth or of a particular sex or, if the State chose, living in specified areas of the State. Were Georgia to find the residents of the Fifth District unqualified to vote for Representatives to the State House of Representatives, they could not vote for Representatives to Congress, according to the express words of Art. I,

§2. Other provisions of the Constitution would, of course, be relevant, *but so far as Art. I, §2, is concerned*, the disqualification would be within Georgia's power. How can it be, then, that this very same sentence prevents Georgia from apportioning its Representatives as it chooses? The truth is that it does not.

The Court purports to find support for its position in the third paragraph of Art. I, §2, which provides for the apportionment of Representatives among the States. The appearance of support in that section derives from the Court's confusion of two issues: direct election of Representatives within the States and the apportionment of Representatives among the States. . . . The delegates did have the former intention and made clear provision for it. Although many, perhaps most, of them also believed generally — but assuredly not in the precise, formalistic way of the majority of the Court — that within the States representation should be based on population, they did not surreptitiously slip their belief into the Constitution in the phrase "by the People," to be discovered 175 years later like a Shakespearian anagram.

Far from supporting the Court, the apportionment of Representatives among the States shows how blindly the Court has marched to its decision. Representatives were to be apportioned among the States on the basis of free population plus three-fifths of the slave population. Since no slave voted, the inclusion of three-fifths of their number in the basis of apportionment gave the favored States representation far in excess of their voting population. If, then, slaves were intended to be without representation, Article I did exactly what the Court now says it prohibited: it "weighted" the vote of voters in the slave States. . . .

There is a further basis for demonstrating the hollowness of the Court's assertion that Article I requires "one man's vote in a congressional election . . . to be worth as much as another's," *ante.* Nothing that the Court does today will disturb the fact that although in 1960 the population of an average congressional district was 410,481, the States of Alaska, Nevada, and Wyoming each have a Representative in Congress, although these respective populations are 226,167, 285,278, and 330,066. In entire disregard of population, Art. I, §2, guarantees each of these States and every other State "at Least one Representative." It is whimsical to assert in the face of this guarantee that an absolute principle of "equal numbers of people" is "solemnly embodied" in Article I. All that there is is a provision which bases representation in the House, generally but not entirely, on the population of the States. The provision for representation of *each State* in the House of Representatives is not a mere exception to the principle framed by the majority; it shows that no such principle is to be found. . . .

As the Court repeatedly emphasizes, delegates to the Philadelphia Convention frequently expressed their view that representation should be based on population. There were also, however, many statements favoring limited monarchy and property qualifications for suffrage and expressions of disapproval for unrestricted democracy. Such expressions prove as little on one side of this case as they do on the other. . . .

The upshot of all this is that the language of Art. I, §§2 and 4, the surrounding text, and the relevant history are all in strong and consistent direct contradiction of the Court's holding. The constitutional scheme vests in the States plenary power to regulate the conduct of elections for Representatives, and, in order to protect the Federal Government, provides for congressional supervision of the States' exercise of their power. Within this scheme, the appellants do not have the right which they assert, in the absence of provision for equal districts by the Georgia Legislature or the Congress. The constitutional right which the Court creates is manufactured out of whole cloth. . . .

What is done today saps the political process. The promise of judicial intervention in matter of this sort cannot but encourage popular inertia in efforts for political reform through the political process, with the inevitable result that the process is itself weakened. By yielding to the demand for a judicial remedy in this instance, the Court in my view does a disservice both to itself and to the broader values of our system of government. . . .

≫ *Malapportionment of State Legislatures.*   Shortly after disposing of congressional malapportionment in *Wesberry*, the Court turned its attention to population disparities at the state legislative level.

Reynolds v. Sims

377 U.S. 533 (1964)

Mr. Chief Justice WARREN delivered the opinion of the Court.

Involved in these cases are an appeal and two cross-appeals from a decision of the Federal District Court for the Middle District of Alabama holding invalid, under the Equal Protection Clause of the Federal Constitution, the existing and two legislatively proposed plans for the apportionment of seats in the two houses of the Alabama Legislature, and ordering into effect a temporary reapportionment plan comprised of parts of the proposed but judicially disapproved measures.

I

Plaintiffs below alleged that the last apportionment of the Alabama Legislature was based on the 1900 federal census, despite the requirement of the State Constitution that the legislature be reapportioned decennially. They asserted that, since the population growth in the State from 1900 to 1960 had been uneven, Jefferson and other counties were now victims of serious discrimination with respect to the allocation of legislative representation.

On July 12, 1962, an extraordinary session of the Alabama Legislature adopted two reapportionment plans to take effect for the 1966 elections. One was a proposed constitutional amendment, referred to as the "67-Senator Amendment." It provided for a House of Representatives consisting of 106 members, apportioned by giving one seat to each of Alabama's 67 counties and distributing the others according to population by the "equal proportions" method. Using this formula, the constitutional amendment specified the number of representatives allotted to each county until a new apportionment could be made on the basis of the 1970 census. The Senate was to be composed of 67 members, one from each county. The legislation provided that the proposed amendment should be submitted to the voters for ratification at the November 1962 general election.

The other reapportionment plan was embodied in a statutory measure adopted by the legislature and signed into law by the Alabama Governor, and was referred to as the "Crawford-Webb Act." . . . The act provided for a Senate consisting of 35 members, representing 35 senatorial districts established along county lines, and altered only a few of the former districts. In apportioning the 106 seats in the Alabama House of Representatives, the statutory measure gave each county one seat, and apportioned the remaining 39 on a rough population basis, under a formula requiring increasingly more population for a county to be accorded additional seats. . . .

Under the existing provisions, applying 1960 census figures, only 25.1% of the State's total population resided in districts represented by a majority of the members of the Senate, and only 25.7% lived in counties which could elect a majority of the members of the House of Representatives. Population-variance ratios of up to about 41-to-1 existed in the Senate, and up to about 16-to-1 in the House. Bullock County, with a population of only 13,462, and Henry County, with a population of only 15,286, each were allocated two seats in the Alabama House, whereas Mobile County, with a population of 314,301, was given only three seats, and Jefferson County, with 634,864 people, had only seven representatives. With respect to senatorial apportionment, since the pertinent Alabama constitutional provisions had been consistently construed as prohibiting the giving of more than one Senate seat to any one county, Jefferson County, with over 600,000 people, was given only one senator, as was Lowndes County, with a 1960 population of only 15,417, and Wilcox County, with only 18,739 people. . . .

Undeniably the Constitution of the United States protects the right of all qualified citizens to vote, in state as well as in federal elections. . . . And history has seen a continuing expansion of the scope of the right of suffrage in this country. The right to vote freely for the candidate of one's choice is of the essence of a democratic society, and any restrictions on that right strike at the heart of representative government. And the right of suffrage can be denied by a debasement or dilution of the weight of a citizen's vote just as effectively as by wholly prohibiting the free exercise of the franchise. . . .

In *Wesberry v. Sanders*, 376 U.S. 1, decided earlier this Term, we . . . determined that the constitutional test for the validity of congressional districting schemes was one of substantial equality of population among the various districts established by a state legislature for the election of members of the Federal House of Representatives. . . . [Our] decision in *Wesberry* was of course grounded on that language of the Constitution which prescribes that members of the Federal House of Representatives are to be chosen "by the People," while attacks on state legislative apportionment schemes, such as that involved in the instant cases, are principally based on the Equal Protection Clause of the Fourteenth Amendment. Nevertheless, *Wesberry* clearly established that the fundamental principle of representative government in this country is one of equal representation for equal numbers of people, without regard to race, sex, economic status, or place of residence within a State. Our problem, then, is to ascertain, in the instant cases, whether there are any constitutionally cognizable principles which would justify departures from the basic standard of equality among voters in the apportionment of seats in state legislatures.

III

A predominant consideration in determining whether a State's legislative apportionment scheme constitutes an invidious discrimination violative of rights asserted under the Equal Protection Clause is that the rights allegedly impaired are individual and personal in nature. . . . Undoubtedly, the right of suffrage is a fundamental matter in a free and democratic society. Especially since the right to exercise the franchise in a free and unimpaired manner is preservative of other basic civil and political rights, any alleged infringement of the right of citizens to vote must be carefully and meticulously scrutinized. Almost a century ago, in *Yick Wo v. Hopkins*, 118 U.S. 356, the Court referred to "the political franchise of voting" as "a fundamental political right, because preservative of all rights." 118 U.S., at 370.

Legislators represent people, not trees or acres. Legislators are elected by voters, not farms or cities or economic interests. As long as ours is a representative form of government, and our legislatures are those instruments of government elected directly by and directly representative of the people, the right to elect legislators in a free and unimpaired fashion is a bedrock of our political system. It could hardly be gainsaid that a constitutional claim had been asserted by an allegation that certain otherwise qualified voters had been entirely prohibited from voting for members of their state legislature. And, if a State should provide that the votes of citizens in one part of the State should be given two times, or five times, or 10 times the weight of votes of citizens in another part of the State, it could hardly be contended that the right to vote of those residing in the disfavored areas had not been effectively diluted. It would appear extraordinary to suggest that a State could be constitutionally permitted to enact a law providing that certain of the State's voters could vote two, five, or 10 times for their legislative representatives, while voters living elsewhere could vote only once. And it is inconceivable that a state law to the effect that, in counting votes for legislators, the votes of citizens in one part of the State would be multiplied by two, five, or 10, while the votes of persons in another area would be counted only at face value, could be constitutionally sustainable.

State legislatures are, historically, the fountainhead of representative government in this country. A number of them have their roots in colonial times, and substantially antedate the creation of our Nation and our Federal Government. . . . But representative government is in essence self-government through the medium of elected representatives of the people, and each and every citizen has an inalienable right to full and effective participation in the political processes of his State's legislative bodies. Most citizens can achieve this participation only as qualified voters through the election of legislators to represent them. Full and effective participation by all citizens in state government requires, therefore, that each citizen have an equally effective voice in the election of members of his state legislature. Modern and viable state government needs, and the Constitution demands, no less.

Logically, in a society ostensibly grounded on representative government, it would seem reasonable that a majority of the people of a State could elect a majority of that State's legislators. To conclude differently, and to sanction minority control of state legislative bodies, would appear to deny majority rights in a way that far surpasses any possible denial of minority rights that might otherwise be thought to result. Since legislatures are responsible for enacting laws by which all citizens are to be governed, they should be bodies which are collectively responsive to the popular will. And the concept of equal protection has been traditionally viewed as requiring the uniform treatment of persons standing in the same relation to the governmental action questioned or challenged. With respect to the allocation of legislative representation, all voters, as citizens of a State, stand in the same relation regardless of where they live. Any suggested criteria for the differentiation of citizens are insufficient to justify any discrimination, as to the weight of their votes, unless relevant to the permissible purposes of legislative apportionment. Since the achieving of fair and effective representation for all citizens is concededly the basic aim of legislative apportionment, we conclude that the Equal Protection Clause guarantees the opportunity for equal participation by all voters in the election of state legislators. . . .

We are told that the matter of apportioning representation in a state legislature is a complex and many-faceted one. We are advised that States can rationally consider factors other than population in apportioning legislative representation. We are admonished not to restrict the power of the States to impose differing views as to political philosophy on their citizens. We are cautioned about the dangers of entering into political thickets and mathematical quagmires. Our answer is this: a denial of constitutionally protected rights demands judicial protection; our oath and our office require no less of us. . . . To the extent that a citizen's right to vote is debased, he is that much less a citizen. A citizen, a qualified voter, is no more nor no less so because he lives in the city or on the farm. This is the clear and strong command of our Constitution's Equal Protection Clause. This is an essential part of the concept of a government of laws and not men. This is at the heart of Lincoln's vision of "government of the people, by the people, [and] for the people." The Equal Protection Clause demands no less than substantially equal state legislative representation for all citizens, of all places as well as of all races.

IV

We hold that, as a basic constitutional standard, the Equal Protection Clause requires that the seats in both houses of a bicameral state legislature must be apportioned on a population basis. Simply stated, an individual's right to vote for state legislators is unconstitutionally impaired when its weight is in a substantial fashion diluted when compared with votes of citizens living in other parts of the State. Since, under neither the existing apportionment provisions nor either of the proposed plans was either of the houses of the Alabama Legislature apportioned on a population basis, the District Court correctly held that all three of these schemes were constitutionally invalid.

V

Since neither of the houses of the Alabama Legislature, under any of the three plans considered by the District Court, was apportioned on a population basis, we would be justified in proceeding no further. However, one of the proposed plans, that contained in the so-called 67-Senator Amendment, at least superficially resembles the scheme of legislative representation followed in the Federal Congress. Under this plan, each of Alabama's 67 counties is allotted one senator, and no counties are given more than one Senate seat. Arguably, this is analogous to the allocation of two Senate seats, in the Federal Congress, to each of the 50 States, regardless of population. Seats in the Alabama House, under the proposed constitutional amendment, are distributed by giving each of the 67 counties at least one, with the remaining 39 seats being allotted among the more populous counties on a population basis. This scheme, at least at first glance, appears to resemble that prescribed for the Federal House of Representatives, where the 435 seats are distributed among the States on a population basis, although each State, regardless of its population, is given at least one Congressman.

. . . We . . . find the federal analogy inapposite and irrelevant to state legislative districting schemes. . . . The original constitutions of 36 of our States provided that representation in both houses of the state legislatures would be based completely, or predominantly, on population. And the Founding Fathers clearly had no intention of establishing a pattern or model for the apportionment of seats in state legislatures when the system of representation in the Federal Congress was adopted.

The system of representation in the two Houses of the Federal Congress is one ingrained in our Constitution, as part of the law of the land. It is one conceived out of compromise and concession indispensable to the establishment of our federal republic. Arising from unique historical circumstances, it is based on the consideration that in establishing our type of federalism a group of formerly independent States bound themselves together under one national government. . . .

The developing history and growth of our republic cannot cloud the fact that, at the time of the inception of the system of representation in the Federal Congress, a compromise between the larger and smaller States on this matter averted a deadlock in the Constitutional Convention which had threatened to abort the birth of our Nation. . . .

Political subdivisions of States—counties, cities, or whatever—never were and never have been considered as sovereign entities. Rather, they have been traditionally regarded as subordinate governmental instrumentalities created by the State to assist in the carrying out of state governmental functions. As stated by the Court in *Hunter v. City of Pittsburgh*, 207 U.S. 161, 178, these governmental units are "created as convenient agencies for exercising such of the governmental powers of the State as may be entrusted to them," and the "number, nature and duration of the powers conferred upon [them] . . . and the territory over which they shall be exercised rests in the absolute discretion of the State." The relationship of the States to the Federal Government could hardly be less analogous. . . .

Since we find the so-called federal analogy inapposite to a consideration of the constitutional validity of state legislative apportionment schemes, we necessarily hold that the Equal Protection Clause requires both houses of a state legislature to be apportioned on a population basis. . . .

We do not believe that the concept of bicameralism is rendered anachronistic and meaningless when the predominant basis of representation in the two state legislative bodies is required to be the same—population. A prime reason for bicameralism, modernly considered, is to insure mature and deliberate consideration of, and to prevent precipitate action on, proposed legislative measures. Simply because the controlling criterion for apportioning representation is required to be the same in both houses does not mean that there will be no differences in the composition and complexion of the two bodies. Different constituencies can be represented in the two houses. One body could be composed of single-member districts while the other could have at least some multimember districts. The length of terms of the legislators in the separate bodies could differ. The numerical size of the two bodies could be made to differ, even significantly, and the geographical size of districts from which legislators are elected could also be made to differ. And apportionment in one house could be arranged so as to balance off minor inequities in the representation of certain areas in the other house. In summary, these and other factors could be, and are presently in many States, utilized to engender differing complexions and collective attitudes in the two bodies of a state legislature, although both are apportioned substantially on a population basis.

VI

By holding that as a federal constitutional requisite both houses of a state legislature must be apportioned on a population basis, we mean that the Equal Protection Clause requires that a State make an honest and good faith effort to construct districts, in both houses of its legislature, as nearly of equal population as is practicable. We realize that it is a practical impossibility to arrange legislative districts so that each one has an identical number of residents, or citizens, or voters. Mathematical exactness or precision is hardly a workable constitutional requirement.

. . . For the present, we deem it expedient not to attempt to spell out any precise constitutional tests. . . . So long as the divergences from a strict population standard are based on legitimate considerations incident to the effectuation of a rational state policy, some deviations from the equal-population principle are constitutionally permissible with respect to the apportionment of seats in either or both of the two houses of a bicameral state legislature. But neither history alone, nor economic or other sorts of group interests, are permissible factors in attempting to justify disparities from population-based representation. . . . A consideration that appears to be of more substance in justifying some deviations from population-based representation in state legislatures is that of insuring some voice to political subdivisions, as political subdivisions. . . .

VIII

That the Equal Protection Clause requires that both houses of a state legislature be apportioned on a population basis does not mean that States cannot adopt some reasonable plan for periodic revision of their apportionment schemes. Decennial reapportionment appears to be a rational approach to readjustment of legislative representation in order to take into account population shifts and growth. . . .

Mr. Justice HARLAN, dissenting.

Since it can, I think, be shown beyond doubt that state legislative apportionments, as such, are wholly free of constitutional limitations, save such as may be imposed by the Republican Form of Government Clause (Const., Art. IV, §4), the Court's action now bringing them within the purview of the Fourteenth Amendment amounts to nothing less than an exercise of the amending power by this Court. . . .

The Court relies exclusively on that portion of §1 of the Fourteenth Amendment which provides that no State shall "deny to any person within its jurisdiction the equal protection of the laws," and disregards entirely the significance of §2, which reads:

> Representatives shall be apportioned among the several States according to their respective numbers, counting the whole number of persons in each State, excluding Indians not taxed. *But when the right to vote at any election for* the choice of electors for President and Vice President of the United States, Representatives in Congress, *the Executive and Judicial officers of a State, or the members of the Legislature thereof, is denied* to any of the male inhabitants of such State, being twenty-one years of age, and citizens of the United States, *or in any way abridged,* except for participation in rebellion, or other crime, the basis of representation therein shall be reduced in the proportion which the number of such male citizens shall bear to the whole number of male citizens twenty-one years of age in such State.

(Emphasis added.) . . . I am unable to understand the Court's utter disregard of the second section which expressly recognizes the States' power to deny "or in any way" abridge the right of their inhabitants to vote for "the members of the [State] Legislature," and its express provision of a remedy for such denial or abridgment. The comprehensive scope of the second section and its particular reference to the state legislatures preclude the suggestion that the first section was intended to have the result reached by the Court today. . . .

The history of the adoption of the Fourteenth Amendment provides conclusive evidence that neither those who proposed nor those who ratified the Amendment believed that the Equal Protection Clause limited the power of the States to apportion their legislatures as they saw fit. . . . In the House, Thaddeus Stevens . . . explained . . . the second section, which he said he considered "the most important in the article." Its effect, he said, was to fix "the basis of representation in Congress." In unmistakable terms, he recognized the power of a State to withhold the right to vote:

> If any State shall exclude any of her adult male citizens from the elective franchise, or abridge that right, she shall forfeit her right to representation in the same proportion. The effect of this provision will be either to compel the States to grant universal suffrage or so to shear them of their power as to keep them forever in a hopeless minority in the national Government, both legislative and executive. . . .

Toward the end of the debate three days later, Mr. Bingham, the author of the first section in the Reconstruction Committee and its leading proponent, concluded his discussion of it with the following:

> To be sure we all agree, and the great body of the people of this country agree, and the committee thus far in reporting measures of reconstruction

agree, that *the exercise of the elective franchise, though it be one of the privileges of a citizen of the Republic, is exclusively under the control of the States.*

(Emphasis added.). . .

In the Senate, it was fully understood by everyone that neither the first nor the second section interfered with the right of the States to regulate the elective franchise. . . .

Reports of the debates in the state legislatures on the ratification of the Fourteenth Amendment are not generally available. There is, however, compelling indirect evidence. Of the 23 loyal States which ratified the Amendment before 1870, five had constitutional provisions for apportionment of at least one house of their respective legislatures which wholly disregarded the spread of population. Ten more had constitutional provisions which gave primary emphasis to population, but which applied also other principles, such as partial ratios and recognition of political subdivisions, which were intended to favor sparsely settled areas. Can it be seriously contended that the legislatures of these States, almost two-thirds of those concerned, would have ratified an amendment which might render their own States' constitutions unconstitutional?. . .

The Court's elaboration of its new "constitutional" doctrine indicates how far—and how unwisely—it has strayed from the appropriate bounds of its authority. The consequence of today's decision is that in all but the handful of States which may already satisfy the new requirements the local District Court or, it may be, the state courts, are given blanket authority and the constitutional duty to supervise apportionment of the State Legislatures. It is difficult to imagine a more intolerable and inappropriate interference by the judiciary with the independent legislatures of the States. . . .

Generalities cannot obscure the cold truth that cases of this type are not amenable to the development of judicial standards. No set of standards can guide a court which has to decide how many legislative districts a State shall have, or what the shape of the districts shall be, or where to draw a particular district line. No judicially manageable standard can determine whether a State should have single-member districts or multimember districts or some combination of both. No such standard can control the balance between keeping up with population shifts and having stable districts. In all these respects, the courts will be called upon to make particular decisions with respect to which a principle of equally populated districts will be of no assistance whatsoever. . . .

What is done today deepens my conviction that judicial entry into this realm is profoundly ill-advised and constitutionally impermissible. . . . [T]hese decisions give support to a current mistaken view of the Constitution and the constitutional function of this Court. This view, in a nutshell, is that every major social ill in this country can find its cure in some constitutional "principle," and that this Court should "take the lead" in promoting reform when other branches of government fail to act. The Constitution is not a panacea for every blot upon the public welfare, nor should this Court, ordained as a judicial body, be thought of as a general haven for reform movements. The Constitution is an instrument of government, fundamental to which is the premise that in a diffusion of governmental authority lies the greatest promise that this Nation will realize liberty for all its citizens. This Court, limited in function in accordance with that premise, does not serve its

high purpose when it exceeds its authority, even to satisfy justified impatience with
the slow workings of the political process. For when, in the name of constitutional
interpretation, the Court *adds* something to the Constitution that was deliberately
excluded from it, the Court in reality substitutes its view of what should be so for
the amending process. . . .

_____

>> *What Is the Harm from Malapportionment?*   The Court clearly thinks in these
cases that malapportionment is a bad thing—but why? What precisely is the harm
that arises from unequally sized districts? Is it inequality in the relative ability to
influence elected officials? Is it a dignitary affront to citizenship? Does malapportionment have any concrete political consequences?

One obvious consequence of malapportionment is that it can freeze relative
partisan power in the legislature by ignoring changes in the number and distribution of party supporters in a jurisdiction, thereby reducing the political responsiveness of the legislature. In extreme cases, malapportionment over long periods of
time can place control of the legislature permanently in the hands of a political
minority. As the Baltimore-based journalist and satirist H.L. Mencken complained
nearly a century ago, "[t]he yokels hang on because old apportionments give them
unfair advantages. The vote of a malarious peasant on the lower Eastern Shore
counts as much as the votes of twelve Baltimoreans." H.L. MENCKEN, A CARNIVAL
OF BUNCOMBE 160 (Malcolm Moos ed., 1956). More recent and more scientific
studies confirm this intuition. *See* Andrew Gelman and Gary King, *Enhancing Democracy Through Legislative Redistricting*, 88 AM. POL. SCI. REV. 541 (1994), which finds,
perhaps unsurprisingly, that redistricting increases legislative responsiveness and
reduces partisan bias compared to no redistricting.

So who actually benefitted from the Supreme Court's one-person, one-vote
cases? Since malapportionment typically favored representation of sparsely settled
rural areas at the expense of densely settled urban areas, one might have expected
reapportionment in the wake of the one-person, one-vote rulings to favor Democrats over Republicans, thereby causing an overall liberal shift in public policy.
This turns out to have been the case in some regions of the country, but not in all.
According to one study, the effect of eliminating malapportionment varied from
region to region:

> In the South, malapportionment advantaged the Democrats, because rural
> areas voted much more Democratic than urban areas. In the Northeast
> and North Central, malapportionment tended to advantage Republicans,
> because rural areas in those regions voted heavily Republican while urban
> areas voted Democratic. In the West, a more mixed picture emerges, and
> the differences between urban and rural are less pronounced than in
> other regions.

Stephen Ansolabehere and James M. Snyder, Jr., *Reapportionment and Party Realignment in the American States*, 153 U. PA. L. REV. 433, 436-437 (2004). Overall, however,
the authors find that the one-person, one-vote revolution contributed to the left-
ward movement of the Democratic Party and strengthened the position of advocates of racial integration and the civil rights movement. Ironically, though, the

reapportionment revolution also "increased representation of wealthier areas at the expense of poor areas" because reapportionment decreased the overrepresentation of rural areas, nationally the poorest parts of the country, in favor not just of urban areas, but also of suburban areas, which were the wealthiest. *Id.* at 453-457.

In another study, the same authors examined the intrastate distribution of state transfers of resources (otherwise known, perhaps, as "pork") to more than three thousand counties around the nation both before and after the Supreme Court's one-person, one-vote decisions. In the period immediately preceding *Reynolds*, they found a strong relationship between legislative seats per person and the amount of "intergovernmental transfers" per person. Counties with a disproportionately high number of state legislators in comparison to their populations received, perhaps unsurprisingly, more revenue from the state than counties whose populations were comparatively underrepresented. Following the introduction of one-person, one-vote, and the subsequent equalization of representation ratios in state legislatures, the distribution of state funds among counties also equalized. The result was that in

> the most underrepresented counties . . . equal votes increased state revenues by $88 per person per year. In the most overrepresented counties, the rule of one person, one vote reduced state revenues by $268 per person per year. The cumulative effect on the distribution of funds was to . . . shift . . . approximately $7 billion annually of state transfers to local governments from counties that had previously been overrepresented to counties that had previously been underrepresented.

STEPHEN ANSOLABEHERE AND JAMES M. SNYDER, JR., THE END OF INEQUALITY: ONE PERSON, ONE VOTE AND THE TRANSFORMATION OF AMERICAN POLITICS 208-209 (2009).

Is this kind of economic harm from malapportionment sufficient by itself to justify constitutional invalidation of unequally sized districts?

≫ *How Equal Is Equal?* If the Equal Protection Clause requires that legislative districts contain approximately equal voting populations, just how exact must this correspondence be? The Court has complicated this inquiry by holding that the Constitution mandates different standards for state and congressional apportionment.

Congressional Districting. In *Kirkpatrick v. Preisler*, 394 U.S. 542 (1969), the Court held that Article I, §2 "permits only the limited population variances which are unavoidable despite a good-faith effort to achieve absolute equality, or for which justification is shown." Thus, by and large, where congressional apportionment is concerned, absolute equality is required except where it is impossible in good faith to achieve, or where the state can show that population variations are "necessary to achieve some legitimate state objective," *id.* at 741, a high standard that states have rarely bothered to attempt to satisfy. In *Karcher v. Daggett*, 462 U.S. 725 (1983), the Court addressed in greater detail the application of the equal-population principle to congressional apportionment. Under New Jersey's 1982 reapportionment plan, the population of the largest congressional district exceeded that of the smallest by less than 1 percent. New Jersey contended that this degree of equality was sufficiently close to absolute equality to absolve the state of any responsibility to justify what minimal deviations the plan presented. The Court rejected this contention and struck down the plan.

The Court began by holding that under Article I, §2,

> two basic questions shape litigation over population deviations in state legislation apportioning congressional districts. First, the court must consider whether the population differences among districts could have been reduced or eliminated altogether by a good-faith effort to draw districts of equal population. Parties challenging apportionment legislation must bear the burden of proof on this issue, and if they fail to show that the differences could have been avoided the apportionment scheme must be upheld. If, however, the plaintiffs can establish that the population differences were not the result of a good-faith effort to achieve equality, the State must bear the burden of proving that each significant variance between districts was necessary to achieve some legitimate goal.

New Jersey argued that its plan should be regarded per se as a good faith effort to achieve equality because "the maximum population deviation among districts is smaller than the predictable undercount in available census data"; in other words, the state's plan fell within the margin of error of the best available figures. The Court, however, rejected the notion that there is a *de minimis* level of deviation in congressional apportionments. Equal representation would be eroded, the Court said, by such a principle because "[i]f state legislators knew that a certain *de minimis* level of population differences was acceptable, they would doubtless strive to achieve that level rather than equality." Moreover, problems with the data, the Court explained, apply equally to any population-based standard the Court might choose, and only the absolute equality standard "reflects the aspirations of Art. I, §2."

Because the plaintiffs had shown at trial that lines could be drawn that produced even smaller deviations than those produced by the state's plan, the burden then shifted to New Jersey to justify its deviations. The Court held that such justifications must be evaluated on a case-by-case basis, including consideration of "the size of the deviations, the importance of the State's interests, the consistency with which the plan as a whole reflects those interests, and the availability of alternatives that might substantially vindicate those interests yet approximate population equality more closely." New Jersey attempted to justify its plan as necessary to preserve the voting strength of racial minority groups, but the Court found this an inadequate explanation for the plan's deviations.

In a concurring opinion, Justice Stevens suggested that an examination of the bizarre shape of the district boundaries suggested gerrymandering (see Section C.2 below), which cast significant doubt on the good faith of the legislature.

Most recently, in *Tennant v. Jefferson County Commission*, 567 U.S. 758 (2012) (per curiam), the Court surprised observers by upholding a West Virginia congressional districting plan with a 0.79 percent population variance. The state did not contend that drawing districts with a lower population variance was infeasible; instead, it argued that the variance was justified by the state's goals of avoiding splitting counties among congressional districts and preserving the "core of existing districts." The Court found that no alternative districting plan available to the legislature could have satisfied its goals while also producing a lower population variance.

State Legislative Districting. The Court has taken a different approach when a state redistricts its own legislature rather than Congress. In *Mahan v. Howell*, 410 U.S. 315 (1973), the Court held that the Equal Protection Clause does not require application of the *Kirkpatrick* standard to state apportionment decisions. Rather, the correct test is the one enunciated in *Reynolds*, which requires only that districts in state reapportionments be "as nearly of equal population as practicable." This test is more lenient because it allows a state to diverge from the equal-population principle "incident to the effectuation of a rational state policy." What might such a policy be? In *Mahan*, the Court held that the state's policy of "maintaining the integrity of political subdivision lines" — that is, a desire to place entire political units such as towns and villages completely within the same legislative district — justified deviations from absolute equality of up to 9.6 percent from the ideal distribution in individual districts, and an overall average deviation in all districts of 3.89 percent.

Because of the uncertainty as to what degree of inequality in state apportionment was tolerable and the types of justifications that would suffice to sustain inequality, the federal courts soon became inundated with state apportionment litigation. In an effort to permit lower courts to rid themselves of some of these cases, the Court in *Gaffney v. Cummings*, 412 U.S. 735 (1973), held that "minor deviations from mathematical equality among state legislative districts are insufficient to make out a prima facie case of invidious discrimination under the Fourteenth Amendment so as to require justification by the State." By so holding, the Court made it easier for defendant states to have apportionment cases dismissed for failure to state a claim.

The Court explained this decision by noting that

> the basic statistical materials which legislatures and courts usually have to work with are the results of the United States census taken at 10-year intervals. . . . These figures may be as accurate as such immense undertakings can be, but they are inherently less than absolutely accurate. . . . The "population" of a legislative district is just not that knowable to be used for such refined judgments.

Furthermore, the Court observed, "[t]he United States census is more of an event than a process. It measures population at only a single instant in time. District populations are constantly changing, often at different rates in either direction, up or down." Finally, the Court said that the "worthy goal" of "fair and effective representation" is not furthered "by making the standards of reapportionment so difficult to satisfy that the reapportionment task is recurringly removed from legislative hands and performed by federal courts. . . . " The Court then held that the plaintiffs had failed to state a prima facie case of discrimination merely by showing that the deviations from ideal equality under the state's plan were no more than 8 percent for any single district, and averaged only about 2 percent for all districts.

In later cases, the Court has suggested that state apportionment plans with population deviations below 10 percent are prima facie valid under the one-person, one-vote standard. *See, e.g., Brown v. Thomson*, 462 U.S. 835 (1983). Recently, in *Harris v. Arizona Independent Redistricting Commission*, 136 S. Ct. 1301 (2016), a unanimous Court explained that deviations below 10 percent were minor and "do not by themselves, 'make out a prima facie case of invidious discrimination under the Fourteenth Amendment so as to require justification by the State.'" On the other hand, just because a plan's deviations are within 10 percent does not insulate it entirely from judicial review; apparently, such a plan's prima facie validity can be rebutted by evidence that even minor deviations resulted from purely partisan efforts by the party in power to gerrymander the out party into permanent weakness. *Cox v. Larios*, 542 U.S. 947 (2004) (summarily affirming a lower court decision so holding). (Partisan gerrymandering is considered below in Section C.2.) In *Harris v. Arizona Independent Redistricting Commission, supra,* the Court explained that in order to mount a successful attack on state legislative redistricting plans in which the deviation is less than 10 percent, plaintiffs "must show that it is more probable than not that a deviation of less than 10% reflects the predominance of illegitimate reapportionment factors rather than . . . 'legitimate considerations. . . .'" The Court warned that the bar in such challenges is high, noting that "attacks on deviations under 10% will succeed rarely, in unusual cases."

» *What Justifications for Population Deviation Are Valid?*   In both its congressional and state legislative lines of case law, the Court has indicated that some degree of population inequality may be tolerable when the state has a good enough justification for drawing its districts in a way that deviates from strict equality. But what counts as a valid justification for such variance? In *Tennant, supra,* the Court identified several: avoiding splitting political subdivisions (such as counties) among different districts; minimizing population shifts between districts; preserving the cores of prior districts; and "avoiding contests between incumbents." In another branch of case law involving challenges to redistricting plans under the Voting Rights Act, the Court has identified several other valid state interests that apply to the drawing of district lines: compactness, contiguity, keeping communities of interest intact, and compliance with the non-discrimination provisions of the Voting Rights Act itself. These factors are taken up in greater detail in Chapter 5.

» *Local Governments.*   Do the principles of *Wesberry* and *Reynolds* apply to local governments as well as to the state and national legislatures? The Court said yes in *Avery v. Midland County*, 390 U.S. 474 (1968). Midland County, Texas, was governed by a five-person Commissioners Court. One Commissioner was elected at large and the other four from districts. The populations of the districts were: 414, 828, 852, and 67,906. This imbalance resulted from the inclusion in a single district of the entire city of Midland, home of 95 percent of the county's population.

The Court ruled that the Equal Protection Clause "reaches the exercise of state power however manifested, whether exercised directly or through subdivisions of the State. . . . The actions of local government *are* the actions of the State." When a state "delegates lawmaking power to local government and provides for the election of local officials from districts specified by statute . . . it must insure that those qualified to vote have the right to an equally effective voice in the election process." The fact that the state legislature might itself be properly apportioned, the Court held, did not insulate subdivisions from the requirements of the Fourteenth Amendment.

» *Judicial Elections.*   In most states, some or all judges are popularly elected. Typically, the state is laid out into judicial districts, with the voters in each district electing judges who serve locally. In some states, even supreme court justices are elected by district rather than at large. Must such judicial districts satisfy the same equipopulation requirement as legislative districts? In *Wells v. Edwards*, the Supreme Court said no when it summarily affirmed a lower court decision holding judicial elections to be exempt from the requirement of one-person, one-vote. 347 F. Supp. 453 (M.D. La. 1972) (three-judge court), *summarily aff'd*, 409 U.S. 1095 (1973). According to the district court, "[t]he primary purpose of one-man, one-vote apportionment is to make sure that each official member of an elected body speaks for approximately the same number of constituents. But . . . '[j]udges do not represent people, they serve people.' Thus, the rationale behind the one-man, one-vote principle, which evolved out of efforts to preserve a truly representative form of government, is simply not relevant to the makeup of the judiciary."

Is there no sense in which an elected judge "represents" his or her "constituents"? What might explain the following provision of the Michigan Constitution: "The court of appeals shall consist. . .of nine judges who shall be nominated and elected . . . from districts . . . as nearly as possible of equal population. . . ." Or how about this provision from the Illinois Constitution:

> The State is divided into five Judicial Districts for the selection of Supreme and Appellate Court judges. The First Judicial District consists of Cook County [most of which consists of the City of Chicago]. The remainder of the State shall be divided by law into four Judicial Districts of substantially equal population. . . .

Ill. Const. art. VI, §2.

»   *The Relevant Population Base.*   It is easy enough to articulate a standard of one-person, one-vote, but considerably more difficult to implement it in practice. One recurring problem involves the question of who ought to count as a "person" for purposes of satisfying the one-person, one-vote standard. Should a district's population for apportionment purposes be based on its total resident population? The local population may include resident aliens and noncitizens, for example, who are not entitled to vote. Should they be counted for purposes of allocating representation if they are not entitled to representation? What about children or disenfranchised felons? What exactly is the one-person, one-vote standard intended to measure? Population? Citizen population? Voting population?

These questions may seem highly technical, but the courts have been required to answer them because they are often relevant to the actual distribution of political power. For example, in *Burns v. Richardson*, 384 U.S. 73 (1966), the Court confronted a challenge to Hawaii's decision to apportion representation in the state legislature on the basis of registered voters. The plaintiffs claimed that *Reynolds* required the use of total population. The Court framed the problem in the following terms:

> the dispute over use of distribution according to registered voters as a basis for Hawaiian apportionment arises because of the sizable differences in results produced by that distribution in contrast to that produced by the distribution according to the State's total population, as measured by the federal census figures. In 1960 Oahu's share of Hawaii's total population was 79%. Its share of persons actually registered was 73%. On the basis of total population, Oahu would be assigned 40 members of the

51-member house of representatives; on the basis of registered voters it would be entitled to 37 representatives. Probably because of uneven distribution of military residents — largely unregistered — the differences among various districts on Oahu are even more striking. For example, on a total population basis, Oahu's ninth and tenth representative districts would be entitled to 11 representatives, and the fifteenth and sixteenth representative districts would be entitled to eight. On a registered voter basis, however, the ninth and tenth districts claim only six representatives and the fifteenth and sixteenth districts are entitled to 10.

The Court maintained that the Equal Protection Clause does not require any particular method of counting represented populations. No decision of the Court, it said, has

> suggested that the States are required to include aliens, transients, short-term or temporary residents, or persons denied the vote for conviction of crime, in the apportionment base by which their legislators are distributed and against which compliance with the Equal Protection Clause is to be measured. The decision to include or exclude any such group involves choices about the nature of representation with which we have been shown no constitutionally founded reason to interfere.

Nevertheless, the Court noted possible problems with using the actual number of *registered* voters as a basis for apportionment. The number of registered voters is relatively easy to count. However,

> [u]se of a registered voter or actual voter basis presents an additional problem. Such a basis depends not only upon criteria such as govern state citizenship, but also upon the extent of political activity of those eligible to register and vote. Each is thus susceptible to improper influences by which those in political power might be able to perpetuate underrepresentation of groups constitutionally entitled to participate in the electoral process, or perpetuate a "ghost of prior malapportionment." Moreover, "fluctuations in the number of registered voters in a given election may be sudden and substantial, caused by such fortuitous factors as a peculiarly controversial election issue, a particularly popular candidate, or even weather conditions." *Ellis v. Mayor & City Council of Baltimore*, 352 F.2d 123, 130 (4th Cir. 1965). Such effects must be particularly a matter of concern where, as in the case of Hawaii apportionment, registration figures derived from a single election are made controlling for as long as 10 years.

Despite these concerns, the Court upheld the use of registered voters on the ground that "on this record it was found to have produced a distribution of legislators not substantially different from that which would have resulted from the use of a permissible population basis."

The Court did not directly address this problem again for a full half-century, but when it finally returned to the question it reached essentially the same conclusion: the Equal Protection Clause does not require states to use any particular population base, and it permits states considerable (though not unlimited) latitude in choosing how to define the relevant populations. In *Evenwel v. Abbott*, 126 S. Ct. 1120 (2016), Texas drew its state legislative districts on the basis of total population — the population base used by all states for decades. The plaintiffs made the novel argument that drawing districts on the basis of total population violates equal protection by diluting the votes of *eligible voters*. Just because districts contain equal numbers of *people*, the plaintiffs reasoned, does not mean that they contain equal numbers of *voters*. Some districts, they contended, may contain a larger proportion of noncitizens than others, or may contain a larger proportion of people ineligible to vote for other reasons (such as minority). Consequently, the vote of a voter who lives in a district with a large proportion of people ineligible to vote carries greater weight than the votes of voters who live in districts where a greater proportion of the population is eligible to vote. Thus, the plaintiffs argued, equal protection requires equalization of "citizen-voting-age-population" rather than equalization of total population.

The Court, refusing to disturb "decades, even centuries," of "settled practice," rejected this contention, calling the use of total population "plainly permissible." "Nonvoters," the Court explained, "have an important stake in many policy debates — children, their parents, even their grandparents, for example, have a stake in a strong public-education system — and in receiving constituent services, such as help navigating public-benefits bureaucracies. By ensuring that each representative is subject to requests and suggestions from the same number of constituents, total-population apportionment promotes equitable and effective representation."

>> *The Strange Case of Counting Incarcerated Non-Voters.* Where does someone live for purposes of the census? This question is easy to answer in most cases because most people have only one residence and live there permanently. The question can be more difficult to answer in some circumstances — for example, where people have two residences and divide their time between them, or where military personnel are stationed long-term in places other than their permanent residence. One of the strangest circumstances in which this question has lately arisen is with respect to counting incarcerated prisoners. Relatively few people are incarcerated in the same community in which they reside. Prisons often are built in remote rural areas with small populations, whereas most criminals — simply as a matter of mathematical probability — reside in populous areas.

The practice of the Census Bureau is to count prisoners as residents of the district in which they are incarcerated. This can lead to odd situations in which a substantial portion of the population of a rural district can be comprised of prisoners who not only are warehoused in the local prison, but are ineligible to vote. The result can be overrepresentation in Congress and the state or local legislature — in some cases very substantial overrepresentation — of the non-incarcerated population of these prison districts. For example, before redistricting pursuant to the 2010 census, 50 percent of the population in one city council district in Rome, New York, consisted of incarcerated prisoners who were ineligible to vote under state law, who could not travel to the polls to vote, and who predominantly lived downstate when they committed the crimes of which they were convicted. In one Maryland state legislative district, nearly 20 percent of the population consisted of incarcerated prisoners. A city council ward in Anamosa, Iowa, consisted of about 1,320 prisoners and about 60 non-incarcerated residents. *See* Prison Policy Initiative, http://www .prisonersofthecensus.org/; Dale E. Ho, *Captive Constituents: Prison-Based Gerrymandering and the Current Redistricting Cycle*, 22 STAN. L. & POL. REV. 355 (2011).

Recently, however, eleven states have enacted legislation requiring state and local redistricters to count prisoners where they lived before being incarcerated rather than in the community in which they are presently incarcerated: California, Colorado, Connecticut, Delaware, Illinois, Maryland, Nevada, New Jersey, New York, Virginia, and Washington. Many localities have also committed to avoiding prison gerrymandering. The U.S. Census Bureau, however, has shown no interest in counting prisoners as residents of the communities in which they previously lived. However, the Census Bureau has since 2010 agreed to provide data concerning prison populations to states in a way that permits them to avoid counting incarcerated populations at the point of incarceration, if they so wish.

Suppose the legislature does not take such action. Does the practice of counting locally incarcerated prisoners in the population base for redistricting purposes violate the Equal Protection Clause by unconstitutionally diluting the votes of eligible voters? Plaintiffs pressing this argument in litigation have seen mixed results. In *Calvin v. Jefferson County Board of Commissioners*, 172 F.Supp.3d 1292 (N.D. Fla. 2016), the court concluded that the inclusion in the population base of ineligible voters with no connection to the locality constituted illegal vote dilution. In *Davidson v. City of Cranston*, 837 F.3d 135 (1st Cir. 2016), the First Circuit reached the opposite conclusion. Applying *Evenwel*, the court held that the Constitution neither compels nor forbids the inclusion of incarcerated prisoners in the population base for purposes of redistricting. *See also In re Initiative Petition No. 426*, 465 P.3d 1244 (Okla. 2020) (rejecting claim that proposed ballot initiative to bar prison gerrymandering was unconstitutional).

>> *Counting Relevant "Persons": The Problem of Minority Undercounts.* Even once an apportionment decision has been made concerning the relevant population base, a further issue remains: how are the relevant "persons" to be counted? Appropriate, accurate data may not be available. Census data may be obsolete or of marginal usefulness. For example, census data is collected for "census tracts," small geographical units that are convenient for the Census Bureau, but rarely correspond to the boundaries of election districts. Some kinds of population figures must be wholly extrapolated from various kinds of databases. Consider the difficulties in attempting to come up with the number of resident citizens of voting age, for example.

Compounding these counting difficulties is the fact that not every kind of group shows up equally well in census or other population data. Some groups are much more difficult to count than others—illegal immigrants, for example, or the homeless. One of the most consistent, best-documented problems in counting various sub-populations is the phenomenon of the minority undercount. The Census Bureau estimates the 1990 census undercount for the entire U.S. population—the total number of Americans missed by census enumerators—at 1.6 percent. The 1990 undercount for blacks, in contrast, is estimated at 4.57 percent, and for persons of Hispanic origin 4.99 percent. By the time of the 2000 census, improvements in counting techniques lowered the black population undercount, but it was still significant at nearly 2 percent. The Hispanic undercount in 2000 is estimated at

0.71 percent. However, minority populations tend not to be distributed evenly across the country; black populations tend to be disproportionately urban, and Hispanic populations tend to be concentrated either in urban areas or disproportionately in certain geographical regions. This means that a consistent undercount of racial and ethnic minority groups disproportionately affects states (and districts) with large urban populations, such as New York and California, or Southwestern states such as Arizona and California (again). On the national level, this phenomenon can sometimes mean the difference between gaining or losing a seat in Congress. On the state level, it reduces the political influence of urban areas—and of the minority populations they contain—within the state legislature.

The Census Bureau has developed a sophisticated method of correcting undercounts through the use of statistical sampling. In this method, the Bureau targets scientifically selected areas for a far more thorough kind of count than it does in the rest of the nation. Using these results, the Bureau compares data collected by the different methods and from this differential statistically estimates actual populations. The accuracy of this method is apparently quite high, and it could in theory be used to correct for undercounts of all kinds, including minority undercounts. As might be expected, the use of statistical sampling has become politically controversial because of its potential to alter population counts, and thus legislative apportionment, throughout the nation. Although the Census Bureau has been permitted to collect sampled data and to continue refining its sampling and projection techniques, Republicans in Congress have generally prevented federal agencies from utilizing the sampled data for purposes of apportionment or for the allocation of federal programmatic funds. Opponents of the use of sampled data seem to believe, probably correctly, that any correction of minority undercounts will tend to favor Democrats, since blacks in particular vote heavily Democratic.

Legal action to force the use of the more accurate, sampled data has been unsuccessful. In *Wisconsin v. City of New York*, 517 U.S. 1 (1996), the Supreme Court rejected a constitutional challenge to the 1990 census brought by New York City challenging an administrative decision by the Director of the Census Bureau to refrain from using statistically corrected data in the 1990 census. The city argued that the Census Clause of the U.S. Constitution, Art. I, §2, cl. 3, which calls for an "actual enumeration" of the population, requires the Bureau to use the most accurate data possible. It also argued that the equality principle of *Wesberry* and the other one-person, one-vote decisions required apportionments to be conducted as accurately as possible. The Court held that the Director's decision concerning how to conduct and report population statistics was entitled to deference, and rejected any application of *Wesberry*'s heightened standard of review to the use of counting methodology in the apportionment process.

By the time of the 2000 census, a Democratic administration controlled the Census Bureau, and decided, over the objections of the Republican-controlled Congress, that statistical sampling should be used to determine congressional apportionment following the 2000 census. In a reversal of the litigating positions taken with respect to the 1990 census, opponents of sampling sued to block the use of statistically enhanced data. The issue reached the Supreme Court in *Department of Commerce v. United States House of Representatives*, 525 U.S. 316 (1999). In a decision based purely on statutory grounds, the Court held that the Census Act did not authorize the Census Bureau to use sampled data for purposes of determining congressional apportionment.

In a subsequent case, however, the Court rejected a strict reading of the constitutional term "actual enumeration." In *Utah v. Evans*, 536 U.S. 452 (2002), Utah challenged the Bureau's use of a statistical technique known as "hot-deck imputation" to resolve conflicting information about where individuals live, the use of which in 2000 shifted a congressional representative from Utah to North Carolina. After holding that the federal law prohibiting sampling did not apply to this technique, the Court went on to reject a constitutional challenge to the use of this form of estimation. The Constitution uses the word "actual," said the Court, to distinguish an apportionment based on a census from the initial, provisional apportionment written by the Framers into Article I, §2, cl. 2, which was based on relatively uninformed speculation about the populations of the original states. The word "enumeration," the Court held, had a meaning in the eighteenth century synonymous with "counting," and carried no connotation of any particular "counting methodology." In consequence, the Bureau could use the imputation method of counting, at least under the limited circumstances of this case, in which the method was used only as a last resort, and where the only other way to proceed would have been to resolve conflicting information by arbitrarily treating as unoccupied a dwelling that, according to at least some information in the Bureau's possession, was in fact occupied.

Under these decisions, Congress has a great deal of discretion in directing how census figures are to be used by federal government agencies and by Congress itself in apportionment. Congress, however, seems to have no authority to direct states in the use of census figures for purposes of apportionment on the state and local levels. Thus, it appears to be open to states to use adjusted census figures for their own purposes, so long as the Census Bureau continues to make such figures publicly available. This raises the possibility that apportionment in state legislatures could be conducted on the basis of more accurate and potentially fairer data.

This possibility has not always proved welcome to state legislatures. For example, in 2000 the Virginia legislature enacted a statute forbidding the use of adjusted census data for any purpose, including apportionment of the state legislature and local legislative bodies. Federal legal issues concerning this law arose under Section 5 of the Voting Rights Act (considered in the next chapter). The lower court dismissed the case for lack of ripeness without reaching the merits, and the Supreme Court summarily affirmed. *Virginia v. Reno*, 117 F. Supp. 2d 46 (2000) (three-judge court), *summarily aff'd*, 531 U.S. 1062 (2001). Are there any other grounds on which a state law like Virginia's might be subject to challenge?

>> *The Census and Citizenship.* In preparation for the 2020 census, the official responsible for formulating and administering the census questionnaire, U.S. Secretary of Commerce Wilbur Ross, announced that the census would add a new question inquiring about the citizenship of respondents. Secretary Ross claimed that the question was being added at the request of the U.S. Justice Department, which said it would find the data useful for enforcing provisions of the Voting Rights Act (considered below in Chapter 5). Critics of the Trump Administration reacted with immediate skepticism, arguing that the question was in fact being added for the nakedly partisan purpose of depressing the response rate of Latino and other

immigrant groups, which in turn would lower population estimates mainly in Democratic-leaning states and would concurrently depress the transfer of federal programmatic funding to those areas. This view was based on the belief, supported by earlier research by the Census Bureau itself, that immigrant populations would be less inclined to respond to the census if required to disclose their citizenship status. *See* Thomas P. Wolf and Brianna Cea, *A Critical History of the United States Census and Citizenship Questions*, 108 GEO. L.J. ONLINE 1 (2019). A recent study by Harvard's Kennedy School of Government using data from the last census found that asking a question about citizenship would reduce the reported number of Hispanics by 6.1 million, or about 12 percent of that population group. Matthew A. Baum, et al., *Estimating the Effect of Asking about Citizenship on the U.S. Census: Results from a Randomized Control Trial* (HKS Research Working Paper Series, April 2019); Justin Levitt, *Citizenship and the Census*, 119 COLUM. L. REV. 1355 (2019).

In a 5-4 decision, the Supreme Court overturned the Secretary's decision on the ground that the Secretary's proffered reason was "pretextual," and thus an invalid ground under the federal Administrative Procedure Act, which requires agency decisions to be well-grounded, and not "arbitrary and capricious." *Department of Commerce v. New York*, 139 S.Ct. 2551 (2019). Citing factual findings made below, the Court found that the motivation for adding the citizenship question came from Secretary Ross himself, and that the Commerce Department had made unusual efforts to solicit a supporting request from the Justice Department. Thus, the Court held, "[w]e are presented . . . with an explanation for agency action that is incongruent with what the record reveals about the agency's priorities and decisionmaking process."

While the case was pending on appeal, new evidence was uncovered by the plaintiffs strongly supporting their claim that the Administration's decision to add the census question was motivated by purely partisan concerns. The new evidence showed that Thomas Hofeller, a leading Republican mapmaker, had devised and promoted to Republican officials a plan to increase Republican representation in the 2020 redistricting cycle by depressing counts of immigrant populations, and by providing statistics that would facilitate redistricting on the basis of citizen population rather than on the basis of total population — a tactic that would tend to benefit Republicans. *See* Michael Wines, "Deceased G.O.P. Strategist's Hard Drives Reveal New Details on the Census Citizenship Question," *New York Times* (May 30, 2019).

>> *The Remedy: Developing a Redistricting Plan.* When a jurisdiction is malapportioned, or over time becomes malapportioned due to population shifts, it violates the one-person, one-vote principle. The remedy for such a constitutional violation obviously is to redraw district lines to comply with the requirement of population equality. Because a national census is taken only every ten years, shifts in population that lead to malapportionment often slip by unnoticed between censuses. However, the exactitude that the Constitution requires in drawing district lines, along with constant shifts in population distributions, means that every jurisdiction is virtually guaranteed the need to redistrict itself following each decennial census. As a result, the year or two following each census is predictably a busy time for state legislatures as they engage in the redistricting process, with equally predictable litigation over redistricting plans that have been adopted or proposed.

What happens when a jurisdiction is adjudicated to be in violation of the one-person, one-vote principle? Clearly, a redistricting plan is required, but who develops such a plan, and how quickly must it be implemented? The U.S. Supreme Court has consistently taken the position that apportionment is a process committed in the first instance to the discretion of the relevant legislative body.

> [T]he Constitution leaves with the States primary responsibility for apportionment of their federal congressional and state legislative districts. . . . Absent evidence that [the branches of state government] will fail timely to perform that duty, a federal court must neither affirmatively obstruct state reapportionment nor permit federal litigation to be used to impede it.

Growe v. Emison, 507 U.S. 25 (1993). Thus, once a jurisdiction is found to be malapportioned, the first step is generally to order the legislature to develop a redistricting plan that will cure the malapportionment. Redrawing district boundaries is such a politically contentious activity that immediate action by a legislature is rarely to be expected. Consequently, federal courts will typically allow legislatures considerable time to develop a constitutional plan, often allowing the redistricting process to continue through additional election cycles in which the legislature remains malapportioned. There are, of course, a limitless number of ways in which district lines can be drawn that will satisfy the one-person, one-vote principle, and federal courts thus tend to defer, as we have seen, to otherwise legitimate districting decisions made by state governments. In Section C of this chapter and in Chapter 5, we will examine some of the ways in which districting decisions that satisfy the one-person, one-vote principle might nevertheless violate the law.

⯈   *The Judicial Role in Redistricting.*   The Court's one-person, one-vote decisions have thrust the judiciary deeply into the political thicket. By constitutionalizing limitations on apportionment and developing extremely strict criteria, the Supreme Court positioned itself, along with lower federal courts and state courts applying federal law, to be the arbiter of apportionment plans throughout the nation. As a result, legal challenges to apportionment plans are now routine. Following the 2000 round of redistricting, for example, legal challenges were filed to redistricting plans in half the states, and courts invalidated nearly half of the plans they reviewed. A similar eruption of litigation occurred following the 2010 remapping. *See* Justin Levitt, All About Redistricting, http://redistricting.lls.edu/. Is it desirable for courts to engage in such extensive supervision of political activities?

⯈   *Redistricting and Local Community.*   Under the one-person, one-vote doctrine, reapportionment must occur once every decade, following each new national census. Because populations inevitably change to some degree over the course of a decade, some kind of adjustment to election district boundaries every ten years is a virtual certainty. Does all this redrawing of boundaries have any effect on the inhabitants? Consider the following account:

> The process of constantly redrawing electoral district boundaries . . . is one that must deeply stress, if it does not actually erase, the political significance of local boundaries. A boundary that is continually moving is one that is unlikely to serve as any kind of . . . focal point for communal

identity, much less as a dividing line between genuinely distinct political communities. In this way, one-person, one-vote continually impedes the formation (or re-formation) of meaningful local political identity. Moreover, even if some kind of local identity can flourish under these circumstances, the redistricting process would seem to exert a homogenizing pressure by continually linking and unlinking different groups of individuals to particular places and to other groups of individuals. Redistricting thus flattens identity within a jurisdiction by preventing subcommunities from enjoying the kind of stability and sense of permanence that are necessary ingredients for communal self-identification and, ultimately, differentiation. Finally, redistricting inevitably creates a population of political transients — people who, though they never physically relocate, are taken from one district and placed in another to satisfy the demands not of community, but of population equality. Local political bonds of any significance cannot be made and unmade by government fiat, of course, and the process of district reassignment thus can only further weaken the bonds of political and communal affiliation.

James A. Gardner, *One-Person, One-Vote and the Possibility of Political Community*, 80 N.C. L. REV. 1237 (2002).

3. *Nationwide Congressional Apportionment*

Reynolds v. Sims requires that congressional representation be apportioned equally within any individual state. But what about apportionment *across* state lines? To what extent does the Constitution permit deviations in the population represented by congressional delegations from different states? Although the principle of equality applies on an interstate basis, it cannot be applied in precisely the same way due to differences in the constitutional requirements governing interstate apportionment.

Article I, §2, cl. 3, as modified by Section 2 of the Fourteenth Amendment, requires the apportionment of Representatives among the several states "according to their respective numbers." This language, of course, suggests a requirement of proportionality; each state shall have political representation in the House in proportion to its population. However, the Constitution contains other requirements that may prevent the achievement of strict proportionality: first, every state is entitled to a minimum of one Representative in Congress; second, a state can only be entitled to a whole number of Representatives. Obviously, it will probably never happen that the number of representatives each state is entitled to works out exactly to a set of whole numbers. Typically, when Congress does the necessary arithmetic it finds that states are entitled to fractional numbers of representatives. For example, after the first census in 1790, Congress found that Connecticut was entitled, strictly speaking, to 7.89 Representatives, and Rhode Island was entitled to 2.28. The main problem confronting Congress, then, has been what to do with the fractional remainders.

Over the years, Congress has used a variety of methods. From the 1790 through the 1830 reapportionment, Congress used what mathematicians call the "method of greatest divisors," under which fractional remainders are simply disregarded and all figures rounded down to the next whole number. Apparently believing that method to be unfair, Congress in 1842 adopted the "method of major fractions," under which fractional remainders greater than one-half are rounded up and those smaller than one-half rounded down. After further experimentation, Congress settled in 1941 on the current method, the "method of equal proportions," a complex calculation designed to minimize the relative difference across states in the ratio of inhabitants per Representative.

In *Department of Commerce v. Montana*, 503 U.S. 442 (1992), the Court considered a constitutional challenge to this formula by the state of Montana. The 1990 census revealed that eight states would gain additional representatives and thirteen states would lose some of their present representatives. Under the formula used by Congress, Montana would lose one of its two seats in the House. To prevent its political power in Congress from being cut in half, Montana sued, arguing that the method of equal proportions approved by Congress did not achieve the equality in representation required by the Constitution. Montana proposed its own formula, the "Dean Method," which it claimed would produce better results.

The Court began by conceding that "[t]here is some force to the argument that the same historical insights that informed our construction of Article I, §2 in the context of intrastate districting should apply here as well." Even so, the Court said, the equal representation principle is not sufficiently precise to require that any otherwise acceptable mathematical method be used rather than another:

> What is the better measure of inequality—absolute difference in district size, absolute difference in share of a Representative, relative difference in district size or share? Neither mathematical analysis nor constitutional interpretation provides a conclusive answer. In none of these alternative measures of inequality do we find a substantive principle of commanding constitutional significance. The polestar of equal representation does not provide sufficient guidance to allow us to discern a single constitutionally permissible course.

The Court further noted that the

> constitutional guarantee of a minimum of one Representative for each State inexorably compels a significant departure from the ideal. In Alaska, Vermont, and Wyoming, where the statewide districts are less populous than the ideal district, every vote is more valuable than the national average. Moreover, the need to allocate a fixed number of indivisible Representatives among 50 States of varying populations makes it virtually impossible to have the same size district in any pair of States, let alone in all 50.

These considerations led the Court to conclude that the constitutional framework must "delegate to Congress a measure of discretion that is broader than that accorded to the States in the much easier task of determining district sizes within State borders." Here, Congress's good faith choice of a method of apportionment was within the scope of congressional discretion under Article I, §2.

Another interstate apportionment question with consequences for states' representation in Congress arose in *Franklin v. Massachusetts*, 505 U.S. 788 (1992).

In conducting the 1990 census, the federal Bureau of the Census, a division of the Commerce Department, decided to allocate overseas military personnel to the state designated in their personnel files as their "home of record." Previously, the Bureau had not allocated overseas military personnel to any particular state for apportionment purposes. As a result of this decision, enough military personnel were allocated to shift a congressional Representative from Massachusetts to Washington. Massachusetts accordingly sued the Bureau, arguing, among other things, that its decision was unconstitutional.

Article I, §2 requires that the number of Representatives per state be determined by an "actual Enumeration" of "their respective Numbers." Massachusetts argued that this means the census must count only those people actually living "in" each state. The Court rejected this contention and upheld the Bureau's decision. After canvassing the historical record, the Court concluded that the inclusion of military personnel temporarily stationed overseas was not inconsistent with the understanding of the Framers. Moreover, the Bureau's judgment that such personnel "had retained their ties to the States and could and should be counted toward their States' representation in Congress" was within the bounds of allowable government discretion. Finally, Massachusetts was unable to demonstrate that reversing the Bureau's decision would make representation in Congress "more equal."

4. Special Districts

The apportionment cases we have examined so far concern general legislative districts—districts that elect members of a legislature exercising traditional, general governmental powers. But not every elective governmental body exercises this type of power. Particularly on the local level, some governmental bodies exercise very specialized and limited powers, and their actions may not affect every citizen. Others may exercise unusual combinations of legislative, executive, or judicial powers unknown on the state and national level. To what extent do the apportionment principles developed in the context of federal and state elections apply to such governments?

The Court first faced this issue in *Avery v. Midland County*, 390 U.S. 474 (1968). The Commissioners Court of Midland County, Texas, performed a mix of legislative, executive, and judicial functions including setting tax rates, issuing bonds, adopting the county budget, appointing county officers, administering the county's highway and welfare departments, and running the county courthouse. The Court acknowledged the diversity of American local government units and conceded that the Commissioners Court did not fall into any of the "neat categories favored by civics texts." Nevertheless, the Court held, "virtually every American lives within what he and his neighbors regard as a unit of local government with general responsibility and power for local affairs. . . . The Midland County Commissioners Court is such a unit." The Court based this conclusion on the fact that the Commissioners Court had "power to make a large number of decisions having a broad range of impacts on all the citizens of the county."

In *Cipriano v. City of Houma*, 395 U.S. 701 (1969) (per curiam), the Court considered a Louisiana law providing that in referenda called to approve the issuance of bonds by a municipal utility, only property taxpayers were permitted to vote. In

1967, the City of Houma, which owned and operated gas, water, and electric utilities, called a special election to approve the issuance of ten million dollars' worth of utility bonds. The plaintiff, who did not own property and thus paid no property taxes, claimed that the exclusionary voting scheme violated the Equal Protection Clause, and the Court agreed. Applying its decision in *Kramer v. Union Free School District*, 395 U.S. 621 (1969) (Section A above), the Court held that the law failed strict scrutiny. The operation of a municipal utility, the Court said, affected all city residents who use gas, water, and electricity regardless of whether they are property owners, so the exclusion was not sufficiently narrowly tailored. *See also Hill v. Stone*, 421 U.S. 289 (1975) (Court struck down Texas constitutional provision limiting voting in city bond elections to property taxpayers).

Hadley v. Junior College District, 397 U.S. 50 (1970), concerned a Missouri law that provided for an unusual method of selecting officials of a public school district. Under the law, separate school districts could establish a consolidated junior college district. Each junior college district was managed by six elected trustees. The law provided that the trustees should be apportioned among the school districts on the basis of "school enumeration," defined as population in each district between the ages of six and twenty. The Court invalidated the law.

The Court noted that the powers of the trustees included levying and collecting taxes, issuing bonds, hiring and firing teachers, making contracts, acquiring property and managing the junior college. These powers, "while not fully as broad as those of the Midland County Commissioners [in *Avery*], certainly show that the trustees perform important governmental functions within the districts, and we think these powers are general enough and have sufficient impact throughout the district to justify" the application of the equal representation principle. Because apportionment was based on school-age rather than general population, the scheme did not satisfy the one-person, one-vote requirement.

Although the Court had by now struck down every limited purpose election and related voting exclusion it had confronted, it identified a class of cases in which its rulings might be different: "It is of course possible that there might be some case in which a State elects certain functionaries whose duties are so far removed from normal governmental activities and so disproportionately affect different groups that a popular election in compliance with *Reynolds* might not be required, but certainly we see nothing in the present case that indicates that the activities of these trustees fit in that category. Education has traditionally been a vital governmental function, . . . and these trustees, whose election the State has opened to all qualified voters, are governmental officials in every relevant sense of that term."

In the following case, the Court finally confronted this reserved issue.

Salyer Land Co. v. Tulare Lake Basin Water Storage District

410 U.S. 719 (1973)

Mr. Justice REHNQUIST delivered the opinion of the Court.

This is another in the line of cases in which the Court has had occasion to consider the limits imposed by the Equal Protection Clause of the Fourteenth Amendment on legislation apportioning representation in state and local governing

bodies and establishing qualifications for voters in the election of such representatives. *Reynolds v. Sims,* 377 U.S. 533 (1964), enunciated the constitutional standard for apportionment of state legislatures. Later cases such as *Avery v. Midland
County,* 390 U.S. 474 (1968), and *Hadley v. Junior College District,* 397 U.S. 50 (1970),
extended the *Reynolds* rule to the governing bodies of a county and of a junior college district, respectively. We are here presented with the issue expressly reserved
in *Avery, supra:*

> Were the [county's governing body] a special-purpose unit of govern-
> ment assigned the performance of functions affecting definable groups
> of constituents more than other constituents, we would have to confront
> the question whether such a body may be apportioned in ways which
> give greater influence to the citizens most affected by the organization's
> functions.

390 U.S., at 483-484.

The particular type of local government unit whose organization is challenged
on constitutional grounds in this case is a water storage district, organized pursuant
to the California Water Storage District Act, Calif. Water Code §39000 *et seq.* The
peculiar problems of adequate water supplies faced by most of the western third
of the Nation have been described by Mr. Justice Sutherland, who was himself intimately familiar with them, in *California Oregon Power Co. v. Beaver Portland Cement
Co.,* 295 U.S. 142, 156-157 (1935):

> These states and territories comprised the western third of the United
> States — a vast empire in extent, but still sparsely settled. From a line
> east of the Rocky Mountains almost to the Pacific Ocean, and from the
> Canadian border to the boundary of Mexico — an area greater than that
> of the original thirteen states — the lands capable of redemption, in the
> main, constituted a desert, impossible of agricultural use without artificial
> irrigation.
>
> In the beginning, the task of reclaiming this area was left to the
> unaided efforts of the people who found their way by painful effort to
> its inhospitable solitudes. These western pioneers, emulating the spirit of
> so many others who had gone before them in similar ventures, faced the
> difficult problem of wresting a living and creating homes from the raw
> elements about them, and threw down the gage of battle to the forces
> of nature. With imperfect tools, they built dams, excavated canals, con-
> structed ditches, plowed and cultivated the soil, and transformed dry and
> desolate lands into green fields and leafy orchards. . . .

Californians, in common with other residents of the West, found the State's
rivers and streams in their natural state to present the familiar paradox of feast
or famine. With melting snow in the high mountains in the spring, small streams
became roaring freshets, and the rivers they fed carried the potential for destructive
floods. But with the end of the rainy season in the early spring, farmers depended
entirely upon water from such streams and rivers until the rainy season again began
in the fall. Long before that time, however, rivers which ran bank full in the spring
had been reduced to a bare trickle of water.

It was not enough therefore, for individual farmers or groups of farmers to build irrigation canals and ditches which depended for their operation on the natural flow of these streams. Storage dams had to be constructed to impound in their reservoirs the flow of the rivers at flood stage for later release during the dry season regimen of these streams. For the construction of major dams to facilitate the storage of water for irrigation of large areas, the full resources of the State and frequently of the Federal Government were necessary.

But for less costly projects which would benefit a more restricted geographic area, the State was frequently either unable or unwilling to pledge its credit or its resources. The California Legislature, therefore, has authorized a number of instrumentalities, including water storage districts such as the appellee here, to provide a local response to water problems. . . .

Appellee district consists of 193,000 acres of intensively cultivated, highly fertile farm land located in the Tulare Lake Basin. Its population consists of 77 persons, including 18 children, most of whom are employees of one or another of the four corporations that farm 85% of the land in the district.

Such districts are authorized to plan projects and execute approved projects "for the acquisition, appropriation, diversion, storage, conservation, and distribution of water. . . ." Calif. Water Code §42200 *et seq.* Incidental to this general power, districts may "acquire, improve, and operate" any necessary works for the storage and distribution of water as well as any drainage or reclamation works connected therewith, and the generation and distribution of hydroelectric power may be provided for. *Id.*, §§43000, 43025. They may fix tolls and charges for the use of water and collect them from all persons receiving the benefit of the water or other services in proportion to the services rendered. *Id.*, §43006. The costs of the projects are assessed against district land in accordance with the benefits accruing to each tract held in separate ownership. *Id.*, §§46175, 46176. And land that is not benefitted may be withdrawn from the district on petition. *Id.*, §48029.

Governance of the districts is undertaken by a board of directors. *Id.*, §40658. Each director is elected from one of the divisions within the district, *id.*, §39929, and each must take an official oath and execute a bond. *Id.*, §40301. General elections for the directors are to be held in odd-numbered years. *Id.*, §§39027, 41300 *et seq.*

It is the voter qualification for such elections that appellants claim invidiously discriminates against them and persons similarly situated. Appellants are landowners, a landowner-lessee, and residents within the area included in the appellee's water storage district. They brought this action under 42 U.S.C. §1983, seeking declaratory and injunctive relief in an effort to prevent appellee from giving effect to certain provisions of the California Water Code. They allege that §§41000 and 41001 unconstitutionally deny to them the equal protection of the laws guaranteed by the Fourteenth Amendment, in that only landowners are permitted to vote in water storage district general elections, and votes in those elections are apportioned according to the assessed valuation of the land. . . .

It is first argued that §41000, limiting the vote to district landowners, is unconstitutional since nonlandowning residents have as much interest in the operations of a district as landowners who may or may not be residents. Particularly, it is pointed out that the homes of residents may be damaged by floods within the district's boundaries, and that floods may, as with appellant Ellison, cause them to lose their jobs. Support for this position is said to come from the recent decisions of this Court striking down various state laws that limited voting to landowners, *Phoenix v. Kolodziejski*, 399 U.S. 204 (1970), *Cipriano v. City of Houma*, 395 U.S. 701 (1969), and *Kramer v. Union School District*, 395 U.S. 621 (1969). . . .

Cipriano and *Phoenix* involved application of the "one person, one vote" principle to residents of units of local governments exercising general governmental power, as that term was defined in *Avery v. Midland County*, 390 U.S. 474 (1968). *Kramer* and *Hadley v. Junior College District*, 397 U.S. 50 (1970), extended the "one person, one vote" principle to school districts exercising powers which,

> while not fully as broad as those of the Midland County Commissioners, certainly show that the trustees perform important governmental functions within the districts, and we think these powers are general enough and have sufficient impact throughout the district to justify the conclusion that the principle which we applied in *Avery* should also be applied here.

397 U.S., at 53-54. But the Court was also careful to state that:

> It is of course possible that there might be some case in which a State elects certain functionaries whose duties are so far removed from normal governmental activities and so disproportionately affect different groups that a popular election in compliance with *Reynolds*, supra, might not be required, but certainly we see nothing in the present case that indicates that the activities of these trustees fit in that category. Education has traditionally been a vital governmental function, and these trustees, whose election the State has opened to all qualified voters, are governmental officials in every relevant sense of that term.

Id., at 56.

We conclude that the appellee water storage district, by reason of its special limited purpose and of the disproportionate effect of its activities on landowners as a group, is the sort of exception to the rule laid down in *Reynolds* which the quoted language from *Hadley, supra,* and the decision in *Avery, supra,* contemplated.

The appellee district in this case, although vested with some typical governmental powers, has relatively limited authority. Its primary purpose, indeed the reason for its existence, is to provide for the acquisition, storage, and distribution of water for farming in the Tulare Lake Basin. It provides no other general public services such as schools, housing, transportation, utilities, roads, or anything else of the type ordinarily financed by a municipal body. App. 86. There are no towns, shops, hospitals, or other facilities designed to improve the quality of life within the district boundaries, and it does not have a fire department, police, buses, or trains. *Ibid.*

Not only does the district not exercise what might be thought of as "normal governmental" authority, but its actions disproportionately affect landowners. All of the costs of district projects are assessed against land by assessors in proportion to the benefits received. Likewise, charges for services rendered are collectible from persons receiving their benefit in proportion to the services. When such persons are delinquent in payment, just as in the case of delinquency in payments of assessments, such charges become a lien on the land. Calif. Water Code §§47183, 46280.

In short, there is no way that the economic burdens of district operations can fall on residents *qua* residents, and the operations of the districts primarily affect the land within their boundaries.

Under these circumstances, it is quite understandable that the statutory framework for election of directors of the appellee focuses on the land benefitted, rather than on people as such. California has not opened the franchise to all residents, as Missouri had in *Hadley, supra*, nor to all residents with some exceptions, as New York had in *Kramer, supra*. The franchise is extended to landowners, whether they reside in the district or out of it, and indeed whether or not they are natural persons who would be entitled to vote in a more traditional political election. Appellants do not challenge the enfranchisement of nonresident landowners or of corporate landowners for purposes of election of the directors of appellee. Thus, to sustain their contention that all residents of the district must be accorded a vote would not result merely in the striking down of an exclusion from what was otherwise a delineated class, but would instead engraft onto the statutory scheme a wholly new class of voters in addition to those enfranchised by the statute.

We hold, therefore, that the popular election requirements enunciated by *Reynolds, supra*, and succeeding cases are inapplicable to elections such as the general election of appellee Water Storage District.

II

Even though appellants derive no benefit from the *Reynolds* and *Kramer* lines of cases, they are, of course, entitled to have their equal protection claim assessed to determine whether the State's decision to deny the franchise to residents of the district while granting it to landowners was "wholly irrelevant to achievement of the regulation's objectives," *Kotch v. River Port Pilot Comm'rs*, 330 U.S. 552, 556 (1947). No doubt residents within the district may be affected by its activities. But this argument proves too much. Since assessments imposed by the district become a cost of doing business for those who farm within it, and that cost must ultimately be passed along to the consumers of the produce, food shoppers in far away metropolitan areas are to some extent likewise "affected" by the activities of the district. Constitutional adjudication cannot rest on any such "house that Jack built" foundation, however. The California Legislature could quite reasonably have concluded that the number of landowners and owners of sufficient amounts of acreage whose consent was necessary to organize the district would not have subjected their land to the lien of its possibly very substantial assessments unless they had a dominant voice in its control. Since the subjection of the owners' lands to such liens was the basis by which the district was to obtain financing, the proposed district had as a practical matter to attract landowner support. Nor, since assessments against landowners were to be the sole means by which the expenses of the district were to be paid, could it be said to be unfair or inequitable to repose the franchise in landowners but not residents. Landowners as a class were to bear the entire burden of the district's costs, and the State could rationally conclude that they, to the exclusion of residents, should be charged with responsibility for its operation. We conclude, therefore, that nothing in the Equal Protection Clause precluded California from limiting the voting for directors of appellee district by totally excluding those who merely reside within the district. . . .

IV

The last claim by appellants is that §41001, which weights the vote according to assessed valuation of the land, is unconstitutional. They point to the fact that several of the smaller landowners have only one vote per person whereas the J.G. Boswell Company has 37,825 votes, and they place reliance on the various decisions of this Court holding that wealth has no relation to resident-voter qualifications and that equality of voting power may not be evaded. See, *e.g., Gray v. Sanders*, 372 U.S. 368 (1963); *Harper v. Virginia Board of Elections*, 383 U.S. 663 (1966).

Appellants' argument ignores the realities of water storage district operation. Since its formation in 1926, appellee district has put into operation four multi-million-dollar projects. The last project involved the construction of two laterals from the Basin to the California State Aqueduct at a capital cost of about $2,500,000. Three small landowners having land aggregating somewhat under four acres with an assessed valuation of under $100 were given one vote each in the special election held for the approval of the project. The J.G. Boswell Company, which owns 61,665.54 acres with an assessed valuation of $3,782,220 was entitled to cast 37,825 votes in the election. By the same token, however, the assessment commissioners determined that the benefits of the project would be uniform as to all of the acres affected, and assessed the project equally as to all acreage. Each acre has to bear $13.26 of cost and the three small landowners, therefore, must pay a total of $46, whereas the company must pay $817,685 for its part. Thus, as the District Court found, "the benefits and burdens to each landowner...are in proportion to the assessed value of the land." 342 F. Supp. 144, 146. We cannot say that the California legislative decision to permit voting in the same proportion is not rationally based. . . .

Mr. Justice DOUGLAS, with whom Mr. Justice BRENNAN and Mr. Justice MARSHALL concur, dissenting.

I

. . . Provisions authorizing a selective franchise are disfavored, because they "always pose the danger of denying some citizens any effective voice in the governmental affairs which substantially affect their lives." *Kramer v. Union School District*, 395 U.S. 621, 627. In order to overcome this strong presumption, it had to be shown up to now (1) that there is a compelling state interest for the exclusion, and (2) that the exclusions are necessary to promote the State's articulated goal. *Phoenix v. Kolodziejski, supra; Cipriano v. City of Houma*, 395 U.S. 701; *Kramer v. Union School District, supra*. In my view, appellants in this case have made a sufficient showing to invoke the above principles, and the presumption thus established has not been overcome.

Assuming, *arguendo*, that a State may, in some circumstances, limit the franchise to that portion of the electorate "primarily affected" by the outcome of an election, *Kramer v. Union School District, supra*, at 632, the limitation may only be upheld if it is demonstrated that "all those excluded are in fact substantially less interested or affected than those the [franchise] includes." *Ibid*. The majority concludes that "there is no way that the economic burdens of district operations can fall on residents *qua* residents, and the operations of the districts primarily affect the land within their boundaries."

But, with all respect, that is a great distortion. In these arid areas of our Nation a water district seeks water in time of drought and fights it in time of flood. One of the functions of water districts in California is to manage flood control. That is general California statutory policy. It is expressly stated in the Water Code that governs water districts. The California Supreme Court ruled some years back that flood control and irrigation are different but complementary aspects of one problem.

From its inception in 1926, this district has had repeated flood control problems. Four rivers, Kings, Kern, Tule, and Kaweah, enter Tulare Lake Basin. South of Tulare Lake Basin is Buena Vista Lake. In the past, Buena Vista has been used to protect Tulare Lake Basin by storing Kern River water in the former. That is how Tulare Lake Basin was protected from menacing floods in 1952. But that was not done in the great 1969 flood, the result being that 88,000 of the 193,000 acres in respondent district were flooded. The board of the respondent district—dominated by the big landowner J.G. Boswell Co.—voted 6-4 to table the motion that would put into operation the machinery to divert the flood waters to the Buena Vista Lake. The reason is that J.G. Boswell Co. had a long-term agricultural lease in the Buena Vista Lake Basin and flooding it would have interfered with the planting, growing, and harvesting of crops the next season.

The result was that water in the Tulare Lake Basin rose to 192.5 USGS datum. Ellison, one of the appellants who lives in the district, is not an agricultural landowner. But his residence was 15½ feet below the water level of the crest of the flood in 1969.

The appellee district has large levees; and if they are broken, damage to houses and loss of life are imminent.

Landowners—large or small, resident or nonresident lessees or landlords, sharecroppers or owners—all should have a say. But irrigation, water storage, the building of levees, and flood control, implicate the entire community. All residents of the district must be granted the franchise. . . .

The majority, however, would distinguish the water storage district from "units of local government having general governmental powers over the entire geographic area served by the body," *Avery v. Midland County,* 390 U.S. 474, 485, and fit this case within the exception contemplated for "a special-purpose unit of government assigned the performance of functions affecting definable groups of constituents more than other constituents." *Id.,* at 483-484. . . .

[T]he Tulare Lake Basin Water Storage District surely performs "important governmental functions" which "have sufficient impact throughout the district" to justify the application of the *Avery* principle.

Whatever may be the parameters of the exception alluded to in *Avery* and *Hadley,* I cannot conclude that this water storage district escapes the constitutional restraints relative to a franchise within a governmental unit.

II

When we decided *Reynolds v. Sims,* 377 U.S. 533, and discussed the problems of malapportionment we thought and talked about people—of population, of the constitutional right of "qualified citizens to vote," (*id.,* at 554) of "the right of suffrage," (*id.*, at 555) of the comparison of "one man's vote" to that of another man's vote. *Id.*, at 559. We said:

> Legislators represent people, not trees or acres. Legislators are elected by voters, not farms or cities or economic interests. As long as ours is a representative form of government, and our legislatures are those instruments of government elected directly by and directly representative of the people, the right to elect legislators in a free and unimpaired fashion is a bedrock of our political system.

Id., at 562.

It is indeed grotesque to think of corporations voting within the framework of political representation of people. Corporations were held to be "persons" for purposes both of the Due Process Clause of the Fourteenth Amendment and of the Equal Protection Clause. Yet, it is unthinkable in terms of the American tradition that corporations should be admitted to the franchise. Could a State allot voting rights to its corporations, weighting each vote according to the wealth of the corporation? Or could it follow the rule of one corporation, one vote?

It would be a radical and revolutionary step to take, as it would change our whole concept of the franchise. California takes part of that step here by allowing corporations to vote in these water district matters that entail performance of vital governmental functions. One corporation can outvote 77 individuals in this district. Four corporations can exercise these governmental powers as they choose, leaving every individual inhabitant with a weak, ineffective voice. The result is a corporate political kingdom undreamed of by those who wrote our Constitution.

Coda: The Court handed down its decision in *Salyer* in March 1973. In November 1974, California voters approved an amendment to the California Constitution providing, in its entirety: "The right to vote or hold office may not be conditioned by a property qualification."

The Court has decided several other cases involving the applicability of the one-person, one-vote principle to special districts. *See Associated Enterprises, Inc. v. Toltec Watershed Improvement District*, 410 U.S. 743 (1973) (per curiam) (companion case to *Salyer* presenting similar facts); *Ball v. James*, 451 U.S. 355 (1981) (upholding land-based voting scheme for an Arizona agricultural improvement and power district); *New York City Board of Estimate v. Morris*, 489 U.S. 688 (1989) (invalidating composition of New York City Board of Estimate because some members elected on a borough (county) basis without regard to population differences among the boroughs, and rejecting contention that unique set of powers wielded by the Board brought it outside the equal representation principle).

▷▷ *The Variety of Special Districts.* There are over 87,000 local government units in the United States. Of these, about 39,000 are general purpose local governments such as county, municipal, and town governments. The remainder are special district governments that perform an enormous variety of different functions and operate under vastly different structures. About 13,500 of these single-purpose local governmental units are school districts. Of the rest, about 20 percent perform some kind of function relating to natural resources, such as drainage, flood control, irrigation, and soil and water conservation. Another 16 percent provide fire protection. The next most common functions relate to water supplies, housing and community development services, and sewerage. Others include park and recreation districts, hospital districts, highway districts, cemetery districts, library districts, airport districts, and many other kinds. *See* U.S. Bureau of the Census, *Census of Governments* (2002). The San Francisco Bay Area alone, for example, contains about 650 special districts exercising various powers.

Some of the most unusual, and politically touchy, special districts limit representation on the governing board or council according to some sort of financial interest in the district's activities. For example, the California Supreme Court confronted a highly unusual apportionment scheme in *Southern California Rapid Transit District v. Bolen*, 822 P.2d 875 (Cal. 1992). The Southern California Rapid Transit District (SCRTD) is responsible for constructing, financing, and operating a mass rapid transit system ("Metro Rail") in Los Angeles County. The California legislature authorized SCRTD to establish "special benefit assessment districts" surrounding planned Metro Rail subway stations along the route. Voter approval for establishment of such a district was required under certain circumstances. However, because residential property was exempt from any assessments by SCRTD, only commercial property owners were allowed to vote in the referenda. Furthermore, each eligible property owner was entitled to one vote for every $1,000 of assessed real property value. The legislature's reasoning appeared to be that because the Metro Rail would deliver a great windfall to the commercial businesses surrounding each planned station, these businesses should pay a greater share of the cost of the system.

The California Supreme Court upheld this scheme. The court held that the special benefit districts did not exercise general governmental powers, and the result was controlled by *Salyer* rather than by *Avery*. The court distinguished *Cipriano* on the ground that the activities of the special districts would not affect the interests of "nonvoting residents" of the districts in any way "distinguishable from that of every other resident of the multi county area comprising the transit district."

One of the most recent—and controversial—innovations in local government law concerns the creation of Business Improvement Districts (BIDs).

> A BID is a territorial subdivision of a city in which property owners or businesses are subject to additional taxes. The revenues generated by these district-specific taxes are reserved to fund services and improvements within the district and to pay for the administrative costs of BID operations. BIDs' services are provided in addition to those offered by city governments. Most BIDs focus on traditional municipal activities, such as garbage collection, street maintenance, and security patrols. A few provide assistance to the homeless. Some engage in street repairs, undertake landscaping, provide street furniture, maintain parks, and create public amenities. Many sponsor street fairs and special events, produce promotional brochures, and engage in other direct efforts to draw shoppers, tourists, and businesses into their districts.

BIDs are funded primarily by district-specific taxes. . . . As the name implies, the property in a "business improvement district" is primarily devoted to business purposes, although many districts include some residential property. In nearly all states, establishment of a BID requires the approval of the local government, but the impetus for creating a district typically comes from neighborhood property owners or businesses, who also take the lead in mapping the district's boundaries and in developing its service and financing plan. Many states provide for property owner- or business-dominated advisory, administrative, or management boards which implement the BID's program and manage its operations.

Richard Briffault, *A Government for Our Time? Business Improvement Districts and Urban Governance*, 99 COLUM. L. REV. 365, 368-369 (1999). In the typical BID structure, revenues are collected from owners of business property within the district and the use of those revenues is then managed by a board elected predominantly or exclusively by the business property owners who provide the BID's revenue. In *Kessler v. Grand Central District Management Association, Inc.*, 158 F.3d 92 (2d Cir. 1998), the Second Circuit rejected a one-person, one-vote challenge to New York's property qualification for voting for BID managers on the ground that, even though they exercise many of the powers traditionally associated with general governments, a BID is, on balance, a special-purpose government under *Salyer*.

≫ *Voting Equality Abroad.* Not every jurisdiction has taken the view that the right to vote implies a vote that is precisely equally weighted. Consider the view of the Supreme Court of Canada:

[T]he purpose of the right to vote enshrined in [the Canadian Charter of Rights and Freedoms] is not equality of voting power *per se*, but the right to "effective representation." Ours is a representative democracy. Each citizen is entitled to be *represented* in government. Representation comprehends the idea of having a voice in the deliberations of government as well as the idea of the right to bring one's grievances and concerns to the attention of one's government representative. . . . What are the conditions of effective representation? The first is relative parity of voting power. A system which dilutes one citizen's vote unduly as compared with another citizen's vote runs the risk of providing inadequate representation to the citizen whose vote is diluted. The legislative power of the citizen whose vote is diluted will be reduced, as may be access to and assistance from his or her representative. The result will be uneven and unfair representation.

But parity of voting power, though of prime importance, is not the only factor to be taken into account in ensuring effective representation. . . . Notwithstanding the fact that the value of a citizen's vote should not be unduly diluted, it is a practical fact that effective representation often cannot be achieved without taking into account countervailing factors. . . . [S]uch relative parity as may be possible of achievement may prove undesirable because it has the effect of detracting from the primary goal of effective representation. Factors like geography, community history, community interests and minority representation may need to be taken into account to ensure that our legislative assemblies effectively represent the diversity of our social mosaic.

Reference re Prov. Electoral Boundaries (Sask.), [1991] 2 S.C.R. 158. Applying these principles, the court upheld a Saskatchewan provincial law requiring the creation of twenty-nine urban, thirty-five rural, and two northern "ridings," or election districts. The act permitted the southern ridings to vary in population by up to 25 percent of the average district size, and permitted the two northern ridings to vary from the norm by up to 50 percent. These discrepancies, the court held, were "justified on the basis of factors such as geography, community interests and population growth patterns. It was not seriously suggested that the northern boundaries are inappropriate, given the sparse population and the difficulty of communication in the area." *See* Robert W. Behrman, *Equal or Effective Representation: Redistricting Jurisprudence in Canada and the United States*, 51 Am. J. Legal Hist. 277 (2011).

On the other hand, Saskatchewan is a sparsely populated, mainly rural and agricultural province with about 1.2 million residents, of whom fewer than half live in the province's two largest cities, Saskatoon (270,000) and Regina (230,000). What happens when these same, relatively loose principles of apportionment are applied to Ontario, which is home to forty percent of Canada's population, and contains Toronto, North America's fourth largest metropolitan region (7 million)? According to a leading scholar of comparative constitutional law, the result is not only "chronic underrepresentation of major urban centers in key national decision-making fora," but severe underrepresentation of the minority racial, ethnic, and immigrant communities that tend to gravitate to major urban centers. Remarkably, nearly half (48%) of the population of the City of Toronto is foreign born. Ran Hirschl, City, State: Constitutionalism and the Megacity 68-71 (2020).

In Australia, the principle of one-person, one-vote has been rejected by the High Court of Australia, though not out of any principled objection to it. Rather, in *McGinty v. Western Australia* (1996), 134 A.L.R. 289, the court held that nothing in the Australian Constitution compels Australian states to divide their electorates into districts of equal population; to the contrary, history suggests that the drafters of Australian constitutions have been comfortable with substantial population diversity among election districts. *See* Erin Daly, *Idealists, Pragmatists, and Textualists: Judging Electoral Districts in America, Canada, and Australia*, 21 B.C. Int'l & Comp. L. Rev. 261 (1998).

C.   DISCRIMINATORY MANIPULATION OF REPRESENTATION

As we have now seen, the Court's apportionment jurisprudence is designed to secure equal representation to individual voters. The one-person, one-vote requirement prevents the government from discriminating against disfavored groups by weakening them through vote dilution. But suppose everybody's vote is numerically equal to everybody else's; has all opportunity for discrimination then been eliminated?

It should come as no surprise that malapportionment is only one of many tools that may be utilized to engage in discriminatory manipulation of the representation process. In Chapter 3 we examined some of the ways in which the manipulation of voter qualifications has been used to attempt to control the outcomes of elections. In this section, we turn to much more sophisticated methods of manipulating representation, methods that appear on their face to be completely benign and neutral—and are often used for benign and neutral purposes—but which can also be selected for the purpose, and with the effect, of controlling electoral outcomes. We focus on two time-honored techniques: selection of the method of election, and gerrymandering.

1. Methods of Election

To decide that a certain office should be elective, and that some particular set of voters should be eligible to vote in elections for that office, does not end the structural decision-making process. It remains to be determined what method of election should be used, a decision that can greatly affect the outcome of elections for the office in question. The fundamental point here is that the design of electoral districts is a choice, and that choice will almost always affect electoral outcomes. In the United States, we generally use single-member plurality districts, or the first-past-the-post system, for most elective offices. These are districts that elect only one representative, and the candidate who wins the most votes, even if that amounts only to a plurality of votes cast, wins the seat. The next cases involve the use of multimember districts and at-large elections, ordinarily benign features of an electoral system that can nevertheless be used to achieve discriminatory purposes.

An *at-large* election is one in which all voters of the pertinent jurisdiction elect all members of a multimember body, usually a legislature. For example, if a city council contains seven members, in an at-large election every voter in the city can cast votes for all seven members, as if there were seven different elections. At-large elections contrast with districted elections in which the jurisdiction is broken up into as many districts as the legislature has members, and each district elects only one member. Thus, in our hypothetical city with a seven-member council, we would divide the city into seven districts, and voters may cast votes only for those candidates running for their district's seat.

A *multimember district* is an election district in which the voters get to select more than one candidate; it is a sort of at-large election held on a district scale. For example, in our hypothetical city, we could divide the city into two multimember districts, one district that elects four council members and one that elects three council members. Or we could divide the city into three districts, which would include two multimember districts that elect three council members and one single-member district. In some parts of the country legislative bodies may be elected from multimember districts or from a mix of multimember and single member districts.

Many at-large and multimember elections are conducted using a *place system*. In such a system, each seat on a multimember city council, for example, is considered a separate office, and candidates run for a specific seat. Thus, the Democratic and Republican candidates for Seat 1 run against one another, a different Democrat and a different Republican compete for Seat 2, and so on. Unlike a districted election, however, all voters throughout the jurisdiction vote for one candidate for Seat 1, one candidate for Seat 2, etc. This means that in an at-large election using a place system, a city electorate that is 51 percent Republican, for example, can elect a city council that is 100 percent Republican. Depending upon the geographical distribution of Democrats and Republicans, it is often the case that use of a districted electoral system in the same city would result in a city council that is, say, only 60 percent Republican—a potentially significant difference on many political issues. Thus, the choice of electoral system can significantly and consistently influence the way political power is distributed. Moreover, if we substitute race for political affiliation, it is clear that problems of constitutional dimension may arise.

Below are sample ballot arrangements for a hypothetical at-large election run with and without a place system.

1.   Ballot for at-large election to a three-seat city council WITH a place system

Instruction: Vote for ONE candidate in each column

	City Council Seat 1	City Council Seat 2	City Council Seat 3
Democrat	☐ Abigail Adams	☐ David Drake	☐ Frank Forrest
Republican	☐ Bruce Bowman	☐ Edna East	☐ Gina Grant
Independent	☐ Charlotte Case		☐ James Jordan

2.   Ballot for at-large election to a three-seat city council—NO place system

Instruction: Vote for THREE

Abigail Adams (D)	☐
Bruce Bowman (R)	☐
Charlotte Case (I)	☐
David Drake (D)	☐
Edna East (R)	☐
Frank Forrest (D)	☐
Gina Grant (R)	☐
Henry Higgenbottom (I)	☐
Isabelle Isherwood (I)	☐
James Jordan (I)	☐

How do these different formats affect the result in the hypothetical jurisdiction described above? Suppose that the second ballot format instead contains this instruction: Vote for ONE (top three elected). Does that change the result?

≫   *Origins:* **Whitcomb v. Chavis.**   In *Whitcomb v. Chavis*, 403 U.S. 124 (1971), a group of black voters challenged the use of a multimember state legislative district in Marion County, Indiana, which allocated to Marion County fifteen state representatives and eight state senators. The plaintiffs claimed that use of at-large voting in the setting of a multimember district had a tendency to "submerge minorities" by causing them to be underrepresented relative to their numbers within the district. In particular, the plaintiffs in *Whitcomb* argued that poor blacks in certain neighborhoods were unable to elect representatives of their choice to the state legislature under the multimember district system, but would be able to elect three representatives and one senator if the county were subdivided into single-member districts. The Court rejected this claim. It first observed that "there is no suggestion here that Marion County's multi-member district, or similar districts throughout the State, were conceived or operated as purposeful devices to further racial or economic discrimination." Finding no intentional racial discrimination, the Court went on to consider the plaintiffs' more basic claim that the multimember format submerged minority political power:

> We are not insensitive to the objections long voiced to multi-member district plans. Although not as prevalent as they were in our early history, they have been with us since colonial times and were much in evidence both before and after the adoption of the Fourteenth Amendment. Criticism is rooted in their winner-take-all aspects, their tendency to submerge minorities and to overrepresent the winning party as compared with the party's statewide electoral position, a general preference for legislatures reflecting community interests as closely as possible and disenchantment with political parties and elections as devices to settle policy differences between contending interests. The chance of winning or significantly influencing intraparty fights and issue-oriented elections has seemed to some inadequate protection to minorities, political, racial, or economic; rather, their voice, it is said, should also be heard in the legislative forum where public policy is finally fashioned. In our view, however, experience and insight have not yet demonstrated that multi-member districts are inherently invidious and violative of the Fourteenth Amendment. . . . The short of it is that we are unprepared to hold that district-based elections decided by plurality vote are unconstitutional in either single- or multi-member districts simply because the supporters of losing candidates have no legislative seats assigned to them.

Although the Court in *Whitcomb* rejected the submersion claim before it, it used hedging language that appeared to give encouragement to opponents of the use of at-large elections and multimember districts. Two years later, another such challenge came before the Court.

White v. Regester

412 U.S. 755 (1973)

Mr. Justice WHITE delivered the opinion of the Court.

This case raises questions concerning the validity of the reapportionment plan for the Texas House of Representatives adopted in 1970 by the State Legislative Redistricting Board: . . . whether the multimember districts provided for Bexar and Dallas Counties were properly found to have been invidiously discriminatory against cognizable racial or ethnic groups in those counties.

The Texas Constitution requires the state legislature to reapportion the House and Senate at its first regular session following the decennial census. Tex. Const., Art. III, §28. In 1970, . . . pursuant to the requirements of the Texas Constitution, a Legislative Redistricting Board had been formed to begin the task of redistricting. . . .

On October 15, 1971, the Redistricting Board's . . . House plan was promulgated. . . . That plan divided the 150-member body among 79 single-member and 11 multimember districts. . . .

We affirm the District Court's judgment insofar as it invalidated the multimember districts in Dallas and Bexar Counties and ordered those districts to be redrawn into single-member districts. Plainly, under our cases, multimember districts are not *per se* unconstitutional, nor are they necessarily unconstitutional when used in combination with single-member districts in other parts of the State. *Whitcomb v. Chavis*, 403 U.S. 124 (1971); *Reynolds v. Sims.* But we have entertained claims that multimember districts are being used invidiously to cancel out or minimize the voting strength of racial groups. See *Whitcomb v. Chavis, supra; Burns v. Richardson; Fortson v. Dorsey.* To sustain such claims, it is not enough that the racial group allegedly discriminated against has not had legislative seats in proportion to its voting potential. The plaintiffs' burden is to produce evidence to support findings that the political processes leading to nomination and election were not equally open to participation by the group in question—that its members had less opportunity than did other residents in the district to participate in the political processes and to elect legislators of their choice. *Whitcomb v. Chavis, supra*, at 149-150.

With due regard for these standards, the District Court first referred to the history of official racial discrimination in Texas, which at times touched the right of Negroes to register and vote and to participate in the democratic processes. It referred also to the Texas rule requiring a majority vote as a prerequisite to nomination in a primary election and to the so-called "place" rule limiting candidacy for legislative office from a multimember district to a specified "place" on the ticket, with the result being the election of representatives from the Dallas multimember district reduced to a head-to-head contest for each position. These characteristics of the Texas electoral system, neither in themselves improper nor invidious, enhanced the opportunity for racial discrimination, the District Court thought. More fundamentally, it found that since Reconstruction days, there have been only two Negroes in the Dallas County delegation to the Texas House of Representatives and that these two were the only two Negroes ever slated by the Dallas Committee for Responsible Government (DCRG), a white-dominated organization that is in effective control of Democratic Party candidate slating in Dallas County. That organization, the District Court found, did not need the support of the Negro community to win elections in the county, and it did not therefore exhibit good-faith concern for the political and other needs and aspirations of the Negro community. The court found that as recently as 1970 the DCRG was relying upon "racial campaign tactics in white precincts to defeat candidates who had the overwhelming support of the black community." Based on the evidence before it, the District Court concluded that "the black community has been effectively excluded from participation in the Democratic primary selection process," and was therefore generally not permitted to enter into the political process in a reliable and meaningful manner. These findings and conclusions are sufficient to sustain the District Court's judgment with respect to the Dallas multimember district and, on this record, we have no reason to disturb them.

The same is true of the order requiring disestablishment of the multimember district in Bexar County. . . . [T]he District Court considered the Mexican-Americans in Bexar County to be an identifiable class for Fourteenth Amendment purposes and proceeded to inquire whether the impact of the multimember district on this group constituted invidious discrimination. Surveying the historic and present condition of the Bexar County Mexican-American community, which is concentrated for the most part on the west side of the city of San Antonio, the court observed, based upon prior cases and the record before it, that the Bexar community, along with other Mexican-Americans in Texas, had long "suffered from, and continues to suffer from, the results and effects of invidious discrimination and treatment in the fields of education, employment, economics, health, politics and others." The bulk of the Mexican-American community in Bexar County occupied the Barrio, an area consisting of about 28 contiguous census tracts in the city of San Antonio. Over 78% of Barrio residents were Mexican-Americans, making up 29% of the county's total population. The Barrio is an area of poor housing; its residents have low income and a high rate of unemployment. The typical Mexican-American suffers a cultural and language barrier that makes his participation in community processes extremely difficult, particularly, the court thought, with respect to the political life of Bexar County. "[A] cultural incompatibility . . . conjoined with the poll tax and the most restrictive voter registration procedures in the nation have operated to effectively deny Mexican-Americans access to the political processes in Texas even longer than the Blacks were formally denied access by the white primary." The residual impact of this history reflected itself in the fact that Mexican-American voting registration remained very poor in the county and that only five Mexican-Americans since 1880 have served in the Texas Legislature from Bexar County. Of these, only two were from the Barrio area. The District Court also concluded from the evidence that the Bexar County legislative delegation in the House was insufficiently responsive to Mexican-American interests.

Based on the totality of the circumstances, the District Court evolved its ultimate assessment of the multi-member district, overlaid, as it was, on the cultural and economic realities of the Mexican-American community in Bexar County and its relationship with the rest of the county. Its judgment was that Bexar County Mexican-Americans "are effectively removed from the political processes of Bexar [County] in violation of all the *Whitcomb* standards, whatever their absolute numbers may total in that County." Single-member districts were thought required to remedy "the effects of past and present discrimination against Mexican-Americans," *ibid.*, and to bring the community into the full stream of political life of the county and State by encouraging their further registration, voting, and other political activities. . . .

On the record before us, we are not inclined to overturn these findings, representing as they do a blend of history and an intensely local appraisal of the design and impact of the Bexar County multimember district in the light of past and present reality, political and otherwise.

———————

Did *Regester* provide the victory that the plaintiffs in *Whitcomb* had sought?

>> *Disparate Impact vs. Disparate Treatment.*   In *Washington v. Davis*, 426 U.S. 229 (1976), the Court was asked to hold that constitutional principles of equal protection bar government actions that have a discriminatory impact on blacks even when that impact is unintentional. The plaintiffs were black applicants for positions as District of Columbia police officers. Part of the application process involved taking a written examination, which black applicants failed in disproportionately higher numbers than white applicants. The plaintiffs did not contend that the test was intentionally designed to exclude blacks — in the language of employment discrimination, that it provided racially "disparate treatment." Rather, they claimed only that it had a racial "disparate impact." The Court rejected the plaintiffs' claim, holding that the Equal Protection Clause bars only intentional discrimination.

Although it was not a voting rights case, *Washington v. Davis* clearly had the effect of foreclosing equal protection challenges to methods of election based solely on the fact that those methods resulted in white domination of the machinery of government. Under *Washington*, blacks would have to show in an equal protection case that such methods were deliberately maintained for racially discriminatory purposes, a sometimes difficult task.

The Fifteenth Amendment, however, contains separate and distinct protection against racial discrimination in the right to vote, and offered a possible way around the result of *Washington v. Davis*. In the following case, a group of black plaintiffs raised a disparate impact challenge under the Fifteenth Amendment.

City of Mobile v. Bolden

446 U.S. 55 (1980)

Mr. Justice STEWART announced the judgment of the Court and delivered an opinion, in which THE CHIEF JUSTICE, Mr. Justice POWELL, and Mr. Justice REHNQUIST joined.

The city of Mobile, Ala., has since 1911 been governed by a City Commission consisting of three members elected by the voters of the city at large. The question in this case is whether this at-large system of municipal elections violates the rights of Mobile's Negro voters in contravention of federal statutory or constitutional law.

I

[Pursuant to Alabama law], the three Commissioners jointly exercise all legislative, executive, and administrative power in the municipality. They are required after election to designate one of their number as Mayor, a largely ceremonial office, but no formal provision is made for allocating specific executive or administrative duties among the three. As required by the state law enacted in 1911, each candidate for the Mobile City Commission runs for election in the city at large for a term of four years in one of three numbered posts, and may be elected only by a majority of the total vote. This is the same basic electoral system that is followed by literally thousands of municipalities and other local governmental units throughout the Nation. . . .

III

The Court's early decisions under the Fifteenth Amendment established that it imposes but one limitation on the powers of the States. It forbids them to discriminate against Negroes in matters having to do with voting. See *Ex parte Yarbrough*, 110 U.S. 651, 665; *Neal v. Delaware*, 103 U.S. 370, 389-390; *United States v. Cruikshank*, 92 U.S. 542, 555-556; *United States v. Reese*, 92 U.S. 214. The Amendment's command and effect are wholly negative. "The Fifteenth Amendment does not confer the right of suffrage upon any one," but has "invested the citizens of the United States with a new constitutional right which is within the protecting power of Congress. That right is exemption from discrimination in the exercise of the elective franchise on account of race, color, or previous condition of servitude." *Id.* at 217-218.

Our decisions, moreover, have made clear that action by a State that is racially neutral on its face violates the Fifteenth Amendment only if motivated by a discriminatory purpose. . . . In *Gomillion v. Lightfoot*, 364 U.S. 339, the Court held that allegations of a racially motivated gerrymander of municipal boundaries stated a claim under the Fifteenth Amendment. The constitutional infirmity of the state law in that case, according to the allegations of the complaint, was that in drawing the municipal boundaries the legislature was "solely concerned with segregating white and colored voters by fencing Negro citizens out of town so as to deprive them of their pre-existing municipal vote." *Id.*, at 341. The Court made clear that in the absence of such an invidious purpose, a State is constitutionally free to redraw political boundaries in any manner it chooses. *Id.*, at 347. . . .

The Fifteenth Amendment . . . prohibits only purposefully discriminatory denial or abridgment by government of the freedom to vote "on account of race, color, or previous condition of servitude." Having found that Negroes in Mobile "register and vote without hindrance," the District Court and Court of Appeals were in error in believing that the appellants invaded the protection of that Amendment in the present case.

IV

The Court of Appeals also agreed with the District Court that Mobile's at-large electoral system violates the Equal Protection Clause of the Fourteenth Amendment. There remains for consideration, therefore, the validity of its judgment on that score.

A

The claim that at-large electoral schemes unconstitutionally deny to some persons the equal protection of the laws has been advanced in numerous cases before this Court. That contention has been raised most often with regard to multimember constituencies within a state legislative apportionment system. The constitutional objection to multimember districts is not and cannot be that, as such, they depart from apportionment on a population basis in violation of *Reynolds v. Sims*, 377 U.S. 533, and its progeny. Rather the focus in such cases has been on the lack of representation multimember districts afford various elements of the voting population in a system of representative legislative democracy. "Criticism [of multimember districts] is rooted in their winner-take-all aspects, their tendency to submerge minorities . . . , a general preference for legislatures reflecting community interests as closely as possible and disenchantment with political parties and elections as devices to settle policy differences between contending interests." *Whitcomb v. Chavis*, 403 U.S. 124, 158-159.

Despite repeated constitutional attacks upon multimember legislative districts, the Court has consistently held that they are not unconstitutional per se, *e.g.*, *White v. Regester*, 412 U.S. 755; *Whitcomb v. Chavis*, *supra*. We have recognized, however, that such legislative apportionments could violate the Fourteenth Amendment if their purpose were invidiously to minimize or cancel out the voting potential of racial or ethnic minorities. See *White v. Regester*, *supra*; *Whitcomb v. Chavis*, *supra*. To prove such a purpose it is not enough to show that the group allegedly discriminated against has not elected representatives in proportion to its numbers. *White v. Regester*, *supra*, at 765-766; *Whitcomb v. Chavis*, 403 U.S., at 149-150. A plaintiff must prove that the disputed plan was "conceived or operated as [a] purposeful [device] to further racial . . . discrimination," *id.*, at 149.

This burden of proof is simply one aspect of the basic principle that only if there is purposeful discrimination can there be a violation of the Equal Protection Clause of the Fourteenth Amendment. See *Washington v. Davis*, 426 U.S. 229; *Arlington Heights v. Metropolitan Housing Dev. Corp.*, 429 U.S. 252; *Personnel Administrator of Mass. v. Feeney*, 442 U.S. 256. . . . Although dicta may be drawn from a few of the Court's earlier opinions suggesting that disproportionate effects alone may establish a claim of unconstitutional racial vote dilution, the fact is that such a view is not supported by any decision of this Court. More importantly, such a view is not consistent with the meaning of the Equal Protection Clause as it has been understood in a variety of other contexts involving alleged racial discrimination. *Washington v. Davis*, *supra* (employment); *Arlington Heights v. Metropolitan Housing Dev. Corp.*, *supra* (zoning); *Keyes v. School District No. 1, Denver, Colo.*, 413 U.S. 189, 208 (public schools); *Akins v. Texas*, 325 U.S. 398, 403-404 (jury selection).

In only one case has the Court sustained a claim that multimember legislative districts unconstitutionally diluted the voting strength of a discrete group. That case was *White v. Regester*. There the Court upheld a constitutional challenge by Negroes and Mexican-Americans to parts of a legislative reapportionment plan adopted by the State of Texas. The plaintiffs alleged that the multimember districts for the two counties in which they resided minimized the effect of their votes in violation of the Fourteenth Amendment, and the Court held that the plaintiffs had been able to "produce evidence to support findings that the political processes leading to nomination and election were not equally open to participation by the [groups] in question." 412 U.S., at 766, 767. In so holding, the Court relied upon evidence in the record that included a long history of official discrimination against minorities as well as indifference to their needs and interests on the part of white elected officials. The Court also found in each county additional factors that restricted the access of minority groups to the political process. In one county, Negroes effectively were excluded from the process of slating candidates for the Democratic Party, while the plaintiffs in the other county were Mexican-Americans who "[suffered] a cultural and language barrier" that made "participation in community processes extremely difficult, particularly . . . with respect to the political life" of the county. *Id.*, at 768 (footnote omitted).

White v. Regester is thus consistent with "the basic equal protection principle that the invidious quality of a law claimed to be racially discriminatory must ultimately be traced to a racially discriminatory purpose," *Washington v. Davis*, 426 U.S., at 240. . . .

[It] is clear that the evidence in the present case fell far short of showing that the appellants "conceived or operated [a] purposeful [device] to further racial . . . discrimination." *Whitcomb v. Chavis*, 403 U.S., at 149. . . . [The] District Court based its conclusion of unconstitutionality primarily on the fact that no Negro had ever been elected to the City Commission, apparently because of the pervasiveness of racially polarized voting in Mobile. The trial court also found that city officials had not been as responsive to the interests of Negroes as to those of white persons. On the basis of these findings, the court concluded that the political processes in Mobile were not equally open to Negroes, despite its seemingly inconsistent findings that there were no inhibitions against Negroes becoming candidates, and that in fact Negroes had registered and voted without hindrance. . . .

[The] District Court's finding of fact, unquestioned on appeal, make clear that Negroes register and vote in Mobile "without hindrance," and that there are no official obstacles in the way of Negroes who wish to become candidates for election to the Commission. Indeed, it was undisputed that the only active "slating" organization in the city is comprised of Negroes. It may be that Negro candidates have been defeated, but that fact alone does not work a constitutional deprivation. *Whitcomb v. Chavis*, 403 U.S., at 160; see *Arlington Heights*, 429 U.S., at 266, and n.15. . . .

[T]he District Court and the Court of Appeals supported their conclusion by drawing upon the substantial history of official racial discrimination in Alabama. But past discrimination cannot, in the manner of original sin, condemn governmental action that is not itself unlawful. The ultimate question remains whether a discriminatory intent has been proved in a given case. More distant instances of official discrimination in other cases are of limited help in resolving that question.

Finally, the District Court and the Court of Appeals pointed to the mechanics of the at-large electoral system itself as proof that the votes of Negroes were being invidiously canceled out. But those features of that electoral system, such as the majority vote requirement, tend naturally to disadvantage any voting minority, as we noted in *White v. Regester*, 412 U.S. 755. They are far from proof that the at-large electoral scheme represents purposeful discrimination against Negro voters.

B

We turn finally to the arguments advanced in Part I of Mr. Justice Marshall's dissenting opinion. The theory of this dissenting opinion—a theory much more extreme than that espoused by the District Court or the Court of Appeals—appears to be that every "political group," or at least every such group that is in the minority, has a federal constitutional right to elect candidates in proportion to its numbers. Moreover, a political group's "right" to have its candidates elected is said to be a "fundamental interest," the infringement of which may be established without proof that a State has acted with the purpose of impairing anybody's access to the political process. This dissenting opinion finds the "right" infringed in the present case because no Negro has been elected to the Mobile City Commission.

Whatever appeal the dissenting opinion's view may have as a matter of political theory, it is not the law. The Equal Protection Clause of the Fourteenth Amendment does not require proportional representation as an imperative of political organization. . . .

More than 100 years ago the Court unanimously held that "the Constitution of the United States does not confer the right of suffrage upon any one. . . ." *Minor v. Happersett*, 21 Wall. 162, 178. See *Lassiter v. Northampton Election Bd.*, 360 U.S., at 50-51. It is for the States "to determine the conditions under which the right of suffrage may be exercised. . ., absent of course the discrimination which the Constitution condemns," *ibid.* It is true, as the dissenting opinion states, that the Equal Protection Clause confers a substantive right to participate in elections on an equal basis with other qualified voters. See *Dunn v. Blumstein*, 405 U.S. 330, 336; *Reynolds v. Sims*, 377 U.S., at 576. But this right to equal participation in the electoral process does not protect any "political group," however defined, from electoral defeat.

The dissenting opinion erroneously discovers the asserted entitlement to group representation within the "one person, one vote" principle of *Reynolds v. Sims, supra,* and its progeny. Those cases established that the Equal Protection Clause guarantees the right of each voter to "have his vote weighted equally with those of all other citizens." 377 U.S., at 576. The Court recognized that a voter's right to "have an equally effective voice" in the election of representatives is impaired where representation is not apportioned substantially on a population basis. In such cases, the votes of persons in more populous districts carry less weight than do those of persons in smaller districts. There can be, of course, no claim that the "one person, one vote" principle has been violated in this case, because the city of Mobile is a unitary electoral district and the Commission elections are conducted at large. It is therefore obvious that nobody's vote has been "diluted" in the sense in which that word was used in the *Reynolds* case. . . .

V

The judgment is reversed, and the case is remanded to the Court of Appeals for further proceedings.

It is so ordered.

Mr. Justice STEVENS, concurring in the judgment.

. . . While I agree with Mr. Justice Stewart that no violation of respondents' constitutional rights has been demonstrated, my analysis of the issue proceeds along somewhat different lines.

In my view, there is a fundamental distinction between state action that inhibits an individual's right to vote and state action that affects the political strength of various groups that compete for leadership in a democratically governed community.

That distinction divides so-called vote dilution practices into two different categories "governed by entirely different constitutional considerations."

In the first category are practices such as poll taxes or literacy tests that deny individuals access to the ballot. Districting practices that make an individual's vote in a heavily populated district less significant than an individual's vote in a smaller district also belong in that category. See *Baker v. Carr*, 369 U.S. 186; *Reynolds v. Sims*, 377 U.S. 533. Such practices must be tested by the strictest of constitutional standards, whether challenged under the Fifteenth Amendment or under the Equal Protection Clause of the Fourteenth Amendment. See, *e.g., Dunn v. Blumstein*, 405 U.S. 330, 337.

This case does not fit within the first category. The District Court found that black citizens in Mobile "register and vote without hindrance" and there is no claim that any individual's vote is worth less than any other's. Rather, this case draws into question a political structure that treats all individuals as equals but adversely affects the political strength of a racially identifiable group. Although I am satisfied that such a structure may be challenged under the Fifteenth Amendment as well as under the Equal Protection Clause of the Fourteenth Amendment, I believe that under either provision it must be judged by a standard that allows the political process to function effectively.

My conclusion that the Fifteenth Amendment applies to a case such as this rests on this Court's opinion in *Gomillion v. Lightfoot*, 364 U.S. 339. That case established that the Fifteenth Amendment does not simply guarantee the individual's right to vote; it also limits the States' power to draw political boundaries. Although *Gomillion* involved a districting structure that completely excluded the members of one race from participation in the city's elections, it does not stand for the proposition that no racial group can prevail on a Fifteenth Amendment claim unless it proves that an electoral system has the effect of making its members' right to vote, in Mr. Justice Marshall's words, "nothing more than the right to cast meaningless ballots." I agree with Mr. Justice Marshall that the Fifteenth Amendment need not and should not be so narrowly construed. I do not agree, however, with his view that every "showing of discriminatory impact" on a historically and socially disadvantaged racial group is sufficient to invalidate a districting plan.

Neither *Gomillion* nor any other case decided by this Court establishes a constitutional right to proportional representation for racial minorities. What *Gomillion* holds is that a sufficiently "uncouth" or irrational racial gerrymander violates the Fifteenth Amendment. . . . In its prior cases the Court has phrased the standard as being whether the districting practices in question "unconstitutionally operate to dilute or cancel the voting strength of racial or political elements." *Whitcomb v. Chavis*, 403 U.S. 124, 144. . . . Today, the plurality [holds] . . . that the primary, if not the sole, focus of the inquiry must be on the intent of the political body responsible for making the districting decision. . . . I do not believe that it is appropriate to focus on the subjective intent of the decisionmakers. . . .

In my view, the proper standard is suggested by three characteristics of the gerrymander condemned in *Gomillion*: (1) the 28-sided configuration was, in the Court's word, "uncouth," that is to say, it was manifestly not the product of a routine or a traditional political decision; (2) it had a significant adverse impact on a minority group; and (3) it was unsupported by any neutral justification and thus was either totally irrational or entirely motivated by a desire to curtail the political strength of the minority. These characteristics suggest that a proper test should focus on the objective effects of the political decision rather than the subjective motivation of the decisionmaker. . . .

Conversely, I am also persuaded that a political decision that affects group voting rights may be valid even if it can be proved that irrational or invidious factors have played some part in its enactment or retention. The standard for testing the acceptability of such a decision must take into account the fact that the responsibility for drawing political boundaries is generally committed to the legislative process and that the process inevitably involves a series of compromises among different group interests. If the process is to work, it must reflect an awareness of group interests and it must tolerate some attempts to advantage or to disadvantage particular segments of the voting populace. . . . Accordingly, a political decision that is supported by valid and articulable justifications cannot be invalid simply because some participants in the decisionmaking process were motivated by a purpose to disadvantage a minority group.

The decision to retain the commission form of government in Mobile, Ala., is such a decision. I am persuaded that some support for its retention comes, directly or indirectly, from members of the white majority who are motivated by a desire to make it more difficult for members of the black minority to serve in positions of responsibility in city government. I deplore that motivation and wish that neither it nor any other irrational prejudice played any part in our political processes. But I do not believe otherwise legitimate political choices can be invalidated simply because an irrational or invidious purpose played some part in the decisionmaking process. . . . Mobile's basic election system is the same as that followed by literally thousands of municipalities and other governmental units throughout the nation. The fact that these at-large systems characteristically place one or more minority groups at a significant disadvantage in the struggle for political power cannot invalidate all such systems. . . .

Mr. Justice WHITE, dissenting. . . .

The Court's decision is flatly inconsistent with *White v. Regester* and it cannot be understood to flow from our recognition in *Washington v. Davis*, 426 U.S. 229 (1976), that the Equal Protection Clause forbids only purposeful discrimination. Both the District Court and the Court of Appeals properly found that an invidious discriminatory purpose could be inferred from the totality of facts in this case. The Court's cryptic rejection of their conclusions ignores the principles that an invidious discriminatory purpose can be inferred from objective factors of the kind relied on in *White v. Regester* and that the trial courts are in a special position to make such intensely local appraisals. . . .

In the instant case the District Court and the Court of Appeals faithfully applied the principles of *White v. Regester* in assessing whether the maintenance of a system of at-large elections for the selection of Mobile City Commissioners denied Mobile Negroes their Fourteenth and Fifteenth Amendment rights. Scrupulously adhering to our admonition that "[the] plaintiffs' burden is to produce evidence to support findings that the political processes leading to nomination and election were not equally open to participation by the group in question," *id.*, at 766, the

District Court conducted a detailed factual inquiry into the openness of the candidate selection process to blacks. The court noted that "Mobile blacks were subjected to massive official and private racial discrimination until the Voting Rights Act of 1965" and that "[the] pervasive effects of past discrimination still substantially [affect] black political participation." 423 F. Supp. 384, 387 (S.D. Ala. 1976). Although the District Court noted that "[since] the Voting Rights Act of 1965, blacks register and vote without hindrance," the court found that "local political processes are not equally open" to blacks. Despite the fact that Negroes constitute more than 35% of the population of Mobile, no Negro has ever been elected to the Mobile City Commission. The plaintiffs introduced extensive evidence of severe racial polarization in voting patterns during the 1960's and 1970's with "white voting for white and black for black if a white is opposed to a black," resulting in the defeat of the black candidate or, if two whites are running, the defeat of the white candidate most identified with blacks. *Id.*, at 388. Regression analyses covering every City Commission race in 1965, 1969, and 1973, both the primary and general election of the county commission in 1968 and 1972, selected school board races in 1962, 1966, 1970, 1972, and 1974, city referendums in 1963 and 1973, and a countywide legislative race in 1969 confirmed the existence of severe bloc voting. *Id.*, at 388-389. Nearly every active candidate for public office testified that because of racial polarization "it is highly unlikely that anytime in the foreseeable future, under the at-large system, . . . a black can be elected against a white." *Id.*, at 388. After single-member districts were created in Mobile County for state legislative elections, "three blacks of the present fourteen member Mobile County delegation have been elected." *Id.*, at 389. Based on the foregoing evidence, the District Court found "that the structure of the at-large election of city commissioners combined with strong racial polarization of Mobile's electorate continues to effectively discourage qualified black citizens from seeking office or being elected thereby denying blacks equal access to the slating or candidate selection process." *Ibid.*

The District Court also reviewed extensive evidence that the City Commissioners elected under the at-large system have not been responsive to the needs of the Negro community. The court found that city officials have been unresponsive to the interests of Mobile Negroes in municipal employment, appointments to boards and committees, and the provision of municipal services in part because of "the political fear of a white backlash vote when black citizens' needs are at stake." *Id.*, at 392. The court also found that there is no clear-cut state policy preference for at-large elections and that past discrimination affecting the ability of Negroes to register and to vote "has helped preclude the effective participation of blacks in the election system today." *Id.*, at 393. The adverse impact of the at-large election system on minorities was found to be enhanced by the large size of the citywide election district, the majority vote requirement, the provision that candidates run for positions by place or number, and the lack of any provision for at-large candidates to run from particular geographic subdistricts. . . .

A plurality of the Court . . . casts aside the meticulous application of the principles of these cases by both the District Court and the Court of Appeals by concluding that the evidence they relied upon "fell far short of showing" purposeful discrimination. . . . The plurality apparently bases this conclusion on the fact that there are no official obstacles barring Negroes from registering, voting, and

running for office, coupled with its conclusion that none of the factors relied upon
by the courts below would alone be sufficient to support an inference of purposeful
discrimination. The absence of official obstacles to registration, voting, and running for office heretofore has never been deemed to insulate an electoral system
from attack under the Fourteenth and Fifteenth Amendments. [*White v. Regester*,
412 U.S. 755 (1973); *Gomillion v. Lightfoot*, 364 U.S. 339 (1960); *Terry v. Adams*,
345 U.S. 461 (1953).] Thus, even though Mobile's Negro community may register
and vote without hindrance, the system of at-large election of City Commissioners
may violate the Fourteenth and Fifteenth Amendments if it is used purposefully to
exclude Negroes from the political process. . . .

Because I believe that the findings of the District Court amply support an
inference of purposeful discrimination in violation of the Fourteenth and Fifteenth
Amendments, I respectfully dissent.

Mr. Justice MARSHALL, dissenting.

The American ideal of political equality, conceived in the earliest days of our
colonial existence and fostered by the egalitarian language of the Declaration of
Independence, could not forever tolerate the limitation of the right to vote to
white propertied males. Our constitution has been amended six times in the movement toward a democracy for more than the few, and this Court has interpreted the
Fourteenth Amendment to prove that "a citizen has a constitutionally protected
right to participate in elections on an equal basis with other citizens in the jurisdiction," *Dunn v. Blumstein*, 405 U.S. 330, 336 (1972). The Court's decision today is in
a different spirit. Indeed, a plurality of the Court concludes that, in the absence of
proof of intentional discrimination by the State, the right to vote provides the politically powerless with nothing more than the right to cast meaningless ballots. . . .

The plurality would require plaintiffs in vote-dilution cases to meet the stringent burden of establishing discriminatory intent within the meaning of *Washington
v. Davis*, 426 U.S. 229 (1976); *Arlington Heights v. Metropolitan Housing Dev. Corp.*,
429 U.S. 252 (1977); and *Personnel Administrator of Mass. v. Feeney*, 442 U.S. 256
(1979). In my view, our vote-dilution decisions require only a showing of discriminatory impact to justify the invalidation of a multimember districting scheme, and,
because they are premised on the fundamental interest in voting protected by the
Fourteenth Amendment, the discriminatory-impact standard adopted by them is
unaffected by *Washington v. Davis, supra*, and its progeny. . . .

I

The Court does not dispute the proposition that multimember districting can
have the effect of submerging electoral minorities and overrepresenting electoral
majorities. It is for this reason that we developed a strong preference for single-
member districting in court-ordered reapportionment plans. Furthermore, and
more important for present purposes, we decided a series of vote-dilution cases
under the Fourteenth Amendment that were designed to protect electoral minorities from precisely the combination of electoral laws and historical and social factors
found in the present cases. In my view, the plurality's treatment of these cases is fanciful. Although we have held that multimember districts are not unconstitutional

per se, there is simply no basis for the plurality's conclusion that under our prior cases proof of discriminatory intent is a necessary condition for the invalidation of multimember districting. . . .

It is apparent that a showing of discriminatory intent in the creation or mainte-nance of multimember districts is as unnecessary after *White* as it was under our earlier vote-dilution decisions. Under this line of cases, an electoral districting plan is invalid if it has the effect of affording an electoral minority "less opportunity than . . . other residents in the district to participate in the political processes and to elect legislators of their choice," *id.*, at 766. It is also apparent that the Court in *White* considered equal access to the political process as meaning more than merely allowing the minority the opportunity to vote. *White* stands for the proposition that an electoral system may not relegate an electoral minority to political impotence by diminishing the importance of its vote. The plurality's approach requiring proof of discriminatory purpose in the present cases is, then, squarely contrary to *White* and its predecessors. . . .

Reynolds v. Sims and its progeny focused solely on the discriminatory *effects* of malapportionment. They recognize that, when population figures for the repre-sentational districts of a legislature are not similar, the votes of citizens in larger districts do not carry as much weight in the legislature as do votes cast by citizens in smaller districts. The equal protection problem attacked by the "one person, one vote" principle is, then, one of vote dilution. . . . In the present cases, the alleged vote dilution, though caused by the combined effects of the electoral structure and social and historical factors rather than by unequal population distribution, is ana-lytically the same concept: the unjustified abridgment of a fundamental right. It follows, then, that a showing of discriminatory intent is just as unnecessary under the vote-dilution approach adopted in *Fortson v. Dorsey*, 379 U.S. 433 (1965), and applied in *White v. Regester, supra*, as it is under our reapportionment cases.[15]. . .

Our vote-dilution decisions, then, involve the fundamental-interest branch, rather than the antidiscrimination branch, of our jurisprudence under the Equal Protection Clause. They recognize a substantive constitutional right to participate on an equal basis in the electoral process that cannot be denied or diminished

---

15. Proof of discriminatory purpose has been equally unnecessary in our decisions assessing whether various impediments to electoral participation are inconsistent with the fundamental interest in voting. In the seminal case, *Harper v. Virginia Bd. of Elections*, 383 U.S. 663 (1966), we invalidated a $1.50 poll tax imposed as a precondition to voting. Relying on our decision two years earlier in *Reynolds v. Sims*, see *Harper, supra*, at 667-668, 670, we determined that "the right to vote is too precious, too fundamental to be so burdened or conditioned," 383 U.S., at 670. We analyzed the right to vote under the familiar standard that "where fundamental rights and liberties are asserted under the Equal Protection Clause, classifications which might invade or restrain them must be closely scrutinized and care-fully confined." *Ibid.* In accord with *Harper*, we have applied heightened scrutiny in assessing the imposition of filing fees, *e.g., Lubin v. Panish*, 415 U.S. 709 (1974); limitations on who may participate in elections involving specialized governmental entities, *e.g., Kramer v. Union School District*, 395 U.S. 621 (1969); durational residency requirements, *e.g., Dunn v. Blum-stein, supra*; enrollment time limitations for voting in party primary elections, *e.g., Kusper v. Pontikes*, 414 U.S. 51 (1973); and restrictions on candidate access to the ballot, *e.g., Illinois Elections Bd. v. Socialist Workers Party*, 440 U.S. 173 (1979).

for any reason, racial or otherwise, lacking quite substantial justification. They are premised on a rationale wholly apart from that underlying *Washington v. Davis*, 426 U.S. 229 (1976). . . .

The plurality's response is that my approach amounts to nothing less than a constitutional requirement of proportional representation for groups. That assertion amounts to nothing more than a red herring: I explicitly reject the notion that the Constitution contains any such requirement. The constitutional protection against vote dilution found in our prior cases does not extend to those situations in which a group has merely failed to elect representatives in proportion to its share of the population. To prove unconstitutional vote dilution, the group is also required to carry the far more onerous burden of demonstrating that it has been effectively fenced out of the political process. . . .

The plaintiffs in No. 77-1844 proved that no Negro had ever been elected to the Mobile City Commission, despite the fact that Negroes constitute about one-third of the electorate, and that the persistence of severe racial bloc voting made it highly unlikely that any Negro could be elected at large in the foreseeable future. . . . The plaintiffs convinced the District Court that Mobile Negroes were unable to use alternative avenues of political influence. They showed that Mobile Negroes still suffered pervasive present effects of massive historical official and private discrimination, and that the City Commission had been quite unresponsive to the needs of the minority community. The City of Mobile has been guilty of such pervasive racial discrimination in hiring employees that extensive intervention by the Federal District Court has been required. 423 F. Supp., at 389, 400. Negroes are grossly underrepresented on city boards and committees. *Id.*, at 389-390. The city's distribution of public services is racially discriminatory. *Id.*, at 390-391. City officials and police were largely unmoved by Negro complaints about police brutality and a "mock lynching." *Id.*, at 392. The District Court concluded that "[this] sluggish and timid response is another manifestation of the low priority given to the needs of the black citizens and of the [commissioners'] political fear of a white backlash vote when black citizens' needs are at stake." *Ibid.* . . .

IV

The American approach to government is premised on the theory that, when citizens have the unfettered right to vote, public officials will make decisions by the democratic accommodation of competing beliefs, not by deference to the mandates of the powerful. The American approach to civil rights is premised on the complementary theory that the unfettered right to vote is preservative of all other rights. The theoretical foundations for these approaches are shattered where, as in the present cases, the right to vote is granted in form, but denied in substance.

It is time to realize that manipulating doctrines and drawing improper distinctions under the Fourteenth and Fifteenth Amendments, as well as under Congress' remedial legislation enforcing those Amendments, make this Court an accessory to the perpetuation of racial discrimination. The plurality's requirement of proof of *intentional discrimination*, so inappropriate in today's cases, may represent an attempt to bury the legitimate concerns of the minority beneath the soil of a doctrine almost as impermeable as it is specious. If so, the superficial tranquility created by such measures can be but short-lived. If this Court refuses to honor our long-recognized principle that the Constitution "nullifies sophisticated as well as simple-minded modes of discrimination," *Lane v. Wilson*, 307 U.S., at 275, it cannot expect the victims of discrimination to respect political channels of seeking redress. I dissent.

[Justice Blackmun concurred in the result only. He agreed with Justice White that the findings below supported an inference of purposeful discrimination. He nevertheless concurred in the reversal because he believed the District Court's remedy went too far. It was not necessary, he wrote, to replace the commission system with a mayor-council form of government. The lower court should have tried to maintain at least some of the features of the commission system that the people of Mobile adopted for their own self-governance.

[In a two-sentence dissent, Justice Brennan agreed with Justice Marshall that proof of discriminatory impact suffices to make out a claim, and with Justices Marshall and White that such a claim had been proven here.]

>> *The Demise of Multimember Districts.* Congress has by statute prohibited the use of at-large elections and multimember districts in congressional elections since 1842. In contrast, multimember districts used to be quite common in plans apportioning representation in state legislatures. In the 1950s, only nine states relied exclusively on single-member districts. By 1962, when the Court decided *Baker v. Carr*, about half of the members of state legislatures' lower houses were elected from multimember districts, and one-sixth of state senators were so elected.

> Multimember districts with four or more seats were not uncommon in the 1960s. Indeed, at various times in the 1960s, metropolitan counties across the nation elected huge multimember legislative delegations on an at-large basis: Cuyahoga County (Cleveland) elected 17 members to Ohio's lower house; Denver County (Denver), 17 and 8 members, respectively, to the house and senate of Colorado; Marion County (Indianapolis), 15 and 8 members, respectively, to Indiana's house and senate. . . . In general, successive waves of redistricting . . . dramatically reduced the number of states relying on multimember districts. Among lower houses, the number with multimember districts dropped from 41 in 1962 to 23 in 1974 to 15 in 1984; for upper houses, the number slipped from 30 in 1962 to 12 in 1974 to 7 in 1984. . . . Moreover, the size of multimember districts has declined. Most of the very large metropolitan multimember districts noted above had disappeared by the mid-1970s. . . .

Timothy G. O'Rourke, *The Impact of Reapportionment on Congress and State Legislatures, in* Voting Rights and Redistricting in the United States 203 (Mark E. Rush ed., 1998).

Although at-large and multimember districts have all but disappeared from state legislative elections, they are extremely common on the local level. At-large election is the most common format for municipal elections, followed by mixed systems in which some local council members are elected by district and others are elected at-large. *See* Municipal Year Book.

>> *Alternatives to Pure At-Large Elections and Single-Member Electoral Systems.*   All electoral systems have benefits and drawbacks. Therefore, the choice of electoral system is a choice about tradeoffs. As Professor Donald Horowitz explains, no "electoral system simply reflects voter preferences or the existing pattern of cleavages in a society or the prevailing political party configuration. Every electoral system shapes and reshapes these features of the environment, and each does so in different ways." Donald L. Horowitz, *Electoral Systems: A Primer for Decision Makers,* 14 J. DEMOCRACY 115, 115 (2003). Electoral systems both reflect and shape voter preferences. Consequently, the choice of electoral system is also a choice about tradeoffs and the different ways in which electoral systems aggregate voter preferences. It is not enough to ask whether an electoral system will adequately reflect voter preferences; we must choose an electoral system with an eye toward the goals that we would like to pursue in making that choice.

What are the goals that ought to be kept in mind in choosing an electoral system? Consider some possibilities. First, an electoral system might be valued for pursuing proportionality. That is, one might want an electoral system that achieves some rough proportionality between votes and seats so that the composition of the legislature reflects roughly the distribution of political opinion in the community. Second, an electoral system might pursue the value of responsiveness: one might want an electoral system to facilitate voters' ability to hold their representative accountable through periodic elections, thereby promoting their responsiveness to their constituents.

Third, an electoral system might purse the value of political stability. Thus, one might want an electoral system to elevate to office only candidates who enjoy a particularly broad degree of public support. The standard American "first-past-the-post" electoral system, for example, is capable of selecting candidates with relatively narrow but highly intense support, especially when candidates may take office by polling a mere plurality — that is, a minority — of the votes. Candidates who take office with the support only of a narrow group of zealous partisans run the risk of losing political effectiveness and support quickly. Other electoral systems are designed to avoid this risk. A system devised in the eighteenth century by the Marquis de Condorcet is designed expressly to identify candidates who are widely preferred to their competitors by examining voter preferences *below* their first choices. In the Condorcet system, voters rank all the candidates, and the system simulates a series of head-to-head contests between all candidates. The candidate who wins more head-to-head contests than any other is deemed the winner. In this system, A is considered a better choice than B even when few voters rank A as their first choice; it counts in A's favor just as much if a voter ranks A third and B fourth as when a voter ranks A first and B second.

Lastly, for purposes of political peace, we might want an electoral system to reflect and record as best as possible the preferences of political minorities. We thus might want to privilege electoral systems that limit the scope of majoritarian victories over those that provide large governance rewards to majorities. *See* Horowitz, *supra,* at 116-120. What other goals do you think should be pursued by electoral systems?

Although in the United States we have generally used at-large or single-member districting, many jurisdictions in the United States, specifically at the local level, have used proportional or semi-proportional systems, primarily to remedy voting rights violations. The purported benefits of alternative voting systems are that they reduce the opportunity for manipulation by the government officials who are responsible for making the design choices and they are better at taking into account the preferences of political minorities. Scholars and courts have generally considered the following three electoral systems as alternatives to single-member districts and as alternatives to reducing the majoritarian effects of pure at-large systems while still maintaining multimember constituencies.

Limited Voting. In a limited voting system, voters cast fewer votes than there are seats to be filled. For example, in our hypothetical seven-member council, instead of casting all seven votes for the seven members of the city council, our voters would be limited to, say, six or five or four votes for seven seats. The vote limitation diminishes the majority's ability to swamp the political minority and allows the political minority a chance at representation. By limiting the number of votes, a unified majority cannot win every seat. The greater the vote limitation compared to the number of seats, the greater the probability that the political minority will elect their candidate of choice. To determine whether a cohesive political minority—a group or political party—will win at least one seat, we need to determine what mathematicians and political scientists call the "threshold of exclusion" or the "threshold of representation." The threshold of exclusion is the minimum level of support that a cohesive political minority must exceed in order to elect a candidate of its choice, no matter how the majority votes. To arrive at this threshold, we assume that the majority and the minority have different candidate preferences; that the majority casts all of the votes available to it; that the majority votes as a bloc and against the preferences of the minority; and that the majority casts its votes evenly among its preferred candidates. These are worst-case scenario assumptions for the political minority. It assumes that the majority maximizes its electoral advantage. Even under worst-case assumptions, the minority can capture at least one seat, if the minority votes cohesively.

The formula for determining the threshold of exclusion is: (number of votes)/(number of votes) + (number of seats) × 100. Consider a city with 1,000 voters and a seven-member city council. Let us say that 60% of our voters belong to the Jazz Party and 40% belong to the Classical Party. Let us also limit our voters to 3 votes. We would calculate the threshold of exclusion as follows: (3)/(3 + 7) × 100 = 30 percent. This means that out of 1,000 voters if a group consisting of 30% + 1, or 301, voted for the same candidate, giving that candidate 301 votes, that candidate must win one of the seats, no matter what everyone else did. Thus, the Classical Party must win at least one seat, as long as its members vote cohesively for a preferred candidate. If we limited our voters to 1 vote, the threshold would be 12.5%, which means a group of 126 voters can elect their preferred candidate. If we limited them to 4 votes, the threshold would be 36% and if we limited them to 5 votes, the threshold would be 41.6%. Again, recall that this is the worst-case scenario for the political minority, which means that even where we limit voters to 5 votes and the voters of the Classical Party are no longer guaranteed to win a seat, the Party might still be able to elect a preferred candidate if its members vote cohesively and the voters of the Jazz Party do not.

Cumulative Voting. In a cumulative system, voters are given as many votes as there are seats. Cumulative voting systems allow voters not just to express their preferences, but also to register the intensity of their preferences. Thus, a voter is not only given as many votes as there are seats, but the voter is also permitted to concentrate all of her votes on one candidate — that is, "plump" all of her votes on one candidate — or distribute her votes across her preferred candidates in a manner that reflects her intensity of preferences. Because the voter can distribute her votes across multiple candidates, cumulative voting systems enable groups of voters to form coalitions with like-minded others. Lastly, like limited voting, cumulative voting systems also make it easier for numerical minorities to draw a share of representation. This is one reason why many corporations use cumulative voting to elect the company's directors. Just like the more familiar single-member districted election, the winners in cumulative vote system are the candidates who receive the most votes.

As with limited voting, to determine whether a political minority will be able to elect a representative of its choice, we must calculate the threshold of exclusion. Again, as in the limited voting context, the threshold of exclusion for cumulative voting is calculated assuming the worst set of conditions for the political minority, which is essentially that the majority group votes cohesively and attempts to maximize its electoral outcome. The threshold of exclusion for cumulative voting is calculated as $1/1$ + number of seats × 100. Thus, in our seven-seat city council example, the threshold of exclusion is $1/8$ × 100 or 12.5%. This means that out of 1,000 voters, a political minority that constitutes at least 13% of the population, or 130 voters, is guaranteed to elect at least one candidate. Again, this is true no matter how the majority votes. If the majority does not vote as a bloc, but the minority group does, the minority group might be able to elect its representative of choice even with fewer than 13% of the vote. In our hypothetical seven-member city council, the Classical Party is likely to win three seats (400/130 = 3) under a cumulative voting system given that they constitute 40% of the 1,000 voters in the city.

Single Transferable Vote (STV). STV has at least two important properties: it facilitates representation by numerical minorities and it minimizes wasted votes. In a single transferable vote system, voters rank candidates from most to least preferred. Voters often place a "1" by their most preferred candidate, a "2" for next preferred, and so on. Voters may rank all of the candidates or only some of the candidates. A candidate is elected when she meets a certain threshold or quota. Votes are counted in rounds until seats are filled when enough candidates meet the quota for election. The first choice ballots are counted in the first round and candidates that meet the quota or threshold are elected. If no candidate meets the quota, then the candidate that received the least first choice votes is considered the losing candidate of this round, and is eliminated from contention. However, in STV the losing candidate's *ballots* are not discarded; we take from their ballots the voters' second choices and transfer those votes to the second choice candidates. Similarly, we don't throw out the ballots of the winning candidates; we take the second choice votes on those ballots and transfer them to the second choice candidates. We continue to count ballots, moving down the preference ladder, until all of the seats are filled.

There are two commonly used methods to calculate the quota or threshold. The first method, the Hare quota, is named after Thomas Hare, an English political scientist who designed the system. The Hare quota is simply the number of votes divided by the number of seats. The more common quota formula is the Droop quota, which was invented by mathematician Henry Droop. Unlike the Hare quota, the Droop quota guarantees that there will not be more candidates who meet the quota than there are seats. The quota is calculated as follows: (the number of valid votes cast/(seats to fill) + 1) + 1. Take our city council example with 1,000 voters and seven seats. If all of the voters cast valid votes, we would calculate the quota as follows: (1,000/7 + 1) + 1 = 126. Thus, a candidate will be elected with 126 votes. If a candidate receives more than 126 votes, the excess votes are redistributed to the next preferred candidate.

2. Gerrymandering

Gerrymandering refers to the drawing of political district boundaries to achieve a particular outcome in an election. Voters of a preferred political inclination are included within or excluded from the district to the point that a comfortable majority of the district's voters can be relied on to vote in the desired way. The term is named after Elbridge Gerry of Massachusetts, a signer of the Declaration of Independence and a delegate to the constitutional convention. As Governor of Massachusetts in 1810 and 1811, Gerry supervised the redistricting of the state in a way intended to give Republicans continued control of state government. One rambling district was shaped something like a salamander, and was referred to at the time as the "Gerrymander."

The term later came into general use.

1812 cartoon from which the term "gerrymander" got its name.

This section provides an introduction to racial and partisan gerrymandering. Racial gerrymandering will be considered in much greater detail in Chapter 5 when we turn to the Voting Rights Act. Consideration in this chapter is limited to constitutional rather than statutory issues.

Gomillion v. Lightfoot

364 U.S. 339 (1960)

Mr. Justice FRANKFURTER delivered the opinion of the Court.

This litigation challenges the validity, under the United States Constitution, of Local Act No. 140, passed by the Legislature of Alabama in 1957, redefining the boundaries of the City of Tuskegee. Petitioners are Negro citizens of Alabama who were, at the time of this redistricting measure, residents of the City of Tuskegee. Petitioners' claim is that enforcement of the statute, which alters the shape of Tuskegee from a square to an uncouth twenty-eight-sided figure, will constitute a discrimination against them in violation of the Due Process and Equal Protection Clauses of the Fourteenth Amendment to the Constitution and will deny them the right to vote in defiance of the Fifteenth Amendment. . . .

At this stage of the litigation we are not concerned with the truth of the allegations, that is, the ability of petitioners to sustain their allegations by proof. The sole question is whether the allegations entitle them to make good on their claim that they are being denied rights under the United States Constitution. The complaint, charging that Act 140 is a device to disenfranchise Negro citizens, alleges the following facts: Prior to Act 140 the City of Tuskegee was square in shape; the Act transformed it into a strangely irregular twenty-eight-sided figure as indicated in the diagram appended to this opinion. The essential inevitable effect of this redefinition of Tuskegee's boundaries is to remove from the city all save only four or five of its 400 Negro voters while not removing a single white voter or resident. The result of the Act is to deprive the Negro petitioners discriminatorily of the benefits of residence in Tuskegee, including, *inter alia*, the right to vote in municipal elections.

These allegations, if proven, would abundantly establish that Act 140 was not an ordinary geographic redistricting measure even within familiar abuses of gerrymandering. If these allegations upon a trial remained uncontradicted or unqualified, the conclusion would be irresistible, tantamount for all practical purposes to a mathematical demonstration, that the legislation is solely concerned with segregating white and colored voters by fencing Negro citizens out of town so as to deprive them of their pre-existing municipal vote.

It is difficult to appreciate what stands in the way of adjudging a statute having this inevitable effect invalid in light of the principles by which this Court must judge, and uniformly has judged, statutes that, howsoever speciously defined, obviously discriminate against colored citizens. "The [Fifteenth] Amendment nullifies sophisticated as well as simple-minded modes of discrimination." *Lane v. Wilson*, 307 U.S. 268, 275.

The complaint amply alleges a claim of racial discrimination. Against this claim the respondents have never suggested, either in their brief or in oral argument, any countervailing municipal function which Act 140 is designed to serve. The respondents invoke generalities expressing the State's unrestricted power—unlimited, that is, by the United States Constitution—to establish, destroy, or reorganize by contraction or expansion its political subdivisions, to wit, cities, counties, and other local units. We freely recognize the breadth and importance of this aspect of the State's political power. . . .

[T]he Court has never acknowledged that the States have power to do as they will with municipal corporations regardless of consequences. Legislative control of municipalities, no less than other state power, lies within the scope of relevant limitations imposed by the United States Constitution. . . .The opposite conclusion, urged upon us by respondents, would sanction the achievement by a State of any impairment of voting rights whatever so long as it was cloaked in the garb of the realignment of political subdivisions. "It is inconceivable that guaranties embedded in the Constitution of the United States may thus be manipulated out of existence." *Frost & Frost Trucking Co. v. Railroad Commission of California*, 271 U.S. 583, 594. . . .

According to the allegations here made, the Alabama Legislature has not merely redrawn the Tuskegee city limits with incidental inconvenience to the petitioners; it is more accurate to say that it has deprived the petitioners of the municipal franchise and consequent rights and to that end it has incidentally changed the city's boundaries. While in form this is merely an act redefining metes and bounds, if the allegations are established, the inescapable human effect of this essay in geometry and geography is to despoil colored citizens, and only colored citizens, of their theretofore enjoyed voting rights. . . .

APPENDIX TO OPINION OF THE COURT

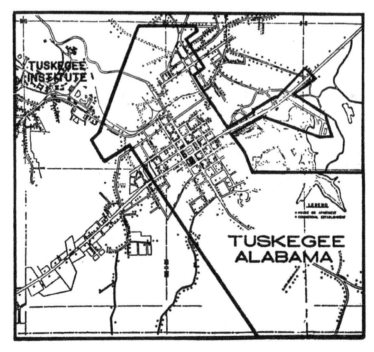

Chart showing Tuskegee, Alabama, before and after Act 140.
(The entire area of the square comprised the City prior to Act 140. The irregular
black-bordered figure within the square represents the post-enactment city.)

Racially discriminatory gerrymandering presents an easy case because of the Fifteenth Amendment. But what about where district lines are drawn not with racial considerations in mind, but to serve partisan political ends such as preserving, or even artificially increasing, a political party's share of seats in a legislature? Here the Fifteenth Amendment plays no role and any constitutional constraint must be found in the Fourteenth Amendment.

≫   *A Half-Century of Judicial Indecision.*   As we have seen, the Supreme Court adopted a strongly interventionist approach in redistricting cases during the 1960s when it developed and applied the one person, one vote standard to invalidate nearly every districting plan in the nation. In the domain of partisan gerrymandering, however, the Court took a different route. From the beginning, many justices expressed reservations about interfering in aspects of the redistricting process that they viewed as inherently political in nature. As a majority wrote for the Court in its first such case, *Gaffney v. Cummings*, 412 U.S. 735 (1973):

> Politics and political considerations are inseparable from districting and apportionment. . . . It is not only obvious, but absolutely unavoidable, that the location and shape of districts may well determine the political complexion of the area. . . . The reality is that districting inevitably has and is intended to have substantial political consequences. [We will not attempt] the impossible task of extirpating politics from what are the essentially political processes of the sovereign States.

In later cases, serious divisions began to appear on the Court, which persist up to the present. On some issues, the justices have generally agreed. They agree, for example, that deliberate manipulation of district boundaries for the purpose of partisan gain is a deeply troubling and anti-democratic practice. Most justices to examine the issue over the last forty years have also agreed that even though partisanship cannot be entirely eliminated from the redistricting process, intentional partisan gerrymandering can rise to the level of unconstitutionality under the Equal Protection Clause when it is sufficiently egregious.

Strong disagreements have emerged, however, over how to distinguish impermissible from permissible consideration of partisanship in the crafting of redistricting maps—when, that is, a redistricting map crosses the line into unconstitutionality. This disagreement has emerged in two ways: first, over the precise constitutional standard that should be used to distinguish constitutional from unconstitutional gerrymanders; and second, over whether it is even possible for courts to develop a standard that is "judicially manageable." Justices in the first group have over the years offered numerous constitutional standards, but no standard has ever commanded a majority. Justices in the second group believe that the reason no majority has coalesced around a standard is because the task itself exceeds judicial competence, and that partisan gerrymandering should be deemed to raise a political question that federal courts are incompetent to answer. This position is the one that finally attracted a bare majority in the Court's 2019 decision in *Rucho v. Common Cause* (below).

≫   *First Attempt:* **Davis v. Bandemer.**   *Gaffney* involved a bipartisan gerrymander in which the two parties collaborated to produce a map that reflected roughly the strength of each party in the electorate. The Court's first engagement with a unilateral gerrymander, in which one party deliberately shores up its own strength at the expense of its competitor, occurred in *Davis v. Bandemer*, 478 U.S. 109 (1986). Following the 1980 census, Republicans in Indiana controlled both chambers of the state legislature and the governor's office. In a process that entirely excluded Democrats from any role in creating district maps, the legislature drew a congressional map that the Speaker of the House candidly described in a deposition as designed to "save as many incumbent Republicans as possible." In the 1982 midterm elections, the map produced Republican majorities in both houses. Most notably, Republicans won 57% of House seats on only 43% of the popular vote. Six justices agreed that the proper constitutional standard required a showing both of (1) intentional discrimination by the in party against the out party, and (2) an actual discriminatory impact. The same six agreed that the plaintiffs had shown the required intent to discriminate; indeed, a plurality thought it reasonable to assume that "those responsible for the legislation will know the likely political composition of the new districts," and that the requirement of intentional discrimination will likely be satisfied "[a]s long as redistricting is done by a legislature."

The Court splintered, however, on the second prong. Two justices thought a discriminatory impact had been proved, but four justices held that a single election in the gerrymandering party's favor is insufficient to show the requisite impact. Indiana, this group observed, is a swing state, and consequently a favorable result in a single election cannot reliably prove that the gerrymandering political party has successfully obtained for itself a persistent and constitutionally improper advantage.

Three justices dissented. Writing for this group, Justice O'Connor argued that the Court's analysis was "flawed from its inception. The Equal Protection Clause does not supply judicially manageable standards for resolving purely political gerrymandering claims." Under the Court's reasoning, she contended, "[t]here is simply no clear stopping point to prevent the gradual evolution of a requirement of roughly proportional representation for every cohesive political group." Yet, she argued, if the Constitution permits legislatures to be elected from single-member districts, then it cannot require proportionality of representation, and such a requirement cannot therefore be read into the Equal Protection Clause. Moreover, she went on, unlike racial minorities, which enjoy special constitutional protection,

> members of the Democratic and Republican Parties cannot claim that they are a discrete and insular group vulnerable to exclusion from the political process by some dominant group: these political parties are the dominant groups, and the Court has offered no reason to believe that they are incapable of fending for themselves through the political process. Indeed, there is good reason to think that political gerrymandering is a self-limiting enterprise. See B. Cain, The Reapportionment Puzzle 151-159 (1984). In order to gerrymander, the legislative majority must weaken some of its safe seats, thus exposing its own incumbents to greater risks of defeat—risks they may refuse to accept past a certain point. *Id.*, at 154-155. Similarly, an overambitious gerrymander can lead to disaster for the legislative majority: because it has created more seats in which it hopes to win relatively narrow victories, the same swing in overall voting strength will tend to cost the legislative majority more and more seats as

the gerrymander becomes more ambitious. *Id.*, at 152. More generally, each major party presumably has ample weapons at its disposal to conduct the partisan struggle that often leads to a partisan apportionment, but also often leads to a bipartisan one. There is no proof before us that political gerrymandering is an evil that cannot be checked or cured by the people or by the parties themselves. Absent such proof, I see no basis for concluding that there is a need, let alone a constitutional basis, for judicial intervention. . . .

⟫   *Partisan Gerrymandering as a "Self-Limiting Enterprise."*   In her *Bandemer* concurrence, Justice O'Connor refers to partisan gerrymandering as a "self-limiting enterprise," a contention that she supports with a brief explanation and a citation to an influential work by Bruce Cain, a political scientist. Cain's fuller explanation of his point appears below. According to Cain, a party that attempts to gerrymander itself into a stronger position can do so only by making more precarious its hold on seats that are presently safe, a risky action. In addition, taking seats away from incumbents through gerrymandering is not always a foregone conclusion.

> [Another] consideration is whether the party has the resources to fight in the more efficient seats it would be creating. The safe seats in the majority party that have been weakened in order to shore up the marginals may cost the gerrymandering party more money in the next election if, by weakening the seats, it inadvertently encourages strong candidates from the opposition to run. Against that consideration are the marginal majority party seats that have been strengthened, which may discourage some strong opposition candidates who would otherwise have run. However, since both of these kinds of seats will have majority party incumbents in them, they will not cost the party nearly so much as will attempts to win weakened minority party seats. Because challengers have to spend more than incumbents, the gerrymandering party has to be prepared to spend a lot of money to unseat the minority party's incumbents. Weakening the opponent by a few registration points will not per se guarantee a victory for the majority party. It must be prepared to overcome the minority party incumbent's natural advantages—name recognition, proven track record, and the like—in order to win the seat in the next election, or wait until the seat becomes open, by which time the gerrymandered advantage may have eroded. . . .
>
> In short, reapportionment cannot make magical transformations in the state's political composition. . . . It can increase the party's delegation, but there are limits to how far it can alter the public's policy preferences. The designs of a majority party can be moderated by the presence of legislators from the opposite party in the legislature or by sizeable blocks of opposition-party voters in its districts. Policy transformations through reapportionment are hindered by the dilemma that heightened power in the legislature can be offset by the changed voter composition in the districts. Partisan gerrymandering can produce a more extreme skew in the distribution of seats in the legislature, but at the price of less skew in the distribution of opinion in individual seats. Parties in their turn can be

moderated in their policies by having fewer representatives in the legislature or internally by having a broader spectrum of voters to represent. For the ideologue, partisan gerrymandering may actually not be worthwhile.

BRUCE CAIN, THE REAPPORTIONMENT PUZZLE (1984).

Two political scientists coined a new term to describe a partisan gerrymander that backfires: a "dummymander." Bernard Grofman and Thomas L. Brunell, *The Art of the Dummymander: The Impact of Recent Redistricting on the Partisan Makeup of Southern House Seats, in* REDISTRICTING IN THE NEW MILLENNIUM 183 (Peter F. Galderisi ed., 2005). Their article describes what they claim were misconceived and overreaching gerrymanders in the 1990 and 2000 redistricting cycles in Alabama, Georgia, Mississippi, North Carolina, and South Carolina.

≫ *Back to the Drawing Board.* The Court did not accept another partisan gerrymandering case for 18 years. During that period, although by all accounts partisan gerrymandering was commonplace, not a single plaintiff prevailed in a constitutional challenge relying on the *Bandemer* standard. Recognizing the confusion in the field, the Court finally returned to the issue in *Vieth v. Jubilirer*, 541 U.S. 267 (2004). There, it made no headway in clarifying the governing law, and indeed succeeded only in further muddying the waters. Four justices argued that partisan gerrymandering presents a political question that federal courts lack jurisdiction to adjudicate. Four justices ruled that partisan gerrymandering is justiciable and that excessive gerrymandering can rise to the level of unconstitutionality, but could not agree on a standard.

Justice Kennedy provided the swing vote, and he split the baby. Although he agreed that the Court lacked a clear constitutional standard by which to identify the line between constitutional and unconstitutional gerrymandering, he refused to conclude that no judicially manageable standard might ever emerge in the give and take of future litigation.

> Our attention has not been drawn to statements of principled, well-accepted rules of fairness that should govern redistricting, or to helpful formulations of the legislator's duty in drawing district lines. . . . There are, then, weighty arguments for holding cases like these to be nonjusticiable; and those arguments may prevail in the long run. In my view, however, the arguments are not so compelling that they require us now to bar all future claims of injury from a partisan gerrymander. . . . That no [constitutional] standard has emerged in this case should not be taken to prove that none will emerge in the future. . . .
>
> The plurality says that 18 years, in effect, prove the negative. [But] by the timeline of the law 18 years is rather a short period. In addition, the rapid evolution of technologies in the apportionment field suggests yet unexplored possibilities. Computer assisted districting has become so routine and sophisticated that legislatures, experts, and courts can use databases to map electoral districts in a matter of hours, not months. Technology is both a threat and a promise. On the one hand, if courts refuse to entertain any claims of partisan gerrymandering, the temptation to use partisan favoritism in districting in an unconstitutional manner will grow. On the other hand, these new technologies may produce new

methods of analysis that make more evident the precise nature of the burdens gerrymanders impose on the representational rights of voters and
parties. That would facilitate court efforts to identify and remedy the burdens, with judicial intervention limited by the derived standards.

If suitable standards with which to measure the burden a gerrymander imposes on representational rights did emerge, hindsight would show
that the Court prematurely abandoned the field. That is a risk the Court
should not take.

For these reasons, Justice Kennedy joined the plurality in voting to dismiss the case,
but not in holding partisan gerrymandering claims nonjusticiable.

Justice Kennedy's opinion set off a wild scramble among litigants, lawyers, and
political scientists to devise a constitutional standard that would satisfy a majority of
the Court. We review some of the more prominent standards later in this section.

Following *Vieth*, the Court took two more partisan gerrymandering cases with
equally dismal results. *LULAC v. Perry*, 548 U.S. 399 (2006), produced no majority for any constitutional approach or standard, and in *Gill v. Whitford*, 138 S.Ct.
1916 (2018), the Court punted the entire issue by dismissing for lack of standing.
Finally, in the case below, after Justice Kennedy retired and was replaced by Brett
Kavanaugh, a five-justice majority finally coalesced on the question of how federal
courts should address claims of unconstitutional gerrymandering under the Equal
Protection Clause.

Rucho v. Common Cause

138 S.Ct. 2484 (2019)

Roberts, C.J., delivered the opinion of the Court, in which Thomas, Alito, Gorsuch, and Kavanaugh, JJ., joined. Kagan, J., filed a dissenting opinion, in which
Ginsburg, Breyer, and Sotomayor, JJ., joined.

Chief Justice ROBERTS delivered the opinion of the Court.

Voters and other plaintiffs in North Carolina and Maryland challenged their
States' congressional districting maps as unconstitutional partisan gerrymanders. . . . These cases require us to consider once again whether claims of excessive
partisanship in districting are "justiciable"—that is, properly suited for resolution
by the federal courts. This Court has not previously struck down a districting plan as
an unconstitutional partisan gerrymander, and has struggled without success over
the past several decades to discern judicially manageable standards for deciding
such claims. The districting plans at issue here are highly partisan, by any measure.
The question is whether the courts below appropriately exercised judicial power
when they found them unconstitutional as well.

I

The first case involves a challenge to the congressional redistricting plan
enacted by the Republican-controlled North Carolina General Assembly in 2016.
The Republican legislators leading the redistricting effort instructed their mapmaker to use political data to draw a map that would produce a congressional

delegation of ten Republicans and three Democrats. As one of the two Republicans chairing the redistricting committee stated, "I think electing Republicans is better than electing Democrats. So I drew this map to help foster what I think is better for the country." He further explained that the map was drawn with the aim of electing ten Republicans and three Democrats because he did "not believe it [would be] possible to draw a map with 11 Republicans and 2 Democrats." One Democratic state senator objected that entrenching the 10–3 advantage for Republicans was not "fair, reasonable, [or] balanced" because, as recently as 2012, "Democratic congressional candidates had received more votes on a statewide basis than Republican candidates." The General Assembly was not swayed by that objection and approved the 2016 Plan by a party-line vote.

In November 2016, North Carolina conducted congressional elections using the 2016 Plan, and Republican candidates won 10 of the 13 congressional districts. In the 2018 elections, Republican candidates won nine congressional districts, while Democratic candidates won three. The Republican candidate narrowly prevailed in the remaining district, but the State Board of Elections called a new election after allegations of fraud. . . .

The plaintiffs challenged the 2016 Plan on multiple constitutional grounds. First, they alleged that the Plan violated the Equal Protection Clause of the Fourteenth Amendment by intentionally diluting the electoral strength of Democratic voters. Second, they claimed that the Plan violated their First Amendment rights by retaliating against supporters of Democratic candidates on the basis of their political beliefs. Third, they asserted that the Plan usurped the right of "the People" to elect their preferred candidates for Congress, in violation of the requirement in Article I, §2, of the Constitution that Members of the House of Representatives be chosen "by the People of the several States." Finally, they alleged that the Plan violated the Elections Clause by exceeding the State's delegated authority to prescribe the "Times, Places and Manner of holding Elections" for Members of Congress.

After a four-day trial, the three-judge District Court unanimously concluded that the 2016 Plan violated the Equal Protection Clause and Article I of the Constitution. The court further held, with Judge Osteen dissenting, that the Plan violated the First Amendment. . . . The court also agreed with the plaintiffs that the 2016 Plan discriminated against them because of their political speech and association, in violation of the First Amendment. . . . Finally, the District Court concluded that the 2016 Plan violated the Elections Clause and Article I, §2. The District Court enjoined the State from using the 2016 Plan in any election after the November 2018 general election. . . .

The second case before us is *Lamone v. Benisek*. In 2011, the Maryland Legislature—dominated by Democrats—undertook to redraw the lines of that State's eight congressional districts. The Governor at the time, Democrat Martin O'Malley, led the process. He appointed a redistricting committee to help redraw the map, and asked Congressman Steny Hoyer, who has described himself as a "serial gerrymanderer," to advise the committee. The Governor later testified that his aim was to "use the redistricting process to change the overall composition of Maryland's congressional delegation to 7 Democrats and 1 Republican by flipping" one district. . . . The map was adopted by a party-line vote. It was used in the 2012 election and succeeded in flipping the Sixth District. A Democrat has held the seat ever since.

In November 2013, three Maryland voters filed this lawsuit. They alleged that the 2011 Plan violated the First Amendment, the Elections Clause, and Article I, §2, of the Constitution. [The] District Court concluded that the plaintiffs' claims were justiciable, and that the Plan violated the First Amendment by diminishing their "ability to elect their candidate of choice" because of their party affiliation and voting history, and by burdening their associational rights. On the latter point, the court relied upon findings that Republicans in the Sixth District "were burdened in fundraising, attracting volunteers, campaigning, and generating interest in voting in an atmosphere of general confusion and apathy.". . .

II

A

Article III of the Constitution limits federal courts to deciding "Cases" and "Controversies." We have understood that limitation to mean that federal courts can address only questions "historically viewed as capable of resolution through the judicial process." *Flast v. Cohen,* 392 U.S. 83 (1968). . . . Chief Justice Marshall famously wrote that it is "the province and duty of the judicial department to say what the law is." *Marbury v. Madison,* 5 U.S. 137, 177(1803). Sometimes, however, "the law is that the judicial department has no business entertaining the claim of unlawfulness — because the question is entrusted to one of the political branches or involves no judicially enforceable rights." *Vieth v. Jubelirer,* 541 U.S. 267, 277 (2004) (plurality opinion). In such a case the claim is said to present a "political question" and to be nonjusticiable — outside the courts' competence and therefore beyond the courts' jurisdiction. *Baker v. Carr,* 369 U.S. 186, 217 (1962). Among the political question cases the Court has identified are those that lack "judicially discoverable and manageable standards for resolving [them]." *Ibid.* . . .

B

Partisan gerrymandering is nothing new. Nor is frustration with it. The practice was known in the Colonies prior to Independence, and the Framers were familiar with it at the time of the drafting and ratification of the Constitution. During the very first congressional elections, George Washington and his Federalist allies accused Patrick Henry of trying to gerrymander Virginia's districts against their candidates — in particular James Madison, who ultimately prevailed over fellow future President James Monroe.

In 1812, Governor of Massachusetts and future Vice President Elbridge Gerry notoriously approved congressional districts that the legislature had drawn to aid the Democratic-Republican Party. The moniker "gerrymander" was born when an outraged Federalist newspaper observed that one of the misshapen districts resembled a salamander. "By 1840, the gerrymander was a recognized force in party politics and was generally attempted in all legislation enacted for the formation of election districts. It was generally conceded that each party would attempt to gain power which was not proportionate to its numerical strength."

The Framers addressed the election of Representatives to Congress in the Elections Clause. Art. I, §4, cl. 1. That provision assigns to state legislatures the power to prescribe the "Times, Places and Manner of holding Elections" for Members of Congress, while giving Congress the power to "make or alter" any such regulations. . . .

Congress has regularly exercised its Elections Clause power, including to address partisan gerrymandering. The Apportionment Act of 1842, which required single-member districts for the first time, specified that those districts be "composed of contiguous territory" in "an attempt to forbid the practice of the gerrymander." Later statutes added requirements of compactness and equality of population. (Only the single member district requirement remains in place today. 2 U.S.C. §2c.) Congress also used its Elections Clause power in 1870, enacting the first comprehensive federal statute dealing with elections as a way to enforce the Fifteenth Amendment. Force Act of 1870. Starting in the 1950s, Congress enacted a series of laws to protect the right to vote through measures such as the suspension of literacy tests and the prohibition of English-only elections.

Appellants suggest that, through the Elections Clause, the Framers set aside electoral issues such as the one before us as questions that only Congress can resolve. We do not agree. In two areas—one-person, one-vote and racial gerrymandering—our cases have held that there is a role for the courts with respect to at least some issues that could arise from a State's drawing of congressional districts.

But the history is not irrelevant. The Framers were aware of electoral districting problems and considered what to do about them. They settled on a characteristic approach, assigning the issue to the state legislatures, expressly checked and balanced by the Federal Congress. As Alexander Hamilton explained, "it will . . . not be denied that a discretionary power over elections ought to exist somewhere. It will, I presume, be as readily conceded that there were only three ways in which this power could have been reasonably modified and disposed: that it must either have been lodged wholly in the national legislature, or wholly in the State legislatures, or primarily in the latter, and ultimately in the former." The Federalist No. 59. At no point was there a suggestion that the federal courts had a role to play. Nor was there any indication that the Framers had ever heard of courts doing such a thing.

C

Courts have nevertheless been called upon to resolve a variety of questions surrounding districting. Early on, doubts were raised about the competence of the federal courts to resolve those questions. See *Colegrove v. Green*, 328 U.S. 549 (1946). In the leading case of *Baker v. Carr*, . . . [t]his Court . . . identified various considerations relevant to determining whether a claim is a nonjusticiable political question, including whether there is "a lack of judicially discoverable and manageable standards for resolving it." 369 U.S. at 217. The Court concluded that the claim of population inequality among districts did not fall into that category, because such a claim could be decided under basic equal protection principles. . . .

Another line of challenges to districting plans has focused on race. Laws that explicitly discriminate on the basis of race, as well as those that are race neutral on their face but are unexplainable on grounds other than race, are of course presumptively invalid. The Court applied those principles to electoral boundaries in *Gomillion v. Lightfoot*, concluding that a challenge to an "uncouth twenty-eight sided" municipal boundary line that excluded black voters from city elections stated a constitutional claim.

Partisan gerrymandering claims have proved far more difficult to adjudicate. The basic reason is that, while it is illegal for a jurisdiction to depart from the one-person, one-vote rule, or to engage in racial discrimination in districting, "a jurisdiction may engage in constitutional political gerrymandering."

To hold that legislators cannot take partisan interests into account when drawing district lines would essentially countermand the Framers' decision to entrust districting to political entities. The "central problem" is not determining whether a jurisdiction has engaged in partisan gerrymandering. It is "determining when political gerrymandering has gone too far." *Vieth*, 541 U.S. at 296 (plurality opinion).

We first considered a partisan gerrymandering claim in *Gaffney v. Cummings* in 1973. There we rejected an equal protection challenge to Connecticut's redistricting plan, which "aimed at a rough scheme of proportional representation of the two major political parties" by "wiggl[ing] and joggl[ing] boundary lines" to create the appropriate number of safe seats for each party. 412 U. S., at 738, 752, n. 18 (internal quotation marks omitted). In upholding the State's plan, we reasoned that districting "inevitably has and is intended to have substantial political consequences." Id., at 753.

Thirteen years later, in *Davis v. Bandemer*, we addressed a claim that Indiana Republicans had cracked and packed Democrats in violation of the Equal Protection Clause. A majority of the Court agreed that the case was justiciable, but the Court splintered over the proper standard to apply. Four Justices would have required proof of "intentional discrimination against an identifiable political group and an actual discriminatory effect on that group." *Id.* at 127. Two Justices would have focused on "whether the boundaries of the voting districts have been distorted deliberately and arbitrarily to achieve illegitimate ends." *Id.* at 165 (Powell, J., concurring in part and dissenting in part). Three Justices, meanwhile, would have held that the Equal Protection Clause simply "does not supply judicially manageable standards for resolving purely political gerrymandering claims." *Id.* at 147 (O'Connor, J., concurring in judgment). At the end of the day, there was "no 'Court' for a standard that properly should be applied in determining whether a challenged redistricting plan is an unconstitutional partisan political gerrymander." *Id.* at 185, n. 25 (opinion of Powell, J.). In any event, the Court held that the plaintiffs had failed to show that the plan violated the Constitution.

Eighteen years later, in *Vieth*, the plaintiffs complained that Pennsylvania's legislature "ignored all traditional redistricting criteria, including the preservation of local government boundaries," in order to benefit Republican congressional candidates. 541 U. S., at 272–273 (plurality opinion). Justice Scalia wrote for a four-Justice plurality. He would have held that the plaintiffs' claims were nonjusticiable because there was no "judicially discernible and manageable standard" for deciding them. *Id.* at 306. Justice Kennedy, concurring in the judgment, noted "the lack of comprehensive and neutral principles for drawing electoral boundaries [and] the absence of rules to limit and confine judicial intervention." *Id.* at 306–307. He nonetheless left open the possibility that "in another case a standard might emerge." Id., at 312. Four Justices dissented.

In *LULAC*, the plaintiffs challenged a mid-decade redistricting map approved by the Texas Legislature. Once again a majority of the Court could not find a justiciable standard for resolving the plaintiffs' partisan gerrymandering claims. See 548 U. S. at 414 (noting that the "disagreement over what substantive standard to apply" that was evident in Bandemer "persists").

As we summed up last Term in *Gill*, our "considerable efforts in *Gaffney, Bandemer, Vieth,* and *LULAC* leave unresolved whether . . . claims [of legal right] may be brought in cases involving allegations of partisan gerrymandering." . . .

III

In considering whether partisan gerrymandering claims are justiciable, we are mindful of Justice Kennedy's counsel in *Vieth*: Any standard for resolving such claims must be grounded in a "limited and precise rationale" and be "clear, manageable, and politically neutral." An important reason for those careful constraints is that . . . "[t]he opportunity to control the drawing of electoral boundaries through the legislative process of apportionment is a critical and traditional part of politics in the United States." An expansive standard requiring "the correction of all election district lines drawn for partisan reasons would commit federal and state courts to unprecedented intervention in the American political process," *Vieth*, 541 U.S. at 306.

As noted, the question is one of degree: How to "provid[e] a standard for deciding how much partisan dominance is too much." *LULAC*, 548 U.S. at 420 (opinion of Kennedy, J.). And it is vital in such circumstances that the Court act only in accord with especially clear standards: "With uncertain limits, intervening courts — even when proceeding with best intentions — would risk assuming political, not legal, responsibility for a process that often produces ill will and distrust." *Vieth*, 541 U.S. at 307 (opinion of Kennedy, J.). . . .

Partisan gerrymandering claims rest on an instinct that groups with a certain level of political support should enjoy a commensurate level of political power and influence. Explicitly or implicitly, a districting map is alleged to be unconstitutional because it makes it too difficult for one party to translate statewide support into seats in the legislature. But such a claim is based on a "norm that does not exist" in our electoral system — "statewide elections for representatives along party lines." *Bandemer*, 478 U.S. at 159 (opinion of O'Connor, J.).

Partisan gerrymandering claims invariably sound in a desire for proportional representation. As Justice O'Connor put it, such claims are based on "a conviction that the greater the departure from proportionality, the more suspect an apportionment plan becomes." "Our cases, however, clearly foreclose any claim that the Constitution requires proportional representation or that legislatures in reapportioning must draw district lines to come as near as possible to allocating seats to the contending parties in proportion to what their anticipated statewide vote will be."

The Founders certainly did not think proportional representation was required. For more than 50 years after ratification of the Constitution, many States elected their congressional representatives through at-large or "general ticket" elections. Such States typically sent single-party delegations to Congress. See E. Engstrom,

Partisan Gerrymandering and the Construction of American Democracy 43–51 (2013). That meant that a party could garner nearly half of the vote statewide and wind up without any seats in the congressional delegation. The Whigs in Alabama suffered that fate in 1840: "their party garnered 43 percent of the statewide vote, yet did not receive a single seat." *Id.*, at 48. When Congress required single-member districts in the Apportionment Act of 1842, it was not out of a general sense of fairness, but instead a (mis)calculation by the Whigs that such a change would improve their electoral prospects.

Unable to claim that the Constitution requires proportional representation outright, plaintiffs inevitably ask the courts to make their own political judgment about how much representation particular political parties *deserve*—based on the votes of their supporters—and to rearrange the challenged districts to achieve that end. But federal courts are not equipped to apportion political power as a matter of fairness, nor is there any basis for concluding that they were authorized to do so. . . .

The initial difficulty in settling on a "clear, manageable and politically neutral" test for fairness is that it is not even clear what fairness looks like in this context. There is a large measure of "unfairness" in any winner-take-all system. Fairness may mean a greater number of competitive districts. Such a claim seeks to undo packing and cracking so that supporters of the disadvantaged party have a better shot at electing their preferred candidates. But making as many districts as possible more competitive could be a recipe for disaster for the disadvantaged party. As Justice White has pointed out, "[i]f all or most of the districts are competitive . . . even a narrow statewide preference for either party would produce an overwhelming majority for the winning party in the state legislature." *Bandemer*, 478 U.S. at 130 (plurality opinion).

On the other hand, perhaps the ultimate objective of a "fairer" share of seats in the congressional delegation is most readily achieved by yielding to the gravitational pull of proportionality and engaging in cracking and packing, to ensure each party its "appropriate" share of "safe" seats. Such an approach, however, comes at the expense of competitive districts and of individuals in districts allocated to the opposing party.

Or perhaps fairness should be measured by adherence to "traditional" districting criteria, such as maintaining political subdivisions, keeping communities of interest together, and protecting incumbents. But protecting incumbents, for example, enshrines a particular partisan distribution. And the "natural political geography" of a State—such as the fact that urban electoral districts are often dominated by one political party—can itself lead to inherently packed districts. . . .

Deciding among just these different visions of fairness . . . poses basic questions that are political, not legal. There are no legal standards discernible in the Constitution for making such judgments, let alone limited and precise standards that are clear, manageable, and politically neutral. Any judicial decision on what is "fair" in this context would be an "unmoored determination" of the sort characteristic of a political question beyond the competence of the federal courts.

And it is only after determining how to define fairness that you can even begin to answer the determinative question: "How much is too much?" At what point does permissible partisanship become unconstitutional? If compliance with traditional districting criteria is the fairness touchstone, for example, how much deviation from those criteria is constitutionally acceptable and how should map-drawers prioritize competing criteria? Should a court "reverse gerrymander" other parts of a State to counteract "natural" gerrymandering caused, for example, by the urban concentration of one party? If a districting plan protected half of the incumbents but redistricted the rest into head to head races, would that be constitutional? A court would have to rank the relative importance of those traditional criteria and weigh how much deviation from each to allow.

If a court instead focused on the respective number of seats in the legislature, it would have to decide the ideal number of seats for each party and determine at what point deviation from that balance went too far. If a 5–3 allocation corresponds most closely to statewide vote totals, is a 6–2 allocation permissible, given that legislatures have the authority to engage in a certain degree of partisan gerrymandering? Which seats should be packed and which cracked? Or if the goal is as many competitive districts as possible, how close does the split need to be for the district to be considered competitive? Presumably not all districts could qualify, so how to choose? Even assuming the court knew which version of fairness to be looking for, there are no discernible and manageable standards for deciding whether there has been a violation. The questions are "unguided and ill suited to the development of judicial standards," *Vieth*, 541 U.S. at 296 (plurality opinion), and "results from one gerrymandering case to the next would likely be disparate and inconsistent," *id.*, at 308 (opinion of Kennedy, J.).

Appellees contend that if we can adjudicate one-person, one-vote claims, we can also assess partisan gerrymandering claims. But the one-person, one-vote rule is relatively easy to administer as a matter of math. The same cannot be said of partisan gerrymandering claims, because the Constitution supplies no objective measure for assessing whether a districting map treats a political party fairly. It hardly follows from the principle that each person must have an equal say in the election of representatives that a person is entitled to have his political party achieve representation in some way commensurate to its share of statewide support.

More fundamentally, "vote dilution" in the one-person, one-vote cases refers to the idea that each vote must carry equal weight. In other words, each representative must be accountable to (approximately) the same number of constituents. That requirement does not extend to political parties. It does not mean that each party must be influential in proportion to its number of supporters. . . .

Nor do our racial gerrymandering cases provide an appropriate standard for assessing partisan gerrymandering. "[N]othing in our case law compels the conclusion that racial and political gerrymanders are subject to precisely the same constitutional scrutiny. In fact, our country's long and persistent history of racial discrimination in voting — as well as our Fourteenth Amendment jurisprudence, which always has reserved the strictest scrutiny for discrimination on the basis of race — would seem to compel the opposite conclusion." *Shaw I*, 509 U.S. at 650. Unlike partisan gerrymandering claims, a racial gerrymandering claim does not ask for a fair share of political power and influence, with all the justiciability conundrums that entails. It asks instead for the elimination of a racial classification. A partisan gerrymandering claim cannot ask for the elimination of partisanship.

IV

Appellees and the dissent propose a number of "tests" for evaluating partisan gerrymandering claims, but none meets the need for a limited and precise standard that is judicially discernible and manageable. And none provides a solid grounding for judges to take the extraordinary step of reallocating power and influence between political parties.

A

The *Common Cause* District Court concluded that all but one of the districts in North Carolina's 2016 Plan violated the Equal Protection Clause by intentionally diluting the voting strength of Democrats. In reaching that result the court first required the plaintiffs to prove "that a legislative mapdrawer's predominant purpose in drawing the lines of a particular district was to 'subordinate adherents of one political party and entrench a rival party in power.'" The District Court next required a showing "that the dilution of the votes of supporters of a disfavored party in a particular district—by virtue of cracking or packing—is likely to persist in subsequent elections such that an elected representative from the favored party in the district will not feel a need to be responsive to constituents who support the disfavored party." Finally, after a prima facie showing of partisan vote dilution, the District Court shifted the burden to the defendants to prove that the discriminatory effects are "attributable to a legitimate state interest or other neutral explanation."

The District Court's "predominant intent" prong is borrowed from the racial gerrymandering context. In racial gerrymandering cases, we rely on a "predominant intent" inquiry to determine whether race was, in fact, the reason particular district boundaries were drawn the way they were. If district lines were drawn for the purpose of separating racial groups, then they are subject to strict scrutiny because "race-based decisionmaking is inherently suspect." *Miller*, 515 U.S. at 915. But determining that lines were drawn on the basis of partisanship does not indicate that the districting was improper. A permissible intent—securing partisan advantage—does not become constitutionally impermissible, like racial discrimination, when that permissible intent "predominates."

The District Court tried to limit the reach of its test by requiring plaintiffs to show, in addition to predominant partisan intent, that vote dilution "is likely to persist" to such a degree that the elected representative will feel free to ignore the concerns of the supporters of the minority party. But "[t]o allow district courts to strike down apportionment plans on the basis of their prognostications as to the outcome of future elections . . . invites 'findings' on matters as to which neither judges nor anyone else can have any confidence." *Bandemer*, 478 U.S. at 160 (opinion of O'Connor, J.). And the test adopted by the *Common Cause* court requires a far more nuanced prediction than simply who would prevail in future political contests. Judges must forecast with unspecified certainty whether a prospective winner will have a margin of victory sufficient to permit him to ignore the supporters of his defeated opponent (whoever that may turn out to be). Judges not only have to pick the winner—they have to beat the point spread.

The appellees assure us that "the persistence of a party's advantage may be shown through sensitivity testing: probing how a plan would perform under other plausible electoral conditions." Experience proves that accurately predicting electoral outcomes is not so simple, either because the plans are based on flawed assumptions about voter preferences and behavior or because demographics and priorities change over time. In our two leading partisan gerrymandering cases themselves, the predictions of durability proved to be dramatically wrong. In 1981, Republicans controlled both houses of the Indiana Legislature as well as the governorship. Democrats challenged the state legislature districting map enacted by the Republicans. This Court in *Bandemer* rejected that challenge, and just months later the Democrats increased their share of House seats in the 1986 elections. Two years later the House was split 50–50 between Democrats and Republicans, and the Democrats took control of the chamber in 1990. Democrats also challenged the Pennsylvania congressional districting plan at issue in *Vieth*. Two years after that challenge failed, they gained four seats in the delegation, going from a 12–7 minority to an 11–8 majority. At the next election, they flipped another Republican seat.

Even the most sophisticated districting maps cannot reliably account for some of the reasons voters prefer one candidate over another, or why their preferences may change. Voters elect individual candidates in individual districts, and their selections depend on the issues that matter to them, the quality of the candidates, the tone of the candidates' campaigns, the performance of an incumbent, national events or local issues that drive voter turnout, and other considerations. Many voters split their tickets. Others never register with a political party, and vote for candidates from both major parties at different points during their lifetimes. For all of those reasons, asking judges to predict how a particular districting map will perform in future elections risks basing constitutional holdings on unstable ground outside judicial expertise.

B

The District Courts also found partisan gerrymandering claims justiciable under the First Amendment, coalescing around a basic three-part test: proof of intent to burden individuals based on their voting history or party affiliation; an actual burden on political speech or associational rights; and a causal link between the invidious intent and actual burden. Both District Courts concluded that the districting plans at issue violated the plaintiffs' First Amendment right to association. . . .

To begin, there are no restrictions on speech, association, or any other First Amendment activities in the districting plans at issue. The plaintiffs are free to engage in those activities no matter what the effect of a plan may be on their district.

The plaintiffs' argument is that partisanship in districting should be regarded as simple discrimination against supporters of the opposing party on the basis of political viewpoint. Under that theory, any level of partisanship in districting would constitute an infringement of their First Amendment rights. But as the Court has explained, "[i]t would be idle . . . to contend that any political consideration taken into account in fashioning a reapportionment plan is sufficient to invalidate it." *Gaffney*, 412 U.S. at 752. The First Amendment test simply describes the act of districting for partisan advantage. It provides no standard for determining when partisan activity goes too far.

As for actual burden, the slight anecdotal evidence found sufficient by the District Courts in these cases shows that this too is not a serious standard for separating constitutional from unconstitutional partisan gerrymandering. The District Courts relied on testimony about difficulty drumming up volunteers and enthusiasm. How much of a decline in voter engagement is enough to constitute a First Amendment burden? How many door knocks must go unanswered? How many petitions unsigned? How many calls for volunteers unheeded? The *Common Cause* District Court held that a partisan gerrymander places an unconstitutional burden on speech if it has more than a "*de minimis*" "chilling effect or adverse impact" on any First Amendment activity. The court went on to rule that there would be an adverse effect "even if the speech of [the plaintiffs] was not *in fact* chilled"; it was enough that the districting plan "makes it easier for supporters of Republican candidates to translate their votes into seats," thereby "enhanc[ing] the[ir] relative voice."

These cases involve blatant examples of partisanship driving districting decisions. But the First Amendment analysis below offers no "clear" and "manageable" way of distinguishing permissible from impermissible partisan motivation. The *Common Cause* court embraced that conclusion, observing that "a judicially manageable framework for evaluating partisan gerrymandering claims need not distinguish an 'acceptable' level of partisan gerrymandering from 'excessive' partisan gerrymandering" because "the Constitution does not authorize state redistricting bodies to engage in such partisan gerrymandering." The decisions below prove the prediction of the *Vieth* plurality that "a First Amendment claim, if it were sustained, would render unlawful *all* consideration of political affiliation in districting," 541 U.S. at 294, contrary to our established precedent.

C

The dissent proposes using a State's own districting criteria as a neutral baseline from which to measure how extreme a partisan gerrymander is. The dissent would have us line up all the possible maps drawn using those criteria according to the partisan distribution they would produce. Distance from the "median" map would indicate whether a particular districting plan harms supporters of one party to an unconstitutional extent. *Post* (opinion of KAGAN, J.).

As an initial matter, it does not make sense to use criteria that will vary from State to State and year to year as the baseline for determining whether a gerrymander violates the Federal Constitution. The degree of partisan advantage that the Constitution tolerates should not turn on criteria offered by the gerrymanderers themselves. It is easy to imagine how different criteria could move the median map toward different partisan distributions. As a result, the same map could be constitutional or not depending solely on what the mapmakers said they set out to do. That possibility illustrates that the dissent's proposed constitutional test is indeterminate and arbitrary.

Even if we were to accept the dissent's proposed baseline, it would return us to "the original unanswerable question (How much political motivation and effect is too much?)." *Vieth*, 541 U.S. at 296–297 (plurality opinion). Would twenty percent away from the median map be okay? Forty percent? Sixty percent? Why or why not? (We appreciate that the dissent finds all the unanswerable questions annoying, see *post*, but it seems a useful way to make the point.) The dissent's answer says it all: "This much is too much." That is not even trying to articulate a standard or rule.

The dissent argues that there are other instances in law where matters of degree are left to the courts. True enough. But those instances typically involve constitutional or statutory provisions or common law confining and guiding the exercise of judicial discretion. For example, the dissent cites the need to determine "substantial anticompetitive effect[s]" in antitrust law. That language, however, grew out of the Sherman Act, understood from the beginning to have its "origin in the common law" and to be "familiar in the law of this country prior to and at the time of the adoption of the [A]ct." Judges began with a significant body of law about what constituted a legal violation. In other cases, the pertinent statutory terms draw meaning from related provisions or statutory context. Here, on the other hand, the Constitution provides no basis whatever to guide the exercise of judicial discretion. Common experience gives content to terms such as "substantial risk" or "substantial harm," but the same cannot be said of substantial deviation from a median map. There is no way to tell whether the prohibited deviation from that map should kick in at 25 percent or 75 percent or some other point. The only provision in the Constitution that specifically addresses the matter assigns it to the political branches. See Art. I, §4, cl. 1.

D

The North Carolina District Court further concluded that the 2016 Plan violated the Elections Clause and Article I, §2. We are unconvinced by that novel approach.

Article I, §2, provides that "[t]he House of Representatives shall be composed of Members chosen every second Year by the People of the several States." The Elections Clause provides that "[t]he Times, Places and Manner of holding Elections for Senators and Representatives, shall be prescribed in each State by the Legislature thereof; but the Congress may at any time by Law make or alter such Regulations, except as to the Places of chusing Senators." Art. I, §4, cl. 1.

The District Court concluded that the 2016 Plan exceeded the North Carolina General Assembly's Elections Clause authority because, among other reasons, "the Elections Clause did not empower State legislatures to disfavor the interests of supporters of a particular candidate or party in drawing congressional districts." The court further held that partisan gerrymandering infringes the right of "the People" to select their representatives. Before the District Court's decision, no court had reached a similar conclusion. In fact, the plurality in *Vieth* concluded—without objection from any other Justice—that neither §2 nor §4 of Article I "provides a judicially enforceable limit on the political considerations that the States and Congress may take into account when districting." 541 U.S. at 305.

The District Court nevertheless asserted that partisan gerrymanders violate "the core principle of [our] republican government" preserved in Art. I, §2, "namely, that the voters should choose their representatives, not the other way around." 318 F.Supp.3d at 940 (quoting *Arizona State Legislature*, 576 U.S., at ——). That seems like an objection more properly grounded in the Guarantee Clause of Article IV, §4, which "guarantee[s] to every State in [the] Union a Republican

Form of Government." This Court has several times concluded, however, that the Guarantee Clause does not provide the basis for a justiciable claim.

V

Excessive partisanship in districting leads to results that reasonably seem unjust. But the fact that such gerrymandering is "incompatible with democratic principles," *Arizona State Legislature*, 576 U.S., at ——, does not mean that the solution lies with the federal judiciary. We conclude that partisan gerrymandering claims present political questions beyond the reach of the federal courts. Federal judges have no license to reallocate political power between the two major political parties, with no plausible grant of authority in the Constitution, and no legal standards to limit and direct their decisions. . . .

What the appellees and dissent seek is an unprecedented expansion of judicial power. We have never struck down a partisan gerrymander as unconstitutional — despite various requests over the past 45 years. The expansion of judicial authority would not be into just any area of controversy, but into one of the most intensely partisan aspects of American political life. That intervention would be unlimited in scope and duration — it would recur over and over again around the country with each new round of districting, for state as well as federal representatives. Consideration of the impact of today's ruling on democratic principles cannot ignore the effect of the unelected and politically unaccountable branch of the Federal Government assuming such an extraordinary and unprecedented role.

Our conclusion does not condone excessive partisan gerrymandering. Nor does our conclusion condemn complaints about districting to echo into a void. The States, for example, are actively addressing the issue on a number of fronts. In 2015, the Supreme Court of Florida struck down that State's congressional districting plan as a violation of the Fair Districts Amendment to the Florida Constitution. The dissent wonders why we can't do the same. The answer is that there is no "Fair Districts Amendment" to the Federal Constitution. Provisions in state statutes and state constitutions can provide standards and guidance for state courts to apply. . . . Indeed, numerous other States are restricting partisan considerations in districting through legislation. One way they are doing so is by placing power to draw electoral districts in the hands of independent commissions. For example, in November 2018, voters in Colorado and Michigan approved constitutional amendments creating multimember commissions that will be responsible in whole or in part for creating and approving district maps for congressional and state legislative districts. See Colo. Const., Art. V, §§44, 46; Mich. Const., Art. IV, §6. Missouri is trying a different tack. Voters there overwhelmingly approved the creation of a new position — state demographer — to draw state legislative district lines. Mo. Const., Art. III, §3.

Other States have mandated at least some of the traditional districting criteria for their mapmakers. Some have outright prohibited partisan favoritism in redistricting. See Fla. Const., Art. III, §20(a) ("No apportionment plan or individual district shall be drawn with the intent to favor or disfavor a political party or an incumbent."); Mo. Const., Art. III, §3 ("Districts shall be designed in a manner that achieves both partisan fairness and, secondarily, competitiveness. 'Partisan fairness' means that parties shall be able to translate their popular support into legislative representation with approximately equal efficiency."); Iowa Code §42.4(5) (2016) ("No district shall be drawn for the purpose of favoring a political party, incumbent legislator or member of Congress, or other person or group."); Del. Code Ann., Tit. xxix, §804 (2017) (providing that in determining district boundaries for the state legislature, no district shall "be created so as to unduly favor any person or political party").

As noted, the Framers gave Congress the power to do something about partisan gerrymandering in the Elections Clause. The first bill introduced in the 116th Congress would require States to create 15-member independent commissions to draw congressional districts and would establish certain redistricting criteria, including protection for communities of interest, and ban partisan gerrymandering. H. R. 1, 116th Cong., 1st Sess., §§2401, 2411 (2019).

Dozens of other bills have been introduced to limit reliance on political considerations in redistricting. In 2010, H. R. 6250 would have required States to follow standards of compactness, contiguity, and respect for political subdivisions in redistricting. It also would have prohibited the establishment of congressional districts "with the major purpose of diluting the voting strength of any person, or group, including any political party," except when necessary to comply with the Voting Rights Act of 1965. H. R. 6250, 111th Cong., 2d Sess., §2 (referred to committee).

Another example is the Fairness and Independence in Redistricting Act, which was introduced in 2005 and has been reintroduced in every Congress since. That bill would require every State to establish an independent commission to adopt redistricting plans. The bill also set forth criteria for the independent commissions to use, such as compactness, contiguity, and population equality. It would prohibit consideration of voting history, political party affiliation, or incumbent Representative's residence. H. R. 2642, 109th Cong., 1st Sess., §4 (referred to subcommittee).

We express no view on any of these pending proposals. We simply note that the avenue for reform established by the Framers, and used by Congress in the past, remains open. . . .

No one can accuse this Court of having a crabbed view of the reach of its competence. But we have no commission to allocate political power and influence in the absence of a constitutional directive or legal standards to guide us in the exercise of such authority. "It is emphatically the province and duty of the judicial department to say what the law is." *Marbury v. Madison*, 1 Cranch at 177. In this rare circumstance, that means our duty is to say "this is not law."

The judgments of the United States District Court for the Middle District of North Carolina and the United States District Court for the District of Maryland are vacated, and the cases are remanded with instructions to dismiss for lack of jurisdiction.

It is so ordered.

Justice KAGAN, with whom Justice GINSBURG, Justice BREYER, and Justice SOTOMAYOR join, dissenting.

For the first time ever, this Court refuses to remedy a constitutional violation because it thinks the task beyond judicial capabilities.

And not just any constitutional violation. The partisan gerrymanders in these cases deprived citizens of the most fundamental of their constitutional rights: the rights to participate equally in the political process, to join with others to advance political beliefs, and to choose their political representatives. In so doing, the partisan gerrymanders here debased and dishonored our democracy, turning upside-down the core American idea that all governmental power derives from the people. These gerrymanders enabled politicians to entrench themselves in office as against voters' preferences. They promoted partisanship above respect for the popular will. They encouraged a politics of polarization and dysfunction. If left unchecked, gerrymanders like the ones here may irreparably damage our system of government.

And checking them is *not* beyond the courts. The majority's abdication comes just when courts across the country, including those below, have coalesced around manageable judicial standards to resolve partisan gerrymandering claims. Those standards satisfy the majority's own benchmarks. They do not require—indeed, they do not permit—courts to rely on their own ideas of electoral fairness, whether proportional representation or any other. And they limit courts to correcting only egregious gerrymanders, so judges do not become omnipresent players in the political process. But yes, the standards used here do allow—as well they should—judicial intervention in the worst-of-the-worst cases of democratic subversion, causing blatant constitutional harms. In other words, they allow courts to undo partisan gerrymanders of the kind we face today from North Carolina and Maryland. In giving such gerrymanders a pass from judicial review, the majority goes tragically wrong.

I

A

The plaintiffs here challenge two congressional districting plans—one adopted by Republicans in North Carolina and the other by Democrats in Maryland—as unconstitutional partisan gerrymanders. As I relate what happened in those two States, ask yourself: Is this how American democracy is supposed to work?

Start with North Carolina. After the 2010 census, the North Carolina General Assembly, with Republican majorities in both its House and its Senate, enacted a new congressional districting plan. That plan governed the two next national elections. In 2012, Republican candidates won 9 of the State's 13 seats in the U.S. House of Representatives, although they received only 49% of the statewide vote. In 2014, Republican candidates increased their total to 10 of the 13 seats, this time based on 55% of the vote. Soon afterward, a District Court struck down two districts in the plan as unconstitutional racial gerrymanders. The General Assembly, with both chambers still controlled by Republicans, went back to the drawing board to craft the needed remedial state map. And here is how the process unfolded:

- The Republican co-chairs of the Assembly's redistricting committee, Rep. David Lewis and Sen. Robert Rucho, instructed Dr. Thomas Hofeller, a Republican districting specialist, to create a new map that would maintain the 10–3 composition of the State's congressional delegation come what might. Using sophisticated technological tools and precinct-level election results selected to predict voting behavior, Hofeller drew district lines to minimize Democrats' voting strength and ensure the election of 10 Republican Congressmen. 2018).

- Lewis then presented for the redistricting committee's (retroactive) approval a list of the criteria Hofeller had employed—including one labeled "Partisan Advantage." That criterion, endorsed by a party-line vote, stated that the committee would make all "reasonable efforts to construct districts" to "maintain the current [10–3] partisan makeup" of the State's congressional delegation.

- Lewis explained the Partisan Advantage criterion to legislators as follows: We are "draw[ing] the maps to give a partisan advantage to 10 Republicans and 3 Democrats because [I] d[o] not believe it['s] possible to draw a map with 11 Republicans and 2 Democrats."

- The committee and the General Assembly later enacted, again on a party-line vote, the map Hofeller had drawn.

- Lewis announced: "I think electing Republicans is better than electing Democrats. So I drew this map to help foster what I think is better for the country."

You might think that judgment best left to the American people. But give Lewis credit for this much: The map has worked just as he planned and predicted. In 2016, Republican congressional candidates won 10 of North Carolina's 13 seats, with 53% of the statewide vote. Two years later, Republican candidates won 9 of 12 seats though they received only 50% of the vote. (The 13th seat has not yet been filled because fraud tainted the initial election.)

Events in Maryland make for a similarly grisly tale. For 50 years, Maryland's 8-person congressional delegation typically consisted of 2 or 3 Republicans and 5 or 6 Democrats. After the 2000 districting, for example, the First and Sixth Districts reliably elected Republicans, and the other districts as reliably elected Democrats. But in the 2010 districting cycle, the State's Democratic leaders, who controlled the governorship and both houses of the General Assembly, decided to press their advantage.

- Governor Martin O'Malley, who oversaw the process, decided (in his own later words) "to create a map that was more favorable for Democrats over the next ten years." Because flipping the First District was geographically next-to-impossible, "a decision was made to go for the Sixth."

- O'Malley appointed an advisory committee as the public face of his effort, while asking Congressman Steny Hoyer, a self-described "serial gerrymanderer," to hire and direct a mapmaker. Hoyer retained Eric Hawkins, an analyst at a political consulting firm providing services to Democrats.

- Hawkins received only two instructions: to ensure that the new map produced 7 reliable Democratic seats, and to protect all Democratic incumbents.

- Using similar technologies and election data as Hofeller, Hawkins produced a map to those specifications. Although new census figures required removing only 10,000 residents from the Sixth District, Hawkins proposed a large-scale population transfer. The map moved about 360,000 voters out of the district and another 350,000 in. That swap decreased the number of registered Republicans in the district by over 66,000 and increased the number of registered Democrats by about 24,000, all to produce a safe Democratic district.

- After the advisory committee adopted the map on a party-line vote, State Senate President Thomas Miller briefed the General Assembly's Democratic caucuses about the new map's aims. Miller told his colleagues that the map would give "Democrats a real opportunity to pick up a seventh seat in the delegation" and that "[i]n the face of Republican gains in redistricting in other states[,] we have a serious obligation to create this opportunity."
- The General Assembly adopted the plan on a party-line vote.

Maryland's Democrats proved no less successful than North Carolina's Republicans in devising a voter-proof map. In the four elections that followed (from 2012 through 2018), Democrats have never received more than 65% of the statewide congressional vote. Yet in each of those elections, Democrats have won (you guessed it) 7 of 8 House seats—including the once-reliably-Republican Sixth District.

B

Now back to the question I asked before: Is that how American democracy is supposed to work? I have yet to meet the person who thinks so.

"Governments," the Declaration of Independence states, "deriv[e] their just Powers from the Consent of the Governed." The Constitution begins: "We the People of the United States." The Gettysburg Address (almost) ends: "[G]overnment of the people, by the people, for the people." If there is a single idea that made our Nation (and that our Nation commended to the world), it is this one: The people are sovereign. The "power," James Madison wrote, "is in the people over the Government, and not in the Government over the people." 4 Annals of Cong. 934 (1794).

Free and fair and periodic elections are the key to that vision. The people get to choose their representatives. And then they get to decide, at regular intervals, whether to keep them. . . . Election day—next year, and two years later, and two years after that—is what links the people to their representatives, and gives the people their sovereign power. That day is the foundation of democratic governance.

And partisan gerrymandering can make it meaningless. At its most extreme . . . the practice amounts to "rigging elections." *Vieth v. Jubelirer*, 541 U.S. 267, 317 (Kennedy, J., concurring in judgment). . . . The "core principle of republican government," this Court has recognized, is "that the voters should choose their representatives, not the other way around." *Arizona State Legislature v. Arizona Independent Redistricting Comm'n*, 576 U.S. ——, —— (2015). Partisan gerrymandering turns it the other way around. By that mechanism, politicians can cherry-pick voters to ensure their reelection. And the power becomes, as Madison put it, "in the Government over the people." 4 Annals of Cong. 934.

The majority disputes none of this. . . . Indeed, the majority concedes (really, how could it not?) that gerrymandering is "incompatible with democratic principles." And therefore what? That recognition would seem to demand a response. The majority offers two ideas that might qualify as such. One is that the political process can deal with the problem[; the] other is that political gerrymanders have always been with us. . . . The majority's idea instead seems to be that if we have lived with partisan gerrymanders so long, we will survive.

That complacency has no cause. Yes, partisan gerrymandering goes back to the Republic's earliest days. (As does vociferous opposition to it.) But big data and modern technology—of just the kind that the mapmakers in North Carolina and Maryland used—make today's gerrymandering altogether different from the crude linedrawing of the past. . . . Mapmakers now have access to more granular data about party preference and voting behavior than ever before. . . . Just as important, advancements in computing technology have enabled mapmakers to put that information to use with unprecedented efficiency and precision. . . . The effect is to make gerrymanders far more effective and durable than before, insulating politicians against all but the most titanic shifts in the political tides. . . .

C

Partisan gerrymandering of the kind before us not only subverts democracy (as if that weren't bad enough). It violates individuals' constitutional rights as well. . . . Partisan gerrymandering operates through vote dilution—the devaluation of one citizen's vote as compared to others. A mapmaker draws district lines to "pack" and "crack" voters likely to support the disfavored party. . . . Whether the person is packed or cracked, his vote carries less weight—has less consequence—than it would under a neutrally drawn (non-partisan) map. In short, the mapmaker has made some votes count for less, because they are likely to go for the other party.

That practice implicates the Fourteenth Amendment's Equal Protection Clause. [Equal protection] "can be denied by a debasement or dilution of the weight of a citizen's vote just as effectively as by wholly prohibiting the free exercise of the franchise." *Reynolds*. Based on that principle, this Court in its one-person-one-vote decisions prohibited creating districts with significantly different populations. . . . The constitutional injury in a partisan gerrymandering case is much the same, except that the dilution is based on party affiliation. In such a case, too, the districters have set out to reduce the weight of certain citizens' votes, and thereby deprive them of their capacity to "full[y] and effective[ly] participat[e] in the political process[]." As Justice Kennedy (in a controlling opinion) once hypothesized: If districters declared that they were drawing a map "so as most to burden [the votes of] Party X's" supporters, it would violate the Equal Protection Clause. *Vieth*, 541 U.S. at 312. . . .

And partisan gerrymandering implicates the First Amendment too. That Amendment gives its greatest protection to political beliefs, speech, and association. Yet partisan gerrymanders subject certain voters to "disfavored treatment"—again, counting their votes for less—precisely because of "their voting history [and] their expression of political views." *Vieth*, 541 U.S. at 314 (opinion of Kennedy, J.). And added to that strictly personal harm is an associational one. Representative democracy is "unimaginable without the ability of citizens to band together in [support of] candidates who espouse their political views." By diluting the votes of certain citizens, the State frustrates their efforts to translate those affiliations into political effectiveness.

Though different Justices have described the constitutional harm in diverse ways, nearly all have agreed on this much: Extreme partisan gerrymandering (as happened in North Carolina and Maryland) violates the Constitution. Once again, the majority never disagrees; it appears to accept the "principle that each person must have an equal say in the election of representatives." And indeed, without this settled and shared understanding that cases like these inflict constitutional injury, the question of whether there are judicially manageable standards for resolving them would never come up.

II

So the only way to understand the majority's opinion is as follows: In the face of grievous harm to democratic governance and flagrant infringements on individuals' rights . . . the majority declines to provide any remedy. For the first time in this Nation's history, the majority declares that it can do nothing about an acknowledged constitutional violation because it has searched high and low and cannot find a workable legal standard to apply.

The majority gives two reasons for thinking that the adjudication of partisan gerrymandering claims is beyond judicial capabilities. First and foremost, the majority says, it cannot find a neutral baseline — one not based on contestable notions of political fairness — from which to measure injury. . . . And second, the majority argues that even after establishing a baseline, a court would have no way to answer "the determinative question: 'How much is too much?' " No "discernible and manageable" standard is available, the majority claims. . . .

[The] majority [correctly notes that judges] should not be apportioning political power based on their own vision of electoral fairness. . . . But in throwing up its hands, the majority misses something under its nose: What it says can't be done *has* been done. Over the past several years, federal courts across the country — including, but not exclusively, in the decisions below — have largely converged on a standard for adjudicating partisan gerrymandering claims. . . . And that standard does what the majority says is impossible. The standard does not use any judge-made conception of electoral fairness — either proportional representation or any other; instead, it takes as its baseline a State's *own* criteria of fairness, apart from partisan gain. And by requiring plaintiffs to make difficult showings relating to both purpose and effects, the standard invalidates the most extreme, but only the most extreme, partisan gerrymanders. . . .

A

. . . Both courts [below] focused on the harm of vote dilution. . . . And both courts (like others around the country) used basically the same three-part test to decide whether the plaintiffs had made out a vote dilution claim: (1) intent; (2) effects; and (3) causation. First, the plaintiffs challenging a districting plan must prove that state officials' "predominant purpose" in drawing a district's lines was to "entrench [their party] in power" by diluting the votes of citizens favoring its rival. *Rucho*, 318 F.Supp.3d at 864 (quoting *Arizona State Legislature*, 576 U.S., at ——). Second, the plaintiffs must establish that the lines drawn in fact have the intended effect by "substantially" diluting their votes. *Lamone*, 348 F.Supp.3d at 498.

And third, if the plaintiffs make those showings, the State must come up with a legitimate, non-partisan justification to save its map. See *Rucho*, 318 F.Supp.3d at 867. If you are a lawyer, you know that this test looks utterly ordinary. It is the sort of thing courts work with every day.

Turn now to the test's application. First, did the North Carolina and Maryland districters have the predominant purpose of entrenching their own party in power? Here, the two District Courts catalogued the overwhelming direct evidence that they did. . . . The majority does not contest the lower courts' findings; how could it? Instead, the majority says that state officials' intent to entrench their party in power is perfectly "permissible," even when it is the predominant factor in drawing district lines. But that is wrong. True enough, that the intent to inject "political considerations" into districting may not raise any constitutional concerns. . . . And true enough that even the naked purpose to gain partisan advantage may not rise to the level of constitutional notice when it is not the driving force in mapmaking or when the intended gain is slight. See *Vieth*, 541 U.S. at 286 (plurality opinion). But when political actors have a specific and predominant intent to entrench themselves in power by manipulating district lines, that goes too far. . . . It cannot be permissible and thus irrelevant, as the majority claims, that state officials have as their purpose the kind of grotesquely gerrymandered map that, according to all this Court has ever said, violates the Constitution.

On to the second step of the analysis, where the plaintiffs must prove that the districting plan substantially dilutes their votes. . . . Consider the sort of evidence used in North Carolina first. There, the plaintiffs demonstrated the districting plan's effects mostly by relying on what might be called the "extreme outlier approach." . . . The approach—which also has recently been used in Michigan and Ohio litigation—begins by using advanced computing technology to randomly generate a large collection of districting plans that incorporate the State's physical and political geography and meet its declared districting criteria, *except for* partisan gain. For each of those maps, the method then uses actual precinct-level votes from past elections to determine a partisan outcome (*i.e.,* the number of Democratic and Republican seats that map produces). Suppose we now have 1,000 maps, each with a partisan outcome attached to it. We can line up those maps on a continuum—the most favorable to Republicans on one end, the most favorable to Democrats on the other. We can then find the median outcome—that is, the outcome smack dab in the center—in a world with no partisan manipulation. And we can see where the State's actual plan falls on the spectrum—at or near the median or way out on one of the tails? The further out on the tail, the more extreme the partisan distortion and the more significant the vote dilution.

Using that approach, the North Carolina plaintiffs offered a boatload of alternative districting plans—all showing that the State's map was an out-out-out-outlier. One expert produced 3,000 maps, adhering in the way described above to the districting criteria that the North Carolina redistricting committee had used, other than partisan advantage. To calculate the partisan outcome of those maps, the expert also used the same election data (a composite of seven elections) that Hofeller had employed when devising the North Carolina plan in the first instance. The results were, shall we say, striking. Every single one of the 3,000 maps would have produced at least one more Democratic House Member than the State's actual map, and 77% would have elected three or four more. A second expert obtained essentially the same results with maps conforming to more generic districting criteria (*e.g.*, compactness and contiguity of districts). Over 99% of that expert's 24,518 simulations would have led to the election of at least one more Democrat, and over 70% would have led to two or three more. Based on those and other findings, the District Court determined that the North Carolina plan substantially dilutes the plaintiffs' votes.

Because the Maryland gerrymander involved just one district, the evidence in that case was far simpler—but no less powerful for that. . . . [A] reversal of the district's partisan composition translated into four consecutive Democratic victories, including in a wave election year for Republicans (2014). In what was once a party stronghold, Republicans now have little or no chance to elect their preferred candidate. The District Court thus found that the gerrymandered Maryland map substantially dilutes Republicans' votes.

The majority claims all these findings are mere "prognostications" about the future, in which no one "can have any confidence." But the courts below did not gaze into crystal balls, as the majority tries to suggest. Their findings about these gerrymanders' effects on voters—both in the past and predictably in the future—were evidence-based, data-based, statistics-based. . . .

B

The majority's broadest claim, as I've noted, is that this is a price we must pay because judicial oversight of partisan gerrymandering cannot be "politically neutral" or "manageable." [Yet that] kind of oversight is not only possible; it's been done.

. . . Contrary to the majority's suggestion, the District Courts did not have to—and in fact did not—choose among competing visions of electoral fairness. That is because they did not try to compare the State's actual map to an "ideally fair" one (whether based on proportional representation or some other criterion). Instead, they looked at the difference between what the State did and what the State would have done if politicians hadn't been intent on partisan gain. Or put differently, the comparator (or baseline or touchstone) is the result not of a judge's philosophizing but of the State's own characteristics and judgments. . . . [T]he courts' analyses used the State's own criteria for electoral fairness—except for naked partisan gain. Under their approach, in other words, the State selected its own fairness baseline in the form of its other districting criteria. All the courts did was determine how far the State had gone off that track because of its politicians' effort to entrench themselves in office. . . .

The majority's sole response misses the point. According to the majority, "it does not make sense to use" a State's own (non-partisan) districting criteria as the baseline from which to measure partisan gerrymandering because those criteria "will vary from State to State and year to year." But that is a virtue, not a vice . . . Using the criteria the State itself has chosen at the relevant time prevents any judicial predilections from affecting the analysis—exactly what the majority claims it wants. At the same time, using those criteria enables a court to measure just what it should: the extent to which the pursuit of partisan advantage . . . has distorted the State's districting decisions. . . .

The majority's "how much is too much" critique fares no better than its neutrality argument. How about the following for a first-cut answer: This much is too much. By any measure, a map that produces a greater partisan skew than any of 3,000 randomly generated maps. . . reflects "too much" partisanship. Think about what I just said: The absolute worst of 3,001 possible maps. The *only one* that could produce a 10–3 partisan split even as Republicans got a bare majority of the statewide vote. And again: How much is too much? This much is too much. . . .

Nor is there any reason to doubt, as the majority does, the competence of courts to determine whether a district map "substantially" dilutes the votes of a rival party's supporters. . . As this Court recently noted, "the law is full of instances" where a judge's decision rests on "estimating rightly . . . some matter of degree"— including the "substantial[ity]" of risk or harm. *Johnson v. United States*, 576 U.S. ——, —— (2015); see, *e.g., Ohio v. American Express Co.*, 585 U.S. ——, —— (determining "substantial anticompetitive effect[s]" when applying the Sherman Act). . . . The majority is wrong to think that these laws typically (let alone uniformly) further "confine[] and guide[]" judicial decisionmaking. . . . To the extent additional guidance has developed over the years (as under the Sherman Act), courts themselves have been its author—as they could be in this context too. And contrary to the majority's suggestion, courts all the time make judgments about the substantiality of harm without reducing them to particular percentages. If courts are no longer competent to do so, they will have to relinquish, well, substantial portions of their docket. . . .

III

This Court has long understood that it has a special responsibility to remedy violations of constitutional rights resulting from politicians' districting decisions. . . . But the need for judicial review is at its most urgent in cases like these. "For here, politicians' incentives conflict with voters' interests, leaving citizens without any political remedy for their constitutional harms." *Gill*, 585 U.S., at —— (KAGAN, J., concurring). Those harms arise because politicians want to stay in office. No one can look to them for effective relief.

The majority disagrees, concluding its opinion with a paean to congressional bills limiting partisan gerrymanders. "Dozens of [those] bills have been introduced," the majority says. One was "introduced in 2005 and has been reintroduced in every Congress since." And might be reintroduced until the end of time. Because what all these *bills* have in common is that they are not *laws*. The politicians who benefit from partisan gerrymandering are unlikely to change partisan gerrymandering. And because those politicians maintain themselves in office through partisan gerrymandering, the chances for legislative reform are slight.

No worries, the majority says; it has another idea. The majority notes that voters themselves have recently approved ballot initiatives to put power over districting in the hands of independent commissions or other non-partisan actors. Some Members of the majority, of course, once thought such initiatives unconstitutional. See *Arizona State Legislature,* 576 U.S., at —— (ROBERTS, C. J., dissenting). But put that aside. Fewer than half the States offer voters an opportunity to put initiatives to direct vote; in all the rest (including North Carolina and Maryland), voters are dependent on legislators to make electoral changes (which for all the reasons already given, they are unlikely to do). And even when voters have a mechanism they can work themselves, legislators often fight their efforts tooth and nail. . . .

The majority's most perplexing "solution" is to look to state courts. "[O]ur conclusion," the majority states, does not "condemn complaints about districting to echo into a void": Just a few years back, "the Supreme Court of Florida struck down that State's congressional districting plan as a violation" of the State Constitution. And indeed, the majority might have added, the Supreme Court of Pennsylvania last year did the same thing. But what do those courts know that this Court does not? If they can develop and apply neutral and manageable standards to identify unconstitutional gerrymanders, why couldn't we? . . .

Of all times to abandon the Court's duty to declare the law, this was not the one. The practices challenged in these cases imperil our system of government. Part of the Court's role in that system is to defend its foundations. None is more important than free and fair elections. With respect but deep sadness, I dissent.

———————

After *Rucho,* state legislatures are free to gerrymander on partisan grounds without fear of interference from the federal judiciary. Does this present a problem for democratic politics? If so, of what kind, and does any possible remedy remain other than the dubious self-restraint of state legislators?

≫ ***What Is So Bad About Partisan Gerrymandering?***   In all the legal back and forth about the evils of partisan gerrymandering, a basic question is often overlooked: what exactly is so bad about it? What harm does it cause, and to whom? If partisan gerrymandering is unfair, to whom is it unfair, and in what way? Critics have tended to identify two broad classes of harms, one emphasizing harm to the political party victimized by partisan gerrymandering, and its members, and the other emphasizing harm to the political system as whole, a kind of harm that is by definition shared by all members of the public.

Distortion of Policy. One view of partisan gerrymandering is that it effectuates a kind of discrimination by the majority party and its members against the minority party and its members by giving the majority party more power in the legislature than it is in some sense "entitled" to exercise. Control of the legislature has obvious advantages in that it allows the party in control to achieve its legislative agenda with greater ease, and the larger the margin of control the more readily the majority party may dominate the legislative agenda. Or, put another way, "as a district plan skews further in a Democratic (Republican) direction, the ideological midpoint of the legislature becomes more liberal (conservative)."

Nicholas O. Stephanopoulos, *The Causes and Consequences of Gerrymandering*, 59 WM. & MARY L. REV. 2115 (2018). This leads to a kind of distortion of public policy in favor of the majority party at the expense of the minority party—that is, the majority party is able to have its way to a degree that would be unlikely were districts drawn more fairly, and as a result the legislature does not enact policy that either does justice to the political views of the minority or fairly represents the political sentiments of the electorate taken as a whole. *See* Thomas W. Gilligan and John G. Matsusaka, *Public Choice Principles of Redistricting*, 129 PUBLIC CHOICE 381 (2006). In this sense, gerrymandering represents a kind of "theft" of public policy.

This kind of distortion of public policy may be magnified by another effect of partisan gerrymandering that is sometimes identified, namely, that legislators elected from gerrymandered districts will be more extreme in their views than legislators elected from more competitive districts: "Those in charge of redistricting . . . have the ability to affect not only which party is favored to win a district, but, by manipulating the proportion of voters in a district on the left or right, the ideological character of the winning candidate as well." Micah Altman and Michael McDonald, *Redistricting and Polarization, in* AMERICAN GRIDLOCK: THE SOURCES, CHARACTER, AND IMPACT OF POLITICAL POLARIZATION (James A. Thurber and Antoine Yoshinaka, eds., 2015). If this is correct, then gerrymandering may doubly distort public policy by not only making it easier for the gerrymandering party to achieve its agenda, but by moving the party's agenda itself further from the center of public opinion.

A related potential effect of gerrymandering—and in a sense an even more concrete form of legislative "theft"—is a distortion of governmental monetary outlays in favor of supporters of the majority party. As the authors of one study put it, "[t]he winning party, it is widely conjectured, rewards its supporters with pork, with a larger share of expenditures from existing programs." Stephen Ansolabehere and James M. Snyder, Jr., *Party Control of State Government and the Distribution of Public Expenditures*, 108 SCAND. J. ECON. 547 (2006). According to this 50-state study, during the period 1957-1997, heavily Democratic areas received on average 9 percent more public money when Democrats controlled the state legislature than when it was under Republican control, and heavily Republican areas received 8 percent less public funds when the legislature was controlled by Democrats than when it was controlled by Republicans. Politically balanced areas of the states received about the same level of public outlays regardless of which party controlled the legislature.

Are these kinds of harms sufficient to give rise to a constitutional violation based on a kind of discrimination theory? Don't these accounts of the harm of gerrymandering rely implicitly on a baseline of proportionality, and a consequent identification of what constitutes a "fair" or "equal" share of public policy outcomes or monetary outlays by reference to the proportional support in the electorate for one party or the other? The Court typically denies the existence of any constitutional right on the part of supporters of a political party to a proportionate share of legislative *seats*. Wouldn't a claim of some entitlement to a proportionate share of legislative policy and outlays be even more attenuated?

Decline in Electoral Competitiveness. Consider the following figures:

> The 2004 House elections may have been the least competitive in American history. . . . Out of 401 contests between incumbents and challengers, only five incumbents were defeated. . . . Astonishingly, only 22 House races in the entire country were decided by a margin of less than 10 percentage points—a record for the postwar era. At the other end of the spectrum, 172 winning candidates in 2004 either had no major party opposition or coasted to victory by a margin of at least 40 percentage points. . . . [C]ompetition in House elections has been declining for more than 50 years. . . . [T]he reelection rate of House incumbents has increased from 87% between 1946 and 1950 to 94% between 1952 and 1980, 97% between 1982 and 2000, and 99% in the 2002-2004 elections. . . . [Similarly,] the proportion of House races decided by less than 10 percentage points fell from 22% between 1946 and 1950 to 21% between 1952 and 1960, 17% between 1962 and 1970, 16% between 1972 and 1980, 12% between 1992 and 2000, and 7% in the 2002-2004 elections.

Alan I. Abramowitz et al., *Incumbency, Redistricting, and the Decline of Competition in U.S. House Elections,* 68 J. POL. 75, 75-76 (2006). A decline in electoral competitiveness may work several different kinds of harms to the political system, and consequently to the public at large.

Lack of Governmental Accountability. One of the advantages of a properly functioning two-party system is usually said to be the ability of the electorate to "fire" the party in power when it does not like that party's performance, and to replace it with the out party at the next election. (The role of parties in a democracy is taken up in greater detail in Chapter 7.) If manipulation of the rules of competition by the party in power makes it impossible to dislodge that party, then democracy itself may be thwarted:

> [E]lectoral accountability can exist only when effective political competition generates genuine political choices. Yet the power to design and revise the ground rules of democracy itself must reside somewhere. As long as some of that power rests with self-interested political actors, as it almost inevitably will, electoral accountability will be fragile. . . . The justification for judicial review in contexts such as malapportionment is to address the structural risk of political self-entrenchment.

Richard H. Pildes, *Foreword: The Constitutionalization of Democratic Politics,* 118 HARV. L. REV. 29, 43-44 (2004).

Is the electorate any less able now than in the past to "throw the bums out" and replace the party in power with the opposition party? In the nineteenth century, partisan control of the House of Representatives changed hands 16 times. In the first half of the twentieth century, partisan control of the House changed hands seven more times—in 1910, 1918, 1930, 1946, 1948, 1952, and 1954. Beginning in 1954, however, the Democrats retained control of the House for 40 years, until the

Republicans took it back in 1994 — an unprecedented period of stability in which partisan control of the House changed only once in a half century.

But is the decline in competitive district elections and in partisan turnover in the House attributable to *gerrymandering*? There is at least some reason to be skeptical. In one study, two political scientists isolated the effect of redistricting on reelection by comparing reelection rates in the U.S. House of Representatives to reelection rates for U.S. Senators and state governors, officials who are elected from fixed districts the boundaries of which cannot be altered. According to the authors, "[t]he central pattern is that incumbency advantages in *all* statewide offices, as well as the U.S. House and Senate, have trended up from about 2 percent [i.e., incumbents receive a 2 percent bump in the popular vote compared to challengers] in the 1940s to, on average, 8 percent in the 1990s." Stephen Ansolabehere and James M. Snyder, Jr., *The Incumbency Advantage in U.S. Elections: An Analysis of State and Federal Offices, 1942-2000*, 1 ELECTION L.J. 315, 317 (2002). For similar results, see Abramowitz et al., *supra*. In other words, the upward trend in congressional reelection rates is attributable not to self-entrenchment by incumbents, but to some other advantage of incumbency that accrues to all office-holders, whether elected from districts or not.

In a later work, the same authors refer to "[t]he argument that redistricting causes the incumbency advantage" as "the Freddy Krueger of American politics," an argument that, "seemingly vanquished, returns to haunt again and again." STEPHEN ANSOLABEHERE AND JAMES M. SNYDER, JR., THE END OF INEQUALITY: ONE PERSON, ONE VOTE AND THE TRANSFORMATION OF AMERICAN POLITICS 263 (2009). In their most recent study, these authors conclude firmly that "redistricting is not a cause of incumbency effects, nor does it increase vote margins [for incumbent legislators]." Instead, they found, the opposite is true: "redistricting lowers vote margins, and the more a legislator's district changes, the worse he or she can expect to do at the polls." Stephen Ansolabehere and James M. Snyder, Jr., *The Effects of Redistricting on Incumbents*, 11 ELECTION L.J. 490, 499 (2012). Redistricting, in other words, by changing the boundaries of existing electoral districts, actually disrupts settled relations between incumbent legislators and their constituents, thereby weakening the ties between them and costing the incumbent votes in the ensuing elections.

Lack of Legislator Responsiveness. A second charge lodged against partisan gerrymandering looks not at the ability of the voters to cast out the entire government, but focuses instead on the responsiveness of individual legislators to their constituents. If legislators are assured of reelection by careful gerrymandering, do they have the same incentives to listen and respond to the concerns of *any* of their constituents, even those in the majority? If not, is this a bad thing? Do legislators who hold a safe seat use their freedom to exercise their best judgment for the public good in a Burkean way? Or is the real prospect of electoral punishment at the polls necessary to keep legislators from becoming corrupt or being captured by special interests? (The material in Chapter 6 on legislative term limits may be of relevance here.) Even if a legislator in a safe seat can't realistically be challenged by someone of the opposition party, might not that legislator face at least some kind of potential discipline from the prospect of a challenge in his or her party's primary election? Although the empirical evidence has been mixed, for a study concluding that legislators from competitive districts *are* more responsive to their constituents, see John D. Griffin, *Electoral Competition and Democratic Responsiveness: A Defense of the Marginality Hypothesis*, 68 J. POL. 911 (2006).

A closely related question is: if legislators are responsive at all, to whom do they respond? Normally, one would assume that legislators in unsafe, politically competitive (marginal) seats would be most likely to gravitate toward the political center of their districts because they may need to pick up votes from centrist independents or moderates from the other party. One would similarly assume that legislators holding safe seats would be most likely to respond to their core partisan supporters, moving them away from the political center. The only recent study to address these questions found, contrary to theoretical predictions, that U.S. Senators with safe seats tend to cast votes closer to the ideological center of the state electorate as a whole than do Senators from politically competitive states, i.e., those who face potential electoral challenge. The latter tend to cast senatorial votes in ways better calculated to appeal to their own partisan supporters. In other words, "marginal legislators position themselves among their core constituencies rather than pursue an electoral strategy that rests on attracting moderates, independents, and other swing voters. It seems as if marginal incumbents are concerned that appealing to voters in the center will alienate more of their core supporters than they would gain in new voters from the center." Girish J. Gulati, *Revisiting the Link Between Electoral Competition and Policy Extremism in the U.S. Congress*, 32 AM. POL. RES. 495, 510 (2004).

Voter Alienation. A third possible problem with partisan gerrymandering is that, by creating safe seats, it turns many people away from politics, stoking alienation and depressing participation. If voters in a district know that the incumbent will win the seat come what may, they may decide that voting and other forms of political participation are wastes of their time, thereby reinforcing the incumbent's already significant advantage. This kind of political alienation may be corrosive to the public good will and support necessary to sustain democracy in the long run.

On the other hand, might it be possible that it is *competition* that drives people away from politics? Might uncompetitive elections held in safe districts ultimately create a happier electorate? Some have argued that this might indeed be the case. In one of the most important political science studies published this century, the authors conducted a large-scale survey of public attitudes toward politics. They found that

> even though Americans say they want democratic decision making, they do not believe standard elements of it, such as debate and compromise, are either helpful or necessary. . . . In fact, people believe the existence of conflict is a sign that elected officials are out of touch with ordinary Americans. . . . The notion that debating among elected officials may actually be necessitated by their responsibility to represent the interests of diverse

constituencies across the country is rejected by most Americans. The important point in the people's thinking is that anybody *not* connected with biased special interests and self-serving elected officials would basically arrive at the same place.

JOHN R. HIBBING AND ELIZABETH THEISS-MORSE, STEALTH DEMOCRACY: AMERICANS' BELIEFS ABOUT HOW GOVERNMENT SHOULD WORK 137, 142 (2002). According to this theory, the very kind of debate among citizens and candidates associated with vigorously contested, highly competitive elections might be just what large numbers of citizens don't want to hear.

In a provocative book, Thomas Brunell makes precisely this argument. "[V]oters who cast a vote for the candidate who wins the election," Brunell argues, "are systematically happier with their representative, evaluate Congress as an institution more positively, and feel more efficacious than losing voters." Moreover, those who vote for a winner have an increased likelihood that they will be "well represented in the [legislature] and see public policy enacted that is closer to their own ideal point than are the losers." From this premise, Brunell reaches the obvious conclusion: "homogeneous districts, with as many Democrats or Republicans packed into each district as possible, are going to maximize voter satisfaction and improve representation and attitudes toward government." Brunell further argues that representatives are more likely to represent the dominant opinion among their constituents when districts are homogeneous, that gerrymandering through bizarre boundaries will be minimized, and that communities of interest will be better preserved, when districts are drawn deliberately to be uncompetitive. THOMAS L. BRUNELL, REDISTRICTING AND REPRESENTATION: WHY COMPETITIVE ELECTIONS ARE BAD FOR AMERICA 29-30 (2008).

Legislative Polarization. A final critique that has been leveled at partisan gerrymandering is that it has increased the degree of polarization in Congress, leading to the kind of ugly and bitter partisanship now displayed in congressional politics, and to a consequent inability of Congress to perform its legislative duties responsibly.

The two charts on the next page show the distribution of members of the House, by party, across a left-right ideological spectrum. The horizontal axis displays political ideology (grouped, for convenience of display, into deciles) from most liberal, on the left, to most conservative, on the right. Each bar shows the number of Representatives falling into each of the ten ideological groupings. The dark bars represent Democrats and the light ones Republicans. During the 91st Congress (1969-1970), there was substantial ideological overlap between the parties; although most Democrats were liberal and most Republicans were conservative, many Democrats were just as conservative, or even more conservative, than many Republicans, and many Republicans were just as liberal, or even more liberal, than many Democrats. The second chart shows the same information for the 105th Congress (1997-1998). By this period, ideological overlap between the two parties had all but disappeared. Over this 30-year period, not only did each party become much more ideologically homogeneous, but the two parties moved away from one another ideologically.

Member Ideology
91st Congress (1969-70)

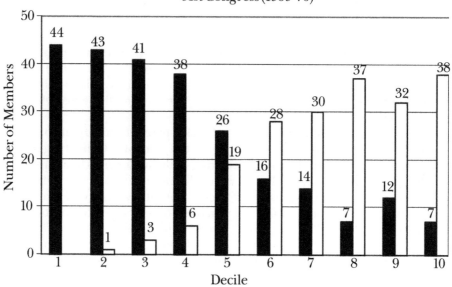

Member Ideology
105th Congress (1997-98)

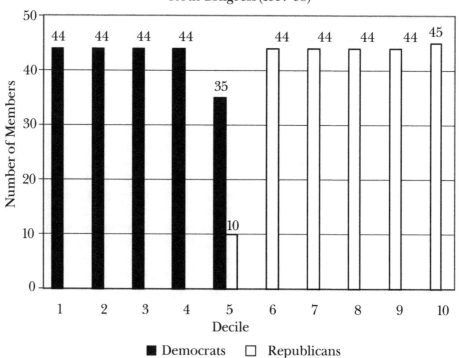

Source: John H. Aldrich and David W. Rohde, *The Logic of Conditional Party Government, in* LAWRENCE
C. DODD AND BRUCE I. OPPENHEIMER, CONGRESS RECONSIDERED (7th ed. 2001).

How, if at all, is the polarization of Congress linked to a decline in electoral competition produced by gerrymandering? Consider the following account:

> By making individual districts noncompetitive, partisan gerrymandering also frustrates the representation of centrist views in the House. Safe districts are drawn to be either more conservative or more liberal than a non-gerrymandered district would be; their average voter is intended to be reliably off the overall median. Artificially skewing districts in this way ensures the election of candidates from particular parties, but also makes it less likely that candidates who reflect the views of these median voters will be elected. In advantaging one political party, then, partisan gerrymandering not only disadvantages the other major political party and makes districts uncompetitive, but it also makes the representation of centrist views more difficult.
>
> Another feature of elections exacerbates this effect. Deadening competition between the major parties shifts any real political competition in the district into one party's primary, where ideological activists dominate. Centrist candidates of both parties have trouble surviving in safe districts because in the primaries they must appeal to a group of voters representative neither of the district as a whole, nor of the party as a whole—rather, the group of voters at primaries represents only the party's more partisan members. More sharply ideological candidates appeal to this primary electorate. Democratic primary voters vote for more left-leaning candidates than the average Democrat, let alone the average voter, would, and Republican primary voters vote for more right-leaning candidates than the average Republican or average voter would. As a result, districts elect candidates more extreme than the general population of voters in the district, and the House has become bipolar even though the country has stayed largely in the middle. Making districts safe thus silences the center.

Daniel R. Ortiz, *Got Theory?*, 153 U. Pa. L. Rev. 459, 489 (2004).

On the other hand, party polarization similar to that shown above has also occurred in the U.S. Senate, a trend for which partisan gerrymandering cannot account. Political scientists seem increasingly to agree that gerrymandering is not responsible for legislative polarization. *See* Alan I. Abramowitz, The Disappearing Center ch. 7 (2010); Seth E. Masket et al., *The Gerrymanders Are Coming! Legislative Redistricting Won't Affect Competition or Polarization Much, No Matter Who Does It*, 45 PS: Pol. Sci. & Pol. 39 (2012); James E. Campbell, Polarized: The Reality of American Politics (2016).

Might some other social or political trend be responsible independently for both party polarization and partisan gerrymandering? One simple explanation is that the American electorate has become more ideologically polarized during this period, and polarization among representatives is merely an accurate reflection of polarization among the represented. Abramowitz, *supra*; Campbell, *supra*. A variant of this account holds that Americans have not become more ideologically polarized in the sense of holding more extreme views—the great majority remain centrists—but that they have sorted themselves more homogeneously into the two major parties. Thus, whereas in the past some moderate conservatives might be Democrats and some moderate liberals might be Republicans, today the great majority of liberals and conservatives have affiliated with the party that better represents the totality of their views. Pew Research Center, *Political Polarization in the American Public* (2014).

Another, related explanation is that voluntary residential segregation by the electorate along ideological lines (the so-called Big Sort) causes legislative polarization. BILL BISHOP AND ROBERT G. CUSHING, THE BIG SORT: WHY THE CLUSTERING OF LIKE-MINDED AMERICA IS TEARING US APART (2009). On this account, Americans increasingly prefer to live in communities of the ideologically like-minded, and increasingly have the means to do so; as a result, more and more Americans live in geographically compact ideological enclaves. If this is true, then compactly drawn territorial districts will inevitably be more ideologically homogeneous, and thus less centrist, than would be the case if people lived in ideologically heterogeneous groupings (as apparently they used to).

A final possibility is that gerrymandering, though not the primary cause of ideological polarization, is nonetheless a contributing factor. For example, by one estimate a "gerrymandering effect" accounts for perhaps 10 to 15 percent of ideological polarization during the 1970s. Nolan McCarty, Keith T. Poole, and Howard Rosenthal, *Does Gerrymandering Cause Polarization?*, 53 AM. J. POL. SCI. 666 (2009). A more recent study similarly concludes that "not all congressional districts, and likely not even a majority, can be made competitive, and . . . redistricting is but one piece of a greater polarization puzzle." Nevertheless, the authors argue, reducing gerrymandering may ameliorate polarization to an extent worth pursuing. Micah Altman and Michael McDonald, *Redistricting and Polarization, in* AMERICAN GRIDLOCK: THE SOURCES, CHARACTER, AND IMPACT OF POLITICAL POLARIZATION (James A. Thurber and Antoine Yoshinaka eds., 2015).

➤➤ *How Bad Is It?*   We conclude this review of the harms of partisan gerrymandering with a reality check: assuming that partisan gerrymandering causes some degree of any of the harms reviewed above, just how bad is it? Here, there is a surprising amount of disagreement. A recent study by the Brennan Center for Justice concludes that partisan gerrymandering in the most populous states resulted in a net benefit to Republicans of 16 or 17 seats in Congress. Laura Royden and Michael Li, *Extreme Maps* (Brennan Ctr. 2017). In contrast, a contemporaneous study by two political scientists found that "if districts were drawn randomly with respect to partisanship and race, Republicans would only expect to lose a single seat in Congress to Democrats." Jowei Chen and David Cottrell, *Evaluating Partisan Gains from Congressional Gerrymandering*, 44 ELECTORAL STUD. 329, 338 (2016). Another study, which did not quantify its results in terms of seats, found that partisan gerrymandering in the 2010 cycle created a 5 percent bias in congressional elections favoring Republicans. ANTHONY McGANN, ET AL., GERRYMANDERING IN AMERICA (2016). All three studies, however, agree that the bulk of gerrymandering effects, whatever their magnitude, are concentrated in a small number of battleground states controlled mainly by Republicans, including most prominently Florida, Michigan, North Carolina, Ohio, Pennsylvania, and Virginia.

Another frequently advanced hypothesis is that partisan bias in the makeup of Congress and state legislatures is real, but it is not attributable to intentional gerrymandering by parties in control of the redistricting process; it is, instead, a natural result of the application of a single-member district system of representation to the way in which Democrats and Republicans happen to distribute themselves on the landscape. The idea here is that people who tend to vote Democratic also happen to have a preference for living in densely populated urban areas, whereas people who tend to vote Republican prefer to live in rural and suburban settings. As a result, "Democratic voters in some states are less efficiently distributed across districts, leading to electoral bias favoring Republican control." Chen & Cottrell, *supra*, at 331. The mechanism by which this occurs is that "Democrats win districts in [urban] areas by far greater margins than they need, leaving the Republicans to win a greater number of nonurban districts by smaller margins." McGANN, ET AL., *supra*, at 97. This effect is thought to contribute to the fact that, over the last twenty years, Republicans have won 52 percent of all congressional seats on 48 percent of the popular vote, and 55-56 percent of all state house and senate seats on 52 percent of the popular vote, Nicholas Eubank and Jonathan Rodden, *Who Is My Neighbor? The Spatial Efficiency of Partisanship*, 7 STATS. & PUB. POL'Y 87 (2020), though it appears to be possible to compensate for this effect through careful districting. McGANN, ET AL., *supra*, at 97-145.

» *Partisan Gerrymandering under State Constitutions.* With the Supreme Court in *Rucho* having taken the federal courts out of the business of policing constitutional limits to partisan gerrymandering, attention has now focused on state courts. Every state has its own constitution, and each state constitution provides at least some and, in most cases, extensive protection for individual rights. For the most part, state constitutional rights provisions tend to resemble counterpart provisions in the U.S. Constitution, and consequently tend to protect more or less the same rights that appear in the federal document. Moreover, state courts often look to the U.S. Supreme Court for guidance in interpreting parallel provisions of their own constitutions, and consequently the dominant pattern among state bills of rights is one of similar provisions, similarly interpreted.

There are, however, important exceptions to the general pattern. First, state constitutions frequently contain provisions that have no counterpart in the U.S. Constitution. Such provisions sometimes include the right to an adequate education, the right to a judicial remedy for injuries and other wrongs, and, perhaps significantly, the rights to vote and to free and fair elections. Second, even when state constitutional rights provisions bear a textual similarity to provisions of the U.S. Constitution, state courts are free to interpret them differently, and have sometimes done so.

League of Women Voters v. Commonwealth

178 A.3d 737 (Pa. 2018)

[In 2011, the Republican-controlled Pennsylvania legislature enacted a congressional redistricting plan that was widely viewed as an egregious case of partisan gerrymandering. Under this plan, even though the statewide congressional vote was more or less evenly divided between the two major parties, Republicans consistently won the same 13 seats and Democrats the same 5 seats. Plaintiffs challenged the plan under Article I, Section 5 of the Pennsylvania Constitution, which provides: "Elections shall be free and equal; and no power, civil or military, shall at any time interfere to prevent the free exercise of the right of suffrage."]

Upon review, . . . we are persuaded . . . that the 2011 Plan clearly, plainly, and palpably violates the Free and Equal Elections Clause of our Constitution.

Pennsylvania's Constitution, when adopted in 1776, was widely viewed as "the most radically democratic of all the early state constitutions." Ken Gormley, "Overview of Pennsylvania Constitutional Law," as appearing in Ken Gormley, ed., The Pennsylvania Constitution A Treatise on Rights and Liberties, 3 (2004). Indeed, our Constitution, which was adopted over a full decade before the United States Constitution, served as the foundation—the template—for the federal charter. *Id.* Our autonomous state Constitution, rather than a "reaction" to federal constitutional jurisprudence, stands as a self-contained and self-governing body of constitutional law, and acts as a wholly independent protector of the rights of the citizens of our Commonwealth. . . .

[The present] Pa. Const. art. I, §5 . . . first appeared, albeit in different form, in our Commonwealth's first organic charter of governance adopted in 1776, 11 years before the United States Constitution was adopted. By contrast, the United States Constitution—which furnishes no explicit protections for an individual's electoral rights, nor sets any minimum standards for a state's conduct of the electoral process—does not contain, nor has it ever contained, an analogous provision.

The broad text of the first clause of this provision mandates clearly and unambiguously, and in the broadest possible terms, that all elections conducted in this Commonwealth must be "free and equal." In accordance with the plain and expansive sweep of the words "free and equal," we view them as indicative of the framers' intent that all aspects of the electoral process, to the greatest degree possible, be kept open and unrestricted to the voters of our Commonwealth, and, also, conducted in a manner which guarantees, to the greatest degree possible, a voter's right to equal participation in the electoral process for the selection of his or her representatives in government. Thus, Article I, Section 5 guarantees our citizens an equal right, on par with every other citizen, to elect their representatives. Stated another way, the actual and plain language of Section 5 mandates that all voters have an equal opportunity to translate their votes into representation. This interpretation is consistent with both the historical reasons for the inclusion of this provision in our Commonwealth's Constitution and the meaning we have ascribed to it through our case law. . . .

[The phrase initially appeared in Pennsylvania's 1776 constitution.] This section reflected the delegates' desire to secure access to the election process by all people with an interest in the communities in which they lived—universal suffrage—by prohibiting exclusion from the election process of those without property or financial means. It, thus, established a critical "leveling" protection in an effort to establish the uniform right of the people of this Commonwealth to select their representatives in government. It sought to ensure that this right of the people would forever remain equal no matter their financial situation or social class. . . .

[It was then carried forward into the revised constitution of 1790. Because the 1798-90 constitutional convention met under circumstances of] regional, ideological, and sectarian strife . . . , which bitterly divided the people of various regions of our state, this provision must be understood then as a salutary effort by the learned delegates to the 1790 convention to end, once and for all, the primary cause of popular dissatisfaction which undermined the governance of Pennsylvania: namely, the dilution of the right of the people of this Commonwealth to select representatives to govern their affairs based on considerations of the region of the state in which they lived, and the religious and political beliefs to which they adhered. . . .

[Nearly 150 years ago, in] answering the question of how elections must be made equal, we stated: "Clearly by laws which shall arrange all the qualified electors into suitable districts, and make their votes equally potent in the election; so that some shall not have more votes than others, and that all shall have an equal share in filling the offices of the Commonwealth." Thus, with this decision, our Court established that any legislative scheme which has the effect of impermissibly diluting the potency of an individual's vote for candidates for elective office relative to that of other voters will violate the guarantee of "free and equal" elections afforded by Article I, Section 5. This interpretation is wholly consonant with the intent of the framers of the 1790 Constitution to ensure that each voter will have an equally effective power to select the representative of his or her choice, free from any discrimination on the basis of his or her particular beliefs or views. [We have followed this interpretation in subsequent cases.]. . . .

In addition to the occasion for the adoption of the Free and Equal Elections Clause, the circumstances in which the provision was adopted, the mischief to be remedied, and the object to be obtained, as described above, the consequences of a particular interpretation are also relevant in our analysis. Specifically, partisan gerrymandering dilutes the votes of those who in prior elections voted for the party not in power to give the party in power a lasting electoral advantage. By placing voters preferring one party's candidates in districts where their votes are wasted on candidates likely to lose (cracking), or by placing such voters in districts where their votes are cast for candidates destined to win (packing), the non-favored party's votes are diluted. It is axiomatic that a diluted vote is not an equal vote, as all voters do not have an equal opportunity to translate their votes into representation. This is the antithesis of a healthy representative democracy.

Indeed, for our form of government to operate as intended, each and every Pennsylvania voter must have the same free and equal opportunity to select his or her representatives. As our foregoing discussion has illustrated, our Commonwealth's commitment to neutralizing factors which unfairly impede or dilute individuals' rights to select their representatives was borne of our forebears' bitter personal experience suffering the pernicious effects resulting from previous electoral schemes that sanctioned such discrimination. Furthermore, adoption of a broad interpretation guards against the risk of unfairly rendering votes nugatory, artificially entrenching representative power, and discouraging voters from participating in the electoral process because they have come to believe that the power of their individual vote has been diminished to the point that it "does not count." A broad and robust interpretation of Article I, Section 5 serves as a bulwark against the adverse consequences of partisan gerrymandering.

The above analysis of the Free and Equal Elections Clause—its plain language, its history, the occasion for the provision and the circumstances in which it was adopted, the case law interpreting this clause, and consideration of the consequences of our interpretation—leads us to conclude the Clause should be given the broadest interpretation, one which governs all aspects of the electoral process, and which provides the people of this Commonwealth an equally effective power to select the representative of his or her choice, and bars the dilution of the people's power to do so.

[Accordingly, we hold that] an essential part of . . . an inquiry [under Article I, Section 5] is an examination of whether the congressional districts created under a redistricting plan are: composed of compact and contiguous territory; as nearly equal in population as practicable; and which do not divide any county, city, incorporated town, borough, township, or ward, except where necessary to ensure equality of population. . . .

[The court then applied this standard to the evidence, which it held showed a clear violation. In general, the court accepted evidence mounted by the plaintiff that the plan was drawn deliberately to favor Republicans over Democrats, and that an alternative plan could easily have been drawn which would have created more compact districts and split fewer counties and local jurisdictions.]

————————

In 2022, the Ohio Supreme Court invalidated the state's redistricting plan under a section of the Ohio Constitution, approved by voters in 2015, which expressly provided:

> (A) No general assembly district plan shall be drawn primarily to favor or disfavor a political party.
> (B) The statewide proportion of districts whose voters, based on state-wide state and federal partisan general election results during the last ten years, favor each political party shall correspond closely to the statewide preferences of the voters of Ohio.

League of Women Voters of Ohio v. Ohio Redistricting Commission, __ N.E.3d __ (Ohio, Jan. 12, 2022). One month later, the North Carolina Supreme Court invalidated the state's congressional and state legislative maps under sections of the state constitution providing that "all persons are created equal"; "[a]ll political power is vested in and derived from the people"; and "[a]ll elections shall be free." The court construed these provisions together to commit the state to a system of popular sovereignty in which "each voter must have substantially equal voting power and the state may not diminish or dilute that voting power on a partisan basis." *Harper v. Hall*, __ S.E.2d __(N.C. Feb. 14, 2022).

On the other hand, many state courts have either imported federal doctrinal analyses into their state constitutional rulings, or have read relevant state constitutional clauses weakly. *See* James A. Gardner, *Representation without Party: Lessons from State Constitutional Attempts to Control Gerrymandering*, 37 RUTGERS L. J. 881 (2006). For example, in a challenge to Wisconsin redistricting maps arguing that the state constitutions forbids partisan gerrymandering, the Wisconsin Supreme Court held:

> Claims of political unfairness in the maps present political questions, not legal ones. Such claims have no basis in the constitution or any other law and therefore must be resolved through the political process and not by the judiciary. The United States Supreme Court recently declared there are no legal standards by which judges may decide whether maps are politically "fair." *Rucho v. Common Cause*, 139 S. Ct. 2484, 2499-500 (2019). We agree. The Wisconsin Constitution requires the legislature—a political body—to establish the legislative districts in this state. Just as the laws enacted by the legislature reflect policy choices, so will the maps drawn by that political body. Nothing in the constitution empowers this court to second-guess those policy choices, and nothing in the constitution vests

this court with the power of the legislature to enact new maps. Our role in redistricting remains a purely judicial one, which limits us to declaring what the law is and affording the parties a remedy for its violation.

Johnson v. Wisconsin Election Comm'n, 967 N.W.2d 469 (Wis. 2021). Do state constitutions provide a reasonable alternative to federal judicial policing of partisan gerrymandering after *Rucho*? Note that most state judges are elected, subjecting them to possible electoral retaliation for unpopular rulings (see Chapter 10). After the Pennsylvania Supreme Court issued the ruling above, Republican leaders in the state legislature introduced a motion to impeach the four Democrats on the court who had ruled to invalidate the gerrymander, though the motions went nowhere. Does this kind of tactic nevertheless exert pressure on judges in attempting to check coordinate branches?

>> *Partisan Gerrymandering Standards.* If state courts do step up to take over from federal courts the job of enforcing constitutional constraints on partisan gerrymandering, they will in most instances be developing for the first time a jurisprudence of partisan fairness in districting under their respective state constitutions. This puts state courts in a position similar to the one in which federal courts found themselves between *Bandemer* and *Rucho*—in need of a standard that will help them distinguish normal partisan pushing and shoving from unfairness that rises to the level of unconstitutionality.

Two leading standards that were developed by political scientists and legal academics to assist federal courts, and which after *Rucho* have become irrelevant to federal jurisprudence, may nevertheless furnish guidance to state courts that decide to take up the challenge.

Partisan Bias. This standard predates *Vieth* and was developed by political scientists Andrew Gelman and Gary King. *See* Andrew Gelman and Gary King, *A Unified Method of Evaluating Electoral Systems and Redistricting Plans*, 38 AM. J. POL. SCI. 514 (1992); *see also* Bernard Grofman and Gary King, *The Future of Partisan Gerrymandering After* LULAC v. Perry, 6 ELECTION L.J. 2 (2007). Partisan bias is based upon the concept of partisan symmetry—the idea that similarly situated parties ought to be treated similarly—and is therefore a theory and measure of partisan fairness. Parties are treated equally (or fairly or symmetrically) where the percentage of votes received (for example, 55 percent) would translate into a certain percentage of seats, no matter which party won the share of votes. For example, if the Republican Party in an election won 55 percent of the votes and received 60 percent of the seats, the symmetry and fairness criteria are met if the Democrats would have received 60 percent of the seats had they won 55 percent of the votes. The relationship that is of interest here is not the one between votes and seats—political scientists call this relationship electoral responsiveness, which is about how well votes translates into seats. The idea of partisan bias or symmetry gets at how well the parties are treated vis-à-vis each other.

To make this intuitive, consider how we sometimes think about the problem of racial fairness. Assume that a black person claims that she was treated unfairly because she was denied a particular benefit, such as admission to a school. To determine whether the black person was treated fairly we often look at the problem in two related ways. First, we can ask whether the benefit is something that the person was entitled to. That is, we're interested in the relationship between the person and the benefit. The complainant might say, "I'm entitled to the benefit because I met the relevant criteria and having met the criteria the only reason I was denied the benefit is because of my race." Second and alternatively, we can ask a counterfactual, whether a white person would have been similarly treated under identical circumstances. Our fairness assessment is not the relationship between the person and the benefit—not whether our complainant met the relevant criteria—but the relationship between the two individuals of different races and whether they were (or would have been) treated similarly or differently under the same circumstances. If a black person is denied a benefit that would be awarded to her if she were white, we would say that the process is biased against her because of her race. This second, comparative, approach is particularly useful where the first approach can't tell us whether the complainant was treated fairly because, for example, the criteria are indeterminate. Sometimes people are awarded benefits when they meet the criteria and sometimes they are not. (For example, not everyone who meets the baseline criteria for admissions to universities is awarded admission.) Thus, if we want to assess fairness, assessing the relationship between the person and the benefit is not helpful.

This reasoning is analogous to the context of assessing partisan fairness. We cannot simply assess fairness by looking at electoral responsiveness—the relationship between votes and seats. While we think that there ought to be a somewhat linear relationship between votes and seats, there are good reasons why more votes do not always translate proportionately into more seats. So, to assess fairness, we have to beyond a direct assessment of the seats-to-votes relationship. The partisan symmetry standard does just that. Like the race example, it asks a counterfactual: whether the losing party would have been similarly treated under identical circumstances—i.e., won the same number of seats given its vote share under the same electoral system—had it won the election. If the Republican Party won 55 percent of the votes and received 60 percent of the seats, but the Democratic Party would have received 45 percent of the seats if it had won 60 percent of the votes, we would say that the system is biased against the Democrats (and vice versa). The partisan symmetry standard was favorably cited by Justice Stevens in his opinion, concurring in part and dissenting in part, in *LULAC v. Perry*, 548 U.S. 399, 466-467 (2006). Justice Stevens noted that partisan symmetry is a "reliable standard" that is "widely accepted by scholars as providing a measure of partisan fairness in electoral systems." He also noted that it was a "helpful (though certainly not talismanic) tool in this type of litigation," *id.* at 468 & n.9, and that it could be one of eight objective factors that courts could use to assess the constitutionality of a statewide political gerrymander. *Id.* at 473 & n.11.

Efficiency Gap. Competing with the Gelman and King model is another understanding of partisan fairness called the "efficiency gap," developed by political scientist Eric McGhee and law professor Nicholas Stephanopoulos. *See* Nicholas O. Stephanopoulos and Eric M. McGhee, *Partisan Gerrymandering and the Efficiency Gap*, 82 U. Chi. L. Rev. 831 (2015). Like the Gelman and King model, the efficiency gap is also a conception and measure of partisan symmetry. That is, it too is interested in whether the parties are treated similarly under the same circumstances. But unlike the Gelman/King approach to partisan symmetry, which focuses directly on the relationship between votes and seats through a comparative assessment, the efficiency gap focuses on a specific way in which parties create partisan advantage by looking at how the party in control of the redistricting process creates partisan advantage by the way it groups voters in districts. The efficiency gap assumes that the strategy of the dominant party, the party in control of districting, is to group its voters as efficiently as possible and to group the voters of the out party as inefficiently as possible. Put differently, the dominant party wants to maximize the impact of the votes of its voters and "waste" the votes of voters from the other party. McGhee and Stephanopoulos define as wasted votes any votes cast for a losing candidate as well as votes cast for a winning candidate in excess of the margin needed to win.

To make this more intuitive and concrete, suppose we have a city with four districts and 100 voters. Suppose that half of the voters are registered as Sky Party members and the other half as Ground Party members. And suppose that registration perfectly predicted voting behavior and that the Sky Party oversees redistricting in a first-past-the-post system governed by the one-person one-vote principle. The Sky Party wants to capture as many seats as possible. To do so, it must waste the least number of votes from Sky Party voters and the most number of votes from Ground Party voters. Thus we would expect the following distribution of voters:

District	Sky Party	Ground Party	Wasted Votes
1	13	12	0 SP; 12 GP
2	13	12	0 SP; 12 GP
3	13	12	0 SP; 12 GP
4	11	14	11 SP; 2 GP
Total	50	50	11 SP; 38 GP

As you can see, the Sky Party distributed its voters very efficiently. Sky received 50 percent of the votes but 75 percent of the seats. It did not waste any votes in District 1, 2, or 3. In contrast, the Ground Party wasted 12 votes, as per the McGhee and Stephanopoulos definition of wasted votes, in each district except for District 4, where it wasted 2. The Sky Party only wasted 11 votes total, in District 4. To calculate the efficiency gap, we determine the total net wasted votes between two parties ($38 - 11 = 27$) and we divide the sum by the total number of votes cast ($27/100 = .27$). Expressed as a percentage, the efficiency gap is 27 percent, which means that the Sky Party, since it wasted fewer votes than the Ground Party, was better able to convert its votes to legislative seats and won 27 percent more seats than it would have if both parties had wasted an equal number of votes. Functionally, this means that the Sky Party won one more seat ($.27 \times 4$ seats $= 1.08$) than it would have if both parties were similarly inefficient in the distribution of voters.

»   *Re-Redistricting.*   If redistricting once per decade is not exciting enough for you, how about redistricting twice, or even three times? Prior to the one-person, one-vote decisions of the 1960s, state practice varied widely:

> [I]n the 19th century, states redistricted almost whenever they wanted. In every year from 1862 and 1896, with one exception, at least one state redrew its congressional district boundaries. Ohio, for example, redrew its congressional district boundaries six times between 1878 and 1890. Other states went long stretches with the same boundaries. . . . Connecticut, for instance, kept the exact same congressional district lines for 70 years (1842-1912).

ERIK J. ENGSTROM, PARTISAN GERRYMANDERING AND THE CONSTRUCTION OF AMER-
ICAN DEMOCRACY 8 (2013). The Court's one-person, one-vote rulings produced
a convergence in state practice. Under those rulings, it became clear that states
would have to redistrict themselves following each new census in order to avoid
a virtually certain constitutional violation. For 40 years, an unofficial consensus
existed that redistricting was something to be undertaken immediately following
each decennial census, but not more frequently. This consensus fell apart in 2003
when Republicans in Colorado and Texas, finding themselves in control of their
respective state legislatures following the 2002 elections, decided to redraw election
districts that had been created immediately following the 2000 census. These new
plans were much more favorable to Republicans than the plans they replaced. In
Texas, the Republican drive to replace the first post-2000 plan caused an unseemly
and somewhat comical midnight run across the New Mexico border by 11 Democratic senators who holed up in a motel there to deprive the Texas Senate of a
quorum sufficient to enact the new redistricting plan. When one senator finally
returned, the Senate enacted the plan into law.

Are these multiple redistrictings legal? Multiple redistricting might be
restricted by either state or federal law. About ten states have constitutional provisions that limit redistricting to once per decade. In *Colorado General Assembly
v. Salazar*, 79 P.3d 1221 (Colo. 2003), the Colorado Supreme Court ruled that the
Colorado Legislature's second redistricting plan of 2003 violated an implicit state
constitutional prohibition on multiple redistrictings. As for federal law, Congress
could probably use its Article I, §4 power to regulate elections to prohibit multiple redistricting between censuses, but such a restriction would apply only to congressional redistricting and not state legislative redistricting. Congress has thus
far not shown any inclination to get involved. That leaves the question of the U.S.
Constitution.

Because the Texas Constitution does not prohibit redistricting more than
once in a decade, Democrats challenging the Texas re-redistricting were forced to
argue that multiple reapportionment is implicitly prohibited by the federal Constitution. In *Session v. Perry*, 298 F. Supp. 451, 458-459 (E.D. Tex. 2004) (three-judge
court), a three-judge District Court rejected this claim.

> Plaintiffs argue that Texas lacks the power . . . to redraw congressional
> districts in the middle of the decade. . . . Although there are compelling
> arguments why it would be good policy for states to abstain from drawing
> district lines mid-decade, Plaintiffs ultimately fail to provide any authority—
> constitutional, statutory, or judicial—demonstrating that mid-decade
> redistricting is forbidden in Texas. . . .
>
> [The] Elections Clause of the Constitution grants states broad power
> to regulate the "time, place, and manner of holding elections for Senator
> and Representatives." [Art. I, §4.] . . . This provision delegates to state leg-
> islatures both the power and responsibility to redraw congressional voting
> districts. . . . While states may only enact "time, places and manner" regu-
> lations, the text does not define or otherwise limit the states' discretion.
> Nonetheless, Congress may, if it chooses, make regulations governing
> the "times, places and manner" of holding elections or alter regulations
> enacted by state legislatures. This reservation to Congress, however, is not
> a direct limitation on the scope of the states' authority; rather, it allows

Congress to override state election decisions or to enact regulations of its own. Unless and until Congress chooses to act, the states' power to redistrict remains unlimited by constitutional text. . . .

The case eventually worked its way up to the Supreme Court, but the plaintiffs declined on appeal to pursue directly the issue of state authority to redistrict in the middle of a decade, and the Court did not decide the issue. For a discussion of policy reasons disfavoring multiple redistricting between censuses, see Adam Cox, *Partisan Fairness and Redistricting Politics*, 79 N.Y.U. L. Rev. 751 (2004).

≫   *The Call for Independent Districting Commissions.*   Continuing frustration with the Supreme Court's inability to provide a workable standard for judicial policing of partisan gerrymandering has prompted many to believe that the only feasible solution to the problem lies in taking the job of drawing election district lines away from legislatures and giving it to some other entity structured so as to insulate it from partisan impulses. The most frequently mentioned candidate is an independent nonpartisan or bipartisan commission.

Sixteen states now employ some sort of independent districting commission to draw districts for at least some legislative offices. Such commissions typically are structured to achieve impartiality in one of two ways. One method is to create an evenly split, bipartisan commission and require majority or supermajority agreement to redistricting plans. In New Jersey, for example, the majority and minority leaders of each state legislative chamber appoint two members each; the chairs of the two major political parties appoint two members each; and these twelve members jointly appoint a thirteenth, and presumably tie-breaking member. If the twelve members cannot agree on a thirteenth, the New Jersey Supreme Court makes the appointment. It is assumed in this scheme that the people appointed to the commission by partisans will themselves be either politicians or strong partisans. New York's commission is similarly constituted, and no plan can be reported to the legislature without a two-thirds vote of commission members.

A different strategy is to remove politicians altogether from the decision making process. Perhaps the most ambitious attempt of this type is California's. Adopted by initiatives in 2008 and 2010, California's system creates a redistricting commission whose members are citizens and are selected through an elaborate process intended to assure their individual and collective independence from partisan politics. Eight of the fourteen members are chosen through a process that includes open applications, interviews, strikes by legislative leaders, and a random drawing. These eight then choose the final six members from the remaining finalists. By law, no one is eligible for the commission who has in the preceding ten years been a candidate for office, worked for a campaign, served as a paid consultant to a campaign, or contributed more than $2,000 to certain campaigns. In addition, five members of the commission must be Republicans, five must be Democrats, and four must be either affiliated with a minor party or unaffiliated with any party. *See* Karin MacDonald, *Adventures in Redistricting: A Look at the California Redistricting Commission*, 11 Election L.J. 472 (2012).

But do such commissions really solve the problems of partisan self-dealing presented by legislative self-redistricting?

> [I]t is almost impossible to design institutions to be authentically nonpartisan and politically disinterested. . . . Whoever draws the lines

must get authority from somewhere—the person will either be appointed or elected. Elected officials, as former Florida Secretary of State Katherine Harris [who presided over the 2000 Florida recount] demonstrated, are almost certainly conflicted. And appointed officials will be beholden to those appointing them or at least selected because their intentions are well-known. . . .

Even Iowa's "nonpartisan" Legislative Services Bureau . . . is appointed by and serves at the pleasure of the Legislative Council, which the majority party in the legislature controls. Moreover, the legislature can veto the plans submitted by the Legislative Services Bureau, as it did to the initial plan proposed [in 2001] and did twice in 1980. The Legislative Services Bureau certainly has a reputation of nonpartisanship quite similar to that of boundary commissions in other countries, and the Iowa legislature has agreed to plans that promote competition. This tradition may have more to do with Iowa's political culture, however, than with features inherent to the institutional form that the state has chosen. One can only wonder if the civil service of more politically confrontational or polarized states would be similarly nonpartisan or receive the mutual assent of all government officials. . . .

Even if nonpartisan redistricting were feasible, would it be desirable? The assumption that guides [such proposals] is that the redistricting process would be better if politics were taken out of it. As with election regulation more generally, we should ask whether we would really want a world in which unaccountable and disinterested officials make the fundamental decisions concerning representation. . . . [P]oliticians should be in charge of politics. [R]edistricting can be part of substantive policymaking and administration. Legislative bargains in the redistricting process are not completely detached from others that occur throughout a legislative session. Through redistricting, legislatures not only make the tough value-laden decisions as to how communities should be represented, but they create service relationships between representatives and constituents that fit into larger public policy programs. The removal of politics from redistricting seeks to break these relationships. . . .

Nathaniel Persily, *In Defense of Foxes Guarding Henhouses: The Case for Judicial Acquiescence to Incumbent-Protecting Gerrymanders*, 116 HARV. L. REV. 649, 674-675 (2002). Who has the best of this argument? Do independent commissions present the prospect for a solution to the problems of partisan-dominated gerrymandering? If not a solution, at least some improvement? What about the difficulty of holding appointed independent commissions democratically accountable? Would increasing reliance on such commissions simply trade one kind of unaccountability for another?

To answer at least some of these questions, political scientists have begun to compare the work of independent redistricting commissions to that of state legislatures. The early results do not provide much support for the contention that commissions do a better and less partisan job, or that they create fewer safe seats and more competitive ones.

Our evidence shows that control of redistricting had no effect on change in the proportions of safe and marginal districts between 2000 and

2002. . . . In states in which redistricting was done by nonpartisan commissions or courts, the proportion of marginal districts decreased from 25% in 2000 to 24% in 2002 while the proportion of safe districts increased from 44% in 2000 to 51% in 2002; in states in which redistricting was done by partisan state legislatures, the proportion of marginal districts decreased from 29% in 2000 to 28% in 2002 while the proportion of safe districts decreased from 46% in 2000 to 45% in 2002. There is no evidence that redistricting by nonpartisan redistricting commission or courts resulted in more competitive districts than redistricting by partisan state legislatures.

Alan I. Abramowitz et al., *Incumbency, Redistricting, and the Decline of Competition in U.S. House Elections*, 68 J. POL. 75, 79 (2006). A more recent study covering 1992-2012 found that maps drawn by independent commissions produced, at best, only modestly more electoral competition than maps produced by legislatures. Peter Miller and Bernard Grofman, *Redistricting Commissions in the Western United States*, 3 U.C. IRVINE L. REV. 637 (2013). The authors also found that "the 2012 elections were business as usual. . . . Even in California it appears that eighty-five percent of the seats are solidly held by one of the parties, regardless of who draws the lines." *Id.* at 684.

Another study focusing on competitiveness in state legislative elections during 2000 and 2004 found that redistricting maps prepared by *courts* produced a substantially greater number of competitive districts than plans prepared by state legislatures. David Lublin and Michael P. McDonald, *Is It Time to Draw the Line? The Impact of Redistricting on Competition in State House Elections*, 5 ELECTION L.J. 144 (2006). The studies discussed above are not directly comparable, but it is worth considering whether judges might be more "neutral" than commissions in drafting districting plans. Would you expect to find a difference in the neutrality of elected state judges compared to appointed federal judges? A recent study did not address this precise question, but it found no evidence that maps drawn by courts, whether federal or state, favor the political party of the judges who drew them. The study also confirmed the finding that judge-drawn maps are more competitive than maps drawn by legislatures. James B. Cottrill and Terri J. Peretti, *Gerrymandering from the Bench? The Electoral Consequences of Judicial Redistricting*, 12 ELECTION L.J. 261 (2013).

And just how "independent" of politics are independent commissions? In Arizona, for example, the governor removed for alleged misconduct the chair of an independent redistricting panel that had been created by popular initiative, and the state senate confirmed the removal on a party-line vote. The chair was reinstated by order of the Arizona Supreme Court. Intense partisan attacks were launched against independent commissions in California and Idaho. In the current round of redistricting following the 2020 census, independent redistricting commissions appear to have been complete flops. In Ohio, two Republican commissioners, the sitting state House Speaker and Senate President, drew maps in secret, excluding even other Republican commissioners from participating. In New York, Democratic and Republican commissioners were so far from reaching agreement that each group submitted its own map to the legislature, in violation of binding legal procedures. In Utah, Republicans in the state legislature adopted their own maps, ignoring proposals from a redistricting commission created by voter initiative in 2018. In Virginia, commissioners were unable to reach agreement; Republicans rejected any compromise with Democrats, and Democrats walked out. As a result, the commission produced no maps, triggering the backup procedure of line-drawing by the state supreme court.

Arizona State Legislature v. Arizona Independent Redistricting Commission

135 S. Ct. 2652 (2015)

Justice GINSBURG delivered the opinion of the Court.

In 2000, Arizona voters adopted an initiative, Proposition 106, aimed at "ending the practice of gerrymandering and improving voter and candidate participation in elections." Proposition 106 amended Arizona's Constitution to remove redistricting authority from the Arizona Legislature and vest that authority in an independent commission, the Arizona Independent Redistricting Commission (AIRC or Commission). After the 2010 census, as after the 2000 census, the AIRC adopted redistricting maps for congressional as well as state legislative districts.

The Arizona Legislature challenged the map the Commission adopted in January 2012 for congressional districts, . . . seeking a declaration that the Commission and its map for congressional districts violated the "Elections Clause" of the U.S. Constitution. That Clause, critical to the resolution of this case, provides:

> The Times, Places and Manner of holding Elections for Senators and Representatives, shall be prescribed in each State by the Legislature thereof; but the Congress may at any time by Law make or alter such Regulations. . . .

Art. I, §4, cl. 1. The Arizona Legislature's complaint alleged that "[t]he word 'Legislature' in the Elections Clause means [specifically and only] the representative body which makes the laws of the people"; so read, the Legislature urges, the Clause precludes resort to an independent commission, created by initiative, to accomplish redistricting. The AIRC responded that, for Elections Clause purposes, "the Legislature" is not confined to the elected representatives; rather, the term encompasses all legislative authority conferred by the State Constitution, including initiatives adopted by the people themselves.

We hold . . . that lawmaking power in Arizona includes the initiative process, and that . . . the Elections Clause permit[s] use of the AIRC in congressional districting in the same way the Commission is used in districting for Arizona's own Legislature.

I

A

Direct lawmaking by the people was "virtually unknown when the Constitution of 1787 was drafted." There were obvious precursors or analogues to the direct lawmaking operative today in several States, notably, New England's town hall meetings and the submission of early state constitutions to the people for ratification. But it was not until the turn of the 20th century, as part of the Progressive agenda of the era, that direct lawmaking by the electorate gained a foothold, largely in Western States.

The two main "agencies of direct legislation" are the initiative and the referendum. The initiative operates entirely outside the States' representative assemblies; it allows "voters [to] petition to propose statutes or constitutional amendments to be adopted or rejected by the voters at the polls." While the initiative allows the electorate to adopt positive legislation, the referendum serves as a negative check. It allows "voters [to] petition to refer a legislative action to the voters [for approval or disapproval] at the polls." "The initiative [thus] corrects sins of omission" by representative bodies, while the "referendum corrects sins of commission."

B

For the delegates to Arizona's constitutional convention, direct lawmaking was a "principal issu[e]." By a margin of more than three to one, the people of Arizona ratified the State's Constitution, which included, among lawmaking means, initiative and referendum provisions. In the runup to Arizona's admission to the Union in 1912, those provisions generated no controversy.

In particular, the Arizona Constitution "establishes the electorate [of Arizona] as a coordinate source of legislation" on equal footing with the representative legislative body.

C

Proposition 106, vesting redistricting authority in the AIRC, was adopted by citizen initiative in 2000 against a "background of recurring redistricting turmoil" in Arizona. Redistricting plans adopted by the Arizona Legislature sparked controversy in every redistricting cycle since the 1970's, and several of those plans were rejected by a federal court or refused preclearance by the Department of Justice under the Voting Rights Act of 1965.

Aimed at "ending the practice of gerrymandering and improving voter and candidate participation in elections," Proposition 106 amended the Arizona Constitution to remove congressional redistricting authority from the state legislature, lodging that authority, instead, in a new entity, the AIRC. The AIRC convenes after each census, establishes final district boundaries, and certifies the new districts to the Arizona Secretary of State. The legislature may submit nonbinding recommendations to the AIRC, and is required to make necessary appropriations for its operation. The highest ranking officer and minority leader of each chamber of the legislature each select one member of the AIRC from a list compiled by Arizona's Commission on Appellate Court Appointments. The four appointed members of the AIRC then choose, from the same list, the fifth member, who chairs the Commission. A Commission's tenure is confined to one redistricting cycle.

Holders of, or candidates for, public office may not serve on the AIRC, except candidates for or members of a school board. No more than two members of the Commission may be members of the same political party, and the presiding fifth member cannot be registered with any party already represented on the Commission. Subject to the concurrence of two-thirds of the Arizona Senate, AIRC members may be removed by the Arizona Governor for gross misconduct, substantial neglect of duty, or inability to discharge the duties of office.

D

On January 17, 2012, the AIRC approved final congressional and state legislative maps based on the 2010 census. Less than four months later, on June 6, 2012, the Arizona Legislature filed suit in the United States District Court for the District of Arizona, naming as defendants the AIRC, its five members, and the Arizona Secretary of State. The Legislature sought both a declaration that Proposition 106 and congressional maps adopted by the AIRC are unconstitutional, and, as affirmative relief, an injunction against use of AIRC maps for any congressional election after the 2012 general election.

III

Before focusing directly on the . . . constitutional prescriptions in point, we summarize this Court's precedent relating to appropriate state decisionmakers for redistricting purposes. Three decisions compose the relevant case law: *Ohio ex rel. Davis v. Hildebrant*, 241 U.S. 565 (1916); *Hawke v. Smith (No. 1)*, 253 U.S. 221 (1920); and *Smiley v. Holm*, 285 U.S. 355 (1932).

A

Davis v. Hildebrant involved an amendment to the Constitution of Ohio vesting in the people the right, exercisable by referendum, to approve or disapprove by popular vote any law enacted by the State's legislature. A 1915 Act redistricting the State for the purpose of congressional elections had been submitted to a popular vote, resulting in disapproval of the legislature's measure. State election officials asked the State's Supreme Court to declare the referendum void. That court rejected the request, holding that the referendum authorized by Ohio's Constitution, "was a part of the legislative power of the State," and "nothing in [federal statutory law] or in [the Elections Clause] operated to the contrary." This Court affirmed the Ohio Supreme Court's judgment. In upholding the state court's decision, we recognized that the referendum was "part of the legislative power" in Ohio, legitimately exercised by the people to disapprove the legislation creating congressional districts. For redistricting purposes, *Hildebrant* thus established, "the Legislature" did not mean the representative body alone. Rather, the word encompassed a veto power lodged in the people.

Hawke v. Smith involved the Eighteenth Amendment to the Federal Constitution. Ohio's Legislature had ratified the Amendment, and a referendum on that ratification was at issue. Reversing the Ohio Supreme Court's decision upholding the referendum, we held that "ratification by a State of a constitutional amendment is not an act of legislation within the proper sense of the word." Instead, Article V governing ratification had lodged in "the legislatures of three-fourths of the several States" sole authority to assent to a proposed amendment. *Id.* at 226. The Court contrasted the ratifying function, exercisable exclusively by a State's legislature, with "the ordinary business of legislation." *Davis v. Hildebrant*, the Court explained, involved the enactment of legislation, *i.e.*, a redistricting plan, and properly held that "the referendum [was] part of the legislative authority of the State for [that] purpose."

Smiley v. Holm raised the question whether legislation purporting to redistrict Minnesota for congressional elections was subject to the Governor's veto. The

Minnesota Supreme Court had held that the Elections Clause placed redistricting authority exclusively in the hands of the State's legislature, leaving no role for the Governor. We reversed that determination and held, for the purpose at hand, Minnesota's legislative authority includes not just the two houses of the legislature; it includes, in addition, a make-or-break role for the Governor. In holding that the Governor's veto counted, we distinguished instances in which the Constitution calls upon state legislatures to exercise a function other than lawmaking.

[W]e observed, redistricting "involves lawmaking in its essential features and most important aspect." Lawmaking, we further noted, ordinarily "must be in accordance with the method which the State has prescribed for legislative enactments." In Minnesota, the State's Constitution had made the Governor "part of the legislative process." And the Elections Clause, we explained, respected the State's choice to include the Governor in that process, although the Governor could play no part when the Constitution assigned to "the Legislature" a ratifying, electoral, or consenting function.

In sum, our precedent teaches that redistricting is a legislative function, to be performed in accordance with the State's prescriptions for lawmaking, which may include the referendum and the Governor's veto. The exercise of the initiative, we acknowledge, was not at issue in our prior decisions. But as developed below, we see no constitutional barrier to a State's empowerment of its people by embracing that form of lawmaking.

C

[W]e hold that the Elections Clause permits the people of Arizona to provide for redistricting by independent commission. To restate the key question in this case, the issue centrally debated by the parties: Absent congressional authorization, does the Elections Clause preclude the people of Arizona from creating a commission operating independently of the state legislature to establish congressional districts? The history and purpose of the Clause weigh heavily against such preclusion, as does the animating principle of our Constitution that the people themselves are the originating source of all the powers of government.

We note, preliminarily, that dictionaries, even those in circulation during the founding era, capaciously define the word "legislature." Samuel Johnson defined "legislature" simply as "[t]he power that makes laws." 2 A Dictionary of the English Language (1st ed. 1755); ibid. (6th ed. 1785); ibid. (10th ed. 1792); ibid. (12th ed. 1802). Thomas Sheridan's dictionary defined "legislature" exactly as Dr. Johnson did: "The power that makes laws." 2 A Complete Dictionary of the English Language (4th ed. 1797). Noah Webster defined the term precisely that way as well. Compendious Dictionary of the English Language 174 (1806). And Nathan Bailey similarly defined "legislature" as "the Authority of making Laws, or Power which makes them." An Universal Etymological English Dictionary (20th ed. 1763).

As to the "power that makes laws" in Arizona, initiatives adopted by the voters legislate for the State just as measures passed by the representative body do. See Ariz. Const., Art. IV, pt. 1, §1 ("The legislative authority of the state shall be vested in the legislature, consisting of a senate and a house of representatives, but the people reserve the power to propose laws and amendments to the constitution and to enact or reject such laws and amendments at the polls, independently of the legislature."). As well in Arizona, the people may delegate their legislative authority over redistricting to an independent commission just as the representative body may choose to do.

1

The dominant purpose of the Elections Clause, the historical record bears out, was to empower Congress to override state election rules, not to restrict the way States enact legislation. As this Court explained in *Arizona v. Inter Tribal Council of Ariz., Inc.*, 570 U.S. 1 (2013), the Clause "was the Framers' insurance against the possibility that a State would refuse to provide for the election of representatives to the Federal Congress."

The Clause was also intended to act as a safeguard against manipulation of electoral rules by politicians and factions in the States to entrench themselves or place their interests over those of the electorate. As Madison urged, without the Elections Clause, "[w]henever the State Legislatures had a favorite measure to carry, they would take care so to mould their regulations as to favor the candidates they wished to succeed." 2 Records of the Federal Convention 241 (M. Farrand rev. 1966). Madison spoke in response to a motion by South Carolina's delegates to strike out the federal power. Those delegates so moved because South Carolina's coastal elite had malapportioned their legislature, and wanted to retain the ability to do so.

While attention focused on potential abuses by state-level politicians, and the consequent need for congressional oversight, the legislative processes by which the States could exercise their initiating role in regulating congressional elections occasioned no debate. That is hardly surprising. Recall that when the Constitution was composed in Philadelphia and later ratified, the people's legislative prerogatives—the initiative and the referendum—were not yet in our democracy's arsenal. The Elections Clause, however, is not reasonably read to disarm States from adopting modes of legislation that place the lead rein in the people's hands.

2

The Arizona Legislature maintains that, by specifying "the Legislature thereof," the Elections Clause renders the State's representative body the sole "component of state government authorized to prescribe . . . regulations . . . for congressional redistricting." The Chief Justice, in dissent, agrees. But it is characteristic of our federal system that States retain autonomy to establish their own governmental processes.

We resist reading the Elections Clause to single out federal elections as the one area in which States may not use citizen initiatives as an alternative legislative process. Nothing in that Clause instructs, nor has this Court ever held, that a state legislature may prescribe regulations on the time, place, and manner of holding federal elections in defiance of provisions of the State's constitution. See *Shiel*, H.R. Misc. Doc. No. 57, at 349-352 (concluding that Oregon's Constitution prevailed over any conflicting legislative measure setting the date for a congressional election).

3

The Framers may not have imagined the modern initiative process in which the people of a State exercise legislative power coextensive with the authority of an institutional legislature. But the invention of the initiative was in full harmony with the Constitution's conception of the people as the font of governmental power. As Madison put it: "The genius of republican liberty seems to demand . . . not only that all power should be derived from the people, but that those intrusted with it should be kept in dependence on the people." *Id.* No. 37, at 223.

4

Banning lawmaking by initiative to direct a State's method of apportioning congressional districts would do more than stymie attempts to curb partisan gerrymandering, by which the majority in the legislature draws district lines to their party's advantage. It would also cast doubt on numerous other election laws adopted by the initiative method of legislating.

The people, in several States, functioning as the lawmaking body for the purpose at hand, have used the initiative to install a host of regulations governing the "Times, Places and Manner" of holding federal elections. Art. I, §4. For example, the people of California provided for permanent voter registration, specifying that "no amendment by the Legislature shall provide for a general biennial or other periodic reregistration of voters." The people of Ohio banned ballots providing for straight-ticket voting along party lines. The people of Oregon shortened the deadline for voter registration to 20 days prior to an election. None of those measures permit the state legislatures to override the people's prescriptions. The Arizona Legislature's theory—that the lead role in regulating federal elections cannot be wrested from "the Legislature," and vested in commissions initiated by the people—would endanger all of them.

The list of endangered state elections laws, were we to sustain the position of the Arizona Legislature, would not stop with popular initiatives. Almost all state constitutions were adopted by conventions and ratified by voters at the ballot box, without involvement or approval by "the Legislature." Core aspects of the electoral process regulated by state constitutions include voting by "ballot" or "secret ballot," voter registration, absentee voting, vote counting, and victory thresholds. Again, the States' legislatures had no hand in making these laws and may not alter or amend them.

The importance of direct democracy as a means to control election regulations extends beyond the particular statutes and constitutional provisions installed by the people rather than the States' legislatures. The very prospect of lawmaking by the people may influence the legislature when it considers (or fails to consider) election-related measures. Turning the coin, the legislature's responsiveness to the people its members represent is hardly heightened when the representative body can be confident that what it does will not be overturned or modified by the voters themselves.

Invoking the Elections Clause, the Arizona Legislature instituted this lawsuit to disempower the State's voters from serving as the legislative power for redistricting purposes. But the Clause surely was not adopted to diminish a State's authority to determine its own lawmaking processes. Article I, §4, stems from a different view. Both parts of the Elections Clause are in line with the fundamental premise that all political power flows from the people. So comprehended, the Clause doubly empowers the people. They may control the State's lawmaking processes in the first instance, as Arizona voters have done, and they may seek Congress' correction of regulations prescribed by state legislatures. . . .

For the reasons stated, the judgment of the United States District Court for the District of Arizona is

Affirmed.

Chief Justice ROBERTS, with whom Justice SCALIA, Justice THOMAS, and Justice ALITO join, dissenting.

I

The Elections Clause both imposes a duty on States and assigns that duty to a particular state actor: In the absence of a valid congressional directive to the contrary, States must draw district lines for their federal representatives. And that duty "shall" be carried out "in each State by the Legislature thereof."

In Arizona, however, redistricting is not carried out by the legislature. Instead, as the result of a ballot initiative, an unelected body called the Independent Redistricting Commission draws the lines. The key question in the case is whether the Commission can conduct congressional districting consistent with the directive that such authority be exercised "by the Legislature."

The majority concedes that the unelected Commission is not "the Legislature" of Arizona. The Court contends instead that the people of Arizona as a whole constitute "the Legislature" for purposes of the Elections Clause, and that they may delegate the congressional districting authority conferred by that Clause to the Commission. The majority provides no support for the delegation part of its theory, and I am not sure whether the majority's analysis is correct on that issue. But even giving the Court the benefit of the doubt in that regard, the Commission is still unconstitutional. Both the Constitution and our cases make clear that "the Legislature" in the Elections Clause is the representative body which makes the laws of the people.

A

The majority devotes much of its analysis to establishing that the people of Arizona may exercise lawmaking power under their State Constitution. Nobody doubts that. This case is governed, however, by the Federal Constitution. The States do not, in the majority's words, "retain autonomy to establish their own governmental processes," if those "processes" violate the United States Constitution. . . .

The relevant question in this case is how to define "the Legislature" under the Elections Clause. The Court seems to conclude, based largely on its understanding of the "history and purpose" of the Elections Clause, that "the Legislature" encompasses any entity in a State that exercises legislative power. That circular definition lacks any basis in the text of the Constitution or any other relevant legal source.

The majority's textual analysis consists, in its entirety, of one paragraph citing founding era dictionaries. The majority points to various dictionaries that follow Samuel Johnson's definition of "legislature" as the "power that makes laws." The notion that this definition corresponds to the entire population of a State is strained to begin with, and largely discredited by the majority's own admission that "[d]irect lawmaking by the people was virtually unknown when the Constitution of 1787 was drafted. . . ."

Any ambiguity about the meaning of "the Legislature" is removed by other founding era sources. "[E]very state constitution from the Founding Era that used the term legislature defined it as a distinct multimember entity comprised of representatives." Morley, The Intratextual Independent "Legislature" and the Elections Clause, 109 Nw. U. L. Rev. Online 131, 147, and n. 101 (2015) (citing eleven State Constitutions). The Federalist Papers are replete with references to "legislatures" that can only be understood as referring to representative institutions.

I could go on, but the Court has said this before. As we put it nearly a century ago, "Legislature" was "not a term of uncertain meaning when incorporated into the Constitution." *Hawke*, 253 U.S., at 227. "What it meant when adopted it still means for the purpose of interpretation." "A Legislature" is "the representative body which ma[kes] the laws of the people."

B

The Constitution includes seventeen provisions referring to a State's "Legislature." Every one of those references is consistent with the understanding of a legislature as a representative body. More importantly, many of them are only consistent with an institutional legislature—and flatly incompatible with the majority's reading of "the Legislature" to refer to the people as a whole.

Start with the Constitution's first use of the term: "The House of Representatives shall be composed of Members chosen every second Year by the People of the several States, and the Electors in each State shall have the Qualifications requisite for Electors of the most numerous Branch of the State Legislature." Art. I, §2, cl. 1. This reference to a "Branch of the State Legislature" can only be referring to an institutional body, and the explicit juxtaposition of "the State Legislature" with "the People of the several States" forecloses the majority's proposed reading.

The list goes on. . . .

Each of these provisions offers strong structural indications about what "the Legislature" must mean. But the most powerful evidence of all comes from the Seventeenth Amendment. Under the original Constitution, Senators were "chosen by the Legislature" of each State, Art. I, §3, cl. 1, while Members of the House of Representatives were chosen "by the People," Art. I, §2, cl. 1. That distinction was critical to the Framers. As James Madison explained, the Senate would "derive its powers from the States," while the House would "derive its powers from the people of America." The Federalist No. 39, at 244. George Mason believed that the power of state legislatures to select Senators would "be a reasonable guard" against "the Danger . . . that the national, will swallow up the State Legislatures." Not everyone agreed. James Wilson proposed allowing the people to elect Senators directly. His proposal was rejected ten to one. Debates in the Federal Convention of 1787, S. Doc. No. 404, 57th Cong., 1st Sess., 8 (1902).

Before long, reformers took up Wilson's mantle and launched a protracted campaign to amend the Constitution. That effort began in 1826, when Representative Henry Storrs of New York proposed—but then set aside—a constitutional amendment transferring the power to elect Senators from the state legislatures to the people. Over the next three-quarters of a century, no fewer than 188 joint resolutions proposing similar reforms were introduced in both Houses of Congress.

At no point in this process did anyone suggest that a constitutional amendment was unnecessary because "Legislature" could simply be interpreted to mean "people." In fact, as the decades rolled by without an amendment, 28 of the 45 States settled for the next best thing by holding a popular vote on candidates for Senate, then pressuring state legislators into choosing the winner. All agreed that cutting the state legislature out of senatorial selection entirely would require nothing less than to "Strike out" the original words in the Constitution and "insert, 'elected by the people'" in its place.

Yet that is precisely what the majority does to the Elections Clause today—amending the text not through the process provided by Article V, but by judicial decision. The majority's revision renders the Seventeenth Amendment an 86-year waste of time, and singles out the Elections Clause as the only one of the Constitution's seventeen provisions referring to "the Legislature" that departs from the ordinary meaning of the term.

C

The history of the Elections Clause further supports the conclusion that "the Legislature" is a representative body. The first known draft of the Clause to appear at the Constitutional Convention provided that "Each state shall prescribe the time and manner of holding elections." 1 Debates on the Federal Constitution 146 (J. Elliot ed. 1836). After revision by the Committee of Detail, the Clause included the important limitation at issue here: "The times and places, and the manner, of holding the elections of the members of each house, shall be prescribed *by the legislature of each state*, but their provisions concerning them may, at any time, be altered *by the legislature of the United States.*" *Id.* at 225 (emphasis added). The insertion of "the legislature" indicates that the Framers thought carefully about which entity within the State was to perform congressional districting. And the parallel between "the legislature of each state" and "the legislature of the United States" further suggests that they meant "the legislature" as a representative body. . . .

I respectfully dissent.

» *Are the People Sovereign?* *Arizona Independent Redistricting Commission* addresses a fundamental question that has been an underlying consideration in this chapter: who is the ultimate sovereign, the people or their representatives? Justice Ginsburg's majority opinion is based upon the notion that the Constitution reflects the principle "of the people as the font of governmental power." But is Justice Ginsburg retroactively reading that principle, through the lens of the Progressive movement, into the constitutional structure? That is, though Justice Ginsburg is likely right that in modern American representative democracy our conception of sovereignty is fundamentally populist—sovereignty lies with the people—that conception is not necessarily reflective of the Constitution's text or design. Isn't it the case that Chief Justice Roberts has the better argument here on the basis not just of the text but on the basis of constitutional design: the structural logic of the Constitution is republicanism, which rests authority, judgment, and independence in certain contexts on the elected representatives of the people, the legislature? Put differently, the Constitution reflects a joint conception of sovereignty—sometimes the people are sovereign, sometimes their representatives are sovereign. Thus, is it not the case that desire of the people of Arizona to bypass their state legislature (and grant themselves more sovereignty) is forbidden by both the text and design of a constitution that divided sovereignty between the people and representatives?

For an originalist critique of the majority's analysis, see Saikrishna Bangalore Prakash and John Yoo, *People ≠ Legislature*, 39 Harv. J.L. & Pub. Pol'y 351 (2016).

≫ *Public Participation and Transparency as a Solution?* A different approach to minimizing partisan gerrymandering might be to rely on disclosure and public participation in the redistricting process. Here the idea is that by making information about contemplated redistricting plans available to the public in a readily accessible format, public input can be obtained and public knowledge harnessed in ways that will allow mapmakers to draw better and fairer plans. For example, a bill introduced in Congress, the Redistricting Transparency Act of 2010, H.R. 4918, 111th Cong., 2d Sess., would have required state redistricting authorities, when engaged in congressional redistricting, to maintain a website, provide the public notice of and opportunities to comment on initial plans, and to hold public hearings on proposed plans. The advent of open-source software, widely and cheaply available, has greatly enhanced the ability of the public to participate in redistricting proceedings by allowing individuals to draw and offer for consideration their own maps, created with the same degree of precision, and relying on the same data, as those drawn by redistricting professionals. *See* Micah Altman and Michael P. McDonald, *Public Participation GIS: The Case of Redistricting, in* Proceedings of the 47th Annual Hawaii International Conference on System Sciences (IEEE/Computer Society Press 2014).

The authority to make decisions must be lodged somewhere. What are the institutional arrangements that will most reliably lead final decision makers to behave in the ways we wish them to behave? In the case of redistricting, does publicity furnish better incentives against gerrymandering than regulating the identity of those who draw the lines? How would we know? *See generally* Justin Levitt, *Weighing the Potential of Citizen Redistricting*, 43 Loy. L.A. L. Rev. 513 (2011).

≫ *Discerning the Popular Will: The Aggregation Problem.* In most contemporary theories of democracy, the legitimacy of democratic rule depends upon its consistency with the popular will. It is necessary to democratic legitimacy for the government that rules to be the one in fact preferred by the people; rule by any other government is by hypothesis a kind of usurpation, and thus illegitimate. Elections, in short, must express the will of the people.

This principle is elementary, yet the preceding materials undermine it severely. The choice of electoral system or district lines, it seems, can affect the way in which the popular will is expressed. Even in a presumptively fair system of universal suffrage, majority rule, and equally weighted voting, choosing one electoral method or set of district lines will result in the election of one legislature, and choosing another method or set of lines may produce a quite different legislature. The preferences of individual voters have not changed; all that has changed is the method of counting and adding up their votes.

Consider the following analysis:

We can only say that "the people" has a will if it is organized by some sort of voting procedure, which operates to decide only questions of certain understood types. But then, whether "the people" (or the electorate) wills to be governed by the Labour or the Conservative Party may well depend on what methods are used for voting and counting votes and on how the constituencies are drawn. The will of the people cannot be determined independently of the particular procedure employed, for it is not a natural will, nor is it a sum of similar wills of persons sharing common interests, but the result of going through a procedure which weighs some wills against others. . . .

    To say . . . that the majority has its way in any given election or referendum, means only that a given number express a preference for one course, a smaller number for another, and that by the rules of the game the former course must be adopted. Majority and minority are not necessarily competing interests, but aggregates of individuals in a certain arithmetical relation. The relation is significant as a way of arriving at decisions only because of the rule that makes it so. To say, then, that the will of the majority of citizens rules is only another way of describing election or referendum procedure. It is not something else which this procedure brings about. . . . Until the count is made, there may be no way of telling which interest *is* the majority, and which, therefore, will "rule."

S.I. BENN AND R.S. PETERS, PRINCIPLES OF POLITICAL THOUGHT 397-399 (1959). Do you agree?

CHAPTER 5

RACIAL DISCRIMINATION AND THE RIGHT TO VOTE

A. INTRODUCTION

The United States aspires to be a multiracial and multicultural democracy in which its people are entitled to vote free from racial discrimination. If successful, this would be its greatest accomplishment since the founding. At the time of the founding, the new American republic was thought to be the greatest experiment in self-government known to humankind. The founding generation set in motion a liberal democratic order in which the people were sovereign and self-governing. Yet, notwithstanding its expressed commitments to both liberalism and democratic self-government, these commitments were severely undermined by the new republic's bargain with white supremacy.

For most of this country's history, "We the people of the United States," the opening phrase of the Constitution of the United States, really meant "We the white people of the United States." The constitutional order at the dawn of the American republic did not include people of color, particularly black and native peoples, among those who would or could participate in the exercise of self-government. Scholars of race have long understood that the promises of liberalism and democracy have been severely tested by the realities of racial subordination and white supremacy.

Those inconvenient realities have existed alongside our loftier commitments since the very beginning of the American republic because racial equality was not among the new republic's founding principles. Among the many examples that could be marshalled, the Constitution protected chattel slavery by forbidding Congress from regulating the international slave trade for twenty years after the ratification of the Constitution. The Constitution also allocated political power based upon a formula, the three-fifths compromise, which granted greater power to the Southern states by authorizing them to count enslaved people of the South as three-fifths of a person for purposes of enumeration and representation, notwithstanding the fact that enslaved persons were not allowed to vote. The Constitution protected the discriminatory grant of suffrage rights even with respect to free people of color by delegating voting qualifications and election administration to the states, which, not surprisingly, limited suffrage rights to white men, and in many cases to white men who owned some measure of property. And even when property restrictions were repealed, most states continued to deny the right to vote to free men of color. Of course, few states contemplated extending the right of suffrage to women and none to black women.

As a formal constitutional and legal matter, the Reconstruction Amendments addressed the fundamental deficiencies of the Constitution of 1789 and ostensibly abandoned white supremacy. The Thirteenth Amendment abolished chattel slavery. The Fourteenth made citizenship in the republic contingent upon birth and voluntary association rather than race. The Fifteenth Amendment, ratified in 1870, explicitly prohibited denial of the right to vote on account of race, color, or previous condition of servitude, and therefore, at least for black men, established a right to vote free from racial discrimination. Taken together, the Reconstruction Amendments — the Thirteenth, Fourteenth, and Fifteenth Amendments — were thought finally and formally to extend the promises of a liberal democratic republic to all. Equal citizenship and equality of political participation were shorn of their racial restrictions.

Of course, the mere say-so of the Constitution has never been enough to change the behavior of everyone. In anticipation of the need for legislation to enforce the Fifteenth Amendment, Congress in 1870 and 1871 enacted legislation under Section 2 of the Fifteenth Amendment. Congress passed three statutes, one in 1870 and two in 1871, collectively known as the Enforcement Acts. One can think of the Enforcement Acts as early precursors to the Voting Rights Act of 1965 (VRA), though the Enforcement Acts were much more extensive in terms of their ambition and scope than the VRA. Section 1 of the 1870 Act guaranteed the right to vote "at any election" "without distinction of race, color, or previous condition of servitude." Section 2 required state officials "charged with the performance of duties in furnishing to citizens an opportunity to vote," "to give to all citizens of the United States the same and equal opportunity . . . to become qualified to vote without distinction of race, color, or previous condition of servitude." If the state officials failed to provide an equal opportunity for voters to become qualified without regard to race, they were to "forfeit and pay the sum of five hundred dollars to the person aggrieved" for every offense. The victim was also entitled to attorney's fees. Section 8 provided for exclusive jurisdiction in the federal courts. Other sections of the statute provided for criminal penalties for violations of the statute, including violations for threatening or intimidating those trying to exercise their right to vote. The statutes' usefulness was impaired by unfavorable court rulings, and most of their provisions were repealed in 1894, when Republicans lost control of Congress.

For the next 80 years, white supremacy reigned. Little progress was made in securing the rights promised by the Fifteenth Amendment. As we have seen, it was not unusual up until the middle of the last century, especially in the South, for state and local governments simply to ignore the Fifteenth Amendment and continue officially and openly to deny black people the right to vote. In earlier chapters, we have encountered numerous methods by which black voting and registration was suppressed and, where black voters managed both to register and vote, black voting power was diluted: literacy tests, poll taxes, grandfather clauses, white primaries, racial gerrymandering, at-large voting systems, felon disfranchisement laws, and even outright violence. Judicial invalidation of some of these practices, such as the white primary, made some inroads into the toolkit of segregationists, but black registration and voting continued to lag badly.

Congress finally turned its attention to this problem in 1957 when it enacted the first voting rights enforcement measure since Reconstruction. The Civil Rights Act of 1957 made interference with voting rights a federal offense and authorized the United States Attorney General to prosecute violations. However, the Act was aimed primarily at vindicating the civil rights of individuals, and the extensive amount of work required to prove a violation in even a single case made the Act a clumsy tool to achieve real reform. Congress made some minor adjustments in the Civil Rights Act of 1960 by authorizing the appointment of federal referees to oversee elections where a pattern and practice of voting discrimination was proved, but courts frequently declined to appoint referees. The inefficacy of these measures can be gauged by their results: between 1957 and 1963, the U.S. Department of Justice brought more than 40 suits under these statutes, yet this effort resulted in the registration of only 6,000 or so new black voters.

Although black registration nationwide rose from about 3 percent in 1940 to about 43 percent in 1964, in Alabama, Georgia, Mississippi, North Carolina, and South Carolina only about 20 percent of black residents were registered, and in Mississippi the number was less than 7 percent. In Louisiana, 32 percent of black residents were registered in 1964, compared to more than 80 percent of whites. In some local jurisdictions, the figures were truly shocking. In Terrell County, Georgia, a jurisdiction where in 1958 black citizens made up 64 percent of the population, only 48 black people in the entire county were registered to vote, compared to 2,810 whites. Moreover, due to strengthened Southern resistance to nationally led efforts to desegregate schools and other civil rights enforcement measures, the number of registered black voters actually declined between 1964 and 1965 in Alabama, Arkansas, Florida, Georgia, South Carolina, and Virginia following measures such as purges of voter registration rolls.

It was not until 1965 that Congress acted again. Responding to pressure from constituents, from President Lyndon B. Johnson, and perhaps most significantly from galvanizing national and worldwide photographic and television coverage of civil rights protests in Selma and Birmingham, Alabama, Congress passed the Voting Rights Act. In an address to Congress on March 15, 1965, President Johnson asked Congress to pass the VRA:

> Mr. Speaker, Mr. President, members of the Congress. I speak tonight for the dignity of man and the destiny of democracy. . . . At times, history and fate meet at a single time in a single place, to shape a turning point in man's unending search for freedom. So it was at Lexington and Concord. So it was a century ago at Appomattox. So it was last week in Selma, Alabama. There, long-suffering men and women peacefully protested the denial of their rights as Americans. Many were brutally assaulted. One good man, a man of God, was killed. There is no cause for pride in what has happened in Selma. There is no cause for self-satisfaction in the long denial of equal rights of millions of Americans. But there is cause for hope and for faith in our democracy in what is happening here tonight. . . . Our

mission is at once the oldest and the most basic of this country: to right
wrong, to do justice, to serve man. . . .

There is no Negro problem. There is no Southern problem. There
is no Northern problem. There is only an American problem. And we are
met here tonight as Americans, not as Democrats or Republicans, we are
met here as Americans to solve that problem. . . . [T]o deny a man his
hopes because of his color or race, his religion or the place of his birth,
is not only to do injustice, it is to deny America and to dishonor the dead
who gave their lives for American freedom.

Many of the issues of civil rights are very complex and most difficult.
But about this there can and should be no argument. Every American
citizen must have an equal right to vote. . . . Yet the harsh fact is that in
many places in this country men and women are kept from voting simply
because they are Negroes. Every device of which human ingenuity is capable has been used to deny this right. The Negro citizen may go to register
only to be told that the day is wrong, or the hour is late, or the official in
charge is absent. And if he persists, and if he manages to present himself
to the registrar, he may be disqualified because he did not spell out his
middle name or because he abbreviated a word on the application.

And if he manages to fill out an application, he is given a test. The
registrar is the sole judge of whether he passes this test. He may be asked
to recite the entire Constitution, or explain the most complex provisions
of State law. And even a college degree cannot be used to prove that he
can read and write. For the fact is that the only way to pass these barriers
is to show a white skin. . . .

As a man whose roots go deeply into Southern soil, I know how
agonizing racial feelings are. I know how difficult it is to reshape the attitudes and the structure of our society. But a century has passed, more
than a hundred years, since the Negro was freed. And he is not fully free
tonight. . . . The time of justice has now come. And I tell you that I believe
sincerely that no force can hold it back. It is right, in the eyes of man and
God, that it should come. And when it does, I think that day will brighten
the lives of every American.

For additional reading, see, among many possible works, U.S. COMMISSION ON
CIVIL RIGHTS, VOTING: 1961 COMMISSION ON CIVIL RIGHTS REPORT (1961); U.S.
House of Representatives, *Voting Rights Act of 1965*, H.R. REP. No. 439, 89th Cong.,
1st Sess. (1965); J. MORGAN KOUSSER, THE SHAPING OF SOUTHERN POLITICS: SUF-
FRAGE RESTRICTION AND THE ESTABLISHMENT OF THE ONE-PARTY SOUTH (1974);
STEVEN F. LAWSON, BLACK BALLOTS: VOTING RIGHTS IN THE SOUTH, 1944-1969
(1976); DAVID J. GARROW, PROTEST AT SELMA: MARTIN LUTHER KING, JR., AND
THE VOTING RIGHTS ACT OF 1965 (1978); QUIET REVOLUTION IN THE SOUTH: THE
IMPACT OF THE VOTING RIGHTS ACT, 1965-1990 (Chandler Davidson and Bernard
Grofman eds., 1994); TAYLOR BRANCH, AT CANAAN'S EDGE: AMERICA IN THE KING
YEARS, 1965-68 (2006); GARY MAY, BENDING TOWARD JUSTICE: THE VOTING RIGHTS
ACT AND THE TRANSFORMATION OF AMERICAN DEMOCRACY (2013). For a helpful
annotated bibliography of works on the Voting Rights Act, see Terrye Conroy, *The
Voting Rights Act of 1965: A Selected Annotated Bibliography*, 98 LAW LIBR. J. 663 (2006).

In 2008, the country elected its first black president, Barack Hussein Obama, in what was truly a watershed moment, one noted, and in many cases celebrated, the world over. Obama was reelected in 2012. Obama was viewed by many as the cosmopolitan embodiment of liberal democracy, and his election as the fulfillment of the aims of the civil rights movement, all made possible by the Voting Rights Act. It may have seemed then that the country turned the page on white supremacy, never to return to those dark chapters. Liberal democracy seemed triumphant, and white supremacy put to the sword by the VRA.

But in 2016, Americans elected Donald J. Trump, who came to national political prominence by questioning whether Obama was born in America. His campaign, captured by the slogan "Make American Great Again," explicitly deployed xenophobic and racist tropes. Trump's appeal to white supremacy and reliance on white supremacists for his support was not furtive or subtle; it was there for all to see. *See, e.g.,* Evan Osnos, *The Fearful and the Frustrated: Donald Trump's Nationalist Coalition Takes Shape — For Now,* THE NEW YORKER (August 24, 2015). As Law Professor Joshua Sellers has argued, Trump's campaign and election relied upon "white identity politics," which Sellers defines as "the creation of beliefs and alliances intended to advance the collective political interest of white voters." Professor Sellers concludes that "white identity politics is more than just an aberrational feature of partisan politics; it is a recurrent durable driver of political outcomes." Joshua S. Sellers, *Election Law and White Identity Politics,* 87 FORDHAM L. REV. 1515, 1519, 1532 (2019). *See also,* ASHLEY JARDINA, WHITE IDENTITY POLITICS (2019); JOHN SIDES, LYNN VAVRECK, & MICHAEL TESLER, IDENTITY CRISIS (2018); MARISA HABRAJANO & ZOLTAN HAJNAL, WHITE BACKLASH: IMMIGRATION, RACE & AMERICAN POLITICS (2015).

A fundamental question for Americans in the twenty-first century is whether American democracy has final resolved its struggle between liberal democracy and white supremacy in favor of liberal democracy, or whether that struggle continues. For a course on election law within the context of the American political system, our inquiry is about the role that election law has played and continues to play in mediating that struggle. The Voting Rights Act has served as the quintessential representation of our nation's commitment to racial equality and against white supremacy in the domain of electoral politics. The materials for this chapter examine both the rise and fall of the VRA. The materials also explicitly ask whether the fall of the VRA represents the end of the nation's commitment to combatting white supremacy, the triumph of liberal democracy, or something between the two.

B. *THE SOUTH AS AN "AUTHORITARIAN ENCLAVE"?*

There is a tendency to see a statute titled, "The Voting Rights Act," and think that it will provide a set of positive rights that an individual can wield against his or her government. For the most part, that is not the 1965 Act. As a general matter, the Voting Rights Act of 1965 was a codification of the Fifteenth Amendment's prohibition against racial discrimination, which meant that it followed the Constitution's negative rights approach to voting and political participation. That is, it neither granted any rights nor required governments to take any particular actions; it simply, though importantly, prohibited the states from discriminating based on race.

Additionally, and more pertinently, Congress, through the VRA, largely conceived racial discrimination in voting as a very specific regional problem. Both the VRA and the country viewed racial discrimination in voting as a particularly Southern malady. It is not that the drafters of the Act believed that racism or racial discrimination did not exist in the rest of the country; they, particularly civil rights activists, were not so deluded. It is more the case that the drafters of the VRA thought the South was peculiar with respect to both the extent of its racial caste system and its political oligarchy. Of course, the South objected to being painted as particularly loathsome. Congress and President Johnson attempted to be responsive to the South's sensitivities while also attempting to address an issue that they viewed as primarily a Southern problem. The agility required to walk that tightrope can be seen in Johnson's speech excerpted above. Johnson referenced his Southern roots, while disclaiming that racial discrimination is a "Southern problem." He claimed instead that it is an American problem, while at the same time alluding to his belief that racial discrimination is "deeply rooted" in "the structure of our society." Opponents of the VRA objected to the Act, in part, on the ground that the South was not any more undemocratic than the rest of the country.

Scholars of comparative democracy have broadly disagreed with the self-serving assessments of the Southern opponents of the VRA. Their writings have confirmed the undemocratic nature of the American South during the antebellum and Jim Crow eras. The analysis begins with the observation that the transition from authoritarianism to democracy often does not occur at a uniform pace, and that it is common for democratizing states to contain lingering enclaves of authoritarian rule long after much or most of the country has become democratic. On this account, the South was "a regional bloc of authoritarian states that was firmly integrated into the structure of national political life. The political regimes of these states were unambiguously undemocratic by any definition of the concept. Political competition was severely restricted, and so was voting." EDWARD L. GIBSON, BOUNDARY CONTROL: SUBNATIONAL AUTHORITARIANISM IN FEDERAL DEMOCRACIES 35 (2012). The Civil War constituted a massive national intervention to promote local democratization. It was followed by a second phase in which Southern politicians for nearly a century successfully sealed off their enclave from further national interference not by imposing isolation, but by participating with great effectiveness in the national political system. This tactic allowed Southern leaders to maintain local authoritarian rule without fear of national intervention. In short, Southern rulers created "institutions to demobilize white electorates, extrude blacks from electoral politics, and forestall workers' challenges to state institutions and policies. Enclave rulers carefully protected their polity's conditional autonomy and skillfully deployed federal officeholders to block potential interference, especially concerning voting rights and state-sponsored violence." ROBERT MICKEY, PATHS OUT OF DIXIE: THE DEMOCRATIZATION OF AUTHORITARIAN ENCLAVES IN AMERICA'S DEEP SOUTH, 1944-1972 (2015), at 34. On this view, democracy was not consolidated in the United States until late in the twentieth century.

C. *THE VRA AND THE POWER OF CONGRESS*

The VRA brought democracy and equality of representation to the South. It attacked the South's racial inequality and flattened its political hierarchy. For more than thirty years after Congress passed the statute, starting with the landmark case of *South Carolina v. Katzenbach*, the Court broadly interpreted the Act and routinely reaffirmed the power of Congress to enact its various provisions. Moreover, Congress has periodically amended the statute, often building upon the Court's prior broad interpretations of previous provisions, and, less frequently, overruling the Court's prior interpretations of particular provisions that Congress thought were erroneous. The statute that we call "the VRA" is the result of a partnership between Congress and the Court aligned together because both institutions believed that racial discrimination in voting is the fundamental problem that ailed American democracy. The Court filled the gaps in the statute and interpreted the Act to address developments that Congress did not or could not anticipate.

But as we will see in the latter part of this chapter, over the past fifteen years or so, the Court has played a very different role. It has increasingly interpreted the statute narrowly and limited the scope of the Act. Necessarily, it has as well constrained the power of Congress to address the problem of racial discrimination in voting as Congress understands the problem. The main reason for this change is because the Court no longer believes that the type of racial discrimination that characterized the pre-VRA political practices in the South continues to be a problem. As a doctrinal matter, the Court is increasingly imposing a "colorblind" jurisprudence upon a race-conscious statute.

The current question for VRA law and policy is whether, and if so to what extent, racial discrimination continues to shape American electoral practices. Are we seeing a return to the type of racial discrimination and voter suppression that we saw pre-1965 as voting rights activists claim? What explains the retreat that we see on voting rights? Is it white supremacy? Partisanship? Ideology? Is the United States, even now, a fully democratic nation? Has the nation become the South? Is there a different model for thinking about voting equality beyond the race-based model of the VRA?

In order to set a framework for thinking about these questions, we first look at the provisions of the Act in greater detail. The Voting Rights Act of 1965 is one of the strongest civil rights measures ever enacted. It has also been the fundamental regulatory framework that Congress has used to combat racial discrimination in voting. Since the inception of the Act, its provisions have been regarded as unusual and inventive. The structure of the Act is more like an engineering manual than a code of rights. One fundamental question raised by the Act is whether Congress has the power to enact the Act's regulatory provisions. We thus begin with a detailed examination of the statute and the power of Congress to enact the Act.

The VRA's most important provisions are Sections 2, 4, and 5. Section 2 prohibits a state and its political subdivisions from imposing any voting qualification or using any voting procedure that discriminatorily abridges the right to vote. We discuss Section 2 in more detail below. Prior to 1982, before Congress amended Section 2 to expand the scope of its coverage and prior to the Supreme Court's 2013 decision in *Shelby County v. Holder*, Sections 4 and 5 of the Act were the cornerstones of a complex statutory scheme that provided for the identification of states with a history of racial discrimination in voting, and federal oversight of the voting systems of those states. As originally enacted, Section 4(b) of the Act, 42 U.S.C. §1973b(b), provided:

> The provisions of subsection (a) of this section shall apply in any State or in any political subdivision of a State which
>
> > (1) the Attorney General determines maintained on November 1, 1964, any test or device, and with respect to which
> >
> > (2) the Director of the Census determines that less than 50 per centum of the persons of voting age residing therein were registered on November 1, 1964, or that less than 50 per centum of such persons voted in the presidential election of November 1964.
>
> A determination or certification of the Attorney General or of the Director of the Census under this section or under section 1973f or 1973k of this title shall not be reviewable in any court and shall be effective upon publication in the Federal Register.

Section 4(b) required that the Attorney General identify those states that (1) maintained any voting "test or device" as of November 1, 1964, and (2) had a voter registration rate of less than 50 percent, or in which less than 50 percent of eligible voters voted in the 1964 presidential election. This is generally referred to as the "coverage formula." Section 4(c) defines "test or device" to include legal requirements that the voter demonstrate (a) literacy, (b) educational achievement or knowledge of any particular subject, (c) good moral character, or (d) qualification to vote by the vouching of other voters. The purpose of this section was to identify the states that were discriminating most against black voters without calling them out by name.

Sections 4 and 5 were intended as temporary measures. They were originally enacted for five years. Congress renewed both provisions in 1970 for another five years and extended the coverage formula to jurisdictions that maintained a test or device in 1968 and in which less than 50 percent of eligible voters voted in the election of 1968. In 1975 Congress renewed both Sections 4 and 5 for seven years and modified the coverage formula to include jurisdictions that used a test or device and in which less than 50 percent of eligible voters voted. Congress renewed both provisions in 1982, this time for 25 years, though it did not modify the coverage formula.

The Attorney General determined that the following states meet the Section 4(b) test: Alabama, Alaska, Arizona, Georgia, Louisiana, Mississippi, South Carolina, Texas, and Virginia (except for a handful of counties and cities, which have been released from VRA oversight). In addition, the Attorney General determined that certain individual counties and towns in California, Florida, Michigan, New Hampshire (no longer covered), New York,[1] North Carolina, and South Dakota

---

1. The covered counties in New York State were Bronx County, Kings County (Brooklyn), and New York County (Manhattan).

meet the standards of Section 4(b). *See* 28 C.F.R. §51.4 app. These jurisdictions are generally known as "covered jurisdictions."

In addition to establishing the conditions under which jurisdictions become covered by the VRA, Section 4 also establishes the conditions under which covered jurisdictions can become free from the provisions of the VRA. This is commonly referred to as "bailout." Section 4(a) of the VRA provides that the U.S. District Court for the District of Columbia can lift the obligation of a jurisdiction to comply with the VRA's preclearance requirements by issuing a declaratory judgment if the jurisdiction can show that, for a period of ten years:

> **(A)** no such test or device has been used within such State or political subdivision for the purpose or with the effect of denying or abridging the right to vote on account of race or color . . . ;
>
> **(B)** no final judgment of any court of the United States . . . has determined that denials or abridgements of the right to vote on account of race or color have occurred anywhere in the territory of such State or political subdivision . . . ;
>
> **(D)** such State or political subdivision and all governmental units within its territory have complied with section 1973c [Section 5] of this title . . . ;
>
> **(E)** the Attorney General has not interposed any objection . . . ; and
>
> **(F)** such State or political subdivision and all governmental units within its territory—
>
> **(i)** have eliminated voting procedures and methods of election which inhibit or dilute equal access to the electoral process;
>
> **(ii)** have engaged in constructive efforts to eliminate intimidation and harassment of persons exercising rights protected under subchapters I-A to I-C of this chapter; and
>
> **(iii)** have engaged in other constructive efforts, such as expanded opportunity for convenient registration and voting for every person of voting age and the appointment of minority persons as election officials throughout the jurisdiction and at all stages of the election and registration process.

Between 1982 and 2013, when the Court struck down the coverage formula, more than 200 separate jurisdictions bailed out, although the number of successful bailout proceedings is fewer than 50 because many proceedings have included multiple jurisdictions. Successfully bailed out jurisdictions include, in addition to many cities and counties in Virginia, counties, cities, and special districts in Alabama, California, Connecticut, Colorado, Georgia, Hawaii, Idaho, North Carolina, and Texas. For a complete listing, see the Section 4 web page of the Civil Rights Division, at http://www.justice.gov/crt/about/vot/misc/sec_4.php.

The Act subjected covered jurisdictions to two principal restrictions. First, under Section 4(a), 42 U.S.C. §1973b(a), no citizen of any covered state or of its political subdivisions "shall be denied the right to vote in any Federal, State, or local election because of his failure to comply with any test or device. . . ." In other words, the Act automatically invalidates the four kinds of voting tests listed in Section 4(c).

Much more far-reaching, however, is Section 5, 42 U.S.C. §1973c. This section, as most recently amended, provides:

> Whenever a [covered jurisdiction] . . . shall enact or seek to administer any voting qualification or prerequisite to voting, or standard, practice, or procedure with respect to voting different from that in force or effect on November 1, 1964 . . . such State or subdivision may institute an action in the United States District Court for the District of Columbia for a declaratory judgment that such qualification, prerequisite, standard, practice, or procedure neither has the purpose nor will have the effect of denying or abridging the right to vote on account of race or color . . . : Provided, That such qualification, prerequisite, standard, practice, or procedure may be enforced without such proceeding if the qualification, prerequisite, standard, practice, or procedure has been submitted . . . to the Attorney General and the Attorney General has not interposed an objection within sixty days. . . .

Section 5 thus prohibits any covered jurisdiction from changing any voting qualifications, standards, or procedures that were in place on November 1, 1964 without first obtaining advance approval, either from a federal court or from the U.S. Attorney General. Under Section 5, such approval is to be granted only if the proposed change has neither the purpose nor the effect of abridging the right to vote on account of race.

The requirement of obtaining advance administrative or judicial approval under Section 5 is known as "preclearance." Although covered jurisdictions may go directly to court to obtain judicial preclearance of proposed changes to voting procedures, typically they attempt first to obtain administrative approval from the Justice Department. This function is administered by the Civil Rights Division. Administrative preclearance is thought to be more expeditious and less expensive than judicial preclearance. Section 5 is structured so that if the Department objects to a proposed change, the covered jurisdiction may still go to court to obtain judicial approval.

>> *The Scope and Standard of Section 5.*   Two issues have tended to arise in Section 5 preclearance proceedings and litigation. The first issue is whether the proposed change is a change to a "standard, practice, or procedure with respect to voting" within the meaning of the Act. In other words, does Section 5 cover the proposed change in the law? States understandably do not wish to submit their laws to the Attorney General of the United States for advance approval, and thus frequently argue that this language should be narrowly construed. The second issue is whether a proposed change in the law covered by Section 5 has "the purpose [or] the effect of denying or abridging the right to vote on account of race or color." Each of these questions is examined further below.

Section 5 clearly is considerably broader than Section 4(a) because it covers *any* proposed change in a state's laws "with respect to voting," and not merely the particular "tests" and "devices" specified by Section 4(c). But what exactly is a "standard, practice, or procedure with respect to voting" such that the restrictions of the VRA apply to a covered jurisdiction?

In *Allen v. State Board of Elections*, 393 U.S. 544 (1969), the Court held that this language of Section 5 should be read broadly. The case involved four different changes to voting laws in Mississippi and Virginia. The changes were a change from district to at-large voting; a change from election to appointment of certain officials; a change in the requirements for independent candidates to get on the ballot; and a change in the way that ballots could be marked. The Court held: "We must reject a narrow construction [of] §5. The Voting Rights Act was aimed at the subtle, as well as the obvious, state regulations which have the effect of denying citizens their right to vote because of their race." The Court therefore held that the legal changes at issue were subject to the preclearance requirements of Section 5.

The Court further elucidated the contours of Section 5 coverage in *Presley v. Etowah County Commission*, 502 U.S. 491 (1992). *Presley* addressed changes to the decision-making authority of two different county commissions in Alabama. County commissions are elected bodies in Alabama and their primary responsibility is "to supervise and control the maintenance, repair, and construction of the county roads." *Presley v. Etowah County* is a consolidation of two cases. In the first case, as the result of a consent decree, the Etowah County Commission expanded from a five-member commission to a six-member commission. Prior to the consent decree, four members of the commission were elected from the districts in which they resided and one member was elected at large. After the consent decree, each member was elected from a residential district. In addition to four holdover commissioners who had been on the commission prior to the enactment of the consent decree, the commission added two new members, including the county's first black commissioner, elected from a majority-black district. After the addition of the two new members, the commission adopted a resolution, with the two new commissioners dissenting, which deprived the two new members of any authority to supervise and control the maintenance of the roads in their district. The resolution transferred that power to the four holdover commissioners and assigned the two new commissioners minor responsibilities. In the second case, involving Russell County, a consent decree resulted in districted elections; provided individual county commissioners with responsibility for their districts; and produced the county's first black commissioner. Following the consent decree, the state of Alabama abolished individual road districts and transferred responsibility for road operations to the county engineer.

The question presented by *Presley* was whether these changes ought to be precleared pursuant to Section 5. Though the Court noted that Section 5 ought to be interpreted broadly, it stated that "changes subject to section 5 pertain only to voting." These include "changes that involve the manner of voting"; changes that involve "candidacy requirements and qualifications"; "changes in the composition of the electorate that may vote for candidates for a given office"; and "changes that affect the creation or abolition of an elective office." The Court concluded that neither change at issue in the case was a change pertaining to voting. With respect to Etowah County, the Court noted that the change "has no connection to voting procedures: It does not affect the manner of holding elections. . . . Rather [it] concerns the internal operations of an elected body." With respect to Russell County, the Court concluded that the "making or unmaking of an appointive post will result in the erosion or accretion of the powers of some official responsible to the electorate, but it does not follow that those changes are covered by section 5."

The Court did identify in *Presley* numerous covered actions, including changes from districted to at-large elections and from elective to appointive offices; changes in municipal boundary lines through annexation or other means; and changes to rules concerning ballot access, the marking of ballots, campaigning, filing deadlines, and the size of elected bodies.

In addition, lower courts have construed Section 5 to reach changes concerning absentee ballots; candidate qualifications; voter registration; term limits; and the date, time, and location of voting. Note, however, that ordinary misconduct under or maladministration of existing laws is not considered to be a covered change in practices and procedures.

Under the VRA, if a proposed change in the law is subject to the Section 5 preclearance requirement, preclearance will be forthcoming if the proposed change is one that "does not have the purpose and will not have the effect of denying or abridging the right to vote on account of race or color." (In 2006, Congress altered this language slightly; it now reads: "neither has the purpose nor will have the effect." The significance of this change is discussed below.) Application of this standard requires courts to identify some standard against which to judge whether the proposed change *abridges* the right to vote. What is the appropriate standard of measurement under Section 5? The Court addressed that question in *Beer v. United States*, 425 U.S. 130 (1976).

Beer involved the drawing of city council districts for the City of New Orleans. At the time, 55 percent of the city's population and 65 percent of the city's registered voters were white, and 45 percent of the total population and 35 percent of registered voters were black. The city council consisted of seven members, five of whom were elected from districts and two of whom were elected at large. The city submitted a plan that created two districts in which African Americans were the majority of the population and one district in which they were the majority of registered voters. The Attorney General objected to the city's redistricting plan on the ground that the manner in which the city drew districts prevented it from drawing an additional majority-black district. The city sought a declaratory judgment from the United States District Court in the District of Columbia. That court agreed with the Attorney General.

The United States Supreme Court disagreed. The Court articulated a "non-retrogression standard," by which a covered jurisdiction is entitled to implement a proposed change in its election laws if the change will not make a racial group worse off than it was under the laws in place before the change—that is, under laws enacted before passage of the Voting Rights Act itself. Applying the nonretrogression standard to the facts of the case, the Court concluded that the redistricting plan did not make black voters worse off compared to the previous redistricting plan, and in fact they were better off compared to the previous redistricting plan because that plan provided only one majority-black district. Consequently, there was no retrogression.

>> *Intentional Discrimination and Nonretrogression.* What happens under Section 5 if a covered jurisdiction's proposed change is *intended* to discriminate against black people, yet is nonretrogressive—in other words, that it is purposely

calculated to suppress black voting strength, yet does not do so as egregiously (or does so no more egregiously) than did the voting procedures previously in place? Or, to put this another way, what if the jurisdiction's purpose is merely to continue and extend the same discrimination that produced existing discriminatory laws? In *Reno v. Bossier Parish*, 528 U.S. 320 (2000), the Court held that an intention to discriminate does not by itself establish a violation of Section 5 (even though it may serve to establish a violation of Section 2 or of the Fifteenth Amendment) unless that intention also includes an intent to retrogress, i.e., to make things worse than they were under the previous regime. The Court addressed what seemed to be an incongruity. Under the Court's interpretation of the statute, federal officials would have to preclear a voting change that has a discriminatory purpose or effect. The Court stated:

> [A]ppellants [also] object that our reading of §5 would require the District Court or Attorney General to preclear proposed voting changes with a discriminatory effect or purpose, or even with both. That strikes appellants as an inconceivable prospect only because they refuse to accept the limited meaning that we have said preclearance has in the vote-dilution context. It does not represent approval of the voting change; it is nothing more than a determination that the voting change is no more dilutive than what it replaces, and therefore cannot be stopped in advance under the extraordinary burden-shifting procedures of §5, but must be attacked through the normal means of a §2 action. As we have repeatedly noted, in vote-dilution cases §5 prevents nothing but backsliding, and preclearance under §5 affirms nothing but the absence of backsliding. This explains why the sole consequence of failing to obtain preclearance is continuation of the status quo. To deny preclearance to a plan that is not retrogressive — *no matter how unconstitutional it may be* — would risk leaving in effect a status quo that is even worse. For example, in the case of a voting change with a discriminatory but nonretrogressive purpose and a discriminatory but ameliorative effect, the result of denying preclearance would be to preserve a status quo with more discriminatory effect than the proposed change.

In an opinion joined by Justices Stevens, Ginsburg, and Breyer, Justice Souter concluded bluntly that *Beer* was wrongly decided. The Court in *Beer* misread the legislative history, he argued, which is "replete with references to the need to block changes in voting practices that would perpetuate existing discrimination and stand in the way of truly nondiscriminatory alternatives." Congress was well aware, he wrote, that " '[b]arring one contrivance too often has caused no change in result, only in methods.' H.R. Rep. No. 439, 89th Cong., 1st Sess. 10 (1965)," and it intended to deal with "the frustration of running to stay in place." Thus, said Justice Souter, the legislative history shows that the VRA "contains no reservation in favor of customary abridgment grown familiar after years of relentless discrimination, and the preclearance requirement was not enacted to authorize covered jurisdictions to pour old poison into new bottles."

>> *Judging Retrogression by the Baseline Plan.* To decide whether retrogression has occurred in violation of Section 5, it is necessary to identify a point of reference

against which retrogression can be measured. In most areas of election law, this presents no difficulty, as there is no question as to what the law was before some proposed change. In some cases, however, the basis of comparison can be more difficult to discern, usually because the law changes rapidly. This is probably most true of redistricting, where several plans can follow rapidly one upon the next, and where judicial intervention may invalidate redistricting plans at some point after they have already taken effect. For purposes of identifying retrogression in redistricting plans, the U.S. Department of Justice applies the following regulation:

> In determining whether a submitted change is retrogressive the Attorney General will normally compare the submitted change to the voting practice or procedure in effect at the time of the submission. If the existing practice or procedure upon submission . . . is not otherwise legally enforceable under section 5, it cannot serve as a benchmark, and . . . the comparison shall be with the last legally enforceable practice or procedure used by the jurisdiction.

28 C.F.R. §51.54(b)(1). Under this definition, then, DOJ will look to the most recent *validly enacted* plan, whether or not it is still in effect. Another way to say this is as follows. Section 5 makes the law as it stood in 1964, at the time the VRA first was enacted, the presumptive baseline for purposes of comparison in a preclearance proceeding. Thus, the baseline for comparison is either the plan in effect in 1964 or the last lawfully enacted plan, which usually means the one most recently precleared by DOJ. The Supreme Court approved this definition in *Abrams v. Johnson*, 521 U.S. 74 (1997).

>>   *The Three-Judge Court.*   One odd feature of the Voting Rights Act is that it requires judicial proceedings under Section 5 to be heard by a three-judge U.S. district court. 42 U.S.C. §1973b(a)(5). A three-judge court consists of one judge of the Court of Appeals for the relevant circuit and two district court judges from the relevant district. Appeal from the judgment of a three-judge district court is directly to the U.S. Supreme Court. Three-judge courts are also convened to hear reapportionment challenges. 28 U.S.C. §2284. The reason for using such courts appears to lie in the perceived significance of reapportionment and voting rights challenges for state-federal relations. There was some sentiment in Congress that a state's political practices should not be susceptible to invalidation at the hands of a single federal district court judge. *See* Michael E. Solimine, *The Three-Judge District Court in Voting Rights Litigation*, 30 U. MICH. J.L. REFORM 79 (1996).

>>   *Bail-in.*   Sections 4(a) and 5 identify the covered jurisdictions and require them to preclear. To escape coverage a covered jurisdiction must bail out. The Act also provides for a bail-in or an opt-in mechanism. Section 3(c) of the VRA provides:

> If in any proceeding instituted by the Attorney General or an aggrieved person under any statute to enforce the voting guarantees of the fourteenth or fifteenth amendment in any State or political subdivision the court finds that violations of the fourteenth or fifteenth amendment justifying equitable relief have occurred within the territory of such State or

political subdivision, the court, in addition to such relief as it may grant, shall retain jurisdiction for such period as it may deem appropriate and during such period no voting qualification or prerequisite to voting or standard, practice, or procedure with respect to voting different from that in force or effect at the time the proceeding was commenced shall be enforced unless and until the court finds that such qualification, prerequisite, standard, practice, or procedure does not have the purpose and will not have the effect of denying or abridging the right to vote on account of race or color, or in contravention of the voting guarantees [that protect individuals who are members of language minority groups.]

52 U.S.C. §10302. This provision is known as the "pocket trigger" or "bail-in." Section 3(c) enables a court to bail in a jurisdiction where the court finds that the jurisdiction engaged in intentional discrimination. Once bailed in, the jurisdiction must either preclear future changes with the court or with the DOJ. Arkansas and New Mexico, along with twelve counties, two cities, and two school districts, have been bailed in through Section 3(c). *See* Travis Crum, *The Voting Rights Act's Secret Weapon: Pocket Trigger Litigation and Dynamic Preclearance*, 119 YALE L.J. 1993 (2010).

≫ *The Constitutionality of Sections 4 and 5.* Ever since its promulgation in 1965, critics of the VRA have ceaselessly questioned Congress's power to pass the Act. Critics have particularly focused on Section 5's preclearance requirement and most recently the Section 4(b) coverage formula. The following material explores the Supreme Court's different answers to the constitutional attacks on the Act's central provisions. Until the Court's 2013 decision in *Shelby County v. Holder*, its 1966 decision in *South Carolina v. Katzenbach* expressed the Court's doctrinal understanding of the power of Congress to enact the VRA.

South Carolina v. Katzenbach

383 U.S. 301 (1966)

Chief Justice WARREN delivered the opinion of the Court.

. . . South Carolina has filed a bill of complaint, seeking a declaration that selected provisions of the Voting Rights Act of 1965 violate the Federal Constitution, and asking for an injunction against enforcement of these provisions by the Attorney General. . . .

The Voting Rights Act was designed by Congress to banish the blight of racial discrimination in voting, which has infected the electoral process in parts of our country for nearly a century. The Act creates stringent new remedies for voting discrimination where it persists on a pervasive scale, and in addition the statute strengthens existing remedies for pockets of voting discrimination elsewhere in the country. Congress assumed the power to prescribe these remedies from §2 of the Fifteenth Amendment, which authorizes the National Legislature to effectuate by "appropriate" measures the constitutional prohibition against racial discrimination in voting. We hold that the sections of the Act which are properly before us are an appropriate means for carrying out Congress' constitutional responsibilities and are consonant with all other provisions of the Constitution. We therefore deny South Carolina's request that enforcement of these sections of the Act be enjoined.

I

The constitutional propriety of the Voting Rights Act of 1965 must be judged with reference to the historical experience which it reflects. Before enacting the measure, Congress explored with great care the problem of racial discrimination in voting. The House and Senate Committees on the Judiciary each held hearings for nine days and received testimony from a total of 67 witnesses. More than three full days were consumed discussing the bill on the floor of the House, while the debate in the Senate covered 26 days in all. At the close of these deliberations, the verdict of both chambers was overwhelming. The House approved the bill by a vote of 328-74, and the measure passed the Senate by a margin of 79-18.

Two points emerge vividly from the voluminous legislative history of the Act contained in the committee hearings and floor debates. First: Congress felt itself confronted by an insidious and pervasive evil which had been perpetuated in certain parts of our country through unremitting and ingenious defiance of the Constitution. Second: Congress concluded that the unsuccessful remedies which it had prescribed in the past would have to be replaced by sterner and more elaborate measures in order to satisfy the clear commands of the Fifteenth Amendment. . . .

In recent years, Congress has repeatedly tried to cope with the problem by facilitating case-by-case litigation against voting discrimination. The Civil Rights Act of 1957 authorized the Attorney General to seek injunctions against public and private interference with the right to vote on racial grounds. Perfecting amendments in the Civil Rights Act of 1960 permitted the joinder of States as parties defendant, gave the Attorney General access to local voting records, and authorized courts to register voters in areas of systematic discrimination. Title I of the Civil Rights Act of 1964 expedited the hearing of voting cases before three-judge courts and outlawed some of the tactics used to disqualify Negroes from voting in federal elections.

Despite the earnest efforts of the Justice Department and of many federal judges, these new laws have done little to cure the problem of voting discrimination. According to estimates by the Attorney General during hearings on the Act, registration of voting-age Negroes in Alabama rose only from 14.2% to 19.4% between 1958 and 1964; in Louisiana it barely inched ahead from 31.7% to 31.8% between 1956 and 1965; and in Mississippi it increased only from 4.4% to 6.4% between 1954 and 1964. In each instance, registration of voting-age whites ran roughly 50 percentage points or more ahead of Negro registration.

The previous legislation has proved ineffective for a number of reasons. Voting suits are unusually onerous to prepare, sometimes requiring as many as 6,000 man-hours spent combing through registration records in preparation for trial. Litigation has been exceedingly slow, in part because of the ample opportunities for delay afforded voting officials and others involved in the proceedings. Even when favorable decisions have finally been obtained, some of the States affected have merely switched to discriminatory devices not covered by the federal decrees or have enacted difficult new tests designed to prolong the existing disparity between white and Negro registration. Alternatively, certain local officials have defied and evaded court orders or have simply closed their registration offices to freeze the voting rolls. The provision of the 1960 law authorizing registration by federal officers has had little impact on local maladministration because of its procedural complexities.

During the hearings and debates on the Act, Selma, Alabama, was repeatedly referred to as the pre-eminent example of the ineffectiveness of existing legislation. In Dallas County, of which Selma is the seat, there were four years of litigation by the Justice Department and two findings by the federal courts of widespread voting discrimination. Yet in those four years, Negro registration rose only from 156 to 383, although there are approximately 15,000 Negroes of voting age in the county. Any possibility that these figures were attributable to political apathy was dispelled by the protest demonstrations in Selma in the early months of 1965. . . .

III

[South Carolina challenged many provisions of the Act.] These provisions of the Voting Rights Act of 1965 are challenged on the fundamental ground that they exceed the powers of Congress and encroach on an area reserved to the States by the Constitution. . . .

[The] basic question presented by the case [is: has] Congress exercised its powers under the Fifteenth Amendment in an appropriate manner with relation to the States?

The ground rules for resolving this question are clear. The language and purpose of the Fifteenth Amendment, the prior decisions construing its several provisions, and the general doctrines of constitutional interpretation, all point to one fundamental principle. As against the reserved powers of the States, Congress may use any rational means to effectuate the constitutional prohibition of racial discrimination in voting. . . .

Section 1 of the Fifteenth Amendment declares that "[t]he right of citizens of the United States to vote shall not be denied or abridged by the United States or by any State on account of race, color, or previous condition of servitude." This declaration has always been treated as self-executing and has repeatedly been construed, without further legislative specification, to invalidate state voting qualifications or procedures which are discriminatory on their face or in practice. . . . The gist of the matter is that the Fifteenth Amendment supersedes contrary exertions of state power. "When a State exercises power wholly within the domain of state interest, it is insulated from federal judicial review. But such insulation is not carried over when state power is used as an instrument for circumventing a federally protected right." *Gomillion v. Lightfoot,* 364 U.S., at 347.

South Carolina contends that the cases cited above are precedents only for the authority of the judiciary to strike down state statutes and procedures — that to allow an exercise of this authority by Congress would be to rob the courts of their rightful constitutional role. On the contrary, §2 of the Fifteenth Amendment expressly declares that "Congress shall have power to enforce this article by appropriate legislation." By adding this authorization, the Framers indicated that Congress was to be chiefly responsible for implementing the rights created in §1. "It is the power of Congress which has been enlarged. Congress is authorized to *enforce* the prohibitions by appropriate legislation. Some legislation is contemplated to make the [Civil War] amendments fully effective." *Ex parte Virginia,* 100 U.S. 339, 345. Accordingly, in addition to the courts, Congress has full remedial powers to effectuate the constitutional prohibition against racial discrimination in voting. . . .

The basic test to be applied in a case involving §2 of the Fifteenth Amendment is the same as in all cases concerning the express powers of Congress with relation to the reserved powers of the States. Chief Justice Marshall laid down the classic formulation, 50 years before the Fifteenth Amendment was ratified:

> Let the end be legitimate, let it be within the scope of the constitution, and all means which are appropriate, which are plainly adapted to that end, which are not prohibited, but consist with the letter and spirit of the constitution, are constitutional.

McCulloch v. Maryland, 4 Wheat. 316, 421.

We therefore reject South Carolina's argument that Congress may appropriately do no more than to forbid violations of the Fifteenth Amendment in general terms — that the task of fashioning specific remedies or of applying them to particular localities must necessarily be left entirely to the courts. Congress is not circumscribed by any such artificial rules under §2 of the Fifteenth Amendment. In the oft-repeated words of Chief Justice Marshall, referring to another specific legislative authorization in the Constitution, "This power, like all others vested in Congress, is complete in itself, may be exercised to its utmost extent, and acknowledges no limitations, other than are prescribed in the constitution." *Gibbons v. Ogden,* 9 Wheat. 1, 196.

. . . We here hold that the portions of the Voting Rights Act properly before us are a valid means for carrying out the commands of the Fifteenth Amendment. Hopefully, millions of non-white Americans will now be able to participate for the first time on an equal basis in the government under which they live. We may finally look forward to the day when truly "[t]he right of citizens of the United States to vote shall not be denied or abridged by the United States or by any State on account of race, color, or previous condition of servitude."

>> *Congressional Reauthorization of Section 5.* The VRA is widely regarded as one of the most successful — perhaps the single most successful — piece of civil rights legislation ever enacted. Sometimes called the "second Reconstruction," the VRA is largely responsible for eliminating obstacles to black registration, voting, and representation in the South, and in the process giving blacks a voice in the processes of democratic self-government. *See, e.g.,* Quiet Revolution in the South: The Impact of the Voting Rights Act, 1965-1990 (Chandler Davidson and Bernard Grofman eds., 1994).

Under previous legislation, Section 5 was scheduled to sunset in 2007. In 2006, Congress enacted the Fannie Lou Hamer, Rosa Parks, and Coretta Scott King Voting Rights Act Reauthorization and Amendments Act of 2006, a statute that extended the Section 5 preclearance requirement to covered jurisdictions for another 25 years. In extending the Act, Congress praised the *Beer* retrogression standard as having been responsible for considerable improvement in the voting influence and electoral success of racial minorities. House Committee on the Judiciary, H.R. Rep. No. 109-478 (2006), at 69-70.

The Act also made some small amendments to Section 5 to overrule some Supreme Court decisions with which Congress disagreed. One decision that Congress legislatively overruled was *Bossier Parish*, which Congress invalidated by changing the purpose-and-effect language of Section 5 from "does not have the purpose and will not have the effect" to "neither has the purpose nor will have the effect." In explaining this amendment, the House Judiciary Committee said its purpose was to restore the intended meaning of the statute: "Through the 'purpose' requirement, Congress sought to prevent covered jurisdictions from enacting and enforcing voting changes made with a clear racial animus, regardless of the measurable impact of such discriminatory changes." It pointed out that in the 20 years prior to *Bossier*, the Justice Department had denied preclearance to 224 requested changes, accounting for about one-third of all denials, on the ground of discriminatory purpose alone. "Voting changes that 'purposefully' keep minority groups 'in their place,'" the Committee went on, "have no role in our electoral process and are precisely the types of changes Section 5 is intended to bar." *Id.* at 66-68.

Wholly apart from the question whether Congress should have reauthorized Section 5 is the intriguing question whether it had the power to do so. Since the Supreme Court first upheld Section 5 of the VRA in *South Carolina v. Katzenbach*, the Court has charted a very different course concerning congressional power under Section 5 of the Fourteenth Amendment. In a string of cases, including *City of Boerne v. Flores*, 521 U.S. 507 (1997); *United States v. Morrison*, 529 U.S. 598 (2000); *Board of Trustees v. Garrett*, 531 U.S. 356 (2001); and *Nevada v. Hibbs*, 538 U.S. 271 (2003), the Court has been far less deferential to congressional invocations of the Section 5 power. In these cases, the Court has aggressively reviewed the factual record before Congress to determine whether congressional use of the Section 5 power is truly "remedial," meaning that the legislative remedy must be demonstrably "congruent" and "proportional" to the documented harm Congress intends it to redress. Using this analysis, the Court has invalidated several federal statutes on the ground that Congress had not adequately documented a harm requiring the use of legislative power to the extent that Congress invoked it.

In 1965, when Congress initially enacted Section 5 of the VRA, it presumably could easily have satisfied even the much stricter standard of the *Boerne* line of cases. The central question following *Boerne* was whether the statute remained necessary, providing a justification for Congress to continue to reauthorize it. In the committee report accompanying the Section 5 extension, Congress took great pains to document the facts giving rise to what Congress determined to be a need for reauthorization. In its report, the House Judiciary Committee acknowledged the successes of Section 5, but also claimed that "substantial discrimination continues to exist in 2006." It defended this contention by reference to data on (1) continuing disparities in minority voter registration and turnout; (2) continuing disparities in the number of whites and blacks elected to office in covered jurisdictions; (3) the general lack of electoral support for Latino, Asian-American, Native American, and Alaskan native candidates; (4) continued patterns of racially polarized voting; and (5) actual discriminatory conduct over the last 40 years. Is this kind of a showing sufficient to satisfy the Court's new analysis under the *Boerne* line of cases of a problem sufficient to require the radical solution offered by Section 5 of state submission to highly intrusive federal oversight and authority?

≫ *Constitutionality Redux.*   In May 2008, a three-judge panel of the U.S. District Court for the District of Columbia considered a broad-based constitutional challenge to the renewed VRA on precisely these grounds. In a lengthy opinion, the court unanimously sustained the authority of Congress to enact the 2006 extension. Holding that the constitutionality of the VRA extension was governed by *Katzenbach* rather than by *Boerne*, the court applied a rationality standard and found the massive evidentiary record assembled by Congress more than sufficient to satisfy the Fifteenth Amendment. For good measure, the court in the alternative applied the *Boerne* "congruence and proportionality" standard and still found the evidentiary record sufficient to sustain the congressional judgment to reauthorize the VRA. *Northwest Austin Municipal Utility District Number One (Northwest Austin) v. Mukasey*, 557 F. Supp. 2d 9 (D.D.C. 2008).

On appeal, the Supreme Court ducked the constitutional question altogether, deciding the case instead on statutory grounds. Along the way, however, the Court had this to say about the issue of congressional power:

> The historic accomplishments of the Voting Rights Act are undeniable. When it was first passed, unconstitutional discrimination was rampant and the "registration of voting-age whites ran roughly 50 percentage points or more ahead" of black registration in many covered States. *Katzenbach, supra*, at 313. Today, the registration gap between white and black voters is in single digits in the covered States; in some of those States, blacks now register and vote at higher rates than whites. . . . At the same time, §5, "which authorizes federal intrusion into sensitive areas of state and local policymaking, imposes substantial 'federalism costs.' " *Lopez*, 525 U.S. at 282. These federalism costs have caused Members of this Court to express serious misgivings about the constitutionality of §5. . . . Some of the conditions that we relied upon in upholding this statutory scheme in *Katzenbach* and *City of Rome* have unquestionably improved. Things have changed in the South. Voter turnout and registration rates now approach parity. Blatantly discriminatory evasions of federal decrees are rare. And minority candidates hold office at unprecedented levels. See generally H. R. Rep. No. 109-478, at 12-18.
>
> These improvements are no doubt due in significant part to the Voting Rights Act itself, and stand as a monument to its success. Past success alone, however, is not adequate justification to retain the preclearance requirements. It may be that these improvements are insufficient and that conditions continue to warrant preclearance under the Act. But the Act imposes current burdens and must be justified by current needs. . . .
>
> The evil that §5 is meant to address may no longer be concentrated in the jurisdictions singled out for preclearance. The statute's coverage formula is based on data that is now more than 35 years old, and there is considerable evidence that it fails to account for current political conditions. For example, the racial gap in voter registration and turnout is lower in the States originally covered by §5 than it is nationwide. E. BLUM

& L. CAMPBELL, ASSESSMENT OF VOTING RIGHTS PROGRESS IN JURISDIC-
TIONS COVERED UNDER SECTION FIVE OF THE VOTING RIGHTS ACT 3-
6 (2006). Congress heard warnings from supporters of extending §5
that the evidence in the record did not address "systematic differences
between the covered and the non-covered areas of the United States[,] . . .
and, in fact, the evidence that is in the record suggests that there is more
similarity than difference." The Continuing Need for Section 5 Pre-
Clearance: Hearing before the Senate Committee on the Judiciary, 109th
Cong., 2d Sess., 10 (2006) (statement of Richard H. Pildes). . . . The Act's
preclearance requirements and its coverage formula raise serious constitutional questions under [any contemporary] test.

This seems like a much more skeptical account of the underlying merits question than that given by the D.C. District Court. In the following case, *Shelby County
v. Holder*, the Court squared up to the constitutional question that it avoided in
Northwest Austin.

Shelby County, Alabama v. Holder

133 S. Ct. 2612 (2013)

Chief Justice ROBERTS delivered the opinion of the Court.

The Voting Rights Act of 1965 employed extraordinary measures to address
an extraordinary problem. Section 5 of the Act required States to obtain federal
permission before enacting any law related to voting—a drastic departure from
basic principles of federalism. And §4 of the Act applied that requirement only
to some States—an equally dramatic departure from the principle that all States
enjoy equal sovereignty. This was strong medicine, but Congress determined it was
needed to address entrenched racial discrimination in voting, "an insidious and
pervasive evil which had been perpetuated in certain parts of our country through
unremitting and ingenious defiance of the Constitution." *South Carolina v. Katzenbach*, 383 U.S. 301, 309 (1966). As we explained in upholding the law, "exceptional
conditions can justify legislative measures not otherwise appropriate." *Id.*, at 334.
Reflecting the unprecedented nature of these measures, they were scheduled to
expire after five years.

Nearly 50 years later, they are still in effect; indeed, they have been made more
stringent, and are now scheduled to last until 2031. There is no denying, however,
that the conditions that originally justified these measures no longer characterize
voting in the covered jurisdictions. By 2009, "the racial gap in voter registration and
turnout [was] lower in the States originally covered by §5 than it [was] nationwide."
Northwest Austin Municipal Util. Dist. No. One v. Holder, 557 U.S. 193, 203-204 (2009).
Since that time, Census Bureau data indicate that African-American voter turnout
has come to exceed white voter turnout in five of the six States originally covered
by §5, with a gap in the sixth State of less than one half of one percent.

At the same time, voting discrimination still exists; no one doubts that. The
question is whether the Act's extraordinary measures, including its disparate treatment of the States, continue to satisfy constitutional requirements. As we put it a

short time ago, "the Act imposes current burdens and must be justified by current needs." *Northwest Austin*, 557 U.S., at 203.

I

A

In 2006, Congress . . . reauthorized the Voting Rights Act for 25 years, . . . without change to its coverage formula. Fannie Lou Hamer, Rosa Parks, and Coretta Scott King Voting Rights Act Reauthorization and Amendments Act, 120 Stat. 577. Congress also amended §5 to prohibit more conduct than before. Section 5 now forbids voting changes with "any discriminatory purpose" as well as voting changes that diminish the ability of citizens, on account of race, color, or language minority status, "to elect their preferred candidates of choice." 42 U.S.C. §§1973c(b)-(d).

Shortly after this reauthorization, a Texas utility district brought suit, seeking to bail out from the Act's coverage and, in the alternative, challenging the Act's constitutionality. See *Northwest Austin*, 557 U.S., at 200-201. A three-judge District Court explained that only a State or political subdivision was eligible to seek bailout under the statute, and concluded that the utility district was not a political subdivision, a term that encompassed only "counties, parishes, and voter-registering subunits." *Northwest Austin Municipal Util. Dist. No. One v. Mukasey*, 573 F. Supp. 2d 221, 232 (D.D.C. 2008). The District Court also rejected the constitutional challenge. *Id.*, at 283.

We reversed. We explained that " 'normally the Court will not decide a constitutional question if there is some other ground upon which to dispose of the case.' " *Northwest Austin, supra*, at 205. Concluding that "underlying constitutional concerns," among other things, "compel[led] a broader reading of the bailout provision," we construed the statute to allow the utility district to seek bailout. *Northwest Austin*, 557 U.S., at 207. In doing so we expressed serious doubts about the Act's continued constitutionality.

We explained that §5 "imposes substantial federalism costs" and "differentiates between the States, despite our historic tradition that all the States enjoy equal sovereignty." We also noted that "[t]hings have changed in the South. Voter turnout and registration rates now approach parity. Blatantly discriminatory evasions of federal decrees are rare. And minority candidates hold office at unprecedented levels." Finally, we questioned whether the problems that §5 meant to address were still "concentrated in the jurisdictions singled out for preclearance."

Eight Members of the Court subscribed to these views, and the remaining Member would have held the Act unconstitutional. Ultimately, however, the Court's construction of the bailout provision left the constitutional issues for another day.

B

Shelby County is located in Alabama, a covered jurisdiction. It has not sought bailout, as the Attorney General has recently objected to voting changes proposed from within the county. Instead, in 2010, the county sued the Attorney General in Federal District Court in Washington, D.C., seeking a declaratory judgment that sections 4(b) and 5 of the Voting Rights Act are facially unconstitutional, as well as a permanent injunction against their enforcement. The District Court ruled against the county and upheld the Act.

The Court of Appeals for the D.C. Circuit affirmed. We granted certiorari.

II

In *Northwest Austin*, we stated that "the Act imposes current burdens and must be justified by current needs." 557 U.S., at 203. And we concluded that "a departure from the fundamental principle of equal sovereignty requires a showing that a statute's disparate geographic coverage is sufficiently related to the problem that it targets." *Ibid.* These basic principles guide our review of the question before us.[1]

A

The Constitution and laws of the United States are "the supreme Law of the Land." U.S. Const., Art. VI, cl. 2. State legislation may not contravene federal law. The Federal Government does not, however, have a general right to review and veto state enactments before they go into effect.

Outside the strictures of the Supremacy Clause, States retain broad autonomy in structuring their governments and pursuing legislative objectives. Indeed, the Constitution provides that all powers not specifically granted to the Federal Government are reserved to the States or citizens. Amdt. 10. This "allocation of powers in our federal system preserves the integrity, dignity, and residual sovereignty of the States." *Bond v. United States*, 131 S. Ct. 2355, 2364 (2011). But the federal balance "is not just an end in itself: Rather, federalism secures to citizens the liberties that derive from the diffusion of sovereign power." *Ibid.* (internal quotation marks omitted).

More specifically, " 'the Framers of the Constitution intended the States to keep for themselves, as provided in the Tenth Amendment, the power to regulate elections.' " *Gregory v. Ashcroft*, 501 U.S. 452, 461-462 (1991).

Not only do States retain sovereignty under the Constitution, there is also a "fundamental principle of *equal* sovereignty" among the States. *Northwest Austin, supra,* at 203. Over a hundred years ago, this Court explained that our Nation "was and is a union of States, equal in power, dignity and authority." At the same time, as we made clear in *Northwest Austin*, the fundamental principle of equal sovereignty remains highly pertinent in assessing subsequent disparate treatment of States. 557 U.S., at 203.

The Voting Rights Act sharply departs from these basic principles. It suspends "*all* changes to state election law—however innocuous—until they have been precleared by federal authorities in Washington, D.C." States must beseech the Federal Government for permission to implement laws that they would otherwise have the right to enact and execute on their own, subject of course to any injunction in a §2 action. The Attorney General has 60 days to object to a preclearance request,

---

1. Both the Fourteenth and Fifteenth Amendments were at issue in *Northwest Austin*, see Juris. Statement i, and Brief for Federal Appellee 29-30, in *Northwest Austin Municipal Util. Dist. No. One v. Holder*, O.T. 2008, No. 08-322, and accordingly *Northwest Austin* guides our review under both Amendments in this case.

longer if he requests more information. If a State seeks preclearance from a three-judge court, the process can take years.

And despite the tradition of equal sovereignty, the Act applies to only nine States (and several additional counties). While one State waits months or years and expends funds to implement a validly enacted law, its neighbor can typically put the same law into effect immediately, through the normal legislative process. Even if a noncovered jurisdiction is sued, there are important differences between those proceedings and preclearance proceedings; the preclearance proceeding "not only switches the burden of proof to the supplicant jurisdiction, but also applies substantive standards quite different from those governing the rest of the nation." 679 F.3d, at 884 (Williams, J., dissenting) (case below).

All this explains why, when we first upheld the Act in 1966, we described it as "stringent" and "potent." *Katzenbach*, 383 U.S., at 308, 315, 337. We recognized that it "may have been an uncommon exercise of congressional power," but concluded that "legislative measures not otherwise appropriate" could be justified by "exceptional conditions." We have since noted that the Act "authorizes federal intrusion into sensitive areas of state and local policymaking," *Lopez*, 525 U.S., at 282, and represents an "extraordinary departure from the traditional course of relations between the States and the Federal Government," *Presley v. Etowah County Comm'n*, 502 U.S. 491, 500-501 (1992). As we reiterated in *Northwest Austin*, the Act constitutes "extraordinary legislation otherwise unfamiliar to our federal system."

B

In 1966, we found these departures from the basic features of our system of government justified. The "blight of racial discrimination in voting" had "infected the electoral process in parts of our country for nearly a century." Several States had enacted a variety of requirements and tests "specifically designed to prevent" African-Americans from voting. Case-by-case litigation had proved inadequate to prevent such racial discrimination in voting, in part because States "merely switched to discriminatory devices not covered by the federal decrees," "enacted difficult new tests," or simply "defied and evaded court orders." Shortly before enactment of the Voting Rights Act, only 19.4 percent of African-Americans of voting age were registered to vote in Alabama, only 31.8 percent in Louisiana, and only 6.4 percent in Mississippi. *Id.*, at 313. Those figures were roughly 50 percentage points or more below the figures for whites.

At the time, the coverage formula—the means of linking the exercise of the unprecedented authority with the problem that warranted it—made sense. We found that "Congress chose to limit its attention to the geographic areas where immediate action seemed necessary." The areas where Congress found "evidence of actual voting discrimination" shared two characteristics: "the use of tests and devices for voter registration, and a voting rate in the 1964 presidential election at least 12 points below the national average." We explained that "[t]ests and devices are relevant to voting discrimination because of their long history as a tool for perpetrating the evil; a low voting rate is pertinent for the obvious reason that widespread disenfranchisement must inevitably affect the number of actual voters." We therefore concluded that "the coverage formula [was] rational in both practice and theory." It accurately reflected those jurisdictions uniquely characterized by voting discrimination "on a pervasive scale," linking coverage to the devices used to effectuate discrimination and to the resulting disenfranchisement. The formula ensured that the "stringent remedies [were] aimed at areas where voting discrimination ha[d] been most flagrant."

C

Nearly 50 years later, things have changed dramatically. Shelby County contends that the preclearance requirement, even without regard to its disparate coverage, is now unconstitutional. Its arguments have a good deal of force. In the covered jurisdictions, "[v]oter turnout and registration rates now approach parity. Blatantly discriminatory evasions of federal decrees are rare. And minority candidates hold office at unprecedented levels." *Northwest Austin*, 557 U.S., at 202. The tests and devices that blocked access to the ballot have been forbidden nationwide for over 40 years.

The following chart, compiled from the Senate and House Reports, compares voter registration numbers from 1965 to those from 2004 in the six originally covered States. These are the numbers that were before Congress when it reauthorized the Act in 2006:

	1965			2004		
	White	Black	Gap	White	Black	Gap
Alabama	69.2	19.3	49.9	73.8	72.9	0.9
Georgia	62.[6]	27.4	35.2	63.5	64.2	-0.7
Louisiana	80.5	31.6	48.9	75.1	71.1	4.0
Mississippi	69.9	6.7	63.2	72.3	76.1	-3.8
South Carolina	75.7	37.3	38.4	74.4	71.1	3.3
Virginia	61.1	38.3	22.8	68.2	57.4	10.8

See S. Rep. No. 109-295, p. 11 (2006); H.R. Rep. No. 109-478, at 12. The 2004 figures come from the Census Bureau. Census Bureau data from the most recent election indicate that African-American voter turnout exceeded white voter turnout in five of the six States originally covered by §5, with a gap in the sixth State of less than one half of one percent. The preclearance statistics are also illuminating. In the first decade after enactment of §5, the Attorney General objected to 14.2 percent of proposed voting changes. In the last decade before reenactment, the Attorney General objected to a mere 0.16 percent.

There is no doubt that these improvements are in large part *because of* the Voting Rights Act. The Act has proved immensely successful at redressing racial discrimination and integrating the voting process.

Yet the Act has not eased the restrictions in §5 or narrowed the scope of the coverage formula in §4(b) along the way. Those extraordinary and unprecedented features were reauthorized—as if nothing had changed. In fact, the Act's unusual remedies have grown even stronger. When Congress reauthorized the Act in 2006, it did so for another 25 years on top of the previous 40—a far cry from the initial

346

five-year period. Congress also expanded the prohibitions in §5. We had previously interpreted §5 to prohibit only those redistricting plans that would have the purpose or effect of worsening the position of minority groups. See *Bossier II,* 528 U.S., at 324, 335-336. In 2006, Congress amended §5 to prohibit laws that could have favored such groups but did not do so because of a discriminatory purpose, even though we had stated that such broadening of §5 coverage would "exacerbate the substantial federalism costs that the preclearance procedure already exacts, perhaps to the extent of raising concerns about §5's constitutionality," *Bossier II, supra,* at 336. In addition, Congress expanded §5 to prohibit any voting law "that has the purpose of or will have the effect of diminishing the ability of any citizens of the United States," on account of race, color, or language minority status, "to elect their preferred candidates of choice." §1973c(b). In light of those two amendments, the bar that covered jurisdictions must clear has been raised even as the conditions justifying that requirement have dramatically improved.

Respondents do not deny that there have been improvements on the ground, but argue that much of this can be attributed to the deterrent effect of §5, which dissuades covered jurisdictions from engaging in discrimination that they would resume should §5 be struck down. Under this theory, however, §5 would be effectively immune from scrutiny; no matter how "clean" the record of covered jurisdictions, the argument could always be made that it was deterrence that accounted for the good behavior.

The provisions of §5 apply only to those jurisdictions singled out by §4. We now consider whether that coverage formula is constitutional in light of current conditions.

III

A

When upholding the constitutionality of the coverage formula in 1966, we concluded that it was "rational in both practice and theory." *Katzenbach,* 383 U.S., at 330. The formula looked to cause (discriminatory tests) and effect (low voter registration and turnout), and tailored the remedy (preclearance) to those jurisdictions exhibiting both.

By 2009, however, we concluded that the "coverage formula raise[d] serious constitutional questions." *Northwest Austin,* 557 U.S., at 204. As we explained, a statute's "current burdens" must be justified by "current needs," and any "disparate geographic coverage" must be "sufficiently related to the problem that it targets." *Id.,* at 203. The coverage formula met that test in 1965, but no longer does so.

Coverage today is based on decades-old data and eradicated practices. The formula captures States by reference to literacy tests and low voter registration and turnout in the 1960s and early 1970s. But such tests have been banned nationwide for over 40 years. And voter registration and turnout numbers in the covered States have risen dramatically in the years since. Racial disparity in those numbers was compelling evidence justifying the preclearance remedy and the coverage formula. There is no longer such a disparity.

In 1965, the States could be divided into two groups: those with a recent history of voting tests and low voter registration and turnout, and those without those characteristics. Congress based its coverage formula on that distinction. Today the Nation is no longer divided along those lines, yet the Voting Rights Act continues to treat it as if it were.

B

The Government's defense of the formula is limited. First, the Government contends that the formula is "reverse-engineered": Congress identified the jurisdictions to be covered and *then* came up with criteria to describe them. Under that reasoning, there need not be any logical relationship between the criteria in the formula and the reason for coverage; all that is necessary is that the formula happen to capture the jurisdictions Congress wanted to single out.

[T]he Government's reverse-engineering argument does not even attempt to demonstrate the continued relevance of the formula to the problem it targets. And in the context of a decision as significant as this one — subjecting a disfavored subset of States to "extraordinary legislation otherwise unfamiliar to our federal system," that failure to establish even relevance is fatal.

The Government falls back to the argument that because the formula was relevant in 1965, its continued use is permissible so long as any discrimination remains in the States Congress identified back then — regardless of how that discrimination compares to discrimination in States unburdened by coverage. This argument does not look to "current political conditions," but instead relies on a comparison between the States in 1965.

But history did not end in 1965. By the time the Act was reauthorized in 2006, there had been 40 more years of it. In assessing the "current need[]" for a preclearance system that treats States differently from one another today, that history cannot be ignored. During that time, largely because of the Voting Rights Act, voting tests were abolished, disparities in voter registration and turnout due to race were erased, and African-Americans attained political office in record numbers. And yet the coverage formula that Congress reauthorized in 2006 ignores these developments, keeping the focus on decades-old data relevant to decades-old problems, rather than current data reflecting current needs.

C

In defending the coverage formula, the Government, the intervenors, and the dissent also rely heavily on data from the record that they claim justify disparate coverage. Congress compiled thousands of pages of evidence before reauthorizing the Voting Rights Act. The court below and the parties have debated what that record shows — they have gone back and forth about whether to compare covered to noncovered jurisdictions as blocks, how to disaggregate the data State by State, how to weigh §2 cases as evidence of ongoing discrimination, and whether to consider evidence not before Congress, among other issues. Regardless of how to look at the record, however, no one can fairly say that it shows anything approaching the "pervasive," "flagrant," "widespread," and "rampant" discrimination that faced Congress in 1965, and that clearly distinguished the covered jurisdictions from the rest of the Nation at that time.

But a more fundamental problem remains: Congress did not use the record it compiled to shape a coverage formula grounded in current conditions. It instead reenacted a formula based on 40-year-old facts having no logical relation to the present day. The dissent relies on "second-generation barriers," which are not impediments to the casting of ballots, but rather electoral arrangements that affect the weight of minority votes. That does not cure the problem. Viewing the preclearance requirements as targeting such efforts simply highlights the irrationality of continued reliance on the §4 coverage formula, which is based on voting tests and access to the ballot, not vote dilution. We cannot pretend that we are reviewing an updated statute, or try our hand at updating the statute ourselves, based on the new record compiled by Congress. Contrary to the dissent's contention, we are not ignoring the record; we are simply recognizing that it played no role in shaping the statutory formula before us today.

The dissent also turns to the record to argue that, in light of voting discrimination in Shelby County, the county cannot complain about the provisions that subject it to preclearance. *Post*, at 23-30. But that is like saying that a driver pulled over pursuant to a policy of stopping all redheads cannot complain about that policy, if it turns out his license has expired. Shelby County's claim is that the coverage formula here is unconstitutional in all its applications, because of how it selects the jurisdictions subjected to preclearance. The county was selected based on that formula, and may challenge it in court.

D

The dissent proceeds from a flawed premise. It quotes the famous sentence from *McCulloch v. Maryland*, 4 Wheat. 316, 421, 4 L. Ed. 579 (1819), with the following emphasis: "Let the end be legitimate, let it be within the scope of the constitution, and *all means which are appropriate, which are plainly adapted to that end*, which are not prohibited, but consist with the letter and spirit of the constitution, are constitutional." But this case is about a part of the sentence that the dissent does not emphasize — the part that asks whether a legislative means is "consist[ent] with the letter and spirit of the constitution." The dissent states that "[i]t cannot tenably be maintained" that this is an issue with regard to the Voting Rights Act, but four years ago, in an opinion joined by two of today's dissenters, the Court expressly stated that "[t]he Act's preclearance requirement and its coverage formula raise serious constitutional questions." *Northwest Austin, supra*, at 204. The dissent does not explain how those "serious constitutional questions" became untenable in four short years.

In other ways as well, the dissent analyzes the question presented as if our decision in *Northwest Austin* never happened. For example, the dissent refuses to consider the principle of equal sovereignty, despite *Northwest Austin*'s emphasis on its significance. *Northwest Austin* also emphasized the "dramatic" progress since 1965, but the dissent describes current levels of discrimination as "flagrant," "widespread," and "pervasive." Despite the fact that *Northwest Austin* requires an Act's "disparate geographic coverage" to be "sufficiently related" to its targeted problems, the dissent maintains that an Act's limited coverage actually eases Congress's burdens, and suggests that a fortuitous relationship should suffice. Although *Northwest Austin* stated definitively that "current burdens" must be justified by "current needs," the dissent argues that the coverage formula can be justified by history, and that the required showing can be weaker on reenactment than when the law was first passed.

There is no valid reason to insulate the coverage formula from review merely because it was previously enacted 40 years ago. If Congress had started from scratch in 2006, it plainly could not have enacted the present coverage formula. It would have been irrational for Congress to distinguish between States in such a fundamental way based on 40-year-old data, when today's statistics tell an entirely different story. And it would have been irrational to base coverage on the use of voting tests 40 years ago, when such tests have been illegal since that time. But that is exactly what Congress has done.

Striking down an Act of Congress "is the gravest and most delicate duty that this Court is called on to perform." We do not do so lightly. That is why, in 2009, we took care to avoid ruling on the constitutionality of the Voting Rights Act when asked to do so, and instead resolved the case then before us on statutory grounds. But in issuing that decision, we expressed our broader concerns about the constitutionality of the Act. Congress could have updated the coverage formula at that time, but did not do so. Its failure to act leaves us today with no choice but to declare §4(b) unconstitutional. The formula in that section can no longer be used as a basis for subjecting jurisdictions to preclearance.

Our decision in no way affects the permanent, nationwide ban on racial discrimination in voting found in §2. We issue no holding on §5 itself, only on the coverage formula. Congress may draft another formula based on current conditions. Such a formula is an initial prerequisite to a determination that exceptional conditions still exist justifying such an "extraordinary departure from the traditional course of relations between the States and the Federal Government." *Presley*, 502 U.S., at 500-501. Our country has changed, and while any racial discrimination in voting is too much, Congress must ensure that the legislation it passes to remedy that problem speaks to current conditions.

The judgment of the Court of Appeals is reversed.

Justice THOMAS, concurring.

I join the Court's opinion in full but write separately to explain that I would find §5 of the Voting Rights Act unconstitutional as well.

Justice GINSBURG, with whom Justice BREYER, Justice SOTOMAYOR, and Justice KAGAN join, dissenting.

In the Court's view, the very success of §5 of the Voting Rights Act demands its dormancy. Congress was of another mind. Recognizing that large progress has been made, Congress determined, based on a voluminous record, that the scourge of discrimination was not yet extirpated. The question this case presents is who decides whether, as currently operative, §5 remains justifiable,[1] this Court, or a Congress charged with the obligation to enforce the post-Civil War Amendments

---

1. The Court purports to declare unconstitutional only the coverage formula set out in §4(b). But without that formula, §5 is immobilized.

"by appropriate legislation." With overwhelming support in both Houses, Congress concluded that, for two prime reasons, §5 should continue in force, unabated. First, continuance would facilitate completion of the impressive gains thus far made; and second, continuance would guard against backsliding. Those assessments were well within Congress' province to make and should elicit this Court's unstinting approbation.

I

"[V]oting discrimination still exists; no one doubts that." *Ante.* But the Court today terminates the remedy that proved to be best suited to block that discrimination. The Voting Rights Act of 1965 (VRA) has worked to combat voting discrimination where other remedies had been tried and failed. Particularly effective is the VRA's requirement of federal preclearance for all changes to voting laws in the regions of the country with the most aggravated records of rank discrimination against minority voting rights.

A century after the Fourteenth and Fifteenth Amendments guaranteed citizens the right to vote free of discrimination on the basis of race, the "blight of racial discrimination in voting" continued to "infec[t] the electoral process in parts of our country." *South Carolina v. Katzenbach,* 383 U.S. 301, 308. Early attempts to cope with this vile infection resembled battling the Hydra. Whenever one form of voting discrimination was identified and prohibited, others sprang up in its place. This Court repeatedly encountered the remarkable "variety and persistence" of laws disenfranchising minority citizens. To take just one example, the Court, in 1927, held unconstitutional a Texas law barring black voters from participating in primary elections, *Nixon v. Herndon,* in 1944, the Court struck down a "reenacted" and slightly altered version of the same law, *Smith v. Allwright;* and in 1953, the Court once again confronted an attempt by Texas to "circumven[t]" the Fifteenth Amendment by adopting yet another variant of the all-white primary, *Terry v. Adams.*

During this era, the Court recognized that discrimination against minority voters was a quintessentially political problem requiring a political solution. As Justice Holmes explained: If "the great mass of the white population intends to keep the blacks from voting," "relief from [that] great political wrong, if done, as alleged, by the people of a State and the State itself, must be given by them or by the legislative and political department of the government of the United States." *Giles v. Harris,* 189 U.S. 475 (1903).

Congress learned from experience that laws targeting particular electoral practices or enabling case-by-case litigation were inadequate to the task. In the Civil Rights Acts of 1957, 1960, and 1964, Congress authorized and then expanded the power of "the Attorney General to seek injunctions against public and private interference with the right to vote on racial grounds." *Katzenbach,* 383 U.S., at 313. But circumstances reduced the ameliorative potential of these legislative Acts.

Although the VRA wrought dramatic changes in the realization of minority voting rights, the Act, to date, surely has not eliminated all vestiges of discrimination against the exercise of the franchise by minority citizens. Jurisdictions covered by the preclearance requirement continued to submit, in large numbers, proposed changes to voting laws that the Attorney General declined to approve, auguring that barriers to minority voting would quickly resurface were the preclearance remedy eliminated. Congress also found that as "registration and voting of minority citizens increas[ed], other measures may be resorted to which would dilute increasing minority voting strength." Efforts to reduce the impact of minority votes, in contrast to direct attempts to block access to the ballot, are aptly described as "second-generation barriers" to minority voting.

Second-generation barriers come in various forms. One of the blockages is racial gerrymandering, the redrawing of legislative districts in an "effort to segregate the races for purposes of voting." *Id.*, at 642. Another is adoption of a system of at-large voting in lieu of district-by-district voting in a city with a sizable black minority. By switching to at-large voting, the overall majority could control the election of each city council member, effectively eliminating the potency of the minority's votes. A similar effect could be achieved if the city engaged in discriminatory annexation by incorporating majority-white areas into city limits, thereby decreasing the effect of VRA-occasioned increases in black voting. Whatever the device employed, this Court has long recognized that vote dilution, when adopted with a discriminatory purpose, cuts down the right to vote as certainly as denial of access to the ballot. *Shaw.*

In response to evidence of these substituted barriers, Congress reauthorized the VRA for five years in 1970, for seven years in 1975, and for 25 years in 1982. Each time, this Court upheld the reauthorization as a valid exercise of congressional power. As the 1982 reauthorization approached its 2007 expiration date, Congress again considered whether the VRA's preclearance mechanism remained an appropriate response to the problem of voting discrimination in covered jurisdictions.

Congress did not take this task lightly. Quite the opposite. The 109th Congress that took responsibility for the renewal started early and conscientiously. In October 2005, the House began extensive hearings, which continued into November and resumed in March 2006. In April 2006, the Senate followed suit, with hearings of its own. In May 2006, the bills that became the VRA's reauthorization were introduced in both Houses. The House held further hearings of considerable length, as did the Senate, which continued to hold hearings into June and July. In mid-July, the House considered and rejected four amendments, then passed the reauthorization by a vote of 390 yeas to 33 nays. The bill was read and debated in the Senate, where it passed by a vote of 98 to 0. President Bush signed it a week later, on July 27, 2006, recognizing the need for "further work . . . in the fight against injustice," and calling the reauthorization "an example of our continued commitment to a united America where every person is valued and treated with dignity and respect."

In the long course of the legislative process, Congress "amassed a sizable record." *Northwest Austin Municipal Util. Dist. No. One v. Holder.* The House and Senate Judiciary Committees held 21 hearings, heard from scores of witnesses, received a number of investigative reports and other written documentation of continuing discrimination in covered jurisdictions. In all, the legislative record Congress compiled filled more than 15,000 pages. The compilation presents countless "examples of flagrant racial discrimination" since the last reauthorization; Congress also brought to light systematic evidence that "intentional racial discrimination in voting remains so serious and widespread in covered jurisdictions that section 5 preclearance is still needed."

After considering the full legislative record, Congress made the following findings: The VRA has directly caused significant progress in eliminating first-generation barriers to ballot access, leading to a marked increase in minority voter registration and turnout and the number of minority elected officials. But despite this progress, "second generation barriers constructed to prevent minority voters from fully participating in the electoral process" continued to exist, as well as racially polarized voting in the covered jurisdictions, which increased the political vulnerability of racial and language minorities in those jurisdictions. Extensive "[e]vidence of continued discrimination," Congress concluded, "clearly show[ed] the continued need for Federal oversight" in covered jurisdictions. The overall record demonstrated to the federal lawmakers that, "without the continuation of the Voting Rights Act of 1965 protections, racial and language minority citizens will be deprived of the opportunity to exercise their right to vote, or will have their votes diluted, undermining the significant gains made by minorities in the last 40 years."

Based on these findings, Congress reauthorized preclearance for another 25 years, while also undertaking to reconsider the extension after 15 years to ensure that the provision was still necessary and effective. The question before the Court is whether Congress had the authority under the Constitution to act as it did.

II

In answering this question, the Court does not write on a clean slate. It is well established that Congress' judgment regarding exercise of its power to enforce the Fourteenth and Fifteenth Amendments warrants substantial deference. The VRA addresses the combination of race discrimination and the right to vote, which is "preservative of all rights." *Yick Wo v. Hopkins*, 118 U.S. 356, 370 (1886). When confronting the most constitutionally invidious form of discrimination, and the most fundamental right in our democratic system, Congress' power to act is at its height.

The basis for this deference is firmly rooted in both constitutional text and precedent. The Fifteenth Amendment, which targets precisely and only racial discrimination in voting rights, states that, in this domain, "Congress shall have power to enforce this article by appropriate legislation."[2] In choosing this language, the Amendment's framers invoked Chief Justice Marshall's formulation of the scope of Congress' powers under the Necessary and Proper Clause:

> Let the end be legitimate, let it be within the scope of the constitution, and *all means which are appropriate, which are plainly adapted to that end,*

---

2. The Constitution uses the words "right to vote" in five separate places: the Fourteenth, Fifteenth, Nineteenth, Twenty-Fourth, and Twenty-Sixth Amendments. Each of these Amendments contains the same broad empowerment of Congress to enact "appropriate legislation" to enforce the protected right. The implication is unmistakable: Under our constitutional structure, Congress holds the lead rein in making the right to vote equally real for all U.S. citizens. These Amendments are in line with the special role assigned to Congress in protecting the integrity of the democratic process in federal elections. U.S. Const., Art. I, §4 ("[T]he Congress may at any time by Law make or alter" regulations concerning the "Times, Places and Manner of holding Elections for Senators and Representatives."); *Arizona v. Inter Tribal Council of Ariz., Inc.* (2013).

which are not prohibited, but consist with the letter and spirit of the constitution, are constitutional.

McCulloch v. Maryland, 4 Wheat. 316, 421 (emphasis added). It cannot tenably be maintained that the VRA, an Act of Congress adopted to shield the right to vote from racial discrimination, is inconsistent with the letter or spirit of the Fifteenth Amendment, or any provision of the Constitution read in light of the Civil War Amendments. Nowhere in today's opinion, or in *Northwest Austin*,[3] is there clear recognition of the transformative effect the Fifteenth Amendment aimed to achieve. Notably, "the Founders' first successful amendment told Congress that it could 'make no law' over a certain domain"; in contrast, the Civil War Amendments used "language [that] authorized transformative new federal statutes to uproot all vestiges of unfreedom and inequality" and provided "sweeping enforcement powers . . . to enact 'appropriate' legislation targeting state abuses." A. Amar, America's Constitution: A Biography 361, 363, 399 (2005).

The stated purpose of the Civil War Amendments was to arm Congress with the power and authority to protect all persons within the Nation from violations of their rights by the States. In exercising that power, then, Congress may use "all means which are appropriate, which are plainly adapted" to the constitutional ends declared by these Amendments. *McCulloch*, 4 Wheat., at 421. So when Congress acts to enforce the right to vote free from racial discrimination, we ask not whether Congress has chosen the means most wise, but whether Congress has rationally selected means appropriate to a legitimate end. "It is not for us to review the congressional resolution of [the need for its chosen remedy]. It is enough that we be able to perceive a basis upon which the Congress might resolve the conflict as it did." *Katzenbach v. Morgan.*

Until today, in considering the constitutionality of the VRA, the Court has accorded Congress the full measure of respect its judgments in this domain should garner. *South Carolina v. Katzenbach* supplies the standard of review: "As against the reserved powers of the States, Congress may use any rational means to effectuate the constitutional prohibition of racial discrimination in voting." 383 U.S., at 324. Faced with subsequent reauthorizations of the VRA, the Court has reaffirmed this standard. *E.g., City of Rome.* Today's Court does not purport to alter settled precedent establishing that the dispositive question is whether Congress has employed "rational means."

For three reasons, legislation *re*authorizing an existing statute is especially likely to satisfy the minimal requirements of the rational-basis test. First, when reauthorization is at issue, Congress has already assembled a legislative record justifying the initial legislation. Congress is entitled to consider that preexisting record as well as the record before it at the time of the vote on reauthorization. This is especially true where, as here, the Court has repeatedly affirmed the statute's constitutionality and Congress has adhered to the very model the Court has upheld.

Second, the very fact that reauthorization is necessary arises because Congress has built a temporal limitation into the Act. It has pledged to review, after a span of

---

3. Acknowledging the existence of "serious constitutional questions". . . does not suggest how those questions should be answered.

years (first 15, then 25) and in light of contemporary evidence, the continued need for the VRA.

Third, a reviewing court should expect the record supporting reauthorization to be less stark than the record originally made. Demand for a record of violations equivalent to the one earlier made would expose Congress to a catch-22. If the statute was working, there would be less evidence of discrimination, so opponents might argue that Congress should not be allowed to renew the statute. In contrast, if the statute was not working, there would be plenty of evidence of discrimination, but scant reason to renew a failed regulatory regime.

This is not to suggest that congressional power in this area is limitless. It is this Court's responsibility to ensure that Congress has used appropriate means. The question meet for judicial review is whether the chosen means are "adapted to carry out the objects the amendments have in view." *Ex parte Virginia*, 100 U.S. 339, 346 (1880). The Court's role, then, is not to substitute its judgment for that of Congress, but to determine whether the legislative record sufficed to show that "Congress could rationally have determined that [its chosen] provisions were appropriate methods." *City of Rome.*

In summary, the Constitution vests broad power in Congress to protect the right to vote, and in particular to combat racial discrimination in voting. This Court has repeatedly reaffirmed Congress' prerogative to use any rational means in exercise of its power in this area. And both precedent and logic dictate that the rational-means test should be easier to satisfy, and the burden on the statute's challenger should be higher, when what is at issue is the reauthorization of a remedy that the Court has previously affirmed, and that Congress found, from contemporary evidence, to be working to advance the legislature's legitimate objective.

[The dissent goes on in Part III to examine in detail the record before Congress when it reauthorized Section 5 in 2006, and in Part IV it argues that the majority should not have addressed Shelby County's facial challenge.]

≫   *What Does* Shelby County *Mean for Section 5?*   Notwithstanding the majority's statement that it only holds the coverage formula unconstitutional, the Court's opinion effectively renders Section 5 inoperative. As we saw at the beginning of this chapter, the purpose of the coverage formula is to determine which jurisdictions ought to preclear their voting changes. If there is no coverage formula, there is no work for Section 5 to do. Consequently, though Section 5 remains constitutional, it is essentially inoperative.

Bailout Under Section 4. Why wasn't bailout an effective remedy? The Court in *Northwest Austin* interpreted the bailout provision in a way that made it much easier for covered jurisdictions to bail out from coverage. This raises questions about why more jurisdictions have not sought bailout. If the preclearance requirements of Section 5 are really so onerous, why haven't jurisdictions that are qualified to seek bailout done so? The obvious possibility is that bailout is so difficult that jurisdictions have been deterred from seeking it. Yet this possibility is in some tension with the fact that jurisdictions seeking bailout have a perfect record. Gerry Hebert, the civil rights lawyer who has represented every jurisdiction that since 1982 has sought bailout, argues that many smaller covered jurisdictions don't know the bailout option exists. He also argues that seeking preclearance has become so routinized in covered jurisdictions that compliance is not in practice either costly or burdensome, and that covered jurisdictions therefore lack an incentive to seek bailout, which does involve incurring new and additional costs. J. Gerald Hebert, *An Assessment of the Bailout Provisions of the Voting Rights Act, in* VOTING RIGHTS ACT REAUTHORIZATION OF 2006: PERSPECTIVES ON DEMOCRACY, PARTICIPATION, AND POWER (ANA HENDERSON ED., 2007).

Dignity of the States. The Court's decision in *Shelby County* is premised on the proposition that Sections 4 and 5 treat the states differently in a manner that is constitutionally significant. The constitutional harm appears to be the fact that the differential treatment offends the equal dignity or sovereignty of the states. What does this principle mean? Consider the following critical assessment:

> According to the argument advanced by Shelby County, Alabama, the heart of the problem with the Act is that its differential treatment of covered and non-covered states offends the "equal dignity" of the covered states.
>
> The equal dignity of the states, this argument runs, obligates Congress either to treat all states equally, or to have a strong justification for doing otherwise.
>
> The dignitary harm here lies in treating the South—the former Confederacy—differently from most of the rest of the nation in a particular way that carries with it an implication that the past is not dead. Section 5 holds that the states with the worst histories of Jim Crow disenfranchisement from the middle part of the twentieth century remain, even today, under a cloud of suspicion that other states are not under, a cloud that can be lifted only through a formal judicial bailout process. Section 5 thus places the Southern states under a regime of regional federal oversight that is a faint echo, especially in its geographic outline, of Reconstruction itself. The chief indignity of this regime, for the Southern states, is its implication, which Chief Justice Roberts so forthrightly brought to the surface at oral argument: "General," he asked, "is it the government's submission that the citizens in the South are more racist than citizens in the North?"
>
> A historical memory of a "War Between the States," followed by a reunion between noble blue and gray on equal terms—with Reconstruction a best-forgotten corrupt interregnum in between—might well yield the conclusion that antebellum understandings of state sovereignty remain largely intact, even today. However, such a conclusion cannot be sustained if we instead remember the Civil War and Reconstruction as a radical transformation of the South through federal military and civilian power, with a series of amendments specifically ratifying the use of that federal power to establish the equal citizenship of Southern blacks.
>
> The latter story is not as kind to the Southern states. It is not as protective of their dignity. To remember what actually happened between 1861 and 1870 is to remember a shattered nation reconstructed on new

foundations, where the terms of readmission of the conquered South were based, fundamentally, not on principles of equal sovereignty, but on military conquest, surrender, and occupation. It is to remember a series of amendments that remade the Constitution, shifting weighty new powers to the federal government, above all in the enforcement of the rights of racial minorities. . . . Those states alone were forced to adopt the Fourteenth Amendment as a condition of readmission, remaking the constitutional order on new terms far less amenable to claims of either the sovereign dignity or the equality of the Southern states.

Joseph Fishkin, *The Dignity of the South*, 123 YALE L.J. ONLINE 175 (2013).

For a qualified defense of the Court's equal sovereignty analysis, see Thomas B. Colby, *In Defense of the Equal Sovereignty Principle*, 65 DUKE L.J. 1087 (2016).

Congressional Incentives. How does the ruling in *Shelby County* affect congressional incentives to manage civil rights legislation? Ordinarily, obsolete statutes that were constitutional when enacted remain valid, and courts have no authority later on to strike them down just because they have become obsolete. For example, in *Walters v. National Association of Radiation Survivors*, 473 U.S. 305 (1985), the Court sustained a Civil War–era statute limiting to ten dollars the fee a veteran could pay to an attorney to represent him in an action seeking veterans' benefits for service-related injuries. The plaintiff argued that the passage of time had made the fee limitation so low as to violate due process. The Court rejected the argument, declining the implicit invitation to engage in judicial updating of statutory law. The prominent legal scholar Guido Calabresi shocked the establishment by arguing in a 1982 book that courts should update statutes in common law fashion, GUIDO CALABRESI, A COMMON LAW FOR THE AGE OF STATUTES (1982), a position that has gained no traction in the more than 40 years since its publication.

Congress reconsidered the Voting Rights Act in 2006 only because the original legislation contained a sunset provision — an approach usually deemed to be consistent with sound legislative practice. Yet if Congress had not provided for sunset, and the Court's decision in *South Carolina v. Katzenbach* upholding the VRA had been the last word on its constitutionality, Sections 4 and 5 would still be standing. Does the Court's ruling in *Shelby County* punish Congress for engaging in sound legislative practices? Does it furnish Congress with the perverse incentive to avoid sunset provisions in civil rights legislation out of fear that some future Supreme Court populated with different judges might someday come to different conclusions about an act's constitutionality than the present Court?

>> **State Responses to Shelby County.** Did the Court's ruling in *Shelby County* influence the behavior of formerly covered jurisdictions? The available evidence suggests strongly that it did. Several previously covered states and localities made significant changes to their voting laws that the Justice Department might well have blocked under an active Section 5, or at the least would have given significant scrutiny.

Alabama enacted a law requiring voters to present photo identification when they show up to vote at the polls or by absentee ballot. Though the law was passed two years before the Court decided *Shelby County*, which coincidentally or not arose out of Alabama, the state decided not to implement the law while it was litigating the *Shelby County* case. The day after the Court announced its decision in *Shelby County*, Alabama declared that it would be enforcing its voter identification law.

North Carolina amended its voting laws immediately following the Court's ruling in *Shelby County*. Prior to the Court's decision in *Shelby County*, the state of North Carolina was contemplating very modest changes to its voting laws. Following the Court's decision, the state made significant changes to its voting laws. These changes included implementing a fairly strict photo voter identification requirement, eliminating same-day registration, curtailing the number of days for early voting, eliminating pre-registration for 17-year-olds, and rescinding the provision that allowed voters to cast a provisional ballot when they voted in the wrong polling station.

Texas also responded to the Court's decision in *Shelby County* by passing a strict photo identification law. The law was previously blocked by a federal court, which concluded that it was discriminatory.

In other areas, states and localities reduced the number of polling places serving populations of color; initiated purges of voter rolls; and enacted voter ID requirements. *See Democracy Diminished: State and Local Threats to Voting Post*-Shelby County, Alabama v. Holder (NAACP Legal Defense Fund 2016). During this period, lower courts in North Carolina, Texas, and Virginia made factual findings after full trials that the legislatures of these states intentionally discriminated on the basis of race in the process of drawing new legislative district maps. Such cases have begun to filter up to the Supreme Court, which, although it has taken a critical eye toward such findings, has nevertheless upheld several of them. *See North Carolina v. Covington*, 585 U.S. __ (2018) (affirming lower court finding that race was the predominant factor in North Carolina districts); *Abbott v. Perez*, 585 U.S. ___ (2018) (upholding one such finding while invalidating numerous others).

These highly visible and significant changes post–*Shelby County* by states that were previously subject to the coverage formula fueled the fears of the Act's supporters that previously covered states and localities were reverting back to their discriminatory behavior. Proponents of these changes of course denied that they were racially discriminatory. They defended the voting changes on the ground that the changes were necessary to protect the integrity of the voting process and minimize voting fraud; to reduce costs and duplicative services; and in some cases some lawmakers defended their state's voting changes on partisan grounds. Do you view these changes as evidence that Sections 4 and 5 of the VRA are still needed?

▶▶ *What Now?* Is there a remedy for the defects the Court identified? Can Congress amend the Section 4 coverage formula to satisfy the Court? If so, what kind of formula would suffice? Legal commentators have offered a plethora of options. For example, Professor Ellen Katz and her students have suggested using past violations of Section 2 of the VRA as the basis for a new coverage formula. *See* Ellen D. Katz et al., *Documenting Discrimination in Voting: Judicial Findings Under Section 2 of the Voting Rights Act Since 1982*, 39 U. MICH. J.L. REFORM 643 (2007). *See also*, Morgan Kousser, *Gutting the Landmark Civil Rights Legislation*, Reuters, EverythingNews (Jun. 26, 2013). Professor Kousser notes that outcomes of Section 2 lawsuits can be used to craft a new formula. Professor Spencer Overton has also endorsed a

similar idea. Spencer Overton, *How to Update the Voting Rights Act*, http://www.huf
fingtonpost.com/spencer-overton/how-to-update-the-voting_b_3497350.html. *But
see*, Adam B. Cox and Thomas J. Miles, *Documenting Discrimination?*, 108 COLUM.
L. REV. SIDEBAR 31 (2008) (arguing that cases that go to court are not representative of the universe of voting rights cases, and that one therefore cannot draw
reliable inferences about the prevalence of discrimination in one jurisdiction as
against another.). Professors Christopher Elmendorf and Douglas Spencer propose
"a new, legally defensible coverage approach based on between-state differences in
the proportion of voting age citizens who subscribe to negative stereotypes about
racial minorities and vote accordingly." Christopher Elmendorf and Douglas Spencer, *The Geography of Racial Stereotyping: Evidence and Implications for VRA Preclearance
After* Shelby County, 102 CAL. L. REV. 1123 (2014).

Academics are not the only ones wrestling with a *Shelby County* fix. There have
been many proposals in Congress to respond to *Shelby County*. The latest and most
significant one is the John Lewis Voting Rights Advancement Act of 2021, which
was passed by the House of Representatives on August 24, 2021, on partisan lines.
Every Democrat voted for the bill and every Republican, save one, voted against
it. Among its provisions, the Act would require preclearance for: (a) any state that
had 15 or more voting rights violations in the past ten years; (b) any state that
committed ten or more voting rights violations in the past 25 years if one of the
violations was committed by the state itself, as opposed to a subdivision within the
state; (c) any subdivision of the state that committed three or more voting rights
violations within the past twenty-five years. The Act defined voting rights violations
as court decisions, including injunctions, concluding that the state or jurisdiction violated the Fourteenth or Fifteenth Amendments by abridging or denying
the right to vote on the basis of race; court decisions finding that the state or one
of its subdivisions violated the VRA as amended by the John Lewis Voting Rights
Advancement Act; objections by the Attorney General under the VRA as amended;
and consent decrees between the government and a jurisdiction in which the jurisdiction admitted to violating voting rights laws and the constitutional provisions
against racial discrimination in voting. According to Benjamin Barber of the Institute for Southern Studies, the bill would have covered the states of Alabama, California, Georgia, Louisiana, Mississippi, New York, North Carolina, South Carolina,
Texas, and Virginia. https://www.facingsouth.org/2019/03/states-facing-federal-
preclearance-under-proposed-voting-rights-act-fix. The bill also would have
required more states to preclear in comparison to the preclearance regime in place
before *Shelby County*. For a full text of the bill, see https://www.congress.gov/bill/
117th-congress/house-bill/4/text. Is the John Lewis Voting Rights Advancement
Act constitutional? How do you think it would fare given what you know about the
voting rights jurisprudence of the Roberts Court?

Even though the Democratic Party controlled both houses of Congress and the
White House, the bill died in the Senate on November 3, 2021. The Democrats did
not have enough votes to overcome a filibuster. The Democrats tried again on January 19, 2022. This time, they merged the bill with a more comprehensive election
law, the Freedom to Vote Act. Once again, the attempt was unsuccessful. Democratic
Senators Joe Manchin of West Virginia and Kyrsten Sinema of Arizona blocked their
party's efforts to create an exception to the filibuster for voting rights legislation.

What can we conclude from Congress' failure to amend the VRA in response to *Shelby County*? Notwithstanding proposals by academics, activists, and legislators, there has been no significant legislative action on fixing the VRA after the Court's *Shelby County* decision. What accounts for this lack of legislative activity a few years removed from *Shelby County*? Professors Guy-Uriel Charles and Luis Fuentes-Rohwer have argued that voting rights law and policy are unlikely to change substantially in a post-*Shelby County* world unless there is new consensus about the importance of voting as a fundamental right. They maintain that the VRA was the product of a social movement, the civil rights movement, which made the case to the nation that racial discrimination in voting was the central problem of American democracy. Today, Americans disagree fundamentally about what ails American democracy, if anything. The authors argue that voting rights policy has now become ideological and partisan and that change in this area can come about only if there is a new consensus to replace one ideological view over a rival view. *See* Guy-Uriel E. Charles and Luis Fuentes-Rohwer, *Voting Rights Law and Policy in Transition*, 127 HARV. L. REV. F. 243 (2014).

D. SECTION 2

As we have seen, Section 5 of the VRA applies only to covered jurisdictions. Section 2, in contrast, contains no such limitation: its proscription of racial discrimination in voting extends to all jurisdictions, regardless of their voting rights history and regardless of their status under Section 5. The materials in this section explore the meaning and administration of Section 2 of the Act.

———————————

The Fifteenth Amendment provides that the right to vote "shall not be denied or abridged by the United States or by any State on account of race [or] color. . . ." In *Mobile v. Bolden*, 446 U.S. 55 (1980) (see Chapter 4), the Court held that the Fifteenth Amendment bars only intentional discrimination in voting. As originally enacted in 1965, Section 2 of the Voting Rights Act closely tracked the language of the Fifteenth Amendment: "No voting qualification or prerequisite to voting, or standard, practice or procedure, shall be imposed or applied by any State or political subdivision to deny or abridge the right of any citizen of the United States to vote on account of race or color." The question thus arose whether Section 2, like the Fifteenth Amendment, also barred only intentional racial discrimination, or whether its protection of voting rights extended to unintentionally created disparate impacts.

The Court addressed this issue in *Bolden*:

> [I]t is apparent that the language of §2 no more than elaborates upon that of the Fifteenth Amendment, and the sparse legislative history of §2 makes clear that it was intended to have an effect no different from that of the Fifteenth Amendment.

Section 2 was an uncontroversial provision in proposed legislation whose other provisions engendered protracted dispute. The House Report on the bill simply recited that §2 "grants . . . a right to be free from enactment or enforcement of voting qualifications . . . or practices which deny or abridge the right to vote on account of race or color." H.R. Rep. No. 439, 89th Cong., 1st Sess., 23 (1965). The view that this section simply restated the prohibitions already contained in the Fifteenth Amendment was expressed without contradiction during the Senate hearings. Senator Dirksen indicated at one point . . . [that §2 was] "almost a rephrasing of the 15th [A]mendment." Attorney General Katzenbach agreed.

In view of the section's language and its sparse but clear legislative history, it is evident that this statutory provision adds nothing to the appellees' Fifteenth Amendment claim.

446 U.S. at 60-61.

Two years after the Court's decision in *Bolden*, Congress amended Section 2 for the express purpose of overruling the Court's interpretation of the 1965 language. The key change to Section 2 was the addition of the following language: "No voting qualification or prerequisite to voting or standard, practice, or procedure shall be imposed or applied by any State *in a manner which results in* a denial or abridgment of the right of any citizen of the United States to vote on account of race or color. . . ." In the following case, the Court interpreted this new, so-called results test for the first time. *Gingles* is the analogue to *Katzenbach*. Though *Katzenbach* is a constitutional case and *Gingles* is a statutory case interpreting section 2 of the Act, both cases represent the highwater mark of judicial cooperation and deference to Congress in their respective areas. As you will see below, a majority of the Court, against sharp dissents, attempts valiantly to give meaning to and to operationalize Congress's command that a state cannot abridge the right of any citizen to vote on account of race. Section 2 prohibits both the denial of the right to vote based upon race and the dilution of the right to vote based upon race. *Gingles* is a vote dilution case.

Thornburg v. Gingles

478 U.S. 30 (1986)

Justice BRENNAN announced the judgment of the Court and delivered the opinion of the Court with respect to Parts I, II, III-A, III-B, IV-A, and V, an opinion with respect to Part III-C, in which Justice MARSHALL, Justice BLACKMUN, and Justice STEVENS join, and an opinion with respect to Part IV-B, in which Justice WHITE joins.

This case requires that we construe for the first time §2 of the Voting Rights Act of 1965, as amended June 29, 1982. 42 U.S.C. §1973. The specific question to be decided is whether the three-judge District Court, convened in the Eastern District of North Carolina pursuant to 28 U.S.C. §2284(a) and 42 U.S.C. §1973c, correctly held that the use in a legislative redistricting plan of multimember districts in five North Carolina legislative districts violated §2 by impairing the opportunity of black voters "to participate in the political process and to elect representatives of their choice." §2(b), 96 Stat. 134.

I. BACKGROUND

In April 1982, the North Carolina General Assembly enacted a legislative redistricting plan for the State's Senate and House of Representatives. Appellees, black citizens of North Carolina who are registered to vote, challenged seven districts, one single-member and six multimember districts, alleging that the redistricting scheme impaired black citizens' ability to elect representatives of their choice in violation of §2 of the Voting Rights Act.

After appellees brought suit, but before trial, Congress amended §2. The amendment was largely a response to this Court's plurality opinion in *Mobile v. Bolden*, 446 U.S. 55 (1980), which had declared that, in order to establish a violation either of §2 or of the Fourteenth or Fifteenth Amendments, minority voters must prove that a contested electoral mechanism was intentionally adopted or maintained by state officials for a discriminatory purpose. Congress substantially revised §2 to make clear that a violation could be proved by showing discriminatory effect alone and to establish as the relevant legal standard the "results test," applied by this Court in *White v. Regester*, 412 U.S. 755 (1973), and by other federal courts before *Bolden, supra.* S. Rep. No. 97-417, p. 28 (1982) (hereinafter S. Rep.).

Section 2, as amended, reads as follows:

> (a) No voting qualification or prerequisite to voting or standard, practice, or procedure shall be imposed or applied by any State or political subdivision in a manner which results in a denial or abridgement of the right of any citizen of the United States to vote on account of race or color, or in contravention of the guarantees set forth in section 4(f)(2), as provided in subsection (b).
>
> (b) A violation of subsection (a) is established if, based on the totality of circumstances, it is shown that the political processes leading to nomination or election in the State or political subdivision are not equally open to participation by members of a class of citizens protected by subsection (a) in that its members have less opportunity than other members of the electorate to participate in the political process and to elect representatives of their choice. The extent to which members of a protected class have been elected to office in the State or political subdivision is one circumstance which may be considered: *Provided*, That nothing in this section establishes a right to have members of a protected class elected in numbers equal to their proportion in the population.

Codified at 42 U.S.C. §1973.

The Senate Judiciary Committee majority Report accompanying the bill that amended §2 elaborates on the circumstances that might be probative of a §2 violation, noting the following "typical factors":

1. the extent of any history of official discrimination in the state or political subdivision that touched the right of the members of the minority group to register, to vote, or otherwise to participate in the democratic process;

2. the extent to which voting in the elections of the state or political subdivision is racially polarized;

3. the extent to which the state or political subdivision has used unusually large election districts, majority vote requirements, anti-single shot provisions, or other voting practices or procedures that may enhance the opportunity for discrimination against the minority group;

4. if there is a candidate slating process, whether the members of the minority group have been denied access to that process;

5. the extent to which members of the minority group in the state or political subdivision bear the effects of discrimination in such areas as education, employment and health, which hinder their ability to participate effectively in the political process;

6. whether political campaigns have been characterized by overt or subtle racial appeals;

7. the extent to which members of the minority group have been elected to public office in the jurisdiction.

Additional factors that in some cases have had probative value as part of plaintiffs' evidence to establish a violation are:

whether there is a significant lack of responsiveness on the part of elected officials to the particularized needs of the members of the minority group.

whether the policy underlying the state or political subdivision's use of such voting qualification, prerequisite to voting, or standard, practice or procedure is tenuous.

S. Rep., at 28-29.

The District Court applied the "totality of the circumstances" test set forth in §2(b) to appellees' statutory claim, and, relying principally on the factors outlined in the Senate Report, held that the redistricting scheme violated §2 because it resulted in the dilution of black citizens' votes in all seven disputed districts. In light of this conclusion, the court did not reach appellees' constitutional claims.

Preliminarily, the court found that black citizens constituted a distinct population and registered-voter minority in each challenged district. The court noted that at the time the multimember districts were created, there were concentrations of black citizens within the boundaries of each that were sufficiently large and contiguous to constitute effective voting majorities in single-member districts lying wholly within the boundaries of the multimember districts. . . .

The District Court then proceeded to find that the following circumstances combined with the multimember districting scheme to result in the dilution of black citizens' votes.

First, the court found that North Carolina had officially discriminated against its black citizens with respect to their exercise of the voting franchise from approximately 1900 to 1970 by employing at different times a poll tax, a literacy test, a prohibition against bullet (single-shot) voting,[5] and designated seat plans[6] for multimember districts. The court observed that even after the removal of direct barriers to black voter registration, such as the poll tax and literacy test, black voter registration remained relatively depressed; in 1982 only 52.7% of age-qualified blacks statewide were registered to vote, whereas 66.7% of whites were registered. The District Court found these statewide depressed levels of black voter registration to be present in all of the disputed districts and to be traceable, at least in part, to the historical pattern of statewide official discrimination.

Second, the court found that historic discrimination in education, housing, employment, and health services had resulted in a lower socioeconomic status for North Carolina blacks as a group than for whites. The court concluded that this lower status both gives rise to special group interests and hinders blacks' ability to participate effectively in the political process and to elect representatives of their choice.

Third, the court considered other voting procedures that may operate to lessen the opportunity of black voters to elect candidates of their choice. It noted that North Carolina has a majority vote requirement for primary elections and, while acknowledging that no black candidate for election to the State General Assembly had failed to win solely because of this requirement, the court concluded that it nonetheless presents a continuing practical impediment to the opportunity of black voting minorities to elect candidates of their choice. . . .

Fourth, the court found that white candidates in North Carolina have encouraged voting along color lines by appealing to racial prejudice. It noted that the record is replete with specific examples of racial appeals, ranging in style from overt and blatant to subtle and furtive, and in date from the 1890's to the 1984 campaign for a seat in the United States Senate. The court determined that the use of racial appeals in political campaigns in North Carolina persists to the present day and that its current effect is to lessen to some degree the opportunity of black citizens to participate effectively in the political processes and to elect candidates of their choice.

Fifth, the court examined the extent to which blacks have been elected to office in North Carolina, both statewide and in the challenged districts. It found, among other things, that prior to World War II, only one black had been elected to public

---

5. Bullet (single-shot) voting has been described as follows: " 'Consider [a] town of 600 whites and 400 blacks with an at-large election to choose four council members. Each voter is able to cast four votes. Suppose there are eight white candidates, with the votes of the whites split among them approximately equally, and one black candidate, with all the blacks voting for him and no one else. The result is that each white candidate receives about 300 votes and the black candidate receives 400 votes. The black has probably won a seat. This technique is called single-shot voting. Single-shot voting enables a minority group to win some at-large seats if it concentrates its vote behind a limited number of candidates and if the vote of the majority is divided among a number of candidates.' " *City of Rome v. United States*, 446 U.S. 156, 184, n.19 (1980), quoting United States Commission on Civil Rights, The Voting Rights Act: Ten Years After, pp. 206-207 (1975).

6. Designated (or numbered) seat schemes require a candidate for election in multimember districts to run for specific seats, and can, under certain circumstances, frustrate bullet voting. See, *e.g., City of Rome, supra*, at 185, n.21.

office in this century. While recognizing that "it has now become possible for black citizens to be elected to office at all levels of state government in North Carolina," 590 F. Supp., at 367, the court found that, in comparison to white candidates running for the same office, black candidates are at a disadvantage in terms of relative probability of success. It also found that the overall rate of black electoral success has been minimal in relation to the percentage of blacks in the total state population. For example, the court noted, from 1971 to 1982 there were at any given time only two-to-four blacks in the 120-member House of Representatives—that is, only 1.6% to 3.3% of House members were black. From 1975 to 1983 there were at any one time only one or two blacks in the 50-member State Senate—that is, only 2% to 4% of State Senators were black. By contrast, at the time of the District Court's opinion, blacks constituted about 22.4% of the total state population. . . .

The court did acknowledge the improved success of black candidates in the 1982 elections, in which 11 blacks were elected to the State House of Representatives, including 5 blacks from the multimember districts at issue here. However, the court pointed out that the 1982 election was conducted after the commencement of this litigation. The court found the circumstances of the 1982 election sufficiently aberrational and the success by black candidates too minimal and too recent in relation to the long history of complete denial of elective opportunities to support the conclusion that black voters' opportunities to elect representatives of their choice were not impaired.

Finally, the court considered the extent to which voting in the challenged districts was racially polarized. Based on statistical evidence presented by expert witnesses, supplemented to some degree by the testimony of lay witnesses, the court found that all of the challenged districts exhibit severe and persistent racially polarized voting.

Based on these findings, the court declared the contested portions of the 1982 redistricting plan violative of §2 and enjoined appellants from conducting elections pursuant to those portions of the plan. . . .

II. SECTION 2 AND VOTE DILUTION THROUGH USE OF MULTIMEMBER DISTRICTS

An understanding both of §2 and of the way in which multimember districts can operate to impair blacks' ability to elect representatives of their choice is prerequisite to an evaluation of appellants' contentions. First, then, we review amended §2 and its legislative history in some detail. Second, we explain the theoretical basis for appellees' claim of vote dilution.

A. Section 2 and Its Legislative History

Subsection 2(a) prohibits all States and political subdivisions from imposing *any* voting qualifications or prerequisites to voting, or any standards, practices, or procedures which result in the denial or abridgment of the right to vote of any citizen who is a member of a protected class of racial and language minorities. . . .

The Senate Report which accompanied the 1982 amendments elaborates on the nature of §2 violations and on the proof required to establish these violations. First and foremost, the Report dispositively rejects the position of the plurality in *Mobile v. Bolden*, 446 U.S. 55 (1980), which required proof that the contested electoral practice or mechanism was adopted or maintained with the intent to discriminate against minority voters.[7] See, *e.g.*, S. Rep., at 2, 15-16, 27. The intent test was repudiated for three principal reasons—it is "unnecessarily divisive because it involves charges of racism on the part of individual officials or entire communities," it places an "inordinately difficult" burden of proof on plaintiffs, and it "asks the wrong question." *Id.*, at 36. The "right" question, as the Report emphasizes repeatedly, is whether "as a result of the challenged practice or structure plaintiffs do not have an equal opportunity to participate in the political processes and to elect candidates of their choice." *Id.*, at 28.

In order to answer this question, a court must assess the impact of the contested structure or practice on minority electoral opportunities "on the basis of objective factors." *Id.*, at 27. The Senate Report specifies factors which typically may be relevant to a §2 claim: [these factors are set out in the previous section of the opinion]. The Report stresses, however, that this list of typical factors is neither comprehensive nor exclusive. While the enumerated factors will often be pertinent to certain types of §2 violations, particularly to vote dilution claims, other factors may also be relevant and may be considered. *Id.*, at 29-30. Furthermore, the Senate Committee observed that "there is no requirement that any particular number of factors be proved, or that a majority of them point one way or the other." *Id.*, at 29. Rather, the Committee determined that "the question whether the political processes are 'equally open' depends upon a searching practical evaluation of the 'past and present reality,' " *id.*, at 30 (footnote omitted), and on a "functional" view of the political process. *Id.*, at 30, n.120.

Although the Senate Report espouses a flexible, fact-intensive test for §2 violations, it limits the circumstances under which §2 violations may be proved in three ways. First, electoral devices, such as at-large elections, may not be considered *per se* violative of §2. Plaintiffs must demonstrate that, under the totality of the circumstances, the devices result in unequal access to the electoral process. *Id.*, at 16. Second, the conjunction of an allegedly dilutive electoral mechanism and the lack of proportional representation alone does not establish a violation. *Ibid.* Third, the results test does not assume the existence of racial bloc voting; plaintiffs must prove it. *Id.*, at 33.

B. Vote Dilution Through the Use of Multimember Districts

Appellees contend that the legislative decision to employ multimember, rather than single-member, districts in the contested jurisdictions dilutes their

---

7. The Senate Report states that amended §2 was designed to restore the "results test"—the legal standard that governed voting discrimination cases prior to our decision in *Mobile v. Bolden*, 446 U.S. 55 (1980). S. Rep., at 15-16. The Report notes that in pre-*Bolden* cases such as *White v. Regester*, 412 U.S. 755 (1973), and *Zimmer v. McKeithen*, 485 F.2d 1297 (CA5 1973), plaintiffs could prevail by showing that, under the totality of the circumstances, a challenged election law or procedure had the effect of denying a protected minority an equal chance to participate in the electoral process. Under the "results test," plaintiffs are not required to demonstrate that the challenged electoral law or structure was designed or maintained for a discriminatory purpose. S. Rep., at 16.

votes by submerging them in a white majority,[11] thus impairing their ability to elect representatives of their choice.[12] We note also that we have no occasion to consider whether the standards we apply to respondents' claim that multimember districts operate to dilute the vote of geographically cohesive minority groups that are large enough to constitute majorities in single-member districts and that are contained within the boundaries of the challenged multimember districts, are fully pertinent to other sorts of vote dilution claims, such as a claim alleging that the splitting of a large and geographically cohesive minority between two or more multimember or single-member districts resulted in the dilution of the minority vote.

The essence of a §2 claim is that a certain electoral law, practice, or structure interacts with social and historical conditions to cause an inequality in the opportunities enjoyed by black and white voters to elect their preferred representatives. This Court has long recognized that multimember districts and at-large voting schemes may " 'operate to minimize or cancel out the voting strength of racial [minorities in] the voting population.' " The theoretical basis for this type of impairment is that where minority and majority voters consistently prefer different candidates, the majority, by virtue of its numerical superiority, will regularly defeat the choices of minority voters. . . .

While many or all of the factors listed in the Senate Report may be relevant to a claim of vote dilution through submergence in multimember districts, unless there is a conjunction of the following circumstances, the use of multimember districts generally will not impede the ability of minority voters to elect representatives of their choice.[15]

---

11. Dilution of racial minority group voting strength may be caused by the dispersal of blacks into districts in which they constitute an ineffective minority of voters or from the concentration of blacks into districts where they constitute an excessive majority.

12. The claim we address in this opinion is one in which the plaintiffs alleged and attempted to prove that their ability *to elect* the representatives of their choice was impaired by the selection of a multimember electoral structure. We have no occasion to consider whether §2 permits, and if it does, what standards should pertain to, a claim brought by a minority group, that is not sufficiently large and compact to constitute a majority in a single-member district, alleging that the use of a multimember district impairs its ability to *influence* elections.

15. Under a "functional" view of the political process mandated by §2, S. Rep., at 30, n.120, the most important Senate Report factors bearing on §2 challenges to multimember districts are the "extent to which minority group members have been elected to public office in the jurisdiction" and the "extent to which voting in the elections of the state or political subdivision is racially polarized." *Id.*, 28-29. If present, the other factors, such as the lingering effects of past discrimination, the use of appeals to racial bias in election campaigns, and the use of electoral devices which enhance the dilutive effects of multimember districts when substantial white bloc voting exists—for example antibullet voting laws and majority vote requirements, are supportive of, but not essential to, a minority voter's claim.

In recognizing that some Senate Report factors are more important to multimember district vote dilution claims than others, the Court effectuates the intent of Congress. It is obvious that unless minority group members experience substantial difficulty electing representatives of their choice, they cannot prove that a challenged electoral mechanism impairs their ability "to elect." §2(b). And, where the contested electoral structure is a multimember district, commentators and courts agree that in the absence of significant white bloc voting

Consequently, if difficulty in electing and white bloc voting are not proved, minority voters have not established that the multimember structure interferes with their ability to elect their preferred candidates. Minority voters may be able to prove that they still suffer social and economic effects of past discrimination, that appeals to racial bias are employed in election campaigns, and that a majority vote is required to win a seat, but they have not demonstrated a substantial inability to elect caused by the use of a multimember district. Stated succinctly, a bloc voting majority must *usually* be able to defeat candidates supported by a politically cohesive, geographically insular minority group.

. . . These circumstances are necessary preconditions for multimember districts to operate to impair minority voters' ability to elect representatives of their choice for the following reasons. First, the minority group must be able to demonstrate that it is sufficiently large and geographically compact to constitute a majority in a single-member district. If it is not, as would be the case in a substantially integrated district, the *multimember form* of the district cannot be responsible for minority voters' inability to elect its candidates.[17]

Second, the minority group must be able to show that it is politically cohesive. If the minority group is not politically cohesive, it cannot be said that the selection of a multimember electoral structure thwarts distinctive minority group interests. Third, the minority must be able to demonstrate that the white majority votes sufficiently as a bloc to enable it—in the absence of special circumstances, such as the minority candidate running unopposed—usually to defeat the minority's preferred candidate. In establishing this last circumstance, the minority group demonstrates that submergence in a white multimember district impedes its ability to elect its chosen representatives.

---

it cannot be said that the ability of minority voters to elect their chosen representatives is inferior to that of white voters.

17. The reason that a minority group making such a challenge must show, as a threshold matter, that it is sufficiently large and geographically compact to constitute a majority in a single-member district is this: Unless minority voters possess the *potential* to elect representatives in the absence of the challenged structure or practice, they cannot claim to have been injured by that structure or practice. The single-member district is generally the appropriate standard against which to measure minority group potential to elect because it is the smallest political unit from which representatives are elected. Thus, if the minority group is spread evenly throughout a multimember district, or if, although geographically compact, the minority group is so small in relation to the surrounding white population that it could not constitute a majority in a single-member district, these minority voters cannot maintain that they would have been able to elect representatives of their choice in the absence of the multimember electoral structure. As two commentators have explained:

> To demonstrate [that minority voters are injured by at-large elections], the minority voters must be sufficiently concentrated and politically cohesive that a putative districting plan would result in districts in which members of a racial minority would constitute a majority of the voters, whose clear electoral choices are in fact defeated by at-large voting. If minority voters' residences are substantially integrated throughout the jurisdiction, the at-large district cannot be blamed for the defeat of minority-supported candidates. . . . [This standard] thus would only protect racial minority votes from diminution proximately caused by the districting plan; *it would not assure racial minorities proportional representation.*

Blacksher & Menefee 55-56 (footnotes omitted; emphasis added).

Finally, we observe that the usual predictability of the majority's success distinguishes structural dilution from the mere loss of an occasional election.

III. RACIALLY POLARIZED VOTING

Having stated the general legal principles relevant to claims that §2 has been violated through the use of multimember districts, we turn to the arguments of appellants and of the United States as *amicus curiae* addressing racially polarized voting. . . .

A. The District Court's Treatment of Racially Polarized Voting

The investigation conducted by the District Court into the question of racial bloc voting credited some testimony of lay witnesses, but relied principally on statistical evidence presented by appellees' expert witnesses, in particular that offered by Dr. Bernard Grofman. Dr. Grofman collected and evaluated data from 53 General Assembly primary and general elections involving black candidacies. These elections were held over a period of three different election years in the six originally challenged multimember districts. Dr. Grofman subjected the data to two complementary methods of analysis—extreme case analysis and bivariate ecological regression analysis—in order to determine whether blacks and whites in these districts differed in their voting behavior. These analytic techniques yielded data concerning the voting patterns of the two races, including estimates of the percentages of members of each race who voted for black candidates.

. . . The District Court found that blacks and whites generally preferred different candidates and, on that basis, found voting in the districts to be racially correlated. The court accepted Dr. Grofman's expert opinion that the correlation between the race of the voter and the voter's choice of certain candidates was statistically significant. Finally, adopting Dr. Grofman's terminology, see Tr. 195, the court found that in all but 2 of the 53 elections the degree of racial bloc voting was "so marked as to be substantively significant, in the sense that the results of the individual election would have been different depending upon whether it had been held among only the white voters or only the black voters." 590 F. Supp., at 368.

The court also reported its findings . . . that a high percentage of black voters regularly supported black candidates and that most white voters were extremely reluctant to vote for black candidates. The court then considered the relevance to the existence of legally significant white bloc voting of the fact that black candidates have won some elections. It determined that in most instances, special circumstances, such as incumbency and lack of opposition, rather than a diminution in usually severe white bloc voting, accounted for these candidates' success. The court also suggested that black voters' reliance on bullet voting was a significant factor in their successful efforts to elect candidates of their choice. Based on all of the evidence before it, the trial court concluded that each of the districts experienced racially polarized voting "in a persistent and severe degree." *Id.*, at 367.

B. The Degree of Bloc Voting That Is Legally Significant Under §2

2. The Standard for Legally Significant Racial Bloc Voting

The Senate Report states that the "extent to which voting in the elections of the state or political subdivision is racially polarized," S. Rep., at 29, is relevant to a vote dilution claim. Further, courts and commentators agree that racial bloc voting is a key element of a vote dilution claim. . . . Because, as we explain below, the extent of bloc voting necessary to demonstrate that a minority's ability to elect its preferred representatives is impaired varies according to several factual circumstances, the degree of bloc voting which constitutes the threshold of legal significance will vary from district to district. Nonetheless, it is possible to state some general principles and we proceed to do so.

The purpose of inquiring into the existence of racially polarized voting is twofold: to ascertain whether minority group members constitute a politically cohesive unit and to determine whether whites vote sufficiently as a bloc usually to defeat the minority's preferred candidates. Thus, the question whether a given district experiences legally significant racially polarized voting requires discrete inquiries into minority and white voting practices. A showing that a significant number of minority group members usually vote for the same candidates is one way of proving the political cohesiveness necessary to a vote dilution claim, Blacksher & Menefee 59-60, and n.344, and, consequently, establishes minority bloc voting within the context of §2. And, in general, a white bloc vote that normally will defeat the combined strength of minority support plus white "crossover" votes rises to the level of legally significant white bloc voting. *Id.*, at 60. The amount of white bloc voting that can generally "minimize or cancel," S. Rep., at 28; *Regester*, 412 U.S., at 765, black voters' ability to elect representatives of their choice, however, will vary from district to district according to a number of factors, including the nature of the allegedly dilutive electoral mechanism; the presence or absence of other potentially dilutive electoral devices, such as majority vote requirements, designated posts, and prohibitions against bullet voting; the percentage of registered voters in the district who are members of the minority group; the size of the district; and, in multimember districts, the number of seats open and the number of candidates in the field. . . .

Because loss of political power through vote dilution is distinct from the mere inability to win a particular election, *Whitcomb*, 403 U.S., at 153, a pattern of racial bloc voting that extends over a period of time is more probative of a claim that a district experiences legally significant polarization than are the results of a single election. . . . Also for this reason, in a district where elections are shown usually to be polarized, the fact that racially polarized voting is not present in one or a few individual elections does not necessarily negate the conclusion that the district experiences legally significant bloc voting. Furthermore, the success of a minority candidate in a particular election does not necessarily prove that the district did not experience polarized voting in that election; special circumstances, such as the absence of an opponent, incumbency, or the utilization of bullet voting, may explain minority electoral success in a polarized contest.

3. Standard Utilized by the District Court

. . . While the court did not phrase the standard for legally significant racial bloc voting exactly as we do, a fair reading of the court's opinion reveals that the court's analysis conforms to our view of the proper legal standard.

The District Court's findings concerning black support for black candidates in the five multimember districts at issue here clearly establish the political cohesiveness of black voters. . . . In all but 5 of 16 primary elections, black support for black candidates ranged between 71% and 92%; and in the general elections, black support for black Democratic candidates ranged between 87% and 96%.

In sharp contrast to its findings of strong black support for black candidates, the District Court found that a substantial majority of white voters would rarely, if ever, vote for a black candidate. In the primary elections, white support for black candidates ranged between 8% and 50%, and in the general elections it ranged between 28% and 49%. The court also determined that, on average, 81.7% of white voters did not vote for any black candidate in the primary elections. In the general elections, white voters almost always ranked black candidates either last or next to last in the multicandidate field, except in heavily Democratic areas where white voters consistently ranked black candidates last among the Democrats, if not last or next to last among all candidates. The court further observed that approximately two-thirds of white voters did not vote for black candidates in general elections, even after the candidate had won the Democratic primary and the choice was to vote for a Republican or for no one.

While the District Court did not state expressly that the percentage of whites who refused to vote for black candidates in the contested districts would, in the usual course of events, result in the defeat of the minority's candidates, that conclusion is apparent both from the court's factual findings and from the rest of its analysis. . . .

We conclude that the District Court's approach, which tested data derived from three election years in each district, and which revealed that blacks strongly supported black candidates, while, to the black candidates' usual detriment, whites rarely did, satisfactorily addresses each facet of the proper legal standard.

C. Evidence of Racially Polarized Voting

1. Appellants' Argument

North Carolina and the United States also contest the evidence upon which the District Court relied in finding that voting patterns in the challenged districts were racially polarized. They argue that the term "racially polarized voting" must, as a matter of law, refer to voting patterns for which the *principal cause* is race. They contend that the District Court utilized a legally incorrect definition of racially polarized voting by relying on bivariate statistical analyses which merely demonstrated a *correlation* between the race of the voter and the level of voter support for certain candidates, but which did not prove that race was the primary determinant of voters' choices. . . .[31]

---

31. Appellants argue that plaintiffs must establish that race was the primary determinant of voter behavior as part of their prima facie showing of polarized voting; the United

2. Causation Irrelevant to Section 2 Inquiry

The first reason we reject appellants' argument that racially polarized voting refers to voting patterns that are in some way *caused by race*, rather than to voting patterns that are merely *correlated with the race of the voter*, is that the reasons black and white voters vote differently have no relevance to the central inquiry of §2. By contrast, the correlation between race of voter and the selection of certain candidates is crucial to that inquiry.

Both §2 itself and the Senate Report make clear that the critical question in a §2 claim is whether the use of a contested electoral practice or structure results in members of a protected group having less opportunity than other members of the electorate to participate in the political process and to elect representatives of their choice. . . . It is the *difference* between the choices made by blacks and whites—not the reasons for that difference—that results in blacks having less opportunity than whites to elect their preferred representatives. Consequently, we conclude that under the "results test" of §2, only the correlation between race of voter and selection of certain candidates, not the causes of the correlation, matters.

3. Race of Voter as Primary Determinant of Voter Behavior

Appellants and the United States contend that the legal concept of "racially polarized voting" refers not to voting patterns that are merely *correlated with the voter's race*, but to voting patterns that are *determined primarily by the voter's race*, rather than by the voter's other socioeconomic characteristics.

The first problem with this argument is that it ignores the fact that members of geographically insular racial and ethnic groups frequently share socioeconomic characteristics, such as income level, employment status, amount of education, housing and other living conditions, religion, language, and so forth. . . . Where such characteristics are shared, race or ethnic group not only denotes color or place of origin, it also functions as a shorthand notation for common social and economic characteristics. Appellants' definition of racially polarized voting is even more pernicious where shared characteristics are causally related to race or ethnicity. The opportunity to achieve high employment status and income, for example, is often influenced by the presence or absence of racial or ethnic discrimination. A definition of racially polarized voting which holds that black bloc voting does not exist when black voters' choice of certain candidates is most strongly influenced by the fact that the voters have low incomes and menial jobs—when the reason most of those voters have menial jobs and low incomes is attributable to past or present racial discrimination—runs counter to the Senate Report's instruction to conduct a searching and practical evaluation of past and present reality, S. Rep., at 30, and interferes with the purpose of the Voting Rights Act to eliminate the negative effects of past discrimination on the electoral opportunities of minorities. *Id.,* at 5, 40.

States suggests that plaintiffs make out a prima facie case merely by showing a correlation between race and the selection of certain candidates, but that defendants should be able to rebut by showing that factors other than race were the principal causes of voters' choices. We reject both arguments.

Furthermore, under appellants' theory of racially polarized voting, even uncontrovertible evidence that candidates strongly preferred by black voters are always defeated by a bloc voting white majority would be dismissed for failure to prove racial polarization whenever the black and white populations could be described in terms of other socioeconomic characteristics. . . .

4. Race of Candidate as Primary Determinant of Voter Behavior

North Carolina's and the United States' suggestion that racially polarized voting means that voters select or reject candidates *principally* on the basis of the *candidate's race* is also misplaced.

First, both the language of §2 and a functional understanding of the phenomenon of vote dilution mandate the conclusion that the race of the candidate *per se* is irrelevant to racial bloc voting analysis. Section 2(b) states that a violation is established if it can be shown that members of a protected minority group "have less opportunity than other members of the electorate to . . . elect representatives *of their choice.*" (Emphasis added.) Because both minority and majority voters often select members of their own race as their preferred representatives, it will frequently be the case that a black candidate is the choice of blacks, while a white candidate is the choice of whites. Indeed, the facts of this case illustrate that tendency—blacks preferred black candidates, whites preferred white candidates. Thus, as a matter of convenience, we and the District Court may refer to the preferred representative of black voters as the "black candidate" and to the preferred representative of white voters as the "white candidate." Nonetheless, the fact that race of voter and race of candidate is often correlated is not directly pertinent to a §2 inquiry. Under §2, it is the status of the candidate as the *chosen representative of a particular racial group*, not the race of the candidate, that is important. . . .

5. Racial Animosity as Primary Determinant of Voter Behavior

Finally, we reject the suggestion that racially polarized voting refers only to white bloc voting which is caused by white voters' *racial hostility* toward black candidates. To accept this theory would frustrate the goals Congress sought to achieve by repudiating the intent test of *Mobile v. Bolden*, and would prevent minority voters who have clearly been denied an opportunity to elect representatives of their choice from establishing a critical element of a vote dilution claim.

In amending §2, Congress rejected the requirement announced by this Court in *Bolden* that §2 plaintiffs must prove the discriminatory intent of state or local governments in adopting or maintaining the challenged electoral mechanism. . . .

The Senate Report states that one reason the Senate Committee abandoned the intent test was that "the Committee . . . heard persuasive testimony that the intent test is unnecessarily divisive because it involves charges of racism on the part of individual officials or entire communities." S. Rep., at 36. The Committee found the testimony of Dr. Arthur S. Flemming, Chairman of the United States Commission on Civil Rights, particularly persuasive. He testified:

> [Under an intent test] [litigators] representing excluded minorities will have to explore the motivations of individual council members, mayors, and other citizens. The question would be whether their decisions were

motivated by invidious racial considerations. Such inquiries can only be divisive, threatening to destroy any existing racial progress in a community. It is the intent test, not the results test, that would make it necessary to brand individuals as racist in order to obtain judicial relief. . . .

A second reason Congress rejected the old intent test was that in most cases it placed an "inordinately difficult burden" on §2 plaintiffs. The new intent test would be equally, if not more, burdensome. In order to prove that a *specific factor*—racial hostility—*determined* white voters' ballots, it would be necessary to demonstrate that other potentially relevant *causal factors*, such as socioeconomic characteristics and candidate expenditures, do not correlate better than racial animosity with white voting behavior. . . .

The final and most dispositive reason the Senate Report repudiated the old intent test was that it "asks the wrong question." S. Rep., at 36. Amended §2 asks instead "whether minorities have equal access to the process of electing their representatives." *Ibid.*

Focusing on the discriminatory intent of the voters, rather than the behavior of the voters, also asks the wrong question. All that matters under §2 and under a functional theory of vote dilution is voter behavior, not its explanations. . . .

6. Summary

In sum, we would hold that the legal concept of racially polarized voting, as it relates to claims of vote dilution, refers only to the existence of a correlation between the race of voters and the selection of certain candidates. Plaintiffs need not prove causation or intent in order to prove a prima facie case of racial bloc voting and defendants may not rebut that case with evidence of causation or intent.

IV. THE LEGAL SIGNIFICANCE OF SOME BLACK CANDIDATES' SUCCESS

A

North Carolina and the United States maintain that the District Court failed to accord the proper weight to the success of some black candidates in the challenged districts. Black residents of these districts, they point out, achieved improved representation in the 1982 General Assembly election. . . . Essentially, appellants and the United States contend that if a racial minority gains proportional or nearly proportional representation in a single election, that fact alone precludes, as a matter of law, finding a §2 violation.

Section 2(b) provides that "[the] extent to which members of a protected class have been elected to office . . . is one circumstance which may be considered." 42 U.S.C. §1973(b). The Senate Committee Report also identifies the extent to which minority candidates have succeeded as a pertinent factor. S. Rep., at 29. However, the Senate Report expressly states that "the election of a few minority candidates does not 'necessarily foreclose the possibility of dilution of the black vote,'" noting that if it did, "the possibility exists that the majority citizens might evade [§2] by manipulating the election of a 'safe' minority candidate." *Id.*, at 29, n.115. . . . Thus, the language of §2 and its legislative history plainly demonstrate that proof that some minority candidates have been elected does not foreclose a §2 claim. . . .

The District Court in this case carefully considered the totality of the circumstances and found that in each district racially polarized voting; the legacy of official discrimination in voting matters, education, housing, employment, and health services; and the persistence of campaign appeals to racial prejudice acted in concert with the multimember districting scheme to impair the ability of geographically insular and politically cohesive groups of black voters to participate equally in the political process and to elect candidates of their choice. It found that the success a few black candidates have enjoyed in these districts is too recent, too limited, and, with regard to the 1982 elections, perhaps too aberrational, to disprove its conclusion. . . . We cannot say that the District Court, composed of local judges who are well acquainted with the political realities of the State, clearly erred. . . .

Justice WHITE, concurring.

I join Parts I, II, III-A, III-B, IV-A, and V of the Court's opinion and agree with Justice Brennan's opinion as to Part IV-B. I disagree with Part III-C of Justice Brennan's opinion.

Justice Brennan states in Part III-C that the crucial factor in identifying polarized voting is the race of the voter and that the race of the candidate is irrelevant. Under this test, there is polarized voting if the majority of white voters vote for different candidates than the majority of the blacks, regardless of the race of the candidates. I do not agree. Suppose an eight-member multimember district that is 60% white and 40% black, the blacks being geographically located so that two safe black single-member districts could be drawn. Suppose further that there are six white and two black Democrats running against six white and two black Republicans. Under Justice Brennan's test, there would be polarized voting and a likely §2 violation if all the Republicans, including the two blacks, are elected, and 80% of the blacks in the predominantly black areas vote Democratic. I take it that there would also be a violation in a single-member district that is 60% black, but enough of the blacks vote with the whites to elect a black candidate who is not the choice of the majority of black voters. This is interest-group politics rather than a rule hedging against racial discrimination. I doubt that this is what Congress had in mind in amending §2 as it did. . . .

Justice O'CONNOR, with whom THE CHIEF JUSTICE, Justice POWELL, and Justice REHNQUIST join, concurring in the judgment.

I

In order to explain my disagreement with the Court's interpretation of §2, it is useful to illustrate the impact that alternative districting plans or types of districts typically have on the likelihood that a minority group will be able to elect candidates it prefers, and then to set out the critical elements of a vote dilution claim as they emerge in the Court's opinion.

Consider a town of 1,000 voters that is governed by a council of four representatives, in which 30% of the voters are black, and in which the black voters are concentrated in one section of the city and tend to vote as a bloc. It would be possible to draw four single-member districts, in one of which blacks would constitute an overwhelming majority. The black voters in this district would be assured of electing a representative of their choice, while any remaining black voters in the other districts would be submerged in large white majorities. This option would give the minority group roughly proportional representation.

Alternatively, it would usually be possible to draw four single-member districts in *two* of which black voters constituted much narrower majorities of about 60%. The black voters in these districts would often be able to elect the representative of their choice in each of these two districts, but if even 20% of the black voters supported the candidate favored by the white minority in those districts the candidates preferred by the majority of black voters might lose. This option would, depending on the circumstances of a particular election, sometimes give the minority group more than proportional representation, but would increase the risk that the group would not achieve even roughly proportional representation.

It would also usually be possible to draw four single-member districts in each of which black voters constituted a minority. In the extreme case, black voters would constitute 30% of the voters in each district. Unless approximately 30% of the white voters in this extreme case backed the minority candidate, black voters in such a district would be unable to elect the candidate of their choice in an election between only two candidates even if they unanimously supported him. This option would make it difficult for black voters to elect candidates of their choice even with significant white support, and all but impossible without such support.

Finally, it would be possible to elect all four representatives in a single at-large election in which each voter could vote for four candidates. Under this scheme, white voters could elect all the representatives even if black voters turned out in large numbers and voted for one and only one candidate. To illustrate, if only four white candidates ran, and each received approximately equal support from white voters, each would receive about 700 votes, whereas black voters could cast no more than 300 votes for any one candidate. If, on the other hand, eight white candidates ran, and white votes were distributed less evenly, so that the five least favored white candidates received fewer than 300 votes while three others received 400 or more, it would be feasible for blacks to elect one representative with 300 votes even without substantial white support. If even 25% of the white voters backed a particular minority candidate, and black voters voted only for that candidate, the candidate would receive a total of 475 votes, which would ensure victory unless white voters also concentrated their votes on four of the eight remaining candidates, so that each received the support of almost 70% of white voters. As these variations show, the at-large or multimember district has an inherent tendency to submerge the votes of the minority. The minority group's prospects for electoral success under such a district heavily depend on a variety of factors such as voter turnout, how many candidates run, how evenly white support is spread, how much white support is given to a candidate or candidates preferred by the minority group, and the extent to which minority voters engage in "bullet voting" (which occurs when voters refrain from casting all their votes to avoid the risk that by voting for their lower ranked choices they may give those candidates enough votes to defeat their higher ranked choices).

There is no difference in principle between the varying effects of the alternatives outlined above and the varying effects of alternative single-district plans and multimember districts. The type of districting selected and the way in which district lines are drawn can have a powerful effect on the likelihood that members of a geographically and politically cohesive minority group will be able to elect candidates of their choice.

Although §2 does not speak in terms of "vote dilution," I agree with the Court that proof of vote dilution can establish a violation of §2 as amended. The phrase "vote dilution," in the legal sense, simply refers to the impermissible discriminatory effect that a multimember or other districting plan has when it operates "to cancel out or minimize the voting strength of racial groups." *White*, 412 U.S., at 765. See also *Fortson v. Dorsey*, 379 U.S. 433, 439 (1965). This definition, however, conceals some very formidable difficulties. Is the "voting strength" of a racial group to be assessed solely with reference to its prospects for electoral success, or should courts look at other avenues of political influence open to the racial group? Insofar as minority voting strength is assessed with reference to electoral success, how should undiluted minority voting strength be measured? How much of an impairment of minority voting strength is necessary to prove a violation of §2? What constitutes racial bloc voting and how is it proved? What weight is to be given to evidence of actual electoral success by minority candidates in the face of evidence of racial bloc voting?

The Court resolves the first question summarily: minority voting strength *is* to be assessed solely in terms of the minority group's ability to elect candidates it prefers. Under this approach, the essence of a vote dilution claim is that the State has created single-member or multimember districts that unacceptably impair the minority group's ability to elect the candidates its members prefer.

In order to evaluate a claim that a particular multimember district or single-member district has diluted the minority group's voting strength to a degree that violates §2, however, it is also necessary to construct a measure of "undiluted" minority voting strength. "[The] phrase [vote dilution] itself suggests a norm with respect to which the fact of dilution may be ascertained." *Mississippi Republican Executive Committee v. Brooks*, 469 U.S. 1002, 1012 (1984) (Rehnquist, J., dissenting from summary affirmance). Put simply, in order to decide whether an electoral system has made it harder for minority voters to elect the candidates they prefer, a court must have an idea in mind of how hard it "should" be for minority voters to elect their preferred candidates under an acceptable system.

Several possible measures of "undiluted" minority voting strength suggest themselves. First, a court could simply use proportionality as its guide: if the minority group constituted 30% of the voters in a given area, the court would regard the minority group as having the potential to elect 30% of the representatives in that area. Second, a court could posit some alternative districting plan as a "normal" or "fair" electoral scheme and attempt to calculate how many candidates preferred by the minority group would probably be elected under that scheme. There are, as we have seen, a variety of ways in which even single-member districts could be drawn, and each will present the minority group with its own array of electoral risks and benefits; the court might, therefore, consider a range of acceptable plans in attempting to estimate "undiluted" minority voting strength by this method. Third, the court could attempt to arrive at a plan that would maximize feasible minority electoral success, and use this degree of predicted success as its measure of "undiluted" minority voting strength. If a court were to employ this third alternative, it would often face hard choices about what would truly "maximize" minority electoral success. An example is the scenario described above, in which a minority group could be concentrated in one completely safe district or divided among two districts in each of which its members would constitute a somewhat precarious majority.

The Court today has adopted a variant of the third approach, to wit, undiluted minority voting strength means the maximum feasible minority voting strength. . . . The Court's definition of the elements of a vote dilution claim is simple and invariable: a court should calculate minority voting strength by assuming that the minority group is concentrated in a single-member district in which it constitutes a voting majority. . . .

The Court's statement of the elements of a vote dilution claim also supplies an answer to another question posed above: *how much* of an impairment of undiluted minority voting strength is necessary to prove vote dilution. The Court requires the minority group that satisfies the threshold requirements of size and cohesiveness to prove that it will *usually* be unable to elect as many representatives of its choice under the challenged districting scheme as its undiluted voting strength would permit. This requirement, then, constitutes the true test of vote dilution. Again, no reason appears why this test would not be applicable to a vote dilution claim challenging single-member as well as multimember districts.

This measure of vote dilution, taken in conjunction with the Court's standard for measuring undiluted minority voting strength, creates what amounts to a right to *usual, roughly* proportional representation on the part of sizable, compact, cohesive minority groups. . . .

To appreciate the implications of this approach, it is useful to return to the illustration of a town with four council representatives given above. Under the Court's approach, if the black voters who constitute 30% of the town's voting population do not usually succeed in electing one representative of their choice, then regardless of whether the town employs at-large elections or is divided into four single-member districts, its electoral system violates §2. Moreover, if the town had a black voting population of 40%, on the Court's reasoning the black minority, so long as it was geographically and politically cohesive, would be entitled usually to elect two of the four representatives, since it would normally be possible to create two districts in which black voters constituted safe majorities of approximately 80%.

To be sure, the Court also requires that plaintiffs prove that racial bloc voting by the white majority interacts with the challenged districting plan so as usually to defeat the minority's preferred candidate. In fact, however, this requirement adds little that is not already contained in the Court's requirements that the minority group be politically cohesive and that its preferred candidates usually lose. As the Court acknowledges, under its approach, "in general, a white bloc vote that normally will defeat the combined strength of minority support plus white 'crossover' votes rises to the level of legally significant white bloc voting." *Ante*, at 56. But this is to define legally significant bloc voting by the racial majority in terms of the extent of the racial minority's electoral success. If the minority can prove that it could constitute a majority in a single-member district, that it supported certain candidates, and that those candidates have not usually been elected, then a finding that there is "legally significant white bloc voting" will necessarily follow. Otherwise, by definition, those candidates would usually have won rather than lost.

. . . If a minority group is politically and geographically cohesive and large enough to constitute a voting majority in one or more single-member districts, then unless white voters usually support the minority's preferred candidates in sufficient numbers to enable the minority group to elect as many of those candidates as it could elect in such hypothetical districts, it will routinely follow that a vote dilution claim can be made out, and the multimember district will be invalidated. There is simply no need for plaintiffs to establish "the history of voting-related discrimination in the State or political subdivision," *ante,* or "the extent to which the State or political subdivision has used voting practices or procedures that tend to enhance the opportunity for discrimination against the minority group," *ante,* or "the exclusion of members of the minority group from candidate slating processes," *ibid.,* or "the extent to which minority group members bear the effects of past discrimination in areas such as education, employment, and health," *ibid.,* or "the use of overt or subtle racial appeals in political campaigns," *ibid.,* or that "elected officials are unresponsive to the particularized needs of the members of the minority group." *Ibid.* Of course, these other factors may be supportive of such a claim, because they may strengthen a court's confidence that minority voters will be unable to overcome the relative disadvantage at which they are placed by a particular districting plan, or suggest a more general lack of opportunity to participate in the political process. But the fact remains that electoral success has now emerged, under the Court's standard, as the linchpin of vote dilution claims, and that the elements of a vote dilution claim create an entitlement to roughly proportional representation within the framework of single-member districts.

II

In my view, the Court's test for measuring minority voting strength and its test for vote dilution, operating in tandem, come closer to an absolute requirement of proportional representation than Congress intended when it codified the results test in §2. . . .

In my view, we should refrain from deciding in this case whether a court must invariably posit as its measure of "undiluted" minority voting strength single-member districts in which minority group members constitute a majority. There is substantial doubt that Congress intended "undiluted minority voting strength" to mean "maximum feasible minority voting strength." Even if that is the appropriate definition in some circumstances, there is no indication that Congress intended to mandate a single, universally applicable standard for measuring undiluted minority voting strength, regardless of local conditions and regardless of the extent of past discrimination against minority voters in a particular State or political subdivision. Since appellants have not raised the issue, I would assume that what the District Court did here was permissible under §2, and leave open the broader question whether §2 *requires* this approach. . . .

On the same reasoning, I would reject the Court's test for vote dilution. The Court measures undiluted minority voting strength by reference to the possibility of creating single-member districts in which the minority group would constitute a majority, rather than by looking to raw proportionality alone. The Court's standard for vote dilution, when combined with its test for undiluted minority voting strength, makes actionable every deviation from usual, rough proportionality in representation for any cohesive minority group as to which this degree of proportionality is feasible within the framework of single-member districts. Requiring that every minority group that could possibly constitute a majority in a single-member district be assigned to such a district would approach a requirement of proportional representation as nearly as is possible within the framework of single-member districts. Since the Court's analysis entitles every such minority group usually to elect as many representatives under a multimember district as it could elect under the most favorable single-member district scheme, it follows that the Court is requiring a form of proportional representation. This approach is inconsistent with the results test and with §2's disclaimer of a right to proportional representation. . . .

I would adhere to the approach outlined in *Whitcomb* and *White* and followed, with some elaboration, in *Zimmer* and other cases in the Courts of Appeals prior to *Bolden*. Under that approach, a court should consider all relevant factors bearing on whether the minority group has "less opportunity than other members of the electorate to participate in the political process *and* to elect representatives of their choice." 42 U.S.C. §1973 (emphasis added). The court should not focus solely on the minority group's ability to elect representatives of its choice. Whatever measure of undiluted minority voting strength the court employs in connection with evaluating the presence or absence of minority electoral success, it should also bear in mind that "the power to influence the political process is not limited to winning elections." *Davis v. Bandemer.* Of course, the relative lack of minority electoral success under a challenged plan, when compared with the success that would be predicted under the measure of undiluted minority voting strength the court is employing, can constitute powerful evidence of vote dilution. Moreover, the minority group may in fact lack access to or influence upon representatives it did not support as candidates. *Cf. Davis v. Bandemer.* Nonetheless, a reviewing court should be required to find more than simply that the minority group does not usually attain an undiluted measure of electoral success. The court must find that even substantial minority success will be highly infrequent under the challenged plan before it may conclude, on this basis alone, that the plan operates "to cancel out or minimize the voting strength of [the] racial [group]." *White, supra,* at 765.

III

Only three Justices of the Court join Part III-C of Justice Brennan's opinion, which addresses the validity of the statistical evidence on which the District Court relied in finding racially polarized voting in each of the challenged districts. Insofar as statistical evidence of divergent racial voting patterns is admitted solely to establish that the minority group is politically cohesive and to assess its prospects for electoral success, I agree that defendants cannot rebut this showing by offering evidence that the divergent racial voting patterns may be explained in part by causes other than race, such as an underlying divergence in the interests of minority and white voters. I do not agree, however, that such evidence can never affect the overall vote dilution inquiry. Evidence that a candidate preferred by the minority group in a particular election was rejected by white voters for reasons other than those which made that candidate the preferred choice of the minority group would seem clearly relevant in answering the question whether bloc voting by white voters will consistently defeat minority candidates. Such evidence would suggest that another candidate, equally preferred by the minority group, might be able to attract greater white support in future elections.

I believe Congress also intended that explanations of the reasons why white voters rejected minority candidates would be probative of the likelihood that candidates elected without decisive minority support would be willing to take the minority's interests into account. In a community that is polarized along racial lines, racial hostility may bar these and other indirect avenues of political influence to a much greater extent than in a community where racial animosity is absent although the interests of racial groups diverge. . . .

V

When members of a racial minority challenge a multimember district on the grounds that it dilutes their voting strength, I agree with the Court that they must show that they possess such strength and that the multimember district impairs it. A court must therefore appraise the minority group's undiluted voting strength in order to assess the effects of the multimember district. I would reserve the question of the proper method or methods for making this assessment. But once such an assessment is made, in my view the evaluation of an alleged impairment of voting strength requires consideration of the minority group's access to the political processes generally, not solely consideration of the chances that its preferred candidates will actually be elected. Proof that white voters withhold their support from minority-preferred candidates to an extent that consistently ensures their defeat is entitled to significant weight in plaintiffs' favor. However, if plaintiffs direct their proof solely towards the minority group's prospects for electoral success, they must show that substantial minority success will be highly infrequent under the challenged plan in order to establish that the plan operates to "cancel out or minimize" their voting strength. *White*, 412 U.S., at 765.

Compromise is essential to much if not most major federal legislation, and confidence that the federal courts will enforce such compromises is indispensable to their creation. I believe that the Court today strikes a different balance than Congress intended to when it codified the results test and disclaimed any right to proportional representation under §2. For that reason, I join the Court's judgment but not its opinion.

>> *The "*Gingles *Factors."*   In later cases, the Court has refined and clarified the analytic requirements of *Gingles*, summarizing the test for vote dilution under Section 2 as requiring analysis of three factors:

Our decision in *Thornburg v. Gingles*, 478 U.S. 30 (1986), set out the basic framework for establishing a vote dilution claim. . . . Plaintiffs must show three threshold conditions: first, the minority group "is sufficiently large and geographically compact to constitute a majority in a single-member district"; second, the minority group is "politically cohesive"; and third, the majority "votes sufficiently as a bloc to enable it . . . to defeat the minority's preferred candidate." 478 U.S. at 50-51. Once plaintiffs establish these conditions, the court considers whether, "on the totality of circumstances," minorities have been denied an "equal opportunity" to "participate in the political process and to elect representatives of their choice." 42 U.S.C. §1973(b).

Abrams v. Johnson, 521 U.S. 74, 90-91 (1997).

» *Participation in the Political Process.* Section 2 provides that covered groups must not have "less opportunity than other members of the electorate to participate in the political process *and* to elect representatives of their choice." What is the relationship between the two parts of this key statutory phrase?

The Court's decision in *Gingles* focuses closely on the ability to elect representatives. But what exactly is "participation"? Unless participation is defined narrowly (and perhaps redundantly) as the successful election of representatives, Section 2's language suggests that participation in the political process is something different from electing representatives.

In *Gingles*, the Court focused exclusively on the electoral portion of the section's guarantee, ignoring the statute's apparent protection of participation in other facets of the political process. The Court protected the opportunity of minority voters "to elect representatives of their choice" by articulating a standard that compares electoral performance in the challenged district with performance in a hypothetical single-member district. Although *Gingles* reserves the question of whether other types of political activity are protected by amended section 2, its subsequent construction by the lower courts suggests that its logic may make it more difficult for plaintiffs to assert, and courts to elaborate, such rights.

In the aftermath of *Gingles*, it is crucial to reconsider the meaning of "political opportunity" under section 2. While the Court may have intended the opinion as a cautious first foray into ill-charted waters, *Gingles*'s electoral focus threatens to rigidify into an approach that employs a misleadingly simple measure of political effectiveness. It may therefore leave minorities who suffer subtler forms of political impairment without legal remedy. One way to combat this danger is to reexamine the reasons for enhancing minority political participation, and the way in which minority interests—and those of other participants—are vindicated through the political process. Such a reevaluation suggests that the opportunity to elect candidates, while important, is not the sole or even the most crucial element of political efficacy. Important political goals such as expression of preferences and alteration of substantive policies are accomplished not simply by pulling a lever, but by engaging in activities such as discussion, lobbying, and coalition-building with others. Minority voters can be barred from these kinds of interaction by the present effects of past discrimination, gerrymandering, and other electoral devices that perpetuate these effects. Enforcement under section 2 should address these forms of impairment as well. Although enhancing the ability of minority voters to elect candidates of their choice is an important means of reducing disaffection and ensuring a voice for minority voters in the political process, over the long run, enforcement must secure opportunities for interaction and political coalescence as well.

Kathryn Abrams, *"Raising Politics Up": Minority Political Participation and Section 2 of the Voting Rights Act*, 63 N.Y.U. L. Rev. 449, 452-453 (1988).

In the preceding passage, Abrams takes the position that the "participation" prong of Section 2 is broader than and independent of the "election" prong. Do you agree? Might equal participation alone, in Abrams' broader sense, satisfy Section 2 if not accompanied by the successful election of representatives? *Can* participation be equal if it does not lead to the election of representatives?

» *The "Opportunity" to Participate and Elect.* Section 2 does not require that covered groups actually participate and elect representatives on an equal footing with other groups, only that they have the "opportunity" to do so. What is the significance of this qualification? What counts as an "opportunity" to participate, and an "opportunity" to elect? How would we know whether such opportunities exist other than by examining *actual* participation and election of representatives? Does the Court in *Gingles* give adequate consideration to these questions?

» *Maximization of Minority Voting Power.* After *Gingles*, Section 2 prohibits the minimization of minority voting power, but is the converse proposition also true — does Section 2 require minority influence to be maximized? In *Johnson v. DeGrandy*, 512 U.S. 997 (1994), the Court said no. The plaintiffs in *DeGrandy* challenged Florida's districting of Dade County. Hispanics constituted 50 percent of the voting-age population of the county. The challenged districting plan created Hispanic majorities in nine of the eighteen House districts within the county (50 percent) and in nine of the twenty Senate districts (45 percent). Thus, the challenged plan allowed Hispanics nearly proportional representation. Nevertheless, the Hispanic plaintiffs argued that Hispanics were subjected to continuing discrimination in Dade County, and that the districts could be redrawn to create additional majority-minority districts.

The Court held that Section 2 had not been violated, even in the presence of discrimination and even given the possibility of creating a greater number of cohesive, majority-Hispanic districts. "Treating equal political opportunity as the focus of the enquiry," wrote Justice Souter for a six-Justice majority, "we do not see how these district lines, apparently providing political effectiveness in proportion to voting-age numbers, deny equal political opportunity."

However, the Court also rejected the opposite contention, advanced by the state: that any Section 2 claim can automatically be defeated where the districting plan provides proportional representation. Creating a proportionality "safe harbor," the Court held, would be contrary to the text and purpose of the VRA, which require reviewing courts to consider the "totality of the circumstances."

>> *Section 2 and Proportional Representation.*   As the Court's decision in *Gingles* makes clear, if Section 2 means anything, it means that minority voting strength cannot be discriminatorily minimized. Conversely, *DeGrandy* tells us that Section 2 does not require that minority voting strength be maximized. Where, then, between minimization and maximization, does Section 2 require minority voting strength be set to satisfy its proscription of racial discrimination in election practices?

One possible benchmark is proportionality; one might say that minority voting strength is set fairly when it is likely to lead to minority representation in rough proportion to minority population. Yet the proviso of Section 2 expressly rules out using proportionality as a baseline against which to measure the presence or absence of discrimination: "nothing in this section establishes a right to have members of a protected class elected in numbers equal to their proportion in the population." The majority in *Gingles* purports to follow the statutory instruction to avoid using proportionality as the relevant benchmark. Does it successfully do so? Justice O'Connor argues in her concurrence that the Court's analysis does essentially what the statute disavows as its objective. Do you agree?

If a lack of proportionality in representation is not an acceptable measure against which to judge racial discrimination in voting under Section 2, what could or ought to serve as such a measure? Abigail Thernstrom, a prominent academic critic of the VRA and now a member of the U.S. Civil Rights Commission, argues that "the proper test for electoral exclusion is the presence of legislative seats largely *reserved* for whites — not legislative seats *occupied disproportionately* by whites." ABIGAIL THERNSTROM, WHOSE VOTES COUNT? 225 (1987). Is this a workable standard?

Does Section 2 contain an inherent and irresolvable tension between "the rejection of proportional representation and the focus on the number of minority elected officials"? Pamela S. Karlan, *Maps and Misreadings: The Role of Geographic Compactness in Racial Vote Dilution Litigation*, 24 HARV. C.R.-C.L. L. REV. 173, 179 (1989). Are the goals of Section 2 capable of being satisfied by any arrangement *other than* proportionality?

What is the basis for the congressional and judicial hostility toward forms of proportional representation?

>> *"Safe," "Coalitional," and "Influence" Districts.*   Commentators sometimes distinguish between different types of districts according to the ability of black voters to affect the outcome of elections held within the district.

> Safe districts are those in which a majority of the voting-age population is made up of minority voters. By making a minority the actual majority in an election district, safe districting can ensure that minority voters control the outcome in such districts. Coalitional districts, instead, are those with a significant minority population and white voters who are willing to form interracial political coalitions in support of minority candidates. When coalitional districts exist or can be created, they can also elect minority candidates, but through interracial coalitions.

Richard H. Pildes, *Is Voting Rights Law Now at War with Itself? Social Science and Voting Rights in the 2000s*, 80 N.C. L. REV. 1517 (2002). In contrast, an influence district is one in which black voters are not only a minority, but are also unable, either alone or in coalition with any sufficiently sizable group of white voters, to elect the candidates of their choice. They are sufficiently numerous to influence the outcomes of elections in the direction they favor, but not in any decisive way.

In *Georgia v. Ashcroft*, 539 U.S. 461 (2003), a case decided under Section 5 of the VRA, the Court considered a state legislative redistricting plan enacted by Georgia in 2001. The state legislature, controlled by Democrats, had decided that the political influence of Georgia's black population could be enhanced by unpacking heavily black districts and spreading black voters more thinly, an approach it implemented by substituting a larger number of slightly risky influence districts for a smaller number of safe ones. The question was whether this move amounted to "retrogression" in the position of black voters within the meaning of Section 5. The Court held that the plan did not result in prohibited retrogression:

> The ability of minority voters to elect a candidate of their choice is important but often complex in practice to determine. In order to maximize the electoral success of a minority group, a State may choose to create a certain number of "safe" districts, in which it is highly likely that minority voters will be able to elect the candidate of their choice. . . . Alternatively, a State may choose to create a greater number of districts in which it is likely — although perhaps not quite as likely as under the benchmark plan — that minority voters will be able to elect candidates of their choice.

> Section 5 does not dictate that a State must pick one of these methods of redistricting over another. Either option "will present the minority group with its own array of electoral risks and benefits," and presents "hard choices about what would truly 'maximize' minority electoral success." *Thornburg v. Gingles*, at 89. On one hand, a smaller number of safe majority-minority districts may virtually guarantee the election of a minority group's preferred candidate in those districts. Yet even if this concentration of minority voters in a few districts does not constitute the unlawful packing of minority voters, such a plan risks isolating minority voters from the rest of the state, and risks narrowing political influence to only a fraction of political districts. . . .

> On the other hand, spreading out minority voters over a greater number of districts creates more districts in which minority voters may have the opportunity to elect a candidate of their choice. Such a strategy has the potential to [create] coalitions of voters who together will help to achieve the electoral aspirations of the minority group. It also, however, creates the risk that the minority group's preferred candidate may lose. . . . Section 5 gives States the flexibility to choose one theory of effective representation over the other. . . . The State may choose, consistent with §5, that it is better to risk having fewer minority representatives in order to achieve greater overall representation of a minority group by increasing the number of representatives sympathetic to the interests of minority voters.

Do you agree with the majority that blacks can be made better off by spreading rather than concentrating their influence? According to one prominent critic of the decision, the Court was essentially talking about ex ante probabilities and making the claim that the absolute ability to control the outcome in, say, ten districts was the functional equivalent of having an even chance of winning, say, twenty districts. As a matter of arithmetic that is of course true; as a practical matters, it seems far more dubious. It ignores, for example, the importance of legislative seniority; winning several elections in a row from the same district may be preferable to winning the same number of seats spread among several districts if in the latter case one's representative is always a first-termer. Moreover, making sure that one's group *always* has at least some representation in the room where legislative deals are being made might be far more beneficial than occasionally having superrepresentation and occasionally being absent altogether.

Pamela S. Karlan, Georgia v. Ashcroft *and the Retrogression of Retrogression*, 3 ELECTION L.J. 21 (2004). Do you agree?

Karlan also criticized *Ashcroft* on the ground that the Court "seemed to treat coalitional and influence districts as fungible":

Being part of a winning coalition in which a sufficient number of white voters support a candidate sponsored by the black community may be quite different from having some less direct effect on election outcomes. . . . [I]nfluence cannot really be understood as a linear concept. It will depend on two factors: the size of the minority group and its position relative to the political fault line that separates other voters within the district. . . . [Consequently, r]acial bloc voting may make coalitional districts impossible: at the limit, if black and white voters prefer entirely different candidates, then black voters will be unable to elect their candidate of choice unless they are an electoral majority. . . . Without having a firm empirical handle on the existence and extent of racial bloc voting, it is simply impossible to make any intelligent assessment of the extent to which a redistricting plan allows minority voters an effective exercise of the electoral franchise.

Do you agree?

Congress overruled *Georgia v. Ashcroft* in the Voting Rights Reauthorization and Amendments Act of 2006, expressing the view that the Court's decision "would allow the minority community's own choice of preferred candidates to be trumped by political deals struck by State legislators purporting to give 'influence' to the minority community while removing that community's ability to elect candidates. . . . The majority opinion in *Georgia* turns Section 5 on its head. . . . Its purpose is to . . . ensure that minority voters are not discriminated against and that gains made by minority voters over the course of decades are not eroded. . . . " H.R. Rep. No. 109-478 (2006), at 69.

≫ *Influence Districts Under Section 2.* *Georgia v. Ashcroft*, described above, suggested that a legislature could create minority influence districts as a reasonable, nonretrogressive substitute for majority-minority districts, but it was overruled by congressional amendment to Section 5. What is the status of influence districts under Section 2? *Gingles* suggests that no violation can be proved in the districting context unless the minority group in question can comprise a majority of a geographically compact district. But what if the minority group is insufficiently numerous to constitute a majority, but is sufficiently compact to be able to form a significant influence bloc, if it were not dispersed among multiple districts? Would that violate Section 2? Should it?

The Court faced this question in *Bartlett v. Strickland*, 556 U.S. 1 (2009), and in a splintered 5-4 opinion held that no violation of Section 2 could occur unless the protected minority group were large enough and compact enough to form a numerical majority in a well-drawn district. The plaintiffs argued that the ability of black voters to form politically effective coalitions with like-minded white voters was compromised on account of North Carolina's failure to group them in a single district in which they would be, if not an outright majority, nevertheless the dominant political bloc. Writing for a plurality of three Justices, Justice Kennedy rejected this claim. "Nothing in §2," he wrote, "grants special protection to a minority group's right to form political coalitions. . . . Section 2 does not impose on those who draw election districts a duty to give minority voters the most potential, or the best potential, to elect a candidate by attracting crossover voting." Construing *Gingles* to require an outright majority, he went on, has the added benefit of providing "workable standards" conducive to "sound judicial and legislative administration" because it "relies on an objective, numerical test: Do minorities make up more than 50 percent of the voting-age population in the relevant geographic area?" Justice Kennedy observed, however, that the Court's ruling would not preclude legislatures from creating coalitional and influence districts where feasible; the creation of such districts simply was not required by Section 2. Justice Thomas, joined by Justice Scalia, concurred in the judgment that the case should be dismissed on the more expansive ground that *Gingles* itself was wrongly decided, and that vote dilution is not a cognizable injury under Section 2 of the VRA.

Justice Souter, joined by Justices Stevens, Ginsburg, and Breyer, dissented. He argued that the majority's approach gives states a perverse incentive to pack black voters into majority-minority districts, thereby narrowing their potential influence when the purpose of Section 2 is to prevent the kind of packing that had previously been used to minimize black voting strength. The "baseline" for measuring black opportunity to elect, he said, is "the minority's rough proportion of the relevant population." Furthermore, "[t]here is nothing in the statutory text to suggest that Congress meant to protect minority opportunity to elect solely by the creation of majority-minority districts. . . . Recognizing crossover districts has the value of giving States greater flexibility to draw districting plans with a fair number of minority-opportunity districts, and this in turn allows for a beneficent reduction in the number of majority-minority districts with their 'quintessentially race-conscious calculus,' thereby moderating reliance on race as an exclusive determinant in districting decisions."

What is the effect of the electorate's increasing partisan polarization on the ability of black voters to form successful influence or coalitional districts? Partisan cleavages in the electorate largely coincide with racial ones — that is, black voters reliably, and overwhelmingly, register and vote Democratic. This means that in some areas of the country, especially in the South, black Democrats can find few opportunities to partner with white Democrats because white voters in those areas have so thoroughly aligned themselves with the Republican Party. *See* Harry Enten, *It's Much Harder to Protect Southern Black Voters' Influence Than It Was 10 Years Ago*, www .fivethirtyeight.com (Dec. 5, 2016). Does this mean that the VRA's historic emphasis on majority-minority districts is becoming better justified or less well justified than it was just 20 years ago? Is the problem race or is it partisanship?

⟩⟩   *Judicial Elections.*   Under Section 2(b), a violation of Section 2(a) is established if the plaintiffs show that the members of their class have "less opportunity to participate in the political process and to elect *representatives* of their choice." Although they are elected in many states, judges are not normally thought of as "representatives" in the same way as legislators or executive branch officials. In light of Congress's use of the word "representatives" in Section 2, does the Act cover judicial elections? In *Chisom v. Roemer*, 501 U.S. 380 (1991), the Court held that it does. Rejecting a claim that Section 2's language limits its coverage to legislative and executive elections, the Court said: "We think . . . that the better reading of the word 'representatives' describes the winners of representative, popular elections." *See also Houston Lawyers' Association v. Attorney General*, 501 U.S. 419 (1991) (holding that Section 2 applies to election of Texas trial judges).

⟩⟩   *The Impact of Breaking Up At-Large Systems in the South.*   Section 2 has most often been applied, as in *Gingles*, to require the replacement of at-large or multimember districts with single-member districts. How has this affected black representation on the local level? Consider the following data from Alabama, which examines black representation on municipal councils in cities (a) with populations exceeding 6,000, (b) with black populations of at least 10 percent, and (c) that employed an at-large electoral system in 1970 but later switched to single-member districts. The data compares the percentage of black elected legislators in 1970, under the at-large system, and in 1989, under single-member districting:

% Black in City	Number of Cities	Mean % Black in City	Mean % Black on City Council (1970)	Mean % Black on City Council (1989)
10–29	23	19	0	20
30–49	13	37	0	38
50 or higher	1	74	0	80

As the fourth column indicates, in 1970 not a single black person had been elected as a municipal legislator in any city of over 6,000 in the entire state of Alabama. By 1989, black representatives on city councils had been elected in numbers roughly proportionate to black municipal populations. The authors of this study attribute this change entirely to the Voting Rights Act. *See* Peyton McCrary et al., *Alabama, in* QUIET REVOLUTION IN THE SOUTH: THE IMPACT OF THE VOTING RIGHTS ACT 1965-1990 (Chandler Davidson and Bernard Grofman eds., 1994).

⟩⟩   *Can Section 2 Do the Work of Section 5?*   Although the Court struck down Section 4, it effectively rendered Section 5 useless, for now. Until and unless Congress amends the coverage formula under Section 4, Section 2 stands as the primary operative component of the VRA. One question being explored by voting rights lawyers and scholars is whether Section 2 can do much of the work previously performed by Section 5.

At oral argument for *Shelby County*, Justice Kennedy joined a chorus of Section 5's critics in stating that "it's not clear to me that there's that much difference [between] a Section 2 suit now and preclearance." Certainly the language of Section 2 is almost identical that of to Section 5, but whether or not these provisions have resulted in similar outcomes is far from clear.

As a preliminary matter, there are clear procedural differences between preclearance and bringing a suit under Section 2. Most obviously, Section 2 limits judicial scrutiny to the back end of alleged voter discrimination, that is, "the default is that a challenged policy goes into effect under Section 2 but that it does not under Section 5." Nicholas Stephanopoulos, *The South After* Shelby County, 2013 SUP. CT. REV. 55, 57. Relatedly, under Section 5, covered jurisdictions bear the burden of proving non-infringement, whereas Section 2 places the burden of proving infringement on the plaintiff. Finally, litigation under Section 2 tends to prove more expensive than under Section 5, and this financial burden is often placed on individual plaintiffs rather than on the Department of Justice. *Id.* at 57-58.

One of the biggest differences between Sections 2 and 5 is Section 5's burden-shifting device. Recall that Section 5 shifts the burden of proof from would-be plaintiffs, likely to be minority voters, to the covered jurisdiction, which must prove that its proposed changes would not be retrogressive. By contrast, in a Section 2 lawsuit, the complaining party bears the burden of proof. This may be the biggest difference between Section 2 and Section 5.

》 *Section 2 and Felon Disenfranchisement.*   Recall from Chapter 3 that the disenfranchisement of convicted felons, although constitutional under Section 2 of the Fourteenth Amendment, *Richardson v. Ramirez*, can violate the Fourteenth Amendment if it is intentional. *Hunter v. Underwood.* Section 2 of the VRA does not, of course, require a showing of intentional discrimination. However, given both the racial impact of felon disenfranchisement and its political effects, might a policy of felon disenfranchisement violate Section 2? As indicated in Chapter 3, such challenges were for many years routinely rejected. En banc panels of the Second, Ninth, and Eleventh Circuits have reached similar results, rejecting Section 2 challenges to state felon disenfranchisement provisions as a matter of law.

According to the Second Circuit, although the plain language of Section 2 appears to encompass felony disqualification of voters, it was not the intention of Congress in Section 2 to reach these kinds of provisions. The court pointed to seven factors supporting this conclusion:

> (1) the explicit approval given such laws in the Fourteenth Amendment; (2) the long history and continuing prevalence of felon disenfranchisement provisions throughout the United States; (3) the statements in the House and Senate Judiciary Committee Reports; (4) the absence of any affirmative consideration of felon disenfranchisement laws during either the 1965 passage of the Act or its 1982 revision; (5) the introduction thereafter of bills specifically intended to include felon disenfranchisement

provisions within the VRA's coverage; (6) the enactment of a felon disenfranchisement statute for the District of Columbia by Congress soon after the passage of the Voting Rights Act; and (7) the subsequent passage of statutes designed to facilitate the removal of convicted felons from the voting rolls. We therefore conclude that §1973 was not intended to—thus does not—encompass felon disenfranchisement provisions.

Hayden v. Pataki, 449 F.3d 305, 315-316 (2d Cir. 2006) (en banc). The Eleventh Circuit reached a similar conclusion in *Johnson v. Governor of the State of Florida*, 405 F.3d 1214 (11th Cir. 2005) (en banc), as did the First Circuit in *Simmons v. Galvin*, 575 F.3d 24 (1st Cir. 2009). After a panel decision going the other way, the en banc Ninth Circuit also fell into line. *Farrakhan v. Gregoire*, 623 F.3d 990 (9th Cir. 2010) (en banc).

E.   RACE, REPRESENTATION, AND THE CONSTITUTION

In *Thornburg v. Gingles*, the Court addressed a statutory question, the circumstances pursuant to which the VRA requires the states to take race into account when constructing electoral districts. The materials that follow address the constitutional question: whether the Constitution imposes limits on when and how the state may take race into account for the purpose of providing representation for voters of color. We know that the Constitution forbids the government from discriminating based on race, as does the VRA. The question is whether the Constitution allows the states to take race into account for the purposes of ensuring adequate representation for voters of color. We begin with the 1977 case of *United Jewish Organizations v. Carey (UJO)*. We will then turn to a set of cases from the mid-1990s and close with some cases from the Roberts Court.

Before we begin, we provide a quick-and-dirty primer on the Court's broader equal protection doctrine and how it intersects with the constitutional questions that arise under Section 2 of the VRA. The Court decided *UJO v. Carey* in 1977. The following year, it decided *Regents of University of California v. Bakke*, 438 U.S. 265 (1978). In *Bakke*, the Court struck down a state medical school's affirmative action admissions program on equal protection grounds, while simultaneously affirming in principle that a properly framed affirmative action program could survive constitutional challenge. In a divided set of opinions, four Justices ruled that race could never be a legitimate criterion in allocating seats in a medical school's entering class; and a different four Justices ruled that race could be a legitimate criterion when racial criteria were used for the purpose of rectifying societal discrimination and achieving greater racial balance among students and doctors. Justice Powell wrote the swing opinion in which he agreed that the state could make benignly motivated racial distinctions. In particular, the state could take race into account to attain a broadly diverse class where race is one of the many criteria considered by the state. But Powell also agreed that the admissions program at issue in the case ought to be struck down because it used a quota system, which was too rigid to survive constitutional scrutiny. Two years later, in *Fullilove v. Klutznick*, 448 U.S. 448

(1980), the Court upheld a federal program under which 10 percent of federal construction funds on any project had to be allocated to minority-owned businesses.

Within a decade, a newly composed Court began a rapid retreat from the positions staked out in those cases. In *Wygant v. Jackson Board of Education*, 476 U.S. 267 (1986), a divided Court invalidated a school board hiring plan that, for purposes of deciding which teachers to lay off, took into account the racial balance of the teaching staff and the race of individual teachers. *Richmond v. J.A. Croson Co.*, 488 U.S. 469 (1989), represented something of a watershed case. There, a firm majority of the Court for the first time decided that race was not a permissible consideration — not even in principle — in governmental decision making. In *Croson,* the Court struck down a minority business set-aside program run by the city of Richmond, Virginia, that was identical to the one upheld in *Klutznick.* The Court distinguished *Klutznick* on the ground that states are situated differently under the Fourteenth Amendment than Congress, which under Section 5 has specific authority to enact legislation designed to promote racial equality. Applying strict scrutiny to Richmond's program, a majority of the Court suggested in *Croson* that the only legitimate reason why a state might ever be able to take race into account would be to rectify the results of past, proven discrimination. In finding that Richmond had failed to demonstrate the existence of such past discrimination in the construction industry, the Court established a rigorous standard of proof.

The following year, Justice Brennan, in his last year on the Court, managed to cobble together a majority to uphold an FCC minority preference policy in awarding broadcast licenses. Seizing on *Croson's* distinction between the powers of state governments and the national government, the majority in *Metro Broadcasting, Inc. v. FCC*, 497 U.S. 547 (1990), held that federal affirmative action policies should be subjected to a less rigorous standard of intermediate scrutiny. Applying that standard, the majority held that the FCC's interest in promoting a diversity of viewpoints among broadcasters was a sufficiently important interest to justify taking race into account. Justices O'Connor, Rehnquist, Scalia, and Kennedy dissented, arguing that all racial categorizing by government should be subjected to strict scrutiny, and that the government's interest in promoting diversity did not make the grade, at least where it sought to use race as a proxy for viewpoint.

In 1995, shortly after Clarence Thomas replaced Thurgood Marshall, a newly configured majority overruled *Metro Broadcasting.* In *Adarand Constructors, Inc. v. Pena*, 515 U.S. 200 (1995), the Court struck down a federal minority set-aside program in highway construction. The Court ruled that strict scrutiny applied to any use of racial criteria by a government, whether federal, state, or local, and that the desire to help certain racial groups on the theory that they were economically disadvantaged was not a compelling government interest.

In 2003 the Court decided a pair of affirmative action cases, *Grutter v. Bollinger*, 539 U.S. 206 (2003), and *Gratz v. Bollinger*, 539 U.S. 244 (2003). In *Grutter*, the Court upheld the University of Michigan Law School's race-conscious affirmative action program. In an opinion for the Court by Justice Sandra Day O'Connor, the Court held that even though strict scrutiny applied to all racial classifications, racial classifications that are necessary to further a compelling interest and are narrowly tailored do not violate the Constitution. The Court reaffirmed Powell's reasoning in Bakke that diversity is a compelling state interest. The Court upheld the Law School's affirmative action program on the ground that it furthered a compelling state interest, diversity, and it was narrowly tailored. In *Gratz*, the Court struck down the University of Michigan's undergraduate affirmative action program on the ground that it was not narrowly tailored. Chief Justice William Rehnquist, who authored the Court's opinion, concluded that race was the decisive factor in the University's admissions decisions and that the University's affirmative action program was not sufficiently distinguishable from a quota system.

In 2006, in *Parents Involved in Community Schools v. Seattle School District*, 551 U.S. 701 (2006), consolidated with *Meredith v. Jefferson County*, Chief Justice John Roberts, writing for the Court, struck down race conscious school assignment plans in Seattle, Washington and in Louisville, Kentucky. The Seattle school district took race into account, as one consideration among many, for assigning students to oversubscribed high schools. The Louisville school district took race into account in assigning students to elementary schools. The Court held that the diversity rationale was only relevant in the context of higher education and therefore did not serve as a compelling state interest outside of that context. Roberts concluded that the schools were engaged in racial balancing, which is not a compelling government interest. Moreover, he added, even if it was, the school assignment plans were not narrowly tailored.

A question that is always implicit and sometimes explicit in voting rights cases below is whether race consciousness in the domain of voting is subject to the Court's broader colorblindness-infused equal protection jurisprudence or whether the domain of voting is an exception to that jurisprudence. Put differently, will the Court apply its jurisprudence in *Parents Involved, Grutter, Gratz, Croson*, and *Adarand* to the VRA, particularly Section 2, or will the Court view the VRA as an exception to its race jurisprudence?

1.   Section 5: Race as a Redistricting Criterion

United Jewish Organizations of Williamsburgh, Inc. v. Carey

430 U.S. 144 (1977)

Mr. Justice WHITE announced the judgment of the Court and filed an opinion in which Mr. Justice STEVENS joined; Parts I, II, and III of which are joined by Mr. Justice BRENNAN and Mr. Justice BLACKMUN; and Parts I and IV of which are joined by Mr. Justice REHNQUIST.

The question presented is whether, in the circumstances of this case, the use of racial criteria by the State of New York in its attempt to comply with §5 of the Voting Rights Act and to secure the approval of the Attorney General violated the Fourteenth or Fifteenth Amendment.

I

On April 1, 1974, the Attorney General concluded that, as to certain districts in Kings County covering the Bedford-Stuyvesant area of Brooklyn, the State had not met the burden placed on it by §5 and the regulations thereunder to demonstrate that [its 1972] redistricting had neither the purpose nor the effect of abridging the right to vote by reason of race or color. . . .

Under the 1972 plan, Kings County had three state senate districts with nonwhite majorities of approximately 91%, 61%, and 53%; under the revised 1974 plan, there were again three districts with nonwhite majorities, but now all three were between 70% and 75% nonwhite. As for state assembly districts, both the 1972 and the 1974 plans provided for seven districts with nonwhite majorities. However, under the 1972 plan, there were four between 85% and 95% nonwhite, and three were approximately 76%, 61%, and 52%, respectively; under the 1974 plan, the two smallest nonwhite majorities were increased to 65% and 67.5%, and the two largest nonwhite majorities were decreased from greater than 90% to between 80% and 90%. The report of the legislative committee on reapportionment stated that these changes were made "to overcome Justice Department objections" by creating more "substantial nonwhite majorities" in two assembly districts and two senate districts.

One of the communities affected by these revisions in the Kings County reapportionment plan was the Williamsburgh area, where about 30,000 Hasidic Jews live.[*] Under the 1972 plan, the Hasidic community was located entirely in one assembly district (61% nonwhite) and one senate district (37% nonwhite); in order to create substantial nonwhite majorities in these districts, the 1974 revisions split the Hasidic community between two senate and two assembly districts. A staff member of the legislative reapportionment committee testified that in the course of meetings and telephone conversations with Justice Department officials, he "got the feeling . . . that 65 percent would be probably an approved figure" for the nonwhite population in the assembly district in which the Hasidic community was located, a district approximately 61% nonwhite under the 1972 plan. To attain the 65% figure, a portion of the white population, including part of the Hasidic community, was reassigned to an adjoining district.

Shortly after the State submitted this revised redistricting plan for Kings County to the Attorney General, petitioners sued on behalf of the Hasidic Jewish community of Williamsburgh, alleging that the 1974 plan "would dilute the value of each plaintiff's franchise by halving its effectiveness," solely for the purpose of achieving a racial quota and therefore in violation of the Fourteenth Amendment. Petitioners also alleged that they were assigned to electoral districts solely on the basis of race, and that this racial assignment diluted their voting power in violation of the Fifteenth Amendment. . . .

---

* [According to 1970 census data, state senate districts for this redistricting cycle had an average population of about 304,000, and state assembly districts had an average population of about 102,000. — Eds.]

II

Petitioners argue that the New York Legislature, although seeking to comply with the Voting Rights Act as construed by the Attorney General, has violated the Fourteenth and Fifteenth Amendments by deliberately revising its reapportionment plan along racial lines. In rejecting petitioners' claim, we address four propositions: First, that whatever might be true in other contexts, the use of racial criteria in districting and apportionment is never permissible; second, that even if racial considerations may be used to redraw district lines in order to remedy the residual effects of past unconstitutional reapportionments, there are no findings here of prior discriminations that would require or justify as a remedy that white voters be reassigned in order to increase the size of black majorities in certain districts; third, that the use of a "racial quota" in redistricting is never acceptable; and fourth, that even if the foregoing general propositions are infirm, what New York actually did in this case was unconstitutional, particularly its use of a 65% nonwhite racial quota for certain districts. The first three arguments, as we now explain, are foreclosed by our cases construing and sustaining the constitutionality of the Voting Rights Act; the fourth we address in Parts III and IV.

[White concludes that "neither the Fourteenth nor the Fifteenth Amendment mandates any per se rule against using racial factors in districting and apportionment." White also rejects the plaintiffs' second objection on the ground that the "permissible use of racial criteria is not confined to eliminating the effects of past discriminatory districting or apportionment" and the fact that the VRA permissibly mandates race conscious is implicit in the Court's past VRA cases. White argues that the plaintiffs' third objection is also unpersuasive because "in the process of drawing black majority districts in order to comply with §5, the State must decide how substantial those majorities must be in order to satisfy the Voting Rights Act." White reasoned, "whatever the specific percentage, the State will inevitably arrive at it as a necessary means to ensure the opportunity for the election of a black representative and to obtain approval of its reapportionment plan."]

III

Having rejected these three broad objections to the use of racial criteria in redistricting under the Voting Rights Act, we turn to the fourth question, which is whether the racial criteria New York used in this case the revision of the 1972 plan to create 65% nonwhite majorities in two additional senate and two additional assembly districts were constitutionally infirm. We hold they are not. . . .

IV

. . . Whether or not the plan was authorized by or was in compliance with §5 of the Voting Rights Act, New York was free to do what it did as long as it did not violate the Constitution, particularly the Fourteenth and Fifteenth Amendments; and we are convinced that neither Amendment was infringed.

There is no doubt that in preparing the 1974 legislation the State deliberately used race in a purposeful manner. But its plan represented no racial slur or stigma with respect to whites or any other race, and we discern no discrimination violative of the Fourteenth Amendment nor any abridgment of the right to vote on account of race within the meaning of the Fifteenth Amendment.

It is true that New York deliberately increased the nonwhite majorities in certain districts in order to enhance the opportunity for election of nonwhite representatives from those districts. Nevertheless, there was no fencing out the white population from participation in the political processes of the county, and the plan did not minimize or unfairly cancel out white voting strength. Compare *White v. Regester*, 412 U.S., at 765-767, and *Gomillion v. Lightfoot*, 364 U.S. 339 (1960), with *Gaffney v. Cummings*, 412 U.S. 735, 751-754 (1973). Petitioners have not objected to the impact of the 1974 plan on the representation of white voters in the county or in the State as a whole. As the Court of Appeals observed, the plan left white majorities in approximately 70% of the assembly and senate districts in Kings County, which had a countywide population that was 65% white. Thus, even if voting in the county occurred strictly according to race, whites would not be underrepresented relative to their share of the population.

In individual districts where nonwhite majorities were increased to approximately 65%, it became more likely, given racial bloc voting, that black candidates would be elected instead of their white opponents, and it became less likely that white voters would be represented by a member of their own race; but as long as whites in Kings County, as a group, were provided with fair representation, we cannot conclude that there was a cognizable discrimination against whites or an abridgment of their right to vote on the grounds of race.[24] Furthermore, the individual voter in the district with a nonwhite majority has no constitutional complaint merely because his candidate has lost out at the polls and his district is represented by a person for whom he did not vote. Some candidate, along with his supporters, always loses. See *Whitcomb v. Chavis*, 403 U.S. at 153-160.

Where it occurs, voting for or against a candidate because of his race is an unfortunate practice. But it is not rare; and in any district where it regularly happens, it is unlikely that any candidate will be elected who is a member of the race that is in the minority in that district. However disagreeable this result may be, there is no authority for the proposition that the candidates who are found racially unacceptable by the majority, and the minority voters supporting those candidates, have had their Fourteenth or Fifteenth Amendment rights infringed by this process. Their position is similar to that of the Democratic or Republican minority that is submerged year after year by the adherents to the majority party who tend to vote a straight party line. . . . New York's 1974 plan . . . can be viewed as seeking to alleviate the consequences of racial voting at the polls and to achieve a fair allocation of political power between white and nonwhite voters in Kings County.

---

24. We also note that the white voter who as a result of the 1974 plan is in a district more likely to return a nonwhite representative will be represented, to the extent that voting continues to follow racial lines, by legislators elected from majority white districts. The effect of the reapportionment on whites in districts where nonwhite majorities have been increased is thus mitigated by the preservation of white majority districts in the rest of the county. See Note, 25 Stan. L. Rev. 84, 87 (1972). Of course, if voting does not follow racial lines, the white voter has little reason to complain that the percentage of nonwhites in his district has been increased.

In this respect New York's revision of certain district lines is little different in kind from the decision by a State in which a racial minority is unable to elect representatives from multimember districts to change to single-member districting for the purpose of increasing minority representation. This change might substantially increase minority representation at the expense of white voters, who previously elected all of the legislators but who with single-member districts could elect no more than their proportional share. If this intentional reduction of white voting power would be constitutionally permissible, as we think it would be, we think it also permissible for a State, employing sound districting principles such as compactness and population equality, to attempt to prevent racial minorities from being repeatedly outvoted by creating districts that will afford fair representation to the members of those racial groups who are sufficiently numerous and whose residential patterns afford the opportunity of creating districts in which they will be in the majority.

Mr. Justice MARSHALL took no part in the consideration or decision of this case.

Mr. Justice BRENNAN, concurring in part.

I join Parts I, II, and III of Mr. Justice White's opinion. . . .

If we were presented here with a classification of voters motivated by racial animus, *City of Richmond v. United States*, 422 U.S. 358, 378 (1975); *Wright v. Rockefeller*, 376 U.S. 52, 58 (1964); *Gomillion v. Lightfoot*, 364 U.S. 339, 347 (1960), or with a classification that effectively downgraded minority participation in the franchise, *Georgia v. United States, supra*, 411 U.S., at 534; *Whitcomb v. Chavis*, 403 U.S. 124, 144 (1971), we promptly would characterize the resort to race as "suspect" and prohibit its use. Under such circumstances, the tainted apportionment process would not necessarily be saved by its proportional outcome, for the segregation of voters into "separate but equal" blocs still might well have the intent or effect of diluting the voting power of minority voters. . . .

[Here,] . . . the challenged race assignment may be permissible because it is cast in a remedial context with respect to a disadvantaged class rather than in a setting that aims to demean or insult any racial group. . . . Such a decision, in my view, raises particularly sensitive issues of doctrine and policy. Unlike Part IV of Mr. Justice White's opinion, I am wholly content to leave this thorny question until another day, for I am convinced that the existence of the Voting Rights Act makes such a decision unnecessary and alone suffices to support an affirmance of the judgment before us.

I begin with the settled principle that not every remedial use of race is forbidden. . . . In my view, if and when a decisionmaker embarks on a policy of benign racial sorting, he must weigh the concerns [justifying remediation] . . . against the need for effective social policies promoting racial justice in a society beset by deeprooted racial inequities. But I believe that Congress here adequately struck that balance in enacting the carefully conceived remedial scheme embodied in the Voting Rights Act. . . .

Mr. Justice STEWART, with whom Mr. Justice POWELL joins, concurring in the judgment.

The petitioners' contention is essentially that racial awareness in legislative reapportionment is unconstitutional per se. Acceptance of their position would mark an egregious departure from the way this Court has in the past analyzed the constitutionality of claimed discrimination in dealing with the elective franchise on the basis of race.

The petitioners have made no showing that a racial criterion was used as a basis for denying them their right to vote, in contravention of the Fifteenth Amendment. See *Gomillion v. Lightfoot*, 364 U.S. 339. They have made no showing that the redistricting scheme was employed as part of a "contrivance to segregate"; to minimize or cancel out the voting strength of a minority class or interest; or otherwise to impair or burden the opportunity of affected persons to participate in the political process. See *Wright v. Rockefeller*, 376 U.S. 52, 58; *White v. Regester*, 412 U.S. 755; *Louisiana v. United States*, 380 U.S. 145; *Fortson v. Dorsey*, 379 U.S. 433.

Under the Fourteenth Amendment the question is whether the reapportionment plan represents purposeful discrimination against white voters. *Washington v. Davis*, 426 U.S. 229. Disproportionate impact may afford some evidence that an invidious purpose was present. *Arlington Heights v. Metropolitan Housing Dev. Corp.*, 429 U.S. 252, 256. But the record here does not support a finding that the redistricting plan undervalued the political power of white voters relative to their numbers in Kings County. Cf. *City of Richmond v. United States*, 422 U.S. 358. That the legislature was aware of race when it drew the district lines might also suggest a discriminatory purpose. Such awareness is not, however, the equivalent of discriminatory intent. The clear purpose with which the New York Legislature acted in response to the position of the United States Department of Justice under the Voting Rights Act forecloses any finding that it acted with the invidious purpose of discriminating against white voters.

Having failed to show that the legislative reapportionment plan had either the purpose or the effect of discriminating against them on the basis of their race, the petitioners have offered no basis for affording them the constitutional relief they seek. Accordingly, I join the judgment of the Court.

Mr. Chief Justice BURGER, dissenting.

. . . If *Gomillion* teaches anything, I had thought it was that drawing of political boundary lines with the sole, explicit objective of reaching a predetermined racial result cannot ordinarily be squared with the Constitution. The record before us reveals and it is not disputed that this is precisely what took place here. In drawing up the 1974 reapportionment scheme, the New York Legislature did not consider racial composition as merely one of several political characteristics; on the contrary, race appears to have been the one and only criterion applied.

. . . In *Allen* and *Katzenbach* the Court acknowledged that the Voting Rights Act contemplated that the Attorney General and the affected state legislatures would be obliged to think in racial terms. . . . The present case, however, presents a quite different situation. Faced with the straightforward obligation to redistrict so as to avoid "a retrogression in the position of racial minorities with respect to their effective exercise of the electoral franchise," *Beer v. United States*, 425 U.S. 130, 141, the state legislature mechanically adhered to a plan designed to maintain without tolerance for even a 1.6% deviation a "nonwhite" population of 65% within several of the new districts. There is no indication whatever that use of this rigid figure was in any way related much less necessary to fulfilling the State's obligation under the Voting Rights Act as defined in *Beer.* . . .

The assumption that "whites" and "nonwhites" in the County form homogeneous entities for voting purposes is entirely without foundation. The "whites" category consists of a veritable galaxy of national origins, ethnic backgrounds, and religious denominations. It simply cannot be assumed that the legislative interests of all "whites" are even substantially identical. In similar fashion, those described as "nonwhites" include, in addition to Negroes, a substantial portion of Puerto Ricans. Memorandum of Decision, U.S. Dept. of Justice Nos. V6541-47, July 1, 1974, p. 13 (App. 294).[3] The Puerto Rican population, for whose protection the Voting Rights Act was "triggered" in Kings County, has expressly disavowed any identity of interest with the Negroes, and, in fact, objected to the 1974 redistricting scheme because it did not establish a Puerto Rican controlled district within the county. . . . While petitioners certainly have no constitutional right to remain unified within a single political district, they do have, in my view, the constitutional right not to be carved up so as to create a voting bloc composed of some other ethnic or racial group through the kind of racial gerrymandering the Court condemned in *Gomillion v. Lightfoot.* . . .

The result reached by the Court today in the name of the Voting Rights Act is ironic. The use of a mathematical formula tends to sustain the existence of ghettos by promoting the notion that political clout is to be gained or maintained by marshaling particular racial, ethnic, or religious groups in enclaves. It suggests to the voter that only a candidate of the same race, religion, or ethnic origin can properly represent that voter's interests, and that such candidate can be elected only from a district with a sufficient minority concentration. The device employed by the State of New York and endorsed by the Court today, moves us one step farther away from a truly homogeneous society. This retreat from the ideal of the American "melting pot" is curiously out of step with recent political history and indeed with what the Court has said and done for more than a decade. The notion that Americans vote in firm blocs has been repudiated in the election of minority members as mayors and legislators in numerous American cities and districts overwhelmingly white. Since I cannot square the mechanical racial gerrymandering in this case with the mandate of the Constitution, I respectfully dissent from the affirmance of the judgment of the Court of Appeals.

>> *Creating a "Safe" Minority-Controlled Seat.*   In redistricting, the main response to the VRA's prohibition of submersion of minority political power has been the creation of so-called majority-minority districts — districts that are controlled by members of the group in question. One issue that confronts redistricters, then,

---

3. The Puerto Rican population constitutes 10.4% of the entire county population and one-third of the "nonwhite" population.

is how many members of the relevant minority group must be drawn into the district in order to assure that group's control over the district's electoral politics. For many years, voting rights lawyers had generally set the necessary degree of minority control at 65 percent (the benchmark apparently used in *UJO*). According to this standard, a district was not deemed to be reliably under black control unless its voting population was 65 percent black.

> The belief that super-majorities were needed if districts were to elect African-Americans rested on three premises: blacks register at lower rates than whites; among registrants, blacks are less likely to turn out and vote than are whites; and white voters are less likely to vote for a black candidate than black voters are to cast ballots for a white candidate. Along with these assumptions came the understandable desire among prospective candidates in these majority-minority districts to stack the odds in their favor. If the minority population were sufficiently large, then the choice of a candidate would be confined to the Democratic party, thereby avoiding a serious general election campaign. Moreover, the black vote constitutes a greater share of the vote in a Democratic primary than in a general election, so prospects for electing African-Americans rise when the determination is made in the primary. . . .
>
> [However, contemporary research shows that the] sixty-five percent rule that once guided districting efforts sets too high a standard today for congressional districts. As long as white crossover rates outpace black crossovers, and black and white registration rates are roughly equal, African-Americans will not need majority-black districts to win. With black Democratic candidates able to muster almost universal support from the African-American electorate, the crossover advantage will not likely be imperiled even as more southern whites shift support to the GOP. Currently, black Democrats, although not performing as well with the white electorate as do white Democrats, attract about a third of the white vote. Support at this level, often coupled with near universal black support, should enable blacks to win in congressional districts in which African-Americans are numerous but less than a majority.

Charles S. Bullock, III and Richard E. Dunn, *The Demise of Racial Redistricting and the Future of Black Representation*, 48 EMORY L.J. 1209 (1999). If Bullock and Dunn's conclusion is correct, black voting power could be maintained, and probably increased, by spreading black voters more thinly than the 65-percent rule would have allowed.

>> *The Problem of "Filler People."* The plaintiffs in *UJO* complained that their own voting strength as a group had been diluted by being spread across too many districts. The force of this claim was enhanced by the fact that the plaintiffs were not merely "undifferentiated" white voters, but Hasidic Jews, members of a discrete and extremely cohesive religious community. But did the plaintiffs' claim of injury depend upon their membership in such a group? Every time a district is drawn so as to give control to one group within its borders, other voters in the district are placed in a position where their ability to influence the selection of representatives is intentionally compromised. Consider the following account:

[F]or the state to create viable minority districts, . . . the state must create two groups of voters . . . on the basis of their race or ethnicity. First, the state must assign black voters to compact, majority-black districts on the basis of their race. Second, the state must assign some group of voters to nondiluted, nonpacked districts to balance out the numerical mandates of one person, one vote. These additional individuals must not be of the relevant demographic group (in order to avoid claims of packing); and, in the interest of minority representation, they should not be expected to compete in any genuine sense for electoral representation in the district to which they are assigned lest they undo the preference given to the specified minority group. It is the status of this precarious group — the filler people — that raises extraordinarily troubling problems under current voting-rights jurisprudence. . . .

The majority in *UJO* had no problem rejecting the claims of the filler people because the Court assumed that filler people were not subjected to a dilution of their aggregate group strength, and the Court found no stigma associated with the state's classification. . . . Filler people are by their very nature electoral fodder, means to others' ends. . . . [But it might be said that w]henever districts are drawn to create a designated group beneficiary, the nonpreferred group is essentialized or, worse, denied their dignitary right to equal treatment and respect by having their welfare discounted.

The Court's apparent response is that there is no reason to assume that a representative will not represent all residents of the district. That is, once an election is held, "filler people" become "constituents" and command the same attention from their representative as other members of the district. But this view seems mere wishful thinking, particularly in districts drawn to comply with the Voting Rights Act. In such cases, polarized voting is a proven fact, and there is little reason to believe that a representative will not pay primary attention to the majority group in the district — a group expressly brought together to elect the representative of its choice. This point can be generalized beyond voting-rights cases. If we do not think that there are predictable consequences from the way we draw district lines, then any lines will do. But just the opposite is true. Line drawers invariably know who stands to gain or lose when pencil meets map, and winners, not surprisingly, use their power to elect representatives responsive to their concerns.

T. Alexander Aleinikoff and Samuel Issacharoff, *Race and Redistricting: Drawing Constitutional Lines After* Shaw v. Reno, 92 MICH. L. REV. 588, 630-633 (1993).

>> ***Race and the Problem of "Authentic" Representation.*** The point of assuring any group electoral control over a legislative district is, obviously, to assure that group the ability to elect the representative of its choice. But given such control, how should the favored group choose among possible candidates? Should it take the opportunity presented by electoral control to elect one of its own members? Or is it sufficient to elect a person whom group members feel will represent them and their interests effectively? Is someone who is not a member of the underrepresented

group *capable* of representing it? Can whites adequately represent blacks? Can blacks adequately represent Hasidic Jews? Can Anglos adequately represent Latinos?

A theory of representation that requires the representative to share some relevant characteristic of the represented is often called a theory of "descriptive representation." *See* HANNA FENICHEL PITKIN, THE CONCEPT OF REPRESENTATION ch. 4 (1967). During the Revolutionary period, John Adams argued that a legislature "should be an exact portrait, in miniature, of the people at large, as it should think, feel, reason and act like them." John Adams, *Letter to John Penn, in* 4 WORKS 205. Does sharing a trait of race, ethnicity or religion enable a representative to "think, feel, reason and act" like his or her constituents? A more sophisticated defense of descriptive representation has been worked out by Anne Phillips, who calls it a "politics of presence":

> If we were to be strict in our definitions, we would have to say that representatives only "really" represent their constituents on the issues that were explicitly debated in the course of the election campaign. On everything else, the representatives have to fall back on their own judgement or their own prejudice. And though some of this could be averted by fuller discussion of a wider range of issues, citizens have neither the time nor the knowledge to extract a comprehensive statement of what candidates might think on every issue that might conceivably arise. They then have to fall back on some more general notion of the ways in which they are being represented. . . . Whether these candidates are male or female, black or white, recent or long-ago migrants, can then become of major significance.
>
> [Another argument] is that people from disadvantaged groups need more aggressive advocates on the public stage. Not that people never act for anyone other than themselves: some of the existing political parties have established a worthy record of policies against discrimination or programmes for disadvantaged groups; and wherever such policies are implemented, it is by legislative assemblies in which those discriminated against have a negligible presence. Politicians are elected on party commitments, which might include any number of policies relating to sexual or racial equality or the fairer treatment of minority groups. If there is a clear mandate for these policies, does it really matter who the politicians are? Why not put the effort into establishing the commitments, rather than bothering about the characteristics of the people who implement them?
>
> Part of the answer to this refers back to symbolic representation, for there is something distinctly odd about a democracy that accepts a responsibility for redressing disadvantage, but never sees the disadvantaged as the appropriate people to carry this through. The other part is grounded in a rather sober pessimism about the limits to binding mandates. As any reasonably diligent observer of the political process will confirm, policy decisions are not settled in advance by party programmes or election commitments. New problems and issues always emerge alongside unanticipated constraints, and in the subsequent weighing of interpretations and priorities it can matter immensely who the representatives are. When there is a significant under-representation of disadvantaged groups at the

point of final decision, this can and does have serious consequences. However strong our attachment to the politics of binding mandates (people of
course vary in this), representatives *do* have considerable autonomy, which
is part of why it matters who those representatives are.

[A final argument] stresses those ideas or concerns that have not
even reached the political agenda The problem of representation is not
just that preferences refuse to cluster around a neat set of political alternatives, or that the enforced choice between only two packages can leave
major interest groups without any voice. There is an additional problem
of the preferences not yet legitimated, the views not even formulated,
much less expressed. . . . In the market-place paradigm which sees citizens
choosing between packages of political ideas, there is little space for further development. People become consumers of existing products, and
cannot do much to alter the range. They can pressure political parties
to take up issues that no one party has so far addressed, and once these
issues are on the agenda they can use the ballot box to "punish" those
who still ignore them. They may not, however, even be able to formulate
these new issues if they are not first drawn into the political process. It is
only when people are more consistently present in the process of working out alternatives that they have much chance of challenging dominant
conventions. The argument for a more equitable distribution of representative positions is very much bound up with this.

ANNE PHILLIPS, THE POLITICS OF PRESENCE 43-45 (1995). *See also* Jane Mansbridge,
Should Blacks Represent Blacks and Women Represent Women? A Contingent "Yes," 61 J.
POL. 628 (1999).

Consider the following response by Carol Swain, a more empirically oriented
political scientist:

White representatives who support the goals of blacks, however
these goals are defined, are a further source of black representation. . . .
[The evidence shows that many white representatives take] seriously their
mandate to represent black interests even when their districts were still
majority-white. They supported and helped push civil rights legislation
and Great Society programs through a reluctant Congress at a time when
the few blacks in Congress lacked the seniority, clout, experience, and
other resources to take on leadership roles. . . . [D]escriptive representation of blacks guarantees only black faces and is, at best, an intangible
good; substantive representation is by definition real and color blind. Substantive representation can be measured by a politician's performance on
indicators such as voting and casework.

Many white members of Congress perform as well or better on the
indicators . . . than some black representatives. Many of the white associate
members of the Black Caucus have already shown that they are prepared
to and can serve the interests of blacks by actively working to frame legislation that will benefit disadvantaged groups and by supporting causes
that the majority of African Americans consider in their interest. Some of
them, moreover, are high in seniority and hold congressional leadership

positions that enable them to act effectively on advancing their legislative agendas. . . .

What difference does the race of the representative make for the representation of black policy preferences? . . . It is evident that partisanship and region are far more important than race in predicting whether representatives will pursue black interests. . . . [Nevertheless, a]lthough a white representative can "think, act, and talk black," he or she can never *be* black. White representation of blacks will never replace black representation. . . . The presence of black representatives in Congress, regardless of their political party, fulfills a host of psychological needs that are no less important for being intangible. One need only attend an annual Black Caucus legislative weekend to see the pride that the hundreds of blacks who attend the affair have in the group of congressional black representatives. Black representatives are celebrities — icons for their group. . . .

Although black Republicans do not represent the substantive interests of the majority of African Americans, they have something valuable to contribute to both whites and blacks. Their counterintuitive positions help to remind people that blacks are not monolithic. Confronted with this information, as Americans were in the case of the Clarence Thomas confirmation hearings, when impressive blacks testified for both sides, white Americans may be more likely to treat blacks as individuals and less likely to succumb to racial polarization.

CAROL SWAIN, BLACK FACES, BLACK INTERESTS: THE REPRESENTATION OF AFRICAN AMERICANS IN CONGRESS 211-217 (1993). Swain goes on to conclude that black voters might be better served by attending more closely to the interests representatives commit to advancing rather than their race.

Empirical social science research tends to support the contention that descriptive representation does, under certain circumstances, make a small but measurable difference in the likelihood of a state legislature acting favorably on matters of interest to the black community. One study examining the behavior of state legislatures between 1971 and 1994 found that increases in the proportion of black legislators resulted in modest increases in spending in policy areas of interest to black constituents. Chris T. Owens, *Black Substantive Representation in State Legislatures from 1971-1994*, 86 SOC. SCI. Q. 779 (2005). The effect, however, can vary with the circumstances. Where legislative politics are "racialized" in a negative and antagonistic way, black descriptive representation accomplishes little and may even be counterproductive, as black representatives are likely to be marginalized. Where legislative politics are not racialized, however, descriptive representation can produce a legislature somewhat more responsive to minority policy interests than it would otherwise be. *See* Robert R. Preuhs, *The Conditional Effect of Minority Descriptive Representation: Black Legislators and Policy Influence in the American States*, 68 J. POL. 585 (2006).

What explains this effect? The evidence is fragmented. One obvious possibility is politics as usual: like any politicians, black legislators may be more likely to reward their active supporters with policy benefits, and when their supporters are black, black politicians funnel benefits in that direction. One study that provides support for this possibility found that black employment and labor force participation tend to rise following the election of a black mayor. This effect is most pronounced in the municipal employment sector, suggesting that black officials are more willing than whites to hire black employees, or at least expect more strongly to benefit politically from doing so. John V.C. Nye, Ilia Rainer, and Thomas Stratmann, *Do Black Mayors Improve Black Employment Outcomes? Evidence from Large U.S. Cities*, 31 J.L. Econ. & Org. 383 (2014). Another possibility is that black legislators are simply more interested than white legislators in advancing the welfare of the black community. A recent study supporting this possibility found that black legislators were twice as likely as non-black legislators to respond to correspondence from black citizens living outside their election districts — that is, in circumstances where there could be no possible political reward for doing so. David E. Broockman, *Black Politicians Are More Intrinsically Motivated to Advance Blacks' Interests: A Field Experiment Manipulating Political Incentives*, 57 Am. J. Pol. Sci. 521 (2013). A third possible explanation is a communication effect. On this account, black voters feel more comfortable communicating their views to black legislators, and consequently communicate much less freely with their representative when he or she is white. As a result, even white politicians of good will who are willing to listen obtain a distorted understanding of the views of their constituents, leading them to pursue a legislative agenda that overweighs the interests of white constituents. David E. Broockman, *Distorted Communication, Unequal Representation: Constituents Communicate Less to Representatives Not of Their Race*, 58 Am. J. Pol. Sci. 307 (2013).

Even assuming that some kind of descriptive representation is necessary or desirable, does it follow that *each* election district must have a representative who descriptively represents the majority of voters *in that district*? In footnote 24 of the *UJO* opinion, the Court wrote:

> the white voter who as a result of the 1974 plan is in a district more likely to return a nonwhite representative will be represented, to the extent that voting continues to follow racial lines, by legislators elected from majority white districts. The effect of the reapportionment on whites in districts where nonwhite majorities have been increased is thus mitigated by the preservation of white majority districts in the rest of the county.

In other words, whites (and by implication blacks and other groups) can be descriptively represented by legislators other than their own — a kind of "virtual descriptive representation." Can the desire for descriptive representation, to the extent it is legitimate, be satisfied by virtual representation offered by other representatives elected from other districts? Even if voters' desire for a descriptive representative of their own cannot be satisfied virtually, might virtual descriptive representation nonetheless confer any substantive benefits? A recent comparative study found that the presence in a legislature of even a single LGBT legislator can have a significant impact on the positions taken by the legislature as a whole on issues of interest to the LGBT community: "a country that has elected an LGBT member to parliament is 14 times more likely to have marriage equality or civil union/registered partner laws than a country without an elected gay MP." Andrew Reynolds, *Representation and Rights: The Impact of LGBT Legislators in Comparative Perspective*, 107 AM. POL. SCI. REV. 259 (2013). Why? Does the presence of minority legislators in the body alter the legislature's discourse? Its beliefs?

There is also a robust literature on the relationship between descriptive representation and political efficacy, which political scientists largely define as a sense of trust in the system and influence. On average, for African American voters, descriptive representation is positively correlated with political efficacy. *See, e.g,* Emily A. West, *Descriptive Representation and Political Efficacy: Evidence from Obama and Clinton*, 79 J. POL. 351 (2017); Susan A. Banduci, Todd Donovan, & Jeffrey A. Karp, *Minority Representation, Empowerment, and Participation*, 66 J. POL. 534 (2004); and Claudine Gay, *Spirals of Trust?: The Effect of Descriptive Representation on the Relationship between Citizens and Their Government*, 46 AM. J. POL. SCI. 717 (2002). Interestingly, the correlation between descriptive representation and efficacy is weaker for women voters.

>> ***Representation Quotas.***   In the United States, legally enforced racial, ethnic, and gender quotas for public office are typically unconstitutional. That is not the case abroad, and many societies have turned to quotas to force their legislatures more closely to resemble the general population. One of the most popular kinds of quotas is gender-based: more than 130 nations around the world require national or local legislatures to include some minimum proportion of women among the representatives. Such quotas are often imposed by regulating the nominees of political parties. In France, parties that fail to nominate the required quota of women lose some public funding. In Brazil, parties failing to comply must forfeit seats. *See* Amanda Clayton, *How Do Electoral Gender Quotas Affect Policy?*, 24 ANN. REV. POL. SCI. 235 (2021); Patricia Popelier, *A Constitutional Perspective on Electoral Gender Quotas, in* COMPARATIVE ELECTION LAW (James A. Gardner, ed., 2022).

What is the effect of such quotas on politics in the nations where they have been adopted? According to one study, the interest of adolescent girls and women in politics, and the likelihood that they will participate in politics as adults, increases along with the proportion of women holding legislative office. Christina Wolbrecht and David E. Campbell, *Leading by Example: Female Members of Parliament as Political Role Models*, 51 AM. J. POL. SCI. 921 (2007). Other studies have found that the presence of female representatives has a substantive effect on policies considered and adopted by the legislature. For example, a study of Norwegian local legislatures found a correlation between the number of female representatives and the generosity of child care policies adopted by the legislature. Health care and elimination of poverty rise higher on the legislative agenda when more women are in the legislature. Clayton, *supra.* In other words, descriptive representation had substantive ramifications. Kathleen A. Bratton and Leonard P. Ray, *Descriptive Representation, Policy Outcomes, and Municipal Day-Care Coverage in Norway*, 46 AM. J. POL. SCI. 428 (2002).

In New York City, party officials known as "district leaders" "shall be of opposite sexes, if the rules of the county [party] committee so provide." Under this provision, political parties in New York City can establish gender quotas for certain kinds of party leadership positions. New York Election Law §2-110(2). Is this provision constitutional? Does the answer depend on whether the party is more like an arm of the government or more like a private association? See Chapter 7 for more on the nature of political parties.

2. *Section 2: Race, Redistricting, and the* Shaw *Cases*

Although the Court has never directly addressed the constitutionality of Section 2 of the Voting Rights Act, it seemed implicitly to validate the constitutionality of Section 2 in *UJO*, and the question did not come up in *Gingles*. The issue has never been squarely raised by litigants or by the Justices, but in a 1993 decision that caught many people by surprise, the Court suggested, somewhat obliquely, that Section 2, or at least the prevailing interpretation of Section 2, might be unconstitutional.

>> *The* Shaw *Decision.*   *Shaw v. Reno,* 509 U.S. 630 (1993), concerned the constitutionality of North Carolina's Twelfth Congressional District, a majority-black district created in response to objections from the United States Justice Department that North Carolina had drawn its election districts in a way that failed to provide black voters with adequate voting strength.

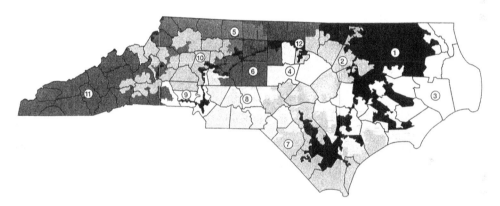

Calling the district's shape "bizarre," the Court described it in the following terms:

> District 12 is . . . unusually shaped. It is approximately 160 miles long and, for much of its length, no wider than the I-85 corridor. It winds in snake-like fashion through tobacco country, financial centers, and manufacturing areas "until it gobbles in enough enclaves of black neighborhoods." Northbound and southbound drivers on I-85 sometimes find themselves in separate districts in one county, only to "trade" districts when they enter the next county. Of the 10 counties through which District 12 passes, five are cut into three different districts; even towns are divided. At one point the district remains contiguous only because it intersects at a single point with two other districts before crossing over them. One state legislator has remarked that " 'if you drove down the interstate with both car doors open, you'd kill most of the people in the district.' "

The district was challenged by a group of *white* voters on constitutional grounds:

> Appellants alleged not that the revised plan constituted a political gerrymander, nor that it violated the "one person, one vote" principle, see *Reynolds v. Sims*, 377 U.S. 533 (1964), but that the State had created an unconstitutional *racial* gerrymander. . . . That argument strikes a powerful historical chord: It is unsettling how closely the North Carolina plan resembles the most egregious racial gerrymanders of the past.
>
> An understanding of the nature of appellants' claim is critical to our resolution of the case. In their complaint, appellants did not claim that the General Assembly's reapportionment plan unconstitutionally "diluted" white voting strength. They did not even claim to be white. Rather, appellants' complaint alleged that the deliberate segregation of voters into separate districts on the basis of race violated their constitutional right to participate in a "color-blind" electoral process.

The Court proved receptive to this claim. "Classifications of citizens solely on the basis of race," the Court said, are "odious" because they "stigmatize individuals by reason of their membership in a racial group [and] incite racial hostility." Consequently, the Court decided to apply strict scrutiny to "redistricting legislation that is so bizarre on its face that it is 'unexplainable on grounds other than race.'" In language that proved highly confusing to civil rights lawyers and lower courts, the Court seemed to place great emphasis on the shape of the district:

> In some exceptional cases, a reapportionment plan may be so highly irregular that, on its face, it rationally cannot be understood as anything other than an effort to "segregate . . . voters" on the basis of race. *Gomillion, supra*, at 341. *Gomillion*, in which a tortured municipal boundary line was drawn to exclude black voters, was such a case.
>
> Put differently, we believe that reapportionment is one area in which appearances do matter. A reapportionment plan that includes in one district individuals who belong to the same race, but who are otherwise widely separated by geographical and political boundaries, and who may have little in common with one another but the color of their skin, bears an uncomfortable resemblance to political apartheid. It reinforces the perception that members of the same racial group—regardless of their age, education, economic status, or the community in which they live—think alike, share the same political interests, and will prefer the same candidates at the polls. We have rejected such perceptions elsewhere as impermissible racial stereotypes. By perpetuating such notions, a racial gerrymander may exacerbate the very patterns of racial bloc voting that majority-minority districting is sometimes said to counteract.
>
> The message that such districting sends to elected representatives is equally pernicious. When a district obviously is created solely to effectuate the perceived common interests of one racial group, elected officials are more likely to believe that their primary obligation is to represent only the members of that group, rather than their constituency as a whole. This is altogether antithetical to our system of representative democracy.

The Court limited its decision to holding that the plaintiffs had stated a claim under the Fourteenth Amendment, and remanded the case for further proceedings.

>> *What Harm Did the Plaintiffs Suffer in* **Shaw?**   As the Court notes, the plaintiffs in *Shaw* "did not even claim to be white." By failing to allege any particular group membership, they thereby renounced any ability to raise the kind of claim made by the plaintiffs in *UJO*—that they were members of a distinct group that had been gerrymandered into a minority status within the challenged district and whose votes were therefore impermissibly rendered ineffective through some kind of group-based vote dilution. Nor could whites as a statewide group challenge the districting plan on vote dilution grounds because the plan actually provided roughly proportionate representation in North Carolina's congressional delegation to whites and blacks. What, then, was the harm suffered by the plaintiffs and recognized by the Court?

In an influential article, Richard Pildes, a law professor, and Richard Niemi, a political scientist, argued that *Shaw* recognized an entirely new kind of constitutional injury that involves "expressive" harms. "The theory of voting rights [*Shaw*] endorses," they wrote, "centers on the perceived legitimacy of structures of political representation, rather than on the distribution of actual political power between racial or political groups." Claims of vote dilution and claims of bizarre district appearance "share no common conceptual elements. They recognize distinct kinds of injuries, implicate different constitutional values, and reflect differing conceptions of the relationship between law and politics." Pildes and Niemi went on to explain:

> When race becomes the single dominant value to which the process subordinates all others . . . , it triggers *Shaw*. For the Court, what distinguishes "bizarre" race-conscious districts is the signal they send out that, to government officials, race has become paramount and dwarfed all other, traditionally relevant criteria. This view is the foundation of the qualitative distinction central to *Shaw*: at a certain point, the use of race . . . creates the social impression that one legitimate value has come to dominate all others.
>
> In resisting the use of race in this specific way, *Shaw* requires that redistricting continue to be understood—and, perhaps more importantly, perceived—as implicating multiple values. . . . [I]n the Court's eyes, oddly shaped race-conscious districts compromise the values of political integrity and legitimacy. . . . When political bodies devise extremely contorted districting schemes, the violation of these standards suggests politicians are engaged in manipulation of public institutions for their own ends. . . .
>
> One can only understand *Shaw*, we believe, in terms of a view that what we call expressive harms are constitutionally cognizable. An expressive harm is one that results from the ideas or attitudes expressed through a governmental action, rather than from the more tangible or material consequences the action brings about. On this view, the meaning of a governmental action is just as important as what that action does. Public policies can violate the Constitution not only because they bring about concrete costs, but because the very meaning they convey demonstrates

inappropriate respect for relevant public values. On this unusual conception of constitutional harm, when a governmental action expresses disrespect for such values, it can violate the Constitution. . . . Expressive harms are therefore, in general, social rather than individual. Their primary effect is not as much the tangible burdens they impose on particular individuals, but the way in which they undermine collective understandings.

Richard H. Pildes and Richard G. Niemi, *Expressive Harms, "Bizarre Districts," and Voting Rights: Evaluating Election-District Appearances After* Shaw v. Reno, 92 MICH. L. REV. 483 (1993). In a later ruling, *Bush v. Vera*, 517 U.S. 952, 984 (1996), Justice O'Connor adopted the term "expressive harms" for the Court.

Do you agree that race-conscious districting inflicts an expressive harm on society? Isn't the idea behind race-conscious districting undertaken pursuant to the Voting Rights Act a good one—namely, to redress past racial discrimination in voting and to prevent such discrimination in the future? Why wouldn't the "message" sent by extreme efforts to assure black representation be the benign one of official pursuit of racial harmony? It has been argued that *Shaw* is better characterized as a capitulation by the Court to an incorrect social understanding of race-conscious districting:

> [T]here is no good reason for the Supreme Court to give those who misinterpret a policy a kind of constitutional veto power over it. Instead, the Court should be in the business of setting straight those who misconstrue the meaning of a policy that is under constitutional challenge and issuing its ruling on the basis of an adequate understanding of that meaning.

Andrew Altman, *Expressive Meaning, Race and the Law: The Racial Gerrymandering Cases*, 5 LEGAL THEORY 75, 90-91 (1999). Do you agree?

>> **Standing to Challenge Racial Gerrymandering.**   In *United States v. Hays*, 515 U.S. 737 (1995), a group of voters sought to challenge Louisiana's legislative apportionment plan on the ground that it involved the kind of purely racial gerrymandering condemned in *Shaw*. However, the challengers did not reside within the district that was "the primary focus of their racial gerrymandering claim." The Court dismissed the case because the plaintiffs lacked standing to bring a *Shaw* claim. "Where a plaintiff resides in a racially gerrymandered district," the Court explained, "the plaintiff has been denied equal treatment because of the legislature's reliance on racial criteria, and therefore has standing to challenge the legislature's action." On the other hand, if the plaintiff does not live in the gerrymandered district, the Court said, the plaintiff cannot have suffered the stigmatization and impairment of representation at issue in *Shaw*.

Is the result in *Hays* consistent with the Court's articulation of the injury in *Shaw*? If the constitutionally relevant injury is the "expressive harm" communicated when a government makes race the main consideration in drawing district lines, wouldn't the injury be suffered by anyone who receives the harmful message? Is there any reason to think that the message communicated by excessively race-oriented districting is received only by people who live in the challenged district? If *Hays* is correct about limitations on standing, must not the relevant injury be some kind of dilution of the votes of whites living in the gerrymandered district rather than a broad communicative harm to the public? For commentary, see Samuel Issacharoff and Pamela S. Karlan, *Standing and Misunderstanding in Voting Rights Law*, 111 HARV. L. REV. 2276 (1998); Judith Reed, *Sense and Nonsense: Standing in the Racial Districting Cases as a Window on the Supreme Court's View of the Right to Vote*, 4 MICH. J. RACE & L. 389 (1999).

———————

The immediate result of *Shaw* was to sow immense confusion in the lower courts. The Supreme Court soon realized that it would have to clarify its ruling in that case, and attempted to do so in the case below.

Miller v. Johnson

515 U.S. 900 (1995)

Justice KENNEDY delivered the opinion of the Court.

The constitutionality of Georgia's congressional redistricting plan is at issue here. In *Shaw v. Reno*, 509 U.S. 630 (1993), we held that a plaintiff states a claim under the Equal Protection Clause by alleging that a state redistricting plan, on its face, has no rational explanation save as an effort to separate voters on the basis of race. The question we now decide is whether Georgia's new Eleventh District gives rise to a valid equal protection claim under the principles announced in *Shaw*, and, if so, whether it can be sustained nonetheless as narrowly tailored to serve a compelling governmental interest.

I

A

The Equal Protection Clause of the Fourteenth Amendment provides that no State shall "deny to any person within its jurisdiction the equal protection of the laws." U.S. Const., Amdt. 14, §1. Its central mandate is racial neutrality in governmental decisionmaking. Though application of this imperative raises difficult questions, the basic principle is straightforward: "Racial and ethnic distinctions of any sort are inherently suspect and thus call for the most exacting judicial examination. . . . This perception of racial and ethnic distinctions is rooted in our Nation's constitutional and demographic history." *Regents of Univ. of California v. Bakke*, 438 U.S. 265 (1978) (opinion of Powell, J.). This rule obtains with equal force regardless of "the race of those burdened or benefitted by a particular classification." *Richmond v. J. A. Croson Co.*, 488 U.S. 469, 494 (1989) (plurality opinion). Laws classifying citizens on the basis of race cannot be upheld unless they are narrowly tailored to achieving a compelling state interest.

In *Shaw v. Reno* we recognized that these equal protection principles govern a State's drawing of congressional districts, though, as our cautious approach there discloses, application of these principles to electoral districting is a most delicate task. Our analysis began from the premise that "laws that explicitly distinguish between individuals on racial grounds fall within the core of [the Equal Protection Clause's] prohibition." *Id.* This prohibition extends not just to explicit racial classifications, but also to laws neutral on their face but " 'unexplainable on grounds other than race.' " *Id.* (quoting *Arlington Heights v. Metropolitan Housing Development Corp.*, 429 U.S. 252, 266 (1977)). Applying this basic Equal Protection analysis in the voting rights context, we held that "redistricting legislation that is so bizarre on its face that it is 'unexplainable on grounds other than race,' . . . demands the same close scrutiny that we give other state laws that classify citizens by race."

This case requires us to apply the principles articulated in *Shaw* to the most recent congressional redistricting plan enacted by the State of Georgia.

B

In 1965, the Attorney General designated Georgia a covered jurisdiction under §4(b) of the Voting Rights Act. In consequence, §5 of the Act requires Georgia to obtain either administrative preclearance by the Attorney General or approval by the United States District Court for the District of Columbia of any change in a "standard, practice, or procedure with respect to voting" made after November 1, 1964. 42 U.S.C. §1973c. The preclearance mechanism applies to congressional redistricting plans, and requires that the proposed change "not have the purpose and will not have the effect of denying or abridging the right to vote on account of race or color." 42 U.S.C. §1973c. "The purpose of §5 has always been to insure that no voting-procedure changes would be made that would lead to a retrogression in the position of racial minorities with respect to their effective exercise of the electoral franchise."

Between 1980 and 1990, one of Georgia's 10 congressional districts was a majority-black district, that is, a majority of the district's voters were black. The 1990 Decennial Census indicated that Georgia's population of 6,478,216 persons, 27% of whom are black, entitled it to an additional eleventh congressional seat, App. 9, prompting Georgia's General Assembly to redraw the State's congressional districts. Both the House and the Senate adopted redistricting guidelines which, among other things, required single-member districts of equal population, contiguous geography, nondilution of minority voting strength, fidelity to precinct lines where possible, and compliance with §§2 and 5 of the Act, 42 U.S.C. §§1973, 1973c. Only after these requirements were met did the guidelines permit drafters to consider other ends, such as maintaining the integrity of political subdivisions, preserving the core of existing districts, and avoiding contests between incumbents.

A special session opened in August 1991, and the General Assembly submitted a congressional redistricting plan to the Attorney General for preclearance on October 1, 1991. The legislature's plan contained two majority-minority districts, the Fifth and Eleventh, and an additional district, the Second, in which blacks comprised just over 35% of the voting age population. Despite the plan's increase in the number of majority-black districts from one to two and the absence of any evidence of an intent to discriminate against minority voters, 864 F. Supp. 1354, 1363, and n.7 (S.D. Ga. 1994), the Department of Justice refused preclearance on January 21, 1992. The Department's objection letter noted a concern that Georgia had created only two majority-minority districts, and that the proposed plan did not "recognize" certain minority populations by placing them in a majority-black district.

The General Assembly returned to the drawing board. A new plan was enacted and submitted for preclearance. This second attempt assigned the black population in Central Georgia's Baldwin County to the Eleventh District and increased the black populations in the Eleventh, Fifth and Second Districts. The Justice Department refused preclearance again, relying on alternative plans proposing three majority-minority districts. *Id.*, 120-126. One of the alternative schemes relied on by the Department was the so-called "max-black" plan, 864 F. Supp. at 1360, 1362-1363, drafted by the American Civil Liberties Union (ACLU) for the General Assembly's black caucus. The key to the ACLU's plan was the "Macon/Savannah trade." The dense black population in the Macon region would be transferred from the Eleventh District to the Second, converting the Second into a majority-black district, and the Eleventh District's loss in black population would be offset by extending the Eleventh to include the black populations in Savannah. *Id.*, at 1365-1366. Pointing to the General Assembly's refusal to enact the Macon/Savannah swap into law, the Justice Department concluded that Georgia had "failed to explain adequately" its failure to create a third majority-minority district. App. 125. The State did not seek a declaratory judgment from the District Court for the District of Columbia. 864 F. Supp. at 1366, n.11.

Twice spurned, the General Assembly set out to create three majority-minority districts to gain preclearance. *Id.*, at 1366. Using the ACLU's "max-black" plan as its benchmark, *id.*, at 1366-1367, the General Assembly enacted a plan that

> bore all the signs of [the Justice Department's] involvement: The black population of Meriwether County was gouged out of the Third District and attached to the Second District by the narrowest of land bridges; Effingham and Chatham Counties were split to make way for the Savannah extension, which itself split the City of Savannah; and the plan as a whole split 26 counties, 23 more than the existing congressional districts.

Id., at 1367. The new plan also enacted the Macon/Savannah swap necessary to create a third majority-black district. The Eleventh District lost the black population of Macon, but picked up Savannah, thereby connecting the black neighborhoods of metropolitan Atlanta and the poor black populace of coastal Chatham County, though 260 miles apart in distance and worlds apart in culture. In short, the social, political and economic makeup of the Eleventh District tells a tale of disparity, not community. The Almanac of American Politics has this to say about the Eleventh District: "Geographically, it is a monstrosity, stretching from Atlanta to Savannah. Its core is the plantation country in the center of the state, lightly populated, but heavily black. It links by narrow corridors the black neighborhoods in Augusta, Savannah and southern DeKalb County." M. Barone & G. Ujifusa, Almanac of American Politics 356 (1994). Georgia's plan included three majority-black districts, though, and received Justice Department preclearance on April 2, 1992.

Elections were held under the new congressional redistricting plan on November 4, 1992, and black candidates were elected to Congress from all three majority-black districts. *Id.*, at 1369. On January 13, 1994, appellees, five white voters from the Eleventh District, filed this action against various state officials (Miller

Appellants) in the United States District Court for the Southern District of Georgia. . . . Their suit alleged that Georgia's Eleventh District was a racial gerrymander and so a violation of the Equal Protection Clause as interpreted in *Shaw v. Reno*. . . . A majority of the District Court panel agreed that the Eleventh District was invalid under Shaw. . . .

II

A

Finding that the "evidence of the General Assembly's intent to racially gerrymander the Eleventh District is overwhelming, and practically stipulated by the parties involved," the District Court held that race was the predominant, overriding factor in drawing the Eleventh District. 864 F. Supp., at 1374; see *id.*, at 1374-1378. Appellants do not take issue with the court's factual finding of this racial motivation. Rather, they contend that evidence of a legislature's deliberate classification of voters on the basis of race cannot alone suffice to state a claim under *Shaw*. They argue that, regardless of the legislature's purposes, a plaintiff must demonstrate that a district's shape is so bizarre that it is unexplainable other than on the basis of race, and that appellees failed to make that showing here. Appellants' conception of the constitutional violation misapprehends our holding in *Shaw* and the Equal Protection precedent upon which *Shaw* relied.

Shaw recognized a claim "analytically distinct" from a vote dilution claim. 509 U.S. (slip op., at 21). Whereas a vote dilution claim alleges that the State has enacted a particular voting scheme as a purposeful device "to minimize or cancel out the voting potential of racial or ethnic minorities," *Mobile v. Bolden*, 446 U.S. 55, 66 (1980), an action disadvantaging voters of a particular race, the essence of the equal protection claim recognized in *Shaw* is that the State has used race as a basis for separating voters into districts. Just as the State may not, absent extraordinary justification, segregate citizens on the basis of race in its public parks, buses, golf courses, beaches, and schools, so did we recognize in *Shaw* that it may not separate its citizens into different voting districts on the basis of race. The idea is a simple one: "At the heart of the Constitution's guarantee of equal protection lies the simple command that the Government must treat citizens 'as individuals, not "as simply components of a racial, religious, sexual or national class." ' " When the State assigns voters on the basis of race, it engages in the offensive and demeaning assumption that voters of a particular race, because of their race, "think alike, share the same political interests, and will prefer the same candidates at the polls." *Shaw*, *supra*, (slip op., at 16). Race-based assignments "embody stereotypes that treat individuals as the product of their race, evaluating their thoughts and efforts—their very worth as citizens—according to a criterion barred to the Government by history and the Constitution." They also cause society serious harm. As we concluded in *Shaw*:

> Racial classifications with respect to voting carry particular dangers. Racial gerrymandering, even for remedial purposes, may balkanize us into competing racial factions; it threatens to carry us further from the goal of a political system in which race no longer matters—a goal that the Fourteenth and Fifteenth Amendments embody, and to which the Nation

continues to aspire. It is for these reasons that race-based districting by our state legislatures demands close judicial scrutiny.

Shaw, supra, (slip op., at 26).

Our observation in *Shaw* of the consequences of racial stereotyping was not meant to suggest that a district must be bizarre on its face before there is a constitutional violation. Nor was our conclusion in *Shaw* that in certain instances a district's appearance (or, to be more precise, its appearance in combination with certain demographic evidence) can give rise to an equal protection claim, a holding that bizarreness was a threshold showing, as appellants believe it to be. . . . Shape is relevant not because bizarreness is a necessary element of the constitutional wrong or a threshold requirement of proof, but because it may be persuasive circumstantial evidence that race for its own sake, and not other districting principles, was the legislature's dominant and controlling rationale in drawing its district lines. The logical implication, as courts applying *Shaw* have recognized, is that parties may rely on evidence other than bizarreness to establish race-based districting. . . .

Appellants and some of their *amici* argue that the Equal Protection Clause's general proscription on race-based decisionmaking does not obtain in the districting context because redistricting by definition involves racial considerations. Underlying their argument are the very stereotypical assumptions the Equal Protection Clause forbids. It is true that redistricting in most cases will implicate a political calculus in which various interests compete for recognition, but it does not follow from this that individuals of the same race share a single political interest. The view that they do is "based on the demeaning notion that members of the defined racial groups ascribe to certain 'minority views' that must be different from those of other citizens," *Metro Broadcasting,* 497 U.S. at 636 (Kennedy, J., dissenting), the precise use of race as a proxy the Constitution prohibits. . . .

In sum, we make clear that parties alleging that a State has assigned voters on the basis of race are neither confined in their proof to evidence regarding the district's geometry and makeup nor required to make a threshold showing of bizarreness. Today's case requires us further to consider the requirements of the proof necessary to sustain this equal protection challenge.

B

Federal court review of districting legislation represents a serious intrusion on the most vital of local functions. . . . Electoral districting is a most difficult subject for legislatures, and so the States must have discretion to exercise the political judgment necessary to balance competing interests. Although race-based decisionmaking is inherently suspect, until a claimant makes a showing sufficient to support that allegation the good faith of a state legislature must be presumed, see *Bakke, supra,* at 318-319 (opinion of Powell, J.). The courts, in assessing the sufficiency of a challenge to a districting plan, must be sensitive to the complex interplay of forces that enter a legislature's redistricting calculus. Redistricting legislatures will, for example, almost always be aware of racial demographics; but it does not follow that race predominates in the redistricting process. *Shaw, supra,* see *Personnel Administrator of Mass. v. Feeney,* 442 U.S. 256, 279, 282 (1979) ("'Discriminatory purpose' . . . implies more than intent as volition or intent as awareness of consequences. It implies that the decisionmaker . . . selected or reaffirmed a particular course of action at least in part 'because of,' not merely 'in spite of,' its adverse effects"). The distinction between being aware of racial considerations and being motivated by them may be difficult to make. This evidentiary difficulty, together with the sensitive nature of redistricting and the presumption of good faith that must be accorded legislative enactments, requires courts to exercise extraordinary caution in adjudicating claims that a state has drawn district lines on the basis of race. The plaintiff's burden is to show, either through circumstantial evidence of a district's shape and demographics or more direct evidence going to legislative purpose, that race was the predominant factor motivating the legislature's decision to place a significant number of voters within or without a particular district. To make this showing, a plaintiff must prove that the legislature subordinated traditional race-neutral districting principles, including but not limited to compactness, contiguity, respect for political subdivisions or communities defined by actual shared interests, to racial considerations. . . .

In our view, the District Court applied the correct analysis, and its finding that race was the predominant factor motivating the drawing of the Eleventh District was not clearly erroneous. The court found it was "exceedingly obvious" from the shape of the Eleventh District, together with the relevant racial demographics, that the drawing of narrow land bridges to incorporate within the District outlying appendages containing nearly 80% of the district's total black population was a deliberate attempt to bring black populations into the district. 864 F. Supp. at 1375. Although by comparison with other districts the geometric shape of the Eleventh District may not seem bizarre on its face, when its shape is considered in conjunction with its racial and population densities, the story of racial gerrymandering seen by the District Court becomes much clearer. . . .

The court found that "it became obvious," both from the Justice Department's objection letters and the three preclearance rounds in general, "that [the Justice Department] would accept nothing less than abject surrender to its maximization agenda." *Id.*, at 1366. It further found that the General Assembly acquiesced and as a consequence was driven by its overriding desire to comply with the Department's maximization demands. . . . The State . . . conceded . . . that "to the extent that precincts in the Eleventh Congressional District are split, a substantial reason for their being split was the objective of increasing the black population of that district." And in its brief to this Court, the State concedes that "it is undisputed that Georgia's eleventh is the product of a desire by the General Assembly to create a majority black district." Brief for Miller Appellants 30. . . . On this record, we fail to see how the District Court could have reached any conclusion other than that race was the predominant factor in drawing Georgia's Eleventh District; and in any event we conclude the court's finding is not clearly erroneous. . . .

Nor can the State's districting legislation be rescued by mere recitation of purported communities of interest. The evidence was compelling "that there are no tangible 'communities of interest' spanning the hundreds of miles of the Eleventh District." *Id.*, at 1389-1390. A comprehensive report demonstrated the fractured political, social, and economic interests within the Eleventh District's black population. See Plaintiff's Exh. No. 85, pp. 10-27 (report of Timothy G. O'Rourke, Ph.D.). It is apparent that it was not alleged shared interests but rather the object of maximizing the District's black population and obtaining Justice Department approval that in fact explained the General Assembly's actions. 864 F. Supp. at 1366, 1378, 1380. . . .

Race was, as the District Court found, the predominant, overriding factor explaining the General Assembly's decision to attach to the Eleventh District various appendages containing dense majority-black populations. 864 F. Supp. at 1372, 1378. As a result, Georgia's congressional redistricting plan cannot be upheld unless it satisfies strict scrutiny, our most rigorous and exacting standard of constitutional review.

III

To satisfy strict scrutiny, the State must demonstrate that its districting legislation is narrowly tailored to achieve a compelling interest. There is a "significant state interest in eradicating the effects of past racial discrimination." The State does not argue, however, that it created the Eleventh District to remedy past discrimination, and with good reason: there is little doubt that the State's true interest in designing the Eleventh District was creating a third majority-black district to satisfy the Justice Department's preclearance demands. Whether or not in some cases compliance with the Voting Rights Act, standing alone, can provide a compelling interest independent of any interest in remedying past discrimination, it cannot do so here. As we suggested in *Shaw*, compliance with federal antidiscrimination laws cannot justify race-based districting where the challenged district was not reasonably necessary under a constitutional reading and application of those laws. The congressional plan challenged here was not required by the Voting Rights Act under a correct reading of the statute. . . .

We do not accept the contention that the State has a compelling interest in complying with whatever preclearance mandates the Justice Department issues. When a state governmental entity seeks to justify race-based remedies to cure the effects of past discrimination, we do not accept the government's mere assertion that the remedial action is required. Rather, we insist on a strong basis in evidence of the harm being remedied. See, *e.g.*, *Shaw, supra; Croson, supra.* "The history of racial classifications in this country suggests that blind judicial deference to legislative or executive pronouncements of necessity has no place in equal protection analysis." *Croson, supra*, at 501. Our presumptive skepticism of all racial classifications prohibits us as well from accepting on its face the Justice Department's conclusion that racial districting is necessary under the Voting Rights Act. Where a State relies on the Department's determination that race-based districting is necessary to comply with the Voting Rights Act, the judiciary retains an independent obligation in adjudicating consequent equal protection challenges to ensure that the State's actions are narrowly tailored to achieve a compelling interest. Were we to accept the Justice Department's objection itself as a compelling interest adequate to insulate racial districting from constitutional review, we would be surrendering to the Executive Branch our role in enforcing the constitutional limits on race-based official action. We may not do so. . . .

Georgia's drawing of the Eleventh District was not required under the Act because there was no reasonable basis to believe that Georgia's earlier enacted plans violated §5. Wherever a plan is "ameliorative," a term we have used to describe plans increasing the number of majority-minority districts, it "cannot violate §5 unless the new apportionment itself so discriminates on the basis of race or color as to violate the Constitution." *Beer*, 425 U.S. at 141. Georgia's first and second proposed plans increased the number of majority-black districts from 1 out of 10 (10%) to 2 out of 11 (18.18%). These plans were "ameliorative" and could not have violated §5's non-retrogression principle. *Ibid.* . . .

Instead of grounding its objections on evidence of a discriminatory purpose, it would appear the Government was driven by its policy of maximizing majority-black districts. Although the Government now disavows having had that policy, see Brief for United States 35, and seems to concede its impropriety, see Tr. of Oral Arg. 32-33, the District Court's well-documented factual finding was that the Department did adopt a maximization policy and followed it in objecting to Georgia's first two plans. . . .

[W]e recognized in *Beer* that "the purpose of §5 has always been to insure that no voting-procedure changes would be made that would lead to a retrogression in the position of racial minorities with respect to their effective exercise of the electoral franchise." 425 U.S. at 141. The Justice Department's maximization policy seems quite far removed from this purpose. . . .

IV

The Voting Rights Act, and its grant of authority to the federal courts to uncover official efforts to abridge minorities' right to vote, has been of vital importance in eradicating invidious discrimination from the electoral process and enhancing the legitimacy of our political institutions. Only if our political system and our society cleanse themselves of that discrimination will all members of the polity share an equal opportunity to gain public office regardless of race. As a Nation we share both the obligation and the aspiration of working toward this end. The end is neither assured nor well served, however, by carving electorates into racial blocs. "If our society is to continue to progress as a multiracial democracy, it must recognize that the automatic invocation of race stereotypes retards that progress and causes continued hurt and injury." *Edmonson v. Leesville Concrete Co.*, 500 U.S. 614, 630-631 (1991). It takes a shortsighted and unauthorized view of the Voting Rights Act to invoke that statute, which has played a decisive role in redressing some of our worst forms of discrimination, to demand the very racial stereotyping the Fourteenth Amendment forbids.

The judgment of the District Court is affirmed, and the case is remanded for further proceedings consistent with this decision.

It is so ordered.

Justice GINSBURG, with whom Justices STEVENS and BREYER join, and with whom Justice SOUTER joins except as to Part III-B, dissenting.

I

At the outset, it may be useful to note points on which the Court does not divide. . . . [T]o meet statutory requirements, state legislatures must sometimes consider race as a factor highly relevant to the drawing of district lines. . . . Therefore, the fact that the Georgia General Assembly took account of race in drawing district lines — a fact not in dispute — does not render the State's plan invalid. To offend the Equal Protection Clause, all agree, the legislature had to do more than consider race. How much more, is the issue that divides the Court today. . . .

II

A

Before *Shaw v. Reno*, this Court invoked the Equal Protection Clause to justify intervention in the quintessentially political task of legislative districting in two circumstances: to enforce the one-person-one-vote requirement, see *Reynolds v. Sims*, and to prevent dilution of a minority group's voting strength. See *Regester*.

In *Shaw*, the Court recognized a third basis for an equal protection challenge to a State's apportionment plan. The Court wrote cautiously, emphasizing that judicial intervention is exceptional: "Strict [judicial] scrutiny" is in order, the Court declared, if a district is "so extremely irregular on its face that it rationally can be viewed only as an effort to segregate the races for purposes of voting." 509 U.S. (slip op., at 10).

"Extrem[e] irregularity" was evident in *Shaw*. . . . The problem in *Shaw* was not the plan architects' consideration of race as relevant in redistricting. Rather, in the Court's estimation, it was the virtual exclusion of other factors from the calculus. Traditional districting practices were cast aside, the Court concluded, with race alone steering placement of district lines.

B

The record before us does not show that race similarly overwhelmed traditional districting practices in Georgia. Although the Georgia General Assembly prominently considered race in shaping the Eleventh District, race did not crowd out all other factors, as the Court found it did in North Carolina's delineation of the *Shaw* district.

In contrast to the snake-like North Carolina district inspected in *Shaw*, Georgia's Eleventh District is hardly "bizarre," "extremely irregular," or "irrational on its face." Instead, the Eleventh District's design reflects significant consideration of "traditional districting factors (such as keeping political subdivisions intact) and the usual political process of compromise and trades for a variety of nonracial reasons.". . .

Nor does the Eleventh District disrespect the boundaries of political subdivisions. Of the 22 counties in the District, 14 are intact and 8 are divided. That puts the Eleventh District at about the state average in divided counties. . . .

Evidence at trial similarly shows that considerations other than race went into determining the Eleventh District's boundaries. For a "political reason" — to accommodate the request of an incumbent State Senator regarding the placement of the precinct in which his son lived — the DeKalb County portion of the Eleventh District was drawn to include a particular (largely white) precinct. 2 Tr. 187, 202. The corridor through Effingham County was substantially narrowed at the request of a (white) State Representative. 2 Tr. 189-190, 212-214. In Chatham County, the District was trimmed to exclude a heavily black community in Garden City because a State

Representative wanted to keep the city intact inside the neighboring First District. 2 Tr. 218-219. The Savannah extension was configured by "the narrowest means possible" to avoid splitting the city of Port Wentworth. 4 Tr. 172-174, 175-178, 181-183.

Georgia's Eleventh District, in sum, is not an outlier district shaped without reference to familiar districting techniques. . . .

D

Along with attention to size, shape, and political subdivisions, the Court recognizes as an appropriate districting principle, "respect for . . . communities defined by actual shared interests." The Court finds no community here, however, because a report in the record showed "fractured political, social, and economic interests within the Eleventh District's black population."

But ethnicity itself can tie people together, as volumes of social science literature have documented—even people with divergent economic interests. For this reason, ethnicity is a significant force in political life. . . . N. Glazer & D. Moynihan, Beyond the Melting Pot 19-20 (1963). See also, *e.g.*, E. Litt, Beyond Pluralism: Ethnic Politics in America 2 (1970); Ethnic Group Politics, Preface ix (H. Bailey & E. Katz eds. 1969).

To accommodate the reality of ethnic bonds, legislatures have long drawn voting districts along ethnic lines. Our Nation's cities are full of districts identified by their ethnic character—Chinese, Irish, Italian, Jewish, Polish, Russian, for example. See, *e.g.*, S. Erie, Rainbow's End: Irish-Americans and the Dilemmas of Urban Machine Politics, 1840-1985, p. 91 (1988) (describing Jersey City's "Horseshoe district" as "lumping most of the city's Irish together"); Coveted Landmarks Add a Twist to Redistricting Task, L.A. Times, Sept. 10, 1991, pp. A1, A24 ("In San Francisco in 1961, . . . an Irish Catholic [State Assembly member] 'wanted his district drawn following [Catholic] parish lines so all the parishes where he went to baptisms, weddings and funerals would be in his district.'. . ."); Stone, Goode: Bad and Indifferent, Washington Monthly, July-August 1986, pp. 27, 28 (discussing "The Law of Ethnic Loyalty—. . . a universal law of politics," and identifying "predominantly Italian wards of South Philadelphia," a "Jewish Los Angeles district," and a "Polish district in Chicago"). The creation of ethnic districts reflecting felt identity is not ordinarily viewed as offensive or demeaning to those included in the delineation.

III

To separate permissible and impermissible use of race in legislative apportionment, the Court orders strict scrutiny for districting plans "predominantly motivated" by race. No longer can a State avoid judicial oversight by giving—as in this case—genuine and measurable consideration to traditional districting practices. Instead, a federal case can be mounted whenever plaintiffs plausibly allege that other factors carried less weight than race. This invitation to litigate against the State seems to me neither necessary nor proper.

A

The Court derives its test from diverse opinions on the relevance of race in contexts distinctly unlike apportionment. The controlling idea, the Court says, is

" 'the simple command [at the heart of the Constitution's guarantee of equal protection] that the Government must treat citizens as individuals, not as simply components of a racial, religious, sexual or national class.' "

In adopting districting plans, however, States do not treat people as individuals. Apportionment schemes, by their very nature, assemble people in groups. States do not assign voters to districts based on merit or achievement, standards States might use in hiring employees or engaging contractors. Rather, legislators classify voters in groups—by economic, geographical, political, or social characteristics—and then "reconcile the competing claims of [these] groups." *Davis v. Bandemer*, 478 U.S. 109, 147 (1986) (O'Connor, J., concurring in judgment).

That ethnicity defines some of these groups is a political reality. Until now, no constitutional infirmity has been seen in districting Irish or Italian voters together, for example, so long as the delineation does not abandon familiar apportionment practices. If Chinese-Americans and Russian-Americans may seek and secure group recognition in the delineation of voting districts, then African-Americans should not be dissimilarly treated. Otherwise, in the name of equal protection, we would shut out "the very minority group whose history in the United States gave birth to the Equal Protection Clause." See *Shaw*, 509 U.S. (slip op., at 4) (Stevens, J., dissenting).

B

Under the Court's approach, judicial review of the same intensity, *i.e.*, strict scrutiny, is in order once it is determined that an apportionment is predominantly motivated by race. It matters not at all, in this new regime, whether the apportionment dilutes or enhances minority voting strength. . . .

Special circumstances justify vigilant judicial inspection to protect minority voters—circumstances that do not apply to majority voters. A history of exclusion from state politics left racial minorities without clout to extract provisions for fair representation in the lawmaking forum. The equal protection rights of minority voters thus could have remained unrealized absent the Judiciary's close surveillance. The majority, by definition, encounters no such blockage. White voters in Georgia do not lack means to exert strong pressure on their state legislators. The force of their numbers is itself a powerful determiner of what the legislature will do that does not coincide with perceived majority interests.

State legislatures like Georgia's today operate under federal constraints imposed by the Voting Rights Act—constraints justified by history and designed by Congress to make once-subordinated people free and equal citizens. But these federal constraints do not leave majority voters in need of extraordinary judicial solicitude. The Attorney General, who administers the Voting Rights Act's preclearance requirements, is herself a political actor. She has a duty to enforce the law Congress passed, and she is no doubt aware of the political cost of venturing too far to the detriment of majority voters. Majority voters, furthermore, can press the State to seek judicial review if the Attorney General refuses to preclear a plan that the voters favor. Finally, the Act is itself a political measure, subject to modification in the political process.

C

The Court's disposition renders redistricting perilous work for state legis-latures. Statutory mandates and political realities may require States to consider race when drawing district lines. . . . Only after litigation—under either the Voting Rights Act, the Court's new *Miller* standard, or both—will States now be assured that plans conscious of race are safe. Federal judges in large numbers may be drawn into the fray. This enlargement of the judicial role is unwarranted. The reappor-tionment plan that resulted from Georgia's political process merited this Court's approbation, not its condemnation. Accordingly, I dissent.

APPENDIX A GEORGIA CONGRESSIONAL DISTRICTS 1992

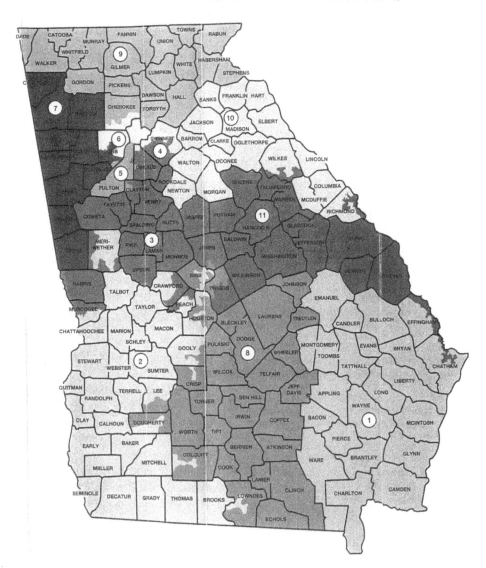

>> *What Interests Are Compelling?* Following *Shaw*, the Court in *Miller* found that the use of race in redistricting decisions demands strict scrutiny. Where creating a majority-minority district is not required to remedy a demonstrable history of racial discrimination, what kinds of interests can satisfy the Equal Protection Clause? In *Miller*, Georgia claimed that it was affirmatively required to take race into consideration in order to comply with the Voting Rights Act. Shouldn't compliance with a valid federal civil rights law constitute a compelling interest for purposes of strict scrutiny? Why does the Court reject that contention? Here is Justice Kennedy's language again:

> Whether or not in some cases compliance with the Voting Rights Act, standing alone, can provide a compelling interest independent of any interest in remedying past discrimination, it cannot do so here. As we suggested in *Shaw*, compliance with federal antidiscrimination laws cannot justify race-based districting where the challenged district was not reasonably necessary under a constitutional reading and application of those laws. The congressional plan challenged here was not required by the Voting Rights Act under a correct reading of the statute. . . .

What is the meaning of this language? Is Justice Kennedy saying that Section 2 of the VRA is unconstitutional? Or that it has been unconstitutionally applied in this case? If the latter, who is guilty of the unconstitutional application? Is it Georgia or the Justice Department? If the latter, why is the state being held accountable for an administrative action of the Justice Department when it is not a party to the suit and when the validity of its action is not before the Court?

In *League of United Latin American Citizens v. Perry*, 548 U.S. 399 (2006), a majority of the Justices held, in passing, that compliance with Section 5 of the VRA *is* a compelling interest for purposes of strict scrutiny. In subsequent cases, the Court has explicitly assumed, though without authoritatively deciding, that compliance with the VRA is a compelling interest. *E.g., Bethune-Hill v. Virginia State Board of Elections*, 580 U.S. 178 (2017). Does this clarify the holding in *Miller*? Or does it muddy the waters further?

>> *When Is Race the "Predominant Factor" in Redistricting?* *Miller* altered the focus in *Shaw* cases from the shape of the district to the influence of race on districting decisions. Presumably, the Court believed that a "predominant factor" standard would be easier to manage judicially than a "bizarrely shaped district" standard. Is it? How do we know when race is the "predominant" factor in districting rather than merely a "subordinate" factor, or one among several equally weighted factors?

> To appreciate both the intractability of a predominant motive test for redistricting and the way any such test is likely to be applied in practice, assume initially that it is possible with respect to any one specific line-location decision to say that one factor motivated it exclusively. One line was drawn for partisan reasons; another was drawn to protect constituencies of the existing officeholder; still another, to raise the percentage of minority voters; still others, to respect the demands of incumbents in adjoining districts. Even if we could assign a single pure or dominant motive to the drawing of any one particular line, how would we assign a dominant motive to the location of the district as a whole? Should we

assign a motive to each discrete line-location decision, then aggregate them quantitatively to see which motivation accounts for the largest number of specific decisions? Or should we try to assess how many people in the district actually were affected by each specific line-location decision, add these up, and then treat as predominant the motive that affected the largest number of residents? Should it be the motive that appeared to be most important to those with political power, that is, the goal they were least willing to compromise? Or should it be the motives chronologically addressed first in the sequence of redistricting, as the cases sometimes seem to suggest?

In other words, even if we could treat each specific line-location decision as resting on one exclusive motive whose role we could know with certainty, there still seems no intelligible way to determine the "predominant motive" for the design of an election district. [Furthermore], it is unrealistic to treat even discrete line-location decisions as stemming from one exclusive motivation. Any one decision can itself reflect a complex mix of racial, partisan, and candidate-specific considerations. As soon as the redistricting problem is confronted on its own terms, the intractability of trying to determine the predominant motive for the location of a district becomes readily apparent.

Richard H. Pildes, *Principled Limitations on Racial and Partisan Redistricting,* 106 YALE L.J. 2505, 2546 (1997).

In *Bethune-Hill v. Virginia State Board of Elections,* 580 U.S. 178 (2017), the Supreme Court provided additional guidance on application of the predominant factor test. There, black plaintiffs challenged 12 Virginia congressional districts as racially gerrymandered. A three-judge district court rejected the challenge on the ground that the plaintiffs could not, as a matter of law, prove that race was the predominant factor in drawing district lines unless they could show that the legislature had faced a choice between adhering to traditional districting criteria and grouping voters by race, and had resolved the conflict in favor of racial criteria. The Supreme Court rejected this analysis:

> [A] conflict between the enacted plan and traditional redistricting criteria is not a threshold requirement or a mandatory precondition . . . to establish a claim of racial gerrymandering. . . . As a practical matter, in many cases, . . . challengers will be unable to prove an unconstitutional racial gerrymander without evidence that the enacted plan conflicts with traditional redistricting criteria. In general, legislatures that engage in impermissible race-based redistricting will find it necessary to depart from traditional principles in order to do so. And, in the absence of a conflict with traditional principles, it may be difficult for challengers to find other evidence.

Instead, the Court held, lower courts should consider "the districtwide context" and conduct a "holistic analysis" so as to give "proper weight" to evidence showing undue consideration of race. Do these clarifications meet the concerns expressed above by Professor Pildes?

⟫   *Extending the "Predominant Factor" Test to Partisan Gerrymandering?*   You will recall from Chapter 4 that the Supreme Court failed, in its 1986 ruling in *Davis v. Bandemer*, to agree on a workable standard by which to assess the constitutionality of partisan gerrymandering. In *Vieth v. Jubelirer*, 541 U.S. 267 (2004), the Court's first partisan gerrymandering case since *Bandemer*, the plaintiffs argued that the Court could simply use the "predominant factor" test from *Miller* when assessing the constitutionality of a purely partisan gerrymander. Writing for the plurality, Justice Scalia declined to adopt this solution:

> Appellants contend that their [predominant] intent test *must* be discernible and manageable because it has been borrowed from our racial gerrymandering cases. *See Miller v. Johnson*, 515 U.S. 900 (1995). To begin with, in a very important respect that is not so. In the racial gerrymandering context, the predominant intent test has been applied to the challenged district in which the plaintiffs voted. Here, however, appellants do not assert that an apportionment fails their intent test if any single district does so. . . . Vague as the "predominant motivation" test might be when used to evaluate single districts, it all but evaporates when applied statewide. Does it mean, for instance, that partisan intent must outweigh all other goals — contiguity, compactness, preservation of neighborhoods, etc. — *statewide*? And how is the statewide "outweighing" to be determined? If three-fifths of the map's districts forgo the pursuit of partisan ends in favor of strictly observing political-subdivision lines, and only two-fifths ignore those lines to disadvantage the plaintiffs, is the observance of political subdivisions the "predominant" goal between those two? We are sure appellants do not think so.
>
> Even within the narrower compass of challenges to a single district, applying a "predominant intent" test to *racial* gerrymandering is easier and less disruptive. The Constitution clearly contemplates districting by political entities, see Article I, §4, and unsurprisingly that turns out to be root-and-branch a matter of politics. By contrast, the purpose of segregating voters on the basis of race is not a lawful one, and is much more rarely encountered. Determining whether the shape of a particular district is so substantially affected by the presence of a rare and constitutionally suspect motive as to invalidate it is quite different from determining whether it is so substantially affected by the excess of an ordinary and lawful motive as to invalidate it. Moreover, the fact that partisan districting is a lawful and common practice means that there is almost *always* room for an election-impeding lawsuit contending that partisan advantage was the predominant motivation; not so for claims of racial gerrymandering. Finally, courts might be justified in accepting a modest degree of unmanageability to enforce a constitutional command which (like the Fourteenth Amendment obligation to refrain from racial discrimination) is clear; whereas they are not justified in inferring a judicially enforceable constitutional obligation (the obligation not to apply *too much* partisanship in districting) which is both dubious and severely unmanageable. For these reasons, to the extent that our racial gerrymandering cases represent a model of discernible and manageable standards, they provide no comfort here.

Has Justice Scalia succeeded in explaining why the predominant factor test is both mandatory and judicially manageable in the racial gerrymandering context, yet so unworkable that it must be rejected as judicially unmanageable where the gerrymandering in question is based on partisanship?

>>   *The Search for Neutrality in Districting.*   If race cannot be the predominant factor in districting decisions, what *can* be the predominant factor? The *Shaw* cases treat the use of race as raising great suspicion, although they do not go so far as to banish it entirely from the districting calculus. After *Miller*, how can a redistricting state legislature defend itself from charges that it relied predominantly on race? What factors can a legislature point to as its actual motivations and influences that will be considered legitimate under Section 2 (or for that matter under constitutional standards barring intentional racial discrimination under the Fifteenth Amendment, or intentional partisan discrimination under the Fourteenth Amendment)?

Generally, the Court has identified five criteria in districting that are "objective factors that may serve to defeat a claim that a district has been gerrymandered on racial lines." *Shaw*, 509 U.S. at 647. These factors, which the Court has often referred to as "traditional" factors in districting decisions, are compactness, contiguity, observance of existing political boundaries, preservation of communities of interest, and protection of incumbent office-holders. The Court seems to considers the application of these criteria in redistricting to be legitimate in the sense that they raise no legal concerns under the Constitution or the VRA; and neutral in that their use in no way suggests reliance on undue racial or partisan considerations in drawing district lines.

Compactness and Contiguity. Compactness and contiguity refer to the physical shape of the district. If a district is conceived as a geometric shape, it is generally more compact the fewer sides it has. A square or rectangular district would be considered highly compact; a district that bends, twists, or throws out tentacles is less compact. Political scientists sometimes measure compactness by calculating the ratio of a district's area to its perimeter. *See* Richard H. Pildes and Richard G. Niemi, *Expressive Harms, "Bizarre Districts," and Voting Rights: Evaluating Election-District Appearance After* Shaw v. Reno, 92 MICH. L. REV. 483 (1993). A district is contiguous if it forms a single solid shape such that one can travel from any part of the district to any other part of the district without crossing into a different district. A district is contiguous, but not compact, if it is longer to travel from one part of the district to another part by staying within the district than by cutting through a different district. What is the value of insisting upon compactness and contiguity? Consider the following explanation:

> The objections to bizarre-looking reapportionment maps are not aesthetic (except for those who prefer Mondrian to Pollock). They are based on a recognition that representative democracy cannot be achieved merely by assuring population equality across districts. To be an effective representative, a legislator must represent a district that has a reasonable homogeneity of needs and interests; otherwise the policies he supports will not represent the preferences of most of his constituents. There is some although of course not a complete correlation between geographical

propinquity and community of interests, and therefore compactness and contiguity are desirable features in a redistricting plan. Compactness and contiguity also reduce travel time and costs, and therefore make it easier for candidates for the legislature to campaign for office and once elected to maintain close and continuing contact with the people they represent. Viewing legislators as agents and the electorate as their principal, we can see that compactness and contiguity reduce the "agency costs" of representative democracy. But only up to a point, for the achievement of perfect contiguity and compactness would imply ruthless disregard for other elements of homogeneity; would require breaking up counties, towns, villages, wards, even neighborhoods. If compactness and contiguity are proxies for homogeneity of political interests, so is making district boundaries follow (so far as possible) rather than cross the boundaries of the other political subdivisions in the state.

Prosser v. Elections Board, 793 F. Supp. 859, 863 (W.D. Wis. 1992) (three-judge court) (per curiam). Does this account strike you as accurate?

Requirements of compactness and contiguity are often written into state constitutions. For example, 36 state constitutions provide expressly that election districts for at least some legislative chambers be "contiguous." State courts have tended to interpret this requirement deferentially, particularly where districts contain or detour around bodies of water. Twenty-four states require election districts to be "compact." Michigan additionally requires certain senatorial districts to be "as rectangular" and "as nearly uniform in shape as possible." Mich. Const. art. IV, §2. It is not clear, however, that provisions restricting allowable district shape have had any appreciable constraining effect on redistricting practices. *See* Richard H. Pildes and Richard G. Niemi, *Expressive Harms, "Bizarre Districts," and Voting Rights: Evaluating Election-District Appearances After* Shaw v. Reno, 92 Mich. L. Rev. 483, 528 (1993).

Even if compactness is desirable, what is so important about contiguity? Isn't it possible that the values served by compactness could sometimes be better served by including several compact but noncontiguous areas in the same district than by stringing them artificially into a contiguous area by using assorted tentacles and pseudopods? In 2002, the Canadian provincial Boundaries Commission for New Brunswick proposed including all First Nations reservations within the province in a single, non-contiguous election district: "Regrouping all Indian reserves in one electoral district would allow the currently dispersed communities to interface with only one MP instead of several as is currently the case. It would also give strength to these communities because their numbers would no longer be fragmented. This innovative approach to electoral participation would be a first in Canada." The proposal was ultimately rejected not only by majority political forces, but also by the Indian groups themselves: "First Nations communities preferred to retain a presence in multiple electoral districts, citing travel challenges, the preservation of existing relationships and the advantages of access to multiple and varied federal party representatives." Federal Electoral Boundaries Commission for New Brunswick, Federal Representation 2004.

Respect for Political Boundaries and Communities of Interest. The Court has consistently held that a state's wish to avoid carving up established political subdivisions in the districting process is entitled to respect. This position explains in part the Court's decision to allow states greater leeway in departing from the principle of one-person, one-vote when drawing state legislative districts than when drawing congressional districts: allowing states greater freedom to deviate from exact mathematical equality allows districters the freedom to route election district borders along political boundaries between established subdivisions such as towns and counties. *Mahan v. Howell,* 410 U.S. 315 (1973) (see Chapter 4). The Court suggested some of the advantages of respecting established political boundaries in *Bush v. Vera,* 517 U.S. 952, 974 (1996):

> Not only are the shapes of the districts bizarre; they also exhibit utter disregard of city limits, local election precincts, and voter tabulation district lines. *See, e.g.,* 861 F. Supp. at 1340 (60% of District 18 and District 29 residents live in split precincts). This caused a severe disruption of traditional forms of political activity. Campaigners seeking to visit their constituents "had to carry a map to identify the district lines, because so often the borders would move from block to block"; voters "did not know the candidates running for office" because they did not know which district they lived in. In light of Texas' requirement that voting be arranged by precinct, with each precinct representing a community that shares local, state, and federal representatives, it also created administrative headaches for local election officials: "The effect of splitting dozens of [voter tabulation districts] to create Districts 18 and 29 was an electoral nightmare. Harris County estimated that it must increase its number of precincts from 672 to 1,225 to accommodate the new Congressional boundaries. Polling places, ballot forms, and the number of election employees are correspondingly multiplied. Voters were thrust into new and unfamiliar precinct alignments, a few with populations as low as 20 voters." *Id.,* at 1325.

The Court's solicitude for established political groupings is not, however, confined to those demarcated by formal political boundaries: the Court has also approved districting decisions that respect "communities of interest" even when those communities do not coincide with established political boundaries. Unlike established political subdivisions, however, communities of interest are difficult to identify with precision. Legislatures have sometimes attempted to establish the existence of a community of interest by reference to shared demographic factors such as income, or the character of the relevant neighborhoods as urban or rural. The Court, however, has closely scrutinized district lines that rest on claims concerning communities of interest, often finding such claims unconvincing. For example, in one case the Texas Legislature defended the integrity of one district on the grounds that it circumscribed a community of interest, but the Court rejected the claim:

> Appellants highlight the facts that the district has a consistently urban character and has common media sources throughout, and that its tentacles include several major transportation lines into the city of Dallas. These factors, which implicate traditional districting principles, do

correlate to some extent with the district's layout. But we see no basis in the record for displacing the District Court's conclusion that race predominated over them, particularly in light of the court's findings that the State's supporting data were not "available to the Legislature in any organized fashion before District 30 was created," 861 F. Supp. at 1338, and that they do not "differentiate the district from surrounding areas," *ibid.*, with the same degree of correlation to district lines that racial data exhibit. . . .

Bush v. Vera, 517 U.S. at 966. Similarly, in *Miller,* the Georgia Legislature attempted to defend its inclusion within a single district of geographically dispersed black populations on the ground that they comprised a community of interest. The Court was unconvinced:

> Nor can the State's districting legislation be rescued by mere recitation of purported communities of interest. The evidence was compelling "that there are no tangible 'communities of interest' spanning the hundreds of miles of the Eleventh District." A comprehensive report demonstrated the fractured political, social, and economic interests within the Eleventh District's black population. See Plaintiff's Exh. No. 85, pp. 10-27 (report of Timothy G. O'Rourke, Ph.D.). . . . A State is free to recognize communities that have a particular racial makeup, provided its action is directed toward some common thread of relevant interests. "When members of a racial group live together in one community, a reapportionment plan that concentrates members of the group in one district and excludes them from others may reflect wholly legitimate purposes." *Shaw,* 509 U.S. at 646. But where the State assumes from a group of voters' race that they "think alike, share the same political interests, and will prefer the same candidates at the polls," it engages in racial stereotyping at odds with equal protection mandates. *Id.,* at 647.

Miller v. Johnson, 515 U.S. at 919-920. Consider the reaction of the Fifth Circuit to the Court's treatment of communities of interest in districting cases: "Because of the inherently subjective nature of the concept, it would seem that reasonable people might disagree as to what constitutes a community. We thus caution against general over-reliance on the communities of interest factor." *Chen v. City of Houston,* 206 F.3d 502, 517 n.9 (5th Cir. 2000).

The Alaska Constitution provides that legislative districts should contain "as nearly as practicable a relatively integrated socio-economic area." Alaska Const. art. VI, §6. The Hawaii Constitution similarly provides: "submergence of an area in a larger district wherein substantially different socio-economic interests predominate shall be avoided." Hawaii Const. art. IV, §6(8). The Colorado Constitution provides for the preservation of "whole communities of interest." Colo. Const. art. V, §48-1. Do these provisions meaningfully constrain the discretion of legislators engaged in redistricting? If not, would other language be more effective?

The California Citizens Redistricting Commission has adopted an innovative, evidence-based approach to determining the location of communities of interest. Instead of merely analyzing data, it has held extensive hearings and actively solicited public testimony and opinion concerning the nature and extent of such communities. In this process, ordinary citizens described the affinities they felt (or did not feel) for neighboring people and communities. Karin MacDonald and Bruce E. Cain, *Community of Interest Methodology and Public Testimony*, 3 U.C. IRVINE L. REV. 609 (2013). Is this a more objective way to determine communities of interest? More reliable? Are there any downside risks to this method?

———————

In *League of United Latin American Citizens (LULAC) v. Perry*, 548 U.S. 399 (2006), the Texas re-redistricting case, the Court may have caused even further confusion by blurring the distinction between the compactness and community-of-interest analyses. In *LULAC*, the plaintiffs challenged the composition of the Twenty-Fifth Congressional District under a 2003 Texas redistricting plan. The problems with the Twenty-Fifth District originated with changes made to the Twenty-Third Congressional District, a district along the Mexican border dominated by Latino voters. A redistricting plan imposed by court order in 2001 made the district more competitive, threatening the hold of long-time Republican incumbent Henry Bonilla. Upon gaining control of both houses of the legislature in 2002, Texas Republicans redrew the district to protect Bonilla. The new plan split the city of Laredo, where most of the district's population was concentrated, shifting about 100,000 mostly Latino voters to a neighboring district. To make up the lost population, the legislative mapmakers turned the district north, away from the border, to include a largely Anglo, Republican area in the central part of the state. This reduced the Latino share of the voting-age population of the district to 46 percent. To maintain compliance with the VRA, the legislature redrew District 25 to make a new majority-Latino district. Because it had divided the Latino population along the Mexican border to protect Bonilla, mapmakers needed to bring other Latino populations into the district, which was accomplished by stretching the district 300 miles north to take in substantial Latino communities in the Austin metropolitan area.

In an otherwise splintered opinion, the Court ruled, by a 5-4 vote, that the newly configured District 25 failed to comply with the compactness requirement of the first *Gingles* factor. The Court identified the district's lack of compactness, however, not in terms of its geographical shape, but in terms of the lack of community of interest of the Latino population groups drawn into the same district. "[T]here is no basis," the Court held, "to believe a district that combines two far-flung segments of a racial group with disparate interests provides the opportunity that §2 requires or that the first *Gingles* condition contemplates." (Opinion of Kennedy, J.). The Latino populations along the Mexican border and in the Austin area had "different characteristics, needs, and interests. . . . The practical consequence of drawing a district to cover two distant, disparate communities is that one or both groups will be unable to achieve their political goals." The only common link, in the majority's view, was the residents' race, which was, as in *Miller*, an insufficient basis for grouping voters because it made unwarranted and demeaning assumptions about the similarity of political interests and opinions of two distinct subgroups. This ruling required the invalidation of Districts 23 and 25.

Chief Justice Roberts, joined by Justice Alito, dissented from the Court's invalidation of the redrawn Latino districts.

> The District Court, far from "assum[ing]" that Latino voters in District 25 would "prefer the same candidate at the polls," concluded that they were likely to do so based on statistical evidence of historic voting patterns. . . . It is the majority that is indulging in unwarranted "assumption[s]" about voting, contrary to the facts found at trial. . . . What is blushingly ironic is that the district preferred by the majority — former District 23 — suffers from the same "flaw" the majority ascribes to District 25, except to a greater degree. . . . Latino communities joined to form the voting majority in old District 23 are nearly twice as far apart [as the Latino communities in new District 25]. . . . [P]erhaps the majority is willing to "assume" that Latinos around San Antonio have common interests with those on the Rio Grande rather than those around Austin, even though San Antonio and Austin are a good bit closer to each other (less than 80 miles) than either is to the Rio Grande. . . .

Why don't Latino voters in Laredo and Austin comprise a community of interest if they tend to vote the same way? If the linkages that constitute a community of interest are so subtle that they are not reflected in voting decisions, is it proper to view the VRA as concerned with them? Or is *LULAC* better understood as an instance of the Court's liberal wing turning doctrines created by the Court's conservative wing (in *Miller* and *Vera*) against them? Has the community-of-interest analysis become entirely result-oriented in this area of law?

Protection of Incumbents. The Court has also held repeatedly that a legitimate, neutral redistricting criterion is the protection of incumbents, "at least in the limited form of 'avoiding contests between incumbent[s].'" *Bush v. Vera*, 517 U.S. 952, 964 (1996), quoting *Karcher v. Daggett*, 462 U.S. 725, 740 (1983). The Court has never explained the reasons for its position, but in applying this doctrine the Court seems to mean that it is legitimate for redistricters to draw lines so as to avoid placing two incumbents in the same district. Although the Court's language does not go so far as to explicitly approve drawing district lines so as to assure incumbents reelection, in its cases the Court has never raised an objection to this practice, which seems to have gone on frequently in districting plans approved by the Court. The Court's reference to avoiding contests between incumbents may refer to the Court's belief that a state has a legitimate interest in avoiding electoral structures that lead to destructive political battles, a position it has staked out in cases dealing with state regulation of political parties (see Chapter 7).

Do you agree that protecting incumbents should be viewed as a legitimate goal in the redistricting process? As a "neutral" goal? Why is drawing district lines around a group of people identified by their support for a particular incumbent official less objectionable than drawing district lines around a group of people on account of their race? Are the two kinds of groups necessarily distinct?

» **The Indeterminacy Problem, Again.** Professors Aleinikoff and Issacharoff have well described the redistricting process:

> In a democratic society, the purpose of voting is to allow the electors to select their governors. Once a decade, however, that process is inverted, and the governors and their political agents are permitted to select their electors.

T. Alexander Aleinikoff and Samuel Issacharoff, *Race and Redistricting: Drawing Constitutional Lines After* Shaw v. Reno, 92 MICH. L. REV. 588 (1993). Section 2 of the VRA is obviously designed to help assure that this process is conducted fairly. Compactness, contiguity, and the other considerations set out above are, to be sure, "traditional" and "objective" considerations in redistricting, as the Court observes—but are they fair or neutral?

To answer this question, we would need to have some concept of what a fair and neutral redistricting plan would look like. Here, however, we begin to run into the indeterminacy problem we encountered in Chapter 4 when considering constitutional requirements regarding electoral systems. Clearly, the goal of districting prescribed by most democratic theories would be to achieve a districting system that results in the "true" or "accurate" expression of the will of the voters. As with the choice among electoral systems, however, it seems equally clear that the will of the voters cannot be determined independently of some procedure designed to determine it. The problem with districting is that lines can be drawn so as to produce a great variety of results, and there is no obvious way to decide which outcome from among the many possibilities represents the true will of the people. As one prominent commentator once put it, "[all] districting is gerrymandering." ROBERT G. DIXON, JR., DEMOCRATIC REPRESENTATION: REAPPORTIONMENT IN LAW AND POLITICS 462 (1968). Thus, we may well ask: in what sense is a districting plan that contains compact and contiguous districts, but results in a legislature that is overwhelmingly Democratic (or white, or male, or Anglo) more "fair" or "neutral"—or a more accurate expression of the people's will—than one which contains oddly shaped districts but results in a legislature that is politically, or racially, or ethnically balanced?

> Whatever criteria are used to construct a district system, some interests will be advantaged and others disadvantaged in comparison to what their prospects would have been in a system constructed according to different criteria. If there is any point of view from which outcomes matter—as obviously there is—and if the political circumstances warrant any definite predictions about the relationship between districting arrangements and outcomes, then this is not something to which we should be indifferent.

> Of course, there are other ways to defend impartial or neutral districting criteria than to hold that they are intrinsically fair. One might think that the use of impartial criteria, perhaps in conjunction with some nonpartisan (or bipartisan) scheme for making apportionment decisions, would be the best way to avoid the substantive evils associated with gerrymandering. For example, impartial methods might be minimally vulnerable to self-serving manipulation by the party in power. As a practical matter, there is doubtless much to recommend this idea. But we must note that on this view, there is no claim that neutral criteria are intrinsically

fairer than others; it simply happens that the use of politically neutral criteria helps to avoid outcomes that we have independent reasons to want to avoid. The theoretically interesting question is what kinds of reasons these might be; but any answer to this question must invoke result-oriented considerations (for example, concerns about the inequitable character of the outcomes likely to be produced when the dominant party manipulates the structure of representation in order to insulate itself from competitive electoral pressures). This invites the further question why these considerations rather than others should determine judgments about fair representation. The idea of procedural impartiality simply cannot answer this question; a more substantive conception of the aims of representation is needed.

CHARLES BEITZ, POLITICAL EQUALITY: AN ESSAY IN DEMOCRATIC THEORY 148-149 (1989).

If Beitz is correct, we must choose among competing districting plans not merely by examining the procedure used to produce them, but also by examining — and evaluating — their substantive results. We must be willing to say, in other words, that one outcome is better or more desirable than another. On what basis might courts make such a judgment? Has Justice Frankfurter turned out to be right in his warning, in *Colegrove v. Green*, that the courts should not enter this "political thicket"? Perhaps this problem is what Lani Guinier refers to when she claims that the VRA is "a statute in search of a theory." Lani Guinier, *[E]racing Democracy: The Voting Rights Cases*, 108 HARV. L. REV. 109, 113 (1994).

>> *Can Districting Be Eliminated?*   One way out of the redistricting mess might be to eliminate election districts altogether. This could be done by moving to a system of proportional representation (PR) in a predominantly at-large electoral system. In such a system, voters would not be grouped in advance into electoral units; instead, they would group themselves by supporting and voting for any of a wide variety of candidates running throughout the at-large political unit:

> Semiproportional [and proportional] systems permit shifting coalitions to form based on voters' own determinations of their interests or their group identity. In other words, geography and race rely on representational assumptions about group association but do not suggest the necessity, standing alone, of representing or defining group interests a particular way. Modified at-large systems, such as cumulative voting, could be viewed as preferable alternatives that allow members of racial groups, politically cohesive groups, and strategically motivated individuals to be both self-defined and represented, while minimizing the problem of wasted votes for *all* voters.

LANI GUINIER, THE TYRANNY OF THE MAJORITY 137 (1994). The problem of wasted votes that Guinier refers to is another artifact of territorial districting under a winner-take-all system: those who vote for the losing candidate may feel unrepresented, except perhaps virtually, by like-minded candidates elected from other districts, if there are any. Proportional systems tend to award some legislative seats to candidates who might not be able to win a majority of the popular vote in any particular district.

But even if districting were eliminated by using proportional representation, would this eliminate the problem of gerrymandering? Not necessarily. Perhaps surprisingly, proportional representation systems often rely on districting to carve a jurisdiction into subdivisions of manageable size. In a large, populous nation, the national legislature may contain hundreds of seats. It is usually thought to be infeasible to ask individual voters to select at-large among hundreds of candidates, and consequently nations that use PR typically divide the nation into numerous districts, each of which elects multiple representatives using PR. For example, the lower house of the Irish Legislature, the Dail, contains 166 seats; members are elected from districts that select three, four, or five members each. In Tasmania, Malta, and the Australian Capital Territory, districts send either five or seven members. How one draws the district lines can affect how many seats a party wins because, even though the system is proportional, individual seats can only be won as whole units. Thus, it is possible with modern techniques to gerrymander in or out supporters of particular parties to manipulate whether the number of votes cast for that party's candidates reaches the fractional threshold necessary to elect an additional candidate.

This result could be avoided, but to do so it would be necessary to abandon voting for individual legislators in favor of a "party list" system. In such a system, used in Israel, all voters throughout the nation vote together for the entire national legislature, the Knesset, but vote only for the party they prefer — they have no opportunity to select individuals to fill legislative seats. After the voting, each party learns what proportion of the vote it earned, and thus how many seats it is entitled to fill. For this purpose, each party maintains a list of putative legislators, and it works down its list until it has filled all the seats to which the vote tally entitles it. Gerrymandering is impossible in such a system, but there is a tradeoff in the loss of direct voter control over the identities of legislators.

For an interesting argument on grounds of democratic theory that the ideal congressional district is not only nonterritorial but populated by random assignment of citizens, see ANDREW REHFELD, THE CONCEPT OF CONSTITUENCY: POLITICAL REPRESENTATION, DEMOCRATIC LEGITIMACY, AND INSTITUTIONAL DESIGN (2005).

3.   Easley: *Détente & Equilibrium*

Between 1995, following its decision in *Miller*, and 2000, the Court decided a string of cases striking down redistricting plans for relying excessively on race. In two of those cases, *Shaw v. Hunt*, 517 U.S. 899 (1996), and *Hunt v. Cromartie*, 526 U.S. 541 (1999), the Court invalidated subsequent attempts by the North Carolina legislature to remedy the defects found by the Court in *Shaw v. Reno*. In another case, *Abrams v. Johnson*, 521 U.S. 711 (1997), the Court invalidated a subsequent attempt by the Georgia legislature to correct the problems that led to invalidation in *Miller v. Johnson*. And in *Bush v. Vera*, 517 U.S. 952 (1996), the Court invalidated aspects of a Texas redistricting plan on the ground that race was the predominant

factor in drawing certain districts. State legislatures, understandably, were beginning to despair for guidance about how to comply with both the requirements of
Section 2 and Section 5 of the VRA that they not engage in racial discrimination
against blacks, and the Court's insistence in the *Shaw* line of cases that they not discriminate against whites or other voters in violation of the Fourteenth Amendment.

Indeed, in a set of highly splintered opinions in *Bush*, five Justices suggested
(without actually holding) that there may be no way to reconcile Section 2 with the
commands of the Fourteenth Amendment as interpreted by *Shaw*. In *Bush*, a plurality consisting of Justices O'Connor, Rehnquist, and Kennedy held that the Texas
districts at issue were subject to strict scrutiny, and that the district court's factual
findings amply supported its conclusion that the district could not survive because
race had been the predominant factor in drawing the districts. The plurality did not
address the constitutionality of Section 2. However, in a concurring opinion joined
by Justice Scalia, Justice Thomas ruled that the intentional creation of any majority-
minority district requires strict scrutiny. In view of Justices Thomas and Scalia's
position in *Adarand Constructors, Inc. v. Pena*, 515 U.S. 200 (1995), that the only justification for any kind of race-conscious treatment is to rectify demonstrated, past
discrimination, their position in *Bush* may well be taken as an indication that they
view Section 2 as unconstitutional because it authorizes the creation of majority-
minority districts for other reasons. Finally, in a dissenting opinion, Justice Souter,
joined by Justices Ginsburg and Breyer, argued that the Court had boxed itself into
a corner and "[t]he only way to avoid this conflict would be to declare the Voting
Rights Act unconstitutional." In a bizarre twist that may have revealed just how far
the Court had lost its way, Justice O'Connor responded to the dissent by filing an
opinion concurring *with herself* in which she pleaded that the Court "allow States to
assume the constitutionality of §2 of the VRA, including the 1982 amendments."

The Court did, however, decide one case during this period upholding a redistricting plan, *Lawyer v. Department of Justice*, 521 U.S. 567 (1997). There, the Court
affirmed a district court finding that race had not predominated in the drawing
of one of Florida's state senatorial districts. The brief 5-4 affirmance offered little
substantive guidance, however, holding only that the district court's factual findings
were not clearly erroneous.

At the dawn of the twenty-first century, it seemed that the Court found an
equilibrium and made peace between two commitments that appeared to be on
a collision course: an increasingly colorblind interpretation of the Constitution
hurtling at full speed against a race-conscious remedial statute. As the case below
shows, the Court achieved this détente by relying upon an artifact of our politics,
the correlation between racial and partisan identity, to make it harder on evidentiary grounds for plaintiffs bringing *Shaw* claims to prevail.

Easley v. Cromartie

532 U.S. 234 (2001)

BREYER, J., delivered the opinion of the Court, in which STEVENS, O'CONNOR,
SOUTER, and GINSBURG, JJ., joined. THOMAS, J., filed a dissenting opinion, in which
REHNQUIST, C.J., and SCALIA and KENNEDY, JJ., joined.

Justice BREYER delivered the opinion of the Court.

In this appeal, we review a three-judge District Court's determination that North Carolina's legislature used race as the "predominant factor" in drawing its 12th Congressional District's 1997 boundaries. The court's findings, in our view, are clearly erroneous. We therefore reverse its conclusion that the State violated the Equal Protection Clause. U.S. Const., Amdt. 14, §1.

I

This "racial districting" litigation is before us for the fourth time. Our first two holdings addressed North Carolina's *former* Congressional District 12, one of two North Carolina congressional districts drawn in 1992 that contained a majority of African-American voters. See *Shaw v. Reno*, 509 U.S. 630 (1993) (*Shaw I*); *Shaw v. Hunt*, 517 U.S. 899 (1996) (*Shaw II*).

A

In *Shaw I*, the Court considered whether plaintiffs' factual allegation—that the legislature had drawn the former district's boundaries for race-based reasons—if true, could underlie a legal holding that the legislature had violated the Equal Protection Clause. The Court held that it could.

In *Shaw II*, the Court reversed a subsequent three-judge District Court's holding that the boundary-drawing law in question did not violate the Constitution. This Court found that the district's "unconventional," snakelike shape, the way in which its boundaries split towns and counties, its predominately African-American racial make-up, and its history, together demonstrated a deliberate effort to create a "majority-black" district in which race "could not be compromised," not simply a district designed to "protec[t] Democratic incumbents." And the Court concluded that the legislature's use of racial criteria was not justified.

B

Our third holding focused on a new District 12, the boundaries of which the legislature had redrawn in 1997. *Hunt v. Cromartie*, 526 U.S. 541 (1999). A three-judge District Court, with one judge dissenting, had granted summary judgment in favor of those challenging the district's boundaries. The court found that the legislature again had "used criteria . . . that are facially race driven," in violation of the Equal Protection Clause. It based this conclusion upon "uncontroverted material facts" showing that the boundaries created an unusually shaped district, split counties and cities, and in particular placed almost all heavily Democratic-registered, predominantly African-American voting precincts, inside the district while locating some heavily Democratic-registered, predominantly white precincts, outside the district. This latter circumstance, said the court, showed that the legislature was trying to maximize new District 12's African-American voting strength, not the district's Democratic voting strength.

This Court reversed. We agreed with the District Court that the new district's shape, the way in which it split towns and counties, and its heavily African-American voting population all helped the plaintiffs' case. But neither that evidence by itself, nor when coupled with the evidence of Democratic registration, was sufficient to show, on summary judgment, the unconstitutional race-based objective that plaintiffs claimed. That is because there was a genuine issue of material fact as to whether the evidence also was consistent with a constitutional political objective, namely, the creation of a safe Democratic seat.

We pointed to the affidavit of an expert witness for defendants, Dr. David W. Peterson. Dr. Peterson offered to show that, because North Carolina's African-American voters are overwhelmingly Democratic voters, one cannot easily distinguish a legislative effort to create a majority-African-American district from a legislative effort to create a safely Democratic district. *Id.*, at 550. And he also provided data showing that *registration* did not indicate how voters would actually vote. We agreed that data showing how voters actually behave, not data showing only how those voters are registered, could affect the outcome of this litigation. We concluded that the case was "not suited for summary disposition" and we reversed the District Court.

C

On remand, the parties undertook additional discovery. The three-judge District Court held a 3-day trial. And the court again held (over a dissent) that the legislature had unconstitutionally drawn District 12's new 1997 boundaries. It found that the legislature had tried "(1) [to] cur[e] the [previous district's] constitutional defects" while also "(2) drawing the plan to maintain the existing partisan balance in the State's congressional delegation." It added that to "achieve the second goal," the legislature "drew the new plan (1) to avoid placing two incumbents in the same district and (2) to preserve the partisan core of the existing districts." *Ibid.* The court concluded that the "plan as enacted largely reflects these directives." *Ibid.* But the court also found "as a matter of fact that the General Assembly . . . used criteria . . . that are facially race driven" without any compelling justification for doing so. *Id.*, at 28a.

The court based its latter, constitutionally critical, conclusion in part upon the district's snakelike shape, the way in which it split cities and towns, and its heavily African-American (47%) voting population, *id.*, at 11a-17a — all matters that this Court had considered when it found summary judgment inappropriate, *Cromartie, supra*, at 544. The court also based this conclusion upon a specific finding — absent when we previously considered this litigation — that the legislature had drawn the boundaries in order "to collect precincts with *high racial identification rather than political identification.*"

This last-mentioned finding rested in turn upon five subsidiary determinations:

(1)   that "the legislators excluded many heavily-Democratic precincts from District 12, even when those precincts immediately border the Twelfth and would have established a far more compact district," *id.*, at 25a; see also *id.*, at 29a ("more heavily Democratic precincts . . . were bypassed . . . in favor of precincts with a higher African-American population");

(2)   that "[a]dditionally, Plaintiffs' expert, Dr. Weber, showed time and again how race trumped party affiliation in the construction of the 12th District and how political explanations utterly failed to explain the composition of the district," *id.*, at 26a;

(3) that Dr. Peterson's testimony was "'unreliable' and not relevant," *id.*, at 27a (citing testimony of Dr. Weber);

(4) that a legislative redistricting leader, Senator Roy Cooper, had alluded at the time of redistricting "to a need for 'racial and partisan' balance," *ibid.*; and

(5) that the Senate's redistricting coordinator, Gerry Cohen, had sent Senator Cooper an e-mail reporting that Cooper had "moved Greensboro Black community into the 12th, and now need[ed] to take [about] 60,000 out of the 12th," App. 369; App. to Juris. Statement 27a-28a.

We now reverse.

II

The issue in this case is evidentiary. We must determine whether there is adequate support for the District Court's key findings, particularly the ultimate finding that the legislature's motive was predominantly racial, not political. In making this determination, we are aware that, under *Shaw I* and later cases, the burden of proof on the plaintiffs (who attack the district) is a "demanding one." *Miller v. Johnson.* The Court has specified that those who claim that a legislature has improperly used race as a criterion, in order, for example, to create a majority-minority district, must show at a minimum that the "legislature subordinated traditional race-neutral districting principles . . . to racial considerations." *Id.*, at 916 (majority opinion). Race must not simply have been "*a* motivation for the drawing of a majority minority district," *Bush v. Vera*, 517 U.S. 952, 959 (1996) (O'Connor, J., principal opinion) (emphasis in original), but "the '*predominant* factor' motivating the legislature's districting decision," *Cromartie*, 526 U.S., at 547 (quoting *Miller, supra*, at 916) (emphasis added). Plaintiffs must show that a facially neutral law "is 'unexplainable on grounds other than race.'" *Cromartie, supra*, at 546 (quoting *Shaw I*, 509 U.S., at 644, in turn quoting *Arlington Heights v. Metropolitan Housing Development Corp.*, 429 U.S. 252, 266 (1977)).

The Court also has made clear that the underlying districting decision is one that ordinarily falls within a legislature's sphere of competence. *Miller*, 515 U.S., at 915. Hence, the legislature "must have discretion to exercise the political judgment necessary to balance competing interests," *ibid.*, and courts must "exercise *extraordinary caution* in adjudicating claims that a State has drawn district lines on the basis of race," *id.*, at 916 (emphasis added). Caution is especially appropriate in this case, where the State has articulated a legitimate political explanation for its districting decision, and the voting population is one in which race and political affiliation are highly correlated. See *Cromartie, supra*, at 551-552 (noting that "[e]vidence that blacks constitute even a supermajority in one congressional district while amounting to less than a plurality in a neighboring district will not, by itself, suffice to prove that a jurisdiction was motivated by race in drawing its district lines when the evidence also shows a high correlation between race and party preference").

We also are aware that we review the District Court's findings only for "clear error." In applying this standard, we, like any reviewing court, will not reverse a lower court's finding of fact simply because we "would have decided the case differently." *Anderson v. Bessemer City*, 470 U.S. 564, 573 (1985). Rather, a reviewing court must ask whether "on the entire evidence," it is "left with the definite and firm conviction that a mistake has been committed." *United States v. United States Gypsum Co.*, 333 U.S. 364 (1948).

Where an intermediate court reviews, and affirms, a trial court's factual findings, this Court will not "lightly overturn" the concurrent findings of the two lower courts. *E.g., Neil v. Biggers*, 409 U.S. 188, 193, n.3 (1972). But in this instance there is no intermediate court, and we are the only court of review. Moreover, the trial here at issue was not lengthy and the key evidence consisted primarily of documents and expert testimony. Credibility evaluations played a minor role. Accordingly, we find that an extensive review of the District Court's findings, for clear error, is warranted. That review leaves us "with the definite and firm conviction," *United States Gypsum Co., supra*, at 395, that the District Court's key findings are mistaken.

III

The critical District Court determination—the matter for which we remanded this litigation—consists of the finding that race *rather than* politics *predominantly* explains District 12's 1997 boundaries. That determination rests upon three findings (the district's shape, its splitting of towns and counties, and its high African-American voting population) that we previously found insufficient to support summary judgment. *Cromartie, supra*, at 547-549. Given the undisputed evidence that racial identification is highly correlated with political affiliation in North Carolina, these facts in and of themselves cannot, as a matter of law, support the District Court's judgment. See *Vera*, 517 U.S., at 968 (O'Connor, J., principal opinion) ("If district lines merely correlate with race because they are drawn on the basis of political affiliation, which correlates with race, there is no racial classification to justify"). The District Court rested, however, upon five new subsidiary findings to conclude that District 12's lines are the product of no "mer[e] correlat[ion]," *ibid.*, but are instead a result of the predominance of race in the legislature's line-drawing process. See *supra*, at 1458.

In considering each subsidiary finding, we have given weight to the fact that the District Court was familiar with this litigation, heard the testimony of each witness, and considered all the evidence with care. Nonetheless, we cannot accept the District Court's findings as adequate for reasons which we shall spell out in detail and which we can summarize as follows:

First, the primary evidence upon which the District Court relied for its "race, not politics," conclusion is evidence of voting registration, not voting behavior; and that is precisely the kind of evidence that we said was inadequate the last time this case was before us. Second, the additional evidence to which appellees' expert, Dr. Weber, pointed, and the statements made by Senator Cooper and Gerry Cohen, simply do not provide significant additional support for the District Court's conclusion. Third, the District Court, while not accepting the contrary conclusion of appellants' expert, Dr. Peterson, did not (and as far as the record reveals, could not) reject much of the significant supporting factual information he provided. Fourth, in any event, appellees themselves have provided us with charts summarizing evidence of voting behavior and those charts tend to refute the court's "race not politics" conclusion.

A

The District Court primarily based its "race, not politics," conclusion upon its finding that "the legislators excluded many heavily-Democratic precincts from District 12, even when those precincts immediately border the Twelfth and would have established a far more compact district." This finding, however—insofar as it differs from the remaining four—rests solely upon evidence that the legislature excluded heavily white precincts with high Democratic Party *registration*, while including heavily African-American precincts with equivalent, or lower, Democratic Party registration.

As we said before, the problem with this evidence is that it focuses upon party registration, not upon voting behavior. And we previously found the same evidence, compare *ibid.* (District Court's opinion after trial) with *id.*, at 249a-250a (District Court's summary judgment opinion), inadequate because registration figures do not accurately predict preference at the polls. In part this is because white voters registered as Democrats "cross-over" to vote for a Republican candidate more often than do African-Americans, who register and vote Democratic between 95% and 97% of the time. A legislature trying to secure a safe Democratic seat is interested in Democratic voting behavior. Hence, a legislature may, by placing reliable Democratic precincts within a district without regard to race, end up with a district containing more heavily African-American precincts, but the reasons would be political rather than racial.

Insofar as the District Court relied upon voting registration data, particularly data that were previously before us, it tells us nothing new; and the data do not help answer the question posed when we previously remanded this litigation. *Cromartie, supra,* at 551.

B

The District Court wrote that "[a]dditionally, [p]laintiffs' expert, Dr. Weber, showed time and again how race trumped party affiliation in the construction of the 12th District and how political explanations utterly failed to explain the composition of the district." App. to Juris. Statement 26a. In support of this conclusion, the court relied upon six different citations to Dr. Weber's trial testimony. We have examined each reference.

[The Court undertook an extensive review of Dr. Weber's testimony.]

We do not see how Dr. Weber's testimony, taken as a whole, could have provided more than minimal support for the District Court's conclusion that race predominantly underlay the legislature's districting decision.

C

The District Court found that the testimony of the State's primary expert, Dr. Peterson, was " 'unreliable' and not relevant." App. to Juris. Statement 27a (quoting Dr. Weber and citing Tr. 222-224, 232). Dr. Peterson's testimony was designed to show that African-American Democratic voters were more reliably Democratic and that District 12's boundaries were drawn to include reliable Democrats. Specifically, Dr. Peterson compared precincts immediately within District 12 and those immediately without to determine whether the boundaries of the district corresponded better with race than with politics. The principle underlying Dr. Peterson's analysis is that if the district were drawn with race predominantly in mind, one would expect the boundaries of the district to correlate with race more than with politics.

[The Court reviewed Dr. Peterson's testimony.]

The District Court's criticism of Dr. Peterson's testimony at most affects the reliability of the fourth element of Dr. Peterson's testimony, his special boundary segment analysis. The District Court's criticism of Dr. Peterson's boundary segment analysis does not undermine the data related to the split communities. The criticism does not undercut Dr. Peterson's presentation of statistical evidence showing that registration was a poor indicator of party preference and that African-Americans are much more reliably Democratic voters, nor have we found in the record any significant evidence refuting that data. . . .

D

The District Court also relied on two pieces of "direct" evidence of discriminatory intent.

1

The court found that a legislative redistricting leader, Senator Roy Cooper, when testifying before a legislative committee in 1997, had said that the 1997 plan satisfies a "need for 'racial and partisan' balance." The court concluded that the words "racial balance" referred to a 10-to-2 Caucasian/African-American balance in the State's 12-member congressional delegation. *Ibid.* Hence, Senator Cooper had admitted that the legislature had drawn the plan with race in mind.

Senator Cooper's full statement reads as follows:

Those of you who dealt with Redistricting before realize that you cannot solve each problem that you encounter and everyone can find a problem with this Plan. However, I think that overall it provides for a fair, geographic, racial and partisan balance throughout the State of North Carolina. I think in order to come to an agreement all sides had to give a little bit, but I think we've reached an agreement that we can live with.

App. 460.

We agree that one can read the statement about "racial . . . balance" as the District Court read it—to refer to the current congressional delegation's racial balance. But even as so read, the phrase shows that the legislature considered race, along with other partisan and geographic considerations; and as so read it says little or nothing about whether race played a *predominant* role comparatively speaking.

2

The second piece of "direct" evidence relied upon by the District Court is a February 10, 1997, e-mail sent from Gerry Cohen, a legislative staff member responsible for drafting districting plans, to Senator Cooper and Senator Leslie Winner. Cohen wrote: "I have moved Greensboro Black community into the 12th, and now need to take [about] 60,000 out of the 12th. I await your direction on this." App. 369.

The reference to race—*i.e.*, "Black community"—is obvious. But the e-mail does not discuss the point of the reference. It does not discuss why Greensboro's African-American voters were placed in the 12th District; it does not discuss the political consequences of failing to do so; it is addressed only to two members of the legislature; and it suggests that the legislature paid less attention to race in respect to the 12th District than in respect to the 1st District, where the e-mail provides a far more extensive, detailed discussion of racial percentages. It is less persuasive than the kinds of direct evidence we have found significant in other redistricting cases. See *Vera, supra,* at 959 (O'Connor, J., principal opinion) (State conceded that one of its goals was to create a majority-minority district); *Miller, supra,* at 907 (State set out to create majority-minority district); *Shaw II,* 517 U.S., at 906 (recounting testimony by Cohen that creating a majority-minority district was the "principal reason" for the 1992 version of District 12). Nonetheless, the e-mail offers some support for the District Court's conclusion. . . .

IV

We concede the record contains a modicum of evidence offering support for the District Court's conclusion. That evidence includes the Cohen e-mail, Senator Cooper's reference to "racial balance," and to a minor degree, some aspects of Dr. Weber's testimony. The evidence taken together, however, does not show that racial considerations predominated in the drawing of District 12's boundaries. That is because race in this case correlates closely with political behavior. The basic question is whether the legislature drew District 12's boundaries because of race *rather than* because of political behavior (coupled with traditional, nonracial districting considerations). It is not, as the dissent contends, whether a legislature may defend its districting decisions based on a "stereotype" about African-American voting behavior. And given the fact that the party attacking the legislature's decision bears the burden of proving that racial considerations are "dominant and controlling," *Miller,* 515 U.S., at 913, given the "demanding" nature of that burden of proof, *id.,* at 929 (O'Connor, J., concurring), and given the sensitivity, the "extraordinary caution," that district courts must show to avoid treading upon legislative prerogatives, *id.,* at 916 (majority opinion), the attacking party has not successfully shown that race, rather than politics, predominantly accounts for the result. The record leaves us with the "definite and firm conviction," that the District Court erred in finding to the contrary. And we do not believe that providing appellees a further opportunity to make their "precinct swapping" arguments in the District Court could change this result.

We can put the matter more generally as follows: In a case such as this one where majority-minority districts (or the approximate equivalent) are at issue and where racial identification correlates highly with political affiliation, the party attacking the legislatively drawn boundaries must show at the least that the legislature could have achieved its legitimate political objectives in alternative ways that are comparably consistent with traditional districting principles. That party must also show that those districting alternatives would have brought about significantly greater racial balance. Appellees failed to make any such showing here. We conclude that the District Court's contrary findings are clearly erroneous. Because of this disposition, we need not address appellants' alternative grounds for reversal.

The judgment of the District Court is
Reversed.

Justice THOMAS, with whom THE CHIEF JUSTICE, Justice SCALIA, and Justice KENNEDY join, dissenting.

The issue for the District Court was whether racial considerations were predominant in the design of North Carolina's Congressional District 12. The issue for this Court is simply whether the District Court's factual finding—that racial considerations did predominate—was clearly erroneous. Because I do not believe the court below committed clear error, I respectfully dissent. . . .

Reviewing for clear error, I cannot say that the District Court's view of the evidence was impermissible. First, the court relied on objective measures of compactness, which show that District 12 is the most geographically scattered district in North Carolina, to support its conclusion that the district's design was not dictated by traditional districting concerns. . . .

Second, the court relied on the expert opinion of Dr. Weber, who interpreted statistical data to conclude that there were Democratic precincts with low black populations excluded from District 12, which would have created a more compact district had they been included. . . . Third, the court credited Dr. Weber's testimony that the districting decisions could not be explained by political motives. . . . Fourth, the court discredited the testimony of the State's witness, Dr. Peterson. . . .

Finally, the court found that other evidence demonstrated that race was foremost on the legislative agenda: an e-mail from the drafter of the 1992 and 1997 plans to senators in charge of legislative redistricting, the computer capability to draw the district by race, and statements made by Senator Cooper that the legislature was going to be able to avoid *Shaw's* majority-minority trigger by ending just short of the majority. App. to Juris. Statement in No. 99-1864, p. 28a. The e-mail, in combination with the indirect evidence, is evidence ample enough to support the District Court's finding for purposes of clear error review. The drafter of the redistricting plans reported in the bluntest of terms: "I have moved Greensboro Black community into the 12th [District], and now need to take . . . 60,000 out of the 12th [District]." App. 369. Certainly the District Court was entitled to believe that the drafter was targeting voters and shifting district boundaries purely on the basis of race. The Court tries to belittle the import of this evidence by noting that the e-mail does not discuss *why* blacks were being targeted. See *ante*, at 1464-1465. However, the District Court was assigned the task of determining *whether*, not *why*, race predominated. As I see it, this inquiry is sufficient to answer the constitutional question because racial gerrymandering offends the Constitution whether the motivation is malicious or benign. It is not a defense that the legislature merely may have drawn the district based on the stereotype that blacks are reliable Democratic voters. And regardless of whether the e-mail tended to show that the legislature was operating under an even stronger racial motivation when it was drawing District 1 than when it was drawing District 12, cf. *ante*, at 1464-1465, I am convinced that the District Court permissibly could have accorded great weight to this e-mail as direct evidence of a racial motive. Surely, a decision can be racially motivated even if another decision was also racially motivated.

If I were the District Court, I might have reached the same conclusion that the Court does, that "[t]he evidence taken together . . . does not show that racial considerations predominated in the drawing of District 12's boundaries," *ante*, at 1466. But I am not the trier of fact, and it is not my role to weigh evidence in the first instance. The only question that this Court should decide is whether the District Court's finding of racial predominance was clearly erroneous. In light of the direct evidence of racial motive and the inferences that may be drawn from the circumstantial evidence, I am satisfied that the District Court's finding was permissible, even if not compelled by the record.

»   *Understanding* **Cromartie II**.   Isn't Justice Thomas correct that given the applicable standard of review—an appellate court must defer to the trial court's factual determinations unless the trial's courts findings of fact are clearly erroneous—the Court was obligated to defer to the trial's court's factual conclusions that race predominated in the construction of the district? If there is evidence in favor of both race and partisanship, how can the trial's court's findings be clearly erroneous? What is the justification for the majority's opinion?

Consider one explanation that argues that the Court's aim in *Cromartie II* was to ease the tension between the colorblindness impulse of its equal protection jurisprudence and the race consciousness command of Section 2 and 5 of the VRA by putting an end to *Shaw*-type claims. "The Court sent a clear message to legislatures drawing majority-minority districts that they would have a safe harbor from such claims so long as they could plausibly claim they were motivated by political considerations as opposed to racial considerations when they drew the district lines. Given the relationship between political and racial identity, it was not hard for state legislatures to plausibly claim that their redistricting lines were motivated by politics and not race." Guy-Uriel E. Charles & Luis Fuentes-Rohwer, *Race and Representation Revisited: The New Racial Gerrymandering Cases and Section 2 of the VRA*, 59 Wm. & Mary L. Rev. 1559, 1564 (2018). They argue that the Court's decision in *Cromartie II* buried "*Shaw* claims . . . for well over a decade" allowing "states . . . free[dom] to pursue descriptive representation unburdened by strict judicial supervision." Do you find this explanation persuasive?

»   *Polarization, Partisanship, and Race.*   As we have seen, the American electorate has become more politically polarized in recent years. What implications might that continued polarization have for the VRA?

In *Easley*, the majority found that racial considerations did not predominate in the drawing of district lines; rather, partisan considerations predominated. To the extent that race was considered, the Court found, it was used only, or at least mainly, as a proxy for partisan affiliation. But what if (1) the electorate continues to sort itself by partisanship, and (2) racial cleavages align increasingly with partisan ones? This means that virtually all *partisan* manipulation of district lines will have *racial* consequences. How, then, will courts be able to distinguish racial gerrymandering that is actionable under the VRA from partisan gerrymandering, which is not?

Conjoined polarization [in which partisan and racial cleavages coincide] renders futile any attempt under section 2 to distinguish between race and politics. . . . A section 2 violation can be established based only on racially disparate results, without racially discriminatory intent. . . . Doctrinally, it is sufficient that those district lines do in fact dilute minority voting strength. But . . . [i]f section 2's prohibition against vote dilutions of minorities becomes interchangeable with a prohibition against vote dilutions of *Democrats*, it will face strong resistance from the federal judiciary.

Bruce E. Cain and Emily R. Zhang, *Blurred Lines: Conjoined Polarization and Voting Rights*, 77 Ohio St. L.J. 867, 890 (2016). Does this analysis suggest that racial discrimination can always be completely disguised by partisan discrimination? Or does it suggest that racial discrimination will become unnecessary because all its goals can be achieved through discrimination on the basis of partisanship?

In an early article on these issues Professor Richard Hasen argued:

When a legislature passes an election-administration law (outside of the redistricting context) discriminating against a party's voters or otherwise burdening voters, that fact should not be a defense. Instead, courts should read the Fourteenth Amendment's Equal Protection Clause to require the legislature to produce substantial evidence that it has a good reason for burdening voters and that its means are closely connected to achieving those ends. The achievement of partisan ends would not be considered a good reason (as it appears to be in the redistricting context). This rule would both discourage party power grabs and protect voting rights of minority voters. In short, it would inhibit discrimination on the basis of both race and party, and protect all voters from unnecessary burdens on the right to vote.

Richard L. Hasen, *Race or Party?: How Should Courts Think about Republican Efforts to Make it Harder to Vote in North Carolina and Elsewhere*, 127 Harv. L. Rev. F. 58, 62 (2014). Note that Professor Hasen excludes redistricting from his approach. Is racial gerrymandering different? What should courts do in the redistricting context?

>> ***Does the VRA Produce Mere Token Representation?*** There can be no doubt that the VRA, taken as a whole, has contributed significantly to the political strength and electoral successes of black Americans. Many long-standing patterns of discrimination in voting that artificially depressed black registration and voting, and consequently the election of blacks to office, were destroyed by the Act. *See* Quiet Revolution in the South: The Impact of the Voting Rights Act 1965-1990 (Chandler Davidson and Bernard Grofman eds., 1994).

While no one denies that the freedom of blacks to register and vote is a valuable achievement, some have questioned whether the increasingly bitter fight to guarantee the election of black representatives should be the proper focus of efforts to increase black political strength. Lani Guinier, for example, has argued that the election of black representatives is essentially meaningless if they become token and ineffectual members of the legislative bodies in which they sit. Guinier argues that the same forces of racial polarization prevalent in the electoral arena often conspire to isolate and neutralize black legislators in the legislature, and that the same kinds of remedies the VRA applies in voting must also be applied to legislative activity:

> Because marginalization occurs in the legislative body, it is impossible to determine whether it has, in fact, occurred unless the analysis of racial polarization is extended to see if white representatives in the legislature consistently coalesce in opposition to minority voters' interests. . . . In making this inquiry, "prejudice" could be inferred from the presence of a majoritarian bloc that consistently exercises disproportionate power to exclude dissenting viewpoints associated with economically disadvantaged, socially isolated, and physically or culturally identifiable numerical minorities. . . . [R]acial bloc voting that leads predictably to perennial minority losses constitutes a violation of the norms of a fair legislative process. . . .

LANI GUINIER, THE TYRANNY OF THE MAJORITY 105 (1994). To remedy these problems, Guinier suggests supermajority voting requirements within the legislature, or the approximation of a system of proportional voting by allocating to each legislator multiple votes that could be cast as the legislator saw fit across several pieces of legislation. Does Guinier's analysis make sense to you? How do we distinguish between losing legislative (or electoral) contests due to racial discrimination, and losing such contests due to legitimate ideological disagreement?

>> *Black Interests and Black Legislators.* Much of the dispute in the Section 2 cases arises from attempts by either the litigants or the Justice Department to maximize the number of majority-minority districts within a jurisdiction. Clearly, advocates of this strategy have proceeded on the assumption that blacks are best off when they can control directly the largest number of seats. Some recent research disputes this assumption.

In order to make blacks a majority in the largest number of districts, black populations must be concentrated into those districts. While the targeted districts become blacker, other districts necessarily become whiter. Consequently, while blacks gain great influence in the districts where they predominate, they exercise virtually no influence in other districts. In one study, David Lublin, a political scientist, found that this pattern, while increasing the number of black representatives in Congress, has actually reduced the overall responsiveness of Congress to the interests and concerns of black voters. DAVID LUBLIN, THE PARADOX OF REPRESENTATION: RACIAL GERRYMANDERING AND MINORITY INTERESTS IN CONGRESS (1997).

According to Lublin, drawing fewer racially integrated districts where blacks constituted a significant minority caused many such districts to swing dramatically in a conservative direction. This trend was most noticeable in Southern suburban districts. Previously, many districts had combined black urban and white suburban populations. Because blacks were a substantial minority in those districts, only politically moderate candidates were able to carry them. Thus, although such districts might not elect blacks to Congress, they often elected white Democrats who were responsive to the interests of their black constituents. When district lines were redrawn to give urban blacks outright control over the districts in which they lived, suburban districts became much more white and conservative. Many such districts switched from Democratic to Republican, and many of these Republicans were extremely conservative (Newt Gingrich, elected from a suburban district of Atlanta, is probably the prime example).

Lublin argues that this trend caused Democrats to lose control of Congress in 1994. He also found that this kind of districting decision has made the House of Representatives less likely to adopt legislative proposals favored by blacks than it was when its membership was whiter, but more Democratic. Lublin suggests that black political strength is maximized not by the creation of majority-minority districts, but by the creation of influence districts in which blacks make up about 40 percent of the population. In this way, black populations may be spread more thinly, but can exercise a significant influence over the politics of many more districts. *See also* CAROL M. SWAIN, BLACK FACES, BLACK INTERESTS: THE REPRESENTATION OF AFRICAN AMERICANS IN CONGRESS (1993). For a critique of Lublin's analysis, see Richard L. Engstrom, *Race and Southern Politics: The Special Case of Congressional Redistricting, in* WRITING SOUTHERN POLITICS (Robert P. Steed and Laurence W. Moreland eds., University Press of Kentucky 2006). For a study providing empirical support for Lublin's argument, see David Epstein et al., *Estimating the Effect of Redistricting on Minority Substantive Representation*, 23 J.L. ECON. & ORG. 499 (2007) (arguing that the 1990 redistricting in South Carolina led to the election of a legislature with more black representatives, but which was more hostile overall to the interests of black voters).

If there really is a tradeoff between them, which do you think is more important: descriptive representation, and the racial integration of the legislature; or interest representation, and legislative responsiveness to the political positions of racial minorities?

>> *Descriptive Representation Revisited.* Also, does it follow from the possibility of descriptive representation that the interests of *all* members of a group will be equally advanced? According to one study, "representation by an African American Member of Congress (MC) will boost the probability that ideologically liberal African Americans will participate in elections, while more conservative African Americans will be less likely to vote when they are descriptively represented." John D. Griffin and Michael Keane, *Descriptive Representation and the Composition of African American Turnout*, 50 AM. J. POL. SCI. 998, 999 (2006). This suggests not only that some subgroups of the black community prefer descriptive representation to substantive representation, but that the difference between the two kinds of representation may in the end collapse into pure interest representation because those blacks who prefer to be represented by blacks tend to do so because black representatives are more likely to support liberal policy positions.

At the same time, it is not clear that policy positions and a preference for descriptive representation are completely independent variables. In another study, the authors found that black voters report a higher level of satisfaction with municipal services and schools when elected local and school board officials are black. Melissa J. Marschall and Anirudh V.S. Ruhil, *Substantive Symbols: The Attitudinal Dimension of Black Political Incorporation in Local Government*, 51 AM. J. POL. SCI. 17 (2007). The complexities of evaluating these questions can get quite mind-bending!

4.   *The New* Shaw *Cases*

The Court's decision in *Cromartie II* essentially put an end to *Shaw* cases. This meant that voting rights plaintiffs who were voters of color could vindicate their rights under the VRA and compel states to draw majority-minority districts, where doing so was necessary to comply with Sections 2 and 5 of the VRA, without worrying that the Court would strike down the statute as unconstitutional. *Shaw* suits were typically regarded as cases in which white plaintiffs use the Fourteenth Amendment to constrain the extent to which the state can use the VRA, under Section 2 or 5, to draw majority-minority districts. Recall that in the *Shaw* case itself, white plaintiffs sought to employ the Fourteenth Amendment to preclude the state from drawing majority-minority districts, which the state wanted to do pursuant to Section 2 of the VRA. To the extent that a state used Section 2 or Section 5 as a justification for drawing majority-minority districts and to the extent that majority-minority districts provided greater political representation for voters of color, *Shaw* claims are thus thought to be inimical to the interests of voters of color, who are generally thought to favor a broad scope for Section 2 and greater political representation under Section 2. Moreover, black plaintiffs and other plaintiffs of color seeking to challenge racial discrimination in districting have always done so directly under the Fourteenth or Fifteenth Amendments, as *Gomillion v. Lightfoot* attests.

But the jurisprudential landscape changed after 2013, following the Court's decision in *Shelby County v. Holder*. The absence of preclearance pushed civil rights plaintiffs to use all the tools at their disposal, including using the *Shaw* doctrine to challenge racially gerrymandered districts. The first of the new *Shaw* cases to reach the Court was *Alabama Legislative Black Caucus v. Alabama*, 575 U.S. 254 (2015).

The plaintiffs in *Alabama Legislative Black Caucus* were political organizations in Alabama that represent black legislators and Democrats, respectively. They challenged Alabama's 2012 state legislative redistricting, arguing that many of the districts were racial gerrymanders in violation of the Fourteenth Amendment. Their specific complaint appeared to be that the state diluted the votes of African-American voters by packing them into majority-minority districts. Their complaint was not that Alabama created too many majority-minority districts, but that Alabama put more black voters than necessary into those districts. Alabama defended its state legislative redistricting plan on the grounds that it sought to comply with the equipopulation principle as precisely as possible and that it sought to comply with Section 5 of the VRA by maintaining both the same number of majority-minority districts as well as the same percentage of black voters in those districts as in the prior redistricting plan. A three-judge court ruled against the plaintiffs.

The Supreme Court, in an opinion by Justice Breyer, reversed the lower court, though it did not decide the case on the merits. Justice Breyer concluded that the district court committed four errors as a matter of law. First, the district court failed to recognize that a racial gerrymandering claim does not apply to a state considered as a whole but must be a district-by-district claim. In order to state a claim, a plaintiff must allege and eventually prove that "race was improperly used in the drawing of the boundaries of one or more *specific electoral districts.*" The plaintiff cannot assert that the state improperly used race in the state as a whole. Second, the Court held that the district court was wrong in its conclusion that one of the organizations did not have standing to file the racial gerrymandering claim. Third, the Court clarified what it means for race to predominate in the drawing of a district. In *Miller v. Johnson*, the Court stated that in order to make out a *Shaw* claim, a plaintiff must allege and show that race predominated in the drawing of the district and that racial considerations were subordinated to traditional redistricting criteria, such as compactness, contiguity, and respect for political subdivisions. In *Alabama Legislative Black Caucus*, the majority held that complying with the one-person, one vote requirement (the equipopulation principle) is "a background rule against which redistricting takes place" and is not "a factor to be treated like other nonracial factors when a court determines" racial predominance. Thus, the state cannot use compliance with the equipopulation principle to defend against a charge of racial gerrymandering. Lastly, the Court held that Section 5 does not require a state to maintain a specific percentage of black voters in each district. Section 5 "requires the jurisdiction to maintain a minority's ability to elect a preferred candidate of choice," not a "particular numerical minority percentage." Consequently, the Court remanded the case to the district court to apply the correct legal standards, giving the plaintiffs another opportunity to prevail on the merits.

On remand, the District Court issued a mixed ruling. In a highly fact-intensive analysis in which the court said it had "no mechanical formula or system of weights for considering [the] evidence," the court found that race did not predominate in twenty-two of the thirty-six challenged districts, but that it did predominate in the remaining fourteen. The court went on to find that Alabama had satisfied strict scrutiny in two of the fourteen districts, but not in the others.

The most significant case of the new *Shaw* cases, so far, is from North Carolina. Coincidentally, it is the same district that gave rise to *Cromartie II*. As you read the case below, consider whether there is any difference between a new *Shaw* claim and a run-of-the-mill equal protection claim.

Cooper v. Harris

137 S.Ct. 1455 (2017)

Justice KAGAN delivered the opinion of the Court.

The Constitution entrusts States with the job of designing congressional districts. But it also imposes an important constraint: A State may not use race as the predominant factor in drawing district lines unless it has a compelling reason. In this case, a three-judge District Court ruled that North Carolina officials violated that bar when they created two districts whose voting-age populations were majority black. Applying a deferential standard of review to the factual findings underlying that decision, we affirm.

I

A

The Equal Protection Clause of the Fourteenth Amendment limits racial gerrymanders in legislative districting plans. It prevents a State, in the absence of "sufficient justification," from "separating its citizens into different voting districts on the basis of race." *Bethune–Hill v. Virginia State Bd. of Elections*, 137 S.Ct. 788, 797 (2017). When a voter sues state officials for drawing such race-based lines, our decisions call for a two-step analysis.

First, the plaintiff must prove that "race was the predominant factor motivating the legislature's decision to place a significant number of voters within or without a particular district." *Miller v. Johnson*, 515 U.S. 900, 916 (1995). That entails demonstrating that the legislature "subordinated" other factors—compactness, respect for political subdivisions, partisan advantage, what have you—to "racial considerations." The plaintiff may make the required showing through "direct evidence" of legislative intent, "circumstantial evidence of a district's shape and demographics," or a mix of both.

Second, if racial considerations predominated over others, the design of the district must withstand strict scrutiny. The burden thus shifts to the State to prove that its race-based sorting of voters serves a "compelling interest" and is "narrowly tailored" to that end. This Court has long assumed that one compelling interest is complying with operative provisions of the Voting Rights Act of 1965 (VRA or Act). See, *e.g., Shaw v. Hunt*, 517 U.S. 899, 915 (1996) (*Shaw II*).

Two provisions of the VRA—§ 2 and § 5—are involved in this case. Section 2 prohibits any "standard, practice, or procedure" that "results in a denial or abridgement of the right . . . to vote on account of race." We have construed that ban to extend to "vote dilution"—brought about, most relevantly here, by the "dispersal of [a group's members] into districts in which they constitute an ineffective minority of voters." *Thornburg v. Gingles*, 478 U.S. 30, 46, n. 11 (1986). Section 5, at the time of the districting in dispute, worked through a different mechanism. Before this Court invalidated its coverage formula, *see Shelby County v. Holder*, 133 S.Ct. 2612 (2013), that section required certain jurisdictions (including various North Carolina counties) to pre-clear voting changes with the Department of Justice, so as to forestall "retrogression" in the ability of racial minorities to elect their preferred candidates, *Beer v. United States*, 425 U.S. 130, 141 (1976).

When a State invokes the VRA to justify race-based districting, it must show (to meet the "narrow tailoring" requirement) that it had "a strong basis in evidence" for concluding that the statute required its action. *Alabama Legislative Black Caucus v. Alabama*, 135 S.Ct. 1257, 1274 (2015). Or said otherwise, the State must establish that it had "good reasons" to think that it would transgress the Act if it did *not* draw race-based district lines. That "strong basis" (or "good reasons") standard gives States "breathing room" to adopt reasonable compliance measures that may prove, in perfect hindsight, not to have been needed.

A district court's assessment of a districting plan, in accordance with the two-step inquiry just described, warrants significant deference on appeal to this Court. We of course retain full power to correct a court's errors of law, at either stage of the analysis. But the court's findings of fact—most notably, as to whether racial considerations predominated in drawing district lines—are subject to review only for clear error. Under that standard, we may not reverse just because we "would have decided the [matter] differently." A finding that is "plausible" in light of the full record—even if another is equally or more so—must govern.

B

This case concerns North Carolina's most recent redrawing of two congressional districts, both of which have long included substantial populations of black voters. In its current incarnation, District 1 is anchored in the northeastern part of the State, with appendages stretching both south and west (the latter into Durham). District 12 begins in the south-central part of the State (where it takes in a large part of Charlotte) and then travels northeast, zig-zagging much of the way to the State's northern border. Both have quite the history before this Court.

We first encountered the two districts, in their 1992 versions, in [*Shaw I*]. There, we held that voters stated an equal protection claim by alleging that Districts 1 and 12 were unwarranted racial gerrymanders. After a remand to the District Court, the case arrived back at our door. See *Shaw II,* 517 U.S. 899. That time, we dismissed the challenge to District 1 for lack of standing, but struck down District 12. The design of that "serpentine" district, we held, was nothing if not race-centric, and could not be justified as a reasonable attempt to comply with the VRA.

The next year, the State responded with a new districting plan, including a new District 12—and residents of that district brought another lawsuit alleging an impermissible racial gerrymander. A District Court sustained the claim twice, but both times this Court reversed. See *Hunt v. Cromartie,* 526 U.S. 541 (1999) (*Cromartie I*); *Cromartie II,* 532 U.S. 234. Racial considerations, we held, did not predominate in designing the revised District 12. Rather, that district was the result of a *political* gerrymander—an effort to engineer, mostly "without regard to race," a safe Democratic seat.

The State redrew its congressional districts again in 2001, to account for population changes revealed in the prior year's census. Under the 2001 map, which went unchallenged in court, neither District 1 nor District 12 had a black voting-age population (called a "BVAP") that was a majority of the whole: The former had a BVAP of around 48%, the latter a BVAP of around 43%. Nonetheless, in five successive general elections conducted in those reconfigured districts, all the candidates preferred by most African–American voters won their contests—and by some handy margins. In District 1, black voters' candidates of choice garnered as much as 70% of the total vote, and never less than 59%. And in District 12, those candidates won with 72% of the vote at the high end and 64% at the low.

Another census, in 2010, necessitated yet another congressional map— (finally) the one at issue in this case. State Senator Robert Rucho and State Representative David Lewis, both Republicans, chaired the two committees jointly responsible for preparing the revamped plan. They hired Dr. Thomas Hofeller, a veteran political mapmaker, to assist them in redrawing district lines. Several hearings, drafts, and revisions later, both chambers of the State's General Assembly adopted the scheme the three men proposed.

The new map (among other things) significantly altered both District 1 and District 12. The 2010 census had revealed District 1 to be substantially underpopulated: To comply with the Constitution's one-person-one-vote principle, the State needed to place almost 100,000 new people within the district's boundaries. Rucho, Lewis, and Hofeller chose to take most of those people from heavily black areas of Durham, requiring a finger-like extension of the district's western line. With that addition, District 1's BVAP rose from 48.6% to 52.7%. District 12, for its part, had no need for significant total-population changes: It was overpopulated by fewer than 3,000 people out of over 730,000. Still, Rucho, Lewis, and Hofeller decided to reconfigure the district, further narrowing its already snakelike body while adding areas at either end—most relevantly here, in Guilford County. Those changes appreciably shifted the racial composition of District 12: As the district gained some 35,000 African–Americans of voting age and lost some 50,000 whites of that age, its BVAP increased from 43.8% to 50.7%.

Registered voters in the two districts (David Harris and Christine Bowser, here called "the plaintiffs") brought this suit against North Carolina officials, complaining of impermissible racial gerrymanders. After a bench trial, a three-judge District Court held both districts unconstitutional. All the judges agreed that racial considerations predominated in the design of District 1. And in then applying strict scrutiny, all rejected the State's argument that it had a "strong basis" for thinking that the VRA compelled such a race-based drawing of District 1's lines. As for District 12, a majority of the panel held that "race predominated" over all other factors, including partisanship. And the court explained that the State had failed to put forward any reason, compelling or otherwise, for its attention to race in designing that district. . . .

III

[W]e turn to the merits of this case, beginning (appropriately enough) with District 1. As noted above, the court below found that race furnished the predominant rationale for that district's redesign. And it held that the State's interest in complying with the VRA could not justify that consideration of race. We uphold both conclusions.

A

Uncontested evidence in the record shows that the State's mapmakers, in considering District 1, purposefully established a racial target: African–Americans should make up no less than a majority of the voting-age population. Senator Rucho and Representative Lewis were not coy in expressing that goal. They repeatedly told their colleagues that District 1 had to be majority-minority, so as to comply with the VRA. During a Senate debate, for example, Rucho explained that District 1 "must include a sufficient number of African–Americans" to make it "a majority black district." Similarly, Lewis informed the House and Senate redistricting committees that the district must have "a majority black voting age population." And that objective was communicated in no uncertain terms to the legislators' consultant. Dr. Hofeller testified multiple times at trial that Rucho and Lewis instructed him "to draw [District 1] with a [BVAP] in excess of 50 percent."

Hofeller followed those directions to the letter, such that the 50%-plus racial target "had a direct and significant impact" on District 1's configuration. In particular, Hofeller moved the district's borders to encompass the heavily black parts of Durham (and only those parts), thus taking in tens of thousands of additional African–American voters. That change and similar ones, made (in his words) to ensure that the district's racial composition would "add[] up correctly," deviated from the districting practices he otherwise would have followed. Hofeller candidly admitted that point: For example, he testified, he sometimes could not respect county or precinct lines as he wished because "the more important thing" was to create a majority-minority district. The result is a district with stark racial borders: Within the same counties, the portions that fall inside District 1 have black populations two to three times larger than the portions placed in neighboring districts.

Faced with this body of evidence — showing an announced racial target that subordinated other districting criteria and produced boundaries amplifying divisions between blacks and whites — the District Court did not clearly err in finding that race predominated in drawing District 1.

B

The more substantial question is whether District 1 can survive the strict scrutiny applied to racial gerrymanders. As noted earlier, we have long assumed that complying with the VRA is a compelling interest. And we have held that race-based districting is narrowly tailored to that objective if a State had "good reasons" for thinking that the Act demanded such steps. North Carolina argues that District 1 passes muster under that standard: The General Assembly (so says the State) had "good reasons to believe it needed to draw [District 1] as a majority-minority district to avoid Section 2 liability" for vote dilution. We now turn to that defense.

This Court identified, in *Thornburg v. Gingles,* three threshold conditions for proving vote dilution under § 2 of the VRA. First, a "minority group" must be "sufficiently large and geographically compact to constitute a majority" in some reasonably configured legislative district. Second, the minority group must be "politically cohesive." And third, a district's white majority must "vote [] sufficiently as a bloc" to usually "defeat the minority's preferred candidate." Those three showings, we have explained, are needed to establish that "the minority [group] has the potential to elect a representative of its own choice" in a possible district, but that racially polarized voting prevents it from doing so in the district as actually drawn because it is "submerg[ed] in a larger white voting population." If a State has good reason to think that all the "*Gingles* preconditions" are met, then so too it has good reason to believe that § 2 requires drawing a majority-minority district. But if not, then not.

Here, electoral history provided no evidence that a § 2 plaintiff could demonstrate the third *Gingles* prerequisite — effective white bloc-voting. For most of the twenty years prior to the new plan's adoption, African–Americans had made up less than a majority of District 1's voters; the district's BVAP usually hovered between 46% and 48%. Yet throughout those two decades, as the District Court noted, District 1 was "an extraordinarily safe district for African–American preferred candidates." In the *closest* election during that period, African–Americans' candidate of choice received 59% of the total vote; in other years, the share of the vote garnered by those candidates rose to as much as 70%. Those victories (indeed, landslides) occurred because the district's white population did *not* "vote [] sufficiently as a bloc" to thwart black voters' preference; rather, a meaningful number of white voters joined a politically cohesive black community to elect that group's favored candidate. In the lingo of voting law, District 1 functioned, election year in and election year out, as a "crossover" district, in which members of the majority help a "large enough" minority to elect its candidate of choice. When voters act in that way, "[i]t is difficult to see how the majority-bloc-voting requirement could be met"—and hence how § 2 liability could be established. So experience gave the State no reason to think that the VRA required it to ramp up District 1's BVAP.

The State counters that, in this context, past performance is no guarantee of future results. Recall here that the State had to redraw its whole congressional map following the 2010 census. And in particular, the State had to add nearly 100,000 new people to District 1 to meet the one-person-one-vote standard. That meant about 13% of the voters in the new district would never have voted there before. So, North Carolina contends, the question facing the state mapmakers was not whether the *then-existing* District 1 violated § 2. Rather, the question was whether the *future* District 1 would do so if drawn without regard to race. And that issue, the State claims, could not be resolved by "focusing myopically on past elections."

But that reasoning, taken alone, cannot justify North Carolina's race-based redesign of District 1. True enough, a legislature undertaking a redistricting must assess whether the new districts it contemplates (not the old ones it sheds) conform to the VRA's requirements. And true too, an inescapable influx of additional voters into a district may suggest the possibility that its former track record of compliance can continue only if the legislature intentionally adjusts its racial composition. Still, North Carolina too far downplays the significance of a longtime pattern of white crossover voting in the area that would form the core of the redrawn District 1. And even more important, North Carolina can point to no meaningful legislative inquiry into what it now rightly identifies as the key issue: whether a new, enlarged District 1, created without a focus on race but however else the State would choose, could lead to § 2 liability. To have a strong basis in evidence to conclude that § 2 demands such race-based steps, the State must carefully evaluate whether a plaintiff could establish the *Gingles* preconditions—including effective white bloc-voting—in a new district created without those measures. We see nothing in the legislative record that fits that description.

In sum: Although States enjoy leeway to take race-based actions reasonably judged necessary under a proper interpretation of the VRA, that latitude cannot rescue District 1. We by no means "insist that a state legislature, when redistricting, determine *precisely* what percent minority population [§ 2 of the VRA] demands." But neither will we approve a racial gerrymander whose necessity is supported by no evidence. Accordingly, we uphold the District Court's conclusion that North Carolina's use of race as the predominant factor in designing District 1 does not withstand strict scrutiny.

IV

We now look west to District 12, making its fifth(!) appearance before this Court. This time, the district's legality turns, and turns solely, on which of two possible reasons predominantly explains its most recent reconfiguration. The plaintiffs contended at trial that the General Assembly chose voters for District 12, as for District 1, because of their race; more particularly, they urged that the Assembly intentionally increased District 12's BVAP in the name of ensuring preclearance under the VRA's § 5. But North Carolina declined to mount any defense (similar to the one we have just considered for District 1) that § 5's requirements in fact justified race-based changes to District 12—perhaps because § 5 could not reasonably be understood to have done so. Instead, the State altogether denied that racial considerations accounted for (or, indeed, played the slightest role in) District 12's redesign. According to the State's version of events, Senator Rucho, Representative Lewis, and Dr. Hofeller moved voters in and out of the district as part of a "strictly" political gerrymander, without regard to race. The mapmakers drew their lines, in other words, to "pack" District 12 with Democrats, not African-Americans.

Getting to the bottom of a dispute like this one poses special challenges for a trial court. In the more usual case alleging a racial gerrymander — where no one has raised a partisanship defense — the court can make real headway by exploring the challenged district's conformity to traditional districting principles, such as compactness and respect for county lines. But such evidence loses much of its value when the State asserts partisanship as a defense, because a bizarre shape — as of the new District 12 — can arise from a "political motivation" as well as a racial one. And crucially, political and racial reasons are capable of yielding similar oddities in a district's boundaries. That is because, of course, "racial identification is highly correlated with political affiliation." As a result of those redistricting realities, a trial court has a formidable task: It must make "a sensitive inquiry" into all "circumstantial and direct evidence of intent" to assess whether the plaintiffs have managed to disentangle race from politics and prove that the former drove a district's lines.

Our job is different — and generally easier. As described earlier, we review a district court's finding as to racial predominance only for clear error, except when the court made a legal mistake. In light of those principles, we uphold the District Court's finding of racial predominance respecting District 12.

A

Begin with some facts and figures, showing how the redistricting of District 12 affected its racial composition. As explained above, District 12 (unlike District 1) was approximately the right size as it was: North Carolina did not — indeed, could not — much change its total population. But by further slimming the district and adding a couple of knobs to its snakelike body (including in Guilford County), the General Assembly incorporated tens of thousands of new voters and pushed out tens of thousands of old ones. And those changes followed racial lines: To be specific, the new District 12 had 35,000 more African-Americans of voting age and 50,000 fewer whites of that age. (The difference was made up of voters from other racial categories.) Those voter exchanges produced a sizable jump in the district's BVAP, from 43.8% to 50.7%. The Assembly thus turned District 12 (as it did District 1) into a majority-minority district.

As the plaintiffs pointed out at trial, Rucho and Lewis had publicly stated that racial considerations lay behind District 12's augmented BVAP. In a release issued along with their draft districting plan, the two legislators ascribed that change to the need to achieve preclearance of the plan under § 5 of the VRA. At that time, § 5 covered Guilford County and thus prohibited any "retrogression in the [electoral] position of racial minorities" there. And part of Guilford County lay within District 12, which meant that the Department of Justice would closely scrutinize that district's new lines. In light of those facts, Rucho and Lewis wrote: "Because of the presence of Guilford County in the Twelfth District, we have drawn our proposed Twelfth District at a [BVAP] level that is above the percentage of

[BVAP] found in the current Twelfth District." According to the two legislators, that race-based "measure w[ould] ensure preclearance of the plan." Thus, the District Court found, Rucho's and Lewis's own account "evince[d] intentionality" as to District 12's racial composition: *Because of* the VRA, they increased the number of African–Americans.

Hofeller confirmed that intent in both deposition testimony and an expert report. Before the redistricting, Hofeller testified, some black residents of Guilford County fell within District 12 while others fell within neighboring District 13. The legislators, he continued, "decided to reunite the black community in Guilford County into the Twelfth." Why? Hofeller responded, in language the District Court emphasized: "[I]n order to be cautious and draw a plan that would pass muster under the Voting Rights Act."

The State's preclearance submission to the Justice Department indicated a similar determination to concentrate black voters in District 12. "One of the concerns of the Redistricting Chairs," North Carolina there noted, had to do with the Justice Department's years-old objection to "a failure by the State to create a second majority minority district" (that is, in addition to District 1). The submission then went on to explain that after considering alternatives, the redistricters had designed a version of District 12 that would raise its BVAP to 50.7%. Thus, concluded the State, the new District 12 "increases[] the African–American community's ability to elect their candidate of choice." In the District Court's view, that passage once again indicated that making District 12 majority-minority was no "mere coincidence," but a deliberate attempt to avoid perceived obstacles to preclearance.

And still there was more: Perhaps the most dramatic testimony in the trial came when Congressman Mel Watt (who had represented District 12 for some 20 years) recounted a conversation he had with Rucho in 2011 about the district's future make-up. According to Watt, Rucho said that "his leadership had told him that he had to ramp the minority percentage in [District 12] up to over 50 percent to comply with the Voting Rights Law." And further, that it would then be Rucho's "job to go and convince the African–American community" that such a racial target "made sense" under the Act. The District Court credited Watt's testimony about the conversation, citing his courtroom demeanor and "consistent recollection" under "probing cross-examination."

The State's contrary story—that politics alone drove decisionmaking—came into the trial mostly through Hofeller's testimony. Hofeller explained that Rucho and Lewis instructed him, first and foremost, to make the map as a whole "more favorable to Republican candidates." One agreed-on stratagem in that effort was to pack the historically Democratic District 12 with even more Democratic voters, thus leaving surrounding districts more reliably Republican. To that end, Hofeller recounted, he drew District 12's new boundaries based on political data—specifically, the voting behavior of precincts in the 2008 Presidential election between Barack Obama and John McCain. Indeed, he claimed, he displayed only this data, and no racial data, on his computer screen while mapping the district. In part of his testimony, Hofeller further stated that the Obama–McCain election data explained (among other things) his incorporation of the black, but not the white, parts of Guilford County then located in District 13. Only *after* he drew a politics-based line between those adjacent areas, Hofeller testified, did he "check[]" the racial data and "f[ind] out" that the resulting configuration of District 12 "did not have a[§ 5] issue."

The District Court, however, disbelieved Hofeller's asserted indifference to the new district's racial composition. The court recalled Hofeller's contrary deposition testimony—his statement (repeated in only slightly different words in his expert report) that Rucho and Lewis "decided" to shift African–American voters into District 12 "in order to" ensure preclearance under § 5. And the court explained that even at trial, Hofeller had given testimony that undermined his "blame it on politics" claim. Right after asserting that Rucho and Lewis had told him "[not] to use race" in designing District 12, Hofeller added a qualification: "except perhaps with regard to Guilford County." As the District Court understood, that is the kind of "exception" that goes pretty far toward swallowing the rule. District 12 saw a net increase of more than 25,000 black voters in Guilford County, relative to a net gain of fewer than 35,000 across the district: So the newly added parts of that county played a major role in pushing the district's BVAP over 50%. The District Court came away from Hofeller's self-contradictory testimony unpersuaded that this decisive influx of black voters was an accident. Whether the racial make-up of the county was displayed on his computer screen or just fixed in his head, the court thought, Hofeller's denial of race-based districting "r[ang] hollow."

The District Court's assessment that all this evidence proved racial predominance clears the bar of clear error review. The court emphasized that the districting plan's own architects had repeatedly described the influx of African–Americans into District 12 as a § 5 compliance measure, not a side-effect of political gerrymandering. And those contemporaneous descriptions comported with the court's credibility determinations about the trial testimony—that Watt told the truth when he recounted Rucho's resolve to hit a majority-BVAP target; and conversely that Hofeller skirted the truth (especially as to Guilford County) when he claimed to have followed only race-blind criteria in drawing district lines. We cannot disrespect such credibility judgments. [W]e are far from having a "definite and firm conviction" that the District Court made a mistake in concluding from the record before it that racial considerations predominated in District 12's design.

B

The State mounts a final, legal rather than factual, attack on the District Court's finding of racial predominance. When race and politics are competing explanations of a district's lines, argues North Carolina, the party challenging the district must introduce a particular kind of circumstantial evidence: "an alternative [map] that achieves the legislature's political objectives while improving racial balance." That is true, the State says, irrespective of what other evidence is in the case—so even if the plaintiff offers powerful direct proof that the legislature adopted the map it did for racial reasons. Because the plaintiffs here (as all agree) did not present such a counter-map, North Carolina concludes that they cannot prevail. The dissent echoes that argument.

We have no doubt that an alternative districting plan, of the kind North Carolina describes, can serve as key evidence in a race-versus-politics dispute. One, often highly persuasive way to disprove a State's contention that politics drove a district's lines is to show that the legislature had the capacity to accomplish all its partisan goals without moving so many members of a minority group into the district.

But they are hardly the *only* means. Suppose that the plaintiff in a dispute like this one introduced scores of leaked emails from state officials instructing their mapmaker to pack as many black voters as possible into a district, or telling him to make sure its BVAP hit 75%. Based on such evidence, a court could find that racial rather than political factors predominated in a district's design, with or without an alternative map. And so too in cases lacking that kind of smoking gun, as long as the evidence offered satisfies the plaintiff's burden of proof.

A plaintiff's task, in other words, is simply to persuade the trial court—without any special evidentiary prerequisite—that race (not politics) was the "predominant consideration in deciding to place a significant number of voters within or without a particular district."

North Carolina insists, however, that we have already said to the contrary—more particularly, that our decision in *Cromartie II* imposed a non-negotiable "alternative-map requirement." But the reasoning of *Cromartie II* belies that reading. The Court's opinion nowhere attempts to explicate or justify the categorical rule that the State claims to find there. And given the strangeness of that rule—which would treat a mere form of evidence as the very substance of a constitutional claim—we cannot think that the Court adopted it without any explanation.

Rightly understood, the passage from *Cromartie II* had a different and narrower point, arising from and reflecting the evidence offered in that case. The direct evidence of a racial gerrymander, we thought, was extremely weak: We said of one piece that it "says little or nothing about whether race played a predominant role" in drawing district lines; we said of another that it "is less persuasive than the kinds of direct evidence we have found significant in other redistricting cases." Nor did the report of the plaintiffs' expert impress us overmuch: In our view, it "offer[ed] little insight into the legislature's true motive." That left a set of arguments of the would-have-could-have variety. In a case like *Cromartie II*—that is, one in which the plaintiffs had meager direct evidence of a racial gerrymander and needed to rely on evidence of forgone alternatives—only maps [that show what the state should have done] could carry the day.

But this case is most unlike *Cromartie II*, even though it involves the same electoral district some twenty years on. This case turned not on the possibility of creating more optimally constructed districts, but on direct evidence of the General Assembly's intent in creating the actual District 12, including many hours of trial testimony subject to credibility determinations. That evidence, the District Court plausibly found, itself satisfied the plaintiffs' burden of debunking North Carolina's "it was really politics" defense; there was no need for an alternative map to do the same job. And we pay our precedents no respect when we extend them far beyond the circumstances for which they were designed.

V

Applying a clear error standard, we uphold the District Court's conclusions that racial considerations predominated in designing both District 1 and District 12. For District 12, that is all we must do, because North Carolina has made no attempt to justify race-based districting there. For District 1, we further uphold the

District Court's decision that § 2 of the VRA gave North Carolina no good reason to reshuffle voters because of their race. We accordingly affirm the judgment of the District Court.

Justice GORSUCH took no part in the consideration or decision of this case.

Justice THOMAS, concurring.

I join the opinion of the Court because it correctly applies our precedents under the Constitution and the Voting Rights Act of 1965 (VRA), 52 U.S.C. § 10301 *et seq.* I write briefly to explain the additional grounds on which I would affirm the three-judge District Court and to note my agreement, in particular, with the Court's clear-error analysis.

As to District 1, I think North Carolina's concession that it created the district as a majority-black district is by itself sufficient to trigger strict scrutiny. I also think that North Carolina cannot satisfy strict scrutiny based on its efforts to comply with § 2 of the VRA. In my view, § 2 does not apply to redistricting and therefore cannot justify a racial gerrymander. See *Holder v. Hall,* 512 U.S. 874, 922–923 (1994) (Thomas, J., concurring in judgment).

As to District 12, I agree with the Court that the District Court did not clearly err when it determined that race was North Carolina's predominant motive in drawing the district. This is the same conclusion I reached when we last reviewed District 12. *Easley v. Cromartie,* 532 U.S. 234, 267 (2001) (*Cromartie II*) (dissenting opinion). The Court reached the contrary conclusion in *Cromartie II* only by misapplying our deferential standard for reviewing factual findings. Today's decision does not repeat *Cromartie II's* error, and indeed it confines that case to its particular facts. It thus represents a welcome course correction to this Court's application of the clear-error standard.

Justice ALITO, with whom Chief Justice ROBERTS and Justice KENNEDY join, concurring in the judgment in part and dissenting in part.

A precedent of this Court should not be treated like a disposable household item — say, a paper plate or napkin — to be used once and then tossed in the trash. But that is what the Court does today in its decision regarding North Carolina's 12th Congressional District: The Court junks a rule adopted in a prior, remarkably similar challenge to this very same congressional district.

In *Easley v. Cromartie* (*Cromartie II*), the Court considered the constitutionality of the version of District 12 that was adopted in 1997. That district had the same basic shape as the district now before us, and the challengers argued that the legislature's predominant reason for adopting this configuration was race. The State responded that its motive was not race but politics. Its objective, the State insisted, was to create a district in which the Democratic candidate would win. Rejecting that explanation, a three-judge court found that the legislature's predominant motive was racial, specifically to pack African–Americans into District 12.

A critical factor in our analysis was the failure of those challenging the district to come forward with an alternative redistricting map that served the legislature's political objective as well as the challenged version without producing the same racial effects. . . . The failure to produce an alternative map doomed the challengers in *Cromartie II*, and the same should be true now. Partisan gerrymandering is always unsavory, but that is not the issue here. The issue is whether District 12 was drawn predominantly because of race. The record shows that it was not.

Reviewing the evidence, two themes emerge. First, District 12's borders and racial composition are readily explained by political considerations and the effects of the legislature's political strategy on the demographics of District 12. Second, the majority largely ignores this explanation, as did the court below, and instead adopts the most damning interpretation of all available evidence.

Both of these analytical maneuvers violate our clearly established precedent. Our cases say that we must "exercise extraordinary caution where the State has articulated a legitimate political explanation for its districting decision," [yet] the majority ignores that political explanation. Our cases say that "the good faith of a state legislature must be presumed," [yet] the majority presumes the opposite. And *Cromartie II* held that plaintiffs in a case like this are obligated to produce a map showing that the legislature could have achieved its political objectives without the racial effect seen in the challenged plan; here, the majority junks that rule and says that the plaintiffs' failure to produce such a map simply "does not matter."

⟫   *Effect of the New **Shaw** Cases?*   What is the effect of the Supreme Court's analysis in the new *Shaw* cases? The implicit accusation in Justice Alito's dissent is that the Court is interpreting its doctrine to make it easier for civil rights plaintiffs to win new *Shaw* claims, just as it did in *Cromartie II* to make it harder for those challenging majority-minority districts to do so, thereby protecting civil rights plaintiffs. Do you agree with this criticism?

Faustian Bargain? Is it tactically wise for voting rights plaintiffs to file *Shaw* claims using the new *Shaw* cases? Are they trading short-term gains for long-term losses, or is it too soon to worry? How should we understand the import of these cases? Professors Guy-Uriel Charles and Luis Fuentes-Rowher argue that it is a mistake because the new racial gerrymandering cases are not like the old racial gerrymandering cases. They argue that:

> the best way to make sense of *Shaw* and the *Shaw* cases is to simply recognize them as cases that are about representational rights and the Court's hesitant, clumsy, and groping attempt to work its way through two concepts of representation. Specifically, *Shaw* forced the Court to think about the constitutional limits on the state's authority when the state is arbitrating between descriptive representation and substantive representation. While *Shaw* and the racial gerrymandering cases certainly favored substantive over descriptive representation, *Shaw* also attempted to preserve the ability of state legislatures to pursue descriptive representation for voters of color so long as they did so within the relative parameters established by the Court. *Shaw* sought to cabin, not eliminate, the state's pursuit of descriptive representation.

Guy-Uriel E. Charles & Luis Fuentes-Rohwer, *Race & Representation Revisited: The New Racial Gerrymandering Cases & Section 2 of the VRA*, 59 Wm. & Mary L. Rev. 1559, 1579 (2018). By contrast, they argue, the new racial gerrymandering cases are more consistent with colorblindness than race consciousness. "Racial gerrymandering cases are now adjudicated exclusively through the anticlassification framework.

Just like other areas of equal protection law, what matters in the districting context is determining whether the government has classified on the basis of race and whether it has good reason for doing so. This is the consensus of the new racial gerrymandering cases." *Id.* at 1593. Dale E. Ho, Director of the American Civil Liberties Voting Rights Project, sees the cases differently. Though he also views them as two different sets of cases, he sees the new racial gerrymandering more favorably than the *Shaw* cases. The *Shaw* cases "sought to turn the redistricting process away from race." But the new racial gerrymandering cases "root out intentional efforts to discriminate on the basis of race." Dale E. Ho, *Something Old, Something New, or Something Really Old? Second Generation Racial Gerrymandering Litigation as Intentional Racial Discrimination Cases*, 59 WM. & MARY L. REV. 1887, 1891-1892 (2018). Who has the better of the argument?

On August 1, 2018, Justice Kennedy, who provided the fifth vote in *Cooper v. Harris*, retired from the Court. He was replaced by Brett Kavanaugh, formerly a judge on the D.C. Circuit and regarded then as one of the most conservative judges on that court. On October 26, 2020, Amy Coney Barrett replaced Ruth Bader Ginsburg, who died on September 18, 2020. On June 20, 2022, Ketanji Brown Jackson was sworn in as the 116th Supreme Court Justice and the first black woman to sit on the nation's highest court. The Supreme Court is now composed of six Justices appointed by Republican presidents and three appointed by Democratic presidents. By one account, this is one of the most conservative Supreme Courts in almost a century. https://www.npr.org/2022/07/05/1109444617/the-supreme-court-conservative. How does the composition of the Court affect its rulings in this domain?

Racial Discrimination and the Presumption of Legislative Good Faith. Litigation that proceeds simultaneously under the Constitution and the VRA can be extraordinarily protracted and complex. In a recent decision, the Supreme Court issued a stern reminder to lower courts presiding over such litigation that they cannot simplify their tasks by taking procedural shortcuts. Specifically, lower courts must proceed in a way that places the burden of proof at every phase of the proceedings on plaintiffs challenging government actions and that at every step correspondingly accords the legislature a presumption of good faith — even when, in an earlier phase of the litigation, the lower court had found the legislature to be guilty of intentional racial discrimination, a circumstance that might be thought to relieve the court of the need to presume the legislature's good faith in subsequent phases of the same case. *Abbott v. Perez*, 585 U.S. __ (2018).

5. *The End of Section 2?*

In the wake of *Shelby County* and following the Court's decisions in the new racial gerrymandering cases, several lower courts used Section 2 of the VRA or the Fourteenth Amendment to strike down state laws burdening the right to vote. For example, in *NC State Conference of the NAACP v. McCrory*, 831 F.3d 204 (4th Cir. 2016), the Fourth Circuit struck down North Carolina's omnibus voting rights law, including the voter photo identification requirement, the provision abolishing same day registration, and the elimination of the first week of early voting. The court concluded that the law's provisions "target African Americans with almost surgical precision, . . . constitute inapt remedies for the problems assertedly justifying them, and in fact impose cures for problems that did not exist." The court concluded that the state "enacted the challenged provisions of the law with discriminatory intent." In *Veasey v. Abbott*, 830 F.3rd 216 (5th Cir. 2016) (en banc), the Fifth Circuit affirmed the district court's ruling that Texas's voter identification law violated Section 2 of the VRA. In *One Wisconsin Institute Inc. v. Nichol*, 186 F.Supp.3rd 968 (W.D. Wis. 2016), a federal district court judge in Wisconsin struck down a number of provisions of that state's electoral changes, including a restriction on absentee ballots and a provision limiting early voting.

These cases provided a path for litigants to challenge laws that they thought were discriminatory because they had either a racial impact or intent. The cases showed that the federal courts were willing to use Section 2 of the VRA as well as the Fourteenth Amendment to address what they perceive to be violations of voting rights, and particularly to enjoin voting laws that have a racially discriminatory intent or effect. But the Court has sent some strong signals that Section 2 may provide much less of a path than both litigants and courts may have thought.

In *Abbott v. Perez*, 585 U.S. __ (2018), the Court reviewed a decision of the U.S. District Court for the Western District of Texas invalidating legislative maps drawn by the Texas Legislature. Following the 2010 census and reapportionment, Texas in 2011 drew new maps. Because *Shelby County v. Holder* had not yet been decided, Texas was required under the VRA to obtain preclearance from the D.C. District Court. Before that court could rule, the 2011 maps were challenged in Texas federal court on the grounds that they were intentional racial gerrymanders. With the 2012 election impending, the Texas District Court drew up interim maps. Texas appealed the interim ruling to the Supreme Court, which reversed on the ground that the lower court, in drawing the map, had not given sufficient deference to the legislative judgments embodied in the 2011 maps. *Perry v. Perez*, 565 U.S. 388 (2012) (per curiam). The Supreme Court accordingly ordered the District Court to draw new maps that retained as much as possible the decisions of the Texas Legislature, and to redraw districts only to the extent necessary to avoid legal defects. On remand, the District Court drew maps that differed significantly from the state's 2011 plan.

At this point, in August 2012, the D.C. District Court denied preclearance to the 2011 maps. The state then held its 2012 elections under the interim maps prepared by the Texas District Court. The state still needed legally valid maps, however, and in 2013 the governor called a special session of the legislature which repealed the 2011 maps and adopted as its own the interim maps drawn by the Texas District Court. The next day, the Supreme Court handed down *Shelby County*, and Texas quickly obtained vacatur of the earlier decision of the D.C. District Court. Meanwhile, the plaintiffs in the Texas District Court amended their complaint to add challenges to the 2013 map, while continuing their challenges to the 2011 plans.

Texas conducted its 2014 and 2016 elections under the 2013 legislative maps. In 2017, after a full trial, the Texas District Court held the original 2011 plans unconstitutional racial gerrymanders. In a subsequent ruling, the court held that the same districts found unconstitutional in the 2011 plan were still unconstitutional under the 2013 plan on the ground that the state legislature had merely carried forward the discriminatory intent initially manifested in the 2011 plan. The state, in other words, despite enacting new plans, had not in so doing "purged" the unconstitutional motivations that "tainted" the 2011 maps.

In a 5-4 ruling written by Justice Alito and joined by Chief Justice Roberts and Justices Kennedy, Thomas, and Gorsuch, the Court reversed. "The allocation of the burden of proof and the presumption of legislative good faith," the Court held, "are not changed by a finding of past discrimination." The Texas legislature, the Court observed, did not simply reenact the same law that had already been invalidated; instead, it enacted a new law, and the only intentions relevant to that law's constitutionality were those of the 2013 legislature, not its 2011 predecessor. By demanding that the 2013 legislature "purge the taint" of its predecessor's discriminatory intent, the lower court improperly shifted the burden of proof from the plaintiffs to the defendants, and failed to accord the new legislature the presumption of good faith to which it was entitled.

This error, in the Court's view, invalidated the District Court's findings of discriminatory intent on most of the challenged districts. The court's findings regarding four districts did not share this flaw, however, because they rested on different grounds. Nevertheless, the Court reversed three of these on the merits as clear error, leaving the District Court's finding of intentional racial gerrymandering in place against only one state house district.

Justice Sotomayor, joined by Justices Ginsburg, Breyer, and Kagan, dissented. The lower court did not, she argued, shift the burden of proof but rather engaged in a meticulous *Arlington Heights* analysis of the record, resting its rulings on firm evidence of discrimination in the 2013 districting cycle.

As much of a warning as *Abbott* was for voting rights plaintiffs, the case that sounded the alarm is the one reproduced below, *Brnovich v. Democratic National Committee*. Most of the cases about Section 2, such as *Abbott*, are vote dilution cases. *Brnovich* is a vote denial case. Does the fact that this is a case alleging a denial of the right to vote because of the state regulations at issue justify the Court's decision below?

Brnovich v. Democratic National Committee

594 U.S. __ (2021)

ALITO, J., delivered the opinion of the Court, in which ROBERTS, C. J., and THOMAS, GORSUCH, KAVANAUGH, and BARRETT, JJ., joined. GORSUCH, J., filed a concurring opinion, in which THOMAS, J., joined. KAGAN, J., filed a dissenting opinion, in which BREYER and SOTOMAYOR, JJ., joined.

JUSTICE ALITO delivered the opinion of the Court.

In these cases, we are called upon for the first time to apply §2 of the Voting Rights Act of 1965 to regulations that govern how ballots are collected and counted. Arizona law generally makes it very easy to vote. All voters may vote by mail or in person for nearly a month before election day, but Arizona imposes two restrictions that are claimed to be unlawful. First, in some counties, voters who choose to cast a ballot in person on election day must vote in their own precincts or else their ballots will not be counted. Second, mail in ballots cannot be collected by anyone other than an election official, a mail carrier, or a voter's family member, household member, or caregiver. After a trial, a District Court upheld these rules, as did a panel of the United States Court of Appeals for the Ninth Circuit. But an en banc court, by a divided vote, found them to be unlawful. It relied on the rules' small disparate impacts on members of minority groups, as well as past discrimination dating back to the State's territorial days. And it overturned the District Court's finding that the Arizona Legislature did not adopt the ballot-collection restriction for a discriminatory purpose. We now hold that the en banc court misunderstood and misapplied §2 and that it exceeded its authority in rejecting the District Court's factual finding on the issue of legislative intent.

I

A

Congress enacted the landmark Voting Rights Act of 1965, in an effort to achieve at long last what the Fifteenth Amendment had sought to bring about 95 years earlier: an end to the denial of the right to vote based on race. Ratified in 1870, the Fifteenth Amendment provides in §1 that "[t]he right of citizens of the United States to vote shall not be denied or abridged by the United States or by any State on account of race, color, or previous condition of servitude." Section 2 of the Amendment then grants Congress the "power to enforce [the Amendment] by appropriate legislation."

Despite the ratification of the Fifteenth Amendment, the right of African-Americans to vote was heavily suppressed for nearly a century. States employed a variety of notorious methods, including poll taxes, literacy tests, property qualifications, "'white primar[ies],'" and "'grandfather clause[s].'" Challenges to some blatant efforts reached this Court and were held to violate the Fifteenth Amendment.

Invoking the power conferred by §2 of the Fifteenth Amendment, Congress enacted the Voting Rights Act to address this entrenched problem. The Act and its amendments in the 1970s specifically forbade some of the practices that had been used to suppress black voting. Section 2 stated simply that "[n]o voting qualification or prerequisite to voting, or standard, practice, or procedure shall be imposed or applied by any State or political subdivision to deny or abridge the right of any citizen of the United States to vote on account of race or color."

Unlike other provisions of the VRA, §2 attracted relatively little attention during the congressional debates and was "little-used" for more than a decade after its passage. But during the same period, this Court considered several cases involving "vote-dilution" claims asserted under the Equal Protection Clause of the Fourteenth Amendment. In these and later vote-dilution cases, plaintiffs claimed that features of legislative districting plans, including the configuration of legislative districts and the use of multi-member districts, diluted the ability of particular voters to affect the outcome of elections.

One Fourteenth Amendment vote-dilution case, *White* v. *Regester*, came to have outsized importance in the development of our VRA case law. In *White*, the Court . . . explained what a vote dilution plaintiff must prove, and the words the Court chose would later assume great importance in VRA §2 matters. According to *White*, a vote-dilution plaintiff had to show that "the political processes leading to nomination and election were not *equally open* to participation by the group in question—that its members had *less opportunity* than did other residents in the district to participate in the political processes and to elect legislators of their choice." The decision in *White* predated *Washington* v. *Davis*, 426 U. S. 229 (1976), where the Court held that an equal-protection challenge to a facially neutral rule requires proof of discriminatory purpose or intent, and the *White* opinion said nothing one way or the other about purpose or intent.

A few years later, the question whether a VRA §2 claim required discriminatory purpose or intent came before this Court in *Mobile* v. *Bolden*, 446 U. S. 55 (1980). The plurality opinion for four Justices concluded first that §2 of the VRA added nothing to the protections afforded by the Fifteenth Amendment. *Id.*, at 60– 61. The plurality then observed that prior decisions "ha[d] made clear that action by a State that is racially neutral on its face violates the Fifteenth Amendment only if motivated by a discriminatory purpose." *Id.*, at 62. The obvious result of those premises was that facially neutral voting practices violate §2 only if motivated by a discriminatory purpose.

Shortly after *Bolden* was handed down, Congress amended §2 of the VRA. The oft-cited Report of the Senate Judiciary Committee accompanying the 1982 Amendment stated that the amendment's purpose was to repudiate *Bolden* and establish a new vote-dilution test based on what the Court had said in *White*. The bill that was initially passed by the House of Representatives included what is now §2(a). In place of the phrase "to deny or abridge the right . . . to vote on account of race or color," the amendment substituted "in a manner which *results in* a denial or abridgement of the right . . . to vote on account of race or color."

The House bill "originally passed . . . under a loose understanding that §2 would prohibit all discriminatory 'effects' of voting practices, and that intent would be 'irrelevant,'" but "[t]his version met stiff resistance in the Senate." *Mississippi Republican Executive Committee* v. *Brooks*, 469 U. S. 1002, 1010 (1984) (Rehnquist, J., dissenting) (quoting H. R. Rep. No. 97–227, at 29). The House and Senate compromised, and the final product included language proposed by Senator Dole. 469 U. S., at 1010–1011; S. Rep. No. 97– 417, at 3–4; 128 Cong. Rec. 14131–14133 (1982) (Sen. Dole describing his amendment).

What is now §2(b) was added, and that provision sets out what must be shown to prove a §2 violation. It requires consideration of "the totality of circumstances" in each case and demands proof that "the political processes leading to nomination or election in the State or political subdivision are not *equally open* to participation" by members of a protected class "*in that its members have less opportunity* than other members of the electorate to participate in the political process and to elect representatives of their choice." 52 U. S. C. §10301(b) (emphasis added). Reflecting the Senate Judiciary Committee's stated focus on the issue of vote dilution, this language was taken almost verbatim from *White*.

This concentration on the contentious issue of vote dilution reflected the results of the Senate Judiciary Committee's extensive survey of what it regarded as Fifteenth Amendment violations that called out for legislative redress. That survey listed many examples of what the Committee took to be unconstitutional vote dilution, but the survey identified only three isolated episodes involving the outright denial of the right to vote, and none of these concerned the equal application of a facially neutral rule specifying the time, place, or manner of voting. These sparse results were presumably good news. They likely showed that the VRA and other efforts had achieved a large measure of success in combating the previously widespread practice of using such rules to hinder minority groups from voting.

This Court first construed the amended §2 in *Thornburg* v. *Gingles*, 478 U.S. 30 (1986) — another vote-dilution case. In the years since *Gingles*, we have heard a steady stream of §2 vote-dilution cases, but until today, we have not considered how §2 applies to generally applicable time, place, or manner voting rules. In recent years, however, such claims have proliferated in the lower courts.

B

The present dispute concerns two features of Arizona voting law, which generally makes it quite easy for residents to vote. All Arizonans may vote by mail for 27 days before an election using an "early ballot." No special excuse is needed, and any voter may ask to be sent an early ballot automatically in future elections. In addition, during the 27 days before an election, Arizonans may vote in person at an early voting location in each county.

And they may also vote in person on election day. Each county is free to conduct election-day voting either by using the traditional precinct model or by setting up "voting centers." Voting centers are equipped to provide all voters in a county with the appropriate ballot for the precinct in which they are registered, and this allows voters in the county to use whichever vote center they prefer.

The regulations at issue in this suit govern precinct based election-day voting and early mail-in voting. Voters who choose to vote in person on election day in a county that uses the precinct system must vote in their assigned precincts. If a voter goes to the wrong polling place, poll workers are trained to direct the voter to the right location. If a voter finds that his or her name does not appear on the register at what the voter believes is the right precinct, the voter ordinarily may cast a provisional ballot. That ballot is later counted if the voter's address is determined to be within the precinct. But if it turns out that the voter cast a ballot at the wrong precinct, that vote is not counted.

For those who choose to vote early by mail, Arizona has long required that "[o]nly the elector may be in possession of that elector's unvoted early ballot." In 2016, the state legislature enacted House Bill 2023 (HB 2023), which makes it a crime for any person other than a postal worker, an elections official, or a voter's caregiver, family member, or household member to knowingly collect an early ballot — either before or after it has been completed.

In 2016, the Democratic National Committee and certain affiliates brought this suit and named as defendants (among others) the Arizona attorney general and secretary of state in their official capacities. Among other things, the plaintiffs claimed that both the State's refusal to count ballots cast in the wrong precinct and its ballot-collection restriction "adversely and disparately affect Arizona's American Indian, Hispanic, and African American citizens," in violation of §2 of the VRA. In addition, they alleged that the ballot-collection restriction was "enacted with discriminatory intent" and thus violated both §2 of the VRA and the Fifteenth Amendment.

III

A

We start with the text of VRA §2. It now provides:

> (a) No voting qualification or prerequisite to voting or standard, practice, or procedure shall be imposed or applied by any State or political subdivision in a manner which results in a denial or abridgement of the right of any citizen of the United States to vote on account of race or color, or in contravention of the guarantees set forth in section 10303(f)(2) of this title, as provided in subsection (b).
>
> (b) A violation of subsection (a) is established if, based on the totality of circumstances, it is shown that the political processes leading to nomination or election in the State or political subdivision are not equally open to participation by members of a class of citizens protected by subsection (a) in that its members have less opportunity than other members of the electorate to participate in the political process and to elect representatives of their choice. The extent to which members of a protected class have been elected to office in the State or political subdivision is one circumstance which may be considered.

In *Gingles*, our seminal §2 vote-dilution case, the Court quoted the text of amended §2 and then jumped right to the Senate Judiciary Committee Report, which focused on the issue of vote dilution. But because this is our first §2 time, place, or manner case, a fresh look at the statutory text is appropriate. Today, our statutory interpretation cases almost always start with a careful consideration of the text, and there is no reason to do otherwise here.

B

Section 2(a), as noted, omits the phrase "to deny or abridge the right . . . to vote on account of race or color," which the *Bolden* plurality had interpreted to require proof of discriminatory intent. In place of that language, §2(a) substitutes the phrase "in a manner which *results in* a denial or abridgement of the right . . . to vote on account of race or color." (Emphasis added.) We need not decide what this text would mean if it stood alone because §2(b), which was added to win Senate approval, explains what must be shown to establish a §2 violation. Section 2(b) states that §2 is violated only where "the political processes leading to nomination or election" are not "*equally open* to participation" by members of the relevant protected group "*in that its members have less opportunity* than other members of the electorate to participate in the political process and to elect representatives of their choice." (Emphasis added.) The key requirement is that the political processes leading to nomination and election (here, the process of voting) must be "equally open" to minority and non-minority groups alike, and the most relevant definition of the term "open," as used in §2(b), is "without restrictions as to who may participate," Random House Dictionary of the English Language 1008 (J. Stein ed. 1966), or "requiring no special status, identification, or permit for entry or participation," Webster's Third New International Dictionary 1579 (1976). What §2(b) means by voting that is not "equally open" is further explained by this language: "in that its members have less opportunity than other members of the electorate to participate in the political process and to elect representatives of their choice." The phrase "in that" is "used to specify the respect in which a statement is true." Thus, equal openness and equal opportunity are not separate requirements. Instead, equal opportunity helps to explain the meaning of equal openness. And the term "opportunity" means, among other things, "a combination of circumstances, time, and place suitable or favorable for a particular activity or action." Putting these terms together, it appears that the core of §2(b) is the requirement that voting be "equally open." The statute's reference to equal "opportunity" may stretch that concept to some degree to include consideration of a person's ability to *use* the means that are equally open. But equal openness remains the touchstone.

C

One other important feature of §2(b) stands out. The provision requires consideration of "the totality of circumstances." Thus, any circumstance that has a logical bearing on whether voting is "equally open" and affords equal "opportunity" may be considered. We will not attempt to compile an exhaustive list, but several important circumstances should be mentioned.

1

1. First, the size of the burden imposed by a challenged voting rule is highly relevant. The concepts of "open[ness]" and "opportunity" connote the absence of obstacles and burdens that block or seriously hinder voting, and therefore the size of the burden imposed by a voting rule is important. After all, every voting rule imposes a burden of some sort. Voting takes time and, for almost everyone, some travel, even if only to a nearby mailbox. But because voting necessarily requires some effort and compliance with some rules, the concept of a voting system that is "equally open" and that furnishes an equal "opportunity" to cast a ballot must tolerate the "usual burdens of voting." *Crawford* v. *Marion County Election Bd.*, 553 U. S. 181, 198 (2008) (opinion of Stevens, J.). Mere inconvenience cannot be enough to demonstrate a violation of §2.[1]

2. For similar reasons, the degree to which a voting rule departs from what was standard practice when §2 was amended in 1982 is a relevant consideration. Because every voting rule imposes a burden of some sort, it is useful to have benchmarks

---

1. There is a difference between openness and opportunity, on the one hand, and the absence of inconvenience, on the other. For example, suppose that an exhibit at a museum in a particular city is open to everyone free of charge every day of the week for several months. Some residents of the city who have the opportunity to view the exhibit may find it inconvenient to do so for many reasons—the problem of finding parking, dislike of public transportation, anticipation that the exhibit will be crowded, a plethora of weekend chores and obligations, etc. Or, to take another example, a college course may be open to all students and all may have the opportunity to enroll, but some students may find it inconvenient to take the class for a variety of reasons. For example, classes may occur too early in the morning or on Friday afternoon; too much reading may be assigned; the professor may have a reputation as a hard grader; etc.

with which the burdens imposed by a challenged rule can be compared. The burdens associated with the rules in widespread use when §2 was adopted are therefore useful in gauging whether the burdens imposed by a challenged rule are sufficient to prevent voting from being equally "open" or furnishing an equal "opportunity" to vote in the sense meant by §2. Therefore, it is relevant that in 1982 States typically required nearly all voters to cast their ballots in person on election day and allowed only narrow and tightly defined categories of voters to cast absentee ballots. We doubt that Congress intended to uproot facially neutral time, place, and manner regulations that have a long pedigree or are in widespread use in the United States.

3. The size of any disparities in a rule's impact on members of different racial or ethnic groups is also an important factor to consider. Small disparities are less likely than large ones to indicate that a system is not equally open. To the extent that minority and non-minority groups differ with respect to employment, wealth, and education, even neutral regulations, no matter how crafted, may well result in some predictable disparities in rates of voting and noncompliance with voting rules. But the mere fact there is some disparity in impact does not necessarily mean that a system is not equally open or that it does not give everyone an equal opportunity to vote. What are at bottom very small differences should not be artificially magnified.

4. Next, courts must consider the opportunities provided by a State's entire system of voting when assessing the burden imposed by a challenged provision. This follows from §2(b)'s reference to the collective concept of a State's "political processes" and its "political process" as a whole. Thus, where a State provides multiple ways to vote, any burden imposed on voters who choose one of the available options cannot be evaluated without also taking into account the other available means.

5. Finally, the strength of the state interests served by a challenged voting rule is also an important factor that must be taken into account. As noted, every voting rule imposes a burden of some sort, and therefore, in determining "based on the totality of circumstances" whether a rule goes too far, it is important to consider the reason for the rule. Rules that are supported by strong state interests are less likely to violate §2.

One strong and entirely legitimate state interest is the prevention of fraud. Fraud can affect the outcome of a close election, and fraudulent votes dilute the right of citizens to cast ballots that carry appropriate weight. Fraud can also undermine public confidence in the fairness of elections and the perceived legitimacy of the announced outcome. Ensuring that every vote is cast freely, without intimidation or undue influence, is also a valid and important state interest.

D

The interpretation set out above follows directly from what §2 commands: consideration of "the totality of circumstances" that have a bearing on whether a State makes voting "equally open" to all and gives everyone an equal "opportunity" to vote. The dissent, by contrast, would rewrite the text of §2 and make it turn almost entirely on just one circumstance—disparate impact.

That is a radical project, and the dissent strains mightily to obscure its objective. It discusses all sorts of voting rules that are not at issue here. And it dwells on points of law that nobody disputes: that §2 applies to a broad range of voting rules, practices, and procedures; that an "abridgement" of the right to vote under §2 does not require outright denial of the right; that §2 does not demand proof of discriminatory purpose; and that a "facially neutral" law or practice may violate that provision.

Only after this extended effort at misdirection is the dissent's aim finally unveiled: to undo as much as possible the compromise that was reached between the House and Senate when §2 was amended in 1982.

IV

A

In light of the principles set out above, neither Arizona's out-of-precinct rule nor its ballot-collection law violates §2 of the VRA. Arizona's out-of-precinct rule enforces the requirement that voters who choose to vote in person on election day must do so in their assigned precincts. Having to identify one's own polling place and then travel there to vote does not exceed the "usual burdens of voting." On the contrary, these tasks are quintessential examples of the usual burdens of voting.

Not only are these unremarkable burdens, but the District Court's uncontested findings show that the State made extensive efforts to reduce their impact on the number of valid votes ultimately cast.

Polling place information is also made available by other means. The secretary of state's office operates websites that provide voter-specific polling place information and allow voters to make inquiries to the secretary's staff. The burdens of identifying and traveling to one's assigned precinct are also modest when considering Arizona's "political processes" as a whole. But even if it is marginally harder for Arizona voters to find their assigned polling places, the State offers other easy ways to vote. Any voter can request an early ballot without excuse. Any voter can ask to be placed on the permanent early voter list so that an early ballot will be mailed automatically. Voters may drop off their early ballots at any polling place, even one to which they are not assigned. And for nearly a month before election day, any voter can vote in person at an early voting location in his or her county. The availability of those options likely explains why out-of-precinct votes on election day make up such a small and apparently diminishing portion of overall ballots cast—0.47% of all ballots in the 2012 general election and just 0.15% in 2016.

Next, the racial disparity in burdens allegedly caused by the out-of-precinct policy is small in absolute terms. The District Court accepted the plaintiffs' evidence that, of the Arizona counties that reported out-of-precinct ballots in the 2016 general election, a little over 1% of Hispanic voters, 1% of African-American voters, and 1% of Native American voters who voted on election day cast an out-of-precinct ballot. For non-minority voters, the rate was around 0.5%. A policy that appears to work for 98% or more of voters to whom it applies—minority and non-minority alike—is unlikely to render a system unequally open.

Section 2 does not require a State to show that its chosen policy is absolutely necessary or that a less restrictive means would not adequately serve the State's objectives.

In light of the modest burdens allegedly imposed by Arizona's out-of-precinct policy, the small size of its disparate impact, and the State's justifications, we conclude the rule does not violate §2 of the VRA.

B

HB 2023 likewise passes muster under the results test of §2. Arizonans who receive early ballots can submit them by going to a mailbox, a post office, an early ballot drop box, or an authorized election official's office within the 27-day early voting period. They can also drop off their ballots at any polling place or voting center on election day, and in order to do so, they can skip the line of voters waiting to vote in person. Making any of these trips—much like traveling to an assigned polling place—falls squarely within the heartland of the "usual burdens of voting." And voters can also ask a statutorily authorized proxy—a family member, a household member, or a caregiver—to mail a ballot or drop it off at any time within 27 days of an election.

The plaintiffs were unable to provide statistical evidence showing that HB 2023 had a disparate impact on minority voters. Instead, they called witnesses who testified that third-party ballot collection tends to be used most heavily in disadvantaged communities and that minorities in Arizona—especially Native Americans—are disproportionately disadvantaged. But from that evidence the District Court could conclude only that prior to HB 2023's enactment, "minorities generically were more likely than non-minorities to return their early ballots with the assistance of third parties." How much more, the court could not say from the record. Neither can we. And without more concrete evidence, we cannot conclude that HB 2023 results in less opportunity to participate in the political process.

Even if the plaintiffs had shown a disparate burden caused by HB 2023, the State's justifications would suffice to avoid §2 liability. "A State indisputably has a compelling interest in preserving the integrity of its election process." *Purcell v. Gonzalez*, 549 U. S. 1, 4 (2006). Limiting the classes of persons who may handle early ballots to those less likely to have ulterior motives deters potential fraud and improves voter confidence. That was the view of the bipartisan Commission on Federal Election Reform chaired by former President Jimmy Carter and former Secretary of State James Baker.

But prevention of fraud is not the only legitimate interest served by restrictions on ballot collection. As the Carter-Baker Commission recognized, third-party ballot collection can lead to pressure and intimidation. And it should go without saying that a State may take action to prevent election fraud without waiting for it to occur and be detected within its own borders. Section 2's command that the political processes remain equally open surely does not demand that "a State's political system sustain some level of damage before the legislature [can] take corrective action." *Munro v. Socialist Workers Party*, 479 U. S. 189, 195 (1986). Fraud is a real risk that accompanies mail-in voting even if Arizona had the good fortune to avoid it. Election fraud has had serious consequences in other States. For example, the North Carolina Board of Elections invalidated the results of a 2018 race for a seat in the House of Representatives for evidence of fraudulent mail-in ballots. The Arizona Legislature was not obligated to wait for something similar to happen closer to home.

As with the out-of-precinct policy, the modest evidence of racially disparate burdens caused by HB 2023, in light of the State's justifications, leads us to the conclusion that the law does not violate §2 of the VRA.

V

We also granted certiorari to review whether the Court of Appeals erred in concluding that HB 2023 was enacted with a discriminatory purpose.

The District Court's finding on the question of discriminatory intent had ample support in the record. Applying the familiar approach outlined in *Arlington Heights* v. *Metropolitan Housing Development Corp.*, 429 U. S. 252, 266–268 (1977), the District Court considered the historical background and the sequence of events leading to HB 2023's enactment; it looked for any departures from the normal legislative process; it considered relevant legislative history; and it weighed the law's impact on different racial groups.

The court noted, among other things, that HB 2023's enactment followed increased use of ballot collection as a Democratic get-out-the-vote strategy and came "on the heels of several prior efforts to restrict ballot collection, some of which were spearheaded by former Arizona State Senator Don Shooter." . . . Shooter's own election in 2010 had been close and racially polarized. Aiming in part to frustrate the Democratic Party's get-out-the-vote strategy, Shooter made what the court termed "unfounded and often far-fetched allegations of ballot collection fraud."

We are more than satisfied that the District Court's interpretation of the evidence is permissible.

***

Arizona's out-of-precinct policy and HB 2023 do not violate §2 of the VRA, and HB 2023 was not enacted with a racially discriminatory purpose. The judgment of the Court of Appeals is reversed, and the cases are remanded for further proceedings consistent with this opinion.

It is so ordered.

JUSTICE GORSUCH, with whom JUSTICE THOMAS joins, concurring.

I join the Court's opinion in full, but flag one thing it does not decide. Our cases have assumed—without deciding—that the Voting Rights Act of 1965 furnishes an implied cause of action under §2. See *Mobile* v. *Bolden*, 446 U. S. 55, 60, and n. 8 (1980) (plurality opinion). Lower courts have treated this as an open question. *E.g., Washington* v. *Finlay*, 664 F. 2d 913, 926 (CA4 1981). Because no party argues that the plaintiffs lack a cause of action here, and because the existence (or not) of a cause of action does not go to a court's subject-matter jurisdiction, see *Reyes Mata* v. *Lynch*, 576 U. S. 143, 150 (2015), this Court need not and does not address that issue today.

JUSTICE KAGAN, with whom JUSTICE BREYER and JUSTICE SOTOMAYOR join, dissenting.

If a single statute represents the best of America, it is the Voting Rights Act. It marries two great ideals: democracy and racial equality. And it dedicates our country to carrying them out. Section 2, the provision at issue here, guarantees that members of every racial group will have equal voting opportunities. Citizens of every race will have the same shot to participate in the political process and to elect representatives of their choice. They will all own our democracy together—no one more and no one less than any other.

If a single statute reminds us of the worst of America, it is the Voting Rights Act. Because it was—and remains—so necessary. Because a century after the Civil War was fought, at the time of the Act's passage, the promise of political equality remained a distant dream for African American citizens. The Voting Rights Act is ambitious, in both goal and scope. When President Lyndon Johnson sent the bill to Congress, ten days after John Lewis led marchers across the Edmund Pettus Bridge, he explained that it was "carefully drafted to meet its objective—the end of discrimination in voting in America." He was right about how the Act's drafting reflected its aim. "The end of discrimination in voting" is a far-reaching goal. And the Voting Rights Act's text is just as far-reaching. A later amendment, adding the provision at issue here, became necessary when this Court construed the statute too narrowly. And in the last decade, this Court assailed the Act again, undoing its vital Section 5. See *Shelby County* v. *Holder*, 570 U. S. 529 (2013). But Section 2 of the Act remains, as written, as expansive as ever—demanding that every citizen of this country possess a right at once grand and obvious: the right to an equal opportunity to vote.

Today, the Court undermines Section 2 and the right it provides. The majority fears that the statute Congress wrote is too "radical"—that it will invalidate too many state voting laws. So the majority writes its own set of rules, limiting Section 2 from multiple directions. Wherever it can, the majority gives a cramped reading to broad language. And then it uses that reading to uphold two election laws from Arizona that discriminate against minority voters. I could say—and will in the following pages—that this is not how the Court is supposed to interpret and apply statutes. But that ordinary critique woefully undersells the problem. What is tragic here is that the Court has (yet again) rewritten—in order to weaken—a statute that stands as a monument to America's greatness, and protects against its basest impulses. What is tragic is that the Court has damaged a statute designed to bring about "the end of discrimination in voting." I respectfully dissent.

I

[T]he Court decides this Voting Rights Act case at a perilous moment for the Nation's commitment to equal citizenship. It decides this case in an era of voting-rights retrenchment—when too many States and localities are restricting access to voting in ways that will predictably deprive members of minority groups of equal access to the ballot box. If "any racial discrimination in voting is too much," as the *Shelby County* Court recited, then the Act still has much to do. Or more precisely, the fraction of the Act remaining—the Act as diminished by the Court's hand. Congress never meant for Section 2 to bear all of the weight of the Act's commitments. That provision looks to courts, not to the Executive Branch, to restrain discriminatory voting practices. And litigation is an after-the-fact remedy, incapable of providing relief until an election—usually, more than one election—has come and gone.

See *id.*, at 572 (Ginsburg, J., dissenting). So Section 2 was supposed to be a back-up, for all its sweep and power. But after *Shelby County*, the vitality of Section 2—a "permanent, nationwide ban on racial discrimination in voting"—matters more than ever. For after *Shelby County*, Section 2 is what voters have left.

II

Section 2, as drafted, is well-equipped to meet the challenge. Congress meant to eliminate all "discriminatory election systems or practices which operate, designedly or otherwise, to minimize or cancel out the voting strength and political effectiveness of minority groups." S. Rep. No. 97–417, p. 28 (1982) (S. Rep.). And that broad intent is manifest in the provision's broad text. As always, this Court's task is to read that language as Congress wrote it—to give the section all the scope and potency Congress drafted it to have. So I start by showing how Section 2's text requires courts to eradicate voting practices that make it harder for members of some races than of others to cast a vote, unless such a practice is necessary to support a strong state interest. I then show how far from that text the majority strays. Its analysis permits exactly the kind of vote suppression that Section 2, by its terms, rules out of bounds.

A

Section 2, as relevant here, has two interlocking parts. Subsection (a) states the law's basic prohibition:

> No voting qualification or prerequisite to voting or standard, practice, or procedure shall be imposed or applied by any State or political subdivision in a manner which results in a denial or abridgement of the right of any citizen of the United States to vote on account of race or color.

Subsection (b) then tells courts how to apply that bar—or otherwise said, when to find that an infringement of the voting right has occurred:

> A violation of subsection (a) is established if, based on the totality of circumstances, it is shown that the political processes leading to nomination or election in the State or political subdivision are not equally open to participation by members of [a given race] in that [those] members have less opportunity than other members of the electorate to participate in the political process and to elect representatives of their choice.

Those provisions have a great many words, and I address them further below. But their essential import is plain: Courts are to strike down voting rules that contribute to a racial disparity in the opportunity to vote, taking all the relevant circumstances into account.

The first thing to note about Section 2 is how far its prohibitory language sweeps. The provision bars any "voting qualification," any "prerequisite to voting," or any "standard, practice, or procedure" that "results in a denial or abridgement of the right" to "vote on account of race." The overlapping list of covered state actions makes clear that Section 2 extends to every kind of voting or election rule. Congress carved out nothing pertaining to "voter qualifications or the manner in which elections are conducted." *Holder* v. *Hall*, 512 U. S. 874, 922 (1994)

(THOMAS, J., concurring in judgment). So, for example, the provision "covers all manner of registration requirements, the practices surrounding registration," the "locations of polling places, the times polls are open, the use of paper ballots as opposed to voting machines, and other similar aspects of the voting process that might be manipulated to deny any citizen the right to cast a ballot and have it properly counted." All those rules and more come within the statute — so long as they result in a race-based "denial or abridgement" of the voting right. And the "denial or abridgement" phrase speaks broadly too. "[A]bridgment necessarily means something more subtle and less drastic than the complete denial of the right to cast a ballot, denial being separately forbidden." *Bossier*, 528 U. S., at 359 (SOUTER, J., concurring in part and dissenting in part). It means to "curtail," rather than take away, the voting right. American Heritage Dictionary 4 (1969).

The "results in" language, connecting the covered voting rules to the prohibited voting abridgement, tells courts that they are to focus on the law's effects. Rather than hinge liability on state officials' motives, Congress made it ride on their actions' consequences.

So the text of Section 2, as applied in our precedents, tells us the following, every part of which speaks to the ambition of Congress's action. Section 2 applies to any voting rule, of any kind. The provision prohibits not just the denial but also the abridgment of a citizen's voting rights on account of race. The inquiry is focused on effects: It asks not about why state officials enacted a rule, but about whether that rule results in racial discrimination. The discrimination that is of concern is inequality of voting opportunity. That kind of discrimination can arise from facially neutral (not just targeted) rules. There is a Section 2 problem when an election rule, operating against the backdrop of historical, social, and economic conditions, makes it harder for minority citizens than for others to cast ballots.

And strong state interests may save an otherwise discriminatory rule, but only if that rule is needed to achieve them — that is, only if a less discriminatory rule will not attain the State's goal. That is a lot of law to apply in a Section 2 case. Real law — the kind created by Congress. (A strange thing, to hear about it all only in a dissent.) None of this law threatens to "take down," as the majority charges, the mass of state and local election rules. Here is the flipside of what I have said above, now from the plaintiff's perspective: Section 2 demands proof of a statistically significant racial disparity in electoral opportunities (not outcomes) resulting from a law not needed to achieve a government's legitimate goals. That showing is hardly insubstantial; and as a result, Section 2 vote denial suits do not often succeed (even with lower courts applying the law as written, not the majority's new, concocted version). But Section 2 was indeed meant to do something important — crucial to the operation of our democracy. The provision tells courts — however "radical" the majority might find the idea — to eliminate facially neutral (as well as targeted) electoral rules that unnecessarily create inequalities of access to the political process. That is the very project of the statute, as conceived and as written — and now as damaged by this Court.

B

The majority's opinion mostly inhabits a law-free zone. It congratulates itself in advance for giving Section 2's text "careful consideration." And then it leaves that language almost wholly behind. The "important circumstances" it invents all cut in one direction—toward limiting liability for race-based voting inequalities.

III

Just look at Arizona. Two of that State's policies disproportionately affect minority citizens' opportunity to vote. The first—the out-of-precinct policy—results in Hispanic and African American voters' ballots being thrown out at a statistically higher rate than those of whites. And whatever the majority might say about the ordinariness of such a rule, Arizona applies it in extra-ordinary fashion: Arizona is *the* national outlier in dealing with out-of-precinct votes, with the next-worst offender nowhere in sight. The second rule—the ballot-collection ban—makes voting meaningfully more difficult for Native American citizens than for others. And nothing about how that ban is applied is "usual" either—this time because of how many of the State's Native American citizens need to travel long distances to use the mail. Both policies violate Section 2, on a straightforward application of its text. Considering the "totality of circumstances," both "result in" members of some races having "less opportunity than other members of the electorate to participate in the political process and to elect a representative of their choice." §10301(b). The majority reaches the opposite conclusion because it closes its eyes to the facts on the ground.

A

Arizona's out-of-precinct policy requires discarding any Election Day ballot cast elsewhere than in a voter's assigned precinct. Under the policy, officials throw out every choice in every race—including national or statewide races (*e.g.*, for President or Governor) that appear identically on every precinct's ballot. The question is whether that policy unequally affects minority citizens' opportunity to cast a vote.

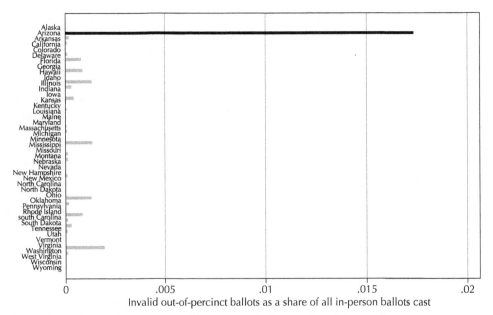

Invalid out-of-percinct ballots as a share of all in-person ballots cast

Votes in such numbers can matter—enough for Section 2 to apply.

And the out-of-precinct policy operates unequally: Ballots cast by minorities are more likely to be discarded. In 2016, Hispanics, African Americans, and Native Americans were about twice as likely—or said another way, 100% more likely—to have their ballots discarded than whites. And it is possible to break that down a bit. Sixty percent of the voting in Arizona is from Maricopa County. There, Hispanics were 110% more likely, African Americans 86% more likely, and Native Americans 73% more likely to have their ballots tossed. Pima County, the next largest county, provides another 15% of the statewide vote. There, Hispanics were 148% more likely, African Americans 80% more likely, and Native Americans 74% more likely to lose their votes. Assessing those disparities, the plaintiffs' expert found, and the District Court accepted, that the discriminatory impact of the out-of-precinct policy was statistically significant—meaning, again, that it was highly unlikely to occur by chance.

The majority is wrong to assert that those statistics are "highly misleading." In the majority's view, they can be dismissed because the great mass of voters are unaffected by the out-of-precinct policy. But Section 2 is less interested in "absolute terms" (as the majority calls them) than in relative ones.

B

Arizona's law mostly banning third-party ballot collection also results in a significant race-based disparity in voting opportunities. The problem with that law again lies in facts nearly unique to Arizona—here, the presence of rural Native American communities that lack ready access to mail service. Given that circumstance, the Arizona statute discriminates in just the way Section 2 proscribes. The majority once more comes to a different conclusion only by ignoring the local conditions with which Arizona's law interacts. The critical facts for evaluating the ballot-collection rule have to do with mail service. Most Arizonans vote by mail. But many rural Native American voters lack access to mail service, to a degree hard for most of us to fathom. Only 18% of Native voters in rural counties receive home mail delivery, compared to 86% of white voters living in those counties. And for many or most, there is no nearby post office. Native Americans in rural Arizona "often must travel 45 minutes to 2 hours just to get to a mailbox." And between a quarter to a half of households in these Native communities do not have a car. So getting ballots by mail and sending them back poses a serious challenge for Arizona's rural Native Americans.

For that reason, an unusually high rate of Native Americans used to "return their early ballots with the assistance of third parties."

Put all of that together, and Arizona's ballot-collection ban violates Section 2. The ban interacts with conditions on the ground—most crucially, disparate access to mail service—to create unequal voting opportunities for Native Americans. And the State has shown no need for the law to go so far. Arizona, as noted above, already has statutes in place to deter fraudulent collection practices. Those laws give every sign of working.

IV

Congress enacted the Voting Rights Act to address a deep fault of our democracy—the historical and continuing attempt to withhold from a race of citizens their fair share of influence on the political process. For a century, African Americans had struggled and sacrificed to wrest their voting rights from a resistant Nation. The statute they and their allies at long last attained made a promise to all Americans. From then on, Congress demanded, the political process would be equally open to every citizen, regardless of race.

One does not hear much in the majority opinion about that promise. One does not hear much about what brought Congress to enact the Voting Rights Act, what Congress hoped for it to achieve, and what obstacles to that vision remain today. One would never guess that the Act is, as the President who signed it wrote, "monumental." For all the opinion reveals, the majority might be considering any old piece of legislation—say, the Lanham Act or ERISA.

This Court has no right to remake Section 2. Maybe some think that vote suppression is a relic of history—and so the need for a potent Section 2 has come and gone. Cf. *Shelby County*, 570 U. S., at 547 ("[T]hings have changed dramatically"). But Congress gets to make that call. Because it has not done so, this Court's duty is to apply the law as it is written. The law that confronted one of this country's most enduring wrongs; pledged to give every American, of every race, an equal chance to participate in our democracy; and now stands as the crucial tool to achieve that goal. That law, of all laws, deserves the sweep and power Congress gave it. That law, of all laws, should not be diminished by this Court.

>> *Evaluating* **Brnovich: *Much Ado About Nothing*?**   What, if anything, is wrong with the majority's decision in *Brnovich*? From the majority's perspective, Arizona adopted some modest and reasonable voting statutes, an out-of-precinct policy, and a third-party ban on ballot collection, that may or may not have had an impact on the State's voters of color. But it certainly did not deny them the right to vote, in violation of the statute, particularly as compared to the State's overall election law facilitating access to the ballot for its voters. This seems like a reasonable and justifiable way to look at the case. Much ado about nothing? Consider the following assessment:

> The Court's opinion in *Brnovich* is deeply problematic, but not because the majority reached the wrong result. Reasonable people can disagree as to whether the specific electoral rules at issue — the wrong-precinct rule or denial-of-assistance-by-third-parties rule — impose un due burdens on voters of color. One could understand an opinion concluding that the challenged laws do not make it sufficiently harder for voters of color to exercise their right to cast a ballot, which would make them okay under the VRA. To see what a reasonable opinion that ruled against the plaintiffs would look like, read the district-court opinion in the case, which found that the Arizona laws were not enacted with a discriminatory intent and the laws did not have disparate impact on voters of color.

> Had the Supreme Court followed the district court's lead, one could disagree, even vigorously, with that opinion. But that would be a legitimate and reasonable disagreement among people who share a joint

enterprise: How should we, the legal and political system, protect voters of color from having to disproportionately bear burdens in our voting system? The problem with Justice Alito's opinion in *Brnovich* is that the majority seems wholly uninterested in participating in that joint enterprise.

. . . . *Brnovich* is so troubling and potentially destructive because it is not operating within the confines of the VRA project. The decision is a repudiation of the core aims of that project. Rather than engage productively in the collective enterprise of figuring out how to protect voters of color against the states, the Court majority is more interested in protecting the electoral rules of the states from undue intrusion by voters of color. The majority's opinion sends a clear message that voter fraud, not racial discrimination, is a threat to the American system of representation. Of course, the majority rejects that characterization. Without feeling or effect, the majority notes that Section 2 "provides vital protection against discriminatory voting rules and no one suggests that discrimination in voting has been extirpated or that the threat has been eliminated." This is a standard line in the Court's VRA cases.

But that line is meaningless. In order to protect the states from voters of color, the Court has to make bringing Section 2 claims harder. As a consequence, the opinion is best understood as setting up a series of legal obstacles designed to protect the supposedly vulnerable states. The majority articulates five factors that courts must address when confronted with a Section 2 claim. First, the size of the burden imposed by the state is important. Second, they must look to the extent of the differential burden borne by voters of color as compared with white voters. Third, voting rules with a long pedigree, or those already in place when the substantive version of Section 2 was enacted by Congress, are presumptively allowed. Fourth, in order to determine whether a voting rule is impermissible, "courts must consider the opportunities provided by a State's entire system of voting." And finally, courts must defer to the strength of a state's justification, particularly when the state asserts voter fraud as a justification, which the Court pronounced as a "strong and entirely legitimate state interest." These factors are intended to, and will, protect the states against many Section 2 lawsuits. They will make Section 2 claims less likely to be filed by plaintiffs, and more likely to be lost when they are.

Guy-Uriel E. Charles & Luis E. Fuentes-Rhower, *The Court's Voting Rights Decision Was Worse Than People Think*, https://www.theatlantic.com/ideas/archive/2021/07/brnovich-vra-scotus-decision-arizona-voting-right/619330. Do you agree with that assessment? Is the Court no longer interested in protected voters of color against racial discrimination? Does *Brnovich* signal the end of the VRA project?

Voter Fraud and the Big Lie. One of the perhaps surprising aspects of the majority opinion in *Brnovich* is its emphasis on voter fraud as a legitimate state interest. This emphasis is potentially disconcerting not only because there is very little evidence to support allegations of voter fraud, but also because it comes in the wake of former President Donald Trump's repeated falsehoods that the 2020 presidential election was marred by voter fraud and that President Joseph Biden was not lawfully elected. More than 15 months after the 2020 Presidential election, 70%

of Republican voters still believed that the election was stolen, and that Biden was not the lawful winner. https://www.poynter.org/fact-checking/2022/70-percent-republicans-falsely-believe-stolen-election-trump/. Studies have concluded that there is a relationship between perceptions of voter fraud and ideology or partisanship. On average, voters who are more conservative, or Republican, tend to perceive voter fraud as affecting elections and worry more about it than voters who are more liberal, or Democrat. *See, e.g.,* Adriano Udani, David C. Campbell, Brian Fogarty, *How Local Media Coverage of Voter Fraud Influences Partisan Perceptions in the United States,* 18 STATE POL. & POL. Q. 193 (2013); Charles Stewart III, Stephen Ansolabehere, & Nathaniel Persily, *Revisiting Public Opinion on Voter Identification and Voter Fraud in an Era of Increasing Partisan Polarization,* 68 STAN. L. REV. 1455 (2016); and Stephen Ansolabehere and Nathaniel Persily, *Voter Fraud in the Eye of the Beholder: The Role of Public Opinion in the Challenge to Voter Identification Requirements,* 121 HARV. L. REV. 1737 (2008). There is also a correlation between perceptions of voter fraud and racial resentment. *See, e.g.,* David C. Wilson & Paul R. Brewer, *The Foundations of Public Opinion on Voter ID Laws: Political Predispositions, Racial Resentment, and Information Effects,* 77 Pub. Op. Q. 962 (2013). Given the role that the Big Lie has played in destabilizing American democracy, and given the partisan and racial implications of voter fraud allegations, should the majority opinion have been more careful in giving support to the argument that the State was legitimately worried about voter fraud, notwithstanding the lack of any evidence to buttress that worry?

Does Section 2 Allow Private Rights of Action? Justice Gorsuch notes in his concurrence that the Court has never decided whether Section 2 allows a private right of action — that is, whether Section 2 allows private parties, such as civil rights groups, individual plaintiffs, or partisan groups, to challenge violations of the provision. If no private right of action is permitted, only the Attorney General of the United States can file suit to vindicate rights under Section 2. In *Arkansas State Conference NAACP v. Arkansas Board of Apportionment,* ___ F. Supp.3d___ (E.D. Ark., Feb. 17, 2022) a lower court took the hint from Justice Gorsuch and declared that Section 2 does not provide a private right of action. Voting rights activists have argued that such a conclusion would effectively kill the provision, given that most Section 2 lawsuits are filed by private parties and not by the Attorney General. There is a circuit split on the issue, which means that the Court will eventually resolve the question. For a very thoughtful analysis of the terrain, see Dan Tokaji, *Public Rights and Private Rights of Action: The Enforcement of Federal Election Laws,* 44 IND. L. REV. 113 (2010). For a very useful review of the lower court decisions, see Megan Hurd, *Promoting Private Enforcement of the Voting Rights Act and the Materiality Provision: Contrasting Northeast Ohio Coalition for the Homeless v. Husted and Schweir v. Cox,* 87 U. CIN. L. REV. 1379 (2018).

The Future of the VRA? The Supreme Court has granted two consolidated challenges to Alabama's new congressional maps, *Merrill v. Milligan* and *Merrill v. Caster.* The plaintiffs in the cases argue that the maps violate Section 2 of the Voting Rights Act by diminishing the power of black voters. A federal district judge agreed with the plaintiffs and issued an injunction. The Court stayed the order and allowed the maps to go into effect for Alabama's primary elections. The Court will hear the cases in the 2022-2023 Supreme Court term.

Justice Roberts joined the liberals in dissent from the order staying the injunction, in which Justice Kagan stated, "[I]t does a disservice to Black Alabamians who under that precedent have had their electoral power diminished—in violation of a law this Court once knew to buttress all of American democracy."

Fear of a Multiracial Future; Fear of a Liberal Democratic Future? In a series of articles, social scientists have documented the social, psychological and political angst that white voters are feeling as they contemplate living in a country which, they are constantly being told, is becoming increasingly multiracial and multicultural. According to a growing body of research, white Americans experience their growing minority status, or the perception of their growing minority status, as a threat to their political, economic, and cultural hegemony. *See, e.g,* Dowell Myers and Morris Levy, *Racial Population Projections and Reactions to Alternative News Accounts of Growing Diversity,* 677 ANN. AM. ACAD. 215 (2018); Maureen Craig, Julian M. Rucker, and Jennifer A. Richeson; *Racial and Political Dynamics of an Approaching "Majority-Minority" United States,* 677 ANN. AM. ACAD. 204 (2018); Maureen Craig, Julian M. Rucker, and Jennifer A. Richeson, *The Pitfalls and Promise of Increasing Racial Diversity; Threat, Contact, and Race Relations in the 21st Century,* 27 CUR. DIR. PSY. SCI. 188 (2017); H. Robert Outten, Michael T. Schmitt, Daniel A. Miller, and Amber L. Garcia, *Feeling Threatened about the Future: Whites' Emotional Reaction to Anticipated Ethnic Demographic Changes,* 38 PERS. SOC. PSYCHOL. BUL. 14 (2012). These demographic fears and worries are layered atop a polity that is polarized by race, ideology, culture, and partisanship. That is, as our political parties have become more homogenous by ideology, race, and culture, our partisan divisions are also identically ideological, racial, and cultural. Moreover, and more alarmingly, partisans really dislike the other side, more than they like their side. This is a development that scholars have termed affective polarization. *See, e.g.,* Alan Abramowitz and Jennifer McCoy, *United States: Racial Resentment, Negative Partisanship, and Polarization in Trump's America,* 681 ANN. AM. ACAD. 137 (2019); Joshua Robison and Rachel L. Moskowitz, *The Group Basis of Partisan Affective Polarization,* 81 J. POL. 1075 (2019); Shanto Iyengar et. al., *The Origins and Consequences of Affective Polarization in the United States,* 22 ANN. REV. POL. SCI.7.1 (2019); and Lilliana Mason, *A Cross-Cutting Calm: How Social Sorting Drives Affective Polarization,* 80 PUB. OP. Q. 351 (2016). What are the prospects for a liberal democratic future given these political conditions?

Hope: Election Law Federalism? The news is not all bad. In 2021, 25 states enacted 62 laws expanding access to the voting booth, and so far in 2022, four states have passed five more. The most common provisions contained within these bills are: expanding early voting opportunities (Indiana, Kentucky, Louisiana, Massachusetts, Maryland, New Jersey, Oklahoma, Virginia); easing access to mail-in voting (California, Connecticut, Illinois, Indiana, Kentucky, Massachusetts, Maryland, Maine, Minnesota, North Dakota, Nevada, New York, Oregon, Virginia, Vermont); expanding access to ballot drop-off locations (California, Connecticut, Hawai'i, Illinois, Kentucky, Maryland, Maine, Nevada, Virginia, Vermont); easing voter registration (Connecticut, Delaware, Hawai'i, Illinois, Maine, North Dakota, Nevada, New York, Virginia); and increasing access to voters with disabilities (Connecticut, Hawai'i, Illinois, Indiana, Kentucky, Massachusetts, Maine, Montana, North Dakota, Nevada, Virginia). And even though the John Lewis Voting Rights Act did not get through Congress, the State of New York passed its own version. Will election law federalism save us?

CHAPTER 6

CANDIDATES AND THE IDEAL OF IMPARTIAL PUBLIC SERVICE

This chapter turns from voters and their relation with their representatives to focus on those who wish to do the representing: candidates for elective office. What kind of people should be permitted to run for office? What kinds of restrictions might be implemented to narrow the field in appropriate ways, and what powers do the various levels of government have to impose qualifications and conditions on running for office? And what options are available to a democratic polity when events reveal that they have made a mistake, and elevated to office someone unworthy of their trust?

A. POLITICS AND THE CHARACTERISTICS OF ELECTED OFFICIALS

If governance is a means to an end rather than an end in itself, then any consideration of the appropriate characteristics of government officials must begin with some notion of the kind of governance a political society desires. To answer this question, we must ask what we want government officials to do, how they ought to do it, and who, in consequence, is best suited to perform the desired functions in the appropriate ways.

This chapter focuses on an important thread in American political thought: the idea that government officials ought to be benign, virtuous, and impartial rulers, a conception of governance closely associated with republicanism, which we examined in some detail in Chapter 2.

Henry St. John Bolingbroke

The Idea of a Patriot King (1738)

It seems to me, upon the whole matter, that to save or redeem a nation . . . from perdition, nothing less is necessary than . . . the concurrence, and the

481

influence, of a Patriot King, the most uncommon of all phenomena in the physical or moral world. Nothing can so surely and so effectually restore the virtue and public spirit essential to the preservation of liberty and national prosperity, as the reign of such a prince. . . .

The good of the people is the ultimate and true end of government. Governors are, therefore, appointed for this end, and the civil constitution which appoints them, and invests them with their power, is determined to do so by that law of nature and reason, which has determined the end of government, and which admits this form of government as the proper means of arriving at it. Now, the greatest good of a people is their liberty . . . and, in the case here referred to, the people has judged it so, and provided for it accordingly. Liberty is to the collective body, what health is to every individual body. Without health no pleasure can be tasted by man: without liberty no happiness can be enjoyed by society. The obligation, therefore, to defend and maintain the freedom of such constitutions will appear most sacred to a Patriot King.

Kings who have weak understandings, bad hearts, and strong prejudices, and all these, as it often happens, inflamed by their passions, and rendered incurable by their self-conceit and presumption; such kings are apt to imagine, and they conduct themselves so as to make many of their subjects imagine, that the king and the people in free governments are rival powers, who stand in competition with one another, who have different interests, and must of course have different views: that the rights and privileges of the people are so many spoils taken from the right and prerogative of the crown; and that the rules and laws, made for the exercise and security of the former, are so many diminutions of their dignity, and restraints on their power.

A Patriot King will see all this in a far different and much truer light. The constitution will be considered by him as one law, consisting of two tables, containing the rule of his government, and the measure of his subjects' obedience; or as one system, composed of different parts and powers, but all duly proportioned to one another, and conspiring by their harmony to the perfection of the whole. He will make one, and but one, distinction between his rights, and those of his people: he will look on his to be a trust, and theirs a property. He will discern, that he can have a right to no more than is trusted to him by the constitution: and that his people, who had an original right to the whole by the law of nature, can have the sole indefeasible right to any part; and really have such a right to that part which they have reserved to themselves. In fine, the constitution will be reverenced by him as the law of God and of man; the force of which binds the king as much as the meanest subject, and the reason of which binds him much more. . . .

Just so our Patriot King must be a patriot from the first. He must be such in resolution, before he grows such in practice. He must fix at once the general principles and ends of all his actions, and determine that his whole conduct shall be regulated by them, and directed to them. When he has done this, he will have turned, by one great effort, the bent of his mind so strongly towards the perfection of a kingly character, that he will exercise with ease, and as it were by a natural determination, all the virtues of it; which will be suggested to him on every occasion by the principles wherewith his mind is imbued, and by those ends that are the constant objects of his attention. . . .

As soon as corruption ceases to be an expedient of government, and it will cease to be such as soon as a Patriot King is raised to the throne, the panacea is applied; the spirit of the constitution revives of course: and, as fast as it revives, the orders and forms of the constitution are restored to their primitive integrity, and become what they were intended to be, real barriers against arbitrary power, not blinds nor masks under which tyranny may lie concealed. . . .

To espouse no party, but to govern like the common father of his people, is so essential to the character of a Patriot King, that he who does otherwise forfeits the title. It is the peculiar privilege and glory of this character, that princes who maintain it, and they alone, are so far from the necessity, that they are not exposed to the temptation, of governing by a party; which must always end in the government of a faction: the faction of the prince, if he has ability; the faction of his ministers, if he has not; and, either one way or other, in the oppression of the people. For faction is to party what the superlative is to the positive: party is a political evil, and faction is the worst of all parties. The true image of a free people, governed by a Patriot King, is that of a patriarchal family, where the head and all the members are united by one common interest, and animated by one common spirit: and where, if any are perverse enough to have another, they will be soon borne down by the superiority of those who have the same; and, far from making a division, they will but confirm the union of the little state. That to approach as near as possible to these ideas of perfect government, and social happiness under it, is desirable in every state, no man will be absurd enough to deny. The sole question is, therefore, how near to them it is possible to attain? For, if this attempt be not absolutely impracticable, all the views of a Patriot King will be directed to make it succeed. Instead of abetting the divisions of his people, he will endeavour to unite them, and to be himself the centre of their union: instead of putting himself at the head of one party in order to govern his people, he will put himself at the head of his people in order to govern, or more properly to subdue, all parties. Now, to arrive at this desirable union, and to maintain it, will be found more difficult in some cases than in others, but absolutely impossible in none, to a wise and good prince. . . .

———————

Lord Bolingbroke's analysis deeply influenced the founding generation. According to one account, George Washington "so completely embodied the patriot king model that had Lord Bolingbroke been able to observe his conduct as general and president he surely would have listed Washington along with Elizabeth . . . as an ideal leader. . . . [H]istorians ever since have portrayed Washington as attempting, at least, to live up to his own self-conception: the patriot leader above faction, working for national unity, and seeking to reign as well as to rule." RALPH KETCHAM, PRESIDENTS ABOVE PARTY: THE FIRST AMERICAN PRESIDENCY, 1789-1829 (1984), at 89.

The following excerpt describes political thought concerning leadership qualities during a much later but no less influential period: the Progressive Era around the turn of the twentieth century.

Robert Wiebe

The Search for Order 1877-1920 (1967)

Systematic thinkers of all kinds early in the twentieth century gravitated to political theory in an effort to explain what seemed the most pressing problems of their time. Here an immediate heritage offered them practically nothing of value. The economic principles in the original classical theory had relegated government to the role of a small, wasteful necessity. Cooperative utopias such as those of Bellamy and Lloyd had moved the final step and effectively dissolved the government. Less systematically, commentators of all sorts late in the nineteenth century had approved a simple government of moral men whose good sense would keep it out of society's affairs. When the maintenance of order and balance required an occasional intervention, it should act promptly and then withdraw at once. Precise lines of authority separating the branches of government and close limitations surrounding each official task would help preserve these virtues.

A strikingly different conception of government arrived with the new century, a conception that received at least some support from almost every prominent theorist of the time. . . . A blend of many ideas, the new political theory borrowed its most revolutionary qualities from bureaucratic thought, and the heart of these was continuity. Trained, professional servants would staff a government broadly and continuously involved in society's operations. In order to meet problems as they arose, these officials should hold flexible mandates, ones that perforce would blur the conventional distinctions among executive, legislature, and judiciary. Above them stood the public man, a unique and indispensable leader. Although learned enough to comprehend the details of a modern, specialized government, he was much more than an expert among experts. His vision encompassed the entire nation, his impartiality freed him from all prejudices, and his detached wisdom enabled him to devise an equitable and progressive policy for the whole society. Corps of servants received his general directives and translated them into their particular areas. At the same time, they channeled basic information back to the public man, so that all government activity was ultimately coordinated in his mind. Because he could best determine where and how the government should expand or contract, he should have the broadest discretionary power, including the right to bend unnecessarily rigid constitutional limitations.

As the nation's leader, the public man would be an educator-extraordinary. He bore the greatest responsibility for raising mass intelligence to the level of true public opinion. That, as Franklin Giddings explained, "is rational like-mindedness. . . . Public feeling, public sentiment, the most ardent conviction of belief, may exist with scarcely an admixture of real public opinion. We can derive . . . no assurance that a stable popular government can be maintained in a nation which ceases to be hourly creative of genuine public opinion—the fruit of rational discourse." Thus the very future of democracy rested with the public man's instructional talents. In time, after a "long tutelage in public affairs," the electorate would come to participate directly in certain aspects of government through the initiative, referendum, and recall. The proper use of such mechanisms, however, depended upon the prior existence of that rational public.

The political theorist from 1880 could recognize a good deal of familiar terminology: good men in high office, minimum waste, a rational electorate, civil service, direct democracy, a harmonious, growing society. In a new setting, however, words could play strange tricks. The good men were no longer moral exemplars but leaders of broad power; minimum waste implied a smoothly functioning bureaucracy, not a handful of honest men on low salaries; a rational electorate presupposed the eventual inclusion of all citizens, instead of its restriction to one class; civil service promised increasing government service throughout the nation rather than its further withdrawal; direct democracy no longer replaced the government in Washington, but strengthened it; and the harmonious society, now usually composed of interacting groups instead of isolated individuals, depended upon the government's presence, not its absence.

The theory was immediately and persistently attacked as undemocratic, an accusation that never ceased to sting its defenders. Sensitive to the traditional suspicion of an overweening government, uneasy as they trod so close to elitist rule, they still believed they were only modernizing, not destroying democracy. In fact the theory was not as boldly authoritarian as it sometimes appeared. It assumed, first of all, a frictionless bureaucracy. The theory's advocates were convinced that the process of becoming an expert, of immersing oneself in the scientific method, eradicated petty passions and narrow ambitions, just as it removed faults in reasoning. The product was the perfect bureaucrat, whose flawlessly wired inner box guaranteed precisely accurate responses within his specialty. The latitude he enjoyed in administration existed only because no one could predict the course of a fluid society and the expert would require a freedom sufficient to follow it. At this level, the theory purported to describe government by science, not by men.

Second, the theory also presupposed an ethereal communion between leaders and citizens. As all citizens became rational, they would naturally arrive at the same general answers. Experts, of course, would always know more in their particular fields, and the public man would always see the whole more clearly; but national rationality would assure consensus on the big issues, the matters of principle. Here the question of who led and who followed became academic. All were moving reasonably, scientifically, in the same direction, with power distributed merely to ensure a smooth, efficient operation of the whole society.

Finally, the entire realm of leadership was left exceptionally vague. All of the theory's exponents envisaged some form of instructions welling up from below and then transmuted, or translated, or transmitted by the government into public policy. Viewed in one way, that left the public man an ominous freedom of action, and his communion with the masses suggested the lockstep of totalitarianism. In another light, however, leaders served as little more than highly intelligent coordinators who responded to all manner of rational public demands, integrated them, and arranged for their fulfillment. In this sense, the public man was chief of a huge bureau of service, bound at one end by the citizen's initiative and at the other by the discipline of science. The theory itself never indicated which way the balance might tip.

In fact, fuzziness in crucial matters constituted its gravest weakness. How could the electorate recognize a public man? Did the government require only one such man or a sizable cadre? However one might interpret the theory, these questions were fundamental. Not only was government inoperative without its public men, but with false leaders the whole system turned into a nightmare. Nevertheless, its spokesmen waited until the public man was in office before acknowledging him. In the end, the public man remained a mystical, self-evident truth, and countless Americans simply made it an article of faith that at the right time he would materialize and lead.

Idealism supplied most of the new theory's superstructure — the philosopher-kings, the rational public, the social consensus. Bureaucratic thought filled the interior — the beautifully functioning administration, the perfect administrative types, the interacting groups, the society in indeterminate process. Many men never accepted any of the theory. Others borrowed only a piece here and there. No candidate ever won high office on such a platform. Yet this revolutionary approach to government, incomplete as it was, eventually dominated the politics of the early twentieth century.

For more on Progressive beliefs concerning impartial, scientific principles of leadership and governance, see RICHARD HOFSTADTER, THE AGE OF REFORM: FROM BRYAN TO F.D.R. (1955); SAMUEL HABER: EFFICIENCY AND UPLIFT: SCIENTIFIC MANAGEMENT IN THE PROGRESSIVE ERA, 1890-1920 (1964).

As you read the materials that follow, consider the extent to which republican or Progressive notions of leadership might be reflected in assumptions underlying constitutional and statutory qualifications imposed on office holding.

B.   QUALIFICATIONS FOR OFFICE

The history of American thought about the qualifications that individuals ought to possess to hold public office largely parallels the history of American thought about the qualifications people needed to vote. During the eighteenth and early nineteenth centuries, qualifications for office tended to focus on age, citizenship, residency, and property requirements. Typically, these requirements were significantly more stringent for holding office than for voting. For example, under the Georgia Constitution of 1777, eligible voters needed to possess a freehold of "ten pounds value," Ga. Const. (1777), Art. IX, while candidates for the legislature needed 250 acres of land or property in the amount of 250 pounds. *Id.*, Art. VI. The South Carolina Constitution of 1778 went the furthest in this regard: candidates for governor had to possess a freehold of "at least ten thousand pounds currency, clear of debt," S.C. Const. (1778), Art. V, an amount that probably limited the choice of governor to perhaps 25 prominent South Carolinians. *See* James A. Gardner, *Southern Character, Confederate Nationalism, and the Interpretation of State Constitutions: A Case Study in Constitutional Argument,* 76 TEX. L. REV. 1219, 1273 n.275 (1998). Similarly, the Arkansas Constitution of 1836 required voters to have resided in the state for six months, but legislators had to be residents for a year, and candidates for governor had to be either native-born citizens of the state or the United States, or if not, residents of the state for ten years. Ark. Const. (1836), art. IV, §§2, 4, 6; art. V, §4.

The rationales for these qualifications also tracked the imposition of similar qualifications on voters. Age was thought to bring maturity, stability, and wisdom. Citizenship was thought to signal membership in, and thus loyalty to, the political community. A residency period assured familiarity with local values and a stake in the community. Property qualifications assured the independence necessary to develop political judgment before assuming office, and the ability while in office to avoid temptations toward self-enrichment.

➤➤ *The Exclusivity of Constitutional Qualifications.* The United States Constitution creates only four elective offices—President, Vice President, Senator and Representative—and sets the qualifications for each of them. The President and the Vice President each must be 35 years old and a natural born citizen. U.S. Const. Art. II, §1, cl. 5. A Senator must be 30 years old, a U.S. citizen for nine years, and an inhabitant of the state represented. *Id.*, Art. I, §3, cl. 3. A Representative must be 25 years old, a U.S. citizen for seven years, and an inhabitant of the state represented. *Id.*, Art. I, §2, cl. 2. Do these exhaust the qualifications that can be imposed on candidates for federal office?

The Supreme Court first considered this question in *Powell v. McCormack*, 395 U.S. 486 (1969). In 1966, Adam Clayton Powell, Jr., won reelection to the House of Representatives from a congressional district in New York City. During his previous term, Powell had been accused of various kinds of misconduct as chair of a House committee. At the opening of the 90th Congress, the House leadership refused to administer the oath of office to Powell, instead referring his case to a special Select Committee for consideration. The Select Committee concluded that Powell had engaged in misconduct and recommended that he be seated, fined, and deprived of his seniority. The full House rejected the committee's recommendation and voted 307 to 116 to exclude him from his seat, which was declared vacant. In so doing, the House relied on Article I, §5, cl. 1 of the Constitution, which provides: "Each House shall be the Judge of the Elections, Returns and Qualifications of its own Members." Powell sued, contesting his exclusion.

In a lengthy and historically detailed opinion tracing legislative membership practices back to the sixteenth century, the Supreme Court concluded that Powell had been wrongfully excluded. The Court conceded that Article I, §5 granted the House unreviewable power to determine a member's qualifications, but held that the qualifications committed to the House's judgment were limited to the three expressly mentioned in Article I, §2: age, citizenship, and residency. Consequently, the House could not decide for itself the qualifications for House membership, and thus could not exclude a duly elected person on the basis of prior misconduct.

The Framers, the Court held, clearly intended to limit the qualifications on House membership to those enumerated in the Constitution. Moreover, the Court felt itself in any event

> compelled to resolve any ambiguity in favor of a narrow construction of the scope of Congress' power to exclude members-elect. A fundamental principle of our representative democracy is, in Hamilton's words, "that the people should choose whom they please to govern them." As Madison

pointed out at the Convention, this principle is undermined as much by limiting whom the people can select as by limiting the franchise itself.

Id. at 548. Ironically, the Court also suggested in dicta that the House was free to *expel* Powell under Article I, §5, cl. 2 upon a two-thirds vote, a proportion the House had exceeded in voting to exclude Powell from the chamber in the first place.

Although *Powell* seemed to foreclose the possibility of the imposition of additional qualifications by the *federal* government, it did not directly address the constitutionality of additional qualifications imposed by the *states.* The Court confronted this question in the following case.

U.S. Term Limits, Inc. v. Thornton

514 U.S. 779 (1995)

STEVENS, J., delivered the opinion of the Court, in which KENNEDY, SOUTER, GINSBURG, and BREYER, JJ., joined.

The Constitution sets forth qualifications for membership in the Congress of the United States. Article I, §2, cl. 2, which applies to the House of Representatives, provides:

> No Person shall be a Representative who shall not have attained to the Age of twenty five Years, and been seven Years a Citizen of the United States, and who shall not, when elected, be an Inhabitant of that State in which he shall be chosen.

Article I, §3, cl. 3, which applies to the Senate, similarly provides:

> No Person shall be a Senator who shall not have attained to the Age of thirty Years, and been nine Years a Citizen of the United States, and who shall not, when elected, be an Inhabitant of that State for which he shall be chosen.

Today's cases present a challenge to an amendment to the Arkansas State Constitution that prohibits the name of an otherwise-eligible candidate for Congress from appearing on the general election ballot if that candidate has already served three terms in the House of Representatives or two terms in the Senate. The Arkansas Supreme Court held that the amendment violates the Federal Constitution. We agree. . . .

I

At the general election on November 3, 1992, the voters of Arkansas adopted Amendment 73 to their State Constitution. Proposed as a "Term Limitation Amendment," its preamble stated:

> The people of Arkansas find and declare that elected officials who remain in office too long become preoccupied with reelection and ignore their duties as representatives of the people. Entrenched incumbency has reduced voter participation and has led to an electoral system that is less free, less competitive, and less representative than the system established by the Founding

Fathers. Therefore, the people of Arkansas, exercising their reserved powers, herein limit the terms of the elected officials.

The limitations in Amendment 73 apply to three categories of elected officials. Section 1 provides that no elected official in the executive branch of the state government may serve more than two 4-year terms. Section 2 applies to the legislative branch of the state government; it provides that no member of the Arkansas House of Representatives may serve more than three 2-year terms and no member of the Arkansas Senate may serve more than two 4-year terms. Section 3, the provision at issue in these cases, applies to the Arkansas Congressional Delegation. It provides:

> (a) Any person having been elected to three or more terms as a member of the United States House of Representatives from Arkansas shall not be certified as a candidate and shall not be eligible to have his/her name placed on the ballot for election to the United States House of Representatives from Arkansas.
>
> (b) Any person having been elected to two or more terms as a member of the United States Senate from Arkansas shall not be certified as a candidate and shall not be eligible to have his/her name placed on the ballot for election to the United States Senate from Arkansas.

Amendment 73 states that it is self-executing and shall apply to all persons seeking election after January 1, 1993.

II

[T]he constitutionality of Amendment 73 depends critically on the resolution of [the following question:] whether the Constitution forbids States from adding to or altering the qualifications specifically enumerated in the Constitution. . . . Our resolution of [this] issue draws upon our prior resolution of a related but distinct issue: whether Congress has the power to add to or alter the qualifications of its Members.

Twenty-six years ago, in *Powell v. McCormack*, 395 U.S. 486 (1969), we reviewed the history and text of the Qualifications Clauses in a case involving an attempted exclusion of a duly elected Member of Congress. The principal issue was whether the power granted to each House in Art. I, §5, to judge the "Qualifications of its own Members" includes the power to impose qualifications other than those set forth in the text of the Constitution. [W]e held that it does not. . . .

We started our analysis in *Powell* by examining the British experience with qualifications for membership in Parliament, focusing in particular on the experience of John Wilkes. While serving as a member of Parliament, Wilkes had published an attack on a peace treaty with France. This literary endeavor earned Wilkes a conviction for seditious libel and a 22-month prison sentence. In addition, Parliament declared Wilkes ineligible for membership and ordered him expelled. Despite (or perhaps because of) these difficulties, Wilkes was reelected several times. Parliament, however, persisted in its refusal to seat him. After several years of Wilkes' efforts, the House of Commons voted to expunge the resolutions that had expelled Wilkes and had declared him ineligible, labeling those prior actions " 'subversive of the rights of the whole body of electors of this kingdom.' " *Id.*, at 528, quoting

22 Parliamentary History England 1411 (1782) (Parl. Hist. Eng.). After reviewing Wilkes' "long and bitter struggle for the right of the British electorate to be represented by men of their own choice," 395 U.S. at 528, we concluded in *Powell* that "on the eve of the Constitutional Convention, English precedent stood for the proposition that 'the law of the land had regulated the qualifications of members to serve in parliament' and those qualifications were 'not occasional but fixed.'" *Ibid.*, at 528.

Against this historical background, we viewed the Convention debates as manifesting the Framers' intent that the qualifications in the Constitution be fixed and exclusive. We found particularly revealing the debate concerning a proposal made by the Committee of Detail that would have given Congress the power to add property qualifications. James Madison argued that such a power would vest " 'an improper & dangerous power in the Legislature,' " by which the Legislature " 'can by degrees subvert the Constitution.' " 395 U.S. at 533-534, quoting 2 Records of the Federal Convention of 1787, pp. 249-250 (M. Farrand ed. 1911) (hereinafter Farrand).[7] Madison continued: " 'A Republic may be converted into an aristocracy or oligarchy as well by limiting the number capable of being elected, as the number authorised to elect.' " 395 U.S. at 534, quoting 2 Farrand 250. . . .

The Framers further revealed their concerns about congressional abuse of power when Gouverneur Morris suggested modifying the proposal of the Committee of Detail to grant Congress unfettered power to add qualifications. We noted that Hugh Williamson "expressed concern that if a majority of the legislature should happen to be 'composed of any particular description of men, of lawyers for example, . . . the future elections might be secured to their own body.' " *Id.*, at 535, quoting 2 Farrand 250. . . . We also recognized in *Powell* that the post-Convention ratification debates confirmed that the Framers understood the qualifications in the Constitution to be fixed and unalterable by Congress. . . . The exercise by Congress of its power to judge the qualifications of its Members further confirmed this understanding. We concluded that, during the first 100 years of its existence, "Congress strictly limited its power to judge the qualifications of its members to those enumerated in the Constitution." 395 U.S. at 542.

As this elaborate summary reveals, our historical analysis in *Powell* was both detailed and persuasive. We thus conclude now, as we did in *Powell*, that history shows that, with respect to Congress, the Framers intended the Constitution to establish fixed qualifications.

In *Powell*, of course, we did not rely solely on an analysis of the historical evidence, but instead complemented that analysis with "an examination of the basic principles of our democratic system." *Id.*, at 548. We noted that allowing Congress to impose additional qualifications would violate that "fundamental principle of our representative democracy . . . 'that the people should choose whom they please to govern them.' " *Id.*, at 547, quoting 2 Elliot's Debates 257 (A. Hamilton, New York).

---

7. Though we recognized that Madison was responding to a proposal that would have allowed Congress to impose property restrictions, we noted that "Madison's argument was not aimed at the imposition of a property qualification as such, but rather at the delegation to the Congress of the discretionary power to establish any qualifications." *Id.*, at 534.

Our opinion made clear that this broad principle incorporated at least two fundamental ideas. First, we emphasized the egalitarian concept that the opportunity to be elected was open to all.[11] . . . Second, we recognized the critical postulate that sovereignty is vested in the people, and that sovereignty confers on the people the right to choose freely their representatives to the National Government. . . . Thus, in *Powell*, we agreed with the sentiment expressed on behalf of Wilkes' admission to Parliament: " 'That the right of the electors to be represented by men of their own choice, was so essential for the preservation of all their other rights, that it ought to be considered as one of the most sacred parts of our constitution.' " 395 U.S. at 534, n. 65, quoting 16 Parl. Hist. Eng. 589-590 (1769).

Powell thus establishes two important propositions: first, that the "relevant historical materials" compel the conclusion that, at least with respect to qualifications imposed by Congress, the Framers intended the qualifications listed in the Constitution to be exclusive; and second, that that conclusion is equally compelled by an understanding of the "fundamental principle of our representative democracy . . . 'that the people should choose whom they please to govern them.' " 395 U.S. at 547.

In sum, after examining *Powell*'s historical analysis and its articulation of the "basic principles of our democratic system," we reaffirm that the qualifications for service in Congress set forth in the text of the Constitution are "fixed," at least in the sense that they may not be supplemented by Congress.

III

Our reaffirmation of *Powell*, does not necessarily resolve the specific questions presented in these cases. For petitioners argue that whatever the constitutionality of additional qualifications for membership imposed by Congress, the historical and textual materials discussed in *Powell* do not support the conclusion that the Constitution prohibits additional qualifications imposed by States. In the absence of such a constitutional prohibition, petitioners argue, the Tenth Amendment and the principle of reserved powers require that States be allowed to add such qualifications.

Before addressing these arguments, we find it appropriate to take note of the striking unanimity among the courts that have considered the issue. None of the overwhelming array of briefs submitted by the parties and *amici* has called to our attention even a single case in which a state court or federal court has approved of a State's addition of qualifications for a member of Congress. To the contrary, an impressive number of courts have determined that States lack the authority to add qualifications [the Court cited 21 state and federal decisions].

Petitioners argue that the Constitution contains no express prohibition against state-added qualifications, and that Amendment 73 is therefore an appropriate exercise of a State's reserved power to place additional restrictions on the choices

---

11. Contrary to the dissent's suggestion, we do not understand *Powell* as reading the Qualifications Clauses "to create a personal right to be a candidate for Congress." The Clauses did, however, further the interest of the people of the entire Nation in keeping the door to the National Legislature open to merit of every description.

that its own voters may make. We disagree for two independent reasons. First, we conclude that the power to add qualifications is not within the "original powers" of the States, and thus is not reserved to the States by the Tenth Amendment. Second, even if States possessed some original power in this area, we conclude that the Framers intended the Constitution to be the exclusive source of qualifications for members of Congress, and that the Framers thereby "divested" States of any power to add qualifications. . . .

Contrary to petitioners' assertions, the power to add qualifications is not part of the original powers of sovereignty that the Tenth Amendment reserved to the States. Petitioners' Tenth Amendment argument misconceives the nature of the right at issue because that Amendment could only "reserve" that which existed before. As Justice Story recognized, "the states can exercise no powers whatsoever, which exclusively spring out of the existence of the national government, which the constitution does not delegate to them. . . . No state can say, that it has reserved, what it never possessed." 1 Story §627. . . .

With respect to setting qualifications for service in Congress, no such right existed before the Constitution was ratified. . . . [T]he Framers envisioned a uniform national system, rejecting the notion that the Nation was a collection of States, and instead creating a direct link between the National Government and the people of the United States. In that National Government, representatives owe primary allegiance not to the people of a State, but to the people of the Nation. As Justice Story observed, each Member of Congress is "an officer of the union, deriving his powers and qualifications from the constitution, and neither created by, dependent upon, nor controllable by, the states. . . . Those officers owe their existence and functions to the united voice of the whole, not of a portion, of the people." 1 Story §627. Representatives and Senators are as much officers of the entire union as is the President. States thus "have just as much right, and no more, to prescribe new qualifications for a representative, as they have for a president. . . . It is no original prerogative of state power to appoint a representative, a senator, or president for the union." *Ibid.*[16]

. . . In short, as the Framers recognized, electing representatives to the National Legislature was a new right, arising from the Constitution itself. The Tenth Amendment thus provides no basis for concluding that the States possess reserved power to add qualifications to those that are fixed in the Constitution. Instead, any state power to set the qualifications for membership in Congress must derive not from the reserved powers of state sovereignty, but rather from the delegated powers of national sovereignty. In the absence of any constitutional delegation to the States of power to add qualifications to those enumerated in the Constitution, such a power does not exist. . . .

---

16. The Constitution's provision for election of Senators by the state legislatures, see Art. I, §3, cl. 1, is entirely consistent with this view. The power of state legislatures to elect Senators comes from an express delegation of power from the Constitution, and thus was not at all based on some aspect of original state power. Of course, with the adoption of the Seventeenth Amendment, state power over the election of Senators was eliminated, and Senators, like Representatives, were elected directly by the people.

Finally, state-imposed restrictions, unlike the congressionally imposed restrictions at issue in *Powell*, violate a third idea central to [the] basic principle [that the people should be able to choose whom they please to represent them]: that the right to choose representatives belongs not to the States, but to the people. From the start, the Framers recognized that the "great and radical vice" of the Articles of Confederation was "the principle of LEGISLATION for STATES or GOVERNMENTS, in their CORPORATE or COLLECTIVE CAPACITIES, and as contradistinguished from the INDIVIDUALS of whom they consist." The Federalist No. 15, at 108 (Hamilton). Thus the Framers, in perhaps their most important contribution, conceived of a Federal Government directly responsible to the people, possessed of direct power over the people, and chosen directly, not by States, but by the people. . . . The Congress of the United States, therefore, is not a confederation of nations in which separate sovereigns are represented by appointed delegates, but is instead a body composed of representatives of the people. As Chief Justice John Marshall observed: "The government of the union, then, . . . is, emphatically, and truly, a government of the people. In form and in substance it emanates from them. Its powers are granted by them, and are to be exercised directly on them, and for their benefit." *McCulloch v. Maryland*, 4 Wheat. at 404-405. Ours is a "government of the people, by the people, for the people." A. Lincoln, Gettysburg Address (1863). . . .

Permitting individual States to formulate diverse qualifications for their representatives would result in a patchwork of state qualifications, undermining the uniformity and the national character that the Framers envisioned and sought to ensure. Such a patchwork would also sever the direct link that the Framers found so critical between the National Government and the people of the United States. . . .

In sum, the available historical and textual evidence, read in light of the basic principles of democracy underlying the Constitution and recognized by this Court in *Powell*, reveal the Framers' intent that neither Congress nor the States should possess the power to supplement the exclusive qualifications set forth in the text of the Constitution. . . .

V

The merits of term limits, or "rotation," have been the subject of debate since the formation of our Constitution, when the Framers unanimously rejected a proposal to add such limits to the Constitution. . . . Over half the States have adopted measures that impose such limits on some offices either directly or indirectly, and the Nation as a whole, notably by constitutional amendment, has imposed a limit on the number of terms that the President may serve.[49] Term limits, like any other qualification for office, unquestionably restrict the ability of voters to vote for whom they wish. On the other hand, such limits may provide for the infusion of fresh ideas and new perspectives, and may decrease the likelihood that representatives will lose touch with their constituents. It is not our province to resolve this longstanding debate.

---

49. See U.S. Const., Amdt. 22 (1951) (limiting Presidents to two 4-year terms).

We are, however, firmly convinced that allowing the several States to adopt term limits for congressional service would effect a fundamental change in the constitutional framework. Any such change must come not by legislation adopted either by Congress or by an individual State, but rather — as have other important changes in the electoral process[50] — through the Amendment procedures set forth in Article V. . . . In the absence of a properly passed constitutional amendment, allowing individual States to craft their own qualifications for Congress would thus erode the structure envisioned by the Framers, a structure that was designed, in the words of the Preamble to our Constitution, to form a "more perfect Union."

The judgment is affirmed.

It is so ordered.

Justice THOMAS, with whom THE CHIEF JUSTICE, Justice O'CONNOR, and Justice SCALIA join, dissenting.

I dissent. Nothing in the Constitution deprives the people of each State of the power to prescribe eligibility requirements for the candidates who seek to represent them in Congress. The Constitution is simply silent on this question. And where the Constitution is silent, it raises no bar to action by the States or the people.

I

Because the majority fundamentally misunderstands the notion of "reserved" powers, I start with some first principles. Contrary to the majority's suggestion, the people of the States need not point to any affirmative grant of power in the Constitution in order to prescribe qualifications for their representatives in Congress, or to authorize their elected state legislators to do so.

A

Our system of government rests on one overriding principle: all power stems from the consent of the people. To phrase the principle in this way, however, is to be imprecise about something important to the notion of "reserved" powers. The ultimate source of the Constitution's authority is the consent of the people of each individual State, not the consent of the undifferentiated people of the Nation as a whole. . . .

In short, the notion of popular sovereignty that undergirds the Constitution does not erase state boundaries, but rather tracks them. The people of each State obviously did trust their fate to the people of the several States when they consented to the Constitution; not only did they empower the governmental institutions of the United States, but they also agreed to be bound by constitutional amendments that they themselves refused to ratify. See Art. V (providing that proposed amendments shall take effect upon ratification by three-quarters of the States). At the same time, however, the people of each State retained their separate political identities. As

---

50. See, *e.g.*, Amdt. 17 (1913) (direct elections of Senators); Amdt. 19 (1920) (extending suffrage to women); Amdt. 22 (1951) (Presidential term limits); Amdt. 24 (1964) (prohibition against poll taxes); Amdt. 26 (1971) (lowering age of voter eligibility to 18).

Chief Justice Marshall put it, "no political dreamer was ever wild enough to think of breaking down the lines which separate the States, and of compounding the American people into one common mass." *McCulloch v. Maryland*, 17 U.S. 316, 403 (1819). . . .

B

1

The majority begins by announcing an enormous and untenable limitation on the principle expressed by the Tenth Amendment. According to the majority, the States possess only those powers that the Constitution affirmatively grants to them or that they enjoyed before the Constitution was adopted; the Tenth Amendment "could only 'reserve' that which existed before." . . . But it was not the state governments that were doing the reserving. The Constitution derives its authority instead from the consent of the people of the States. Given the fundamental principle that all governmental powers stem from the people of the States, it would simply be incoherent to assert that the people of the States could not reserve any powers that they had not previously controlled. . . .

2

The majority also sketches out what may be an alternative (and narrower) argument. Again citing Story, the majority suggests that it would be inconsistent with the notion of "national sovereignty" for the States or the people of the States to have any reserved powers over the selection of Members of Congress. . . .

Political scientists can debate about who commands the "primary allegiance" of Members of Congress once they reach Washington. From the framing to the present, however, the *selection* of the Representatives and Senators from each State has been left entirely to the people of that State or to their state legislature. See Art. I, §2, cl. 1 (providing that members of the House of Representatives are chosen "by the People of the several States"); Art. I, §3, cl. 1 (originally providing that the Senators from each State are "chosen by the Legislature thereof"); Amdt. 17 (amending §3 to provide that the Senators from each State are "elected by the people thereof"). The very name "congress" suggests a coming together of representatives from distinct entities. In keeping with the complexity of our federal system, once the representatives chosen by the people of each State assemble in Congress, they form a national body and are beyond the control of the individual States until the next election. But the selection of representatives in Congress is indisputably an act of the people of each State, not some abstract people of the Nation as a whole. . . .

3

In a final effort to deny that the people of the States enjoy "reserved" powers over the selection of their representatives in Congress, the majority suggests that the Constitution expressly delegates to the States certain powers over congressional elections. Such delegations of power, the majority argues, would be superfluous if the people of the States enjoyed reserved powers in this area.

Only one constitutional provision — the Times, Places and Manner Clause of Article I, §4 — even arguably supports the majority's suggestion. . . . [But] the Clause grants power exclusively to Congress, not to the States. If the Clause did not exist at all, the States would still be able to prescribe the times, places, and manner of holding congressional elections; the deletion of the provision would simply deprive Congress of the power to override these state regulations. . . .

II

I take it to be established, then, that the people of Arkansas do enjoy "reserved" powers over the selection of their representatives in Congress. Purporting to exercise those reserved powers, they have agreed among themselves that the candidates covered by §3 of Amendment 73 — those whom they have already elected to three or more terms in the House of Representatives or to two or more terms in the Senate — should not be eligible to appear on the ballot for reelection, but should nonetheless be returned to Congress if enough voters are sufficiently enthusiastic about their candidacy to write in their names. Whatever one might think of the wisdom of this arrangement, we may not override the decision of the people of Arkansas unless something in the Federal Constitution deprives them of the power to enact such measures.

The majority settles on "the Qualifications Clauses" as the constitutional provisions that Amendment 73 violates. [But] the Qualifications Clauses are merely straightforward recitations of the minimum eligibility requirements that the Framers thought it essential for every Member of Congress to meet. They restrict state power only in that they prevent the States from abolishing all eligibility requirements for membership in Congress.

Because the text of the Qualifications Clauses does not support its position, the majority turns instead to its vision of the democratic principles that animated the Framers. But the majority's analysis goes to a question that is not before us: whether Congress has the power to prescribe qualifications for its own members.

A

. . . The Qualifications Clauses . . . prevent the individual States from abolishing all eligibility requirements for Congress. This restriction on state power reflects the fact that when the people of one State send immature, disloyal, or unknowledgeable representatives to Congress, they jeopardize not only their own interests but also the interests of the people of other States. Because Congress wields power over all the States, the people of each State need some guarantee that the legislators elected by the people of other States will meet minimum standards of competence. The Qualifications Clauses provide that guarantee: they list the requirements that the Framers considered essential to protect the competence of the National Legislature.[11]

----

11. Thus, the age requirement was intended to ensure that Members of Congress were people of mature judgment and experience. See, *e.g.*, 1 Farrand 375 (remarks of George Mason at the Philadelphia Convention); 3 *id.*, at 147 (remarks of James McHenry before the Maryland House of Delegates). The citizenship requirement was intended both to ensure

If the people of a State decide that they would like their representatives to possess additional qualifications, however, they have done nothing to frustrate the policy behind the Qualifications Clauses. Anyone who possesses all of the constitutional qualifications, plus some qualifications required by state law, still has all of the federal qualifications. Accordingly, the fact that the Constitution specifies certain qualifications that the Framers deemed necessary to protect the competence of the National Legislature does not imply that it strips the people of the individual States of the power to protect their own interests by adding other requirements for their own representatives. . . .

The majority responds that "a patchwork of state qualifications" would "undermine the uniformity and the national character that the Framers envisioned and sought to ensure." Yet the Framers thought it perfectly consistent with the "national character" of Congress for the Senators and Representatives from each State to be chosen by the legislature or the people of that State. The majority never explains why Congress' fundamental character permits this state-centered system, but nonetheless prohibits the people of the States and their state legislatures from setting any eligibility requirements for the candidates who seek to represent them. . . .

B

Although the Qualifications Clauses neither state nor imply the prohibition that it finds in them, the majority infers from the Framers' "democratic principles" that the Clauses must have been generally understood to preclude the people of the States and their state legislatures from prescribing any additional qualifications for their representatives in Congress. But the majority's evidence on this point establishes only two more modest propositions: (1) the Framers did not want the Federal Constitution itself to impose a broad set of disqualifications for congressional office, and (2) the Framers did not want the Federal Congress to be able to supplement the few disqualifications that the Constitution does set forth. The logical conclusion is simply that the Framers did not want the people of the States and their state legislatures to be constrained by too many qualifications imposed at the national level. The evidence does not support the majority's more sweeping conclusion that the Framers intended to bar the people of the States and their state legislatures from adopting additional eligibility requirements to help narrow their own choices. . . .

The fact that the Framers did not grant a qualification-setting power to Congress does not imply that they wanted to bar its exercise at the state level. One reason why the Framers decided not to let Congress prescribe the qualifications of its own members was that incumbents could have used this power to perpetuate themselves or their ilk in office. . . . But neither the people of the States nor the

---

that Members of Congress were familiar with the country and that they were not unduly susceptible to foreign influence. See, *e.g.*, 2 *id.*, at 216 (remarks of George Mason). The inhabitancy requirement was intended to produce a National Legislature whose Members, collectively, had a local knowledge of all the States. See, *e.g.*, The Federalist No. 56 (Madison). The Ineligibility Clause was intended to guard against corruption. See, *e.g.*, 1 Farrand 381 (remarks of Alexander Hamilton).

state legislatures would labor under the same conflict of interest when prescribing qualifications for Members of Congress, and so the Framers would have had to use a different calculus in determining whether to deprive them of this power. . . .

Congressional power over qualifications would have enabled the representatives from some States, acting collectively in the National Legislature, to prevent the people of another State from electing their preferred candidates. The John Wilkes episode in 18th-century England illustrates the problems that might result. As the majority mentions, Wilkes's district repeatedly elected him to the House of Commons, only to have a majority of the representatives of other districts frustrate their will by voting to exclude him. Americans who remembered these events might well have wanted to prevent the National Legislature from fettering the choices of the people of any individual State (for the House of Representatives) or their state legislators (for the Senate).

Yet this is simply to say that qualifications should not be set at the national level for offices whose occupants are selected at the state level. The majority never identifies the democratic principles that would have been violated if a state legislature, in the days before the Constitution was amended to provide for the direct election of Senators, had imposed some limits of its own on the field of candidates that it would consider for appointment. Likewise, the majority does not explain why democratic principles forbid the people of a State from adopting additional eligibility requirements to help narrow their choices among candidates seeking to represent them in the House of Representatives. . . .

The majority appears to believe that restrictions on eligibility for office are inherently undemocratic. But the Qualifications Clauses themselves prove that the Framers did not share this view; eligibility requirements to which the people of the States consent are perfectly consistent with the Framers' scheme. In fact, we have described "the authority of the people of the States to determine the qualifications of their most important government officials" as "an authority that lies at the heart of representative government." *Gregory v. Ashcroft*, 501 U.S. 452, 463 (1991) (refusing to read federal law to preclude States from imposing a mandatory retirement age on state judges who are subject to periodic retention elections). When the people of a State themselves decide to restrict the field of candidates whom they are willing to send to Washington as their representatives, they simply have not violated the principle that "the people should choose whom they please to govern them." See 2 Elliot 257 (remarks of Alexander Hamilton at the New York convention). . . .

▶▶ *Subsequent Efforts to Establish Congressional Term Limits.*   Thwarted in *Thornton*, advocates of congressional term limits nevertheless persevered by devoting their attention to marshaling support for a constitutional amendment. One strategy, adopted in about a dozen states, was to apply intense pressure to candidates and incumbent officials to support such an amendment through the adoption of a so-called Scarlet Letter provision. A Scarlet Letter provision is a state law or state constitutional provision that requires information about a candidate's position on a term limit amendment to be printed on the election ballot. Typically, such a provision would first require candidates to take a public pledge to support a federal term limit amendment. If a candidate refused to do so, state election officials were directed to print on the ballot next to the candidate's name, often in capital letters, "DECLINED TO PLEDGE TO SUPPORT TERM LIMITS." In the case of incumbents, the pledge typically required the official, while in office, to make certain specific efforts to introduce a constitutional amendment concerning term limits. Incumbents who failed to take the required steps received a ballot notation stating: "DISREGARDED VOTERS' INSTRUCTION ON TERM LIMITS."

In *Cook v. Gralike*, 531 U.S. 510 (2001), the Supreme Court struck down a Scarlet Letter provision from Missouri, as applied to candidates for Congress. The Court held that state power under Article I, §4 to regulate the "manner" of elections did not extend to the kind of ballot notations at issue.

≫ ***Term Limits for State Officials.***   If *Thornton* precludes state-imposed term limits on federal officials, what about state-imposed term limits on *state* officials? Many states have enacted such limitations, typically by amending the state constitution. Obviously, a term limit imposed by a state constitution cannot violate that constitution, so the only conceivable obstacle to term limits on state officials would arise from federal constitutional law. In *Legislature of the State of California v. Eu*, 816 P.2d 1309 (Cal. 1991), the California Supreme Court rejected First and Fourteenth Amendment challenges to California's Proposition 140, which limited most state officials, including the Governor and state Senators, to two terms, and members of the Assembly to three terms.

The court held that Proposition 140 implicated the federally guaranteed right to vote by impairing "the voters' right to reelect the incumbent," but that the First Amendment implications of this impairment were small because "[v]oters retain the ability to vote for any qualified candidate holding the beliefs or possessing the attributes they may desire in a public officeholder." The court held, however, that these considerations were outweighed by the "state's strong interests in protecting against an entrenched, dynastic legislative bureaucracy, and in thereby encouraging new candidates to seek public office."

Furthermore, nothing short of disqualifying incumbents would have achieved the state's goal: "Whether by reason of superior fund raising ability, greater media coverage, larger and more experienced staffs, greater name recognition among the voters, favorably drawn voting districts, or other factors, incumbents do indeed appear to enjoy considerable advantages over other candidates." Opponents of the term limits argued that a lifetime limit of two or three terms was unnecessary to prevent entrenchment, and that a limit on consecutive terms would accomplish the state's objectives. The court disagreed:

> we believe the framers [of the amendment] might well have reasonably concluded that a mere ban on consecutive terms could encourage popular "career politicians" to trade terms with each other, or to attempt to arrange for a "caretaker" candidate, such as a spouse or relative, to hold office for them during the interrupted term. For example, when in 1966 George Wallace became legally ineligible to run for reelection as Governor of Alabama because of state term limitations applicable to that office, his wife Lureen successfully ran in his place, and served as Governor until

her death in 1968. George Wallace was reelected as Governor in 1970 and again in 1974.

See also Citizens for Legislative Choice v. Miller, 144 F.3d 916 (6th Cir. 1998) (upholding amendment to Michigan Constitution imposing lifetime legislative term limits).

» *The Effect of Term Limits.*   The state-level movement for term limits obtained some rapid successes in the early 1990s; 15 states currently impose term limits on state legislators, and 35 impose term limits on at least some elected executive branch officials. Term limit provisions in these states have by now resulted in the "terming out" of thousands of elected officials. As a result, we now have considerable data about the real-world impact of term limits on state governance. What has been their actual impact?

One goal often mentioned by advocates of term limits is changing the kind of people who are elected to state office — replacing career politicians, who enter politics for the long haul, perhaps for their own self-interest, with citizen legislators who enter politics briefly to accomplish specific policy goals and then leave to resume their former lives. According to one study, there is no evidence of such a substitution effect, at least when measured by the income, religious affiliation, age, and ideology of elected officials: "In short, there is no evidence at all that term limits changed the ideological makeup of legislatures or even of the candidate pool from which they were selected." John M. Carey et al., *The Effects of Term Limits on State Legislatures: A New Survey of the 50 States*, 31 Legis. Q. 105, 114 (2006). In fact, the effect of term limits seems to have been the opposite of what was intended: state legislative candidates in states with term limits were *more* likely than candidates in non–term limit states to have held some prior elective office. The authors of the study speculate that "with less assurance that state legislative office will be a continuing source of employment, those seeking such a career path require even more political ambition or self-confidence than before, and this trait is reflected in these individuals' levels of prior officeholding." *Id.* at 117.

Proponents of term limits also expected them, by eliminating a class of career politicians, to improve the quality of representation by producing legislators who were less beholden to special interests and correspondingly more attentive to their ordinary constituents; and who, because they did not need to worry about reelection, would spend less time raising funds and more time on the public business. These expectations, too, have apparently failed to materialize. Legislators in term limit states report spending no less time on fundraising than legislators in non–term limit states, with the exception of those legislators who are in their last possible term. Moreover, term limited legislators report spending *less* time than non–term limited legislators in keeping in touch with their constituents and in securing government money and projects for their districts. *Id.* at 118-119. This behavioral change need not, however, run to the public detriment. It appears that term limits produce what the study authors call a "Burkean shift": term limited legislators "are more inclined to favor their own conscience and the interests of the state over those of the district." *Id.* at 123.

Finally, as critics of term limits have long predicted, the evidence suggests that term limits effect a transfer of power from the legislative to the executive branch by weakening the legislature's ability to stand up to the governor. *Id.* at 123-128.

This result is confirmed by another study, whose author concludes: "When term limits have removed a legislature's veteran leaders, less experienced members who replace them will lack the political savvy to bargain effectively." THAD KOUSSER, TERM LIMITS AND THE DISMANTLING OF STATE LEGISLATIVE PROFESSIONALISM 176 (2005). The Kousser study also finds that term limits redistribute power within the term limited legislature from the minority to the majority, and diminish the ability of the legislature to develop innovative policy solutions to social problems.

>> *District Residency Requirements.* In 1842, Congress legislatively required that states elect Representatives by district. The Constitution, however, requires only that a Representative be a resident of "that State in which he shall be chosen"—not of the election district. Is it constitutionally permissible for a state to require that candidates for Representative reside in the district from which they seek election? Although the Supreme Court has never considered this issue, several lower courts have concluded that states may not add a district residency requirement to the constitutional list of qualifications. *See Dillon v. Fiorina,* 340 F. Supp. 729 (D.N.M. 1972); *Exon v. Tiemann,* 279 F. Supp. 609 (D. Neb. 1968); *State ex rel. Chavez v. Evans,* 446 P.2d 445 (N.M. 1968); *Hellmann v. Collier,* 141 A.2d 908 (Md. 1958).

Moreover, the Constitution requires only that candidates for Representative be residents of the state from which they are elected at the time of election, not earlier: "No Person shall be a Representative who shall not . . . *when elected,* be an Inhabitant of that State in which he shall be chosen." Art. I, §2, cl. 2 (emphasis added). May a state require a candidate to be an inhabitant of the state at some earlier period—may it, in other words, establish a durational residency requirement? In *Schaefer v. Townsend,* 215 F.3d 1031 (9th Cir. 2000), the Ninth Circuit invalidated a California statute requiring candidates for Congress to reside in the state at the time they file nomination papers, a residency period that could range, depending upon the election, from 43 to 88 days. The court applied *Thornton* to find that the residency requirement added improperly to the qualifications laid out in the Constitution.

Some states have approached these concerns from another direction, by requiring that candidates for office be registered voters in the district from which they wish to run. Such provisions have similarly been invalidated as applied to congressional elections as adding a residency (or durational residency) requirement. *See Campbell v. Davidson,* 233 F.3d 1229 (10th Cir. 2000).

What about state establishment of a durational residency requirement in *state* elections? Every state imposes such requirements for at least some offices, and in some cases the required period of residency can be long. Missouri and Oregon, for example, require candidates for governor to have resided in the state for ten years, and eight states require gubernatorial candidates to have been residents for seven years. For an overview, see Eugene D. Mazo, *Residency and Democracy,* 42 FLA. ST. U. L. REV. 611 (2016).

Do state residency requirements for candidates raise any issues under the *federal* constitution? *Compare Akron v. Bell,* 660 F.2d 166 (6th Cir. 1981) (upholding one-year residency requirement for city council candidates), *with Zeilenga v. Nelson,* 428 P.2d 578 (Cal. 1971) (invalidating five-year residency requirement for candidates for county board of supervisors), and *Robertson v. Bartels,* 150 F. Supp. 2d 691 (D.N.J. 2001) (striking down a one-year residency requirement for candidates for the state assembly, as applied to a candidate who, without moving his residence, had been redistricted out of his former district and into a new one within the one-year district residency period).

▶▶ *Other Candidate Qualifications.*   States have attempted to impose numerous other qualifications on candidates for Congress. None has survived. Courts have struck down state-imposed requirements that candidates for Congress take a loyalty oath, *see Shub v. Simpson*, 76 A.2d 332 (Md. 1950); *In re O'Connor*, 17 N.Y.S.2d 758 (Super. Ct. 1940), and that they be free from felony convictions. *Application of Ferguson*, 294 N.Y.S.2d 174 (Super. Ct. 1968); *Danielson v. Fitzsimmons*, 44 N.W.2d 484 (Minn. 1950). Under these latter decisions, ex-felons may be barred from voting, but may not be barred from running for and holding national office. What could justify this anomalous result?

In *Chandler v. Miller*, 520 U.S. 305 (1997), the Court invalidated a Georgia law requiring all candidates for state office to produce a negative urinalysis drug test from a state-approved laboratory as a condition for having their name placed on the ballot. The requirement was challenged, appropriately enough, by candidates from the Libertarian Party. The Court held that the drug test requirement constituted a warrantless, suspicionless search in violation of the Fourth Amendment.

Finally, the Court held in *Gregory v. Ashcroft*, 501 U.S. 452 (1991), that federal law creates no obstacle to a state's imposition of age requirements on state office-holders. At issue in *Gregory* was a provision of the Missouri Constitution requiring state judges to retire at age 70. The Court found no equal protection violation, and further held that the federal Age Discrimination in Employment Act did not bar the age limit. Although the judges in question were appointed rather than elected, the Court's analysis suggests that it would not reach a different result regarding elected officials.

On the other hand, qualifications established by states for candidates for *state* office have often fared better. As noted earlier, the California Supreme Court upheld term limits for California legislative offices in *Legislature of the State of California v. Eu, supra.* The Arizona Supreme Court sustained a state law disqualifying from public office any person "who cannot write and read in the English language." *Escamilla v. Cuello*, 282 P.3d 403 (Ariz. 2012). The plaintiff, a candidate for city council in San Luis, was disqualified under this standard because she could read and write English at only a ninth- or tenth-grade level. The court held that the state had a legitimate interest in the ability of public officers to "communicate with their constituents and the public." It also observed that the statutory bar was not permanent, but would lift should the plaintiff improve her English proficiency. Is this a literacy requirement for office-holding? If so, why should literacy requirements be illegal for voters but legal for candidates?

In 2018, Louisiana voters approved an amendment to the state constitution barring felons from running for office for five years following completion of their sentences. La. Const. art. I, §10.1. In 2016, Alabama voters approved a constitutional amendment lifting all maximum age limits on office holders. Ala. Amdt. 13 (2016).

▶▶ **Additional Presidential Qualifications.**   In 2016, Donald Trump became the first presidential candidate in 40 years to refuse publicly to disclose his tax returns. In response, legislation was introduced in more than 20 states that would require presidential candidates to release their most recent tax returns as a condition of having their names printed on the election ballot. In 2019, California became the first state to enact such legislation, the Presidential Tax and Transparency Act. Litigation challenging its constitutionality was brought in both federal and state court. A federal district court granted a preliminary injunction against the act on the grounds that it unconstitutionally adds an additional qualification to the constitutional qualifications for president, and it is preempted by the federal Ethics in Government Act, which requires no such disclosure. *Griffin v. Padilla*, 417 F.Supp.3d 1291 (E.D. Cal. 2019). In parallel litigation in state court, the California Supreme Court struck down the act on the ground that it conflicted with a provision of the California Constitution requiring placement on the presidential ballot of all candidates "found by the Secretary of State to be recognized candidates throughout the nation . . . for the office of President of the United States." The court held that the statute "would exclude from the ballot even someone who is actively seeking the presidential nomination of a political party that participates in the primary election, and is widely regarded as leading contender for that nomination — precisely the sort of presidential candidate that Article II, section 5(c) [of the California Constitution] specifies *must* appear on the ballot." *Patterson v. Padilla*, 451 P.3d 1171 (Cal. 2019). The Ninth Circuit then vacated the federal district court opinion as moot.

>>   *Qualifications for Nonelective Offices.*   The cases examined so far concern the qualifications to run for elective office. Not every office, however, is elective, and issues occasionally arise concerning the types of qualifications that a state can impose on those who seek to hold an appointive or other nonelective office. The Court has addressed this issue several times. In *Turner v. Fouche*, 396 U.S. 346 (1970), the Court struck down a requirement that members of a local school board own real property. The Court held that the requirement was not rationally related to any legitimate state interest. A property ownership requirement for membership on a local airport commission was also invalidated in *Chappelle v. Greater Baton Rouge Airport District*, 431 U.S. 159 (1977), *summarily reversing* 329 So. 2d 801 (La. App. 1976).

A property ownership requirement was before the Court again in *Quinn v. Milsap*, 491 U.S. 95 (1989). The Missouri Constitution provided for the following method for reorganizing the governments of St. Louis City and County. Upon the filing of a petition signed by a certain number of voters, the mayor of St. Louis and the county executive of St. Louis County were required to appoint a 19-member "Board of Freeholders." The Board would then draft a proposed reorganization plan, which would be submitted to the voters for approval. The state constitution limited membership on the Board to owners of real property.

The Court struck down the property requirement under the Equal Protection Clause on the grounds of irrationality. The Court rejected Missouri's argument that real property owners had a greater stake and interest in the long-term future of the area. As in *Turner*, the Court also rejected the contention that the property requirement was rational because the Board made decisions that affected land. Furthermore, the Court found that the Board had the power to recommend reorganization plans that affected far more than just land, which meant that the land ownership requirement was not sufficiently well tailored to meet equal protection requirements.

C.   *CONDITIONS OF CANDIDACY*

The previous section considered candidate qualifications—those minimum requirements that any person must satisfy to be eligible to hold the office to which he or she seeks election. A "qualification" for office is sometimes defined as a factor the absence of which serves as an absolute bar to office-holding. *See, e.g., State v. Crane,* 197 P.2d 864, 871 (Wyo. 1948); *Hopfmann v. Connolly,* 746 F.2d 97, 103 (1st Cir. 1984), *vacated in part on other grounds,* 471 U.S. 459 (1985). Yet not all candidate eligibility requirements take this all-or-nothing form. Some eligibility requirements permit an otherwise qualified person to run for office, but only upon satisfaction of some condition that is within the person's power to satisfy. When the government imposes such conditions on candidacy, a qualified person is in a sense free to stand for office, but only if he or she is willing to make whatever sacrifice is necessary to satisfy the conditions. Because some conditions can create powerful disincentives to candidacy, conditions on candidacy have generally been thought to raise constitutional questions.

1.   *Resign-to-Run Requirements*

American constitutions have long included provisions barring multiple office-holding. The U.S. Constitution, for example, provides: "no Person holding any Office under the United States, shall be a Member of either House during his Continuance in Office." U.S. Const. Art. I, §6, cl. 1. That is why Senators or Representatives who are appointed to cabinet positions must resign their seats in Congress. State constitutions often contain similar provisions. Clearly, one significant purpose of these restrictions is to maintain the constitutional separation of powers. Is that the only purpose?

Some provisions, however, go further, not only barring people from simultaneously holding more than one public office, but also barring them from simultaneously *holding* office and *running* for any office other than the one they already hold. What could justify such a requirement? And how significant a justification is the government required to produce? Is there a constitutional right to run for office that a resign-to-run law infringes? The Court considered these questions in the following case.

Clements v. Fashing

457 U.S. 957 (1982)

Justice REHNQUIST delivered the opinion of the Court with respect to Parts I, II, and V, and delivered an opinion with respect to Parts III and IV, in which THE CHIEF JUSTICE, Justice POWELL, and Justice O'CONNOR joined.

Appellees in this case challenge two provisions of the Texas Constitution that limit a public official's ability to become a candidate for another public office. The primary question in this appeal is whether these provisions violate the Equal Protection Clause of the Fourteenth Amendment.

I

Article III, §19, of the Texas Constitution provides:

No judge of any court, Secretary of State, Attorney General, clerk of any court of record, or any person holding a lucrative office under the United States, or this State, or any foreign government shall during the term for which he is elected or appointed, be eligible to the Legislature.

Section 19 renders an officeholder ineligible for the Texas Legislature if his current term of office will not expire until after the legislative term to which he aspires begins. *Lee v. Daniels*, 377 S.W.2d 618 (Tex. 1964). Resignation is ineffective to avoid §19 if the officeholder's current term of office overlaps the term of the legislature to which he seeks election. *Ibid.* In other words, §19 requires an officeholder to complete his current term of office before he may be eligible to serve in the legislature.

Article XVI, §65, is commonly referred to as a "resign-to-run" or "automatic resignation" provision. Section 65 covers a wide range of state and county offices.[1] It provides in relevant part:

[I]f any of the officers named herein shall announce their candidacy, or shall in fact become a candidate, in any General, Special or Primary Election, for any office of profit or trust under the laws of this State or the United States other than the office then held, at any time when the unexpired term of the office then held shall exceed one (1) year, such announcement or such candidacy shall constitute an automatic resignation of the office then held.

Four of the appellees are officeholders subject to the automatic resignation provision of §65. Fashing is a County Judge, Baca and McGhee are Justices of the Peace, and Ybarra is a Constable. Each officeholder-appellee alleged in the complaint that he is qualified under Texas law to be a candidate for higher judicial office, and that the reason he has not and will not announce his candidacy is that such an announcement will constitute an automatic resignation from his current position. Appellee Baca alleged in addition that he could not become a candidate for the legislature because of §19. The remaining appellees are 20 voters who allege that they would vote for the officeholder-appellees were they to become candidates.

The District Court for the Western District of Texas held that §19 and §65 denied appellees equal protection. . . . We . . . now reverse. . . .

III

The Equal Protection Clause allows the States considerable leeway to enact legislation that may appear to affect similarly situated people differently. Legislatures

---

1. Section 65 covers District Clerks, County Clerks, County Judges, County Treasurers, Criminal District Attorneys, County Surveyors, Inspectors of Hides and Animals, County Commissioners, Justices of the Peace, Sheriffs, Assessors and Collectors of Taxes, District Attorneys, County Attorneys, Public Weighers, and Constables. Section 65 altered the terms of these offices.

are ordinarily assumed to have acted constitutionally. Under traditional equal protection principles, distinctions need only be drawn in such a manner as to bear some rational relationship to a legitimate state end. Classifications are set aside only if they are based solely on reasons totally unrelated to the pursuit of the State's goals and only if no grounds can be conceived to justify them. We have departed from traditional equal protection principles only when the challenged statute places burdens upon "suspect classes" of persons or on a constitutional right that is deemed to be "fundamental." *San Antonio Independent School Dist. v. Rodriguez,* 411 U.S. 1, 17 (1973).

Thus, we must first determine whether the provisions challenged in this case deserve "scrutiny" more vigorous than that which the traditional principles would require.

Far from recognizing candidacy as a "fundamental right," we have held that the existence of barriers to a candidate's access to the ballot "does not of itself compel close scrutiny." *Bullock v. Carter,* 405 U.S. 134, 143 (1972). "In approaching candidate restrictions, it is essential to examine in a realistic light the extent and nature of their impact on voters." *Ibid.* In assessing challenges to state election laws that restrict access to the ballot, this Court has not formulated a "litmus-paper test for separating those restrictions that are valid from those that are invidious under the Equal Protection Clause." *Storer v. Brown,* 415 U.S. 724, 730 (1974). Decision in this area of constitutional adjudication is a matter of degree, and involves a consideration of the facts and circumstances behind the law, the interests the State seeks to protect by placing restrictions on candidacy, and the nature of the interests of those who may be burdened by the restrictions. *Ibid.; Williams v. Rhodes,* 393 U.S. 23, 30 (1968).

. . . Thus, it is necessary to examine the provisions in question in terms of the extent of the burdens that they place on the candidacy of current holders of public office.

IV

A

. . . Section 19 merely prohibits officeholders from cutting short their current term of office in order to serve in the legislature. In Texas, the term of office for a Justice of the Peace is four years, while legislative elections are held every two years. See Tex. Const. Art. V, §18; Art. III, §§3, 4. Therefore, §19 simply requires Baca to complete his 4-year term as Justice of the Peace before he may be eligible for the legislature. At most, therefore, Baca must wait two years—one election cycle— before he may run as a candidate for the legislature. . . .

In establishing a maximum "waiting period" of two years for candidacy by a Justice of the Peace for the legislature, §19 places a *de minimis* burden on the political aspirations of a *current* officeholder. Section 19 discriminates neither on the basis of political affiliation nor on any factor not related to a candidate's qualifications to hold political office. . . . We conclude that this sort of insignificant interference with access to the ballot need only rest on a rational predicate in order to survive a challenge under the Equal Protection Clause.

Section 19 clearly rests on a rational predicate. That provision furthers Texas' interests in maintaining the integrity of the State's Justices of the Peace.[5] By prohibiting candidacy for the legislature until completion of one's term of office, §19 seeks to ensure that a Justice of the Peace will neither abuse his position nor neglect his duties because of his aspirations for higher office. The demands of a political campaign may tempt a Justice of the Peace to devote less than his full time and energies to the responsibilities of his office. A campaigning Justice of the Peace might be tempted to render decisions and take actions that might serve more to further his political ambitions than the responsibilities of his office. The State's interests are especially important with regard to judicial officers. It is a serious accusation to charge a judicial officer with making a politically motivated decision. By contrast, it is to be expected that a legislator will vote with due regard to the views of his constituents.

Texas has a legitimate interest in discouraging its Justices of the Peace from vacating their current terms of office. By requiring Justices of the Peace to complete their current terms of office, the State has eliminated one incentive to vacate one's office prior to the expiration of the term. The state may act to avoid the difficulties that accompany interim elections and appointments. . . .

Finally, it is no argument that §19 is invalid because it burdens only those officeholders who desire to run for the legislature. . . .

The Equal Protection Clause allows the State to regulate "one step at a time, addressing itself to the phase of the problem which seems most acute." *Williamson v. Lee Optical Co.*, 348 U.S., at 489. The State "need not run the risk of losing an entire remedial scheme simply because it failed, through inadvertence or otherwise, to cover every evil that might conceivably have been attacked." *McDonald v. Board of Election Comm'rs*, 394 U.S., at 809.

B

Article XVI, §65, of the Texas Constitution provides that the holders of certain offices automatically resign their positions if they become candidates for any other elected office, unless the unexpired portion of the current term is one year or less. The burdens that §65 imposes on candidacy are even less substantial than those imposed by §19. The two provisions, of course, serve essentially the same state interests. . . .

. . . Section 65 was enacted in 1954 as a transitional provision applying only to the 1954 election. 2 G. Braden, The Constitution of the State of Texas: An Annotated and Comparative Analysis 812 (1977). Section 65 extended the terms of those offices enumerated in the provision from two to four years. The provision also staggered the terms of other offices so that at least some county and local offices would be contested at each election. *Ibid.* The automatic resignation proviso to §65 was not added until 1958. . . .

---

5. The State's particular interest in maintaining the integrity of the judicial system could support §19, even if such a restriction could not survive constitutional scrutiny with regard to any other officeholder.

Thus, the automatic resignation provision in Texas is a creature of the State's electoral reforms of 1958. That the State did not go further in applying the automatic resignation provision to those officeholders whose terms were not extended by §11 or §65, absent an invidious purpose, is not the sort of malfunctioning of the State's lawmaking process forbidden by the Equal Protection Clause. A regulation is not devoid of a rational predicate simply because it happens to be incomplete. See *Williamson v. Lee Optical Co., supra,* at 489. The Equal Protection Clause does not forbid Texas to restrict one elected officeholder's candidacy for another elected office unless and until it places similar restrictions on other officeholders. *Broadrick v. Oklahoma,* 413 U.S., at 607, n.5. *Cf. Minnesota v. Clover Leaf Creamery Co.,* 449 U.S. 456, 466 (1981). The provision's language and its history belie any notion that §65 serves the invidious purpose of denying access to the political process to identifiable classes of potential candidates.

V

As an alternative ground to support the judgments of the courts below, appellees contend that §19 and §65 violate the First Amendment. Our analysis of appellees' challenge under the Equal Protection Clause disposes of this argument. We have concluded that the burden on appellees' First Amendment interests in candidacy are so insignificant that the classifications of §19 and §65 may be upheld consistent with traditional equal protection principles. The State's interests in this regard are sufficient to warrant the *de minimis* interference with appellees' interests in candidacy.

There is another reason why appellees' First Amendment challenge must fail. Appellees are *elected* state officeholders who contest restrictions on partisan political activity. Section 19 and §65 represent a far more limited restriction on political activity than this Court has upheld with regard to *civil servants.* See *CSC v. Letter Carriers,* 413 U.S. 548 (1973); *Broadrick v. Oklahoma, supra; United Public Workers v. Mitchell,* 330 U.S. 75 (1947)....

Neither the Equal Protection Clause nor the First Amendment authorizes this Court to review in cases such as this the manner in which a State has decided to govern itself. Constitutional limitations arise only if the classification scheme is invidious or if the challenged provision significantly impairs interests protected by the First Amendment. Our view of the wisdom of a state constitutional provision may not color our task of constitutional adjudication.

The judgment of the Court of Appeals is *Reversed.*

[Justice Stevens concurred in the judgment and joined Parts I, II, and V of Justice Rehnquist's opinion.]

Justice BRENNAN, with whom Justice MARSHALL and Justice BLACKMUN join, and with whom Justice WHITE joins as to Part I, dissenting. . . .

I

Putting to one side the question of the proper level of equal protection scrutiny to be applied to these restrictions on candidacy for public office, I find it clear that no genuine justification exists that might support the classifications embodied in either Art. III, §19, or Art. XVI, §65.

The State seeks to justify both provisions on the basis of its interest in discouraging abuse of office and neglect of duties by current officeholders campaigning for higher office during their terms. The plurality posits an additional justification not asserted by the State for §19: That section also discourages certain officeholders "from vacating their current terms of office." But neither the State nor the plurality offers any justification for *differential* treatment of various classes of officeholders, and the search for such justification makes clear that the classifications embodied in these provisions lack any meaningful relationship to the State's asserted or supposed interests.

. . . What relationship does the plurality find between the burden placed on the class of all state, federal, and foreign officeholders seeking legislative seats and the asserted state interests? If it faced the question, the plurality would of course have to acknowledge that Texas has no interest in protecting, for example, federal officials—particularly those serving the electorate of another State—from the corrupting influence of a state legislative campaign. The only conceivable state interest in barring these candidacies would be the purely impermissible one of protecting Texas legislative seats against outside competition. . . .

The plurality cannot, in the same manner that it avoids the overbreadth of the class, avoid the irrationality in the fact that §19 applies *only* to candidacy for the Texas Legislature. Officeholders are free to run for President, the United States Senate, governor, mayor, city council, and many other offices. The distracting and corrupting effects of campaigning are obviously present in *all* campaigns, not only those for the legislature. The plurality responds to this characteristic of the legislative scheme by stating that "[t]he Equal Protection Clause allows the State to regulate 'one step at a time. . . .'" But the record in this case belies any assertion by the State that it is proceeding "one step at a time." Article III, §29, has existed in its present form since 1876. There is no legislative history to explain its intended purpose or to suggest that it is part of a larger, more equitable regulatory scheme. And in the 106 years that have passed since §19's adoption, the Texas Legislature has adopted no comparable bar to candidacy for other offices. . . .

Appellants, unlike the plurality, at least attempt to justify the distinction between legislative campaigns and other campaigns. They argue that an officeholder-candidate will not enforce *legislative* policy if he or she is campaigning for a legislative seat. Brief for Appellants 9. But this attempted justification is unpersuasive. Appellants' argument apparently rests on the tenuous premise that a candidate is likely to choose the strategy of undermining the program of an incumbent opponent in order to advance his own prospects. It is plain that whatever force there is to this premise cannot be limited to a candidate for the legislature; it may as logically be argued that a judge will further his ambition for higher judicial office by failing to follow judicial decisions of a higher court, or that a state legislator with gubernatorial aspirations will use his present position to sabotage the program of the present administration. . . .

I turn now to Art. XVI, §65. That section applies only to persons holding any of approximately 16 enumerated offices. . . . Other officeholders, performing similar if not identical duties, are not within the reach of this or any similar restriction and are thus free to campaign for one office while holding another. . . . Neither appellants nor the plurality offer any explanation why the State has a greater interest in having the undivided attention of a "Public Weigher" than of a state criminal court judge, or any reason why the State has a greater interest in preventing the abuse of office by an "Inspector of Hides and Animals," than by a justice of the Texas Supreme Court. Yet in each instance §65 applies to the former office and not to the latter. Again the plurality opines that the State is legislating "one step at a time." But while Art. XVI, §65, is of more recent vintage than Art. III, §19, it has been part of the Texas Constitution for 24 years without prompting any corresponding rule applicable to holders of statewide office. Thus §65, like §19, cannot in any realistic sense be upheld as one step in an evolving scheme. . . .

II

I also believe that Art. III, §19, violates the First Amendment. The Court dismisses this contention by stating that this provision is a more limited restriction on political activities of public employees than we have upheld in prior cases. But none of our precedents presented a restriction on campaigning that applied even *after* an official had resigned from public office or to officials who did not serve in the regulating government. Moreover, the Court does not go on to address what is for me the crucial question: What justification does the State have for this restriction and how does this provision address the State's asserted interests?

The Court acknowledges that Art. III, §19, restrains government employees' pursuit of political office. Such pursuit is clearly protected by the First Amendment and restrictions on it must be justified by the State's interest in ensuring the continued proper performance of current public duties. . . .

. . . [T]his Court has unequivocally rejected the premise that one surrenders the protection of the First Amendment by accepting the responsibilities of public employment. *Elrod v. Burns,* 427 U.S. 347 (1976); *Pickering v. Board of Education, supra.* And the Court has clearly recognized that restrictions on candidacy impinge on First Amendment rights. See, *e.g., Illinois State Bd. of Elections v. Socialist Workers Party,* 440 U.S. 173 (1979); *Lubin v. Panish,* 415 U.S. 709 (1974); *American Party of Texas v. White,* 415 U.S. 767 (1974); *Bullock v. Carter,* 405 U.S. 134, 142-143 (1972); *Williams v. Rhodes,* 393 U.S. 23, 34 (1968). Our precedents establish the guiding principle for applying the strictures of the First Amendment to restrictions of expressional conduct of state employees: The Court must arrive at an accommodation " 'between the interests of the [employee] . . . and the interest of the [government], as an employer.' " *CSC v. Letter Carriers, supra,* at 564, quoting *Pickering v. Board of Education, supra,* at 568. And in striking the required balance, "[t]he gain to the subordinating interest provided by the means must outweigh the incurred loss of protected rights." *Elrod v. Burns, supra,* at 362 (plurality opinion). In undertaking this balance, I acknowledge, of course, that the State has a vital interest in ensuring that public officeholders perform their duties properly, and that a State requires substantial flexibility to develop both direct and indirect methods of serving that interest. But if the State's interest is not substantially furthered by the challenged restrictions, then the restrictions are an unnecessary intrusion into employee rights. If the restriction is effective, but interferes with protected activity more than is reasonably necessary to further the asserted state interest, then the overintrusive aspects of the restriction lack constitutional justification. In short, to survive scrutiny under the First Amendment, a restriction on political campaigning by government employees must be narrowly tailored and substantially related to furthering the State's asserted interests.

It is clear to me that Art. III, §19, is not narrowly tailored to conform to the State's asserted interests. Nor does it further those interests in a meaningful way. . . .

Not all states, of course, prohibit incumbents from running for other offices, and some states even permit candidates to run for more than one office at once. During the 2000 election, for example, the Democratic candidate for Vice President, Senator Joseph Lieberman of Connecticut, was sometimes criticized for running in Connecticut simultaneously for election as Vice President and for reelection as Senator, though Connecticut law allowed him to do so. Is that a better arrangement than in Texas? Is it more important that an able and popular public servant hold *some* office than that he or she hold a *particular* office?

2. Forgoing Government Employment

One of the most significant conditional restrictions on political candidacy is imposed by the Hatch Act, which bars federal employees from engaging in most kinds of partisan political activity, including running for any partisan political office. The Hatch Act applies to every federal employee except the highest-level political appointees, and to any state employee whose position is funded by the federal government under any of several federal benefit programs, such as the food stamp program. In addition, many states have enacted Hatch Act equivalents for state employees. Collectively, the Hatch Act and equivalent state restrictions apply to millions of government workers.

In the *Letter Carriers* case set out below, federal employees challenged the constitutionality of the Hatch Act. Although the Court focused on the provisions of the Act that restricted federal employees' ability to participate in political *campaigning*, the Court used the same rationales to justify the ban on running for office.

Letter Carriers was not the first case to consider the constitutionality of the Hatch Act. In *United Public Workers v. Mitchell*, 330 U.S. 75 (1947), the Court sustained the Act against constitutional attack. The Court apparently reconsidered the issue in *Letter Carriers* for two reasons. First, it was arguable that the holding of *Mitchell* was narrow enough so as not to dispose of all the issues raised in *Letter Carriers*. Second, the District Court was under the impression that subsequent decisions of the Supreme Court had so eroded *Mitchell's* holding that the decision could no longer be viewed as controlling.

United States Civil Service Commission v. National Association of Letter Carriers, AFL-CIO

413 U.S. 548 (1973)

Mr. Justice WHITE delivered the opinion of the Court.

[This case presents] the single question whether the prohibition in §9(a) of the Hatch Act, now codified in 5 U.S.C. §7324(a)(2), against federal employees taking "an active part in political management or in political campaigns," is unconstitutional on its face. Section 7324(a) provides:

> **(a)** An employee in an Executive agency or an individual employed by the government of the District of Columbia may not—
>
> > **(1)** use his official authority or influence for the purpose of interfering with or affecting the result of an election; or
> >
> > **(2)** take an active part in political management or in political campaigns. . . .

I

The case began when the National Association of Letter Carriers, six individual federal employees and certain local Democratic and Republican political committees filed a complaint, asserting on behalf of themselves and all federal employees that 5 U.S.C. §7324(a)(2) was unconstitutional on its face and seeking an injunction against its enforcement.

Each of the plaintiffs alleged that the Civil Service Commission was enforcing, or threatening to enforce, the Hatch Act's prohibition against active participation in political management or political campaigns with respect to certain defined activity in which that plaintiff desired to engage. The Union, for example, stated among other things that its members desired to campaign for candidates for public office. The Democratic and Republican Committees complained of not being able to get federal employees to run for state and local offices. Plaintiff Hummel stated that he was aware of the provision of the Hatch Act and that the activities he desired to engage in would violate that Act as, for example, his participating as a delegate in a party convention or holding office in a political club. . . .

II

As the District Court recognized, the constitutionality of the Hatch Act's ban on taking an active part in political management or political campaigns has been here before. This very prohibition was attacked in the *Mitchell* case by a labor union and various federal employees as being violative of the First, Ninth, and Tenth Amendments and as contrary to the Fifth Amendment. . . .

We unhesitatingly reaffirm the *Mitchell* holding that . . . neither the First Amendment nor any other provision of the Constitution invalidates a law barring this kind of partisan political conduct by federal employees.

A

Such decision on our part would no more than confirm the judgment of history, a judgment made by this country over the last century that it is in the best interest of the country, indeed essential, that federal service should depend upon meritorious performance rather than political service, and that the political influence of federal employees on others and on the electoral process should be limited. That this judgment eventuated is indisputable, and the major steps in reaching it may be simply and briefly set down.

Early in our history, Thomas Jefferson was disturbed by the political activities of some of those in the Executive Branch of the Government. See 10 J. Richardson, Messages and Papers of the Presidents 98 (1899). The heads of the executive departments, in response to his directive, issued an order stating in part that "the right of any officer to give his vote at elections as a qualified citizen is not meant to be restrained, nor, however given, shall it have any effect to his prejudice; but it is expected that he will not attempt to influence the votes of others nor take any part in the business of electioneering, that being deemed inconsistent with the spirit of the Constitution and his duties to it." *Id.*, at 98-99.

There were other voices raised in the 19th century against the mixing of partisan politics and routine federal service. But until after the Civil War, the spoils system under which federal employees came and went, depending upon party service and changing administrations, rather than meritorious performance, was much the vogue and the prevalent basis for governmental employment and advancement. 1 Report of Commission on Political Activity of Government Personnel, Findings and Recommendations 7-8 (1968). That system did not survive. Congress authorized the President to prescribe regulations for the creation of a civil service of federal employees in 1871, 16 Stat. 514; but it was the Civil Service Act of 1883, c. 27, 22 Stat. 403, known as the Pendleton Act, H. Kaplan, The Law of Civil Service 9-10 (1958), that declared that "no person in the public service is for that reason under any obligations to contribute to any political fund, or to render any political service" and that "no person in said service has any right to use his official authority or influence to coerce the political action of any person or body." . . .

The experience of the intervening years, particularly that of the 1936 and 1938 political campaigns, convinced a majority in Congress that the prohibition against taking an active part in political management and political campaigns should be extended to the entire federal service. . . . This was the so-called Hatch Act, named after the Senator who was its chief proponent. In its initial provisions, §§1 and 2, it forbade anyone from coercing or interfering with the vote of another person and prohibited federal employees from using their official positions to influence or interfere with or affect the election or nomination of certain federal officials. Sections 3 and 4 of the Act prohibited the promise of, or threat of termination of, employment or compensation for the purpose of influencing or securing political activity, or support or opposition for any candidate. . . .

On the day prior to signing the bill, President Franklin Roosevelt sent a message to Congress stating his conviction that the bill was constitutional and recommending that Congress at its next session consider extending the Act to state and local government employees. 84 Cong. Rec. 10745-10747 and 10875. This, Congress quickly proceeded to do. The Act of July 19, 1940, c. 640, 54 Stat. 767, extended the Hatch Act to officers and employees of state and local agencies "whose principal employment is in connection with any activity which is financed in whole or in part by loans or grants made by the United States. . . ." The Civil Service Commission was empowered under §12 (b) to investigate and adjudicate violations of the Act by state and local employees. Also relevant for present purposes, §9 (a) of the Hatch Act was amended so that all persons covered by the Act were free to "express their opinions on all political subjects *and candidates*." (Emphasis added.) . . .

This account of the efforts by the Federal Government to limit partisan political activities by those covered by the Hatch Act should not obscure the equally relevant fact that all 50 States have restricted the political activities of their own employees.

B

Until now, the judgment of Congress, the Executive, and the country appears to have been that partisan political activities by federal employees must be limited if the Government is to operate effectively and fairly, elections are to play their proper part in representative government, and employees themselves are to be sufficiently free from improper influences. The restrictions so far imposed on federal employees are not aimed at particular parties, groups, or points of view, but apply equally to all partisan activities of the type described. They discriminate against no racial, ethnic, or religious minorities. Nor do they seek to control political opinions or beliefs, or to interfere with or influence anyone's vote at the polls.

But, as the Court held in *Pickering v. Board of Education*, 391 U.S. 563, 568 (1968), the government has an interest in regulating the conduct and "the speech of its employees that differ[s] significantly from those it possesses in connection with regulation of the speech of the citizenry in general. The problem in any case is to arrive at a balance between the interests of the [employee], as a citizen, in commenting upon matters of public concern and the interest of the [government], as an employer, in promoting the efficiency of the public services it performs through its employees." Although Congress is free to strike a different balance than it has, if it so chooses, we think the balance it has so far struck is sustainable by the obviously important interests sought to be served by the limitations on partisan political activities now contained in the Hatch Act.

It seems fundamental in the first place that employees in the Executive Branch of the Government, or those working for any of its agencies, should administer the law in accordance with the will of Congress, rather than in accordance with their own or the will of a political party. They are expected to enforce the law and execute the programs of the Government without bias or favoritism for or against any political party or group or the members thereof. A major thesis of the Hatch Act is that to serve this great end of Government—the impartial execution of the laws—it is essential that federal employees, for example, not take formal positions in political parties, not undertake to play substantial roles in partisan political campaigns, and not run for office on partisan political tickets. Forbidding activities like these will reduce the hazards to fair and effective government.

There is another consideration in this judgment: it is not only important that the Government and its employees in fact avoid practicing political justice, but it is also critical that they appear to the public to be avoiding it, if confidence in the system of representative Government is not to be eroded to a disastrous extent.

Another major concern of the restriction against partisan activities by federal employees was perhaps the immediate occasion for enactment of the Hatch Act in 1939. That was the conviction that the rapidly expanding Government work force should not be employed to build a powerful, invincible, and perhaps corrupt political machine. The experience of the 1936 and 1938 campaigns convinced Congress that these dangers were sufficiently real that substantial barriers should be raised against the party in power—or the party out of power, for that matter—using the thousands or hundreds of thousands of federal employees, paid for at public expense, to man its political structure and political campaigns.

A related concern, and this remains as important as any other, was to further serve the goal that employment and advancement in the Government service not depend on political performance, and at the same time to make sure that Government employees would be free from pressure and from express or tacit invitation to vote in a certain way or perform political chores in order to curry favor with their superiors rather than to act out their own beliefs. It may be urged that prohibitions against coercion are sufficient protection; but for many years the joint judgment of the Executive and Congress has been that to protect the rights of federal employees with respect to their jobs and their political acts and beliefs it is not enough merely to forbid one employee to attempt to influence or coerce another. . . .

Mr. Justice DOUGLAS, with whom Mr. Justice BRENNAN and Mr. Justice MARSHALL concur, dissenting.

The Hatch Act by §9(a) prohibits federal employees from taking "an active part in political management or in political campaigns." Some of the employees, whose union is speaking for them, want to run in state and local elections for the school board, for city council, for mayor:

> to write letters on political subjects to newspapers;
> to be a delegate in a political convention;
> to run for an office and hold office in a political party or political club;
> to campaign for candidates for political office;
> to work at polling places in behalf of a political party. . . .

The District Court felt that the prohibitions in the Act are "worded in generalities that lack precision," 346 F. Supp. 578, 582, with the result that it is hazardous for an employee "if he ventures to speak on a political matter since he will not know when his words or acts relating to political subjects will offend." Id., at 582-583.

The chilling effect of these vague and generalized prohibitions is so obvious as not to need elaboration. That effect would not be material to the issue of constitutionality if only the normal contours of the police power were involved. On the run of social and economic matters the "rational basis" standard which United Public Workers v. Mitchell, 330 U.S. 75, applied would suffice. But what may have been unclear to some in Mitchell should by now be abundantly clear to all. We deal here with a First Amendment right to speak, to propose, to publish, to petition Government, to assemble. Time and place are obvious limitations. Thus no one could object if employees were barred from using office time to engage in outside activities whether political or otherwise. But it is of no concern of Government what an employee does in his spare time, whether religion, recreation, social work, or politics is his hobby—unless what he does impairs efficiency or other facets of the merits of his job. Some things, some activities do affect or may be thought to affect the employee's job performance. But his political creed, like his religion, is irrelevant. In the areas of speech, like religion, it is of no concern what the employee says in private to his wife or to the public in Constitution Hall. . . .

Free discussion of governmental affairs is basic in our constitutional system. Laws that trench on that area must be narrowly and precisely drawn to deal with precise ends. Overbreadth in the area of the First Amendment has a peculiar evil, the evil of creating chilling effects which deter the exercise of those freedoms. . . .

Mitchell is of a different vintage from the present case. Since its date, a host of decisions have illustrated the need for narrowly drawn statutes that touch First Amendment rights.

The present Act cannot be appropriately narrowed to meet the need for narrowly drawn language not embracing First Amendment speech or writing without substantial revision. . . .

A nursing assistant at a veterans' hospital put an ad in a newspaper reading:

To All My Many Friends of Poplar Bluff and Butler County I want to take this opportunity to ask your vote and support in the election, TUESDAY, AUGUST 7th. A very special person is seeking the Democratic nomination for Sheriff. I do not have to tell you of his qualifications, his past records stand.

This person is my dad, Lester (Less) Massingham.

THANK YOU
WALLACE (WALLY) MASSINGHAM

He was held to have violated the Act. *Massingham,* 1 Political Activity Reporter 792, 793 (1959).

Is a letter a permissible "expression" of views or a prohibited "solicitation?" The Solicitor General says it is a "permissible" expression; but the Commission ruled otherwise. For an employee who does not have the Solicitor General as counsel great consequences flow from an innocent decision. He may lose his job. Therefore the most prudent thing is to do nothing. Thus is self-imposed censorship imposed on many nervous people who live on narrow economic margins.

I would strike this provision of the law down as unconstitutional so that a new start may be made on this old problem that confuses and restricts nearly five million federal, state, and local public employees today that live under the present Act.

———————

In 1993, Congress significantly amended the Hatch Act, loosening some of its most burdensome restrictions on political activity by government employees. However, the ban on becoming a candidate for partisan political office remains in effect. 5 U.S.C. §7323(a)(3). Additionally, employees of the Federal Election Commission, FBI, Secret Service, CIA, National Security Council, National Security Agency, and a few other agencies are still barred from taking "an active part in political management or political campaigns." *Id.* §7323(b)(2)(B). All federal employees remain barred from engaging in political activities while on duty. *Id.* §7324.

In 2012, Congress again enacted slight relaxations of Hatch Act prohibitions. Under the Hatch Act, state and local employees whose salaries are funded in whole or in part by the federal government (as through federal grants or loans) may not run for elective office. Under the Hatch Act Modernization Act of 2012, the restriction now applies only to state or local employees whose positions are funded fully by federal dollars. The Act also eases penalties for violations. However, it extends Hatch Act prohibitions to employees of the government of the District of Columbia.

»   *Coercion by Private Employers.*   Civil service laws like the Hatch Act preclude the government from coercing the political activity of its employees. But what about *private* employers? Can Microsoft or General Motors — or the local ice cream shop — demand that their employees actively support particular parties or candidates? As a general rule, the answer is yes: under the traditional doctrine of employment at will, employers can fire their employees for any reason at all, including failure to knock on doors to support the reelection of Mayor X. To the extent employees of private firms have relief, it comes either from (1) a common-law public policy exception to the employment-at-will doctrine, which varies from state to state, or (2) state civil rights statutes that constrain the permissible grounds for firing or disciplining employees. For example, New York Labor Law §201(d)(2) provides:

> Unless otherwise provided by law, it shall be unlawful for any employer or employment agency to refuse to hire, employ or license, or to discharge from employment or otherwise discriminate against an individual in compensation, promotion or terms, conditions or privileges of employment because of . . . (a) an individual's political activities outside of working hours, off of the employer's premises and without use of the employer's equipment or other property, if such activities are legal. . . .

See also Novosel v. Nationwide Ins. Co., 721 F.2d 894 (3d Cir. 1983) (holding that an employee who was discharged for refusing to participate in a company-wide initiative to lobby the state legislature stated a claim for wrongful discharge on a theory of violation of state public policy). For an overview of statutory protections for employees' political activities, see Eugene Volokh, *Private Employees' Speech and Political Activity: Statutory Protection Against Employer Retaliation,* 16 Tex. Rev. L. & Pol. 297 (2012).

3. Disclosure of Personal Financial Information

Section 101(c) of the federal Ethics in Government Act of 1978, 5 U.S.C. App. 4, provides:

> Within thirty days of becoming a candidate . . . in a calendar year for nomination or election to the office of President, Vice President, or Member of Congress, or on or before May 15 of that calendar year, whichever is later, but in no event later than 30 days before the election, and on or before

May 15 of each successive year an individual continues to be a candidate, an individual other than an incumbent President, Vice President, or Member of Congress shall file a report containing the information described in section 102[(a) and] (b).

Section 102(a), which applies to all filers, including incumbent office-holders and covered federal employees as well as candidates, provides:

Each report . . . shall include a full and complete statement with respect to the following:

(1)(A) The source, type, and amount or value of income . . . from any source . . . and the source, date, and amount of honoraria from any source, received during the preceding calendar year, aggregating $200 or more in value. . . . (B) The source and type of income which consists of dividends, rents, interest, and capital gains, received during the preceding calendar year which exceeds $200 in amount or value. . . .

(2)(A) The identity of the source, a brief description, and the value of all gifts aggregating more than . . . $250 . . . received from any source other than a relative of the reporting individual during the preceding calendar year, except that any food, lodging, or entertainment received as personal hospitality of an individual need not be reported, and any gift with a fair market value of $100 or less . . . need not be aggregated for purposes of this subparagraph. . . .

(3) The identity and category of value of any interest in property held during the preceding calendar year in a trade or business, or for investment or the production of income, which has a fair market value which exceeds $1,000 as of the close of the preceding calendar year. . . .

(4) The identity and category of value of the total liabilities owed to any creditor other than a spouse, or a parent, brother, sister, or child of the reporting individual or of the reporting individual's spouse which exceed $10,000 at any time during the preceding calendar year, excluding [certain mortgages and loans].

(5) Except as provided in this paragraph, a brief description, the date, and category of value of any purchase, sale or exchange during the preceding calendar year which exceeds $1,000 [in real property, stocks, bonds, or other securities].

(6)(A) The identity of all positions held on or before the date of filing during the current calendar year (and, for the first report filed by an individual, during the two-year period preceding such calendar year) as an officer, director, trustee, partner, proprietor, representative, employee, or consultant of any corporation, company, firm, partnership, or other business enterprise, any nonprofit organization, any labor organization, or any educational or other institution other than the United States. . . . (B) If any person, other than the United States Government, paid a nonelected reporting individual compensation in excess of $5,000 in any of the two calendar years prior to the calendar year during which the individual files his first report under this title, the individual shall include in the report— (i) the identity of each source of such compensation; and (ii) a brief description of the nature of the duties performed or services rendered by the reporting individual for each such source. . . .

Those subject to the Act typically need not report exact amounts for each item required to be disclosed, but must instead indicate its rough value by designating a range of values within which it falls. For example, values of many kinds of assets may be reported in one of the following ranges:

(i)   not more than $1,000,
(ii)   greater than $1,000 but not more than $2,500,
(iii) greater than $2,500 but not more than $5,000,
(iv)   greater than $5,000 but not more than $15,000,
(v)   greater than $15,000 but not more than $50,000,
(vi)   greater than $50,000 but not more than $100,000,
(vii) greater than $100,000 but not more than $1,000,000,
(viii) greater than $1,000,000 but not more than $5,000,000, or
(ix)   greater than $5,000,000.

Section 102(a)(1)(B). A sample page from the disclosure form that presidential candidates must file appears on the next page.

What is the point of requiring candidates for federal office to disclose this kind of information? Do voters learn anything significant?

Making the kind of financial disclosure required by the Ethics in Government Act is not only burdensome, but also requires candidates to expose intimate details of their personal lives to public scrutiny. State and federal financial disclosure laws have been challenged many times on a variety of constitutional grounds, and have generally been upheld. Courts have typically acknowledged that financial disclosure requirements impose significant burdens on constitutionally protected privacy interests, and may expose filers to financial and even physical risks by revealing information that may be used in attempts to harm them. Yet most courts have held that the great public interest in disclosure justifies the substantial burdens imposed. *See Plante v. Gonzalez*, 575 F.2d 1119 (5th Cir. 1978), *cert. denied*, 439 U.S. 1129 (1979) (upholding Florida constitutional provision requiring financial disclosure of most state and local elected and appointed officials and candidates for elected office); *Barry v. City of New York*, 712 F.2d 1554 (2d Cir. 1983) (upholding New York City's financial disclosure law for city officials and candidates for city offices); *Duplantier v. United States*, 606 F.2d 654 (5th Cir. 1979) (upholding federal Ethics in Government Act disclosure requirements as applied to federal judges).

≫ *Even More Disclosure?*   Is the amount of financial disclosure now required of candidates for office sufficient? Should candidates be required to make other kinds of disclosures in addition to financial ones? For example, some candidates for office disclose information about their physical health, and sometimes their mental health, either by revealing it themselves or by authorizing their physicians to give interviews to the press. Should such disclosure be made mandatory? Should

SF 278 (Rev. 03/2000)
5 C.F.R. Part 2634
U.S. Office of Government Ethics

SCHEDULE A

Reporting Individual's Name

Page Number ____ of ____

BLOCK A — Assets and Income

For you, your spouse, and dependent children, report each asset held for investment or the production of income which had a fair market value exceeding $1,000 at the close of the reporting period, or which generated more than $200 in income during the reporting period, together with such income.

For yourself, also report the source and actual amount of earned income exceeding $200 (other than from the U.S. Government). For your spouse, report the source but not the amount of earned income of more than $1,000 (except report the actual amount of any honoraria over $200 of your spouse).

None ☐

Examples:
- Central Airlines Common
- Doe Jones & Smith, Hometown, State
- Kempstone Equity Fund
- IRA: Heartland 500 Index Fund

BLOCK B — Valuation of Assets at close of reporting period

BLOCK C — Income: type and amount. If "None (or less than $201)" is checked, no other entry is needed in Block C for that item.

	Valuation of Assets (Block B)													Income Type (Block C)				Income Amount (Block C)												Other Income (Specify Type & Actual Amount)	Date (Mo., Day, Yr.) Only if Honoraria
	None (or less than $1,001)	$1,001 - $15,000	$15,001 - $50,000	$50,001 - $100,000	$100,001 - $250,000	$250,001 - $500,000	$500,001 - $1,000,000	Over $1,000,000*	$1,000,001 - $5,000,000	$5,000,001 - $25,000,000	$25,000,001 - $50,000,000	Over $50,000,000	Excepted Investment Fund	Excepted Trust	Qualified Trust	Dividends	Rent and Royalties	Interest	Capital Gains	None (or less than $201)	$201 - $1,000	$1,001 - $2,500	$2,501 - $5,000	$5,001 - $15,000	$15,001 - $50,000	$50,001 - $100,000	$100,001 - $1,000,000	Over $1,000,000*	$1,000,001 - $5,000,000	Over $5,000,000		
Central Airlines Common			x													x							x									
Doe Jones & Smith, Hometown, State				x																												Law Partnership Income $1,500,000	
Kempstone Equity Fund						x							x										x									
IRA: Heartland 500 Index Fund													x								x												
1																																	
2																																	
3																																	
4																																	
5																																	
6																																	

* This category applies only if the asset/income is solely that of the filer's spouse or dependent children. If the asset/income is either that of the filer or jointly held by the filer with the spouse or dependent children, mark the other higher categories of value, as appropriate.

Prior Editions Cannot Be Used.

OGE/Adobe Acrobat version 1.0.1 (3/29/01)

candidates be required to submit to mandatory criminal and background checks? If you can't get hired to work the cashier at Walmart without a background check, shouldn't the voters have similar background information about candidates for high elective office, where the stakes are immeasurably higher?

For arguments in favor of expanded disclosure along these additional dimensions, see Megha Dharia, et al., *What Should Presidential Candidates Tell Us About Themselves? Proposals for Improving Transparency in Presidential Campaigns* (Fordham University School of Law, Democracy and the Constitution Clinic, Jan. 2020).

D.   DISQUALIFICATION AND REMOVAL

Thus far, we have focused on qualifications for office, the primary mechanism by which the people screen out candidates who are in principle least likely to possess the qualities voters want in their elected officials. Indeed, a not uncommon view at the time of the founding was that "if elections brought to office men distinguished by reason and virtue, ex-post control over their actions would not be necessary." ADAM PRZEWORSKI, WHY BOTHER WITH ELECTIONS? 16 (2018). A different view is that candidate qualifications tend to set the bar quite low, and from time to time individuals who meet the basic qualifications might be elected to offices for which they are not well qualified and in which they perform incompetently or, worse, corruptly. Alternatively, candidates qualified at the time of election might undergo changes during their time in office that render them incompetent, or they might unexpectedly adopt behaviors inconsistent with the electorate's expectations based on officials' prior records of service or campaign commitments. In these circumstances, the public might think it best to remove such officials from office before the next opportunity to oust them electorally rolls around. In this section, we explore briefly some of the avenues the law provides for disqualifying or removing underperforming government officials.

>> *Vote of No Confidence.*   The simplest and procedurally cleanest way to remove an executive branch official from office is the method available in parliamentary systems: a legislative vote of no confidence. In Westminster-style parliamentary systems, the prime minister is not elected by the people, but by the parliament. The prime minister, and members of his or her cabinet, thus serve solely at the sufferance of the legislature. When an incumbent prime minister begins to lose support among legislators, he or she then becomes vulnerable to a motion for a vote of no confidence, which can be brought for any reason.

Nevertheless, successful parliamentary removal of a prime minister through a vote of no confidence is rare. In Britain, the birthplace of the modern parliament, the last successful ouster of a prime minister on a no-confidence vote was in 1979, and the most recent one before that was in 1924. Only one Australian prime minister has ever been removed by a vote of no confidence. On the other hand, the credible threat of a no-confidence vote has sometimes functioned as the equivalent of an actual vote, causing prime ministers to resign or political parties to change leadership.

Presidential constitutions like that of the U.S. lack such a mechanism, for the most part substituting impeachment as the sole method for removing an underperforming president, cabinet official, or judge.

》 *Impeachment.* The U.S. Constitution provides for removal of officials by impeachment, but addresses it in the sparest possible language. Article I, §2, provides: "The House of Representatives . . . shall have the sole power of impeachment." Article I, §3, provides: "The Senate shall have the sole power to try all impeachments . . . [a]nd no person shall be convicted without the concurrence of two thirds of the members present." Section 3 goes on to explain that "Judgment in cases of impeachment shall not extend further than to removal from office, and disqualification to hold and enjoy any office of honor, trust or profit under the United States." Finally, Article II, §4 provides: "The President, Vice President and all civil officers of the United States, shall be removed from office on impeachment for, and conviction of, treason, bribery, or other high crimes and misdemeanors."

These spare provisions leave open a number of important questions, including what precisely counts as an impeachable "high crime" or "misdemeanor" and what procedures apply during impeachment proceedings. Both questions have been answered almost entirely by reference to history and actual practice rather than judicial interpretation. Indeed, it seems unlikely that federal courts will ever address these questions on the merits, as they are likely to be considered nonjusticiable political questions. In *Nixon v. United States*, 506 U.S. 224 (1993), an impeached federal judge challenged the procedures used by the Senate to convict him. The Supreme Court dismissed the question as nonjusticiable, holding that the Constitution textually commits to the Senate procedural decisions concerning how to try an impeachment.

Impeachable Offenses. Like many principles written into the Constitution, impeachment was known to the Framers from longstanding English and American colonial practices. In England, according to a leading scholar, "any person, whether an official or not, could be impeached by the Parliament for anything." MICHAEL J. GERHARDT, IMPEACHMENT: WHAT EVERYONE NEEDS TO KNOW 11 (2018). By the seventeenth century, however, impeachment had become primarily a tool for addressing "misconduct in high places." PETER CHARLES HOFFER AND N.E.H. HULL, IMPEACHMENT IN AMERICA, 1635-1805 (1984), at 6. This remained the focus in the American colonies, and later in the post-Revolutionary independent states, where impeachment was conceived mainly as "a mechanism for the maintenance of a healthy politics and the preservation of constitutional governance." FRANK O. BOWMAN III, HIGH CRIMES AND MISDEMEANORS: A HISTORY OF IMPEACHMENT FOR THE AGE OF TRUMP 235 (2019).

Legal historians thus generally agree that the constitutional term "high crimes and misdemeanors" is exceedingly broad, and capacious enough to encompass any kind of serious abuse of power, regardless of whether the abuse in question is prohibited independently by a criminal statute. During the Virginia ratifying convention, for example, a delegate questioned the allocation to the president of the power to pardon, arguing that it was susceptible to abuse. James Madison responded that a president who abused the pardon power, say by pardoning his own subordinates after directing them to act illegally, would be subject to impeachment. *Id.* at 264.

Clearly, there is no statute criminalizing abuse of the pardon power. The potentially infinite and unforeseeable ways in which a president might abuse power, combined with the capacious constitutional language, means, according to one scholar, "that *we can impeach a president whenever we should." Id.* (emphasis in original).

In the most recent presidential impeachment proceedings relating to President Trump (2019 and 2021), however, lawyers defending the president took the position that the term "high crimes and misdemeanors" must be construed narrowly, and understood to refer only to conduct that is actually criminal under existing law. On this view, a president's "mere" abuse of power, or breach of some political rather than criminal norm, does not furnish a constitutionally sufficient ground for impeachment. This argument appeared to gain traction with some senators, although it is difficult in this context to disentangle partisan motivations from deliberative legal judgments. However, it seems clear that if Congress does come to understand the scope of impeachable offenses in this narrower way, the utility of impeachment as a check on the misuse of official power will be greatly reduced, if not entirely undermined.

Uses of Impeachment. Impeachment has been used rarely throughout American history. On the federal level, in the entirety of American history, the House has voted to impeach only twenty individuals—fifteen judges, a senator, a cabinet secretary, and three presidents (Andrew Johnson, Bill Clinton, and Donald Trump, twice). Of these, only eight were convicted by the Senate, all of them judges. GERHARDT, *supra*, at 24-25. On the state level, although every state constitution provides for impeachment, nationwide only thirty state officials have been impeached and removed. Among more recent proceedings, these include the governors of Arizona (1988) and Illinois (2009), both on charges related to corruption in office.

Sometimes a credible threat of impeachment can produce a resignation, obviating the need to mount a full proceeding. In 1974, following the Watergate scandal, the House Judiciary Committee voted to adopt and refer to the full House articles of impeachment against President Richard Nixon. Two weeks later, before the House could vote on the referred articles, Nixon resigned.

In other countries that, like the United States, have adopted a presidential rather than a parliamentary system, even presidents have from time to time been impeached and removed from office. In 2016, Dilma Rousseff, the president of Brazil, was impeached on corruption charges, convicted, and removed. That same year, the president of South Korea, Park Geunhye, was impeached, and later removed, also on corruption charges. Eight other heads of state have been impeached and removed in the last four decades. *Id.* at 141-143.

Procedures. Over the years, Congress has worked out a procedure for impeachment proceedings. On the House side, articles of impeachment are generally developed by a committee after investigation and hearings, and then referred to the full House for a vote. The Senate has developed a set of trial-like procedures to assess guilt or innocence, involving lawyers, testimony, submission of evidence, and questioning. Although in some cases involving lower-level officials the Senate has delegated the conduct of an impeachment trial to a committee, in cases involving the president the Senate assigns the trial to the full chamber sitting as a whole. This of course means that an impeachment trial consumes enormous legislative resources, and during such a trial virtually all other business of Congress is deferred. This procedural burden furnishes an additional deterrent to the initiation of impeachment proceedings.

>> *Automatic Removal for Misbehavior.*   In many U.S. jurisdictions, certain government officials, including elected ones, are removed automatically from office upon being convicted of a crime. For example, in Kansas,

> Every person holding any office of trust or profit, under and by virtue of any of the laws of the state of Kansas, either state, district, county, township or city office, . . . who shall commit any act constituting a violation of any penal statute involving moral turpitude, shall forfeit such person's office and shall be ousted from such office in the manner hereinafter provided.

Kan. Code §60-1205. The statute goes on to create a procedure in which removal is initiated by petition of the state's Attorney General. In other jurisdictions, public ethics laws provide that removal from office is added automatically to punishments imposed by a court when sentencing a defendant who holds public office. E.g., Ark. Code §21-12-302.

Automatic removal can be triggered by conviction of traditional felonies like murder, assault, or larceny, but in many states it can also be triggered by types of misconduct that are specific to public officials. In Georgia, for instance, an official may be removed for "[m]alpractice, misfeasance, or malfeasance in office" or "[u]sing oppression or tyrannical partiality in the administration or under the color of his or her office." Ga. Code §45-11-4(b). In Washington, a public official commits a removal-triggering misdemeanor if "[h]e or she intentionally commits an unauthorized act under color of law; or . . . intentionally refrains from performing a duty imposed upon him or her by law." Wash. Code §9A.80.010.

Automatic removal provisions generally do not apply to a state's highest elected officials, such as the governor or lieutenant governor, because state constitutions typically specify impeachment as the vehicle for removal from those offices.

>> *Removal for Incompetence.*   At its adoption, the U.S. Constitution provided that the duties of the presidency "shall devolve on the Vice President" in case of the president's "inability to discharge the powers and duties of the said office." Art. II, §1, cl. 6. However, the document provided no guidance as to what counted as "inability," nor any procedure for determining when and how to apply the provision. This uncertainty, combined with the understandable fear among presidential aides and congressional leaders of being perceived as usurpers should they relieve a sitting president of his or her duties, has led government officials on several occasions to ignore or simply to tolerate the apparent incompetence of presidents. The most notable incident occurred in 1919, when Woodrow Wilson suffered a debilitating stroke. His condition was not disclosed to the public for a considerable period, and the White House maintained a façade of normalcy, although it is believed that his wife, Edith Wilson, performed many of his duties behind the scenes.

After John F. Kennedy's assassination in 1963, it became clear to Congress that medical technology might be able to keep presidents alive but unconscious or incapacitated, and that constitutional ambiguities about how to approach these situations needed to be resolved. The result was the Twenty-Fifth Amendment, ratified in 1965, which provides:

> Whenever the Vice President and a majority of either the principal officers of the executive departments or of such other body as Congress may by law provide, transmit to the President pro tempore of the Senate and the Speaker of the House of Representatives their written declaration that the President is unable to discharge the powers and duties of his office, the Vice President shall immediately assume the powers and duties of the office as Acting President.
>
> Thereafter, when the President transmits to the President pro tempore of the Senate and the Speaker of the House of Representatives his written declaration that no inability exists, he shall resume the powers and duties of his office unless the Vice President and a majority of either the principal officers of the executive department or of such other body as Congress may by law provide, transmit within four days to the President pro tempore of the Senate and the Speaker of the House of Representatives their written declaration that the President is unable to discharge the powers and duties of his office. Thereupon Congress shall decide the issue, assembling within forty-eight hours for that purpose if not in session. If the Congress, within twenty-one days after receipt of the latter written declaration, or, if Congress is not in session, within twenty-one days after Congress is required to assemble, determines by two-thirds vote of both Houses that the President is unable to discharge the powers and duties of his office, the Vice President shall continue to discharge the same as Acting President; otherwise, the President shall resume the powers and duties of his office.

The existence of the Amendment has not, however, made the possibility of its invocation less politically controversial, and it has never been used. Toward the end of his second term (1985–1989), Ronald Reagan, then in his late seventies, was thought by many to be suffering from early signs of dementia, yet those with authority under the Twenty-Fifth Amendment seemed to have no stomach for pursuing the possibility. Early in the Trump Administration, media reports claimed that discussions had been initiated in the Justice Department over whether Trump was exhibiting signs of incompetence sufficient to trigger removal under the Amendment, but nothing ever went beyond the discussion stage. According to the congressional committee investigating the January 6, 2021, insurrection at the U.S. Capitol, several cabinet-level officials again contemplated invoking the Twenty-Fifth Amendment when Trump repeatedly refused to accept the results of the election; again, nothing ever went beyond the discussion stage.

Is the Twenty-Fifth Amendment adequate to its task? Does it resolve only the easiest cases, such as when a president is unconscious and hospitalized, but leave beyond reach the more ambiguous and potentially concerning cases, such as when a president begins to suffer a decline in mental health or acuity? In a parliamentary system, a vote of no confidence is always available in such situations. Do presidential systems need a similarly flexible procedure? Is the stigma associated with being ousted from office on a vote of no confidence comparable to the stigma associated with being ousted from office under an incompetence provision?

>> *Recall Elections.*   A recall election is a special election held outside the ordinary sequence for the purpose of removing an incumbent official from office before the conclusion of his or her term. Recall elections first appeared in the early twentieth century, usually as part of a package of reforms sought by Progressives designed to enhance the democratic accountability of government officials. Other such reforms often included the initiative, referendum, and primary election. Progressives commonly held the view that state and local politics were dominated by party machines that monopolized candidate selection and then corrupted elected officials by demanding that they use their offices to deliver material benefits to party members in exchange for votes. Recall was thought to provide voters with the ability to bypass machine control over the electoral process and thus essentially to fire officials who were not behaving consistent with the public trust.

Nineteen states currently provide for recall elections. Most provisions for recall elections are contained in state constitutions. Generally, a recall election is held only if a petition circulated for that purpose gathers a sufficient number of signatures. For example, Article II, §14(b), of the California Constitution provides:

A petition to recall a statewide officer must be signed by electors equal in number to 12 percent of the last vote for the office, with signatures from each of 5 counties equal in number to 1 percent of the last vote for the office in the county. Signatures to recall Senators, members of the Assembly, members of the Board of Equalization, and judges of courts of appeal and trial courts must equal in number 20 percent of the last vote for the office.

Note the different signature requirements for statewide officials and those representing districts or other limited jurisdictions. Provisions for recall elections generally do not prescribe the grounds upon which a recall may be predicated; the California Constitution, for example, specifically provides: "Sufficiency of reason is not reviewable." Art. II, §14(a). Thus, voters may recall an official for any reason, or for no reason at all.

Recall elections have been rare, generally because proponents of recall have been unable to gather the requisite number of signatures. Among statewide officials, only four governors have been subjected to a recall election, and only two of those recall attempts have been successful. The most recent instance occurred in California in 2021, when Governor Gavin Newsom successfully fought off a recall attempt. The previous California gubernatorial recall attempt, however, in 2003 to recall Governor Gray Davis, was successful, and resulted in the election to the governorship of the actor and bodybuilder Arnold Schwarzenegger.

Fewer than thirty recall proceedings have been held to remove state legislators, with about half successful. However, the frequency of recall petitions and elections has been increasing, suggesting that the recall may be evolving into a tool of partisan disruption rather than a mechanism by which the public enforces expectations of good governance.

>> *Expulsion.* Article I, §5, cl.2 of the U.S. Constitution provides: "Each House may determine the rules of its proceedings, punish its members for disorderly behavior, and, with the concurrence of two thirds, expel a member." The language is obviously open-ended, suggesting that the grounds for expulsion are within the discretion of each chamber to decide. In what appears to be its only comment concerning the scope of the expulsion power, the Supreme Court said only that "[t]he right to expel extends to all cases where the offense is such as in the judgment of the [chamber] is inconsistent with the trust and duty of a member." *In re Chapman,* 166 U.S. 661 (1897).

Congress has used the power of expulsion rarely. Only five members of the House have been expelled, along with fifteen senators. Most of the expulsions occurred in the mid-nineteenth century and were based on charges of treason arising from secession and the Civil War. The most recent expulsion was of Rep. Jim Traficant of Ohio in 2002, following his conviction for bribery, racketeering, and tax evasion. Many more members of Congress have engaged in serious misbehavior of one kind or another over the years; often they have resigned or lost bids for re-election before the congressional machinery of expulsion might have been put into motion.

How useful as a practical matter is expulsion? To what extent might partisanship enter into the calculations of congressional leadership? Does any political benefit accrue to Senators or Representatives who vote to expel a colleague?

>> *Lustration.* Rooted in the Latin for "purification," *lustration* refers to the cleansing of the body politic by excluding from political participation officials and supporters of a prior regime. It is most often invoked as a principle of transitional justice when a liberal democratic form of government replaces an illiberal one. Lustration is generally justified as a kind of "ritual cleansing" that "paves the way for a moral and political renaissance." Luc Huyse, *Justice after Transition: On the Choices Successor Elites Make in Dealing with the Past,* 20 LAW & SOC. INQ. 51, 55 (1995). It also is understood to help assure the survival of the new regime against the threat of subversion from within by adherents of the prior regime. Lustration is typically applied to classes of people rather than specific individuals, and is retrospective in that it is triggered by past misbehavior.

In modern times, lustration has most often been invoked in transitions from communism to democracy. For example, when Germany was reunited following the fall of the Iron Curtain, lustration provisions disqualified nearly 55,000 former members of the East German regime from holding office in the reunited—and liberally democratic—nation. Tom Ginsburg, et al., *The Law of Democratic Disqualification,* 111 CAL. L. REV. ___ (forthcoming 2023). In many cases, lustration restrictions are temporary; Bulgaria disqualified certain Communist collaborators for a period of five years during its transition from communism, and Lithuania did so for ten years. *Id.*

A considerably older lustration provision is the comparatively little-known third section of the Fourteenth Amendment (1868):

No person shall be a Senator or Representative in Congress, or elector of President and Vice President, or hold any office, civil or military, under the United States, or under any state, who, having previously taken an oath, as a member of Congress, or as an officer of the United States, or as a member of any state legislature, or as an executive or judicial officer of any state, to support the Constitution of the United States, shall have engaged in insurrection or rebellion against the same, or given aid or comfort to the enemies thereof. But Congress may by a vote of two-thirds of each House, remove such disability.

This provision, adopted following the Civil War, was designed to prevent officials of the former Confederacy from holding public office in the future. It did not impose this disability on ordinary citizens who supported secession and the war, and in this sense was "narrow but deep. The exclusion from office embraced a theory that the political and military elites of the South were the only people who should bear the constitutional responsibility for the Civil War." Gerard N. Maglicocca, *Amnesty and Section Three of the Fourteenth Amendment*, 36 CONST. COMM. 87, 99 (2021).

Following ratification of the Fourteenth Amendment, Congress enacted the Ku Klux Klan Act, one provision of which imposed on federal prosecutors a duty to bring disqualification actions against state officials barred from service by Section Three. The Grant Administration promptly complied, bringing numerous *quo warranto* enforcement proceedings. In 1871, the Senate itself enforced Section 3 by refusing to seat Zebulon Vance, governor of North Carolina during the Civil War, who had been elected to the Senate. *Id.* at 108-111.

However, the main focus of congressional attention soon turned from the first sentence of Section 3, imposing disqualification, to the second sentence, permitting Congress to relieve the disability by legislation. Initially, amnesty was provided on a case-by-case basis through private bills introduced by individual legislators. Eventually, however, Congress began to stagger under the weight of thousands of such individual relief bills, and in 1872 enacted a broad amnesty law that lifted the effect of Section 3 for all but the highest officials of the Confederacy. 17 Stat. 142 (1872).

Section 3 would likely be of only historical interest today if not for the January 6, 2021, insurrection at the U.S. Capitol by supporters of outgoing president Donald Trump, who rioted in an attempt to prevent the counting of electoral votes that would formalize the victory of Joe Biden. Several lawsuits have been filed around the country in advance of the 2022 election cycle seeking to disqualify those who either participated directly in the insurrection or "have . . . given aid or comfort" to those who did. Application of Section 3 in these circumstances raises numerous legal questions. Was the January 6 riot an "insurrection or rebellion" within the meaning of Section 3? If so, is the disqualification imposed by Section 3 self-executing, or does it require implementing legislation by Congress? What counts as giving "aid or comfort" to the insurrectionists? Does it include making public statements in support of the rioters? Does it include, among incumbent members of Congress, opposing certification of the Electoral College vote count on false or frivolous grounds? Among those seeking state office, does it include making false claims about state election returns, or conspiring to alter them in Trump's favor, or pressuring election officials to do so?

In the 2022 election cycle, challenges have been brought under Section Three against the eligibility of a handful of Republican candidates on the ground that they actively encouraged or supported the January 6 insurrection. As of this writing, the only cases to proceed to adjudication have generated federal judicial rulings holding that the 1872 federal amnesty law operated only retrospectively rather than prospectively, and allowing the eligibility challenges to go forward through state administrative processes. See *Cawthorn v. Amalfi*, No. 22-1251 (4th Cir., May 24, 2022); *Greene v. Raffensberger*, 22-cv-1294-AT (N.D. Ga., Apr. 18, 2022). The Arizona Supreme Court dismissed a challenge to a candidate's eligibility under Section Three on the ground that it was not among the grounds for disqualification provided by Arizona law; the opinion suggested, without deciding, that disqualification under Section Three is reserved for Congress alone. *Hansen v. Finchem*, No. CV-22-0099-AP/EL (Ariz. S.Ct., May 9, 2022).

>> *Techniques of Militant Democracy: Party Bans and Individual Disqualification.* The term *militant democracy* is used by political theorists to describe the deployment by liberal democracies of illiberal tactics for their own self-preservation. More specifically, it refers to measures intended to exclude from participation in politics individuals or political parties that are opposed to democracy, yet compete democratically to gain power with the intent of using it, should they attain it, to destroy democracy. On this view, "[d]emocracy and democratic tolerance have been used for their own destruction." Karl Lowenstein, *Militant Democracy and Fundamental Rights, I*, 31 AM. POL. SCI. REV. 417, 423 (1937). The paradigm most often invoked is Weimar Germany of the 1930s, in which a democratic regime was overthrown by the Nazi Party from within, after it came to power legally by working within the system's rules. Once in power, it worked energetically to ensure it would remain perpetually in power, which required destroying democracy and replacing it with fascism.

Following the defeat of Germany in World War II, "[t]he major Allied heads of state committed themselves not only to the restoration of democracy, but to the complete elimination of the Nazi Party from German political life." SAMUEL ISSACHAROFF, FRAGILE DEMOCRACIES 44 (2015). The result is Article 21 of the German Basic Law (Constitution), which provides: "Parties that, by reason of their aims or the behavior of their adherents, seek to undermine or abolish the free democratic basic order or to endanger the existence of the Federal Republic of Germany shall be unconstitutional." This provision is judicially enforceable, and has been deployed to ban political parties which, like the Nazi Party, oppose liberal democracy, the foundation of the German constitutional order. Similar provisions banning anti-democratic or illiberal political parties, or those seeking to undermine the state through violence or terrorism, may be found in the constitutions or laws of Australia, Canada, Israel, New Zealand, Spain, and the United Kingdom, among others. *See, e.g.*, MILITANT DEMOCRACY (András Sajó, ed., 2004). In addition, the relevant laws sometimes permit similar restrictions to be placed on individuals, thereby barring them from political participation.

The principal difference between lustration provisions and party bans motivated by principles of militant democracy is that the former are retrospective, punishing only anti-democratic behavior that occurred in the past, usually under a prior regime, while the latter are prospective, holding out the prospect of civic disqualification for any future anti-democratic behavior.

Should militant democracy measures like these be applied in the United States? A recent study analyzing positions taken by the Republican Party finds that it has "retreated from upholding democratic norms in recent years," and that "[i]ts rhetoric is closer to authoritarian parties" such as those in Turkey, Poland, and Hungary. V-Dem Institute, *New Global Data on Political Parties* (Oct. 26, 2020). To the extent that the Trump wing of the party continues to control it, should it be considered an anti-democratic party, and subject, at least in principle, to sanctions, either as an organization or on its leaders? It seems doubtful that the First Amendment would permit such measures. Should it? Does the First Amendment work to protect democracy, or might it in some cases work to undermine it? Or might it at least create a domain of vulnerability that authoritarian-minded parties might exploit?

CHAPTER 7
THE PARTY SYSTEM

A. *INTRODUCTION: WHAT IS A POLITICAL PARTY?*

To many democratic polities, the idea that political parties play a significant role in democratic self-governance seems so obvious and normal that it is written expressly into the national constitution. The Swiss Constitution, for example, provides: "The political parties shall contribute to forming the opinion and will of the People." Art. 137. The German Constitution similarly provides: "Political parties shall participate in the formation of the political will of the people. They may be freely established. Their internal organisation must conform to democratic principles. . . ." Art. 21(1).

In the United States, in contrast, political parties have always occupied an uncertain role. The Constitution neither mentions nor makes any provision for political parties as mechanisms of governance, yet U.S. political parties, like parties elsewhere, have come to occupy an important role in political life both formally and informally. It is parties, not government, that recruit candidates for office. Parties, not government, mobilize citizens to vote. Parties inform voters about policy choices during elections, and they help translate citizen preferences into workable platforms of policy commitments suitable for actual governance. *See* Russell J. Dalton et al., Political Parties and Democratic Linkage: How Parties Organize Democracy 7 (2011). Parties even occupy a formal role in government itself: Congress has organized itself for many official purposes along party lines, writing into law the positions of Majority and Minority Leader of the Senate and House of Representatives, as well as the majority and minority Whips, and conferring on them various forms of legal authority. *See, e.g.,* 2 U.S.C. §§4501, 6134. Yet there is nothing in the Constitution that requires political parties to exist at all. Why have parties arisen? What functions do they serve?

George Washington

Farewell Address (Sept. 19, 1796)

. . . Let me now . . . warn you in the most solemn manner against the baneful effects of the spirit of party generally.

This spirit, unfortunately, is inseparable from our nature, having its root in the strongest passions of the human mind. It exists under different shapes in all governments, more or less stifled, controlled, or repressed; but in those of the popular form it is seen in its greatest rankness and is truly their worst enemy.

The alternate domination of one faction over another, sharpened by the spirit of revenge natural to party dissension, which in different ages and countries has perpetrated the most horrid enormities, is itself a frightful despotism. But this leads at length to a more formal and permanent despotism. The disorders and miseries which result gradually incline the minds of men to seek security and repose in the absolute power of an individual, and sooner or later the chief of some prevailing faction, more able or more fortunate than his competitors, turns this disposition to the purposes of his own elevation on the ruins of public liberty.

Without looking forward to an extremity of this kind (which nevertheless ought not to be entirely out of sight), the common and continual mischiefs of the spirit of party are sufficient to make it the interest and duty of a wise people to discourage and restrain it.

It serves always to distract the public councils and enfeeble the public administration. It agitates the community with ill-founded jealousies and false alarms; kindles the animosity of one part against another; foments occasional riot and insurrection. It opens the door to foreign influence and corruption, which find a facilitated access to the government itself through the channels of party passion. Thus the policy and the will of one country are subjected to the policy and will of another.

There is an opinion that parties in free countries are useful checks upon the administration of the government, and serve to keep live the spirit of liberty. This within certain limits is probably true; and in governments of monarchical cast patriotism may look with indulgence, if not with favor, upon the spirit of party, but in those of the popular character, in governments purely elective, it is a spirit not to be encouraged. From their natural tendency it is certain there will always be enough of that spirit for every salutary purpose; and there being constant danger of excess, the effort ought to be by force of public opinion to mitigate and assuage it. A fire not to be quenched, it demands a uniform vigilance to prevent its bursting into a flame, lest, instead of warming, it should consume.

———————————

>> *Republicanism and Anti-Party Politics.*   The generation of Americans that founded the United States and wrote its Constitution feared and despised political parties. The "root idea" of Anglo-American political thought concerning parties was that "parties are evil." RICHARD HOFSTADTER, THE IDEA OF A PARTY SYSTEM: THE RISE OF LEGITIMATE OPPOSITION IN THE UNITED STATES, 1780-1840 (1970), at 9. Thomas Jefferson denounced party affiliation as "the last degradation of a free and moral agent." Alexander Hamilton claimed that the goal of the Constitution was "to abolish factions, and to unite all parties for the general welfare." George Washington, as we have just seen, warned in his Farewell Address against "the baneful effects of the Spirit of Party." Even James Madison, one of the least dogmatic of the founders, thought that political parties were, at best, unavoidable evils in a free society, forces to be condemned, yet patiently endured.

The founders' antipathy toward political parties rested on their belief that parties were the vehicles by which self-interested groups and individuals—"factions," in their terminology—coordinated and pressed their efforts to seize political power. Once in possession of power, factions could be expected to use it to pursue their own private self-interest at the expense of the common good, a course of behavior that political theorists since Aristotle have judged to be a defining characteristic of bad government. These beliefs led the founders to hope, naively as it turns out, that political parties would not emerge on the American political scene, or if they did emerge, that their appearances would be infrequent and evanescent.

The eighteenth-century American conception of parties was heavily influenced by classical and medieval notions of the "balanced" or "mixed" constitution:

> Looked to as the guarantee of England's unrivaled freedom, the constitution was "mixed" or "balanced" in the sense that it incorporated the three distinct estates or constitutional orders into a single governing structure. The crown, the nobility, and the commoners were not just constitutional abstractions but easily recognized, discrete elements of both society and polity. By institutionalizing the three constitutional orders in the monarch, the House of Lords, and the House of Commons, each limiting the others' ability to engross power, history had presented eighteenth-century England with a constitution that offered the hope of eternal liberty. This far, nearly all the English polity was in agreement. . . .
>
> The conditions of society in the colonies encouraged their inhabitants to embrace the theory and practice of the constitutional party as an antidote to their own apparent instability. The absence of a fixed aristocracy or hierarchy, the wide availability of land, and the scarcity and high price of labor produced an unusual level of sociopolitical competition. The consequence was a broad unwillingness to defer to the social or political leadership of the moment. But democratization and division did not reflect a desire to do away with hierarchy and unity. Rather, instability prompted efforts to restore an order of unity and hierarchy in each colony. . . .
>
> [For example, in Massachusetts, resistance to royal] officeholders knew itself as the "popular party." Its unifying assumptions were that officeholding was just a species of avarice and that the king's first constitutional obligation was to protect his sworn subjects from his officers, especially in the colonies, where patronage went not to a local elite but instead to a transient class of ministerial favorites. . . . [This "popular party"] claimed to be the party of the entire legitimate polity. . . . The "popular party" was not a party in any modern sense; it had no institutional life or organization, and it disappeared when the crisis passed. . . . Revolution and the move from monarchy to republicanism were, then, a grand effort by a constitutional party to again eliminate party [of the factional variety] from the polity.

GERALD LEONARD, THE INVENTION OF PARTY POLITICS 22-25 (2002).

By the 1790s, the Federalist and Democratic-Republican parties were sufficiently well organized to serve, albeit weakly, as organizing forces in contesting the presidency in the post-Washington era. Upon the election of the Federalist candidate John Adams in 1796, the Democratic-Republican Party came to occupy the role of a Jeffersonian opposition party. Nevertheless, within the conceptual framework of the period, even Democratic-Republican opposition to the incumbent Federalist administration was understood by Jeffersonians not as the opposition by one faction to the dominance of another, but as an attempt by the "true" and organically complete polity to assert itself against an illegitimate seizure of power by an aristocratic, antipopular faction. *Id.* at 33. When Jefferson won the presidency in the bitterly contested election of 1800, Democratic-Republicans generally assumed that there would be no continuing need for party structure and organization now that the people's true representatives had regained power.

Notwithstanding the ideological commitments of eighteenth-century republicans, contemporary political scientists, unlike historians, tend to see the activities of Federalists and Jeffersonians as little more than early examples of the use of party organizations to facilitate ideologically driven contests for control over the policy-making apparatus of government. According to one influential account, political parties emerged during this period in response to "the attempts of Hamiltonians and Jeffersonians to win a consistent pattern of victories on policy . . . and to establish undeniable precedents" on the great ideological issues of the day, most significantly the degree of power to be exercised by the national government. Parties, according to this account, were merely organizational innovations that enabled opposing groups of committed ideologues to overcome the organizational problems inherent in collective action. JOHN ALDRICH, WHY PARTIES? THE ORIGIN AND TRANSFORMATION OF POLITICAL PARTIES IN AMERICA 77 (1995).

≫ *Jacksonian Democracy and the Rise of the Modern Party.* The Jacksonian Democrats of the 1820s and '30s are generally credited with inventing the modern, national political party. Under the leadership of Martin Van Buren, perhaps the nation's first "political operative," the Democrats used party resources and organizational structures as a means to promote and contest public policies, identify and support candidates, mobilize public opinion, and turn out voters at elections for offices at every level. The Democrats under Jackson also became enthusiastic dispensers of political patronage for the purpose of securing the support and loyalty of party members. The effectiveness of Democratic Party organization and tactics contributed greatly to the demise of its main opponent, the Whig Party, and forced all other subsequent political parties to pursue similar tactics to compete effectively.

The idea of organizing essentially permanent structures for the purpose of effectively contesting political offices represented a substantial departure from the republican model of politics, in which all-inclusive popular parties arose, spontaneously and temporarily, to assert the people's sovereignty and then disappeared from the scene, their services no longer required. The individuals behind this change in organizational mode — upstate New Yorkers who, with Van Buren at their head, became known as the "Albany Regency" —

> came from a social class for which the perquisites and connections, the marginal advantages and limited prominence of small offices were much esteemed as means of making one's way toward the top. What they

had was, by and large, hard earned, and there was a distinct edge of class resentment in their attitude toward patrician politicians who assumed that office was a prerogative of social rank that could be claimed without the expenditure of years of work in party-building and without the exacting discipline of party loyalty. . . . They were . . . outside and somewhat estranged from political leadership by inherited wealth and position or personal brilliance and glamour. They thought that negotiation and the management of opinion were better than leadership through deference. . . .

As a combat organization, the party would demand discipline of an almost military severity. . . . Personal careers, like personal views, were to be sacrificed to the common interest. The politician was expected to pursue his personal advancement, but not aggressively, and certainly not outside the pattern settled by his political associates. Humility, Van Buren later suggested . . . , ought to be the governing rule. . . . The central value of party unity to an organization of men of their origins seems to have been quite clear to the Regency spokesmen. Party unity was the democrat's answer to the aristocrat's wealth, prestige, and connections. In these they could never match him, but by presenting a united front in party affairs, they could give democracy a more than compensating foundation of strength.

Hofstadter, *supra*, at 241-246.

Despite their organization and active contestation of office, Jacksonian Democrats did not see themselves as dedicated to advancing the interests of any particular segment of society against any other segment, and in that sense they did not conceive of themselves as a "faction" in the republican sense.

Van Buren did not conceive of this party organization that he celebrated as a mere electoral machine or as an agent of a particular set of social or economic measures or even ideologies. Such a party he would have regarded as factious. His party was the constitutional party of the sovereign people. . . . But in Van Buren's hands the constitutional party [of earlier times] became a mass party, organized down to the last democrat in the land. It anticipated no single millennial victory but permanent triumph through permanent constitutional struggle, every election a ratification election for Van Buren's partyist Constitution of pure majoritarianism and strict construction.

Leonard, *supra*, at 43. In this sense, however, the Jacksonian conception of party took a significant step in the direction of the modern model:

most remarkable, and most novel, in the Regency defense of parties . . . was their forthright commitment to the idea . . . that permanent competition between parties is of positive social value. "The spirit of party," one member said, was "the vigilant watchman over the conduct of those in power." . . . Active party competition would thus inform the people, cure apathy, check dishonesty and corruption, and become conducive to the larger social peace.

Hofstadter, *supra*, at 251. Thus, party competition, far from being destructive and antithetical to achievement of the common good, could now be seen as a productive and reliable method of assuring the common good.

>> *Progressivism and Nonpartisanship.* For the most part, the ideology of parties worked out in the Jacksonian era has continued to provide the dominant framework for thinking about political parties. A significant exception, however, is the Progressive Era of the late nineteenth and early twentieth centuries, during which an updated form of republicanism held sway: the ideology of nonpartisanship.

In the typical nonpartisan election, candidates do not take up party labels and there is no overt party competition. Candidates are to be chosen not on the basis of their policy views, but on the basis of their general competence and qualifications for the office in question. Indeed, nonpartisanship is premised on the Progressive belief that most issues of governance — and particularly of local governance — are inherently apolitical because they admit of only one correct answer, a belief that makes ideologically oriented political competition superfluous. As New York City's reformist mayor Fiorello LaGuardia once put it, "there is no Democratic or Republican way of cleaning the streets." Any centralized nominating organization that functions like a party in a partisan system is, in nonpartisanship, conceived to be more like a committee of the electorate-at-large, acting on behalf of the entire group in exercising a limited, delegated responsibility, and in this sense harkens back noticeably to the republican conception of a political party as representing the unified and organic interests of the entire populace. *See* Samuel Haber, Efficiency and Uplift: Scientific Management in the Progressive Era, 1890-1920 (1964), at 102-103; Leon Weaver, Nonpartisan Elections in Local Government: Some Key Issues and Suggested Guide Lines for Decision-Making 20 (Citizens Research Council of Michigan 1971).

Indeed, it has been suggested that the ideal of nonpartisanship has so thoroughly infiltrated American political culture that, quite contrary to earlier periods, there is now a widely recognized social benefit to declaring oneself an "independent" for purposes of political self-identification. "Political independents . . . are viewed more positively than are partisans: independents are perceived as 'free thinkers' who are 'more open to the truth' and able to set aside the 'dogma' of partisanship." Samara Klar and Yanna Krupnikov, Independent Politics: How American Disdain for Parties Leads to Political Inaction 8 (2016).

During the ascendancy of Progressivism, which did not fully decline until the 1950s, Progressive activists made significant headway in institutionalizing nonpartisanship as a method of electoral politics. As a result, nonpartisan elections are presently used in a majority of local American jurisdictions. On the state level, Nebraska remains to this day the great exemplar of Progressive experimentation. Unlike any other state, Nebraska has a unicameral state legislature, and election to the legislature is on a nonpartisan ticket. Neb. Const. art. III, §7.

The merits of nonpartisanship as an electoral system have long been debated. One common complaint is that nonpartisanship "demobilizes" the electorate — i.e., discourages its participation — by flattening the terrain of contestation, making politics more technocratic and thus less interesting, and depriving voters of the motivation to turn out and vote that has historically been present in elections that are contested by competing political parties. *See* Neal Caren, *Big City, Big Turnout?*

Participation in American Cities, 29 J. URBAN AFF. 31 (2007) (concluding that non-partisanship is associated with lower turnout). Another unintended consequence of nonpartisan elections may be that voters, deprived of party cues to help them locate candidates on the spectrum of partisan views, tend to place undue weight on incumbency. Brian F. Schaffner, et al., *Teams without Uniforms: The Nonpartisan Ballot in State and Local Elections*, 54 POL. RES. Q. 7 (2001).

Austin Ranney

The Doctrine of Responsible Party Government (1954)

The doctrine of party government rests upon the belief that, in a modern, thickly populated society like that of the United States, democracy should be conceived of as popular *control* over government, and not as popular *participation* in the day-to-day activities of government. In such a society, the argument runs, governmental problems are so complex that the great bulk of the people can have neither the leisure nor the special training required to formulate specific and workable measures for their solution. . . . In a democratic society, therefore, the people, through some kind of "institutional midwifery," make known their wants to the government's rulers, i.e., those who at the moment are carrying on its day-to-day activities. They also exercise *control* over the government in this sense: If half-plus-one of the people feel their wants are not being satisfied, they can, in peaceful and orderly elections coming at frequent intervals, replace the set of rulers in power with an alternate set, an "opposition," which all along has been "keeping its ear to the ground" to learn and anticipate the people's wants, pointing out the errors and deficiencies of the rulers in power, and which now stands ready itself to assume power. Thus the people control the government by determining who shall carry on its activities. There is plenty of popular participation in government, but not in the delusive sense of participation in the specific work of governmental agencies. . . .

The second major contention of the doctrine of party government is that the popular control over government which is the essence of democracy can best be established by the popular choice between and control over alternate responsible political parties; for only such parties can provide the coherent, unified sets of rulers who will assume collective responsibility to the people for the manner in which government is carried on. Only in the alternation in office of such parties can the popular will be translated into governmental action.

Party government in its most ideal form, according to its proponents, should work in the following manner: There must exist at least two (and preferable only two) unified, disciplined political parties. Each has its conception of what the people want and a program of various measures designed to satisfy those wants. In a pre-election campaign each attempts to convince a majority of the people that its program will best do what the people want done. In the election each voter votes for a particular candidate in his district, primarily because that candidate is a member of the party which the voter wants to take power, and only secondarily because he prefers the individual qualities of one candidate to those of the other. The party which secures a majority of the offices of government in the election then takes over the entire power of the government and the entire responsibility for what the government does. It then proceeds to put its program into effect. Or perhaps unforeseen circumstances arise which make the party decide to alter or even abandon its program. In any event, at the next election the people decide whether, on the whole, they approve of the general direction that the party in power has been taking — in short, whether their wants are being satisfied. If the answer is yes, they return that party to power; if the answer is no, they replace it with the opposition party.

This is what is meant by "responsible party government." Such a government, its proponents argue, would perform at least three indispensable functions in a truly democratic society. In the first place, by selecting from the myriad public issues the particular ones upon which elections are to be fought, parties would enable the people to express themselves effectively upon those issues. . . .

To be sure, parties, by choosing only certain issues to debate, deprive the people of the chance to express their will on other issues. This point, however, involves a less severe criticism of the party-government system than one may think; for it is highly doubtful whether, in the absence of parties and their channelizing function, there would often exist anything approaching a majority-opinion on the issues which parties leave alone. In any event, party government would enable the people to choose effectively a general program, a general direction for government to take, as embodied in a set of leaders committed to that program. It might limit the people's theoretical (but, in the absence of any organizing agency, meaningless) freedom of choice among the almost infinite number of possible specific measures; but it would give them the *effective* choice between alternative general programs.

In the second place, the advocates of responsible party government argue that it would accomplish the important function of energizing and activating public opinion. How this function might be accomplished did not concern the classical theorists of democracy. The antidemocrats seem to have believed that under any conditions the people were incapable of displaying the concern with public affairs required by democracy; and the democrats apparently assumed that, if given the power, the people would automatically take up the responsibility for their government. . . . The experience of some two-hundred years of popular government, maintain the party-government theorists, has indicated that some sort of extragovernmental agency is needed to energize and activate public opinion. Party government, they believe, would provide such an agency. . . .

Finally, its friends believe, party government would establish popular control over government by making the group of rulers in power *collectively* responsible to the people. . . .

To complete the picture of what is involved in the doctrine of party government, it must be observed that its proponents warn that several conditions must be fulfilled if it is to exist. In the absence of any of these conditions, parties cannot be expected to do their job. First and foremost, they say, party government requires the existence of parties which have sufficient coherence and discipline for their members to display solidarity on all great questions of public policy. After all, party government is based upon the substitution of *party* for individual responsibility. If the members of each party frequently desert their party's line on questions of public policy, then the people cannot effectively either blame or reward either party, *as a party* for what it does or does not do. Party responsibility, upon which party government depends, cannot exist in such a situation.

The problem then becomes: How do we go about getting parties whose members *will* stick together on public questions? And that, in turn, leads to the examination of the further questions: What should constitute party membership? Just who should be considered as the party members from whom we may expect this solidarity and discipline? . . .

Those who advance the party-government position agree, although some stress this point much more than others, that the existing political parties are performing a significant and valuable role in the American system, and that the nation is notably better off with them than it would be with no parties at all. They also agree, however, that measured by the standard outlined above, American parties do not provide anything like "responsible party government." They document this judgment by pointing to certain characteristics of the existing party system.

In the first place, they point out, American major parties do not have any real programs—they do not "stand" for anything. Their platforms are for the most part merely collections of generalities designed primarily with an eye to offending as few people as possible. It is standard practice for them either to equivocate on or to ignore completely the pressing and divisive issues of the day. Almost never is there any important difference between the programs of the two parties. In consequence their propaganda beclouds the issues and befuddles the voters. Seldom does it clarify or educate, as the doctrine of party government says it should.

In the second place, the party-government writers charge that American parties seldom display unity upon matters of public policy. Legislative votes or any other governmental action is very rarely along strict party lines. Thus, in terms of who does what, it is often very difficult for the voter to determine what *the* position of either party on such questions is. Since party lines break down so easily, one party is about as "responsible" as the other for what the government does or does not do, regardless of which party is in "power." This means that the people can for the most part vote negatively: They can turn the party in power out of office as a punishment for its failure to satisfy their wants, but they cannot reasonably expect the opposition party to stand behind its announced program, nor can they reasonably expect a significant change in the way things are going. This, in turn, means that the people are deprived of the chance to make a clear and effective choice at the polls. It means that the American party system is not doing the job of translating the popular will into governmental action.

These writers conclude that the deficiencies of the existing American party system, when measured by the standard of responsible party government, add up to this: In a system of party government the parties seek power, not as an end in itself, but in order that they may put their programs into governmental action. They therefore conceive of their job as having two aspects: winning elections in order to get power and using the power they win to carry out their programs. Thus each party organizes its forces with the unity and discipline necessary *before* elections in the campaigning activities necessary to win power and *after* elections in the governmental activities necessary to put their programs into law.

In the American system, on the other hand, the parties consider winning power to be their sole end. When power is won, their job is completed. Thus each

party demonstrates a considerable measure of unity and discipline in the campaigning activities necessary to elect the party ticket; but neither demonstrates (or apparently feels under any real obligation to demonstrate) such unity and discipline *after*
winning power as it would need to put its program into law. In their capacity as
agencies for organizing and conducting elections, they are highly developed; and
in their capacity as agencies for carrying on government, they are underdeveloped.
Yet no political party, these writers argue, can deny its obligations as an agency for
carrying on government; and the result of the deficiencies of American parties is
not that they completely fail to fulfill these obligations, but only that they fulfill
them inadequately and with a minimum of responsibility.

The responsible party model came to prominence in the 1940s and 1950s, particularly after an influential special panel of the American Political Science Association elaborated the theory in *Toward a More Responsible Two-Party System*, 44 AM. POL.
SCI. REV. SUPP. (1950). Does this model accurately capture contemporary public
ideas about the party system? How different is it from the ideas of party developed
during the republican and Jacksonian periods?

>> *Interest Pluralism, Political Parties, and Factions.*   Another view of political par-
ties is advanced by the interest pluralism approach to democracy. Reread the selection by Anthony Downs in Chapter 1. Recall that interest pluralism conceives of
parties as representatives of the interests of their members. On this model, voters
vote for candidates from particular parties because they believe that those parties,
when in office, will use their power in ways that provide more benefits to the voter
than would competing parties. Parties, in turn, compete with one another for the
power and prestige that office-holding brings rather than due to any ideological
commitment.

This view of parties accords well with the republican suspicion of parties as
mere factions. Yet, according to interest pluralism, this kind of factional behavior actually is beneficial because, in the end, social utility is maximized when and
because political parties compete actively with one another to satisfy the selfish
interests of their members. Thus, the criticisms of the responsible party model to
which Ranney alludes become virtues of the party system rather than weaknesses.

This theory, however, depends upon the responsiveness of parties' policy commitments to the preferences of voters. If, as Downs maintained, parties are essentially teams of politicians competing with one another for public office, and gaining
office requires catering to public opinion, then the utility-maximizing potential of
party competition might be realized. But what if interest pluralism characterizes
not only relations *between* parties, but the internal organization of parties themselves? On this view, parties are so *internally* pluralistic that they are generally incapable of generating coherent policy packages upon which to compete for votes.
Instead, American parties tend to be loose coalitions of "organized policy demanders," each of which seeks first to gain control of the party and its commitments, and
then to win office – not to satisfy the public, but to "capture and use government
for [its] particular goals." Kathleen Bawn, et al., *A Theory of Political Parties: Groups,
Policy Demands and Nominations in American Politics*, 10 PERSP. POLS. 571, 571, 575

(2012). These kinds of factionalized parties, on this view, are able to succeed not by figuring out what the public wants and then providing it, but by exploiting the ignorance and apathy of a substantial segment of the electorate.

More recently, it has been suggested that the preceding model no longer characterizes American political parties in the age of Trump, in which parties have indeed differentiated themselves in broad, ideological terms. Alternatively, it has been argued that the model of parties as coalitions of "intense policy demanders" still characterizes the Democratic Party, which is little more than "a coalition of discrete identity groups that lack an overarching political structure to tie their policy demands together," but not the Republican Party, which is in fact united by "an overarching ideology based on a set of principles about the role of government and the role of the United States in world affairs." Nolan McCarty and Eric Schickler, *On the Theory of Parties*, 21 Ann. Rev. Pol. Sci. 175, 188-189 (2018).

⟫ *Where Are Political Parties?* In one of the most important works of political science written in the twentieth century, V.O. Key elaborated an important aspect of political parties that complicates any attempt to generalize about their behavior. The term "party," Key observed, is applied to describe at least three different phenomena. First, the term "party" is often used to describe those who, "[w]ithin the body of voters as a whole, . . . regard themselves as party members." These individuals "react in characteristic partisan ways to public issues," but are not highly organized. This group may be termed the "party-in-the-electorate." A second usage of the term refers to "the group of more or less professional political workers. The Republican national committeemen, the Republican state central committees, the Republican county chairmen, and all the men and women who do the work of the political organization." This group is the professional political party, the party organization itself. Finally, a third group consists of party members who actually hold public office: the "party-in-the-government," which may include "the President, groups of his party in both House and Senate, and the heads of executive departments." V.O. Key, Jr., Politics, Parties, and Pressure Groups (1958).

These three groups need not and often do not work together in a coordinated way. Given this disjunction, does it make sense to speak of parties as being accountable to the electorate? To speak of parties as carrying out governmental policies? What ramifications, if any, might Key's view have for the legal regulation of parties?

⟫ *What Kind of Party System Do We Have?* In the 1950s, American political scientists bemoaned what they claimed was the failure of the American party system to live up to the responsible party model. The parties, they complained, did not present clear and distinct choices, but instead overlapped considerably in their ideological commitments and in the ideology of their memberships and elected officials. Party loyalty and discipline was poor. Party leadership was dispersed and ineffective rather than clear and commanding. As a result, the party system was not working to achieve the necessary degree of electoral accountability. *Toward a More Responsible Two-Party System*, 44 Am. Pol. Sci. Rev. Supp. (1950).

How are things today? In the words of one observer, "Be careful what you wish for." Alan Abramowitz, The Disappearing Center: Engaged Citizens, Polarization, and American Democracy ix (2010). In the early twenty-first century, political parties are more ideologically distinct than they have been in half a century, and American politics is sharper, louder, more divisive, more polarized, and nastier than most people can remember—more so than many people like it. Bipartisanship seems dead; where cooperation used to be routine, now it is news-worthy. Does this give us the kind of government accountability that the responsi-ble party model predicts?

Few seem to think so. According to one account, effective party-based account-ability, no matter how desirable in theory, is rendered impossible in the United States by other aspects of the constitutional plan. On this view, responsible party government requires "strongly majoritarian political institutions that allow the winning party team to implement the policies chosen by the voters." This result is blocked, however, by "a number of important antimajoritarian features" such as lifetime appointment of judges, overrepresentation of minorities in the Senate and the Electoral College, bicameralism, and separation of powers. ABRAMOWITZ, *supra*, at 6, 160-165.

Another account suggests that the dispersed nature of the American party system interferes with both its responsiveness to public opinion, particularly at the political center, and the linkage that should exist in theory between electoral results and policy accountability. Here, the argument is that highly local and fre-quently informal organizations operating under the umbrella of national parties so thoroughly control access to candidacy that they exercise undue—and unsystem-atic and unpredictable—influence over the ideological and policy commitments of the national parties. SETH E. MASKET, NO MIDDLE GROUND: HOW INFORMAL PARTY ORGANIZATIONS CONTROL NOMINATIONS AND POLARIZE LEGISLATURES (2009). A variant of this account argues that parties have not just been weakened and dis-persed, but have been for many purposes essentially replaced by other kinds of organizations with far less democratic pedigree.

> "Outside" groups—groups that are neither official party entities nor can-didate campaigns—have taken over a startling array of core party func-tions. These groups do not just run campaign ads. They mobilize voters, test messages, organize donors, maintain comprehensive voter databases, employ long-term campaign workers, and make major strategic choices in individual campaigns and across multiple races.

Joseph Fishkin and Heather K. Gerken, *The Party's Over:* McCutcheon, *Shadow Par-ties, and the Future of the Party System*, 2014 SUP. CT. REV. 175, 176. According to this view, the modern party is not a free-standing, independent organization, but one intertwined with all manner of private organizations such as "the NRA, the teach-ers' unions, and the Heritage Foundation." *Id.* at 187. In these private organiza-tions, moreover, large monetary donors can acquire considerably more influence than they ordinarily can in a traditional party organization. *Id.* at 194.

How is it possible for American parties to be simultaneously more ideologi-cally organized and polarized than they have been for decades, *and* weak, function-ally dispersed, and thoroughly colonized by private organizations?

>> ***The Legal Treatment of Parties: The First Amendment Right of Association.***   Even though the Constitution makes no mention of political parties, it is in some ways highly relevant to parties and their operations. Most importantly, a political party is, in at least some of its aspects and functions, a prominent example of an expressive

association within the meaning of the First Amendment: it is a group of people who associate in order to advance their beliefs. Any government attempt to regulate political parties must therefore comport with the First Amendment freedom of association.

One of the earliest cases to recognize an expressive right of association was *NAACP v. Button*, 371 U.S. 415 (1963), in which the Court invalidated several Virginia rules governing attorney behavior that were designed to thwart the NAACP's ability to locate potential plaintiffs to bring racial discrimination challenges to segregated school systems. The Court said: "In the context of NAACP objectives, litigation is not a technique of resolving private differences; it is a means for [achieving] equality of treatment. . . . It is [a] form of political expression." The Court observed that "the First and Fourteenth Amendments protect certain forms of orderly group activity. Thus we have affirmed the right 'to engage in association for the advancement of beliefs and ideas.'" Even though the NAACP is not "a conventional political party," for the NAACP, "litigation may be the most effective form of political association." The Court has gone on to recognize the First Amendment associational interests of many private organizations including clubs like the Jaycees and Rotary Club. *See Roberts v. U.S. Jaycees*, 468 U.S. 609 (1984); *Board of Directors of Rotary International v. Rotary Club of Duarte*, 481 U.S. 537 (1987).

Where political parties are concerned, the Court has applied the First Amendment right of association in the following terms:

> For more than [three] decades, this Court has recognized the constitutional right of citizens to create and develop new political parties. The right derives from the First and Fourteenth Amendments and advances the constitutional interest of likeminded voters to gather in pursuit of common political ends, thus enlarging the opportunities of all voters to express their own political preferences. See *Anderson v. Celebrezze*, 460 U.S. 780, 793-794 (1983); *Williams v. Rhodes*, 393 U.S. 23, 30-31 (1968). To the degree that a State would thwart this interest by [regulating the activities of political parties], we have called for the demonstration of a corresponding interest sufficiently weighty to justify the limitation, see *Anderson, supra,* at 789, and we have accordingly required any severe restriction to be narrowly drawn to advance a state interest of compelling importance. . . .

Norman v. Reed, 502 U.S. 279, 288 (1992).

>>   ***Party Control over Membership.***   If a political party is, for constitutional purposes, akin to a private club, may it restrict membership to those it considers desirable? In *Duke v. Cleland*, 954 F.2d 1526 (11th Cir.), *cert. denied*, 502 U.S. 1086 (1992), the Eleventh Circuit said yes. In the 1992 presidential election campaign, David Duke, a former leader of the Ku Klux Klan, announced his candidacy for the Republican Party's presidential nomination. Under Georgia law, presidential primary candidates are selected in a two-step process. The Secretary of State first draws up a list of candidates nationally recognized through news media reports as "aspirants" for President and who are members of political parties holding a primary election. This list is then submitted to a party committee that selects the candidates to appear on the party's primary election ballot. The Republican Party's committee declined to place Duke's name on the party's primary ballot. The committee defended its decision on the ground that Duke was "ideologically outside the party." Duke challenged the Georgia law permitting the party leadership to remove his name from the ballot.

The court upheld the challenged law. The party's First Amendment right of association, the court held, "encompasses its decision to exclude Duke as a candidate on the Republican Primary ballot because Duke's political beliefs are inconsistent with those of the Republican Party. . . . [P]arty procedures to guard against intrusion by those with inconsistent ideologies are legitimate." The court was careful to note, however, that Georgia law did not prohibit Duke from running for President as an independent candidate.

Less dramatically, but perhaps more importantly, a political party may control its membership through the pedestrian expedient of controlling the use of its name. In *Norman v. Reed*, 502 U.S. 279 (1992), the Supreme Court held that a state may prohibit new political associations of citizens from using the name of an established political party without obtaining formal permission from the established party. By permitting parties to police the use of their names, such a regulatory scheme would allow parties to conduct as well a kind of ideological policing of those who wish to run as party candidates.

B.   *BALLOT ACCESS AND THE TWO-PARTY SYSTEM*

In turning now to the constitutional jurisprudence governing the regulation of political parties, we begin with the issue of political competition. Before the twentieth century, legal questions regarding who could run for office — questions that today are addressed under the legal heading of "ballot access" — never arose because partisan politics was essentially unregulated. Although the state controlled polling places and provided officials to receive and count ballots, anyone could run for office because the ballot itself was unregulated: any piece of paper that indicated a vote for a particular person for a particular office counted as an acceptable ballot. As a result, political parties exercised a great degree of control over elections. Each party printed its own ballots listing its own candidates for all offices to be filled at the election. Voters thus tended to choose their candidates simply by accepting ballots from agents of the parties of their choice, who diligently patrolled polling places, offering ballots to prospective voters. Voters who wished to vote a split ticket generally had to accept a ballot from one party and physically scratch out the names of candidates for whom they did not wish to vote, and then write in the names of the candidates they supported. Because many more offices were elective during the nineteenth century than is now the case, ballots were often very long, frequently listing dozens of offices. Voters rarely had sufficient information to form preferences for all but the most prominent offices on party ballots, and so tended to take the path of least resistance and vote a straight ticket. Also, nineteenth-century polling places were often anarchic by contemporary standards, with party agents offering alcohol or cash bribes to voters who took their ballots, frequently accompanied by a healthy dose of veiled physical intimidation. Ballots were exchanged in full public view, and it was difficult for a voter either to hide his ballot from the crowd, or to conceal the making of any alterations to the ballot. At some polling places, mobs of partisans patrolled the area around the voting window, threatening violence against those who voted for the opposing party, and in some cases following through on the threat.

Progressive reformers of the late nineteenth and early twentieth century disapproved intensely of virtually every aspect of this voting process, especially the degree to which it was controlled by parties. These reformers believed that elections should be controlled by the state, an impartial entity that could take partisan passions out of the act of voting, and mounted a highly successful reform campaign to do just that. The centerpiece of this reform was the introduction of the secret (or "Australian") ballot. Under this system, familiar to contemporary voters, the state—not the parties—prepares a single, uniform, official ballot. Voters then cast these ballots secretly, in the privacy of a voting booth. Once the state began to control the ballot, however, it had to make decisions that in the past took care of themselves: who, precisely, could appear on the ballot? And by what criteria were these decisions to be informed? The introduction of the secret ballot thus inserted the government deeply into the political process.

1. Access to the Official Ballot

Every state has some sort of rules governing whose names can be placed on the official election ballot and under what circumstances. One might ask: why are such rules necessary? Why can't everyone who is eligible and who wants to be considered by the electorate get his or her name on the ballot? The Court addressed these questions in a line of decisions beginning with *Williams v. Rhodes*, 393 U.S. 23 (1968). There, the Ohio American Independent Party and the Socialist Labor Party both sought to place their presidential nominees on the general election ballot. Under Ohio law, to secure a spot on the ballot, a new party had to obtain signatures from qualified voters in a number equal to 15 percent of the number of ballots cast in the immediately preceding gubernatorial election. The Republican and Democratic Parties, in contrast, were allowed by law to retain their positions on the ballot so long as their candidates attracted at least 10 percent of the votes cast in the last gubernatorial election. Neither party was required to collect any signatures at all. Furthermore, Ohio law did not permit candidates to run as independents; they were required to run as the nominee of a political party. These requirements were challenged as a violation of equal protection.

Writing for the Court, Justice Black invalidated the minor party ballot access provisions:

> The State . . . contends that it has absolute power to put any burdens it pleases on the selection of electors because of the First Section of the Second Article of the Constitution, providing that "Each State shall appoint, in such Manner as the Legislature thereof may direct, a Number of Electors . . ." to choose a President and Vice President. There, of course, can be no question but that this section does grant extensive power to the States to pass laws regulating the selection of electors. But . . . we must

reject the notion that Art. II, §1, gives the States power to impose burdens [in violation of] the Fourteenth Amendment. . . .

In the present situation the state laws place burdens on two different, although overlapping, kinds of rights — the right of individuals to associate for the advancement of political beliefs, and the right of qualified voters, regardless of their political persuasion, to cast their votes effectively. Both of these rights, of course, rank among our most precious freedoms. . . .

The Ohio laws before us give the two old, established parties a decided advantage over any new parties struggling for existence and thus place substantially unequal burdens on both the right to vote and the right to associate. The right to form a party for the advancement of political goals means little if a party can be kept off the election ballot and thus denied an equal opportunity to win votes. So also, the right to vote is heavily burdened if that vote may be cast only for one of two parties at a time when other parties are clamoring for a place on the ballot.

Applying strict scrutiny, the Court found the government interests insufficiently compelling:

The State . . . claims that [it] may validly promote a two-party system in order to encourage compromise and political stability. The fact is, however, that the Ohio system does not merely favor a "two-party system"; it favors two particular parties — the Republicans and the Democrats — and in effect tends to give them a complete monopoly. . . . Competition in ideas and governmental policies is at the core of our electoral process and of the First Amendment freedoms. New parties struggling for their place must have the time and opportunity to organize in order to meet reasonable requirements for ballot position, just as the old parties have had in the past.

Ohio [also] points out . . . that if three or more parties are on the ballot, it is possible that no one party would obtain 50% of the vote, and the runner-up might have been preferred to the plurality winner by a majority of the voters. Concededly, the State does have an interest in attempting to see that the election winner be the choice of a majority of its voters. But to grant the State power to keep all political parties off the ballot until they have enough members to win would stifle the growth of all new parties working to increase their strength from year to year. . . .

Why would a state require as a condition of ballot access that a candidate for office be the designated candidate of an established political party? What kind of an interest does a state have in promoting any kind of party system, much less a two-party system? Why should the state have to confer upon a party an imprimatur of official recognition before that party's nominees can qualify for a place on the ballot?

» *Filing Fees.* Signature requirements are not the only way that states regulate access to the ballot; sometimes filing fees have been used. In *Bullock v. Carter*, 405 U.S. 134 (1972), the Court invalidated a Texas filing fee statute that required candidates for County Commissioner to pay a filing fee of over $1,400, and candidates for County Judge to pay $6,300. The challenge was brought by otherwise qualified candidates who were unable to afford the fees. Relying on *Harper v. Virginia Board of Elections*, 383 U.S. 663 (1966), the Court analyzed the filing fee as a disfavored wealth restriction on the right to vote of supporters of the plaintiff candidates. "The initial and direct impact of filing fees," the Court explained, "is felt by aspirants for office, rather than voters, and the Court has not heretofore attached such fundamental status to candidacy as to invoke a rigorous standard of review." However, the Court said,

> the rights of voters and the rights of candidates do not lend themselves to neat separation; laws that affect candidates always have at least some theoretical, correlative effect on voters. . . . Many potential office seekers lacking both personal wealth and affluent backers are in every practical sense precluded from seeking the nomination of their chosen party, no matter how qualified they might be, and no matter how broad or enthusiastic their popular support. The effect of this exclusionary mechanism on voters is neither incidental nor remote. Not only are voters substantially limited in their choice of candidates, but also there is the obvious likelihood that this limitation would fall more heavily on the less affluent segment of the community, whose favorites may be unable to pay the large costs required by the Texas system. To the extent that the system requires candidates to rely on contributions from voters in order to pay the assessments, a phenomenon that can hardly be rare in light of the size of the fees, it tends to deny some voters the opportunity to vote for a candidate of their choosing; at the same time it gives the affluent the power to place on the ballot their own names or the names of persons they favor.

Applying strict scrutiny, the Court invalidated the fees. The Court recognized that Texas had valid reasons for imposing filing fees:

> The Court has recognized that a State has a legitimate interest in regulating the number of candidates on the ballot. In so doing, the State understandably and properly seeks to prevent the clogging of its election machinery, avoid voter confusion, and assure that the winner is the choice of a majority, or at least a strong plurality, of those voting, without the expense and burden of runoff elections. Although we have no way of gauging the number of candidates who might enter primaries in Texas if access to the ballot were unimpeded by the large filing fees in question here, we are bound to respect the legitimate objectives of the State in avoiding overcrowded ballots. Moreover, a State has an interest, if not a duty, to protect the integrity of its political processes from frivolous or fraudulent candidacies.

However, the fees at issue here bore an insufficiently close relation to the legislative goals:

> To say that the filing fee requirement tends to limit the ballot to the more serious candidates is not enough. There may well be some rational relationship between a candidate's willingness to pay a filing fee and the

seriousness with which he takes his candidacy, but the candidates in this case affirmatively alleged that they were unable, not simply unwilling, to pay the assessed fees, and there was no contrary evidence. It is uncontested that the filing fees exclude legitimate as well as frivolous candidates. And even assuming that every person paying the large fees required by Texas law takes his own candidacy seriously, that does not make him a "serious candidate" in the popular sense. If the Texas fee requirement is intended to regulate the ballot by weeding out spurious candidates, it is extraordinarily ill-fitted to that goal; other means to protect those valid interests are available.

>> *The Reign of Equal Protection in Ballot Access Cases.*   For more than a decade, the Court's approach in *Williams* and *Bullock,* in which it analyzed ballot access regulation under the Equal Protection Clause, prevailed in cases challenging state restrictions on ballot access. *See Lubin v. Panish,* 415 U.S. 709 (1974) (invalidating filing fees); *Storer v. Brown,* 415 U.S. 727 (1974) (upholding California's complex system of ballot access); and *American Party of Texas v. White,* 415 U.S. 767 (1974) (sustaining a complex system of ballot access used by Texas). However, in *Anderson v. Celebrezze,* which follows, the Court set off in a strikingly new direction, abandoning the established equal protection analysis for one based on First Amendment considerations.

Anderson v. Celebrezze

460 U.S. 780 (1983)

Justice STEVENS delivered the opinion of the Court.

On April 24, 1980, petitioner John Anderson announced that he was an independent candidate for the office of President of the United States. Thereafter, his supporters—by gathering the signatures of registered voters, filing required documents, and submitting filing fees—were able to meet the substantive requirements for having his name placed on the ballot for the general election in November 1980 in all 50 States and the District of Columbia. On April 24, however, it was already too late for Anderson to qualify for a position on the ballot in Ohio and certain other States because the statutory deadlines for filing a statement of candidacy had already passed. The question presented by this case is whether Ohio's early filing deadline placed an unconstitutional burden on the voting and associational rights of Anderson's supporters.

The facts are not in dispute. [The following facts are taken from the lower court opinion, 664 F.2d 554 (6th Cir. 1981).]

[On June 8, 1979, Congressman John B. Anderson, Jr. of Illinois began his campaign to become the Republican Party candidate for the Presidency in the November, 1980 general election. Between June 9, 1979 and April 24, 1980, he raised over $7,700,000 and arranged to appear in 27 Republican primaries, actually appearing in nine. The results of these nine primaries showed that Anderson's attempt to become the Republican party nominee was doomed to failure. On April 24, 1980, Anderson announced that he would instead campaign as an independent.

He requested those states in which he was still scheduled to appear in a Republican primary, including Ohio, to remove his name from the primary ballot, and began the formidable task of complying with the various state requirements for placing an independent candidate's name on the November general election ballot.

[Ohio offers alternative routes to the general election ballot. Candidates who pursue the independent path are governed by Ohio Rev. Code §3513.257, which requires that a statement of candidacy and nominating petitions bearing the signatures of 5,000 qualified voters be filed by the 75th day before the first Tuesday after the first Monday in June immediately preceding the general election. Thus, Congressman Anderson had to have filed no later than March 20, 1980 in order to appear on the November, 1980 general election ballot. Candidates who chose instead to vie for a political party's nomination for the Presidency by seeking delegates to the national convention in Ohio's June primary had to file, also by March 20, a declaration of candidacy and nominating petitions bearing signatures from 1,000 members of the candidate's party. Ohio Rev. Code §3513.05. . . .

[Ohio does not require that the person ultimately chosen as a political party's presidential nominee have participated in the state's June primary. Thus, while an independent must declare his candidacy by March 20, theoretically at least a partisan candidate need take no action and make no commitment until after his party's convention (or 75 days before the general election in the case of a minor political party — Ohio Rev. Code §3505.01). As a result, the official deadline for a partisan candidate's announcement is approximately five months after an independent must declare his or her candidacy.

[Anderson gathered approximately 16,000 signatures for his nominating petitions in Ohio between May 10 and May 15. He tendered the nominating petitions and a statement of candidacy to the Secretary of State's office on May 16, but appellant refused to accept them or to put Anderson's name on the ballot solely on the ground that the petitions and statement were not timely filed under section 3513.257.]

I

After a date toward the end of March, even if intervening events create unanticipated political opportunities, no independent candidate may enter the Presidential race and seek to place his name on the Ohio general election ballot. Thus the direct impact of Ohio's early filing deadline falls upon aspirants for office. Nevertheless, as we have recognized, "the rights of voters and the rights of candidates do not lend themselves to neat separation; laws that affect candidates always have at least some theoretical, correlative effect on voters." *Bullock v. Carter*, 405 U.S. 134, 143 (1972). Our primary concern is with the tendency of ballot access restrictions "to limit the field of candidates from which voters might choose." Therefore, "[in] approaching candidate restrictions, it is essential to examine in a realistic light the extent and nature of their impact on voters." *Ibid.*

The impact of candidate eligibility requirements on voters implicates basic constitutional rights.[7] . . . As we have repeatedly recognized, voters can assert their

---

7. In this case, we base our conclusions directly on the First and Fourteenth Amendments and do not engage in a separate Equal Protection Clause analysis. We rely, however, on

preferences only through candidates or parties or both. "It is to be expected that a voter hopes to find on the ballot a candidate who comes near to reflecting his policy preferences on contemporary issues." *Lubin v. Panish*, 415 U.S. 709, 716 (1974). The right to vote is "heavily burdened" if that vote may be cast only for major-party candidates at a time when other parties or other candidates are "clamoring for a place on the ballot." *Ibid.*; *Williams v. Rhodes, supra*, at 31. The exclusion of candidates also burdens voters' freedom of association, because an election campaign is an effective platform for the expression of views on the issues of the day, and a candidate serves as a rallying point for like-minded citizens.

Although these rights of voters are fundamental, not all restrictions imposed by the States on candidates' eligibility for the ballot impose constitutionally suspect burdens on voters' rights to associate or to choose among candidates. We have recognized that, "as a practical matter, there must be a substantial regulation of elections if they are to be fair and honest and if some sort of order, rather than chaos, is to accompany the democratic processes." *Storer v. Brown*, 415 U.S. 724, 730 (1974). To achieve these necessary objectives, States have enacted comprehensive and sometimes complex election codes. Each provision of these schemes, whether it governs the registration and qualifications of voters, the selection and eligibility of candidates, or the voting process itself, inevitably affects — at least to some degree — the individual's right to vote and his right to associate with others for political ends. Nevertheless, the State's important regulatory interests are generally sufficient to justify reasonable, nondiscriminatory restrictions.

Constitutional challenges to specific provisions of a State's election laws therefore cannot be resolved by any "litmus-paper test" that will separate valid from invalid restrictions. *Storer, supra*, at 730. Instead, a court must resolve such a challenge by an analytical process that parallels its work in ordinary litigation. It must first consider the character and magnitude of the asserted injury to the rights protected by the First and Fourteenth Amendments that the plaintiff seeks to vindicate. It then must identify and evaluate the precise interests put forward by the State as justifications for the burden imposed by its rule. In passing judgment, the Court must not only determine the legitimacy and strength of each of those interests, it also must consider the extent to which those interests make it necessary to burden the plaintiff's rights. Only after weighing all these factors is the reviewing court in a position to decide whether the challenged provision is unconstitutional. . . .

II

An early filing deadline may have a substantial impact on independent-minded voters. In election campaigns, particularly those which are national in

---

the analysis in a number of our prior election cases resting on the Equal Protection Clause of the Fourteenth Amendment. These cases, applying the "fundamental rights" strand of equal protection analysis, have identified the First and Fourteenth Amendment rights implicated by restrictions on the eligibility of voters and candidates, and have considered the degree to which the State's restrictions further legitimate state interests. See, *e.g.*, *Williams v. Rhodes*, 393 U.S. 23 (1968); *Bullock v. Carter*, 405 U.S. 134 (1972); *Lubin v. Panish*, 415 U.S. 709 (1974).

scope, the candidates and the issues simply do not remain static over time. Various candidates rise and fall in popularity; domestic and international developments bring new issues to center stage and may affect voters' assessments of national problems. Such developments will certainly affect the strategies of candidates who have already entered the race; they may also create opportunities for new candidacies. See A. Bickel, Reform and Continuity 87-89 (1971). Yet Ohio's filing deadline prevents persons who wish to be independent candidates from entering the significant political arena established in the State by a Presidential election campaign—and creating new political coalitions of Ohio voters—at any time after mid to late March. At this point developments in campaigns for the major-party nominations have only begun, and the major parties will not adopt their nominees and platforms for another five months. Candidates and supporters within the major parties thus have the political advantage of continued flexibility; for independents, the inflexibility imposed by the March filing deadline is a correlative disadvantage because of the competitive nature of the electoral process.

If the State's filing deadline were later in the year, a newly emergent independent candidate could serve as the focal point for a grouping of Ohio voters who decide, after mid-March, that they are dissatisfied with the choices within the two major parties. As we recognized in *Williams v. Rhodes*, 393 U.S., at 33, "[since] the principal policies of the major parties change to some extent from year to year, and since the identity of the likely major party nominees may not be known until shortly before the election, this disaffected 'group' will rarely if ever be a cohesive or identifiable group until a few months before the election." Indeed, several important third-party candidacies in American history were launched after the two major parties staked out their positions and selected their nominees at national conventions during the summer. But under §3513.25.7, a late-emerging Presidential candidate outside the major parties, whose positions on the issues could command widespread community support, is excluded from the Ohio general election ballot. The "Ohio system thus denies the 'disaffected' not only a choice of leadership but a choice on the issues as well." *Williams v. Rhodes, supra*, at 33.

Not only does the challenged Ohio statute totally exclude any candidate who makes the decision to run for President as an independent after the March deadline, it also burdens the signature-gathering efforts of independents who decide to run in time to meet the deadline. When the primary campaigns are far in the future and the election itself is even more remote, the obstacles facing an independent candidate's organizing efforts are compounded. Volunteers are more difficult to recruit and retain, media publicity and campaign contributions are more difficult to secure, and voters are less interested in the campaign.

It is clear, then, that the March filing deadline places a particular burden on an identifiable segment of Ohio's independent-minded voters. As our cases have held, it is especially difficult for the State to justify a restriction that limits political participation by an identifiable political group whose members share a particular viewpoint, associational preference, or economic status. . . .

A burden that falls unequally on new or small political parties or on independent candidates impinges, by its very nature, on associational choices protected by the First Amendment. It discriminates against those candidates and—of particular importance—against those voters whose political preferences lie outside the existing political parties. *Clements v. Fashing, supra,* at 964-965 (plurality opinion). By limiting the opportunities of independent-minded voters to associate in the electoral arena to enhance their political effectiveness as a group, such restrictions threaten to reduce diversity and competition in the marketplace of ideas. Historically political figures outside the two major parties have been fertile sources of new ideas and new programs; many of their challenges to the status quo have in time made their way into the political mainstream. In short, the primary values protected by the First Amendment— "a profound national commitment to the principle that debate on public issues should be uninhibited, robust, and wide-open," *New York Times Co. v. Sullivan,* 376 U.S. 254, 270 (1964) — are served when election campaigns are not monopolized by the existing political parties.

Furthermore, in the context of a Presidential election, state-imposed restrictions implicate a uniquely important national interest. For the President and the Vice President of the United States are the only elected officials who represent all the voters in the Nation. Moreover, the impact of the votes cast in each State is affected by the votes cast for the various candidates in other States. Thus in a Presidential election a State's enforcement of more stringent ballot access requirements, including filing deadlines, has an impact beyond its own borders. Similarly, the State has a less important interest in regulating Presidential elections than statewide or local elections, because the outcome of the former will be largely determined by voters beyond the State's boundaries. . . . The Ohio filing deadline challenged in this case does more than burden the associational rights of independent voters and candidates. It places a significant state-imposed restriction on a nationwide electoral process.

III

The State identifies three separate interests that it seeks to further by its early filing deadline for independent Presidential candidates: voter education, equal treatment for partisan and independent candidates, and political stability. We now examine the legitimacy of these interests and the extent to which the March filing deadline serves them.

Voter Education

There can be no question about the legitimacy of the State's interest in fostering informed and educated expressions of the popular will in a general election. Moreover, the Court of Appeals correctly identified that interest as one of the concerns that motivated the Framers' decision not to provide for direct popular election of the President. We are persuaded, however, that the State's important and legitimate interest in voter education does not justify the specific restriction on participation in a Presidential election that is at issue in this case.

The passage of time since the Constitutional Convention in 1787 has brought about two changes that are relevant to the reasonableness of Ohio's statutory requirement that independents formally declare their candidacy at least seven months in advance of a general election. First, although it took days and often weeks for even the most rudimentary information about important events to be transmitted from one part of the country to another in 1787, today even trivial details about national candidates are instantaneously communicated nationwide in both verbal and visual form. Second, although literacy was far from universal in 18th-century America, today the vast majority of the electorate not only is literate but also is informed on a day-to-day basis about events and issues that affect election choices and about the ever-changing popularity of individual candidates. In the modern world it is somewhat unrealistic to suggest that it takes more than seven months to inform the electorate about the qualifications of a particular candidate simply because he lacks a partisan label. . . .

This reasoning applies with even greater force to a Presidential election, which receives more intense publicity. Nor are we persuaded by the State's assertion that, unless a candidate actually files a formal declaration of candidacy in Ohio by the March deadline, Ohio voters will not realize that they should pay attention to his candidacy. Brief for Respondent 38. The validity of this asserted interest is undermined by the State's willingness to place major-party nominees on the November ballot even if they never campaigned in Ohio.

It is also by no means self-evident that the interest in voter education is served at all by a requirement that independent candidates must declare their candidacy before the end of March in order to be eligible for a place on the ballot in November. Had the requirement been enforced in Ohio, petitioner Anderson might well have determined that it would be futile for him to allocate any of his time and money to campaigning in that State. The Ohio electorate might thereby have been denied whatever benefits his participation in local debates could have contributed to an understanding of the issues. A State's claim that it is enhancing the ability of its citizenry to make wise decisions by restricting the flow of information to them must be viewed with some skepticism. As we observed in another First Amendment context, it is often true "that the best means to that end is to open the channels of communication rather than to close them." *Virginia Pharmacy Board v. Virginia Citizens Consumer Council, Inc.*, 425 U.S. 748, 770 (1976).

Equal Treatment

We also find no merit in the State's claim that the early filing deadline serves the interest of treating all candidates alike. Brief for Respondent 33. It is true that a candidate participating in a primary election must declare his candidacy on the same date as an independent. But both the burdens and the benefits of the respective requirements are materially different, and the reasons for requiring early filing for a primary candidate are inapplicable to independent candidates in the general election.

The consequences of failing to meet the statutory deadline are entirely different for party primary participants and independents. The name of the nominees of the Democratic and Republican Parties will appear on the Ohio ballot in November even if they did not decide to run until after Ohio's March deadline had passed, but the independent is simply denied a position on the ballot if he waits too long. Thus, under Ohio's scheme, the major parties may include all events preceding their national conventions in the calculus that produces their respective nominees and campaign platforms, but the independent's judgment must be based on a history that ends in March. The early filing deadline for a candidate in a party's primary election is adequately justified by administrative concerns. Seventy-five days appears to be a reasonable time for processing the documents submitted by candidates and preparing the ballot.

Neither the administrative justification nor the benefit of an early filing deadline is applicable to an independent candidate. . . . After filing his statement of candidacy, the independent does not participate in a structured intraparty contest to determine who will receive organizational support; he must develop support by other means. In short, "equal treatment" of partisan and independent candidates simply is not achieved by imposing the March filing deadline on both. . . .

Political Stability

Respondent's brief explains that the State has a substantial interest in protecting the two major political parties from "damaging intraparty feuding." Brief for Respondent 41. According to respondent, a candidate's decision to abandon efforts to win the party primary and to run as an independent "can be very damaging to state political party structure." Anderson's decision to run as an independent, respondent argues, threatened to "splinter" the Ohio Republican Party "by drawing away its activists to work in his 'independent' campaign." *Id.*, at 37.

Ohio's asserted interest in political stability amounts to a desire to protect existing political parties from competition—competition for campaign workers, voter support, and other campaign resources—generated by independent candidates who have previously been affiliated with the party.

In *Williams v. Rhodes* we squarely held that protecting the Republican and Democratic Parties from external competition cannot justify the virtual exclusion of other political aspirants from the political arena. . . .

More generally, the early filing deadline is not precisely drawn to protect the parties from "intraparty feuding," whatever legitimacy that state goal may have in a Presidential election. If the deadline is designed to keep intraparty competition within the party structure, its coverage is both too broad and too narrow. It is true that in this case §3513.25.7 was applied to a candidate who had previously competed in party primaries and then sought to run as an independent. But the early deadline applies broadly to independent candidates who have not been affiliated in the recent past with any political party. On the other hand, as long as the decision to run is made before the March deadline, Ohio does not prohibit independent candidacies by persons formerly affiliated with a political party, or currently participating in intraparty competition in other States—regardless of the effect on the political party structure. . . .

IV

We began our inquiry by noting that our primary concern is not the interest of candidate Anderson, but rather, the interests of the voters who chose to associate together to express their support for Anderson's candidacy and the views he espoused. Under any realistic appraisal, the "extent and nature" of the burdens Ohio has placed on the voters' freedom of choice and freedom of association, in an election of nationwide importance, unquestionably outweigh the State's minimal interest in imposing a March deadline.

The judgment of the Court of Appeals is
Reversed.

Justice REHNQUIST, with whom Justice WHITE, Justice POWELL, and Justice
O'CONNOR join, dissenting.

Article II of the Constitution provides that "[each] State shall appoint, in such
Manner as the Legislature thereof may direct, a Number of Electors" who shall
select the President of the United States. U.S. Const., Art. II, §1, cl. 2. This provision, one of few in the Constitution that grants an express plenary power to the
States, conveys "the broadest power of determination" and "[it] recognizes that [in
the election of a President] the people act through their representatives in the legislature, and *leaves it to the legislature exclusively to define the method of effecting the object.*"
McPherson v. Blacker, 146 U.S. 1, 27 (1892) (emphasis added).

[T]he Constitution does not require that a State allow any particular Presidential candidate to be on its ballot, and so long as the Ohio ballot access laws are rational and allow nonparty candidates reasonable access to the general election ballot,
this Court should not interfere with Ohio's exercise of its Art. II, §1, cl. 2, power.
Since I believe that the Ohio laws meet these criteria, I dissent. . . .

Anderson makes no claim, and thus has offered no evidence to show, that the
early filing deadline impeded his "signature-gathering efforts." That alone should
be enough to prevent the Court from finding that the deadline has such an impact.
A statute "is not to be upset upon hypothetical and unreal possibilities, if it would
be good upon the facts as they are."

The Court's intimation that the Ohio filing deadline infringes on a nonparty
candidate who makes the decision to run for President after the March deadline is
similarly without support in the record. Certainly, if such candidates emerge, the
Ohio deadline will prevent their running in the general election as nonparty candidates. Just as certainly, however, Anderson was not such a candidate. Anderson
formally announced his candidacy for the Presidency on June 8, 1979 — over nine
months before Ohio's March 20 deadline. . . .

On the record before us, the effect of the Ohio filing deadline is quite easily summarized: it requires that a candidate, who has already decided to run for
President, decide by March 20 which route his candidacy will take. He can become
a nonparty candidate by filing a nominating petition with 5,000 signatures and
assure himself a place on the general election ballot. Or he can become a party
candidate and take his chances in securing a position on the general election ballot
by seeking the nomination of a party's national convention. Anderson chose the
latter route and submitted in a timely fashion his nominating petition for Ohio's
Republican Primary. Then, realizing that he had no chance for the Republican
nomination, Anderson sought to change the form of this candidacy. The Ohio filing deadline prevented him from making this change. Quite clearly, rather than
prohibiting him from seeking the Presidency, the filing deadline only prevented
Anderson from having two shots at it in the same election year.

Thus, Ohio's filing deadline does not create a restriction "denying the franchise to citizens," such as those faced by the Court in *Kramer v. Union School District,*
395 U.S. 621, 626 (1969) (emphasis omitted), *Cipriano v. City of Houma,* 395 U.S. 701
(1969) (per curiam), *Evans v. Cornman,* 398 U.S. 419 (1970), *Phoenix v. Kolodziejski,*

399 U.S. 204 (1970), and *Dunn v. Blumstein*, 405 U.S. 330 (1972). Likewise, Ohio's filing deadline does not create a restriction that makes it "virtually impossible" for new-party candidates or nonparty candidates to qualify for the ballot, such as those addressed in *Williams v. Rhodes*, 393 U.S. 23, 25 (1968), *Bullock v. Carter*, 405 U.S. 134 (1972), and *Lubin v. Panish*, 415 U.S. 709 (1974). . . .

The point the Court misses is that in cases like this and *Storer*, we have never required that States meet some kind of "narrowly tailored" standard in order to pass constitutional muster. In reviewing election laws like Ohio's filing deadline, we have said before that a court's job is to ensure that the State "in no way freezes the status quo, but implicitly recognizes the potential fluidity of American political life." *Jenness v. Fortson*, 403 U.S. 431, 439 (1971). If it does not freeze the status quo, then the State's laws will be upheld if they are "tied to a particularized legitimate purpose, and [are] in no sense invidious or arbitrary.". . .

The Ohio filing deadline easily meets the test described above. In the interest of the "stability of its political system," *Storer v. Brown*, 415 U.S., at 736, Ohio must be "free to assure itself that [a nonparty] candidate is a serious contender, *truly independent*, and with a satisfactory level of community support." *Id.*, at 746. This interest alone is sufficient to support Ohio ballot access laws which require that candidates for Presidential electors choose their route early, thus preventing a person who has decided to run for a party nomination from switching to a nonparty candidacy after he discovers that he is not the favorite of his party. . . .

>> *The Individual Rights Model.*   By grounding its decision in the First Amendment in *Anderson*, the Court commits itself strongly to adjudicating ballot access cases using a classic individual rights model: the issues in these cases are resolved in a familiar way, by deciding first whose rights are at stake, whether and how much those rights have been infringed, and whether the state has offered a sufficient justification for the infringement to satisfy the applicable level of judicial scrutiny. But is the individual rights model the best model to resolve cases like these? Is the problem with restrictive ballot access laws really the infringement of the rights of individual voters or candidates, or is it better conceived as a deviation from some kind of *structure* established by the Constitution for the contestation of elective office? Consider the following critique:

> [T]he conventional understanding of individual rights and equality cannot readily be transferred to the domain of democracy. First, state action that would be impermissible viewpoint discrimination in other domains is inevitable in the construction of democratic institutions. States must choose the forms through which representation will occur . . . , [meaning that] states must inevitably act on the basis of substantive visions of the kind of democratic politics they seek to encourage. . . .

> Second, elections and related democratic processes are pervasively regulated (far more so than the general realm of public debate). In the more visible foreground, states print ballots, determine the conditions under which candidates and parties attain ballot access, and organize and

structure the process of voting. In the background, prior decisions have been made about the underlying structure of elections and representative institutions. Because the "rights" at stake in political cases are already structured and conditioned by these prior institutional-design choices, these rights cannot be understood as general, intrinsic liberties. The content of political rights must instead derive from the purposes of the institutional structures within which those rights exist. Even if such reasoning is implicit or hidden from a judge, the content of such rights will necessarily depend upon judgments concerning which aims to attribute to a country's democratic institutional structures. Democracy is a "heavily regulated industry," and . . . the rights of democracy [are] inevitably conditioned by the entire institutional structure within which these rights exist. . . . Yet as cases involving political parties show, the Court nonetheless often reverts to rights analysis imported from other spheres to address issues involving democratic institutions.

Third, politics involves, at its core, the organization and mobilization of groups and coalitions for effective concerted action. In the context of democratic governance, individual interests can frequently be realized effectively only through these organizations, coalitions, and intermediaries. Yet American political culture resists the essentially collective nature of politics. Indeed, a myth of romantic individualism — an illusion that the ideal politics is one in which individuals are the key agents in democratic life — has long had a distinct and powerful hold over American conceptions of democracy. That vision is manifest in the exceptional hostility American culture and law have shown to the central organizational entities of politics, the parties. . . . The central fact of democratic politics in modern societies is that effective individual participation depends upon collective organizational forms, such as political parties, interest groups, and coalitions. Emasculating these organizations in the name of empowering individuals or isolated groups is confused at best and political suicide at worst. . . .

These same considerations apply when courts face rights and equality claims concerning politics. Indeed, the American judicial system, so oriented toward rights and equality, faces the same risk of romanticism that has long shaped the broader American political culture: absent judicial appreciation of how recognizing these claims will affect the system of organizations and coalitions central to political success, judicial decisions can undermine the very interests courts believe themselves to be securing. Rights and equality doctrines can focus too readily on atomized individuals or disaggregated groups in isolation from the overall organizational and coalitional matrix that determines actual political power. . . .

Insufficiently attentive at times to the differences between politics and other domains, the Court has reflexively applied to politics understandings of rights inappropriately borrowed from other domains. The result has been constraints on what should be acceptable experimentation in the design of democracy. The current constitutional law of democracy thus does both too little — by not applying constitutional law aggressively enough to address the structural dangers of incumbent and partisan self-entrenchment—and too much—by formally and analogically relying on individual and associational rights from other domains without a functional analysis that would diminish the role of such rights in the context of democratic politics.

Richard H. Pildes, *Foreword: The Constitutionalization of Democratic Politics,* 118 HARV. L. REV. 29, 50-55 (2004).

2. *Write-In Votes*

The Court's ballot access cases make clear that the state may constitutionally keep some candidates off the ballot. But even the absence of a candidate's name from the ballot need not preclude that candidate's running for office and, at least in theory, winning the election, if the state permits the use of write-in votes. In this sense, the write-in vote could be characterized as a last line of defense for popular sovereignty, an ultimate check on the ability of the state to misuse its acknowledged power to limit who gets on the ballot. Does a candidate, then, have a "right" to wage a write-in campaign? Does a voter have a "right" to cast a write-in vote? The Court addressed these questions in the following case.

Burdick v. Takushi

504 U.S. 428 (1992)

Justice WHITE delivered the opinion of the Court.

The issue in this case is whether Hawaii's prohibition on write-in voting unreasonably infringes upon its citizens' rights under the First and Fourteenth Amendments. Petitioner contends that the Constitution requires Hawaii to provide for the casting, tabulation, and publication of write-in votes. The Court of Appeals for the Ninth Circuit disagreed, holding that the prohibition, taken as part of the State's comprehensive election scheme, does not impermissibly burden the right to vote. 937 F.2d 415, 422 (1991). We affirm.

I

Petitioner is a registered voter in the city and County of Honolulu. In 1986, only one candidate filed nominating papers to run for the seat representing petitioner's district in the Hawaii House of Representatives. Petitioner wrote to state officials inquiring about Hawaii's write-in voting policy and received a copy of an opinion letter issued by the Hawaii Attorney General's Office stating that the State's election law made no provision for write-in voting.

Petitioner then filed this lawsuit, claiming that he wished to vote in the primary and general elections for a person who had not filed nominating papers and that he wished to vote in future elections for other persons whose names were not and might not appear on the ballot. . . .

II

Petitioner proceeds from the erroneous assumption that a law that imposes any burden upon the right to vote must be subject to strict scrutiny. Our cases do not so hold.

It is beyond cavil that "voting is of the most fundamental significance under our constitutional structure." It does not follow, however, that the right to vote in any manner and the right to associate for political purposes through the ballot are absolute. The Constitution provides that States may prescribe "the Times, Places and Manner of holding Elections for Senators and Representatives," Art. I, §4, cl. 1, and the Court therefore has recognized that States retain the power to regulate their own elections. *Sugarman v. Dougall*, 413 U.S. 634, 647 (1973); *Tashjian v. Republican Party of Connecticut*, 479 U.S. 208, 217 (1986). Common sense, as well as constitutional law, compels the conclusion that government must play an active role in structuring elections; "as a practical matter, there must be a substantial regulation of elections if they are to be fair and honest and if some sort of order, rather than chaos, is to accompany the democratic processes." *Storer v. Brown*, 415 U.S. 724, 730 (1974).

Election laws will invariably impose some burden upon individual voters. Each provision of a code, "whether it governs the registration and qualifications of voters, the selection and eligibility of candidates, or the voting process itself, inevitably affects—at least to some degree—the individual's right to vote and his right to associate with others for political ends." *Anderson v. Celebrezze*, 460 U.S. 780, 788 (1983). Consequently, to subject every voting regulation to strict scrutiny and to require that the regulation be narrowly tailored to advance a compelling state interest, as petitioner suggests, would tie the hands of States seeking to assure that elections are operated equitably and efficiently. See Brief for Petitioner 32-37. Accordingly, the mere fact that a State's system "creates barriers . . . tending to limit the field of candidates from which voters might choose . . . does not of itself compel close scrutiny." *Bullock v. Carter*, 405 U.S. 134, 143 (1972); *Anderson, supra*, at 788.

Instead, as the full Court agreed in *Anderson, supra*, at 788-789; *id.*, at 808, 817 (Rehnquist, J., dissenting), a more flexible standard applies. A court considering a challenge to a state election law must weigh "the character and magnitude of the asserted injury to the rights protected by the First and Fourteenth Amendments that the plaintiff seeks to vindicate" against "the precise interests put forward by the State as justifications for the burden imposed by its rule," taking into consideration "the extent to which those interests make it necessary to burden the plaintiff's rights." *Id.*, at 789.

Under this standard, the rigorousness of our inquiry into the propriety of a state election law depends upon the extent to which a challenged regulation burdens First and Fourteenth Amendment rights. Thus, as we have recognized when those rights are subjected to "severe" restrictions, the regulation must be narrowly drawn to advance a state interest of compelling importance." But when a state election law provision imposes only "reasonable, nondiscriminatory restrictions" upon the First and Fourteenth Amendment rights of voters, "the State's important regulatory interests are generally sufficient to justify" the restrictions. *Anderson, supra*, at 788. We apply this standard in considering petitioner's challenge to Hawaii's ban on write-in ballots.

A

There is no doubt that the Hawaii election laws, like all election regulations, have an impact on the right to vote, *Anderson, supra,* at 788, but it can hardly be said that the laws at issue here unconstitutionally limit access to the ballot by party or independent candidates or unreasonably interfere with the right of voters to associate and have candidates of their choice placed on the ballot. Indeed, petitioners understandably do not challenge the manner in which the State regulates candidate access to the ballot.

To obtain a position on the November general election ballot, a candidate must participate in Hawaii's open primary, "in which all registered voters may choose in which party primary to vote." See Haw. Rev. Stat. §12-31 (1985). The State provides three mechanisms through which a voter's candidate-of-choice may appear on the primary ballot.

First, a party petition may be filed 150 days before the primary by any group of persons who obtain the signatures of one percent of the State's registered voters. Haw. Rev. Stat. §11-62 (Supp. 1991). . . .

The second method through which candidates may appear on the Hawaii primary ballot is the established party route. Established parties that have qualified by petition for three consecutive elections and received a specified percentage of the vote in the preceding election may avoid filing party petitions for 10 years. Haw. Rev. Stat. §11-61 (1985). The Democratic, Republican, and Libertarian Parties currently meet Hawaii's criteria for established parties. Like new party candidates, established party contenders are required to file nominating papers 60 days before the primary. Haw. Rev. Stat. §§12-2.5 to 12-7 (1985 and Supp. 1991). . . .

The third mechanism by which a candidate may appear on the ballot is through the designated nonpartisan ballot. Nonpartisans may be placed on the nonpartisan primary ballot simply by filing nominating papers containing 15 to 25 signatures, depending upon the office sought, 60 days before the primary. §§12-3 to 12-7. To advance to the general election, a nonpartisan must receive 10 percent of the primary vote or the number of votes that was sufficient to nominate a partisan candidate, whichever number is lower. . . .

Although Hawaii makes no provision for write-in voting in its primary or general elections, the system outlined above provides for easy access to the ballot until the cutoff date for the filing of nominating petitions, two months before the primary. Consequently, any burden on voters' freedom of choice and association is borne only by those who fail to identify their candidate of choice until days before the primary. But in *Storer v. Brown,* we gave little weight to "the interest the candidate and his supporters may have in making a late rather than an early decision to seek independent ballot status." 415 U.S., at 736. We think the same reasoning applies here and therefore conclude that any burden imposed by Hawaii's write-in vote prohibition is a very limited one. "To conclude otherwise might sacrifice the political stability of the system of the State, with profound consequences for the entire citizenry, merely in the interest of particular candidates and their supporters having instantaneous access to the ballot." *Storer, supra,* at 736.

Because he has characterized this as a voting rights rather than ballot access case, petitioner submits that the write-in prohibition deprives him of the opportunity to cast a meaningful ballot, conditions his electoral participation upon the waiver of his First Amendment right to remain free from espousing positions that he does not support, and discriminates against him based on the content of the message he seeks to convey through his vote. Brief for Petitioner 19. At bottom, he claims that he is entitled to cast and Hawaii required to count a "protest vote" for Donald Duck, Tr. of Oral Arg. 5, and that any impediment to this asserted "right" is unconstitutional.

Petitioner's argument is based on two flawed premises. First, in *Bullock v. Carter*, we minimized the extent to which voting rights cases are distinguishable from ballot access cases, stating that "the rights of voters and the rights of candidates do not lend themselves to neat separation." 405 U.S., at 143. Second, the function of the election process is "to winnow out and finally reject all but the chosen candidates," *Storer*, 415 U.S., at 735, not to provide a means of giving vent to "short-range political goals, pique, or personal quarrels." Ibid. Attributing to elections a more generalized expressive function would undermine the ability of States to operate elections fairly and efficiently. *Id.*, at 730.

Accordingly, we have repeatedly upheld reasonable, politically neutral regulations that have the effect of channeling expressive activity at the polls. Petitioner offers no persuasive reason to depart from these precedents. Reasonable regulation of elections does not require voters to espouse positions that they do not support; it does require them to act in a timely fashion if they wish to express their views in the voting booth. And there is nothing content based about a flat ban on all forms of write-in ballots.

The appropriate standard for evaluating a claim that a state law burdens the right to vote is set forth in *Anderson*. Applying that standard, we conclude that, in light of the adequate ballot access afforded under Hawaii's election code, the State's ban on write-in voting imposes only a limited burden on voters' rights to make free choices and to associate politically through the vote.

B

We turn next to the interests asserted by Hawaii to justify the burden imposed by its prohibition of write-in voting. Because we have already concluded that the burden is slight, the State need not establish a compelling interest to tip the constitutional scales in its direction. Here, the State's interests outweigh petitioner's limited interest in waiting until the eleventh hour to choose his preferred candidate.

Hawaii's interest in "avoiding the possibility of unrestrained factionalism at the general election" provides adequate justification for its ban on write-in voting in November. The primary election is "an integral part of the entire election process," *Storer, supra*, at 735, and the State is within its rights to reserve "the general election ballot . . . for major struggles . . . [and] not a forum for continuing intraparty feuds." *Ibid*. The prohibition on write-in voting is a legitimate means of averting divisive sore-loser candidacies. Hawaii further promotes the two-stage, primary-general election process of winnowing out candidates, see *Storer, supra*, at 735, by permitting the unopposed victors in certain primaries to be designated office holders. See Haw. Rev. Stat. §§12-41, 12-42 (1985). This focuses the attention of voters upon contested races in the general election. This would not be possible, absent the write-in voting ban. . . .

We think these legitimate interests asserted by the State are sufficient to outweigh the limited burden that the write-in voting ban imposes upon Hawaii's voters. . . .

Justice KENNEDY, with whom Justice BLACKMUN and Justice STEVENS join, dissenting.

. . . The record demonstrates the significant burden that Hawaii's write-in ban imposes on the right of voters such as petitioner to vote for the candidates of their choice. In the election that triggered this lawsuit, petitioner did not wish to vote for the one candidate who ran for state representative in his district. Because he could not write in the name of a candidate he preferred, he had no way to cast a meaningful vote. Petitioner's dilemma is a recurring, frequent phenomenon in Hawaii because of the State's ballot access rules and the circumstance that one party, the Democratic Party, is predominant. It is critical to understand that petitioner's case is not an isolated example of a restriction on the free choice of candidates. The very ballot access rules the Court cites as mitigating his injury in fact compound it systemwide.

Democratic candidates often run unopposed, especially in state legislative races. In the 1986 general election, 33 percent of the elections for state legislative offices involved single candidate races. The comparable figures for 1984 and 1982 were 39 percent and 37.5 percent. Large numbers of voters cast blank ballots in uncontested races, that is, they leave the ballots blank rather than vote for the single candidate listed. In 1990, 27 percent of voters who voted in other races did not cast votes in uncontested state Senate races. Twenty-nine percent of voters did not cast votes in uncontested state house races. Even in contested races in 1990, 12 to 13 percent of voters cast blank ballots.

Given that so many Hawaii voters are dissatisfied with the choices available to them, it is hard to avoid the conclusion that at least some voters would cast write-in votes for other candidates if given this option. The write-in ban thus prevents these voters from participating in Hawaii elections in a meaningful manner.

This evidence also belies the majority's suggestion that Hawaii voters are presented with adequate electoral choices because Hawaii makes it easy to get on the official ballot. To the contrary, Hawaii's ballot access laws taken as a whole impose a significant impediment to third-party or independent candidacies. The majority suggests that it is easy for new parties to petition for a place on the primary ballot because they must obtain the signatures of only one percent of the State's registered voters. This ignores the difficulty presented by the early deadline for gathering these signatures: 150 days (5 months) before the primary election. Meeting this deadline requires considerable organization at an early stage in the election, a condition difficult for many small parties to meet. . . .

The dominance of the Democratic Party magnifies the disincentive because the primary election is dispositive in so many races. In effect, a Hawaii voter who wishes to vote for any independent candidate must choose between doing so and participating in what will be the dispositive election for many offices. This dilemma imposes a substantial burden on voter choice. It explains also why so few independent candidates secure enough primary votes to advance to the general election. As the majority notes, only eight independent candidates have succeeded in advancing to the general election in the past 10 years. That is, less than one independent candidate per year on average has in fact run in a general election in Hawaii.

The majority's approval of Hawaii's ban is ironic at a time when the new democracies in foreign countries strive to emerge from an era of sham elections in which the name of the ruling party candidate was the only one on the ballot. Hawaii does not impose as severe a restriction on the right to vote, but it imposes a restriction that has a haunting similarity in its tendency to exact severe penalties for one who does anything but vote the dominant party ballot.

Aside from constraints related to ballot access restrictions, the write-in ban limits voter choice in another way. Write-in voting can serve as an important safety mechanism in those instances where a late-developing issue arises or where new information is disclosed about a candidate late in the race. In these situations, voters may become disenchanted with the available candidates when it is too late for other candidates to come forward and qualify for the ballot. The prohibition on write-in voting imposes a significant burden on voters, forcing them either to vote for a candidate whom they no longer support, or to cast a blank ballot. Write-in voting provides a way out of the quandary, allowing voters to switch their support to candidates who are not on the official ballot. Even if there are other mechanisms to address the problem of late-breaking election developments (unsuitable candidates who win an election can be recalled), allowing write-in voting is the only way to preserve the voters' right to cast a meaningful vote in the general election. . . .

The majority's analysis ignores the inevitable and significant burden a write-in ban imposes upon some individual voters by preventing them from exercising their right to vote in a meaningful manner. The liberality of a state's ballot access laws is one determinant of the extent of the burden imposed by the write-in ban; it is not, though, an automatic excuse for forbidding all write-in voting. In my view, a state that bans write-in voting in some or all elections must justify the burden on individual voters by putting forth the precise interests that are served by the ban. A write-in prohibition should not be presumed valid in the absence of any proffered justification by the State. The standard the Court derives from *Anderson v. Celebrezze*, 460 U.S. 780 (1983), means at least this. . . . The interests proffered by the State, some of which are puzzling, are not advanced to any significant degree by the write-in prohibition. . . .

>> *The* **Anderson-Burdick** *Framework.* If *Anderson* and *Burdick* had applied only to ballot access cases their impact might have been slight. In fact, these cases essentially refounded the right to vote, in virtually all of its applications, from principles of equal treatment to principles of free speech and association. Under this reformulation, courts "considering a challenge to a state election law" must weigh the burden on a plaintiff's "First and Fourteenth Amendment [rights]" against the government's justifications, and then apply either strict scrutiny or rational basis review depending on the outcome of that balancing. The result is that all claims alleging infringement of a constitutionally grounded right to vote have been shifted presumptively from the Equal Protection Clause to the First Amendment, and that the

constitutionally relevant interests of plaintiffs are now redefined from interests in equal treatment to interests in speaking freely and associating.

The reach of this reformulation is evident from the enormous variety of problems to which the *Anderson-Burdick* framework has since been applied. The Supreme Court itself has applied the analysis to adjudicate the validity of laws regulating eligibility to vote in party primary elections, the presentation of photo identification at the polls, and disclosure of the identity of initiative petition signers. Lower courts have applied the *Anderson-Burdick* framework to problems as disparate as the availability and content of voting procedures, the qualifications of election officials, the details of electoral management, and many other issues. The *Anderson-Burdick* test has thus become the principal vehicle for adjudicating all election law issues except those dealing with racial discrimination — handled under the Fourteenth and Fifteenth Amendments — and those raising issues of restrictions on speech, which are handled under conventional First Amendment principles.

>> ***Write-In Votes in the Real World.***   Can a write-in candidate actually win an election? Generally, no. But that does not mean it never happens. Most successful write-in campaigns are for very local offices, such as school board, for which the number of voters is so small that an organized write-in campaign can make a difference in the outcome.

Very occasionally, however, a write-in campaign can succeed for higher office. On November 2, 2010, Lisa Murkowski, a Republican Senator from the state of Alaska, became the first United States Senator in 50 years to win an election with a write-in campaign. Senator Murkowski, who was the incumbent, lost in the Republican primary to a more conservative candidate, Joe Miller. Instead of bowing out, she waged a write-in campaign in the general election and defeated the nominees of both major parties. The Miller campaign challenged many of Murkowski's write-in votes, alleging misspelling of "Murkowski" or other irregularities. For example, some voters wrote in the Senator's last name but not her first name and did not fill in the oval for the write-in candidate. Alaska law provides that "a vote for a write-in candidate . . . shall be counted if the oval is filled in for that candidate and if the name, as it appears on the write-in declaration of candidacy, of the candidate or the last name of the candidate is written in the space provided." Alaska Stat. §15.15.360(a)(11). The Alaska Supreme Court ultimately held that under the Alaska statute it is the voter's intent that counts. A vote is not disqualified if the voter misspells a candidate's name. *See Miller v. Treadwell*, 245 P.3d 867 (Alaska 2010). For an analysis of the issues raised by the race, see Chad Flanders, *How Do You Spell M-U-R-K-O-W-S-K-I? Part I: The Question of Assistance to the Voter*, 28 ALASKA L. REV. 1 (2011).

>> ***Other Expressive Ballot Options.***   Voters typically cast write-in votes because they are unhappy with the sanctioned choices. In a few jurisdictions, voters are offered an additional way to express their dissatisfaction. In Nevada, ballots for statewide and national office are required by law to include a line allowing voters to cast a vote for "None of these candidates." Such votes are tallied and the total reported, but they do not count for purposes of deciding which candidate won the election. Nev. Rev. Stat. §293.269. In India, voters are entitled to cast a vote for "None of

the Above" (NOTA). In other jurisdictions, such as Spain and Australia, voters may express their displeasure by turning in a blank ballot.

Should voting systems permit voters to express their rejection of all candidates in this way? What is the value of permitting them to do so? Are there any risks? Why shouldn't voters be limited to expressing a preference for candidates who have made it through an arduous process of vetting via party nomination?

3. State Institutionalization of the Two-Party System

Timmons v. Twin Cities Area New Party

520 U.S. 351 (1997)

Chief Justice REHNQUIST delivered the opinion of the Court.

Most States prohibit multiple-party, or "fusion," candidacies for elected office.[1] The Minnesota laws challenged in this case prohibit a candidate from appearing on the ballot as the candidate of more than one party. Minn. Stat. §§204B.06, subd. 1(b), and 204B.04, subd. 2 (1994). We hold that such a prohibition does not violate the First and Fourteenth Amendments to the United States Constitution.

Respondent is a chartered chapter of the national New Party. Petitioners are Minnesota election officials. In April 1994, Minnesota State Representative Andy Dawkins was running unopposed in the Minnesota Democratic-Farmer-Labor Party's (DFL) primary.[2] That same month, New Party members chose Dawkins as their candidate for the same office in the November 1994 general election. Neither Dawkins nor the DFL objected, and Dawkins signed the required affidavit of candidacy for the New Party. Minn. Stat. §204B.06 (1994). Minnesota, however, prohibits fusion candidacies. Because Dawkins had already filed as a candidate for the DFL's nomination, local election officials refused to accept the New Party's nominating petition.

The New Party filed suit in United States District Court, contending that Minnesota's antifusion laws violated the party's associational rights under the First and Fourteenth Amendments. . . . [The Court of Appeals invalidated the statute.] We now reverse.

Fusion was a regular feature of Gilded Age American politics. Particularly in the West and Midwest, candidates of issue-oriented parties like the Grangers,

---

1. "Fusion," also called "cross-filing" or "multiple-party nomination," is "the electoral support of a single set of candidates by two or more parties." Argersinger, "A Place on the Ballot": Fusion Politics and Antifusion Laws, 85 Am. Hist. Rev. 287, 288 (1980); see also Twin Cities Area New Party v. McKenna, 73 F.3d 196, 197-198 (C.A.8 1996) (Fusion is "the nomination by more than one political party of the same candidate for the same office in the same general election").

2. The DFL is the product of a 1944 merger between Minnesota's Farmer-Labor Party and the Democratic Party, and is a "major party" under Minnesota law. Minn. Stat. §200.02, subd. 7(a) (1994) (major parties are parties that have won five percent of a statewide vote and therefore participate in the state primary elections).

Independents, Greenbackers, and Populists often succeeded through fusion with the Democrats, and vice versa. Republicans, for their part, sometimes arranged fusion candidacies in the South, as part of a general strategy of encouraging and exploiting divisions within the dominant Democratic Party. See generally Argersinger, *"A Place on the Ballot": Fusion Politics and Antifusion Laws*, 85 Am. Hist. Rev. 287, 288-290 (1980).

Fusion was common in part because political parties, rather than local or state governments, printed and distributed their own ballots. These ballots contained only the names of a particular party's candidates, and so a voter could drop his party's ticket in the ballot box without even knowing that his party's candidates were supported by other parties as well. But after the 1888 presidential election, which was widely regarded as having been plagued by fraud, many States moved to the "Australian ballot system." Under that system, an official ballot, containing the names of all the candidates legally nominated by all the parties, was printed at public expense and distributed by public officials at polling places. *Id.*, at 290-292; *Burdick v. Takushi*, 504 U.S. 428, 446-447 (1992) (Kennedy, J., dissenting) (States' move to the Australian ballot system was a "progressive reform to reduce fraudulent election practices"). By 1896, use of the Australian ballot was widespread. During the same period, many States enacted other election-related reforms, including bans on fusion candidacies. See Argersinger, *supra*, at 288, 295-298. Minnesota banned fusion in 1901. This trend has continued and, in this century, fusion has become the exception, not the rule. Today, multiple-party candidacies are permitted in just a few States, and fusion plays a significant role only in New York.[7]

The First Amendment protects the right of citizens to associate and to form political parties for the advancement of common political goals and ideas. *Colorado Republican Federal Campaign Comm'n v. Federal Election Comm.*, 518 U.S. 604, 616 (1996) ("The independent expression of a political party's views is 'core' First Amendment activity no less than is the independent expression of individuals, candidates, or other political committees"); *Norman v. Reed*, 502 U.S. 279, 288 (1992) ("constitutional right of citizens to create and develop new political parties . . . advances the constitutional interest of like-minded voters to gather in pursuit of common political ends"); *Tashjian v. Republican Party of Conn.*, 479 U.S. 208, 214 (1986). As a result, political parties' government, structure, and activities enjoy constitutional protection. *Eu v. San Francisco County Democratic Central Comm.*, 489 U.S. 214, 230 (1989) (noting political party's "discretion in how to organize itself, conduct its affairs, and select its leaders"); *Tashjian, supra*, at 224 (Constitution protects a party's "determination . . . of the structure which best allows it to pursue its political goals").

On the other hand, it is also clear that States may, and inevitably must, enact reasonable regulations of parties, elections, and ballots to reduce election- and campaign-related disorder. *Burdick, supra*, at 433 (" '[A]s a practical matter, there

---

7. See N.Y. Elec. Law §§6-120, 6-146(1) (McKinney 1978 and Supp. 1996). Since 1936, when fusion was last relegalized in New York, several minor parties, including the Liberal, Conservative, American Labor, and Right to Life Parties, have been active and influential in New York politics. See Burnham Declaration, App. 15-16; Cobble & Siskind, *supra* n. 6, at 3-4.

must be a substantial regulation of elections if they are to be fair and honest and if some sort of order, rather than chaos, is to accompany the democratic process'") (quoting *Storer v. Brown*, 415 U.S. 724, 730 (1974)); *Tashjian, supra*, at 217 (The Constitution grants States "broad power to prescribe the 'Time, Places and Manner of holding Elections for Senators and Representatives,' Art. I, §4, cl. 1, which power is matched by state control over the election process for state offices").

When deciding whether a state election law violates First and Fourteenth Amendment associational rights, we weigh the "'character and magnitude'" of the burden the State's rule imposes on those rights against the interests the State contends justify that burden, and consider the extent to which the State's concerns make the burden necessary. *Burdick, supra*, at 434 (quoting *Anderson v. Celebrezze*, 460 U.S. 780, 789 (1983)). Regulations imposing severe burdens on plaintiffs' rights must be narrowly tailored and advance a compelling state interest. Lesser burdens, however, trigger less exacting review, and a State's "'important regulatory interests'" will usually be enough to justify "'reasonable, nondiscriminatory restrictions.'" *Burdick, supra*, at 434 (quoting *Anderson, supra*, at 788); *Norman, supra*, at 288-289 (requiring "corresponding interest sufficiently weighty to justify the limitation"). No bright line separates permissible election-related regulation from unconstitutional infringements on First Amendment freedoms. *Storer, supra*, at 730 ("[N]o litmus-paper test . . . separat[es] those restrictions that are valid from those that are invidious. . . . The rule is not self-executing and is no substitute for the hard judgments that must be made").

The New Party's claim that it has a right to select its own candidate is uncontroversial, so far as it goes. See, *e.g., Cousins v. Wigoda*, 419 U.S. 477 (1975) (party, not State, has right to decide who will be State's delegates at party convention). That is, the New Party, and not someone else, has the right to select the New Party's "standard bearer." It does not follow, though, that a party is absolutely entitled to have its nominee appear on the ballot as that party's candidate. A particular candidate might be ineligible for office, unwilling to serve, or, as here, another party's candidate. That a particular individual may not appear on the ballot as a particular party's candidate does not severely burden that party's associational rights. *See Burdick*, 504 U.S., at 440, n.10 ("It seems to us that limiting the choice of candidates to those who have complied with state election law requirements is the prototypical example of a regulation that, while it affects the right to vote, is eminently reasonable"); *Anderson*, 460 U.S. at 792, n.12 ("Although a disaffiliation provision may preclude . . . voters from supporting a particular ineligible candidate, they remain free to support and promote other candidates who satisfy the State's disaffiliation requirements").

The New Party relies on *Eu v. San Francisco County Democratic Central Comm., supra*, and *Tashjian v. Republican Party of Conn., supra*. In *Eu*, we struck down California election provisions that prohibited political parties from endorsing candidates in party primaries and regulated parties' internal affairs and structure. And in *Tashjian*, we held that Connecticut's closed-primary statute, which required voters in a party primary to be registered party members, interfered with a party's associational rights by limiting "the group of registered voters whom the Party may invite to participate in the basic function of selecting the Party's candidates." 479 U.S., at

215-216. But while *Tashjian* and *Eu* involved regulation of political parties' internal affairs and core associational activities, Minnesota's fusion ban does not. The ban, which applies to major and minor parties alike, simply precludes one party's candidate from appearing on the ballot, as that party's candidate, if already nominated by another party. Respondent is free to try to convince Representative Dawkins to be the New Party's, not the DFL's, candidate. Whether the party still wants to endorse a candidate who, because of the fusion ban, will not appear on the ballot as the party's candidate, is up to the party.

The Court of Appeals also held that Minnesota's laws "keep the New Party from developing consensual political alliances and thus broadening the base of public participation in and support for its activities." *McKenna*, 73 F.3d at 199. The burden on the party was, the court held, severe because "[h]istory shows that minor parties have played a significant role in the electoral system where multiple party nomination is legal, but have no meaningful influence where multiple party nomination is banned." *Ibid.* In the view of the Court of Appeals, Minnesota's fusion ban forces members of the New Party to make a "no-win choice" between voting for "candidates with no realistic chance of winning, defect[ing] from their party and vot[ing] for a major party candidate who does, or declin[ing] to vote at all." *Ibid.*

But Minnesota has not directly precluded minor political parties from developing and organizing. *Cf. Norman*, 502 U.S. at 289 (statute "foreclose[d] the development of any political party lacking the resources to run a statewide campaign"). Nor has Minnesota excluded a particular group of citizens, or a political party, from participation in the election process. *Cf. Anderson, supra,* at 792-793 (filing deadline "places a particular burden on an identifiable segment of Ohio's independent-minded voters"); *Bullock v. Carter,* 405 U.S. 134 (1972) (striking down Texas statute requiring candidates to pay filing fees as a condition to having their names placed on primary-election ballots). The New Party remains free to endorse whom it likes, to ally itself with others, to nominate candidates for office, and to spread its message to all who will listen.

The Court of Appeals emphasized its belief that, without fusion-based alliances, minor parties cannot thrive. This is a predictive judgment which is by no means self-evident. But, more importantly, the supposed benefits of fusion to minor parties do not require that Minnesota permit it. *See Tashjian, supra,* at 222 (refusing to weigh merits of closed and open primaries). Many features of our political system — *e.g.,* single-member districts, "first past the post" elections, and the high costs of campaigning — make it difficult for third parties to succeed in American politics. But the Constitution does not require States to permit fusion any more than it requires them to move to proportional-representation elections or public financing of campaigns.

The New Party contends that the fusion ban burdens its "right . . . to communicate its choice of nominees on the ballot on terms equal to those offered other parties, and the right of the party's supporters and other voters to receive that information," and insists that communication on the ballot of a party's candidate choice is a "critical source of information for the great majority of voters . . . who . . . rely upon party 'labels' as a voting guide." Brief for Respondent 22-23.

It is true that Minnesota's fusion ban prevents the New Party from using the ballot to communicate to the public that it supports a particular candidate who is already another party's candidate. In addition, the ban shuts off one possible avenue a party might use to send a message to its preferred *candidate* because, with fusion, a candidate who wins an election on the basis of two parties' votes will likely know more — if the parties' votes are counted separately — about the particular wishes and ideals of his constituency. We are unpersuaded, however, by the party's contention that it has a right to use the ballot itself to send a particularized message, to its candidate and to the voters, about the nature of its support for the candidate. Ballots serve primarily to elect candidates, not as forums for political expression. *See Burdick*, 504 U.S. at 438. Like all parties in Minnesota, the New Party is able to use the ballot to communicate information about itself and its candidate to the voters, so long as that candidate is not already someone else's candidate. The party retains great latitude in its ability to communicate ideas to voters and candidates through its participation in the campaign, and party members may campaign for, endorse, and vote for their preferred candidate even if he is listed on the ballot as another party's candidate.

In sum, Minnesota's laws do not restrict the ability of the New Party and its members to endorse, support, or vote for anyone they like. The laws do not directly limit the party's access to the ballot. They are silent on parties' internal structure, governance, and policymaking. Instead, these provisions reduce the universe of potential candidates who may appear on the ballot as the party's nominee only by ruling out those few individuals who both have already agreed to be another party's candidate and also, if forced to choose, themselves prefer that other party. They also limit, slightly, the party's ability to send a message to the voters and to its preferred candidates. We conclude that the burdens Minnesota imposes on the party's First and Fourteenth Amendment associational rights — though not trivial — are not severe. . . .

Relatedly, petitioners urge that permitting fusion would undercut Minnesota's ballot-access regime by allowing minor parties to capitalize on the popularity of another party's candidate, rather than on their own appeal to the voters, in order to secure access to the ballot. Brief for Petitioners 45-46. That is, voters who might not sign a minor party's nominating petition based on the party's own views and candidates might do so if they viewed the minor party as just another way of nominating the same person nominated by one of the major parties. Thus, Minnesota fears that fusion would enable minor parties, by nominating a major party's candidate, to bootstrap their way to major-party status in the next election and circumvent the State's nominating-petition requirement for minor parties. See Minn. Stat. §§200.02, subd. 7 (defining "major party"), and 204D.13 (1994) (describing ballot order for major and other parties). The State surely has a valid interest in making sure that minor and third parties who are granted access to the ballot are bona fide and actually supported, on their own merits, by those who have provided the statutorily required petition or ballot support. *Anderson*, 460 U.S. at 788, n.9; *Storer*, 415 U.S. at 733.

States also have a strong interest in the stability of their political systems. *Eu, supra*, at 226; *Storer, supra*, at 736. This interest does not permit a State to completely insulate the two-party system from minor parties' or independent candidates' competition and influence, *Anderson, supra*, at 802; *Williams v. Rhodes*, 393 U.S. 23 (1968), nor is it a paternalistic license for States to protect political parties from the consequences of their own internal disagreements. *Eu, supra*, at 227; *Tashjian*, 479 U.S. at 224. That said, the States' interest permits them to enact reasonable election regulations that may, in practice, favor the traditional two-party system, and that temper the destabilizing effects of party-splintering and excessive factionalism. The Constitution permits the Minnesota Legislature to decide that political stability is best served through a healthy two-party system. . . .

We conclude that the burdens Minnesota's fusion ban imposes on the New Party's associational rights are justified by "correspondingly weighty" valid state interests in ballot integrity and political stability. In deciding that Minnesota's fusion ban does not unconstitutionally burden the New Party's First and Fourteenth Amendment rights, we express no views on the New Party's policy-based arguments concerning the wisdom of fusion. It may well be that, as support for new political parties increases, these arguments will carry the day in some States' legislatures. But the Constitution does not require Minnesota, and the approximately 40 other States that do not permit fusion, to allow it. The judgment of the Court of Appeals is reversed.

Justice STEVENS, with whom Justice GINSBURG joins, and with whom Justice SOUTER joins as to Parts I and II, dissenting.

I

The members of a recognized political party unquestionably have a constitutional right to select their nominees for public office and to communicate the identity of their nominees to the voting public. Both the right to choose and the right to advise voters of that choice are entitled to the highest respect. . . .

[T]he State contends that the fusion ban in fact limits by only a few candidates the range of individuals a party may nominate, and that the burden is therefore quite small. But the *number* of candidates removed from the Party's reach cannot be the determinative factor. The ban leaves the Party free to nominate any eligible candidate except the particular "'standard bearer who best represents the party's ideologies and preferences.'" *Eu v. San Francisco County Democratic Central Comm.*, 489 U.S. 214 (1989).

The Party could perhaps choose to expend its resources supporting a candidate who was not in fact the best representative of its members' views. But a party's choice of a candidate is the most effective way in which that party can communicate to the voters what the party represents and, thereby, attract voter interest and support.[1] Political parties "exist to advance their members' shared political beliefs,"

---

1. The burden on the Party's right to nominate its first-choice candidate, by limiting the Party's ability to convey through its nominee what the Party represents, risks impinging on another core element of any political party's associational rights — the right to "broaden the base of public participation in and support for its activities." *Tashjian v. Republican Party of Conn.*, 479 U.S. 208, 214 (1986). The Court of Appeals relied substantially on this right

and "in the context of particular elections, candidates are necessary to make the party's message known and effective, and vice versa." *Colorado Republican Federal Campaign Comm. v. Federal Election Comm'n*, 518 U.S. 604, 629 (1996) (Kennedy, J., dissenting). *See also Anderson v. Celebrezze*, 460 U.S. 780, 821 (1983) (Rehnquist, J., dissenting) ("Political parties have, or at least hope to have, a continuing existence, representing particular philosophies. Each party has an interest in finding the best candidate to advance its philosophy in each election").

The State next argues that — instead of nominating a second-choice candidate — the Party could remove itself from the ballot altogether, and publicly endorse the candidate of another party. But the right to be on the election ballot is precisely what separates a political party from any other interest group. The Court relies on the fact that the Party remains free "to spread its message to all who will listen," *ante*, through forums other than the ballot. Given the limited resources available to most minor parties, and the less-than-universal interest in the messages of third parties, it is apparent that the Party's message will, in this manner, reach a much smaller audience than that composed of all voters who can read the ballot in the polling booth.

The majority rejects as unimportant the limits that the fusion ban may impose on the Party's ability to express its political views, relying on our decision in *Burdick v. Takushi*, 504 U.S. 428, 445 (1992), in which we noted that "the purpose of casting, counting, and recording votes is to elect public officials, not to serve as a general forum for political expression." But in *Burdick* we concluded simply that an individual voter's interest in expressing his disapproval of the single candidate running for office in a particular election did not require the State to finance and provide a mechanism for tabulating write-in votes. Our conclusion that the ballot is not principally a forum for the individual expression of political sentiment through the casting of a vote does not justify the conclusion that the ballot serves no expressive purpose for the parties who place candidates on the ballot. Indeed, the long-recognized right to choose a " 'standard bearer who best represents the party's ideologies and preferences,' " *Eu*, 489 U.S. at 224, is inescapably an expressive right. "To the extent that party labels provide a shorthand designation of the views of party candidates on matters of public concern, the identification of candidates with particular parties plays a role in the process by which voters inform themselves for the exercise of the franchise." *Tashjian v. Republican Party of Conn.*, 479 U.S. 208, 220 (1986).

---

in concluding that the fusion ban impermissibly burdened the New Party, but its focus was somewhat different. *See Twin Cities Area New Party v. McKenna*, 73 F.3d 196, 199 (C.A.8 1996). A fusion ban burdens the right of a minor party to broaden its base of support because of the political reality that the dominance of the major parties frequently makes a vote for a minor party or independent candidate a "wasted" vote. When minor parties can nominate a candidate also nominated by a major party, they are able to present their members with an opportunity to cast a vote for a candidate who will actually be elected. Although this aspect of a party's effort to broaden support is distinct from the ability to nominate the candidate who best represents the party's views, it is important to note that the party's right to broaden the base of its support is burdened in both ways by the fusion ban.

In this case, and presumably in most cases, the burden of a statute of this kind is imposed upon the members of a minor party, but its potential impact is much broader. Popular candidates like Andy Dawkins sometimes receive nation-wide recognition. Fiorello LaGuardia, Earl Warren, Ronald Reagan, and Franklin D. Roosevelt are names that come readily to mind as candidates whose reputations and political careers were enhanced because they appeared on election ballots as fusion candidates. See Note, *Fusion and the Associational Rights of Minor Political Parties*, 95 Colum. L. Rev. 683 (1995). A statute that denied a political party the right to nominate any of those individuals for high office simply because he had already been nominated by another party would, in my opinion, place an intolerable burden on political expression and association.

II

Minnesota argues that the statutory restriction on the Party's right to nominate the candidate of its choice is justified by the State's interests in avoiding voter confusion, preventing ballot clutter and manipulation, encouraging candidate competition, and minimizing intraparty factionalism. None of these rationales can support the fusion ban because the State has failed to explain how the ban actually serves the asserted interests. . . .

While the State describes some imaginative theoretical sources of voter confusion that could result from fusion candidacies, in my judgment the argument that the burden on First Amendment interests is justified by this concern is meritless and severely underestimates the intelligence of the typical voter. We have noted more than once that "[a] State's claim that it is enhancing the ability of its citizenry to make wise decisions by restricting the flow of information to them must be viewed with some skepticism." *Eu*, 489 U.S. at 228; *Tashjian*, 479 U.S. at 221; *Anderson*, 460 U.S. at 798.

The State's concern about ballot manipulation, readily accepted by the majority, is similarly farfetched. The possibility that members of the major parties will begin to create dozens of minor parties with detailed, issue-oriented titles for the sole purpose of nominating candidates under those titles, is entirely hypothetical. The majority dismisses out-of-hand the Party's argument that the risk of this type of ballot manipulation and crowding is more easily averted by maintaining reasonably stringent requirements for the creation of minor parties. In fact, though, the Party's point merely illustrates the idea that a State can place some kinds — but not every kind — of limitation on the abilities of small parties to thrive. If the State wants to make it more difficult for any group to achieve the legal status of being a political party, it can do so within reason and still not run up against the First Amendment. . . .

The State argues that the fusion ban promotes political stability by preventing intraparty factionalism and party raiding. States do certainly have an interest in maintaining a stable political system. *Eu*, 489 U.S. at 226. But the State has not convincingly articulated how the fusion ban will prevent the factionalism it fears. Unlike the law at issue in *Storer v. Brown*, 415 U.S. 724 (1974), for example, this law would not prevent sore-loser candidates from defecting with a disaffected segment of a major party and running as an opposition candidate for a newly formed minor party. Nor does this law, like those aimed at requiring parties to show a modicum of support in order to secure a place on the election ballot, prevent the formation of numerous small parties. Indeed, the activity banned by Minnesota's law is the formation of coalitions, not the division and dissension of "splintered parties and unrestrained factionalism." *Id.*, at 736.

As for the State's argument that the fusion ban encourages candidate competition, this claim treats "candidates" as fungible goods, ignoring entirely each party's interest in nominating not just any candidate, but the candidate who best represents the party's views. Minnesota's fusion ban simply cannot be justified with reference to this or any of the above-mentioned rationales. I turn, therefore, to what appears to be the true basis for the Court's holding—the interest in preserving the two-party system.

III

. . . In most States, perhaps in all, there are two and only two major political parties. It is not surprising, therefore, that most States have enacted election laws that impose burdens on the development and growth of third parties. The law at issue in this case is undeniably such a law. The fact that the law was both intended to disadvantage minor parties and has had that effect is a matter that should weigh against, rather than in favor of, its constitutionality.

Our jurisprudence in this area reflects a certain tension: On the one hand, we have been clear that political stability is an important state interest and that incidental burdens on the formation of minor parties are reasonable to protect that interest, *see Storer*, 415 U.S., at 736; on the other, we have struck down state elections laws specifically because they give "the two old, established parties a decided advantage over any new parties struggling for existence," *Williams v. Rhodes*, 393 U.S. 23, 31 (1968). Between these boundaries, we have acknowledged that there is "no litmus-paper test for separating those restrictions that are valid from those that are invidious. . . . The rule is not self-executing and is no substitute for the hard judgments that must be made." *Storer*, 415 U.S., at 730.

Nothing in the Constitution prohibits the States from maintaining single-member districts with winner-take-all voting arrangements. And these elements of an election system do make it significantly more difficult for third parties to thrive. But these laws are different in two respects from the fusion bans at issue here. First, the method by which they hamper third-party development is not one that impinges on the associational rights of those third parties; minor parties remain free to nominate candidates of their choice, and to rally support for those candidates. The small parties' relatively limited likelihood of ultimate success on election day does not deprive them of the right to try. Second, the establishment of single-member districts correlates directly with the States' interests in political stability. Systems of proportional representation, for example, may tend toward factionalism and fragile coalitions that diminish legislative effectiveness. In the context of fusion candidacies, the risks to political stability are extremely attenuated. Of course, the reason minor parties so ardently support fusion politics is because it allows the parties to build up a greater base of support, as potential minor party members realize that a vote for the smaller party candidate is not necessarily a "wasted" vote.

Eventually, a minor party might gather sufficient strength that—were its members so inclined—it could successfully run a candidate not endorsed by any major party, and legislative coalition building will be made more difficult by the presence of third-party legislators. But the risks to political stability in that scenario are speculative at best.

In some respects, the fusion candidacy is the best marriage of the virtues of the minor party challenge to entrenched viewpoints and the political stability that the two-party system provides. The fusion candidacy does not threaten to divide the legislature and create significant risks of factionalism, which is the principal risk proponents of the two-party system point to. But it does provide a means by which voters with viewpoints not adequately represented by the platforms of the two major parties can indicate to a particular candidate that—in addition to his support for the major party views—he should be responsive to the views of the minor party whose support for him was demonstrated where political parties demonstrate support—on the ballot. . . .

In my opinion legislation that would otherwise be unconstitutional because it burdens First Amendment interests and discriminates against minor political parties cannot survive simply because it benefits the two major parties. Accordingly, I respectfully dissent.

    Justice SOUTER, dissenting.

    I join Parts I and II of Justice Stevens's dissent. . . . I am, however, unwilling to go the further distance of considering and rejecting the majority's "preservation of the two-party system" rationale. . . . There is considerable consensus that party loyalty among American voters has declined significantly in the past four decades, see, *e.g.,* W. Crotty, American Parties in Decline 26-34 (2d ed. 1984); Jensen, The Last Party System: Decay of Consensus, 1932-1980, in The Evolution of American Electoral Systems 219-225 (P. Kleppner et al. eds. 1981), and that the overall influence of the parties in the political process has decreased considerably, see, *e.g.,* Cutler, Party Government Under the American Constitution, 134 U. Penn. L. Rev. 25 (1987); Sundquist, Party Decay and the Capacity to Govern, in The Future of American Political Parties: The Challenge of Governance 42-69 (J. Fleishman ed. 1982). In the wake of such studies, it may not be unreasonable to infer that the two-party system is in some jeopardy. See, *e.g.,* Lowi, N.Y. Times, Aug. 23, 1992, Magazine, p. 28 ("[H]istorians will undoubtably focus on 1992 as the beginning of the end of America's two-party system").

    Surely the majority is right that States "have a strong interest in the stability of their political systems," *ante,* that is, in preserving a political system capable of governing effectively. If it could be shown that the disappearance of the two-party system would undermine that interest, and that permitting fusion candidacies poses a substantial threat to the two-party scheme, there might well be a sufficient predicate for recognizing the constitutionality of the state action presented by this case. Right now, however, no State has attempted even to make this argument, and I would therefore leave its consideration for another day.

>> *Origins of the Two-Party System.* As the Court observes in *Timmons*, the two-party system is the nearly universal form of political organization throughout the United States. How did this occur? Did institutional designers make a deliberate choice to create two and only two major political parties? As we have seen, the Framers of the U.S. Constitution did not want *any* parties, much less two, much less two permanent parties locked in perpetual opposition; this seems to rule out a conscious choice, at least on the federal level.

The common wisdom among political scientists is that the two-party system was not deliberately chosen, but is rather an unforeseen consequence of a different choice that was deliberate: the choice to select legislative bodies from single-member districts using a plurality-vote rule for determining winners. This system, sometimes referred to as a "plurality," "winner-take-all," or "first-past-the-post" system, is the familiar one in which different candidates compete head-to-head for the legislative seats from each district, and the winner in each district is the one who polls the most votes (a plurality). In some variations, the winner must poll a majority of votes cast, sometimes requiring a subsequent runoff election between the top two contenders.

In a comparative study performed in the 1950s, the political scientist Maurice Duverger became the first to notice that jurisdictions that use Anglo-American style, districted, winner-take-all electoral systems tend to have only two parties, whereas jurisdictions that use forms of proportional representation tend to have strong and stable multiparty political systems. *See* MAURICE DUVERGER, POLITICAL PARTIES: THEIR ORIGINS AND ACTIVITY IN THE MODERN STATE (1954). This empirical connection is now thought to reflect a causal connection between the structure of electoral systems and the structure of the party system, a principle that has since become known as "Duverger's Law." According to Duverger's Law, different requirements for winning legislative seats create different incentives, in turn resulting in different party structures:

> If winning is defined as receiving the most votes; that is, as a plurality, then one might reasonably expect a two-party system owing to the necessity under this definition of maximizing votes. Since the best way, in the long run, to get the most votes is to get more than half, each of two parties might be expected to structure a coalition in the hope, *before the election*, of getting a majority. . . . And if winning is defined as the achievement of some number of votes less than half (as is necessarily the case under proportional representation), then the necessity of maximizing disappears entirely.

William H. Riker, *Duverger's Law Revisited, in* ELECTORAL LAWS AND THEIR POLITICAL CONSEQUENCES 21 (Bernard Grofman and Arend Lijphart eds., 1986). In other words, the rules of the game in a districted, winner-take-all system give parties an incentive to appeal to the widest possible spectrum of voters in the hope of winning a majority of votes cast in single-member districts. A plethora of parties cannot successfully compete for this advantageous kind of broad appeal, because a plethora of parties will by definition split the vote. As a result, parties that are initially less successful at appealing broadly will find themselves squeezed out by the two parties that are more successful. Moreover, the two major parties will then enjoy a significant advantage in maintaining their competitive primacy: these parties can easily fend off challenges from smaller parties simply by altering their positions slightly so as to broaden their appeal just enough to capture support from those who would otherwise support minor party candidates. This makes the two-party system a stable one. This dynamic has played out many times in American politics. In a typical pattern, major parties co-opt positions taken by minor party challengers:

> Minor parties often advocate policies not embraced by the major parties. Frequently, the major parties respond rationally to this signal that there are disgruntled voters and adopt the third parties' positions as their own. Often these new positions can be accommodated with relatively little discomfort to the party. Indeed, a major party's very survival depends on its ability to build a broad, heterogeneous coalition. Only third parties with the most extreme beliefs or narrowest of constituencies are immune from these raids.

STEVEN J. ROSENSTONE, ROY L. BEHR, AND EDWARD H. LAZARUS, THIRD PARTIES IN AMERICA: CITIZEN RESPONSE TO MAJOR PARTY FAILURE 43 (rev. 2d ed. 1984).

Is a conscious preference for single-member districts and outright plurality or majoritarian elections the same as a preference for a two-party system?

So-called sore loser laws—laws that prohibit candidates who lose party primaries from later running in the general election as the candidate of a different party or as an independent—further lock the political process into a two-party model by requiring that pre-election conflict be resolved in the forum of major party primaries. Is this kind of reinforcement of the two-party model advisable? Does it marginalize candidates and voters lying outside the main currents of opinion with their parties? And if so, does that mechanism contribute to the polarization of parties and partisan officials? *See* Michael S. Kang, *Sore Loser Laws and Democratic Contestation*, 99 GEO. L.J. 1013 (2011).

⏭ *Two-Party vs. Multiparty Systems.*   Proponents of the two-party system typically make several arguments in its favor. Perhaps the most common argument is that a two-party system produces strong leadership and a concomitant capacity to govern. Because in a two-party system one party is necessarily rewarded with control over the legislative chamber (though not necessarily, in a bicameral system, over both chambers), a two-party system is more likely to result in majoritarian control over the government, in turn ensuring that the government will be able to act decisively and pursuant to a single, coherent plan. This is said to distinguish a government in a two-party system from a government in a multiparty system, which must constantly compromise to bring along its coalition partners. Another common and related argument is that two-party systems enhance democratic accountability. The tendency of such systems to award seats disproportionately to the majority party makes them extremely sensitive to small changes in public opinion:

> The leaders of a political party that can remain in power despite considerable loss of electoral support will clearly find less need to take account of popular opinion than the leaders of a party who realize that only a relatively small reduction in their electoral strength will remove them from office. One of the most criticized consequences of the plurality system,

> the wide variation in votes cast to seats won, therefore becomes a positive advantage for the development of responsive governments. Within a plurality system a relatively small loss of votes will result in a disproportionately large loss of seats for the largest parliamentary parties and will be likely to threaten their ability to form part of a government.

J.A. Chandler, *The Plurality Vote: A Reappraisal*, 30 POL. STUD. 87, 92 (1982). Moreover, a governing party that does not respond effectively to changes in public opinion will, on this view, be more vulnerable to "expulsion" from office; winner-take-all systems thus provide voters with a more effective "means of ousting" than does proportional representation. Michael Pinto-Duschinsky, *Send the Rascals Packing: Defects of Proportional Representation and the Virtues of the Westminster Model*, 25 TIMES LITERARY SUPP. 10 (Sept. 25, 1998).

Yet another argument in favor of the two-party system is that governments formed under it will be more moderate than those formed under multiparty systems. Because a two-party system places such a premium on majority support, it "encourages the competing parties to adopt a majority-forming attitude. The parties incline to be moderate, to seek conciliation." Quentin L. Quade, *PR and Democratic Statecraft*, 2 J. DEMOCRACY 36, 41 (Summer 1991). This forces the parties "to coalesce before the balloting occurs," a process that requires them to "synthesize the divergent interests and opinions" of voters. Guy Lardeyret, *The Problem with PR*, 2 J. DEMOCRACY 30, 33 (Summer 1991). The result is a majority government of moderate views.

Are these arguments sufficient to support the maintenance of a two-party system? What about the lack of choice presented to voters? Does a two-party system impose excessive costs on voters who are dissatisfied with the existing party choices by essentially forcing them either to work for change within one of the two major parties or to waste their effort and votes on minor parties with no realistic chance to win elections? For an argument that the defense of the two-party system has been overtaken by changes in contemporary campaigning, which subordinate the interests of parties to those of individual marquee candidates, see Richard L. Hasen, *Entrenching the Duopoly: Why the Supreme Court Should Not Allow the States to Protect the Democrats and Republicans from Political Competition*, 1997 SUP. CT. REV. 331.

Do we have a two-party system because we prefer it, or do we prefer a two-party system because we have it? For the latter view, see LISA JANE DISCH, THE TYRANNY OF THE TWO-PARTY SYSTEM (2002).

>> *A Two-Party System vs. Two Specific Parties.* As the Court made clear in *Williams v. Rhodes*, preferring a two-party system is not the same as preferring any two particular parties; the critical criterion is that there be two parties, not that they have a certain identity or take any particular positions on public policy. Nevertheless, how likely is it in practice that a minor party will be able to overtake and replace one of the existing major parties? On the national level, the odds are low. The last major national party to lose its advantaged position was the Whig Party, which began to decline after Winfield Scott's devastating loss to Franklin Pierce in 1852, and failed to field a presidential candidate in any subsequent election. The Democratic and Republican parties have been the two major parties in the United States since 1856.

Here are the most successful third-party runs at the U.S. presidency by date, candidate, party name, and percentage of the popular vote:

1912	Theodore Roosevelt	Progressive	27.4%
1856	Millard Fillmore	Whig-American	21.5
1992	H. Ross Perot	Independent	18.9
1860	John C. Breckinridge	Southern Democrat	18.1
1924	Robert LaFollette	Progressive	16.6
1968	George Wallace	American Independent	13.5
1860	John Bell	Constitutional Union	12.6
1848	Martin Van Buren	Free Soil	10.1
1892	James B. Weaver	Populist	8.5
1980	John B. Anderson	Independent	6.6

Source: Rosenstone et al., *supra*, App. A.

Note that several of these candidacies occurred between 1848 and 1860, while the Whigs were in decline and before the new Republican Party had consolidated its status as a major party. Although identifiable minor party candidates have been present in every presidential election since the solidification of the modern political party as an institution in the late 1830s, few have polled as well as the candidates listed above. Between LaFollette's showing in 1924 and Wallace's in 1968, for example, no minor party candidate earned as much as 3 percent of the popular vote.

Third parties also had considerable success for much of American history in electing candidates to Congress. In all but two federal elections between 1828 and 1944, minor parties elected at least one member of the House.

>> *The Two-Party System as One-Party System.* Although the two-party system has produced reasonably competitive presidential elections for the last 150 years, its reliability on the national level does not necessarily imply the same reliability on the local level. In fact, during some periods in some areas of the country, one of the two major parties has been so far ascendant over the other as to render the idea of two-party competition on the state and local levels something of an exaggeration, if not an outright sham. This was so in the American South, for example, from about the 1920s through the 1990s, when the Democratic Party was the only game in town. In consequence, the only elections that really mattered in the South during this period were Democratic primary elections: whoever got the Democratic nomination was virtually assured of winning the general election.

One might think that a functionally one-party system might nevertheless operate much as a two-party system would in that all significant political competition within the jurisdiction would simply be funneled into the only party organization available, and would reassert itself in the form of spirited intraparty contests for the Democratic nomination. In some cases something like this did occur. For example, in Florida between 1920 and 1948, the median percentage of the Democratic vote polled by the winner of the Democratic gubernatorial primary was 57 percent, with a low of 30 percent, suggesting that, over the long run, Democratic primaries were reasonably competitive. On the other hand, the median winning percentage in Democratic gubernatorial primaries during the same period in Tennessee and Virginia was over 98 percent. This latter figure reveals an exceptional degree of factional dominance within the Democratic Party in those states, suggesting that the kind of competition supposedly fostered by the two-party system was not occurring under the umbrella of the single dominant party. *See* V.O. KEY, JR., SOUTHERN POLITICS 17 (1950). According to Key, this situation severely distorted politics in the South from the models contemplated by party-friendly political theories:

> In the conduct of campaigns for the control of legislatures, for the control of governorships, and for representatives in the national Congress, the South must depend for political leadership, not on political parties, but on lone-wolf operators, on fortuitous groups of individuals usually of a transient nature, on spectacular demagogues odd enough to command the attention of considerable numbers of voters, on men who have become persons of political consequence in their own little bailiwicks, and on other types of leaders whose methods to attract electoral attention serve as substitutes of leadership of a party organization. . . .
>
> [This kind of f]actional fluidity and discontinuity probably makes a government especially susceptible to individual pressures and especially disposed toward favoritism. . . . In a loose, catch-as-catch-can politics highly unstable coalitions must be held together by whatever means is available. This contract goes to that contractor, this distributor is dealt with by the state liquor board, that group of attorneys have an "in" at the statehouse, this bond house is favored. Such practices occur in organized politics, to be sure, but an organized politics is also better able to establish general standards, to resist individual claims for preference, and to consider individual actions in the light of general policy. . . .

Id. at 16, 305.

C.   CANDIDATE SELECTION

Having secured access to the ballot for its candidates, a qualifying party must choose those candidates. It is generally agreed that candidate selection is "one of the central defining functions of a political party in a democracy."

> This is true not only in the sense that selection of candidates to contest elections is one of the functions that separates parties from other organizations that may try to influence electoral outcomes and governmental decisions, but also in the sense that the candidates it nominates play an important role in defining what the party is. . . . [A] party's candidates in large measure define and constitute its public face in elections . . . . They articulate and interpret the party's record from the past and its program

and promises for the future. . . . [C]andidacy is one of the main recruit-
ment routes for membership in the [public] face of the party. . . .

Richard S. Katz, *The Problem of Candidate Selection and Models of Party Democracy,* 7
PARTY POLS. 277, 278 (2001).

In most of the world, parties are free to adopt whatever methods of candidate
selection they prefer. In the United States, however, procedures of candidate
selection have long been regulated by law, meaning that party procedures of
candidate selection tend to be a mixture of government regulation and party self-
regulation. Because the selection of candidates is so deeply bound up with a party's
identity and capacity to communicate its message effectively and persuasively, government regulation inevitably affects the constitutionally protected associational
interests of party members.

Today, virtually all major elective offices in the United States are filled in
a two-step process. In the first phase, each political party chooses its candidate
from a field of contenders; in the second phase, the nominees of the various
parties compete against each other. Until not long ago, political parties typically
chose their nominees in the proverbial "smoke-filled room." That is, party officers assembled at a caucus or convention and bargained among themselves to
select a candidate. This type of selection process was criticized on at least two
grounds. First, the convention process largely excluded the party's rank-and-
file members from participating in the crucial decision of whom to nominate,
making the process undemocratic. Second, nominations often were arranged
through a process of exchanging promises, favors, and patronage that left nominees with large political "debts" to repay and could lead to corruption and favoritism, in addition to an undemocratic result. Particularly during the Progressive
Era, reformers worked, with considerable success, to institute primary elections
for the purpose of giving party members greater control over the selection of
party nominees.

1.   *Eligibility to Vote in Primaries: The White Primary Cases*

For most political parties, the essence of party membership involves participation in the selection of a candidate for office. Consequently, voting in party
primaries seems to be an area in which any party interest in autonomy would be
strongest. On the other hand, voting, even in a primary, implicates the voting rights
of citizens, a traditional area of state concern. What happens when these two interests collide and the state tries to regulate voting eligibility in political primaries?

In *Nixon v. Herndon,* 273 U.S. 536 (1927), the Supreme Court invalidated a
Texas statute forbidding blacks to vote in any primary election conducted by the
Democratic Party. Because the state itself was the source of the prohibition, the
Court had no trouble striking down the law as a violation of equal protection,
observing that it was "hard to imagine a more direct and obvious infringement."
But what happens if such a rule is enacted by a political party itself? That is just
what the Texas Democratic Party subsequently did; the issue reached the Court in
the following case.

Smith v. Allwright

321 U.S. 649 (1944)

Mr. Justice REED delivered the opinion of the Court.

This writ of certiorari brings here for review a claim for damages in the sum of $5,000 on the part of petitioner, a Negro citizen of the 48th precinct of Harris County, Texas, for the refusal of respondents, election and associate election judges respectively of that precinct, to give petitioner a ballot or to permit him to cast a ballot in the primary election of July 27, 1940, for the nomination of Democratic candidates for the United States Senate and House of Representatives, and Governor and other state officers. The refusal is alleged to have been solely because of the race and color of the proposed voter.

The actions of respondents are said to violate §§31 and 43 of Title 8 of the United States Code in that petitioner was deprived of rights secured by §§2 and 4 of Article I and the Fourteenth, Fifteenth and Seventeenth Amendments to the United States Constitution.[1]

The State of Texas by its Constitution and statutes provides that every person, if certain other requirements are met which are not here in issue, qualified by residence in the district or county "shall be deemed a qualified elector." Constitution of Texas, Article VI, §2; Vernon's Civil Statutes (1939 ed.), Article 2955. Primary elections for United States Senators, Congressmen and state officers are provided for by Chapters Twelve and Thirteen of the statutes. Under these chapters, the Democratic party was required to hold the primary which was the occasion of the alleged wrong to petitioner. . . .

The Democratic party on May 24, 1932, in a state convention adopted the following resolution, which has not since been "amended, abrogated, annulled or avoided":

> Be it resolved that all white citizens of the State of Texas who are qualified to vote under the Constitution and laws of the State shall be eligible to membership in the Democratic party and, as such, entitled to participate in its deliberations.

---

1. 8 U.S.C. §31:

   "All citizens of the United States who are otherwise qualified by law to vote at any election by the people in any State, Territory, district, county, city, parish, township, school district, municipality, or other territorial subdivision, shall be entitled and allowed to vote at all such elections, without distinction of race, color, or previous condition of servitude; any constitution, law, custom, usage, or regulation of any State or Territory, or by or under its authority, to the contrary notwithstanding."

   §43:

   "Every person who, under color of any statute, ordinance, regulation, custom, or usage, of any State or Territory, subjects, or causes to be subjected, any citizen of the United States or other person within the jurisdiction thereof to the deprivation of any rights, privileges, or immunities secured by the Constitution and laws, shall be liable to the party injured in an action at law, suit in equity, or other proper proceeding for redress." . . .

It was by virtue of this resolution that the respondents refused to permit the petitioner to vote.

Texas is free to conduct her elections and limit her electorate as she may deem wise, save only as her action may be affected by the prohibitions of the United States Constitution or in conflict with powers delegated to and exercised by the National Government. The Fourteenth Amendment forbids a State from making or enforcing any law which abridges the privileges or immunities of citizens of the United States and the Fifteenth Amendment specifically interdicts any denial or abridgement by a State of the right of citizens to vote on account of color. Respondents appeared in the District Court and the Circuit Court of Appeals and defended on the ground that the Democratic party of Texas is a voluntary organization with members banded together for the purpose of selecting individuals of the group representing the common political beliefs as candidates in the general election. As such a voluntary organization, it was claimed, the Democratic party is free to select its own membership and limit to whites participation in the party primary. Such action, the answer asserted, does not violate the Fourteenth, Fifteenth or Seventeenth Amendment as officers of government cannot be chosen at primaries and the Amendments are applicable only to general elections where governmental officers are actually elected. Primaries, it is said, are political party affairs, handled by party, not governmental, officers. . . .

It may now be taken as a postulate that the right to vote in such a primary for the nomination of candidates without discrimination by the State, like the right to vote in a general election, is a right secured by the Constitution. *United States v. Classic*, 313 U.S. at 314; *Ex parte Yarbrough*, 110 U.S. 651, 663 *et seq.* By the terms of the Fifteenth Amendment that right may not be abridged by any State on account of race. Under our Constitution the great privilege of the ballot may not be denied a man by the State because of his color.

We are thus brought to an examination of the qualifications for Democratic primary electors in Texas, to determine whether state action or private action has excluded Negroes from participation. . . .

Texas requires by the law the election of the county officers of a party. These compose the county executive committee. The county chairmen so selected are members of the district executive committee and choose the chairman for the district. Precinct primary election officers are named by the county executive committee. Statutes provide for the election by the voters of precinct delegates to the county convention of a party and the selection of delegates to the district and state conventions by the county convention. The state convention selects the state executive committee. No convention may place in platform or resolution any demand for specific legislation without endorsement of such legislation by the voters in a primary. Texas thus directs the selection of all party officers.

Primary elections are conducted by the party under state statutory authority. The county executive committee selects precinct election officials and the county, district or state executive committees, respectively, canvass the returns. These party committees or the state convention certify the party's candidates to the appropriate officers for inclusion on the official ballot for the general election. No name which has not been so certified may appear upon the ballot for the general election as a candidate of a political party. No other name may be printed on the ballot which has not been placed in nomination by qualified voters who must take oath that they did not participate in a primary for the selection of a candidate for the office for which the nomination is made.

The state courts are given exclusive original jurisdiction of contested elections and of mandamus proceedings to compel party officers to perform their statutory duties.

We think that this statutory system for the selection of party nominees for inclusion on the general election ballot makes the party which is required to follow these legislative directions an agency of the State in so far as it determines the participants in a primary election. The party takes its character as a state agency from the duties imposed upon it by state statutes; the duties do not become matters of private law because they are performed by a political party. . . .

When primaries become a part of the machinery for choosing officials, state and national, as they have here, the same tests to determine the character of discrimination or abridgement should be applied to the primary as are applied to the general election. If the State requires a certain electoral procedure, prescribes a general election ballot made up of party nominees so chosen and limits the choice of the electorate in general elections for state offices, practically speaking, to those whose names appear on such a ballot, it endorses, adopts and enforces the discrimination against Negroes, practiced by a party entrusted by Texas law with the determination of the qualifications of participants in the primary. This is state action within the meaning of the Fifteenth Amendment. *Guinn v. United States*, 238 U.S. 347, 362.

The United States is a constitutional democracy. Its organic law grants to all citizens a right to participate in the choice of elected officials without restriction by any State because of race. This grant to the people of the opportunity for choice is not to be nullified by a State through casting its electoral process in a form which permits a private organization to practice racial discrimination in the election. Constitutional rights would be of little value if they could be thus indirectly denied. *Lane v. Wilson*, 307 U.S. 268, 275.

The privilege of membership in a party may be, as this Court said in *Grovey v. Townsend*, 295 U.S. 45, 55, no concern of a State. But when, as here, that privilege is also the essential qualification for voting in a primary to select nominees for a general election, the State makes the action of the party the action of the State.

Terry v. Adams

345 U.S. 461 (1953)

Mr. Justice BLACK announced the judgment of the Court and an opinion in which Mr. Justice DOUGLAS and Mr. Justice BURTON join.

In *Smith v. Allwright*, 321 U.S. 649, we held that rules of the Democratic Party of Texas excluding Negroes from voting in the party's primaries violated the Fifteenth Amendment. While no state law directed such exclusion, our decision pointed out that many party activities were subject to considerable statutory control. This case raises questions concerning the constitutional power of a Texas county political organization called the Jaybird Democratic Association or Jaybird Party to exclude Negroes from its primaries on racial grounds. The Jaybirds deny that their racial exclusions violate the Fifteenth Amendment. They contend that the Amendment applies only to elections or primaries held under state regulation, that their association is not regulated by the state at all, and that it is not a political party but a self-governing voluntary club. . . .

The Jaybird Association or Party was organized in 1889. Its membership was then and always has been limited to white people; they are automatically members if their names appear on the official list of county voters. It has been run like other political parties with an executive committee named from the county's voting precincts. Expenses of the party are paid by the assessment of candidates for office in its primaries. Candidates for county offices submit their names to the Jaybird Committee in accordance with the normal practice followed by regular political parties all over the country. Advertisements and posters proclaim that these candidates are running subject to the action of the Jaybird primary. While there is no legal compulsion on successful Jaybird candidates to enter Democratic primaries, they have nearly always done so and with few exceptions since 1889 have run and won without opposition in the Democratic primaries and the general elections that followed. Thus the party has been the dominant political group in the county since organization, having endorsed every county-wide official elected since 1889.

It is apparent that Jaybird activities follow a plan purposefully designed to exclude Negroes from voting and at the same time to escape the Fifteenth Amendment's command that the right of citizens to vote shall neither be denied nor abridged on account of race. These were the admitted party purposes according to the following testimony of the Jaybird's president:

Q. . . . Now Mr. Adams, will you tell me specifically what is the specific purpose of holding these elections and carrying on this organization like you do?

A. Good government.

Q. Now I will ask you to state whether or not it is the opinion and policy of the Association that to carry on good government they must exclude negro citizens?

A. Well, when we started it was and it is still that way, I think.

Q. And then one of the purposes of your organization is for the specific purpose of excluding negroes from voting, isn't it?

A. Yes.

Q. And that is your policy?

A. Yes.

Q. I will ask you, that is the reason you hold your election in May rather than in June or July, isn't it?

A. Yes.

Q. Because if you held it in July you would have to abide by the statutes and the law by letting them vote?

A. They do vote in July.

Q. And if you held yours at that time they would have to vote too, wouldn't they?

A. Why sure.

Q. And you hold it in May so they won't have to?
A. Well, they don't vote in ours but they can vote on anybody in the July election they want to.
Q. But you are not answering my question. My question is that you hold yours in May so you won't have to let them vote, don't you?
A. Yes.
Q. And that is your purpose?
A. Yes.
Q. And your intention?
A. Yes.
Q. And to have a vote of the white population at a time when the negroes can't vote, isn't that right?
A. That's right.
Q. That is the whole policy of your Association?
A. Yes.
Q. And that is its purpose?
A. Yes. . . .

[T]he Fifteenth Amendment . . . bans racial discrimination in voting by both state and nation. It thus establishes a national policy, obviously applicable to the right of Negroes not to be discriminated against as voters in elections to determine public governmental policies or to select public officials, national, state, or local. . . .

It is significant that precisely the same qualifications as those prescribed by Texas entitling electors to vote at county-operated primaries are adopted as the sole qualifications entitling electors to vote at the county-wide Jaybird primaries with a single proviso—Negroes are excluded. Everyone concedes that such a proviso in the county-operated primaries would be unconstitutional. The Jaybird Party thus brings into being and holds precisely the kind of election that the Fifteenth Amendment seeks to prevent. When it produces the equivalent of the prohibited election, the damage has been done.

For a state to permit such a duplication of its election processes is to permit a flagrant abuse of those processes to defeat the purposes of the Fifteenth Amendment. The use of the county-operated primary to ratify the result of the prohibited election merely compounds the offense. It violates the Fifteenth Amendment for a state, by such circumvention, to permit within its borders the use of any device that produces an equivalent of the prohibited election.

The only election that has counted in this Texas county for more than fifty years has been that held by the Jaybirds from which Negroes were excluded. The Democratic primary and the general election have become no more than the perfunctory ratifiers of the choice that has already been made in Jaybird elections from which Negroes have been excluded. It is immaterial that the state does not control that part of this elective process which it leaves for the Jaybirds to manage. The Jaybird primary has become an integral part, indeed the only effective part, of the elective process that determines who shall rule and govern in the county. The effect of the whole procedure, Jaybird primary plus Democratic primary plus general election, is to do precisely that which the Fifteenth Amendment forbids—strip

Negroes of every vestige of influence in selecting the officials who control the local county matters that intimately touch the daily lives of citizens. . . .

Mr. Justice FRANKFURTER.

. . . To find a denial or abridgment of the guaranteed voting right to colored citizens of Texas solely because they are colored, one must find that the State has had a hand in it. . . . As the action of the entire white voting community, the Jaybird primary is as a practical matter the instrument of those few in this small county who are politically active—the officials of the local Democratic party and, we may assume, the elected officials of the county. . . . They join the white voting community in proceeding with elaborate formality, in almost all respects parallel to the procedures dictated by Texas law for the primary itself, to express their preferences in a wholly successful effort to withdraw significance from the State-prescribed primary, to subvert the operation of what is formally the law of the State for primaries in this county. . . .

The State of Texas has entered into a comprehensive scheme of regulation of political primaries, including procedures by which election officials shall be chosen. The county election officials are thus clothed with the authority of the State to secure observance of the State's interest in "fair methods and a fair expression" of preferences in the selection of nominees. *Cf. Waples v. Marrast*, 108 Tex. 5, 12, 184 S.W. 180, 183. If the Jaybird Association, although not a political party, is a device to defeat the law of Texas regulating primaries, and if the electoral officials, clothed with State power in the county, share in that subversion, they cannot divest themselves of the State authority and help as participants in the scheme. . . . This is a case in which county election officials have participated in and condoned a continued effort effectively to exclude Negroes from voting. . . .

Mr. Justice CLARK, with whom THE CHIEF JUSTICE, Mr. Justice REED, and Mr. Justice JACKSON join, concurring.

We agree that . . . the Jaybird Democratic Association is a political party whose activities fall within the Fifteenth Amendment's self-executing ban. Not every private club, association or league organized to influence public candidacies or political action must conform to the Constitution's restrictions on political parties. Certainly a large area of freedom permits peaceable assembly and concerted private action for political purposes to be exercised separately by white and colored citizens alike. More, however, is involved here.

The record discloses that the Jaybird Democratic Association operates as part and parcel of the Democratic Party, an organization existing under the auspices of Texas law. . . . Quite evidently the Jaybird Democratic Association operates as an auxiliary of the local Democratic Party organization, selecting its nominees and using its machinery for carrying out an admitted design of destroying the weight and effect of Negro ballots in Fort Bend County. To be sure, the Democratic primary and the general election are nominally open to the colored elector. But his must be an empty vote cast after the real decisions are made. And because the Jaybird-indorsed nominee meets no opposition in the Democratic primary, the Negro minority's vote is nullified at the sole stage of the local political process where the bargaining and interplay of rival political forces would make it count.

The Jaybird Democratic Association device, as a result, strikes to the core of the electoral process in Fort Bend County. Whether viewed as a separate political organization or as an adjunct of the local Democratic Party, the Jaybird Democratic Association is the decisive power in the county's recognized electoral process. Over the years its balloting has emerged as the locus of effective political choice. . . . [W]hen a state structures its electoral apparatus in a form which devolves upon a political organization the uncontested choice of public officials, that organization itself, in whatever disguise, takes on those attributes of government which draw the Constitution's safeguards into play. *Smith v. Allwright, supra,* at 664.

2. Federal and State Power to Regulate Partisan Primaries

Because the Constitution contains unique provisions dealing directly with racial discrimination, the foregoing cases do not necessarily shed much light on the power of the state and federal governments to regulate, on non-racial grounds, the main features of primary elections. We turn now to that question.

Most primary elections are conducted in a way that is indistinguishable from the general election: voters go to the same official polling place, deal with the same election officials, and use the same official ballots or voting machines as for the general election. This is because government has undertaken to regulate primary elections in much the same way as it regulates general elections. However, there is an important difference between the two types of elections. Unlike a general election, which determines authoritatively and for all the people who gets to hold offices created by law, a primary election is simply a vehicle by which a private association of individuals decides whom to put up as a candidate. If a primary election is merely a private decision by a private group—much like the selection of officers by a chapter of the Rotary Club or the Elks—a question arises as to the power of the government to regulate it.

≫ *Federal Power to Regulate Primaries.*   The Supreme Court first addressed the question of federal power in *Newberry v. United States,* 256 U.S. 232 (1921). Truman Newberry sought the Republican nomination for the 1918 Senate race in Michigan. Newberry spent a huge sum of money to obtain his party's nomination, thereby violating a federal law that imposed a cap on the amount that any Senate candidate could spend in a primary election. Upon his indictment, Newberry moved to dismiss on the ground that the federal cap was unconstitutional; he contended that Congress lacked the constitutional power to regulate primary elections. A plurality of the Court agreed.

The government argued that Congress had the power to regulate primary elections under Article I, §4, which provides: "The times, places and manner of holding elections for Senators and Representatives, shall be prescribed in each State by the Legislature thereof; but the Congress may at any time by law make or alter such regulations. . . ." Justice McReynolds wrote for four Justices that the word "elections" must be given the meaning it had

when the Constitution came into existence—final choice of an officer by the duly qualified electors. Primaries were then unknown. Moreover, they are in no sense elections for an office, but merely methods by which party adherents agree upon candidates whom they intend to offer and support for ultimate choice by all qualified electors. General provisions touching elections in constitutions or statutes are not necessarily applicable to primaries — the two things are radically different.

Twenty years later, in *United States v. Classic,* 313 U.S. 299 (1941), the Court reversed field and held that Congress may regulate primary elections. The case concerned federal criminal charges against Louisiana election officials who had altered and miscounted ballots cast in a Democratic primary election for Congress. As in the *White Primary Cases,* the Court found the level of state involvement significant: the state required primary elections by law, paid for them, and limited ballot access to primary winners. "Interference with the right to vote in the Congressional primary," the Court held, "is thus, as a matter of law and in fact, an interference with the effective choice of the voters at the only stage of the election procedure when their choice is of significance, since it is at the only stage when such interference could have any practical effect on the ultimate result, the choice of the Congressman to represent the district." The kind of manipulation of a primary election with which the defendants were charged, if true, deprived primary voters of a right secured by the Constitution.

In a departure from its approach in *Newberry,* the Court took a generous view of the congressional power to regulate elections:

> We may assume that the framers of the Constitution . . . did not have specifically in mind the selection and elimination of candidates for Congress by the direct primary any more than they contemplated the application of the commerce clause to interstate telephone, telegraph and wireless communication, which are concededly within it. But in determining whether a provision of the Constitution applies to a new subject matter, it is of little significance that it is one with which the framers were not familiar. . . .

> [W]e think that the authority of Congress, given by [Article I,] §4, includes the authority to regulate primary elections when, as in this case, they are a step in the exercise by the people of their choice of representatives in Congress. . . .

> Unless the constitutional protection of the integrity of "elections" extends to primary elections, Congress is left powerless to effect the constitutional purpose, and the popular choice of representatives is stripped of its constitutional protection save only as Congress, by taking over the control of state elections, may exclude from them the influence of the state primaries. Such an expedient would end that state autonomy with respect to elections which the Constitution contemplated that Congress should be free to leave undisturbed, subject only to such minimum regulation as it should find necessary to insure the freedom and integrity of the choice. Words, especially those of a constitution, are not to be read with such stultifying narrowness. The words of §§2 and 4 of Article I, read in the sense which is plainly permissible and in the light of the constitutional purpose, require us to hold that a primary election which involves

a necessary step in the choice of candidates for election as representatives in Congress, and which in the circumstances of this case controls that choice, is an election within the meaning of the constitutional provision and is subject to congressional regulation as to the manner of holding it. . . .

>> *State Regulatory Power.*   If the power of Congress to regulate primaries in federal elections is now established, it is equally well established that the authority of *states* to regulate primary elections is subject to constitutional limitations. In *Cousins v. Wigoda*, 419 U.S. 477 (1975), for example, the Court invalidated an Illinois law that purported to control which slate of delegates of the state Democratic Party could be seated at the 1972 national Democratic Party convention to choose presidential and vice presidential candidates. The national party had ruled that the Illinois delegation had been selected in violation of national party rules, and refused to seat it, choosing instead to seat a different Illinois delegation chosen by other means. An Illinois court issued an injunction directing the national party to seat the rejected delegation, and the party sued. "The National Democratic Party and its adherents," said the Court, "enjoy a constitutionally protected right of political association," a right that entitled them to decide for themselves the procedures by which to choose presidential candidates.

> The States themselves have no constitutionally mandated role in the great task of the selection of Presidential and Vice-Presidential candidates. . . . [T]he National Party Convention [is] a concerted enterprise engaged in the vital process of choosing Presidential and Vice-Presidential candidates — a process which usually involves coalitions cutting across state lines. The Convention serves the pervasive national interest in the selection of candidates for national office, and this national interest is greater than any interest of an individual State.

Consequently, the state could not demonstrate a regulatory interest sufficient to justify its infringement of party members' rights of association.

The power of a state to influence the outcome of a primary election was again raised in *Democratic Party of Wisconsin v. La Follette*, 450 U.S. 107 (1981). Rule 2A of the National Democratic Party provided: "Participation in the delegate selection process in primaries or caucuses shall be restricted to Democratic voters only who publicly declare their party preference and have that preference publicly recorded." This rule meant that delegates to the national convention, at which the party nominated its candidates for President and Vice President, would be seated only if they were selected exclusively by registered Democrats; the party, understandably enough, wanted its candidates to be chosen by its own members. Wisconsin, however, had created by law a system of "open" or "crossover" primaries in which any eligible voter could vote in the primary election of any party without regard to the voter's own party affiliation. Further, the state by law required any delegates ultimately chosen to vote in accordance with the results of the open primary. The national party accordingly announced in 1979 that it would not seat delegates from Wisconsin at the 1980 nominating convention.

The Wisconsin Attorney General then filed suit seeking a declaration that the national party could not lawfully refuse to seat the Wisconsin delegates. The Wisconsin Supreme Court issued the requested declaration, and the Supreme Court reversed. Relying on *Cousins*, the Court found that Wisconsin's exercise of its authority to require the Democratic Party to seat representatives chosen and required to vote under a method disapproved by the party imposed a substantial burden on the party's rights of association. No state interest was found sufficient to justify the burden.

EU v. San Francisco County Democratic Central Committee

489 U.S. 214 (1989)

Justice MARSHALL delivered the opinion of the Court.

I

The State of California heavily regulates its political parties. Although the laws vary in extent and detail from party to party, certain requirements apply to all "ballot-qualified" parties. The California Elections Code (Code) provides that the "official governing bodies" for such a party are its "state convention," "state central committee," and "county central committees," Cal. Elec. Code Ann. §11702 (West 1977), and that these bodies are responsible for conducting the party's campaigns. At the same time, the Code provides that the official governing bodies "shall not endorse, support, or oppose, any candidate for nomination by that party for partisan office in the direct primary election." *Ibid.* It is a misdemeanor for any primary candidate, or a person on her behalf, to claim that she is the officially endorsed candidate of the party. §29430.

Although the official governing bodies of political parties are barred from issuing endorsements, other groups are not. Political clubs affiliated with a party, labor organizations, political action committees, other politically active associations, and newspapers frequently endorse primary candidates. With the official party organizations silenced by the ban, it has been possible for a candidate with views antithetical to those of her party nevertheless to win its primary.[4]

In addition to restricting the primary activities of the official governing bodies of political parties, California also regulates their internal affairs. Separate statutory provisions dictate the size and composition of the state central committees; set forth rules governing the selection and removal of committee members; fix the maximum term of office for the chair of the state central committee; require that the chair rotate between residents of northern and southern California; specify the time and place of committee meetings; and limit the dues parties may impose on members. Violations of these provisions are criminal offenses punishable by fine and imprisonment.

---

4. In 1980, for example, Tom Metzger won the Democratic Party's nomination for United States House of Representative from the San Diego area, although he was a Grand Dragon of the Ku Klux Klan and held views antithetical to those of the Democratic Party.

II

A State's broad power to regulate the time, place, and manner of elections "does not extinguish the State's responsibility to observe the limits established by the First Amendment rights of the State's citizens." *Tashjian.* To assess the constitutionality of a state election law, we first examine whether it burdens rights protected by the First and Fourteenth Amendments. *Id.* If the challenged law burdens the rights of political parties and their members, it can survive constitutional scrutiny only if the State shows that it advances a compelling state interest, and is narrowly tailored to serve that interest. *Tashjian, Kusper, Dunn.*

A

We first consider California's prohibition on primary endorsements by the official governing bodies of political parties. California concedes that its ban implicates the First Amendment, but contends that the burden is "minuscule." We disagree. The ban directly affects speech which "is at the core of our electoral process and of the First Amendment freedoms." *Williams v. Rhodes.* . . .

California's ban on primary endorsements . . . prevents party governing bodies from stating whether a candidate adheres to the tenets of the party or whether party official believe that the candidate is qualified for the position sought. This prohibition directly hampers the ability of a party to spread its message and hamstrings voters seeking to inform themselves about the candidates and the campaign issues. A "highly paternalistic approach" limiting what people may hear is generally suspect, *Virginia State Bd. of Pharmacy v. Virginia Citizens Consumer Council, Inc.*, 425 U.S. 748, 770 (1976), but it is particularly egregious where the State censors the political speech a political party shares with its members.

Barring political parties from endorsing and opposing candidates not only burdens their freedom of speech but also infringes upon their freedom of association. . . . Freedom of association means not only that an individual voter has the right to associate with the political party of her choice, *Tashjian, supra*, but also that a political party has a right to "identify the people who constitute the association," *id.*, and to select a "standard bearer who best represents the party's ideologies and preferences." *Ripon Society, Inc. v. National Republican Party*, 525 F.2d 567, 601 (D.C. Cir. 1975) (Tamm, J., concurring in result), *cert. denied*, 424 U.S. 933 (1976). . . .

Because the ban burdens appellees' rights to free speech and free association, it can only survive constitutional scrutiny if it serves a compelling governmental interest. The State offers two: stable government and protecting voters from confusion and undue influence. Maintaining a stable political system is, unquestionably, a compelling state interest. *Storer v. Brown.* California, however, never adequately explains how banning parties from endorsing or opposing primary candidates advances that interest. . . .

The only explanation the State offers is that its compelling interest in stable government embraces a similar interest in party stability. The State relies heavily on *Storer v. Brown, supra*, where we stated that because "splintered parties and unrestrained factionalism may do significant damage to the fabric of government," States may regulate elections to insure that "some sort of order, rather than chaos . . . accompan[ies] the democratic processes." Our decision in *Storer*, however, does not stand for the proposition that a State may enact election laws to mitigate intraparty factionalism during a primary campaign. . . . A primary is not hostile to intraparty feuds; rather it is an ideal forum in which to resolve them. . . . Because preserving party unity during a primary is not a compelling state interest, we must look elsewhere to justify the challenged law.

The State's second justification for the ban on party endorsements and statements of opposition is that it is necessary to protect primary voters from confusion and undue influence. Certainly the State has a legitimate interest in fostering an informed electorate. . . .

However, "'[a] State's claim that it is enhancing the ability of its citizenry to make wise decisions by restricting the flow of information to them must be viewed with some skepticism.'" *Tashjian, supra,* at 221 (quoting *Anderson v. Celebrezze, supra,* at 798). While a State may regulate the flow of information between political associations and their members when necessary to prevent fraud and corruption, see *Buckley v. Valeo,* 424 U.S., at 26-27; *Jenness v. Fortson, supra,* at 442, there is no evidence that California's ban on party primary endorsements serves that purpose.

Because the ban on primary endorsements by political parties burdens political speech while serving no compelling governmental interest, we hold that §§11702 and 29430 violate the First and Fourteenth Amendments.

B

We turn next to California's restrictions on the organization and composition of official governing bodies, the limits on the term of office for state central committee chair, and the requirement that the chair rotate between residents of northern and southern California. These laws directly implicate the associational rights of political parties and their members. As we noted in *Tashjian,* a political party's "determination . . . of the structure which best allows it to pursue its political goals, is protected by the Constitution." 479 U.S., at 224. Freedom of association also encompasses a political party's decisions about the identity of, and the process for electing, its leaders. . . .

The laws at issue burden these rights. By requiring parties to establish official governing bodies at the county level, California prevents the political parties from governing themselves with the structure they think best. And by specifying who shall be the members of the parties' official governing bodies, California interferes with the parties' choice of leaders. A party might decide, for example, that it will be more effective if a greater number of its official leaders are local activists rather than Washington-based elected officials. The Code prevents such a change. . . .

In the instant case, the State has not shown that its regulation of internal party governance is necessary to the integrity of the electoral process. Instead, it contends that the challenged laws serve a compelling "interest in the 'democratic management of the political party's internal affairs.'" Brief for Appellants 43. This, however, is not a case where intervention is necessary to prevent the derogation of the civil rights of party adherents. *Cf. Smith v. Allwright,* 321 U.S. 649 (1944). Moreover, as we have observed, the State has no interest in "protect[ing] the integrity of the Party against the Party itself." *Tashjian,* 479 U.S., at 224. The State further claims that limiting the term of the state central committee chair and requiring that the chair rotate between residents of northern and southern California helps "prevent regional friction from reaching a 'critical mass.'" Brief for Appellants 48. However, a State cannot substitute its judgment for that of the party as to the desirability of a particular internal party structure, any more than it can tell a party that its proposed communication to party members is unwise. *Tashjian, supra*, at 224.

In sum, a State cannot justify regulating a party's internal affairs without showing that such regulation is necessary to ensure an election that is orderly and fair. Because California has made no such showing here, the challenged laws cannot be upheld. . . .

>> *Political Parties: Public or Private Entities?*   Parties clearly play a significant role in the electoral process. In this sense they serve important public, even quasi-governmental functions, thereby justifying extensive government regulation. On the other hand, political parties are at the same time clearly voluntary organizations created by private individuals to serve their private interests. In this sense they are more like private clubs, and like clubs are entitled to assert various constitutional rights to be free from government regulation. This paradoxical duality of political parties complicates the resolution of questions concerning the appropriate treatment of parties under the law.

Democratic nations have struck this balance in many different ways, though the recent trend globally has been to stress the public functions of parties, thereby justifying greater state regulatory oversight of party activities, but also correspondingly greater state financial support of those activities. For example, as we have seen, some constitutions expressly identify a significant role for parties in democratic self-governance, providing them with a potentially significant degree of constitutional protection. But the same constitutional provisions sometimes impose regulatory requirements on political parties; the Constitution of Portugal, for example, provides that a party "must be governed by the principles of transparency, democratic organization and management and the participation of all of its members." Art. 51(5). This requirement, found also in the constitutions of Germany and Spain, among others, means that parties must be internally democratic in their organization and procedures. Parties generally must register with and enjoy official state recognition before they will be permitted to compete for office. Worldwide, nearly 70 percent of democratic states provide public funding directly to political parties. In Europe, public subsidies provide more than half of total party income. In exchange for the provision of funds, such states often demand compliance with regulatory requirements. Anika Gauja, *Political Parties: Private Associations or Public Utilities? in* COMPARATIVE ELECTION LAW (James A. Gardner, ed., 2022).

As is often the case, the United States is something of an outlier, denying that parties play an official role in democratic processes, while acknowledging that they play a critical informal role, and providing no public financial support to parties to facilitate their performance of that role, but occasionally providing public subsidies directly to candidates rather than the parties that support them (see Chapter 9.G below). This has resulted in a lack of jurisprudential clarity. As one scholar has observed, "The patently integral role of political parties in partisan competition contrasts rather strikingly with the ambivalent treatment given to political parties in the law. The principal cases . . . alternatively treat them as the political equivalent of common carriers subject to ordinary regulatory oversight, or as rights-bearing entities entitled to protection from state incursion." Samuel Issacharoff, *Private Parties with Public Purposes: Political Parties, Associational Freedoms, and Partisan Competition,* 101 COLUM. L. REV. 274, 278 (2001).

>> *The Associational Coherence of Political Parties.*   Political parties tend to present themselves as tightly knit, ideologically coherent advocacy groups, no different in kind from the Sierra Club or the Elks, and thus entitled to similar treatment under the First Amendment. But are parties like clubs? What does it take to join? What are the requirements of continuing membership? How involved in the activities of the party are the great mass of its members? As the political scientist Frank Sorauf has asked, "Are then the major American parties nothing more than great, formless aggregates of people who say they are Democrats or Republicans? Are they nothing more than vague, often poorly articulated political labels that people attach themselves to?" FRANK J. SORAUF, PARTY POLITICS IN AMERICA 7 (2d ed. 1972). Yet Sorauf concludes parties are more than this: "It *is* possible to join them, to work within them, to become officers in them, to participate in setting their goals and strategies—much as one would within a local fraternal organization or machinists' union. They do have the characteristics of stable, patterned personal relationships, the banding together of individuals to seek goals, which we associate with social organizations." *Id.* at 7-8.

Political theorist Nancy Rosenblum goes further, arguing that political parties are not only meaningful associations, but associations serving a unique and vital function in the coordination of collective social life:

> First, major American parties bridge local and national citizenship. . . . In a country with fragmented government and a shifting array of political associations, major parties are reasonably omnipresent, federated structures. . . . It follows that parties alone deal with a comprehensive range of local, state, and national issues and bring local organizations in touch with national political affairs, and vice versa. . . . With this, parties bring some coalescence if not unity to our understanding of political life.
>
> The second defining characteristic of parties is that they are *inclusive* and *integrative.* American parties draw support from every socioeconomic group. No other political association pulls together such large and diverse segments of the population. . . . Parties are not well organized interests with predetermined preferences, then. But neither are they simply the voice of heterogeneous unorganized voters; their inclusiveness is not a matter of giving expression to diffuse majority sentiment. Rather, parties are *dynamically integrative.* . . . They are mini-associative democracies. . . .
>
> [The third defining characteristic of parties is] their *comprehensiveness.* Parties are preoccupied with wide-ranging agenda-setting at both regional and national levels. Unlike interest and advocacy groups whose agendas are often restricted to a single (sometimes uncompromisable) principle or policy, party agendas are broad and open-ended. . . . Some minor parties are more like interest groups . . . [b]ut the major parties have comprehensive and necessarily flexible aims. . . . Alone among associations,

then, parties offer a comprehensive map of the political world—cues and symbols and framing devices that extend across issues and candidates and over time. And active membership exposes men and women to a distinctive form of political socialization. . . .

Nancy L. Rosenblum, *Political Parties as Membership Groups*, 100 COLUM. L. REV. 813, 824-826 (2000). Does Rosenblum make an effective case for according political parties preferred treatment under the First Amendment?

Consider an alternative account of the Progressive hostility to political parties:

> The target of Progressive ire was the party machine, accused of excessive patronage, graft, wasteful spending, extortion and intimidation, rigging elections, and a host of other unseemly acts. Parties impeded democracy, it was thought, by turning elections into sham competitions while the true kingmakers decided the winner behind closed doors in the prototypical smoke-filled room. . . . For [the] modern-day Progressives, parties remain obstructive forces for the realization of the general will of the electorate. Progressives therefore tend to favor state regulations that vitiate party autonomy or freedom of association and make parties less relevant for electoral purposes. . . .

Nathaniel Persily and Bruce E. Cain, *The Legal Status of Political Parties: A Reassessment of Competing Paradigms*, 100 COLUM. L. REV. 775, 786 (2000).

>> ***Parties, Government, and Party Regulation by Government.*** Underlying the extension to parties of constitutional protection against intrusive government regulation lies an account of parties as private expressive organizations. One may contest this account by contesting the similarity of parties to other kinds of protected expressive organizations, but one may also dispute it from the other end: by contesting what the government is when it regulates parties.

> [T]he doctrinal approach, exemplified by [cases like] *Eu*, . . . channels attention toward fruitless debates, such as whether parties are "public" or "private entities," and . . . obscures more pertinent questions by making naive and oversimplified assumptions about the nature of parties, of the state, and of the relationship between the two. . . . A deficiency of [this and similar approaches] is that what they portray as conflicts between parties and the state are more often than not intraparty disputes in disguise. . . .
>
> [C]onventional [constitutional] doctrine . . . treats the state *as if* it were entirely autonomous. . . . The doctrine is not concerned with, and in that sense does not recognize, the operations of private-sector individuals and groups upon the government. . . . [But p]arties' major interactions with the government are not as objects of government actions. To the contrary, it is the parties that operate upon and actually constitute the government. . . . [Thus,] when the government "regulates" the parties, to a very large extent the parties are regulating themselves. . . . [U]nlike any other private groups, political parties routinely, pervasively, and legitimately exercise their influence from *within* the government. . . . Statutes passed by a state legislature are passed by party politicians. When these

statutes are challenged in court by other party members or party entities, the invisible issue in the litigation is: Who gets to speak for "the party"?

Daniel Hays Lowenstein, *Associational Rights of Major Political Parties: A Skeptical Inquiry*, 71 Tex. L. Rev. 1741, 1743, 1754-1758, 1777 (1993). Do you agree that government regulation of political parties cannot be meaningfully distinguished from disputes between different segments of the party system? Does Lowenstein go too far in conflating governments with parties? If he does, in what sense are they distinct? Lowenstein uses his critique as a basis for arguing that courts should be much less aggressive in protecting parties from unwanted government regulation. But mightn't his analysis equally support the opposite conclusion? Suppose one party controls the government. Must we not, on Lowenstein's assumptions, be suspicious that any regulation of parties enacted by such a government is really a disguised attempt by the party in power to use the apparatus of government to permanently disadvantage its competitor, thereby justifying heightened and skeptical judicial review?

New York State Board of Elections v. Lopez Torres

552 U.S. 196 (2008)

Justice SCALIA delivered the opinion of the Court.

The State of New York requires that political parties select their nominees for Supreme Court Justice at a convention of delegates chosen by party members in a primary election. We consider whether this electoral system violates the First Amendment rights of prospective party candidates.

I

A

The Supreme Court of New York is the State's trial court of general jurisdiction, with an Appellate Division that hears appeals from certain lower courts. . . . Over the years, New York has changed the method by which Supreme Court Justices are selected several times. Under the New York Constitution of 1821, Art. IV, §7, all judicial officers, except Justices of the Peace, were appointed by the Governor with the consent of the Senate. *See* 7 Sources and Documents of the U.S. Constitutions 181, 184 (W. Swindler ed. 1978). In 1846, New York amended its Constitution to require popular election of the Justices of the Supreme Court (and also the Judges of the New York Court of Appeals). *Id.* at 192, 200 (N.Y. Const. of 1846, Art. VI, §12). In the early years under that regime, the State allowed political parties to choose their own method of selecting the judicial candidates who would bear their endorsements on the general-election ballot. The major parties opted for party conventions, the same method then employed to nominate candidates for other state offices.

In 1911, the New York Legislature enacted a law requiring political parties to select Supreme Court nominees (and most other nominees who did not run statewide) through direct primary elections. Act of Oct. 18, 1911, ch. 891, §45(4), 1911

N.Y. Laws 2657, 2682. The primary system came to be criticized as a "device capable of astute and successful manipulation by professionals," Editorial, *The State Convention*, N.Y. Times, May 1, 1917, p 12, and the Republican candidate for Governor in 1920 campaigned against it as "a fraud" that "offered the opportunity for two things, for the demagogue and the man with money," *Miller Declares Primary a Fraud*, N.Y. Times, Oct. 23, 1920, p 4. A law enacted in 1921 required parties to select their candidates for the Supreme Court by a convention composed of delegates elected by party members. Act of May 2, 1921, ch. 479, §§45(1), 110, 1921 N.Y. Laws 1451, 1454, 1471.

New York retains this system of choosing party nominees for Supreme Court Justice to this day. Section 6-106 of New York's election law sets forth its basic operation: "Party nominations for the office of justice of the supreme court shall be made by the judicial district convention." N.Y. Elec. Law Ann. §6-106 (West 2007). A "party" is any political organization whose candidate for Governor received 50,000 or more votes in the most recent election. §1-104(3). In a September "delegate primary," party members elect delegates from each of New York's 150 assembly districts to attend the party's judicial convention for the judicial district in which the assembly district is located. *See* N.Y. State Law Ann. §121 (West 2003); N.Y. Elec. Law Ann. §§6-124, 8-100(1)(a) (West 2007). An individual may run for delegate by submitting to the Board of Elections a designating petition signed by 500 enrolled party members residing in the assembly district, or by five percent of such enrolled members, whichever is less. §§6-136(2)(i), (3). These signatures must be gathered within a 37-day period preceding the filing deadline, which is approximately two months before the delegate primary. §§6-134(4), 6-158(1). The delegates elected in these primaries are uncommitted; the primary ballot does not specify the judicial nominee whom they will support. §7-114.

The nominating conventions take place one to two weeks after the delegate primary. §§6-126, 6-158(5). Each of the 12 judicial districts has its own convention to nominate the party's Supreme Court candidate or candidates who will run at large in that district in the general election. §§6-124, 6-156. The general election takes place in November. §8-100(1)(c). The nominees from the party conventions appear automatically on the general-election ballot. §7-104(5). They may be joined on the general-election ballot by independent candidates and candidates of political organizations that fail to meet the 50,000 vote threshold for "party" status; these candidates gain access to the ballot by submitting timely nominating petitions with (depending on the judicial district) 3,500 or 4,000 signatures from voters in that district or signatures from five percent of the number of votes cast for Governor in that district in the prior election, whichever is less. §§6-138, 6-142(2).

B

Respondent Lopez Torres was elected in 1992 to the civil court for Kings County—a court with more limited jurisdiction than the Supreme Court—having gained the nomination of the Democratic Party through a primary election. She claims that soon after her election, party leaders began to demand that she make patronage hires, and that her consistent refusal to do so caused the local party to oppose her unsuccessful candidacy at the Supreme Court nominating conventions in 1997, 2002, and 2003. The following year, Lopez Torres . . . brought suit in federal court against the New York Board of Elections, [contending] that New York's election law burdened the rights of challengers seeking to run against candidates favored by the party leadership, and deprived voters and candidates of their rights to gain access to the ballot and to associate in choosing their party's candidates. . . . .

II

A

A political party has a First Amendment right to limit its membership as it wishes, and to choose a candidate-selection process that will in its view produce the nominee who best represents its political platform. *Democratic Party of United States v. Wisconsin ex rel. La Follette*, 450 U.S. 107, 122 (1981); *California Democratic Party v. Jones*, 530 U.S. 567, 574-575 (2000). These rights are circumscribed, however, when the State gives the party a role in the election process — as New York has done here by giving certain parties the right to have their candidates appear with party endorsement on the general-election ballot. Then . . . the State acquires a legitimate governmental interest in assuring the fairness of the party's nominating process, enabling it to prescribe what that process must be. We have, for example, considered it to be "too plain for argument" that a State may prescribe party use of primaries or conventions to select nominees who appear on the general-election ballot. *American Party of Tex. v. White*, 415 U.S. 767, 781 (1974). That prescriptive power is not without limits. In *Jones*, for example, we invalidated on First Amendment grounds California's blanket primary, reasoning that it permitted non-party members to determine the candidate bearing the party's standard in the general election. 530 U.S. at 577.

In the present case, however, the party's associational rights are at issue (if at all) only as a shield and not as a sword. Respondents are in no position to rely on the right that the First Amendment confers on political parties to structure their internal party processes and to select the candidate of the party's choosing. Indeed, both the Republican and Democratic state parties have intervened from the very early stages of this litigation to defend New York's electoral law. The weapon wielded by these plaintiffs is their *own* claimed associational right not only to join, but to have a certain degree of influence in, the party. They contend that New York's electoral system does not go far enough — does not go as far as the Constitution demands — in assuring that they will have a fair chance of prevailing in their parties' candidate-selection process.

This contention finds no support in our precedents. We have indeed acknowledged an individual's associational right to vote in a party primary without undue state-imposed impediment. . . . [But just as] States may require persons to demonstrate "a significant modicum of support" before allowing them access to the general-election ballot, lest it become unmanageable, *Jenness v. Fortson*, 403 U.S. 431, 442 (1971), they may similarly demand a minimum degree of support for candidate access to a primary ballot. The signature requirement here is far from excessive. See, e.g., *Norman v. Reed*, 502 U.S. 279, 295 (1992) (approving requirement of 25,000 signatures, or approximately two percent of the electorate); *White, supra*, at 783 (approving requirement of one percent of the vote cast for Governor in the preceding general election, which was about 22,000 signatures).

Respondents' real complaint is not that they cannot vote in the election for delegates, nor even that they cannot run in that election, but that the convention process that follows the delegate election does not give them a realistic chance to secure the party's nomination. The party leadership, they say, inevitably garners more votes for its slate of delegates (delegates uncommitted to any judicial nominee) than the unsupported candidate can amass for himself. And thus the leadership effectively determines the nominees. But this says nothing more than that the party leadership has more widespread support than a candidate not supported by the leadership. No New York law compels election of the leadership's slate—or, for that matter, compels the delegates elected on the leadership's slate to vote the way the leadership desires. And no state law prohibits an unsupported candidate from attending the convention and seeking to persuade the delegates to support her. Our cases invalidating ballot-access requirements have focused on the requirements themselves, and not on the manner in which political actors function under those requirements. Here respondents complain not of the state law, but of the voters' (and their elected delegates') preference for the choices of the party leadership.

To be sure, we have, as described above, permitted States to set their faces against "party bosses" by requiring party-candidate selection through processes more favorable to insurgents, such as primaries. But to say that the State can require this is a far cry from saying that the Constitution demands it. None of our cases establishes an individual's constitutional right to have a "fair shot" at winning the party's nomination. And with good reason. What constitutes a "fair shot" is a reasonable enough question for legislative judgment, which we will accept so long as it does not too much infringe upon the party's associational rights. But it is hardly a manageable constitutional question for judges—especially for judges in our legal system, where traditional electoral practice gives no hint of even the existence, much less the content, of a constitutional requirement for a "fair shot" at party nomination. Party conventions, with their attendant "smoke-filled rooms" and domination by party leaders, have long been an accepted manner of selecting party candidates. "National party conventions prior to 1972 were generally under the control of state party leaders" who determined the votes of state delegates. *American Presidential Elections: Process, Policy, and Political Change* 14 (H. Schantz ed. 1996). Selection by convention has never been thought unconstitutional, even when the delegates were not selected by primary but by party caucuses. See *ibid.* . . . .

B

Respondents put forward, as a special factor which gives them a First Amendment right to revision of party processes in the present case, the assertion that party loyalty in New York's judicial districts renders the general-election ballot "uncompetitive." They argue that the existence of entrenched "one-party rule" demands that the First Amendment be used to impose additional competition in the nominee-selection process of the parties. (The asserted "one-party rule," we may observe, is that of the Democrats in some judicial districts, and of the Republicans in others. *See* 411 F. Supp. 2d at 230.) This is a novel and implausible reading of the First Amendment.

To begin with, it is hard to understand how the competitiveness of the general election has anything to do with respondents' associational rights in the party's selection process. It makes no difference to the person who associates with a party and seeks its nomination whether the party is a contender in the general election, an underdog, or the favorite. Competitiveness may be of interest to the voters in the general election, and to the candidates who choose to run *against* the dominant party. But we have held that those interests are well enough protected so long as all candidates have an adequate opportunity to appear on the general-election ballot. In *Jenness* we upheld a petition-signature requirement for inclusion on the general-election ballot of five percent of the eligible voters, *see* 403 U.S. at 442, and in *Munro v. Socialist Workers Party*, 479 U.S. 189, 199 (1986), we upheld a petition-signature requirement of one percent of the vote in the State's primary. New York's general-election balloting procedures for Supreme Court Justice easily pass muster under this standard. Candidates who fail to obtain a major party's nomination via convention can still get on the general-election ballot for the judicial district by providing the requisite number of signatures of voters resident in the district. N.Y. Elec. Law Ann. §6-142(2). To our knowledge, outside of the Fourteenth and Fifteenth Amendment contexts, no court has ever made "one-party entrenchment" a basis for interfering with the candidate-selection processes of a party.

The reason one-party rule is entrenched may be (and usually is) that voters approve of the positions and candidates that the party regularly puts forward. It is no function of the First Amendment to require revision of those positions or candidates. The States can, within limits (that is, short of violating the parties' freedom of association), discourage party monopoly — for example, by refusing to show party endorsement on the election ballot. But the Constitution provides no authority for federal courts to prescribe such a course. The First Amendment creates an open marketplace where ideas, most especially political ideas, may compete without government interference. See *Abrams v. United States*, 250 U.S. 616, 630 (1919) (Holmes, J., dissenting). It does not call on the federal courts to manage the market by preventing too many buyers from settling upon a single product....

New York State has thrice (in 1846, 1911, and 1921) displayed a willingness to reconsider its method of selecting Supreme Court Justices. If it wishes to return to the primary system that it discarded in 1921, it is free to do so; but the First Amendment does not compel that. We reverse the Second Circuit's contrary judgment.

Justice STEVENS, with whom Justice SOUTER joins, concurring.

While I join Justice Scalia's cogent resolution of the constitutional issues raised by this case, I think it appropriate to emphasize the distinction between constitutionality and wise policy. Our holding with respect to the former should not be misread as endorsement of the electoral system under review, or disagreement with the findings of the District Court that describe glaring deficiencies in that system and even lend support to the broader proposition that the very practice of electing judges is unwise. But as I recall my esteemed former colleague, Thurgood Marshall, remarking on numerous occasions: "The Constitution does not prohibit legislatures from enacting stupid laws."

3. Eligibility to Vote in Primaries: Party Membership

The laws regulating political primaries can be fairly complex, so it is helpful at the outset to have a clear idea of the different kinds of primary elections that various states do or may hold. Primary elections fall into two basic categories: those with restricted ballots and those with unrestricted ballots.

Where the primary ballot is restricted, only candidates of a particular party are listed on any given ballot. The ballot thus becomes the primary election ballot of a single party, and the candidate who polls the most votes becomes the party's endorsed candidate in the general election. Restricted primaries fall generally into three types:

1. *Closed.* Only established, registered members of the party may vote in that party's primary. Voters registered as members of other parties or as independents may not vote in the party's primary election.
2. *Semiclosed.* Same as a closed primary, with one exception: established, registered members *and independents* may vote in a party's primary. Members of other parties may not vote, except in the primary of their own party.
3. *Open.* All voters, regardless of prior registration, and whether registered members of a party or independents, may vote in any party's primary by requesting the appropriate ballot on primary day. Sometimes same-day party membership registration is required, but it has no constraining effect for future elections.

The other class of primary elections uses an unrestricted ballot. On such a ballot, *all* candidates, regardless of party affiliation or endorsement, are listed on every ballot. There is no differentiation among ballots received by Democrats, Republicans, or any other voters, regardless of registration; all voters use precisely the same ballot. There are two types of unrestricted ballot primaries:

1. *Blanket.* All voters, regardless of prior registration, may vote for any candidate of any party. The candidate from each party with the most votes is the endorsed party candidate in the general election.
2. *Nonpartisan.* All voters, regardless of prior registration, may vote for any candidate of any party. The top two (or other number) vote-getters are the candidates in the general election, and they run against one another, but they are not the endorsed candidates of any party. It is possible that two candidates from the same party may end up running against one another in the general election.

The obvious difference among the different kinds of primaries lies in the composition of the party electorate. In a closed primary, the membership of each party separately and independently selects a nominee. This model conforms most closely to the responsible party model of closed, rigorously ideological and ideologically differentiated parties. The further a party moves from the closed primary model, the more non-party members it permits to vote in its primary, and thus to have a say in determining the identity of the party's nominee. By the time we reach a nonpartisan primary, the primary is so thoroughly open that the very idea of distinctive party candidates has dissolved away, and the election is more about individuals and their qualities than partisan ideology and partisanship.

Tashjian v. Republican Party of Connecticut

479 U.S. 208 (1986)

Justice MARSHALL delivered the opinion of the Court.

Appellee Republican Party of the State of Connecticut (Party) in 1984 adopted a Party rule which permits independent voters — registered voters not affiliated with any political party — to vote in Republican primaries for federal and state-wide offices. Appellant Julia Tashjian, the Secretary of the State of Connecticut, is charged with the administration of the State's election statutes, which include a provision requiring voters in any party primary to be registered members of that party. Conn. Gen. Stat. §9-431 (1985). Appellees, who in addition to the Party include the Party's federal officeholders and the Party's state chairman, challenged this eligibility provision on the ground that it deprives the Party of its First Amendment right to enter into political association with individuals of its own choosing. The District Court granted summary judgment in favor of appellees. The Court of Appeals affirmed. We noted probable jurisdiction, and now affirm.

I

The statute challenged in these proceedings, §9-431, has remained substantially unchanged since the adoption of the State's primary system. . . . Motivated in part by the demographic importance of independent voters in Connecticut politics,[3] in September 1983 the Party's Central Committee recommended calling a state convention to consider altering the Party's rules to allow independents to vote in Party primaries. In January 1984 the state convention adopted the Party rule now at issue, which provides:

> Any elector enrolled as a member of the Republican Party and any elector not enrolled as a member of a party shall be eligible to vote in primaries for nomination of candidates for the offices of United States Senator, United States Representative, Governor, Lieutenant Governor, Secretary of the State, Attorney General, Comptroller and Treasurer.

During the 1984 session, the Republican leadership in the state legislature, in response to the conflict between the newly enacted Party rule and §9-431, proposed to amend the statute to allow independents to vote in primaries when permitted by Party rules. The proposed legislation was defeated, substantially along party lines, in both houses of the legislature, which at that time were controlled by the Democratic Party. . . .

II

We begin from the recognition that "[constitutional] challenges to specific provisions of a State's election laws . . . cannot be resolved by any 'litmus-paper test'

---

3. The record shows that in October 1983 there were 659,268 registered Democrats, 425,695 registered Republicans, and 532,723 registered and unaffiliated voters in Connecticut.

that will separate valid from invalid restrictions." *Anderson v. Celebrezze*, 460 U.S. 780, 789 (1983) (quoting *Storer v. Brown*, 415 U.S. 724, 730 (1974)). "Instead, a court . . . must first consider the character and magnitude of the asserted injury to the rights protected by the First and Fourteenth Amendments that the plaintiff seeks to vindicate. It then must identify and evaluate the precise interests put forward by the State as justifications for the burden imposed by its rule. In passing judgment, the Court must not only determine the legitimacy and strength of each of those interests, it also must consider the extent to which those interests make it necessary to burden the plaintiff's rights." 460 U.S., at 789.

The nature of appellees' First Amendment interest is evident. "It is beyond debate that freedom to engage in association for the advancement of beliefs and ideas is an inseparable aspect of the 'liberty' assured by the Due Process Clause of the Fourteenth Amendment, which embraces freedom of speech." *NAACP v. Alabama*, 357 U.S. 449, 460 (1958); see *NAACP v. Button*, 371 U.S. 415, 430 (1963); *Bates v. Little Rock*, 361 U.S. 516, 522-523 (1960). The freedom of association protected by the First and Fourteenth Amendments includes partisan political organization. "The right to associate with the political party of one's choice is an integral part of this basic constitutional freedom." *Kusper v. Pontikes*, 414 U.S. 51, 57 (1973).

The Party here contends that §9-431 impermissibly burdens the right of its members to determine for themselves with whom they will associate, and whose support they will seek, in their quest for political success. The Party's attempt to broaden the base of public participation in and support for its activities is conduct undeniably central to the exercise of the right of association. As we have said, the freedom to join together in furtherance of common political beliefs "necessarily presupposes the freedom to identify the people who constitute the association." *Democratic Party of United States v. Wisconsin ex rel. La Follette*, 450 U.S. 107, 122 (1981).

A major state political party necessarily includes individuals playing a broad spectrum of roles in the organization's activities. Some of the Party's members devote substantial portions of their lives to furthering its political and organizational goals, others provide substantial financial support, while still others limit their participation to casting their votes for some or all of the Party's candidates. Considered from the standpoint of the Party itself, the act of formal enrollment or public affiliation with the Party is merely one element in the continuum of participation in Party affairs, and need not be in any sense the most important. . . .

The statute here places limits upon the group of registered voters whom the Party may invite to participate in the "basic function" of selecting the Party's candidates. *Kusper v. Pontikes, supra*, at 58. The State thus limits the Party's associational opportunities at the crucial juncture at which the appeal to common principles may be translated into concerted action, and hence to political power in the community.[7] This is not a satisfactory response to the Party's contentions for two reasons.

---

7. Appellant contends that any infringement of the associational right of the Party or its members is *de minimis*, because Connecticut law, as amended during the pendency of this litigation, provides that any previously unaffiliated voter may become eligible to vote in the Party's primary by enrolling as a Party member as late as noon on the last business day preceding the primary. Conn. Gen. Stat. §9-56 (1985). Thus, appellant contends, any independent voter wishing to participate in any Party primary may do so.

First, as the Court of Appeals noted, the formal affiliation process is one which individual voters may employ in order to associate with the Party, but it provides no means by which the members of the Party may choose to broaden opportunities for joining the association by their own act, without any intervening action by potential voters. Second, and more importantly, the requirement of public affiliation with the Party in order to vote in the primary conditions the exercise of the associational right upon the making of a public statement of adherence to the Party which the State requires regardless of the actual beliefs of the individual voter. . . .

III

Appellant contends that §9-431 is a narrowly tailored regulation which advances the State's compelling interests by ensuring the administrability of the primary system, preventing raiding, avoiding voter confusion, and protecting the responsibility of party government.

A

Although it was not presented to the Court of Appeals as a basis for the defense of the statute, appellant argues here that the administrative burden imposed by the Party rule is a sufficient ground on which to uphold the constitutionality of §9-431. Appellant contends that the Party's rule would require the purchase of additional voting machines, the training of additional poll workers, and potentially the printing of additional ballot materials specifically intended for independents voting in the Republican primary. In essence, appellant claims that the administration of the system contemplated by the Party rule would simply cost the State too much.

Even assuming the factual accuracy of these contentions, which have not been subjected to any scrutiny by the District Court, the possibility of future increases in the cost of administering the election system is not a sufficient basis here for infringing appellees' First Amendment rights. Costs of administration would likewise increase if a third major party should come into existence in Connecticut, thus requiring the State to fund a third major-party primary. Additional voting machines, poll workers, and ballot materials would all be necessary under these circumstances as well. But the State could not forever protect the two existing major parties from competition solely on the ground that two major parties are all the public can afford. *Cf. Anderson v. Celebrezze,* 460 U.S. 780 (1983); *Williams v. Rhodes,* 393 U.S. 23 (1968). While the State is of course entitled to take administrative and financial considerations into account in choosing whether or not to have a primary system at all, it can no more restrain the Republican Party's freedom of association for reasons of its own administrative convenience than it could on the same ground limit the ballot access of a new major party.

B

Appellant argues that §9-431 is justified as a measure to prevent raiding, a practice "whereby voters in sympathy with one party designate themselves as voters of another party so as to influence or determine the results of the other party's primary." While we have recognized that "a State may have a legitimate interest in seeking to curtail 'raiding,' since that practice may affect the integrity of the electoral process," *Kusper v. Pontikes*, 414 U.S., at 59-60, that interest is not implicated here. The statute as applied to the Party's rule prevents independents, who otherwise cannot vote in any primary, from participating in the Republican primary. Yet a raid on the Republican Party primary by independent voters, a curious concept only distantly related to the type of raiding discussed in *Kusper* and *Rosario*, is not impeded by §9-431; the independent raiders need only register as Republicans and vote in the primary. Indeed, under Conn. Gen. Stat. §9-56 (1985), which permits an independent to affiliate with the Party as late as noon on the business day preceding the primary, see n.7, *supra*, the State's election statutes actually *assist* a "raid" by independents, which could be organized and implemented at the 11th hour. The State's asserted interest in the prevention of raiding provides no justification for the statute challenged here.

C

Appellant's next argument in support of §9-431 is that the closed primary system avoids voter confusion. Appellant contends that "[the] legislature could properly find that it would be difficult for the general public to understand what a candidate stood for who was nominated in part by an unknown amorphous body outside the party, while nevertheless using the party name." Brief for Appellant 59. Appellees respond that the State is attempting to act as the ideological guarantor of the Republican Party's candidates, ensuring that voters are not misled by a "Republican" candidate who professes something other than what the State regards as true Republican principles. Brief for Appellees 28.

As we have said, "[there] can be no question about the legitimacy of the State's interest in fostering informed and educated expressions of the popular will in a general election." *Anderson v. Celebrezze*, 460 U.S., at 796. To the extent that party labels provide a shorthand designation of the views of party candidates on matters of public concern, the identification of candidates with particular parties plays a role in the process by which voters inform themselves for the exercise of the franchise. Appellant's argument depends upon the belief that voters can be "misled" by party labels. But "[our] cases reflect a greater faith in the ability of individual voters to inform themselves about campaign issues." *Id.*, at 797. . . .

In arguing that the Party rule interferes with educated decisions by voters, appellant also disregards the substantial benefit which the Party rule provides to the Party and its members in seeking to choose successful candidates. Given the numerical strength of independent voters in the State, one of the questions most likely to occur to Connecticut Republicans in selecting candidates for public office is how can the Party most effectively appeal to the independent voter? By inviting independents to assist in the choice at the polls between primary candidates selected at the Party convention, the Party rule is intended to produce the candidate and platform most likely to achieve that goal. The state statute is said to decrease voter confusion, yet it deprives the Party and its members of the opportunity to inform themselves as to the level of support for the Party's candidates among a critical group of electors. "A State's claim that it is enhancing the ability of its citizenry to make wise decisions by restricting the flow of information to them must be viewed with some skepticism." *Anderson v. Celebrezze, supra*, at 798. The State's legitimate interests in preventing voter confusion and providing for educated and responsible voter decisions in no respect "make it necessary to burden the [Party's] rights." 460 U.S., at 789.

D

Finally, appellant contends that §9-431 furthers the State's compelling interest in protecting the integrity of the two-party system and the responsibility of party government. Appellant argues vigorously and at length that the closed primary system chosen by the state legislature promotes responsiveness by elected officials and strengthens the effectiveness of the political parties.

The relative merits of closed and open primaries have been the subject of substantial debate since the beginning of this century, and no consensus has as yet emerged.[11] . . . But our role is not to decide whether the state legislature was acting wisely in enacting the closed primary system in 1955, or whether the Republican Party make a mistake in seeking to depart from the practice of the past 30 years. . . .

The Party's determination of the boundaries of its own association, and of the structure which best allows it to pursue its political goals, is protected by the Constitution. "And as is true of all expressions of First Amendment freedoms, the courts may not interfere on the ground that they view a particular expression as unwise or irrational.". . .

Justice SCALIA, with whom THE CHIEF JUSTICE and Justice O'CONNOR join, dissenting.

Both the right of free political association and the State's authority to establish arrangements that assure fair and effective party participation in the election process are essential to democratic government. Our cases make it clear that the accommodation of these two vital interests does not lend itself to bright-line rules but requires careful inquiry into the extent to which the one or the other interest is inordinately impaired under the facts of the particular case. . . .

In my view, the Court's opinion exaggerates the importance of the associational interest at issue, if indeed it does not see one where none exists. There is no question here of restricting the Republican Party's ability to recruit and enroll Party members by offering them the ability to select Party candidates; Conn. Gen. Stat. §9-56 (1985) permits an independent voter to join the Party as late as the day before the primary. *Cf. Kusper v. Pontikes*, 414 U.S. 51 (1973). Nor is there any question of restricting the ability of the Party's members to select whatever candidate they desire. Appellees' only complaint is that the Party cannot leave the selection of its candidate to persons who are not members of the Party, and are unwilling to become members. It seems to me fanciful to refer to this as an interest in freedom of association between the members of the Republican Party and the putative independent voters. The Connecticut voter who, while steadfastly refusing to register as

---

11. At the present time, 21 States provide for "closed" primaries of the classic sort, in which the primary voter must be registered as a member of the party for some period of time prior to the holding of the primary election. . . . Sixteen States allow a voter previously unaffiliated with any party to vote in a party primary if he affiliates with the party at the time of, or for the purpose of, voting in the primary. . . .

a Republican, casts a vote in the Republican primary, forms no more meaningful an "association" with the Party than does the independent or the registered Democrat who responds to questions by a Republican Party pollster. If the concept of freedom of association is extended to such casual contacts, it ceases to be of any analytic use. . . .

The ability of the members of the Republican Party to select their own candidate, on the other hand, unquestionably implicates an associational freedom — but it can hardly be thought that that freedom is unconstitutionally impaired here. The Party is entirely free to put forward, if it wishes, that candidate who has the highest degree of support among Party members and independents combined. The State is under no obligation, however, to let its party primary be used, instead of a party-funded opinion poll, as the means by which the party identifies the relative popularity of its potential candidates among independents. Nor is there any reason apparent to me why the State cannot insist that this decision to support what might be called the independents' choice be taken *by the party membership in a democratic fashion*, rather than through a process that permits the members' votes to be diluted — and perhaps even absolutely outnumbered — by the votes of outsiders. . . .

California Democratic Party v. Jones

530 U.S. 567 (2000)

Justice SCALIA delivered the opinion of the Court.

This case presents the question whether the State of California may, consistent with the First Amendment to the United States Constitution, use a so-called "blanket" primary to determine a political party's nominee for the general election.

I

Under California law, a candidate for public office has two routes to gain access to the general ballot for most state and federal elective offices. He may receive the nomination of a qualified political party by winning its primary, *see* Cal. Elec. Code Ann. §§15451, 13105(a) (West 1996); or he may file as an independent by obtaining (for a statewide race) the signatures of one percent of the State's electorate or (for other races) the signatures of three percent of the voting population of the area represented by the office in contest, see §8400.

Until 1996, to determine the nominees of qualified parties California held what is known as a "closed" partisan primary, in which only persons who are members of the political party — *i.e.*, who have declared affiliation with that party when they register to vote, see Cal. Elec. Code Ann. §§2150, 2151 (West 1996 and Supp. 2000) — can vote on its nominee, see Cal. Elec. Code Ann. §2151 (West 1996). In 1996 the citizens of California adopted by initiative Proposition 198. Promoted largely as a measure that would "weaken" party "hard-liners" and ease the way for "moderate problem-solvers," App. 89-90 (reproducing ballot pamphlet distributed to voters), Proposition 198 changed California's partisan primary from a closed primary to a blanket primary. Under the new system, "[a]ll persons entitled

to vote, including those not affiliated with any political party, shall have the right
to vote . . . for any candidate regardless of the candidate's political affiliation."
Cal. Elec. Code Ann. §2001 (West Supp. 2000); see also §2151. Whereas under the
closed primary each voter received a ballot limited to candidates of his own party,
as a result of Proposition 198 each voter's primary ballot now lists every candidate
regardless of party affiliation and allows the voter to choose freely among them. It
remains the case, however, that the candidate of each party who wins the greatest
number of votes "is the nominee of that party at the ensuing general election." Cal.
Elec. Code Ann. §15451 (West 1996).[2]

Petitioners in this case are four political parties—the California Democratic
Party, the California Republican Party, the Libertarian Party of California, and the
Peace and Freedom Party—each of which has a rule prohibiting persons not members of the party from voting in the party's primary. Petitioners brought suit in the
United States District Court for the Eastern District of California against respondent California Secretary of State, alleging, *inter alia,* that California's blanket primary violated their First Amendment rights of association, and seeking declaratory
and injunctive relief. . . .

II

Respondents rest their defense of the blanket primary upon the proposition
that primaries play an integral role in citizens' selection of public officials. As a consequence, they contend, primaries are public rather than private proceedings, and
the States may and must play a role in ensuring that they serve the public interest.
Proposition 198, respondents conclude, is simply a rather pedestrian example of a
State's regulating its system of elections.

We have recognized, of course, that States have a major role to play in structuring and monitoring the election process, including primaries. *Burdick v. Takushi,*
504 U.S. 428, 433 (1992); *Tashjian v. Republican Party of Conn.,* 479 U.S. 208, 217
(1986). . . . What we have not held, however, is that the processes by which political parties select their nominees are, as respondents would have it, wholly public
affairs that States may regulate freely. To the contrary, we have continually stressed
that when States regulate parties' internal processes they must act within limits
imposed by the Constitution. See, *e.g., Eu v. San Francisco County Democratic Central
Comm.,* 489 U.S. 214 (1989); *Democratic Party of United States v. Wisconsin ex rel. La
Follette,* 450 U.S. 107 (1981). In this regard, respondents' reliance on *Smith v. Allwright,* 321 U.S. 649 (1944), and *Terry v. Adams,* 345 U.S. 461 (1953), is misplaced.
In *Allwright,* we invalidated the Texas Democratic Party's rule limiting participation
in its primary to whites; in *Terry,* we invalidated the same rule promulgated by the

2. California's new blanket primary system does not apply directly to the apportionment of presidential delegates. See Cal. Elec. Code Ann. §§15151, 15375, 15500 (West
Supp. 2000). Instead, the State tabulates the presidential primary in two ways: according to
the number of votes each candidate received from the entire voter pool and according to
the amount each received from members of his own party. The national parties may then
use the latter figure to apportion delegates. Nor does it apply to the election of political
party central or district committee members; only party members may vote in these elections. See Cal. Elec. Code Ann. §2151 (West 1996 and Supp. 2000).

Jaybird Democratic Association, a "self-governing voluntary club," 345 U.S. at 463. These cases held only that, when a State prescribes an election process that gives a special role to political parties, it "endorses, adopts and enforces the discrimination against Negroes," that the parties (or, in the case of the Jaybird Democratic Association, organizations that are "part and parcel" of the parties, see *id.*, at 482 (Clark, J., concurring)) bring into the process—so that the parties' discriminatory action becomes state action under the Fifteenth Amendment. *Allwright, supra,* at 664. They do not stand for the proposition that party affairs are public affairs, free of First Amendment protections—and our later holdings make that entirely clear. *See, e.g., Tashjian, supra.*

Representative democracy in any populous unit of governance is unimaginable without the ability of citizens to band together in promoting among the electorate candidates who espouse their political views. The formation of national political parties was almost concurrent with the formation of the Republic itself. *See* Cunningham, *The Jeffersonian Republican Party, in* 1 History of U.S. Political Parties 239, 241 (A. Schlesinger ed., 1973). Consistent with this tradition, the Court has recognized that the First Amendment protects "the freedom to join together in furtherance of common political beliefs," *Tashjian, supra,* at 214-215, which "necessarily presupposes the freedom to identify the people who constitute the association, and to limit the association to those people only," *La Follette,* 450 U.S. at 122. That is to say, a corollary of the right to associate is the right not to associate. " 'Freedom of association would prove an empty guarantee if associations could not limit control over their decisions to those who share the interests and persuasions that underlie the association's being.' " *Id.,* at 122, n.22 (quoting L. Tribe, American Constitutional Law 791 (1978)). *See also Roberts v. United States Jaycees,* 468 U.S. 609 (1984).

In no area is the political association's right to exclude more important than in the process of selecting its nominee. That process often determines the party's positions on the most significant public policy issues of the day, and even when those positions are predetermined it is the nominee who becomes the party's ambassador to the general electorate in winning it over to the party's views. *See Timmons v. Twin Cities Area New Party,* 520 U.S. 351, 372 (1997) (Stevens, J., dissenting) ("But a party's choice of a candidate is the most effective way in which that party can communicate to the voters what the party represents and, thereby, attract voter interest and support"). Some political parties—such as President Theodore Roosevelt's Bull Moose Party, the La Follette Progressives of 1924, the Henry Wallace Progressives of 1948, and the George Wallace American Independent Party of 1968—are virtually inseparable from their nominees (and tend not to outlast them). *See generally* E. Kruschke, Encyclopedia of Third Parties in the United States (1991).

Unsurprisingly, our cases vigorously affirm the special place the First Amendment reserves for, and the special protection it accords, the process by which a political party "select[s] a standard bearer who best represents the party's ideologies and preferences." *Eu, supra,* at 224. The moment of choosing the party's nominee, we have said, is "the crucial juncture at which the appeal to common principles may be translated into concerted action, and hence to political power in the community." *Tashjian,* 479 U.S. at 216. . . .

California's blanket primary violates the principles set forth in these cases. Proposition 198 forces political parties to associate with—to have their nominees, and hence their positions, determined by—those who, at best, have refused to affiliate with the party, and, at worst, have expressly affiliated with a rival. In this respect, it is qualitatively different from a closed primary. Under that system, even when it is made quite easy for a voter to change his party affiliation the day of the primary, and thus, in some sense, to "cross over," at least he must formally *become a member of the party;* and once he does so, he is limited to voting for candidates of that party.

The evidence in this case demonstrates that under California's blanket primary system, the prospect of having a party's nominee determined by adherents of an opposing party is far from remote—indeed, it is a clear and present danger. For example, in one 1997 survey of California voters 37 percent of Republicans said that they planned to vote in the 1998 Democratic gubernatorial primary, and 20 percent of Democrats said they planned to vote in the 1998 Republican United States Senate primary. Tr. 668-669. Those figures are comparable to the results of studies in other States with blanket primaries. One expert testified, for example, that in Washington the number of voters crossing over from one party to another can rise to as high as 25 percent, *id.,* at 511, and another that only 25 to 33 percent of all Washington voters limit themselves to candidates of one party throughout the ballot, App. 136. The impact of voting by nonparty members is much greater upon minor parties, such as the Libertarian Party and the Peace and Freedom Party. In the first primaries these parties conducted following California's implementation of Proposition 198, the total votes cast for party candidates in some races was more than *double* the total number of *registered party members.* California Secretary of State, Statement of Vote, Primary Election, June 2, 1998.

The record also supports the obvious proposition that these substantial numbers of voters who help select the nominees of parties they have chosen not to join often have policy views that diverge from those of the party faithful. The 1997 survey of California voters revealed significantly different policy preferences between party members and primary voters who "crossed over" from another party. One expert went so far as to describe it as "inevitable [under Proposition 198] that parties will be forced in some circumstances to give their official designation to a candidate who's not preferred by a majority or even plurality of party members." Tr. 421 (expert testimony of Bruce Cain). . . .

In any event, the deleterious effects of Proposition 198 are not limited to altering the identity of the nominee. Even when the person favored by a majority of the party members prevails, he will have prevailed by taking somewhat different positions—and, should he be elected, will continue to take somewhat different positions in order to be *re*nominated. As respondents' own expert concluded, "[t]he policy positions of Members of Congress elected from blanket primary states are . . . more moderate, both in an absolute sense and relative to the other party, and so are more reflective of the preferences of the mass of voters at the center of the ideological spectrum." App. 109 (expert report of Elisabeth R. Gerber). It is unnecessary to cumulate evidence of this phenomenon, since, after all, the whole *purpose* of Proposition 198 was to favor nominees with "moderate" positions. *Id.* at 89. It encourages candidates—and officeholders who hope to be renominated— to curry favor with persons whose views are more "centrist" than those of the party base. In effect, Proposition 198 has simply moved the general election one step earlier in the process, at the expense of the parties' ability to perform the "basic function" of choosing their own leaders. *Kusper*, 414 U.S. at 58. . . .

In sum, Proposition 198 forces petitioners to adulterate their candidate-selection process — the "basic function of a political party," *ibid.* — by opening it up to persons wholly unaffiliated with the party. Such forced association has the likely outcome — indeed, in this case the *intended* outcome — of changing the parties' message. We can think of no heavier burden on a political party's associational freedom. Proposition 198 is therefore unconstitutional unless it is narrowly tailored to serve a compelling state interest. *See Timmons*, 520 U.S. at 358 ("Regulations imposing severe burdens on [parties'] rights must be narrowly tailored and advance a compelling state interest"). It is to that question which we now turn.

III

Respondents proffer seven state interests they claim are compelling. Two of them — producing elected officials who better represent the electorate and expanding candidate debate beyond the scope of partisan concerns — are simply circumlocution for producing nominees and nominee positions other than those the parties would choose if left to their own devices. Indeed, respondents admit as much. For instance, in substantiating their interest in "representativeness," respondents point to the fact that "officials elected under blanket primaries stand closer to the median policy positions of their districts" than do those selected only by party members. Brief for Respondents 40. And in explaining their desire to increase debate, respondents claim that a blanket primary forces parties to reconsider long standing positions since it "compels [their] candidates to appeal to a larger segment of the electorate." *Id.*, at 46. Both of these supposed interests, therefore, reduce to nothing more than a stark repudiation of freedom of political association: Parties should not be free to select their own nominees because those nominees, and the positions taken by those nominees, will not be congenial to the majority. . . .

Respondents' third asserted compelling interest is that the blanket primary is the only way to ensure that disenfranchised persons enjoy the right to an effective vote. By "disenfranchised," respondents do not mean those who cannot vote; they mean simply independents and members of the minority party in "safe" districts. These persons are disenfranchised, according to respondents, because under a closed primary they are unable to participate in what amounts to the determinative election — the majority party's primary; the only way to ensure they have an "effective" vote is to force the party to open its primary to them. This also appears to be nothing more than reformulation of an asserted state interest we have already rejected — recharacterizing nonparty members' keen desire to participate in selection of the party's nominee as "disenfranchisement" if that desire is not fulfilled. We have said, however, that a "nonmember's desire to participate in the party's affairs is overborne by the countervailing and legitimate right of the party to determine its own membership qualifications." *Tashjian*, 479 U.S. at 215-216, n.6. The voter's desire to participate does not become more weighty simply because the State supports it. Moreover, even if it were accurate to describe the plight of the non-party-member in a safe district as "disenfranchisement," Proposition 198 is not needed to solve the problem. The voter who feels himself disenfranchised should simply join the party. That may put him to a hard choice, but it is not a state-imposed restriction upon *his* freedom of association, whereas compelling party members to accept his selection of their nominee *is* a state-imposed restriction upon theirs.

Respondents' remaining four asserted state interests—promoting fairness, affording voters greater choice, increasing voter participation, and protecting privacy—are not, like the others, automatically out of the running; but neither are they, *in the circumstances of this case*, compelling. That determination is not to be made in the abstract, by asking whether fairness, privacy, etc., are highly significant values; but rather by asking whether the *aspect* of fairness, privacy, etc., addressed by the law at issue is highly significant. And for all four of these asserted interests, we find it not to be.

The aspect of fairness addressed by Proposition 198 is presumably the supposed inequity of not permitting nonparty members in "safe" districts to determine the party nominee. If that is unfair at all (rather than merely a consequence of the eminently democratic principle that—except where constitutional imperatives intervene—the majority rules), it seems to us less unfair than permitting nonparty members to hijack the party. As for affording voters greater choice, it is obvious that the net effect of this scheme—indeed, its avowed purpose—is to *reduce* the scope of choice, by assuring a range of candidates who are all more "centrist." This may well be described as broadening the range of choices *favored by the majority*—but that is hardly a compelling state interest, if indeed it is even a legitimate one. The interest in increasing voter participation is just a variation on the same theme (more choices favored by the majority will produce more voters), and suffers from the same defect. As for the protection of privacy: The specific privacy interest at issue is not the confidentiality of medical records or personal finances, but confidentiality of one's party affiliation. Even if (as seems unlikely) a scheme for administering a closed primary could not be devised in which the voter's declaration of party affiliation would not be public information, we do not think that the State's interest in assuring the privacy of this piece of information in all cases can conceivably be considered a "compelling" one. If such information were generally so sacrosanct, federal statutes would not require a declaration of party affiliation as a condition of appointment to certain offices. *See, e.g.,* 47 U.S.C. §154(b)(5) ("[M]aximum number of commissioners [of the Federal Communications Commission] who may be members of the same political party shall be a number equal to the least number of commissioners which constitutes a majority of the full membership of the Commission"); 47 U.S.C. §396(c)(1) (1994 ed., Supp. III) (no more than five members of Board of Directors of Corporation for Public Broadcasting may be of same party); 42 U.S.C. §2000e-4(a) (no more than three members of Equal Employment Opportunity Commission may be of same party).

Finally, we may observe that even if all these state interests were compelling ones, Proposition 198 is not a narrowly tailored means of furthering them. Respondents could protect them all by resorting to a *nonpartisan* blanket primary. Generally speaking, under such a system, the State determines what qualifications it requires for a candidate to have a place on the primary ballot—which may include nomination by established parties and voter-petition requirements for independent candidates. Each voter, regardless of party affiliation, may then vote for any candidate, and the top two vote getters (or however many the State prescribes) then move on to the general election. This system has all the characteristics of the partisan blanket primary, save the constitutionally crucial one: Primary voters are not choosing a party's nominee. Under a nonpartisan blanket primary, a State may ensure more choice, greater participation, increased "privacy," and a sense of "fairness"—all without severely burdening a political party's First Amendment right of association.

Respondents' legitimate state interests and petitioners' First Amendment rights are not inherently incompatible. To the extent they are in this case, the State of California has made them so by forcing political parties to associate with those who do not share their beliefs. And it has done this at the "crucial juncture" at which party members traditionally find their collective voice and select their spokesman. *Tashjian*, 479 U.S. at 216. The burden Proposition 198 places on petitioners' rights of political association is both severe and unnecessary. The judgment for the Court of Appeals for the Ninth Circuit is reversed.

Justice STEVENS, with whom Justice GINSBURG joins as to Part I, dissenting.

I

. . . The blanket primary system instituted by Proposition 198 does not abridge "the ability of citizens to band together in promoting among the electorate candidates who espouse their political views." *Ante.* The Court's contrary conclusion rests on the premise that a political party's freedom of expressive association includes a "right not to associate," which in turn includes a right to exclude voters unaffiliated with the party from participating in the selection of that party's nominee in a primary election. *Ante.* In drawing this conclusion, however, the Court blurs two distinctions that are critical: (1) the distinction between a private organization's right to define itself and its messages, on the one hand, and the State's right to define the obligations of citizens and organizations performing public functions, on the other; and (2) the distinction between laws that abridge participation in the political process and those that encourage such participation.

When a political party defines the organization and composition of its governing units, when it decides what candidates to endorse, and when it decides whether and how to communicate those endorsements to the public, it is engaged in the kind of private expressive associational activity that the First Amendment protects. . . . [However,] the associational rights of political parties are neither absolute nor as comprehensive as the rights enjoyed by wholly private associations. I think it clear—though the point has never been decided by this Court—"that a State may require parties to use the primary format for selecting their nominees." *Ante.* The reason a State may impose this significant restriction on a party's associational freedoms is that both the general election and the primary are quintessential forms of state action. It is because the primary is state action that an organization—whether it calls itself a political party or just a "Jaybird" association—may not deny non-Caucasians the right to participate in the selection of its nominees. *Terry v. Adams*, 345 U.S. 461 (1953); *Smith v. Allwright*, 321 U.S. 649, 663-664 (1944). The Court is quite right in stating that those cases "do not stand for the proposition that party affairs are [*wholly*] public affairs, free of First Amendment protections." They do, however, stand for the proposition that primary elections, unlike most "party affairs," are state action. The protection that the first amendment affords to the "internal processes" of a political party, do not encompass a right to exclude non-members from voting in a state-required, state-financed primary election.

The so-called "right not to associate" that the Court relies upon, then, is simply inapplicable to participation in a state election. A political party, like any other association, may refuse to allow non-members to participate in the party's decisions when it is conducting its own affairs; California's blanket primary system does not infringe this principle. *Ante,* at 2406, n.2. But an election, unlike a convention or caucus, is a public affair. Although it is true that we have extended First Amendment protection to a party's right to invite independents to participate in its primaries, *Tashjian v. Republican Party of Conn.,* 479 U.S. 208 (1986), neither that case nor any other has held or suggested that the "right not to associate" imposes a limit on the State's power to open up its primary elections to all voters eligible to vote in a general election. In my view, while state rules abridging participation in its elections should be closely scrutinized, the First Amendment does not inhibit the State from acting to broaden voter access to state-run, state-financed elections. When a State acts not to limit democratic participation but to expand the ability of individuals to participate in the democratic process, it is acting not as a foe of the First Amendment but as a friend and ally. . . .

In my view, the First Amendment does not mandate that a putatively private association be granted the power to dictate the organizational structure of state-run, state-financed primary elections. It is not this Court's constitutional function to choose between the competing visions of what makes democracy work — party autonomy and discipline versus progressive inclusion of the entire electorate in the process of selecting their public officials — that are held by the litigants in this case. *Luther v. Borden,* 7 How. 1, 40-42 (1849). That choice belongs to the people. *U.S. Term Limits, Inc. v. Thornton,* 514 U.S. 779, 795 (1995).

Even if the "right not to associate" did authorize the Court to review the State's policy choice, its evaluation of the competing interests at stake is seriously flawed. For example, the Court's conclusion that a blanket primary severely burdens the parties' associational interests in selecting their standard bearers does not appear to be borne out by experience with blanket primaries in Alaska and Washington. See, *e.g.,* 169 F.3d, at 656-659, and n.23. Moreover, that conclusion rests substantially upon the Court's claim that "[t]he evidence before the District Court" disclosed a "clear and present danger" that a party's nominee may be determined by adherents of an opposing party. This hyperbole is based upon the Court's liberal view of its appellate role, not upon the record and the District Court's factual findings. Following a bench trial and the receipt of expert witness reports, the District Court found that "there is little evidence that raiding [by members of an opposing party] will be a factor under the blanket primary. On this point there is almost unanimity among the political scientists who were called as experts by the plaintiffs and defendants." 169 F.3d, at 656. While the Court is entitled to test this finding by making an independent examination of the record, the evidence it cites — including the results of the June 1998 primaries, which should not be considered because they are not in the record — does not come close to demonstrating that the District Court's factual finding is clearly erroneous.

As to the Court's concern that benevolent crossover voting impinges on party associational interests, the District Court found that experience with a blanket primary in Washington and other evidence "suggest[ed] that there will be particular elections in which there will be a substantial amount of cross-over voting . . . although the cross-over vote will rarely change the outcome of any election and in the typical contest will not be at significantly higher levels than in open primary states." 169 F.3d, at 657. In my view, an empirically debatable assumption about the relative number and effect of likely crossover voters in a blanket primary, as opposed to an open primary or a nominally closed primary with only a brief pre-registration requirement, is too thin a reed to support a credible First Amendment distinction. See *Tashjian*, 479 U.S., at 219 (rejecting State's interest in keeping primary closed to curtail benevolent crossover voting by independents given that independents could easily cross over even under closed primary by simply registering as party members).

On the other side of the balance, I would rank as "substantial, indeed compelling," just as the District Court did, California's interest in fostering democratic government by "[i]ncreasing the representativeness of elected officials, giving voters greater choice, and increasing voter turnout and participation in [electoral processes]." 169 F.3d, at 662; *cf. Timmons*, 520 U.S. at 364 ("[W]e [do not] require elaborate, empirical verification of the weightiness of the State's asserted justifications"). The Court's glib rejection of the State's interest in increasing voter participation, *ante*, at 2413, is particularly regrettable. In an era of dramatically declining voter participation, States should be free to experiment with reforms designed to make the democratic process more robust by involving the entire electorate in the process of selecting those who will serve as government officials. Opening the nominating process to all and encouraging voters to participate in any election that draws their interest is one obvious means of achieving this goal. I would also give some weight to the First Amendment associational interests of nonmembers of a party seeking to participate in the primary process, to the fundamental right of such nonmembers to cast a meaningful vote for the candidate of their choice, *Burdick v. Takushi*, 504 U.S. 428, 445 (1992) (Kennedy, J., dissenting), and to the preference of almost 60% of California voters—including a majority of registered Democrats and Republicans—for a blanket primary. 169 F.3d, at 649. In my view, a State is unquestionably entitled to rely on this combination of interests in deciding who may vote in a primary election conducted by the State. It is indeed strange to find that the First Amendment forecloses this decision. . . .

[Part II omitted.]

Before the *Jones* ruling, Alaska had employed a blanket primary since 1947—before statehood. In 1996, the state's Republican Party challenged the blanket primary format on First Amendment grounds. The Alaska Supreme Court upheld the law, emphasizing the weak role that formal party affiliation had historically played in Alaska politics:

> In 1994 there were 340,464 registered voters in Alaska. Of these more than 182,000 voters were registered as nonpartisan or undeclared. By contrast,

there were 78,212 registered Republicans, 59,782 registered Democrats, 12,936 registered Alaskan Independence Party members, 2,558 Green Party members, and 4,595 "other" party members. Thus approximately fifty-four percent of all registered voters in Alaska were nonpartisan or undeclared, whereas approximately twenty-three percent were registered Republicans and approximately eighteen percent were registered Democrats.

Against this backdrop, the state's interest in using a blanket primary format seemed sufficiently important to the court to satisfy the First Amendment:

> In Alaska, where a majority of voters are not affiliated with any party, a closed or partially-closed primary system can plausibly be viewed as bestowing on a minority of the electorate a disproportionately powerful role in the selection of public officeholders. If political parties and politically affiliated voters are to have more power in the election process, that is power taken from unaffiliated voters.

O'Callaghan v. State, 914 P.2d 1250 (Alaska 1996). Following the Supreme Court's decision in *Jones,* however, the Alaska Supreme Court reversed its prior ruling and invalidated the state's blanket primary. *O'Callaghan v. State,* 6 P.3d 728 (Alaska 2000). Does *Jones* require the invalidation of all blanket primaries, or might differing local circumstances permit different results in different states?

The Ninth Circuit applied *Jones* to invalidate Washington's blanket primary in *Democratic Party of Washington v. Reed,* 343 F.3d 1198 (9th Cir. 2003).

———————

In *Clingman v. Beaver,* 544 U.S. 581 (2005), the Supreme Court considered yet another variation, a "semiclosed" primary system, in which voter eligibility is limited to party members, plus registered independents. Under Oklahoma law, parties were given the option of restricting eligibility to vote in primaries to registered members of their own parties, or in addition allowing registered Independents to participate. The Libertarian Party of Oklahoma (LPO), however, petitioned to open its primary to all registered voters, a request that the State Election Board denied. The LPO sued, claiming a violation of its associational rights.

In an opinion by Justice Thomas, the Court rejected the LPO's challenge. "We are persuaded," the Court held, "that any burden Oklahoma's semiclosed primary imposes is minor and justified by legitimate state interests."

> A voter who is unwilling to disaffiliate from another party to vote in the LPO's primary forms little "association" with the LPO—nor the LPO with him. That same voter might wish to participate in numerous party primaries, or cast ballots for several candidates, in any given race. . . . As in *Timmons,* Oklahoma's law does not regulate the LPO's internal processes, its authority to exclude unwanted members, or its capacity to communicate with the public. And just as in *Timmons,* . . . Oklahoma conditions the party's ability to welcome a voter into its primary on the voter's willingness to dissociate from his current party of choice.

> *Tashjian* is distinguishable. . . . Connecticut's closed primary limited citizens' freedom of political association [in] that it required Independent voters to affiliate publicly with a party to vote in its primary. That is not true in this case. At issue here are voters who have *already* affiliated publicly with one of Oklahoma's political parties. These voters need not register as Libertarians to vote in the LPO's primary; they need only declare themselves Independents, which would leave them free to participate in any party primary that is open to registered Independents. . . .

Because the burden was minor, the Court applied rational basis review and sustained the restriction. The law, it held, was justified by the state's important regulatory interest in "preserv[ing] the political parties as viable and identifiable interest groups, insuring that the results of a primary election, in a broad sense, accurately reflect the voting of the party members." Oklahoma's system also "aids in parties' electioneering and party-building efforts," and helps prevent "party raiding." Consequently, the restriction was upheld as valid.

>> ***Party Autonomy in Primary Elections.*** Should political parties be able to define their own membership for purposes of deciding who may vote in primary elections? Consistent with standard First Amendment doctrine, the Court has approached this question by treating parties as rights-bearing organizations and inquiring into the justifications for abridging those rights. But is this the right approach?

> [A]s a purely doctrinal matter, the claim of the major political parties to formal institutional autonomy from state regulation is at best a weak rights claim. . . . [Parties'] ability to make a full-throated demand for autonomy from state regulation is compromised by the fact that the present party system is so fundamentally the product of a heavily regulated electoral arena. . . . [T]he tension in *Jones* flows directly from the desire to strike down the blanket primary as a constitutionally unacceptable intrusion upon party autonomy, while at the same time leaving essentially untouched an extraordinary regulatory framework that defines the electoral arena. [A better approach would] focus on what measure of constitutional protection political parties require to be able to play their proper role in a democratic system based on partisan competition. . . . [T]he core of this argument is that the alterations of the party candidate selection processes threaten to thwart the parties' ability to carry forth as the indispensable organizational vehicles for republican politics, and they threaten as well the incentive to undertake voter education and mobilization in the political process. It is not the parties' right of autonomy that is jeopardized, but the parties' ability to play a role that is crucial to republican government. . . .

Samuel Issacharoff, *Private Parties with Public Purposes: Political Parties, Associational Freedoms, and Partisan Competition*, 101 COLUM. L. REV. 274, 276, 278, 308 (2001). Issacharoff goes on to conclude that the evidence presented by the state in *Jones* was insufficient to demonstrate any significant interference with the ability of parties to play their necessary role in democratic government.

Consider the following response:

[G]iving the party as organization the broadest degree of autonomy is functionally important for several reasons. First, it protects against dominant party abuse. Dominant party abuse commonly occurs when one party controls the governorship and state legislature and uses that legislative control to pass measures that confer on it political advantage . . . , such as when one party tries to prevent another party from adopting the nomination process most beneficial to the other party. This is arguably what the *Tashjian* case was about: the dominant party trying to prevent the other party from opening its nomination process to independents to gain electoral advantage. . . . Since the greatest dangers in a two-party system are the possible collapse into a one-party system (e.g., Southern politics from 1948 to 1964) and the general loss of a second viable choice across the board (e.g., strong incumbency effects), autonomy from other party control assures that rules and procedures are set in the best interests of party members, and not in the interests of their opposition.

A second argument for party autonomy, which I would call protection from majority abuse, is more relevant to the facts in *Jones* than in *Tashjian*. . . . It should be assumed in any discussion that people all along the ideological spectrum would prefer to have their views predominate. If the two parties drift in a more polarized direction, those in the middle will be unhappy. . . . If the parties drift toward the center, voters on the ends become alienated. . . . The history of party nomination processes is that the parties tinker with rules in response to their varying inclinations either to please the base or to entice more independent and crossover voters into their ranks. In this framework, we can recharacterize the facts in *Jones* as a centrist majority (independents and moderate partisans) fixing the rules to give themselves an advantage over a much smaller minority of ideologues in the selection of candidates. . . . Even though the U.S. two-party system already has strong centripetal forces and fields relatively non-ideological and centrist candidates as compared to European democracies, the blanket primary supporters sought to eliminate the [possibility of parties attempting to appeal to the extremes] with a procedural coup d'etat. This is no less an abuse of power than the partisan case.

Aside from these two protective functions, party autonomy has other roles. One is that it facilitates the coalition-building process for broadly based parties. Since the logic of winner-take-all election systems works against factions striking out on their own and fielding a separate slate of candidates, groups have incentives to make compromises in order to build alliances. The product of those compromises can move the party away from the median voter ideal, but the extent of this movement constantly varies with the political context and recent electoral experiences. The flexibility to move away from an electorally dominant position is important to keeping coalition partners under the big tent. It may be necessary for a party to go through a cycle of loss until new terms of compromise are offered by the groups that feel most intensely about a given issue position. . . .

Finally, there is the ultimate irony of two-party systems with enhanced median voter incentives; namely, that in equilibrium, they converge to the same point. The reason is quite simple: the median voter position is dominant and no position to the left or right can defeat it. . . . A two-party system becomes noncompetitive when it produces only one viable choice for extended periods of time and at various levels of the system. A virtually noncompetitive system is one in which both choices are effectively the same choice; in which technically there is a choice between two labels, but substantively there is little or no difference between them. For those at or near the median position, this describes a political nirvana, [but] for all others, the already limited representational coverage of the two-party system becomes more limited. Giving parties autonomy saves the two-party system from becoming a meaningless exercise in labeling, and further prevents a descent into personality and character assassination politics (because that is all that is left to argue about).

Bruce E. Cain, *Party Autonomy and Two-Party Electoral Competition*, 149 U. PA. L. REV. 793, 807-810 (2001). Is Cain correct when he suggests that all government regulation of political parties should be presumed to be the product of a desire by the party temporarily in power to entrench itself by disadvantaging the party out of power? Does the public have no legitimate interest in how the major parties campaign for votes and to whom they appeal? Do you agree with Cain that a party nomination process that produces ideologically similar, centrist candidates is tantamount to a one-party system?

» *The Consequences of* Jones *for Other Kinds of Primaries.* The Court suggests in *Jones* that its ruling has no implications for open primaries, which states may presumably continue to require. An open primary differs from a blanket primary in that voters may vote only for candidates of one party; they must affiliate with a single party for purposes of voting in the primary, unlike in the case of the blanket primary, where they need not confine themselves to voting for the candidates of any single party. However, an open primary differs from a traditional closed primary in that voters typically may declare a party affiliation when they arrive at the polls; they need not have joined, or registered with, a party in advance of the election. Why should a state be permitted to require an open primary any more than a blanket primary? The Court also suggests that California could still accomplish most of its objectives by resorting to a nonpartisan primary. Is a nonpartisan system really the equivalent of a centrist-oriented two-party system?

» *Party Control over Candidate "Branding".* The traditional closed primary format seems to provide the strongest link between a party and its candidates. In that format, the party's ability to exercise some degree of control over who runs, who can vote, and the ideological commitments of its candidates seems greatest. As the primary format moves further from the closed model, the ability of the party to influence these factors declines—although the ability of a candidate affiliated with the party to win the general election may correspondingly increase. Is this a trade worth making? Is it more important for a party's candidates to win office, or to implement the party's ideological and policy agenda once they get there?

Another way to think about this is in terms of party "branding." To what degree is it important that a party establish a distinctive and consistent brand? And how important is it for a party to be able to control the use and meaning of its political brand?

The power of the state to regulate primary elections in ways that weaken the parties' control over their brands was tested in *Washington State Grange v. Washington State Republican Party*, 552 U.S. 442 (2008). After Washington's blanket primary was invalidated in the wake of *Jones*, it adopted by initiative (I-872) a "top-two" primary. In this format, all candidates from all parties run against one another in a single primary in which voters may vote for any candidate on the ballot, regardless of the voter's party affiliation. The two candidates with the highest totals then go on to face each other in the general election, even if they happen to be of the same party. In this system internal party primaries are thus eliminated. Parties do not nominate their own standard-bearer; instead, the entire electorate chooses from the entire field of candidates from all parties (as well as independents), and the general election serves the function of a runoff contest between the two most popular candidates, again without regard to party affiliation.

Because in this system parties do not formally choose a nominee in a separate proceeding, a question necessarily arises about how candidates in a top-two primary should be permitted to brand themselves on the ballot. In Washington, a decision was made to leave this decision up to the candidates themselves. Under state law, a candidate for office had only to state his or her "party preference" (e.g., Democrat, Republican, Right to Life, Green, etc.) and the candidate's name and indicated party preference would then appear on the ballot. This meant, however, as the Court observed, that "[a] political party cannot prevent a candidate who is unaffiliated with, or even repugnant to, the party from designating it as his party of preference." Before the new primary law could be implemented, the Washington Republican Party brought a facial challenge in federal court on the ground that the law deprived parties of control over their associational rights to define membership and choose a standard-bearer.

In an opinion by Justice Thomas, the Court chose to duck the constitutional question.

> Respondents argue that I-872 is unconstitutional under *Jones* because it . . . allows primary voters who are unaffiliated with a party to choose the party's nominee. Respondents claim that candidates who progress to the general election under I-872 will become the *de facto* nominees of the parties they prefer, thereby violating the parties' right to choose their own standard-bearers and altering their messages. . . . The flaw in this argument is that, unlike the California primary, the I-872 primary does not, by its terms, choose parties' nominees. The essence of nomination — the choice of a party representative — does not occur under I-872. The law never refers to the candidates as nominees of any party, nor does it treat them as such. To the contrary, the election regulations specifically provide that the primary "does not serve to determine the nominees of a political party but serves to winnow the number of candidates to a final list of two for the general election." Wash. Admin. Code §434-262-012. . . .

Respondents counter that, even if the I-872 primary does not actually choose parties' nominees, it nevertheless burdens their associational rights because voters will assume that candidates on the general election ballot are the nominees of their preferred parties. This brings us to the heart of respondents' case — and to the fatal flaw in their argument. At bottom, respondents' objection to I-872 is that voters will be confused by candidates' party-preference designations. Respondents' arguments are largely variations on this theme. Thus, they argue that even if voters do not assume that candidates on the general election ballot are the nominees of their parties, they will at least assume that the parties associate with, and approve of, them. This, they say, compels them to associate with candidates they do not endorse, alters the messages they wish to convey, and forces them to engage in counterspeech to disassociate themselves from the candidates and their positions on the issues.

We reject each of these contentions for the same reason: They all depend, not on any facial requirement of I-872, but on the possibility that voters will be confused as to the meaning of the party-preference designation. But . . . [t]here is simply no basis to presume that a well-informed electorate will interpret a candidate's party-preference designation to mean that the candidate is the party's chosen nominee or representative or that the party associates with or approves of the candidate. . . . Of course, it is *possible* that voters will misinterpret the candidates' party-preference designations as reflecting endorsement by the parties. But these cases involve a facial challenge, and we cannot strike down I-872 on its face based on the mere possibility of voter confusion.

Justice Scalia, joined by Justice Kennedy, dissented. Allowing candidates to self-identify as members of a political party, he said, inevitably

color[s] perception of the party's message, and that self-identification on the ballot, with no space for party repudiation or party identification of its own candidate, impairs the party's advocacy of its standard bearer. Because Washington has not demonstrated that this severe burden upon parties' associational rights is narrowly tailored to serve a compelling interest — indeed, because it seems to me Washington's only plausible interest is precisely to reduce the effectiveness of political parties — I would find the law unconstitutional. . . . There is no state interest behind this law except the Washington Legislature's dislike for bright-colors partisanship, and its desire to blunt the ability of political parties with noncentrist views to endorse and advocate their own candidates.

Following the Court's decision, Washington adopted rules to implement I-872. Under those rules, the ballot is to contain a "prominent, unambiguous, explicit statement that a candidate's party preference does not imply a nomination, endorsement, or association with the political party. . . . Ballot inserts and the Voters' Pamphlet further explain the new system," as does a statewide voter education initiative. On remand, the lower courts rejected the contention that voters were in fact confused by the new ballot format. *Washington State Republican Party v. Washington State Grange*, No. 11-35122 (9th Cir., Jan. 19, 2012).

» *Post-Jones Developments in California.*   In 2010, California voters approved an initiative, Proposition 14, that implemented the nonpartisan primary recommended by the Supreme Court in *Jones*. Like Washington's, California's new system lists all candidates on the ballot, regardless of their party affiliation, and each candidate may state a "party preference" that is understood not to indicate a formal party affiliation or endorsement. The two candidates who poll the most votes in the primary go on to compete in the general election.

In each of the general elections since adoption of Proposition 14, somewhere between 15 and 20 percent of congressional races have featured two members of the same party (usually two Democrats) competing for office. These races are usually in heavily Democratic districts. In such a district, does an election contest between two Democrats provide voters with a better or worse set of options than a contest between a Democrat and a Republican?

You will recall that the motivation that set California off on its search for a more inclusive primary format was to produce candidates and elected officials who were more centrist and moderate. Has the "top-two" primary format achieved that goal? A recent study of the top-two format in California and Washington reaches equivocal results, finding "virtually no effect" on candidate moderation, though the authors caution that the impact of other reforms, such as redistricting and term limits, complicate the analysis. Eric McGhee and Boris Shor, *Has the Top Two Primary Elected More Moderates?*, 15 Persp. on Pols. 1053 (2017).

Another justification for the top-two primary was to promote participation by offering the electorate two centrist candidates with broad appeal, thus reducing abstention by voters turned off by extremist candidates. If California accomplished this goal, it may have been more than offset by voter abstention for other reasons. In 2016, a presidential election year, one in six California voters who turned out at the polls (16.2%) nevertheless did not cast a vote in the U.S. Senate race, the largest proportion of comparable ballot drop-off in at least 70 years. The reason may well have been that the top-two primary pitted two Democrats against one another in the Senate race. Can you offer an explanation for why a voter might prefer abstention to voting in these circumstances?

» *Judicial Review of Constitutional Claims by Parties.*   If there is a problem with the Court's jurisprudence of political parties, does the problem arise from the substance of the Court's rulings, or does it arise from more basic problems associated with judicial entry into the political thicket?

> [T]he Constitution provides no guidance about how to resolve these conflicts. Moreover, several different outcomes are often consistent with plausible visions of democratic institutions. Thus, to decide political party cases, judges are very likely to rely on their own views of the best governance structures for a stable democracy. This means that one contested view of the role of political parties in a democracy is constitutionalized, thereby eliminating the opportunity for states and the federal government to experiment over time with other democratic forms. [In *Jones*,] the Court's decision locked out a choice made by the people of California about their election process. . . . Moreover, the Court eliminated a choice that is consistent with a reasonable vision of democracy that emphasizes

the views of voters in the center of the ideological spectrum and moderates an increasingly partisan system. One may argue that this is not the best vision of democracy, but nothing in the Constitution mandates that it be rejected.

Elizabeth Garrett, *Is the Party Over? Courts and the Political Process*, 2002 SUP. CT. REV. 95, 131, 134-135.

≫   *Party Nominations in Presidential Elections.*   How to choose a president proved to be the most difficult issue the Philadelphia Convention addressed. After much debate, the Founders settled on the Electoral College as the electing body, but devoted little attention to the question of how qualified candidates for the presidency would come to the attention of the Electoral College. In the absence of any kind of formal nominating system, they appeared to assume that leading candidates for the presidency would simply be known, either personally or by reputation, to the members of the Electoral College, quite possibly a reasonable assumption in a world in which the ruling elite in any state might have numbered only a few dozen.

The lack of a constitutionally prescribed nominating process created an opening that was soon exploited once parties began to appear on the scene. For the election of 1800, the Jeffersonians sought to control proceedings in the Electoral College by first forming a congressional caucus of like-minded members, preselecting their preferred presidential candidate, and then promoting themselves or their allies through ground-level political mobilization as candidates for appointment to the Electoral College. This tactic extraconstitutionally transferred the task of candidate selection from the College to the congressional caucus, and transformed the Electoral College from a body of wise men exercising independent judgment into a ministerial body that ratifies choices made elsewhere in the system.

As American parties grew in organizational capacity and discipline, the system was changed again, during the Jacksonian period, from informal nomination by congressional caucus to formal nomination by national conventions of party delegates. The convention system persisted until the mid-twentieth century, when it was replaced by a system of state-by-state presidential primary elections.

Although primary elections began to appear as early as the late nineteenth century, early primaries counted very little in the parties' calculus of nomination. Not all state parties held primaries, running in a primary was considered optional, and the results were viewed as merely advisory. As late as 1952, the Democratic nominee, Adlai Stevenson, did not run in a single primary; nominations were still tightly controlled by party insiders. In 1960, John F. Kennedy demonstrated his appeal as a candidate by winning several primaries, but still had to rely on the judgment of party leaders to secure the nomination.

This system changed radically after the 1968 Democratic convention, when the party nominated an insider, Vice President Hubert Humphrey, who had not run in a single primary, over Senator Eugene McCarthy, a popular, anti-war progressive who had won several primaries. Humphrey was trounced by Richard Nixon in the general election. Rank-and-file Democrats raised an enormous ruckus over the practice of insider candidate selection, leading the party to appoint a commission to recommend how to open up the process. The commission recommended moving to a system of binding primary elections, and the party quickly implemented the recommended changes. This proved so popular that the Republicans eventually followed suit. The result is that the choice of presidential candidates has been transferred from party professionals to the mass electorate.

This system is more democratic, but is it better? Does it produce better-quality candidates than nomination processes that rely on what is sometimes called "peer review"—i.e., the judgment of seasoned professionals who not only know what it takes to win elections, but are presumably committed to the party's policy commitments? Many have argued that the democratization of presidential nomination has produced worse candidates, leading in turn to a lack of voter enthusiasm, followed by voter alienation—exactly what the democratizing, participatory reforms to the nomination process were meant to prevent. Extrusion of party elites from the nomination process has also been blamed for weakening the capacity of parties to control or discipline their own nominees, a development that may offer an advantage to celebrity candidates whom old party hands might very likely reject as unqualified due to a lack of prior political or governmental experience. It has thus been suggested, paradoxically, that political parties in a democracy are best able to fulfill their democratic functions when they are organized hierarchically, which is to say, undemocratically. Do you agree?

For commentary, *see, e.g.,* The Best Candidate (Eugene D. Mazo and Michael R. Dimino, eds., 2020); Frances McCall Rosenbluth and Ian Shapiro, Responsible Parties: Saving Democracy from Itself (2018); Raymond J. LaRaja and Jonathan Rauch, *Voters Need Help: How Party Insiders Can Make Presidential Primaries Safer, Fairer, and More Democratic* (Brookings Inst., Jan. 31, 2020).

D. POLITICAL PATRONAGE

No discussion of the party system would be complete without a brief examination of political patronage, the process by which political parties dispense favors to party loyalists. We have already seen in *CSC v. Letter Carriers*, 413 U.S. 548 (1973) (Chapter 6), that the patronage system caused Congress sufficient concern to prompt the introduction of a civil service system granting significant job protection to government employees. In the Hatch Act, moreover, Congress barred federal employees from running for office or from participating in partisan political campaigns in order to prevent an incumbent administration from using its employees as a gigantic campaign army paid for at public expense.

This section digresses briefly to consider the workings of the patronage system as they relate to the internal personnel decisions of the government.

Elrod v. Burns

427 U.S. 347 (1976)

Mr. Justice Brennan announced the judgment of the Court and delivered an opinion in which Mr. Justice White and Mr. Justice Marshall joined.

This case presents the question whether public employees who allege that they were discharged or threatened with discharge solely because of their partisan political affiliation or nonaffiliation state a claim for deprivation of constitutional rights secured by the First and Fourteenth Amendments. . . .

II

In December 1970, the Sheriff of Cook County, a Republican, was replaced by Richard Elrod, a Democrat. At that time, respondents, all Republicans, were employees of the Cook County Sheriff's Office. They were non-civil-service employees and, therefore, not covered by any statute, ordinance, or regulation protecting them from arbitrary discharge. One respondent, John Burns, was Chief Deputy of the Process Division and supervised all departments of the Sheriff's Office working on the seventh floor of the building housing that office. Frank Vargas was a bailiff and security guard at the Juvenile Court of Cook County. Fred L. Buckley was employed as a process server in the office. Joseph Dennard was an employee in the office.

It has been the practice of the Sheriff of Cook County, when he assumes office from a Sheriff of a different political party, to replace non-civil-service employees of the Sheriff's Office with members of his own party when the existing employees lack or fail to obtain requisite support from, or fail to affiliate with, that party. Consequently, subsequent to Sheriff Elrod's assumption of office, respondents, with the exception of Buckley, were discharged from their employment solely because they did not support and were not members of the Democratic Party and had failed to obtain the sponsorship of one of its leaders. Buckley is in imminent danger of being discharged solely for the same reasons. Respondents allege that the discharges were ordered by Sheriff Elrod under the direction of the codefendants in this suit. . . .

IV

The Cook County Sheriff's practice of dismissing employees on a partisan basis is but one form of the general practice of political patronage. The practice also includes placing loyal supporters in government jobs that may or may not have been made available by political discharges. Nonofficeholders may be the beneficiaries of lucrative government contracts for highway construction, buildings, and supplies. Favored wards may receive improved public services. Members of the judiciary may even engage in the practice through the appointment of receiverships, trusteeships, and refereeships. Although political patronage comprises a broad range of activities, we are here concerned only with the constitutionality of dismissing public employees for partisan reasons.

Patronage practice is not new to American politics. It has existed at the federal level at least since the Presidency of Thomas Jefferson, although its popularization and legitimation primarily occurred later, in the Presidency of Andrew Jackson. The practice is not unique to American politics. It has been used in many European countries, and in darker times, it played a significant role in the Nazi rise to power in Germany and other totalitarian states. More recent times have witnessed a strong decline in its use, particularly with respect to public employment. Indeed, only a few decades after Andrew Jackson's administration, strong discontent with the corruption and inefficiency of the patronage system of public employment eventuated in the Pendleton Act, the foundation of modern civil service. And on the state and local levels, merit systems have increasingly displaced the practice. This trend led the Court to observe in *CSC v. Letter Carriers*, 413 U.S. 548, 564 (1973), that "the judgment of Congress, the Executive, and the country appears to have been that partisan political activities by federal employees must be limited if the Government is to operate effectively and fairly, elections are to play their proper part in representative government, and employees themselves are to be sufficiently free from improper influences."

The decline of patronage employment is not, of course, relevant to the question of its constitutionality. It is the practice itself, not the magnitude of its occurrence, the constitutionality of which must be determined. Nor for that matter does any unacceptability of the practice signified by its decline indicate its unconstitutionality. Our inquiry does not begin with the judgment of history, though the actual operation of a practice viewed in retrospect may help to assess its workings with respect to constitutional limitations.

V

The cost of the practice of patronage is the restraint it places on freedoms of belief and association. In order to maintain their jobs, respondents were required to pledge their political allegiance to the Democratic Party, work for the election of other candidates of the Democratic Party, contribute a portion of their wages to the Party, or obtain the sponsorship of a member of the Party, usually at the price of one of the first three alternatives. Regardless of the incumbent party's identity, Democratic or otherwise, the consequences for association and belief are the same. An individual who is a member of the out-party maintains affiliation with his own party at the risk of losing his job. He works for the election of his party's candidates and espouses its policies at the same risk. The financial and campaign assistance that he is induced to provide to another party furthers the advancement of that party's policies to the detriment of his party's views and ultimately his own beliefs, and any assessment of his salary is tantamount to coerced belief. Even a pledge of allegiance to another party, however ostensible, only serves to compromise the individual's true beliefs. Since the average public employee is hardly in the financial position to support his party and another, or to lend his time to two parties, the individual's ability to act according to his beliefs and to associate with others of his political persuasion is constrained, and support for his party is diminished.

It is not only belief and association which are restricted where political patronage is the practice. The free functioning of the electoral process also suffers. Conditioning public employment on partisan support prevents support of competing political interests. Existing employees are deterred from such support, as well as the multitude seeking jobs. As government employment, state or federal, becomes more pervasive, the greater the dependence on it becomes, and therefore the greater becomes the power to starve political opposition by commanding partisan support, financial and otherwise. Patronage thus tips the electoral process in favor of the incumbent party, and where the practice's scope is substantial relative to the size of the electorate, the impact on the process can be significant.

Our concern with the impact of patronage on political belief and association does not occur in the abstract, for political belief and association constitute the core of those activities protected by the First Amendment. Regardless of the nature of the inducement, whether it be by the denial of public employment or, as in *Board of Education v. Barnette*, 319 U.S. 624 (1943), by the influence of a teacher over students, "[i]f there is any fixed star in our constitutional constellation, it is that no official, high or petty, can prescribe what shall be orthodox in politics, nationalism, religion, or other matters of opinion or force citizens to confess by word or act their faith therein." *Id.*, at 642. And, though freedom of belief is central, "[t]he First Amendment protects political association as well as political expression." *Buckley*, 424 U.S. at 15. . . . "The right to associate with the political party of one's choice is an integral part of this basic constitutional freedom." *Kusper v. Pontikes*, 414 U.S. 51, 56-57 (1973).

These protections reflect our "profound national commitment to the principle that debate on public issues should be uninhibited, robust, and wide-open," *New York Times Co. v. Sullivan*, 376 U.S. 254, 270 (1964), a principle itself reflective of the fundamental understanding that "[c]ompetition in ideas and governmental policies is at the core of our electoral process. . . ." *Williams v. Rhodes*, 393 U.S., at 32. Patronage, therefore, to the extent it compels or restrains belief and association, is inimical to the process which undergirds our system of government and is "at war with the deeper traditions of democracy embodied in the First Amendment."

VI

Although the practice of patronage dismissals clearly infringes First Amendment interests, our inquiry is not at an end, for the prohibition on encroachment of First Amendment protections is not an absolute. Restraints are permitted for appropriate reasons. . . . It is firmly established that a significant impairment of First Amendment rights must survive exacting scrutiny. . . .

The interest advanced must be paramount, one of vital importance, and the burden is on the government to show the existence of such an interest. In the instant case, care must be taken not to confuse the interest of partisan organizations with governmental interests. Only the latter will suffice. . . . In short, if conditioning the retention of public employment on the employee's support of the in-party is to survive constitutional challenge, it must further some vital government end by a means that is least restrictive of freedom of belief and association in achieving that end, and the benefit gained must outweigh the loss of constitutionally protected rights.

One interest which has been offered in justification of patronage is the need to insure effective government and the efficiency of public employees. It is argued that employees of political persuasions not the same as that of the party in control of public office will not have the incentive to work effectively and may even be motivated to subvert the incumbent administration's efforts to govern effectively. We are not persuaded. The inefficiency resulting from the wholesale replacement of large numbers of public employees every time political office changes hands belies this justification. And the prospect of dismissal after an election in which the incumbent party has lost is only a disincentive to good work. Further, it is not clear that dismissal in order to make room for a patronage appointment will result in replacement by a person more qualified to do the job, since appointment often occurs in exchange for the delivery of votes, or other party service, not job capability. More fundamentally, however, the argument does not succeed because it is doubtful that the mere difference of political persuasion motivates poor performance; nor do we think it legitimately may be used as a basis for imputing such behavior. The Court has consistently recognized that mere political association is an inadequate basis for imputing disposition to ill-willed conduct. . . . At all events, less drastic means for insuring government effectiveness and employee efficiency are available to the State. Specifically, employees may always be discharged for good cause, such as insubordination or poor job performance, when those bases in fact exist. . . .

The lack of any justification for patronage dismissals as a means of furthering government effectiveness and efficiency distinguishes this case from *CSC v. Letter Carriers,* 413 U.S. 548 (1973), and *United Public Workers v. Mitchell,* 330 U.S. 75 (1949). In both of those cases, legislative restraints on political management and campaigning by public employees were upheld despite their encroachment on First Amendment rights because, inter alia, they did serve in a necessary manner to foster and protect efficient and effective government. Interestingly, the activities that were restrained by the legislation involved in those cases are characteristic of patronage practices.

A second interest advanced in support of patronage is the need for political loyalty of employees, not to the end that effectiveness and efficiency be insured, but to the end that representative government not be undercut by tactics obstructing the implementation of policies of the new administration, policies presumably sanctioned by the electorate. The justification is not without force, but is nevertheless inadequate to validate patronage wholesale. Limiting patronage dismissals to policymaking positions is sufficient to achieve this governmental end. Nonpolicymaking individuals usually have only limited responsibility and are therefore not in a position to thwart the goals of the in-party.

No clear line can be drawn between policymaking and nonpolicymaking positions. While nonpolicymaking individuals usually have limited responsibility, that is not to say that one with a number of responsibilities is necessarily in a policymaking position. The nature of the responsibilities is critical. Employee supervisors, for example, may have many responsibilities, but those responsibilities may have only limited and well-defined objectives. An employee with responsibilities that are not well defined or are of broad scope more likely functions in a policymaking position. In determining whether an employee occupies a policymaking position, consideration should also be given to whether the employee acts as an adviser or formulates plans for the implementation of broad goals. . . .

It is argued that a third interest supporting patronage dismissals is the preservation of the democratic process. According to petitioners, " 'we have contrived no system for the support of party that does not place considerable reliance on patronage. The party organization makes a democratic government work and charges a price for its services.'" The argument is thus premised on the centrality of partisan politics to the democratic process.

Preservation of the democratic process is certainly an interest protection of which may in some instances justify limitations on First Amendment freedoms. But however important preservation of the two-party system or any system involving a fixed number of parties may or may not be, we are not persuaded that the elimination of patronage practice or, as is specifically involved here, the interdiction of patronage dismissals, will bring about the demise of party politics. Political parties existed in the absence of active patronage practice prior to the administration of Andrew Jackson, and they have survived substantial reduction in their patronage power through the establishment of merit systems. . . .

In summary, patronage dismissals severely restrict political belief and association. Though there is a vital need for government efficiency and effectiveness, such dismissals are on balance not the least restrictive means for fostering that end. There is also a need to insure that policies which the electorate has sanctioned are effectively implemented. That interest can be fully satisfied by limiting patronage dismissals to policymaking positions. Finally, patronage dismissals cannot be justified by their contribution to the proper functioning of our democratic process through their assistance to partisan politics since political parties are nurtured by other, less intrusive and equally effective methods. More fundamentally, however, any contribution of patronage dismissals to the democratic process does not suffice to override their severe encroachment on First Amendment freedoms. We hold, therefore, that the practice of patronage dismissals is unconstitutional under the First and Fourteenth Amendments, and that respondents thus stated a valid claim for relief. . . .

Mr. Justice STEWART, with whom Mr. Justice BLACKMUN joins, concurring in the judgment.

Although I cannot join the plurality's wide-ranging opinion, I can and do concur in its judgment. . . . The single substantive question involved in this case is whether a nonpolicymaking, nonconfidential government employee can be discharged or threatened with discharge from a job that he is satisfactorily performing upon the sole ground of his political beliefs. I agree with the plurality that he cannot. . . .

Mr. Justice POWELL, with whom THE CHIEF JUSTICE and Mr. Justice REHNQUIST join, dissenting.

The Court holds unconstitutional a practice as old as the Republic, a practice which has contributed significantly to the democratization of American politics. This decision is urged on us in the name of First Amendment rights, but in my view the judgment neither is constitutionally required nor serves the interest of a representative democracy. It also may well disserve—rather than promote—core values of the First Amendment. I therefore dissent. . . .

As the plurality opinion recognizes, patronage practices of the sort under consideration here have a long history in America. . . . The observation that patronage in employment received its primary popularization and legitimation during Jackson's Presidency understates the historical antecedents of the practice, which stretch back to Washington's Presidency. . . .

It is recognized that patronage in employment played a significant role in democratizing American politics. See, *e.g.*, C. Fish, The Civil Service and the Patronage 156-157 (1905); Sorauf, *Patronage and Party*, 3 Midwest J. Pol. Sci. 115-116

(1959). Before patronage practices developed fully, an "aristocratic" class dominated political affairs, a tendency that persisted in areas where patronage did not become prevalent. C. Fish, *supra*, at 157. Patronage practices broadened the base of political participation by providing incentives to take part in the process, thereby increasing the volume of political discourse in society. Patronage also strengthened parties, and hence encouraged the development of institutional responsibility to the electorate on a permanent basis.

. . . It is difficult to disagree with the view, as an abstract proposition, that government employment ordinarily should not be conditioned upon one's political beliefs or activities. But we deal here with a highly practical and rather fundamental element of our political system, not the theoretical abstractions of a political science seminar. In concluding that patronage hiring practices are unconstitutional, the plurality seriously underestimates the strength of the government interest—especially at the local level—in allowing some patronage hiring practices, and it exaggerates the perceived burden on First Amendment rights. . . .

The complaining parties are or were employees of the Sheriff. In many communities, the sheriff's duties are as routine as process serving, and his election attracts little or no general public interest. In the States, and especially in the thousands of local communities, there are large numbers of elective offices, and many are as relatively obscure as that of the local sheriff or constable. Despite the importance of elective offices to the ongoing work of local governments, election campaigns for lesser offices in particular usually attract little attention from the media, with consequent disinterest and absence of intelligent participation on the part of the public. Unless the candidates for these offices are able to dispense the traditional patronage that has accrued to the offices, they also are unlikely to attract donations of time or money from voluntary groups. In short, the resource pools that fuel the intensity of political interest and debate in "important" elections frequently "could care less" about who fills the offices deemed to be relatively unimportant. Long experience teaches that at this local level traditional patronage practices contribute significantly to the democratic process. The candidates for these offices derive their support at the precinct level, and their modest funding for publicity, from cadres of friends and political associates who hope to benefit if their "man" is elected. The activities of the latter are often the principal source of political information for the voting public. The "robust" political discourse that the plurality opinion properly emphasizes is furthered—not restricted—by the time-honored system.

Patronage hiring practices also enable party organizations to persist and function at the local level. Such organizations become visible to the electorate at large only at election time, but the dull periods between elections require ongoing activities: precinct organizations must be maintained; new voters registered; and minor political "chores" performed for citizens who otherwise may have no practical means of access to officeholders. In some communities, party organizations and clubs also render helpful social services.

It is naive to think that these types of political activities are motivated at these levels by some academic interest in "democracy" or other public service impulse. For the most part, as every politician knows, the hope of some reward generates a major portion of the local political activity supporting parties. . . . Parties generally are stable, high-profile, and permanent institutions. When the names on a long ballot are meaningless to the average voter, party affiliation affords a guidepost by which voters may rationalize a myriad of political choices. *Cf. Buckley v. Valeo*, 424 U.S., at 66-68. Voters can and do hold parties to long-term accountability, and it is not too much to say that, in their absence, responsive and responsible performance in low-profile offices, particularly, is difficult to maintain.

It is against decades of experience to the contrary, then, that the plurality opinion concludes that patronage hiring practices interfere with the "free functioning of the electoral process." This *ad hoc* judicial judgment runs counter to the judgments of the representatives of the people in state and local governments, representatives who have chosen, in most instances, to retain some patronage practices in combination with a merit oriented civil service. . . .

I thus conclude that patronage hiring practices sufficiently serve important state interests, including some interests sought to be advanced by the First Amendment, to justify a tolerable intrusion on the First Amendment interests of employees or potential employees.

>> ***Developments Following* Elrod.** *Elrod*'s distinction between policy-making and non-policy-making employees caused some confusion. In *Branti v. Finkel*, 445 U.S. 507 (1980), the Court attempted to clarify the categories of employees who could and could not be discharged because of their political affiliation. *Branti* involved the discharge for political reasons of two lawyers who were assistant public defenders. In overturning the discharge on First Amendment grounds, the Court said: "the ultimate inquiry is not whether the label 'policymaker' or 'confidential' fits a particular position; rather, the question is whether the hiring authority can demonstrate that party affiliation is an appropriate requirement for the effective performance of the public office involved." The Court went on to hold that the discharge of the lawyers was improper because "[t]he primary, if not the only, responsibility of an assistant public defender is to represent individual citizens in controversy with the State." Any policy making, the Court said, "must relate to the needs of individual clients and not to any partisan political interests."

The Court extended the reach of *Elrod* in *Rutan v. Republican Party of Illinois*, 497 U.S. 62 (1990), where it held that governmental refusals to hire, transfer, and promote on the basis of political affiliation should be treated the same for constitutional purposes as dismissals. The case is especially notable, however, for a scathing dissent by Justice Scalia, who was joined by Chief Justice Rehnquist, Justice Kennedy, and, in part, by Justice O'Connor. In his opinion, Scalia challenged the premises on which the Court based its hostility to the patronage system, arguing that the Court's decisions "may well have disastrous consequences for our political system." Far from finding the government's interest in maintaining a patronage system constitutionally improper, Scalia thought that interest to be compelling. The Court's view, he said, "reflects a naive vision of politics and an inadequate appreciation of the systemic effects of patronage in promoting political stability and facilitating the social and political integration of previously powerless groups."

Party strength requires the efforts of the rank-and-file, especially in
"the dull periods between elections," to performs such tasks as organizing
precincts, registering new voters, and providing constituent services. Even
the most enthusiastic supporter will shrink before such drudgery, and it
is folly to think that ideological conviction alone will motivate sufficient
numbers to keep the party going through the off-years. . . . Patronage is
" 'a necessary evil if you want a strong organization, because the patronage system permits of discipline, and without discipline, there's no party
organization.' " . . .

The patronage system does not, of course, merely foster political
parties in general; it fosters the two-party system in particular. When getting a job, as opposed to effectuating a particular substantive policy, is an
available incentive for party-workers, those attracted by that incentive are
likely to work for the party that has the best chance of displacing the "ins,"
rather than for some splinter group that has a more attractive political
philosophy but little hope of success. Not only is a two-party system more
likely to emerge, but the differences between those parties are more likely
to be moderated, as each has a relatively greater interest in appealing to
a majority of the electorate and a relatively lesser interest in furthering
philosophies or programs that are far from the mainstream. The stabiliz-
ing effects of such a system are obvious. . . .

Patronage, moreover, has been a powerful means of achieving the
social and political integration of excluded groups. By supporting and
ultimately dominating a particular party "machine," racial and ethnic
minorities have—on the basis of their politics rather than their race or
ethnicity—acquired the patronage awards the machine had power to
confer. . . . The abolition of patronage, however, prevents groups that
have only recently obtained political power, especially blacks, from following this path to economic and social advancement.

▶▶ *How Effective Is Patronage?*   Political parties in the United States may have a
long history of using patronage tactics to attempt to retain power, but has patronage actually been an effective tool for doing so? A study examining the period 1885
to 1995 finds that it has. Examining the transition from patronage to civil service
employment systems in the states, the authors find that the probability of a party
retaining control over the legislature is 25 percent higher under patronage systems
than under civil service systems. Thus, "entrenched parties have an electoral advantage under the patronage system relative to nonentrenched parties." Olle Folke
et al., *Patronage and Elections in U.S. States*, 105 Am. Pol. Sci. Rev. 567, 568 (2011).

E.   FINAL THOUGHTS ON PARTIES

The cases set out in this chapter, and the legislation they adjudicate, assume
implicitly that law is a necessary and effective element in regulating political parties
and, presumably, in structuring the political process. Are these assumptions warranted? Consider the following account:

E.E. Schattschneider

Party Government (1942)

The rise of political parties is indubitably one of the principal distinguishing marks of modern government. The parties, in fact, have played a major role as *makers* of governments, more especially they have been the makers of democratic government. It should be stated flatly at the outset that . . . the political parties created democracy and that modern democracy is unthinkable save in terms of the parties. As a matter of fact, the condition of the parties is the best possible evidence of the nature of any regime. The most important distinction in modern political philosophy, the distinction between democracy and dictatorship, can be made best in terms of party politics. The parties are not therefore merely appendages of modern government; they are in the center of it and play a determinative and creative role in it. . . .

American parties are important in view of their accomplishments. It can be said justly that they have transformed the American Constitution. They have substantially abolished the electoral college, created a plebiscitary presidency, and contributed powerfully to the extraconstitutional growth of that office. As a result of the efforts of the political parties the President of the United States today receives a mandate to govern the nation and is responsible for the safety and welfare of the Republic. The parties have greatly simplified the most complex system of government in the world, and we may be certain that the work of reconstruction will continue as long as the party system endures. More important than all other changes the parties have wrought in the system of government is the fact that they have democratized it. They took over an eighteenth-century constitution and made it function to satisfy the needs of modern democracy in ways not contemplated by the authors. As the political entrepreneurs who have mobilized and organized the dynamic forces of American public life, these parties have presided over the transformation of the government of the United States from a small experiment in republicanism to the most powerful regime on earth, vastly more liberal and democratic than it was in 1789. They have supervised or adapted themselves to the conquest of a continent, the transformation of the economic system, the absorption of the largest immigrant population in the history of the world, a series of great economic crises, and the rise of the modern administrative state, to mention only a few of the developments in which the parties have participated.

The significance of the parties in this system of government is illustrated by the fact that the fall of a major party or a major shift of power within one of the great parties is likely to be followed by the gravest consequences. . . .

[T]he convention at Philadelphia produced a constitution with a dual attitude: it was proparty in one sense and antiparty in another. The authors of the Constitution refused to suppress the parties by destroying the fundamental liberties in which parties originate. They or their immediate successors accepted amendments that guaranteed civil rights and thus established a system of party tolerance, i.e., the right to agitate and to organize. This is the proparty aspect of the system. On the other hand, the authors of the Constitution set up an elaborate division and balance of powers within an intricate governmental structure designed to make parties ineffective. It was hoped that the parties would lose and exhaust themselves in futile attempts to fight their way through the labyrinthine framework of the government, much as an attacking army is expected to spend itself against the defensive works of a fortress. This is the antiparty part of the constitutional scheme. To quote Madison, the "great object" of the Constitution was "to preserve the public good and private rights against the danger of such a faction [party] and at the same time to preserve the spirit and form of popular government." . . .

Everyone who has thought about it at all has recognized that the parties and the law are nonassimilable. The extralegal character of political parties is one of their most notable qualities. In a highly legalistic system of government such as the government of the United States, therefore, the parties seem to be a foreign substance. It is profoundly characteristic that the fundamental party arrangements are unknown to the law.

The law, it is well recognized, cannot control public authorities perfectly. It is precisely through this breach in the rule of law that the parties make their way to the citadel of government. That is to say, they undertake to control the decisions of public authorities at the points at which the law cannot control them. Furthermore, by political devices which are far more subtle than the devices of the law, they are able to establish refinements of control of which the law is incapable. (Compare, for instance, the delicacy of political responsibility depending on confidence with legal responsibility based on the kind of evidence that can be used in a court of law.) The parties are able to compel public officers to behave in ways that the law does not contemplate, by methods of which the law is ignorant, without in any way affecting the validity of their official acts. What goes on behind the formal act, the official seals, and public documents the law refuses to know. Since the parties operate in a legal no man's land they are able to produce startling effects: in effect, they may empty an office of its contents, transfer the authority of one magistrate to another magistrate, or to persons unknown to the constitution and laws of the land. It follows that though politicians may know something about the law, it is completely unnecessary for a lawyer to know anything about politics. . . .

»   *The Nature of Contemporary Partisanship*   If parties themselves are not the problem, and indeed are a necessary part of any meaningfully democratic state, might the trouble lie instead in the nature of contemporary partisanship? Consider this account:

> Traditional partisanship is motivated fundamentally not by selfish interests but by . . . an understanding of how to live. . . . Modern politics [in contrast] does not seek to generalize the highest goods or virtues about which people will always disagree. . . . What defines a liberal politics is not an agreement only to disagree within certain bounds . . . , but to disagree in a certain *way*: according to constitutional procedures, in a certain manner. In particular, it is an agreement to engage in disagreement without threatening to exit or to destroy the constitutional process of disagreement.
>
> The logic of [contemporary] partisanship does not fix only on winning *this* election. To follow the logic to an extreme is to see that partisans strive to put their opposition out of business. . . . The problem

with partisans of the moment is not that their ideal preferences are too extreme, but rather that they hold to these preferences with uncompromising certitude. It is not their principles but their tactics that give today's partisans the look of fanatics.

RUSSELL MUIRHEAD, THE PROMISE OF PARTY IN A POLARIZED AGE (2014).

CHAPTER 8

FREE SPEECH, POLITICAL INFORMATION, AND THE LIBERAL DEMOCRATIC ORDER

A. INTRODUCTION

1. Free Speech and the Liberal Democratic Equilibrium

Free speech and the free flow of political information are hallmarks of liberal democracies. A first-order operating assumption of liberal democracies is that political representatives, or those seeking to wield political power, must be allowed to speak and campaign freely so that voters can have access to the political information necessary to make decisions that are in their best interest. A second-order assumption of liberal democracies is that political actors generally will speak truthfully and provide accurate information to voters, and that the provision of truthful information in turn facilitates political accountability, an indispensable component of self-government. We, as a self-governing people, need to hear from our political leaders and we need to have accurate information about our political leaders, our political system, our government, and the political beliefs of our fellow citizens. Otherwise, we will not be able properly to assess whether our political leaders are serving us well and whether to keep them or throw out the rascals.

Liberal democracies have generally used law to address these two assumptions in different, though complementary, ways. Liberal democracies generally and broadly protect free speech, especially political speech, through law and custom. In the American context, the First Amendment is both symbol and right. Americans often talk about the freedom of speech, by which they mean to refer to a customary principle, not always a legal right. By contrast, with exceptions at the margins, liberal democracies have generally refused to use law to arbitrate the truthfulness of political speech, leaving that task to the political marketplace. Political actors have a legal right to speak, campaign, advertise, and the like. But citizens and the public are tasked with the responsibility of deciding among competing truth claims. It is inconsistent with the fundamental principles of political liberalism — it is in fact illiberal — for the government to tell the citizens what political information they ought to believe. That general equilibrium has, for the most part, served liberal democracies well.

However, in the last few years, that equilibrium has come under severe stress. The rise of social media systems has lowered the costs of mass communication and decentralized information networks. While that is a good thing, the social media ecosystem has made it easier to disseminate false and misleading political information. Of course, change in media technology is nothing new. The printing press, radio, and television were once technological innovations, and they also lowered the costs of information. But the modern social media landscape has presented what some researchers regard as a set of unforeseen challenges to liberal democracy. As one recent report put it, "social media are playing a role in the development of a new political culture animated by a wilful disregard for the truth." If this process continues, it "will make it more difficult for societies to operate on the basis of important liberal democratic principles: authenticity, rationality, tolerance, trust, and the recognition and institutional integration of political differences." Online Civic Culture Center, *News Sharing on UK Social Media: Misinformation, Disinformation & Correction* (2019), https://www.lboro.ac.uk/research/online-civic-culture-centre/news-events/articles/o3c-1-survey-report-news-sharing-misinformation/.

In 2016, the Oxford Dictionaries named the adjective "post-truth" word of the year. They defined post-truth "as 'relating to or denoting circumstances in which objective facts are less influential in shaping public opinion than appeals to emotion and personal belief.'" They chose "post-truth" because they have "seen a spike in frequency this year in the context of the EU referendum in the United Kingdom and the presidential election in the United States. It has also become associated with a particular noun, in the phrase post-truth politics."

Post-truth is not just a term; it also represents a particular phenomenon: the deliberate circulation of intentionally false news articles that are intended to influence political decision making. This is what some researchers have defined as "fake news" – false information propagated with a particular purpose, deception, and with a particular intent, to influence political belief or political behavior. *See, e.g,* Hunt Allcott & Matthew Gentzkow, *Social Media and Fake News in the 2016 Election,* 31 J. ECON. PERSP. 211, 213-14 (2017); *see also* Brett G. Johnson & Kimberly Kelling, *Placing Facebook: "Trending," Napalm Girl, and Journalistic Boundary Work,* 12 JOURN. PRAC. 817 (2018). "Across democracies, 'fake news' has flourished in current political climates, producing misinformation on social media platforms. It has served to diminish the credibility of mainstream news networks, dividing the general public further, both ideologically and on the mere acceptance of the fact, providing credence to ideological claims of 'fake news.'" Terry Lee, *The Global Rise of "Fake News" and the Threat to Democratic Elections in the USA,* 22 PUB. ADMIN. & POLC'Y, 16 (2019).

Fake news, like technological change in the mass media ecosystem, is not new. The phrase itself has been in use for over 125 years. Its contemporary manifestation has historical antecedents. *See, e.g.,* Joanna M. Burkhardt, *History of Fake News,* 53 LIB. TECH. REP. 5 (2017). However, our modern social media landscape has influenced the prevalence of fake news tremendously and exaggerated its significance. Compared to traditional media, fake news is particularly dominant on social media platforms—Facebook, Twitter, Tiktok, and the like. "Leading up to the 2016 US presidential election, the public's engagement with 'fake news' through Facebook was higher than through mainstream sources." Lee, *supra.* In their analysis of the 2016 presidential election, Johnson and Kelling concluded that there were "about three times more fake pro-Trump articles than pro-Clinton articles, and the average pro-Trump article was shared more on Facebook than the average pro-Clinton article." Johnson & Kelling, *supra,* at 223.

The new media environment has also worsened the problems of misinformation and disinformation by allowing citizens and voters to silo their information environments. Social media networks have made it easier for voters to create information silos and echo chambers in which voters are exposed primarily to information that reinforces their prior beliefs. Indeed, studies have shown that voters seek information that is consistent with what they believe and avoid information that challenges their preexisting beliefs. *See, e.g.,* Matteo Cinelli et. al., *The Echo Chamber Effect on Social Media,* 118 PNAS 1 (2017); Eytan Bakshy *et. al., Exposure to Ideologically Diverse News and Opinion On Facebook,* 348 SCIENCE 1130 (2015). *See generally,* CASS R. SUNSTEIN, REPUBLIC.COM (2011).

Fundamentally, the practice of free speech and the prevalence of disinformation, instead of facilitating the ends of liberal democracy, threatens to undermine its fundamental aims. The problem of disinformation, misinformation, fake news, and even newer developments, such as deep fakes—artificial intelligence technological innovations that make it extremely hard to distinguish between real and fake videos and media—have also called into question the previous equilibrium of liberal democracies. It is no longer clear that a liberal speech regime and a private market for truth facilitates self-government and individual liberty. If a liberal speech regime simply produces as much false political information as it does truthful political information, if voters are uninterested in truth because they are more interested in information that confirms their prior beliefs, and if citizens, because of innovations in deep fake technology, simply cannot differentiate a real campaign ad from a fake one, a liberal speech regime may as easily serve illiberal ends as liberal ones.

In fact, one could argue that the 2020 Trump campaign and its so-called "stop the steal" campaign, was both an early warning and demonstration of how a liberal free speech regime can be put to illiberal ends in a social media environment rife with political disinformation and misinformation. Following the January 6 attack on the United States Capitol by Trump loyalists seeking to prevent the certification of the 2020 presidential election, a number of social media platforms banned Trump from their networks. Before eventually banning Trump, some platforms attempted less drastic measures such as deleting some of his social media posts or labelling them as false. But in the wake of the violent attack on the Capitol, Twitter and Snapchat banned Trump permanently. Facebook, Instagram, YouTube, and Twitch suspended his accounts. Should social media companies have such power?

The central question raised by this chapter is whether (and if so, the extent to which) the government can influence the type of information that voters receive during political campaigns by prohibiting or compelling certain types of political speech. The cases and materials presented in this chapter reflect the state of the law outside of the new social media landscape. Legal doctrine in the context of campaign speech has not yet come to terms with the problems for speech and liberal democracy raised by the change in political communication caused by advances in our technology. As you read through the materials that follow, consider whether the traditional legal framework can meet the challenges presented by how social media mediate political communication. Can the liberal democracy equilibrium—strong defense of free speech and private arbitration of truth—continue to serve us well in our current political environment? Or do we need a new equilibrium? Given the tremendous power of social media platforms, do we trust these private actors to determine what political speech ought to be permitted or prohibited? Are there functionally any differences between the major social media companies and the government? Given technological advances, the psychological predispositions of the public, and the populist impulses of our era, can ordinary citizens be trusted to choose between political information that is comforting and political information that is disconcerting? Fact from fiction? Real from deep fake?

2.   *Short History of Political Campaigns*

To provide some context for the materials that follow, we first explore the purposes of political campaigns. What information should political campaigns provide? Perhaps if we could develop some consensus on the purpose and objective of political campaigns, we might also develop some agreement on the constitutional and legal limits of the regulation of political speech. Fundamentally, campaigns and their attendant institutions, such as newspapers and other media, provide information to voters, presumably to enable voters to make informed electoral choices. We begin with a historical overview of American campaign practices. Then we turn to various kinds of restrictions imposed by government on political speech.

» *Eighteenth-Century Campaigns.*   Campaigns have performed different functions at different times in American history. Democratic practices at the founding were built upon an ideological foundation of republicanism (see Chapter 2), which conceived of popular sovereignty as a process in which ordinary citizens selected the individuals who would rule over them. As a result, eighteenth-century electoral practices contemplated a different role for the citizen-elector than do modern practices. Eighteenth-century Americans possessed a narrower understanding of democracy and self-government. For most eighteenth-century Americans, the average American was not capable of self-government. The task of the citizen-elector was not to select candidates on the basis of the candidate's substantive policy decisions or on a determination that the politician would advance the substantive interests of the voter—the eighteen-century citizen was not thought to possess the capacity to evaluate substance. Rather, the citizen-elector selected candidates on the basis of the candidate's character. "Although the people could not judge a man on the basis of what he might do in office, they were nevertheless well-qualified to judge whether he was likely to do it honestly and virtuously." James A. Gardner, What Are Campaigns For?: The Role of Persuasion in Electoral Law and Politics 14 (2009). Consequently, election to office confirmed one's moral character. Politicians were gentlemen, and office-holding confirmed their social standing. Social standing and office-holding were thus mutually reinforcing mechanisms.

Consistent with these premises, the eighteenth-century politician did not campaign for elected office, and offices were not contested—at least not in the manner that we understand electoral contestation today. "Virtually no activity took place that contemporary voters would recognize as campaigning. Gentlemen did not 'run' but 'stood' for office. Any kind of overt electioneering was looked upon with disfavor and alarm, for it suggested an unseemly and potentially dangerous degree of personal ambition." *Id.* at 17. Personal ambition was channeled through surrogates. Men from socially prominent families nominated other men from socially prominent families for office. "Election to office constituted a kind of recognition of the station of local leading men and a reaffirmation of the social hierarchy, and therefore frequently went uncontested." *Id.* at 16. Elections were a species of gentlemen's agreements assented to — really deferred to — by the people.

The republican ideal was evident in the democratic practices of the day. Consider the act of voting itself.

> At the nation's founding, the concrete procedures for voting varied widely from state to state and even from town to town. In some locales, particularly in the South, voting was still an oral and public act: men assembled before election judges, waited for their names to be called, and then announced which candidates they supported; in one variant of this process common in Virginia, men inscribed their names in a poll book underneath the name of the candidate they preferred.

ALEXANDER KEYSSAR, THE RIGHT TO VOTE: THE CONTESTED HISTORY OF DEMOCRACY IN THE UNITED STATES 23-24 (2000).

» *Nineteenth-Century Campaigns.* If the eighteenth century was the era of the gentleman-politician, the nineteenth century was the era of the political party. Politics and campaigns came to be organized by and around political parties, first in the form of the Democratic Party and later the Whigs, the two dominant political parties by the mid-1830s. These changes coincided with significant changes in the extension of the franchise. As property requirements and other laws constraining the franchise swelled the ranks of the "voteless," "significant and growing clusters of men who were full participants in economic and social life . . . lacked political rights." KEYSSAR, *supra*, at 29. Paradoxically, this led many states and localities to do away with property requirements and extend the franchise to a broader segment of the population.

Parties and candidates communicated directly to this growing electorate on substantive issues. They sponsored rallies, speeches, parades, and debates, and competed fiercely for votes. In consequence, the nineteenth century was an era of remarkable political participation.

> Between 1800 and 1824, about one-quarter of the eligible electorate turned out to vote in presidential elections. . . . By 1840, in contrast, turnout suddenly spiked to over 80 percent — and this of an electorate greatly expanded by the relaxation during the Jacksonian period of state voter eligibility laws. In every presidential election for the balance of the nineteenth century, voter turnout ranged between roughly 70 and 80 percent before beginning a slow decline during the twentieth century.

GARDNER, *supra*, at 19. Moreover, the electorate "identified strongly with political parties, participated in party activities, attended speeches and rallies, marched in or cheered their candidates at parades, and belonged to political clubs." *Id.* at 19. Thus, these voters "not only turned out at the polls, but participated in politics with a depth of intensity unmatched during any other period in American history." *Id.*

Whether nineteenth-century Americans were truly engaged in the political process is debated by historians. Americans voted in tremendous numbers, but it is unclear the extent to which nineteenth-century voters were aware of the issues of their day, understood the significance of the issues that were being debated, and were truly knowledgeable on the issues. What then accounts for the high level of political participation? Gardner provides three explanations. Fundamentally, political participation performed important functions separate from the acquisition of political information and deliberation. "First, politics was simply an enjoyable form of public entertainment." GARDNER, *supra*, at 27. Few entertainment opportunities were available to the average nineteenth-century citizen. Political gatherings and their accompanying spectacle and hoopla were critical sources of diversion from mundane life. "Second, participation in politics provided an affirming experience of social solidarity. Many writers have likened the kind of enthusiasm with which nineteenth-century Americans supported their political parties to the kind of enthusiasm with which contemporary Americans support their home football or baseball teams." *Id.* Third, parties relied on a combination of motivation and social pressure to engender political participation.

> [N]ineteenth-century political parties relied heavily on effective mobilization of their supporters. Party agents were numerous, and in an era of unregulated partisan political activity, they resorted without compunction to favors, bribery, and if necessary to physical force to get their charges to the polls. But social pressures may have played an equally important role in maintaining high levels of voter turnout. . . . If in the age of republicanism the main obligation of political citizenship was deference, during the period from about 1840 through roughly the 1880s or 1890s, the primary obligation of political citizenship was partisan loyalty.

Id. at 28-29.

»   *The Twentieth Century and the Modern Era.*   If the nineteenth century was an era of enthusiastic partisanship, the twentieth century was an era of individualism and rationality. The Progressives, in particular, reacted against the patronage-driven politics of the nineteenth century and called for a new focus on civic rationality and the common good. "At the heart of Progressive thought lay the belief that public affairs in a complex world must be conducted rationally and for the common good." GARDNER, *supra*, at 30-31. Citizens could no longer blindly follow the preferences of their party, but were expected to support policies that were in the best interest of the polity. "To discharge this responsibility required of citizens something that had not previously demanded of them: hard work, discipline, and self-denial." *Id.* at 31. Citizens were expected actively to engage the political process — to be informed, to attend political events, and to make substantive decisions.

Concomitantly, Progressives also expected more of political campaigns. Campaigns could no longer simply entertain voters; they were expected to perform an educative role. They were expected to present substantive choices so that the voters, as rational decision makers, could perform their function. Progressives also enacted many electoral reforms to reduce the electorate's dependence on political parties, to clean up electoral politics, and to facilitate informed decision making. These reforms included the secret or Australian ballot, nonpartisan local elections, the replacement of party patronage with a civil service system, the direct primary, and a broadening of the franchise to include women.

Although the Progressive Era provided the framework within which our political campaigns are conducted by raising the bar for civic citizenship, it also gave rise to a crisis of voter competence:

> The Progressive conceptions of the voter as a rational, independent sovereign, and of the campaign as a civic forum for informing and persuading an intelligent and critical public, invested individual voters with a power and elevated them to a status they had never before enjoyed. Yet paradoxically, this change in public conceptions precipitated a crisis of democracy from which the nation has never recovered. By raising the bar — by setting for candidates and voters a demanding standard of knowledge, attentiveness, diligent reflection, and impartial self-sacrifice — Progressivism opened the door to a new phenomenon in the history of American democracy: the possibility that our actual practice of politics might fall short of our ideals.

GARDNER, *supra*, at 36.

3. Restrictions on Speech

>> *First Amendment Doctrine.*   The Supreme Court has turned frequently to the First Amendment to guide it in its evaluation of the constitutionality of laws and practices pertaining to democratic processes. Most of our exposure thus far to the regulatory role of the First Amendment has come in the context of the right to association, a right derivative of the basic right to speak freely. This chapter, in contrast, turns to much more direct restrictions on speech itself, requiring a more direct confrontation with basic principles of free speech jurisprudence.

First Amendment doctrine is notoriously complex. Because this is a course in election law, you should not become bogged down in the minutiae of free speech law. Nevertheless, a brief overview of the relevant doctrine may help you place in context the Supreme Court's treatment of political speech and campaign-finance restrictions.

When evaluating the constitutionality of a speech-restrictive law, a court typically first asks whether the law restricts speech on the basis of its content — that is, whether the regulatory sanction attached to the law applies to speech only when the speaker takes a particular position or speaks on some particular topic. This inquiry determines the appropriate standard of review. Content-based restrictions are subject to strict scrutiny, under which the law must serve a compelling government interest and be narrowly tailored to achieve that interest. Laws that discriminate not only on the basis of content, but also on the basis of the speaker's viewpoint, are almost certainly unconstitutional.

Content-neutral restrictions—those that apply to speech regardless of what the speaker is saying—are permissible if they are reasonable restrictions on the time, place, or manner of speech. In many circumstances, though not all, content-neutral restrictions on speech are subject to a form of intermediate scrutiny—that is, review that applies a standard somewhere between the very lenient constitutional standard of rational basis review and the most demanding strict scrutiny standard. One common formulation of this standard is the *O'Brien* test, so named after *United States v. O'Brien*, 391 U.S. 367 (1968), in which the Court held that a content-neutral regulation of the time, place, or manner of speech may be upheld if "it furthers an important or substantial governmental interest; if the governmental interest is unrelated to the suppression of free expression; and if the incidental restriction on alleged First Amendment freedoms is no greater than is essential to the furtherance of that interest." In more recent cases arising in the election law area, the Court has also developed a test of "exacting scrutiny" under which laws restricting speech will be upheld if the law bears a "substantial relation" to a "sufficiently important" governmental interest.

Political speech has often been said by the Court to lie at the heart of free-speech protections. When you read the cases in this chapter, consider whether the Court's evaluation of the value of a particular speaker and its potential speech might be somehow influencing the Court's rulings.

>> *Underlying Theories.*   Theories of free speech can help bring some order to the case law, though no single theory is capable of explaining all the Court's many decisions across First Amendment law. One conventionally prominent theory of the First Amendment is the concept of the "marketplace of ideas." This theory derives from Justice Holmes's contention a century ago that "the best test of truth is the power of the thought to get itself accepted in the competition of the market and that truth is the only ground upon which [our] wishes safely can be carried out." *Abrams v. United States*, 250 U.S. 616 (1919) (Holmes, J., dissenting). On this view, suppression of speech inhibits the ability of a society to find the truth—the grounds upon which we should build our lives.

Another commonly accepted theory of free speech flows more directly from a model of politics. On this view, decisions in a democratic polity are made ideally through debate and rational deliberation. The philosopher Alexander Meiklejohn advanced this contention forcefully, arguing that such a model of politics was institutionalized in the First Amendment.

> The Constitution [ordains] that all authority to exercise control, to determine common action, belongs to "We, the People." [Under this system, free men are governed] by themselves. [What,] then, does the First Amendment forbid? [The] town meeting suggests an answer. That meeting is called to discuss and, on the basis of such discussion, to decide matters of public policy. [The] voters, therefore, must be made as wise as possible. [And] this, in turn, requires that so far as time allows, all facts and interests relevant to the problem shall be fully and fairly presented to the meeting [so] that all the alternative lines of action can be wisely measured in relation to one another. . . .

> The First Amendment . . . [requires] that no suggestion of policy shall be denied a hearing because it is one side of the issue rather than another. [Citizens] may not be barred [from speaking] because their views are thought to be false or dangerous. [The] reason for this equality of ideas lies deep in the very foundation of the self-governing process. When men govern themselves it is they—and no one else—who must pass judgment on the unwisdom and unfairness and danger. . . . [Thus,] the unlimited guarantee of the freedom of public discussion, which is given by the First Amendment, [protects the speech] of a citizen who is planning for the general welfare.

ALEXANDER MEIKLEJOHN, FREE SPEECH AND ITS RELATION TO SELF-GOVERNMENT (1948). The Supreme Court has been greatly influenced by this thesis, holding, for example, that the First Amendment "has its fullest and most urgent application precisely to the conduct of campaigns for political office." *Monitor Patriot Co. v. Roy* (see below).

However, the Court has not always been consistent, and one way of making sense of its cases on political speech is to recognize that the Court's campaign-speech jurisprudence has sometimes vacillated between a nineteenth- and twentieth-century understanding of citizenship and the role of campaigns. The dominant approach, which we can call individualism, would have been generally familiar to the Progressives. Under that theory, the individual is the critical democratic actor and decision maker. The individual is regarded as a rational actor and the best judge of his or her preferences. The individualist model privileges voter autonomy and voter information. If individuals are to make informed political choices, they need as much information as possible, from as many sources as possible. From this perspective, restrictions on speech are disfavored and the Court uses strict scrutiny to strike down political-speech limitations. Doctrinally, the Court relies heavily on a robust theory of the First Amendment to enforce this worldview. There is no weighing of competing values. The analysis is often fairly straightforward and fairly formalistic.

The second approach reflects a structural or institutionalist understanding of American politics. In this model, democratic outcomes are the product of structural arrangements, and the individual voter's choices and decisions both influence and are influenced by structural arrangements. Whereas individualists view the voter as a rational actor who is capable of sorting through complex political information to make an independent and informed choice, structuralists view the voter as vulnerable to elite manipulation. Structuralists have less faith in the capacity of the individual voter to make sense of political information. Moreover, structuralists understand that democratic outcomes are mediated through institutions such as political parties or the news media. Consequently, structuralists are more willing to entertain government regulation of campaign speech, especially where the aim of the regulation is to reduce the opportunities for elite manipulation of political information and to maintain pride of place for the institutions that are thought to play an important role in American politics. Doctrinally, the First Amendment plays a reduced role under this approach. For example, a court proceeding on a structural model might weigh First Amendment values against other democratic values, such as the right to vote or political equality. The analysis is often less predictable and more nuanced.

As you read the cases below, consider the underlying assumptions they make about the operation of American politics. Which worldview do they reflect? Do they reflect the worldview of democratic individualism, structuralism, or some other conception of democratic practice?

B.   RESTRICTIONS ON THE CONTENT OF CAMPAIGN SPEECH

1.   False Statements

The Supreme Court has said that "there is no constitutional value in false statements of fact," *Gertz v. Robert Welch, Inc.*, 418 U.S. 323, 340 (1974), but has never actually declared that false statements of fact are presumptively unprotected by the First Amendment. Rather, it has identified specific types of false statements that are accorded less constitutional protection. The Court, for example, has long recognized the constitutionality of libel laws, though it has cabined these laws by requiring a showing of "actual malice" to impose liability on newspapers for printing false statements about public figures. *New York Times Co. v. Sullivan*, 376 U.S. 254, 283 (1964). Similarly, the Court has affirmed the constitutionality of civil liability for fraud. *Illinois ex rel. Madigan v. Telemarketing Assocs.*, 538 U.S. 600, 621 (2003). The First Amendment stature of other false statements is unknown. *See* Julia K. Wood, Note, *Truth, Lies, and Stolen Valor: A Case for Protecting False Statements of Fact Under the First Amendment*, 61 DUKE L.J. 469, 479-485 (2011).

As a normative matter, if political information is critical to the electorate's choice, shouldn't the information be truthful? What is the best method of producing truthful information so that voters can make an informed choice? Is true speech best achieved, as some supporters of the marketplace of ideas argue, through the unrestricted freedom of listeners to make and identify false statements? How concerned should the electorate be that a government's prohibition on election-related speech is likely to deter worthy speech?

▶▶ ***Libel Law as a Mechanism for Policing Falsehoods.***   Traditionally, the remedy for false statements about a person has been the common law tort of libel. Libel law typically provides that a person who suffers injury as the result of a false and defamatory statement can recover actual damages and, if the statement is made maliciously, punitive damages, in a civil lawsuit. Actionable injuries can include injury to reputation, loss of business or other economic opportunities, and pain and suffering. A statement is usually considered defamatory only if it casts the plaintiff in a bad light. Finally, in the United States, truth has long been a defense to a charge of libel.

Because libel laws restrict speech, however, the Supreme Court has held that the First Amendment limits their reach. In the seminal case of *New York Times v. Sullivan*, 376 U.S. 254 (1964), the Court held that a plaintiff who is a public official cannot maintain a libel action based on criticism of his or her official conduct unless the plaintiff can show that the statement was made with "actual malice"—that is, "with knowledge that it was false or with reckless disregard of whether it was false or not." Sullivan was a commissioner of Montgomery, Alabama, with supervisory responsibilities over the police department. In 1960, the New York Times carried an advertisement placed by civil rights advocates criticizing the behavior of the Montgomery police during a civil rights rally. The advertisement contained several minor factual errors. Sullivan brought a libel suit in the Alabama courts, contending that the advertisement's indirect criticism of him in his role as supervisor of the police department had damaged his reputation. The jury awarded actual and punitive damages of $500,000.

In an opinion by Justice Brennan, the Court overturned this verdict. It observed that the First Amendment reflects "a profound national commitment to the principle that debate on public issues should be uninhibited, robust, and wide-open, and that it may well include vehement, caustic, and sometimes unpleasantly sharp attacks on government and public officials." Moreover, error, the Court said, "is inevitable in free debate[;] it must be protected if the freedoms of expression are to have the 'breathing space' that they 'need . . . to survive.'" The Court specifically rejected the notion that false criticism of government officials should be dealt with strongly: "Criticism of their official conduct does not lose its constitutional protection merely because it is effective criticism and hence diminishes their official reputations." Finally, the Court rejected the argument that Alabama's libel law was constitutional because it offered truth as a defense:

> The state rule of law is not saved by its allowance of the defense of truth. [A] rule compelling the critic of official conduct to guarantee the truth of all his factual assertions—and to do so on pain of libel judgments virtually unlimited in amount—leads to . . . "self-censorship." Allowance of the defense of truth, with the burden of proving it on the defendant, does not mean that only false speech will be deterred. [Under] such a rule, would-be critics of official conduct may be deterred from voicing their criticism, even though it is believed to be true and even though it is in fact true, because of doubt whether it can be proved in court or fear of the expense of having to do so. They tend to make only statements which "steer far wider of the unlawful zone." [The] rule thus dampens the vigor and limits the variety of public debate.

The notion that legal rules prohibiting false statements will deter not only false speech but also true speech that might approach the boundaries of truth is known as the "chilling effect." In *Sullivan,* and in many subsequent cases, the Court thus took the view that the chilling effect of a law on presumptively valuable speech is a factor to be considered in determining its constitutionality. As a result, in some circumstances a law restricting speech on the basis of its falsity cannot be successfully defended on the ground that it prohibits *only* speech that is false. If its operation might chill permitted speech because of uncertainty about the law's reach or anxiety about flirting with its boundaries, the law may nevertheless be unconstitutional.

In *Curtis Publishing Co. v. Butts,* 388 U.S. 130 (1967), the Court extended the *Sullivan* "actual malice" rule to plaintiffs who, though they are not "public officials" in the sense of holding government office, are nevertheless "public figures." In *Butts*, the Court held that the athletic director of the University of Georgia was a public figure, and that free public discussion of public figures was as important as free discussion of public officials in the marketplace of ideas. As a result, plaintiffs who are public figures can recover in libel actions only if false statements about them were made with "actual malice." This rule applies to national and local celebrities, and others less famous whose quasi-public stature brings them within the rule.

In the case that follows, the Court considered the application of these constitutional rules to an unsuccessful candidate for the United States Senate who claimed that his election chances were gravely damaged by what he contended were false statements made by a newspaper columnist.

Monitor Patriot Co. v. Roy

401 U.S. 265 (1971)

Mr. Justice STEWART delivered the opinion of the Court.

On September 10, 1960, three days before the New Hampshire Democratic Party's primary election of candidates for the United States Senate, the Concord Monitor, a daily newspaper in Concord, New Hampshire, published a syndicated "D.C. Merry-Go-Round" column discussing the forthcoming election. The column spoke of political maneuvering in the primary campaign, referred to the criminal records of several of the candidates, and characterized Alphonse Roy, one of the candidates, as a "former small-time bootlegger." Roy was not elected in the primary, and he subsequently sued the Monitor Patriot Co. and the North American Newspaper Alliance (NANA), the distributor of the column, for libel.

The newspaper and NANA offered "truth" as their primary defense at trial, and evidence was presented on the issue of whether or not Roy had in fact been a bootlegger during the prohibition era. The defendants also alleged that they had published in good faith, without malice, with a reasonable belief in the probable truth of the charge. . . . At the close of the evidence, the trial judge instructed the jury at great length on the law to be applied to the case. Three possible defenses emerged from these jury instructions.

First, the trial judge told the jury that Roy was a "public official" by virtue of his candidacy in the primary. As a consequence, a special rule, requiring a showing that the article was false and had been published with "knowledge of its falsity or with a reckless disregard of whether it was false or true," would apply so long as the libel concerned "official conduct" as opposed to "private conduct." This private-public distinction was elaborated as follows: "Is it more probable than otherwise that the publication that the plaintiff was a former small-time bootlegger was a public affair on a par with official conduct of public officials?" The trial judge went on:

> As a candidate for the United State[s] Senate, the plaintiff was within the public official concept, and a candidate must surrender to public scrutiny and discussion so much of his private character as affects his fitness for office. That is, anything which might touch on Alphonse Roy's fitness for

the office of United States Senator would come within the concept of official conduct. If it would not touch upon or be relevant to his fitness for the office for which he was a candidate but was rather a bringing forward of the plaintiff's long forgotten misconduct in which the public had no interest, then it would be a private matter in the private sector.

The judge then instructed the jury that if it found the libel to be in the "public sector" it must bring in a verdict for NANA, since there had been no evidence that NANA had engaged in knowing or reckless falsehood, but that it still had to decide on the "preponderance of the evidence" whether the newspaper was liable.

Supposing the publication to be in the "private sector," the trial judge instructed the jury that there were two possible defenses available to the newspaper and NANA. The first was "justification," which would prevail if the jury found that the article was both true and published on a "lawful occasion." The second defense was "conditional privilege," which could prevail even if the jury found the article to be false, but only if it also found that its publication was "on a lawful occasion, in good faith, for a justifiable purpose, and with a belief founded on reasonable grounds of the truth of the matter published."

The jury returned a verdict of $20,000, of which $10,000 was against the newspaper and $10,000 against NANA. On appeal, the New Hampshire Supreme Court affirmed the judgment. . . . We granted certiorari in order to consider the constitutional issues presented by the case.

I

In *New York Times Co. v. Sullivan,* 376 U.S. 254 (1964), we held that the First and Fourteenth Amendments require "a federal rule that prohibits a public official from recovering damages for a defamatory falsehood relating to his official conduct unless he proves that the statement was made with 'actual malice' — that is, with knowledge that it was false or with reckless disregard of whether it was false or not." . . . The approach of *New York Times* was to identify a class of person — there public officials — and a type of activity — there official conduct — and to require as to defamations respecting them a particularly high standard of liability — knowing falsehood or reckless disregard of the truth. . . .

[I]t is abundantly clear that . . . publications concerning candidates must be accorded at least as much protection under the First and Fourteenth Amendments as those concerning occupants of public office. . . . And if it be conceded that the First Amendment was "fashioned to assure the unfettered interchange of ideas for the bringing about of political and social changes desired by the people," *Roth v. United States,* 354 U.S. 476 (1957), then it can hardly be doubted that the constitutional guarantee has its fullest and most urgent application precisely to the conduct of campaigns for political office.

II

The respondent argues that under *New York Times* a plaintiff has a special burden of proof only as to libels "relating to official conduct," that for a candidate "official conduct" means "conduct relevant to fitness for office," and that the public–private issue is one of fact for the jury. In our view, however, the syllogistic manipulation of distinctions between "private sectors" and "public sectors," or matters of fact and matters of law, is of little utility in resolving questions of First Amendment protection.

In *Garrison v. Louisiana*, 379 U.S. 64 (1964), we reversed a conviction for criminal libel of a man who had charged that a group of state court judges were inefficient, took excessive vacations, opposed official investigations of vice, and were possibly subject to "racketeer influences." The Louisiana Supreme Court had held that these statements were not "criticisms . . . of the manner in which any one of the eight judges conducted his court when in session, but rather were accusations of crime" and "personal attacks upon the integrity and honesty" of the judges. This Court rejected the proposed distinction:

> Of course, any criticism of the manner in which a public official performs his duties will tend to affect his private, as well as his public, reputation. The *New York Times* rule is not rendered inapplicable merely because an official's private reputation, as well as his public reputation, is harmed. The public-official rule protects the paramount public interest in a free flow of information to the people concerning public officials, their servants. To this end, anything which might touch on an official's fitness for office is relevant. Few personal attributes are more germane to fitness for office than dishonesty, malfeasance, or improper motivation, even though these characteristics may also affect the official's private character.

The considerations that led us thus to reformulate the "official conduct" rule of *New York Times* in terms of "anything which might touch on an official's fitness for office" apply with special force to the case of the candidate. . . . The principal activity of a candidate in our political system, his "office," so to speak, consists in putting before the voters every conceivable aspect of his public and private life that he thinks may lead the electorate to gain a good impression of him. A candidate who, for example, seeks to further his cause through the prominent display of his wife and children can hardly argue that his qualities as a husband or father remain of "purely private" concern. And the candidate who vaunts his spotless record and sterling integrity cannot convincingly cry "Foul!" when an opponent or an industrious reporter attempts to demonstrate the contrary. . . .

Given the realities of our political life, it is by no means easy to see what statements about a candidate might be altogether without relevance to his fitness for the office he seeks. The clash of reputations is the staple of election campaigns, and damage to reputation is, of course, the essence of libel. But whether there remains some exiguous area of defamation against which a candidate may have full recourse is a question we need not decide in this case. The trial judge presented the issue to the jury in the form of the question: "Is it more probable than otherwise that the publication that the plaintiff was a former small-time bootlegger was a public affair on a par with official conduct of public officials?" This instruction, and the others like it, left the jury far more leeway to act as censors than is consistent with the protection of the First and Fourteenth Amendments in the setting of a political campaign. . . .

It is perhaps unavoidable that in the area of tension between the Constitution and the various state laws of defamation there will be some uncertainty as to what publications are and what are not protected. The mental element of "knowing or reckless disregard" required under the *New York Times* test, for example, is not always easy of ascertainment. . . . But there is a major, and in this case decisive, difference between liability based on a standard of care, and liability based on a judgment of the "relevance" of a past incident of criminal conduct to an official's or a candidate's fitness for office. A standard of care "can be neutral with respect to content of the speech involved, free of historical taint, and adjusted to strike a fair balance between the interests of the community in free circulation of information and those of individuals in seeking recompense for harm done by the circulation of defamatory falsehood." *Curtis Publishing Co. v. Butts*, 388 U.S. 130 (1967). A standard of "relevance," on the other hand, especially such a standard applied by a jury under the preponderance-of-the-evidence test, is unlikely to be neutral with respect to the content of speech and holds a real danger of becoming an instrument for the suppression of those "vehement, caustic, and sometimes unpleasantly sharp attacks," *New York Times*, 376 U.S. at 270, which must be protected if the guarantees of the First and Fourteenth Amendments are to prevail.

We therefore hold as a matter of constitutional law that a charge of criminal conduct, no matter how remote in time or place, can never be irrelevant to an official's or a candidate's fitness for office for purposes of application of the "knowing falsehood or reckless disregard" rule of *New York Times Co. v. Sullivan*. Since the jury in this case was permitted to make its own unguided determination that the charge of prior criminal activity was not "relevant," and that the *New York Times* standard was thus inapplicable, the judgment must be reversed and the case remanded for further proceedings not inconsistent with this opinion.

It is so ordered.

———

Do you agree that a charge of criminal conduct, "no matter how remote in time or place," can *never* be irrelevant to a candidate's fitness for office? Should declaring one's candidacy for public office constitute a declaration of open season on one's character? How should we weigh the public's interest in assembling what amounts to complete public dossiers on candidates against the public's interest in encouraging runs for office by the best people available?

⬗ *The Efficacy of Libel Suits.* How effective a tool are libel lawsuits for ensuring the truth of statements made during campaigns? Consider that the reach of libel suits is limited to punishing only those falsehoods that cause concrete harm to individual reputation. Moreover, after *New York Times* and *Monitor Patriot*, libel suits brought by incumbent officials and challengers can succeed only for reputation-damaging falsehoods made with "actual malice." What proportion of false campaign statements is made with such malice, rather than out of ignorance or incompetence? Would an attitude of willful ignorance—i.e., purposefully ignoring the truth when it is available—count as actual malice? For discussion, see Gerald G. Ashdown, *Distorting Democracy: Campaign Lies in the 21st Century*, 20 WM. & MARY BILL RTS. J. 1085 (2012).

>> *Fair Campaign Codes.*   At times, usually in response to prominent local or national instances of dirty campaigning, state legislatures have enacted codes intended to prescribe, and in many cases to enforce, rules of fair campaigning. Many of these codes proscribe false statements. Here are some examples:

Mass. Laws ch. 56, §42

No person shall make or publish, or cause to be made or published, any false statement in relation to any candidate for nomination or election to public office, which is designed or tends to aid or to injure or defeat such candidate.

No person shall publish or cause to be published in any letter, circular, advertisement, poster or in any other writing any false statement in relation to any question submitted to the voters, which statement is designed to affect the vote on said question.

Whoever knowingly violates any provision of this section shall be punished by a fine of not more than one thousand dollars or by imprisonment for not more than six months.

Wis. Stat. §12.05

No person may knowingly make or publish, or cause to be made or published, a false representation pertaining to a candidate or referendum which is intended or tends to affect voting at an election.

Are laws such as these constitutional under the First Amendment? The next case takes up this issue.

Vanasco v. Schwartz

401 F. Supp. 87 (E.D.N.Y. 1976) (three-judge court)

WERKER, District Judge.

The New York State Board of Elections ("Board") was created as part of the recently enacted "New York State Campaigns, elections and procedures law." Pursuant to its authorized power, the Board promulgated a Fair Campaign Code ("Code") for the purpose, *inter alia*, of "stimulating just debate" in political campaigns. Plaintiffs . . . have challenged the constitutionality of those sections of the Code which prohibit "during the course of any campaign for nomination or election to public office or party position," by means of "campaign literature, media advertisements or broadcasts, public speeches, press releases, writings or otherwise," "attacks on a candidate based on race, sex, religion or ethnic background"; any "misrepresentation of any candidate's qualifications" including the use of "personal vilification" and "scurrilous attacks"; any "misrepresentation of a candidate's position"; and any "misrepresentation of any candidate's party affiliation or party endorsement." The State argues that the Code and the statute constitute a narrowly drawn regulatory scheme covering an area of unprotected expression. We disagree and hold that the challenged sections of the Code and of the statute are repugnant to the right of freedom of speech guaranteed by the First Amendment and are unconstitutional on their face.

I.

Roy Vanasco was [an] unsuccessful Republican party candidate for the New York State Assembly. . . . His incumbent opponent filed a complaint with the Board in which he claimed that Vanasco had distributed palm cards using the phrase "Republican-Liberal" when in fact Vanasco was only on the ballot as a candidate of the Republican party. . . . After a hearing . . . the Board issued a decision in which it found that the use of the phrase "Republican-Liberal" "misrepresented [Vanasco's] party endorsement, since he was not the candidate of the Liberal Party" (a violation of Sec. 6201.1(f) of the Code). . . . The Board then ordered Vanasco to surrender all campaign literature which contained the phrase "Republican-Liberal" or to submit a plan for re-marking the literature. Vanasco complied with the Board's order by re-marking his campaign literature.

Joseph Ferris was the Democratic-Liberal candidate for an Assembly seat in the 51st Assembly District. Ferris was elected to office. His incumbent opponent, Vincent Riccio, complained to the Board that Ferris had misrepresented Riccio's voting record in a leaflet . . . and by making certain remarks which had been quoted in a newspaper article. . . . A hearing was held and a decision filed . . . one day before the election wherein the Board found that Ferris had misrepresented Riccio's voting record (a violation of Sec. 6201.1(e)) and had done so "with actual knowledge of its falsity or with reckless disregard of its falsity." Like Vanasco, Ferris was ordered to surrender his campaign literature or submit a plan for re-marking it. Ferris complied with the Board's order.

On October 29, 1974 Vanasco and Ferris filed suit against the Board in the Eastern District of New York. . . .

II.

[T]he fundamental question which must be answered is: To what extent may a state regulate the speech of those persons who are seeking public office? The plaintiffs argue that only those "well-defined and narrowly limited" classes of speech including the "lewd and obscene, the profane, the libelous, and the insulting or 'fighting' words — those which by their very utterance inflict injury or intend to incite an immediate breach of the peace" fall outside the protection of the First Amendment. . . . According to plaintiffs, the answer to false campaign speech does not lie in regulation by the state but rather in criticism and rebuttal in the "marketplace of ideas." Far from enhancing the political process, regulation of campaign speech will in plaintiffs' words "undermine its most powerful safeguard."

While recognizing that the First Amendment enjoys a "preferred position" among those rights guaranteed by the Constitution, the Board contends that the statute and the Code prohibit only that expression which is unprotected by the First Amendment. Unprotected speech, the Board argues, would include those statements made "with 'actual malice' — that is, with knowledge that (they were) false or with reckless disregard of whether [they were] false or not." . . . *New York Times v. Sullivan*, 376 U.S. 254, 280 (1964). We agree with this position.

Garrison v. Louisiana, in our view, answers plaintiffs' argument that the deliberate false statement is constitutionally protected speech when uttered during the course of a political campaign. There the Court noted:

> That speech is used as a tool for political ends does not automatically bring it under the protective mantle of the Constitution. For the use of the known lie as a tool is at once at odds with the premises of democratic government and with the orderly manner in which economic, social, or political change is to be effected. Calculated falsehood falls into that class of utterances which "are no essential part of any exposition of ideas, and are of such slight social value as a step to truth that any benefit that may be derived from them is clearly outweighed by the social interest in order and morality. Hence the knowingly false statement and the false statement made with the reckless disregard of the truth, do not enjoy constitutional protection." *Garrison,* 379 U.S. at 75.

The decisions in *Times* and *Garrison* and other related cases emphasize the necessity for statements concerning public issues to command a high degree of constitutional protection so that debate may be "uninhibited, robust, and wide open." It is that standard of protection and not the narrow area of unprotected speech which they define that constitutes the real significance of the *Times* line of cases. . . .

It is important to emphasize here a proposition with which the Board agrees, i.e., that any state regulation of campaign speech must be premised on proof and application of a *Times* "actual malice" standard. We are not dealing with defamation suits brought by "private individuals" where a standard somewhat less than that required by *Times* would be appropriate. To the contrary, Board proceedings concern regulation of the speech . . . during campaigns for political office where the constitutional guarantee of freedom of speech "has its fullest and most urgent application." *Monitor Patriot Co.,* 401 U.S. 265, 272 (1970). With this proposition in mind, we can agree with the Board's argument that calculated falsehoods are of such slight social value that no matter what the context in which they are made, they are not constitutionally protected. . . .

III.

The Board admits that [the section of the Code concerning attacks on a candidate based on race, sex, religion, or ethnic background] was not intended to be, and is not, limited by a *Times* "actual malice" standard. It is a blanket prohibition against any attacks on a candidate's race, sex, religion or ethnic background. Justification for such a sweeping prohibition rests on the assumption that this Code section focuses only on attributes which are completely unrelated to any candidate's "fitness for office." Such an assumption is an exercise in self-delusion. . . . It would be a retreat from reality to hold that voters do not consider race, religion, sex or ethnic background when choosing political candidates. Speech is often provocative and indeed offensive, but unless it falls into one of those "well defined and narrowly limited classes" of unprotected speech it enjoys constitutional protection. New York's attempt to eliminate an entire segment of protected speech from the arena of public debate is clearly unconstitutional.

Three sections of the Code specifically challenged by plaintiffs prohibit misrepresentations. . . . As to these sections the Board contends that the statute and the Code are narrowly drafted so that only the deliberate calculated falsehood—unprotected speech—is the subject of regulation. We disagree and hold that these sections of the Code . . . have not been so carefully drawn or authoritatively construed so as to regulate only unprotected expression. These sections cast a substantial chill on the expression of protected speech and are unconstitutionally overbroad and vague on their face. . . .

Overbreadth review is based on a determination of whether the language of the statute in question or the construction it has been given is susceptible of application to protected expression. In effect, it is a doctrine which recognizes that despite any legitimate state interest involved, the chilling effect on protected expression is too high a price to pay when the regulatory scheme has not been narrowly drawn. . . . The Board argues that the Code sections are narrowly drawn to regulate only unprotected calculated falsehoods. . . . [But the] sweeping nature of those sections is exemplified by their provisions. For example, "misrepresentation of any candidate's qualifications" includes among its prohibitions the use of "personal vilification" and "scurrilous attacks." Like "attacks based on race, sex, religion or ethnic background," such expression may be offensive but by that fact alone it does not lose its constitutional protection. . . .

It is not hard to see then, given the often difficult task of trying to define, for example, what a political candidate's "position" is on issues discussed during a campaign, that the term "misrepresentation" could be applied to almost all campaign speech. The candidate who wishes to avoid the consequences of a Code proceeding—including the adverse publicity such as a proceeding would generate—might very well be "chilled" from the expression of protected First Amendment speech. . . .

In our view, the Code creates a "substantial chill" and has a significant likelihood of deterring . . . important First Amendment speech. We cannot agree with the Board's contentions that any chill on protected expression is "minor or purely speculative," and that the chill of unlimited liability for damages or imprisonment under the *Times* and *Garrison* decisions is "much more significant than any chill that might result from the Code's existence." . . .

Nothing in our decision downgrades the state's legitimate interest in insuring fair and honest elections. Undoubtedly, deliberate calculated falsehoods when used by political candidates can lead to public cynicism and apathy toward the electoral process. However, when the State through the guise of protecting the citizen's right to a fair and honest election tampers with what it will permit the citizen to see and hear even that important state interest must give way to the irresistible force of protected expression under the First Amendment.

We conclude that sections 6201.1(c), (d), (e), (f) of the New York Fair Campaign Code and section 472(a) of the New York Election Law are unconstitutional on their face. . . .

What is the best defense of the courts' decisions in *Monitor* and *Vanasco*? Are these cases justified on the theory that the political marketplace will inevitably provide truthful information? Are you convinced by the courts' arguments about the potential for chilling speech? Don't political campaigns have a strong incentive to fact check their statements, for fear of having their claims exposed as false or misrepresentative?

>> *Why Regulate Deceptive Campaign Speech?*   According to a leading account, the reasons include: (1) "[F]alse statements can distort the electoral process. Democracy is premised on an informed electorate." (2) "[F]alse statements can . . . lower the quality of campaign discourse and debate [if] campaigns degenerate into cycles of attack and denial rather than serious engagement on major issues." (3) "[F]alse statements can lead or add to voter alienation by fostering voter cynicism and distrust of the political process." (4) "[F]alse statements against an opponent's character can inflict reputation and emotional injury, [and] attack ads can deter qualified individuals from seeking public office." William P. Marshall, *False Campaign Speech and the First Amendment*, 153 U. Pa. L. Rev. 285, 294-297 (2004). On the other hand, the same author observes, "the arguments in favor of regulation may overstate the harms"; "sanctioning false campaign speech may not . . . be an effective way of informing the public"; "restricting campaign speech . . . is in tension with basic free speech principles"; government regulation may "open[] the door to partisan abuse"; and such regulation may transform courts or regulatory agencies into "political weapons." *Id.* at 297-300.

>> *Post–*New York Times *Fair Campaign Codes.*   The fair campaign statutes below are of more recent vintage. Would they survive constitutional review?

Alaska Stat. §15.13.095

(a) A candidate who is damaged as the result of a false statement about the candidate made with knowledge that it was false, or with reckless disregard for whether it was false or not, made as part of a telephone poll or an organized series of calls, and made with the intent to convince potential voters concerning the outcome of an election in which the candidate is running may recover damages in an action in superior court under this section against the individual who made the telephone call, the individual's employer, and the person who contracted for or authorized the poll or calls to convince. However, the employer of the individual or the person who contracted for or authorized the poll or calls to convince is liable to the defamed candidate only if the employer or person authorized the statement to be made, knowing that it was false or with reckless disregard for whether it was false or not, as part of the poll or calls to convince.

(b) The court may award damages, including punitive damages. If the court finds that the result of the statement places the integrity of the election process in substantial doubt, the eligibility of the successful candidate to hold the office to which elected shall be determined as provided in AS 15.56.110(b) or, in the case of a candidate for governor or lieutenant governor, by impeachment under art. II, sec. 20, Constitution of the State of Alaska.

Colo. Rev. Stat. §1-13-109

(1) (a) No person shall knowingly make, publish, broadcast, or circulate or cause to be made, published, broadcasted, or circulated in any letter, circular, advertisement, or poster or in any other communication any false statement designed to affect the vote on any issue submitted to the electors at any election or relating to any candidate for election to public office.

(b) Any person who violates any provision of paragraph (a) of this subsection (1) commits a class 1 misdemeanor. . . .

(2) (a) No person shall recklessly make, publish, broadcast, or circulate or cause to be made, published, broadcasted, or circulated in any letter, circular, advertisement, or poster or in any other communication any false statement designed to affect the vote on any issue submitted to the electors at any election or relating to any candidate for election to public office. Notwithstanding any other provision of law, for purposes of this subsection (2), a person acts "recklessly" when he or she acts in conscious disregard of the truth or falsity of the statement made, published, broadcasted, or circulated.

(b) Any person who violates any provision of paragraph (a) of this subsection (2) commits a class 2 misdemeanor. . . .

Why would Alaska limit the reach of its statute to false statements made by telephone?

Even recently enacted or amended fair campaign codes, which have been tailored to reach only statements made with actual malice, have not fared well in the lower courts. Since 2014, code provisions from Ohio, Massachusetts, Minnesota, and Washington have been invalidated on First Amendment grounds. *See Susan B. Anthony List v. Driehaus*, 814 F.3d 466 (6th Cir. 2016). On the other hand, the Ohio Supreme Court upheld a fair campaign code provision that prohibited candidates in judicial elections from "conveying information concerning the judicial candidate or an opponent knowing the information to be false." *In re Judicial Campaign Complaint Against O'Toole*, 24 N.E.3d 1114 (Ohio 2014).

>> *Campaign Speech by Words or by Money.* In the next chapter, we will see that the Supreme Court considers the expenditure of money in support of campaign speech to be afforded constitutional protections similar to those afforded to campaign speech itself. For now, though, consider the following account:

At first glance, corporate campaign expenditures would seem to present greater First Amendment issues than deceptive campaign speech. After all, while the Court has held that there is no First Amendment value in false statements of fact, it has stated that campaign money implicates substantial First Amendment concern. Upon closer review, however, the question is more complex. First, corporate expenditures can also be seen as having little First Amendment value if they are, as the Court suggests, distortive and thus of little worth in the search for truth. Second, the First Amendment claim for false campaign speech can be based on concerns unrelated to the value of falsity, namely that regulating such speech would chill the give-and-take inherent in election battles and open the door to partisan abuse. Seen in this light, the claim for First Amendment protection for false campaign speech may be stronger than for corporate campaign expenditures. But the comparison is still not complete because the regulation of corporate campaign expenditures also raises concerns of political misdealing, as campaign finance regulation is inherently susceptible to the problems of legislative entrenchment. As such, its regulation also calls for careful scrutiny. In the end, then, the First Amendment case for protecting deceptive speech and the one for protecting corporate expenditures are not easily distinguished.

Marshall, *supra*, at 314. Do you agree with Professor Marshall's conclusion that both false campaign speech and campaign expenditures should be protected? What distinguishing features can you find between campaign speech and campaign expenditures? Are candidates more likely to be politically accountable for the things they say than the expenditures they make? If you can't easily identify the "speaker" in the case of expenditures, does that undermine a claim for First Amendment protection?

≫   *New Forms of Voter Deception.*   A series of unfavorable federal court decisions suppressed for some time further interest in government regulation of false campaign speech. More recently, however, an emerging new set of tactics has stirred interest in a regulatory response. Earlier forms of campaign falsity tended to target candidates; competing candidates might make false claims about each other, or their supporters might do so in negative campaign advertising. The newer forms of deception are targeted not at candidates but at voters, and contain apparently deliberate misstatements not about the merits or demerits of candidates for office, but about details of voting and voter eligibility in a way that seems calculated to interfere with voting itself.

For example, in 2004, a flyer appeared on the streets of Franklin County, Ohio, claiming to be from the Franklin County Board of Elections. It read, in its entirety:

> Because [of] the confusion caused by unexpected heavy voter registration, voters are asked to apply to the following schedule:
>
> Republican voters are asked to vote at your assigned location on Tuesday.
> Democratic voters are asked to vote at your assigned location on Wednesday.
> Thank you for your cooperation, and remember voting is a privilege.

The flyer was not from the Board of Elections, and it provided obviously false information, given that Election Day was a single Tuesday. Its only conceivable purpose was to induce ill-informed Democratic voters to miss their opportunity to vote. *See*

Gilda R. Daniels, *Voter Deception*, 43 IND. L. REV. 343 (2010). In another example, from Milwaukee, flyers claiming to be from the "Milwaukee Black Voters League" — a non-existent organization — turned up in minority neighborhoods claiming: "If you've already voted in any election this year, you can't vote in the presidential election; If anybody in your family has ever been found guilty of anything, you can't vote in the presidential election; If you violate any of these laws, you can get ten years in prison and your children will get taken away from you." *See* COMMON CAUSE ET AL., DECEPTIVE PRACTICES 2.0: LEGAL AND POLICY RESPONSES 3 (n.d.). This information, too, is clearly false. Many of these deceptive publications are disseminated in, and targeted toward, minority communities. *See also* Nicole Rustin-Paschal, *Online Behavioral Advertising and Deceptive Campaign Tactics: Policy Issues*, 19 WM. & MARY BILL RTS. J. 907 (2011).

Given that statements like these seemingly can be made only with knowledge or reckless disregard for their falsity, is there any constitutional impediment to punishing them? Where they are targeted at minority communities might the VRA itself supply a remedy? Some states have statutes on the books that might cover the kinds of deception described above. Virginia law, for example, provides: "It shall be unlawful for any person to communicate to a registered voter, by any means, false information, knowing the same to be false, intended to impede the voter in the exercise of his right to vote. The provisions of this section shall apply to information only about the date, time, and place of the election or the voter's precinct, polling place, or voter registration status." Va. Code Ann. §24.2-1005.1. Is this statute broad enough to cover the kinds of deliberate deception that voters might encounter?

▶▶   *"Fake News."*   The 2016 presidential election focused public attention on yet another development in campaign misbehavior: the dissemination of "fake news." Reports of fake news are written to resemble reports by legitimate news agencies, but often contain either severely misleading distortions or even outright fabrications. One notorious example was a story circulated on right-wing websites and propagated through social media contending that Democratic presidential candidate Hillary Clinton had been running a child sex ring out of the back of a popular Washington, D.C. pizzeria. Shortly after the election, police arrested a man who came to the pizzeria with a gun, apparently to liberate Mrs. Clinton's sex slaves. Eric Lipton, *Man Motivated by "Pizzagate" Conspiracy Theory Arrested in Washington Gunfire*, N.Y. TIMES, Dec. 5, 2016.

Under classic First Amendment law, the preferred remedy for bad speech is more speech — i.e., speech that exposes and corrects the error. *Whitney v. California*, 274 U.S. 357, 377 (1927) (Brandeis, J., concurring) ("If there be time to expose through discussion the falsehood and fallacies, to avert the evil by the processes of education, the remedy to be applied is more speech, not enforced silence"). Is so-called counterspeech an adequate remedy for the problems posed by fake news? If not, can the production of fake news be regulated by government consistent with the First Amendment?

▶▶   *Indirect Regulation of Campaign Speech by Treating It as Evidence.*   Candidates for office clearly have great latitude to speak in that capacity, and the government's ability to constrain their speech through direct regulation is correspondingly limited. But campaign speech may also be regulated indirectly if it can later be used against candidates who win office. This possibility was tested in *Trump v. Hawaii*, 585 U.S. __ (2018), a case challenging the constitutionality of President Trump's order severely restricting entry into the United States by nationals of six countries, five of which are predominantly Muslim. Mr. Trump campaigned hard on this issue, making numerous statements on the campaign trail that could plausibly be construed as demonstrating an anti-Muslim animus. For example, he called for "a total and complete shutdown of Muslims entering the United States." Speaking of Muslims, Mr. Trump claimed "it is obvious to anybody the hatred [they feel for Americans] is beyond comprehension." All Muslims, he suggested, are "people that believe only in Jihad, and have no sense of reason or respect of human life."

The plaintiffs, which included the state of Hawaii representing its state university system, which admits students from the banned countries, argued that the travel restriction order should be struck down as an unconstitutional act of religious discrimination, and offered Mr. Trump's campaign statements as evidence of his motivations. The Court declined to consider them, however, instead sustaining the order on the ground that, regardless of what other grounds it might rest upon, it had a sufficient basis in national security concerns to pass rational basis review.

2.   *Campaign Promises*

Candidates say many things during the course of campaigns for office. Traditionally, some of these things consist of promises or representations that candidates make about what they will do once in office. One problem with campaign promises, of course, may be that they are false, even deliberately so, in which case significant First Amendment obstacles might nevertheless impede a regulatory response, as the preceding materials show. Here, though, we focus on the opposite problem: campaign promises that are true, sincerely meant, and so understood by voters. In that case, a different kind of problem may arise, one sounding in bribery. After all, any time candidates promise to save taxpayer dollars, cut taxes, or introduce measures that benefit the public, they offer something of value to voters. Legislatures have sometimes expressed concern that such promises could have a corrupting influence on the electorate. This concern about corruption underlies many campaign-finance restrictions as well. We will return to this question in that context, but for purposes of this chapter, we focus here on prohibitions of speech.

Brown v. Hartlage

456 U.S. 45 (1982)

Justice BRENNAN delivered the opinion of the Court.

The question presented is whether the First Amendment, as applied to the States through the Fourteenth Amendment, prohibits a State from declaring an election void because the victorious candidate had announced to the voters during his campaign that he intended to serve at a salary less than that "fixed by law."

I

The parties were opposing candidates in the 1979 general election for the office of Jefferson County Commissioner, "C" District. Petitioner, Carl Brown, was the challenger; respondent, Earl Hartlage, was the incumbent. On August 15, 1979, in the course of the campaign, Brown [and his running mate, Creech,] held a televised press conference [pledging that, if elected, he would lower county commissioners' salaries by $3,000 a year]. Shortly after the press conference, Brown and Creech learned that their commitment to lower their salaries arguably violated the Kentucky Corrupt Practices Act. On August 19, 1979, they issued a joint statement retracting their earlier pledge:

> We are men enough to admit when we've made a mistake. We have discovered that there are Kentucky court decisions and Attorney General opinions which indicate that our pledge to reduce our salaries if elected may be illegal. . . . [W]e do hereby formally rescind our pledge to reduce the County Commissioners' salary if elected and instead pledge to seek corrective legislation in the next session of the General Assembly, to correct this silly provision of State Law.

In the November 6, 1979, election, Brown defeated Hartlage by 10,151 votes. Hartlage then filed this action in the Jefferson Circuit Court, alleging that Brown had violated the Corrupt Practices Act and seeking to have the election declared void and the office of Jefferson County Commissioner, "C" District, vacated by Brown. Section 121.055, upon which Hartlage based his claim, provides:

> Candidates prohibited from making expenditure, loan, promise, agreement, or contract as to action when elected, in consideration for vote.— No candidate for nomination or election to any state, county, city or district office shall expend, pay, promise, loan or become pecuniarily liable in any way for money or other thing of value, either directly or indirectly, to any person in consideration of the vote or financial or moral support of that person. No such candidate shall promise, agree or make a contract with any person to vote for or support any particular individual, thing or measure, in consideration for the vote or the financial or moral support of that person in any election, primary or nominating convention, and no person shall require that any candidate make such a promise, agreement or contract. Ky. Rev. Stat. §121.055 (1982).

In *Sparks v. Boggs*, 339 S.W.2d 480 (1960), the Kentucky Court of Appeals held that candidates' promises to serve at yearly salaries of $1, and to vote to distribute the salary savings to specified charitable organizations, violated the Corrupt Practices Act where the salaries had been "fixed by law." In the instant case, the trial court found that Brown's prospective salary had been fixed by law and that, under the reasoning of *Sparks*, Brown's promise violated the Act. Nevertheless, the court concluded that in light of Brown's retraction, the defeat of his running mate, who had joined in the pledge, and the presumption that the will of the people had been revealed through the election process, Brown had been "fairly elected." . . . The Kentucky Court of Appeals reversed. . . .

II

We begin our analysis of §121.055 by acknowledging that the States have a legitimate interest in preserving the integrity of their electoral processes. Just as a State may take steps to ensure that its governing political institutions and officials properly discharge public responsibilities and maintain public trust and confidence, a State has a legitimate interest in upholding the integrity of the electoral process itself. But when a State seeks to uphold that interest by restricting speech, the limitations on state authority imposed by the First Amendment are manifestly implicated.

At the core of the First Amendment are certain basic conceptions about the manner in which political discussion in a representative democracy should proceed. . . . The free exchange of ideas provides special vitality to the process traditionally at the heart of American constitutional democracy — the political campaign. "[I]f it be conceded that the First Amendment was 'fashioned to assure the unfettered interchange of ideas for the bringing about of political and social changes desired by the people,' then it can hardly be doubted that the constitutional guarantee has its fullest and most urgent application precisely to the conduct of campaigns for political office." *Monitor Patriot Co. v. Roy*, 401 U.S. 265, 271-272 (1971) (citation omitted). The political candidate does not lose the protection of the First Amendment when he declares himself for public office. Quite to the contrary:

> The candidate, no less than any other person, has a First Amendment right to engage in the discussion of public issues and vigorously and tirelessly to advocate his own election and the election of other candidates. Indeed, it is of particular importance that candidates have the unfettered opportunity to make their views known so that the electorate may intelligently evaluate the candidates' personal qualities and their positions on vital public issues before choosing among them on election day. . . .

Buckley v. Valeo, 424 U.S. 1, 52-53 (1976) (per curiam). When a State seeks to restrict directly the offer of ideas by a candidate to the voters, the First Amendment surely requires that the restriction be demonstrably supported by not only a legitimate state interest, but a compelling one, and that the restriction operate without unnecessarily circumscribing protected expression.

III

On its face, §121.055 prohibits a candidate from offering material benefits to voters in consideration for their votes, and, conversely, prohibits candidates from accepting payments in consideration for the manner in which they serve their public function. . . . We discern three bases upon which the application of the statute to Brown's promise might conceivably be justified: first, as a prohibition on buying votes; second, as facilitating the candidacy of persons lacking independent wealth; and third, as an application of the State's interests and prerogatives with respect to factual misstatements. We consider these possible justifications in turn.

A

The first sentence of §121.055 prohibits a political candidate from giving, or promising to give, anything of value to a voter in exchange for his vote or support. In many of its possible applications, this provision would appear to present little constitutional difficulty, for a State may surely prohibit a candidate from buying votes. No body politic worthy of being called a democracy entrusts the selection of leaders to a process of auction or barter. And as a State may prohibit the giving of money or other things of value to a voter in exchange for his support, it may also declare unlawful an agreement embodying the intention to make such an exchange. . . . The fact that such an agreement necessarily takes the form of words does not confer upon it, or upon the underlying conduct, the constitutional immunities that the First Amendment extends to speech. . . .

It is thus plain that *some* kinds of promises made by a candidate to voters, and *some* kinds of promises elicited by voters from candidates, may be declared illegal without constitutional difficulty. But it is equally plain that there are constitutional limits on the State's power to prohibit candidates from making promises in the course of an election campaign. . . . Candidate commitments enhance the accountability of government officials to the people whom they represent, and assist the voters in predicting the effect of their vote. The fact that some voters may find their self-interest reflected in a candidate's commitment does not place that commitment beyond the reach of the First Amendment. We have never insisted that the franchise be exercised without taint of individual benefit; indeed, our tradition of political pluralism is partly predicated on the expectation that voters will pursue their individual good through the political process, and that the summation of these individual pursuits will further the collective welfare. So long as the hoped-for personal benefit is to be achieved through the normal processes of government, and not through some private arrangement, it has always been, and remains, a reputable basis upon which to cast one's ballot.

It remains to determine the standards by which we might distinguish between those "private arrangements" that are inconsistent with democratic government, and those candidate assurances that promote the representative foundation of our political system. We hesitate before attempting to formulate some test of constitutional legitimacy: the precise nature of the promise, the conditions upon which it is given, the circumstances under which it is made, the size of the audience, the nature and size of the group to be benefited, all might, in some instance and to varying extents, bear upon the constitutional assessment. But acknowledging the difficulty of rendering a concise formulation, or recognizing the possibility of borderline cases, does not disable us from identifying cases far from any troublesome border.

It is clear that the statements of petitioner Brown in the course of the August 15 press conference were very different in character from the corrupting agreements and solicitations historically recognized as unprotected by the First Amendment. Notably, Brown's commitment to serve at a reduced salary was made openly, subject to the comment and criticism of his political opponent and to the scrutiny of the voters. We think the fact that the statement was made in full view of the electorate offers a strong indication that the statement contained nothing fundamentally at odds with our shared political ethic.

The Kentucky Court of Appeals analogized Brown's promise to a bribe. But however persuasive that analogy might be as a matter of state law, there is no *constitutional* basis upon which Brown's pledge to reduce his salary might be equated with a candidate's promise to pay voters for their support from his own pocketbook. Although upon election Brown would undoubtedly have had a valid claim to the salary that had been "fixed by law," Brown did not offer the voters a payment from his personal funds. His was a declaration of intention to exercise the fiscal powers of government office within what he believed (albeit erroneously) to be the recognized framework of office. At least to outward appearances, the commitment was fully in accord with our basic understanding of legitimate activity by a government body. Before any implicit monetary benefit to the individual taxpayer might have been realized, public officials — among them, of course, Brown himself — would have had to approve that benefit in accordance with the good faith exercise of their public duties. Although Brown may have been incorrect in suggesting that his salary could have been lawfully reduced, this cannot, in itself, transform his promise into an invitation to engage in a private and politically corrupting arrangement. . . .

In sum, Brown did not offer some private payment or donation in exchange for voter support; Brown's statement can only be construed as an expression of his intention to exercise public power in a manner that he believed might be acceptable to some class of citizens. If Brown's expressed intention had an individualized appeal to some taxpayers who felt themselves the likely beneficiaries of his form of fiscal restraint, that fact is of little constitutional significance. The benefits of most public policy changes accrue not only to the undifferentiated "public," but more directly to particular individuals or groups. Like a promise to lower taxes, to increase efficiency in government, or indeed to increase taxes in order to provide some group with a desired public benefit or public service, Brown's promise to reduce his salary cannot be deemed beyond the reach of the First Amendment, or considered as inviting the kind of corrupt arrangement the appearance of which a State may have a compelling interest in avoiding. . . .

IV

Because we conclude that §121.055 has been applied in this case to limit speech in violation of the First Amendment, we reverse the judgment of the Kentucky Court of Appeals and remand for proceedings not inconsistent with this opinion.

>> *Promises and Bribes.*   Is a promise the same thing as a bribe? Why do candidates make promises to voters? Is there a difference between candidate promises made to the entire electorate as a group, those made to proven or likely supporters, and those made to individual voters? Should courts enforce candidate promises, and if so, by what means? If not, why not? *See generally* Daniel H. Lowenstein, *Political Bribery and the Intermediate Theory of Politics*, 32 UCLA L. Rev. 784 (1985).

Do we have a theory of campaign promises? Do they have any binding force? If so, what is the nature of the commitment, and what is the appropriate sanction, if any, for breach of a campaign promise? If they are not binding, what legitimate purpose do they serve?

3. Constraints of Office

Not all restrictions on the content of campaign speech are motivated by concerns about maintaining the truthfulness of information presented to voters. In some cases, there may be reasons to suppress the circulation of concededly *true* (and non-corrupting) information, indeed to do so deliberately as a method of controlling what voters hear, and thus influencing the grounds upon which voters make decisions. The most common example is the case of nonpartisan elections. Candidates for nonpartisan office are prohibited from indicating any partisan affiliation on the ballot, and historically they have often been prohibited from campaigning based on party affiliation, and political parties have reciprocally been prohibited from endorsing such candidates.

Such restrictions on campaign speech clearly are not motivated by concerns about truth. Rather, the rationale for nonpartisanship lies in the normative belief that partisanship ought to play no role in the selection of individuals to fill certain kinds of offices, typically officials at the local level where, as the Progressives maintained, there is no Democratic or Republican way to pave a street. Nonpartisan elections were to be contested, therefore, solely on the basis of the technical skills and merits of individual citizen-candidates.

Restrictions on truthful campaign speech have been even more severe and comprehensive in the case of judicial elections. In *Republican Party of Minnesota v. White*, 536 U.S. 765 (2002) (set out in full in Chapter 10), Minnesota enacted restrictions on the speech of candidates for elective judicial office which barred them from "announcing" their views on "disputed legal or political issues." The state defended the law on the grounds that a candidate for judicial office could campaign and compete on the basis of " 'character,' 'education,' 'work habits,' and 'how [he] would handle administrative duties if elected.' " Candidates could discuss issues, but only those related to judicial administration, such as "how the candidate feels about cameras in the courtroom, how he would go about reducing the caseload, how the costs of judicial administration can be reduced, and how he proposes to ensure that minorities and women are treated more fairly by the court system." Minnesota justified these restrictions based on a particular conception of the judicial office; permitting candidates to campaign on other kinds of grounds would compromise "the impartiality of the state judiciary and . . . the appearance of the impartiality of the state judiciary."

The Court invalidated these restrictions on First Amendment grounds. The state's interest in regulating the *kind* of office that a judge holds was insufficient to overcome the state's burden of strict scrutiny. If campaigning on the same range of considerations that candidates for legislative and executive offices might deem relevant was incompatible with the nature of the judicial office, the First Amendment nonetheless did not permit the state to preserve the character of the office by limiting campaign speech. Justice Ginsburg, joined by Justices Stevens, Souter, and Breyer, disagreed: "I would differentiate elections for political offices, in which the First Amendment holds full sway, from elections designed to select those whose office it is to administer justice without respect to persons. Minnesota's choice to elect its judges, I am persuaded, does not preclude the State from installing an election process geared to the judicial office."

C.   RESTRICTIONS ON THE TIME, PLACE, AND MANNER OF CAMPAIGN SPEECH

The previous section considered direct regulation of campaign speech on the basis of its content. We turn now to a different kind of restriction on campaign speech, one that is indifferent to its content, but places great weight on the circumstances in which it is made. Such restrictions typically regulate on the basis of the time, place, or manner of the speech in question. Because such regulation is not content-based, it typically receives a more lenient form of constitutional scrutiny. Yet many such regulations fail constitutional review nonetheless. In *Mills v. Alabama*, 384 U.S. 214 (1965) (set out in full in Section D, below), for example, the Court invalidated a state law prohibiting the publication on Election Day of newspaper editorials counseling voting for or against particular candidates. The state defended the law on the ground that it protected candidates from charges and countercharges made so late as to preclude rebuttal before the electorate voted. Finding the law ineffective to achieve this purpose, and expressing a deep suspicion of a law that "makes it a crime . . . to do no more than urge people to vote one way or another in a publicly held election," the Court struck down the statute.

The following case deals with a much more commonplace kind of regulatory restriction, a state statute that prohibits electioneering, here defined as engaging in political speech within 100 feet of a polling place.

Burson v. Freeman

504 U.S. 191 (1992)

Justice BLACKMUN announced the judgment of the Court and delivered an opinion, in which THE CHIEF JUSTICE [REHNQUIST], Justice WHITE, and Justice KENNEDY join.

The question presented is whether a provision of the Tennessee Code, which prohibits the solicitation of votes and the display or distribution of campaign materials within 100 feet of the entrance to a polling place, violates the First and Fourteenth Amendments.

I

The State of Tennessee has carved out an election-day "campaign-free zone" through §2-7-111(b) of its election code. That section reads in pertinent part:

Within the appropriate boundary as established in subsection (a) [100 feet from the entrances], and the building in which the polling place is located, the display of campaign posters, signs or other campaign materials, distribution of campaign materials, and solicitation of votes for or against any person or political party or position on a question are prohibited.

Tenn. Code Ann. §2-7-111(b) (Supp. 1991). Violation of §2-7-111(b) is a Class C misdemeanor punishable by a term of imprisonment not greater than 30 days or a fine not to exceed $50, or both. Tenn. Code Ann. §§2-19-119 and 40-35-111(e)(3) (1990).

II

Respondent Mary Rebecca Freeman has been a candidate for office in Tennessee, has managed local campaigns, and has worked actively in statewide elections. In 1987, she was the treasurer for the campaign of a city-council candidate in Metropolitan Nashville-Davidson County.

Asserting that §§2-7-111(b) and 2-19-119 limited her ability to communicate with voters, respondent brought a facial challenge to these statutes in Davidson County Chancery Court. She sought a declaratory judgment that the provisions were unconstitutional under both the United States and the Tennessee Constitutions. She also sought a permanent injunction against their enforcement. . . .

III

The First Amendment provides that "Congress shall make no law . . . abridging the freedom of speech." This Court in *Thornhill v. Alabama*, 310 U.S. 88, 95 (1940), said: "The freedom of speech . . . which [is] secured by the First Amendment against abridgment by the United States, [is] among the fundamental personal rights and liberties which are secured to all persons by the Fourteenth Amendment against abridgment by a State."

The Tennessee statute implicates three central concerns in our First Amendment jurisprudence: regulation of political speech, regulation of speech in a public forum, and regulation based on the content of the speech. The speech restricted by §2-7-111(b) obviously is political speech. . . .

The second important feature of §2-7-111(b) is that it bars speech in quintessential public forums. These forums include those places "which by long tradition or by government fiat have been devoted to assembly and debate," such as parks, streets, and sidewalks. *Perry Ed. Assn. v. Perry Local Educators' Assn.*, 460 U.S. 37, 45 (1983). "Such use of the streets and public places has, from ancient times, been a part of the privileges, immunities, rights, and liberties of citizens." *Hague v. CIO*, 307 U.S. 496, 515 (1939) (opinion of Roberts, J.). At the same time, however, expressive activity, even in a quintessential public forum, may interfere with other important activities for which the property is used. Accordingly, this Court has held that the government may regulate the time, place, and manner of the expressive activity, so long as such restrictions are content neutral, are narrowly tailored to serve a significant governmental interest, and leave open ample alternatives for communication. *United States v. Grace*, 461 U.S. 171, 177 (1983).

The Tennessee restriction under consideration, however, is not a facially content-neutral time, place, or manner restriction. Whether individuals may exercise their free speech rights near polling places depends entirely on whether their speech is related to a political campaign. The statute does not reach other categories of speech, such as commercial solicitation, distribution, and display. This Court has held that the First Amendment's hostility to content-based regulation extends not only to a restriction on a particular viewpoint, but also to a prohibition of public discussion of an entire topic.

As a facially content-based restriction on political speech in a public forum, §2-7-111(b) must be subjected to exacting scrutiny: The State must show that the "regulation is necessary to serve a compelling state interest and that it is narrowly drawn to achieve that end." *Perry Ed. Assn. v. Perry Local Educators' Assn.,* 460 U.S., at 45.

Despite the ritualistic ease with which we state this now-familiar standard, its announcement does not allow us to avoid the truly difficult issues involving the First Amendment. Perhaps foremost among these serious issues are cases that force us to reconcile our commitment to free speech with our commitment to other constitutional rights embodied in government proceedings. This case presents us with a particularly difficult reconciliation: the accommodation of the right to engage in political discourse with the right to vote—a right at the heart of our democracy.

IV

Tennessee asserts that its campaign-free zone serves two compelling interests. First, the State argues that its regulation serves its compelling interest in protecting the right of its citizens to vote freely for the candidates of their choice. Second, Tennessee argues that its restriction protects the right to vote in an election conducted with integrity and reliability.

The interests advanced by Tennessee obviously are compelling ones. This Court has recognized that the "right to vote freely for the candidate of one's choice is of the essence of a democratic society." *Reynolds v. Sims,* 377 U.S. 533, 555 (1964). Indeed, "[n]o right is more precious in a free country than that of having a voice in the election of those who make the laws under which, as good citizens, we must live. Other rights, even the most basic, are illusory if the right to vote is undermined." *Wesberry v. Sanders,* 376 U.S. 1, 17 (1964).

Accordingly, this Court has concluded that a State has a compelling interest in protecting voters from confusion and undue influence.

The Court also has recognized that a State "indisputably has a compelling interest in preserving the integrity of its election process." *Eu,* 489 U.S. at 231. The Court thus has "upheld generally applicable and evenhanded restrictions that protect the integrity and reliability of the electoral process itself." *Anderson v. Celebrezze,* 460 U.S. 780, 788, n. 9 (1983). In other words, it has recognized that a State has a compelling interest in ensuring that an individual's right to vote is not undermined by fraud in the election process.

To survive strict scrutiny, however, a State must do more than assert a compelling state interest—it must demonstrate that its law is necessary to serve the asserted interest. While we readily acknowledge that a law rarely survives such scrutiny, an examination of the evolution of election reform, both in this country and abroad, demonstrates the necessity of restricted areas in or around polling places.

During the colonial period, many government officials were elected by the *viva voce* method or by the showing of hands, as was the custom in most parts of Europe. That voting scheme was not a private affair, but an open, public decision, witnessed by all and improperly influenced by some. The opportunities that the *viva voce* system gave for bribery and intimidation gradually led to its repeal.

Within 20 years of the formation of the Union, most States had incorporated the paper ballot into their electoral system. Initially, this paper ballot was a vast improvement. Individual voters made their own handwritten ballots, marked them in the privacy of their homes, and then brought them to the polls for counting. But the effort of making out such a ballot became increasingly more complex and cumbersome.

Wishing to gain influence, political parties began to produce their own ballots for voters. These ballots were often printed with flamboyant colors, distinctive designs, and emblems so that they could be recognized at a distance. State attempts to standardize the ballots were easily thwarted—the vote buyer could simply place a ballot in the hands of the bribed voter and watch until he placed it in the polling box. Thus, the evils associated with the earlier *viva voce* system reinfected the election process; the failure of the law to secure secrecy opened the door to bribery and intimidation.

Approaching the polling place under this system was akin to entering an open auction place. . . .

After several failed attempts to adopt the Australian system [of official ballots and private polling booths] in Michigan and Wisconsin, the Louisville, Kentucky, municipal government, the Commonwealth of Massachusetts, and the State of New York adopted the Australian system in 1888. . . . The success achieved through these reforms was immediately noticed and widely praised. . . . Today, all 50 States limit access to the areas in or around polling places. . . .

In sum, an examination of the history of election regulation in this country reveals a persistent battle against two evils: voter intimidation and election fraud. After an unsuccessful experiment with an unofficial ballot system, all 50 States, together with numerous other Western democracies, settled on the same solution: a secret ballot secured in part by a restricted zone around the voting compartments. We find that this widespread and time-tested consensus demonstrates that some restricted zone is necessary in order to serve the States' compelling interests in preventing voter intimidation and election fraud.

Respondent and the dissent advance three principal challenges to this conclusion. First, respondent argues that restricted zones are overinclusive because States could secure these same compelling interests with statutes that make it a misdemeanor to interfere with an election or to use violence or intimidation to prevent voting. We are not persuaded. Intimidation and interference laws fall short of serving a State's compelling interests because they deal with only the most blatant and specific attempts to impede elections. Moreover, because law enforcement officers generally are barred from the vicinity of the polls to avoid any appearance of coercion in the electoral process, many acts of interference would go undetected. These undetected or less than blatant acts may nonetheless drive the voter away before remedial action can be taken.

Second, respondent and the dissent argue that Tennessee's statute is underinclusive because it does not restrict other types of speech, such as charitable and commercial solicitation or exit polling, within the 100-foot zone. We agree that distinguishing among types of speech requires that the statute be subjected to strict scrutiny. We do not, however, agree that the failure to regulate all speech renders the statute fatally underinclusive. In fact, as one early commentator pointed out, allowing members of the general public access to the polling place makes it more difficult for political machines to buy off all the monitors. But regardless of the need for such additional monitoring, there is . . . ample evidence that political candidates have used campaign workers to commit voter intimidation or electoral fraud. In contrast, there is simply no evidence that political candidates have used other forms of solicitation or exit polling to commit such electoral abuses. States adopt laws to address the problems that confront them. The First Amendment does not require States to regulate for problems that do not exist.

Finally, the dissent argues that we confuse history with necessity. Yet the dissent concedes that a secret ballot was necessary to cure electoral abuses. Contrary to the dissent's contention, the link between ballot secrecy and some restricted zone surrounding the voting area is not merely timing—it is common sense. The only way to preserve the secrecy of the ballot is to limit access to the area around the voter. Accordingly, we hold that *some* restricted zone around the voting area is necessary to secure the State's compelling interest.

The real question then is *how large* a restricted zone is permissible or sufficiently tailored. Respondent and the dissent argue that Tennessee's 100-foot boundary is not narrowly drawn to achieve the State's compelling interest in protecting the right to vote. We disagree.

As a preliminary matter, the long, uninterrupted and prevalent use of these statutes makes it difficult for States to come forward with the sort of proof the dissent wishes to require. The majority of these laws were adopted originally in the 1890s, long before States engaged in extensive legislative hearings on election regulations. . . . The fact that these laws have been in effect for a long period of time also makes it difficult for the States to put on witnesses who can testify as to what would happen without them. Finally, it is difficult to isolate the exact effect of these laws on voter intimidation and election fraud. Voter intimidation and election fraud are successful precisely because they are difficult to detect.

Furthermore, because a government has such a compelling interest in securing the right to vote freely and effectively, this Court never has held a State "to the burden of demonstrating empirically the objective effects on political stability that [are] produced" by the voting regulation in question. *Munro v. Socialist Workers Party*, 479 U.S. 189, 195 (1986). Elections vary from year to year, and place to place. It is therefore difficult to make specific findings about the effects of a voting regulation. Moreover, the remedy for a tainted election is an imperfect one. Rerunning an election would have a negative impact on voter turnout. Thus, requiring proof that a 100-foot boundary is perfectly tailored to deal with voter intimidation and election fraud

> would necessitate that a State's political system sustain some level of damage before the legislature could take corrective action. Legislatures, we think, should be permitted to respond to potential deficiencies in the electoral process with foresight rather than reactively, provided that the response is reasonable and does not *significantly impinge* on constitutionally protected rights. *Id.*, at 195-196 (emphasis added).

We do not think that the minor geographic limitation prescribed by §2-7-111(b) constitutes such a significant impingement. Thus, we simply do not view the question whether the 100-foot boundary line could be somewhat tighter as a question of constitutional dimension. Reducing the boundary to 25 feet, as suggested by the Tennessee Supreme Court is a difference only in degree, not a less restrictive alternative in kind. As was pointed out in the dissenting opinion in the Tennessee Supreme Court, it "takes approximately 15 seconds to walk 75 feet." The State of Tennessee has decided that these last 15 seconds before its citizens enter the polling place should be their own, as free from interference as possible. We do not find that this is an unconstitutional choice.

At some measurable distance from the polls, of course, governmental regulation of vote solicitation could effectively become an impermissible burden akin to the statute struck down in *Mills v. Alabama*, 384 U.S. 214 (1966). In reviewing challenges to specific provisions of a State's election laws, however, this Court has not employed any "'litmus-paper test' that will separate valid from invalid restrictions." *Anderson v. Celebrezze*, 460 U.S., at 789. Accordingly, it is sufficient to say that in establishing a 100-foot boundary, Tennessee is on the constitutional side of the line.

In conclusion, we reaffirm that it is the rare case in which we have held that a law survives strict scrutiny. This, however, is such a rare case. Here, the State, as recognized administrator of elections, has asserted that the exercise of free speech rights conflicts with another fundamental right, the right to cast a ballot in an election free from the taint of intimidation and fraud. A long history, a substantial consensus, and simple common sense show that some restricted zone around polling places is necessary to protect that fundamental right. Given the conflict between these two rights, we hold that requiring solicitors to stand 100 feet from the entrances to polling places does not constitute an unconstitutional compromise.

The judgment of the Tennessee Supreme Court is reversed, and the case is remanded for further proceedings not inconsistent with this opinion.

[Justice Scalia concurred only in the judgment, applying a different standard based on public forum analysis, and finding the law "a reasonable, viewpoint-neutral regulation of a nonpublic forum." Justice Thomas did not participate.]

Justice STEVENS, with whom Justice O'CONNOR and Justice SOUTER join, dissenting.

The speech and conduct prohibited in the campaign-free zone created by Tenn. Code Ann. §2-7-111 (Supp. 1991) is classic political expression. . . .

Statutes creating campaign-free zones outside polling places serve two quite different functions—they protect orderly access to the polls and they prevent last-minute campaigning. There can be no question that the former constitutes a compelling state interest and that, in light of our decision in *Mills v. Alabama*, 384 U.S. 214 (1966), the latter does not. Accordingly, a State must demonstrate that the particular means it has fashioned to ensure orderly access to the polls do not unnecessarily hinder last-minute campaigning.

Campaign-free zones are noteworthy for their broad, antiseptic sweep. The Tennessee zone encompasses at least 30,000 square feet around each polling place; in some States, such as Kentucky and Wisconsin, the radius of the restricted zone is

500 feet—silencing an area of over 750,000 square feet. Even under the most sanguine scenario of participatory democracy, it is difficult to imagine voter turnout so complete as to require the clearing of hundreds of thousands of square feet simply to ensure that the path to the polling-place door remains open and that the curtain that protects the secrecy of the ballot box remains closed.

The fact that campaign-free zones cover such a large area in some States unmistakably identifies censorship of election-day campaigning as an animating force behind these restrictions. That some States have no problem maintaining order with zones of 50 feet or less strongly suggests that the more expansive prohibitions are not necessary to maintain access and order. . . .

Moreover, the Tennessee statute does not merely regulate conduct that might inhibit voting; it bars the simple "display of campaign posters, signs, or other campaign materials." §2-7-111(b). Bumper stickers on parked cars and lapel buttons on pedestrians are taboo. The notion that such sweeping restrictions on speech are necessary to maintain the freedom to vote and the integrity of the ballot box borders on the absurd.

The evidence introduced at trial to demonstrate the necessity for Tennessee's campaign-free zone was exceptionally thin. . . . Perhaps in recognition of the poverty of the record, the plurality—without briefing, or legislative or judicial factfinding—looks to history to assess whether Tennessee's statute is in fact necessary to serve the State's interests. . . .

This analysis is deeply flawed; it confuses history with necessity, and mistakes the traditional for the indispensable. The plurality's reasoning combines two logical errors: First, the plurality assumes that a practice's long life itself establishes its necessity; and second, the plurality assumes that a practice that was once necessary remains necessary until it is ended.

With regard to the first, the fact that campaign-free zones were, as the plurality indicates, introduced as part of a broader package of electoral reforms does not demonstrate that such zones were necessary. . . . In my opinion, more than mere timing is required to infer necessity from tradition. . . .

Even if we assume that campaign-free zones were once somehow "necessary," it would not follow that, 100 years later, those practices remain necessary. Much in our political culture, institutions, and practices has changed since the turn of the century: Our elections are far less corrupt, far more civil, and far more democratic today than 100 years ago. These salutary developments have substantially eliminated the need for what is, in my opinion, a sweeping suppression of core political speech. . . .

Minnesota Voters Alliance v. Mansky

585 U.S. ___ (2018)

Chief Justice ROBERTS delivered the opinion of the Court.

Under Minnesota law, voters may not wear a political badge, political button, or anything bearing political insignia inside a polling place on Election Day. The question presented is whether this ban violates the Free Speech Clause of the First Amendment.

I

A

Today, Americans going to their polling places on Election Day expect to wait in a line, briefly interact with an election official, enter a private voting booth, and cast an anonymous ballot. Little about this ritual would have been familiar to a voter in the mid-to-late nineteenth century. For one thing, voters typically deposited privately prepared ballots at the polls instead of completing official ballots on-site. . . . The physical arrangement confronting the voter was also different. The polling place often consisted simply of a "voting window" through which the voter would hand his ballot to an election official situated in a separate room with the ballot box. . . .

As documented in *Burson v. Freeman*, 504 U. S. 191 (1992), "[a]pproaching the polling place under this system was akin to entering an open auction place." *Id.*, at 202 (plurality opinion). The room containing the ballot boxes was "usually quiet and orderly," but "[t]he public space outside the window . . . was chaotic." R. Bensel *The American Ballot Box in the Mid-Nineteenth Century* 13 (2004). Electioneering of all kinds was permitted. Crowds would gather to heckle and harass voters who appeared to be supporting the other side. Indeed, "[u]nder the informal conventions of the period, election etiquette required only that a 'man of ordinary courage' be able to make his way to the voting window." Bensel 20–21. "In short, these early elections were not a very pleasant spectacle for those who believed in democratic government." *Burson*, 504 U. S. at 202 (plurality opinion).

By the late nineteenth century, States began implementing reforms to address these vulnerabilities and improve the reliability of elections. Between 1888 and 1896, nearly every State adopted the secret ballot. Because voters now needed to mark their state-printed ballots on-site and in secret, voting moved into a sequestered space where the voters could "deliberate and make a decision in . . . privacy." Rusk, *The Effect of the Australian Ballot Reform on Split Ticket Voting: 1876-1908*, Am. Pol. Sci. Rev. 1221 (1970). . . . In addition, States enacted "viewpoint-neutral restrictions on election-day speech" in the immediate vicinity of the polls. *Burson*, 504 U. S., at 214–215 (Scalia, J., concurring in judgment). Today, all 50 States and the District of Columbia have laws curbing various forms of speech in and around polling places on Election Day.

Minnesota's such law contains [one such] prohibition[]. . . . Minn. Stat. §211B.11(1) (Supp. 2017). The first sentence of §211B.11(1) forbids any person to "display campaign material, post signs, ask, solicit, or in any manner try to induce or persuade a voter within a polling place or within 100 feet of the building in which a polling place is situated" to "vote for or refrain from voting for a candidate or ballot question." The second sentence prohibits the distribution of "political badges, political buttons, or other political insignia to be worn at or about the polling place." The third sentence — the "political apparel ban" — states that a "political badge, political button, or other political insignia may not be worn at or about the polling place." Versions of all three prohibitions have been on the books in Minnesota for over a century.

There is no dispute that the political apparel ban applies only within the polling place, and covers articles of clothing and accessories with "political insignia" upon them. Minnesota election judges—temporary government employees working the polls on Election Day—have the authority to decide whether a particular item falls within the ban. If a voter shows up wearing a prohibited item, the election judge is to ask the individual to conceal or remove it. If the individual refuses, the election judge must allow him to vote, while making clear that the incident "will be recorded and referred to appropriate authorities." Violators are subject to an administrative process before the Minnesota Office of Administrative Hearings, which, upon finding a violation, may issue a reprimand or impose a civil penalty. Minn. Stat. §§211B.32, 211B.35(2) (2014). That administrative body may also refer the complaint to the county attorney for prosecution as a petty misdemeanor; the maximum penalty is a $300 fine. §§211B.11(4) (Supp. 2017), 211B.35(2) (2014), 609.02(4a) (2016).

B

Petitioner Minnesota Voters Alliance (MVA) is a nonprofit organization that "seeks better government through election reforms." Pet. for Cert. 5. Petitioner Andrew Cilek is a registered voter in Hennepin County and the executive director of MVA; petitioner Susan Jeffers served in 2010 as a Ramsey County election judge. Five days before the November 2010 election, MVA, Jeffers, and other likeminded groups and individuals filed a lawsuit in Federal District Court challenging the political apparel ban on First Amendment grounds. The groups—calling themselves "Election Integrity Watch" (EIW)—planned to have supporters wear buttons to the polls printed with the words "Please I.D. Me," a picture of an eye, and a telephone number and web address for EIW. (Minnesota law does not require individuals to show identification to vote.) One of the individual plaintiffs also planned to wear a "Tea Party Patriots" shirt. The District Court denied the plaintiffs' request for a temporary restraining order and preliminary injunction and allowed the apparel ban to remain in effect for the upcoming election.

In response to the lawsuit, officials for Hennepin and Ramsey Counties distributed to election judges an "Election Day Policy," providing guidance on the enforcement of the political apparel ban. The Minnesota Secretary of State also distributed the Policy to election officials throughout the State. The Policy specified that examples of apparel falling within the ban "include, but are not limited to":

- Any item including the name of a political party in Minnesota, such as the Republican, [Democratic-Farmer-Labor], Independence, Green or Libertarian parties.
- Any item including the name of a candidate at any election.
- Any item in support of or opposition to a ballot question at any election.
- Issue oriented material designed to influence or impact voting (including specifically the 'Please I.D. Me' buttons).
- Material promoting a group with recognizable political views (such as the Tea Party, MoveOn.org, and so on)." App. to Pet. for Cert. I–1 to I–2.

As alleged in the plaintiffs' amended complaint and supporting declarations, some voters associated with EIW ran into trouble with the ban on Election Day. One individual was asked to cover up his Tea Party shirt. Another refused to conceal his "Please I.D. Me" button, and an election judge recorded his name and address for possible referral. And petitioner Cilek—who was wearing the same button and a T-shirt with the words "Don't Tread on Me" and the Tea Party Patriots logo—was twice turned away from the polls altogether, then finally permitted to vote after an election judge recorded his information.

Back in court, MVA and the other plaintiffs (now joined by Cilek) argued that the ban was unconstitutional both on its face and as applied to their apparel. The District Court granted the State's motions to dismiss, and the Court of Appeals for the Eighth Circuit affirmed in part and reversed in part. Minnesota Majority v. Mansky, 708 F. 3d 1051 (2013). . . .

II

The First Amendment prohibits laws "abridging the freedom of speech." Minnesota's ban on wearing any "political badge, political button, or other political insignia" plainly restricts a form of expression within the protection of the First Amendment.

But the ban applies only in a specific location: the interior of a polling place. It therefore implicates our " 'forum based' approach for assessing restrictions that the government seeks to place on the use of its property." *International Soc. for Krishna Consciousness, Inc. v. Lee*, 505 U. S. 672, 678 (1992) (ISKCON). Generally speaking, our cases recognize three types of government-controlled spaces: traditional public forums, designated public forums, and nonpublic forums. In a traditional public forum—parks, streets, sidewalks, and the like—the government may impose reasonable time, place, and manner restrictions on private speech, but restrictions based on content must satisfy strict scrutiny, and those based on viewpoint are prohibited. *See Pleasant Grove City v. Summum*, 555 U. S. 460, 469 (2009). The same standards apply in designated public forums—spaces that have "not traditionally been regarded as a public forum" but which the government has "intentionally opened up for that purpose." *Id.*, at 469–470. In a nonpublic forum, on the other hand—a space that "is not by tradition or designation a forum for public communication"—the government has much more flexibility to craft rules limiting speech. *Perry Ed. Assn. v. Perry Local Educators' Assn.*, 460 U. S. 37, 46 (1983). The government may reserve such a forum "for its intended purposes, communicative or otherwise, as long as the regulation on speech is reasonable and not an effort to suppress expression merely because public officials oppose the speaker's view." *Ibid.*

This Court employs a distinct standard of review to assess speech restrictions in nonpublic forums because the government, "no less than a private owner of property," retains the "power to preserve the property under its control for the use to which it is lawfully dedicated." *Adderley v. Florida*, 385 U. S. 39, 47 (1966). "Nothing in the Constitution requires the Government freely to grant access to all who wish to exercise their right to free speech on every type of Government property without regard to the nature of the property or to the disruption that might be caused by the speaker's activities." *Cornelius v. NAACP Legal Defense & Ed. Fund, Inc.*, 473 U. S. 788, 799–800 (1985). Accordingly, our decisions have long recognized that the government may impose some content-based restrictions on speech in nonpublic forums, including restrictions that exclude political advocates and forms of political advocacy. *See id.* at 806–811. . . .

A polling place in Minnesota qualifies as a nonpublic forum. It is, at least on Election Day, government-controlled property set aside for the sole purpose of voting. . . . Rules strictly govern who may be present, for what purpose, and for how long. *See* Minn. Stat. §204C.06 (2014). And while the four-Justice plurality in *Burson* and Justice Scalia's concurrence in the judgment parted ways over whether the public sidewalks and streets surrounding a polling place qualify as a nonpublic forum, neither opinion suggested that the interior of the building was anything but.

We therefore evaluate MVA's First Amendment challenge under the nonpublic forum standard. The text of the apparel ban makes no distinction based on the speaker's political persuasion, so MVA does not claim that the ban discriminates on the basis of viewpoint on its face. The question accordingly is whether Minnesota's ban on political apparel is "reasonable in light of the purpose served by the forum": voting. *Cornelius*, 473 U. S., at 806.

III

A

We first consider whether Minnesota is pursuing a permissible objective in prohibiting voters from wearing particular kinds of expressive apparel or accessories while inside the polling place. The natural starting point for evaluating a First Amendment challenge to such a restriction is this Court's decision in *Burson*, which upheld a Tennessee law imposing a 100-foot campaign-free zone around polling place entrances. Under the Tennessee law—much like Minnesota's buffer-zone provision—no person could solicit votes for or against a candidate, party, or ballot measure, distribute campaign materials, or "display . . . campaign posters, signs or other campaign materials" within the restricted zone. 504 U.S. at 193–194 (plurality opinion). The plurality found that the law withstood even the strict scrutiny applicable to speech restrictions in traditional public forums. *Id.* at 211. In his opinion concurring in the judgment, Justice Scalia argued that the less rigorous "reasonableness" standard of review should apply, and found the law "at least reasonable" in light of the plurality's analysis. *Id.* at 216.

That analysis emphasized the problems of fraud, voter intimidation, confusion, and general disorder that had plagued polling places in the past. *See id.* at 200–204 (plurality opinion). Against that historical backdrop, the plurality and Justice Scalia upheld Tennessee's determination, supported by overwhelming consensus among the States and "common sense," that a campaign-free zone outside the polls was "necessary" to secure the advantages of the secret ballot and protect the right to vote. *Id.* at 200, 206–208, 211. As the plurality explained, "[t]he State of Tennessee has decided that [the] last 15 seconds before its citizens enter the polling place should be their own, as free from interference as possible." *Id.* at 210. That was not "an unconstitutional choice." *Ibid.*

MVA disputes the relevance of *Burson* to Minnesota's apparel ban. On MVA's reading, Burson considered only "active campaigning" outside the polling place by campaign workers and others trying to engage voters approaching the polls.

Brief for Petitioners 36–37. Minnesota's law, by contrast, prohibits what MVA characterizes as "passive, silent" self-expression by voters themselves when voting. Reply Brief 17. MVA also points out that the plurality focused on the extent to which the restricted zone combated "voter intimidation and election fraud," 504 U. S., at 208 — concerns that, in MVA's view, have little to do with a prohibition on certain types of voter apparel. . . .

[W]e see no basis for rejecting Minnesota's determination that some forms of advocacy should be excluded from the polling place, to set it aside as "an island of calm in which voters can peacefully contemplate their choices." Brief for Respondents 43. Casting a vote is a weighty civic act, akin to a jury's return of a verdict, or a representative's vote on a piece of legislation. It is a time for choosing, not campaigning. The State may reasonably decide that the interior of the polling place should reflect that distinction. . . . Members of the public are brought together at that place, at the end of what may have been a divisive election season, to reach considered decisions about their government and laws. The State may reasonably take steps to ensure that partisan discord not follow the voter up to the voting booth, and distract from a sense of shared civic obligation at the moment it counts the most. That interest may be thwarted by displays that do not raise significant concerns in other situations. . . .

Thus, in light of the special purpose of the polling place itself, Minnesota may choose to prohibit certain apparel there because of the message it conveys, so that voters may focus on the important decisions immediately at hand.

B

But the State must draw a reasonable line. Although there is no requirement of narrow tailoring in a nonpublic forum, the State must be able to articulate some sensible basis for distinguishing what may come in from what must stay out. Here, the unmoored use of the term "political" in the Minnesota law, combined with haphazard interpretations the State has provided in official guidance and representations to this Court, cause Minnesota's restriction to fail even this forgiving test.

Again, the statute prohibits wearing a "political badge, political button, or other political insignia." It does not define the term "political." And the word can be expansive. It can encompass anything "of or relating to government, a government, or the conduct of governmental affairs," *Webster's Third New International Dictionary* 1755 (2002), or anything "[o]f, relating to, or dealing with the structure or affairs of government, politics, or the state," *American Heritage Dictionary* 1401 (3d ed. 1996). Under a literal reading of those definitions, a button or T-shirt merely imploring others to "Vote!" could qualify.

The State argues that the apparel ban should not be read so broadly. According to the State, the statute does not prohibit "any conceivably 'political' message" or cover "all 'political' speech, broadly construed." Brief for Respondents 21, 23. Instead, the State interprets the ban to proscribe "only words and symbols that an objectively reasonable observer would perceive as conveying a message about the electoral choices at issue in [the] polling place." *Id.* at 13. . . .

At the same time, the State argues that the category of "political" apparel is not limited to campaign apparel. After all, the reference to "campaign material" in the first sentence of the statute — describing what one may not "display" in the buffer zone as well as inside the polling place—implies that the distinct term "political" should be understood to cover a broader class of items. As the State's counsel explained to the Court, Minnesota's law "expand[s] the scope of what is prohibited from campaign speech to additional political speech." Tr. of Oral Arg. 50. We consider a State's "authoritative constructions" in interpreting a state law. *Forsyth County v. Nationalist Movement*, 505 U. S. 123, 131 (1992). But far from clarifying the indeterminate scope of the political apparel provision, the State's "electoral choices" construction introduces confusing line-drawing problems.

For specific examples of what is banned under its standard, the State points to the 2010 Election Day Policy—which it continues to hold out as authoritative guidance regarding implementation of the statute. See Brief for Respondents 22–23. The first three examples in the Policy are clear enough: items displaying the name of a political party, items displaying the name of a candidate, and items demonstrating "support of or opposition to a ballot question." App. to Pet. for Cert. I–2.

But the next example—"[i]ssue oriented material designed to influence or impact voting," *id.*, at I–2—raises more questions than it answers. What qualifies as an "issue"? The answer, as far as we can tell from the State's briefing and argument, is any subject on which a political candidate or party has taken a stance. . . . For instance, the Election Day Policy specifically notes that the "Please I.D. Me" buttons are prohibited. App. to Pet. for Cert. I–2. But a voter identification requirement was not on the ballot in 2010, *see* Brief for Respondents 47, n. 24, so a Minnesotan would have had no explicit "electoral choice" to make in that respect. The buttons were nonetheless covered, the State tells us, because the Republican candidates for Governor and Secretary of State had staked out positions on whether photo identification should be required. Ibid.; see App. 58–60.

A rule whose fair enforcement requires an election judge to maintain a mental index of the platforms and positions of every candidate and party on the ballot is not reasonable. Candidates for statewide and federal office and major political parties can be expected to take positions on a wide array of subjects of local and national import. . . . Would a "Support Our Troops" shirt be banned, if one of the candidates or parties had expressed a view on military funding or aid for veterans? What about a "#MeToo" shirt, referencing the movement to increase awareness of sexual harassment and assault? At oral argument, the State indicated that the ban would cover such an item if a candidate had "brought up" the topic.

The next broad category in the Election Day Policy—any item "promoting a group with recognizable political views," App. to Pet. for Cert. I–2—makes matters worse. The State construes the category as limited to groups with "views" about "the issues confronting voters in a given election." Brief for Respondents 23. The State does not, however, confine that category to groups that have endorsed a candidate or taken a position on a ballot question.

Any number of associations, educational institutions, businesses, and religious organizations could have an opinion on an "issue[] confronting voters in a given election." For instance, the American Civil Liberties Union, the AARP, the World Wildlife Fund, and Ben & Jerry's all have stated positions on matters of public concern. If the views of those groups align or conflict with the position of a candidate or party on the ballot, does that mean that their insignia are banned? . . . Take another example: In the run-up to the 2012 election, Presidential candidates of both major parties issued public statements regarding the then-existing policy of the Boy Scouts of America to exclude members on the basis of sexual orientation. Should a Scout leader in 2012 stopping to vote on his way to a troop meeting have been asked to cover up his uniform?

The State emphasizes that the ban covers only apparel promoting groups whose political positions are sufficiently "well-known." Tr. of Oral Arg. 37. But that requirement, if anything, only increases the potential for erratic application. Well known by whom? The State tells us the lodestar is the "typical observer" of the item. Brief for Respondents 21. But that measure may turn in significant part on the background knowledge and media consumption of the particular election judge applying it. . . .

"[P]erfect clarity and precise guidance have never been required even of regulations that restrict expressive activity." *Ward v. Rock Against Racism*, 491 U. S. 781, 794 (1989). But the State's difficulties with its restriction go beyond close calls on borderline or fanciful cases. And that is a serious matter when the whole point of the exercise is to prohibit the expression of political views.

It is "self-evident" that an indeterminate prohibition carries with it "[t]he opportunity for abuse, especially where [it] has received a virtually open-ended interpretation." *Jews for Jesus*, 482 U.S. at 576. . . . We do not doubt that the vast majority of election judges strive to enforce the statute in an evenhanded manner, nor that some degree of discretion in this setting is necessary. But that discretion must be guided by objective, workable standards. Without them, an election judge's own politics may shape his views on what counts as "political." And if voters experience or witness episodes of unfair or inconsistent enforcement of the ban, the State's interest in maintaining a polling place free of distraction and disruption would be undermined by the very measure intended to further it.

That is not to say that Minnesota has set upon an impossible task. Other States have laws proscribing displays (including apparel) in more lucid terms. See, e.g., Cal. Elec. Code Ann. §319.5 (West Cum. Supp. 2018) (prohibiting "the visible display . . . of information that advocates for or against any candidate or measure," including the "display of a candidate's name, likeness, or logo," the "display of a ballot measure's number, title, subject, or logo," and "[b]uttons, hats," or "shirts" containing such information); Tex. Elec. Code Ann. §61.010(a) (West 2010) (prohibiting the wearing of "a badge, insignia, emblem, or other similar communicative device relating to a candidate, measure, or political party appearing on the ballot, or to the conduct of the election"). We do not suggest that such provisions set the outer limit of what a State may proscribe, and do not pass on the constitutionality of laws that are not before us. But we do hold that if a State wishes to set its polling places apart as areas free of partisan discord, it must employ a more discernible approach than the one Minnesota has offered here. . . . Minnesota has not supported its good intentions with a law capable of reasoned application.

The judgment of the Court of Appeals is reversed, and the case is remanded for further proceedings consistent with this opinion.

Justice SOTOMAYOR, with whom Justice BREYER joins, dissenting.

I would certify this case to the Minnesota Supreme Court for a definitive interpretation of the political apparel ban under Minn. Stat. §211B.11(1) (Supp. 2017), which likely would obviate the hypothetical line-drawing problems that form the basis of the Court's decision today. . . . It is at least "fairly possible" that the state court could "ascertain . . . a construction . . . that will contain the statute within constitutional bounds." . . .

≫ *Campaign-Free Election Days.*   In *Mills,* the Court invalidated a statute that banned campaign editorializing on Election Day. The state chose to defend on the relatively weak ground of preventing unanswerable last-minute attacks. But is that really the basis for such a restriction? Isn't the real basis of the law a desire to put a halt to campaigning on Election Day itself—to create a kind of enforced period of repose and reflection as voters make their way to the polls? In other words, to create the same kind of campaign-free zone as an electioneering statute, but to extend its boundaries throughout the community? Is that an illegitimate goal? In New Zealand, all campaigning on Election Day is banned by law. In Spain, the entire day before the election is an official "day of reflection" on which all campaigning is prohibited. Is there anything wrong with a political community's desire to impose upon itself a certain discipline of thoughtfulness and reflection preceding a democratically significant event?

≫ *Speech on the Ballot.*   An election ballot is itself a form of political speech, though typically of very limited scope. At a minimum, the ballot identifies the candidates for office, and in most cases it announces both the party affiliations of the candidates and the fact that they are the endorsed candidates of the various competing political parties. Sometimes, however, ballots contain additional information—they speak more, and on different topics. How does the law deal with speech that takes place on the very face of the ballot?

Racial Designations. In *Anderson v. Martin,* 375 U.S. 399 (1964), the Court invalidated a Louisiana law that required the ballot to designate the race of all candidates for office. The Court began by observing that the law did not prohibit anyone from either voting or running for office.

> In the abstract, Louisiana imposes no restriction upon anyone's candidacy nor upon an elector's choice in the casting of his ballot. But by placing a racial label on a candidate at the most crucial stage in the electoral process—the instant before the vote is cast—the State furnishes a vehicle by which racial prejudice may be so aroused as to operate against one group because of race and for another. This is true because by directing the citizen's attention to the single consideration of race or color, the State indicates that a candidate's race or color is an important—perhaps paramount—consideration in the citizen's choice, which may decisively influence the citizen to cast his ballot along racial lines.

Consequently, the Court struck down the law under the Equal Protection Clause.

Designation of Substantive Issue Position. After the Supreme Court held in *U.S. Term Limits, Inc. v. Thornton* (see Chapter 6) that members of Congress could be subjected to mandatory term limits only upon amendment of the United States Constitution, Arkansas amended its constitution, through a citizen initiative, to require candidates for office to pledge to support a constitutional amendment limiting congressional terms. Satisfaction of the pledge required incumbent officials to take, and non-incumbent candidates for office to pledge to take, a series of designated steps intended to advance the possibility of an amendment to the U.S. Constitution to overturn *Thornton*. In the case of incumbents who failed to take the necessary steps, the Arkansas law directed that the phrase "DISREGARDED VOTERS' INSTRUCTION ON TERM LIMITS" be printed on the ballot adjacent to the name of the candidate. In the case of non-incumbents who declined to take the pledge, the law directed that the phrase "DECLINED TO PLEDGE TO SUPPORT TERM LIMITS" be printed on the ballot adjacent to the candidate's name.

In *Cook v. Gralike*, 531 U.S. 510 (2001), the Court invalidated the Arkansas provision on the ground that it exceeded the state's power under Article I, §4 of the U.S. Constitution to regulate the "Times, Places and Manner of holding Elections for Senators and Representatives." The constitutional difficulty with the Arkansas law, the Court explained, is that Arkansas had improperly used its power to regulate elections to "'dictate electoral outcomes.'" The provision did so by disfavoring candidates who oppose term limits. The ballot labels, said the Court, impose "substantial political risk" on candidates who fail to comply. The Arkansas provision also contained another flaw. Invoking *Anderson*, the Court said: "'by directing the citizen's attention to the single consideration' of the candidates' fidelity to term limits, the labels imply that the issue is 'an important — perhaps paramount — consideration in the citizen's choice, which may decisively influence the citizen to cast his ballot' against candidates branded as unfaithful."

Does such a ballot notation "dictate electoral outcomes"? Do voters lack any agency or critical distance?

Suggestive Wording of Ballot Measures. Other than the names of candidates, offices, and political parties, no text except voting instructions normally appears on ballots. A significant exception is ballot measures. In virtually all states, voters can be asked to vote on complex financial measures related to the acquisition of government indebtedness through bonding, or on the acquisition or disposition of public property. In initiative states, complex measures relating to subjects as diverse as insurance, gay marriage, the use of evidence in court, restructuring of the judicial system, and many other subjects may appear on the ballot. These measures must be explained on the ballot for the benefit of voters who have not come to the polling place fully prepared and informed, yet the choice of language can critically affect the way an underinformed voter assesses the proposal.

In New Jersey, for example, the Attorney General is authorized by law to place on the ballot an "interpretive statement" describing ballot measures for the benefit of voters. As a government official charged with impartial execution of the law, the Attorney General must word the statement neutrally. Yet as an official appointed by a partisan governor to serve in a partisan administration, the Attorney General may prefer a particular outcome. Occasionally, the Attorney General has been found to have engaged in electioneering by sneaking loaded language onto the ballot. As one court put it, "[The state] may not, through the medium of an allegedly 'interpretive statement,' invade the polling place and enter the election booth to urge the voter to cast his vote for its cause." *Guernsey v. Allen*, 164 A.2d 496, 499 (N.J. Super. 1960).

Should ballots contain *more* information? Some have argued that information about the substantive positions of candidates should be printed routinely on the ballot in order to provide generally uninformed voters with useful cues about how to decide among candidates about whom they might know very little upon walking into the voting booth. *See* Elizabeth Garrett, *The Law and Economics of "Informed Voter" Ballot Notations*, 85 VA. L. REV. 1533 (1999); Christopher S. Elmendorf and David Schleicher, *Informing Consent: Voter Ignorance, Political Parties, and Election Law*, 2013 U. ILL. L. REV. 363 (2013).

Note also that information provided on ballots, and in some kinds of campaign literature, such as official voter guides, is speech by the government. Are there special risks to the democratic process when the government itself is the speaker? Many states restrict the authority of state and local governments to advocate for or against ballot measures, even measures that have been officially referred to the voters by those governments, presumably with an implicit recommendation of approval. Why should government be subject to such a limitation?

At the same time, the First Amendment is typically understood to place fewer restrictions on government speakers than on private ones. Often this is because the places in which governments speak are created and managed by them—such places are "limited public forums" rather than "public forums," and the owner of such a forum therefore enjoys considerable authority to determine what is said there, and by whom, even when the forum owner is a government. For example, an official voter guide, written, published, and disseminated by the government, is a limited public forum such that the government has great freedom to decide what goes in the guide and what is excluded. *E.g., Cogswell v. City of Seattle*, 347 F.3d 809 (9th Cir. 2003).

How should we balance the legitimate interest of government in informing the electorate against the risk that incumbent officials might manipulate what voters learn in order to influence the outcome of the election? *Compare* Stephen Shiffrin, *Government Speech*, 27 UCLA L. REV. 565 (1980), *with* Helen Norton, *Campaign Speech Law with a Twist: When the Government Is the Speaker, Not the Regulator*, 61 EMORY L.J. 209 (2011).

≫   *Agenda-Setting and Framing.*   In cases, such as *Mills* and *Burson*, dealing with regulation of the time, place, and manner of campaign speech, the Court has typically evaluated the state interest in regulation in terms of preserving order or avoiding confusion of voters. But are these the best terms in which to describe the state interests at stake?

If campaign speech actually influences the electoral decisions that voters make, how does it do so? Two possible effects seem relevant in this context: agenda-setting and framing. Agenda-setting refers to the capacity of speakers to bring an issue to public attention in the first place. Voters rarely have their own, independent sources of information about public affairs, and must consequently rely on information provided by others to stay informed. In so doing, voters not only submit themselves to judgments made by others about the facts, but also about which facts are important. *See, e.g.*, SHANTO IYENGAR AND DONALD R. KINDER, NEWS THAT MATTERS: TELEVISION AND AMERICAN OPINION (1987).

The fact that an issue comes to public attention does not, however, dictate how it will be received. Framing deals with the evaluative component of public political decision making. Facts and issues do not carry intrinsic moral or political content; such evaluations must be supplied by the voter through a process of interpretation. To frame an issue, then, is to present it in such a way as to influence the voter to reach one interpretation rather than another. Framing therefore generally weaves facts into a consistent and easily understood narrative that increases the likelihood that voters will reach one evaluation of the facts rather than another. *See, e.g.,* Dennis Chong and James N. Druckman, *Framing Theory*, 10 ANN. REV. POL. SCI. 103 (2007).

Might state laws prohibiting speech on Election Day, in the polling place, or on the ballot, be best understood as attempts to minimize opportunities for interested political actors to engage in last-minute agenda-setting or framing for the purpose of gaining an advantage for their own positions? Does the state have an interest in permitting voters a period of repose in which to get into better touch with their own inner sentiments and beliefs? Or is that view too naïve? Is it more accurate to say that no one has his or her own, inner, "true" or "uninfluenced" beliefs; that no one is anything more than a collection of external influences? If the latter is true, might the state have an interest in restricting speech in such a way as to at least give everyone an equal chance to set the agenda and frame the choices for fundamentally malleable voters? *See* James A. Gardner, *Neutralizing the Incompetent Voter: A Comment on* Cook v. Gralike, 1 ELECTION L.J. 49 (2002).

One study found that the effects of exposure to political advertising decay quickly — within about four days — when those exposed to the advertising received it passively, without paying it much attention. In contrast, the effects of exposure to such advertising could be long-lasting when the recipients engaged in "effortful processing," i.e., when people consciously engaged the message of the ads. Most people, however, the authors argue, do not actively engage the advertising to which they are exposed. In examining advertising aired during the 2000 election, the authors found that "ads aired on the day before election day in 2000 had about 28 times more impact . . . than ads aired in the previous 42 days." Seth J. Hill et al., *How Quickly We Forget: The Duration of Persuasion Effects from Mass Communication*, 30 POL. COMM. 521 (2013). Are findings such as these relevant to the legal treatment of electioneering at the polling place and in the days preceding an election?

▶▶ *Prohibition of Exit Polling.* Republican challenger Ronald Reagan won the 1980 presidential election in a landslide over Democratic incumbent Jimmy Carter. Major news networks covering the election "projected" states for either Reagan or Carter based on exit polling of voters conducted throughout the day. As the voting proceeded in Eastern states, where the polls opened earliest, the networks found themselves in a position reliably to project those states for Reagan, and at an earlier hour than they had previously expected. As the Reagan snowball proceeded from east to west, the networks started calling the election for Reagan — before the polls had closed in Western states. Many voters on the West Coast, hearing these projections, felt they had little reason to go to the polls since the election was all but over, and there were at least some anecdotal reports of voters turning around their cars to head home after hearing the news on their car radios. Many people were deeply disturbed by the networks' audacity to project a winner before the last polls had closed. And although no one suggested afterward that the outcome of the presidential race might have been changed by the projections, many state and local officials complained that down-ticket races (for state and local office) might very well have been affected by suppressed turnout resulting from the calling of the race at the top at the ticket.

In response, some states enacted corrective legislation. Knowing that they could not prohibit truthful speech about the election on Election Day, and knowing that they *did* have approved authority to regulate the polling place, some jurisdictions enacted laws to prohibit exit polling itself in an attempt to prevent news organizations from collecting the information enabling them to make early projections. Such laws have not fared well in the courts. *See Daily Herald Co. v. Munro*, 838 F.2d 380 (9th Cir. 1988) (invalidating Washington ban on exit polling within 300 feet of a polling place). Congress considered legislation creating a uniform time for poll closing across the nation, but the legislation was not enacted. Eventually, the problem was solved by voluntary agreement among news organizations not to project a winner in presidential contests until after 9:00 P.M. Pacific Time, when the last polls close in the continental United States.

As is often the case, the law is different elsewhere. The Canada Elections Act, 2000, prohibits publication of poll results on Election Day before the closing of the polls in any given time zone. Publication of polls or surveys is prohibited during the month prior to the election in Luxembourg, during the two weeks prior to an election in Bulgaria and Peru, during the week prior to an election in the Czech Republic, and during the day preceding the election in France. *See* Article 19 Global Campaign for Free Expression, *Comparative Study of Laws and Regulations Restricting the Publication of Electoral Opinion Polls* (Jan. 2003); Graeme Orr and Ron Levy, *Regulating Opinion Polling: A Deliberative Democracy Perspective*, 39 UNSW L.J. 318, 327 (2016).

>> ***Robocalls.***   A classic example of permissible regulation of the time, place, and manner of speech is the measure that prohibits otherwise unobjectionable speech from being communicated in an objectionable way: too loudly, too late at night, on the property of a homeowner over his or her objections, and so forth. *See, e.g., Kovacs v. Cooper*, 336 U.S. 77 (1949) (upholding local ban on loud sound trucks); *Frisby v. Schultz*, 487 U.S. 474 (1986) (recognizing a state interest in protecting the tranquility and privacy of the home from picketing targeting individual private residences). Lately, politicians and advocacy groups have become increasingly fond of the use of automated telephonic communications, often known as "robocalls," that permit a recorded message to be communicated quickly and cheaply by telephone to thousands of homes without human intervention. Automated calls to residences are prohibited under the federal Telephone Consumer Protection Act of 1991, 47 U.S.C. §227, but Congress exempted political calls from the reach of the law.

Can Congress or the states ban the use of robocalls during political campaigns without running afoul of the First Amendment? Could a legislature restrict their use — for example, regulate the frequency or time of calls? Could it offer phone owners an opportunity to opt out of receiving political robocalls through a mechanism like the federal Do Not Call Registry? In *State v. Economic Freedom Fund*, 959 N.E.2d 794 (Ind. 2011), the Indiana Supreme Court upheld the application of the state's autodialer law to an advocacy organization that communicated political messages through robocall technology. Under the law, automated phone messages may not be played without the consent of the recipient, which must be obtained by an initial contact by a live operator. Although the live operator requirement imposed a financial burden on the plaintiff's speech, the court found the law supported by a sufficient government interest in protecting "the privacy, tranquility, and efficiency of telephone customers." The Eighth Circuit upheld a similar requirement under a Minnesota law in *Van Bergen v. Minnesota*, 59 F.3d 1541 (8th Cir. 1995).

Challenges in federal court to state and federal robocall prohibitions have mainly failed. *See Van Bergen v. Minnesota*, 59 F.3d 1541 (8th Cir. 1995) (sustaining federal and state restrictions); *Bland v. Fessler*, 88 F.3d 729 (9th Cir. 1996) (sustaining California law); *Gomez v. Campbell-Ewald Co.*, 768 F.3d 871 (9th Cir. 2014) (upholding federal restrictions); *Patriotic Veterans v. Zoeller*, 845 F.3d 303 (7th Cir. 2017) (upholding Indiana law). *But see Cahaly v. LaRosa*, 796 F.3d 399 (4th Cir. 2015) (striking down South Carolina's law as impermissibly content-based). However, a challenge to a Montana statute imposing a wide-ranging ban on robocalls and including a prohibition on political ones was invalidated in *Victory Processing v. Fox*, 937 F.3d 1218 (9th Cir. 2019). The court found that the state had a compelling interest in protecting the privacy of the home, but that the state's inclusion of political robocalls exceeded the permissible reach of the ban.

≫   *Ballot Selfies.*   The latest clash between new technology and customary ways of conducting elections concerns "ballot selfies." A ballot selfie is a self-portrait taken by a voter in the polling place that shows the voter with his or her completed ballot. The photo is taken after the voter has filled out the ballot but before he or she submits it for counting. Typically, the photo is uploaded to social media, either immediately or shortly after it is taken. Voters engaging in this behavior evidently wish not merely to communicate to their friends, or to the world, how they have voted, but to back up that assertion with photographic evidence.

The difficulty with ballot selfies, of course, is that they contravene long-standing norms of secret balloting. Although voters have always had the ability after leaving the polling place to reveal their votes to others, until the advent of smart-phones they have lacked the ability to offer any proof except their own word. Laws in many jurisdictions, often in place for more than a century, prohibit the exposure of voted ballots. States enacted such prohibitions to protect the secrecy of the vote. The theory of these laws is that vote buying can be deterred by depriving vote buyers of any ability to verify that they have received the benefit of their bargain. Apparently, these laws have enjoyed some success, as organized vote buying seems to have all but disappeared in the United States.

Ballot selfie cases have begun to percolate through the lower courts, which at the moment are split. In 2016, the First Circuit invalidated a recently enacted New Hampshire law providing: "No voter shall take a photograph or a digital image of his or her marked ballot." The court held that the law failed intermediate scrutiny because it did not respond to any actual problem in New Hampshire of vote buying, and because the statute reached innocent as well as venal ballot photography. *Rideout v. Gardner*, 838 F.3d 65 (1st Cir. 2016). A month later, the Sixth Circuit refused to preliminarily enjoin a Michigan law providing: "If an elector shows his or her ballot . . . after that ballot has been marked . . . the ballot shall not be deposited in the ballot box, but shall be marked 'rejected for exposure' . . . and the elector shall not be allowed to vote at the election." *Crookston v. Johnson*, 841 F.3d 396 (6th

Cir. 2016). The court held that the law "seems to be a content-neutral regulation that reasonably protects voters' privacy—and honors a long tradition of protecting the secret ballot." Lower courts in New York and Illinois have also upheld state laws banning ballot selfies. *Silberberg v. Board of Elections*, 274 F.Supp.3d 454 (S.D.N.Y. 2017); *Oettle v. Guthrie*, 2020 Ill. App. 190306 (5th Dist. 2020).

How would you rule in such a case? Is the government interest in preventing vote buying a strong one? Do ballot selfie prohibitions advance that interest? What is the speech value added by a ballot selfie compared to a verbal self-report of how one voted? In what circumstances would verifiable evidence of how one voted be desirable or useful?

D.   CAMPAIGN SPEECH IN THE MASS MEDIA

The First Amendment guarantees not only free speech; it also guarantees freedom of the press. The Supreme Court has held that the Press Clause does not confer on the press any special right to speak or to gather information not available to the general public. *See, e.g., Branzburg v. Hayes*, 408 U.S. 665 (1972); *Pell v. Procunier*, 417 U.S. 817 (1974). Nevertheless, the Court (or at least various members of the Court) has acknowledged from time to time that the language of the Press Clause suggests that the Framers may have contemplated a certain institutional role for the press in the workings of democratic self-government. For example, Justice Powell once wrote that an

> informed public depends on accurate and effective reporting by news media. No individual can obtain for himself the information needed for the intelligent discharge of his political responsibilities. For most citizens the prospect of personal familiarity with newsworthy events is hopelessly unrealistic. In seeking out the news the press therefore acts as an agent of the public at large. It is the means by which the people receive that free flow of information and ideas essential to intelligent self-government. By enabling the public to assert meaningful control over the political process, the press performs a crucial function in effecting the societal purpose of the First Amendment.

Saxbe v. Washington Post Co., 417 U.S. 843 (1974) (Powell, J., dissenting).

Although the mass media is no longer the informational power-broker it was when Justice Powell wrote, it is still impossible today to think about campaigns without thinking about the role of the news media, which remains an important conduit of information to the voter. Given the importance of its role, the kind and amount of information the organized press furnishes can influence the proper functioning of democratic processes. Can the government, consistent with the First Amendment, regulate the amount or type of political information that the media may provide to voters? Should the medium through which news is communicated affect its First Amendment protection? The following set of cases confronts these questions.

Mills v. State of Alabama

384 U.S. 214 (1966)

Mr. Justice BLACK delivered the opinion of the Court.

The question squarely presented here is whether a State, consistently with the United States Constitution, can make it a crime for the editor of a daily newspaper to write and publish an editorial on election day urging people to vote a certain way on issues submitted to them.

On November 6, 1962, Birmingham, Alabama, held an election for the people to decide whether they preferred to keep their existing city commission form of government or replace it with a mayor-council government. On election day the Birmingham Post-Herald, a daily newspaper, carried an editorial written by its editor, appellant, James E. Mills, which strongly urged the people to adopt the mayor-council form of government. Mills was later arrested on a complaint charging that by publishing the editorial on election day he had violated §285 of the Alabama Corrupt Practices Act, which makes it a crime "to do any electioneering or to solicit any votes . . . in support of or in opposition to any proposition that is being voted on the day on which the election affecting such candidates or propositions is being held." The . . . Alabama Supreme Court held that publication of the editorial on election day undoubtedly violated the state law and . . . sustained it as a valid exercise of the State's police power. . . .

The First Amendment, which applies to the States through the Fourteenth, prohibits laws "abridging the freedom of speech, or of the press." The question here is whether it abridges freedom of the press for a State to punish a newspaper editor for doing no more than publishing an editorial on election day urging people to vote a particular way in the election. We should point out at once that this question in no way involves the extent of a State's power to regulate conduct in and around the polls in order to maintain peace, order and decorum there. The sole reason for the charge that Mills violated the law is that he wrote and published an editorial on election day urging Birmingham voters to cast their votes in favor of changing their form of government.

Whatever differences may exist about interpretations of the First Amendment, there is practically universal agreement that a major purpose of that Amendment was to protect the free discussion of governmental affairs. This of course includes discussions of candidates, structures and forms of government, the manner in which government is operated or should be operated, and all such matters relating to political processes. The Constitution specifically selected the press, which includes not only newspapers, books, and magazines, but also humble leaflets and circulars, to play an important role in the discussion of public affairs. Thus the press serves and was designed to serve as a powerful antidote to any abuses of power by governmental officials and as a constitutionally chosen means for keeping officials elected by the people responsible to all the people whom they were selected to serve. Suppression of the right of the press to praise or criticize governmental agents and to clamor and contend for or against change, which is all that this editorial did, muzzles one of the very agencies the Framers of our Constitution thoughtfully and deliberately selected to improve our society and keep it free. The Alabama Corrupt

Practices Act by providing criminal penalties for publishing editorials such as the one here silences the press at a time when it can be most effective. It is difficult to conceive of a more obvious and flagrant abridgment of the constitutionally guaranteed freedom of the press.

Admitting that the state law restricted a newspaper editor's freedom to publish editorials on election day, the Alabama Supreme Court nevertheless sustained the constitutionality of the law on the ground that the restrictions on the press were only "reasonable restrictions" or at least "within the field of reasonableness." The court reached this conclusion because it thought the law imposed only a minor limitation on the press—restricting it only on election days—and because the court thought the law served a good purpose. It said:

> It is a salutary legislative enactment that protects the public from confusive last-minute charges and countercharges and the distribution of propaganda in an effort to influence voters on an election day; when as a practical matter, because of lack of time, such matters cannot be answered or their truth determined until after the election is over.

This argument, even if it were relevant to the constitutionality of the law, has a fatal flaw. The state statute leaves people free to hurl their campaign charges up to the last minute of the day before election. The law held valid by the Alabama Supreme Court then goes on to make it a crime to answer those "last-minute" charges on election day, the only time they can be effectively answered. Because the law prevents any adequate reply to these charges, it is wholly ineffective in protecting the electorate "from confusive last-minute charges and countercharges." We hold that no test of reasonableness can save a state law from invalidation as a violation of the First Amendment when that law makes it a crime for a newspaper editor to do no more than urge people to vote one way or another in a publicly held election.

The judgment of the Supreme Court of Alabama is reversed and the case is remanded for further proceedings not inconsistent with this opinion.

It is so ordered.

Red Lion Broadcasting Co. v. Federal Communications Commission

395 U.S. 367 (1969)

Mr. Justice WHITE delivered the opinion of the Court.

The Federal Communications Commission has for many years imposed on radio and television broadcasters the requirement that discussion of public issues be presented on broadcast stations, and that each side of those issues must be given fair coverage. This is known as the fairness doctrine, which originated very early in the history of broadcasting and has maintained its present outlines for some time. . . . Two aspects of the fairness doctrine, relating to personal attacks in the context of controversial public issues and to political editorializing, were codified more precisely in the form of FCC regulations in 1967. The two cases before us now, which were decided separately below, challenge the constitutional and statutory bases of the doctrine and component rules. *Red Lion* involves the application of the fairness doctrine to a particular broadcast, and *RTNDA* arises as an action to review the FCC's 1967 promulgation of the personal attack and political editorializing regulations, which were laid down after the *Red Lion* litigation had begun.

I

A

The Red Lion Broadcasting Company is licensed to operate a Pennsylvania radio station, WGCB. On November 27, 1964, WGCB carried a 15-minute broadcast by the Reverend Billy James Hargis as part of a "Christian Crusade" series. A book by Fred J. Cook entitled "Goldwater — Extremist on the Right" was discussed by Hargis, who said that Cook had been fired by a newspaper for making false charges against city officials; that Cook had then worked for a Communist-affiliated publication; that he had defended Alger Hiss and attacked J. Edgar Hoover and the Central Intelligence Agency; and that he had now written a "book to smear and destroy Barry Goldwater." When Cook heard of the broadcast he concluded that he had been personally attacked and demanded free reply time, which the station refused. After an exchange of letters among Cook, Red Lion, and the FCC, the FCC declared that the Hargis broadcast constituted a personal attack on Cook; that Red Lion had failed to meet its obligation under the fairness doctrine . . . to send a tape, transcript, or summary of the broadcast to Cook and offer him reply time; and that the station must provide reply time whether or not Cook would pay for it. On review in the Court of Appeals for the District of Columbia Circuit, the FCC's position was upheld as constitutional and otherwise proper.

B

Not long after the *Red Lion* litigation was begun, the FCC issued a Notice of Proposed Rule Making, with an eye to making the personal attack aspect of the fairness doctrine more precise and more readily enforceable, and to specifying its rules relating to political editorials. . . . Twice amended, the rules were held unconstitutional in the *RTNDA* litigation by the Court of Appeals for the Seventh Circuit, on review of the rulemaking proceeding, as abridging the freedoms of speech and press. . . .

C

Believing that the specific application of the fairness doctrine in *Red Lion*, and the promulgation of the regulations in *RTNDA*, are both authorized by Congress and enhance rather than abridge the freedoms of speech and press protected by the First Amendment, we hold them valid and constitutional. . . .

II

The history of the emergence of the fairness doctrine and of the related legislation shows that the Commission's action in the *Red Lion* case did not exceed its authority, and that in adopting the new regulations the Commission was implementing congressional policy rather than embarking on a frolic of its own.

A

Before 1927, the allocation of frequencies was left entirely to the private sector, and the result was chaos. It quickly became apparent that broadcast frequencies constituted a scarce resource whose use could be regulated and rationalized only by the Government. Without government control, the medium would be of little use because of the cacophony of competing voices, none of which could be clearly and predictably heard. Consequently, the Federal Radio Commission was established to allocate frequencies among competing applicants in a manner responsive to the public "convenience, interest, or necessity."

Very shortly thereafter the Commission expressed its' view that the "public interest requires ample play for the free and fair competition of opposing views, and the commission believes that the principle applies . . . to all discussions of issues of importance to the public." This doctrine was applied through denial of license renewals or construction permits, both by the FRC and its successor FCC. After an extended period during which the licensee was obliged not only to cover and to cover fairly the views of others, but also to refrain from expressing his own personal views, the latter limitation on the licensee was abandoned and the doctrine developed into its present form.

There is a twofold duty laid down by the FCC's decisions and described by the 1949 Report on Editorializing by Broadcast Licensees. The broadcaster must give adequate coverage to public issues, and coverage must be fair in that it accurately reflects the opposing views. This must be done at the broadcaster's own expense if sponsorship is unavailable. Moreover, the duty must be met by programming obtained at the licensee's own initiative if available from no other source. The Federal Radio Commission had imposed these two basic duties on broadcasters since the outset, and in particular respects the personal attack rules and regulations at issue here have spelled them out in greater detail.

When a personal attack has been made on a figure involved in a public issue both the doctrine of cases such as *Red Lion* and *Times-Mirror Broadcasting Co.*, and also the 1967 regulations at issue in *RTNDA* require that the individual attacked himself be offered an opportunity to respond. Likewise, where one candidate is endorsed in a political editorial, the other candidates must themselves be offered reply time to use personally or through a spokesman. These obligations differ from the general fairness requirement that issues be presented, and presented with coverage of competing views, in that the broadcaster does not have the option of presenting the attacked party's side himself or choosing a third party to represent that side. But insofar as there is an obligation of the broadcaster to see that both sides are presented, and insofar as that is an affirmative obligation, the personal attack doctrine and regulations do not differ from the preceding fairness doctrine. . . . [I]t is not unreasonable for the FCC to conclude that the objective of adequate presentation of all sides may best be served by allowing those most closely affected to make the response, rather than leaving the response in the hands of the station which has attacked their candidacies, endorsed their opponents, or carried a personal attack upon them. . . .

III

The broadcasters challenge the fairness doctrine and its specific manifestations in the personal attack and political editorial rules on conventional First Amendment grounds, alleging that the rules abridge their freedom of speech and press. Their contention is that the First Amendment protects their desire to use their allotted frequencies continuously to broadcast whatever they choose, and to exclude whomever they choose from ever using that frequency. No man may be prevented from saying or publishing what he thinks, or from refusing in his speech or other utterances to give equal weight to the views of his opponents. This right, they say, applies equally to broadcasters.

A

Although broadcasting is clearly a medium affected by a First Amendment interest, differences in the characteristics of new media justify differences in the First Amendment standards applied to them. For example, the ability of new technology to produce sounds more raucous than those of the human voice justifies restrictions on the sound level, and on the hours and places of use, of sound trucks so long as the restrictions are reasonable and applied without discrimination.

Just as the Government may limit the use of sound-amplifying equipment potentially so noisy that it drowns out civilized private speech, so may the Government limit the use of broadcast equipment. The right of free speech of a broadcaster, the user of a sound truck, or any other individual does not embrace a right to snuff out the free speech of others.

When two people converse face to face, both should not speak at once if either is to be clearly understood. But the range of the human voice is so limited that there could be meaningful communications if half the people in the United States were talking and the other half listening. Just as clearly, half the people might publish and the other half read. But the reach of radio signals is incomparably greater than the range of the human voice and the problem of interference is a massive reality. The lack of know-how and equipment may keep many from the air, but only a tiny fraction of those with resources and intelligence can hope to communicate by radio at the same time if intelligible communication is to be had, even if the entire radio spectrum is utilized in the present state of commercially acceptable technology. . . .

Where there are substantially more individuals who want to broadcast than there are frequencies to allocate, it is idle to posit an unabridgeable First Amendment right to broadcast comparable to the right of every individual to speak, write, or publish. If 100 persons want broadcast licenses but there are only 10 frequencies to allocate, all of them may have the same "right" to a license; but if there is to be any effective communication by radio, only a few can be licensed and the rest must be barred from the airwaves. It would be strange if the First Amendment, aimed at protecting and furthering communications, prevented the Government from making radio communication possible by requiring licenses to broadcast and by limiting the number of licenses so as not to overcrowd the spectrum. . . .

By the same token, as far as the First Amendment is concerned those who are licensed stand no better than those to whom licenses are refused. A license permits broadcasting, but the licensee has no constitutional right to be the one who holds the license or to monopolize a radio frequency to the exclusion of his fellow citizens. There is nothing in the First Amendment which prevents the Government from requiring a licensee to share his frequency with others and to conduct himself as a proxy or fiduciary with obligations to present those views and voices which are representative of his community and which would otherwise, by necessity, be barred from the airwaves.

This is not to say that the First Amendment is irrelevant to public broadcasting. . . . Because of the scarcity of radio frequencies, the Government is permitted to put restraints on licensees in favor of others whose views should be expressed on this unique medium. But the people as a whole retain their interest in free speech by radio and their collective right to have the medium function consistently with the ends and purposes of the First Amendment. It is the right of the viewers and listeners, not the right of the broadcasters, which is paramount. It is the purpose of the First Amendment to preserve an uninhibited marketplace of ideas in which truth will ultimately prevail, rather than to countenance monopolization of that market, whether it be by the Government itself or a private licensee. . . . It is the right of the public to receive suitable access to social, political, esthetic, moral, and other ideas and experiences which is crucial here. That right may not constitutionally be abridged either by Congress or by the FCC.

B

Rather than confer frequency monopolies on a relatively small number of licensees, in a Nation of 200,000,000, the Government could surely have decreed that each frequency should be shared among all or some of those who wish to use it, each being assigned a portion of the broadcast day or the broadcast week. The ruling and regulations at issue here do not go quite so far. They assert that under specified circumstances, a licensee must offer to make available a reasonable amount of broadcast time to those who have a view different from that which has already been expressed on his station. The expression of a political endorsement, or of a personal attack while dealing with a controversial public issue, simply triggers this time sharing. As we have said, the First Amendment confers no right on licensees to prevent others from broadcasting on "their" frequencies and no right to an unconditional monopoly of a scarce resource which the Government has denied others the right to use. . . .

Nor can we say that it is inconsistent with the First Amendment goal of producing an informed public capable of conducting its own affairs to require a broadcaster to permit answers to personal attacks occurring in the course of discussing controversial issues, or to require that the political opponents of those endorsed by the station be given a chance to communicate with the public. Otherwise, station owners and a few networks would have unfettered power to make time available only to the highest bidders, to communicate only their own views on public issues, people and candidates, and to permit on the air only those with whom they agreed. There is no sanctuary in the First Amendment for unlimited private censorship operating in a medium not open to all.

C

It is strenuously argued, however, that if political editorials or personal attacks will trigger an obligation in broadcasters to afford the opportunity for expression to speakers who need not pay for time and whose views are unpalatable to the licensees, then broadcasters will be irresistibly forced to self-censorship and their coverage of controversial public issues will be eliminated or at least rendered wholly ineffective. Such a result would indeed be a serious matter, for should licensees actually eliminate their coverage of controversial issues, the purposes of the doctrine would be stifled.

At this point, however, as the Federal Communications Commission has indicated, that possibility is at best speculative. The communications industry, and in particular the networks, have taken pains to present controversial issues in the past, and even now they do not assert that they intend to abandon their efforts in this regard. It would be better if the FCC's encouragement were never necessary to induce the broadcasters to meet their responsibility. And if experience with the administration of those doctrines indicates that they have the net effect of reducing rather than enhancing the volume and quality of coverage, there will be time enough to reconsider the constitutional implications. The fairness doctrine in the past has had no such overall effect.

That this will occur now seems unlikely, however, since if present licensees should suddenly prove timorous, the Commission is not powerless to insist that they give adequate and fair attention to public issues. It does not violate the First Amendment to treat licensees given the privilege of using scarce radio frequencies as proxies for the entire community, obligated to give suitable time and attention to matters of great public concern. To condition the granting or renewal of licenses on a willingness to present representative community views on controversial issues is consistent with the ends and purposes of those constitutional provisions forbidding the abridgment of freedom of speech and freedom of the press. Congress need not stand idly by and permit those with licenses to ignore the problems which beset the people or to exclude from the airways anything but their own views of fundamental questions. The statute, long administrative practice, and cases are to this effect.

» *The Fairness Doctrine.* During the 1980s, the Reagan administration put increasing pressure on the FCC to abandon the fairness doctrine. By 1987, legislation that would have statutorily required the FCC to repeal the fairness doctrine made substantial headway in Congress. Rather than see its regulatory discretion limited legislatively, the FCC acquiesced to congressional and executive pressure and later that year promulgated regulations repealing the fairness doctrine. How would the federal courts react to a reenactment of the fairness doctrine? Does the reasoning of *Red Lion* survive the advent of cable television and the internet?

Miami Herald Publishing Co. v. Tornillo

418 U.S. 241 (1974)

Mr. Chief Justice BURGER delivered the opinion of the Court.

The issue in this case is whether a state statute granting a political candidate a right to equal space to reply to criticism and attacks on his record by a newspaper violates the guarantees of a free press.

I

In the fall of 1972, appellee, Executive Director of the Classroom Teachers Association, apparently a teachers' collective-bargaining agent, was a candidate for the Florida House of Representatives. On September 20, 1972, and again on September 29, 1972, appellant printed editorials critical of appellee's candidacy. In response to these editorials appellee demanded that appellant print verbatim his replies. . . . Appellant declined to print the appellee's replies and appellee brought suit in Circuit Court, Dade County. . . . The action was premised on Florida Statute §104.38, a "right of reply" statute which provides that if a candidate for nomination or election is assailed regarding his personal character or official record by any newspaper, the candidate has the right to demand that the newspaper print, free of cost to the candidate, any reply the candidate may make to the newspaper's charges. The reply must appear in as conspicuous a place and in the same kind of type as the charges which prompted the reply, provided it does not take up more space than the charges. Failure to comply with the statute constitutes a first-degree misdemeanor.

Appellant sought a declaration that §104.38 was unconstitutional. . . . [T]he Florida Supreme Court . . . held that free speech was enhanced and not abridged by the Florida right-of-reply statute, which in that court's view, furthered the broad societal interest in the free flow of information to the public. . . .

III

Appellant contends the statute is void on its face because it purports to regulate the content of a newspaper in violation of the First Amendment. Alternatively it is urged that the statute is void for vagueness since no editor could know exactly what words would call the statute into operation. It is also contended that the statute fails to distinguish between critical comment which is and which is not defamatory.

The appellee and supporting advocates of an enforceable right of access to the press vigorously argue that government has an obligation to ensure that a wide variety of views reach the public. . . . It is urged that at the time the First Amendment to the Constitution was ratified in 1791 as part of our Bill of Rights the press was broadly representative of the people it was serving. While many of the newspapers were intensely partisan and narrow in their views, the press collectively presented a broad range of opinions to readers. Entry into publishing was inexpensive; pamphlets and books provided meaningful alternatives to the organized press for the expression of unpopular ideas and often treated events and expressed views not covered by conventional newspapers. A true marketplace of ideas existed in which there was relatively easy access to the channels of communication.

Access advocates submit that although newspapers of the present are superficially similar to those of 1791 the press of today is in reality very different from that known in the early years of our national existence. In the past half century a communications revolution has seen the introduction of radio and television into our lives, the promise of a global community through the use of communications satellites, and the spectre of a "wired" nation by means of an expanding cable television network with two-way capabilities. The printed press, it is said, has not escaped the effects of this revolution. Newspapers have become big business and there are far fewer of them to serve a larger literate population. Chains of newspapers, national newspapers, national wire and news services, and one-newspaper towns, are the dominant features of a press that has become noncompetitive and enormously powerful and influential in its capacity to manipulate popular opinion and change the course of events. Major metropolitan newspapers have collaborated to establish news services national in scope. Such national news organizations provide syndicated "interpretive reporting" as well as syndicated features and commentary, all of which can serve as part of the new school of "advocacy journalism."

The elimination of competing newspapers in most of our large cities, and the concentration of control of media that results from the only newspaper's being owned by the same interests which own a television station and a radio station, are important components of this trend toward concentration of control of outlets to inform the public.

The result of these vast changes has been to place in a few hands the power to inform the American people and shape public opinion. Much of the editorial opinion and commentary that is printed is that of syndicated columnists distributed nationwide and, as a result, we are told, on national and world issues there tends to be a homogeneity of editorial opinion, commentary, and interpretive analysis. The abuses of bias and manipulative reportage are, likewise, said to be the result of the vast accumulations of unreviewable power in the modern media empires. In effect, it is claimed, the public has lost any ability to respond or to contribute in a meaningful way to the debate on issues. The monopoly of the means of communication allows for little or no critical analysis of the media except in professional journals of very limited readership. . . .

The obvious solution, which was available to dissidents at an earlier time when entry into publishing was relatively inexpensive, today would be to have additional newspapers. But the same economic factors which have caused the disappearance of vast numbers of metropolitan newspapers, have made entry into the marketplace of ideas served by the print media almost impossible. It is urged that the claim of newspapers to be "surrogates for the public" carries with it a concomitant fiduciary obligation to account for that stewardship. From this premise it is reasoned that the only effective way to insure fairness and accuracy and to provide for some accountability is for government to take affirmative action. The First Amendment interest of the public in being informed is said to be in peril because the "marketplace of ideas" is today a monopoly controlled by the owners of the market.

Proponents of enforced access to the press take comfort from language in several of this Court's decisions which suggests that the First Amendment acts as a sword as well as a shield, that it imposes obligations on the owners of the press in addition to protecting the press from government regulation. . . .

IV

However much validity may be found in these arguments, at each point the implementation of a remedy such as an enforceable right of access necessarily calls for some mechanism, either governmental or consensual. If it is governmental coercion, this at once brings about a confrontation with the express provisions of the First Amendment and the judicial gloss on that Amendment developed over the years.

The Court foresaw the problems relating to government-enforced access as early as its decision in *Associated Press v. United States.* There it carefully contrasted the private "compulsion to print" called for by the Association's bylaws with the provisions of the District Court decree against appellants which "does not compel AP or its members to permit publication of anything which their 'reason' tells them should not be published. . . ." We see that beginning with *Associated Press,* the Court has expressed sensitivity as to whether a restriction or requirement constituted the compulsion exerted by government on a newspaper to print that which it would not otherwise print. The clear implication has been that any such compulsion to publish that which " 'reason' tells them should not be published" is unconstitutional. A responsible press is an undoubtedly desirable goal, but press responsibility is not mandated by the Constitution and like many other virtues it cannot be legislated.

Appellee's argument that the Florida statute does not amount to a restriction of appellant's right to speak because "the statute in question here has not prevented the Miami Herald from saying anything it wished" begs the core question. Compelling editors or publishers to publish that which " 'reason' tells them should not be published" is what is at issue in this case. The Florida statute operates as a command in the same sense as a statute or regulation forbidding appellant to publish specified matter. Governmental restraint on publishing need not fall into familiar or traditional patterns to be subject to constitutional limitations on governmental powers. The Florida statute exacts a penalty on the basis of the content of a newspaper. . . .

Faced with the penalties that would accrue to any newspaper that published news or commentary arguably within the reach of the right-of-access statute, editors might well conclude that the safe course is to avoid controversy. Therefore, under the operation of the Florida statute, political and electoral coverage would be blunted or reduced. . . .

Even if a newspaper would face no additional costs to comply with a compulsory access law and would not be forced to forgo publication of news or opinion by the inclusion of a reply, the Florida statute fails to clear the barriers of the First Amendment because of its intrusion into the function of editors. A newspaper is more than a passive receptacle or conduit for news, comment, and advertising. The choice of material to go into a newspaper, and the decisions made as to limitations on the size and content of the paper, and treatment of public issues and public officials — whether fair or unfair — constitute the exercise of editorial control and judgment. It has yet to be demonstrated how governmental regulation of this crucial process can be exercised consistent with First Amendment guarantees of a free press as they have evolved to this time. Accordingly, the judgment of the Supreme Court of Florida is reversed.

———————

In *Red Lion*, Congress is permitted to play a paternalistic and protective role. In *Miami Herald*, the Court rejects the types of arguments that it accepted in *Red Lion* to protect the right of the newspaper. What explains the different holdings of *Red Lion* and *Miami Herald*? Does it matter that we are dealing with two different types of media, broadcast and print?

Newspapers have a long and storied tradition in political reporting and editorializing. Do you think the Court just views newspapers as more valuable than television broadcasting? What about the internet? If the reasoning in *Red Lion* is based upon scarcity and the government's role in allocating the spectrum, can any type of political speech restriction of the internet ever be constitutional?

>> *Less Is More?*   In *Red Lion*, the Court asserts that "the people as a whole retain . . . their collective right to have the medium [radio] function consistently with the ends and purposes of the First Amendment. . . . It is the purpose of the First Amendment to preserve an uninhibited marketplace of ideas in which truth will ultimately prevail." Yet in that case, preservation of the truth-seeking function of the marketplace of ideas requires a *reduction* in the amount of speech rather than an increase. When it comes to preserving the value of speech, can less be more?

> When we really do believe that speech can advance truth—or when we value what it can do for other reasons—we normally do not free it from constraint, but instead do the opposite: we regulate it, sometimes with extreme severity, and we do so in ways that directly reflect a collective judgment of usefulness or quality or value. Take the courtroom for example: this is an institution that works almost entirely by words, but in it there is very little of what one would call freedom of speech. . . . [Such] regulation has the aim not of suppressing truth, or some other social value, but of making its discovery or expression possible. . . . [R]egulation works to a large degree through compelled silence. Silence is the sculptor's chisel that shapes the speech. . . .

James Boyd White, *Free Speech and Valuable Speech: Silence, Dante, and the "Marketplace of Ideas,"* 51 UCLA L. Rev. 799, 812 (2004). Is this correct—can regulation of speech make it more effective rather than less? Even if so, should the government be the one to wield the chisel and thus to control the shape of what speech produces in the public sphere?

>> *Regulation of Political Speech Abroad.*   Other nations frequently take quite different approaches to the regulation of political speech. For example, paid political advertising is currently prohibited in Belgium, the Czech Republic, Denmark, France, Germany, Ireland, Malta, Norway, Portugal, Romania, Sweden, Switzerland, and the U.K. In 2013, the European Court of Human Rights (ECHR) upheld by a vote of 9 to 8 the U.K.'s statutory prohibition on paid political broadcasting on radio or television. The plaintiff, an animal rights organization, had been turned

down under British law when it sought to buy a 20-second television advertisement opposing the keeping and exhibition of primates. It challenged the ban under Article 10 of the Convention for the Protection of Human Rights and Fundamental Freedoms, which provides: "Everyone has the right to freedom of expression." The court found that its task was to "balance [the plaintiff's] right to impart information and ideas of general interest which the public is entitled to receive [against] the authorities' desire to protect the democratic debate and process from distortion by powerful financial groups with advantageous access to influential media." This balance was struck in favor of the government's interest in protecting democratic processes. The court found it significant that the organization was still free to speak in other, unregulated forums. *Animal Defenders International v. United Kingdom*, No. 48876/08 (Apr. 22, 2013).

E.   *COMPELLED SPEECH: DISCLOSURE*

Up until now, we have considered the extent to which the state can limit the speech of political actors or institutions. We now turn to the obverse question: whether the state can compel political speech.

The Court first addressed the issue of anonymous political speech and participation in a pair of cases decided in the middle of the last century. In *Bates v. City of Little Rock*, 361 U.S. 516 (1960), the Supreme Court considered a case in which several petitioners were convicted of refusing to supply city officials with a list of the names of the members of the local branch of the National Association for the Advancement of Colored People (NAACP). Little Rock officials demanded the list in order to levy a license tax authorized by Arkansas state law. Local NAACP officials refused to supply the list because they believed the public disclosure of their members' names would endanger those members. Because no reasonable relationship existed between the power of Arkansas municipalities to levy taxes and the compelled disclosure of the NAACP's membership rolls, and because the NAACP members' fear of reprisal was justified, the *Bates* Court found that compelled disclosure of the NAACP's members would unreasonably interfere with their freedom of association.

Similarly, in *NAACP v. State of Alabama ex rel. Patterson*, 357 U.S. 449 (1958), the Court addressed a statute mandating that out-of-state corporations register with the Alabama Secretary of State in order to do business within the state. The NAACP refused to comply with the law, and, during the course of litigation on the issue, the state moved for production of a large number of NAACP business records, including membership lists. The NAACP would not produce its membership list and was held in contempt. The Court's disposition was nearly identical to that in *Bates*. *Bates v. Little Rock* and *NAACP v. Alabama* were civil rights era cases and it was not initially clear to what extent they would serve as precedent for the Court's modern compelled-political-speech cases.

We now turn to those cases involving compelled disclosure of the identity of those who speak during political campaigns, those who contribute money in campaigns, and those who engage in the officially significant act of signing petitions to place initiative measures on the ballot.

1.   Disclosure of the Identity of the Speaker

Are there times when citizens should be able to participate in politics anonymously? Though the two NAACP cases mentioned above allow for an exception to disclosure of identity when the disclosure might lead to serious harm, are there any other times when disclosure should be optional? In the following case, Margaret McIntyre, a concerned parent and taxpayer, distributed anonymous leaflets opposing a levy under contemplation by the local school board. After printing and distributing her leaflets, McIntyre faced punishment under the following Ohio statute:

> No person shall write, print, post, or distribute, or cause to be written, printed, posted, or distributed, a notice, placard, dodger, advertisement, sample ballot, or any other form of general publication which is designed to promote the nomination or election or defeat of a candidate, or to promote the adoption or defeat of any issue, or to influence the voters in any election, or make an expenditure for the purpose of financing political communications through newspapers, magazines, outdoor advertising facilities, direct mailings, or other similar types of general public political advertising, or through flyers, handbills, or other nonperiodical printed matter, unless there appears on such form of publication in a conspicuous place or is contained within said statement the name and residence or business address of the chairman, treasurer, or secretary of the organization issuing the same, or the person who issues, makes, or is responsible therefor. The disclaimer "paid political advertisement" is not sufficient to meet the requirements of this division. When such publication is issued by the regularly constituted central or executive committee of a political party . . . it shall be sufficiently identified if it bears the name of the committee and its chairman or treasurer. No person, firm, or corporation shall print or reproduce any notice, placard, dodger, advertisement, sample ballot, or any other form of publication in violation of this section. This section does not apply to the transmittal of personal correspondence that is not reproduced by machine for general distribution.

Ohio Rev. Code Ann. §3599.09(A) (1988).

McIntyre v. Ohio Elections Commission

514 U.S. 334 (1995)

Justice STEVENS delivered the opinion of the Court.

The question presented is whether an Ohio statute that prohibits the distribution of anonymous campaign literature is a "law . . . abridging the freedom of speech" within the meaning of the First Amendment.

I

On April 27, 1988, Margaret McIntyre distributed leaflets to persons attending a public meeting at the Blendon Middle School in Westerville, Ohio. . . . The leaflets expressed Mrs. McIntyre's opposition to [a proposed] levy. There is no suggestion that the text of her message was false, misleading, or libelous. She had composed and printed it on her home computer and had paid a professional printer to make additional copies. Some of the handbills identified her as the author; others merely purported to express the views of "CONCERNED PARENTS AND TAX PAYERS." Except for the help provided by her son and a friend, who placed some of the leaflets on car windshields in the school parking lot, Mrs. McIntyre acted independently.

While Mrs. McIntyre distributed her handbills, an official of the school district, who supported the tax proposal, advised her that the unsigned leaflets did not conform to the Ohio election laws. Undeterred, Mrs. McIntyre appeared at another meeting on the next evening and handed out more of the handbills.

The proposed school levy . . . finally passed . . . in November 1988. Five months later, the same school official filed a complaint with the Ohio Elections Commission charging that Mrs. McIntyre's distribution of unsigned leaflets violated §3599.09(A) of the Ohio Code. The commission agreed and imposed a fine of $100. . . .

The Franklin County Court of Common Pleas reversed. . . . [T]he court concluded that the statute was unconstitutional as applied to [McIntyre's] conduct. The Ohio Court of Appeals, by a divided vote, reinstated the fine. . . . The Ohio Supreme Court affirmed by a divided vote. . . .

II

Ohio maintains that the statute under review is a reasonable regulation of the electoral process. The State does not suggest that all anonymous publications are pernicious or that a statute totally excluding them from the marketplace of ideas would be valid. This is a wise (albeit implicit) concession, for the anonymity of an author is not ordinarily a sufficient reason to exclude her work product from the protections of the First Amendment.

"Anonymous pamphlets, leaflets, brochures and even books have played an important role in the progress of mankind." *Talley v. California*, 362 U.S. 60, 64 (1960). . . . Despite readers' curiosity and the public's interest in identifying the creator of a work of art, an author generally is free to decide whether or not to disclose his or her true identity. The decision in favor of anonymity may be motivated by fear of economic or official retaliation, by concern about social ostracism, or merely by a desire to preserve as much of one's privacy as possible. Whatever the motivation may be, at least in the field of literary endeavor, the interest in having anonymous works enter the marketplace of ideas unquestionably outweighs any public interest in requiring disclosure as a condition of entry. Accordingly, an author's decision to remain anonymous . . . is an aspect of the freedom of speech protected by the First Amendment.

The freedom to publish anonymously extends beyond the literary realm. In *Talley*, the Court held that the First Amendment protects the distribution of unsigned handbills urging readers to boycott certain Los Angeles merchants who were allegedly engaging in discriminatory employment practices. 362 U.S. 60. Writing for the Court, Justice Black noted that "[p]ersecuted groups and sects from time to time throughout history have been able to criticize oppressive practices and laws either anonymously or not at all." *Id.*, at 64. . . . On occasion, quite apart from any threat of persecution, an advocate may believe her ideas will be more persuasive if her readers are unaware of her identity. Anonymity thereby provides a way for a writer who may be personally unpopular to ensure that readers will not prejudge her message simply because they do not like its proponent. . . .

III

California had defended the Los Angeles ordinance at issue in *Talley* as a law "aimed at providing a way to identify those responsible for fraud, false advertising and libel." 362 U.S., at 64. We rejected that argument because nothing in the text or legislative history of the ordinance limited its application to those evils. . . . The Ohio statute likewise contains no language limiting its application to fraudulent, false, or libelous statements; to the extent, therefore, that Ohio seeks to justify §3599.09(A) as a means to prevent the dissemination of untruths, its defense must fail for the same reason given in *Talley*. As the facts of this case demonstrate, the ordinance plainly applies even when there is no hint of falsity or libel.

Ohio's statute does, however, contain a different limitation: It applies only to unsigned documents designed to influence voters in an election. In contrast, the Los Angeles ordinance prohibited all anonymous handbilling "in any place under any circumstances." 362 U.S., at 60-61. For that reason, Ohio correctly argues that *Talley* does not necessarily control the disposition of this case. We must, therefore, decide whether and to what extent the First Amendment's protection of anonymity encompasses documents intended to influence the electoral process.

Ohio places its principal reliance on cases such as *Anderson v. Celebrezze*, 460 U.S. 780 (1983); *Storer v. Brown*, 415 U.S. 724 (1974); and *Burdick v. Takushi*, 504 U.S. 428 (1992), in which we reviewed election code provisions governing the voting process itself. . . . In those cases we refused to adopt "any 'litmus-paper test' that will separate valid from invalid restrictions." *Anderson*, 460 U.S., at 789, quoting *Storer*, 415 U.S., at 730. Instead, we . . . considered the relative interests of the State and the injured voters, and we evaluated the extent to which the State's interests necessitated the contested restrictions. Applying similar reasoning in this case, the Ohio Supreme Court upheld §3599.09(A) as a "reasonable" and "nondiscriminatory" burden on the rights of voters. . . .

Unlike the statutory provisions challenged in *Storer* and *Anderson*, §3599.09(A) of the Ohio Code does not control the mechanics of the electoral process. It is a regulation of pure speech. Moreover, even though this provision applies evenhandedly to advocates of differing viewpoints, it is a direct regulation of the content of speech. Every written document covered by the statute must contain "the name and residence or business address of the chairman, treasurer, or secretary of the organization issuing the same, or the person who issues, makes, or is responsible therefor" [according to §3599.09(A)]. Furthermore, the category of covered documents is defined by their content—only those publications containing speech designed to influence the voters in an election need bear the required markings. Consequently, we are not faced with an ordinary election restriction; this case "involves a limitation on political expression subject to exacting scrutiny." *Meyer v. Grant*, 486 U.S. 414, 420 (1988).

Indeed, as we have explained on many prior occasions, the category of speech regulated by the Ohio statute occupies the core of the protection afforded by the First Amendment. . . .

Of course, core political speech need not center on a candidate for office. The principles enunciated in *Buckley* extend equally to issue-based elections such as the school tax referendum that Mrs. McIntyre sought to influence. . . . Indeed, the speech in which Mrs. McIntyre engaged—handing out leaflets in the advocacy of a politically controversial viewpoint—is the essence of First Amendment expression. . . . That this advocacy occurred in the heat of a controversial referendum vote only strengthens the protection afforded to Mrs. McIntyre's expression: Urgent, important, and effective speech can be no less protected than impotent speech, lest the right to speak be relegated to those instances when it is least needed. . . . No form of speech is entitled to greater constitutional protection than Mrs. McIntyre's.

When a law burdens core political speech, we apply "exacting scrutiny," and we uphold the restriction only if it is narrowly tailored to serve an overriding state interest. . . . Our precedents thus make abundantly clear that the Ohio Supreme Court applied a significantly more lenient standard than is appropriate in a case of this kind.

IV

Nevertheless, the State argues that, even under the strictest standard of review, the disclosure requirement in §3599.09(A) is justified by two important and legitimate state interests. Ohio judges its interest in preventing fraudulent and libelous statements and its interest in providing the electorate with relevant information to be sufficiently compelling to justify the anonymous speech ban. . . .

Insofar as the interest in informing the electorate means nothing more than the provision of additional information that may either buttress or undermine the argument in a document, we think the identity of the speaker is no different from other components of the document's content that the author is free to include or exclude. . . . The simple interest in providing voters with additional relevant information does not justify a state requirement that a writer make statements or disclosures she would otherwise omit. Moreover, in the case of a handbill written by a private citizen who is not known to the recipient, the name and address of the author add little, if anything, to the reader's ability to evaluate the document's message. Thus, Ohio's informational interest is plainly insufficient to support the constitutionality of its disclosure requirement.

The state interest in preventing fraud and libel stands on a different footing. We agree with Ohio's submission that this interest carries special weight during election campaigns when false statements, if credited, may have serious adverse consequences for the public at large. Ohio does not, however, rely solely on §3599.09(A) to protect that interest. . . . Ohio's prohibition of anonymous leaflets plainly is not its principal weapon against fraud. Rather, it serves as an aid to enforcement of the specific prohibitions and as a deterrent to the making of false statements by unscrupulous prevaricators. Although these ancillary benefits are assuredly legitimate, we are not persuaded that they justify §3599.09(A)'s extremely broad prohibition.

As this case demonstrates, the prohibition encompasses documents that are not even arguably false or misleading. It applies not only to the activities of candidates and their organized supporters, but also to individuals acting independently and using only their own modest resources. It applies not only to elections of public officers, but also to ballot issues that present neither a substantial risk of libel nor any potential appearance of corrupt advantage. It applies not only to leaflets distributed on the eve of an election, when the opportunity for reply is limited, but also to those distributed months in advance. It applies no matter what the character or strength of the author's interest in anonymity. Moreover, as this case also demonstrates, the absence of the author's name on a document does not necessarily protect either that person or a distributor of a forbidden document from being held responsible for compliance with the Election Code. Nor has the State explained why it can more easily enforce the direct bans on disseminating false documents against anonymous authors and distributors than against wrongdoers who might use false names and addresses in an attempt to avoid detection. We recognize that a State's enforcement interest might justify a more limited identification requirement, but Ohio has shown scant cause for inhibiting the leafletting at issue here. . . .

VI

Under our Constitution, anonymous pamphleteering is not a pernicious, fraudulent practice, but an honorable tradition of advocacy and of dissent. Anonymity is a shield from the tyranny of the majority. . . . It thus exemplifies the purpose behind the Bill of Rights, and of the First Amendment in particular: to protect unpopular individuals from retaliation—and their ideas from suppression—at the hand of an intolerant society. The right to remain anonymous may be abused when it shields fraudulent conduct. But political speech by its nature will sometimes have unpalatable consequences, and, in general, our society accords greater weight to the value of free speech than to the dangers of its misuse. . . . Ohio has not shown that its interest in preventing the misuse of anonymous election-related speech justifies a prohibition of all uses of that speech. The State may, and does, punish fraud directly. But it cannot seek to punish fraud indirectly by indiscriminately outlawing a category of speech, based on its content, with no necessary relationship to the danger sought to be prevented. One would be hard pressed to think of a better example of the pitfalls of Ohio's blunderbuss approach than the facts of the case before us.

Justice SCALIA dissenting:

[T]he usefulness of a signing requirement lies not only in promoting observance of the law against campaign falsehoods (though that alone is enough to sustain it). It lies also in promoting a civil and dignified level of campaign debate—which the State has no power to command, but ample power to encourage by such undemanding measures as a signature requirement. Observers of the past few national elections have expressed concern about the increase of character assassination — "mudslinging" is the colloquial term — engaged in by political candidates and their supporters to the detriment of the democratic process. Not all of this, in fact not much of it, consists of actionable untruth; most is innuendo, or demeaning characterization, or mere disclosure of items of personal life that have no bearing upon suitability for office. Imagine how much all of this would increase if it could be done anonymously. The principal impediment against it is the reluctance of most individuals and organizations to be publicly associated with uncharitable and uncivil expression. Consider, moreover, the increased potential for "dirty tricks." It is not unheard-of for campaign operatives to circulate material over the name of their opponents or their opponents' supporters (a violation of election laws) in order to attract or alienate certain interest groups. . . . How much easier — and sanction free! — it would be to circulate anonymous material (for example, a really tasteless, though not actionably false, attack upon one's own candidate) with the hope and expectation that it will be attributed to, and held against, the other side. . . .

>> *Anonymous Statements About Candidates' Character.*   The Ohio statute invalidated in *McIntyre* prohibited anonymity for any and all statements intended "to influence the voters in any election." Might a more narrowly drawn statute survive constitutional review? In *Canon v. Justice Court,* 393 P.2d 428 (Cal. 1964), the California Supreme Court confronted a state law making it a misdemeanor anonymously to print or distribute written material "which is designed to injure or defeat any candidate for nomination or election to any public office by reflecting upon his personal character or political action." Although the court in the end invalidated the statute on other grounds, it was untroubled by the ban on anonymous attacks on candidates for office.

> The statute does not prohibit the communication of ideas, not does it attempt to regulate the content of expression. It forbids only anonymity, on pain of conviction of a misdemeanor, with respect to a limited range of expression. . . . [And] the statute impinges upon full freedom of expression only during a limited period of time, for there can be candidates only during the period preceding an election. More importantly, the section applies only to attacks on candidates, not to writings which are a communication of views about issues.

> The purpose of the statute is clear. It requires identification so that (1) the electorate may be better able to evaluate campaign material by examination of the competence and credibility of its source, (2) irresponsible attacks will be deterred, (3) candidates may be better able to refute or rebut charges so that elections will be the expression of the will of an undeceived, well-informed public. It is clear that the integrity of elections, essential to the very preservation of a free society, is a matter "in which the State may have a compelling regulatory concern." *Gibson v. Florida*

Legislative Investigation Comm., 372 U.S. 539, 546 (1963). It was not the aim of the Legislature to hinder the communication of ideas, and there is nothing to indicate that the disclosure requirement, under the circumstances of present-day California politics, would in fact substantially inhibit expression, even in the limited area to which the statute is applicable. It was intended to deter the scurrilous hit and run smear attacks which are all too common in the course of political campaigns.

The primary concern is not for the candidate, however, although it is clearly in the public interest to create conditions conducive to the encouragement of good citizens to seek public office. The chief harm is that suffered by all the people when, as a result of the public having been misinformed and misled, the election is not the expression of the true public will. . . .

Note that the court links the statute to a belief that anonymous smears distort election results by misleading the voters. Is this true? If it is true, does disclosure of the identity of the speaker address the problem? Will voters be better able to evaluate character assassination if they know its source? Or does the law assist candidates in rebutting such attacks more than it assists voters? Even so, if the claims are truthful, isn't the source irrelevant for purposes of rebutting the charges? After all, claims that the source was biased might confuse voters, who could then be misled into believing that the charge is false. If the claims are false, then candidates can rebut the charges as they would if the charges were made by the most respected newspaper in the country. Finally, does requiring disclosure have a chilling effect on worthy speech that the court is overlooking?

≫ *Disclosure and Deterrence.* Why would anyone wish to speak anonymously? The risk of physical or economic retaliation is an obvious and serious consideration, but short of that, why would a speaker in a political conversation desire to remain anonymous? Because of the possibility of embarrassment or exposure as a hypocrite? Shouldn't hypocrites have to deal with the consequences of their own deceptions? Should a wish for anonymity for its own sake be respected?

According to John Stuart Mill, the answer is no. Indeed, Mill went further, arguing that the ballot itself should not be secret. The vote, Mill argued, is a trust that each voter holds for the benefit of the public. It therefore "is not a thing in which he [the citizen] has an option; it has no more to do with his personal wishes than the verdict of a juryman. It is strictly a matter of duty; he is bound to give it according to his best and most conscientious opinion of the public good." In order to provide voters with incentives to use the vote for the public rather than their own private good, "the duty of voting, like any other public duty, should be performed under the eye and criticism of the public" because "the bare fact of having to give an account of their conduct, is a powerful inducement to adhere to conduct of which at least some decent account can be given." Thus, according to Mill, publicity of voting will lead citizens to vote responsibly to avoid the embarrassment of having to give a public accounting of votes that cannot be adequately justified with legitimate reasons. *See* JOHN STUART MILL, CONSIDERATIONS ON REPUBLICAN GOVERNMENT (1869).

>> *Effects of Anonymity on Behavior.*   Conflicting positions about the desirability of anonymity in politics often seem to depend on conflicting empirical assumptions about the behavior of people when they are anonymous. Everyone seems to agree that anonymity can embolden people, but how do they behave when emboldened? Some seem to believe that anonymity emboldens the meek to speak their minds truthfully, to the general benefit and enrichment of public discourse. Others seem to think that anonymity, by eliminating accountability, emboldens the unethical to make scurrilous and false attacks on their opponents, to engage in smear tactics, and in general to impoverish political debate. Which is correct?

Predicting the effect of anonymity on political behavior is in fact difficult. Consider this summary of what little empirical research exists relevant to the topic:

> [T]heorists often treat anonymity as disinhibiting. Yet how disinhibition affects behavior in any given set of circumstances depends upon both the predispositions of the actor and the kinds of social inhibitions that publicity would otherwise invoke. If anonymity is disinhibiting, then it may facilitate antisocial behavior if the individual is predisposed to such behavior and the social pressures to which he or she ordinarily is publicly exposed are prosocial, but anonymity can also facilitate the opposite kind of behavior if these considerations are reversed. According to one particularly sophisticated model of social behavior, the effect of anonymity depends heavily on the context. Anonymity, on this view, "serves to strengthen the impact of social norms . . . when a social identity is salient," but when a personal identity is salient, "the same anonymity will reduce the impact of social norms, and increase the person's adherence to their [sic] own personal standards" regardless of whether those personal standards are pro- or antisocial. . . . In sum, then, whether and how anonymity affects behavior in any significant way seems to depend very much on particularities of context. Anonymity, in other words, is socially mediated, and as variable as the myriad social contexts in which it might be found.

James A. Gardner, *Anonymity and Democratic Citizenship*, 19 WM. & MARY BILL RTS. J. 927, 948-949 (2011).

2.   *Disclosure of Monetary Contributions*

Thus far, we have considered compelled disclosure of the identity of someone who wishes to enter the general political discourse. What about someone who does not wish to speak on his or her own account, but instead wishes merely to support financially the speech of others, such as candidates for office? Do the same considerations apply? The following case deals with the constitutionality of disclosure requirements mandated under the Federal Election Campaign Act (FECA), a law about which much more will be said in Chapter 9, dealing with campaign finance. Here, we focus solely on the question of disclosure.

Buckley v. Valeo

421 U.S. 1 (1976) (per curiam)

II. REPORTING AND DISCLOSURE REQUIREMENTS

The first federal disclosure law was enacted in 1910. It required political committees, defined as national committees and national congressional campaign committees of parties, and organizations operating to influence congressional elections in two or more States, to disclose names of all contributors of $100 or more; identification of recipients of expenditures of $10 or more was also required. Annual expenditures of $50 or more "for the purpose of influencing or controlling, in two or more States, the result of" a congressional election had to be reported independently if they were not made through a political committee. In 1911 the Act was revised to include prenomination transactions such as those involved in conventions and primary campaigns.

Disclosure requirements were broadened in the Federal Corrupt Practices Act of 1925. That Act required political committees, defined as organizations that accept contributions or make expenditures "for the purpose of influencing or attempting to influence" the Presidential or Vice Presidential elections (a) in two or more States or (b) as a subsidiary of a national committee, §302(c), to report total contributions and expenditures, including the names and addresses of contributors of $100 or more and recipients of $10 or more in a calendar year. §305(a). The Act was upheld against a challenge that it infringed upon the prerogatives of the States in *Burroughs v. United States*, 290 U.S. 534 (1934). The Court held that it was within the power of Congress "to pass appropriate legislation to safeguard (a Presidential) election from the improper use of money to influence the result." *Id.*, at 545. Although the disclosure requirements were widely circumvented, no further attempts were made to tighten them until 1960, when the Senate passed a bill that would have closed some existing loopholes. The attempt aborted because no similar effort was made in the House.

The Act presently under review replaced all prior disclosure laws. Its primary disclosure provisions impose reporting obligations on "political committees" and candidates. "Political committee" is defined in §431(d) as a group of persons that receives "contributions" or makes "expenditures" of over $1,000 in a calendar year. "Contributions" and "expenditures" are defined in lengthy parallel provisions similar to those in Title 18. . . . Both definitions focus on the use of money or other objects of value "for the purpose of . . . influencing" the nomination or election of any person to federal office. §431(e)(1), (f)(1).

Each political committee is required to register with the Commission, and to keep detailed records of both contributions and expenditures. These records must include the name and address of everyone making a contribution in excess of $10, along with the date and amount of the contribution. If a person's contributions aggregate more than $100, his occupation and principal place of business are also to be included. These files are subject to periodic audits and field investigations by the Commission.

Each committee and each candidate also is required to file quarterly reports. The reports are to contain detailed financial information, including the full name, mailing address, occupation, and principal place of business of each person who has contributed over $100 in a calendar year, as well as the amount and date of the contributions. They are to be made available by the Commission "for public inspection and copying." Every candidate for federal office is required to designate a "principal campaign committee," which is to receive reports of contributions and expenditures made on the candidate's behalf from other political committees and to compile and file these reports, together with its own statements, with the Commission.

Every individual or group, other than a political committee or candidate, who makes "contributions" or "expenditures" of over $100 in a calendar year "other than by contribution to a political committee or candidate" is required to file a statement with the Commission. Any violation of these record-keeping and reporting provisions is punishable by a fine of not more than $1,000 or a prison term of not more than a year, or both.

A. General Principles

Unlike the overall limitations on contributions and expenditures, the disclosure requirements impose no ceiling on campaign-related activities. But we have repeatedly found that compelled disclosure, in itself, can seriously infringe on privacy of association and belief guaranteed by the First Amendment.

We long have recognized that significant encroachments on First Amendment rights of the sort that compelled disclosure imposes cannot be justified by a mere showing of some legitimate governmental interest. Since *NAACP v. Alabama* we have required that the subordinating interests of the State must survive exacting scrutiny. We also have insisted that there be a "relevant correlation" or "substantial relation" between the governmental interest and the information required to be disclosed. This type of scrutiny is necessary even if any deterrent effect on the exercise of First Amendment rights arises, not through direct government action, but indirectly as an unintended but inevitable result of the government's conduct in requiring disclosure.

Appellees argue that the disclosure requirements of the Act differ significantly from those at issue in *NAACP v. Alabama* and its progeny because the Act only requires disclosure of the names of contributors and does not compel political organizations to submit the names of their members.

As we have seen, group association is protected because it enhances "(e)ffective advocacy." *NAACP v. Alabama*, 357 U.S., at 460. The right to join together "for the advancement of beliefs and ideas," id., is diluted if it does not include the right to pool money through contributions, for funds are often essential if "advocacy" is to be truly or optimally "effective." Moreover, the invasion of privacy of belief may be as great when the information sought concerns the giving and spending of money as when it concerns the joining of organizations. . . . Our past decisions have not drawn fine lines between contributors and members but have treated them interchangeably. . . .

The strict test established by *NAACP v. Alabama* is necessary because compelled disclosure has the potential for substantially infringing the exercise of First Amendment rights. But we have acknowledged that there are governmental interests sufficiently important to outweigh the possibility of infringement, particularly when the "free functioning of our national institutions" is involved. *Communist Party v. Subversive Activities Control Bd.*, 367 U.S. 1, 97 (1961).

The governmental interests sought to be vindicated by the disclosure requirements are of this magnitude. They fall into three categories. First, disclosure provides the electorate with information "as to where political campaign money comes from and how it is spent by the candidate" in order to aid the voters in evaluating those who seek federal office. It allows voters to place each candidate in the political spectrum more precisely than is often possible solely on the basis of party labels and campaign speeches. The sources of a candidate's financial support also alert the voter to the interests to which a candidate is most likely to be responsive and thus facilitate predictions of future performance in office.

Second, disclosure requirements deter actual corruption and avoid the appearance of corruption by exposing large contributions and expenditures to the light of publicity. This exposure may discourage those who would use money for improper purposes either before or after the election. . . .

Third, and not least significant, recordkeeping, reporting, and disclosure requirements are an essential means of gathering the data necessary to detect violations of the contribution limitations described above.

The disclosure requirements, as a general matter, directly serve substantial governmental interests. In determining whether these interests are sufficient to justify the requirements we must look to the extent of the burden that they place on individual rights.

It is undoubtedly true that public disclosure of contributions to candidates and political parties will deter some individuals who otherwise might contribute. In some instances, disclosure may even expose contributors to harassment or retaliation. These are not insignificant burdens on individual rights, and they must be weighed carefully against the interests which Congress has sought to promote by this legislation. In this process, we note and agree with appellants' concession that disclosure requirements certainly in most applications appear to be the least restrictive means of curbing the evils of campaign ignorance and corruption that Congress found to exist. Appellants argue, however, that the balance tips against disclosure when it is required of contributors to certain parties and candidates. We turn now to this contention.

B. Application to Minor Parties and Independents

Appellants contend that the Act's requirements are overbroad insofar as they apply to contributions to minor parties and independent candidates because the governmental interest in this information is minimal and the danger of significant infringement on First Amendment rights is greatly increased.

1. Requisite Factual Showing

In *NAACP v. Alabama* the organization had "made an uncontroverted showing that on past occasions revelation of the identity of its rank-and-file members (had) exposed these members to economic reprisal, loss of employment, threat of physical coercion, and other manifestations of public hostility," 357 U.S., at 462, and the State was unable to show that the disclosure it sought had a "substantial bearing" on the issues it sought to clarify, id., at 464. Under those circumstances, the Court held that "whatever interest the State may have in (disclosure) has not been shown to be sufficient to overcome petitioner's constitutional objections." *Id.*, at 465. . . .

It is true that the governmental interest in disclosure is diminished when the contribution in question is made to a minor party with little chance of winning an election. As minor parties usually represent definite and publicized viewpoints, there may be less need to inform the voters of the interests that specific candidates represent. Major parties encompass candidates of greater diversity. In many situations the label "Republican" or "Democrat" tells a voter little. The candidate who bears it may be supported by funds from the far right, the far left, or any place in between on the political spectrum. It is less likely that a candidate of, say, the Socialist Labor Party will represent interests that cannot be discerned from the party's ideological position.

The Government's interest in deterring the "buying" of elections and the undue influence of large contributors on officeholders also may be reduced where contributions to a minor party or an independent candidate are concerned, for it is less likely that the candidate will be victorious. But a minor party sometimes can play a significant role in an election. Even when a minor-party candidate has little or no chance of winning, he may be encouraged by major-party interests in order to divert votes from other major-party contenders.

We are not unmindful that the damage done by disclosure to the associational interests of the minor parties and their members and to supporters of independents could be significant. These movements are less likely to have a sound financial base and thus are more vulnerable to falloffs in contributions. In some instances fears of reprisal may deter contributions to the point where the movement cannot survive. The public interest also suffers if that result comes to pass, for there is a consequent reduction in the free circulation of ideas both within and without the political arena.

There could well be a case . . . where the threat to the exercise of First Amendment rights is so serious and the state interest furthered by disclosure so insubstantial that the Act's requirements cannot be constitutionally applied. But . . . [o]n this record, the substantial public interest in disclosure identified by the legislative history of this Act outweighs the harm generally alleged.

2. Blanket Exemption

Appellants . . . argue . . . that a blanket exemption for minor parties is necessary lest irreparable injury be done before the required evidence can be gathered.

Those parties that would be sufficiently "minor" to be exempted from the requirements of §434 could be defined, appellants suggest, along the lines used for public-financing purposes, see Part III-A, *infra*, as those who received less than 25% of the vote in past elections. . . . They suggest as an alternative defining "minor parties" as those that do not qualify for automatic ballot access under state law. Presumably, other criteria, such as current political strength (measured by polls or petition), age, or degree of organization, could also be used.

The difficulty with these suggestions is that they reflect only a party's past or present political strength and that is only one of the factors that must be considered. Some of the criteria are not precisely indicative of even that factor. Age, or past political success, for instance, may typically be associated with parties that have a high probability of success. But not all long-established parties are winners [—] some are consistent losers and a new party may garner a great deal of support if it can associate itself with an issue that has captured the public's imagination. None of the criteria suggested is precisely related to the other critical factor that must be considered, the possibility that disclosure will impinge upon protected associational activity.

An opinion dissenting in part from the Court of Appeals' decision . . . argues, however, that a flat exemption for minor parties must be carved out, even along arbitrary lines, if groups that would suffer impermissibly from disclosure are to be given any real protection. An approach that requires minor parties to submit evidence that the disclosure requirements cannot constitutionally be applied to them offers only an illusory safeguard, the argument goes, because the "evils" of "chill and harassment . . . are largely incapable of formal proof." This dissent expressed its concern that a minor party, particularly a new party, may never be able to prove a substantial threat of harassment, however real that threat may be, because it would be required to come forward with witnesses who are too fearful to contribute but not too fearful to testify about their fear. A strict requirement that chill and harassment be directly attributable to the specific disclosure from which the exemption is sought would make the task even more difficult.

We recognize that unduly strict requirements of proof could impose a heavy burden, but it does not follow that a blanket exemption for minor parties is necessary. Minor parties must be allowed sufficient flexibility in the proof of injury to assure a fair consideration of their claim. The evidence offered need show only a reasonable probability that the compelled disclosure of a party's contributors' names will subject them to threats, harassment, or reprisals from either Government officials or private parties. . . .

C. Section 434(e)

Section 434(e) requires "(e)very person (other than a political committee or candidate) who makes contributions or expenditures" aggregating over $100 in a calendar year "other than by contribution to a political committee or candidate" to file a statement with the Commission. Unlike the other disclosure provisions, this section does not seek the contribution list of any association. Instead, it requires direct disclosure of what an individual or group contributes or spends.

In considering this provision we must apply the same strict standard of scrutiny, for the right of associational privacy developed in *NAACP v. Alabama* derives from the rights of the organization's members to advocate their personal points of view in the most effective way. 357 U.S., at 458, 460.

Appellants attack §434(e) as a direct intrusion on privacy of belief, in violation of *Talley v. California*, 362 U.S. 60 (1960), and as imposing "very real, practical burdens . . . certain to deter individuals from making expenditures for their independent political speech" analogous to those held to be impermissible in *Thomas v. Collins*, 323 U.S. 516 (1945).

1. The Role of §434(e) . . .

We have found that §608(e)(1) unconstitutionally infringes upon First Amendment rights. If the sole function of §434(e) were to aid in the enforcement of that provision, it would no longer serve any governmental purpose.

But the two provisions are not so intimately tied. The legislative history on the function of §434(e) is bare, but it was clearly intended to stand independently of §608(e)(1). . . . The provision is responsive to the legitimate fear that efforts would be made, as they had been in the past, to avoid the disclosure requirements by routing financial support of candidates through avenues not explicitly covered by the general provisions of the Act. . . .

D. Thresholds

Appellants' [next] contention, based on alleged overbreadth, is that the monetary thresholds in the record-keeping and reporting provisions lack a substantial nexus with the claimed governmental interests, for the amounts involved are too low even to attract the attention of the candidate, much less have a corrupting influence.

The provisions contain two thresholds. Records are to be kept by political committees of the names and addresses of those who make contributions in excess of $10, §432(c)(2), and these records are subject to Commission audit, §438(a)(8). If a person's contributions to a committee or candidate aggregate more than $100, his name and address, as well as his occupation and principal place of business, are to be included in reports filed by committees and candidates with the Commission, §434(b)(2), and made available for public inspection, §438(a)(4). . . .

The $10 and $100 thresholds are indeed low. Contributors of relatively small amounts are likely to be especially sensitive to recording or disclosure of their political preferences. These strict requirements may well discourage participation by some citizens in the political process, a result that Congress hardly could have intended. . . . But we cannot require Congress to establish that it has chosen the highest reasonable threshold. The line is necessarily a judgmental decision, best left in the context of this complex legislation to congressional discretion. We cannot say, on this bare record, that the limits designated are wholly without rationality.

We are mindful that disclosure serves informational functions, as well as the prevention of corruption and the enforcement of the contribution limitations. Congress is not required to set a threshold that is tailored only to the latter goals. In addition, the enforcement goal can never be well served if the threshold is so high that disclosure becomes equivalent to admitting violation of the contribution limitations.

The $10 recordkeeping threshold, in a somewhat similar fashion, facilitates the enforcement of the disclosure provisions by making it relatively difficult to aggregate secret contributions in amounts that surpass the $100 limit. . . .

In summary, we find no constitutional infirmities in the recordkeeping reporting, and disclosure provisions of the Act. . . .

Justice BURGER, concurring in part and dissenting in part:

The Court's theory . . . goes beyond permissible limits. Under the Court's view, disclosure serves broad informational purposes, enabling the public to be fully informed on matters of acute public interest. Forced disclosure of one aspect of a citizen's political activity, under this analysis, serves the public right to know. This open-ended approach is the only plausible justification for the otherwise irrationally low ceilings of $10 and $100 for anonymous contributions. The burdens of these low ceilings seem to me obvious. . . .

The public right to know ought not be absolute when its exercise reveals private political convictions. Secrecy, like privacy, is not per se criminal. On the contrary, secrecy and privacy as to political preferences and convictions are fundamental in a free society. . . . For me it is far too late in the day to recognize an ill-defined "public interest" to breach the historic safeguards guaranteed by the First Amendment. . . .

The balancing test used by the Court requires that fair recognition be given to competing interests. With respect, I suggest the Court has failed to give the traditional standing to some of the First Amendment values at stake here. Specifically, it has failed to confine the particular exercise of governmental power within limits reasonably required. "In every case the power to regulate must be so exercised as not, in attaining a permissible end, unduly to infringe the protected freedom." *Cantwell v. Connecticut*, 310 U.S. 296, 304 (1940).

"Unduly" must mean not more than necessary, and until today, the Court has recognized this criterion in First Amendment cases. . . . [I]t seems to me that the threshold limits fixed at $10 and $100 for anonymous contributions are constitutionally impermissible on their face. As the Court's opinion notes, Congress gave little or no thought, one way or the other, to these limits. . . . To argue that a 1976 contribution of $10 or $100 entails a risk of corruption or its appearance is simply too extravagant to be maintained. No public right to know justifies the compelled disclosure of such contributions, at the risk of discouraging them. There is, in short, no relation whatever between the means used and the legitimate goal of ventilating possible undue influence. Congress has used a shotgun to kill wrens as well as hawks. In saying that the lines drawn by Congress are "not wholly without rationality," the Court plainly fails to apply the traditional test. . . .

>> *Developments in Disclosure Since* **Buckley.**   The Court most recently addressed the constitutionality of campaign contribution disclosure in *Citizens United v. FEC*, 558 U.S. 310 (2010). Under Section 311 of BCRA, television ads paid for by anyone other than a candidate must include a disclaimer noting that the ad "is not authorized by any candidate or candidate's committee," and must identify the person or group that funded the advertisement. In rejecting a challenge on First Amendment grounds to this provision, the Court affirmed the analysis of *Buckley*:

> In [*Buckley* and *McConnell*], the Court explained that disclosure could be justified based on a governmental interest in "'provid[ing] the electorate with information' about the sources of election-related spending." . . . Although [disclosure] provisions were facially upheld [in both cases], the Court acknowledged that as-applied challenges would be available if a group could show a "'reasonable probability'" that disclosure of its

contributors' names "'will subject them to threats, harassment, or reprisals from either Government officials or private parties.'" Citizens United argues that the disclaimer requirements in §311 are unconstitutional as applied to its ads. It contends that the governmental interest in providing information to the electorate does not justify requiring disclaimers for any commercial advertisements, including the ones at issue here. We disagree. . . . The disclaimers required by §311 "provid[e] the electorate with information," *McConnell, supra,* at 196, and "insure that the voters are fully informed" about the person or group who is speaking, *Buckley, supra,* at 76. At the very least, the disclaimers avoid confusion by making clear that the ads are not funded by a candidate or political party. . . . The Court has explained that disclosure is a less restrictive alternative to more comprehensive regulations of speech.

Citizens United argues that disclosure requirements can chill donations to an organization by exposing donors to retaliation. Some amici point to recent events in which donors to certain causes were blacklisted, threatened, or otherwise targeted for retaliation. In *McConnell,* the Court recognized that [disclosure] would be unconstitutional as applied to an organization if there were a reasonable probability that the group's members would face threats, harassment, or reprisals if their names were disclosed. 540 U.S., at 198. The examples cited by amici are cause for concern. Citizens United, however, has offered no evidence that its members may face similar threats or reprisals. To the contrary, Citizens United has been disclosing its donors for years and has identified no instance of harassment or retaliation.

. . . With the advent of the Internet, prompt disclosure of expenditures can provide shareholders and citizens with the information needed to hold corporations and elected officials accountable for their positions and supporters. . . . This transparency enables the electorate to make informed decisions and give proper weight to different speakers and messages.

▶▶ *The Likelihood of Retaliation and Harassment.*   The Court's approach in these cases has been to uphold blanket contribution disclosure requirements but to permit as-applied exceptions for individuals or groups when there is a demonstrated risk of harm to specific individuals who may suffer retaliation or harassment if their identities are disclosed. This exception has generally been applied sparingly, and has largely been limited to members of obviously vulnerable and unpopular groups, such as racial minorities or socialists, where there is a demonstrable history of violence against group members. *See Bates, supra; NAACP, supra; Brown v. Socialist Workers '74 Committee,* 459 U.S. 87 (1982).

How likely is retaliation against those who produce or fund political advertisements? In the past, it was often difficult to find and communicate with strangers; today, the internet allows individuals to be located quickly, and it frequently yields a great deal of personal information, making retaliation and harassment undoubtedly easier. Does this change the magnitude of the risks associated with disclosure? And what counts as a level of retaliation that rises to a constitutionally cognizable level? Must there be a threat of violence? Or is social media trolling sufficient to justify exemption? How much civic courage should be demanded of those who wish to participate in politics?

For a skeptical view concerning contemporary demands for as-applied exemptions to disclosure laws, see Richard L. Hasen, *Chill Out: A Qualified Defense of Campaign Finance Disclosure in the Internet Age*, 27 J.L. & POL. 557 (2012).

In *Americans for Prosperity Foundation v. Bonta*, 594 U.S. __ (2021), tax-exempt charitable organizations in California brought suit to invalidate a state regulatory requirement mandating disclosure of the identities of their major donors to the state's Attorney General (AG). The AG's regulation, promulgated to facilitate enforcement of California's rules governing eligibility for tax-exempt status, required all registered charitable organizations to reveal the names and addresses of donors who contribute more than $5,000 in a tax year. The plaintiffs challenged the requirement as an unjustified requirement of compelled speech and the Court agreed.

While acknowledging that the state had important interests in enforcing its tax laws, the Court found "a dramatic mismatch" between the regulatory requirement and the interests at stake. The AG's office, the Court found, had never actually made use of the disclosed donor information in an enforcement action, had never considered a less onerous regulatory approach, and was unable to satisfy the Court that it had taken necessary precautions against accidental disclosure of donor identities to the public.

Even disclosure solely to the state, the majority went on, can chill contributions, a form of protected speech and association. The plaintiffs "introduced evidence that they and their supporters have been subjected to bomb threats, protests, stalking, and physical violence," although the Court did not say whether those threats resulted from public knowledge of donors' contributions to the plaintiff organizations. As a result, the challenged regulation was not sufficiently narrowly tailored to survive "exacting scrutiny."

In a dissent for herself and Justices Breyer and Kagan, Justice Sotomayor argued that the decision represented a significant departure from prior case law, which required the plaintiffs to "plead and prove that disclosure will likely expose them to objective harms, such as threats, harassment, or reprisals." She also pointed out that many large donors to these groups had actively sought public credit for supporting the groups, and were "only too happy to publicize their names across the websites and walls of the organizations they support." The Court, she wrote, "abandons the requirement that plaintiffs demonstrate that they are chilled, much less that they are reasonably chilled. . . . At best, then, a subjective preference for privacy, which previously did not confer standing, now subjects disclosure requirements to close scrutiny." She found the disclosure requirements appropriately narrowly tailored under her understanding of prior case law.

Although *Americans for Prosperity* is not an election law case, does it have implications for the seemingly settled judicial acceptance of compelled disclosure in the political setting? Will large campaign donors no longer be required to prove that they face an unusually high risk of retaliation in order to qualify for exemption from otherwise applicable disclosure requirements? Or is the public interest in disclosure inherently greater when donors are contributing to political campaigns than when they are contributing to charitable organizations?

>> *Identity of Speakers vs. Contributors.*   In *McIntyre*, the Court distinguished *Buckley* as follows:

> Our . . . opinion in *Buckley* . . . stressed the importance of providing "the electorate with information 'as to where political campaign money comes from and how it is spent by the candidate.' " 424 U.S., at 66. We observed that the "sources of a candidate's financial support also alert the voter to the interests to which a candidate is most likely to be responsive and thus facilitate predictions of future performance in office." *Id.*, at 67. Those comments concerned contributions to the candidate or expenditures authorized by the candidate or his responsible agent. They had no reference to the kind of independent activity pursued by Mrs. McIntyre. Required disclosures about the level of financial support a candidate has received from various sources are supported by an interest in avoiding the appearance of corruption that has no application to this case.
>
> Though . . . mandatory reporting [of spending] undeniably impedes protected First Amendment activity, the intrusion is a far cry from compelled self-identification on all election-related writings. A written election-related document—particularly a leaflet—is often a personally crafted statement of a political viewpoint. Mrs. McIntyre's handbills surely fit that description. As such, identification of the author against her will is particularly intrusive; it reveals unmistakably the content of her thoughts on a controversial issue. Disclosure of an expenditure and its use, without more, reveals far less information. It may be information that a person prefers to keep secret, and undoubtedly it often gives away something about the spender's political views. Nonetheless, even though money may "talk," its speech is less specific, less personal, and less provocative than a handbill—and as a result, when money supports an unpopular viewpoint it is less likely to precipitate retaliation. . . .
>
> Ohio's statute . . . rests on different and less powerful state interests. . . . In candidate elections, the Government can identify a compelling state interest in avoiding the corruption that might result from campaign expenditures. Disclosure of expenditures lessens the risk that individuals will spend money to support a candidate as a quid pro quo for special treatment after the candidate is in office. . . . In short, although *Buckley* may permit a more narrowly drawn statute, it surely is not authority for upholding Ohio's open-ended provision.

Is the Court's account persuasive? How robust is the distinction between disclosure of speech and the spending of money that facilitates speech? What if McIntyre wrote the pamphlets, but another concerned citizen paid for them? Should those citizens be treated differently for the purposes of acting anonymously? Why?

>> *How Effective Is Disclosure of Contributions?*   A significant justification supporting mandatory disclosure of political contributions is that it will help inform voters; information about the source of a candidate's financial support, it is said, can help voters locate the candidate on the ideological spectrum and also reveal the kinds of interests to which the candidate may be responsive. Recent empirical studies suggest that such information is meaningful when the contribution in question

comes from prominent, politically active organizations with well-known ideological leanings, such as the Sierra Club or the U.S. Chamber of Commerce. *See* Michael W. Sances, *Is Money in Politics Harming Trust in Government? Evidence from Two Survey Experiments*, 12 ELECTION L.J. 53 (2013). Presumably the same would hold true for famous individuals with well-known public political profiles. But does disclosure of contributions realistically serve a meaningful informational function in cases where the donor is not well known? Consider this account:

> There are several reasons . . . to be skeptical of the proposition that contributor information, at least in its current form, is a helpful heuristic cue [for voters]. First, it is not clear what cues such information provides that is not already provided by other existing and readily accessible heuristic cues such as party affiliation and endorsements. . . . Second, it appears that the vast majority of contributors will not be known to the vast majority of voters, and so the fact of their financial support will not provide any useful information about a candidate to most voters. That is, while a voter might be able to use the fact that, for example, Jane Fonda or Rush Limbaugh contributed to a particular candidate's campaign or to an organization that opposed a particular candidate to intuit correctly something about the relevant candidate's qualifications for office or policy positions, the vast majority of reported contributors are not household names within their local communities, much less for most of the relevant electorate. . . . Third and finally, it is not clear that most voters even know contributor information before they enter the voting booth. While party affiliation is usually listed on the ballot, and interest group, newspaper, and celebrity endorsements are often circulated widely, voters generally gain access to contributor information only by proactively searching for such information, which few voters probably do even with Internet-accessible databases. . . . Indeed, at least some of the efforts by institutions that have the capacity to review and reformat contributor data appear to be designed primarily to inform neighbors, customers, co-workers, employers, and others with relationships to the contributors about the character or positions of the contributors, not to inform voters about the character or positions of the candidates. . . .

Lloyd Hitoshi Mayer, *Disclosures on Disclosure*, 44 IND. L. REV. 255 (2010). *See also* Richard Briffault, *Campaign Finance Disclosure 2.0*, 9 ELECTION L.J. 273 (2010). In addition, the efficacy of disclosure regimes depends upon the accuracy with which donor information is reported. There may be reason to doubt that current contribution disclosure regimes are being administered in a way that routinely provides the public with useful and reliable information. *See* Jennifer A. Heerwig and Katherine Shaw, *Through a Glass Darkly: The Rhetoric and Reality of Campaign Finance Disclosure*, 102 GEO. L.J. 1443 (2014).

>> *The Collateral Consequences of Disclosure.* Disclosure of a person's history of political contributions makes public information that ordinarily would be kept private. How willing are people to bear that cost? The fact that so many contribute even under disclosure regimes suggests that many, and perhaps most, are willing to make the tradeoff. On the other hand, research suggests that this willingness

is not evenly distributed among the electorate. Small donors, in particular, may be more reticent to undergo public disclosure than large donors. Thus, efforts to counterbalance the impact of large donors by expanding the donor base to include many small donors may face additional obstacles. People who hold views that differ from the prevailing political views in their social networks—dissenters—may also be less willing to participate in politics by making monetary donations when disclosure is part of the bargain. Raymond J. La Raja, *Political Participation and Civic Courage: The Negative Effect of Transparency on Making Small Campaign Contributions*, 36 Pol. Behavior 753 (2013).

Even if disclosure of a person's name, identifying information, and political contributions represents an acceptable intrusion on privacy in discrete instances, what about the cumulative effect of such disclosures?

> [A] critical aspect of the modern threat to privacy arises from the aggregation of vast quantities of information about individuals. These "digital dossiers" permit data mining with sophisticated algorithms to search for patterns of behavior and taste. Marketers, creditors, government officials, employers, and many others—including political campaigns—can reach additional inferences about individuals' preferences and proclivities with these tools. Each drop of information added to the mix seems trivial, but the cumulative effect is profound. Digital dossiers contain plentiful data from disclosed public records, including such items as voter turnout, political contributions, and petition signing.

William McGeveran, *Mrs. McIntyre's Persona: Bringing Privacy Theory to Election Law*, 19 Wm. & Mary Bill Rts. J. 859, 873 (2011). Should this kind of cumulative publication of information about the political behavior of individuals raise privacy concerns that are not adequately accounted for in the Court's calculus of disclosure?

≫   ***Disclosure of Contributions for Ballot Measures.***   As *Buckley* makes clear, an important justification for disclosing contributions to candidates is to police the risk of quid pro quo corruption—the kind of deal in which officials do favors for those who have given them money, and contributors give money in whole or in part for the purpose of obtaining such influence. This consideration is not present, however, where contributions are made not to support or oppose candidates for public office, but to support or oppose ballot measures—there is no official who can be corrupted. (For more on this issue, see Chapter 9.) Thus, the only significant justification for requiring disclosure of contributions for and against ballot measures is informational. Is that interest sufficient to sustain them? So far, the answer is yes. Both the First and Ninth Circuits have sustained state laws requiring such disclosure on the ground that the state interest in an informed electorate is sufficient. *See National Organization for Marriage, Inc. v. McKee*, 669 F.3d 34 (1st Cir. 2012); *Family PAC v. McKenna*, 664 F.3d 296 (9th Cir. 2012).

3.   *Disclosure of Petition Signing*

In states that permit initiative lawmaking, proposed constitutional amendments or legislation can be placed on the ballot for popular consideration if enough voters sign a petition so demanding. State law governing petition signatures often requires the collection of information about petition signers—addresses or other contact information, for example—often for the purpose of facilitating verification of their eligibility to sign. Should such information be disclosed publicly? The following case takes up that question.

Doe #1 v. Reed

130 S. Ct. 2811 (2010)

Chief Justice ROBERTS delivered the opinion of the Court.

The State of Washington allows its citizens to challenge state laws by referendum. Roughly four percent of Washington voters must sign a petition to place such a referendum on the ballot. That petition, which by law must include the names and addresses of the signers, is then submitted to the government for verification and canvassing, to ensure that only lawful signatures are counted. The Washington Public Records Act (PRA) authorizes private parties to obtain copies of government documents, and the State construes the PRA to cover submitted referendum petitions.

This case arises out of a state law extending certain benefits to same-sex couples, and a corresponding referendum petition to put that law to a popular vote. Respondent-intervenors invoked the PRA to obtain copies of the petition, with the names and addresses of the signers. Certain petition signers and the petition sponsor objected, arguing that such public disclosure would violate their rights under the First Amendment.

The course of this litigation, however, has framed the legal question before us more broadly. The issue at this stage of the case is not whether disclosure of this particular petition would violate the First Amendment, but whether disclosure of referendum petitions in general would do so. We conclude that such disclosure does not as a general matter violate the First Amendment, and we therefore affirm the judgment of the Court of Appeals. . . .

I

The Washington Constitution reserves to the people the power to reject any bill . . . through the referendum process. Wash. Const., Art. II, §1(b). To initiate a referendum, proponents must file a petition with the secretary of state that contains valid signatures of registered Washington voters equal to or exceeding four percent of the votes cast for the office of Governor at the last gubernatorial election. §§1(b), (d). A valid submission requires not only a signature, but also the signer's address and the county in which he is registered to vote. Wash. Rev. Code §29A.72.130 (2008).

In May 2009, Washington Governor Christine Gregoire signed into law Senate Bill 5688, which "expand[ed] the rights and responsibilities" of state-registered domestic partners, including same-sex domestic partners. 586 F.3d 671, 675 (C.A.9 2009). That same month, Protect Marriage Washington, one of the petitioners here, was organized as a "State Political Committee" for the purpose of collecting the petition signatures necessary to place a referendum on the ballot, which would give the voters themselves an opportunity to vote on SB 5688. If the referendum made it onto the ballot, Protect Marriage Washington planned to encourage voters to reject SB 5688.

On July 25, 2009, Protect Marriage Washington submitted to the secretary of state a petition containing over 137,000 signatures. . . . [T]he referendum (R-71) appeared on the November 2009 ballot. The voters approved SB 5688 by a margin of 53% to 47%.

The PRA, Wash. Rev. Code §42.56.001 et seq., makes all "public records" available for public inspection and copying. §42.56.070(1) (2008). The Act defines "[p]ublic record" as "any writing containing information relating to the conduct of government or the performance of any governmental or proprietary function prepared, owned, used, or retained by any state or local agency." §42.56.010(2). Washington takes the position that referendum petitions are "public records."

By August 20, 2009, the secretary had received requests for copies of the R-71 petition from an individual and four entities, including Washington Coalition for Open Government (WCOG) and Washington Families Standing Together (WFST), two of the respondents here. Two entities, WhoSigned.org and KnowThyNeighbor.org, issued a joint press release stating their intention to post the names of the R-71 petition signers online, in a searchable format.

The referendum petition sponsor and certain signers filed a complaint and a motion for a preliminary injunction in the United States District Court . . . seeking to enjoin the secretary of state from publicly releasing any documents that would reveal the names and contact information of the R-71 petition signers. . . . [The District Court held that the plaintiffs were likely to succeed on the merits of Count I, which alleged that the PRA was unconstitutional as applied to referendum petitions, and therefore granted the preliminary injunction. The Ninth Circuit Court of Appeals reversed.]

III

A

The compelled disclosure of signatory information on referendum petitions is subject to review under the First Amendment. An individual expresses a view on a political matter when he signs a petition under Washington's referendum procedure. In most cases, the individual's signature will express the view that the law subject to the petition should be overturned. Even if the signer is agnostic as to the merits of the underlying law, his signature still expresses the political view that the question should be considered "by the whole electorate." *Meyer v. Grant*, 486 U.S. 414, 421 (1988). In either case, the expression of a political view implicates a First Amendment right. . . .

Respondents counter that signing a petition is a legally operative legislative act and therefore does not involve any significant expressive element. It is true that signing a referendum petition may ultimately have the legal consequence of requiring the secretary of state to place the referendum on the ballot. But we do not see how adding such legal effect to an expressive activity somehow deprives that activity of its expressive component, taking it outside the scope of the First Amendment. . . .

Petition signing remains expressive even when it has legal effect in the electoral process. But that is not to say that the electoral context is irrelevant to the nature of our First Amendment review. We allow States significant flexibility in implementing their own voting systems. To the extent a regulation concerns the legal effect of a particular activity in that process, the government will be afforded substantial latitude to enforce that regulation. Also pertinent to our analysis is the fact that the PRA is not a prohibition on speech, but instead a disclosure requirement . . . [which] do[es] not prevent anyone from speaking.

We have a series of precedents considering First Amendment challenges to disclosure requirements in the electoral context. These precedents have reviewed such challenges under what has been termed "exacting scrutiny." That standard "requires a 'substantial relation' between the disclosure requirement and a 'sufficiently important' governmental interest." *Citizens United*, 130 S. Ct., at 914 (quoting *Buckley, supra*, at 64, 66, 96 S. Ct. 612). To withstand this scrutiny, "the strength of the governmental interest must reflect the seriousness of the actual burden on First Amendment rights."

B

Respondents assert two interests to justify the burdens of compelled disclosure under the PRA on First Amendment rights: (1) preserving the integrity of the electoral process by combating fraud, detecting invalid signatures, and fostering government transparency and accountability; and (2) providing information to the electorate about who supports the petition. Because we determine that the State's interest in preserving the integrity of the electoral process suffices to defeat the argument that the PRA is unconstitutional with respect to referendum petitions in general, we need not, and do not, address the State's "informational" interest.

The State's interest in preserving the integrity of the electoral process is undoubtedly important. "States allowing ballot initiatives have considerable leeway to protect the integrity and reliability of the initiative process, as they have with respect to election processes generally." *Buckley v. American Constitutional Law Foundation*, 525 U.S. 182, 191 (1999). The State's interest is particularly strong with respect to efforts to root out fraud, which not only may produce fraudulent outcomes, but has a systemic effect as well: It "drives honest citizens out of the democratic process and breeds distrust of our government." *Purcell v. Gonzalez*, 549 U.S. 1, 4 (2006) (per curiam). The threat of fraud in this context is not merely hypothetical; respondents and their amici cite a number of cases of petition-related fraud across the country to support the point.

But the State's interest in preserving electoral integrity is not limited to combating fraud. That interest extends to efforts to ferret out invalid signatures caused not by fraud but by simple mistake, such as duplicate signatures or signatures of individuals who are not registered to vote in the State. That interest also extends more generally to promoting transparency and accountability in the electoral process, which the State argues is essential to the proper functioning of a democracy.

Plaintiffs contend that the disclosure requirements of the PRA are not "sufficiently related" to the interest of protecting the integrity of the electoral process. They argue that disclosure is not necessary because the secretary of state is already charged with verifying and canvassing the names on a petition, advocates and opponents of a measure can observe that process, and any citizen can challenge the secretary's actions in court. They also stress that existing criminal penalties reduce the danger of fraud in the petition process.

But the secretary's verification and canvassing will not catch all invalid signatures: The job is large and difficult . . . and the secretary can make mistakes, too. Public disclosure can help cure the inadequacies of the verification and canvassing process.

Disclosure also helps prevent certain types of petition fraud otherwise difficult to detect, such as outright forgery and "bait and switch" fraud, in which an individual signs the petition based on a misrepresentation of the underlying issue. The signer is in the best position to detect these types of fraud, and public disclosure can bring the issue to the signer's attention.

Public disclosure thus helps ensure that the only signatures counted are those that should be, and that the only referenda placed on the ballot are those that garner enough valid signatures. Public disclosure also promotes transparency and accountability in the electoral process to an extent other measures cannot. In light of the foregoing, we reject plaintiffs' argument and conclude that public disclosure of referendum petitions in general is substantially related to the important interest of preserving the integrity of the electoral process.

C

Plaintiffs' more significant objection is that "the strength of the governmental interest" does not "reflect the seriousness of the actual burden on First Amendment rights." According to plaintiffs, the objective of those seeking disclosure of the R-71 petition is not to prevent fraud, but to publicly identify those who had validly signed and to broadcast the signers' political views on the subject of the petition. . . .

Plaintiffs explain that once on the Internet, the petition signers' names and addresses can be combined with publicly available phone numbers and maps, in what will effectively become a blueprint for harassment and intimidation. . . .

In related contexts, we have explained that those resisting disclosure can prevail under the First Amendment if they can show "a reasonable probability that the compelled disclosure [of personal information] will subject them to threats, harassment, or reprisals from either Government officials or private parties." *Buckley, supra*, at 74. The question before us, however, is not whether PRA disclosure violates the First Amendment with respect to those who signed the R-71 petition, or other particularly controversial petitions. The question instead is whether such disclosure in general violates the First Amendment rights of those who sign referendum petitions.

The problem for plaintiffs is that their argument rests almost entirely on the specific harm they say would attend disclosure of the information on the R-71 petition, or on similarly controversial ones. But typical referendum petitions concern tax policy, revenue, budget, or other state law issues. Voters care about such issues, some quite deeply—but there is no reason to assume that any burdens imposed by disclosure of typical referendum petitions would be remotely like the burdens plaintiffs fear in this case.

Plaintiffs have offered little in response. They have provided us scant evidence or argument beyond the burdens they assert disclosure would impose on R-71 petition signers or the signers of other similarly controversial petitions. . . .

Faced with the State's unrebutted arguments that only modest burdens attend the disclosure of a typical petition, we must reject plaintiffs' broad challenge to the PRA. In doing so, we note—as we have in other election law disclosure cases—that upholding the law against a broad-based challenge does not foreclose a litigant's success in a narrower one. . . .

We conclude that disclosure under the PRA would not violate the First Amendment with respect to referendum petitions in general and therefore affirm the judgment of the Court of Appeals.

Justice ALITO, concurring:

In my view, respondents' asserted informational interest will not in any case be sufficient to trump the First Amendment rights of signers and circulators who face a threat of harassment. Respondents maintain that publicly disclosing the names and addresses of referendum signatories provides the voting public with "insight into whether support for holding a vote comes predominantly from particular interest groups, political or religious organizations, or other group[s] of citizens," and thus allows voters to draw inferences about whether they should support or oppose the referendum. Additionally, respondents argue that disclosure "allows Washington voters to engage in discussion of referred measures with persons whose acts secured the election and suspension of state law."

The implications of accepting such an argument are breathtaking. Were we to accept respondents' asserted informational interest, the State would be free to require petition signers to disclose all kinds of demographic information, including the signer's race, religion, political affiliation, sexual orientation, ethnic background, and interest-group memberships. Requiring such disclosures, however, runs headfirst into a half century of our case law, which firmly establishes that individuals have a right to privacy of belief and association. . . .

Respondents' informational interest is no more legitimate when viewed as a means of providing the public with information needed to locate and contact supporters of a referendum. In the name of pursuing such an interest, the State would be free to require petition signers to disclose any information that would more easily enable members of the voting public to contact them and engage them in discussion, including telephone numbers, e-mail addresses, and Internet aliases. Once again, permitting the government to require speakers to disclose such information runs against the current of our associational privacy cases. But more important, when speakers are faced with a reasonable probability of harassment or intimidation, the State no longer has any interest in enabling the public to locate and contact supporters of a particular measure—for in that instance, disclosure becomes a means of facilitating harassment that impermissibly chills the exercise of First Amendment rights. . . .

Respondents also maintain that the State has an interest in preserving the integrity of the referendum process and that public disclosure furthers that interest by helping the State detect fraudulent and mistaken signatures. I agree with the Court that preserving the integrity of the referendum process constitutes a sufficiently important state interest. But I harbor serious doubts as to whether public disclosure of signatory information serves that interest in a way that always "reflect[s] the seriousness of the actual burden on First Amendment rights." *Davis v. Federal Election Comm'n.*

Justice SOTOMAYOR, with whom Justice STEVENS and Justice GINSBURG join, concurring:

In assessing the countervailing interests at stake in this case, we must be mindful of the character of initiatives and referenda. These mechanisms of direct democracy are not compelled by the Federal Constitution. It is instead up to the people of each State, acting in their sovereign capacity, to decide whether and how to permit legislation by popular action. States enjoy "considerable leeway" to choose the subjects that are eligible for placement on the ballot and to specify the requirements for obtaining ballot access. . . . *Buckley v. American Constitutional Law Foundation, Inc.*, 525 U.S. 182, 191 (1999). As the Court properly recognizes, each of these structural decisions "inevitably affects—at least to some degree—the individual's right" to speak about political issues and "to associate with others for political ends." *Anderson v. Celebrezze*, 460 U.S. 780, 788 (1983). For instance, requiring petition signers to be registered voters or to use their real names no doubt limits the ability or willingness of some individuals to undertake the expressive act of signing a petition. Regulations of this nature, however, stand "a step removed from the communicative aspect of petitioning," and the ability of States to impose them can scarcely be doubted. *Buckley*, 525 U.S., at 215 (O'Connor, J., concurring in judgment in part and dissenting in part). It is by no means necessary for a State to prove that such "reasonable, nondiscriminatory restrictions" are narrowly tailored to its interests. *Anderson*, 460 U.S., at 788.

The Court today confirms that the State of Washington's decision to make referendum petition signatures available for public inspection falls squarely within the realm of permissible election-related regulations. Public disclosure of the identity of petition signers, which is the rule in the overwhelming majority of States that use initiatives and referenda, advances States' vital interests in "[p]reserving the integrity of the electoral process, preventing corruption, and sustaining the active, alert responsibility of the individual citizen in a democracy for the wise conduct of government." *First Nat. Bank of Boston v. Bellotti*, 435 U.S. 765, 788-789 (1978) (internal quotation marks and alterations omitted). In a society "in which the citizenry is the final judge of the proper conduct of public business," openness in the democratic process is of "critical importance." *Cox Broadcasting Corp. v. Cohn*, 420 U.S. 469, 495 (1975).

On the other side of the ledger, I view the burden of public disclosure on speech and associational rights as minimal in this context. As this Court has observed with respect to campaign-finance regulations, "disclosure requirements . . . 'do not prevent anyone from speaking.' " *Citizens United*, 130 S. Ct. at 914. When it comes to initiatives and referenda, the impact of public disclosure on expressive interests is even more attenuated. While campaign-finance disclosure injects the government into what would otherwise have been private political activity, the process of legislating by referendum is inherently public. . . . The act of signing typically occurs in public, and the circulators who collect and submit signatures ordinarily owe signers no guarantee of confidentiality. For persons with the "civic courage" to participate in this process, the State's decision to make accessible what they voluntarily place in the public sphere should not deter them from engaging in the expressive act of petition signing. Disclosure of the identity of petition signers, moreover, in no way directly impairs the ability of anyone to speak and associate for political ends either publicly or privately.

Justice SCALIA, concurring in the judgment:

We should not repeat and extend the mistake of *McIntyre v. Ohio Elections Comm'n*, 514 U.S. 334 (1995). There, with neither textual support nor precedents requiring the result, the Court invalidated a form of election regulation that had been widely used by the States since the end of the 19th century. The Court held that an Ohio statute prohibiting the distribution of anonymous campaign literature violated the First and Fourteenth Amendments.

Mrs. McIntyre sought a general right to "speak" anonymously about a referendum. Here, plaintiffs go one step further—they seek a general right to participate anonymously in the referendum itself. Referendum petitions are subject to public disclosure under the Public Records Act (PRA). . . . Plaintiffs contend that disclosure of the names, and other personal information included on the petitions, of those who took this legislative action violates their First Amendment right to anonymity.

When a Washington voter signs a referendum petition subject to the PRA, he is acting as a legislator. The Washington Constitution vests "[t]he legislative authority" of the State in the legislature, but "the people reserve to themselves the power . . . to approve or reject at the polls any act, item, section, or part of any bill, act, or law passed by the legislature." Art. 2, §1. . . .

The filing of a [valid] referendum petition . . . has two legal effects: (1) It requires the secretary to place the measure referred to the people on the ballot at the next general election; and (2) it suspends operation of the measure, causing it only to have effect 30 days after it is approved during that election. A voter who signs a referendum petition is therefore exercising legislative power because his signature, somewhat like a vote for or against a bill in the legislature, seeks to affect the legal force of the measure at issue.

Plaintiffs point to no precedent from this Court holding that legislating is protected by the First Amendment. Nor do they identify historical evidence demonstrating that "the freedom of speech" the First Amendment codified encompassed a right to legislate without public disclosure. This should come as no surprise; the exercise of lawmaking power in the United States has traditionally been public. . . .

The long history of public legislating and voting contradicts plaintiffs' claim that disclosure of petition signatures having legislative effect violates the First Amendment. Just as the century-old practice of States' prohibiting anonymous electioneering was sufficient for me to reject the First Amendment claim to anonymity in *McIntyre*, the many-centuries-old practices of public legislating and voting are sufficient for me to reject plaintiffs' claim.

Plaintiffs raise concerns that the disclosure of petition signatures may lead to threats and intimidation. Of course nothing prevents the people of Washington from keeping petition signatures secret to avoid that—just as nothing prevented the States from moving to the secret ballot. But there is no constitutional basis for this Court to impose that course upon the States—or to insist (as today's opinion does) that it can only be avoided by the demonstration of a "sufficiently important governmental interest." And it may even be a bad idea to keep petition signatures secret. There are laws against threats and intimidation; and harsh criticism, short of unlawful action, is a price our people have traditionally been willing to pay for self-governance. Requiring people to stand up in public for their political acts fosters civic courage, without which democracy is doomed. For my part, I do not look forward to a society which, thanks to the Supreme Court, campaigns anonymously (*McIntyre*) and even exercises the direct democracy of initiative and referendum hidden from public scrutiny and protected from the accountability of criticism. This does not resemble the Home of the Brave.

How much information can the state compel the individual to disclose? Name? Address? Partisan identity? Previous vote history? Financial conflicts of interests? Email address? Social security number?

What are campaigns for and what are the assumptions that we make about the individual voter who is at the heart of the campaign? For Justice Sotomayor, campaigns "sustain[] the active, alert, responsibility of the individual citizen in democracy for the wise conduct of government." To fulfill that responsibility, the individual must have "civic courage." But what if she doesn't have civic courage? Is she not entitled to participate? Is this the view of Justice Scalia? What do you make of his concurrence in this case, in which he relied on historical tradition to reject constitutional limits on public disclosure in this context? Is the search for *homo fort* a futile one?

Trump v. Twitter

___ F.Supp.3d ___, 2022 WL 1443233 (N.D. Cal. 2022)

JAMES DONATO, United States District Judge.

Former President Donald J. Trump, the American Conservative Union, and five individuals have sued Twitter, Inc., and Jack Dorsey (together, Twitter), on behalf of themselves and a putative class of Twitter users who have been "de-platformed" and "censored" by Defendants. Plaintiffs alleged claims under the First Amendment and Florida state consumer and "social media" statutes, and seek a declaration that Section 230 of the Communications Decency Act, which states that online service providers like Twitter cannot be held responsible for content posted by others, is unconstitutional. Twitter has moved to dismiss under Federal Rule of Civil Procedure 12(b)(6). The amended complaint is dismissed.

BACKGROUND

Twitter is the well-known "social networking service that allows its Users to post and interact with each other through short messages known as 'tweets.'" Dorsey co-founded Twitter in 2006, and the company today hosts more than 500 million tweets posted daily by approximately 340 million users worldwide.

Plaintiff Trump opened a Twitter account in May 2009 and was an active user until January 7, 2021. On January 8, 2021, Twitter stated that it had "permanently suspended" the account "due to the risk of further incitement of violence."

The amended complaint alleges that the other named plaintiffs also had their Twitter accounts treated unfavorably.

In plaintiffs' view, these account actions were the result of coercion by members of Congress affiliated with the Democratic Party. Plaintiffs quote Senator Mark Warner (D-VA) as saying on October 28, 2020, that "[w]e can and should have a conversation about Section 230—and the ways in which it has enabled platforms to turn a blind eye as their platforms are used to . . . enable domestic terrorist groups to organize violence in plain sight." Section 230 of the Communications Decency Act is said to have "significantly encouraged defendants' censorship of the plaintiff and the putative class members," and the amended complaint alleges that defendants "willful[ly] participat[ed] in joint activity with federal actors to censor plaintiff and the putative class members."

Plaintiffs allege: (1) a violation of the First Amendment to the United States Constitution; (2) that Section 230 of the Communications Decency Act is unconstitutional; (3) deceptive and misleading practices in violation of the Florida Deceptive and Unfair Trade Practices Act (FDUTPA), Florida Statutes §501.201 et seq.; and (4) a violation of the Stop Social Media Censorship Act (SSMCA), Florida Statutes §501.2041. In the prayer for relief, plaintiffs seek, among other things, compensatory and punitive damages, and injunctive and declaratory relief, including an order for Twitter to "immediately reinstate the Twitter accounts of" plaintiffs.

DISCUSSION

I. TWITTER AND THE FIRST AMENDMENT

Plaintiffs' main claim is that defendants have "censor[ed]" plaintiffs' Twitter accounts in violation of their right to free speech under the First Amendment to the United States Constitution. Plaintiffs are not starting from a position of strength. Twitter is a private company, and "the First Amendment applies only to governmental abridgements of speech, and not to alleged abridgements by private companies." *Williby v. Zuckerberg.*

Plaintiffs' only hope of stating a First Amendment claim is to plausibly allege that Twitter was in effect operating as the government under the "state-action doctrine." This doctrine provides that, in some situations, "governmental authority may dominate an activity to such an extent that its participants must be deemed to act with the authority of the government and, as a result, be subject to constitutional constraints." *Edmonson v. Leesville Concrete Co.* This is not an easy claim to make, for good reasons. Private entities are presumed to act as such, and maintaining the line "between the private sphere and the public sphere, with all its attendant constitutional obligations," is a matter of great importance, as "[o]ne great object of the Constitution is to permit citizens to structure their private relations as they choose subject only to the constraints of statutory or decisional law." *Edmonson.* "As a matter of substantive constitutional law the state-action requirement reflects judicial recognition of the fact that 'most rights secured by the Constitution are protected only against infringement by governments.' " *Lugar v. Edmondson Oil Co., Inc.*

The salient question under the state action doctrine is whether "the conduct allegedly causing the deprivation of a federal right" is "fairly attributable to the State." The answer is determined by a "two-part approach," which requires that "the deprivation must be caused by the exercise of some right or privilege created by the State or by a rule of conduct imposed by the state or by a person for whom the State is responsible"; and that "the party charged with the deprivation must be a person who may fairly be said to be a state actor." *Lugar.* These factors "are not the same," and they "diverge when the constitutional claim is directed . . . against a private party." *Lugar.*

The amended complaint does not plausibly show that plaintiffs' ostensible First Amendment injury was caused by "a rule of conduct imposed by the government." The amended complaint merely offers a grab-bag of allegations to the effect that some Democratic members of Congress wanted Mr. Trump, and "the views he espoused," to be banned from Twitter because such "content and views" were "contrary to those legislators' preferred points of view." But the comments of a handful of elected officials are a far cry from a "rule of decision for which the State is responsible." Legislators are perfectly free to express opinions without being deemed the official voice of "the State." Government in our republic of elected representatives would be impossible otherwise. It is also not plausible to conclude that Twitter or any other listener could discern a clear state rule in such remarks, or even determine what a legislator's "preferred views" might be.

The weakness of the state action theory in the amended complaint is further demonstrated by plaintiffs' own explanation of why their accounts were closed. Twitter is said to have closed Mr. Trump's account because of "the risk of further incitement of violence" and "threats to physical safety."

The amended complaint also does not plausibly allege that Twitter could fairly be deemed to be a state actor. Plaintiffs say they have done so by cataloguing "coercive statements" in paragraph 55 of the amended complaint, and statements made during a March 22, 2021, House Committee on Energy and Commerce hearing on the topic of "Disinformation Nation: Social Media's Role in Promoting Extremism and Misinformation." These statements are said to have compelled Twitter to act as a government entity.

They are again not enough for pleading purposes. Paragraph 55 is said to offer "examples of Democrat legislators threatening new regulations, antitrust breakup, and removal of Section 230 immunity for Defendants and other social media platforms if Twitter did not censor views and content with which these Members of Congress disagreed." The actual quotes do not live up to that billing. The statements attributed to "Bruce Reed, Biden's Top Tech Advisor," and Michelle Obama are of no moment because Reed and Obama were not legislators. Then-Senator Kamala Harris is quoted three times for calling for "Trump's Twitter account [to be] suspended" and calling on Dorsey to "do something about this Tweet" from Trump, but conspicuously missing is any threatening remark directed to Twitter.

The statements attributed to the "Disinformation Nation" congressional hearing may have been more heated, but they are still not enough to satisfy plaintiffs' pleading obligation. Committee Chairman Frank Pallone, Jr., is quoted as saying, "it is time for Congress and this Committee to legislate and realign these companies' incentives to effectively deal with disinformation and extremism. . . . The time for self-regulation is over. It is time we legislate to hold you accountable." Representative Mike Doyle said, "Your companies need to be held accountable . . . and we will legislate to stop this." Id. Representative Janice D. Schakowsky said, "What our witnesses need to take away from this hearing is that self-regulation has come to the end of its road, and that this democratically elected body is prepared to move forward with legislation and regulation. Misinformation regarding the election dropped by 73% across social media platforms after Twitter permanently suspended Trump . . . . The question is, what took so long?"

Even giving plaintiffs every benefit of the doubt, these comments fall short of the mark. Plaintiffs' own case citations show why. Strictly speaking, not all of plaintiffs' cases involve the state action doctrine, as the ensuing discussion makes clear. Nevertheless, plaintiffs argued the cases to that end, and the Court will take those arguments on their own terms.

[The Court discusses a series of cases.]

These cases, which are the centerpieces of plaintiffs' state action argument, are strikingly different from the allegations in the amended complaint. In each of the cases, a concrete and specific government action, or threatened action, was identified. Here, plaintiffs offer only ambiguous and open-ended statements to the effect that "we may legislate" something unfavorable to Twitter or the social media sector. This is a world away from: (1) a state commission sending local police officers for drop-in visits and threatening prosecution by the state attorney general (*Bantam Books*); (2) a city mayor and police superintendent threatening law enforcement action to crack down on sit-in demonstrations (*Lombard*); (3) a deputy county attorney threatening prosecution against a private company under a specific law (Carlin); and (4) a federal administrative commission threatening the suspension of licenses or formal rulemaking if its specified elements for an anti-drug program were not followed voluntarily (*Mathis*).

Plaintiffs also overlook Congress's role as an investigatory body, and the fact that "each House has power 'to secure needed information' in order to legislate." *Trump v. Mazars USA, LLP.* This power "encompasses inquiries into the administration of existing laws, studies of proposed laws, and 'surveys of defects in our social, economic or political system for the purpose of enabling the Congress to remedy them.'"

Much of what plaintiffs challenge fits within the normal boundaries of a congressional investigation, as opposed to threats of punitive state action. Plaintiffs' own submissions indicate that the House Committee was making inquiries and surveying possible problems "for the purpose of enabling the Congress to remedy them." In this respect, the allegations in the amended complaint are much more comparable to the cases plaintiffs cited in which no state action was found.

Overall, the amended complaint does not plausibly allege that Twitter acted as a government entity when it closed plaintiffs' accounts. This resolves the main thrust of plaintiffs' state action theory.

Consequently, the amended complaint does not plausibly allege a First Amendment claim against Twitter. Plaintiffs' first claim is dismissed.

II. SECTION 230

Plaintiffs' claim for a declaratory judgment that Section 230 is unconstitutional is dismissed for lack of standing.

III. THE FDUTPA CLAIM

Twitter says that plaintiffs' third claim under the Florida Deceptive and Unfair Trade Practices Act should be dismissed because plaintiffs have agreed, pursuant to the Twitter Terms of Service (TOS), that California law will govern all disputes that arise between Twitter and its users. Dkt. No. 138 at 14. Plaintiffs do not dispute that the TOS is a valid contract between the parties, or that it includes an express choice of California law.

Although this is enough to dismiss the third claim, some additional observations are useful. A good argument can be made that plaintiffs did not plausibly allege deceptive conduct by Twitter for purposes of either the FDUTPA or the UCL. The TOS expressly states that Twitter may suspend or terminate an account "at any time for any or no reason." It also states that Twitter may remove or refuse to distribute any content. There is nothing cagey or misleading about these provisions, and plaintiffs' suggestion that Twitter may have applied them inconsistently, or at the government's behest, does not change that. The TOS gave Twitter contractual permission to act as it saw fit with respect to any account or content for any or no reason, which makes its ostensible motives irrelevant for a deceptive practices claim.

IV. THE SSMCA CLAIM

Plaintiffs' fourth claim under Florida's Stop Social Media Censorship Act is also due for dismissal. Twitter did not make a choice-of-law argument for this claim, see Dkt. No. 138 at 14-19, and so the Court addresses the SSMCA claim on its own terms.

An initial problem for plaintiffs is that only one named plaintiff was a Florida resident with any active Twitter account at the time the statute took effect on July 1, 2021, and so he is the only plaintiff who might conceivably have a SSMCA claim.

Another problem is that plaintiffs say they are challenging only conduct that occurred after the SSMCA effective date. But the amended complaint focuses on actions affecting plaintiffs' accounts prior to July 1, 2021.

There is also a major concern about the enforceability of the SSMCA. Florida government officials were enjoined from enforcing the SSMCA on June 30, 2021, the day before the law was to take effect, in a well-reasoned decision issued by the Northern District of Florida. *NetChoice, LLC v. Moody*. The Court declines plaintiffs' invitation to disregard this decision, particularly while an appeal is pending, and dismisses the SSMCA claim without prejudice.

CONCLUSION

The amended complaint is dismissed in its entirety.

———————

In earlier litigation, individual Twitter users who had subscribed to President Trump's Twitter account brought suit against Mr. Trump when he blocked them after they posted replies to some of the President's tweets that were critical of him or his policies. Trump defended by arguing that a Twitter account is a private channel of communication even when used by the president himself. In *Knight First Amendment Institute v. Trump,* 928 F.3d 226 (9th Cir. 2019), the Ninth Circuit ruled that Trump's routine use of Twitter as a vehicle for conducting official government business converted decisions about access to his account into state action subject to the First Amendment. Trump's blockage from the account exclusively of critics thus amounted to forbidden viewpoint discrimination. The Supreme Court later issued a summary ruling vacating the decision as moot, presumably because Trump had been blocked from Twitter and no longer controlled his account.

We end this chapter where we started it. Is the traditional legal framework, which prohibits the government from regulating political speech, capable of addressing the challenges posed by the new social media landscape? Is private ordering a viable solution? Are you comfortable with Twitter banning a major American political figure, a former President of the United States, a potential future political candidate, from its indispensable communication platform? Is banning a speaker from the marketplace of ideas consistent with political liberalism?

MONEY, POLITICS, AND LAW

"Our politics are a disgrace," lamented the noted political philosopher Ronald Dworkin, "and money is the root of the problem." RONALD DWORKIN, SOVEREIGN VIRTUE 351 (2000). For Dworkin, money was a problem in American politics because the need for financing political campaigns compels politicians to engage in continual and unceasing fundraising. Politicians are often raising money for their next election soon after their last "and often put more time and industry into that task than into those for which they were elected. They spend the bulk of the campaign money they raise, moreover, on television ads that are often negative and nearly always inane, substituting slogans and jingles for argument." *Id.*

Dworkin's view reflected, more or less, the twentieth-century consensus among reformers that our politics are broken because of how we finance our campaigns. Politicians are too dependent upon rich donors and private interests to fund their campaigns. Once in office, because of this dependency, politicians tend to reward their past and future funders with favorable legislation, at the expense of ordinary voters. From 1976, after the Court decided the landmark campaign finance case of *Buckley v. Valeo* (below), election law framed the problem of money in politics as essentially a problem of campaign financing, particularly the outsized ability of rich entities, people, and corporations to use their disproportionate wealth to get their politicians elected.

In 2016, the financier Donald Trump ran for President, and he ran as a populist—promising to look out for the underdog against the rich elites. Trump declared his independence from wealthy elites, vowed to put struggling Americans first, promised to "drain the swamp," and, to quote his campaign slogan, "Make America Great Again." Consistent with his populist appeal, he also promised to finance his campaign differently. As Lauren Carroll of PolitiFact reported during the race for the Republican nomination, Trump stated, "You know a lot of times you see these really dumb deals. And you'll say that's dumb. It doesn't make sense. But then when you think, it does make sense because these politicians are representing interests, whether it's a country or a company, where doing the stupid deals actually makes sense only for that politician and for that company or country." Trump claimed that he would be different because he would self-finance his campaign. He promised to spend $100 million of his own money on his campaign. https://www.politifact.com/factchecks/2016/feb/10/donald-trump/donald-trump-self-funding-his-campaign-sort.

Trump did not fulfill his campaign promise that he would spend $100 million of his own money, and he reneged on the implication that he would totally self-finance his campaign. But he did self-finance most of his campaign for the Republican nomination. A CNN analysis concluded that Trump's campaign for the Republican nomination received about 25 percent of its funding from private donors and about 75 percent from Trump himself. But Trump largely relied on private financing for the general election campaign. He raised more than 75 percent of his campaign funds from private sources. https://www.wsj.com/articles/BL-WB-66493.

From the point of view of the twentieth-century consensus, Trump's 2016 campaign should have been viewed as a welcome correction to what almost all agreed ailed our politics. Compared to his political opponent, the 2016 Democratic nominee, Hillary Clinton, Trump financed his campaign differently, even if the difference was in degree and not in kind. Trump did not rely as much on ideologically allied super PACs, funded by individuals contributing $1 million or more to the PAC; it did not rely on fundraising by registered lobbyists; it raised less money overall; it spent less overall; and, of course, Trump contributed more of his money to his campaign. The appeal of populism is the contention that the populist will rule in the public interest and a self-financed campaign could indicate an early return on that promise.

From a different vantage point, Trump's 2016 presidential could also illustrate the limitations of the twentieth-century consensus, which focused too narrowly on campaign financing as a critical explanation for what is wrong with American politics. As opposed to illustrating the potential of populism, Trump's campaign might better serve as an illustration of its peril and in some respects a uniquely American one. "In little more than ten months, elections featuring Brexit, Donald Trump and Marine Le Pen took place in three of the world's oldest democracies," the Berkeley political scientist Paul Pierson observed. "Understandably, this combination has intensified an already growing interest in right-wing populism. The evidence that this is a cross-national phenomenon is abundant."

However, Pierson argued, notwithstanding what appears to be a co-occurring phenomenon — emerging populist movements in parts of Europe and the United States that share, superficially, similarities — Trumpian populism, Pierson explained, is "a curious hybrid of populism and plutocracy," in contrast to the emergent European populism. "If one shifts from thinking about populism as a cultural or electoral force to examining its influence on governance — its actual impact on the control of public authority, and the priorities towards which that authority is directed," Pierson argued that "the image of populism as a relatively uniform wave of social change sweeping across the landscape of liberal democracies begins to break apart." In particular, "Trump has filled his administration with a mix of the staggeringly wealthy and the staggeringly reactionary. On the big economic issues of taxes, spending, and regulation — ones that have animated conservative elites for a generation — he has pursued, or supported, an agenda that is extremely friendly to large corporations, wealthy families, and well-positioned rent-seekers." Pierson was writing toward the beginning of the Trump presidency, and he predicted that Trump's "budgetary policies (and those pursued by his Republican allies in Congress) will, if enacted, be devastating to the same rural and moderate-income communities that helped him win office." Paul Pierson, *American Hybrid: Donald Trump and the Strange Merger of Populism and Plutocracy*, 68 Brit. J. Soc. 106, 107 (2017).

Pierson's analysis of Trumpian populism helps us frame the problem with money in politics, as it is presenting itself in the twenty-first century, beyond the twentieth-century consensus. In the twenty-first century, the issue of money in politics is not only about how our campaigns are financed, it is about economic inequality more broadly and the relationship among economic inequality, democratic politics, and law. In the United States, the top 1 percent earn more than 22 percent of the income. By contrast, the top 1 percent in the United Kingdom earn under 14 percent, in Germany 13 percent; in France 12 percent; in Finland 10 percent; and in Sweden 9 percent. The United States is much closer to India, Iraq, Namibia, the United Arab Emirates, Turkey, and Thailand, than it is to most countries in Western Europe. As two political scientists, Jacob Hacker and Paul Pierson, have noted: "Runaway inequality has remade American politics, reorienting power and policy toward corporations and the superrich (particularly the most conservative among them). . . . Over the last forty years, the wealthiest Americans and the biggest financial and corporate interests have amassed wealth on a scale unimaginable to prior generations and without parallel in other western democracies. The richest 0.1 percent of Americans now have roughly as much wealth as the bottom 90 percent combined." Jacob S. Hacker & Paul Pierson, Let Them Eat Tweets: How the Right Rule in an Age of Extreme Inequality 1-2 (2020). The super-rich are, moreover, very willing to invest their resources in politics. Since 2010, the top twelve individual megadonors and their spouses—19 people—have donated about one out of every thirteen dollars contributed in federal elections. Twenty-five percent of all contributions to federal campaigns come from the one hundred richest zip codes. Michael Beckel, *Outsized Influence* (IssueOne 2021).

The extent of economic inequality in the United States raises a critical question for students of democracy: are economic inequality and political equality compatible bedfellows, or must one cede to the other? Or, to put the question differently, how is economic inequality reconcilable with the recent surge of populism that we see around the world and in the United States? Hacker and Pierson offer an intriguing answer. "In other rich countries where right-wing populists are challenging for power," populist appeals, even ones based upon race, "get[] coupled with fervent defense of social benefits for white citizens." *Id.* at 5. In those countries, populism is anti-plutocratic. Hacker and Pierson argue that this is not the case in the United States. Here, "plutocracy and right-wing populism have not been opposing forces." *Id.* They call this hybrid American approach "plutocratic populism." *Id.* Moreover, Hacker and Pierson insist that even though "American plutocracy has transformed both of American's two great political parties," the Republican Party has been affected more than the Democrats. *Id.* at 2. "As the power of the plutocrats has increased, America's conservative party has shifted not just to the right of conservative parties in other nations, but to the right of many right-wing parties. And the rightward movement has occurred precisely on those issues where the party's plutocratic supporters have the most radical goals." *Id.* at 2.

The depth of economic inequality in the United States and its relationship to political inequality also raises profound questions for election law and students of

736 Chapter 9. Money, Politics, and Law

law and democracy: what role does law play in mediating the relationship between economic inequality and political inequality? Our goal in this chapter is to explore the role that law has played in shaping the role of money in American politics. Moreover, we are interested in understanding how the Supreme Court has interpreted the Constitution and federal statutes to make it harder for ordinary voters and their representatives to limit the scope of "plutocratic populism." Before jumping into the cases, we begin this chapter with a short history of campaign finance reform. We will then turn to the landmark case of *Buckley v. Valeo*, where the Supreme Court addressed and dismantled Congress's first comprehensive legislative effort, the Federal Election Campaign Act of 1974, which regulated the flow of money in financing political campaigns. We contrast the Court's approach to the Act with its mostly deferential stance to Congress's second attempt at comprehensive reform in the Bipartisan Campaign Reform Act of 2002. As you read the materials that follow, consider how they promote or inhibit plutocracy and democratic inequality.

A. SHORT HISTORY OF CAMPAIGN FINANCE REFORM

For as long as there have been campaigns, there have been questions about how to finance them. In the United States, concerns over financing campaigns for public office have been around since before the writing of the Constitution. Candidates traded influence, power, and gifts for constituents' money and votes even before the dawn of the Republic. In 1757, George Washington — later President, but at the time, a candidate for the Virginia House of Burgesses — bestowed upon the 391 voters in his district the "customary means" of winning votes: "28 gallons of rum, 50 gallons of rum punch, 34 gallons of wine, 46 gallons of beer, and 2 gallons of cider royal." James Madison lost his reelection campaign to the Virginia legislature 20 years later because he refused to supply voters with the customary whiskey.

Historically, not much money was needed to run campaigns. Eighteenth-century campaigning did not involve the expenditure of significant sums. In fact, campaigning for office was disfavored; gentlemen stood for office, they did not run for office. By the nineteenth century, trading for votes became more commonplace. The patronage system that flourished in the United States became a defining aspect of campaign financing in the 1820s. Under this system, a successful candidate would grant civil-service appointments to his political supporters. The dangers of this system were made abundantly clear on July 2, 1881, when Charles J. Guiteau, a campaign supporter — one unfortunately afflicted with a grave mental illness — shot President James A. Garfield because Garfield had refused to grant Guiteau the ambassadorship to which he felt entitled. In 1883, in response to Garfield's assassination, the Pendleton Civil Service Act was passed, outlawing the patronage system. This effectively ended one long-standing method of campaign finance quid pro quo.

The cost of elections rose precipitously throughout the nineteenth century — particularly after the passage of the Pendleton Act — mirroring the rise of corporations in American economic life. Corporations donated funds to friendly politicians and those politicians quickly turned to extortion to squeeze more money from their corporate donors. Senator Boies Penrose, a prominent Republican from Pennsylvania, was well-known for corruption and famously stated, "I believe in the division of labor. You send us to Congress; we pass laws under which you make money . . . and out of your profits, you further contribute to our campaign funds to send us back again to pass more laws to enable you to make more money." Penrose was infamous for introducing regulatory bills — called "squeeze bills" — that he would only kill in committee in exchange for corporate donations; he once reportedly raised $250,000 in 48 hours, an astounding sum for the time.

Corrupt behavior like Penrose's, along with the wildly expensive 1896 presidential election — in which William McKinley spent almost $7 million — led to the passage of the Tillman Act of 1907. The Tillman Act prohibited

> any national bank, or any corporation organized by authority of any laws of Congress, to make a money contribution in connection with any election to any political office. It shall also be unlawful for any corporation whatever to make a money contribution in connection with any election at which Presidential and Vice-Presidential electors or a Representative in Congress is to be voted for or any election by any State legislature of a United States Senator.

Corporations that violated the Act were subjected to a fine of $5,000. The Tillman Act did little to limit corporate spending on campaigns because it contained no real enforcement mechanism.

In 1910, Congress passed the Federal Corrupt Practices Act (FCPA), which required candidates for the House of Representatives to disclose — 30 days after an election — the names of contributors of $100 or more as well as expenditures of $10 or more. The Act was amended in 1911 to extend reporting requirements to Senate candidates and mandated that preliminary reports be filed between 10 and 15 days before an election and every sixth day until the election. More significantly, the FCPA was amended to tie contribution and expenditure limits of federal candidates to those in the states in which federal candidates were running. The FCPA prohibited candidates running for the House of Representatives to spend more than $5,000 and candidates running for the Senate to spend more than $10,000.

Although the FCPA purported to limit spending throughout the election cycle, the Supreme Court struck down the provisions as to primaries and nominating conventions in its 1921 decision in *Newberry v. United States*. Consequently, the FCPA had little effect in the Democratic-dominated South where the winner of the primaries generally won the election.

The early 1920s also saw the Teapot Dome scandal. In 1921, President Harding issued an executive order transferring certain oil fields, including Teapot Dome, to the Department of the Interior. Secretary of the Interior Albert B. Fall, after gaining control of the fields, moved to lease oil production rights without competitive bidding. Two of the companies that leased rights were Pan American Petroleum and Mammoth Oil, the owners of which gave Fall gifts and no-interest loans of almost $500,000. The Senate launched an investigation and, in 1923, the American public became aware of what had happened. President Harding died shortly after the story broke, and some believe that the news led to the President's fatal stroke.

Largely because of the Teapot Dome Scandal and the Supreme Court decision in *Newberry*, Congress rewrote the FCPA in 1925. The new version included many of the same provisions enacted in 1911 but restricted coverage to "general or special election[s]." Spending limits were raised slightly to $25,000 for Senate candidates and $5,000 for House candidates. Candidates now had to turn in, to the Senate or House clerk, receipts accounting for the expenditures made in the race. Furthermore, both candidates and committees were required to disclose their contributors more often, including the names and addresses of all contributors who gave over $100. The biggest change was a total ban on contributions from corporations and banks.

While this version of the FCPA seemed stronger, the 1925 legislation had three flaws. First, despite the claims of some commentators that *Newberry* did not explicitly overrule Congress's ability to regulate primary elections, Congress did not even attempt to bring primary elections under the purview of the FCPA. Ultimately the lack of primary regulations "arose to plague the Senate in [the elections of] 1926."

Second, the expenditure limits were placed on candidates, not on their committees, unless the committee was an "organization which accept[ed] contributions or ma[de] expenditures for the purpose of influencing or attempting to influence the election of candidates . . . (1) in two or more states . . . (2) whether or not . . . [the committee was] a branch or subsidiary of a national committee, association or organization." By establishing many smaller committees operating solely within one state, the FCPA spending limits were easily avoided.

Finally, although the FCPA included a ban on corporate contributions and a requirement to account for expenditures, the law, according to House Clerk William Tyler Page, "ha[d] no teeth in it." All reports were made to the clerks' offices, where there was no record keeping, formalized procedure, or enforcement mechanism. Furthermore, the offices of the clerks were not even open when Congress was not in session. Most alarming, nearly all of the campaign data remained unanalyzed and unpublished in the offices of the clerks.

The FCPA of 1925 was the primary federal campaign-finance legislation for almost 50 years. Over this nearly 50-year period, only one case was ever brought under the FCPA and it ultimately resulted in an acquittal. There were many further attempts at reform but nothing on the scale of the FCPA. The next major statute was the Hatch Act of 1939, which is now widely known for banning federal employees from using their "official authority for the purposes of interfering with or affecting [a federal] election." But the Hatch Act was not truly intended to be a reform measure; its purpose was to "strike at what its sponsors feared was Franklin Roosevelt's growing political power."

In 1947, Congress passed the Taft-Hartley Act, which outlawed direct contributions from unions and was the first time the federal government had attempted to regulate political speech by a particular speaker. But this ban was circumvented through the creation of the first political action committees. Despite increasing pressure from the public and the rising cost of television and radio advertisements, efforts to replace the faltering FCPA stalled due to congressional wrangling.

Congress eventually enacted the Federal Election Campaign Act (FECA) of 1971 and replaced the FCPA with FECA. Though FECA 1971 failed to usher in a new age of campaign finance reform, it promulgated important innovations in American campaign regulation. Its major provisions consisted of:

1. Tighter disclosure requirements and the imposition of a $1,000 limit on individual contributions. Bradley A. Smith, *A Moderate, Modern Campaign Finance Reform Agenda*, 12 NEXUS 23-24 (2007).

2. Limits on expenditures for campaign communications. FECA 1971 set limits on the amount of money a candidate for federal office could spend on so-called communications media, which included television, radio, newspapers, magazines, billboards, and so on. Candidates could use only 60 percent of the money permitted under this provision on "broadcast media." These provisions applied to candidates in federal primaries, except for presidential primaries. Any money spent on behalf of a candidate was counted against a candidate's spending cap.

3. Limitations on contributions and expenditures. FECA 1971 set limits on the amount of money a candidate and her immediate family could contribute to the candidate's campaign. It also set in stone prohibitions on securing funds for corporate or union political action committees by means of force or economic coercion. It forbade donations to federal campaigns by companies engaged as government contractors.

4. FECA officially recognized political action committees and allowed the use of corporate or union money to set them up. *Id.* FECA 1971 described in great detail requirements for the political committees. Disclosure was required for every individual donation of $100 and for donations from a single person that, when aggregated, equaled $100 or greater in a single calendar year. FECA 1971 also required reporting about the campaign's finances, including expenditures, loans, ticket sales, and so on.

FECA 1971 was the most far-reaching campaign-finance law in the history of the federal government, but it was no silver bullet to cure the ills plaguing American political campaigns. FECA encountered many of the same problems as the FCPA. There was still no independent enforcement agency enforcing the rules of FECA. ROBERT E. MUTCH, CAMPAIGNS, CONGRESSES, AND COURTS: THE MAKING OF FEDERAL CAMPAIGN FINANCE LAW 40-41 (1988). This problem became particularly apparent after the election of Richard Nixon when Attorney General John Mitchell failed to investigate any of the many Nixon contributors who did not file a required disclosure report. *Id.* at 28. The lack of a regulatory body had been a problem throughout the history of the FCPA and FECA. President Kennedy's campaign-finance-reform advisor Alexander Heard lamented that the issue could probably not be remedied "unless some startling scandal appears as a catalyst." *Id.* at 42. He turned out to have been prescient.

On June 17, 1972, five men broke into the Democratic National Committee's office in the Watergate office complex in Washington, D.C. Two months later, the five men — along with two others, E. Howard Hunt and G. Gordon Liddy — were indicted by a grand jury for conspiracy, burglary, and violation of federal wire-tapping laws. By the time they were convicted in January 1973, the five burglars had been connected to the Committee to Re-elect the President, a fundraising organization that had supported Nixon's 1972 reelection campaign, resulting in a landslide victory for the incumbent Nixon.

News reporting—most famously by reporters Bob Woodward and Carl Bernstein—relying heavily on anonymous sources like the famed Deep Throat, revealed connections between the break-in at the Watergate complex and increasingly powerful members of the Nixon administration. This information led to a congressional investigation into the Watergate affair, which resulted in Nixon terminating several presidential staffers and appointing a new Attorney General, who appointed a special counsel to conduct an independent investigation of the Watergate affair. The eventual discovery and release of audio recordings documenting Nixon's awareness of and involvement in the Watergate operation, along with initial impeachment proceedings against the President begun by Congress, led to Nixon's resignation on August 8, 1974. His Vice President, Gerald Ford, assumed the presidency the next day.

The connection between the Watergate scandal and campaign finance is not immediately obvious. But the purpose behind Watergate may have actually been related to the finances of the Nixon presidential campaign. First, the Committee to Re-elect the President—the organization to which the Watergate burglars belonged—was ultimately tasked with raising money for the President's reelection campaign. Second, many believe that the target of the initial break-in was Larry O'Brien, then-Chairman of the Democratic National Committee, who had information about illegal donations made by Howard Hughes to the Nixon campaign. FRED EMERY, WATERGATE: THE CORRUPTION OF AMERICAN POLITICS AND THE FALL OF RICHARD NIXON 30 (1995). It is possible that this donation went on to become part of several secret slush funds revealed to have been controlled by the Nixon camp.

In late 1969, Nixon went to his Chief of Staff, H.R. Haldeman, and told him that "[o]ne of [their] most important projects for 1970 [was] to see that [their] major contributors funnel[ed] their funds" through Nixon and his staff. This, Nixon said, would allow them to "see that [the funds were not] wasted in overheads or siphoned off by some possible venal types on the campaign committees" and to "see that they [we]re used more effectively than would be the case if the candidates receive[d] them directly." RICHARD REEVES, PRESIDENT NIXON: ALONE IN THE WHITE HOUSE 153 (2001). Haldeman went on to arrange meetings with Secretary of Commerce Maurice Stans, political strategist Harry Dent, and Dent's assistant John Gleason in order to set up a secret fundraising operation that would bypass the Republican National Committee. This "Town House Project"—so named because it would have to operate out of private offices—was one of several secret money-drop operations controlled by Nixon. *Id.* These funds became the source of finance for the Watergate affair and revealed that at the highest levels, campaign-finance laws were not controlling illegal contributions.

Thus, almost immediately after the passage of FECA 1971, the improprieties committed by Richard Nixon's reelection committee turned a spotlight on the legislation's weaknesses. Moreover, FECA 1971's introduction of contribution and expenditure limitations increased demand for a public-financing structure to protect non-incumbent and minor party candidates. (S. Rep. 93-689.)

The FECA amendments of 1974 reflected Congress's intention to create a single, "comprehensive and far-reaching" campaign-finance structure "for the purpose of providing complete control over and disclosure of campaign contributions and expenditures in campaigns for Federal elective office." Instead of attempting to regulate each aspect of campaign finance piecemeal, the 1974 FECA amendments created a single framework regulating "all elections, all candidates seeking nomination for election or election to Federal office, and all political committees raising or spending in excess of $1,000." (S. Rep. 93-689.)

Many concerns motivated Congress to pass FECA 1974. The first was created by an unfortunate circumstance of timing and a fact of legal life in the United States: when a law has an effective date, there is a push to act *before* that date to avoid the burdens of the law. FECA 1971 had been "predicated upon the principle of public disclosure." Underlying this was a belief on the part of Congress that "timely and complete disclosure of receipts and expenditures would result in the exercise of prudence by candidates and their committees and that excessive expenditures would incur the displeasure of the electorate." (S. Rep. 93-989.) Unfortunately, FECA 1971 did not become effective until April 7, 1972. Before that date came around, politicians "scramble[d] to raise political funds . . . [in order to] avoid the disclosure provisions of the law," a scramble that led to widespread displeasure with the Act and pressure on Congress to pass a more comprehensive law. (S. Rep. 93-989.)

The second concern, as reflected in Senator Cranston's wish-list described above, revolved around public financing. FECA 1971's public-financing provisions were almost nonexistent, and the law had introduced contribution and expenditure limitations. "[C]oncern developed [in Congress] that major political parties and well-known individuals, including incumbent officeholders, would have greater access and appeal to donors than would minor parties and unknown individuals who desired to enter the political arena." (S. Rep. 93-989.) For this reason, Congress believed that a much more robust public-financing scheme was a necessary corollary to any restrictions on contributions or expenditures. The fundamentals of a public financing scheme were provided by Senator Pell by the beginning of 1974, and Pell's bill was incorporated into the more comprehensive FECA 1974. (S. Rep. 93-989.) In fact, it was this portion of the bill that garnered the most attention and sparked the most debate as FECA 1974 moved through Congress.

Interest in public financing evidenced not only a concern about the ability of unknown candidates to run a successful campaign, but also a concern about the role of political parties. Congress worried that directing too much public money directly to candidates would unreasonably weaken political parties, which Congress saw as the necessary basis of America's "vigorous party system." Essentially, the parties' roles in politics were their capacity to "pool[] resources from many small contributors," and Congress did not want to disrupt this ability. (S. Rep. 93-989.) Thus, in drafting FECA 1971, Congress endeavored "to preserve the place of political parties in the elective process." (S. Rep. 93-989.) At the same time, Congress wanted to take a "balanced approach" that would allow minor parties to participate without "stimulat[ing] a proliferation of splinter parties or independent candidates" because "such a proliferation would undermine the stability provided by a strong two-party system and could polarize voters on the basis of a single volatile issue." (S. Rep. 93-989.) Congress also recognized the vital importance that minor parties can and do play in American politics.

Some of Congress's concerns were purely practical. Under FECA 1971, the number of campaign-contribution disclosure reports that had to be filed had proliferated. Candidates were required to submit reports, as were every one of the growing and unchecked number of political committees. Moreover, each report was required to be filed on multiple dates, adding to the extraordinary number of reports being filed. Governmental staff required to deal with these reports were overwhelmed by the number of reports filed, leading to an inability to determine with any confidence the actual source and disposition of funds in a campaign, particularly large presidential campaigns. (H. Rep. 93-1239.)

Moreover, regulations under FECA 1971 were being issued by several different and uncoordinated bodies — the Clerk of the House of Representatives, the Secretary of the Senate, the Comptroller General, the Civil Aeronautics Board, the Federal Communications Commission, and the Interstate Commerce Commission. Not only were such regulations sometimes inconsistent, but some had actually gone so far, in the House's opinion, as to change the substance of the actual statutory requirements to the detriment of the entire disclosure system. FECA 1974 was intended, therefore, to put the statute back on track and streamline and correct regulations. (H. Rep. 93-1239.)

Congress also recognized that a system that controlled contributions and expenditures but did nothing to regulate so-called independent expenditures was doomed to failure. Independent expenditures are funds spent on behalf of a candidate by someone outside the campaign without the candidate's authorization. If contributions to a campaign were limited, but a wealthy person could spend as much money as she pleased on running advertisements promoting that candidate, then the contributions limitation would have almost no effect. "Such a loophole," the Senate Committee on Rules and Administration opined, "would render direct contribution limits virtually meaningless." (S. Rep. 93-989.) While Congress also recognized that limitations on independent expenditures posed uniquely complex First Amendment problems, it believed that to have limits on contributions that passed First Amendment muster — but no limits on independent expenditures because of the First Amendment — would be a triumph of constitutional form over function. Thus, FECA 1974, at least in the opinion of the Senate, needed to include limitations on independent expenditures.

Above all, Congress seemed worried by the increasing role of large contributors in campaign financing and the diminishing role of both the small donor and the thoughtful voter. The "unchecked rise in campaign expenditures, coupled with the absence of limitations on contributions and expenditures, [had] increased the dependence of candidates on special interest groups and large contributors," a system that was unfair to candidates and to an electorate "entitled to base its judgment on a straightforward presentation of a candidate's qualifications for public office and his programs for the Nation rather than on a sophisticated advertising program." (H. Rep. 93-1239.)

Senator Claiborne Pell wrote thoughtfully about the role he saw FECA 1974 playing in the reinvigoration of American democracy and of the individualistic principles on which that democracy once stood, especially in the wake of the Watergate scandal:

> The [Senate] Committee [on Rules and Administration] is reporting to the Senate legislation of historic significance, in accord with those Jeffersonian principles which place abiding confidence in the wisdom of the

individual and in the individual's fundamental role in the development of an enlightened democracy.

We have witnessed the tragic perversion of these principles — in terms of a misuse and corruption of power and a misguided dependence on the influence of large political contributors.

This legislation is deeply concerned with the ending of such abuses. It removed the temptation of seeking or of accepting the large compromising gift. It returns to our people, to our individual voters a rightful share and a rightful responsibility in the choosing of their candidates. And it can serve to establish that climate of public trust in elected officials which this country so earnestly desires. (S. Rep. 93-989.)

Congress, then, knew that it could not "legislate morality, . . . mandate an end to dishonesty, an end to venality, . . . [or] by public law eliminate all the shocking abuses which have so plagued" the nation. (CONG. REC. §4439, Mar. 26, 1974, Sen. Pell.) But Congress believed that it could, "through enlightened legislative action, create a climate which minimizes the cause of abuse, and . . . return to our voters their rights to choose candidates who are not beholden to the large, and so often compromising, political contribution." (CONG. REC. §4439.) Watergate had taken a vicious toll on public trust in government. In passing FECA 1974, Congress knew it could "not eradicate all future Watergates," but it believed that it could "discourage the perpetuation of a climate in which power is abused by the clever at the expense of the unwary, where power is perverted by a calculated deception which . . . we might call a 'school for scandal.'" (*Id.*) Congress wanted government to become less of a "private preserve of the wealthy and special interest," and instead to "return to a Government responsive to all of the people." (§4460, Sen. Clark.)

In sum, with FECA 1974, Congress aimed to create an "effective and comprehensive" campaign-finance system "to restore and strengthen public confidence in the integrity of the political process." (H. Rep. 93-1239.) No small feat, to be sure.

In 1974, Congress did not, therefore, make small changes to FECA 1971. Congress's 1974 FECA amendments offered a strict, comprehensive, new campaign-finance scheme with five major goals: limiting campaign contributions, limiting campaign expenditures, broadening contribution reporting and disclosure requirements, creating a functional public-financing program for federal office, and organizing a single regulatory body with the power and capacity to monitor the whole of federal election law. The Act also continued and strengthened prohibitions on contributions and expenditures by national banks, corporations, and labor unions.

1. Limitations on Campaign Contributions

At its simplest, campaign-finance regulation is an attempt to control the amount of money that can flow through a campaign for elected office. There are two points at which this money flow can be monitored and, if desired, limited: as the money comes into a campaign and as it leaves the campaign. FECA 1974 sought to control the movement of money at both of these points.

Money flows into a campaign in the form of campaign contributions. Congress replaced FECA 1971's toothless contribution limitation with tough new limitations on contributions by the most likely entities through which money is expected to flow into the campaign: individuals, political committees, and national political parties. Contributions by individuals were limited to $1,000 per candidate in any election cycle. Political committees were limited to $5,000 per candidate. Individuals were also limited to $25,000 in total donations during a single election cycle.

With FECA 1974, Congress endeavored to create a legal scheme without loopholes. There existed, however, an obvious loophole in the contributions limitation framework. If contributions to campaigns were limited, then contributors could instead donate to political parties or political action committees with the intention that their contribution be used for a particular candidate. FECA 1974 closed this loophole by considering as "contributions to [a given] candidate" any "contributions to [that] candidate made to any political committee authorized by such candidate." (§101.) Moreover, "[a]ll contributions made by a person, either directly or indirectly, on behalf of a particular candidate," even if those contributions were "in any way earmarked or otherwise directed through an intermediary or conduit to such candidate," were treated by FECA 1974 as contributions from that person to that candidate.

Congress also broadly defined what was meant by "contributions." FECA 1974 defined a contribution to mean:

> **(1)** "a gift, subscription, loan, advance, or deposit of money or anything of value . . . made for the purpose of influencing the nomination for election, or election, of any person to federal office";
> **(2)** any "contract, promise, or agreement, express or implied, whether or not legally enforceable, to make a contribution for such purposes";
> **(3)** funds transferred from one political committee to a candidate's political committee;
> **(4)** payment, by anyone other than the candidate or a political committee, for the personal services of another person rendered to the candidate free of charge.

2.   *Limitations on Expenditures*

With FECA 1974, Congress attempted to limit three different kinds of campaign expenditures. First, the law limited the amount of money that could be spent by the candidate's campaign itself. Second, the law imposed limitations on so-called independent expenditures. Third, the law limited the amount of money that a candidate could spend from personal funds.

FECA 1974's campaign-expenditure limits differed depending on the office for which the candidate was running. The limits applied were as follows, allowing for annual cost-of-living adjustments:

- $10,000,000 for candidates in presidential primaries;
- $20,000,000 for candidates in the general presidential election;
- The greater of $100,000 or 8 cents per eligible voter for candidates in Senate primaries;

- The greater of $150,000 or 12 cents per eligible voter for candidates in general Senate elections; and
- $70,000 for candidates in House primaries or general elections.

The limits imposed by FECA 1974 did not apply only to expenditures directly made by a candidate's campaign. Included within a candidate's total expenditures—which were required to remain under the above caps—were expenditures made on behalf of the candidate. Expenditures made on a candidate's behalf included any expenditure made by an authorized committee or agent of the candidate and any person requested by the candidate to make an expenditure.

The failures of FECA 1971 had made Congress more aware of potential loopholes in its reform regime. For a candidate, the obvious solution to a limit on campaign expenditures was to have individuals outside of the campaign spend their contributions as individuals, instead of donating money to the candidate's campaign. As long as the candidate did not direct the expenditure, such an expenditure would not run afoul of the campaign-expenditure limits.

To avoid such an outcome, Congress disallowed an individual from making "any expenditure . . . relative to a clearly defined candidate during a calendar year which, when added to all other expenditures made by such person during the year advocating the election or defeat of such candidate, exceeds $1,000." (§101.) The political parties were limited, as well, though the dollar values on their limitations were higher.

Political candidates were also limited in the amount of money they could spend from their personal funds or the personal funds of their immediate family members. FECA 1974 imposed yearly limits on such expenditures. Presidential candidates were limited to $50,000 per year, senatorial candidates to $35,000, and House candidates to $25,000. These totals included loans or advances made from the candidate's personal funds or those of her immediate family.

Like "contribution," the term "expenditure" was specifically defined by Congress. FECA 1974 defined expenditure to include any "purchase, payment, distribution, loan, advance, deposit, or gift of money or anything of value," or any contract, promise, or agreement to make expenditure, "for the purpose of influencing" an election. FECA 1974 also specified a number of items that were not included in the definition, such as news stories, nonpartisan get-out-the-vote efforts, and travel expenses by volunteers.

3. Reporting and Disclosure

The 1974 amendments substantially increased reporting requirements for campaigns and candidates in several key ways.

First, FECA 1974 amended FECA to require that every candidate for federal office designate a "political committee" to serve as her "principal campaign committee." (§202.)

Second, FECA 1974 required that every candidate and every political committee supporting the election of a candidate to federal office make reports to the federal government. These reports were required, as in FECA 1971, to include the names and addresses of donors contributing greater than $10, as well as detailed accounts of any expenditures greater than $100. These reports were required to be submitted 10 days before the date of the election and 30 days after the date of the election. (§204.) It also required reporting no later than the tenth day following the close of a calendar quarter in which the candidate or political committee received contributions or made expenditures greater than $1,000.

Third, FECA 1974 required every person who made contributions or expenditures exceeding $100 in a calendar year to file with the federal government a statement containing various personal information. (§204.) Reporting was also required of any person who expended funds or committed any public act intended to influence the outcome of an election or published certain materials relating to candidates. (§208.)

4.   Public Financing

Though the 1971 Senate version of FECA had included a "presidential checkoff plan" to help finance presidential campaigns through voluntary income tax donations, pressure for a more fully realized public-financing scheme rose in 1973. Senator Alan Cranston of California submitted, on behalf of himself and a bipartisan group of more than one-third of the Senate's leadership, eight principles that they considered essential for any public-financing bill. These included extending the presidential checkoff; providing full funding for major-party candidates and some funding for minor-party candidates; providing matching funding for presidential candidates in presidential primaries; establishing expenditure limits in both primary and general elections; allowing private contributions but only in small amounts; creating a role for political parties to serve as bundlers; and creating an independent agency to administer this new campaign-finance system.

FECA 1974 provided public financing for presidential primaries. "Major parties" were entitled to $2,000,000 from the presidential-nomination-convention fund. "Minor parties" were entitled to funds on the basis of their popular support in comparison to that of major-party candidates. If a minor-party presidential candidate had received one-tenth of the votes the average major-party candidate had received, then he would receive one-tenth of the money the major party candidate could claim, or $200,000.

These funds were permitted for use only to defray the costs of putting on a presidential nominating convention. (§406.)

FECA 1974 also established a public-financing system for presidential elections. (§408.) In order to receive funds from the Presidential Primary Matching Payment Account, a candidate must agree to limitations on expenditures and must raise at least $100,000 on his own in the form of at least $5,000 worth of $250 or smaller contributions from people in at least 20 states. Once the requirements were met, the candidate would be eligible to receive payments matching contributions the candidate was able to raise on his own, up to $250 per contributor.

5.   Federal Election Commission

FECA 1974 established a single government commission to oversee federal elections. Under FECA 1974, the Federal Election Commission (FEC) was to be composed of six voting members. The FEC was tasked with "administer[ing], seek[ing] to obtain compliance with, and formulat[ing] policy with respect to" all federal elections law. FECA 1974 vested in the FEC "primary jurisdiction with respect to the civil enforcement of such provisions." The FEC was given broad powers in order to undertake these responsibilities. The FEC could (1) "require . . . any person to submit in writing such reports and answers to questions as the Commission may prescribe"; (2) subpoena testimony and attendance of witnesses and conduct hearings and investigations; and (3) initiate in its own name civil actions for the purpose of enforcing federal election law. (All in §208.)

6. Prohibition on Contributions and Expenditures by National Banks, Corporations, and Labor Unions

FECA 1974 Section 610 forbade national banks and national corporations from making contributions or expenditures "in connection with any election to any political office." All other corporations and labor unions were prohibited from making contributions or expenditures in federal elections. Section 610 did, however, allow unions and corporations to set up a "separate segregated fund to be utilized for political purposes."

To sum up, Congress in the 1974 amendments to FECA attempted to create a "closed system" of campaign finance in federal elections. The amount of money available for use in political campaigns was controlled under this system first by limiting the amount that could be put directly into the pockets of candidates for their use, and second by limiting the amount that could be spent by candidates on their own election, as well as by all others who might conceivably wish to spend on their behalf. This strategy is illustrated graphically in Figure 1.

To foreshadow the remaining substance of this chapter, the congressional plan implemented in FECA did not survive. On the contrary, it was decimated by three generations of Supreme Court decisions. The Court's first decision concerning the statute, *Buckley v. Valeo* (1976), punched major holes in the plan by invalidating restrictions on spending by candidates and individuals, and by striking down provisions limiting candidates' use of their own personal funds. In a second generation of rulings decided between about 1980 and 2008, the Court issued narrower decisions striking down other pieces of the FECA framework, such as limitations on expenditures by political parties, political committees, and nonprofit advocacy groups. Finally, in *Citizens United* (2010), the Court invalidated provisions prohibiting corporations and unions from spending directly from their general treasuries. As a result, although most (but not all) of FECA's original contribution limitations still stand, none of its expenditures limitations survived. At present, the only surviving limitation on independent expenditures is a post-FECA ban on expenditures by foreign nationals. The current situation is illustrated in Figure 2.

Before proceeding to examine the fate of FECA in the courts, we provide some additional background on some of the many different kinds of actors found in the campaign-finance arena.

Figure 1

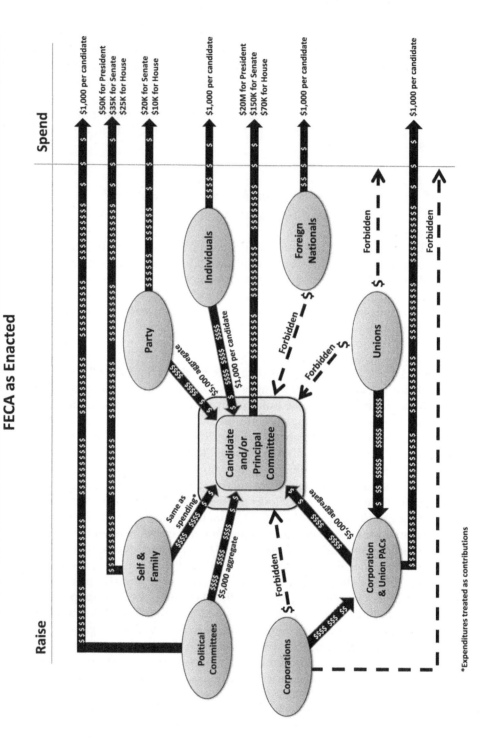

FECA as Enacted

Figure 2

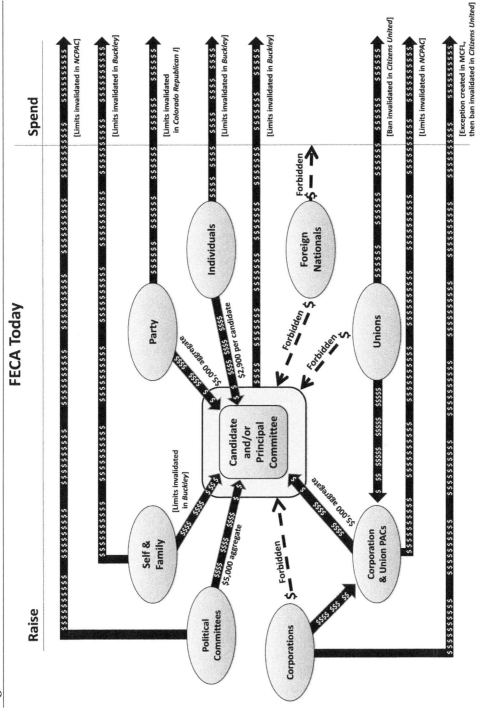

B.   PACs

Many of the groups that raise money to help get candidates elected to office or to finance political campaigns fall into the organizational format of committees. Such organizations commonly take several different forms, described below.

1.   Party Committees

Party committees are the organizational arms of the political parties. They are responsible for the daily operations of the party and for formulating and articulating the party's message and position. They are also responsible for fundraising and funding the party's and its candidates' activities. An advantage of party-committee status is the ability to spend more money in coordinated support of the party's candidates for federal office than other political entities. The Democratic National Committee is the party committee for the Democratic Party and the Republican National Committee is its counterpart in the Republican Party.

2.   PACs: Nonconnected Committees and Separate, Segregated Funds

Chief among these fundraising groups are the political action committees, sometimes called political committees but popularly known as PACs. Political committees are formally the product of the Federal Election Campaign Act, which defined "political committee" as:

> **(A)** any committee, club, association, or other group of persons which receives contributions aggregating in excess of $1,000 during a calendar year or which makes expenditures aggregating in excess of $1,000 during a calendar year; or
>
> **(B)** any separate segregated fund established under section 441b(b) . . . ; or
>
> **(C)** any local committee of a political party which receives contributions aggregating in excess of $5,000 during a calendar year, or makes payments exempted from the definition of contribution or expenditure . . . aggregating in excess of $5,000 during a calendar year, or makes contributions aggregating in excess of $1,000 during a calendar year or makes expenditures aggregating in excess of $1,000 during a calendar year.

PACs are the primary financing mechanism for the political activity of political candidates, office-holders, and all major (and minor) players in the political process. They are the vehicles through which money is collected and through which money is spent. As a formal matter, federal law recognizes two types of PACs. The first type of PAC is the "separate segregated fund," or SSF. Remember that as early as the Tillman Act it had been illegal for corporations, unions, or other similar membership organizations to donate corporate, union, or organizational funds to influence federal elections. These laws did not make it illegal, however, for such groups to put aside donations made by the *members* of the corporation or union into a separate fund, segregated from the rest of the corporate or union coffers. These separate, segregated moneys could then be used to influence federal elections. The actual funds into which this separate money was placed were controlled by political action committees.

The second type of PAC is the "nonconnected political committee" or non-connected PAC. A nonconnected PAC is essentially a political committee that is not a party committee, an authorized committee of a candidate, or an SSF, which means it is unconnected to a corporation or labor organization.

As a practical matter, there are thousands of nonconnected PACs. Some of the best known, and best funded, nonconnected PACs include groups like the Blue Dog PAC, the League of Conservation Voters PAC, the Human Rights Campaign PAC, the National Action Committee, Tuesday Group PAC, Citizens United, and the Family Research Council. There are also a huge number of SSFs. Some well-known SSFs include the PACs of the Service Employees International Union; the American Federation of State, County, and Municipal Employees; the American Federation of Teachers; the National Association of Realtors; the International Brotherhood of Electrical Workers; the Teamsters Union; the Laborers Union; the United Auto Workers; the National Education Association; the Plumbers and Pipefitters Union; the AFL-CIO; and the Operating Engineers Union. The largest total expenditures by PACs during the 2015-2016 election cycle were made by ActBlue, Priorities USA Action, Right to Rise USA, Senate Leadership Fund, and the NextGen Climate Action, which collectively spent more than $1 billion, though more than half of that was spent by ActBlue alone.

3.   *Two Special Kinds of PACs: Leadership PACs and Super PACs*

Two other interesting forms of PACs have developed since the 1970s, when political committees were first defined.

The first is the leadership PAC. Leadership PACs are essentially a special kind of nonconnected PAC, meaning that they raise money from the general population and are not limited to contributions from any particular constituency, as is an SSF. Leadership PACs are distinct in that they are established by members of Congress and other political leaders to support candidates for federal and nonfederal office. A leadership committee is technically defined as a PAC that is directly or indirectly established, financed, maintained, or controlled by a candidate or a person holding federal office that is not the candidate or office-holder's authorized committee or affiliated with the authorized committee.

Unlike nonconnected PACs or SSFs, the names of which usually describe the group or organization behind the committee, the names of leadership PACs are typically more fanciful and less descriptive of who is "behind" the PAC, so to speak. There has not been any real regulation requiring a leadership PAC to disclose the political leader behind the PAC, despite the fact that the leadership PAC must identify itself as such to the FEC. According to opensecrets.org, leadership PACs also spend less than other types of PACs, though the amount of money is still large and may help a politician gain clout among his colleagues. The number of these PACs is also on the rise: in 1998, there were only 120 leadership PACs; in 2004, there were 275; and in 2010, there were 397. There were 536 leadership PACs in 2016. Some of the biggest contributors in the 2015-2016 election cycle among the leadership PACs include the Majority Committee PAC, which is associated with Rep. Kevin McCarthy (R-CA); Prosperity Action, chaired by Rep. Paul Ryan (R-WI); the AmeriPAC: The Fund for a Greater America, chaired by Rep. Steny Hoyer (D-MD); Eye of the Tiger PAC, chaired by Rep. Steve Scalise (R-LA); and More Conservatives PAC, affiliated with Rep. Patrick McHenry (R-NC). Representative McCarthy's PAC made over $2 million in contributions to fellow Republicans.

The second special kind of PAC is a direct result of the D.C. Circuit Court of Appeals decision in *Speechnow.org v. U.S. Federal Election Commission*, which was decided in March 2010 and relied heavily on the Supreme Court's decision in *Citizens United* (and described further below). These new PACs are technically "independent-expenditure only committees" — PACs that make all of their expenditures without consulting with any candidate for federal office — but they are more popularly, and more colorfully, called Super PACs. Super PACs may raise unlimited sums of money from corporations, unions, and individuals and may spend unlimited sums of money to influence federal elections. Super PACs may also engage in express advocacy. They may not, however, coordinate with a candidate or donate any money to a candidate's campaign, unlike regular PACs. Commentators have described Super PACs as falling into one of two categories. The first is the "candidate-specific Super PAC" or the "alter ego" Super PAC "organized to back a specific candidate or formed at the behest of party leaders." Richard Briffault, *Super PACs*, 96 Minn. L. Rev. 1624, 1675-1677 (2012). A Super PAC is another vehicle, and given the lack of contribution limits, a particularly important vehicle, through which wealthy donors could continue to support their candidate financially when they can no longer legally contribute to the candidate directly. A second type of Super PAC is a Super PAC as a shadow party organization. These types of Super PACs are "run by party insiders and broadly served their respective party's campaign agenda and candidates to the extent permissible under the law." Michael S. Kang, *The Year of the Super PAC*, 81 Geo. Wash. L. Rev. 1902 (2013).

One worry about Super PACs is that they will shift control and influence from the candidates and the parties to outside groups. Super PACs have the "legal capacity to channel enormous amounts of money outside contribution limits [which] makes them attractive and useful as instant bases of power for anyone interested in applying financial resources to politics." Kang, *supra*, at 1927. The pre–*Citizens United* world favored the political parties by allowing them to serve as coordinating entities for raising large sums of money for candidates. However, the post–*Citizens United* disruption to the long-standing regulatory regime of campaign finance undermines the value of those strengths in today's candidate politics. Super PACs and 501(c)(4) groups can stockpile vast amounts of campaign money without organizational help or direction from a major party. Kang, *supra*, at 1924. Consequently, "those groups bypass the coordination costs that large-scale campaign fundraising required in the past." *Id.* Super PACs spent more than $1 billion in the 2016 election cycle.

4. 527s

So-called 527 organizations are named after the part of the Tax Code from which they have emerged. Generally, Section 527 sets the tax rules for — and describes the tax-exempt status of — political organizations. A "political organization," under Section 527, is "a party, committee, association, fund, or other organization . . . organized and operated primarily for the purpose of directly or indirectly accepting contributions, or both, for an exempt function." (26 U.S.C. §527(e)(1).) "Exempt function" is defined to include the function of "influencing or attempting to influence the selection, nomination, election, or appointment of any individual to any Federal, State, or local public office." (§527(e)(2).) Thus, a 527 organization is a tax-exempt entity, such as a party committee or a political committee, that is organized for the primary purpose of influencing elections. 527 organizations cannot directly support or oppose a specific candidate. But they can raise unlimited money for general political activities.

While this may sound suspiciously like a "political committee," there are certain organizations that fall within the Section 527 definition of "political organization" but outside the FECA definition of "political committee." Such organizations are not subject to reporting and other requirements imposed by the FEC. As Professor Miriam Galston explains, the disparity between organizations described as "political committees" for the purposes of FECA and those identified as Section 527 groups is a result in large part of differing definitions of "electoral activity." Miriam Galston, *Emerging Constitutional Paradigms and Justifications for Campaign Finance Regulation: The Case of 527 Groups*, 95 GEO. L.J. 1181, 1185 (2007). "[B]ecause federal campaign finance regulations necessarily restrict political speech, the Supreme Court tends to construe narrowly the types of electoral activity that can be subject to particular provisions of FECA." *Id.* She argues that a closer analysis of the functions of 527 groups will be necessary to determine whether such organizations are "actively engaged in the core area of electoral activities that the Constitution allows Congress to restrict." *Id.* at 1187. Independent advocacy, grassroots organizing on political issues, and generic voter mobilization efforts may be more difficult to justify as subject to restriction than would more obvious campaigning or coordinated efforts. *Id.* at 1242.

If an organization is a political committee under FECA, it is subject to FECA's contribution limits. If a 527 organization is not a political committee, it is required to disclose only contributions and expenditures. Unfortunately, the FEC has refused to promulgate clearer rules to help determine when organizations are, in fact, political committees that must register and abide by FEC regulations, preferring to proceed on a case-by-case basis. This approach has left a big and almost unanswerable question: what exactly *is* a Section 527 non-political committee? This question is answered primarily by the organizations themselves, which simply refuse to register if they believe they fall outside of FECA's standard. The best definition that courts have been able to come up with is that a political committee is an organization that has a "major purpose" of influencing a federal election; but how should we determine what constitutes an organization's "major" purpose?

Notwithstanding the difficulty of defining what makes a 527 *not* a political committee, 527s have exploded onto the political scene. In 2004, 527s spent more

than $400 million. (Pub. Citizen, The Last Major Soft Money Loophole: Sec-
tion 527 Groups in the 2004 Election 1.) The best known of these groups was
Swift Vets and POWs for Truth, a conservative 527 that spent nearly $19 million
running commercials opposing John Kerry's presidential bid. (*Swift Vets & POWs
for Truth: Expenditures 2004*, Ctr. for Responsive Politics.) Ultimately, the FEC
determined that Swift Vets—along with other 527s that spent large sums in 2004,
Moveon.org and League of Conservation Voters 527—*should* have registered as
PACs, because they had the "major purpose" of opposing or supporting particular
candidates. Swift Vets was fined about $300,000, which was approximately what the
organization had spent on postage during the 2004 campaign.

While the controversy around 527s has died down since 2004, the amount of
money 527s raise has continued to grow. For example, in the 2010 election cycle,
the non-registered and conservative-leaning 527 American Solutions for Winning
the Future spent more than $28 million. opensecrets.org. In 2016, the left-leaning
ActBlue spent more than $23 million.

5.   501(c)(4) Organizations

A final organizational form for groups hoping to raise money for candidates is the 501(c)(4), named after the section of the tax code under which it is
formed. According to the tax code, 501(c)(4) organizations are civic leagues and
other organizations operated solely for the purpose of promoting social welfare.
They may engage in political campaigns and elections so long as campaigning is
not the organization's primary purpose. That is, 50 percent or less of a 501(c)
(4)'s activities should be political in nature. 501(c)(4) organizations are considered attractive because they do not typically have to reveal the identities of their
donors. More recently, however, 501(c)(4)s have become less attractive, as the
IRS has moved to tax gifts made to such organizations. 501(c)(4) organizations
may not make direct contributions to federal candidates, political parties, or federal PACs. They may, however, make political contributions to expenditure-only
PACs such as Super PACs. *See generally* Gregg D. Polsky and Guy-Uriel E. Charles,
Regulating Section 527 Organizations, 73 Geo. Wash. L. Rev. 1000 (2005). Examples of 501(c)(4) organizations include well-known groups like the AARP and
the NAACP.

C.   *THE* BUCKLEY *SETTLEMENT*

Congress designed FECA 1974 as a single, comprehensive law to regulate
the entirety of federal campaign finance. Only two years after FECA 1974's passage, however, the Supreme Court began to erode this comprehensive regime.
The Court did not view FECA's provisions as integrated components of a comprehensive law, but as a variety of provisions to be considered separately. The *Buckley*
decision considered each of the five aspects of FECA 1974 in turn and exclusive
of one another.

1. FECA in the Court

Buckley v. Valeo

424 U.S. 1 (1976) (per curiam)

These appeals present constitutional challenges to the key provisions of the Federal Election Campaign Act of 1971 (Act), and related provisions of the Internal Revenue Code of 1954, all as amended in 1974. . . .

The statutes at issue, summarized in broad terms, contain the following provisions: (a) individual political contributions are limited to $1,000 to any single candidate per election, with an overall annual limitation of $25,000 by any contributor; independent expenditures by individuals and groups "relative to a clearly identified candidate" are limited to $1,000 a year; campaign spending by candidates for various federal offices and spending for national conventions by political parties are subject to prescribed limits; (b) contributions and expenditures above certain threshold levels must be reported and publicly disclosed; (c) a system for public funding of Presidential campaign activities is established by Subtitle H of the Internal Revenue Code; and (d) a Federal Election Commission is established to administer and enforce the legislation.

This suit was originally filed by appellants in the United States District Court for the District of Columbia. . . . The complaint sought both a declaratory judgment that the major provisions of the Act were unconstitutional and an injunction against enforcement of those provisions. . . . [A] majority of the Court of Appeals rejected, for the most part, appellants' constitutional attacks. . . .

I. CONTRIBUTION AND EXPENDITURE LIMITATIONS

The intricate statutory scheme adopted by Congress to regulate federal election campaigns includes restrictions on political contributions and expenditures that apply broadly to all phases of and all participants in the election process. The major contribution and expenditure limitations in the Act prohibit individuals from contributing more than $25,000 in a single year or more than $1,000 to any single candidate for an election campaign and from spending more than $1,000 a year "relative to a clearly identified candidate." Other provisions restrict a candidate's use of personal and family resources in his campaign and limit the overall amount that can be spent by a candidate in campaigning for federal office.

The . . . critical constitutional questions presented here go . . . to whether the specific legislation that Congress has enacted interferes with First Amendment freedoms or invidiously discriminates against nonincumbent candidates and minor parties in contravention of the Fifth Amendment.

A. General Principles

The Act's contribution and expenditure limitations operate in an area of the most fundamental First Amendment activities. Discussion of public issues and debate on the qualifications of candidates are integral to the operation of the system of government established by our Constitution. The First Amendment affords the broadest protection to such political expression in order "to assure (the) unfettered interchange of ideas for the bringing about of political and social changes desired by the people." *Roth v. United States*, 354 U.S. 476, 484 (1957). . . . In a republic where the people are sovereign, the ability of the citizenry to make informed choices among candidates for office is essential, for the identities of those who are elected will inevitably shape the course that we follow as a nation. . . .

The First Amendment protects political association as well as political expression. The constitutional right of association explicated in *NAACP v. Alabama*, 357 U.S. 449, 460 (1958), stemmed from the Court's recognition that "(e)ffective advocacy of both public and private points of view, particularly controversial ones, is undeniably enhanced by group association." Subsequent decisions have made clear that the First and Fourteenth Amendments guarantee "'freedom to associate with others for the common advancement of political beliefs and ideas,'" a freedom that encompasses "'(t)he right to associate with the political party of one's choice.'" *Kusper v. Pontikes*, 414 U.S. 51, 56, 57 (1973).

It is with these principles in mind that we consider the primary contentions of the parties with respect to the Act's limitations upon the giving and spending of money in political campaigns. Those conflicting contentions could not more sharply define the basic issues before us. Appellees contend that what the Act regulates is conduct, and that its effect on speech and association is incidental at most. Appellants respond that contributions and expenditures are at the very core of political speech, and that the Act's limitations thus constitute restraints on First Amendment liberty that are both gross and direct. . . .

In upholding the constitutional validity of the Act's contribution and expenditure provisions on the ground that those provisions should be viewed as regulating conduct, not speech, the Court of Appeals relied upon *United States v. O'Brien*, 391 U.S. 367 (1968). The *O'Brien* case involved a defendant's claim that the First Amendment prohibited his prosecution for burning his draft card because his act was "'symbolic speech'" engaged in as a "'demonstration against the war and against the draft.'" 391 U.S., at 376. On the assumption that "the alleged communicative element in O'Brien's conduct (was) sufficient to bring into play the First Amendment," the Court sustained the conviction because it found "a sufficiently important governmental interest in regulating the nonspeech element" that was "unrelated to the suppression of free expression" and that had an "incidental restriction on alleged First Amendment freedoms . . . no greater than (was) essential to the furtherance of that interest." Id., at 376-377. . . .

We cannot share the view that the present Act's contribution and expenditure limitations are comparable to the restrictions on conduct upheld in *O'Brien*. The expenditure of money simply cannot be equated with such conduct as destruction of a draft card. Some forms of communication made possible by the giving and spending of money involve speech alone, some involve conduct primarily, and some involve a combination of the two. Yet this Court has never suggested that the dependence of a communication on the expenditure of money operates itself to introduce a nonspeech element or to reduce the exacting scrutiny required by the First Amendment. . . .

Even if the categorization of the expenditure of money as conduct were accepted, the limitations challenged here would not meet the *O'Brien* test because the governmental interests advanced in support of the Act involve "suppressing communication." The interests served by the Act include restricting the voices of people and interest groups who have money to spend and reducing the over-all scope of federal election campaigns. Although the Act does not focus on the ideas expressed by persons or groups subject to its regulations, it is aimed in part at equalizing the relative ability of all voters to affect electoral outcomes by placing a ceiling on expenditures for political expression by citizens and groups. . . . [I]t is beyond dispute that the interest in regulating the alleged "conduct" of giving or spending money "arises in some measure because the communication allegedly integral to the conduct is itself thought to be harmful." 391 U.S., at 382. . . .

A restriction on the amount of money a person or group can spend on political communication during a campaign necessarily reduces the quantity of expression by restricting the number of issues discussed, the depth of their exploration, and the size of the audience reached.[18] This is because virtually every means of communicating ideas in today's mass society requires the expenditure of money. . . . The electorate's increasing dependence on television, radio, and other mass media for news and information has made these expensive modes of communication indispensable instruments of effective political speech.

The expenditure limitations contained in the Act represent substantial rather than merely theoretical restraints on the quantity and diversity of political speech. The $1,000 ceiling on spending "relative to a clearly identified candidate," 18 U.S.C. §608(e)(1) (1970 ed., Supp. IV), would appear to exclude all citizens and groups except candidates, political parties, and the institutional press from any significant use of the most effective modes of communication. Although the Act's limitations on expenditures by campaign organizations and political parties provide substantially greater room for discussion and debate, they would have required restrictions in the scope of a number of past congressional and Presidential campaigns and would operate to constrain campaigning by candidates who raise sums in excess of the spending ceiling.

By contrast with a limitation upon expenditures for political expression, a limitation upon the amount that any one person or group may contribute to a candidate or political committee entails only a marginal restriction upon the contributor's ability to engage in free communication. A contribution serves as a general expression of support for the candidate and his views, but does not communicate the underlying basis for the support. The quantity of communication by the contributor does not increase perceptibly with the size of his contribution, since the expression rests solely on the undifferentiated, symbolic act of contributing. At most, the size of the contribution provides a very rough index of the intensity of the contributor's support for the candidate. A limitation on the amount of money a person may give to a candidate or campaign organization thus involves little direct restraint on his political communication, for it permits the symbolic expression of support evidenced by a contribution but does not in any way infringe

---

18. Being free to engage in unlimited political expression subject to a ceiling on expenditures is like being free to drive an automobile as far and as often as one desires on a single tank of gasoline.

the contributor's freedom to discuss candidates and issues. While contributions may result in political expression if spent by a candidate or an association to present views to the voters, the transformation of contributions into political debate involves speech by someone other than the contributor.

Given the important role of contributions in financing political campaigns, contribution restrictions could have a severe impact on political dialogue if the limitations prevented candidates and political committees from amassing the resources necessary for effective advocacy. There is no indication, however, that the contribution limitations imposed by the Act would have any dramatic adverse effect on the funding of campaigns and political associations. The overall effect of the Act's contribution ceilings is merely to require candidates and political committees to raise funds from a greater number of persons and to compel people who would otherwise contribute amounts greater than the statutory limits to expend such funds on direct political expression, rather than to reduce the total amount of money potentially available to promote political expression.

The Act's contribution and expenditure limitations also impinge on protected associational freedoms. Making a contribution, like joining a political party, serves to affiliate a person with a candidate. In addition, it enables like-minded persons to pool their resources in furtherance of common political goals. The Act's contribution ceilings thus limit one important means of associating with a candidate or committee, but leave the contributor free to become a member of any political association and to assist personally in the association's efforts on behalf of candidates. And the Act's contribution limitations permit associations and candidates to aggregate large sums of money to promote effective advocacy. By contrast, the Act's $1,000 limitation on independent expenditures "relative to a clearly identified candidate" precludes most associations from effectively amplifying the voice of their adherents, the original basis for the recognition of First Amendment protection of the freedom of association. The Act's constraints on the ability of independent associations and candidate campaign organizations to expend resources on political expression "is simultaneously an interference with the freedom of (their) adherents," *Sweezy v. New Hampshire*, 354 U.S. 234, 250 (1957) (plurality opinion).

In sum, although the Act's contribution and expenditure limitations both implicate fundamental First Amendment interests, its expenditure ceilings impose significantly more severe restrictions on protected freedoms of political expression and association than do its limitations on financial contributions.

B. CONTRIBUTION LIMITATIONS

1. The $1,000 Limitation on Contributions by Individuals and Groups to Candidates and Authorized Campaign Committees

Section 608(b) provides, with certain limited exceptions, that "no person shall make contributions to any candidate with respect to any election for Federal office which, in the aggregate, exceed $1,000." . . .

Appellants contend that the $1,000 contribution ceiling unjustifiably burdens First Amendment freedoms, employs overbroad dollar limits, and discriminates against candidates opposing incumbent officeholders and against minor-party candidates in violation of the Fifth Amendment. We address each of these claims of invalidity in turn.

(a)

. . . [T]he primary First Amendment problem raised by the Act's contribution limitations is their restriction of one aspect of the contributor's freedom of political association. The Court's decisions involving associational freedoms establish that the right of association is a "basic constitutional freedom," *Kusper v. Pontikes,* 414 U.S., at 57, that is "closely allied to freedom of speech and a right which, like free speech, lies at the foundation of a free society." *Shelton v. Tucker,* 364 U.S. 479, 486 (1960). In view of the fundamental nature of the right to associate, governmental "action which may have the effect of curtailing the freedom to associate is subject to the closest scrutiny." *NAACP v. Alabama, supra,* 357 U.S., at 460-461. Yet, it is clear that "(n)either the right to associate nor the right to participate in political activities is absolute." *United States Civil Service Commission v. National Association of Letter Carriers AFL-CIO,* 413 U.S. 548, 567 (1973). Even a " 'significant interference' with protected rights of political association" may be sustained if the State demonstrates a sufficiently important interest and employs means closely drawn to avoid unnecessary abridgment of associational freedoms. *Cousins v. Wigoda,* 419 U.S., at 488.

Appellees argue that the Act's restrictions on large campaign contributions are justified by three governmental interests. According to the parties and amici, the primary interest served by the limitations and, indeed, by the Act as a whole, is the prevention of corruption and the appearance of corruption spawned by the real or imagined coercive influence of large financial contributions on candidates' positions and on their actions if elected to office. Two "ancillary" interests underlying the Act are also allegedly furthered by the $1,000 limits on contributions. First, the limits serve to mute the voices of affluent persons and groups in the election process and thereby to equalize the relative ability of all citizens to affect the outcome of elections. Second, it is argued, the ceilings may to some extent act as a brake on the skyrocketing cost of political campaigns and thereby serve to open the political system more widely to candidates without access to sources of large amounts of money.

It is unnecessary to look beyond the Act's primary purpose to limit the actuality and appearance of corruption resulting from large individual financial contributions in order to find a constitutionally sufficient justification for the $1,000 contribution limitation. Under a system of private financing of elections, a candidate lacking immense personal or family wealth must depend on financial contributions from others to provide the resources necessary to conduct a successful campaign. . . . To the extent that large contributions are given to secure a political quid pro quo from current and potential office holders, the integrity of our system of representative democracy is undermined. . . .

Of almost equal concern as the danger of actual quid pro quo arrangements is the impact of the appearance of corruption stemming from public awareness of the opportunities for abuse inherent in a regime of large individual financial contributions. . . .

Appellants contend that the contribution limitations must be invalidated because bribery laws and narrowly drawn disclosure requirements constitute a less restrictive means of dealing with "proven and suspected quid pro quo arrangements." But laws making criminal the giving and taking of bribes deal with only the most blatant and specific attempts of those with money to influence governmental action. And while disclosure requirements serve the many salutary purposes discussed elsewhere in this opinion, Congress was surely entitled to conclude that disclosure was only a partial measure, and that contribution ceilings were a necessary legislative concomitant to deal with the reality or appearance of corruption inherent in a system permitting unlimited financial contributions, even when the identities of the contributors and the amounts of their contributions are fully disclosed.

The Act's $1,000 contribution limitation focuses precisely on the problem of large campaign contributions—the narrow aspect of political association where the actuality and potential for corruption have been identified—while leaving persons free to engage in independent political expression, to associate actively through volunteering their services, and to assist to a limited but nonetheless substantial extent in supporting candidates and committees with financial resources.[31]

Significantly, the Act's contribution limitations in themselves do not undermine to any material degree the potential for robust and effective discussion of candidates and campaign issues by individual citizens, associations, the institutional press, candidates, and political parties.

We find that, under the rigorous standard of review established by our prior decisions, the weighty interests served by restricting the size of financial contributions to political candidates are sufficient to justify the limited effect upon First Amendment freedoms caused by the $1,000 contribution ceiling.

---

31. While providing significant limitations on the ability of all individuals and groups to contribute large amounts of money to candidates, the Act's contribution ceilings do not foreclose the making of substantial contributions to candidates by some major special-interest groups through the combined effect of individual contributions from adherents or the proliferation of political funds each authorized under the Act to contribute to candidates. As a prime example, §610 permits corporations and labor unions to establish segregated funds to solicit voluntary contributions to be utilized for political purposes. Corporate and union resources without limitation may be employed to administer these funds and to solicit contributions from employees, stockholders, and union members. Each separate fund may contribute up to $5,000 per candidate per election so long as the fund qualifies as a political committee under §608(b)(2).

The Act places no limit on the number of funds that may be formed through the use of subsidiaries or divisions of corporations, or of local and regional units of a national labor union. The potential for proliferation of these sources of contributions is not insignificant. In 1972, approximately 1,824,000 active corporations filed federal income tax returns. Internal Revenue Service, Preliminary Statistics of Income 1972, Corporation Income Tax Returns, p. 1 (Pub. 159 (11-74)). (It is not clear whether this total includes subsidiary corporations where the parent filed a consolidated return.) In the same year, 71,409 local unions were chartered by national unions. The Act allows the maximum contribution to be made by each unit's fund provided the decision or judgment to contribute to particular candidates is made by the fund independently of control or direction by the parent corporation or the national or regional union.

(b)

Appellants' first overbreadth challenge to the contribution ceilings rests on the proposition that most large contributors do not seek improper influence over a candidate's position or an officeholder's action. Although the truth of that proposition may be assumed, it does not undercut the validity of the $1,000 contribution limitation. Not only is it difficult to isolate suspect contributions, but, more importantly, Congress was justified in concluding that the interest in safeguarding against the appearance of impropriety requires that the opportunity for abuse inherent in the process of raising large monetary contributions be eliminated.

A second, related overbreadth claim is that the $1,000 restriction is unrealistically low because much more than that amount would still not be enough to enable an unscrupulous contributor to exercise improper influence over a candidate or officeholder, especially in campaigns for statewide or national office. While the contribution limitation provisions might well have been structured to take account of the graduated expenditure limitations for congressional and Presidential campaigns, Congress' failure to engage in such fine tuning does not invalidate the legislation. . . .

C. EXPENDITURE LIMITATIONS

The Act's expenditure ceilings impose direct and substantial restraints on the quantity of political speech. The most drastic of the limitations restricts individuals and groups, including political parties that fail to place a candidate on the ballot, to an expenditure of $1,000 "relative to a clearly identified candidate during a calendar year." §608(e)(1). . . . It is clear that a primary effect of these expenditure limitations is to restrict the quantity of campaign speech by individuals, groups, and candidates. . . .

1. The $1,000 Limitation on Expenditures "Relative to a Clearly Identified Candidate" . . .

Section 608(e)(1) provides that "(n)o person may make any expenditure . . . relative to a clearly identified candidate during a calendar year which, when added to all other expenditures made by such person during the year advocating the election or defeat of such candidate, exceeds $1,000." The plain effect of §608(e)(1) is to prohibit all individuals, who are neither candidates nor owners of institutional press facilities, and all groups, except political parties and campaign organizations, from voicing their views "relative to a clearly identified candidate" through means that entail aggregate expenditures of more than $1,000 during a calendar year. The provision, for example, would make it a federal criminal offense for a person or association to place a single one-quarter page advertisement "relative to a clearly identified candidate" in a major metropolitan newspaper.

Before examining the interests advanced in support of §608(e)(1)'s expenditure ceiling, consideration must be given to appellants' contention that the provision is unconstitutionally vague. . . .

The key operative language of the provision limits "any expenditure . . . relative to a clearly identified candidate." Although "expenditure," "clearly identified," and "candidate" are defined in the Act, there is no definition clarifying what expenditures are "relative to" a candidate. . . . Th[e] context clearly permits, if indeed it does not require, the phrase "relative to" a candidate to be read to mean "advocating the election or defeat of" a candidate.

But while such a construction of §608(e)(1) refocuses the vagueness question, the Court of Appeals was mistaken in thinking that this construction eliminates the problem of unconstitutional vagueness altogether. For the distinction between discussion of issues and candidates and advocacy of election or defeat of candidates may often dissolve in practical application. Candidates, especially incumbents, are intimately tied to public issues involving legislative proposals and governmental actions. Not only do candidates campaign on the basis of their positions on various public issues, but campaigns themselves generate issues of public interest. . . .

[C]onstitutional deficiencies . . . can be avoided only by reading §608(e)(1) as limited to communications that include explicit words of advocacy of election or defeat of a candidate. . . . This is the reading of the provision suggested by the non-governmental appellees in arguing that "(f)unds spent to propagate one's views on issues without expressly calling for a candidate's election or defeat are thus not covered." We agree that in order to preserve the provision against invalidation on vagueness grounds, §608(e)(1) must be construed to apply only to expenditures for communications that in express terms advocate the election or defeat of a clearly identified candidate for federal office.[52]

We turn then to the basic First Amendment question whether §608(e)(1), even as thus narrowly and explicitly construed, impermissibly burdens the constitutional right of free expression. The Court of Appeals summarily held the provision constitutionally valid on the ground that "section 608(e) is a loophole-closing provision only" that is necessary to prevent circumvention of the contribution limitations. We cannot agree.

The . . . Act's expenditure limitations impose far greater restraints on the freedom of speech and association than do its contribution limitations. The markedly greater burden on basic freedoms caused by §608(e)(1) thus cannot be sustained simply by invoking the interest in maximizing the effectiveness of the less intrusive contribution limitations. Rather, the constitutionality of §608(e)(1) turns on whether the governmental interests advanced in its support satisfy the exacting scrutiny applicable to limitations on core First Amendment rights of political expression.

We find that the governmental interest in preventing corruption and the appearance of corruption is inadequate to justify §608(e)(1)'s ceiling on independent expenditures. First, assuming, arguendo, that large independent expenditures pose the same dangers of actual or apparent quid pro quo arrangements as do large contributions, §608(e)(1) does not provide an answer that sufficiently relates to the elimination of those dangers. Unlike the contribution limitations' total ban on the giving of large amounts of money to candidates, §608(e)(1) prevents only some large expenditures. So long as persons and groups eschew expenditures that

---

52. This construction would restrict the application of §608(e)(1) to communications containing express words of advocacy of election or defeat, such as "vote for," "elect," "support," "cast your ballot for," "Smith for Congress," "vote against," "defeat," "reject."

in express terms advocate the election or defeat of a clearly identified candidate, they are free to spend as much as they want to promote the candidate and his views. The exacting interpretation of the statutory language necessary to avoid unconstitutional vagueness thus undermines the limitation's effectiveness as a loophole-closing provision by facilitating circumvention by those seeking to exert improper influence upon a candidate or office-holder. It would naively underestimate the ingenuity and resourcefulness of persons and groups desiring to buy influence to believe that they would have much difficulty devising expenditures that skirted the restriction on express advocacy of election or defeat but nevertheless benefited the candidate's campaign. Yet no substantial societal interest would be served by a loophole-closing provision designed to check corruption that permitted unscrupulous persons and organizations to expend unlimited sums of money in order to obtain improper influence over candidates for elective office.

Second, quite apart from the shortcomings of §608(e)(1) in preventing any abuses generated by large independent expenditures, the independent advocacy restricted by the provision does not presently appear to pose dangers of real or apparent corruption comparable to those identified with large campaign contributions. The parties defending §608(e)(1) contend that it is necessary to prevent would-be contributors from avoiding the contribution limitations by the simple expedient of paying directly for media advertisements or for other portions of the candidate's campaign activities. They argue that expenditures controlled by or coordinated with the candidate and his campaign might well have virtually the same value to the candidate as a contribution and would pose similar dangers of abuse. Yet such controlled or coordinated expenditures are treated as contributions rather than expenditures under the Act. Section 608(b)'s contribution ceilings rather than §608(e)(1)'s independent expenditure limitation prevent attempts to circumvent the Act through prearranged or coordinated expenditures amounting to disguised contributions. By contrast, §608(e)(1) limits expenditures for express advocacy of candidates made totally independently of the candidate and his campaign. Unlike contributions, such independent expenditures may well provide little assistance to the candidate's campaign and indeed may prove counterproductive. The absence of prearrangement and coordination of an expenditure with the candidate or his agent not only undermines the value of the expenditure to the candidate, but also alleviates the danger that expenditures will be given as a quid pro quo for improper commitments from the candidate. Rather than preventing circumvention of the contribution limitations, §608(e)(1) severely restricts all independent advocacy despite its substantially diminished potential for abuse.

While the independent expenditure ceiling thus fails to serve any substantial governmental interest in stemming the reality or appearance of corruption in the electoral process, it heavily burdens core First Amendment expression. . . . Advocacy of the election or defeat of candidates for federal office is no less entitled to protection under the First Amendment than the discussion of political policy generally or advocacy of the passage or defeat of legislation.

It is argued, however, that the ancillary governmental interest in equalizing the relative ability of individuals and groups to influence the outcome of elections serves to justify the limitation on express advocacy of the election or defeat of candidates imposed by §608(e)(1)'s expenditure ceiling. But the concept that government may restrict the speech of some elements of our society in order to enhance the relative voice of others is wholly foreign to the First Amendment. . . . The First Amendment's protection against governmental abridgment of free expression cannot properly be made to depend on a person's financial ability to engage in public discussion.

The Court's decisions in *Mills v. Alabama*, 384 U.S. 214 (1966), and *Miami Herald Publishing Co. v. Tornillo*, 418 U.S. 241 (1974), held that legislative restrictions on advocacy of the election or defeat of political candidates are wholly at odds with the guarantees of the First Amendment. . . . Yet the prohibition of election day-editorials invalidated in *Mills* is clearly a lesser intrusion on constitutional freedom than a $1,000 limitation on the amount of money any person or association can spend during an entire election year in advocating the election or defeat of a candidate for public office. . . .

For the reasons stated, we conclude that §608(e)(1)'s independent expenditure limitation is unconstitutional under the First Amendment. . . .

3. Limitations on Campaign Expenditures

Section 608(c) places limitations on overall campaign expenditures by candidates seeking nomination for election and election to federal office. . . .

No governmental interest that has been suggested is sufficient to justify the restriction on the quantity of political expression imposed by §608(c)'s campaign expenditure limitations. The major evil associated with rapidly increasing campaign expenditures is the danger of candidate dependence on large contributions. The interest in alleviating the corrupting influence of large contributions is served by the Act's contribution limitations and disclosure provisions rather than by §608(c)'s campaign expenditure ceilings. . . .

The interest in equalizing the financial resources of candidates competing for federal office is no more convincing a justification for restricting the scope of federal election campaigns. Given the limitation on the size of outside contributions, the financial resources available to a candidate's campaign, like the number of volunteers recruited, will normally vary with the size and intensity of the candidate's support. There is nothing invidious, improper, or unhealthy in permitting such funds to be spent to carry the candidate's message to the electorate. Moreover, the equalization of permissible campaign expenditures might serve not to equalize the opportunities of all candidates, but to handicap a candidate who lacked substantial name recognition or exposure of his views before the start of the campaign.

The campaign expenditure ceilings appear to be designed primarily to serve the governmental interests in reducing the allegedly skyrocketing costs of political campaigns. . . . [But] the mere growth in the cost of federal election campaigns in and of itself provides no basis for governmental restrictions on the quantity of campaign spending and the resulting limitation on the scope of federal campaigns. The First Amendment denies government the power to determine that spending to promote one's political views is wasteful, excessive, or unwise. In the free society ordained by our Constitution it is not the government, but the people individually as citizens and candidates and collectively as associations and political committees who must retain control over the quantity and range of debate on public issues in a political campaign.

For these reasons we hold that §608(c) is constitutionally invalid. . . .

Chief Justice BURGER, concurring in part and dissenting in part:

I agree fully with that part of the Court's opinion that holds unconstitutional the limitations the Act puts on campaign expenditures which "place substantial and direct restrictions on the ability of candidates, citizens, and associations to engage in protected political expression, restrictions that the First Amendment cannot tolerate." Yet when it approves similarly stringent limitations on contributions, the Court ignores the reasons it finds so persuasive in the context of expenditures. For me contributions and expenditures are two sides of the same First Amendment coin.

By limiting campaign contributions, the Act restricts the amount of money that will be spent on political activity and does so directly. . . . Limiting contributions, as a practical matter, will limit expenditures and will put an effective ceiling on the amount of political activity and debate that the Government will permit to take place. . . .

The Court attempts to separate the two communicative aspects of political contributions [—] the "moral" support that the gift itself conveys, which the Court suggests is the same whether the gift is $10 or $10,000, and the fact that money translates into communication. The Court dismisses the effect of the limitations on the second aspect of contributions. . . . On [the] premise that contribution limitations restrict only the speech of "someone other than the contributor" rests the Court's justification for treating contributions differently from expenditures. The premise is demonstrably flawed; the contribution limitations will, in specific instances, limit exactly the same political activity that the expenditure ceilings limit, and at least one of the "expenditure" limitations the Court finds objectionable operates precisely like the "contribution" limitations.

[I]t seems clear to me that in approving these limitations on contributions the Court must rest upon the proposition that "pooling" money is fundamentally different from other forms of associational or joint activity. I see only two possible ways in which money differs from volunteer work, endorsements, and the like. Money can be used to buy favors, because an unscrupulous politician can put it to personal use; second, giving money is a less visible form of associational activity. With respect to the first problem, the Act does not attempt to do any more than the bribery laws to combat this sort of corruption. In fact, the Act does not reach at all, and certainly the contribution limits do not reach, forms of "association" that can be fully as corrupt as a contribution intended as a quid pro quo such as the eleventh-hour endorsement by a former rival, obtained for the promise of a federal appointment. This underinclusiveness is not a constitutional flaw, but it demonstrates that the contribution limits do not clearly focus on this first distinction. To the extent Congress thought that the second problem, the lesser visibility of contributions, required that money be treated differently from other forms of associational activity, disclosure laws are the simple and wholly efficacious answer; they make the invisible apparent. . . .

Justice WHITE, concurring in part and dissenting in part:

Concededly, neither the limitations on contributions nor those on expenditures directly or indirectly purport to control the content of political speech by candidates or by their supporters or detractors. What the Act regulates is giving and spending money, acts that have First Amendment significance not because they are themselves communicative with respect to the qualifications of the candidate, but because money may be used to defray the expenses of speaking or otherwise communicating about the merits or demerits of federal candidates for election. The act of giving money to political candidates, however, may have illegal or other undesirable consequences: it may be used to secure the express or tacit understanding that the giver will enjoy political favor if the candidate is elected. Both Congress and this Court's cases have recognized this as a mortal danger against which effective preventive and curative steps must be taken.

Since the contribution and expenditure limitations are neutral as to the content of speech and are not motivated by fear of the consequences of the political speech of particular candidates or of political speech in general, this case depends on whether the nonspeech interests of the Federal Government in regulating the use of money in political campaigns are sufficiently urgent to justify the incidental effects that the limitations visit upon the First Amendment interests of candidates and their supporters.

Proceeding from the maxim that "money talks," the Court finds that the expenditure limitations will seriously curtail political expression by candidates and interfere substantially with their chances for election. The Court concludes that the Constitution denies Congress the power to limit campaign expenses; federal candidates and I would suppose state candidates, too are to have the constitutional right to raise and spend unlimited amounts of money in quest of their own election.

As an initial matter, the argument that money is speech and that limiting the flow of money to the speaker violates the First Amendment proves entirely too much. Compulsory bargaining and the right to strike, both provided for or protected by federal law, inevitably have increased the labor costs of those who publish newspapers, which are in turn an important factor in the recent disappearance of many daily papers. Federal and state taxation directly removes from company coffers large amounts of money that might be spent on larger and better newspapers. The antitrust laws are aimed at preventing monopoly profits and price fixing, which gouge the consumer. It is also true that general price controls have from time to time existed and have been applied to the newspapers or other media. But it has not been suggested, nor could it be successfully, that these laws, and many others, are invalid because they siphon off or prevent the accumulation of large sums that would otherwise be available for communicative activities.

In any event, as it should be unnecessary to point out, money is not always equivalent to or used for speech, even in the context of political campaigns. I accept the reality that communicating with potential voters is the heart of an election campaign and that widespread communication has become very expensive. There are, however, many expensive campaign activities that are not themselves communicative or remotely related to speech. Furthermore, campaigns differ among themselves. Some seem to spend much less money than others and yet communicate as much as or more than those supported by enormous bureaucracies with unlimited financing. The record before us no more supports the conclusion that the communicative efforts of congressional and Presidential candidates will be crippled by the expenditure limitations than it supports the contrary. . . . [T]here is no sound basis for invalidating the expenditure limitations, so long as the purposes they serve are legitimate and sufficiently substantial, which in my view they are.

In the first place, expenditure ceilings reinforce the contribution limits and help eradicate the hazard of corruption. . . . Without limits on total expenditures, campaign costs will inevitably and endlessly escalate. Pressure to raise funds will constantly build and with it the temptation to resort in "emergencies" to those sources of large sums, who, history shows, are sufficiently confident of not being caught to risk flouting contribution limits. Congress would save the candidate from this predicament by establishing a reasonable ceiling on all candidates. This is a major consideration in favor of the limitation. . . .

Besides backing up the contribution provisions, which are aimed at preventing untoward influence on candidates that are elected, expenditure limits have their own potential for preventing the corruption of federal elections themselves. For many years the law has required the disclosure of expenditures as well as contributions. . . . There are many illegal ways of spending money to influence elections. One would be blind to history to deny that unlimited money tempts people to spend it on whatever money can buy to influence an election. . . .

I have little doubt in addition that limiting the total that can be spent will ease the candidate's understandable obsession with fundraising, and so free him and his staff to communicate in more places and ways unconnected with the fundraising function. . . .

It is also important to restore and maintain public confidence in federal elections. It is critical to obviate or dispel the impression that federal elections are purely and simply a function of money, that federal offices are bought and sold or that political races are reserved for those who have the facility and the stomach for doing whatever it takes to bring together those interests, groups, and individuals that can raise or contribute large fortunes in order to prevail at the polls.

The ceiling on candidate expenditures represents the considered judgment of Congress that elections are to be decided among candidates none of whom has overpowering advantage by reason of a huge campaign war chest. At least so long as the ceiling placed upon the candidates is not plainly too low, elections are not to turn on the difference in the amounts of money that candidates have to spend. This seems an acceptable purpose and the means chosen a common-sense way to achieve it. The Court nevertheless holds that a candidate has a constitutional right to spend unlimited amounts of money, mostly that of other people, in order to be elected. The holding perhaps is not that federal candidates have the constitutional right to purchase their election, but many will so interpret the Court's conclusion in this case. I cannot join the Court in this respect. . . .

2. *Justifications for Campaign-Finance Regulation*

a. Anti-Corruption Justifications

▶▶ *What Does the Constitution Say About Corruption?*   In *Buckley*, the Court stated that campaign financing can be regulated by the government if the purpose of the regulation is to prevent corruption or the appearance of corruption. The Court treats this anti-corruption principle as an interest that the government might have in regulating how campaigns are financed. However, might the Constitution actually demand this result?

Professor Zephyr Teachout argues that it does, writing that "[t]he Constitution carries within it an anti-corruption principle, much like the separation-of-powers principle, or federalism." Zephyr Teachout, *The Anti-Corruption Principle*, 94 CORNELL L. REV. 341, 341 (2009). Professor Teachout locates this principle in both the history and text of the Constitution. In the context of Article I, for example, Professor Teachout notes that

> [t]he Framers' discussion of the people's house and the elite's house—the House of Representatives and the Senate—was shaped by concerns that the House would be populated by men of weak will, easily corrupted to use their office for venal ends, and that the Senate would become corrupted by vanity and luxury. The size of the houses, the mode of election, the limits on holding multiple offices, the limitations on accepting foreign gifts, and the veto override provision were all considered in light of concerns about corruption, and designed to limit legislators' opportunities to serve themselves.

Id. at 354. Professor Teachout makes similar arguments from Articles II and III and other provisions related to the structure of the federal government.

These anti-corruption ideals, Professor Teachout continues, should not only guide decisions related to interpreting the specific provisions in which they are found, but should enable Congress to enact legislation intended to prevent corruption in any of its guises, including political spending. As she notes:

> I argue that the Court ought to weigh the Framers' anti-corruption principle in their decisions about democratic institutions. Instead of treating the fight against corruption as a "compelling state interest," I argue that it ought to be treated as a fundamental constitutional principle, a principle that Congress should have leeway to pursue absent very strong countervailing constitutional limitations. Instead of strictly scrutinizing anti-corruption efforts, the Courts ought to balance anti-corruption concerns against First Amendment concerns as co-equal considerations. I support this argument by tying the history and structure of the Constitution to several modes of interpretation.

Id. at 345. *See also* ZEPHYR TEACHOUT, CORRUPTION IN AMERICA: FROM BENJAMIN FRANKLIN'S SNUFF BOX TO *CITIZENS UNITED* (2014); Lawrence Lessig, *What an Originalist Would Understand "Corruption" to Mean*, 102 CAL. L. REV. 1 (2014); Seth Barrett Tillman, *The Original Public Meaning of the Emoluments Clause: A Reply to*

Professor Zephyr Teachout, 107 Nw. U. L. Rev. COLLOQUY 180 (2013). Suppose Professor Teachout is correct. Might the risk of corruption arising out of independent expenditures be sufficiently strong to require upholding the $1,000 limitation at issue in *Buckley*? Might it still be found unconstitutional when balanced against other First Amendment concerns?

≫ ***What Is Corruption?*** In upholding limitations on campaign contributions, the Court finds a compelling interest in preventing corruption. But the Court never really defines corruption. What is corruption? This is a question that turns out to be more complicated than we might think. Consider some possibilities.

Public Office for Private Gain? "Corruption," Professor Susan Rose-Ackerman declares, "is the misuse of office for private gain." Susan Rose-Ackerman, *Corruption and Democracy*, 90 PROC. ANN. MEETING AM. SOC'Y INT'L L. 83 (1996). Is this too broad a definition to be useful? The Court in *Buckley* seems to equate corruption to a quid pro quo. But what is a quid pro quo? Consider one definition from the philosophy and political science literature.

> [In] its most generic form a quid pro quo comprises two elements: It involves officials whose judgment is compromised, encumbered, or impaired because (1) they have the official capacity to affect the interests of a private party to whom (2) they are in some way beholden because they have received from that party something of value for which they have provided no private-market consideration in return (so that if the transfer is to be recompensed, it could be recompensed only by an official act).

Andrew Stark, *Beyond Quid Pro Quo: What's Wrong with Private Gain from Public Office?*, 91 AM. POL. SCI. REV. 108 (1997). That definition seems similar to the one provided by Professor Rose-Ackerman.

Dependence Corruption? In a very influential book, Professor Lawrence Lessig has offered what he contends is a different conception of corruption, dependence corruption. *See* LAWRENCE LESSIG, REPUBLIC, LOST: HOW MONEY CORRUPTS CONGRESS—AND A PLAN TO STOP IT (2011). To explain his conception of corruption, Professor Lessig uses an allegory of a fictional country that he calls Lesterland. Lesterland has two kinds of people, a small group of individuals called Lesters and everyone else. Lesterland has two elections, a qualifying election that is like a primary election in which only the Lesters can vote, and a general election in which everyone is allowed to vote.

Professor Lessig analogizes Lesterland to the United States and how we fund our campaigns. As he sees it, there are two elections in the United States. The first election, like the primary election in which only the Lesters are allowed to vote, is a money primary in which only the funders are allowed to participate. The second election is the one in which everyone gets to participate after the funders have decided which candidates are worthy of holding public office.

Dependence corruption is an institutional account of corruption. It does not purport to explain how particular individual political actors are corrupt, but how institutions, particularly legislative bodies, are corrupt. Professor Lessig argues that "the Framers intended Congress to be 'independent.'" *Id.* at 251. By "independent," Professor Lessig does not mean that Congress ought to be free to do whatever it wants; rather, independence means that Congress was meant to be

" 'dependent upon the People alone.' " *Id.* Congress is corrupt when it is no longer
"dependent upon the People alone," but dependent upon a small group of financiers. This dependence upon the financiers, who in Professor Lessig's rendering
are not the People described by the Constitution, causes Congress to align its preferences to the preferences of its small group of funders. *Id.*

How compelling is this definition of corruption? Professor Richard Hasen
argues that even though Professor Lessig "uses the term 'dependence corruption,'
he is writing more about a *distortion* of policy outcomes, or *skew,* caused by the influence of money, channeled through lobbyists, on politics." The problem, therefore,
is not corruption but the fact that "the private system of campaign finance with
lobbyist-arbitrageurs distorts politics and skews political outcomes. That distortion
in turn leads public policy to be out of line with the public's important interest in
efficient government." *See* Richard L. Hasen, *Fixing Washington,* 126 HARV. L. REV.
550, 571, 574 (2012). Is dependence corruption about corruption or distortion? Is
there a difference between the two? For an argument that Lessig's conception is
not about corruption but political participation, see Guy-Uriel E. Charles, *Corruption Temptation,* 102 CAL. L. REV. 25 (2014).

Three Conceptions of Corruption. Professor Deborah Hellman argues that the
Court's campaign-finance jurisprudence reflects three different ideas about corruption. The first conception is "corruption as deformation of judgment." The
point here is that the legislator ought to use her best judgment about the merits
of public policy determinations. She ought not be swayed by campaign contributions or even by the views of others, as such. The second conception is corruption
as the distortion of influence. Here the problem is the failure of the legislator
to be sufficiently responsive to her constituents. Lastly, corruption is the sale of
favors. This last conception is the most familiar conception; it treats monetary
exchanges as outside of the proper role of representation. *See* Deborah Hellman, *Defining Corruption and Constitutionalizing Democracy,* 111 MICH. L. REV. 1385
(2013).

Bribery. What about bribery? The Court also seems to think that corruption
is of a piece with bribery. But it was not convinced by the argument that bribery
laws made campaign-finance contributions unnecessary, apparently because laws
against bribery "deal with only the most blatant and specific attempts of those with
money to influence governmental action." Is corruption different from bribery? 18
U.S.C. §201(c)(1)(A) defines a bribe as a proposal from someone who

> directly or indirectly gives, offers, or promises anything of value to any
> public official, former public official, or person selected to be a public
> official, for or because of any official act performed or to be performed
> by such public official, former public official, or person selected to be a
> public official.

That seems like a fairly broad definition that would cover just about anything. Professor David A. Strauss defines bribery as offers that "go into the officials' pockets" and allowing public officials to convert "authority given to them for public
purposes into private gain." David A. Strauss, *What Is the Goal of Campaign Finance
Reform?,* 1995 U. CHI. LEGAL F. 141, 148. Is that any better? Do we have a concept of
bribery that is different from that of a quid pro quo?

Corruption of Politics. Professor Samuel Issacharoff offers a broader systemic framework that focuses on the corruption of politics itself.

> On this view, the underlying problem is not so much what happens in the electoral arena but what incentives are offered to elected officials while in office. . . . Specifically, the inquiry on officeholding asks whether the electoral system leads the political class to offer private gain from public action to distinct, tightly organized constituencies, which in turn may be mobilized to keep compliant public officials in office.

Samuel Issacharoff, *On Political Corruption*, 124 HARV. L. REV. 118, 126 (2010). Professor Issacharoff seems to think of corruption as patronage. Is patronage a more useful concept?

≫ *The Appearance of Corruption.* Is the appearance of corruption a separate conceptual justification, distinct from corruption itself, for limiting campaign contributions? Consider this view from political scientist Mark Warren, who argues that the appearance of corruption standard is a separate conceptual category.

> Democratic systems of representation depend upon the integrity of appearances, not simply because they are an indication of whether officials are upholding their public trust, but because they provide the means through which citizens can judge whether, in any particular instance, their trust in public officials is warranted. The representative's role is, in part, to provide citizens with the information they need to judge when they should trust and when they should more actively participate in political decision making. The representative can fill this role only if he is worthy of a second-order trust—trust in the veracity of his words and deeds. A representative who is not trustworthy in this sense also denies citizens their rightful participation in public judgments. Likewise, institutions that fail to support citizens' confidence in appearances produce political exclusions and generate a form of disempowerment. Together these failures amount to a corruption of democratic processes. Understanding this dimension of democracy, then, requires that we avoid viewing appearances as mere reflections of underlying realities, and appreciate that they are the grounds upon which democratic judgments are made, and thus part of the constitutive fabric of democracy. Appearance regulations underwrite this key dimension of democracy.

Mark E. Warren, *Democracy and Deceit: Regulating Appearances of Corruption*, 50 AM. J. POL. SCI. 160, 172-173 (2006). Is this conception of corruption as appearances strong enough to serve as an independent basis for regulating campaign finances?

Does it matter to the appearance-of-corruption justification if public opinion is in fact intractable in the belief that politics is corrupt? According to one study, "There can be no doubt that the American people perceive the campaign finance system to be corrupt and, in large numbers, will support almost any restriction on expenditures and contributions." Yet, people's views about the corruption of the finance system often are closely related to, or perhaps parasitic on, their views about "their position in society, the incumbents in office, or their attitudes about how government ought to tax and spend." Nathaniel Persily and Kelli Lammie,

*Perceptions of Corruption and Campaign Finance: When Public Opinion Determines Consti-
tutional Law,* 153 U. Pa. L. Rev. 119, 173 (2004).

Should the strength of the appearance-of-corruption rationale turn on actual
empirical analysis of public perceptions? Or should it have in view some kind of
reasonable or rational hypothetical observer?

The Court in *Buckley* also seemed to define corruption as undue or
improper influence over a candidate or elected official. Of course this is question-
begging: what is undue influence? The concept of undue influence assumes that
there is a baseline around which we can agree that some influence is due, by which
we mean proper, and some influence is undue, by which we mean improper. But
what is that baseline? Should public officials be responsive to the needs of their
constituents? If so, how much? Suppose a bundler (an individual who gathers legal
contributions for a campaign) said to an elected official or candidate for elected
office, "I will raise $500,000 for you if you agree to support our bill." Is that attempt
to influence the politician legitimate or illegitimate? If this is not undue influence,
why are contribution limits constitutional? If this is undue influence, should bun-
dling be outlawed?

≫ ***Extortion.***   Though the Court does not talk about this in *Buckley*, to what
extent might the concern with corruption also include a worry about extortion?
Professor Strauss writes:

> The problem of extortion has received surprisingly little attention in the
> public debate over campaign-finance reform. As a conceptual matter, it
> is the opposite of the concern with corruption (understood as a form of
> bribery): the problem is not the power that contributors have over offi-
> cials, but the power that officials have over potential contributors. Elected
> officials might extract contributions from individuals and groups who
> have no desire to contribute but fear that the official will take actions
> unfavorable to them if they do not.

David A. Strauss, *supra,* at 152. Strauss argues that extortion is a type of an unfair
tax paid by the rich to public officials for the privilege of doing business. He also
argues that extortion is inefficient because it raises the cost of doing business. Is
extortion the best way of understanding the campaign financing problem? If so,
should be the agenda for reform be to protect potential contributors against this
type of tax?

b.   Equality Justifications

Other than preventing corruption through the exchange of money for official
favors, is there any justification for restricting the giving and spending of money in
politics? Over the years, many justifications have been advanced. The group examined immediately below focuses on concerns of equality.

≫ ***"Buying" Office.***   A concern expressed frequently at the time of FECA's enactment was that their wealth allowed the rich simply to "buy" their way into public
office. In floor debates preceding adoption of the 1971 version of FECA, for example, Senators repeatedly linked unlimited campaign spending to the ability of the
rich to dominate electoral contests. "Reasonable limitations must be applied to the

expenditures of a candidate so as to prevent any person with unlimited resources from 'buying' an election," argued one Senator. 117 Cong. Rec. S 29323 (Aug. 4, 1971) (Sen. Symington). "A candidate should not be able to buy off any election in his behalf. Men and women elected to Federal office must be elected and chosen by their constituency and not by themselves," said another. *Id.*, S 26111 (July 20, 1971) (Sen. Prouty). "Media spending," argued another, "should be limited so that no candidate can overwhelm his opponent or the electorate with an advertising campaign of monumental cost, and, in effect, buy his way into office. . . . It is a waste of resources and a distortion of the democratic process." *Id.*, S 29321 (Aug. 4, 1971) (Sen. Muskie). Similar sentiments were expressed during House debates preceding enactment of the 1974 amendments. *See, e.g.,* 117 Cong. Rec. H 7936 (Aug. 8, 1974) (Rep. Kastenmeier) ("one of the primary purposes of this bill . . . is to limit the ability of any candidate to literally buy an election").

What does it mean to "buy" office? Unless the office is literally and corruptly for sale by officials currently in power, people don't actually purchase their office by paying for it directly. To be sure, the literal sale of offices has occurred in the United States, though the practice historically appears to have been associated more with appointive offices than with elective ones. Normally, then, money does not buy office, but it clearly is spent on the presupposition that it buys something that can be exchanged for office. But what? Does it buy votes? Again, unless votes are literally for sale, money doesn't buy votes, but at most something that can be exchanged for votes. What is that something? We explore this question further below.

Regardless of the details of how money might help people "buy" office, it remains true that the U.S. Senate has long been known as a "Millionaire's Club." In 2010, about 80 Senators reported a net worth of over $1 million, and 24 reported a net worth of more than $10 million. In the House, 232 members reported a net worth of more than $1 million, and 42 reported more than $10 million. The richest member of Congress, Rep. Darrell Issa of Southern California, is worth close to $500 million. *See* Center for Responsive Politics, opensecrets.org. These figures diverge grossly from the financial profiles of most Americans. Do they provide evidence that money buys office?

⟩⟩   *Overrepresentation of the Rich.* The sheer cost of mounting a campaign for public office has sometimes been said unfairly to preclude many highly qualified and talented individuals from running for office, a loss to the public and, in many cases, to the representativeness of legislatures. According to a Senate Committee studying campaign finance reform, "[t]he crisis level has been reached in American campaign spending. . . . '[T]here is a danger that the cost of campaigning, chiefly swollen by the cost of television, will exclude the honest poor.'" Senate Committee on Commerce, *Promoting Fair Practices in the Conduct of Election Campaigns for Federal Elective Offices, and for Other Purposes,* S. Rep. 92-96, 92d Cong., 1st Sess. (May 6, 1971), at 22. Indirectly limiting in this way the identity of those who serve in Congress was said in turn to distort the representativeness of the body, and the kinds of interests to which it is responsive: "If our Government is to represent all of America and its diversified economic interests, we must assure that not only the rich have an opportunity to serve." 117 Cong. Rec. S 26111 (July 20, 1977) (Sen. Prouty).

We have previously encountered the notion of "descriptive representation" in Chapter 5, but in the context of racial diversity in the composition of legislatures. Assuming arguments for descriptive representation have any force with respect to the representation of race, or gender, or ethnicity, do they have the same force when it comes to the representation of economic class? Must a legislature contain economic diversity to represent fairly? Or might the wealthy be capable of fairly representing the interests of the working class or the poor? If not, what are the consequences of overrepresentation of the rich?

Aren't there ways to influence legislative policy other than electing a member of your own socioeconomic class? If so, how widely available are those methods, to whom are they available, and how effective are they compared to electing a like-minded or at least sympathetic representative?

>> *Disproportionate Influence of Institutional Entities.*   In a similar vein, campaign finance reform has also been touted as a way of reducing the influence of special interest groups, corporations, PACs, and unions. Institutional entities, such as corporations, unions, and PACs are "[r]elatively small groups whose members are intensely interested in an issue [and thus] have an organizational advantage over much larger groups whose members have a smaller interest. This organizational advantage can translate into an advantage in democratic politics. This is a basic insight of public-choice theory." David A. Strauss, *What Is the Goal of Campaign Finance Reform?*, 1995 U. CHI. LEGAL F. 141 (1995). Thus, entities may be rich in organizational advantage even when they are not necessarily rich in funds. Should we be suspicious of groups in general because they have an inherent organizational advantage? Isn't politics in some degree the enterprise of mobilizing citizens as groups for the purpose of influencing collective political decisions? Recall, on the other hand, from Chapter 7 that Americans of the founding era had a deep-seated suspicion of political parties precisely because they *were* organizations. Is that a sensible objection, and if so, on what grounds?

>> *Equalizing Opportunity to Influence Politics.*   A widely expressed view among supporters of campaign-finance regulation is that restrictions on spending are justified in the service of equalizing the ability of rich and poor to exert influence in the political sphere. Consider this argument from Professor Briffault:

> The most important constitutional value the Court has rejected is, of course, voter equality, which is a central premise of our democratic system. Over the course of our history, the electorate has been expanded from a relatively narrow set of white male property owners or taxpayers to virtually all adult citizens. Modern constitutional developments like the one person, one vote doctrine and the anti-vote-dilution doctrine have sought to ensure not simply that every adult citizen enjoys the right to vote but that each voter has an equally weighted vote, and thus an equal opportunity to influence the outcome of an election. Moreover, modern constitutional law emphatically denies a special place for wealth in voting and elections. Most states long ago scrapped wealth or tax-payment requirements for voting, and the Court made the elimination of such wealth or tax-payment tests constitutionally mandatory. Wealth may not be a criterion for the right to cast a ballot, or to be a candidate, nor may

the wealth of a voter be a factor in deciding how much weight a particular vote may be given.

The role of voter equality in our electoral system has implications beyond the actual casting and counting of ballots. For the election to serve as a mechanism of democratic decision-making, there must be a considerable amount of election-related activity before balloting can occur. Candidates, parties, interest groups, and interested individuals need to be able to attempt to persuade voters as to how to cast their ballots. The election campaign is an integral part of the process of structured choice and democratic deliberation that constitutes an election. The political equality norm that governs the right to vote, the aggregation of votes into election districts, and the right to be a candidate is relevant to the right of voters to present their choices to the general electorate and to attempt to persuade the electorate to support certain candidates or particular positions on ballot propositions. Political equality is undermined when some individuals or interest groups with greater private wealth than others can draw on those resources to make more extensive appeals to the electorate than can those with fewer resources. Indeed, a concern about the tension between greatly unequal private wealth and political equality has long been one of the driving forces behind campaign finance regulation. It is, as Judge Guido Calabresi once put it, "the huge elephant—and donkey—in the living room on all discussions of campaign finance reform."

Richard Briffault, *On Dejudicializing American Campaign Finance Law*, 27 Ga. St. U. L. Rev. 887, 913-914 (2011).

A common objection to this reasoning is that there is nothing illicit about the accumulation of wealth—differences in wealth are innocuous artifacts of a properly functioning and democratically legitimate economic system—whereas the same cannot be said about the accumulation of voting shares, which by definition must be allocated equally if a system is going to deserve to be called democratic. Moreover, many political resources are unequally distributed—intelligence, charisma, persuasiveness, time, and so forth—and nobody seems to think that the distribution of these goods should be regulated. Why should wealth be treated differently?

One possible response is that money is different from other resources: it is a universal unit of exchange, and can thus be converted to any other kind of resource in which an advantage might be useful: "The convertibility of wealth can result in the various sources of influence becoming aligned and reinforcing rather than constraining one another." Jacob Rowbottom, Democracy Distorted: Wealth, Influence and Democratic Politics (2010). Another reason to treat wealth differently might be that it provides a different and more valuable kind of influence than other political resources. Because wealth can be used to "secur[e] access to the channels of communication, wealth determines which views will get a hearing." Citizens thus do not decide freely which candidates and ideas to contemplate; "they do not decide which speakers or views will be funded and disseminated in the first place. The use of economic resources therefore sets the agenda and determines which views will get priority during the pre-voting stages." *Id.* at 26-27. Finally, "the objection to wealth gaining political influence is not that the distribution of wealth is unjust, but that the wealth is distributed according to different values and under different conditions. . . . [R]ewards granted to personal choices in the economic sphere may not be appropriate for the distribution of political power or influence." *Id.* at 29.

c.   Unintended Harm to Representation and Politics

A third group of justifications for restricting the use of money in politics focuses on unintended consequences said to ensue when money plays too prominent a role in the electoral process.

▶▶ *Excessive Time Spent Raising Funds.*   It is frequently said that the amount of money necessary to run a successful campaign for all but the most local offices requires candidates for such offices — including incumbents running for reelection — to spend inordinate amounts of time raising money. Candidates and political operatives even have a name for it — "dialing for dollars," which refers to a period of time that candidates invest daily in cold-calling potential financial donors. This concern was raised frequently during the congressional debates on FECA. Campaign spending, many members of Congress asserted, had degenerated into an "arms race" in which candidates reflexively responded to spending by their opponents with spending of their own, with neither side willing to stand down. This in turn caused incumbents to devote ever-increasing amounts of time to their reelection campaigns, taking time away from actually doing the public's business in the legislature — the reason they were elected in the first place. *See* Vincent Blasi, *Free Speech and the Widening Gyre of Fund-Raising: Why Campaign Spending Limits May Not Violate the First Amendment After All,* 94 COLUM. L. REV. 1281 (1994); David A. Strauss, *What Is the Goal of Campaign Finance Reform?,* 1995 U. CHI. LEGAL F. 141, 155-158.

The problem is even worse today. Raising a billion dollars, as President Obama did in 2012 and Hillary Clinton did in 2016, takes a huge amount of time and effort. Some argue that campaign finance ought to be regulated simply because campaigns cost too much. Campaigns have become remarkably expensive. The 2010 midterm congressional campaign season was the most expensive midterm season in history. The overall price tag for the congressional campaigns approached $4 billion, more than what was spent on presidential campaigns in 2004. The most expensive House race was run by Republican Michele Bachmann of Minnesota; she raised $11 million and spent more than $8 million to get reelected. Ultimately unsuccessful Senate candidate Linda McMahon spent nearly $47 million of her own money on her run. http://news.yahoo.com/blogs/upshot/2010-campaigns-cost-4 -billion-other-fun-election.html. The 2008 election season was even costlier. Candidates, political parties, and interest groups spent about $5.3 billion on campaigns in 2008, 27 percent more than the amount spent during the 2004 campaign season. Presidential candidates alone spent about $2.4 billion, with $1 billion spent by candidates Barack Obama and John McCain alone. http://www.politico.com/ news/stories/1108/15283.html. And in 2012, President Obama's reelection campaign was the first to raise $1 billion. http://www.politico.com/story/2012/10/ team-obama-raises-1-billion-082909. Note that if this criticism is true, the problem arises even when political money is used for entirely proper purposes, and even when no candidate in a race holds a decisive advantage in private wealth.

>> *Coarsening of Campaign Discourse.* Some members of Congress also believed that huge sums pouring into political contests were being spent on low-quality communication that served only to coarsen the quality of political debate. Televised political advertising was still comparatively rare when Congress debated FECA; established politicians of that era had campaigned mainly using personal, grassroots methods that required much labor, but relatively little cash. Few members of Congress liked what they saw of the potential of the new medium.

> In recent years, the promotion of this superficial imagery has been accentuated by candidates of both major parties throughout the Nation. At times it is harmless, but all too often it can be diabolical. Using advertising techniques developed by publicists of detergents, deodorants and automobiles, political candidates have used 30-second and 1-minute advertisements on radio and television to misrepresent facts and create false and baseless impressions about their opponents. . . . No 30-second commercial ever was able to explain how brand X eliminates grease and dirt, and no 30-second commercial will ever be able to allow a political candidate to engage in a rational discussion of a single issue. . . . Today, American are rejecting the politics of superficiality. They demand far more than cliches and invective. What they long for is an honest and frank discussion of the issues which concern them and their country.

117 CONG. REC. S 29317 (Aug. 4, 1971) (Sen. Hartke). However, concern over the use by politicians of techniques of commercial advertising did not arise suddenly in 1971; critics of campaign practices had been making similar complaints since at least the 1920s, with the rise of the so-called merchandising or advertising campaign. RICHARD JENSEN, THE WINNING OF THE MIDWEST: SOCIAL AND POLITICAL CONFLICT, 1888-1896 (1971), ch. 6; ROBERT J. DINKIN, CAMPAIGNING IN AMERICA: A HISTORY OF ELECTION PRACTICES (1989), ch. 6.

Would a reduction in the overall amount of money available for campaigning elevate the quality of political debate? If candidates could not afford television and other forms of mass media, would they campaign differently? Would they engage in more extended and meaningful dialogue? *See* Dennis F. Thompson, *Two Concepts of Corruption: Making Campaigns Safe for Democracy*, 73 GEO. WASH. L. REV. 1036, 1053-1054 (2005).

3. What Does Political Money Buy?

Except in highly anomalous circumstances in which offices or votes are literally for sale, money, notwithstanding the rhetoric of campaign finance reform, does not buy either offices or votes. What, then, does money buy? Since getting votes is the key to winning any election, if the expenditure of money is to make any sense at all, it must buy something that can be exchanged for votes. But what? Most political money is spent on advertising, meaning evidently that money spent during campaigns is spent to obtain, and then presumably to hold, voters' *attention*. The question, then, is: does obtaining the attention of voters influence their votes; and if so, how much, and by what process? These questions are the subject of a lively debate in political science.

⟫ *Observational Data: Winners Spend More.* Candidates for political office, and the parties, individuals, and organizations that support them, spend a lot of money. Total spending on federal elections in 2020 was more than $14 billion. *See* opensecrets.org. Moreover, it is nearly always the case that more spending seems to beat less spending. In the 2008 elections for state offices, the candidate who spent the most won 80 percent of the time. Peter Quist, *The Role of Money and Incumbency in 2007-2008 State Elections* (National Institute on Money in State Politics, May 6, 2010). In California, that figure was 97 percent. Common Cause, *Taking Elections Off the Auction Block* (May 2010).

But does this mean that higher spending *caused* electoral victory? Not necessarily. Although 80 percent of higher spenders won their races, it was better to be an incumbent: incumbents nationwide won 94 percent of 2008 state races. Where incumbents were also the higher fundraiser, they won 97 percent of their races. However, incumbents faced no opponent in 37 percent of their general election races. Quist, *supra.* In California, 86 percent of the winners raised more than five times as much as their opponents. Common Cause, *supra.* It is tautologically true that the higher-spending candidate will prevail when he has no opponent, and it is almost tautologically true that he will do so when he has on hand five times as much money as his opponent who, it may reasonably be inferred, is a weak candidate or otherwise lacking in support from the inception. On the other hand, there is a complex interrelationship between incumbency, fundraising, and the presence of a challenger that may make conclusions harder to draw: incumbents raise funds more easily than challengers, popular incumbents do so even more easily, and a well-funded, popular incumbent discourages potential challengers from even bothering to enter the race. But the fact that the winner spends more than the loser in these situations seems to prove very little about the impact of money.

Or, consider that the candidates who spend the largest sums of all—immense, record-setting sums—rarely win. That is because these tend by and large to be self-financed candidates—rich individuals who, with no established electoral appeal, parachute into races to take on more established opponents. In fact, the more such challengers spend of their own money, the worse they generally perform. According to the definitive study of self-financing candidates, these results have less to do with spending than with the simple fact that self-financing candidates "tend to be inexperienced, low-quality candidates." JENNIFER A. STEEN, SELF-FINANCED CANDIDATES IN CONGRESSIONAL ELECTIONS (2006).

⟫ *The Aggregate View: The Minimal Effects Thesis.* One highly developed branch of political science forecasts election results. Forecasting has reached the point where the best models, usually those forecasting presidential elections, can predict final outcomes closely, routinely within a few percentage points. An interesting feature of these models, however, is that they rely on variables that are in place well before the onset of formal campaigns. The leading studies in this body of work, typically relying on aggregated data concerning large numbers of voters, find that influences such as the condition of the national economy, for example, or the state of voters' personal finances, or whether an incumbent is running for reelection

come very close to fully determining election outcomes. *See, e.g.,* THOMAS M. HOL-
BROOK, DO CAMPAIGNS MATTER? (1996); Gregory B. Markus, *The Impact of Personal
and National Economic Conditions on the Presidential Vote: A Pooled Cross-Sectional Analysis,* 32 AM. J. POL. SCI. 137 (1988).

If a model can correctly forecast the outcome of an election contest without
taking into account a single thing the candidates do or say during the campaign,
or how much they spend, can it really be said that campaigns, much less campaign
spending, play much of a role in deciding elections? This is the so-called minimal
effects thesis—the idea that campaigns are largely irrelevant to electoral outcomes
(at least in high-salience races for high-visibility offices, such as the presidency), or
that their relevance is limited to the margins of extremely close races, the only kind
in which campaigns are capable of making a difference.

Much subsequent political science work has focused on less aggregated levels
of analysis to attempt to understand what complexities might be masked by the very
high level of aggregation required for forecasting national elections.

>> *Effects of Spending on Vote Share.*   The minimal effects thesis seems to stand in
some tension with a substantial body of literature finding a relationship between
campaign spending and "vote share," meaning the percentage of the popular
vote a candidate wins. Many, though not all, of these studies find that spending by
candidates is positively correlated with vote share, i.e., more money means more
votes. Early research in this field initially produced some puzzling results. One well-
known study found that increased campaign spending benefits challengers but not
incumbents, whereas another study found mild benefits from spending for both
challengers and incumbents. *Compare* Gary C. Jacobson, *The Effects of Campaign
Spending in Congressional Elections,* 72 AM. POL. SCI. REV. 469 (1978), *with* Jonathan
S. Krasno and Donald P. Green, *Preempting Quality Challengers in House Elections,* 50
J. POL. 920 (1988). A common explanation for why challengers might benefit more
from campaign spending is that incumbents are already well known, and therefore
do not need to spend much to portray themselves to their constituents, whereas
challengers are less well known, and get a significant advantage from spending to
advertise themselves and their positions. This is consistent, however, with a law of
diminishing marginal utility: after a while, additional campaign spending will not
carry much of a benefit in increasing voter knowledge and receptivity, but it takes a
challenger a longer time to reach the point of diminishing returns than an incumbent. *See* Alan I. Abramowitz, *Incumbency, Campaign Spending, and the Decline of Competition in U.S. House Elections,* 53 J. POL. 34, 37 (1991).

Some studies have gone so far as to attempt to quantify the cost of gaining
additional vote share through campaign spending. Depending on the circumstances, estimates range from $12 to $110 per additional vote for challengers and
between $15 and $367 per additional vote for incumbents. In terms of vote share,
estimates of the effect of spending an additional $100,000 in a U.S. congressio-
nal election vary from between 0.24 percent and 2.17 percent of the vote share
for spending by challengers, and from 0.07 percent to 1.8 percent additional vote
share for incumbents. *See* Alan S. Gerber, *Does Campaign Spending Work?,* 47 AM.
BEHAV. SCIENTIST 541, 546 (2004).

One thing none of these studies claims to show, however, is that campaign
spending can change the final outcome of an election—i.e., that a Democrat

can spend her way to victory in an overwhelmingly Republican district, or that a weak candidate can buy a victory against a much stronger opponent. They purport to show only that a candidate's spending helps, in a rough way, in gathering votes that are in principle available to that candidate. Does this help dissolve the tension with the minimal effects thesis? Could it be that electoral outcomes are determined largely by events exogenous to the campaign, but that campaign spending is necessary for candidates to "draw down" votes that are otherwise theirs for the taking?

>> *Mechanisms: Spending to Persuade.*   If campaign spending has the capacity to attract or draw down votes, how does it do so? One possibility is that the advertising and voter contacts that candidates buy with campaign dollars persuades voters to vote for them. This is a difficult contention to assess, but most of the evidence suggests that campaign speech does not actually persuade voters of anything often enough to count as a significant factor in deciding elections.

In their classic studies of Ohio and New York voters during the 1940s, Berelson and Lazarsfeld found that "the time of final decision, that point after which the voter does not change his intention, occurred *prior* to the campaign for most voters—and thus no 'real decision' was made *in* the campaign in the sense of waiting to consider alternatives." BERNARD R. BERELSON, PAUL F. LAZARSFELD, AND WILLIAM N. McPHEE, VOTING: A STUDY OF OPINION FORMATION IN A PRESIDENTIAL CAMPAIGN 18 (1954). Subsequent research has illuminated why this might be the case. One consideration is that political opinion turns out to be remarkably stable. For example, partisan affiliation is a strong predictor of voting, and partisan affiliation is normally acquired very early in life and generally changes little thereafter. *See, e.g.,* M. KENT JENNINGS AND RICHARD G. NIEMI, GENERATIONS AND POLITICS: A PANEL STUDY OF YOUNG ADULTS AND THEIR PARENTS (1981). In addition, all sorts of cognitive biases and social effects make it unlikely that a person will be persuaded by a candidate to change his political views during the course of a campaign. For example, people tend to exhibit an "attention bias," in which they pay attention selectively to information with which they agree, and a "retention bias" that leads them to forget more readily information inconsistent with what they already believe, should they happen to have acquired any. These are forms of cognitive screening that vastly complicate any attempt to change a person's mind. *See* JAMES A. GARDNER, WHAT ARE CAMPAIGNS FOR? THE ROLE OF PERSUASION IN ELECTORAL LAW AND POLITICS (2009), ch. 3.

Similarly, individual voters are members of social groups, and their interactions with their groups tend constantly to reinforce the group's dominant beliefs, providing a source of resistance to the kind of persuasion that might cause group members to change their views, and thus their votes. As a result, "[t]he rational actor is thus trapped by her place in social and economic structure, and particularly by the distinctive mix of information that attaches to that structural locale." Consequently, the social environment "tends to reproduce the existing distribution of opinion." ROBERT HUCKFELDT AND JOHN SPRAGUE, CITIZENS, POLITICS, AND SOCIAL COMMUNICATION: INFORMATION AND INFLUENCE IN AN ELECTION CAMPAIGN (1995). As the authors of one recent study put it, "The best estimate for the persuasive effects of campaign contact and advertising—such as mail, phone calls, and canvassing—on American candidate choices in general elections is zero." Joshua

L. Kalla and David E. Broockman, *The Minimal Persuasive Effects of Campaign Contact in General Elections: Evidence from 49 Field Experiments*, 112 AM. POL. SCI. REV. 148 (2018).

>> *Mechanisms: Agenda-Setting, Framing, and Priming.* If campaign spending is unlikely to persuade voters in the sense of causing them to change their beliefs, might it nevertheless influence them in less dramatic ways? Political scientists have identified three mechanisms by which campaign speech might influence the behavior of voters. *Agenda-setting* refers to the capacity of certain political actors such as the mass media, politicians, or candidates, to bring an issue to public attention. Because voters generally must rely on others for their information about public affairs, they also must rely on judgments made by others about what information is important. The "agenda-setting hypothesis" holds that "those problems that receive prominent attention on the national news become the problems the viewing public regards as the nation's most important." SHANTO IYENGAR AND DONALD R. KINDER, NEWS THAT MATTERS: TELEVISION AND AMERICAN OPINION 16 (1987).

Merely bringing an issue to public attention does not, however, specify how voters will react to it. *Framing* deals with this question: to frame an issue is to present it in such as way as to influence the interpretation that voters place on the issue. Framing attempts to construct a consistent and easily understood narrative that increases the likelihood that voters will reach the evaluation of the issue preferred by the speaker. *See* Dennis Chong and James N. Druckman, *Framing Theory*, 10 ANN. REV. POL. SCI. 103 (2007).

Finally, *priming* exploits a feature of human cognition, the "availability heuristic." According to researchers, people make decisions not by reviewing everything they know, but by drawing selectively on whatever information or associations happen to be most immediately and readily accessible. As a result, selectively directing voters' attention to some matters rather than others can influence their judgments concerning political issues or candidates. For example, voters exposed to a barrage of media stories about defense policy are more likely to base their evaluation of the President on his performance on defense, whereas voters exposed to stories about environmental policy are more likely to evaluate the President based on his performance on the environment. IYENGAR AND KINDER, *supra*, at 4, 65; Chong and Druckman, *supra*, at 114-115.

That these effects exist, however, does not say much about whether they have an impact in actual electoral contests, and if so, how much. There is evidence that priming and framing effects fade within a matter of days. James N. Druckman and Kjersten R. Nelson, *Framing and Deliberation: How Citizens' Conversations Limit Elite Influence*, 47 AM. J. POL. SCI. 729 (2003). In a contested race, all candidates are likely to be framing and agenda-setting as hard as they can, so these effects may be mutually cancelling outside the laboratory, where the effects have been most reliably identified. Even the strongest proponents of these effects claim only that they might make a difference at the margin, in very close races. In addition, the impact of these effects is inherently limited by the knowledge and predispositions that voters already possess: "Candidates can direct the voters' attention to an issue only if the voters are predisposed to care about that issue to begin with. . . . [T]hey cannot convert nonpartisans and members of the opposite party, and they cannot redirect the interests of most voters and change the substance of the election."

STEPHEN ANSOLABEHERE AND SHANTO IYENGAR, GOING NEGATIVE: HOW ATTACK ADS SHRINK AND POLARIZE THE ELECTORATE 88-89 (1995).

For an argument that such effects can be deployed at the margins successfully in close races by peeling off "cross-pressured partisans"—reliable party voters who are uncomfortable with a small number of their party's salient positions—see D. SUNSHINE HILLYGUS AND TODD G. SHIELDS, THE PERSUADABLE VOTER: WEDGE ISSUES IN PRESIDENTIAL CAMPAIGNS (2008).

>> *Mechanisms: Spending to Mobilize.* A much less ambitious theory of what political spending buys, but one well supported by the evidence, maintains that the point of a well-run campaign is not to persuade but to mobilize those voters who are already predisposed to support a candidate, i.e., induce them to turn out and actually cast a ballot for the candidate they support. Thus, get-out-the-vote (GOTV) activities tend to comprise a significant component in campaign strategy and spending. On this view, the candidate who wins will be the one who most efficiently and effectively mobilizes his or her own base. Campaign spending is thus intended not to persuade the base—the base is already predisposed to vote for the candidate—but to motivate them actually to vote.

Studies suggest that spending money for the purpose of mobilizing existing supporters is a relatively effective use of campaign resources. In local elections, the cost of getting an additional voter to the polls may be as little as a few dollars, up to around $15 per additional vote. *See* Alan S. Gerber and Donald P. Green, *The Effect of a Nonpartisan Get-Out-the-Vote Drive: An Experimental Study of Leafletting*, 62 J. POL. 846 (2000); Donald P. Green, et al., *Getting Out the Vote in Local Elections: Results from Six Door-to-Door Canvassing Experiments*, 65 J. POL. 1083 (2003). In elections for statewide office, the cost may be higher, perhaps $25 or $30 per additional vote. *See* David W. Nickerson, et al., *Partisan Mobilization Campaigns in the Field: Results from a Statewide Turnout Experiment in Michigan*, 59 POL. RES. Q. 85 (2006). One study described the difference between attracting votes from supporters and non-supporters as follows:

> Mobilization of independents is . . . both more difficult (i.e., costlier in resources) and riskier for campaigns. That is, independents need to be persuaded and mobilized, while partisans mainly need to be mobilized. Therefore, campaigns have strategic incentives to target their mobilization efforts on partisans out of fear that the core will stay home without the mobilization effort and that a broader canvass would bring the wrong voters to the polls.

Thomas M. Holbrook and Scott D. McClurg, *The Mobilization of Core Supporters: Campaigns, Turnout, and Electoral Composition in United States Presidential Elections*, 49 AM. J. POL. SCI. 689, 691 (2005). On this view, an election seems to be mainly a competition between the major parties to mobilize reliable supporters, rather than an occasion for public discussion of the issues and persuasion. Gary C. Jacobson, *How Do Campaigns Matter?*, 18 ANN. REV. POL. 31, 38 (2015).

Another component of a mobilization strategy may be to "demobilize" the opponent's base—that is, to demoralize them so they fail to turn out. Negative advertising is often said to have a demobilizing effect: it does not fire up an attacker's supporters to vote for the attacker, but it does have a tendency to induce supporters of the attacked candidate to stay home. STEPHEN ANSOLABEHERE AND SHANTO IYENGAR, GOING NEGATIVE: HOW ATTACK ADS SHRINK AND POLARIZE THE ELECTORATE (1995).

An interesting implication of the mobilization campaign is that it may have a class bias. Who is mobilized by a mobilization campaign? Voters differ in the degree to which they are susceptible to mobilization mainly because they differ in how attentive they are to political campaigns and, concomitantly, how easy they are for candidates to reach. Smart candidates may attempt to conserve resources by reaching out to those voters who are easiest—and thus cheapest—to contact, but those voters are already the most politically engaged, and thus likely to be of higher socioeconomic status. Consequently, rather than bringing new voters to participate in political decisions, mobilization campaigns may exacerbate existing differences in political voice between routine and occasional voters. Jacobson, *supra*, at 41.

⟫   *The Ontology of Citizenship.*   In earlier chapters we examined some of the assumptions that various kinds of democratic theories make about the capacity of citizens. What kinds of assumptions about citizens are made by Congress in FECA? By the Court in *Buckley*?

> [Campaign finance] reform arguments all rest on a single fear: that, left to themselves, various political actors will transform economic power into political power and thereby violate the democratic norm of equal political empowerment. . . . Nevertheless, . . . these theories all violate one of democracy's central normative assumptions: the idea that voters are civically competent. [T]o the extent Americans are the kind of people that democratic theory demands—i.e., engaged, informed voters, who carefully reason through political arguments—we hardly need the kind of protection that campaign finance regulation affords us.

Daniel R. Ortiz, *The Democratic Paradox of Campaign Finance Reform*, 50 STAN. L. REV. 893, 895 (1998).

How, if at all, does the political science data shed light on the assumptions that undergird campaign-finance regulation, or the First Amendment doctrine that requires invalidation of much of it? If voters do not behave rationally, or deliberatively, or otherwise in accordance with the assumptions of democratic theory, might this undermine the rationale for attempting to equalize the influence of rich and poor in the political arena? Would reform efforts be better off focusing on enhancing political engagement, broadly conceived, at the grassroots? *See* Jeremy N. Sheff, *The Myth of the Level Playing Field: Knowledge, Affect, and Repetition in Public Debate*, 75 Mo. L. REV. 143 (2010).

4. Reaction to Buckley

Buckley provoked an enormous reaction, both initially and over the ensuing decades. According to one count, *Buckley* "has been cited in over 2,500 cases, is in the title of 18 books, and is mentioned in 4,000 law review articles." Richard L. Hasen, *The Nine Lives of* Buckley v. Valeo, *in* FIRST AMENDMENT STORIES 367

(Richard W. Garnett and Andrew Koppelman eds., 2011). Among the most frequently debated aspects of the case are the following:

>> *"Wholly Foreign to the First Amendment."*   In the most famous passage in the case, the Court held that "the concept that government may restrict the speech of some elements of our society in order to enhance the relative voice of others is wholly foreign to the First Amendment." Is limiting expenditures for campaign speech — or even campaign speech itself — "wholly foreign" to the First Amendment? The answer to that question depends entirely on one's views about what the First Amendment is designed to accomplish, and how it does so. As we saw in the previous chapter, one commonly advanced view about the First Amendment is that its primary purpose is to secure democratic self-government. Critics and supporters of *Buckley* often differ, however, in how they believe democratic self-government is best secured. One common cleavage lies along the fault line separating an emphasis on the autonomy of speakers from an emphasis on the proper functioning of democratic institutions.

One view — the one to which the Court was sympathetic — is that meaningfully democratic decision making requires that citizens have complete autonomy to decide what messages to hear and what weight to give them. It follows, on this view, that "legislative restrictions on political speech may not be predicated on the ground that the political speaker will have too great a communicative impact, or his competitor too little. Conventional First Amendment norms of individualism, relativism, and antipaternalism preclude any such affirmative equality of influence — not only as an end-state but even as an aspiration." Kathleen M. Sullivan, *Political Money and Freedom of Speech*, 30 U.C. Davis L. Rev. 663, 673 (1997). Others argue, in contrast, that autonomous decision making can sometimes be advanced, not impeded, by government imposition of fair ground rules:

> Those who reduce the first amendment to a limit on state action tend to regard it as a protection of autonomy. The individual is allowed to say what he or she wishes, free from interference from the state. . . . [Under the] public debate principle, . . . [t]he purpose of the first amendment remains what it was under autonomy — to protect the ability of people, as a collectivity, to decide their own fate. Rich public debate also continues to appear as an essential precondition for the exercise of that sovereign prerogative. But now action is judged by its impact on public debate, a social state of affairs, rather than by whether it constrains or otherwise interferes with the autonomy of some individual or institution. The concern is not with the frustration of would-be speakers, but with the quality of public discourse. Autonomy may be protected, but only when it enriches public debate. It might well have to be sacrificed when, for example, the speech of some drowns out the voices of others or systematically distorts the public agenda.

Owen M. Fiss, *Why the State?*, 100 Harv. L. Rev. 781, 785-786 (1987).

Ronald Dworkin makes a similar point, advancing a conception of democracy protected by the First Amendment as "a partnership in collective self-government in which all citizens are given the opportunity to be active and equal partners." Ronald Dworkin, Sovereign Virtue: The Theory and Practice of Equality 354

(2002). This means that citizens play two roles simultaneously, as "judges of political contests," but also as "participants in the political contests they judge. . . . The partnership conception recognizes both roles, because it supposes that in a true democracy citizens must play a part, as equal partners in a collective enterprise, in shaping as well as constituting the public's opinion." *Id.* at 358. According to these views, then, the First Amendment goal of popular self-governance sometimes may be best served when government is restrained from interfering with the autonomously generated political speech of citizens, but at other times self-governance may be best advanced by government intervention designed to promote the quality of public political discourse.

If promoting equality of opportunity among speakers to exercise political influence is "wholly foreign to the First Amendment," on what model of self-governance might the Court implicitly be relying? Should the Court show Congress any deference if Congress believes that the factual conditions underlying a particular model of self-governance are not fulfilled, but could become fulfilled through regulatory intervention?

▶▶ *Equating Spending and Speech.* In constitutional cases, a court's choice of a standard of review can make an immense difference to the outcome of the case. The result in *Buckley* clearly is influenced by the Court's rejection of the *O'Brien* standard, applicable to the regulation of conduct with a communicative impact, and its decision instead to apply "exacting scrutiny," a heightened form of scrutiny reserved for regulation of "core . . . political expression."

One of the earliest critiques of *Buckley*, written by J. Skelly Wright, a judge on the D.C. Circuit Court of Appeals who had joined the opinion the Court overruled, took on the Court for its choice of standard of review. In a rare public rebuke by a lower court judge, Judge Wright attacked the Court's basic doctrinal premise that the giving and spending of money to buy speech should be treated for constitutional purposes the same as if it were speech itself.

> [In a number of decisions, the] Court [has] told us, in effect, that money is speech. This, in my view, misconceives the First Amendment. . . . No one disputes that the money regulated by the campaign reform legislation is closely related to political expression. And no one disputes that the First Amendment applies with special force to the political arena. The legal question is thus not whether the restrictions on giving and spending are subject to First Amendment scrutiny at all. The question is what degree of scrutiny should apply. There are basically two choices. . . . The first is to treat campaign contributions and expenditures as equivalent to pure speech. If this approach is proper, then the giving and spending restrictions enacted in [the FECA amendments of] 1974 should be treated in the same way as laws imposing a prior restraint on speech. . . . Such laws are subject to the most rigorous scrutiny known to constitutional law. . . .
>
> The second legal alternative is to treat political giving and spending as a form of conduct related to speech — something roughly equivalent to the physical act of picketing or to the use of a sound-truck. Alert and careful judicial scrutiny is still warranted, for an ostensibly neutral regulation of conduct may merely disguise an attempt at silencing a particular

viewpoint. Nevertheless, a carefully tailored regulation of the nonspeech element—the picketing or the sound-truck—can survive without being required to pass the rigorous test applied to restrictions on pure speech. The regulation is constitutional if it serves an important governmental interest and if that interest is unrelated to suppression of speech. . . .

The real question in [*Buckley*] was: Can the use of money be regulated . . . where there is an undoubted incidental effect on speech? However, what the Court asked was whether pure speech can be regulated where there is some incidental effect on money. Naturally the answer to the Court's question was "No." But this left untouched the real question in the case. The Court riveted its attention on what the money could buy—be it communication, or communication mixed with conduct. Yet the campaign reform law did not dictate what could be bought. It focused exclusively on the giving and spending itself. In short, the Court turned the congressional telescope around and looked through the wrong end. . . .

The Supreme Court seemed to recognize that "effective political speech" is a multi-dimensional concept. . . . Viewed in this light, the effectiveness of political speakers is not necessarily diminished by reasonable contribution and expenditure ceilings. The giving and spending restrictions may cause candidates and other individuals to rely more on less expensive means of communication. But there is no reason to believe that such a shift in means reduces the number of issues discussed in a campaign. And, by forcing candidates to put more emphasis on local organizing or leafletting or door-to-door canvassing and less on full-page ads and television spot commercials, the restrictions may well generate deeper exploration of the issues raised. . . .

J. Skelly Wright, *Politics and the Constitution: Is Money Speech?*, 85 Yale L.J. 1001 (1976). Do you agree with Judge Wright that the Court treated money as speech in *Buckley* and focused unduly on what money could buy instead of whether the use of money can be regulated?

In a more recent treatment of this issue, Deborah Hellman argues that because money is the universal medium of exchange, and can therefore be used for so many different purposes, exchanging it for speech should not be viewed as raising problems unique to the First Amendment. Instead, she contends, only when a right is itself distributed via market mechanisms should the right to spend money in the exercise of that right be considered part of the right itself. Because rights of political participation are not distributed by market mechanisms, regulation of the use of money to obtain them cannot be considered an integral infringement of such rights. Deborah Hellman, *Money Talks But It Isn't Speech*, 95 Minn. L. Rev. 953 (2011). *See also* Monica Youn, *First Amendment Fault Lines and the* Citizens United *Decision*, 5 Harv. L. & Pol'y Rev. 135 (2011).

Is the Court's analysis here unnecessarily complicated by its resort to an individual rights model for resolving the case? How might the issue be analyzed under a "structural" approach?

≫   *The "Tank of Gas" Metaphor.*   In a famous footnote in *Buckley*, the Court asserts: "Being free to engage in unlimited political expression subject to a ceiling on expenditures is like being free to drive an automobile as far and as often as one desires on a single tank of gasoline." Is this a persuasive account of the impact of expenditure limits? This may depend upon one's assumptions about what a campaign is and how campaign speech operates.

The *Buckley* Court's failure to recognize that political campaigns are interactive competitions, not free-standing exercises of choice, caused the Court to misread the real-world autonomy consequences of its decision, even for the very candidates the Court thought it was freeing. In striking down efforts to impose caps on election expenditures, the *Buckley* Court believed that it was preserving the autonomy of candidates to raise and spend as much (or as little) as they wished in support of their respective candidacies. But eliminating the possibility of a government-imposed cap does not remit candidates to a self-contained world of autonomous choice. Instead, it condemns them to a cyclical prisoners' dilemma, where each candidate must continue to raise and spend more money in order to prevent the other from obtaining an advantage. The reciprocal arms race spiral deprives both candidates of the ability to make an autonomous choice about how much to spend to obtain a full and effective ventilation of a candidate's position. . . . The vast bulk of candidates are no more autonomous under *Buckley* in setting levels of campaign spending than were the Soviet Union and the United States in setting levels of military spending during the height of the Cold War.

The *Buckley* Court's erroneous insistence on viewing election spending as an individual, as opposed to a reciprocal, exercise is reflected in the decision's most successful metaphor. In responding to the argument that regulation of the spending of campaign money was not the same as regulating speech itself, the Court analogized campaign cash to automobile fuel. Since, argued the Court, a car can go only as far as its supply of fuel permits, so a campaign can go only as far as its supply of money permits. But the Court overlooked that an election campaign is not a unilateral effort to go as far as possible, but a race between at least two cars. A race in which one car has seventy-five percent of the fuel is no race at all. And a race in which each car keeps adding fuel just to be sure that the other does not go further, even when neither wishes to go that far, is hardly an exercise in autonomy.

Burt Neuborne, *Is Money Different?*, 77 Tex. L. Rev. 1609, 1617-1618 (1999).

≫   *The Significance of the Campaign Period.*   Everyone seems to agree that there is great significance to the fact that FECA regulated speech occurring during political campaigns. Yet there is disagreement over the significance of that fact for the standard of review and the outcome of the case. One may agree, in other words, that "elections constitute[] a distinct domain for First Amendment purposes," Frederick Schauer and Richard H. Pildes, *Electoral Exceptionalism and the First Amendment*, 77 Tex. L. Rev. 1803, 1808 (1999), yet disagree about the doctrinal significance of that distinctiveness.

The view adopted by the Court, consistent with earlier case law, is that FECA's targeting of speech made during campaigns only makes it more suspect and requires it be subjected to more rigorous constitutional review than might otherwise be the case. The First Amendment, on this view, has it highest and most important application to campaign speech because it is at just this point that the principle of popular sovereignty requires the people to have the most unrestricted access to speech that will or may help them to make democratically significant decisions.

Yet precisely the opposite view also has been expressed: the importance and distinctiveness of elections in a democratic society only provides *more* reason, not less, to tolerate government regulation during the campaign phase.

> The electoral process is in principle distinguishable from ordinary politics in two respects, which together justify subjecting it to stronger or at least different standards. First, unlike ordinary political activity outside government, elections (including the campaigns that precede them) result in decisions that are binding on all citizens. All therefore have an interest in the integrity of the process, and a claim to participate in setting the standards that govern it. Second, . . . campaigns come to a definite and foreseeable conclusion; an election takes place at a particular moment, which until the next election marks an end to the process. . . . [Thus,] elections and the campaigns leading up to them may be considered more a part of government. The standards that control . . . elections should therefore be determined more by collective decision than by individual choice.

DENNIS F. THOMPSON, JUST ELECTIONS: CREATING A FAIR ELECTORAL PROCESS IN THE UNITED STATES 115 (2002). *See also* Dennis F. Thompson, *Election Time: Normative Implications of Temporal Properties of the Electoral Process in the United States*, 98 AM. POL. SCI. REV. 51 (2004); Saul Zipkin, *The Election Period and Regulation of the Democratic Process*, 18 WM. & MARY BILL RTS. J. 533 (2010).

Moreover, if the point of campaigns is to provide the best quality information to voters, a question arises whether that goal will be advanced or impeded by regulations of speech designed to give a fair hearing to all parties. Professor Robert Post argues that on this subject the Supreme Court "has it exactly backward. Informed public decision making is best facilitated by scrupulous rules of procedure, like those we employ in courtrooms, legislative hearings, or classrooms." ROBERT C. POST, CITIZENS DIVIDED: CAMPAIGN FINANCE REFORM AND THE CONSTITUTION 79 (2014).

» *The Balance of Liberties.* Supporters of *Buckley* by and large do not disagree that the goals of FECA and of campaign finance reform generally are desirable ones, at least in the abstract. Nobody argues that the public is better off when elected officials attend more to raising money than to the public's business, or that politics is fairer when political influence depends on wealth, or that campaign discourse is improved when it is dominated by corporations or wealthy individuals. Instead, opponents of campaign regulation tend to argue that *Buckley* was correctly decided for a different reason: because government intervention in the campaign process is a cure worse than the disease. Regulation of campaign finance thus trades off two different kinds of liberty—political equality against freedom of speech—but *Buckley* gets the balance right.

Commentators who defend lenient scrutiny for campaign finance reform legislation uniformly fail to acknowledge that regulation of the political process might be a context warranting distrust of elected officials. In this area, they not only implicitly discount the value of the first amendment rights infringed; they also ignore any systematic possibility that legislators will behave in self- rather than public-interested ways. . . . The political "expertise" of legislators . . . may not be a completely reliable guarantee of their disinterestedness in reforming the political process. Indeed, there are reasons to believe that legislators, given free rein to inhibit political activity, might attempt to restructure the political balance of power so as principally to benefit themselves and their political allies. . . . [T]here is considerable theoretical and anecdotal evidence that elected officials tend to act from other than purely community-regarding motives.

Lillian R. BeVier, *Money and Politics: A Perspective on the First Amendment and Campaign Finance Reform*, 73 CAL. L. REV. 1045, 1076 (1985). *See also* BRADLEY A. SMITH, UNFREE SPEECH: THE FOLLY OF CAMPAIGN FINANCE REFORM (2001).

One response to this position is that the choice is not actually between government intervention and government non-intervention, but between different forms of government intervention. When government refrains from regulating the expenditure of political money, it leaves intact an unequal distribution of wealth resulting from the operation of economic markets. But such markets are not "natural"; they are, on the contrary, created and maintained through exercises of government power. In this sense, the Court's decision in *Buckley* that liberty requires the government to refrain from regulating the expenditure of political money takes the status quo distribution of wealth "as a given, and failure to act—defined as reliance on markets—is treated as no decision at all." Yet in reality, "markets are conspicuously a regulatory system, and reliance on markets for elections is a regulatory choice." CASS R. SUNSTEIN, THE PARTIAL CONSTITUTION 85 (1993). On this view, the decision to favor the market's distribution of wealth available for campaign spending to FECA's distribution is to make a choice to favor market distribution of the relevant resource.

≫ *The Contribution/Expenditure Distinction and Its Consequences.* The Court's analysis in *Buckley* led it to a split decision: limitations on contributions were sustained, whereas limitations on expenditures were invalidated. Not all members of the Court agreed that these two categories of restrictions should receive different treatment: Chief Justice Burger thought all the restrictions should be invalidated whereas Justice White thought all should be upheld. Some present members of the Court have occasionally dropped hints that they too believe the *Buckley* compromise is misguided, but aside from that point of agreement may be just as divided as Burger and White.

The practical result of the Court's split decision, in contrast, seems to be the subject of general agreement: by blowing a huge hole in the closed system of political money that Congress intended to create in FECA, the Court succeeded in creating a system that nobody wanted and that works poorly.

> The result of this split decision is that government may restrict the sup-
> ply of political money flowing to a candidate but not the demand. The
> aftermath is by now familiar: Political candidates need a lot of money
> to compete in American elections. . . . Those costs have escalated with
> the importance of television advertising and the rise of a highly compen-
> sated political consultancy industry. . . . With each contribution capped in
> amount, the candidate seeking to fund his or her formal campaign must
> seek contributions from a larger number of donors. This means spending
> a greater proportion of time fund-raising than would be necessary under
> a system permitting reliance on venture capital from a few fat cats. . . .
> Candidates and their critics alike lament this transformation of our repre-
> sentatives into . . . "mendicants and merchants."

Kathleen M. Sullivan, *Against Campaign Finance Reform*, 1998 UTAH L. REV. 311. It
has also been suggested that by invalidating congressional attempts to relieve candidates from fundraising pressure by capping their spending, yet upholding limits on the flow of funds to candidates, *Buckley* inadvertently increased incentives
for candidates to cheat in their fundraising, i.e., to find ways to circumvent limits.
Since there is no limit on the amounts candidates may spend, and candidates feel
pressure to spend as much as possible, they feel pressure to raise as much money
as possible, as much as they can spend. Thus, a system designed to reduce the possibility of corruption, and that the Court was inclined to uphold principally on the
ground that it reduced corruption and the appearance of corruption, was altered
by the Court in a way that had just the opposite effect. *See, e.g.,* Burt Neuborne, *One
Dollar-One Vote: A Preface to Debating Campaign Finance Reform*, 37 WASHBURN L.J. 1,
34 (1997).

>> *Campaign Finance in Other Countries.*   As is often the case in election law,
things are different elsewhere. In other nations, regulation of campaign finance
is frequently tolerated to a much greater degree. For example, the Supreme Court
of Canada in 2004 sustained a federal law limiting independent campaign expenditures much like the one invalidated in *Buckley*: "The State can restrict the voices
which dominate the political discourse so that others may be heard as well. In Canada, electoral regulation has focused on the latter by regulating electoral spending through comprehensive election finance provisions. These provisions seek to
create a level playing field for those who wish to engage in the electoral discourse.
This, in turn, enables voters to be better informed; no one voice is overwhelmed by
another." *Harper v. Canada* [2004], 1 S.C.R. 827.

For developments in other countries, see, e.g., Samuel Issacharoff, *Campaign
Finance Regulation in the Modern Age: The Constitutional Logic of Campaign Finance Reg-
ulation*, 36 PEPP. L. REV. 373 (2009) (U.K., Canada, Germany); Daniel P. Tokaji, *The
Obliteration of Equality in American Campaign Finance Law: A Transborder Comparison*, 5
J. PARLIAMENTARY & POLITICAL L. 381 (2011) (Canada); Heather K. Gerken, *Mexi-
co's 2007 Election Reforms: A Comparative View*, II MEX. L. REV. 163 (2009).

>> *Campaign Finance in Judicial Elections.*   Are the problems of money in pol-
itics more acute in judicial elections than in elections for other offices? In the
last decade, spending in races for elective state judicial positions has more than
doubled. Perhaps more alarmingly, spending has not increased uniformly among

contributors: the top five spenders in judicial elections in the ten most costly states spent, on average, nearly half a million dollars, while the average investment by all other contributors was about $850. James Sample et al., *The New Politics of Judicial Elections, 2000-2009* (Brennan Center for Justice 2010). Evidence now starting to emerge suggests that judges may be sensitive to the interests of their largest contributors, and that this sensitivity may be expressed in their decisions. *See* Michael S. Kang and Joanna M. Shepherd, *The Partisan Price of Justice: An Empirical Analysis of Campaign Contributions and Judicial Decisions*, 86 N.Y.U. L. REV. 69 (2011). If these findings are correct, might the government have an interest sufficient to justify not just contribution limits in judicial elections, but *spending* limits as well? For such an argument, see James Sample, *Democracy at the Corner of First and Fourteenth: Judicial Campaign Spending and Equality*, 66 N.Y.U. ANN. SURV. AM. L. 727 (2011).

D. *BCRA AND* McCONNELL

In FECA 1974, Congress passed a comprehensive statutory scheme. The Court treated FECA's sections as separate entities. Was that the right approach? Should the Court have struck down the whole statute? Should it have been more respectful of Congress's judgment that the provisions were interdependent? Congress enacted two major and more or less comprehensive campaign-finance statutes in the modern era, the Federal Election Campaign Act of 1974 (FECA 1974) and the Bipartisan Campaign Reform Act (BCRA), the subject of this section. Congress enacted BCRA to address two problems in particular, the problem of "soft money" and the problem of "issue advocacy."

1. *Soft Money*

What is soft money? Consider a description of this problem by Professors Stephen Ansolabehere and James M. Snyder, Jr.:

> American campaign finance law is often described as more loophole than law. Congress and the courts, sometimes working at cross-purposes, continually attempt to clarify and perfect existing regulations, but as campaign practices evolve, candidates, parties, individuals, and groups devise clever, new ways to bend the rules. Today, efforts to reform campaign finance focus on the transfer of national party funds to state and local organizations. Political parties raise large sums from individuals, corporations, and other associations. They then channel these funds to state and local party organizations, which in turn conduct campaign activities that indirectly and sometimes directly affect federal elections. This was an *intended* consequence, a genie that Congress meant to let out of the bottle. Our concern is with the effects of putting the genie back in.

Stephen Ansolabehere and James M. Snyder, Jr., *Soft Money, Hard Money, Strong Parties*, 100 COLUM. L. REV. 598, 598 (2000). Professors Ansolabehere and Snyder refer here to the problem of "soft money." In the 1979 amendments to FECA, Congress specifically excluded state and local party-building activities from federal contribution limitations. *Id.* The term "soft money" is a catchall of sorts. Campaign-finance insiders use the term "hard money" to mean campaign financing that is raised in accordance with the campaign-finance limits of federal campaign-finance law. Soft money is generally everything else. In this case, it refers in particular to exempted state and local expenditures.

In a series of rulings, the FEC went on to clarify this exclusion. For example, in "Allocation of Costs for Voter Registration," FEC Advisory Opinion 1978-10, the FEC determined that when an election included candidates for federal office, expenditures for registration and get-out-the-vote (GOTV) drives would not be considered contributions to those federal candidates so long as the funds were not expended specifically on the federal candidates' behalf. ANTHONY CORRADO, CAMPAIGN FINANCE REFORM: A SOURCEBOOK 190-191 (1997). In "Corporate Support for Party Convention," FEC Advisory Opinion 1978-46, the FEC outlined which convention activities corporate money could and could not be used for, specifically exempting from regulation those funds used for conventions for state and local, but not federal, elections. https://cg-519a459a-0ea3-42c2-b7bc-fa1143481f74.s3-us-gov-west-1.amazonaws.com/legal/aos/62813.pdf. In Advisory Opinion 1978-50, the FEC clarified that GOTV activities that affected elections for state *and* federal elections would have to be apportioned between the state or local party's state and federal coffers; but so long as no specific federal candidates were mentioned, the money did not constitute a contribution to any particular candidate. Because the expenditures are not allocated to any particular candidate, they are not charged against the party's contribution limitations. The FEC went on to issue a number of other advisory opinions further defining the soft money exception.

The problems of soft money have raised concerns among many commentators. Senator Russ Feingold—principal cosponsor, with Senator John McCain, of BCRA (or the McCain-Feingold Act)—argued that the lack of limitations on soft money had led to the replacement of representative democracy with "corporate democracy." In corporate democracy, a shareholder's vote is weighted depending on the number of shares he owns, while in a representative democracy, each person's vote should count equally. Thus, in Senator Feingold's opinion, unlimited soft-money contributions led to an erosion of the principle of "one person, one vote." Russell D. Feingold, *Representative Democracy Versus Corporate Democracy: How Soft Money Erodes the Principle of "One Person, One Vote,"* 35 HARV. J. ON LEGIS. 377 (1998).

Others believe that the soft-money system violates the entirety of campaign-finance regulation in place since the beginning of the twentieth century. That is, soft-money contributions allow corporations, unions, and wealthy individuals to get around campaign-finance regulations that strictly limit their participation in financing campaigns, based on a myth that soft money is spent for "what is euphemistically called 'party building' purposes that are unrelated to influencing federal elections." The reality, for some commentators, is that "[s]oft money is raised by federal candidates and its spending, although done by the parties, is controlled by or coordinated with federal candidates. It is spent by the parties as an adjunct to federal campaigns and for the purpose of influencing federal elections." Donald

J. Simon, *Beyond Post-Watergate Reform: Putting an End to the Soft Money System*, 24 J. LEGIS. 167, 175 (1998).

2. Issue Advocacy

The second problem that motivated Congress to enact BCRA was issue advocacy. *Buckley* addressed the question of limitations on two types of advocacy: express and issue. The Court stated:

> [t]he constitutional deficiencies [of limitations on spending on advocacy] can be avoided only by reading §608(e)(1) as limited to communications that include explicit words of advocacy of election or defeat of a candidate. . . . We agree that in order to preserve the provision against invalidation on vagueness grounds, [it] must be construed to apply only to expenditures for communications that in express terms advocate the election or defeat of a clearly identified candidate for federal office.

To further define what was meant by a communication expressly advocating the election or defeat of a candidate, the Court added a footnote:

> This construction would restrict the application of §608(e)(1) to communications containing express words of advocacy of election or defeat, such as "vote for," "elect," "support," "cast your ballot for," "Smith for Congress," "vote against," "defeat," "reject."

The Court's enumeration of "magic words" that could turn an advertisement from issue advocacy—which is not regulated—to express advocacy—which is regulated—created as many problems as it solved. The list of terms to be avoided provided a simple rubric by which interest groups could judge their advertisements; so long as the group stayed just to the issue side of the issue-express line, it could spend as much money as it could raise on advertisements.

But, as it turns out, advertisements are perhaps not so neatly categorized as pieces of issue or express advocacy. Take, for example, an advertisement that appeared regularly on Montana televisions in the weeks preceding the 1996 election, sponsored by an organization called Citizens for Reform:

> Who is Bill Yellowtail? He preaches family values, but he took a swing at his wife. . . . He talks law and order, but is himself a convicted criminal. And though he talks about protecting children, Yellowtail failed to make his own child support payments, then voted against child support enforcement. Call Bill Yellowtail and tell him we don't approve of his wrongful behavior.

Richard Briffault, *Issue Advocacy: Redrawing the Elections/Politics Line*, 77 TEX. L. REV. 1751, 1751 (1998-1999). In 1992, preceding the presidential elections, the Christian Action Network ran an ad with the following voice-over more than 250 times in 24 major cities across the country:

> Bill Clinton's vision for a better America includes job quotas for homosexuals, giving homosexuals special civil rights, allowing homosexuals in

the armed forces. Al Gore supports homosexual couples' adopting children and becoming foster parents. Is this your vision for a better America? For more information on traditional family values, contact the Christian Action Network.

http://www.insidepolitics.org/ps111/issueads.html. And more recently, in late August of 2010, an ad sponsored by a group called Crossroads Grassroots Policy Strategies ran in Nevada, where sitting Democratic Senator Harry Reid faced a tough reelection bid against Republican Sharron Angle, with the following voice-over:

> With spending already out of control, Harry Reid spearheaded the stimulus spending bill. Harry's stimulus sent nearly two million dollars to California to collect ants in Africa, twenty-five million for new chairlifts and snow-making in Vermont, almost three hundred thousand to Texas to study weather on Venus. Meanwhile, back in Nevada, we still have the highest unemployment and record foreclosures. Really Harry? How about some help for Nevada?

The end plate of the ad included the text, "Help for Nevada? Tell Harry Reid: Nevada needs jobs, not more spending. Vote no on S. Amdt. 4594. Call 775-882-7343." The ad gives no indication that Senate Amendment 4594, a proposed amendment to the Small Business Jobs Act of 2010, was directed at making it easier for small businesses to gain access to credit. https://www.congress.gov/amendment/111th-congress/senate-amendment/4594. Thus, while the text of the ad suggests that the purpose of the advertisement is to encourage Nevadans to vote against Harry Reid, the end plate acts to turn the advertisement into an issue ad that never actually mentions the issue about which it advocates. Crossroads Grassroots Policy Strategies, it bears noting, is a 501(c)(4) organization tied to well-known Republican strategists Karl Rove and Ed Gillespie. http://www.politico.com/news/stories/0810/41327.html#ixzz0zWiKmAeV.

While none of these ads uses *Buckley*'s "magic words" — that is, the ads do not encourage voters to "vote for" anyone or "support" anything — it seems clear that they explicitly target candidates for federal office. Expenditures supporting a clearly identified candidate for federal office are supposed to be regulated by the FEC under FECA, but sham issue ads are a typical tool used to avoid regulation. Courts have been faced with tough questions about the extent to which advertisements that do not use "magic words" can be regulated.

3. The Bipartisan Campaign Reform Act of 2002

In 2001, various members of Congress introduced bills in both the House and Senate to address these two problems, which had become much greater parts of the campaign-finance landscape since FECA 1974 became law. In the House, Representatives Chris Shays (R-CT) and Marty Meehan (D-MA) introduced H.R. 380, the "Bipartisan Campaign Reform Act of 2001," on June 28, 2001. Senators John McCain (R-AZ) and Russell Feingold (D-WI) introduced similar legislation in the Senate. Though the law — which was signed by President George W. Bush on

March 27, 2002—has become known as the McCain-Feingold Act, it was the Shays-Meehan version of the bill that actually passed the two houses of Congress.

BCRA included three main titles. Title I, titled "Reduction of Special Interest Influence," addressed the problem of soft money—also called "nonfederal funds"—in federal elections. It did so in several key ways.

1. *National Parties.* Under BCRA, national-party committees may not solicit, receive, or direct another person to spend soft money. Such committees must also use only hard money—or "federal funds"—to raise funds that are used for federal election activity spending. The national committees also may not solicit funds for, or make direct donations to, tax-exempt 501(c) organizations if the organization spends money in connection with federal elections.

2. *State, District, and Local Parties.* State, district, and local parties generally must spend only hard money to pay for federal election activity. The only other funds that may be used are called "Levin funds," which are donations allowable under state law, raised directly by the state or local party that intends to use them, and limited to no more than $10,000 per year per person. Levin funds can be used for a portion of voter registration activity, voter identification, get-out-the-vote activities, and generic campaign activities so long as they do not refer to a specific candidate and are not used for radio or television communications unless they are communications for only state or local candidates.

   Like national parties, the state, district, and local parties may not solicit funds for or make donations to 501(c) organizations if the organization spends money in connection with federal elections. In addition, the same rules that govern the relationship between national parties and 527 organizations govern the relationship between the state, district, and local parties and 527s.

3. *Federal Candidates and Office-Holders.* BCRA puts limits on the amount and type of funds that can be raised for federal and state candidates by federal candidates and office-holders, their agents, or entities directly or indirectly maintained, established, or controlled by the candidate or office-holder. Such persons cannot solicit, receive, direct, transfer, spend, or disburse funds for a federal election unless the funds are federal funds subject to FECA. For state or local elections, the funds must be consistent with state law, must not exceed FECA's contribution limits, and must be from FECA-approved sources. Federal candidates may, however, speak at and attend fundraising events for state, district, or local party organizations where nonfederal or Levin funds are raised. They may also make general solicitations on behalf of tax-exempt organizations so long as the organization does not engage in activities in connection with federal elections.

Subtitle A of BCRA's Title II concerned "electioneering communications," or issue ads. These are ads that refer to a clearly identified candidate for federal office without explicitly calling for the candidate's election or defeat. Under BCRA as passed in 2002, these ads were reclassified as electioneering communications and thus could no longer be funded by corporations or labor organizations. Over

Chapter 9.   Money, Politics, and Law

certain thresholds, other individuals or groups who funded such ads were required to report the activity and the sources of funds used for the ads. These restrictions applied only to ads on television or radio and did not apply to 501(c)(3) organizations, though these organizations were prohibited by federal law from participating or intervening in a political campaign on behalf of any candidate for public office.

Subtitle B defined when a communication was considered to be "coordinated" between a candidate or political committee and a person making the communication. Rules promulgated under the subtitle provided a three-part test to determine coordination, where satisfaction of all three parts indicated that a communication was coordinated and was made for the purpose of influencing an election. The person who had made such a coordinated communication had made an in-kind contribution or coordinated expenditure on behalf of the candidate. The test asked the following three questions:

1. Who paid for the communication? A coordinated communication is paid for by someone other than the candidate.
2. What is the content of the communication? A coordinated communication is reasonably related to an election. The rules specify four content standards, and if a communication meets any of them, it is considered an election-related communication. In the standards, the phrase "public communication" means "any communication by means of television (including cable and satellite), radio, newspaper, magazine, billboard, mass mailing, telephone bank or any other form of general public political advertising," but does not include communications over the internet. 11 C.F.R. 100.26. The four standards are:
   a. electioneering communications, as described above;
   b. public communications that republish the candidates' campaign materials;
   c. public communications that expressly advocate the election or defeat of a clearly identified candidate; or
   d. public communications that (1) refer to a party or candidate, (2) are publicly disseminated 120 days or fewer before an election, and (3) are directed to voters in the jurisdiction where the candidate or party appears on the ballot.
3. What were the interactions between the person paying for the communication and the candidate? A communication satisfies this prong—called the "conduct prong"—of the test if it meets any of the following five standards. In each, the word "candidate" is shorthand for "candidate, candidate's committee, party committee, or agent of any of the foregoing."

   a. Was it created, produced, or distributed at the request or suggestion of the candidate, or was it created, produced, or distributed at the suggestion of the person paying for the communication and the candidate assented to the suggestion?
   b. Was the candidate materially involved in decisions regarding the content, audience, means, or mode of communication, specific media outlet used, the timing or frequency, size, or prominence of a communication?

    c. Was the communication created, produced, or distributed after one or more substantial discussions about the communication between the person paying for it and the candidate?

    d. Did the person paying for the communication employ a common vendor to create, produce, or distribute the communication and the vendor either works for or communicates information about the candidate?

    e. Did a person who has previously been an employee of the candidate's campaign use or convey information about the plans or needs of the candidate to the person paying for the communication and was that information used in the creation, production, or distribution of the communication?

11 C.F.R. 109.21. BCRA included several other provisions, including contribution limitations and disclaimer prohibitions. More information about BCRA is available at the FEC's website, at https://web.archive.org/web/20170506065504/http://www.fec.gov/press/bkgnd/bcra_overview.shtml.

4. *McConnell v. FEC*

Predictably, the key provisions of BCRA were challenged, in *McConnell v. FEC*, below. As noted above, BCRA was designed to deal with the problems of soft money and issue advertisements. Yet some of the problems Congress addressed in BCRA were created by the way the Supreme Court interpreted FECA in *Buckley*. Might the Court's experience with a comprehensive federal campaign-finance statute in *Buckley* affect the way that it approached BCRA in *McConnell*?

When Congress legislates, it implies that it believes the legislation to be constitutional. Yet the Court's role in the system is often to check the excesses of Congress. How much deference, if any, should the Court give to Congress's attempt to impose restrictions on campaign finance? How much of an obstacle should the Court allow itself to be when Congress is legislating in good faith to address real problems facing the country's elections? As you read *McConnell*, consider the Court's attitude toward Congress's campaign-finance efforts.

McConnell v. Federal Election Commission

540 U.S. 93 (2003)

Justice STEVENS and Justice O'CONNOR delivered the opinion of the Court with respect to BCRA Titles I and II. . . .

I

More than a century ago the "sober-minded Elihu Root" advocated legislation that would prohibit political contributions by corporations in order to prevent "'the great aggregations of wealth, from using their corporate funds, directly or indirectly,' " to elect legislators who would " 'vote for their protection and the advancement of their interests as against those of the public.' " *United States v. Automobile Workers,* 352 U.S. 567, 571 (1957) (quoting E. Root, Addresses on Government and Citizenship 143 (R. Bacon & J. Scott eds. 1916)). . . .

[The Bipartisan Campaign Reform Act of 2002 or] BCRA is the most recent federal enactment designed "to purge national politics of what was conceived to be the pernicious influence of 'big money' campaign contributions." *Id.,* at 572. . . .

Congress' historical concern with the "political potentialities of wealth" and their "untoward consequences for the democratic process," *Automobile Workers, supra,* at 577-578, has long reached beyond corporate money. During and shortly after World War II, Congress reacted to the "enormous financial outlays" made by some unions in connection with national elections. 352 U.S., at 579. Congress first restricted union contributions in the Hatch Act, 18 U.S.C. §610, and it later prohibited "union contributions in connection with federal elections . . . altogether." *National Right to Work, supra,* at 209. Congress subsequently extended that prohibition to cover unions' election-related expenditures as well as contributions, and it broadened the coverage of federal campaigns to include both primary and general elections. Labor Management Relations Act, 1947 (Taft-Hartley Act), 61 Stat. 136. . . . During the consideration of those measures, legislators repeatedly voiced their concerns regarding the pernicious influence of large campaign contributions. . . . As we noted in a unanimous opinion recalling this history, Congress' "careful legislative adjustment of the federal electoral laws, in a 'cautious advance, step by step,' to account for the particular legal and economic attributes of corporations and labor organizations warrants considerable deference." *National Right to Work, supra,* at 209 (citations omitted).

In early 1972 Congress continued its steady improvement of the national election laws by enacting FECA, 86 Stat. 3. . . . As the 1972 Presidential elections made clear, however, FECA's passage did not deter unseemly fundraising and campaign practices. Evidence of those practices persuaded Congress to enact the Federal Election Campaign Act Amendments of 1974, 88 Stat. 1263. Reviewing a constitutional challenge to the amendments, the Court of Appeals for the District of Columbia Circuit described them as "by far the most comprehensive . . . reform legislation [ever] passed by Congress concerning the election of the President, Vice-President and members of Congress." *Buckley v. Valeo,* 519 F.2d 821, 831 (C.A.D.C. 1975) (en banc) (per curiam). . . .

Three important developments in the years after our decision in *Buckley* persuaded Congress that further legislation was necessary to regulate the role that corporations, unions, and wealthy contributors play in the electoral process. As a preface to our discussion of the specific provisions of BCRA, we comment briefly on the increased importance of "soft money," the proliferation of "issue ads," and the disturbing findings of a Senate investigation into campaign practices related to the 1996 federal elections.

Soft Money

Under FECA, "contributions" must be made with funds that are subject to the Act's disclosure requirements and source and amount limitations. Such funds are known as "federal" or "hard" money. FECA defines the term "contribution," however, to include only the gift or advance of anything of value "made by any person for the purpose of influencing any election for *Federal* office." 2 U.S.C. §431(8)(A)(i) (emphasis added). Donations made solely for the purpose of influencing state or local elections are therefore unaffected by FECA's requirements and prohibitions. As a result, prior to the enactment of BCRA, federal law permitted corporations and unions, as well as individuals who had already made the maximum permissible contributions to federal candidates, to contribute "nonfederal money"—also known as "soft money"—to political parties for activities intended to influence state or local elections.

Shortly after *Buckley* was decided, questions arose concerning the treatment of contributions intended to influence both federal and state elections. Although a literal reading of FECA's definition of "contribution" would have required such activities to be funded with hard money, the FEC ruled that political parties could fund mixed-purpose activities—including get-out-the-vote drives and generic party advertising—in part with soft money. In 1995 the FEC concluded that the parties could also use soft money to defray the costs of "legislative advocacy media advertisements," even if the ads mentioned the name of a federal candidate, so long as they did not expressly advocate the candidate's election or defeat. . . .

As the permissible uses of soft money expanded, the amount of soft money raised and spent by the national political parties increased exponentially. Of the two major parties' total spending, soft money accounted for 5% ($21.6 million) in 1984, 11% ($45 million) in 1988, 16% ($80 million) in 1992, 30% ($272 million) in 1996, and 42% ($498 million) in 2000. The national parties transferred large amounts of their soft money to the state parties, which were allowed to use a larger percentage of soft money to finance mixed-purpose activities under FEC rules. In the year 2000, for example, the national parties diverted $280 million—more than half of their soft money—to state parties.

Many contributions of soft money were dramatically larger than the contributions of hard money permitted by FECA. . . . Moreover, the largest corporate donors often made substantial contributions to both parties. Such practices corroborate evidence indicating that many corporate contributions were motivated by a desire for access to candidates and a fear of being placed at a disadvantage in the legislative process relative to other contributors, rather than by ideological support for the candidates and parties.

Not only were such soft-money contributions often designed to gain access to federal candidates, but they were in many cases solicited by the candidates themselves. Candidates often directed potential donors to party committees and tax-exempt organizations that could legally accept soft money. . . .

The solicitation, transfer, and use of soft money thus enabled parties and candidates to circumvent FECA's limitations on the source and amount of contributions in connection with federal elections.

Issue Advertising

In *Buckley* we construed FECA's disclosure and reporting requirements, as well as its expenditure limitations, "to reach only funds used for communications that expressly advocate the election or defeat of a clearly identified candidate." 424 U.S., at 80. As a result of that strict reading of the statute, the use or omission of "magic words" such as "Elect John Smith" or "Vote Against Jane Doe" marked a bright statutory line separating "express advocacy" from "issue advocacy." See *id.*, at 44, n.52. Express advocacy was subject to FECA's limitations and could be financed only using hard money. . . . So-called issue ads, on the other hand, not only could be financed with soft money, but could be aired without disclosing the identity of, or any other information about, their sponsors.

While the distinction between "issue" and express advocacy seemed neat in theory, the two categories of advertisements proved functionally identical in important respects. Both were used to advocate the election or defeat of clearly identified federal candidates, even though the so-called issue ads eschewed the use of magic words. Little difference existed, for example, between an ad that urged viewers to "vote against Jane Doe" and one that condemned Jane Doe's record on a particular issue before exhorting viewers to "call Jane Doe and tell her what you think." Indeed, campaign professionals testified that the most effective campaign ads, like the most effective commercials for products such as Coca-Cola, should, and did, avoid the use of the magic words. . . . Corporations and unions spent hundreds of millions of dollars of their general funds to pay for these ads, and those expenditures, like soft-money donations to the political parties, were unregulated under FECA. . . .

Because FECA's disclosure requirements did not apply to so-called issue ads, sponsors of such ads often used misleading names to conceal their identity. "Citizens for Better Medicare," for instance, was not a grassroots organization of citizens, as its name might suggest, but was instead a platform for an association of drug manufacturers. And "Republicans for Clean Air," which ran ads in the 2000 Republican Presidential primary, was actually an organization consisting of just two individuals. . . .

While the public may not have been fully informed about the sponsorship of so-called issue ads, the record indicates that candidates and officeholders often were. . . . As with soft-money contributions, political parties and candidates used the availability of so-called issue ads to circumvent FECA's limitations. . . .

Senate Committee Investigation

In 1998 the Senate Committee on Governmental Affairs issued a six-volume report summarizing the results of an extensive investigation into the campaign practices in the 1996 federal elections. The report gave particular attention to the effect of soft money on the American political system, including elected officials' practice of granting special access in return for political contributions.

The committee's principal findings relating to Democratic Party fundraising were set forth in the majority's report, while the minority report primarily described Republican practices. The two reports reached consensus, however, on certain central propositions. They agreed that the "soft money loophole" had led to a "meltdown" of the campaign finance system that had been intended "to keep corporate, union and large individual contributions from influencing the electoral process." One Senator stated that "the hearings provided overwhelming evidence that the twin loopholes of soft money and bogus issue advertising have virtually destroyed our campaign finance laws, leaving us with little more than a pile of legal rubble."

The report was critical of both parties' methods of raising soft money, as well as their use of those funds. It concluded that both parties promised and provided special access to candidates and senior Government officials in exchange for large soft-money contributions. . . .

In 1996 both parties began to use large amounts of soft money to pay for issue advertising designed to influence federal elections. The committee found such ads highly problematic for two reasons. Since they accomplished the same purposes as express advocacy (which could lawfully be funded only with hard money), the ads enabled unions, corporations, and wealthy contributors to circumvent protections that FECA was intended to provide. Moreover, though ostensibly independent of the candidates, the ads were often actually coordinated with, and controlled by, the campaigns. The ads thus provided a means for evading FECA's candidate contribution limits.

The report also emphasized the role of state and local parties. While the FEC's allocation regime permitted national parties to use soft money to pay for up to 40% of the costs of both generic voter activities and issue advertising, they allowed state and local parties to use larger percentages of soft money for those purposes. For that reason, national parties often made substantial transfers of soft money to "state and local political parties for 'generic voter activities' that in fact ultimately benefit[ed] federal candidates because the funds for all practical purposes remain[ed] under the control of the national committees." The report concluded that "[t]he use of such soft money thus allow[ed] more corporate, union treasury, and large contributions from wealthy individuals into the system."

The report discussed potential reforms, including a ban on soft money at the national and state party levels and restrictions on sham issue advocacy by nonparty groups. . . .

II

In BCRA, Congress enacted many of the committee's proposed reforms. BCRA's central provisions are designed to address Congress' concerns about the increasing use of soft money and issue advertising to influence federal elections. Title I regulates the use of soft money by political parties, officeholders, and candidates. Title II primarily prohibits corporations and labor unions from using general treasury funds for communications that are intended to, or have the effect of, influencing the outcome of federal elections. . . .

III

Title I is Congress' effort to plug the soft-money loophole. The cornerstone of Title I is new FECA §323(a), which prohibits national party committees and their agents from soliciting, receiving, directing, or spending any soft money. 2 U.S.C. §441i(a) (Supp. II). In short, §323(a) takes national parties out of the soft-money business.

The remaining provisions of new FECA §323 largely reinforce the restrictions in §323(a). . . . Plaintiffs mount a facial First Amendment challenge to new FECA §323, as well as challenges based on the Elections Clause, U.S. Const., Art. I, §4, principles of federalism, and the equal protection component of the Due Process Clause. We address these challenges in turn.

A

In *Buckley* and subsequent cases, we have subjected restrictions on campaign expenditures to closer scrutiny than limits on campaign contributions. . . . In these cases we have recognized that contribution limits, unlike limits on expenditures, "entai[l] only a marginal restriction upon the contributor's ability to engage in free communication." *Buckley*, 424 U.S., at 20. . . .

Like the contribution limits we upheld in *Buckley*, §323's restrictions have only a marginal impact on the ability of contributors, candidates, officeholders, and parties to engage in effective political speech. . . . Complex as its provisions may be, §323, in the main, does little more than regulate the ability of wealthy individuals, corporations, and unions to contribute large sums of money to influence federal elections, federal candidates, and federal officeholders. . . .

Section 323 . . . shows "due regard for the reality that solicitation is characteristically intertwined with informative and perhaps persuasive speech seeking support for particular causes or for particular views." *Schaumburg v. Citizens for a Better Environment*, 444 U.S. 620, 632 (1980). The fact that party committees and federal candidates and officeholders must now ask only for limited dollar amounts or request that a corporation or union contribute money through its PAC in no way alters or impairs the political message "intertwined" with the solicitation. . . . And rather than chill such solicitations . . . the restriction here tends to increase the dissemination of information by forcing parties, candidates, and officeholders to solicit from a wider array of potential donors. As with direct limits on contributions, therefore, §323's spending and solicitation restrictions have only a marginal impact on political speech. . . .

New FECA §323(a)'s Restrictions on National Party Committees

The core of Title I is new FECA §323(a), which provides that "national committee[s] of a political party . . . may not solicit, receive, or direct to another person a contribution, donation, or transfer of funds or any other thing of value, or spend any funds, that are not subject to the limitations, prohibitions, and reporting requirements of this Act." 2 U.S.C. §441i(a)(1) (Supp. II). The prohibition extends to "any officer or agent acting on behalf of such a national committee, and any entity that is directly or indirectly established, financed, maintained, or controlled by such a national committee." §441i(a)(2).

The main goal of §323(a) is modest. In large part, it simply effects a return to the scheme that was approved in *Buckley* and that was subverted by the creation of the FEC's allocation regime. . . . Under that allocation regime, national parties were able to use vast amounts of soft money in their efforts to elect federal candidates. Consequently, as long as they directed the money to the political parties, donors could contribute large amounts of soft money for use in activities designed to influence federal elections. New §323(a) is designed to put a stop to that practice.

1. Governmental Interests Underlying New FECA §323(a)

The Government defends §323(a)'s ban on national parties' involvement with soft money as necessary to prevent the actual and apparent corruption of federal candidates and officeholders. Our cases have made clear that the prevention of corruption or its appearance constitutes a sufficiently important interest to justify political contribution limits. . . .

Of "almost equal" importance has been the Government's interest in combating the appearance or perception of corruption engendered by large campaign contributions. *Buckley, supra,* at 27. Take away Congress' authority to regulate the appearance of undue influence and "the cynical assumption that large donors call the tune could jeopardize the willingness of voters to take part in democratic governance." *Shrink Missouri,* 528 U.S., at 390. . . .

The idea that large contributions to a national party can corrupt or, at the very least, create the appearance of corruption of federal candidates and officeholders is neither novel nor implausible. For nearly 30 years, FECA has placed strict dollar limits and source restrictions on contributions that individuals and other entities can give to national, state, and local party committees for the purpose of influencing a federal election. The premise behind these restrictions has been, and continues to be, that contributions to a federal candidate's party in aid of that candidate's campaign threaten to create—no less than would a direct contribution to the candidate—a sense of obligation. This is particularly true of contributions to national parties, with which federal candidates and officeholders enjoy a special relationship and unity of interest. . . .

The question for present purposes is whether large *soft-money* contributions to national party committees have a corrupting influence or give rise to the appearance of corruption. Both common sense and the ample record in these cases confirm Congress' belief that they do. . . . [T]he FEC's allocation regime has invited widespread circumvention of FECA's limits on contributions to parties for the purpose of influencing federal elections. Under this system, corporate, union, and wealthy individual donors have been free to contribute substantial sums of soft money to the national parties, which the parties can spend for the specific purpose of influencing a particular candidate's federal election. It is not only plausible, but likely, that candidates would feel grateful for such donations and that donors would seek to exploit that gratitude.

The evidence in the record shows that candidates and donors alike have in fact exploited the soft-money loophole, the former to increase their prospects of election and the latter to create debt on the part of officeholders, with the national parties serving as willing intermediaries. Thus, despite FECA's hard-money limits on direct contributions to candidates, federal officeholders have commonly asked donors to make soft-money donations to national and state committees solely in order to assist federal campaigns, including the officeholder's own. . . . National party committees often teamed with individual candidates' campaign committees to create joint fundraising committees, which enabled the candidates to take advantage of the party's higher contribution limits while still allowing donors to give to their preferred candidate. . . . For their part, lobbyists, CEOs, and wealthy individuals alike all have candidly admitted donating substantial sums of soft money to national committees not on ideological grounds, but for the express purpose of securing influence over federal officials. . . .

Particularly telling is the fact that, in 1996 and 2000, more than half of the top 50 soft-money donors gave substantial sums to *both* major national parties, leaving room for no other conclusion but that these donors were seeking influence, or avoiding retaliation, rather than promoting any particular ideology. . . .

The evidence from the federal officeholders' perspective is similar. For example, one former Senator described the influence purchased by nonfederal donations as follows:

> Too often, Members' first thought is not what is right or what they believe, but how it will affect fundraising. Who, after all, can seriously contend that a $100,000 donation does not alter the way one thinks about—and quite possibly votes on—an issue? . . . When you don't pay the piper that finances your campaigns, you will never get any more money from that piper. Since money is the mother's milk of politics, you never want to be in that situation. 251 F. Supp. 2d, at 481 (Kollar-Kotelly, J.) (quoting declaration of former Sen. Alan Simpson ¶10. . . .

[P]laintiffs conceive of corruption too narrowly. Our cases have firmly established that Congress' legitimate interest extends beyond preventing simple cash-for-votes corruption to curbing "undue influence on an officeholder's judgment, and the appearance of such influence." *Colorado* [*Republican*] *II, supra*, at 441, 121 S. Ct. 2351. Many of the "deeply disturbing examples" of corruption cited by this Court in *Buckley*, 424 U.S., at 27, to justify FECA's contribution limits were not episodes of vote buying, but evidence that various corporate interests had given substantial donations to gain access to high-level government officials. . . .

The record in the present cases is replete with similar examples of national party committees peddling access to federal candidates and officeholders in exchange for large soft-money donations. . . . So pervasive is this practice that the six national party committees actually furnish their own menus of opportunities for access to would-be soft-money donors, with increased prices reflecting an increased level of access. . . .

Just as troubling to a functioning democracy as classic *quid pro quo* corruption is the danger that officeholders will decide issues not on the merits or the desires of their constituencies, but according to the wishes of those who have made large financial contributions valued by the officeholder. Even if it occurs only occasionally, the potential for such undue influence is manifest. And unlike straight cash-for-votes transactions, such corruption is neither easily detected nor practical to criminalize. The best means of prevention is to identify and to remove the temptation. . . .

2. New FECA §323(a)'s Restriction on Spending and Receiving Soft Money

Plaintiffs and the Chief Justice contend that §323(a) is impermissibly overbroad because it subjects *all* funds raised and spent by national parties to FECA's hard-money source and amount limits, including, for example, funds spent on purely state and local elections in which no federal office is at stake. Such activities, the Chief Justice asserts, pose "little or no potential to corrupt . . . federal candidates and officeholders." This observation is beside the point. Section 323(a), like the remainder of §323, regulates contributions, not activities. As the record demonstrates, it is the close relationship between federal officeholders and the national parties, as well as the means by which parties have traded on that relationship, that have made all large soft-money contributions to national parties suspect. . . .

[N]ational parties [are] in a position to sell access to federal officeholders in exchange for soft-money contributions that the party can then use for its own purposes. Access to federal officeholders is the most valuable favor the national party committees are able to give in exchange for large donations. The fact that officeholders comply by donating their valuable time indicates either that officeholders place substantial value on the soft-money contribution themselves, without regard to their end use, or that national committees are able to exert considerable control over federal officeholders. Either way, large soft-money donations to national party committees are likely to buy donors preferential access to federal officeholders no matter the ends to which their contributions are eventually put. As discussed above, Congress had sufficient grounds to regulate the appearance of undue influence associated with this practice. The Government's strong interests in preventing corruption, and in particular the appearance of corruption, are thus sufficient to justify subjecting all donations to national parties to the source, amount, and disclosure limitations of FECA. . . .

New FECA §323(b)'s Restrictions on State and Local Party Committees

In constructing a coherent scheme of campaign finance regulation, Congress recognized that, given the close ties between federal candidates and state party committees, BCRA's restrictions on national committee activity would rapidly become ineffective if state and local committees remained available as a conduit for soft-money donations. Section 323(b) is designed to foreclose wholesale evasion of §323(a)'s anticorruption measures by sharply curbing state committees' ability to use large soft-money contributions to influence federal elections. The core of §323(b) is a straightforward contribution regulation: It prevents donors from contributing nonfederal funds to state and local party committees to help finance "Federal election activity." 2 U.S.C. §441i(b)(1) (Supp. II). The term "Federal election activity" encompasses four distinct categories of electioneering: (1) voter registration activity during the 120 days preceding a regularly scheduled federal election; (2) voter identification, get-out-the-vote (GOTV), and generic campaign activity that is "conducted in connection with an election in which a candidate for Federal office appears on the ballot"; (3) any "public communication" that "refers to a clearly identified candidate for Federal office" and "promotes," "supports," "attacks," or "opposes" a candidate for that office; and (4) the services provided by a state committee employee who dedicates more than 25% of his or her time to "activities in connection with a Federal election." §§431(20)(A)(i)-(iv). The Act explicitly excludes several categories of activity from this definition: public communications that refer solely to nonfederal candidates; contributions to nonfederal candidates; state and local political conventions; and the cost of grassroots campaign materials like bumper stickers that refer only to state candidates. §431(20)(B). All activities that fall within the statutory definition must be funded with hard money. §441i(b)(1).

Section 323(b)(2), the so-called Levin Amendment, carves out an exception to this general rule. A refinement on the pre-BCRA regime that permitted parties to pay for certain activities with a mix of federal and nonfederal funds, the Levin Amendment allows state and local party committees to pay for certain types of federal election activity with an allocated ratio of hard money and "Levin funds" — that is, funds raised within an annual limit of $10,000 per person. 2 U.S.C. §441i(b)(2). Except for the $10,000 cap and certain related restrictions to prevent circumvention of that limit, §323(b)(2) leaves regulation of such contributions to the States.

The scope of the Levin Amendment is limited in two ways. First, state and local parties can use Levin money to fund only . . . voter registration activity, voter identification drives, GOTV drives, and generic campaign activities. And not all of these activities qualify: Levin funds cannot be used to pay for any activities that refer to "a clearly identified candidate for Federal office"; they likewise cannot be used to fund broadcast communications unless they refer "solely to a clearly identified candidate for State or local office." §§441i(b)(2)(B)(i)-(ii).

Second, both the Levin funds and the allocated portion of hard money used to pay for such activities must be raised entirely by the state or local committee that spends them. §441i(b)(2)(B)(iv). This means that a state party committee cannot use Levin funds transferred from other party committees to cover the Levin funds portion of a Levin Amendment expenditure. It also means that a state party committee cannot use hard money transferred from other party committees to cover the hard-money portion of a Levin Amendment expenditure. Furthermore, national committees, federal candidates, and federal officeholders generally may not solicit Levin funds on behalf of state committees, and state committees may not team up to raise Levin funds. §441i(b)(2)(C). They can, however, jointly raise the hard money used to make Levin expenditures.

1. Governmental Interests Underlying New FECA §323(b)

We begin by noting that, in addressing the problem of soft-money contributions to state committees, Congress both drew a conclusion and made a prediction. Its conclusion, based on the evidence before it, was that the corrupting influence of soft money does not insinuate itself into the political process solely through national party committees. Rather, state committees function as an alternative avenue for precisely the same corrupting forces. . . . Section 323(b) thus promotes an important governmental interest by confronting the corrupting influence that soft-money donations to political parties already have.

Congress also made a prediction. Having been taught the hard lesson of circumvention by the entire history of campaign finance regulation, Congress knew that soft-money donors would react to §323(a) by scrambling to find another way to purchase influence. It was "neither novel nor implausible," *Shrink Missouri*, 528 U.S., at 391, for Congress to conclude that political parties would react to §323(a) by directing soft-money contributors to the state committees, and that federal candidates would be just as indebted to these contributors as they had been to those who had formerly contributed to the national parties. . . . Preventing corrupting activity from shifting wholesale to state committees and thereby eviscerating FECA clearly qualifies as an important governmental interest.

2. New FECA §323(b)'s Tailoring

Plaintiffs argue that even if some legitimate interest might be served by §323(b), the provision's restrictions are unjustifiably burdensome and therefore cannot be considered "closely drawn" to match the Government's objectives. They advance three main contentions in support of this proposition. . . .

a. §323(b)'s Application to Federal Election Activity

Plaintiffs assert that §323(b) represents a new brand of pervasive federal regulation of state-focused electioneering activities that cannot possibly corrupt or appear to corrupt federal officeholders and thus goes well beyond Congress' concerns about the corruption of the federal electoral process. We disagree.

It is true that §323(b) captures some activities that affect state campaigns for nonfederal offices. But these are the same sorts of activities that already were covered by the FEC's pre-BCRA allocation rules, and thus had to be funded in part by hard money, because they affect federal as well as state elections. As a practical matter, BCRA merely codifies the principles of the FEC's allocation regime while at the same time justifiably adjusting the formulas applicable to these activities in order to restore the efficacy of FECA's longtime statutory restriction—approved by the Court and eroded by the FEC's allocation regime—on contributions to state and local party committees for the purpose of influencing federal elections.

Like the rest of Title I, §323(b) is premised on Congress' judgment that if a large donation is capable of putting a federal candidate in the debt of the contributor, it poses a threat of corruption or the appearance of corruption. . . .

The first two categories of "Federal election activity," voter registration efforts, and voter identification, GOTV, and generic campaign activities conducted in connection with a federal election, clearly capture activity that benefits federal candidates. Common sense dictates, and it was undisputed below, that a party's efforts to register voters sympathetic to that party directly assist the party's candidates for federal office. It is equally clear that federal candidates reap substantial rewards from any efforts that increase the number of like-minded registered voters who actually go to the polls. . . .

Because voter registration, voter identification, GOTV, and generic campaign activity all confer substantial benefits on federal candidates, the funding of such activities creates a significant risk of actual and apparent corruption. Section 323(b) is a reasonable response to that risk. . . .

"Public communications" that promote or attack a candidate for federal office . . . also undoubtedly have a dramatic effect on federal elections. Such ads were a prime motivating force behind BCRA's passage. . . . [A]ny public communication that promotes or attacks a clearly identified federal candidate directly affects the election in which he is participating. . . .

c. New FECA §323(b)'s Impact on Parties' Ability to Engage in Effective Advocacy

Finally, plaintiffs contend that §323(b) is unconstitutional because its restrictions on soft-money contributions to state and local party committees will prevent them from engaging in effective advocacy. . . . If the history of campaign finance regulation discussed above proves anything, it is that political parties are extraordinarily flexible in adapting to new restrictions on their fundraising abilities. Moreover, the mere fact that §323(b) may reduce the relative amount of money available to state and local parties to fund federal election activities is largely inconsequential. The question is not whether §323(b) reduces the amount of funds available over previous election cycles, but whether it is "so radical in effect as to . . . drive the sound of [the recipient's] voice below the level of notice." *Shrink Missouri*, 528 U.S., at 397. If indeed state or local parties can make such a showing, as-applied challenges remain available.

We accordingly conclude that §323(b), on its face, is closely drawn to match the important governmental interests of preventing corruption and the appearance of corruption. . . .

IV

BCRA §201's Definition of "Electioneering Communications"

The first section of Title II, §201, comprehensively amends FECA §304, which requires political committees to file detailed periodic financial reports with the FEC. The amendment coins a new term, "electioneering communications," to replace the narrowing construction of FECA's disclosure provisions adopted by this Court in *Buckley*. . . . [T]he term "electioneering communication" . . . is defined to encompass any "broadcast, cable, or satellite communication" that

> "(I) refers to a clearly identified candidate for Federal office;
> "(II) is made within—
>   "(aa) 60 days before a general, special, or runoff election for the office sought by the candidate; or
>   "(bb) 30 days before a primary or preference election, or a convention or caucus of a political party that has authority to nominate a candidate, for the office sought by the candidate; and
> "(III) in the case of a communication which refers to a candidate for an office other than President or Vice President, is targeted to the relevant electorate." 2 U.S.C. §434(f)(3)(A)(i) (Supp. II).

New FECA §304(f)(3)(C) further provides that a communication is "'targeted to the relevant electorate'" if it "can be received by 50,000 or more persons" in the district or State the candidate seeks to represent. 2 U.S.C. §434(f)(3)(C).

In addition to setting forth this definition, BCRA's amendments to FECA §304 specify significant disclosure requirements for persons who fund electioneering communications. BCRA's use of this new term is not, however, limited to the disclosure context: A later section of the Act . . . restricts corporations' and labor unions' funding of electioneering communications. Plaintiffs challenge the constitutionality of the new term as it applies in both the disclosure and the expenditure contexts.

The major premise of plaintiffs' challenge to BCRA's use of the term "electioneering communication" is that *Buckley* drew a constitutionally mandated line between express advocacy and so-called issue advocacy, and that speakers possess an inviolable First Amendment right to engage in the latter category of speech. Thus, plaintiffs maintain, Congress cannot constitutionally require disclosure of, or regulate expenditures for, "electioneering communications" without making an exception for those "communications" that do not meet *Buckley*'s definition of express advocacy.

That position misapprehends our prior decisions, for the express advocacy restriction was an endpoint of statutory interpretation, not a first principle of constitutional law. . . . [A] plain reading of *Buckley* makes clear that the express advocacy limitation, in both the expenditure and the disclosure contexts, was the product of statutory interpretation rather than a constitutional command. In narrowly reading the FECA provisions in *Buckley* to avoid problems of vagueness and overbreadth, we nowhere suggested that a statute that was neither vague nor overbroad would be required to toe the same express advocacy line. . . .

In short, the concept of express advocacy and the concomitant class of magic words were born of an effort to avoid constitutional infirmities. . . . [O]ur decisions in *Buckley* and *MCFL* were specific to the statutory language before us; they in no way drew a constitutional boundary that forever fixed the permissible scope of provisions regulating campaign-related speech.

Nor are we persuaded, independent of our precedents, that the First Amendment erects a rigid barrier between express advocacy and so-called issue advocacy. That notion cannot be squared with our longstanding recognition that the presence or absence of magic words cannot meaningfully distinguish electioneering speech from a true issue ad. Indeed, the unmistakable lesson from the record in this litigation . . . is that *Buckley*'s magic-words requirement is functionally meaningless. Not only can advertisers easily evade the line by eschewing the use of magic words, but they would seldom choose to use such words even if permitted. And although the resulting advertisements do not urge the viewer to vote for or against a candidate in so many words, they are no less clearly intended to influence the election. *Buckley*'s express advocacy line, in short, has not aided the legislative effort to combat real or apparent corruption, and Congress enacted BCRA to correct the flaws it found in the existing system.

Finally we observe that new FECA §304(f)(3)'s definition of "electioneering communication" raises none of the vagueness concerns that drove our analysis in *Buckley*. The term "electioneering communication" applies only (1) to a broadcast (2) clearly identifying a candidate for federal office, (3) aired within a specific time period, and (4) targeted to an identified audience of at least 50,000 viewers or listeners. These components are both easily understood and objectively determinable. Thus, the constitutional objection that persuaded the Court in *Buckley* to limit FECA's reach to express advocacy is simply inapposite here.

V

Many years ago we observed that "[t]o say that Congress is without power to pass appropriate legislation to safeguard . . . an election from the improper use of money to influence the result is to deny to the nation in a vital particular the power of self protection." *Burroughs v. United States*, 290 U.S., at 545. We abide by that conviction in considering Congress' most recent effort to confine the ill effects of aggregated wealth on our political system. We are under no illusion that BCRA will be the last congressional statement on the matter. Money, like water, will always find an outlet. What problems will arise, and how Congress will respond, are concerns for another day. In the main we uphold BCRA's two principal, complementary

features: the control of soft money and the regulation of electioneering communications. Accordingly, we affirm in part and reverse in part the District Court's
judgment with respect to Titles I and II.

It is so ordered.

Justice SCALIA, concurring in part and dissenting in part:

This is a sad day for the freedom of speech. Who could have imagined that
the same Court which, within the past four years, has sternly disapproved of restrictions upon such inconsequential forms of expression as virtual child pornography,
Ashcroft v. Free Speech Coalition, 535 U.S 234 (2002), tobacco advertising, *Lorillard
Tobacco Co. v. Reilly,* 533 U.S. 525 (2001), dissemination of illegally intercepted communications, *Bartnicki v. Vopper,* 532 U.S. 514 (2001), and sexually explicit cable
programming, *United States v. Playboy Entertainment Group, Inc.,* 529 U.S. 803 (2000),
would smile with favor upon a law that cuts to the heart of what the First Amendment is meant to protect: the right to criticize the government. For that is what the
most offensive provisions of this legislation are all about. We are governed by Congress, and this legislation prohibits the criticism of Members of Congress by those
entities most capable of giving such criticism loud voice: national political parties
and corporations, both of the commercial and the not-for-profit sort. It forbids pre-
election criticism of incumbents by corporations, even not-for-profit corporations,
by use of their general funds; and forbids national-party use of "soft" money to fund
"issue ads" that incumbents find so offensive.

To be sure, the legislation is evenhanded: It similarly prohibits criticism of
the candidates who oppose Members of Congress in their reelection bids. But as
everyone knows, this is an area in which evenhandedness is not fairness. If all electioneering were evenhandedly prohibited, incumbents would have an enormous
advantage. Likewise, if incumbents and challengers are limited to the same quantity of electioneering, incumbents are favored. In other words, any restriction upon
a type of campaign speech that is equally available to challengers and incumbents
tends to favor incumbents.

Beyond that, however, the present legislation targets for prohibition certain
categories of campaign speech that are particularly harmful to incumbents. Is it
accidental, do you think, that incumbents raise about three times as much "hard
money"—the sort of funding generally not restricted by this legislation—as do
their challengers? Or that lobbyists (who seek the favor of incumbents) give 92 percent of their money in "hard" contributions? Is it an oversight, do you suppose,
that the so-called "millionaire provisions" raise the contribution limit for a candidate running against an individual who devotes to the campaign (as challengers
often do) great personal wealth, but do not raise the limit for a candidate running against an individual who devotes to the campaign (as incumbents often do)
a massive election "war chest"? And is it mere happenstance, do you estimate, that
national-party funding, which is severely limited by the Act, is more likely to assist
cash-strapped challengers than flush-with-hard-money incumbents? Was it unintended, by any chance, that incumbents are free personally to receive some soft
money and even to solicit it for other organizations, while national parties are not?

I wish to address . . . fallacious propositions that might be thought to justify
some or all of the provisions of this legislation—only the last of which is explicitly

embraced by the principal opinion for the Court, but all of which underlie, I think, its approach to these cases.

(A) MONEY IS NOT SPEECH

It was said by congressional proponents of this legislation, with support from the law reviews, that since this legislation regulates nothing but the expenditure of money for speech, as opposed to speech itself, the burden it imposes is not subject to full First Amendment scrutiny; the government may regulate the raising and spending of campaign funds just as it regulates other forms of conduct, such as burning draft cards, or camping out on the National Mall. Until today . . . that view has been categorically rejected by our jurisprudence. As we said in *Buckley*, 424 U.S., at 16 "this Court has never suggested that the dependence of a communication on the expenditure of money operates itself to introduce a nonspeech element or to reduce the exacting scrutiny required by the First Amendment."

Our traditional view was correct, and today's cavalier attitude toward regulating the financing of speech (the "exacting scrutiny" test of *Buckley* . . . is not uttered in any majority opinion . . .) frustrates the fundamental purpose of the First Amendment. In any economy operated on even the most rudimentary principles of division of labor, effective public communication requires the speaker to make use of the services of others. An author may write a novel, but he will seldom publish and distribute it himself. A freelance reporter may write a story, but he will rarely edit, print, and deliver it to subscribers. To a government bent on suppressing speech, this mode of organization presents opportunities: Control any cog in the machine, and you can halt the whole apparatus. License printers, and it matters little whether authors are still free to write. Restrict the sale of books, and it matters little who prints them. Predictably, repressive regimes have exploited these principles by attacking all levels of the production and dissemination of ideas. In response to this threat, we have interpreted the First Amendment broadly. Division of labor requires a means of mediating exchange, and in a commercial society, that means is supplied by money. . . .

This, too, presents opportunities for repression: Instead of regulating the various parties to the enterprise individually, the government can suppress their ability to coordinate by regulating their use of money. What good is the right to print books without a right to buy works from authors? Or the right to publish newspapers without the right to pay deliverymen? The right to speak would be largely ineffective if it did not include the right to engage in financial transactions that are the incidents of its exercise.

This is not to say that any regulation of money is a regulation of speech. The government may apply general commercial regulations to those who use money for speech if it applies them evenhandedly to those who use money for other purposes. But where the government singles out money used to fund speech as its legislative object, it is acting against speech as such, no less than if it had targeted the paper on which a book was printed or the trucks that deliver it to the bookstore. . . .

It should be obvious, then, that a law limiting the amount a person can spend to broadcast his political views is a direct restriction on speech. That is no different from a law limiting the amount a newspaper can pay its editorial staff or the amount a charity can pay its leafletters. It is equally clear that a limit on the amount a candidate can raise from any one individual for the purpose of speaking is also a direct limitation on speech. That is no different from a law limiting the amount a publisher can accept from any one shareholder or lender, or the amount a newspaper can charge any one advertiser or customer.

(B) POOLING MONEY IS NOT SPEECH

Another proposition which could explain at least some of the results of today's opinion is that the First Amendment right to spend money for speech does not include the right to combine with others in spending money for speech. . . . The freedom to associate with others for the dissemination of ideas—not just by singing or speaking in unison, but by pooling financial resources for expressive purposes—is part of the freedom of speech. . . .

We have said that "implicit in the right to engage in activities protected by the First Amendment" is "a corresponding right to associate with others in pursuit of a wide variety of political, social, economic, educational, religious, and cultural ends." *Roberts v. United States Jaycees*, 468 U.S. 609, 622 (1984). That "right to associate . . . in pursuit" includes the right to pool financial resources.

If it were otherwise, Congress would be empowered to enact legislation requiring newspapers to be sole proprietorships, banning their use of partnership or corporate form. That sort of restriction would be an obvious violation of the First Amendment, and it is incomprehensible why the conclusion should change when what is at issue is the pooling of funds for the most important (and most perennially threatened) category of speech: electoral speech. The principle that such financial association does not enjoy full First Amendment protection threatens the existence of all political parties. . . .

Which brings me back to where I began: This litigation is about preventing criticism of the government. I cannot say for certain that many, or some, or even any, of the Members of Congress who voted for this legislation did so not to produce "fairer" campaigns, but to mute criticism of their records and facilitate reelection. Indeed, I will stipulate that all those who voted for BCRA believed they were acting for the good of the country. There remains the problem of the Charlie Wilson Phenomenon, named after Charles Wilson, former president of General Motors, who is supposed to have said during the Senate hearing on his nomination as Secretary of Defense that "what's good for General Motors is good for the country." Those in power, even giving them the benefit of the greatest good will, are inclined to believe that what is good for them is good for the country. Whether in prescient recognition of the Charlie Wilson Phenomenon, or out of fear of good old-fashioned, malicious, self-interested manipulation, "[t]he fundamental approach of the First Amendment . . . was to assume the worst, and to rule the regulation of political speech 'for fairness' sake' simply out of bounds." *Austin*, 494 U.S., at 693 (Scalia, J., dissenting). Having abandoned that approach to a limited extent in *Buckley*, we abandon it much further today.

[Chief Justice Rehnquist dissented with respect to BCRA Titles I and V. Justice Stevens dissented with respect to §305.]

Justice KENNEDY, with whom Chief Justice REHNQUIST, Justice SCALIA, and Justice THOMAS join in part, concurring in judgment in part and dissenting in part:

In *Buckley*, the Court held that one, and only one, interest justified the significant burden on the right of association involved there: eliminating, or preventing, actual corruption or the appearance of corruption stemming from contributions to candidates. . . . Thus, the perception of corruption that the majority now asserts is somehow different from the quid pro quo potential discussed in this opinion was created by an exchange featuring quid pro quo potential—contributions directly to a candidate.

In determining whether conduct poses a quid pro quo danger the analysis is functional. In *Buckley*, the Court confronted an expenditure limitation provision that capped the amount of money individuals could spend on any activity intended to influence a federal election (i.e., it reached to both independent and coordinated expenditures). The Court concluded that though the limitation reached both coordinated and independent expenditures, there were other valid FECA provisions that barred coordinated expenditures. Hence, the limit at issue only added regulation to independent expenditures. On that basis it concluded the provision was unsupported by any valid corruption interest. The conduct to which it added regulation (independent expenditures) posed no quid pro quo danger.

Placing *Buckley*'s anticorruption rationale in the context of the federal legislative power yields the following rule: Congress' interest in preventing corruption provides a basis for regulating federal candidates' and officeholders' receipt of quids, whether or not the candidate or officeholder corruptly received them. Conversely, the rule requires the Court to strike down campaign finance regulations when they do not add regulation to "actual or apparent quid pro quo arrangements." Id., at 45.

The Court ignores these constitutional bounds and in effect interprets the anticorruption rationale to allow regulation not just of "actual or apparent quid pro quo arrangements," ibid., but of any conduct that wins goodwill from or influences a Member of Congress. It is not that there is any quarrel between this opinion and the majority that the inquiry since *Buckley* has been whether certain conduct creates "undue influence." On that we agree. The very aim of *Buckley*'s standard, however, was to define undue influence by reference to the presence of quid pro quo involving the officeholder. The Court, in contrast, concludes that access, without more, proves influence is undue. Access, in the Court's view, has the same legal ramifications as actual or apparent corruption of officeholders. This new definition of corruption sweeps away all protections for speech that lie in its path. . . .

To ignore the fact that in *Buckley* the money at issue was given to candidates, creating an obvious quid pro quo danger as much as it led to the candidates also providing access to the donors, is to ignore the Court's comments in *Buckley* that show quid pro quo was of central importance to the analysis. The majority also ignores that in *Buckley*, and ever since, those party contributions that have been subject to congressional limit were not general party-building contributions but were only contributions used to influence particular elections. That is, they were contributions that flowed to a particular candidate's benefit, again posing a quid pro quo danger. . . . Access in itself, however, shows only that in a general sense an officeholder favors someone or that someone has influence on the officeholder. There is no basis, in law or in fact, to say favoritism or influence in general is the same as corrupt favoritism or influence in particular.

By equating vague and generic claims of favoritism or influence with actual or apparent corruption, the Court adopts a definition of corruption that dismantles basic First Amendment rules, permits Congress to suppress speech in the absence of a quid pro quo threat, and moves beyond the rationale that is *Buckley*'s very foundation.

The generic favoritism or influence theory articulated by the Court is at odds with standard First Amendment analyses because it is unbounded and susceptible to no limiting principle. Any given action might be favored by any given person, so by the Court's reasoning political loyalty of the purest sort can be prohibited. There is no remaining principled method for inquiring whether a campaign finance regulation does in fact regulate corruption in a serious and meaningful way. We are left to defer to a congressional conclusion that certain conduct creates favoritism or influence.

Though the majority cites common sense as the foundation for its definition of corruption, in the context of the real world only a single definition of corruption has been found to identify political corruption successfully and to distinguish good political responsiveness from bad—that is quid pro quo. Favoritism and influence are not, as the Government's theory suggests, avoidable in representative politics. It is in the nature of an elected representative to favor certain policies, and, by necessary corollary, to favor the voters and contributors who support those policies. It is well understood that a substantial and legitimate reason, if not the only reason, to cast a vote for, or to make a contribution to, one candidate over another is that the candidate will respond by producing those political outcomes the supporter favors. Democracy is premised on responsiveness. Quid pro quo corruption has been, until now, the only agreed upon conduct that represents the bad form of responsiveness and presents a justiciable standard with a relatively clear limiting principle: Bad responsiveness may be demonstrated by pointing to a relationship between an official and a quid.

From that it follows that the Court today should not ask, as it does, whether some persons, even Members of Congress, conclusorily assert that the regulated conduct appears corrupt to them. Following *Buckley*, it should instead inquire whether the conduct now prohibited inherently poses a real or substantive quid pro quo danger, so that its regulation will stem the appearance of quid pro quo corruption.

» ***Corruption, Again.***   Did the Court in *McConnell* expand the concept of corruption beyond the conceptual confines of *Buckley*? As Professor Dennis Thompson notes:

> We can recognize two distinct concepts in the recent opinions. First, there is the more familiar notion of corruption in which an official provides a governmental benefit or service in return for a payment or favor from a private citizen. The exchange does not require a quid pro quo. It needs only unspoken understandings or implicit expectations. It usually does not involve buying votes, but requires only gaining access to the officials and services of government. This may be called governmental corruption. It can occur in any kind of political system and is not distinctively democratic.

The other, less familiar, concept has begun to show itself only in more recent opinions. It may be called electoral corruption because it refers to the integrity of the elections and the campaigns that lead up to them. It is distinctively democratic, and it is distinct from governmental corruption. As Justice Thomas points out in his dissent in *McConnell*, the majority relies on a "different type of corruption" to uphold the regulation of corporate expenditures. This type of corruption is not really a single coherent idea yet. It expresses several different (though related) dangers to democratic values. One is the risk of distortion of the democratic process by the "corrosive and distorting effects of immense aggregations of wealth . . . that have little or no correlation to the public's support for the corporation's political ideas." Ideas may have more influence than they merit simply because they have more money behind them. More broadly, the *McConnell* majority warns of "untoward consequences for the democratic process." These include practices that undermine the "responsibility of the individual citizen for successful functioning of that process" and obstacles that prevent the electorate from gaining "relevant information about the candidates and their supporters." In all of its various forms, this concept focuses more on the "integrity of the electoral process" than on any subsequent consequences for influence on public officials.

Dennis F. Thompson, *Two Concepts of Corruption: Making Campaigns Safe for Democracy*, 73 GEO. WASH. L. REV. 1036, 1036-1037 (2005).

>> *Deference to Whom?*   In *McConnell*, the Court provides a fair amount of deference to Congress's judgment and to the structural features of the statute that it promulgated. But Justice Scalia retorts that the Court is simply deferring to the judgment of incumbent insiders protecting their positions from challengers. Do you find Justice Scalia's dissent convincing? Consider Robert Bauer's criticism of the majority's deference rationale:

> The Court's attempt to construct [a theory of deference] in *McConnell*, in an awkward relationship to *Buckley*, does not succeed. It does not succeed because a theory of deference tied to *Buckley* is doomed from the start. The Court is seeking to escape the imagined rigors of *Buckley* through a theory of deference, but by insisting on operating within the *Buckley* paradigm of the danger of corruption, it builds the theory on a theoretical foundation that cannot support it. In short, the history of campaign finance reform is by no means a straightforward history of a "resolute" concern with corruption, and that history does not support the claims made by McConnell for congressional "expertise."

Robert F. Bauer, *When "The Pols Make the Calls":* McConnell*'s Theory of Judicial Deference in the Twilight of* Buckley, 153 U. PA. L. REV. 5, 20 (2004). Arguing that much of the history of campaign finance reform was highly politicized, *id.* at 23, and incumbent protective, *id.* at 27-28, Professor Bauer suggests that the Court's focus on the corruption rationale is both suspect and emblematic of the larger problem with the *Buckley* framework. Consider a rejoinder of sorts from Professor Briffault, who is arguing that campaign-finance law ought to be "dejudicialized," by which he means that "courts play a lesser role in determining both the permissible goals of campaign finance law and the proper regulatory techniques." Richard Briffault, *On Dejudicializing American Campaign Finance Law*, 27 Ga. St. U. L. Rev. 887, 929 (2011). Briffault argues:

> It could be argued that aggressive judicial policing of campaign finance law is appropriate because of the danger that elected officials will adopt laws that are self-serving, incumbent-protective, and ruling-party entrenching. After all, campaign finance laws are adopted by elected officials who have a stake in their own re-election and who are certainly unlikely to have any interest in being fair to potential challengers, the party out of power, political newcomers, or other threats to the political status quo. Even if it is true that only politicians can understand campaign finance well enough in practice to produce workable campaign finance laws, it can also be argued that campaign finance is too political to be left to the politicians. Much as the Court's intervention in the political thicket of legislative apportionment was justified by the ongoing unwillingness of elected officials to change the rules under which they had been elected, the Court's extensive intervention into campaign finance law can be justified by a well-founded fear that incumbents will manipulate campaign finance laws in their own interest—that campaign finance regulation can be used as a kind of gerrymandering.
>
> There are four problems with this argument. First, historically relatively little campaign finance regulation reflects the efforts by the party in power to entrench itself. Raymond LaRaja's history of federal campaign finance regulation demonstrates that campaign finance laws are usually enacted by cross-party coalitions, often consisting of a minority faction of the party in power acting in alliance with the party out-of-power. Thus, the first federal campaign finance laws enacted in the period between 1907 and 1925—an era of clear Republican dominance—were pushed through by the Progressive minority within the Republican Party working with the Democratic minority in Congress. These reforms were intended to weaken, not strengthen, the leading party, and according to LaRaja they succeeded. Similarly, the campaign laws adopted in the period between 1939 and 1947 were pushed through by a combination of the conservative minority within the Democratic Party and Republicans and were aimed in large part at weakening the financial role of key groups in the Democratic Party—public employees and unions. In this largely Democratic era, Congress elected "Republican reforms." More recently, BCRA's soft money limits were pushed through by a minority of ideological activists in the Democratic Party, notwithstanding the Democrats' greater dependence on soft money, joined by a reform remnant in the Republican Party clearly out of sync with the majority of the party. BCRA clearly was not an effort by a dominant party to entrench itself as there was no truly dominant party in Congress when BCRA was enacted in 2001-02. Democrats held the narrowest possible majority in the Senate, while Republicans controlled the House and the Presidency. Only the Federal Election Campaign Act of 1971 and the FECA Amendments of 1974 can be seen as

the product of a clear one-party (Democratic) Congressional majority, but even then that majority was not veto-proof and so had to accommodate the concerns of a Republican president, and both measures received considerable Republican support.

Second, it is not at all clear that restrictive campaign finance laws will operate to entrench parties in power. Other countries that have enacted spending limits have witnessed major swings in political control. Canada, for example, limits party campaign spending, independent spending, and spending on broadcast advertising in elections for its federal Parliament. Yet, in the 1993 parliamentary election the dominant Progressive Conservative Party, which entered the election with 169 seats (out of 295), came out of it with just 2 seats, while the previously out-of-power Liberals went from 83 seats to 177 and the brand new Reform Party won 52 seats. Reform eventually merged with the Progressive Conservatives to become the Conservative Party, which garnered 99 seats (out of 308) in 2000, and 124 and control of the government in 2006, while the seats held by the Liberals, who governed from 1993 through 2006, shrank from 172 (in 2000) to 135 (in 2004) to 103 (in 2006) to 77 (in 2008). Spending limits did not lock the Progressive Conservatives into power in 1993, nor did it lock them out of power even after they had fallen to just two seats, much as the limits did not prevent the Liberals from winning in 1993 or prevent them from falling out of power in 2006.

Third, it is far from clear that campaign finance laws are more advantageous to incumbents than no laws at all. Incumbents have built-in advantages in raising money. They can provide benefits to individuals and interests who have a stake in government action. Moreover, given the likelihood that most incumbents will be reelected, those who do business with government have an incentive to donate to incumbents. In the absence of contribution and expenditure limits, incumbents would most likely raise more money and spend more money than their challengers in most elections. Financially, incumbents as a group would almost surely be better off with less rather than more regulation—although, to be sure, regulations can also serve to help incumbents.

Finally, it does not seem that concern about incumbency protection explains the Court's campaign finance decisions. The Court has never provided different constitutional treatment to laws adopted by voter initiative as opposed to those enacted by legislatures, yet surely the former measures are very unlikely to be intended to entrench incumbents. The campaign finance regime that the Court's decisions have produced seems particularly likely to benefit incumbents, since incumbents are best positioned to utilize the PACs, bundlers, and other political intermediaries necessary to collect the large number of dollar-limited contributions needed to finance the unlimited spending the Court permits and many candidates think that the imperatives of politics require. Indeed, PACs have consistently favored incumbents, as well as the party in power or the party thought likely to win the next election, in their campaign donations. Finally, although members of the Court have occasionally criticized certain regulations as likely to be incumbent-protective, the only case where the incumbent-protection concern played a role in a decision was in the three-justice plurality opinion in *Randall.*

Incumbency-entrenchment is a plausible justification for aggressive judicial review of campaign finance law in theory, but it does not hold up that well in practice. At the state and local levels, many campaign finance laws have been adopted by voter initiative, and even federal laws have often been the result of complex coalitions rather than self-serving efforts by the party in power. Electoral results from other countries indicate that restrictive campaign finance laws do not bar dramatic political turnarounds. Nor is there any reason to believe that incumbents are better off with campaign laws than without them.

Most importantly, concern about incumbency protection does not require the rigid, categorical approach the Court has taken to certain campaign finance laws, such as spending limits for candidates or independent committees or special attention to the needs of the opponents of wealthy self-funding candidates. Challenger interests can be vindicated by a close review of the details of particular laws in the relevant political context, rather than by per se rules. That, in fact, has been the approach the Court has taken to the potentially incumbent-protective effects of contribution limits. Such limits are generally constitutional, but will be struck down if so low as to preclude effective competition. The Court has taken a similar stance in considering reporting and disclosure requirements. Disclosure is generally constitutional, but may be invalidated in circumstances where public disclosure of contributions or expenditures exposes vulnerable individuals or groups to threats, harassment, or reprisal.

Id. at 925-929. As we shall see in the next section, the Court's posture of deference proved to be short lived.

So far, *McConnell* has served as the high-water mark of judicial deference to congressional campaign-finance legislation. A mere five years later, in *Davis v. FEC,* 554 U.S. 724 (2008), the Court signaled a change of course. In *Davis,* the Court addressed the so-called millionaire's amendment provision, Section 319(a), of BCRA. Pursuant to Section 319(a), when a candidate spent more than $350,000 of his or her money to finance his or her campaign, the candidate's opponent was entitled to receive additional contributions at three times the usual contribution limits. Thus, in 2008, when the individual contribution limits were $2,300, the contribution limits for contributors to an opponent of a self-financing candidate would be $6,900 instead of $2,300. In addition, the opponent of the self-financing candidate also was entitled to receive unlimited coordinated party expenditures. The plaintiff, Jack Davis, a Democratic Candidate for the House of Representatives in 2006, challenged the provision on the ground that it "burden[ed] his exercise of his First Amendment right to make unlimited expenditures of his personal funds because making expenditures that create the imbalance has the effect of enabling his opponent to raise more money and to use that money to finance speech that counteracts and thus diminishes the effectiveness of Davis' own speech." The Court agreed.

The Court remarked that Section 319(a) would be constitutional if it had "simply raised the contribution limits for all candidates." The constitutional deficiency was Section 319(a)'s "asymmetry" in the differential manner that it treated self-financed candidates and candidates who accepted private contributions to fund their campaigns. The Court disagreed with the government's argument that the asymmetrical treatment of self-financed and privately financed candidates was necessary to level the playing field between extremely wealthy candidates and less wealthy ones. The Court noted that the only legitimate governmental objective permissible under its campaign-finance jurisprudence is preventing corruption or the appearance of corruption. The Court stated that

> in *Buckley*, we held that Congress "may engage in public financing of election campaigns and may condition acceptance of public funds on an agreement by the candidate to abide by specified expenditure limitations" even though we found an independent limit on overall campaign expenditures to be unconstitutional. But the choice involved in *Buckley* was quite different from the choice imposed by §319(a). In *Buckley*, a candidate, by forgoing public financing, could retain the unfettered right to make unlimited personal expenditures. Here, §319(a) does not provide any way in which a candidate can exercise that right without abridgment. Instead, a candidate who wishes to exercise that right has two choices: abide by a limit on personal expenditures or endure the burden that is placed on that right by the activation of a scheme of discriminatory contribution limits. The choice imposed by §319(a) is not remotely parallel to that in *Buckley*.

Consequently, the Court struck down the provision on constitutional grounds.

How was the speech of candidate Davis "burdened" by operation of the millionaire's amendment? Was the amount of speech he would otherwise have made curtailed by law? How plausible is it to think that rich candidates would forgo the opportunity to use their wealth to fund their speech in order to deny their poorer opponents the opportunity to accept larger donations?

E.   *EXPENDITURE LIMITATIONS: PACs, PARTIES, AND CORPORATIONS*

The Court in *Buckley* took the strong position that expenditure limitations are unconstitutional because they violate the First Amendment. The central question following *Buckley* was whether this principle applied only to expenditures by candidates and individuals or whether the principle would be applied to expenditure limitations on political action committees, political parties, nonprofit corporations, unions, and for-profit corporations. As you work through the materials that follow, consider three questions. First, what is the theory of democracy, politics, and constitutional law that guides the Court's analysis? Second, are the values that underlie the principle that expenditure limitations impermissibly infringe upon First Amendment freedoms equally applicable to all the entities to which the Court applies it below? Third, how do you evaluate the effect on American politics that is the consequence of the Court's decisions in the cases below?

1. Independent Expenditures by Ideological but Nonpartisan PACs

In the case below, the Court determines whether a PAC can make independent expenditures on behalf of a presidential candidate who has accepted public financing under the Fund.

Federal Election Commission v. National Conservative Political Action Committee

470 U.S. 480 (1985)

Justice REHNQUIST delivered the opinion of the Court.

The Presidential Election Campaign Fund Act (Fund Act) offers the Presidential candidates of major political parties the option of receiving public financing for their general election campaigns. If a Presidential candidate elects public financing, §9012(f) makes it a criminal offense for independent "political committees," such as appellees National Conservative Political Action Committee (NCPAC) and Fund For A Conservative Majority (FCM), to expend more than $1,000 to further that candidate's election. . . . The present litigation began in May 1983 when the Democratic Party, the DNC, and Edward Mezvinsky, Chairman of the Pennsylvania Democratic State Committee . . . filed suit against NCPAC and FCM (the PACs), who had announced their intention to spend large sums of money to help bring about the reelection of President Ronald Reagan in 1984. Their amended complaint sought a declaration that §9012(f), which they believed would prohibit the PACs' intended expenditures, was constitutional. The FEC intervened for the sole purpose of moving, along with the PACs, to dismiss the complaint for lack of standing.

In June 1983, the FEC brought a separate action against the same defendants seeking identical declaratory relief. . . . After extensive briefing and oral argument, the court issued a comprehensive opinion, holding that . . . the Democrats and the FEC were not entitled to a declaration that §9012(f) is constitutional. The court held that §9012(f) abridges First Amendment freedoms of speech and association, that it is substantially overbroad, and that it cannot permissibly be given a narrowing construction to cure the overbreadth. The court did not, however, declare §9012(f) unconstitutional because the PACs had not filed a counterclaim requesting such a declaration.

II

Both NCPAC and FCM are self-described ideological organizations with a conservative political philosophy. They solicited funds in support of President Reagan's 1980 campaign, and they spent money on such means as radio and television advertisements to encourage voters to elect him President. On the record before us, these expenditures were "independent" in that they were not made at the request of or in coordination with the official Reagan election campaign committee or any of its agents. Indeed, there are indications that the efforts of these organizations were at times viewed with disfavor by the official campaign as counterproductive to its chosen strategy. . . .

[B]oth the Fund Act and FECA play a part in regulating Presidential campaigns. The Fund Act comes into play only if a candidate chooses to accept public funding of his general election campaign, and it covers only the period between the nominating convention and 30 days after the general election. In contrast, FECA applies to all Presidential campaigns, as well as other federal elections, regardless of whether publicly or privately funded. . . . In these cases we consider provisions of the Fund Act that make it a criminal offense for political committees such as NCPAC and FCM to make independent expenditures in support of a candidate who has elected to accept public financing. . . .

There is no question that NCPAC and FCM are political committees and that President Reagan was a qualified candidate, and it seems plain enough that the PACs' expenditures fall within the term "qualified campaign expense." . . . There can be no doubt that the expenditures at issue in this case produce speech at the core of the First Amendment. . . .

The PACs in this case, of course, are not lone pamphleteers or street corner orators in the Tom Paine mold;[21] they spend substantial amounts of money in order to communicate their political ideas through sophisticated media advertisements. And of course the criminal sanction in question is applied to the expenditure of money to propagate political views, rather than to the propagation of those views unaccompanied by the expenditure of money. But for purposes of presenting political views in connection with a nationwide Presidential election, allowing the presentation of views while forbidding the expenditure of more than $1,000 to present them is much like allowing a speaker in a public hall to express his views while denying him the use of an amplifying system. . . .

We also reject the notion that the PACs' form of organization or method of solicitation diminishes their entitlement to First Amendment protection. The First Amendment freedom of association is squarely implicated in these cases. NCPAC and FCM are mechanisms by which large numbers of individuals of modest means can join together in organizations which serve to "amplif[y] the voice of their adherents." *Buckley v. Valeo*, 424 U.S., at 22. It is significant that in 1979-1980 approximately 101,000 people contributed an average of $75 each to NCPAC and in 1980 approximately 100,000 people contributed an average of $25 each to FCM.

Having concluded that the PAC's expenditures are entitled to full First Amendment protection, we now look to see if there is a sufficiently strong governmental interest served by §9012(f)'s restriction on them and whether the section is narrowly tailored to the evil that may legitimately be regulated. The restriction involved here is not merely an effort by the Government to regulate the use of its

---

21. Thomas Paine was a colonial American radical pamphleteer whose most famous work, the anonymously published pamphlet *Common Sense*, argued for American freedom from the British in language understandable by the common people. *See* THOMAS PAINE, COMMON SENSE (Penguin 1986) (1776).

own property. . . . It is a flat, across-the-board criminal sanction applicable to any "committee, association, or organization" which spends more than $1,000 on this particular type of political speech.

We held in *Buckley* . . . that preventing corruption or the appearance of corruption are the only legitimate and compelling government interests thus far identified for restricting campaign finances. . . .

It is contended that, because the PACs may by the breadth of their organizations spend larger amounts than the individuals in *Buckley*, the potential for corruption is greater. But precisely what the "corruption" may consist of we are never told with assurance. The fact that candidates and elected officials may alter or reaffirm their own positions on issues in response to political messages paid for by the PACs can hardly be called corruption, for one of the essential features of democracy is the presentation to the electorate of varying points of view. It is of course hypothetically possible here, as in the case of the independent expenditures forbidden in *Buckley*, that candidates may take notice of and reward those responsible for PAC expenditures by giving official favors to the latter in exchange for the supporting messages. But here, as in *Buckley*, the absence of prearrangement and coordination undermines the value of the expenditure to the candidate, and thereby alleviates the danger that expenditures will be given as a *quid pro quo* for improper commitments from the candidate. On this record, such an exchange of political favors for uncoordinated expenditures remains a hypothetical possibility and nothing more.

Even were we to determine that the large pooling of financial resources by NCPAC and FCM did pose a potential for corruption or the appearance of corruption, §9012(f) is a fatally overbroad response to that evil. It is not limited to multimillion dollar war chests; its terms apply equally to informal discussion groups that solicit neighborhood contributions to publicize their views about a particular Presidential candidate. . . .

Justice WHITE, dissenting.

If the elected Members of the Legislature, who are surely in the best position to know, conclude that large-scale expenditures are a significant threat to the integrity and fairness of the electoral process, we should not second-guess that judgment. Like the expenditure limitations struck down in *Buckley*, §9012(f) serves to back up the limitations on direct campaign contributions, eliminate the danger of corruption, maintain public confidence in the integrity of federal elections, equalize the resources available to the candidates, and hold the overall amount of money devoted to political campaigning down to a reasonable level. I consider these purposes both legitimate and substantial, and more than sufficient to support the challenged provision's incidental and minor burden on actual speech. . . .

⟫ *The Role of PACs.*   Why might we worry about the role of PACs in American politics? In one of the classic books on American politics, *The Semisovereign People: A Realist View of Democracy in America*, E.E. Schattschneider worried that organized interests such as PACs represent mainly a certain segment of American politics— educated, moneyed, privileged, and upper-class. Organized interests are necessarily advantaged as against unorganized interests, which are mainly poor and lower-class. Consequently, organized interests are able to secure for themselves public policy benefits at the expense of the less privileged. One of the most famous lines in *The Semisovereign People* is the observation that the "flaw in the pluralist heaven is that the heavenly chorus sings with a strong upper-class accent." *Id.* at 34-35. Or consider, in a similar vein, John Rawls's criticism of the Court's campaign-finance doctrine. Rawls notes that for the Court, "democracy is a kind of regulated rivalry between economic classes and interest groups in which the outcome should properly depend on the ability and willingness of each to use its financial resources and skills, admittedly very unequal, to make its desired effect." JOHN RAWLS, POLITICAL LIBERALISM 361 (1993). This is not an abstract concern about equality, but a concern about substantive (and biased) public policy outcomes. Should this concern matter to campaign-finance doctrine?

≫ ***Why Do PACs Spend?*** What do PACs get for their contributions to and expenditures in favor of politicians and political candidates? This is one of the most vexing questions in the political science literature on PACs and legislative behavior. Though there is a vast literature in political science on the relationship among money, PACs, and public policy, as two scholars wryly remarked, this is "a body of research infamous for its contradictory studies. Virtually every review of this literature spends time discussing how it is that some researchers have found PACs to be influential, while other researchers have found the opposite." FRANK R. BAUMGARTNER AND BETH L. LEECH, BASIC INTEREST: THE IMPORTANCE OF INTEREST GROUPS IN POLITICS AND IN POLITICAL SCIENCE, 133-134 (1998). The critical question is whether money buys votes or whether PACs contribute to (and spend money on) politicians that share the PAC's ideology or worldview. It is on this question where the literature is most equivocal. Some studies have found a relationship between contributions from PACs and legislators' voting behavior, what some refer to in the literature as vote buying. *See, e.g.*, JAMES B. KAU AND PAUL H. RUBIN, CONGRESSMEN, CONSTITUENTS, AND CONTRIBUTORS: DETERMINANTS OF ROLL CALL VOTING IN THE HOUSE OF REPRESENTATIVES (1982); Thomas Stratmann, *Can Special Interests Buy Congressional Votes? Evidence from Financial Services Legislation*, 45 J.L. & ECON. 345 (2002); Thomas Stratmann, *The Market for Congressional Votes: Is Timing of Contributions Everything?*, 41 J.L. & ECON. 85 (1998); John P. Frendeis and Richard W. Waterman, *PAC Contributions and Legislative Behavior: Senate Voting on Trucking Deregulation*, 66 SOC. SCI. Q. 401 (1985); J.I. Silberman and G.C. Durden, *Determining Legislative Preferences on the Minimum Wage: An Economic Approach*, 84 J. POL. ECON. 317 (1976).

Other studies have reached the opposite conclusion, finding that there is no relationship between the votes of members of Congress and contributions from PACs. *See, e.g.*, JOHN R. WRIGHT, CONTRIBUTIONS, LOBBYING, AND COMMITTEE VOTING IN THE U.S. HOUSE OF REPRESENTATIVES (1989); Stephen G. Bronars and John R. Lott, Jr., *Do Campaign Donations Alter How a Politician Votes? Or, Do Donors Support Candidates Who Value the Same Things That They Do?*, 40 J.L. & ECON. 317 (1997); Janet M. Grenzke, *Shopping in the Congressional Supermarket: The Currency Is Complex*, 33 AM. J. POL. SCI. 1 (1989); John R. Wright, *PACs, Contributions, and Roll Calls: An Organizational Perspective*, 79 AM. POL. SCI. REV. 400 (1985); Henry Chappell, *Campaign Contributions and Congressional Voting: A Simultaneous Probit-Tobit Model*, 62 REV. ECON. & STAT. 77 (1982); William P. Welch, *Campaign Contributions and Legislative Voting: Milk Money and Dairy Price Supports*, 35 W. POL. Q. 267 (1982). Even in the studies that find a positive relationship between campaign contributions and votes, the extent of the influence is not very strong. "Legislators' votes depend almost entirely on their own beliefs and the preferences of their voters and their party. Contributions explain a miniscule fraction of the variation in voting behavior in the U.S. Congress." Stephen Ansolabehere, John M. de Figueiredo, and James M. Snyder Jr., *Why Is There So Little Money in U.S. Politics?*, 17 J. ECON. PERSP. 105, 117 (2003). One explanation for the disagreement among researchers is methodology. The statistical techniques used in many studies enable the researcher to draw a correlation between votes and contributions, but do not enable them to make any conclusions about causation. On this point, see Stratmann, *Can Special Interests Buy Congressional Votes?*, *supra*.

Professors Stephen Ansolabehere, John de Figueiredo, and James Snyder reject the view that campaign contributions are generally quid pro quo investments. They argue that, given how little money is invested in American politics in light of the public policy stakes, it would not be rational to view campaign contributions as investments. From this perspective, the problem is not too much money but too little:

> For example, all defense contracting firms and individuals associated with those firms gave approximately $10.6 million to candidates and parties in 1998 and $13.2 million in 2000. The U.S. government spent approximately $134 billion on defense procurement contracts in fiscal year 2000. . . . Firms, individuals and industry associations of the oil and gas industry gave $21.6 million to candidates and party organizations in 1998 and $33.6 million in 2000. The Energy Information Administration (1999) of the U.S. Department of Energy values subsidies to the energy industry in 1999 at $1.7 billion. . . . The discrepancy between the value of policy and the amounts contributed strains basic economic intuitions. Given the value of policy at stake, firms and other interest groups should give more.

Ansolabehere et al. theorized that either firms receive "astronomically" high returns for their investments or that they are in fact not making investments when they make contributions. Moreover, they argue that "money from organized groups accounts for only a small fraction of overall campaign funds. Since interest groups can get only a little from their contributions, they give only a little. As a result, interest group contributions account for at most a small amount of the variation in voting behavior. In fact, after controlling for legislator ideology, these contributions have no detectable effects on the behavior of legislators." *Id.* at 117.

If campaign contributions and spending do not buy votes, what might PACs, which are presumed to be rational actors, receive in return for their money? There are many reasons that PACs give or spend money. These include access, political ideology, support for a particular piece of legislation, geographical affinity, or partisanship, to list some of the more obvious reasons. According to the literature, PACs are primarily motivated by three justifications. Some PACs seek access and influence. Others are partisan and seek to "maximize the representation of their party within the congressional ranks." Theodore J. Eismeier and Philip H. Pollock III, *Strategy and Choice in Congressional Elections: The Role of Political Action Committees*, 30 AM. J. POL. SCI. 197, 198 (1986). Still others are interested in furthering a particular political ideology. These are of course not mutually exclusive motivations.

>> *The PAC Ecosystem.* The literature generally ascribes dominant tendencies to particular types of PACs. Influenced by the legal framework, researchers divide PACs into four categories: ideological, corporate, labor, and trade associations. *See, e.g.,* Theodore J. Eismeier and Philip H. Pollock III, *Strategy and Choice in Congressional Elections: The Role of Political Action Committees,* 30 Am. J. Pol. Sci. 197, 199-200 (1986). For example, labor and ideological PACs are thought to be motivated primarily by political ideology and partisanship, and corporate and trade union PACs are thought to make contributions and expenditures for access and rent-seeking purposes. Instead of investing in research and development, a firm might make a contribution to secure legislation that might give it an advantage over its competitors. *See, e.g.,* Clyde Wilcox, *Organizational Variables and Contribution Behavior of Large PACs: A Longitudinal Analysis,* 11 Pol. Bev. 157 (1989) ("We now know that PACs sponsored by trade associations are the most likely of all to support incumbents, while nonconnected, ideological PACs are the most likely to invest in challengers or open-seat candidates. Ideological PACs and those sponsored by labor unions are quite partisan, while corporate and trade association PACs usually contribute to incumbents of both parties, directing their nonincumbent contributions to Republicans."). In a paper confirming rent-seeking as one explanation for the political contributions of high-tech corporate firms, Professor Hart noted that firms "with specific material interests in public policy, including government contractors and regulated firms, do seek to preserve these rents by investing in the electoral process." *See* David M. Hart, *Why Do Some Firms Give? Why Do Some Give a Lot?: High-Tech PACs, 1977-1996,* 63 J. Pol. 1230, 1244 (2001).

Other researchers reject the notion that partisanship and ideology do not play a role in corporate PAC contributions and expenditures.

> Interest groups are policy maximizers. Organized interests exist to transmit the policy preferences of their constituents to our elected officials. Groups are interested in passing legislation more favorable to their preferred policy outcomes. . . . I begin with the assumption that interest groups should have no partisan preference at all, given that they are simply looking for votes on specific pieces of legislation.

> However, . . . for three primary reasons, interest groups do have at least a weak party preference. First, the interest group will naturally have an ideological affinity for one party or the other (i.e., no interest group is perfectly indifferent between the two parties). Second, political parties pressure those groups that do lean in their direction to make more donations to candidates from their party and less to candidates from the other party. Third, interest groups understand the importance of majority party status in Congress. . . . The notion that interest groups are formed solely on the basis of showering incumbents from either party with money so that they can have access to [members of Congress] does not comport with the data, nor does it make sense logically.

> The desire for access to elected officials is premised on the notion that these groups have specific policy preferences. If an interest group takes the time and effort to start a PAC, raise money, and distribute those dollars to office-seekers, the group must have some defined policy preferences. This is not to say that groups are not interested in access, they

are. Nonetheless, . . . an interest group's primary concern revolves around policy outputs, which are better effected by a certain set of representatives (i.e., one party or the other) rather than having the ability to have a meeting with a random set of elected officials.

Thomas L. Brunell, *The Relationship Between Political Parties and Interest Groups: Explaining Patterns of PAC Contributions to Candidates for Congress*, 58 POL. RES. Q. 681, 683 (2005).

Should it matter whether rent-seeking or broader public-regarding purposes motivate corporate and labor PACs? *See, e.g.*, Schattschneider's quip that "manufacturers do not join an association to which only manufacturers may belong merely to promote philanthropic or cultural or religious interests." Presumably, they organize to promote their narrow economic self-interest. SCHATTSCHNEIDER, *supra*, at 25. By contrast, Gopoian concluded from his empirical study that while there is ample support for the proposition that some corporate and labor PACs were "self-interested, materially oriented, and narrowly-focused," and this was particularly true for labor PACs, he also found empirical evidence that some PACs, specifically corporate PACs, were motivated by a broader ideological concern than narrow self-interest. They were motivated "by concerns that reflect, if not some vision of what is in the best interests of the nation, then nonetheless something greater than the narrow special interests that many presume to be the only concerns of interest groups." J. David Gopoian, *What Makes PACs Tick? An Analysis of the Allocation Patterns of Economic Interest Groups*, 28 AM. J. POL. SCI. 259, 279 (1984).

≫ *PACs and Access.* Scholars sometimes say that the purpose of campaign contributions and expenditures is to guarantee access to electoral officials. The literature has identified at least three functions of access. We have already explored the first function that access can serve, which is to secure a quid pro quo: access as return on the investment that is the contribution or expenditure. Second, access may simply serve as an external signal of the PAC's importance. PACs seek access "to signal their importance and so maintain and increase their membership. Under this view, access is granted by a legislator purely to secure contributions, and any consequent group influence over legislators is largely incidental." David Austen-Smith, *Campaign Contributions and Access*, 89 AM. POL. SCI. REV. 566, 566 (1995). Third, some scholars have argued that the purpose of the contribution is to secure access so that the PAC can provide information to the legislator. "Officeholders work in complex environments, they are constantly pressured to act (or not act) on myriad issues, and they know their actions may have important consequences. To decide what to do, they engage in a constant search for information." Paul Burstein and C. Elizabeth Hirsh, *Interest Organizations, Information, and Policy Innovation in the U.S. Congress*, 22 SOC. F. 174, 177 (2007). Legislators are particularly interested in information on the public policy problems before them; the potential consequences of proposed solutions; and the electoral consequences of supporting or opposing particular legislative proposals. *Id.*

≫ *Where in the Process Do PACs Have Influence?* In one of the most interesting and classic studies in the literature, Professors Richard Hall and Frank Wayman argued that researchers were missing the connection between PAC money and political outcomes because they were looking for a relationship between contributions and final passage floor votes on legislation. Instead, they argued that PACs get more bang for their buck by mobilizing members of Congress at the committee level. They summarized their findings as follows:

> House members and interest group representatives are parties to an implicit cooperative agreement, but the constraints on member behavior and the rational calculations of group strategists limit the extent to which votes become the basis for exchange. This view suggests expectations about the effects of money on congressional decision making quite different from the ones that motivate the substantial research on the subject. We should find little causal connection between contributions and votes, especially on the floor—an expectation generally supported, although not adequately explained, in the literature. We should expect to find an important connection between contributions and the legislative involvement of sympathetic members, especially in committee—a relationship that empirical research to date has altogether ignored. . . .

> [W]e found solid support for our principal hypothesis: moneyed interests are able to mobilize legislators already predisposed to support the group's position. Conversely, money that a group contributes to its likely opponents has either a negligible or negative effect on their participation. While previous research on these issues provided little evidence that PAC money purchased members' votes, it apparently did buy the marginal time, energy, and legislative resources that committee participation requires. . . .

> The first and most important implication is that moneyed interests do affect the decision-making processes of Congress. . . . In fact, it matters most at that stage of the legislative process that matters most and for a form of legislative behavior likely to have a direct bearing on outcomes. . . . A second and related implication of this investigation, then, is that empirical research should expand its view of the legislative purposes of political money and the other group resources that may accompany it. . . . [W]e believe groups allocate their resources (1) to mobilize strong supporters not only in the House committees but also on the Senate floor, in dealings with executive agencies, and in various other decision-making forums relevant to the group's interests; (2) to demobilize strong opponents; and (3) to effect the support of swing legislators. We require greater knowledge of the frequency and efficacy of such strategies, in any case, before we denigrate the role of moneyed interests in Congress. . . .

Richard L. Hall and Frank W. Wayman, *Buying Time: Moneyed Interests and the Mobilization of Bias in Congressional Committees*, 84 AM. POL. SCI. REV. 797, 814-815 (1990).

One of the more robust findings in the literature is that organized interests give for different reasons. Does it make sense for the Court to treat all organized interests similarly or preclude Congress from treating them differently for campaign-finance purposes?

2. *Independent Expenditures by Political Parties*

Ten years after the Court determined that limitations on independent expenditures by PACs were unconstitutional, the Court was faced with the question of whether independent expenditures by political parties were similarly protected from limitation. The case, *Colorado Republican I*, below, splintered the Court. Justice Breyer, joined by Justices O'Connor and Souter, announced the judgment of the Court. Justice Kennedy filed an opinion concurring in the judgment and dissenting from the plurality opinion. Chief Justice Rehnquist and Justice Scalia joined him. Justice Thomas concurred in the judgment and Chief Justice Rehnquist and Justice Scalia also joined his opinion. Justice Stevens filed a dissenting opinion that was joined by Justice Ginsburg.

Colorado Republican Federal Campaign Committee v. Federal Election Commission [Colorado Republican I]

518 U.S. 604 (1996)

Justice BREYER announced the judgment of the Court and delivered an opinion, in which Justice O'CONNOR and Justice SOUTER join.

In April 1986, before the Colorado Republican Party had selected its senatorial candidate for the fall's election, that Party's Federal Campaign Committee bought radio advertisements attacking Timothy Wirth, the Democratic Party's likely candidate. The Federal Election Commission (FEC) charged that this "expenditure" exceeded the dollar limits that . . . the Federal Election Campaign Act of 1971 (FECA or Act) imposes upon political party "expenditure[s] in connection with" a "general election campaign" for congressional office. 2 U.S.C. §441a(d)(3). This case focuses upon the constitutionality of those limits as applied to this case. We conclude that the First Amendment prohibits the application of this provision to the kind of expenditure at issue here—an expenditure that the political party has made independently, without coordination with any candidate.

I

To understand the issues and our holding, one must begin with FECA as it emerged from Congress in 1974. That Act sought both to remedy the appearance of a "corrupt" political process (one in which large contributions seem to buy legislative votes) and to level the electoral playing field by reducing campaign costs. It consequently imposed limits upon the amounts that individuals, corporations, "political committees" (such as political action committees, or PAC's), and political parties could *contribute* to candidates for federal office, and it also imposed limits upon the amounts that candidates, corporations, labor unions, political committees, and political parties could *spend*, even on their own, to help a candidate win election.

This Court subsequently examined several of the Act's provisions in light of the First Amendment's free speech and association protections. . . . In these cases, the Court essentially weighed the First Amendment interest in permitting candidates (and their supporters) to spend money to advance their political views against a "compelling" governmental interest in assuring the electoral system's legitimacy, protecting it from the appearance and reality of corruption. After doing so, the Court found that the First Amendment prohibited some of FECA's provisions, but permitted others.

Most of the provisions this Court found unconstitutional imposed *expenditure* limits. Those provisions limited candidates' rights to spend their own money, limited a candidate's campaign expenditures, limited the right of individuals to make "independent" expenditures (not coordinated with the candidate or candidate's campaign), and similarly limited the right of political committees to make "independent" expenditures. The provisions that the Court found constitutional mostly imposed *contribution* limits — limits that apply both when an individual or political committee contributes money directly to a candidate and also when they indirectly contribute by making expenditures that they coordinate with the candidate. . . .

FECA also has a special provision, directly at issue in this case, that governs contributions and expenditures by political parties. 2 U.S.C. §441a(d). . . . FECA's special provision, which we shall call the "Party Expenditure Provision," creates a *general exception* from this contribution limitation, and from any other limitation on expenditures. It says: "Notwithstanding any other provision of law with respect to *limitations on expenditures or limitations on contributions,* . . . political party [committees] . . . may make *expenditures* in connection with the general election campaign of candidates for Federal office." §441a(d)(1) (emphasis added). . . . The provision permitted a political party in Colorado in 1986 to spend about $103,000 in connection with the general election campaign of a candidate for the United States Senate.

In January 1986, Timothy Wirth, then a Democratic Congressman, announced that he would run for an open Senate seat in November. In April, before either the Democratic primary or the Republican convention, the Colorado Republican Federal Campaign Committee (Colorado Party or Party), a petitioner here, bought radio advertisements attacking Congressman Wirth. The State Democratic Party complained to the FEC. It pointed out that the Colorado Party had previously assigned its $103,000 general election allotment to the National Republican Senatorial Committee, leaving it without any permissible spending balance. It argued that the purchase of radio time was an "expenditure in connection with the general election campaign of a candidate for Federal office," 2 U.S.C. §441a(d)(3), which, consequently, exceeded the Party Expenditure Provision limits. . . .

II

The summary judgment record indicates that the expenditure in question is what this Court in *Buckley* called an "independent" expenditure, not a "coordinated" expenditure that other provisions of FECA treat as a kind of campaign "contribution." . . . And we therefore treat the expenditure, for constitutional purposes, as an "independent" expenditure, not an indirect campaign contribution.

So treated, the expenditure falls within the scope of the Court's precedents that extend First Amendment protection to independent expenditures. Beginning with *Buckley,* the Court's cases have found a "fundamental constitutional difference between money spent to advertise one's views independently of the candidate's campaign and money contributed to the candidate to be spent on his campaign." *NCPAC, supra,* at 497. This difference has been grounded in the observation that restrictions on contributions impose "only a marginal restriction upon the contributor's ability to engage in free communication," *Buckley, supra,* at 20-21, because the symbolic communicative value of a contribution bears little relation to its size, 424 U.S., at 21, and because such limits leave "persons free to engage in independent political expression, to associate actively through volunteering their services, and to assist to a limited but nonetheless substantial extent in supporting candidates and committees with financial resources," *id.,* at 28. At the same time, reasonable contribution limits directly and materially advance the Government's interest in preventing exchanges of large financial contributions for political favors. *Id.,* at 26-27.

In contrast, the Court has said that restrictions on independent expenditures significantly impair the ability of individuals and groups to engage in direct political advocacy and "represent substantial . . . restraints on the quantity and diversity of political speech." *Id.,* at 19. And at the same time, the Court has concluded that limitations on independent expenditures are less directly related to preventing corruption, since "[t]he absence of prearrangement and coordination of an expenditure with the candidate . . . not only undermines the value of the expenditure to the candidate, but also alleviates the danger that expenditures will be given as a *quid pro quo* for improper commitments from the candidate." *Id.,* at 47.

Given these established principles, we do not see how a provision that limits a political party's independent expenditures can escape their controlling effect. A political party's independent expression not only reflects its members' views about the philosophical and governmental matters that bind them together, it also seeks to convince others to join those members in a practical democratic task, the task of creating a government that voters can instruct and hold responsible for subsequent success or failure. The independent expression of a political party's views is "core" First Amendment activity no less than is the independent expression of individuals, candidates, or other political committees.

We are not aware of any special dangers of corruption associated with political parties that tip the constitutional balance in a different direction. When this Court considered, and held unconstitutional, limits that FECA had set on certain independent expenditures by PAC's, it reiterated *Buckley*'s observation that "the absence of prearrangement and coordination" does not eliminate, but it does help to "alleviate," any "danger" that a candidate will understand the expenditure as an effort to obtain a "*quid pro quo.*" See *NCPAC,* 470 U.S., at 498. The same is true of independent party expenditures.

We recognize that FECA permits individuals to contribute more money ($20,000) to a party than to a candidate ($1,000) or to other political committees ($5,000). 2 U.S.C. §441a(a). We also recognize that FECA permits unregulated "soft money" contributions to a party for certain activities, such as electing candidates for state office or for voter registration and "get out the vote" drives. But the opportunity for corruption posed by these greater opportunities for contributions is, at best, attenuated. . . . A party may not simply channel unlimited amounts of even undesignated contributions to a candidate, since such direct transfers are also considered contributions and are subject to the contribution limits. . . . The greatest danger of corruption, therefore, appears to be from the ability of donors to give sums up to $20,000 to a party which may be used for independent party expenditures for the benefit of a particular candidate. We could understand how Congress, were it to conclude that the potential for evasion of the individual contribution limits was a serious matter, might decide to change the statute's limitations on contributions to political parties. But we do not believe that the risk of corruption present here could justify the markedly greater burden on basic freedoms caused by the statute's limitations on *expenditures*. Contributors seeking to avoid the effect of the $1,000 contribution limit indirectly by donations to the national party could spend that same amount of money (or more) themselves more directly by making their own independent expenditures promoting the candidate. If anything, an independent expenditure made possible by a $20,000 donation, but controlled and directed by a party rather than the donor, would seem less likely to corrupt than the same (or a much larger) independent expenditure made directly by that donor. In any case, the constitutionally significant fact, present equally in both instances, is the lack of coordination between the candidate and the source of the expenditure. This fact prevents us from assuming, absent convincing evidence to the contrary, that a limitation on political parties' independent expenditures is necessary to combat a substantial danger of corruption of the electoral system. . . .

We therefore believe that this Court's prior case law controls the outcome here. We do not see how a Constitution that grants to individuals, candidates, and ordinary political committees the right to make unlimited independent expenditures could deny the same right to political parties. . . .

III

The Government does not deny the force of the precedent we have discussed. Rather, it argue[s] . . . that the expenditure in this case should be treated under those precedents, not as an "independent expenditure," but rather as a "coordinated expenditure," which those cases have treated as "contributions," and which those cases have held Congress may constitutionally regulate. . . .

In support of its argument, the Government points to a set of legal materials, based on FEC interpretations, that seem to say or imply that *all* party expenditures are "coordinated." . . . The Government argues, on the basis of these materials, that the FEC has made an "empirical judgment that party officials will as a matter of course consult with the party's candidates before funding communications intended to influence the outcome of a federal election." The FEC materials, however, do not make this empirical judgment. . . .

The Government does not advance any other legal reason that would require us to accept the FEC's characterization. The FEC has not claimed, for example, that, administratively speaking, it is more difficult to separate a political party's "independent," from its "coordinated," expenditures than, say, those of a PAC. . . . Nor does the fact that the Party Expenditure Provision fails to distinguish between coordinated and independent expenditures indicate a congressional judgment that such a distinction is impossible or untenable in the context of political party spending. Instead, the use of the unmodified term "expenditure" is explained by Congress' desire to limit *all* party expenditures when it passed the 1974 amendments, just as it had limited all expenditures by individuals, corporations, and other political groups.

[T]he Government and supporting *amici* argue that the expenditure is "coordinated" because a party and its candidate are identical, *i.e.*, the party, in a sense, "is" its candidates. We cannot assume, however, that this is so. Congress chose to treat candidates and their parties quite differently under the Act, for example, by regulating contributions from one to the other. And we are not certain whether a metaphysical identity would help the Government, for in that case one might argue that the absolute identity of views and interests eliminates any potential for corruption, as would seem to be the case in the relationship between candidates and their campaign committees.

IV

For these reasons, the judgment of the Court of Appeals is vacated, and the case is remanded for further proceedings.

It is so ordered.

Justice KENNEDY filed an opinion concurring in the judgment and dissenting in part, which Chief Justice REHNQUIST and Justice SCALIA joined:

It makes no sense . . . to ask, as FECA does, whether a party's spending is made "in cooperation, consultation, or concert with" its candidate. The answer in most cases will be yes, but that provides more, not less, justification for holding unconstitutional the statute's attempt to control this type of party spending, which bears little resemblance to the contributions discussed in *Buckley*. Party spending, "in cooperation, consultation, or concert with" its candidates, of necessity "communicate[s] the underlying basis for the support," 424 U.S., at 21, i.e., the hope that he or she will be elected and will work to further the party's political agenda.

The problem is not just the absence of a basis in our First Amendment cases for treating the party's spending as contributions. The greater difficulty posed by the statute is its stifling effect on the ability of the party to do what it exists to do. It is fanciful to suppose that limiting party spending of the type at issue here "does not in any way infringe the contributor's freedom to discuss candidates and issues," id., since it would be impractical and imprudent, to say the least, for a party to support its own candidates without some form of "cooperation" or "consultation." The party's speech, legitimate on its own behalf, cannot be separated from speech on the candidate's behalf without constraining the party in advocating its most essential positions and pursuing its most basic goals. The party's form of organization and the fact that its fate in an election is inextricably intertwined with that of its candidates cannot provide a basis for the restrictions imposed here. . . .

Justice THOMAS filed an opinion concurring in the judgment and dissenting in part, which Chief Justice REHNQUIST and Justice SCALIA joined in part:

The Government asserts that the purpose of §441a(d)(3) is to prevent the corruption of candidates and elected representatives by party officials. . . . As applied in the specific context of campaign funding by political parties, the anti-corruption rationale loses its force. What could it mean for a party to "corrupt" its candidate or to exercise "coercive" influence over him? The very aim of a political party is to influence its candidate's stance on issues and, if the candidate takes office or is reelected, his votes. When political parties achieve that aim, that achievement does not, in my view, constitute "a subversion of the political process." *Federal Election Comm'n v. NCPAC*, 470 U.S., at 497. . . .

In sum, there is only a minimal threat of "corruption," as we have understood that term, when a political party spends to support its candidate or to oppose his competitor, whether or not that expenditure is made in concert with the candidate. Parties and candidates have traditionally worked together to achieve their common goals, and when they engage in that work, there is no risk to the Republic. To the contrary, the danger to the Republic lies in Government suppression of such activity. . . .

Justice STEVENS filed a dissenting opinion, which Justice GINSBURG joined:

A party shares a unique relationship with the candidate it sponsors because their political fates are inextricably linked. That interdependency creates a special danger that the party—or the persons who control the party—will abuse the influence it has over the candidate by virtue of its power to spend. The provisions at issue are appropriately aimed at reducing that threat. . . .

>> *The Treatment of Political Parties.* The plurality rejects the government's argument that a political party's expenditures on behalf a candidate are essentially per se coordinated either because as a matter of fact the party will coordinate with the candidate or as a conceptual matter it does not make political sense to divorce the party from its candidate. The plurality responds by essentially arguing that the Court's precedents on PAC and individual expenditures compel an equivalence between those entities and political parties. Is the plurality's equivalence argument—that a political party is equivalent to a PAC or an individual—compelling? Consider the following argument from Professor Richard Briffault:

But the justifications for constitutional protection for PAC or individual spending are not implicated by spending by party committees. First, individuals and non-party organizations participating in a campaign may have interests other than, or in addition to, the election of the candidate they are backing or the defeat of the candidate they are attacking. They may use their expenditures to highlight an issue in order to send a message, or to persuade the voters to send a message, on that issue. It may be as important to them to make the election a referendum on abortion, or to emphasize that their opposition to a candidate stems from her position on term limits, as to express a position on which candidate should be elected. Their critical issues may include matters candidates prefer to ignore. Indeed, by airing certain messages an independent committee's advertising may be at odds with the campaign strategy of the very candidate it is backing.

The major parties, by contrast, do not have any electoral agenda other than election of their candidates. "The defining mission focus of political parties in the contemporary era is to elect candidates to office." . . .

Second, *Buckley* found . . . that independent expenditures raise little danger of a candidate-financial supporter quid pro quo, which is the constitutional basis for the power to restrict contributions, because the "absence of prearrangement and coordination . . . undermines the value of the expenditure to the candidate." This might be true for an independent expenditure by an individual or interest group that is institutionally distinct from the candidate. In the absence of an ongoing relationship between candidate and independent supporter, the supporter's advertising could hit the wrong themes, or be redundant rather than supplement candidate spending. But there will typically be preexisting ties between the party organization and the candidate who holds the party's nomination.

Party committees frequently aid candidates in hiring campaign managers, consultants, media and pollsters, so that parties and their committees often engage the services of the same political professionals. Party committees provide their candidates with issue and opposition research and poll and focus group data, and they assist candidates with their fundraising. Party committees and candidates share pollsters, campaign strategists, and media consultants; campaign professionals shuttle back and forth among party committees, candidate committees, and consulting firms. Even when they do not sit down to discuss the placement or content of a specific ad, parties and their candidates are structurally integrated, not independent. As a result, party efforts on behalf of a candidate are likely to be quite valuable to the candidate even in the absence of formal coordination. . . .

Certainly, parties are organizationally distinct from their candidates, and it is technically possible, as *Colorado Republican* suggested, for a party committee to support a candidate by engaging in spending that is not coordinated with the candidate's campaign. But the party's relationship to its candidate is very different from that between a PAC and a candidate the PAC is backing. The party includes its candidate. The candidate is typically a member of the party, has been active in the party, and, once nominated, bears the party label, uses the party's place on the ballot, and necessarily benefits from the loyalty and support of party activists. In this way, candidates are far more tightly linked to their respective parties than they are to other politically active organizations that may engage in independent spending.

Richard Briffault, *The Political Parties and Campaign Finance Reform*, 100 COLUM. L. REV. 620, 637-639 (2000).

What follows from the observation that it is difficult if not impossible to disentangle the interest of the party from the interest of the party's candidates? Should campaign-finance law and constitutional doctrine treat parties differently from other entities such as PACs? For example, should parties have a First Amendment right to coordinate political expenditures with candidates even though PACs do not?

>>   **Colorado Republican II.**   In *Colorado Republican I,* the Court held that spending limits in connection with a senatorial campaign were unconstitutional as applied to the Colorado Republican Party. The Court did not address the party's facial challenge—that spending limits on parties were in all circumstances unconstitutional, and that the prohibition on coordinated expenditure was therefore unconstitutional. The Court remanded the case to address the party's facial challenge. That issue eventually returned to the Supreme Court, in *Federal Election Commission v. Colorado Republican Federal Committee (Colorado Republican II),* 533 U.S. 431 (2001).

Justice Souter delivered the opinion of the Court and rejected the argument that restrictions on coordinated expenditures between a party and its candidate were facially unconstitutional. Justice Souter reduced the two parties' positions down to two main arguments. "The first," he wrote, "turns on the relationship of a party to a candidate: a coordinated relationship between them so defines a party that it cannot function as such without coordinated spending, the object of which is a candidate's election." The second argument, Souter went on, "turns on the nature of a party as uniquely able to spend in ways that promote candidate success. We think that this argument is a double-edged sword, and one hardly limited to political parties."

In addressing the first argument, Souter contended that "[t]he assertion that the party is so joined at the hip to candidates that most of its spending must necessarily be coordinated spending is a statement at odds with the history of nearly 30 years under the Act." Because coordinated spending by a party had been limited since FECA 1974 was passed—and only made unlimited by *Colorado Republican I*—the Court believed that "the Party's claim that coordinated spending beyond the limit imposed by the Act is essential to its very function as a party amounts implicitly to saying that for almost three decades political parties have not been functional or have been functioning in systematic violation of the law."

Justice Souter then wrote that the problem with the second argument— that because parties have the purpose of electing candidates, limiting the way parties spend for that purpose is particularly burdensome—was "not so much [a fault of] metaphysics as myopia, a refusal to see how the power of money actually works in the political structure. When we look directly at a party's function in getting and spending money, it would ignore reality to think that the party role is adequately described by speaking generally of electing particular candidates." Rather, the money that parties spend comes from many different contributors with many personal and idiosyncratic interests. Moreover, to reduce the role of parties to simply electing candidates, Souter believed, was unrealistic. Parties "act as agents for spending on behalf of those who seek to produce obligated officeholders. It is this party role, which functionally unites parties with other self-interested political actors, that the Party Expenditure Provision targets."

Souter then addressed the party's argument that "its strong working relationship with candidates and its unique ability to speak in coordination with them should be taken into account in the First Amendment analysis." He acknowledged the power of a party to amplify the messages of its members, but contended that it "does not, however, follow from a party's efficiency in getting large sums and

spending intelligently that limits on a party's coordinated spending should be scrutinized under an unusually high standard." He went on to ask, "If the coordinated
spending of other, less efficient and perhaps less practiced political actors can be
limited consistently with the Constitution, why would the Constitution forbid regulation aimed at a party whose very efficiency in channeling benefits to candidates
threatens to undermine the contribution (and hence coordinated spending) limits
to which those others are unquestionably subject?"

Finally, Souter addressed head on the question of what makes parties different
from other political spenders. It cannot be that the difference is only spending
power, because some individuals have pockets just as deep as parties — or deeper.
"Rich political activists crop up, and the United States has known its Citizens Kane.
Their money speaks loudly, too, and they are therefore burdened by restrictions on
its use just as parties are." And yet, these large individual donors are subjected to
valid coordinated-spending limits according to *Buckley*, as are PACs. In every way,
large political donors and PACs are similar to parties, and a party, like those other
actors, has the "right under *Colorado [Republican] I* to spend money in support of a
candidate without legal limit so long as it spends independently. A party may spend
independently every cent it can raise wherever it thinks its candidate will shine, on
every subject and any viewpoint."

Because of this, Souter applied the same intermediate scrutiny used in other
cases, considering whether the restriction was closely drawn to match the sufficiently important government interest in battling political corruption. Using this
standard, the Court upheld limits on party's coordinated expenditures.

Justice Thomas, joined by Justices Scalia and Kennedy and Chief Justice Rehnquist, countered in dissent that the Court's two conclusions — that "coordinated
expenditures are no different from contributions, and [that] political parties are
no different from individuals and political committees"—were both flawed.

First, Thomas wrote,

> [The Court's] definition [of "coordinated expenditure"] covers a broad
> array of conduct, some of which is akin to an independent expenditure.
> At one extreme, to be sure, are outlays that are virtually indistinguishable
> from simple contributions. But toward the other end of the spectrum are
> expenditures that largely resemble, and should be entitled to the same
> protection as, independent expenditures. Take, for example, a situation
> in which the party develops a television advertising campaign touting a
> candidate's record on education, and the party simply consults with the
> candidate on which time slot the advertisement should run for maximum
> effectiveness. I see no constitutional difference between this expenditure
> and a purely independent one.

This act, Thomas believed, "is not just 'symbolic expression,' but a clear manifestation of the party's most fundamental political views."

Second, Thomas wrote that even if he were "to ignore the breadth of the
statutory text, and to assume that all coordinated expenditures are functionally
equivalent to contributions, [he] still would strike down the Party Expenditure
Provision." When the source of a contribution is an individual or a political committee, a restriction on such contributions entails, in the words of *Buckley*, only a

"marginal restriction." On the other hand, because political parties and candidates are so intertwined, "to break this link between the party and its candidates would impose additional costs and burdens to promote the party message." In fact, "[f]ar from being a mere 'marginal' restraint on speech, the Party Expenditure Provision has restricted the party's most natural form of communication," the coordinated expenditure.

Finally, Thomas took umbrage with the Court's argument that parties are not created simply to elect candidates. "First," he wrote, "no one argues that a party's role is merely to get particular candidates elected. . . . The point is simply that parties and candidates have shared interests, that it is natural for them to work together, and that breaking the connection between parties and their candidates inhibits the promotion of the party's message." Second, he argued that the fact that donors contribute — sometimes to both parties and both candidates — does not put the donors in control of the parties or make the parties agents of the donor. "If the Green Party," he hypothesized, "were to receive a donation from an industry that pollutes, would the Green Party necessarily become, through no choice of its own, an instrument of the polluters? . . . Parties might be the target of the speech of donors, but that does not suggest that parties are influenced (let alone improperly influenced) by the speech."

>> *The Distinctiveness of Parties.*   Is Justice Souter correct that parties are indistinct from other entities? Consider the following argument:

> Political parties play a pivotal role in a republican form of government. Because they are bodies large enough to translate the people's will into action, they bridge the gap between the electors and the government, ensuring that the people have a voice. They also perform a crucial role in the electoral process. . . .

> The American political system has developed through competition between political parties and the regular tradeoffs of power that this entails. Electoral competition enhances democracy and provides the electorate with distinct political alternatives that motivate people to express a preference. To the extent that parties incorporate their differences into their agendas and change their platforms to respond to people's preferences, they facilitate the competition that is central to democratic elections.

> Parties present unique opportunities for speech and association that other organizations cannot provide. Unlike PACs, parties have varied and long-term interests that extend beyond the next election. Parties also represent a broader donor base than PACs. They can help assure that groups without financial access to candidates (either because they lack the funds to personally contribute or because they do not have a PAC representing their interests) are not shut out of the system. Whereas interest groups by definition do not attempt to win a majority, parties provide a means by which the vast majority of people can gain both political identity and political leverage.

> Political institutions are more responsive to majorities when interest groups work together strategically to form coalitions. Strong parties help

develop the coalitions and voting blocs essential to democratic government. They facilitate cohesion by offering alternatives to interest groups
at odds with each other and by informing voters of candidates' positions.
Parties also hold elected officials responsible for their performance.
A politician not facing reelection has much less incentive to be politically
responsible than the party she belongs to, which must justify the actions
of its members in the next election and beyond. Parties are unique institutions in our culture, representing myriad interests in a way that PACs
cannot, and the political speech they provide cannot be found elsewhere
in our electoral system. . . .

PACs present several normative problems. First, by definition
PACs represent a narrow group of interests rather than the public as
a whole. Their real danger arises, however, from the disproportionate
power they wield by virtue of the sums of money they command and
the single issue that unites their members. As a result, candidates and
office holders have difficulty withstanding the onslaught of PAC influence. . . . PACs not only wield disproportionate influence, but their
constituencies change the very tenor of politics. As one journalist
notes, "the preponderance of PACs representing upper-middle-class
donors conspires to tilt the scales of influence heavily against the working middle class and the poor." In recent years, PACs have generated as
much as 47 and 29 percent of total contributions to Senate and House
incumbent races, respectively. Because campaign finance reform did
not limit the total contributions from PACs as it did for individuals and
parties, PACs may donate to an unlimited number of candidates. While
PACs are not subject to limitations on independent expenditures,
they do face caps on the amounts they may contribute to candidates.
The large aggregate sums that FECA allows PACs to spend, however,
increases the possibility that PACs will exert a corrupting influence on
political candidates.

Clarisa Long, *Shouting Down the Voice of the People: Political Parties, Powerful PACs, and
Concerns About Corruption*, 46 STAN. L. REV. 1161, 1175-1180 (1994).

3.   Independent Expenditures by Nonprofit Issue
Advocacy Corporations

In the following case, the Supreme Court dealt with the regulation of "non-
capital amassing corporations," or nonprofit corporations. This case prefigures
one of the more vexing questions in this chapter: the extent to which for-profit
corporations and unions should be allowed to finance federal campaigns. Leaving
aside that question, for now, should we think about nonprofit issue advocacy corporations as separate entities deserving of special First Amendment protection? Put
differently, is campaign-finance law made more or less intelligible if it distinguishes
between for-profit commercial corporations and nonprofit issue advocacy corporations? Is this type of categorization constitutionally sensible?

Federal Election Commission v. Massachusetts Citizens for Life

479 U.S. 238 (1986)

Justice BRENNAN announced the judgment of the Court and delivered the opinion of the Court with respect to Parts I, II, III-B, and III-C, and an opinion with respect to Part III-A, in which Justice MARSHALL, Justice POWELL, and Justice SCALIA join.

I

A

MCFL was incorporated in January 1973 as a nonprofit, nonstock corporation under Massachusetts law. Its corporate purpose as stated in its articles of incorporation is: "To foster respect for human life and to defend the right to life of all human beings, born and unborn, through educational, political and other forms of activities and . . . to engage in any other lawful act or activity for which corporations may be organized."

MCFL does not accept contributions from business corporations or unions. Its resources come from voluntary donations from "members," and from various fund-raising activities such as garage sales, bake sales, dances, raffles, and picnics. The corporation considers its "members" those persons who have either contributed to the organization in the past or indicated support for its activities. . . .

MCFL began publishing a newsletter in January 1973. It was distributed as a matter of course to contributors, and, when funds permitted, to noncontributors who had expressed support for the organization. The total distribution of any one issue has never exceeded 6,000. The newsletter was published irregularly from 1973 through 1978. . . . Each of the newsletters bore a masthead identifying it as the "Massachusetts Citizens for Life Newsletter," as well as a volume and issue number. The publication typically contained appeals for volunteers and contributions and information on MCFL activities, as well as on matters such as the results of hearings on bills and constitutional amendments, the status of particular legislation, and the outcome of referenda, court decisions, and administrative hearings. Newsletter recipients were usually urged to contact the relevant decisionmakers and express their opinion.

B

In September 1978, MCFL prepared and distributed a "Special Edition" prior to the September 1978 primary elections. . . . [M]ore than 100,000 copies of the "Special Edition" were printed for distribution. The front page of the publication was headlined "EVERYTHING YOU NEED TO KNOW TO VOTE PRO-LIFE," and readers were admonished that "[n]o pro-life candidate can win in November without your vote in September." "VOTE PRO-LIFE" was printed in large bold-faced letters on the back page, and a coupon was provided to be clipped and taken to the polls to remind voters of the name of the "pro-life" candidates. Next to the exhortation to vote "pro-life" was a disclaimer: "This special election edition does not represent an endorsement of any particular candidate."

To aid the reader in selecting candidates, the flyer listed the candidates for each state and federal office in every voting district in Massachusetts, and identified each one as either supporting or opposing what MCFL regarded as the correct position on three issues. . . .

The "Special Edition" was edited by an officer of MCFL who was not part of the staff that prepared the MCFL newsletters. The "Special Edition" was mailed free of charge and without request to 5,986 contributors, and to 50,674 others whom MCFL regarded as sympathetic to the organization's purposes. The Commission asserts that the remainder of the 100,000 issues were placed in public areas for general distribution, but MCFL insists that no copies were made available to the general public. The "Special Edition" was not identified on its masthead as a special edition of the regular newsletter, although the MCFL logotype did appear at its top. . . . The corporation spent $9,812.76 to publish and circulate the "Special Edition," all of which was taken from its general treasury funds.

A complaint was filed with the Commission alleging that the "Special Edition" was a violation of §441b [of FECA]. The complaint maintained that the Edition represented an expenditure of funds from a corporate treasury to distribute to the general public a campaign flyer on behalf of certain political candidates. The FEC found reason to believe that such a violation had occurred, initiated an investigation, and determined that probable cause existed to believe that MCFL had violated the Act . . . [and] filed a complaint in the District Court . . . seeking a civil penalty and other appropriate relief.

Both parties moved for summary judgment. The District Court granted MCFL's motion, holding that: (1) the election publications could not be regarded as "expenditures" under §441b(b)(2); (2) the "Special Edition" was exempt from the statutory prohibition by virtue of §431(9)(B)(i), which in general exempts news commentary distributed by a periodical publication unaffiliated with any candidate or political party; and (3) if the statute applied to MCFL, it was unconstitutional as a violation of the First Amendment.

On appeal, the Court of Appeals for the First Circuit held that the statute was applicable to MCFL, but affirmed the District Court's holding that the statute as so applied was unconstitutional. We granted certiorari and now affirm.

II

We agree with the Court of Appeals that the "Special Edition" is not outside the reach of §441b. First, we find no merit in appellee's contention that preparation and distribution of the "Special Edition" does not fall within that section's definition of "expenditure." Section 441b(b)(2) defines "contribution or expenditure" as the provision of various things of value "*to* any candidate, campaign committee, or political party or organization, in connection with any election" (emphasis added). MCFL contends that, since it supplied nothing to any candidate or organization, the publication is not within §441b. However, the general definitions section of the Act contains a broader definition of "expenditure," including within that term the provision of anything of value made "*for the purpose of influencing* any election for Federal office." 2 U.S.C. §431(9)(A)(i) (emphasis added). Since the language of the statute does not alone resolve the issue, we must look to the legislative history of §441b to determine the scope of the term "expenditure."

That history clearly confirms that §441b was meant to proscribe expenditures in connection with an election. We have exhaustively recounted the legislative history of the predecessors of this section in prior decisions. See *Pipefitters v. United States*, 407 U.S. 385, 402-409 (1972); *United States v. Automobile Workers*, 352 U.S. 567, 570-587 (1957). This history makes clear that Congress has long regarded it as insufficient merely to restrict payments made directly to candidates or campaign organizations. . . .

The Federal Election Campaign Act enacted the prohibition now found in §441b. This portion of the Act simply ratified the existing understanding of the scope of §610. Representative Hansen, the sponsor of the provision, declared: "The effect of this language is to carry out the basic intent of section 610, which is to prohibit the use of union or corporate funds for active electioneering directed at the general public on behalf of a candidate in a Federal election." 117 Cong. Rec. 43379 (1971). . . .

Thus, the fact that §441b uses the phrase "to any candidate . . . in connection with any election," while §610 provided "in connection with any primary election," is not evidence that Congress abandoned its restriction, in force since 1947, on expenditures on behalf of candidates. We therefore find no merit in MCFL's argument that only payments to a candidate or organization fall within the scope of §441b.

Appellee next argues that the definition of an expenditure under §441b necessarily incorporates the requirement that a communication "expressly advocate" the election of candidates, and that its "Special Edition" does not constitute express advocacy. The argument relies on the portion of *Buckley v. Valeo* that upheld the disclosure requirement for expenditures by individuals other than candidates and by groups other than political committees. There, in order to avoid problems of overbreadth, the Court held that the term "expenditure" encompassed "only funds used for communications that expressly advocate the election or defeat of a clearly identified candidate." 424 U.S., at 80, 96 S. Ct., at 663 (footnote omitted). The rationale for this holding was:

> [T]he distinction between discussion of issues and candidates and advocacy of election or defeat of candidates may often dissolve in practical application. Candidates, especially incumbents, are intimately tied to public issues involving legislative proposals and governmental actions. Not only do candidates campaign on the basis of their positions on various issues, but campaigns themselves generate issues of public interest. *Id.*, at 42.

We agree with appellee that this rationale requires a similar construction of the more intrusive provision that directly regulates independent spending. We therefore hold that an expenditure must constitute "express advocacy" in order to be subject to the prohibition of §441b. We also hold, however, that the publication of the "Special Edition" constitutes "express advocacy."

Buckley adopted the "express advocacy" requirement to distinguish discussion of issues and candidates from more pointed exhortations to vote for particular persons. We therefore concluded in that case that a finding of "express advocacy" depended upon the use of language such as "vote for," "elect," "support," etc. Just such an exhortation appears in the "Special Edition." The publication not only urges voters to vote for "pro-life" candidates, but also identifies and provides photographs of specific candidates fitting that description. The Edition cannot be regarded as a mere discussion of public issues that by their nature raise the names of certain politicians. Rather, it provides in effect an explicit directive: vote for these (named) candidates. The fact that this message is marginally less direct than "Vote for Smith" does not change its essential nature. The Edition goes beyond issue discussion to express electoral advocacy. The disclaimer of endorsement cannot negate this fact. The "Special Edition" thus falls squarely within §441b, for it represents express advocacy of the election of particular candidates distributed to members of the general public.

In sum, we hold that MCFL's publication and distribution of the "Special Edition" is in violation of §441b. We therefore turn to the constitutionality of that provision as applied to appellee.

III

A

Independent expenditures constitute expression " 'at the core of our electoral process and of the First Amendment freedoms.' " *Buckley*, 424 U.S., at 39 (quoting *Williams v. Rhodes*, 393 U.S. 23, 32 (1968)). We must therefore determine whether the prohibition of §441b burdens political speech, and, if so, whether such a burden is justified by a compelling state interest.

The FEC minimizes the impact of the legislation upon MCFL's First Amendment rights by emphasizing that the corporation remains free to establish a separate segregated fund, composed of contributions earmarked for that purpose by the donors, that may be used for unlimited campaign spending. However, the corporation is *not* free to use its general funds for campaign advocacy purposes. While that is not an absolute restriction on speech, it is a substantial one. Moreover, even to speak through a segregated fund, MCFL must make very significant efforts.

If it were not incorporated, MCFL's obligations under the Act would be those specified by §434(c), the section that prescribes the duties of "[e]very person (other than a political committee)." Section 434(c) provides that any such person that during a year makes independent expenditures exceeding $250 must: (1) identify all contributors who contribute in a given year over $200 in the aggregate in funds to influence elections, §434(c)(1); (2) disclose the name and address of recipients of independent expenditures exceeding $200 in the aggregate, along with an indication of whether the money was used to support or oppose a particular candidate, §434(c)(2)(A); and (3) identify any persons who make contributions over $200 that are earmarked for the purpose of furthering independent expenditures, §434(c)(2)(C). All unincorporated organizations whose major purpose is not campaign advocacy, but who occasionally make independent expenditures on behalf of candidates, are subject only to these regulations.

Because it is incorporated, however, MCFL must establish a "separate segregated fund" if it wishes to engage in any independent spending whatsoever.

§§441b(a), (b)(2)(C). Since such a fund is considered a "political committee" under the Act, §431(4)(B), all MCFL independent expenditure activity is, as a result, regulated as though the organization's major purpose is to further the election of candidates. This means that MCFL must comply with several requirements in addition to those mentioned. Under §432, it must appoint a treasurer; ensure that contributions are forwarded to the treasurer within 10 or 30 days of receipt, depending on the amount of contribution; see that its treasurer keeps an account of every contribution regardless of amount, the name and address of any person who makes a contribution in excess of $50, all contributions received from political committees, and the name and address of any person to whom a disbursement is made regardless of amount; and preserve receipts for all disbursements over $200 and all records for three years. Under §433, MCFL must file a statement of organization containing its name, address, the name of its custodian of records, and its banks, safety deposit boxes, or other depositories; must report any change in the above information within 10 days; and may dissolve only upon filing a written statement that it will no longer receive any contributions nor make disbursements, and that it has no outstanding debts or obligations.

Under §434, MCFL must file either monthly reports with the FEC or reports on the following schedule: quarterly reports during election years, a pre-election report no later than the 12th day before an election, a postelection report within 30 days after an election, and reports every 6 months during nonelection years. These reports must contain information regarding the amount of cash on hand; the total amount of receipts, detailed by 10 different categories; the identification of each political committee and candidate's authorized or affiliated committee making contributions, and any persons making loans, providing rebates, refunds, dividends, or interest or any other offset to operating expenditures in an aggregate amount over $200; the total amount of all disbursements, detailed by 12 different categories; the names of all authorized or affiliated committees to whom expenditures aggregating over $200 have been made; persons to whom loan repayments or refunds have been made; the total sum of all contributions, operating expenses, outstanding debts and obligations, and the settlement terms of the retirement of any debt or obligation. In addition, MCFL may solicit contributions for its separate segregated fund only from its "members," which does not include those persons who have merely contributed to or indicated support for the organization in the past.

It is evident from this survey that MCFL is subject to more extensive requirements and more stringent restrictions than it would be if it were not incorporated. These additional regulations may create a disincentive for such organizations to engage in political speech. Detailed recordkeeping and disclosure obligations, along with the duty to appoint a treasurer and custodian of the records, impose administrative costs that many small entities may be unable to bear. Furthermore, such duties require a far more complex and formalized organization than many small groups could manage. Restriction of solicitation of contributions to "members" vastly reduces the sources of funding for organizations with either few or no formal members, directly limiting the ability of such organizations to engage in core political speech. It is not unreasonable to suppose that, as in this case, an incorporated group of like-minded persons might seek donations to support the dissemination of their political ideas and their occasional endorsement of political candidates, by means of garage sales, bake sales, and raffles. Such persons might well be turned away by the prospect of complying with all the requirements imposed by the Act. . . .

Thus, while §441b does not remove all opportunities for independent spending by organizations such as MCFL, the avenue it leaves open is more burdensome than the one it forecloses. The fact that the statute's practical effect may be to discourage protected speech is sufficient to characterize §441b as an infringement on First Amendment activities. . . .

B

When a statutory provision burdens First Amendment rights, it must be justified by a compelling state interest. *Williams v. Rhodes*, 393 U.S., at 31; *NAACP v. Button*, 371 U.S. 415, 438 (1963). The FEC first insists that justification for §441b's expenditure restriction is provided by this Court's acknowledgment that "the special characteristics of the corporate structure require particularly careful regulation." *National Right to Work Committee*, 459 U.S., at 209-210. The Commission thus relies on the long history of regulation of corporate political activity as support for the application of §441b to MCFL. Evaluation of the Commission's argument requires close examination of the underlying rationale for this longstanding regulation.

We have described that rationale in recent opinions as the need to restrict "the influence of political war chests funneled through the corporate form," *NCPAC*, 470 U.S., at 501; to "eliminate the effect of aggregated wealth on federal elections," *Pipefitters*, 407 U.S., at 416; to curb the political influence of "those who exercise control over large aggregations of capital," *Automobile Workers*, 352 U.S., at 585; and to regulate the "substantial aggregations of wealth amassed by the special advantages which go with the corporate form of organization," *National Right to Work Committee*, 459 U.S., at 207.

This concern over the corrosive influence of concentrated corporate wealth reflects the conviction that it is important to protect the integrity of the marketplace of political ideas. It acknowledges the wisdom of Justice Holmes' observation that "the ultimate good desired is better reached by free trade in ideas—that the best test of truth is the power of the thought to get itself accepted in the competition of the market." *Abrams v. United States*, 250 U.S. 616, 630 (1919) (Holmes, J., joined by Brandeis, J., dissenting).

Direct corporate spending on political activity raises the prospect that resources amassed in the economic marketplace may be used to provide an unfair advantage in the political marketplace. Political "free trade" does not necessarily require that all who participate in the political marketplace do so with exactly equal resources. Relative availability of funds is after all a rough barometer of public support. The resources in the treasury of a business corporation, however, are not an indication of popular support for the corporation's political ideas. They reflect instead the economically motivated decisions of investors and customers. The availability of these resources may make a corporation a formidable political presence, even though the power of the corporation may be no reflection of the power of its ideas.

By requiring that corporate independent expenditures be financed through a political committee expressly established to engage in campaign spending, §441b seeks to prevent this threat to the political marketplace. The resources available to *this* fund, as opposed to the corporate treasury, in fact reflect popular support for the political positions of the committee. . . . The expenditure restrictions of §441b are thus meant to ensure that competition among actors in the political arena is truly competition among ideas.

Regulation of corporate political activity thus has reflected concern not about use of the corporate form *per se*, but about the potential for unfair deployment of wealth for political purposes. Groups such as MCFL, however, do not pose that danger of corruption. MCFL was formed to disseminate political ideas, not to amass capital. The resources it has available are not a function of its success in the economic marketplace, but its popularity in the political marketplace. While MCFL may derive some advantages from its corporate form, those are advantages that redound to its benefit as a political organization, not as a profit-making enterprise. In short, MCFL is not the type of "traditional corporatio[n] organized for economic gain," *NCPAC*, 470 U.S., at 500, that has been the focus of regulation of corporate political activity.

The Commission . . . argues in support of §441b that it prevents an organization from using an individual's money for purposes that the individual may not support. We acknowledged the legitimacy of this concern as to the dissenting stockholder and union member in *National Right to Work Committee*, 459 U.S., at 208, and in *Pipefitters*, 407 U.S., at 414-415. But such persons, as noted, contribute investment funds or union dues for economic gain, and do not necessarily authorize the use of their money for political ends. Furthermore, because such individuals depend on the organization for income or for a job, it is not enough to tell them that any unhappiness with the use of their money can be redressed simply by leaving the corporation or the union. It was thus wholly reasonable for Congress to require the establishment of a separate political fund to which persons can make voluntary contributions.

This rationale for regulation is not compelling with respect to independent expenditures by appellee. Individuals who contribute to appellee are fully aware of its political purposes, and in fact contribute precisely because they support those purposes. It is true that a contributor may not be aware of the exact use to which his or her money ultimately may be put, or the specific candidate that it may be used to support. However, individuals contribute to a political organization in part because they regard such a contribution as a more effective means of advocacy than spending the money under their own personal direction. Any contribution therefore necessarily involves at least some degree of delegation of authority to use such funds in a manner that best serves the shared political purposes of the organization and contributor. In addition, an individual desiring more direct control over the use of his or her money can simply earmark the contribution for a specific purpose, an option whose availability does not depend on the applicability of §441b. Finally, a contributor dissatisfied with how funds are used can simply stop contributing.

Finally, the FEC maintains that the inapplicability of §441b to MCFL would open the door to massive undisclosed political spending by similar entities, and to their use as conduits for undisclosed spending by business corporations and unions.

We see no such danger. Even if §441b is inapplicable, an independent expenditure of as little as $250 by MCFL will trigger the disclosure provisions of §434(c). As a result, MCFL will be required to identify all contributors who annually provide in the aggregate $200 in funds intended to influence elections, will have to specify all recipients of independent spending amounting to more than $200, and will be bound to identify all persons making contributions over $200 who request that the money be used for independent expenditures. These reporting obligations provide precisely the information necessary to monitor MCFL's independent spending activity and its receipt of contributions. The state interest in disclosure therefore can be met in a manner less restrictive than imposing the full panoply of regulations that accompany status as a political committee under the Act.

Furthermore, should MCFL's independent spending become so extensive that the organization's major purpose may be regarded as campaign activity, the corporation would be classified as a political committee. As such, it would automatically be subject to the obligations and restrictions applicable to those groups whose primary objective is to influence political campaigns. In sum, there is no need for the sake of disclosure to treat MCFL any differently than other organizations that only occasionally engage in independent spending on behalf of candidates.

Thus, the concerns underlying the regulation of corporate political activity are simply absent with regard to MCFL. The dissent is surely correct in maintaining that we should not second-guess a decision to sweep within a broad prohibition activities that differ in degree, but not kind. It is not the case, however, that MCFL merely poses less of a threat of the danger that has prompted regulation. Rather, it does not pose such a threat at all. Voluntary political associations do not suddenly present the specter of corruption merely by assuming the corporate form. Given this fact, the rationale for restricting core political speech in this case is simply the desire for a bright-line rule. This hardly constitutes the *compelling* state interest necessary to justify any infringement on First Amendment freedom. While the burden on MCFL's speech is not insurmountable, we cannot permit it to be imposed without a constitutionally adequate justification. In so holding, we do not assume a legislative role, but fulfill our judicial duty—to enforce the demands of the Constitution.

C

Our conclusion is that §441b's restriction of independent spending is unconstitutional as applied to MCFL, for it infringes protected speech without a compelling justification for such infringement. We acknowledge the legitimacy of Congress' concern that organizations that amass great wealth in the economic marketplace not gain unfair advantage in the political marketplace.

Regardless of whether that concern is adequate to support application of §441b to commercial enterprises, a question not before us, that justification does not extend uniformly to all corporations. Some corporations have features more akin to voluntary political associations than business firms, and therefore should not have to bear burdens on independent spending solely because of their incorporated status.

In particular, MCFL has three features essential to our holding that it may not constitutionally be bound by §441b's restriction on independent spending. *First,* it was formed for the express purpose of promoting political ideas, and cannot engage in business activities. If political fundraising events are expressly denominated as requests for contributions that will be used for political purposes, including direct expenditures, these events cannot be considered business activities. This ensures that political resources reflect political support. *Second,* it has no shareholders or other persons affiliated so as to have a claim on its assets or earnings. This ensures that persons connected with the organization will have no economic disincentive for disassociating with it if they disagree with its political activity. *Third,* MCFL was not established by a business corporation or a labor union, and it is its policy not to accept contributions from such entities. This prevents such corporations from serving as conduits for the type of direct spending that creates a threat to the political marketplace.

It may be that the class of organizations affected by our holding today will be small. That prospect, however, does not diminish the significance of the rights at stake. Freedom of speech plays a fundamental role in a democracy; as this Court has said, freedom of thought and speech "is the matrix, the indispensable condition, of nearly every other form of freedom." *Palko v. Connecticut,* 302 U.S. 319, 327 (1937). Our pursuit of other governmental ends, however, may tempt us to accept in small increments a loss that would be unthinkable if inflicted all at once. For this reason, we must be as vigilant against the modest diminution of speech as we are against its sweeping restriction. Where at all possible, government must curtail speech only to the degree necessary to meet the particular problem at hand, and must avoid infringing on speech that does not pose the danger that has prompted regulation. In enacting the provision at issue in this case, Congress has chosen too blunt an instrument for such a delicate task.

The judgment of the Court of Appeals is
Affirmed.

Chief Justice REHNQUIST, with whom Justice WHITE, Justice BLACKMUN, and Justice STEVENS join, concurring in part and dissenting in part:

Because MCFL was formed to disseminate political ideas, we are told, the money it spends — at least in the form of independent expenditures — reflects the political ideas for which it stands without the threat or appearance of corruption. Nor does the Court find any need to protect the interests of contributors to MCFL by requiring the establishment of a separate segregated fund for its political expenditures. Individual contributors can simply withhold their contributions if they disagree with the corporation's choices; those who continue to give will be protected by requiring notice to them that their money might be used for political purposes.

I do not dispute that the threat from corporate political activity will vary depending on the particular characteristics of a given corporation; it is obvious that large and successful corporations with resources to fund a political war chest constitute a more potent threat to the political process than less successful business corporations or nonprofit corporations. It may also be that those supporting some nonbusiness corporations will identify with the corporations' political views more frequently than the average shareholder of General Motors would support the political activities of that corporation. These distinctions among corporations, however, are "distinctions in degree" that do not amount to "differences in kind."

Buckley v. Valeo, 424 U.S. 1, 30 (1976) (per curiam). As such, they are more properly drawn by the Legislature than by the Judiciary. Congress expressed its judgment in §441b that the threat posed by corporate political activity warrants a prophylactic measure applicable to all groups that organize in the corporate form. Our previous cases have expressed a reluctance to fine-tune such judgments; I would adhere to that counsel here. . . .

The distinction between corporate and noncorporate activity was not diminished in *NCPAC*, where we found fatally overbroad the $1,000 limitation in 26 U.S.C. §9012(f) on independent expenditures by "political committees." Our conclusion rested in part on the fact that §9012(f) regulated not only corporations but rather "indiscriminately lump[ed] with corporations any 'committee, association or organization.'" *NCPAC*, 470 U.S., at 500. *NCPAC* accordingly continued to recognize what had been, until today, an acceptable distinction, grounded in the judgment of the political branch, between political activity by corporate actors and that by organizations not benefiting from "the corporate shield which the State [has] granted to corporations as a form of quid pro quo" for various regulations. *Citizens Against Rent Control v. Berkeley*, 454 U.S. 290, 300 (1981) (Rehnquist, J., concurring).

The Court explains the decisions in *NRWC* and *NCPAC* by reference to another distinction found in our decisions—that between contributions and independent expenditures. See *Buckley*, 424 U.S., at 19-23. This . . . distinction . . . does not warrant a different result in view of our longstanding approval of limitations on corporate spending and of the type of regulation involved here. The distinction between contributions and independent expenditures is not a line separating black from white. The statute here—though involving independent expenditures—is not nearly so drastic as the "wholesale restriction of clearly protected conduct" at issue in *NCPAC*, 470 U.S., at 501. It regulates instead the form of otherwise unregulated spending. . . . As the Court correctly notes, the regulation of §441b is not without burdens, but it remains wholly different in character from that which we condemned in *NCPAC*. In these circumstances, I would defer to the congressional judgment that corporations are a distinct category with respect to which this sort of regulation is constitutionally permissible.

The basically legislative character of the Court's decision is dramatically illustrated by its effort to carve out a constitutional niche for "[g]roups such as MCFL." The three-part test gratuitously announced in today's dicta adds to a well-defined prohibition a vague and barely adumbrated exception certain to result in confusion and costly litigation. If we sat as a council of revision to modify legislative judgments, I would hesitate to join the Court's effort because of this fact alone. But we do not sit in that capacity; we are obliged to leave the drawing of lines in cases such as this to Congress if those lines are within constitutional bounds. Believing that the Act of Congress in question here passes this test, I dissent from the Court's contrary conclusion.

The Court in *MCFL* did what it perhaps refused to do in the *Colorado Republican* cases, which is to create constitutional carve-outs from campaign-finance laws for particular entities. In the *Colorado Republican* cases, the Court refused to treat political parties differently from other institutional entities. In *MCFL*, the Court created an exception from the application of Section 441(b) for ideological nonprofit corporations. Is Chief Justice Rehnquist correct that the distinction between commercial and nonprofit advocacy corporations is one of degree and not one of kind? Moreover, is he also right that such a carve-out is best created not by courts but by legislatures? In light of what some might argue is the Court's unsuccessful interventionist posture with FECA in *Buckley*, is Chief Justice Rehnquist correct that the Court should be more respectful of Congress's judgment in this area?

4. *Independent Expenditures by Corporations and Unions*

In the next series of cases, the Court confronts more directly the issues raised by the role of for-profit corporations in financing federal elections. One of the factors you will observe from reading the cases below is the lack of temporal consistency from the Court. Sometimes the Court has concluded that the government can exclude corporations from any direct involvement in financing federal campaigns; sometimes it has held that the First Amendment precludes the federal government from severely limiting the role of corporations in financing campaigns. What accounts for this lack of consistency?

In the following case, Pipefitters Local Union No. 562 and three officers of that union were convicted of conspiracy to violate 18 U.S.C. §610. At the time of trial, Section 610 provided in relevant part:

> It is unlawful . . . for any corporation . . . or any labor organization to make a contribution or expenditure in connection with any [federal] election . . . or in connection with any primary election or political convention . . . held to select candidates for [federal] office. . . .
>
> Every corporation or labor organization which makes any contribution or expenditure in violation of this section shall be fined not more than $5,000; and every officer or director of any corporation, or . . . of any labor organization, who consents to any contribution or expenditure by the corporation or labor organization . . . in violation of this section, shall be fined not more than $1,000 or imprisoned not more than one year, or both; and if the violation was willful, shall be fined not more than $10,000 or imprisoned not more than two years, or both.

Pipefitters Local Union No. 562 v. United States

407 U.S. 385 (1972)

Mr. Justice BRENNAN delivered the opinion of the Court.

Petitioners—Pipefitters Local Union No. 562 and three individual officers of the Union—were convicted by a jury in the United States District Court for the

Eastern District of Missouri of conspiracy under 18 U.S.C. §371 to violate 18 U.S.C. §610. . . .

The indictment charged, in essence, that petitioners had conspired from 1963 to May 9, 1968, to establish and maintain a fund that (1) would receive regular and systematic payments from Local 562 members and members of other locals working under the Union's jurisdiction; (2) would have the appearance, but not the reality of being an entity separate from the Union; and (3) would conceal contributions and expenditures by the Union in connection with federal elections in violation of §610.

The evidence tended to show, in addition to disbursements of about $150,000 by the fund to candidates in federal elections, an identity between the fund and the Union and a collection of well over $1 million in contributions to the fund by a method similar to that employed in the collection of dues or assessments. In particular, it was established that from 1949 through 1962 the Union maintained a political fund to which Union members and others working under the Union's jurisdiction were in fact required to contribute and that the fund was then succeeded in 1963 by the present fund, which was, in form, set up as a separate "voluntary" organization. Yet, a principal Union officer assumed the role of director of the present fund with full and unlimited control over its disbursements. . . .

On the other hand, the evidence also indicated that the political contributions by the fund were made from accounts strictly segregated from Union dues and assessments and that donations to the fund were not, in fact, necessary for employment or Union membership. The fund generally required contributors to sign authorization cards, which contained a statement that their donations were "voluntary . . . [and] no part of the dues or financial obligations of Local Union No. 562 . . . ," and the testimony was overwhelming from both those who contributed and those who did not, as well as from the collectors of contributions, that no specific pressure was exerted, and no reprisals were taken, to obtain donations. Significantly, the Union's attorney who had advised on the organization of the fund testified on cross-examination that his advice had been that payments to the fund could not be made a condition of employment or Local 562 membership, but it was immaterial whether contributions appeared compulsory to those solicited.

Under instructions to determine whether on this evidence the fund was in reality a Union fund or the contributors' fund, the jury found each defendant guilty. The jury also found specially that a willful violation of §610 was not contemplated, and the trial court imposed sentence accordingly. The Union was fined $5,000, while the individual defendants were each sentenced to one year's imprisonment and fined $1,000.

On appeal to the Court of Appeals for the Eighth Circuit, petitioners contended that . . . the evidence was insufficient to sustain a conspiracy to violate §610, and that §610, on its face or as construed and applied, abridged their rights under the First, Fifth, Sixth, and Seventeenth Amendments and Art. I, §2, of the Constitution. . . . The Court of Appeals in a four-to-three en banc decision . . . reject[ed] each of these claims. The gist of the court's decision . . . was that the Pipefitters fund was a subterfuge through which the Union made political contributions of Union monies in violation of §610. . . .

I

We begin with an analysis of §610.

First. The parties are in agreement that §610, despite its broad language, does not prohibit a labor organization from making, through the medium of a political fund organized by it, contributions or expenditures in connection with federal elections, so long as the monies expended are in some sense volunteered by those asked to contribute. . . . This construction of §610 is clearly correct.

The antecedents of §610 have previously been traced. . . . We need recall here only that the prohibition in §313 of the Federal Corrupt Practices Act of 1925, 43 Stat. 1074, on contributions by corporations in connection with federal elections was extended to labor organizations in the War Labor Disputes Act of 1943, 57 Stat. 163, but only for the duration of the war. . . . The prohibition on contributions was then permanently enacted into law in §304 of the Labor Management Relations Act, 1947, 61 Stat. 159, with the addition, however, of a proscription on "expenditures" and an extension of both prohibitions to payments in connection with federal primaries and political conventions as well as federal elections themselves. Yet, neither prohibition applied to payments by union political funds in connection with federal elections so long as the funds were financed in some sense by the voluntary donations of the union membership. Union political funds had come to prominence in the 1944 and 1946 election campaigns and had been extensively studied by special committees of both the House and the Senate. Against the backdrop of the committee findings and recommendations, the Senate debates upon the reach of §304 attached controlling significance to the voluntary source of financing of the funds. The unequivocal view of the proponents of §304 was that the contributions and expenditures of voluntarily financed funds did not violate that provision.

The special committees investigating the 1944 and 1946 campaigns devoted particular attention to the activities of the Political Action Committee (PAC) of the Congress of Industrial Organizations (CIO) because they had stirred considerable public controversy. . . .

Then, in 1947, Congress made permanent the application of §313 of the Corrupt Practices Act to labor organizations and closed the loopholes that were thought to have been exploited in the 1944 and 1946 elections. . . . [D]ebate [on the provision in the Senate] compellingly demonstrates that voluntarily financed union political funds were not believed to be prohibited by the broad wording of §304. Thus, Senator Taft stated:

> [I]t seems to me the conditions are exactly parallel, both as to corporations and labor organizations. [An association of manufacturers] receiving corporation funds and using them in an election would violate the law, in my opinion, exactly as the PAC, if it got its fund from labor unions, would violate the law. If the labor people should desire to set up a political organization and obtain direct contributions for it, there would be nothing unlawful in that. . . .

In response to a question by Senator Magnuson whether unions would be prohibited from publishing a newspaper "favoring a candidate, mentioning his name, or endorsing him for public office," Taft continued:

No; I do not think it means that. The union can issue a newspaper, and can charge the members for the newspaper, that is, the members who buy copies of the newspaper, and the union can put such matters in the newspaper if it wants to. The union can separate the payment of dues from the payment for a newspaper if its members are willing to do so, that is, if the members are willing to subscribe to that kind of a newspaper. I presume the members would be willing to do so. A union can publish such a newspaper, or unions can do as was done last year, organize something like the PAC, a political organization, and receive direct contributions, just so long as members of the union know what they are contributing to, and the dues which they pay into the union treasury are not used for such purpose.

When Magnuson rejoined that "all union members know that a part of their dues in these cases go for the publication of some labor [newspaper] organ," Taft concluded:

Yes. How fair is it? We will assume that 60 percent of a union's employees are for a Republican candidate and 40 percent are for a Democratic candidate. Does the Senator think the union members should be forced to contribute, without being asked to do so specifically, and without having a right to withdraw their payments, to the election of someone whom they do not favor? . . . If they are asked to contribute directly to the support of a newspaper or to the support of a labor political organization, they know what their money is to be used for and presumably approve it. From such contribution the organization can spend all the money it wants to with respect to such matters. But the prohibition is against labor unions using their members' dues for political purposes, which is exactly the same as the prohibition against a corporation using its stockholders' money for political purposes, and perhaps in violation of the wishes of many of its stockholders.

Senator Taft's view that a union cannot violate the law by spending political funds volunteered by its members was consistent with the legislative history of the War Labor Disputes Act and an express interpretation given to that Act by the Attorney General in 1944. His view also reflected concern that a broader application of §610 might raise constitutional questions of invasion of First Amendment freedoms, and he wished particularly to reassure colleagues who had reservations on that score and whose votes were necessary to override a predictable presidential veto. We conclude, accordingly, that his view of the limited reach of §610, entitled in any event to great weight, is in this instance controlling. We therefore hold that §610 does not apply to union contributions and expenditures from political funds financed in some sense by the voluntary donations of employees.

Section 205 of the Federal Election Campaign Act confirms this conclusion by adding at the end of §610 the following paragraph:

As used in this section, the phrase "contribution or expenditure" shall include any direct or indirect payment, distribution, loan, advance, deposit, or gift of money, or any services, or anything of value . . . to any candidate, campaign committee, or political party or organization, in connection with any election to any of the offices referred to in this section; but shall not include communications by a corporation to its stockholders and their families or by a labor organization to its members and their families on any subject; nonpartisan registration and get-out-the-vote campaigns by a corporation aimed at its stockholders and their families, or by a labor organization aimed at its members and their families; the establishment, administration, and solicitation of contributions to a separate segregated fund to be utilized for political purposes by a corporation or labor organization: Provided, That it shall be unlawful for such a fund to make a contribution or expenditure by utilizing money or anything of value secured by physical force, job discrimination, financial reprisals, or the threat of force, job discrimination, or financial reprisal; or by dues, fees, or other monies required as a condition of membership in a labor organization or as a condition of employment, or by monies obtained in any commercial transaction. 86 Stat. 10.

This amendment stemmed from a proposal offered by Representative Hansen on the House floor, to which the Senate acquiesced in conference. Hansen stated that the purpose of his proposal was . . . "to codify the court decisions interpreting (and the legislative history explicating) section 610 . . . and to spell out in more detail what a labor union or corporation can or cannot do in connection with a Federal election." Moreover, there was substantial agreement among his colleagues that the effect of his amendment was, in fact, mere codification and clarification, and even those who disagreed did not dispute that voluntarily financed union political funds are permissible. . . . This consensus that has now been captured in express terms in §610 cannot, of course, by itself conclusively establish what Congress had in mind in 1947. But it does "throw a cross light" on the earlier enactment that, together with the latter's legislative history, demonstrates beyond doubt the correctness of the parties' common ground of interpretation of §610.

Second. Where the litigants part company is in defining precisely when political contributions and expenditures by a union political fund fall outside the ambit of §610. The Government maintains, first, that a valid fund may not be the alter ego of the sponsoring union in the sense of being dominated by it and serving its purposes, regardless of the fund's source of financing. . . . The requirement that the fund be separate from the sponsoring union eliminates, in the Government's view, "the corroding effect of money employed in elections by aggregated power," which this Court has found to be one of the dual purposes underlying §610.

The Government urges, secondly, that in accordance with the legislative intent to protect minority interests from overbearing union leadership, which we have found to be the other purpose of §610, the fund may not be financed by monies actually required for employment or union membership or by payments that are effectively assessed, that is, solicited in circumstances inherently coercive. Petitioners, on the other hand, contend that, to be valid, a political fund need not be distinct from the sponsoring union and, further, that §610 permits the union to exercise institutional pressure, much as recognized charities do, in soliciting donations.

We think that neither side fully and accurately portrays the attributes of legitimate political funds. We hold that such a fund must be separate from the sponsoring union only in the sense that there must be a strict segregation of its monies from union dues and assessments. We hold, too, that although solicitation by union officials is permissible, such solicitation must be conducted under circumstances plainly indicating that donations are for a political purpose and that those solicited may decline to contribute without loss of job, union membership, or any other reprisal within the union's institutional power. Thus, we agree with the second half of the Government's position, but reject the first.

As Senator Taft's remarks quoted above indicate, the test of voluntariness under §610 focuses on whether the contributions solicited for political use are knowing free choice donations. The dominant concern in requiring that contributions be voluntary was, after all, to protect the dissenting stockholder or union member. Whether the solicitation scheme is designed to inform the individual solicited of the political nature of the fund and his freedom to refuse support is, therefore, determinative.

Nowhere, however, has Congress required that the political organization be formally or functionally independent of union control or that union officials be barred from soliciting contributions or even precluded from determining how the monies raised will be spent. The Government's argument to the contrary in the first half of its position is based on a misunderstanding of the purposes of §610. When Congress prohibited labor organizations from making contributions or expenditures in connection with federal elections, it was, of course, concerned not only to protect minority interests within the union but to eliminate the effect of aggregated wealth on federal elections. But the aggregated wealth it plainly had in mind was the general union treasury—not the funds donated by union members of their own free and knowing choice. . . . Indeed, Taft clearly espoused the union political organization merely as an alternative to permissible direct political action by the union itself through publications endorsing candidates in federal elections. The only conditions for that kind of direct electioneering were that the costs of publication be financed through individual subscriptions rather than through union dues and that the newspapers be recognized by the subscribers as political organs that they could refuse to purchase. Neither the absence of even a formally separate organization, the solicitation of subscriptions by the union, nor the method for choosing the candidates to be supported was mentioned as being material. Similarly, the only requirements for permissible political organizations were that they be funded through separate contributions and that they be recognized by the donors as political organizations to which they could refuse support. . . .

This conclusion, too, we find confirmed by §205 of the Federal Election Campaign Act. . . . [Section] 205 plainly permits union officials to establish, administer, and solicit contributions for a political fund. The conditions for that activity are that the fund be "separate" and "segregated" and that its contributions and expenditures not be financed through physical force, job discrimination, or financial reprisal or the "threat" thereof, or through "dues, fees, or other monies required as a condition of membership in a labor organization or as a condition of employment." The quoted language is admittedly subject to contrary interpretations. "Separate" could (and normally when juxtaposed to "segregated" would) be read to mean an apartness beyond "segregated"; "threat" could be construed as referring only to the expression of an actual intention to inflict injury; and "dues, fees, or other monies required as a condition of membership in a labor organization or as a condition of employment" could be interpreted to mean only actual dues or assessments. But we think that the legislative history of §205 establishes that "separate" is synonymous with "segregated"; that "threat" includes the creation of an appearance of an intent to inflict injury even without a design to carry it out; and that "dues, fees, or other monies required as a condition of membership in a labor organization or as a condition of employment" includes contributions effectively assessed even if not actually required for employment or union membership. . . .

Construed as we have done, §205 of the Federal Election Campaign Act does nothing more than accomplish the expressed purpose of its author—that is, codify and clarify prior law. But since we have arrived at our interpretation without reference to prior law, §205 once again throws on §610 as embodied in §304 of the Labor Management Relations Act "a cross light" that confirms our understanding of the law applicable to this prosecution. . . .

Vacated in part, reversed in part, and remanded with directions.

Justice POWELL, with whom Chief Justice BURGER joined, dissenting:

The decision of the Court today will have a profound effect upon the role of labor unions and corporations in the political life of this country. The holding, reversing a trend since 1907, opens the way for major participation in politics by the largest aggregations of economic power, the great unions and corporations. This occurs at a time, paradoxically, when public and legislative interest has focused on limiting—rather than enlarging—the influence upon the elective process of concentrations of wealth and power. . . .

[T]he opinion of the Court today, adopting an interpretation of §610 at variance with its language and purpose, goes a long way toward returning unions and corporations to an unregulated status with respect to political contributions. This opening of the door to extensive corporate and union influence on the elective and legislative processes must be viewed with genuine concern. This seems to me to be a regressive step as contrasted with the numerous legislative and judicial actions in recent years designed to assure that elections are indeed free and representative.

———

Just six years after its decision in *Pipefitters*, the Court was once again called on to determine the validity of a statute limiting campaign contributions and expenditures by corporations. At issue was Massachusetts General Law, Chapter 55, §8 (West Supp. 1977), which provided:

No corporation carrying on the business of a bank, trust, surety, indemnity, safe deposit, insurance, railroad, street railway, telegraph, telephone, gas, electric light, heat, power, canal, aqueduct, or water company, . . . no trustee or trustees owning or holding the majority of the stock of such a corporation, no business corporation incorporated under the laws of or doing business in the commonwealth and no officer or agent acting in behalf of any corporation mentioned in this section, shall directly or indirectly give, pay, expend or contribute, or promise to give, pay, expend or contribute, any money or other valuable thing for the purpose of aiding, promoting or preventing the nomination or election of any person to public office, or aiding, promoting or antagonizing the interests of any political party, or influencing or affecting the vote on any question submitted to the voters, other than one materially affecting any of the property, business or assets of the corporation. No question submitted to the voters solely concerning the taxation of the income, property or transactions of individuals shall be deemed materially to affect the property, business or assets of the corporation. No person or persons, no political committee, and no person acting under the authority of a political committee, or in its behalf, shall solicit or receive from such corporation or such holders of stock any gift, payment, expenditure, contribution or promise to give, pay, expend or contribute for any such purpose. Any corporation violating any provision of this section shall be punished by a fine of not more than fifty thousand dollars and any officer, director or agent of the corporation violating any provision thereof or authorizing such violation, . . . shall be punished by a fine of not more than ten thousand dollars or by imprisonment for not more than one year, or both.

First National Bank of Boston v. Bellotti

435 U.S. 765 (1978)

Mr. Justice POWELL delivered the opinion of the Court. . . .

I

Appellants wanted to spend money to publicize their views on a proposed constitutional amendment that was to be submitted to the voters as a ballot question at a general election on November 2, 1976. The amendment would have permitted the legislature to impose a graduated tax on the income of individuals. After appellee, the Attorney General of Massachusetts, informed appellants that he intended to enforce §8 against them, they brought this action seeking to have the statute declared unconstitutional. . . . Appellants argued that §8 violates the First Amendment, the Due Process and Equal Protection Clauses of the Fourteenth Amendment, and similar provisions of the Massachusetts Constitution. They prayed that the statute be declared unconstitutional on its face and as it would be applied to their proposed expenditures. . . .

III

The court below framed the principal question in this case as whether and to what extent corporations have First Amendment rights. We believe that the court posed the wrong question. The Constitution often protects interests broader than those of the party seeking their vindication. The First Amendment, in particular, serves significant societal interests. The proper question therefore is not whether corporations "have" First Amendment rights and, if so, whether they are coextensive with those of natural persons. Instead, the question must be whether §8 abridges expression that the First Amendment was meant to protect. We hold that it does.

A

The speech proposed by appellants is at the heart of the First Amendment's protection. . . .

If the speakers here were not corporations, no one would suggest that the State could silence their proposed speech. It is the type of speech indispensable to decisionmaking in a democracy, and this is no less true because the speech comes from a corporation rather than an individual. The inherent worth of the speech in terms of its capacity for informing the public does not depend upon the identity of its source, whether corporation, association, union, or individual.

The court below nevertheless held that corporate speech is protected by the First Amendment only when it pertains directly to the corporation's business interests. In deciding whether this novel and restrictive gloss on the First Amendment comports with the Constitution and the precedents of this Court, we need not survey the outer boundaries of the Amendment's protection of corporate speech, or address the abstract question whether corporations have the full measure of rights that individuals enjoy under the First Amendment. The question in this case, simply put, is whether the corporate identity of the speaker deprives this proposed speech of what otherwise would be its clear entitlement to protection. We turn now to that question.

B

The court below found confirmation of the legislature's definition of the scope of a corporation's First Amendment rights in the language of the Fourteenth Amendment. Noting that the First Amendment is applicable to the States through the Fourteenth, and seizing upon the observation that corporations "cannot claim for themselves the liberty which the Fourteenth Amendment guarantees," *Pierce v. Society of Sisters*, 268 U.S. 510, 535 (1925), the court concluded that a corporation's First Amendment rights must derive from its property rights under the Fourteenth.

This is an artificial mode of analysis, untenable under decisions of this Court. . . .

Freedom of speech and the other freedoms encompassed by the First Amendment always have been viewed as fundamental components of the liberty safeguarded by the Due Process Clause, and the Court has not identified a separate source for the right when it has been asserted by corporations. . . . Yet appellee suggests that First Amendment rights generally have been afforded only to corporations engaged in the communications business or through which individuals express themselves, and the court below apparently accepted the "materially affecting" theory as the conceptual common denominator between appellee's position and the precedents of this Court. It is true that the "materially affecting" requirement would have been satisfied in the Court's decisions affording protection to the speech of media corporations and corporations otherwise in the business of communication or entertainment, and to the commercial speech of business corporations. In such cases, the speech would be connected to the corporation's business almost by definition. But the effect on the business of the corporation was not the governing rationale in any of these decisions. None of them mentions, let alone attributes significance to, the fact that the subject of the challenged communication materially affected the corporation's business.

The press cases emphasize the special and constitutionally recognized role of that institution in informing and educating the public, offering criticism, and providing a forum for discussion and debate. *Mills v. Alabama*, 384 U.S., at 219. But the press does not have a monopoly on either the First Amendment or the ability to enlighten. Similarly, the Court's decisions involving corporations in the business of communication or entertainment are based not only on the role of the First Amendment in fostering individual self-expression but also on its role in affording the public access to discussion, debate, and the dissemination of information and ideas. See *Red Lion Broadcasting Co. v. FCC, supra.* Even decisions seemingly based exclusively on the individual's right to express himself acknowledge that the expression may contribute to society's edification. *Winters v. New York*, 333 U.S. 507, 510 (1948).

Nor do our recent commercial speech cases lend support to appellee's business interest theory. They illustrate that the First Amendment goes beyond protection of the press and the self-expression of individuals to prohibit government from limiting the stock of information from which members of the public may draw. A commercial advertisement is constitutionally protected not so much because it pertains to the seller's business as because it furthers the societal interest in the "free flow of commercial information." *Virginia State Bd. of Pharmacy v. Virginia Citizens Consumer Council, Inc.*, 425 U.S. 748, 764 (1976).

C

We thus find no support in the First or Fourteenth Amendment, or in the decisions of this Court, for the proposition that speech that otherwise would be within the protection of the First Amendment loses that protection simply because its source is a corporation that cannot prove, to the satisfaction of a court, a material effect on its business or property. The "materially affecting" requirement is not an identification of the boundaries of corporate speech etched by the Constitution itself. Rather, it amounts to an impermissible legislative prohibition of speech based on the identity of the interests that spokesmen may represent in public debate over controversial issues and a requirement that the speaker have a sufficiently great interest in the subject to justify communication.

Section 8 permits a corporation to communicate to the public its views on certain referendum subjects — those materially affecting its business — but not others. It also singles out one kind of ballot question — individual taxation — as a subject about which corporations may never make their ideas public. The legislature has drawn the line between permissible and impermissible speech according to whether there is a sufficient nexus, as defined by the legislature, between the issue presented to the voters and the business interests of the speaker.

In the realm of protected speech, the legislature is constitutionally disqualified from dictating the subjects about which persons may speak and the speakers who may address a public issue. *Police Dept. of Chicago v. Mosley*, 408 U.S. 92, 96 (1972). If a legislature may direct business corporations to "stick to business," it also may limit other corporations—religious, charitable, or civic—to their respective "business" when addressing the public. Such power in government to channel the expression of views is unacceptable under the First Amendment. Especially where, as here, the legislature's suppression of speech suggests an attempt to give one side of a debatable public question an advantage in expressing its views to the people, the First Amendment is plainly offended. Yet the State contends that its action is necessitated by governmental interests of the highest order. We next consider these asserted interests.

IV

The constitutionality of §8's prohibition of the "exposition of ideas" by corporations turns on whether it can survive the exacting scrutiny necessitated by a state-imposed restriction of freedom of speech. Especially where, as here, a prohibition is directed at speech itself, and the speech is intimately related to the process of governing, "the State may prevail only upon showing a subordinating interest which is compelling," *Bates v. City of Little Rock*, 361 U.S. 516, 524 (1960), "and the burden is on the Government to show the existence of such an interest," *Elrod v. Burns*, 427 U.S. 347, 362 (1976). Even then, the State must employ means "closely drawn to avoid unnecessary abridgment." *Buckley v. Valeo*, 424 U.S., at 25.

The Supreme Judicial Court did not subject §8 to "the critical scrutiny demanded under accepted First Amendment and equal protection principles," *Buckley, supra*, 424 U.S., at 11, because of its view that the First Amendment does not apply to appellants' proposed speech. For this reason the court did not even discuss the State's interests in considering appellants' First Amendment argument. The court adverted to the conceivable interests served by §8 only in rejecting appellants' equal protection claim. Appellee nevertheless advances two principal justifications for the prohibition of corporate speech. The first is the State's interest in sustaining the active role of the individual citizen in the electoral process and thereby preventing diminution of the citizen's confidence in government. The second is the interest in protecting the rights of shareholders whose views differ from those expressed by management on behalf of the corporation. However weighty these interests may be in the context of partisan candidate elections, they either are not implicated in this case or are not served at all, or in other than a random manner, by the prohibition in §8.

A

Preserving the integrity of the electoral process, preventing corruption, and "sustain[ing] the active, alert responsibility of the individual citizen in a democracy for the wise conduct of government" are interests of the highest importance. *United States v. United Automobile Workers*, 352 U.S. 567, 575 (1957). Preservation of the individual citizen's confidence in government is equally important. *Buckley, supra*, 424 U.S., at 27.

Appellee advances a number of arguments in support of his view that these interests are endangered by corporate participation in discussion of a referendum issue. They hinge upon the assumption that such participation would exert an undue influence on the outcome of a referendum vote, and—in the end—destroy the confidence of the people in the democratic process and the integrity of government. According to appellee, corporations are wealthy and powerful and their views may drown out other points of view. If appellee's arguments were supported by record or legislative findings that corporate advocacy threatened imminently to undermine democratic processes, thereby denigrating rather than serving First Amendment interests, these arguments would merit our consideration. But there has been no showing that the relative voice of corporations has been overwhelming or even significant in influencing referenda in Massachusetts, or that there has been any threat to the confidence of the citizenry in government.

Nor are appellee's arguments inherently persuasive or supported by the precedents of this Court. Referenda are held on issues, not candidates for public office. The risk of corruption perceived in cases involving candidate elections simply is not present in a popular vote on a public issue. To be sure, corporate advertising may influence the outcome of the vote; this would be its purpose. But the fact that advocacy may persuade the electorate is hardly a reason to suppress it: The Constitution "protects expression which is eloquent no less than that which is unconvincing." *Kingsley Int'l Pictures Corp. v. Regents*, 360 U.S., at 689. . . . Moreover, the people in our democracy are entrusted with the responsibility for judging and evaluating the relative merits of conflicting arguments. They may consider, in making their judgment, the source and credibility of the advocate. But if there be any danger that the people cannot evaluate the information and arguments advanced by appellants, it is a danger contemplated by the Framers of the First Amendment. In sum, "[a] restriction so destructive of the right of public discussion [as §8], without greater or more imminent danger to the public interest than existed in this case, is incompatible with the freedoms secured by the First Amendment." *Thomas v. Collins*, 323 U.S. 516, 537 (1945).

B

Finally, appellee argues that §8 protects corporate shareholders, an interest that is both legitimate and traditionally within the province of state law. *Cort v. Ash*, 422 U.S. 66, 82-84 (1975). The statute is said to serve this interest by preventing the use of corporate resources in furtherance of views with which some shareholders may disagree. This purpose is belied, however, by the provisions of the statute, which are both underinclusive and overinclusive.

The underinclusiveness of the statute is self-evident. Corporate expenditures with respect to a referendum are prohibited, while corporate activity with respect to the passage or defeat of legislation is permitted, even though corporations may engage in lobbying more often than they take positions on ballot questions submitted to the voters. Nor does §8 prohibit a corporation from expressing its views, by the expenditure of corporate funds, on any public issue until it becomes the subject of a referendum, though the displeasure of disapproving shareholders is unlikely to be any less.

The fact that a particular kind of ballot question has been singled out for special treatment undermines the likelihood of a genuine state interest in protecting shareholders. It suggests instead that the legislature may have been concerned with silencing corporations on a particular subject. . . . Nor is the fact that §8 is limited to banks and business corporations without relevance. Excluded from its provisions and criminal sanctions are entities or organized groups in which numbers of persons may hold an interest or membership, and which often have resources comparable to those of large corporations. Minorities in such groups or entities may have interests with respect to institutional speech quite comparable to those of minority shareholders in a corporation. Thus the exclusion of Massachusetts business trusts, real estate investment trusts, labor unions, and other associations undermines the plausibility of the State's purported concern for the persons who happen to be shareholders in the banks and corporations covered by §8.

The overinclusiveness of the statute is demonstrated by the fact that §8 would prohibit a corporation from supporting or opposing a referendum proposal even if its shareholders unanimously authorized the contribution or expenditure. Ultimately shareholders may decide, through the procedures of corporate democracy, whether their corporation should engage in debate on public issues. Acting through their power to elect the board of directors or to insist upon protective provisions in the corporation's charter, shareholders normally are presumed competent to protect their own interests. . . . Assuming, *arguendo,* that protection of shareholders is a "compelling" interest under the circumstances of this case, we find "no substantially relevant correlation between the governmental interest asserted and the State's effort" to prohibit appellants from speaking. *Shelton v. Tucker,* 364 U.S., at 485.

V

Because that portion of §8 challenged by appellants prohibits protected speech in a manner unjustified by a compelling state interest, it must be invalidated. The judgment of the Supreme Judicial Court is *Reversed.*

Justice WHITE, with whom Justice BRENNAN and Justice MARSHALL join, dissenting:

The Court's fundamental error is its failure to realize that the state regulatory interests in terms of which the alleged curtailment of First Amendment rights accomplished by the statute must be evaluated are themselves derived from the First Amendment. The question posed by this case, as approached by the Court, is whether the State has struck the best possible balance, i.e., the one which it would have chosen, between competing First Amendment interests. Although in my view the choice made by the State would survive even the most exacting scrutiny, perhaps a rational argument might be made to the contrary. What is inexplicable, is for the Court to substitute its judgment as to the proper balance for that of Massachusetts where the State has passed legislation reasonably designed to further First Amendment interests in the context of the political arena where the expertise of legislators is at its peak and that of judges is at its very lowest. . . .

There is now little doubt that corporate communications come within the scope of the First Amendment. This, however, is merely the starting point of analysis, because an examination of the First Amendment values that corporate expression furthers and the threat to the functioning of a free society it is capable of posing reveals that it is not fungible with communications emanating from individuals and is subject to restrictions which individual expression is not. Indeed, what some have considered to be the principal function of the First Amendment, the use of communication as a means of self-expression, self-realization, and self-fulfillment, is not at all furthered by corporate speech. It is clear that the communications of profitmaking corporations are not an integral part of the development of ideas, of mental exploration and of the affirmation of self. They do not represent a manifestation of individual freedom or choice. . . . Shareholders in such entities do not share a common set of political or social views, and they certainly have not invested their money for the purpose of advancing political or social causes or in an enterprise engaged in the business of disseminating news and opinion. . . .

There is an additional overriding interest related to the prevention of corporate domination which is substantially advanced by Massachusetts' restrictions upon corporate contributions: assuring that shareholders are not compelled to support and financially further beliefs with which they disagree where, as is the case here, the issue involved does not materially affect the business, property, or other affairs of the corporation. . . . The interest which the State wishes to protect here is identical to that which the Court has previously held to be protected by the First Amendment: the right to adhere to one's own beliefs and to refuse to support the dissemination of the personal and political views of others, regardless of how large a majority they may compose. . . .

Justice Rehnquist, dissenting:

Since it cannot be disputed that the mere creation of a corporation does not invest it with all the liberties enjoyed by natural persons, our inquiry must seek to determine which constitutional protections are "incidental to its very existence."

There can be little doubt that when a State creates a corporation with the power to acquire and utilize property, it necessarily and implicitly guarantees that the corporation will not be deprived of that property absent due process of law. Likewise, when a State charters a corporation for the purpose of publishing a newspaper, it necessarily assumes that the corporation is entitled to the liberty of the press essential to the conduct of its business. . . .

It cannot be so readily concluded that the right of political expression is equally necessary to carry out the functions of a corporation organized for commercial purposes. A State grants to a business corporation the blessings of potentially perpetual life and limited liability to enhance its efficiency as an economic entity. It might reasonably be concluded that those properties, so beneficial in the economic sphere, pose special dangers in the political sphere. Furthermore, it might be argued that liberties of political expression are not at all necessary to effectuate the purposes for which States permit commercial corporations to exist. So long as the Judicial Branches of the State and Federal Governments remain open to protect the corporation's interest in its property, it has no need, though it may have the desire, to petition the political branches for similar protection. Indeed, the States might reasonably fear that the corporation would use its economic power to obtain further benefits beyond those already bestowed. I would think that any particular form of organization upon which the State confers special privileges or immunities different from those of natural persons would be subject to like regulation, whether the organization is a labor union, a partnership, a trade association, or a corporation.

I can see no basis for concluding that the liberty of a corporation to engage in political activity with regard to matters having no material effect on its business is necessarily incidental to the purposes for which the Commonwealth permitted these corporations to be organized or admitted within its boundaries. . . .

Twelve years later, in *Austin*, below, the Court considered a state statute that included provisions modeled on FECA Section 441b, requiring corporations and labor unions to use segregated funds — or political action committees — to finance independent expenditures made in the course of federal elections. This time the dissenters' views from *Bellotti* constituted the majority rationale.

Austin v. Michigan Chamber of Commerce

494 U.S. 652 (1990)

Justice MARSHALL delivered the opinion of the Court.

In this appeal, we must determine whether §54(1) of the Michigan Campaign Finance Act, violates either the First or the Fourteenth Amendment to the Constitution. Section 54(1) prohibits corporations from using corporate treasury funds for independent expenditures in support of, or in opposition to, any candidate in elections for state office. Corporations are allowed, however, to make such expenditures from segregated funds used solely for political purposes. In response to a challenge brought by the Michigan State Chamber of Commerce (Chamber), the Sixth Circuit held that §54(1) could not be applied to the Chamber, a Michigan nonprofit corporation, without violating the First Amendment. Although we agree that expressive rights are implicated in this case, we hold that application of §54(1) to the Chamber is constitutional because the provision is narrowly tailored to serve a compelling state interest. Accordingly, we reverse the judgment of the Court of Appeals.

I

Section 54(1) of the Michigan Campaign Finance Act prohibits corporations from making contributions and independent expenditures in connection with state candidate elections. . . . The Chamber, a nonprofit Michigan corporation, challenges the constitutionality of this statutory scheme. The Chamber comprises more than 8,000 members, three-quarters of whom are for-profit corporations.

The Chamber's general treasury is funded through annual dues required of all members. . . .

In June 1985 Michigan scheduled a special election to fill a vacancy in the Michigan House of Representatives. Although the Chamber had established and funded a separate political fund, it sought to use its general treasury funds to place in a local newspaper an advertisement supporting a specific candidate. As the Act made such an expenditure punishable as a felony, the Chamber brought suit in District Court for injunctive relief against enforcement of the Act, arguing that the restriction on expenditures is unconstitutional under both the First and the Fourteenth Amendments. The District Court upheld the statute. The Sixth Circuit reversed, reasoning that the expenditure restrictions as applied to the Chamber, violated the First Amendment. . . .

II

To determine whether Michigan's restriction on corporate political expenditures may constitutionally be applied to the Chamber, we must ascertain whether it burdens the exercise of political speech and, if it does, whether it is narrowly tailored to serve a compelling state interest. Certainly, the use of funds to support a political candidate is "speech"; independent campaign expenditures constitute "political expression 'at the core of our electoral process and of the First Amendment freedoms.' " *Buckley v. Valeo*, 424 U.S. 1, 39 (1976) (quoting *Williams v. Rhodes*, 393 U.S. 23, 32 (1968)). The mere fact that the Chamber is a corporation does not remove its speech from the ambit of the First Amendment.

A

This Court concluded in *FEC v. Massachusetts Citizens for Life, Inc.*, 479 U.S. 238 (1986) (*MCFL*), that a federal statute requiring corporations to make independent political expenditures only through special segregated funds burdens corporate freedom of expression. *MCFL*, 479 U.S., at 252. The Court reasoned that the small nonprofit corporation in that case would face certain organizational and financial hurdles in establishing and administering a segregated political fund. . . . These hurdles "impose[d] administrative costs that many small entities [might] be unable to bear" and "create[d] a disincentive for such organizations to engage in political speech." *Id.* at 254.

Despite the Chamber's success in administering its separate political fund, Michigan's segregated fund requirement still burdens the Chamber's exercise of expression because "the corporation is *not* free to use its general funds for campaign advocacy purposes." *MCFL*, 479 U.S., at 252. The Act imposes requirements similar to those in the federal statute involved in *MCFL*: a segregated fund must have a treasurer, and its administrators must keep detailed accounts of contributions, and file with state officials a statement of organization. In addition, a nonprofit corporation like the Chamber may solicit contributions to its political fund only from members, stockholders of members, officers or directors of members, and the spouses of any of these persons. Although these requirements do not stifle corporate speech entirely, they do burden expressive activity. Thus, they must be justified by a compelling state interest.

B

The State contends that the unique legal and economic characteristics of corporations necessitate some regulation of their political expenditures to avoid corruption or the appearance of corruption. State law grants corporations special advantages — such as limited liability, perpetual life, and favorable treatment of the accumulation and distribution of assets — that enhance their ability to attract capital and to deploy their resources in ways that maximize the return on their shareholders' investments. These state-created advantages not only allow corporations to play a dominant role in the Nation's economy, but also permit them to use "resources amassed in the economic marketplace" to obtain "an unfair advantage in the political marketplace." *MCFL*, 479 U.S., at 257. . . . [We] have recognized that "the compelling governmental interest in preventing corruption support[s] the restriction of the influence of political war chests funneled through the corporate form." *NCPAC, supra,* 470 U.S., at 500-501.

The Chamber argues that this concern about corporate domination of the political process is insufficient to justify a restriction on independent expenditures. Although this Court has distinguished these expenditures from direct contributions in the context of federal laws regulating individual donors, it has also recognized that a legislature might demonstrate a danger of real or apparent corruption posed by such expenditures when made by corporations to influence candidate elections. Regardless of whether this danger of "financial *quid pro quo*" corruption may be sufficient to justify a restriction on independent expenditures, Michigan's regulation aims at a different type of corruption in the political arena: the corrosive and distorting effects of immense aggregations of wealth that are accumulated with the help of the corporate form and that have little or no correlation to the public's support for the corporation's political ideas. The Act . . . ensures that expenditures reflect actual public support for the political ideas espoused by corporations.

We emphasize that the mere fact that corporations may accumulate large amounts of wealth is not the justification for §54; rather, the unique state-conferred corporate structure that facilitates the amassing of large treasuries warrants the limit on independent expenditures. Corporate wealth can unfairly influence elections when it is deployed in the form of independent expenditures, just as it can when it assumes the guise of political contributions. We therefore hold that the State has articulated a sufficiently compelling rationale to support its restriction on independent expenditures by corporations.

C

We next turn to the question whether the Act is sufficiently narrowly tailored to achieve its goal. We find that the Act is precisely targeted to eliminate the distortion caused by corporate spending while also allowing corporations to express their political views. . . . [T]he Act does not impose an *absolute* ban on all forms of corporate political spending but permits corporations to make independent political expenditures through separate segregated funds. Because persons contributing to such funds understand that their money will be used solely for political purposes, the speech generated accurately reflects contributors' support for the corporation's political views.

The Chamber argues that §54(1) is substantially overinclusive, because it includes within its scope closely held corporations that do not possess vast reservoirs of capital. . . . Although some closely held corporations, just as some publicly held ones, may not have accumulated significant amounts of wealth, they receive from the State the special benefits conferred by the corporate structure and present the potential for distorting the political process. This potential for distortion justifies §54(1)'s general applicability to all corporations. The section therefore is not substantially overbroad.

III

The Chamber contends that even if the Campaign Finance Act is constitutional with respect to for-profit corporations, it nonetheless cannot be applied to a nonprofit ideological corporation like a chamber of commerce. In *MCFL*, we held that the nonprofit organization there had "features more akin to voluntary political associations than business firms, and therefore should not have to bear burdens on independent spending solely because of [its] incorporated status." 479 U.S., at 263. In reaching that conclusion, we enumerated three characteristics of the corporation that were "essential" to our holding. Because the Chamber does not share these crucial features, the Constitution does not require that it be exempted from the generally applicable provisions of §54(1).

The first characteristic of Massachusetts Citizens for Life, Inc., that distinguished it from ordinary business corporations was that the organization "was formed for the express purpose of promoting political ideas, and cannot engage in business activities." *Id.*, at 264. . . . In contrast, the Chamber's bylaws set forth more varied purposes, several of which are not inherently political. . . .

We described the second feature of MCFL as the absence of "shareholders or other persons affiliated so as to have a claim on its assets or earnings. This ensures that persons connected with the organization will have no economic disincentive for disassociating with it if they disagree with its political activity." 479 U.S., at 264. Although the Chamber also lacks shareholders, many of its members may be similarly reluctant to withdraw as members even if they disagree with the Chamber's political expression, because they wish to benefit from the Chamber's nonpolitical programs and to establish contacts with other members of the business community. The Chamber's political agenda is sufficiently distinct from its educational and outreach programs that members who disagree with the former may continue to pay dues to participate in the latter. . . .

The final characteristic upon which we relied in *MCFL* was the organization's independence from the influence of business corporations. On this score, the Chamber differs most greatly from the Massachusetts organization. MCFL was not established by, and had a policy of not accepting contributions from, business corporations. . . . In striking contrast, more than three-quarters of the Chamber's members are business corporations, whose political contributions and expenditures can constitutionally be regulated by the State. As we read the Act, a corporation's payments into the Chamber's general treasury would not be considered payments to influence an election, so they would not be "contributions" or "expenditures," and would not be subject to the Act's limitations. Business corporations therefore could circumvent the Act's restriction by funneling money through the

Chamber's general treasury. Because the Chamber accepts money from for-profit corporations, it could, absent application of §54(1), serve as a conduit for corporate political spending. In sum, the Chamber does not possess the features that would compel the State to exempt it from restriction on independent political expenditures.

IV

The Chamber also attacks §54(1) as underinclusive because it does not regulate the independent expenditures of unincorporated labor unions. Whereas unincorporated unions, and indeed individuals, may be able to amass large treasuries, they do so without the significant state-conferred advantages of the corporate structure. . . .

Moreover, labor unions differ from corporations in that union members who disagree with a union's political activities need not give up full membership in the organization to avoid supporting its political activities. Although a union and an employer may require that all bargaining unit employees become union members, a union may not compel those employees to support financially "union activities beyond those germane to collective bargaining, contract administration, and grievance adjustment." *Communications Workers v. Beck*, 487 U.S. 735, 745 (1988). An employee who objects to a union's political activities thus can decline to contribute to those activities, while continuing to enjoy the benefits derived from the union's performance of its duties as the exclusive representative of the bargaining unit on labor-management issues. As a result, the funds available for a union's political activities more accurately reflects members' support for the organization's political views than does a corporation's general treasury. . . .

VI

Michigan identified as a serious danger the significant possibility that corporate political expenditures will undermine the integrity of the political process, and it has implemented a narrowly tailored solution to that problem. By requiring corporations to make all independent political expenditures through a separate fund made up of money solicited expressly for political purposes, the Michigan Campaign Finance Act reduces the threat that huge corporate treasuries amassed with the aid of favorable state laws will be used to influence unfairly the outcome of elections. The Michigan Chamber of Commerce does not exhibit the characteristics identified in *MCFL* that would require the State to exempt it from a generally applicable restriction on independent corporate expenditures. We therefore reverse the decision of the Court of Appeals.

It is so ordered.

Justice SCALIA, dissenting:

"Attention all citizens. To assure the fairness of elections by preventing disproportionate expression of the views of any single powerful group, your Government has decided that the following associations of persons shall be prohibited from speaking or writing in support of any candidate: _____." In permitting Michigan to make private corporations the first object of this Orwellian announcement, the

Court today endorses the principle that too much speech is an evil that the democratic majority can proscribe. I dissent because that principle is contrary to our case law and incompatible with the absolutely central truth of the First Amendment: that government cannot be trusted to assure, through censorship, the "fairness" of political debate.

The Court's opinion says that political speech of corporations can be regulated because "[s]tate law grants [them] special advantages," and because this "unique state-conferred corporate structure . . . facilitates the amassing of large treasuries." This analysis seeks to create one good argument by combining two bad ones. Those individuals who form that type of voluntary association known as a corporation are, to be sure, given special advantages . . . that the State is under no obligation to confer. But so are other associations and private individuals given all sorts of special advantages that the State need not confer. . . . It is rudimentary that the State cannot exact as the price of those special advantages the forfeiture of First Amendment rights. The categorical suspension of the right of any person, or of any association of persons, to speak out on political matters must be justified by a compelling state need. That is why the Court puts forward its second bad argument, the fact that corporations "amas[s] large treasuries." But that alone is also not sufficient justification for the suppression of political speech, unless one thinks it would be lawful to prohibit men and women whose net worth is above a certain figure from endorsing political candidates. Neither of these two flawed arguments is improved by combining them. . . .

The contention that prohibiting overt advocacy for or against a political candidate satisfies a "compelling need" to avoid "corruption" is easily dismissed. . . . The Court does not try to defend the proposition that independent advocacy poses a substantial risk of political "corruption," as English speakers understand that term. Rather, it asserts that that concept . . . is really just a narrow subspecies of a hitherto unrecognized genus of political corruption: . . . "the corrosive and distorting effects of immense aggregations of wealth that are accumulated with the help of the corporate form and that have little or no correlation to the public's support for the corporations' political ideas." Under this mode of analysis, virtually anything the Court deems politically undesirable can be turned into political corruption — by simply describing its effects as politically "corrosive," which is close enough to "corruptive" to qualify. It is sad to think that the First Amendment will ultimately be brought down not by brute force but by poetic metaphor. . . .

[Moreover] I doubt that those who framed and adopted the First Amendment would agree that avoiding the New Corruption, that is, calibrating political speech to the degree of public opinion that supports it, is even a desirable objective, much less one that is important enough to qualify as a compelling state interest. Those Founders designed, of course, a system in which popular ideas would ultimately prevail; but also, through the First Amendment, a system in which true ideas could readily become popular. For the latter purpose, the calibration that the Court today endorses is precisely backwards: To the extent a valid proposition has scant public support, it should have wider rather than narrower public circulation. . . .

Despite all the talk about "corruption and the appearance of corruption" — evils that are not significantly implicated and that can be avoided in many other ways — it is entirely obvious that the object of the law we have approved today is not to prevent wrongdoing but to prevent speech. Since those private associations known as corporations have so much money, they will speak so much more, and their views will be given inordinate prominence in election campaigns. This is not an argument that our democratic traditions allow—neither with respect to individuals associated in corporations nor with respect to other categories of individuals whose speech may be "unduly" extensive (because they are rich) or "unduly" persuasive (because they are movie stars) or "unduly" respected (because they are clergymen). The premise of our system is that there is no such thing as too much speech—that the people are not foolish but intelligent, and will separate the wheat from the chaff. . . .

Justice KENNEDY, with whom Justice SCALIA and Justice O'CONNOR joined, dissenting:

We confront here society's interest in free and informed discussion on political issues, a discourse vital to the capacity for self-government. "In the realm of protected speech, the legislature is constitutionally disqualified from dictating the subjects about which persons may speak and the speakers who may address a public issue." *First National Bank of Boston v. Bellotti*, 435 U.S. 765, 784-785 (1978). There is little doubt that by silencing advocacy groups that operate in the corporate form and forbidding them to speak on electoral politics, Michigan's law suffers from both of these constitutional defects.

First, the Act prohibits corporations from speaking on a particular subject, the subject of candidate elections. It is a basic precept that the State may not confine speech to certain subjects. Content-based restrictions are the essence of censorial power. . . .

Second, the Act discriminates on the basis of the speaker's identity. Under the Michigan law, any person or group other than a corporation may engage in political debate over candidate elections; but corporations, even nonprofit corporations that have unique views of vital importance to the electorate, must remain mute. Our precedents condemn this censorship. . . . By using distinctions based upon both the speech and the speaker, the Act engages in the rawest form of censorship: the State censors what a particular segment of the political community might say with regard to candidates who stand for election. . . .

The second censorship scheme validated by today's holding is the one imposed by the Court. . . . Those who thought that the First Amendment exists to protect all points of view in candidate elections will be disillusioned by the Court's opinion today; for that protection is given only to a preferred class of nonprofit corporate speakers: small, single issue nonprofit corporations that pass the Court's own vague test for determining who are the favored participants in the electoral process. . . .

To create second-class speakers that can be stifled on the subject of candidate qualifications is to silence some of the most significant participants in the American public dialogue. . . . I reject any argument based on the idea that these groups and their views are not of importance and value to the self-fulfillment and self-expression of their members, and to the rich public dialogue that must be the mark of any free society. To suggest otherwise is contrary to the American political experience and our own judicial knowledge.

>> *"Distorting Effects."*   Justice Marshall's opinion for the Court in *Austin* seems to rely on three arguments to support the state's regulation. First, using Chief Justice Rehnquist's argument in *Bellotti,* Justice Marshall argued that the state-conferred corporate structure enables corporations to aggregate wealth in a manner that cannot be rivaled by any other institution. Second, corporate wealth can distort election outcomes. Third, limiting this distortion is a compelling state interest. What does "distortion" mean in *Austin,* and does it add anything to the analysis? Is it the worry that corporations have preferences that are different from those of individual citizens? Is it the worry that corporations will drown out the voices of individuals? Is it the worry that corporations will take the side of some citizens and thus tip the balance in public policy disputes between individuals? What is the concept of distortion that animates the Court's opinion?

> A fairly consistent majority position, beginning in *Buckley v. Valeo* itself, had focused on the potential for the corruption of the candidates who aimed to ingratiate themselves to their wealthy backers. Such corruption was defined in terms of actual quid pro quo arrangements, while allowing more expansively for the potential dispiriting influence of the appearance of such arrangements. The alternative perspective viewed corruption as a distortion of political outcomes as a result of the undue influence of wealth. On this view, the source of corruption was large expenditures capturing the marketplace of political ideas, and the corrupted entities were, at bottom, the voters who could only succumb to the entreaties of money. This view defines corruption poorly, and makes corruption appear as a "derivative" problem from broader societal inequalities. As formulated in *Austin v. Michigan State Chamber of Commerce,* the only case to adopt squarely the distortion of electoral outcomes view of corruption, the inequities born of wealth are compounded by the unnatural ability of corporations to amass wealth more readily than can individuals. This argument logically extends to all disparities in electoral influence occasioned by differences in wealth.

Samuel Issacharoff, *On Political Corruption,* 124 HARV. L. REV. 118, 121-122 (2010).

>> *The Source of Corporate Speech Rights.*   A critical point of Justice Marshall's opinion is that corporations are state-created and state-dependent institutions and as such they can be subject to special regulation by campaign-finance law without interference by the First Amendment. Justice Scalia's dissent in *Austin* addresses this point directly, stating that the special advantages provided by states cannot justify states' exacting a "price" in the form of stripping a corporation of First Amendment rights. The difference between Justice Marshall and Justice Scalia can largely be explained by their different conceptions of whether corporations have First Amendment rights from some source other than the state. For Justice Marshall, a corporation comes into existence upon action of the state and that action endows the corporation with its particular sets of rights and responsibilities, rights that do not have to include First Amendment rights. Justice Scalia, however, seems to assume that corporations have some sort of preexisting First Amendment rights that a state would actively be taking away. If corporations do have preexisting First Amendment rights, where do they come from? Do they come from the people who

necessarily operate and own the corporation? Or can these First Amendment rights be explained by a historical tradition under which corporations were permitted to speak?

F. *A NEW CHAPTER:* CITIZENS UNITED

In *Citizens United*, below, its most significant decision since *Buckley*, the Court settled, at least for now, its long-running division between the *Bellotti* and *Austin* approaches to corporate speech rights. This time, it addressed a federal statute, 2 U.S.C. §441b of the Bipartisan Campaign Finance Act (BCRA), which prohibited corporations and unions from making contributions or expenditures in connection with a federal election. The prohibition in question applied to spending funds directly out of corporate and union general treasuries; it did not affect the authority of such entities to contribute funds to PACs or SSFs, subject to applicable limitations.

The prohibition against expenditure also included "electioneering communications," which were defined as "any broadcast, cable, or satellite communication which refer[red] to a clearly identified candidate for Federal office" and was made within 60 days before a general election or 30 days before a primary. The Court concluded that the First Amendment does not permit the government to prohibit corporations from spending money directly out of their general treasuries in federal elections. As you read the majority opinion in *Citizens United*, query whether (a) the Court could not have decided the issue on statutory grounds and (b) whether the Court needed to take such an absolutist position on the issue before it in order to resolve the case.

Citizens United v. Federal Election Commission

558 U.S. 310 (2010)

Justice KENNEDY delivered the opinion of the Court. . . .

In this case we are asked to reconsider *Austin* and, in effect, *McConnell*. It has been noted that "*Austin* was a significant departure from ancient First Amendment principles," *Federal Election Comm'n v. Wisconsin Right to Life, Inc.*, 551 U.S. 449, 490 (2007) (*WRTL*) (Scalia, J., concurring in part and concurring in judgment). We agree with that conclusion and hold that *stare decisis* does not compel the continued acceptance of *Austin*. The Government may regulate corporate political speech through disclaimer and disclosure requirements, but it may not suppress that speech altogether. We turn to the case now before us.

I

A

Citizens United is a nonprofit corporation. . . . Citizens United has an annual budget of about $12 million. Most of its funds are from donations by individuals; but, in addition, it accepts a small portion of its funds from for-profit corporations.

In January 2008, Citizens United released a film entitled *Hillary: The Movie.* . . . It is a 90-minute documentary about then-Senator Hillary Clinton, who was a candidate in the Democratic Party's 2008 Presidential primary elections. *Hillary* mentions Senator Clinton by name and depicts interviews with political commentators and other persons, most of them quite critical of Senator Clinton. *Hillary* was released in theaters and on DVD, but Citizens United wanted to increase distribution by making it available through video-on-demand. . . .

To implement the proposal, Citizens United was prepared to pay for the video-on-demand; and to promote the film, it produced two 10-second ads and one 30-second ad for *Hillary*. Each ad includes a short (and, in our view, pejorative) statement about Senator Clinton, followed by the name of the movie and the movie's Website address. Citizens United desired to promote the video-on-demand offering by running advertisements on broadcast and cable television.

B

Before the Bipartisan Campaign Reform Act of 2002 (BCRA), federal law prohibited — and still does prohibit — corporations and unions from using general treasury funds to make direct contributions to candidates or independent expenditures that expressly advocate the election or defeat of a candidate, through any form of media, in connection with certain qualified federal elections. 2 U.S.C. §441b. BCRA §203 amended §441b to prohibit any "electioneering communication" as well. §441b(b)(2). An electioneering communication is defined as "any broadcast, cable, or satellite communication" that "refers to a clearly identified candidate for Federal office" and is made within 30 days of a primary or 60 days of a general election. §434(f)(3)(A). The Federal Election Commission's (FEC) regulations further define an electioneering communication as a communication that is "publicly distributed." 11 CFR §100.29(a)(2). "In the case of a candidate for nomination for President . . . publicly distributed means" that the communication "[c]an be received by 50,000 or more persons in a State where a primary election . . . is being held within 30 days." §100.29(b)(3)(ii). Corporations and unions are barred from using their general treasury funds for express advocacy or electioneering communications. They may establish, however, a "separate segregated fund" (known as a political action committee, or PAC) for these purposes. §441b(b)(2). The moneys received by the segregated fund are limited to donations from stockholders and employees of the corporation or, in the case of unions, members of the union.

C

Citizens United wanted to make *Hillary* available through video-on-demand within 30 days of the 2008 primary elections. It feared, however, that both the film and the ads would be covered by §441b's ban on corporate-funded independent expenditures, thus subjecting the corporation to civil and criminal penalties under §437g. In December 2007, Citizens United sought declaratory and injunctive relief against the FEC. It argued that (1) §441b is unconstitutional as applied to *Hillary;* and (2) BCRA's disclaimer and disclosure requirements, BCRA §§201 and 311, are unconstitutional as applied to *Hillary* and to the three ads for the movie.

The District Court denied Citizens United's motion for a preliminary injunction and then granted the FEC's motion for summary judgment. The court held that §441b was facially constitutional under *McConnell*, and that §441b was constitutional as applied to *Hillary* because it was "susceptible of no other interpretation than to inform the electorate that Senator Clinton is unfit for office, that the United States would be a dangerous place in a President Hillary Clinton world, and that viewers should vote against her." The court also rejected Citizens United's challenge to BCRA's disclaimer and disclosure requirements. . . .

II

B

Citizens United next argues that §441b may not be applied to *Hillary* under the approach taken in *WRTL*. . . . As explained by The Chief Justice's controlling opinion in *WRTL*, the functional-equivalent test is objective: "a court should find that [a communication] is the functional equivalent of express advocacy only if [it] is susceptible of no reasonable interpretation other than as an appeal to vote for or against a specific candidate." *Id.*, at 469-470.

Under this test, *Hillary* is equivalent to express advocacy. The movie, in essence, is a feature-length negative advertisement that urges viewers to vote against Senator Clinton for President. In light of historical footage, interviews with persons critical of her, and voiceover narration, the film would be understood by most viewers as an extended criticism of Senator Clinton's character and her fitness for the office of the Presidency. The narrative may contain more suggestions and arguments than facts, but there is little doubt that the thesis of the film is that she is unfit for the Presidency. . . .

Citizens United argues that *Hillary* is just "a documentary film that examines certain historical events." We disagree. The movie's consistent emphasis is on the relevance of these events to Senator Clinton's candidacy for President. . . .

As the District Court found, there is no reasonable interpretation of *Hillary* other than as an appeal to vote against Senator Clinton. Under the standard stated in *McConnell* and further elaborated in *WRTL*, the film qualifies as the functional equivalent of express advocacy.

C

Citizens United further contends that §441b should be invalidated as applied to movies shown through video-on-demand, arguing that this delivery system has a lower risk of distorting the political process than do television ads. On what we might call conventional television, advertising spots reach viewers who have chosen a channel or a program for reasons unrelated to the advertising. With video-on-demand, by contrast, the viewer selects a program after taking "a series of affirmative steps": subscribing to cable; navigating through various menus; and selecting the program. See *Reno v. American Civil Liberties Union*, 521 U.S. 844, 867 (1997).

While some means of communication may be less effective than others at influencing the public in different contexts, any effort by the Judiciary to decide which means of communications are to be preferred for the particular type of message and speaker would raise questions as to the courts' own lawful authority. . . .

Courts, too, are bound by the First Amendment. We must decline to draw, and then redraw, constitutional lines based on the particular media or technology used to disseminate political speech from a particular speaker. It must be noted, moreover, that this undertaking would require substantial litigation over an extended time, all to interpret a law that beyond doubt discloses serious First Amendment flaws. The interpretive process itself would create an inevitable, pervasive, and serious risk of chilling protected speech pending the drawing of fine distinctions that, in the end, would themselves be questionable. . . .

E

. . . [T]he Court cannot resolve this case on a narrower ground without chilling political speech, speech that is central to the meaning and purpose of the First Amendment. It is not judicial restraint to accept an unsound, narrow argument just so the Court can avoid another argument with broader implications. Indeed, a court would be remiss in performing its duties were it to accept an unsound principle merely to avoid the necessity of making a broader ruling. Here, the lack of a valid basis for an alternative ruling requires full consideration of the continuing effect of the speech suppression upheld in *Austin*. . . .

III

The First Amendment provides that "Congress shall make no law . . . abridging the freedom of speech." Laws enacted to control or suppress speech may operate at different points in the speech process. . . .

The law before us is an outright ban, backed by criminal sanctions. Section 441b makes it a felony for all corporations—including nonprofit advocacy corporations—either to expressly advocate the election or defeat of candidates or to broadcast electioneering communications within 30 days of a primary election and 60 days of a general election. . . . These prohibitions are classic examples of censorship.

Section 441b is a ban on corporate speech notwithstanding the fact that a PAC created by a corporation can still speak. A PAC is a separate association from the corporation. So the PAC exemption from §441b's expenditure ban, §441b(b)(2), does not allow corporations to speak. Even if a PAC could somehow allow a corporation to speak—and it does not—the option to form PACs does not alleviate the First Amendment problems with §441b. PACs are burdensome alternatives; they are expensive to administer and subject to extensive regulations. . . . PACs have to comply with . . . regulations just to speak. This might explain why fewer than 2,000 of the millions of corporations in this country have PACs. PACs, furthermore, must exist before they can speak. Given the onerous restrictions, a corporation may not be able to establish a PAC in time to make its views known regarding candidates and issues in a current campaign.

Section 441b's prohibition on corporate independent expenditures is thus a ban on speech. As a "restriction on the amount of money a person or group can spend on political communication during a campaign," that statute "necessarily reduces the quantity of expression by restricting the number of issues discussed, the depth of their exploration, and the size of the audience reached." *Buckley v. Valeo*, 424 U.S. 1, 19 (1976) (per curiam). Were the Court to uphold these restrictions, the Government could repress speech by silencing certain voices at any of the various points in the speech process. If §441b applied to individuals, no one would believe that it is merely a time, place, or manner restriction on speech. Its purpose and effect are to silence entities whose voices the Government deems to be suspect.

Speech is an essential mechanism of democracy, for it is the means to hold officials accountable to the people. The right of citizens to inquire, to hear, to speak, and to use information to reach consensus is a precondition to enlightened self-government and a necessary means to protect it. . . .

For these reasons, political speech must prevail against laws that would suppress it, whether by design or inadvertence. Laws that burden political speech are "subject to strict scrutiny," which requires the Government to prove that the restriction "furthers a compelling interest and is narrowly tailored to achieve that interest." *WRTL*, 551 U.S., at 464. While it might be maintained that political speech simply cannot be banned or restricted as a categorical matter, the quoted language from *WRTL* provides a sufficient framework for protecting the relevant First Amendment interests in this case. We shall employ it here.

Premised on mistrust of governmental power, the First Amendment stands against attempts to disfavor certain subjects or viewpoints. Prohibited, too, are restrictions distinguishing among different speakers, allowing speech by some but not others. As instruments to censor, these categories are interrelated: Speech restrictions based on the identity of the speaker are all too often simply a means to control content.

Quite apart from the purpose or effect of regulating content, moreover, the Government may commit a constitutional wrong when by law it identifies certain preferred speakers. By taking the right to speak from some and giving it to others, the Government deprives the disadvantaged person or class of the right to use speech to strive to establish worth, standing, and respect for the speaker's voice. The Government may not by these means deprive the public of the right and privilege to determine for itself what speech and speakers are worthy of consideration. The First Amendment protects speech and speaker, and the ideas that flow from each.

We find no basis for the proposition that, in the context of political speech, the Government may impose restrictions on certain disfavored speakers. Both history and logic lead us to this conclusion.

A

1

The Court has recognized that First Amendment protection extends to corporations. This protection has been extended by explicit holdings to the context of political speech. . . . [P]olitical speech does not lose First Amendment protection "simply because its source is a corporation." *Bellotti, supra,* at 784. The Court has thus rejected the argument that political speech of corporations or other associations should be treated differently under the First Amendment simply because such associations are not "natural persons." *Id.,* at 776.

At least since the latter part of the 19th century, the laws of some States and of the United States imposed a ban on corporate direct contributions to candidates. Yet not until 1947 did Congress first prohibit independent expenditures by corporations and labor unions in §304 of the Labor Management Relations Act 1947. In passing this Act Congress overrode the veto of President Truman, who warned that the expenditure ban was a "dangerous intrusion on free speech." Message from the President of the United States, H.R. Doc. No. 334, 89th Cong., 1st Sess., 9 (1947).

For almost three decades thereafter, the Court did not reach the question whether restrictions on corporate and union expenditures are constitutional. The question was in the background of *United States v. CIO*, 335 U.S. 106 (1948). There, a labor union endorsed a congressional candidate in its weekly periodical. The Court stated that "the gravest doubt would arise in our minds as to [the federal expenditure prohibition's] constitutionality" if it were construed to suppress that writing. *Id.*, at 121. The Court engaged in statutory interpretation and found the statute did not cover the publication. *Id.*, at 121-122, and n.20. Four Justices, however, said they would reach the constitutional question and invalidate the Labor Management Relations Act's expenditure ban. The concurrence explained that any "'undue influence'" generated by a speaker's "large expenditures" was outweighed "by the loss for democratic processes resulting from the restrictions upon free and full public discussion." *Id.*, at 143.

In *United States v. Automobile Workers*, 352 U.S. 567 (1957), the Court again encountered the independent expenditure ban, which had been recodified at 18 U.S.C. §610 (1952 ed.). After holding only that a union television broadcast that endorsed candidates was covered by the statute, the Court "[r]efus[ed] to anticipate constitutional questions" and remanded for the trial to proceed. 352 U.S., at 591. Three Justices dissented, arguing that the Court should have reached the constitutional question and that the ban on independent expenditures was unconstitutional. . . . The dissent concluded that deeming a particular group "too powerful" was not a "justificatio[n] for withholding First Amendment rights from any group—labor or corporate." *Id.*, at 597. The Court did not get another opportunity to consider the constitutional question in that case; for after a remand, a jury found the defendants not guilty.

Later, in *Pipefitters v. United States*, 407 U.S. 385, 400-401 (1972), the Court reversed a conviction for expenditure of union funds for political speech—again without reaching the constitutional question. The Court would not resolve that question for another four years.

2

In *Buckley*, the Court addressed various challenges to the Federal Election Campaign Act of 1971 (FECA) as amended in 1974. These amendments created 18 U.S.C. §608(e) (1970 ed., Supp. V), an independent expenditure ban separate from §610 that applied to individuals as well as corporations and labor unions, *Buckley*, 424 U.S., at 23, 39, and n.45.

Before addressing the constitutionality of §608(e)'s independent expenditure ban, *Buckley* first upheld §608(b), FECA's limits on direct contributions to candidates. The *Buckley* Court recognized a "sufficiently important" governmental interest in "the prevention of corruption and the appearance of corruption." *Id.*, at 25.

This followed from the Court's concern that large contributions could be given "to secure a political *quid pro quo*." *Id.*

The *Buckley* Court explained that the potential for *quid pro quo* corruption distinguished direct contributions to candidates from independent expenditures. . . . *Buckley* invalidated §608(e)'s restrictions on independent expenditures, with only one Justice dissenting.

Buckley did not consider §610's separate ban on corporate and union independent expenditures, the prohibition that had also been in the background in *CIO, Automobile Workers,* and *Pipefitters.* Had §610 been challenged in the wake of *Buckley,* however, it could not have been squared with the reasoning and analysis of that precedent. The expenditure ban invalidated in *Buckley,* §608(e), applied to corporations and unions; and some of the prevailing plaintiffs in *Buckley* were corporations. The *Buckley* Court did not invoke the First Amendment's overbreadth doctrine to suggest that §608(e)'s expenditure ban would have been constitutional if it had applied only to corporations and not to individuals. 424 U.S., at 50. *Buckley* cited with approval the *Automobile Workers* dissent, which argued that §610 was unconstitutional. 424 U.S., at 43.

Notwithstanding this precedent, Congress recodified §610's corporate and union expenditure ban at 2 U.S.C. §441b four months after *Buckley* was decided. Section 441b is the independent expenditure restriction challenged here.

Less than two years after *Buckley, Bellotti,* 435 U.S. 765, reaffirmed the First Amendment principle that the Government cannot restrict political speech based on the speaker's corporate identity. . . .

It is important to note that the reasoning and holding of *Bellotti* did not rest on the existence of a viewpoint-discriminatory statute. It rested on the principle that the Government lacks the power to ban corporations from speaking.

Bellotti did not address the constitutionality of the State's ban on corporate independent expenditures to support candidates. In our view, however, that restriction would have been unconstitutional under *Bellotti*'s central principle: that the First Amendment does not allow political speech restrictions based on a speaker's corporate identity.

3

Thus the law stood until *Austin. Austin* "uph[eld] a direct restriction on the independent expenditure of funds for political speech for the first time in [this Court's] history." 494 U.S., at 695 (Kennedy, J., dissenting). There, the Michigan Chamber of Commerce sought to use general treasury funds to run a newspaper ad supporting a specific candidate. Michigan law, however, prohibited corporate independent expenditures that supported or opposed any candidate for state office. A violation of the law was punishable as a felony. The Court sustained the speech prohibition.

To bypass *Buckley* and *Bellotti,* the *Austin* Court identified a new governmental interest in limiting political speech: an antidistortion interest. *Austin* found a compelling governmental interest in preventing "the corrosive and distorting effects of immense aggregations of wealth that are accumulated with the help of the corporate form and that have little or no correlation to the public's support for the corporation's political ideas." 494 U.S., at 660.

B

The Court is thus confronted with conflicting lines of precedent: a pre-*Austin* line that forbids restrictions on political speech based on the speaker's corporate identity and a post-*Austin* line that permits them. No case before *Austin* had held that Congress could prohibit independent expenditures for political speech based on the speaker's corporate identity. Before *Austin*, Congress had enacted legislation for this purpose, and the Government urged the same proposition before this Court [but in no case] did the Court adopt the proposition.

In its defense of the corporate-speech restrictions in §441b, the Government notes the antidistortion rationale on which *Austin* and its progeny rest in part, yet it all but abandons reliance upon it. It argues instead that two other compelling interests support *Austin*'s holding that corporate expenditure restrictions are constitutional: an anticorruption interest and a shareholder-protection interest. We consider the three points in turn.

1

As for *Austin*'s antidistortion rationale, the Government does little to defend it. And with good reason, for the rationale cannot support §441b.

If the First Amendment has any force, it prohibits Congress from fining or jailing citizens, or associations of citizens, for simply engaging in political speech. If the antidistortion rationale were to be accepted, however, it would permit Government to ban political speech simply because the speaker is an association that has taken on the corporate form. The Government contends that *Austin* permits it to ban corporate expenditures for almost all forms of communication stemming from a corporation. If *Austin* were correct, the Government could prohibit a corporation from expressing political views in media beyond those presented here, such as by printing books. The Government responds "that the FEC has never applied this statute to a book," and if it did, "there would be quite [a] good as-applied challenge." This troubling assertion of brooding governmental power cannot be reconciled with the confidence and stability in civic discourse that the First Amendment must secure.

Political speech is "indispensable to decisionmaking in a democracy, and this is no less true because the speech comes from a corporation rather than an individual." *Bellotti*, 435 U.S., at 777. This protection for speech is inconsistent with *Austin*'s antidistortion rationale. *Austin* sought to defend the antidistortion rationale as a means to prevent corporations from obtaining " 'an unfair advantage in the political marketplace' " by using " 'resources amassed in the economic marketplace.' " 494 U.S., at 659 (quoting *MCFL, supra*, at 257). But *Buckley* rejected the premise that the Government has an interest "in equalizing the relative ability of individuals and groups to influence the outcome of elections." 424 U.S., at 48. *Buckley* was specific in stating that "the skyrocketing cost of political campaigns" could not sustain the governmental prohibition. 424 U.S., at 26. The First Amendment's protections do not depend on the speaker's "financial ability to engage in public discussion." *Id.*, at 49.

Either as support for its antidistortion rationale or as a further argument, the *Austin* majority undertook to distinguish wealthy individuals from corporations on the ground that "[s]tate law grants corporations special advantages—such as limited liability, perpetual life, and favorable treatment of the accumulation and distribution of assets." 494 U.S., at 658-659. This does not suffice, however, to allow laws prohibiting speech. "It is rudimentary that the State cannot exact as the price of those special advantages the forfeiture of First Amendment rights." *Id.*, at 680 (Scalia, J., dissenting).

It is irrelevant for purposes of the First Amendment that corporate funds may "have little or no correlation to the public's support for the corporation's political ideas." *Id.*, at 660 (majority opinion). All speakers, including individuals and the media, use money amassed from the economic marketplace to fund their speech. The First Amendment protects the resulting speech, even if it was enabled by economic transactions with persons or entities who disagree with the speaker's ideas. See *id.*, at 707 (Kennedy, J., dissenting).

Austin's antidistortion rationale would produce the dangerous, and unacceptable, consequence that Congress could ban political speech of media corporations. See *McConnell*, 540 U.S., at 283 (opinion of Thomas, J.) ("The chilling endpoint of the Court's reasoning is not difficult to foresee: outright regulation of the press"). Media corporations are now exempt from §441b's ban on corporate expenditures. See 2 U.S.C. §§431(9)(B)(i), 434(f)(3)(B)(i). Yet media corporations accumulate wealth with the help of the corporate form, the largest media corporations have "immense aggregations of wealth," and the views expressed by media corporations often "have little or no correlation to the public's support" for those views. *Austin*, 494 U.S., at 660. Thus, under the Government's reasoning, wealthy media corporations could have their voices diminished to put them on par with other media entities. There is no precedent for permitting this under the First Amendment. . . .

Austin interferes with the "open marketplace" of ideas protected by the First Amendment. *New York State Bd. of Elections v. Lopez Torres*, 552 U.S. 196, 208 (2008). It permits the Government to ban the political speech of millions of associations of citizens. Most of these are small corporations without large amounts of wealth. This fact belies the Government's argument that the statute is justified on the ground that it prevents the "distorting effects of immense aggregations of wealth." *Austin*, 494 U.S., at 660. It is not even aimed at amassed wealth.

The censorship we now confront is vast in its reach. The Government has "muffle[d] the voices that best represent the most significant segments of the economy." *McConnell, supra*, at 257-258 (opinion of Scalia, J.). And "the electorate [has been] deprived of information, knowledge and opinion vital to its function." *CIO*, 335 U.S., at 144 (Rutledge, J., concurring in result). By suppressing the speech of manifold corporations, both for-profit and nonprofit, the Government prevents their voices and viewpoints from reaching the public and advising voters on which persons or entities are hostile to their interests. Factions will necessarily form in our Republic, but the remedy of "destroying the liberty" of some factions is "worse than the disease." Factions should be checked by permitting them all to speak and by entrusting the people to judge what is true and what is false.

The purpose and effect of this law is to prevent corporations, including small and nonprofit corporations, from presenting both facts and opinions to the public. This makes *Austin*'s antidistortion rationale all the more an aberration. . . . References to massive corporate treasuries should not mask the real operation of this law. Rhetoric ought not obscure reality.

Even if §441b's expenditure ban were constitutional, wealthy corporations could still lobby elected officials, although smaller corporations may not have the resources to do so. And wealthy individuals and unincorporated associations can spend unlimited amounts on independent expenditures. Yet certain disfavored associations of citizens—those that have taken on the corporate form—are penalized for engaging in the same political speech.

When Government seeks to use its full power, including the criminal law, to command where a person may get his or her information or what distrusted source he or she may not hear, it uses censorship to control thought. This is unlawful. The First Amendment confirms the freedom to think for ourselves.

2

What we have said also shows the invalidity of other arguments made by the Government. For the most part relinquishing the antidistortion rationale, the Government falls back on the argument that corporate political speech can be banned in order to prevent corruption or its appearance. In *Buckley,* the Court found this interest "sufficiently important" to allow limits on contributions but did not extend that reasoning to expenditure limits. . . . The *Buckley* Court . . . sustained limits on direct contributions in order to ensure against the reality or appearance of corruption. That case did not extend this rationale to independent expenditures, and the Court does not do so here. . . .

Limits on independent expenditures, such as §441b, have a chilling effect extending well beyond the Government's interest in preventing *quid pro quo* corruption. The anticorruption interest is not sufficient to displace the speech here in question. . . .

A single footnote in *Bellotti* purported to leave open the possibility that corporate independent expenditures could be shown to cause corruption. 435 U.S., at 788, n.26. For the reasons explained above, we now conclude that independent expenditures, including those made by corporations, do not give rise to corruption or the appearance of corruption. Dicta in *Bellotti*'s footnote suggested that "a corporation's right to speak on issues of general public interest implies no comparable right in the quite different context of participation in a political campaign for election to public office." *Id.* . . .

The appearance of influence or access . . . will not cause the electorate to lose faith in our democracy. By definition, an independent expenditure is political speech presented to the electorate that is not coordinated with a candidate. The fact that a corporation, or any other speaker, is willing to spend money to try to persuade voters presupposes that the people have the ultimate influence over elected officials. This is inconsistent with any suggestion that the electorate will refuse " 'to take part in democratic governance' " because of additional political speech made by a corporation or any other speaker. *McConnell, supra,* at 144 (quoting *Nixon v. Shrink Missouri Government PAC,* 528 U.S. 377, 390 (2000)). . . .

3

The Government contends further that corporate independent expenditures can be limited because of its interest in protecting dissenting shareholders from being compelled to fund corporate political speech. This asserted interest, like

Austin's antidistortion rationale, would allow the Government to ban the political speech even of media corporations. Assume, for example, that a shareholder of a corporation that owns a newspaper disagrees with the political views the newspaper expresses. See *Austin*, 494 U.S., at 687 (Scalia, J., dissenting). Under the Government's view, that potential disagreement could give the Government the authority to restrict the media corporation's political speech. The First Amendment does not allow that power. . . .

Those reasons are sufficient to reject this shareholder-protection interest; and, moreover, the statute is both underinclusive and overinclusive. As to the first, if Congress had been seeking to protect dissenting shareholders, it would not have banned corporate speech in only certain media within 30 or 60 days before an election. A dissenting shareholder's interests would be implicated by speech in any media at any time. As to the second, the statute is overinclusive because it covers all corporations, including nonprofit corporations and for-profit corporations with only single shareholders. As to other corporations, the remedy is not to restrict speech but to consider and explore other regulatory mechanisms. The regulatory mechanism here, based on speech, contravenes the First Amendment. . . .

C

Our precedent is to be respected unless the most convincing of reasons demonstrates that adherence to it puts us on a course that is sure error. "Beyond workability, the relevant factors in deciding whether to adhere to the principle of *stare decisis* include the antiquity of the precedent, the reliance interests at stake, and of course whether the decision was well reasoned." *Montejo v. Louisiana*, 129 S. Ct. 2079, 2088-2089 (2009). We have also examined whether "experience has pointed up the precedent's shortcomings." *Pearson v. Callahan*, 129 S. Ct. 808, 816 (2009).

These considerations counsel in favor of rejecting *Austin*, which itself contravened this Court's earlier precedents in *Buckley* and *Bellotti*. "This Court has not hesitated to overrule decisions offensive to the First Amendment." *WRTL*, 551 U.S., at 500 (opinion of Scalia, J.). . . .

For the reasons above, it must be concluded that *Austin* was not well reasoned. The Government defends *Austin*, relying almost entirely on "the quid pro quo interest, the corruption interest or the shareholder interest," and not *Austin*'s expressed antidistortion rationale. When neither party defends the reasoning of a precedent, the principle of adhering to that precedent through *stare decisis* is diminished. *Austin* abandoned First Amendment principles, furthermore, by relying on language in some of our precedents that traces back to the *Automobile Workers* Court's flawed historical account of campaign finance laws.

Austin is undermined by experience since its announcement. Political speech is so ingrained in our culture that speakers find ways to circumvent campaign finance laws. Our Nation's speech dynamic is changing, and informative voices should not have to circumvent onerous restrictions to exercise their First Amendment rights. Speakers have become adept at presenting citizens with sound bites, talking points, and scripted messages that dominate the 24-hour news cycle. Corporations, like individuals, do not have monolithic views. On certain topics corporations may possess valuable expertise, leaving them the best equipped to point out errors or fallacies in speech of all sorts, including the speech of candidates and elected officials.

Rapid changes in technology—and the creative dynamic inherent in the concept of free expression—counsel against upholding a law that restricts political speech in certain media or by certain speakers. Today, 30-second television ads may be the most effective way to convey a political message. Soon, however, it may be that Internet sources, such as blogs and social networking Web sites, will provide citizens with significant information about political candidates and issues. Yet, §441b would seem to ban a blog post expressly advocating the election or defeat of a candidate if that blog were created with corporate funds. The First Amendment does not permit Congress to make these categorical distinctions based on the corporate identity of the speaker and the content of the political speech. . . .

Due consideration leads to this conclusion: *Austin* should be and now is overruled. We return to the principle established in *Buckley* and *Bellotti* that the Government may not suppress political speech on the basis of the speaker's corporate identity. No sufficient governmental interest justifies limits on the political speech of nonprofit or for-profit corporations.

D

Austin is overruled, so it provides no basis for allowing the Government to limit corporate independent expenditures. . . . Section 441b's restrictions on corporate independent expenditures are therefore invalid and cannot be applied to *Hillary.*

Given our conclusion we are further required to overrule the part of *McConnell* that upheld BCRA §203's extension of §441b's restrictions on corporate independent expenditures. The *McConnell* Court relied on the antidistortion interest recognized in *Austin* to uphold a greater restriction on speech than the restriction upheld in *Austin,* and we have found this interest unconvincing and insufficient. This part of *McConnell* is now overruled.

V

When word concerning the plot of the movie *Mr. Smith Goes to Washington* reached the circles of Government, some officials sought, by persuasion, to discourage its distribution. Under *Austin,* though, officials could have done more than discourage its distribution—they could have banned the film. After all, it, like *Hillary,* was speech funded by a corporation that was critical of Members of Congress. *Mr. Smith Goes to Washington* may be fiction and caricature; but fiction and caricature can be a powerful force.

Modern day movies, television comedies, or skits on Youtube.com might portray public officials or public policies in unflattering ways. Yet if a covered transmission during the blackout period creates the background for candidate endorsement or opposition, a felony occurs solely because a corporation, other than an exempt media corporation, has made the "purchase, payment, distribution, loan, advance, deposit, or gift of money or anything of value" in order to engage in political speech. 2 U.S.C. §431(9)(A)(i). Speech would be suppressed in the realm where its necessity is most evident: in the public dialogue preceding a real election. Governments are often hostile to speech, but under our law and our tradition it seems stranger than fiction for our Government to make this political speech a crime. Yet this is the statute's purpose and design.

Some members of the public might consider *Hillary* to be insightful and instructive; some might find it to be neither high art nor a fair discussion on how to set the Nation's course; still others simply might suspend judgment on these points but decide to think more about issues and candidates. Those choices and assessments, however, are not for the Government to make.

The judgment of the District Court is reversed with respect to the constitutionality of 2 U.S.C. §441b's restrictions on corporate independent expenditures. The judgment is affirmed with respect to BCRA's disclaimer and disclosure requirements. The case is remanded for further proceedings consistent with this opinion.

It is so ordered.

Justice SCALIA, with whom Justice ALITO joins, and with whom Justice THOMAS joins in part, concurring.

I write separately to address Justice Stevens' discussion of "Original Understandings." This section of the dissent purports to show that today's decision is not supported by the original understanding of the First Amendment. The dissent attempts this demonstration, however, in splendid isolation from the text of the First Amendment. . . .

Despite the corporation-hating quotations the dissent has dredged up, it is far from clear that by the end of the 18th century corporations were despised. If so, how came there to be so many of them? The dissent's statement that there were few business corporations during the eighteenth century . . . is misleading. . . . [W]hat seems like a small number by today's standards surely does not indicate the relative importance of corporations when the Nation was considerably smaller. . . .

Even if we thought it proper to apply the dissent's approach of excluding from First Amendment coverage what the Founders disliked, and even if we agreed that the Founders disliked founding-era corporations; modern corporations might not qualify for exclusion. Most of the Founders' resentment towards corporations was directed at the state-granted monopoly privileges that individually chartered corporations enjoyed. Modern corporations do not have such privileges, and would probably have been favored by most of our enterprising Founders. . . . Moreover, if the Founders' specific intent with respect to corporations is what matters, why does the dissent ignore the Founders' views about other legal entities that have more in common with modern business corporations than the founding-era corporations? At the time of the founding, religious, educational, and literary corporations were incorporated under general incorporation statutes, much as business corporations are today. . . .

The lack of a textual exception for speech by corporations cannot be explained on the ground that such organizations did not exist or did not speak. . . . Both corporations and voluntary associations actively petitioned the Government and expressed their views in newspapers and pamphlets. . . .

The dissent says that when the Framers "constitutionalized the right to free speech in the First Amendment, it was the free speech of individual Americans that they had in mind." That is no doubt true. All the provisions of the Bill of Rights set forth the rights of individual men and women—not, for example, of trees or polar bears. But the individual person's right to speak includes the right to speak in association with other individual persons. Surely the dissent does not believe that speech by the Republican Party or the Democratic Party can be censored because it is not the speech of "an individual American." It is the speech of many individual Americans, who have associated in a common cause, giving the leadership of the party the right to speak on their behalf. The association of individuals in a business corporation is no different. . . .

But to return to, and summarize, my principal point, which is the conformity of today's opinion with the original meaning of the First Amendment. The Amendment is written in terms of "speech," not speakers. Its text offers no foothold for excluding any category of speaker, from single individuals to partnerships of individuals, to unincorporated associations of individuals, to incorporated associations of individuals—and the dissent offers no evidence about the original meaning of the text to support any such exclusion. We are therefore simply left with the question whether the speech at issue in this case is "speech" covered by the First Amendment. No one says otherwise. . . . Indeed, to exclude or impede corporate speech is to muzzle the principal agents of the modern free economy. We should celebrate rather than condemn the addition of this speech to the public debate.

Justice STEVENS, with whom Justice GINSBURG, Justice BREYER, and Justice SOTOMAYOR join, concurring in part and dissenting in part.

It is . . . distressing that our colleagues have manufactured a facial challenge, because the parties have advanced numerous ways to resolve the case that would facilitate electioneering by nonprofit advocacy corporations such as Citizens United, without toppling statutes and precedents. . . .

Consider just three of the narrower grounds of decision that the majority has bypassed. First, the Court could have ruled, on statutory grounds, that a feature-length film distributed through video-on-demand does not qualify as an "electioneering communication" under §203 of BCRA, 2 U.S.C. §441b. . . .

Second, the Court could have expanded the *MCFL* exemption to cover §501(c)(4) nonprofits that accept only a de minimis amount of money from for-profit corporations. Citizens United professes to be such a group. . . . Numerous Courts of Appeal have held that de minimis business support does not, in itself, remove an otherwise qualifying organization from the ambit of *MCFL*. This Court could have simply followed their lead.

Finally, let us not forget Citizens United's as-applied constitutional challenge. Precisely because Citizens United looks so much like the *MCFL* organizations we have exempted from regulation, while a feature-length video-on-demand film looks so unlike the types of electoral advocacy Congress has found deserving of regulation, this challenge is a substantial one. As the appellant's own arguments show, the Court could have easily limited the breadth of its constitutional holding had it declined to adopt the novel notion that speakers and speech acts must always be treated identically . . . in the political realm. Yet the Court nonetheless turns its back on the as-applied review process that has been a staple of campaign finance litigation since *Buckley* and that was affirmed and expanded just two Terms ago in *WRTL*. . . .

Pervading the Court's analysis is the ominous image of a "categorical ba[n]" on corporate speech. Indeed, the majority invokes the specter of a "ban" on nearly every page of its opinion. This characterization is highly misleading, and needs to be corrected.

In fact it already has been. Our cases have repeatedly pointed out that, "[c]ontrary to the [majority's] critical assumptions," the statutes upheld in *Austin* and *McConnell* do "not impose an absolute ban on all forms of corporate political spending." *Austin*, 494 U.S., at 660; *see also McConnell*, 540 U.S., at 203-204. For starters, both statutes provide exemptions for PACs, separate segregated funds established by a corporation for political purposes. "The ability to form and administer separate segregated funds," we observed in *McConnell*, "has provided corporations and unions with a constitutionally sufficient opportunity to engage in express advocacy. That has been this Court's unanimous view." 540 U.S., at 203.

Under BCRA, any corporation's "stockholders and their families and its executive or administrative personnel and their families" can pool their resources to finance electioneering communications. 2 U.S.C. §441b(b)(4)(A)(i). A significant and growing number of corporations avail themselves of this option; during the most recent election cycle, corporate and union PACs raised nearly a billion dollars. Administering a PAC entails some administrative burden, but so does complying with the disclaimer, disclosure, and reporting requirements that the Court today upholds, and no one has suggested that the burden is severe for a sophisticated for-profit corporation. To the extent the majority is worried about this issue, it is important to keep in mind that we have no record to show how substantial the burden really is, just the majority's own unsupported factfinding. Like all other natural persons, every shareholder of every corporation remains entirely free under *Austin* and *McConnell* to do however much electioneering she pleases outside of the corporate form. The owners of a "mom & pop" store can simply place ads in their own names, rather than the store's. If ideologically aligned individuals wish to make unlimited expenditures through the corporate form, they may utilize an *MCFL* organization that has policies in place to avoid becoming a conduit for business or union interests.

The laws upheld in *Austin* and *McConnell* leave open many additional avenues for corporations' political speech. Consider the statutory provision we are ostensibly evaluating in this case, BCRA §203. It has no application to genuine issue advertising—a category of corporate speech Congress found to be far more substantial than election-related advertising—or to Internet, telephone, and print advocacy. Like numerous statutes, it exempts media companies' news stories, commentaries, and editorials from its electioneering restrictions, in recognition of the unique role played by the institutional press in sustaining public debate. It also allows corporations to spend unlimited sums on political communications with their executives and shareholders, to fund additional PAC activity through trade associations, to distribute voting guides and voting records, to underwrite voter registration and voter turnout activities, to host fundraising events for candidates within certain limits, and to publicly endorse candidates through a press release and press conference.

At the time Citizens United brought this lawsuit, the only types of speech that could be regulated under §203 were: (1) broadcast, cable, or satellite communications; (2) capable of reaching at least 50,000 persons in the relevant electorate;

(3) made within 30 days of a primary or 60 days of a general federal election; (4) by a labor union or a non-*MCFL*, nonmedia corporation; (5) paid for with general treasury funds; and (6) "susceptible of no reasonable interpretation other than as an appeal to vote for or against a specific candidate." The category of communications meeting all of these criteria is not trivial, but the notion that corporate political speech has been "suppress[ed] . . . altogether," that corporations have been "exclu[ded] . . . from the general public dialogue," or that a work of fiction such as Mr. Smith Goes to Washington might be covered is nonsense. Even the plaintiffs in *McConnell*, who had every incentive to depict BCRA as negatively as possible, declined to argue that §203's prohibition on certain uses of general treasury funds amounts to a complete ban.

In many ways, then, §203 functions as a source restriction or a time, place, and manner restriction. It applies in a viewpoint-neutral fashion to a narrow subset of advocacy messages about clearly identified candidates for federal office, made during discrete time periods through discrete channels. . . .

So let us be clear: Neither *Austin* nor *McConnell* held or implied that corporations may be silenced; the FEC is not a "censor"; and in the years since these cases were decided, corporations have continued to play a major role in the national dialogue. Laws such as §203 target a class of communications that is especially likely to corrupt the political process, that is at least one degree removed from the views of individual citizens, and that may not even reflect the views of those who pay for it. Such laws burden political speech, and that is always a serious matter, demanding careful scrutiny. But the majority's incessant talk of a "ban" aims at a straw man. . . .

The second pillar of the Court's opinion is its assertion that "the Government cannot restrict political speech based on the speaker's . . . identity." The case on which it relies for this proposition is *First Nat. Bank of Boston v. Bellotti*, 435 U.S. 765. . . . [T]he holding in that case was far narrower than the Court implies. Like its paeans to unfettered discourse, the Court's denunciation of identity-based distinctions may have rhetorical appeal but it obscures reality.

"Our jurisprudence over the past 216 years has rejected an absolutist interpretation" of the First Amendment. *WRTL*, 551 U.S., at 482 (opinion of Roberts, C.J.). The First Amendment provides that "Congress shall make no law . . . abridging the freedom of speech, or of the press." Apart perhaps from measures designed to protect the press, that text might seem to permit no distinctions of any kind. Yet in a variety of contexts, we have held that speech can be regulated differentially on account of the speaker's identity, when identity is understood in categorical or institutional terms. The Government routinely places special restrictions on the speech rights of students, prisoners, members of the Armed Forces, foreigners, and its own employees. When such restrictions are justified by a legitimate governmental interest, they do not necessarily raise constitutional problems. In contrast to the blanket rule that the majority espouses, our cases recognize that the Government's interests may be more or less compelling with respect to different classes of speakers, and that the constitutional rights of certain categories of speakers, in certain contexts, " 'are not automatically coextensive with the rights' " that are normally accorded to members of our society. *Morse v. Frederick*, 551 U.S. 393, 396-397, 404 (2007) (quoting *Bethel School Dist. No. 403 v. Fraser*, 478 U.S. 675, 682 (1986)).

The free speech guarantee thus does not render every other public interest an illegitimate basis for qualifying a speaker's autonomy; society could scarcely function if it did. It is fair to say that our First Amendment doctrine has "frowned on" certain identity-based distinctions, *Los Angeles Police Dept. v. United Reporting Publishing Corp.*, 528 U.S. 32, 47, n.4 (1999) (Stevens, J., dissenting), particularly those that may reflect invidious discrimination or preferential treatment of a politically powerful group. But it is simply incorrect to suggest that we have prohibited all legislative distinctions based on identity or content. Not even close.

The election context is distinctive in many ways, and the Court, of course, is right that the First Amendment closely guards political speech. But in this context, too, the authority of legislatures to enact viewpoint-neutral regulations based on content and identity is well settled. We have, for example, allowed state-run broadcasters to exclude independent candidates from televised debates. *Arkansas Ed. Television Comm'n v. Forbes*, 523 U.S. 666 (1998). We have upheld statutes that prohibit the distribution or display of campaign materials near a polling place. *Burson v. Freeman*, 504 U.S. 191 (1992). Although we have not reviewed them directly, we have never cast doubt on laws that place special restrictions on campaign spending by foreign nationals. And we have consistently approved laws that bar Government employees, but not others, from contributing to or participating in political activities. These statutes burden the political expression of one class of speakers, namely, civil servants. Yet we have sustained them on the basis of longstanding practice and Congress' reasoned judgment that certain regulations which leave "untouched full participation . . . in political decisions at the ballot box," *Civil Service Comm'n v. Letter Carriers*, 413 U.S. 548, 556 (1973), help ensure that public officials are "sufficiently free from improper influences," *id.*, at 564, and that "confidence in the system of representative Government is not . . . eroded to a disastrous extent," *id.*, at 565.

The same logic applies to this case with additional force because it is the identity of corporations, rather than individuals, that the Legislature has taken into account. As we have unanimously observed, legislatures are entitled to decide "that the special characteristics of the corporate structure require particularly careful regulation" in an electoral context. *NRWC*, 459 U.S., at 209-210. Not only has the distinctive potential of corporations to corrupt the electoral process long been recognized, but within the area of campaign finance, corporate spending is also "furthest from the core of political expression, since corporations' First Amendment speech and association interests are derived largely from those of their members and of the public in receiving information," *Beaumont*, 539 U.S., at 161, n.8. Campaign finance distinctions based on corporate identity tend to be less worrisome, in other words, because the "speakers" are not natural persons, much less members of our political community, and the governmental interests are of the highest order. Furthermore, when corporations, as a class, are distinguished from noncorporations, as a class, there is a lesser risk that regulatory distinctions will reflect invidious discrimination or political favoritism.

If taken seriously, our colleagues' assumption that the identity of a speaker has no relevance to the Government's ability to regulate political speech would lead to some remarkable conclusions. Such an assumption would have accorded the propaganda broadcasts to our troops by "Tokyo Rose" during World War II the same protection as speech by Allied commanders. More pertinently, it would appear to afford the same protection to multinational corporations controlled by foreigners as to individual Americans. . . . Under the majority's view, I suppose it may be a First Amendment problem that corporations are not permitted to vote, given that voting is, among other things, a form of speech.

In short, the Court dramatically overstates its critique of identity-based distinctions, without ever explaining why corporate identity demands the same treatment as individual identity. Only the most wooden approach to the First Amendment could justify the unprecedented line it seeks to draw. . . .

The Court invokes "ancient First Amendment principles" and original understandings to defend today's ruling, yet it makes only a perfunctory attempt to ground its analysis in the principles or understandings of those who drafted and ratified the Amendment. Perhaps this is because there is not a scintilla of evidence to support the notion that anyone believed it would preclude regulatory distinctions based on the corporate form. To the extent that the Framers' views are discernible and relevant to the disposition of this case, they would appear to cut strongly against the majority's position.

This is not only because the Framers and their contemporaries conceived of speech more narrowly than we now think of it, but also because they held very different views about the nature of the First Amendment right and the role of corporations in society. Those few corporations that existed at the founding were authorized by grant of a special legislative charter. . . . Corporations were created, supervised, and conceptualized as quasi-public entities. . . .

The Framers thus took it as a given that corporations could be comprehensively regulated in the service of the public welfare. Unlike our colleagues, they had little trouble distinguishing corporations from human beings, and when they constitutionalized the right to free speech in the First Amendment, it was the free speech of individual Americans that they had in mind. While individuals might join together to exercise their speech rights, business corporations, at least, were plainly not seen as facilitating such associational or expressive ends. . . . In light of these background practices and understandings, it seems to me implausible that the Framers believed "the freedom of speech" would extend equally to all corporate speakers, much less that it would preclude legislatures from taking limited measures to guard against corporate capture of elections.

The Court observes that the Framers drew on diverse intellectual sources, communicated through newspapers, and aimed to provide greater freedom of speech than had existed in England. From these (accurate) observations, the Court concludes that "[t]he First Amendment was certainly not understood to condone the suppression of political speech in society's most salient media." This conclusion is far from certain, given that many historians believe the Framers were focused on prior restraints on publication and did not understand the First Amendment to "prevent the subsequent punishment of such [publications] as may be deemed contrary to the public welfare." *Near v. Minnesota ex rel. Olson*, 283 U.S. 697, 714 (1931). Yet, even if the majority's conclusion were correct, it would tell us only that the First Amendment was understood to protect political speech in certain media. It would tell us little about whether the Amendment was understood to protect general treasury electioneering expenditures by corporations, and to what extent.

As a matter of original expectations, then, it seems absurd to think that the First Amendment prohibits legislatures from taking into account the corporate identity of a sponsor of electoral advocacy. . . .

The truth is we cannot be certain how a law such as BCRA §203 meshes with the original meaning of the First Amendment. I have given several reasons why I believe the Constitution would have been understood then, and ought to be understood now, to permit reasonable restrictions on corporate electioneering, and I will give many more reasons in the pages to come. The Court enlists the Framers in its defense without seriously grappling with their understandings of corporations or the free speech right, or with the republican principles that underlay those understandings.

In fairness, our campaign finance jurisprudence has never attended very closely to the views of the Framers whose political universe differed profoundly from that of today. We have long since held that corporations are covered by the First Amendment, and many legal scholars have long since rejected the concession theory of the corporation. But . . . in light of the Court's effort to cast itself as guardian of ancient values, it pays to remember that nothing in our constitutional history dictates today's outcome. To the contrary, this history helps illuminate just how extraordinarily dissonant the decision is. . . .

In the end, the Court's rejection of *Austin* and *McConnell* comes down to nothing more than its disagreement with their results. Virtually every one of its arguments was made and rejected in those cases, and the majority opinion is essentially an amalgamation of resuscitated dissents. The only relevant thing that has changed since *Austin* and *McConnell* is the composition of this Court. . . .

Today's decision is backwards in many senses. It elevates the majority's agenda over the litigants' submissions, facial attacks over as-applied claims, broad constitutional theories over narrow statutory grounds, individual dissenting opinions over precedential holdings, assertion over tradition, absolutism over empiricism, rhetoric over reality. Our colleagues have arrived at the conclusion that *Austin* must be overruled and that §203 is facially unconstitutional only after mischaracterizing both the reach and rationale of those authorities, and after bypassing or ignoring rules of judicial restraint used to cabin the Court's lawmaking power. Their conclusion that the societal interest in avoiding corruption and the appearance of corruption does not provide an adequate justification for regulating corporate expenditures on candidate elections relies on an incorrect description of that interest, along with a failure to acknowledge the relevance of established facts and the considered judgments of state and federal legislatures over many decades.

In a democratic society, the longstanding consensus on the need to limit corporate campaign spending should outweigh the wooden application of judge-made rules. The majority's rejection of this principle "elevate[s] corporations to a level of deference which has not been seen at least since the days when substantive due process was regularly used to invalidate regulatory legislation thought to unfairly impinge upon established economic interests." *Bellotti*, 435 U.S., at 817, n.13 (WHITE, J., dissenting). At bottom, the Court's opinion is thus a rejection of the common sense of the American people, who have recognized a need to prevent corporations from undermining self-government since the founding, and who have fought against the distinctive corrupting potential of corporate electioneering since the days of Theodore Roosevelt. It is a strange time to repudiate that common sense. While American democracy is imperfect, few outside the majority of this Court would have thought its flaws included a dearth of corporate money in politics. . . .

By removing one of its central components, today's ruling makes a hash out of BCRA's "delicate and interconnected regulatory scheme." *McConnell*, 540 U.S., at 172. Consider just one example of the distortions that will follow: Political parties are barred under BCRA from soliciting or spending "soft money," funds that are not subject to the statute's disclosure requirements or its source and amount limitations. 2 U.S.C. §441i. Going forward, corporations and unions will be free to spend as much general treasury money as they wish on ads that support or attack specific candidates, whereas national parties will not be able to spend a dime of soft money on ads of any kind. The Court's ruling thus dramatically enhances the role of corporations and unions—and the narrow interests they represent—vis-à-vis the role of political parties—and the broad coalitions they represent—in determining who will hold public office.

⟫ *Reaction to* **Citizens United.**   Reaction to *Citizens United* was immediate, widespread, and harsh, in ways that resembled the public and scholarly reactions to *Buckley*. Polls taken immediately following the decision showed it to be widely opposed by those surveyed, including conservatives. The *New York Times* called the decision a "blow to democracy." The *Washington Post* criticized the Court for "toss[ing] out reasonable limits" and making a "mockery" of some Justices' professed commitment to judicial restraint. Ronald Dworkin, writing in the same forum in which he first criticized *Buckley*, called it "the decision that threatens democracy." Jon Stewart, of Comedy Central's "The Daily Show," ridiculed the decision, and his colleague Stephen Colbert performed a recurring satire of the decision involving creating an actual Super PAC, raising money (ostentatiously without disclosure of its sources), and spending it in the 2012 presidential primaries. Never has the esoterica of campaign-finance law been brought more directly and concretely to the masses!

In an unusual move, the President of the United States himself joined in the criticism, issuing a rare, express, and highly public rebuke to the Supreme Court during his State of the Union Address:

> With all due deference to separation of powers, last week the Supreme Court reversed a century of law that I believe will open the floodgates for special interests—including foreign corporations—to spend without limit in our elections. I don't think American elections should be bankrolled by America's most powerful interests, or worse, by foreign entities. They should be decided by the American people. And I'd urge Democrats and Republicans to pass a bill that helps to correct some of these problems.

Barack Obama, *State of the Union Address*, United States Capitol (Jan. 27, 2010).

In a rare spread of public dissent to the judicial system, the Montana Supreme Court—a court not generally known for persnickety independence—strongly criticized the ruling in *Citizens United*, and defiantly upheld a state law prohibiting corporations from making political expenditures. *Western Tradition Partnership v. Attorney General*, 271 P.3d 1 (Mont. 2011). The court attempted to distinguish

Citizens United by reviewing what it characterized as an unusual history of political corruption in Montana associated mainly with the powerful mining industry:

> [T]he State of Montana . . . clearly had a compelling interest to enact the challenged statute in 1912. At that time the State of Montana and its government were operating under a mere shell of legal authority, and the real social and political power was wielded by powerful corporate managers to further their own business interests. The voters had more than enough of the corrupt practices and heavy-handed influence asserted by the special interests controlling Montana's political institutions. Bribery of public officials and unlimited campaign spending by the mining interests were commonplace and well known to the public.

It also held that the state's small size made corporate political spending more effective than in other jurisdictions, and thus more dangerous. In a perfunctory per curiam decision, the Supreme Court reversed, 567 U.S. 516 (2012). Justices Breyer, Ginsburg, Sotomayor, and Kagan dissented, arguing that *Citizens United* should not bar the Montana court from finding on the record before it that "independent expenditures by corporations did in fact lead to corruption or the appearance of corruption in Montana." Montana's experience, the dissenters concluded, "casts grave doubt on the Court's supposition that independent expenditures do not corrupt. . . ."

▶▶ ***The Court's Understanding of "Corruption."*** Some scholars have strongly criticized the Court's understanding of corruption. In *Citizens United*, the Court asserted, "independent expenditures, including those made by corporations, do not give rise to corruption or the appearance of corruption." Do you agree? If there is a danger, acknowledged by the Court since *Buckley*, that legislators can be corrupted by direct contributions, is there no danger at all that they could be corrupted by expenditures made for their benefit, even if those funds do not end up in the legislator's pocket? Much depends upon one's definition of corruption. If one thinks of corruption merely as the outright "sale of favors," then spending independently to advance the political fortunes of a candidate may not be capable of corrupting a candidate. But if one thinks of corruption as including the "deformation of judgment" through impairment of the legislator's ability to legislate impartially, or the "distortion of influence" through inducement of legislators to pay undue attention to the interests of their benefactors, then such expenditures clearly have corrupting potential. Deborah Hellman, *Defining Corruption and Constitutionalizing Democracy*, 111 MICH. L. REV. 1385 (2013). *See also* Zephyr Teachout, *The Anti-Corruption Principle*, 94 CORNELL L. REV. 341 (2009); Samuel Issacharoff, *On Political Corruption*, 124 HARV. L. REV. 118 (2010).

▶▶ ***Who Is the Speaker?*** In *Citizens United*, Justice Kennedy said that Section 441b is an outright ban on speech notwithstanding the fact that corporations can form a segregated PAC to make independent political expenditures. Justice Kennedy remarked that a "PAC is a separate association from the corporation. So the PAC exemption from §441b's expenditure ban, §441b(b)(2), does not allow corporations to speak." Is this a sensible distinction? Consider the following account:

What is the basis for this judgment by Justice Kennedy? . . . How was this conclusion derived and how are we to evaluate it? Is it falsifiable?

Consider some random corporate PACs starting first with the Pfizer Political Action Committee. The Pfizer PAC's webpage is located on the Pfizer Corporation's website and it provides the following description:

> The Pfizer political action committee, Pfizer PAC, is a nonpartisan organization that provides opportunities for employees to participate in the American political process. The Pfizer PAC is an employee-run organization with a steering committee made up of Pfizer employees from around the country. When choosing to make a contribution to a candidate, the Pfizer PAC considers candidates' views on issues that impact Pfizer and its employees as well as the presence of Pfizer facilities or employees in the candidate's district or state. The PAC steering committee reviews and approves all recommendations for PAC contributions on a monthly basis.
>
> Pfizer's procedure that limits Pfizer colleagues' campaign and election activities during working hours also restricts the use of Pfizer resources to support federal and state candidates, political parties and political committees.

Would it be a mistake to conflate the Pfizer PAC with Pfizer Corporation? . . . Would a reasonable observer of the Pfizer PAC be objectively wrong to conclude that when the Pfizer PAC speaks it is Pfizer that is speaking? Consider another corporate PAC, the TargetCitizens Political Forum. Quick, brownie points for the person who can guess the corporation that goes with the PAC. Unlike the Pfizer PAC, the Target PAC did not appear to be on the corporate parent's website. But the presence of the famous Target logo made it very clear that this was a Target PAC. TargetCitizens included the following statement on its website: "The primary benefit of PAC membership is the ability to make a positive impact on legislation affecting our company, team members and communities." Who is the "our" here? Can one sensibly say that the speech emanating from the PAC is not Target's speech?

On July 6, 2010 Target's PAC gave $150,000 to Minnesota Forward, a conservative political action committee. Minnesota Forward used the Target (or should I say the Target PAC) contribution to fund an ad in support of Tom Emmer who was then a candidate for the Republican nomination for Governor in the State of Minnesota. As it turns out, Mr. Emmer is very conservative, an opponent of gay marriage, and his views on gay equality are reflective of the most conservative wing of his party. Many gay rights organizations were outraged and they directed their ire at Target.

Note here a couple of facts. First, it was Minnesota Forward who ran the ad in support of Emmer not Target. Second, it was Target's PAC, TargetCitizens who made the contribution to Minnesota Forward and not Target—that is the money did not come from Target's general treasury. Remarkably, neither the public nor Target thought this was a distinction with a difference. Gay rights supporters as well as it seems the wider public, attributed the speech to Target. Moreover, and more to the point for our purposes, neither the public nor Target distinguished between Target and TargetCitizens. Gregg Steinhafel is Target's CEO and his response to the brouhaha is particularly instructive. Mr. Steinhafel wrote:

> As you know, Target has a history of supporting organizations and candidates, on both sides of the aisle, who seek to advance policies aligned with our business objectives, such as job creation and economic growth. MN Forward is focused specifically on those issues and is committed to supporting candidates from any party who will work to improve the state's job climate. However, it is also important to note that we rarely endorse all advocated positions of the organizations or candidates we support, and we do not have a political or social agenda.

In contrast to the implication from Justice Kennedy, Target clearly believes that it is speaking when it makes contributions through its segregated PAC. Thus, Target's defense was not, "this was not us, but our PAC." Target's defense was "we're not responsible for the speech of the organizations to which we, Target, make contributions." Subjectively, Target clearly viewed TargetCitizens' contribution/speech as Target's contribution/speech and so did everyone else. Where they disagreed was whether Minnesota Forward's speech was also Target's speech. That is, whether Target corporation is responsible for the speech of Minnesota Forward that was made possible, in part, by Target's contribution.

What then should we make of Justice Kennedy's declaration that the corporate PAC's speech is the PAC and not the corporation speaking?

Guy-Uriel E. Charles, *Understanding* Citizens United, 8-9 (2012) (working paper). The Target PAC can be found at https://corporate.target.com/corporate-responsibility/civic-activity/political-contributions. From a subjective perspective, these corporations clearly view their PACs as speaking for the corporation and representing the interests of the corporation. Which way should this subjective view cut?

» ***Do Corporations Have Free Speech Rights to Engage in Political Speech?*** In *Bellotti*, the Court held that independent spending by corporations in the context of a ballot initiative campaign could not be restricted, but rested its ruling on the ground that "the First Amendment goes beyond protection of the press and the self-expression of individuals to prohibit government from limiting the stock of information from which members of the public may draw." In other words, the rationale for prohibiting restrictions on corporate speech rested not so much on vindicating any rights that corporations might hold but on the capacity of information, whatever its source, to inform the public on important political issues. Has the Court shifted ground in *Citizens United*? Does it now conceive of corporations as holders of free speech rights equivalent to those of natural persons? If so, is that position warranted?

» ***How Best to Understand the Court's Decision?*** Is *Citizens United* a results-oriented decision without any basis in law? Or is it a principled application of long-standing First Amendment values? Consider the views of three First Amendment theorists below. Which of the three provides us with the best framework for making sense of the debate on the Court? Let us start first with Professor Kathleen Sullivan, who is generally sympathetic to the views of the majority:

> *Citizens United* has been unjustly maligned as radically departing from settled free speech tradition. In fact, the clashing opinions in the case simply illustrate that free speech tradition has different strands. The libertarian strand from which the majority draws support emphasizes that freedom of speech is a negative command that protects a system of speech, not individual speakers, and thus invalidates government interference with the background system of expression no matter whether a speaker is individual or collective, for-profit or nonprofit, powerful or marginal. The egalitarian strand on which the dissent relies, in contrast, views speech rights as belonging to individual speakers and speech restrictions as subject to a one-way ratchet: impermissible when they create or entrench the subordination of political or cultural minorities, but permissible when aimed at redistributing speaking power to reduce some speakers' disproportionate influence. . . . Finding convergence between the two free speech traditions is key to enacting new legislation that might counteract *Citizens United*'s perceived effects while surviving constitutional challenge. Of the four leading possibilities for reform—invalidating contribution limits, limiting segregated-fund requirements to for-profit corporations, increasing disclosure and disclaimer requirements for corporate political expenditures, and making segregated political funding a condition of the corporate form or the receipt of government benefits—only the disclosure alternative would appear readily capable of uniting both strands. . . . The Court's pronounced willingness to uphold compelled disclosure requirements provides the best guide to future policymaking in the area of campaign finance.

Kathleen M. Sullivan, *Two Concepts of Freedom of Speech*, 124 HARV. L. REV. 143, 176-177 (2010).

Consider a similar intellectual frame, this time from Professor Joshua Cohen, who is much more sympathetic to the dissenters than is Professor Sullivan. Professor Cohen argues that *Citizens United* is best understood as reflecting the majority's and dissenters' "competing theories of democracy [which] are part of constitutional and political argument[s]." Cohen presents two conceptions of democracy, one which he calls Civic Equality and the other which he terms Limited Government Minimalism:

> The Civic Equality conception of democracy comprises four main ideas. The first is that citizens are assumed normally to have conceptions of justice and the common good that shape their political judgments, as well as interests and an assumed competence to understand and protect those interests: these ideas are important in interpreting the notion of citizens as free and politically autonomous. Second, that authoritative collective decision-making among citizens thus conceived has a deliberative aspect: that in a well-functioning democracy, decisions are arrived at through an open and dispersed process of public communication in which individuals can acquire information, express judgments guided by

ideas of justice and the common good, and argue with others about law and policy in light of their conflicting views about justice and the common good. Moreover, third, that citizens are to engage in that process of communication and argument as equals, with equal standing in the processes of collective decision-making. And fourth, that ultimate authority lies in the people, understood as a community of free citizens engaged in public discussion as equals. . . .

Limited Government Minimalism begins with a self-styled *political realism.* . . . Political realism sees competition—especially between and among elites—to control power as a permanent and fundamental fact of political life. Democracy does not transcend that political fact of (elite) competition, but subjects it to a distinctive (and arguably attractive) method of resolution—a peaceful and periodic competition for votes. This view . . . is commonly associated with Joseph Schumpeter's critique of the classical conception of democracy. . . .

Second, a central *purpose* of subjecting (elite) political competition to electoral resolution is that it gives it a more secure protection of personal liberty . . . understood as non-interference with choices, not the self-legislation of politically autonomous citizens. The purpose of elections is not to produce some sort of match of policy to majority preference or to compelling social welfare function. Instead, by subjecting control of state power—as an especially dangerous form of power because it is a monopoly—to the discipline of competitive elections, we do something to check its improper exercise. . . .

Third, Limited Government Minimalism is infused with a mistrust of political power, which is understood, by turns, as ineffective, or as a source of undesirable if unintended consequences, or as dangerous in its effects and self-masking in its intent—a mistrust owing . . . its monopoly character. . . .

Finally, Limited Government Minimalism attaches large importance to unregulated political speech. It is deeply suspicious of such regulation because informed judgment is essential if electoral competition is to work as an effective, thus liberty-protecting check on the threats imposed by political power, and because the regulators cannot be trusted. This conception of political speech—which flows naturally from the previous ideas about politics, liberty, and mistrust of power—is suggested in *Citizens United.*

Joshua Cohen, *Citizens United* v. Democracy?, 9-10, 14-15, 19-21 (2011) (unpublished paper).

Now consider the views of the renowned legal philosopher Ronald Dworkin, who has called *Citizens United* the "decision that threatens democracy." Dworkin argues:

A First Amendment theory is . . . indispensible to responsible adjudication of free speech issues. Many such theories have been offered . . . [but] none of them . . . justifies the damage the five conservative justices have just inflicted on our politics.

The most popular of these theories appeals to the need for an informed electorate. Freedom of political speech is an essential condition of an effective democracy because it ensures that voters have access to as wide and diverse a range of information and political opinion as possible. . . .

Kennedy, who wrote the Court's opinion in *Citizens United* on behalf of the five conservatives, appealed to the "informed electorate" theory. But he offered no reason for supposing that allowing rich corporations to swamp elections with money will in fact produce a better-informed public—and there are many reasons to think it will produce a worse-informed one. Corporations have no ideas of their own. Their ads will promote the opinions of their managers, who could publish or broadcast those opinions on their own or with others of like mind through political action committees (PACs) or other organizations financed through voluntary individual contributions. So though allowing them to use their stockholders' money rather than their own will increase the volume of advertising, it will not add to the diversity of ideas offered to voters.

Corporate advertising will mislead the public, moreover, because its volume will suggest more public support than there actually is for the opinions the ads express. Many of the shareholders who will actually pay for the ads, who in many cases are members of pension and union funds, will hate the opinions they pay to advertise. Obama raised a great deal of money on the Internet, mostly from small contributors, to finance his presidential campaign, and we can expect political parties, candidates, and PACs to tap that source much more effectively in the future. But these contributions are made voluntarily by supporters, not by managers using the money of people who may well be opposed to their opinions. Corporate advertising is misleading in another way as well. It purports to offer opinions about the public interest, but in fact managers are legally required to spend corporate funds only to promote their corporation's own financial interests, which may very well be different.

There is, however, a much more important flaw in the conservative justices' argument. If corporations exercise the power that the Court has now given them, and buy an extremely large share of the television time available for political ads, their electioneering will undermine rather than improve the public's political education. Kennedy declared that speech may not be restricted just to make candidates more equal in their financial resources. But he misunderstood why other nations limit campaign expenditures. This is not just to be fair to all candidates, like requiring a single starting line for runners in a race, but to create the best conditions for the public to make an informed decision when it votes—the main purpose of the First Amendment, according to the marketplace theory. . . .

A second popular theory focuses on the importance of free speech not to educate the public at large but to protect the status, dignity, and moral development of individual citizens as equal partners in the political process. Justice John Paul Stevens summarized this theory in the course of his very long but irresistibly powerful dissenting opinion in *Citizens*

United. . . . Kennedy tried to appeal to this understanding of the First Amendment to justify free speech for corporations. "By taking the right to speak from some and giving it to others," he stated, "the Government deprives the disadvantaged person or class of the right to use speech to strive to establish worth, standing, and respect for the speaker's voice." But this is bizarre. The interests the First Amendment protects, on this second theory, are only the moral interests of individuals who would suffer frustration and indignity if they were censored. Only real human beings can have those emotions or suffer those insults. Corporations, which are only artificial legal inventions, cannot. The right to vote is surely at least as important a badge of equal citizenship as the right to speak, but not even the conservative justices have suggested that every corporation should have a ballot.

Ronald Dworkin, *The Decision That Threatens Democracy*, N.Y. REV. BOOKS, May 13, 2010.

≫   *Rightly Decided for the Wrong Reasons?*   In his dissenting opinion, Justice Stevens noted that the "natural textual home" for the right to produce the documentary at issue in *Citizens United* was, rather than freedom of speech, freedom of the press. *Citizens United*, 558 U.S. at 431 n.57. As one commentator has noted, agreeing with Justice Stevens in this assessment but disagreeing with respect to the Court's judgment,

> [w]hether the government may forbid publication of opinions about officials and candidates is at the very core of the Press Clause. To be sure, in recent decades, the Supreme Court has tended to collapse the various expressive freedoms of the First Amendment (apart from the Religion Clauses) into an undifferentiated "freedom of expression," or more often, simply "freedom of speech." But there are historical and practical reasons why the freedoms of speech, press, assembly, and petition were separately enumerated.

Michael W. McConnell, *Reconsidering* Citizens United *as a Press Clause Case*, 123 YALE L.J. 412, 416 (2013). McConnell notes that such a distinction would "foster analytical clarity" in that "it would help to differentiate the act of publishing one's opinions about a public official or candidate from the act of contributing money to a candidate or political party." *Id.* at 416-417. Is this distinction workable in practice? Would considering *Citizens United* as a Press Clause case have avoided many of the most challenging corporate constitutional rights issues raised by the Court's decision? More importantly, could this reasoning be extended beyond the narrow category of news organizations?

McConnell argues that the freedom of the press should not be so limited. Rather, he notes that historically, and consistent with Supreme Court jurisprudence, "the press" was not limited to "professional news media," but referred instead to "the printing press, meaning the ability of people to disseminate ideas easily and inexpensively to a broad public." *Id.* at 437.

But what effect would understanding documentary films or other corporate political broadcasts as an exercise of the freedom of the press have on our understanding of the larger morass of the Supreme Court's campaign-finance jurisprudence? Would such a doctrinal turn clarify the distinction between expenditures and contributions? Between corporations and individuals? According to McConnell, the freedom of the press covers a much smaller arena of political spending and therefore allows for a more incremental approach to testing the limits of political speech.

> [The Press Clause] says nothing about the right to contribute to candidates, political parties, or PACs. The right to publish belongs to everyone — to natural persons like Thomas Paine, to for-profit corporations like the New York Times Company, and to non-media corporations like Citizens United — but contributing to candidates is not an exercise of the freedom of the press.

Id. at 446. That is, under this account, the freedom of the press extends only to the public dissemination of information and would not extend to either independent expenditures by individuals or PACs or to contributions made directly to candidate committees. Are you convinced? Might it nevertheless be possible to understand expenditures directed to "the press" as subsumed within the rights of the press?

»   *Can Corporate Spending Be Controlled by Other Means?* If, after *Citizens United*, corporate spending cannot be limited by regulatory controls, might it be controlled, or at least deterred, by other means? Two kinds of measures that may hold some potential are remedies internal to corporate rather than election law, and intensified disclosure to bring corporate campaign spending to public attention.

Corporate Democracy Controls. In *Citizens United*, the Court implied that speech by corporations should be treated for constitutional purposes as speech by the association of individuals comprising the corporation. If it is not — if, in other words, speech by the corporation amounts to speech by its management rather than by its shareholders — existing rules of corporate democracy, the Court implies, provide adequate opportunities for shareholders to discipline corporate management. Is this correct? Will management of for-profit corporations be responsive to the political preferences of shareholders?

All corporate decisions, including decisions to spend money on political speech, are subject to traditional corporate rules of fiduciary obligation that bind firm managers to pursue the best interests of the corporation and its shareholders. The question thus arises whether, and if so when, decisions to allocate corporate resources to political expenditures are truly in the interests of the corporation, and what kind of remedies shareholders might possess to influence or block such decisions by management if they disagree with particular investments in political speech.

For the most part, decisions to spend corporate money on political speech are governed by the same deferential rules governing the making of ordinary business decisions. These rules, however, typically provide no opportunity for shareholder input on routine business decisions, nor do they require regular disclosure to investors of the substance of such decisions. Existing rules of corporate law therefore may not adequately align the interests of management with the political preferences of shareholders, or provide sufficient protection for dissenting minority shareholders. *See* Lucian A. Bebchuk and Robert J. Jackson, Jr., *Corporate Political Speech: Who Decides?*, 124 HARV. L. REV. 83 (2010). In addition, "[i]ndividual shareholders generally invest in publicly held corporations through diversified portfolios and through other institutions such as mutual or pension funds. These shareholders may have little idea which stocks they are holding and are concerned only with the total risk and return of their portfolio." Larry E. Ribstein, *The First Amendment and Corporate Governance*, 27 GA. ST. U. L. REV. 1019, 1029 (2011). In these circumstances, the likelihood of effective shareholder control of corporate investments in political speech seems low.

Furthermore, not all corporations may be similarly situated with respect to their interest in political activism. According to a recent study, "family-founded firms have a longer time horizon, with longer-term commitments to non-market activities. . . . Principal-owners are central in selecting the firm's goals and in forming political preferences. . . . Founders define the firm's culture and values, which may include political ideology and partisan leaning. Principal-owners may view the firm as an extension of self and may use the firms' resources to further their own political agendas." Susan Clark Muntean, *Corporate Independent Spending in the Post-BCRA to Pre-Citizens United Era*, 13 BUS. & POL. 1, 7-8 (2011). The data show that founder-controlled and agent-managed firms make political contributions in similar amounts at the lower ranges of corporate political spending, but that corporate "megadonors" are drawn "exclusively" from the ranks of founder-controlled firms. Moreover, family- or founder-controlled firms are much less likely than agent-managed firms to divide their contributions among groups and candidates across the ideological spectrum. *Id.* at 12. Are controls of internal corporate democracy adequate where a powerful founder dominates a corporation's activities and political culture?

According to one account, the roots of early twentieth-century prohibitions on corporate spending in politics lie not, as is conventionally assumed, in the fear of corporate domination of politics, but precisely in the concern that corporate political spending does not adequately advance the interests of shareholders:

> At the turn of the century, when Congress and the states first adopted bans, corporate political contributions were also understood to be . . . a misuse of "other people's money": company executives were opportunistically misappropriating the company owners' money to purchase legislation benefiting the executives themselves. . . . In other words, corporate political corruption was conceptualized as a problem of agency costs within firms.

Adam Winkler, *"Other People's Money": Corporations, Agency Costs, and Campaign Finance Law*, 92 GEO. L.J. 871, 873 (2004).

Intensified Disclosure.   As in earlier decisions, the Court in *Citizens United* expressed approval of disclosure as a substitute for regulation. This has led critics of the decision to look toward a regime of enhanced disclosure of corporate spending as a second-best substitute for the invalidated regulatory ban. In 2010, legislation was introduced in Congress that would have required corporations and unions to disclose publicly and to shareholders all significant independent expenditures. The legislation was not enacted.

In 2011, a group of law professors submitted a proposal for formal rulemaking by the Securities and Exchange Commission (SEC) arguing that publicly traded companies should be required to disclose corporate political activity to shareholders in order for shareholders to respond properly to unwise political spending. Letter from Comm. on Disclosure of Corporate Political Spending to Elizabeth M. Murphy, Sec'y, U.S. Sec. & Exch. Comm'n (Aug. 3, 2011), *available at* http://www.sec.gov/rules/petitions/2011/petn4-637.pdf. Such rulemaking, the professors argued, could be accomplished under the SEC's existing authority and be made through existing facilities of corporate annual reports.* Disclosure to shareholders was necessary, the petition stated, to effectuate the forms of shareholder control specifically envisioned in Justice Kennedy's majority opinion in *Citizens United*. Upholding BCRA's general corporate disclosure requirements, Justice Kennedy wrote that

> [w]ith the advent of the Internet, prompt disclosure of expenditures can provide shareholders and citizens with the information needed to hold corporations and elected officials accountable for their positions. Shareholders can determine whether their corporation's political speech advances the corporation's interest in making profits, and citizens can see whether elected officials are in the pocket of so-called moneyed interests.

Citizens United, 558 U.S. at 370. For this form of corporate control to be effective, "shareholders," the professors asserted, "must have information about the company's political speech; otherwise, shareholders are unable to know whether such speech 'advances the corporation's interest in making profits.'" Disclosure to shareholders was, furthermore, supported by public shareholders: "As early as 2006, polls indicated that 85% of shareholders held the view that there is a lack of transparency surrounding corporate political activity."

The proposal generated a tremendous amount of feedback. As of November 2013, the SEC had received 641,799 form letters and 1,800 other letters commenting on the petition, the vast majority of which supported the proposal. Emily Chasan, *Petition for Disclosure on Political Spending Gains Support*, WALL ST. J., *available at* http://blogs.wsj.com/cfo/2013/11/12/petition-for-disclosure-on-political-spending-gains-support.

Among the critics of the proposal, however, was Professor Stephen Bainbridge, who argued in his own letter to the SEC that

> [t]he proposed rulemaking may not be about transparency at all, but instead be intended as a disincentive for corporations to participate in associations that, among other missions, make political expenditures. That is an illegitimate goal. Political speech is at the core of First Amendment, and the Supreme Court has stated clearly and repeatedly that the corporate source of the speech is not relevant when assessing its protection from regulation.

---

* 15 U.S.C. §78n(a) prohibits the solicitation of proxies "in contravention of such rules and regulations as the Commission may prescribe as necessary or appropriate in the public interest or for the protection of investors."

Letter from Stephen M. Bainbridge et al. to Elizabeth M. Murphy, Sec'y, U.S. Sec. & Exch. Comm'n (Mar. 23, 2012), *available at* http://www.sec.gov/comments/4-637/4637-318.pdf. Furthermore, Bainbridge argues that shareholder disclosure is unnecessary as "[g]enuine political expenditures" are already disclosed.

In contrast to this latter argument, the professors' proposal asserts that political spending information is scattered and "[p]ublic-company investors should not have to bear the costs of assembling this information from these sources when the corporation, which already has the information, can easily provide it to shareholders." Do you agree? Would corporate disclosure to shareholders be duplicative in light of existing disclosure requirements? Does the information gap between corporate managers and shareholders justify this extra layer of disclosure?

Despite the public support of at least one commissioner, the SEC has yet to formally include the proposal as part of its public agenda. Dina ElBoghdady, *SEC Drops Disclosure of Corporate Political Spending from Its Priority List*, WASH. POST (Nov. 30, 2013).

But just how effective would an expanded disclosure remedy be?

> [A]ctually obtaining disclosure of corporate spending has proven difficult in practice. There is considerable evidence that business corporations prefer not to spend directly, that is, through ads taken out by the corporations themselves. Instead, they prefer to act through intermediaries, that is, by donating to other organizations that then sponsor the political ads. This can facilitate the pooling of funds from many like-minded corporate donors and the hiring of political strategists to determine where those funds can be used to the greatest political effect. Under current law, it may also make it possible for corporations to avoid disclosure.

Richard Briffault, *Two Challenges for Campaign Finance Disclosure After* Citizens United *and* Doe v. Reed, 19 WM. & MARY BILL RTS. J. 983, 1006 (2011). In response to this challenge, one of the more controversial aspects of the professors' letter was a proposal for a look-through provision intended to enable shareholders to scrutinize not only the direct recipients of corporate political donations, but also the end uses of funds contributed by the corporation to PACs and other third-party political organizations. *See also* Lucian A. Bebchuk and Robert J. Jackson, Jr., *Shining Light on Corporate Political Spending*, 101 GEO. L.J. 923, 949-953 (2013). Some of the top Super PACs have names such as "American Crossroads" and "Restore Our Future." Does the name reveal anything of value to voters? To shareholders? Are more intrusive look-through disclosure requirements feasible? Constitutional?

Lobbying Reform. It has been suggested that *Citizens United* marks "the nearly complete de-regulation of independent expenditures," and as a result, "[t]he ways forward for campaign finance reform must come from outside of campaign finance law as we have known it." In particular, it has been argued that the only way now open to deal effectively with problems caused by money in the political system is "ex post regulation of money once it is in the political system, rather than ex ante regulation of money to limit its entry in the first place." Michael S. Kang, *The End of Campaign Finance Law*, 98 VA. L. REV. 1 (2012). How might this be accomplished?

One possibility is to exercise heightened regulatory control over lobbying. Suppose that *Citizens United* leads in fact to a reformer's nightmare: a tidal wave of new corporate spending sweeps into office a Congress populated disproportionately by candidates preferred by wealthy corporations. This need not mean, however, that such legislators take office with a legislative agenda in hand, provided by big corporations, which they stand ready to enact. Suppose it means something less — for example, that such legislators are unusually sensitive to the interests of large corporations, or when forced to choose are predisposed to prefer corporate interests over interests of other segments of society. Lobbying access might then be a mechanism by which legislators holding these predispositions are activated to invoke them. It follows that laws restricting or equalizing lobbying access might limit the frequency of signals to legislators from the corporate interests to which they are predisposed to respond in a way that creates opportunities for legislators to perceive and respond to signals arriving from other segments of society through different channels or through their own lobbying. *See* Kang, *supra*; Richard L. Hasen, *Lobbying, Rent Seeking, and the Constitution*, 64 Stan. L. Rev. 191 (2012). Might this be a feasible solution?

» *Political Spending by Foreign Nationals.*   Among the few restrictions on campaign finance that the Supreme Court has not invalidated are those applying to foreign nationals. These restrictions include bans on contributions to candidates or political parties; funding the operation of a PAC; and spending "in connection with" domestic elections. If, as the Court declared in *Citizens United*, the "identity" of a speaker is irrelevant to its First Amendment right to speak freely in the political arena, how can restrictions on foreigners stand? Isn't foreign citizenship an attribute of identity or status? Does the government have a compelling interest in restricting foreign spending in elections that it lacks with respect to spending by domestic actors? If the benefit of speech consists in informing the electorate, why isn't information supplied by foreign corporations of the same value as information supplied by domestic ones? *See* Toni M. Massaro, *Foreign Nationals, Electoral Spending, and the First Amendment*, 34 Harv. J.L. & Pub. Pol'y 663 (2011); Richard L. Hasen, Citizens United *and the Illusion of Coherence*, 109 Mich. L. Rev. 581 (2011).

In *Bluman v. FEC*, the Supreme Court summarily affirmed the ruling of a three-judge district court upholding the constitutionality of restrictions on foreign political spending. 800 F. Supp. 2d 281 (D.D.C., three-judge court), *summarily aff'd*, 132 S. Ct. 1087 (2012). In a brief analysis, the lower court held, based on its study of numerous precedents, that

> [i]t is fundamental to the definition of our national political community that foreign citizens do not have a constitutional right to participate in, and thus may be excluded from, activities of democratic self-government. It follows, therefore, that the United States has a compelling interest for purposes of First Amendment analysis in limiting the participation of foreign citizens in activities of American democratic self-government, and in thereby preventing foreign influence over the U.S. political process.

Id. at 288.

⏩   ***Developments Since* Citizens United.**   Perhaps the most important development following the Court's decision in *Citizens United* was the decision two months later by the D.C. Circuit in *SpeechNow.Org v. FEC*, 599 F.3d 686 (D.C. Cir. 2010). There, the court invalidated a provision of FECA limiting the amount that can be contributed to a PAC organized for the exclusive purpose of making independent expenditures in support of or in opposition to candidates for office. The Court's reasoning drew directly on *Citizens United*:

> The Supreme Court has recognized only one interest sufficiently important to outweigh the First Amendment interests implicated by contributions for political speech: preventing corruption or the appearance of corruption. . . . Because of the Supreme Court's recent decision in *Citizens United v. FEC*, the analysis is straightforward. There, the Court held that the government has *no* anti-corruption interest in limiting independent expenditures. . . . In light of the Court's holding as a matter of law that independent expenditures do not corrupt or create the appearance of quid pro quo corruption, contributions to groups that make only independent expenditures also cannot corrupt or create the appearance of corruption. The Court has effectively held that there is no corrupting "quid" for which a candidate might in exchange offer a corrupt "quo."

As a result, contributions to independent-expenditure-only PACs — so-called Super PACs — are unlimited, as are the amounts these groups can spend.

Although individuals could independently spend unlimited sums following *Buckley* — and after *Citizens United*, corporations and unions could do so too — the option of being able to direct these expenditures through the PAC format made heavy independent spending much more attractive than it had been under the old *Buckley* regime. One reason probably has to do with the ancillary costs of political spending. The average billionaire or Fortune 500 company lacks expertise in how to spend large sums of political money effectively. A PAC offers one-stop shopping: a staff of political experts to determine where the money can best be used and how best to package the desired message; production and distribution resources; access to media; and, no doubt, attentive customer service. Moreover, candidates can raise money for their Super PACs; candidates and their Super PACs can share vendors such as polling and media firms; and Super PACs supporting the candidates are often run by the candidates' former campaign personnel or former political confidants. In addition, recent FEC rulings have made it easier to structure these contributions in ways that evade disclosure requirements, thus maintaining the anonymity of the donor. Service is thus not only effective, but also discreet.

⏩   ***The Impact of* Citizens United.**   Critics of *Citizens United* worried that the Court's decision would dramatically change the political landscape. They feared that the ruling would unleash a flood of corporate money into the political arena, vastly increasing the total amount of money in the system and overwhelming funds provided by political parties and non-corporate actors. This flood of corporate money would in turn, it was feared, have a substantial impact on who gets elected to public office and, eventually, on the content of public policies enacted by state and national elected officials. Moreover, it was feared that *Citizens United* would drive political money from where it is more regulated, as when it is under the control of political parties and candidates, to where it is less regulated—for example, expenditures by 501(c)(4) groups, which do not have to disclose their donors, or contributions by those organizations to Super PACs making independent expenditures.

Have these results come to pass? Yes and no. It is very clear that the amount of money introduced into the national political arena has skyrocketed since the Court's decision in *Citizens United*. For example, in 2000 congressional candidates spent more than $1 billion compared to the $15 million spent by outside groups in independent expenditures. In 2010, outside groups spent more than $540 million, about $715 million in 2012, and well over $1 billion in 2014. *See* Jeff Gulati and Victoria A. Farrar-Myers, *The Impact of Outside Group Expenditures in U.S. House Elections, 2010-2014* (unpublished paper 2017).

But what is the source of this spending? Perhaps surprisingly, it does not appear to be coming from corporations and labor unions, the groups that *Citizens United* freed from long-standing spending restrictions. Perhaps this should not be surprising; according to one analysis, *Citizens United* does nothing to change the basic incentive structure that corporations face, and that structure makes corporate spending in politics very risky. Wendy Hansen et al., *The Effects of* Citizens United *on Corporate Contributions in the 2012 Presidential Election*, 77 J. POL. 535 (2015). Recall the market punishment visited upon the Target corporation, described above, when it donated money to a gubernatorial candidate who had made controversial, anti-gay statements. Corporations and unions might justifiably fear that the consequences of a political misstep may be catastrophic, whereas the potential benefits of successful corporate investment in politics are unduly speculative.

In fact, the rapid rise in "outside" (non-candidate and non-party) electoral spending is coming from individuals and from Super PACs. A report by the Brennan Center for Justice on spending in Senate elections concluded that total spending by Super PACs and outside groups more than doubled in the four years after the Court decided *Citizens United*. Moreover, in the races examined by the Brennan Center, outside groups outspent the political candidates and the political parties. *See* http://www.brennancenter.org/sites/default/files/analysis/Outside%20Spend ing%20Since%20Citizens%20United.pdf. When we think of this kind of spending, we tend to think of it being channeled through groups that are completely unaffiliated with candidates and parties. However, several recent studies suggest caution about this conclusion. A study by the Campaign Finance Institute found that although outside groups were outspending parties and candidates, *see* http://www.cfinst.org/Press/PReleases/17-04-13/POLITICAL_PARTIES_AND_CANDI-DATES_DOMINATED_THE_2016_HOUSE_ELECTIONS_WHILE_HOLDING_THEIR_OWN_IN_THE_SENATE.aspx, such groups tend to be affiliated with parties and their candidates, albeit more loosely than was the case in the past. For example, congressional party leaders have created their own Super PACs and have competed effectively, at least in 2016, with non-party outside groups. At the state level, much of the increase in electoral spending is attributable to the influence of a single organization, the Republican Governors Association, an organization obviously closely affiliated with a national political party. Keith E. Hamm et al., *Independent Spending in State Elections, 2006-2010: Vertically Networked Political Parties Were the Real Story, Not Business*, 12 THE FORUM 305 (2014). *See also* Keith E. Hamm et al., *The*

Impact of Citizens United *in the States: Independent Spending in State Elections, 2006-2010,* 77 J. Pol. 535 (2015).

Another important question is whether the observed increase in political spending by individuals and Super PACs is actually attributable to the Court's decision in *Citizens United.* In an empirical paper, Professors Douglas Spencer and Abby Wood compared independent spending after *Citizens United* between states that did not prohibit corporate and union independent expenditures prior to *Citizens United* and those that did. Because many states did not prohibit independent spending prior to *Citizens United* and some states did, *Citizens United* presented Professors Spencer and Wood with a "natural experiment," which enabled them to gauge the impact of *Citizens United* on independent spending. They found that independent spending rose in both types of states, those that banned independent spending prior to *Citizens United* and those that did not. However, they also found that the spending increase was greater, twice as much, in the states that previously banned independent expenditures by unions and corporations. They also found that, contrary to the expectations of critics of *Citizens United,* the increase in expenditures was not the product of large donations by a few spenders; small expenditures were as likely as large expenditures. *See* Douglas M. Spencer and Abby K. Wood, Citizens United, *States Divided: An Empirical Analysis of Independent Political Spending,* 89 Ind. L.J. 315 (2014). *See also* Hamm et al., *The Impact of* Citizens United, *supra* (reaching similar conclusions).

Perhaps the most critical question is whether the increased spending by outside groups has an impact on electoral outcomes. It is too soon to make any conclusive determinations. Some early studies have found very small to no discernible effects in the elections that they have examined. One study found that *Citizens United* was associated with an increase of approximately 4 percent in the probability of a Republican being elected to a state legislature, with the advantage rising to as much as 10 percent in some states. Tilman Klumpp et al., *The Business of American Democracy:* Citizens United, *Independent Spending, and Elections,* 59 J.L. & Econ. 1 (2016). Another study concluded that outside groups did not have an impact on electoral outcomes of House of Representatives elections, the elections studied by the authors. *See* Gulati and Farrar-Myers, *supra.* Moreover, a historical study of the impact of corporate spending bans in the states from 1935 to 2009 found they have been irrelevant to the content of state policy choices. Raymond J. La Raja and Brian F. Schaffner, *The Effects of Campaign Finance Spending Bans on Electoral Outcomes: Evidence from the States About the Potential Impact of* Citizens United v. FEC, 33 Electoral Stud. 102 (2014).

>> *Counteracting the Effects of* **Citizens United?**   The Court's decision in *Citizens United* has prompted much thinking about how its effects might be counteracted. One response, undertaken by some state legislatures, has been to increase the ceiling on contributions by individuals to candidates and political parties. Jason Torchinsky and Ezra Reese, *State Legislative "Responses" to* Citizens United: *Five Years Later,* 66 Syracuse L. Rev. 273 (2016). By so doing, these states hope to drive money toward more accountable and closely regulated political actors and away from uncontrollable entities like Super PACs. Another possible countermeasure involves private agreements among the candidates not to accept the benefits of third-party spending on their behalf. In the contentious 2012 U.S. Senate contest

between Elizabeth Warren and Scott Brown, the candidates signed what they called a "People's Pledge." The pledge required each candidate to donate to charity an amount equal to one-half the amount spent by outside groups in support of their own candidacy. The results were striking. Out of fear of harming the candidates they wished to support with their own advertising, outside groups instead mainly sat on the sidelines, leaving the candidates in greater control of their own campaigns:

> Outside spending made up only 9% of total spending in Massachusetts, compared to 62%, 47%, and 64% of total spending in Senate races in Virginia, Ohio, and Wisconsin respectively (the second, third, and fifth most expensive races of 2012). Small donors (giving less than $200) had more influence than big donors in Massachusetts, contributing $23.5 million to the big donors' $8 million; in Virginia, Wisconsin, and Ohio combined, the big donors dominated the small donors, $135 million to $23.8 million. Compared to those in Massachusetts, television advertisements in Virginia, Wisconsin, and Ohio were, on average, more than twice as likely to be negative advertisements—36% in Massachusetts, compared to 84% in the other states.

Ganesh Sitaramin, *Contracting Around* Citizens United, 114 COLUM. L. REV. 755, 769 (2014). *See also* Scott P. Bloomberg, *Contracting Around* Citizens United: *A Systemic Solution*, 66 SYRACUSE L. REV. 301 (2016).

McCutcheon v. Federal Election Commission

134 S. Ct. 1434 (2014)

Chief Justice ROBERTS announced the judgment of the Court and delivered an opinion, in which Justice SCALIA, Justice KENNEDY, and Justice ALITO join.

There is no right more basic in our democracy than the right to participate in electing our political leaders. Citizens can exercise that right in a variety of ways: They can run for office themselves, vote, urge others to vote for a particular candidate, volunteer to work on a campaign, and contribute to a candidate's campaign. This case is about the last of those options. . . .

The statute at issue in this case imposes two types of limits on campaign contributions. The first, called base limits, restricts how much money a donor may contribute to a particular candidate or committee. 2 U.S.C. §441a(a)(1). The second, called aggregate limits, restricts how much money a donor may contribute in total to all candidates or committees. §441a(a)(3).

This case does not involve any challenge to the base limits, which we have previously upheld as serving the permissible objective of combatting corruption. We conclude, however, that the aggregate limits do little, if anything, to address that concern, while seriously restricting participation in the democratic process. The aggregate limits are therefore invalid under the First Amendment.

I

For the 2013-2014 election cycle, the base limits in the Federal Election Campaign Act of 1971 (FECA), as amended by the Bipartisan Campaign Reform Act of 2002 (BCRA), permit an individual to contribute up to $2,600 per election to a candidate ($5,200 total for the primary and general elections); $32,400 per year to a national party committee; $10,000 per year to a state or local party committee; and $5,000 per year to a political action committee, or "PAC." 2 U.S.C. §441a(a) (1). A national committee, state or local party committee, or multicandidate PAC may in turn contribute up to $5,000 per election to a candidate. §441a(a)(2). . . .

For the 2013-2014 election cycle, the aggregate limits in BCRA permit an individual to contribute a total of $48,600 to federal candidates and a total of $74,600 to other political committees. Of that $74,600, only $48,600 may be contributed to state or local party committees and PACs, as opposed to national party committees. §441a(a)(3). All told, an individual may contribute up to $123,200 to candidate and noncandidate committees during each two-year election cycle. . . .

In the 2011-2012 election cycle, appellant Shaun McCutcheon contributed a total of $33,088 to 16 different federal candidates, in compliance with the base limits applicable to each. He alleges that he wished to contribute $1,776 to each of 12 additional candidates but was prevented from doing so by the aggregate limit on contributions to candidates. McCutcheon also contributed a total of $27,328 to several noncandidate political committees, in compliance with the base limits applicable to each. He alleges that he wished to contribute to various other political committees, including $25,000 to each of the three Republican national party committees, but was prevented from doing so by the aggregate limit on contributions to political committees. McCutcheon further alleges that he plans to make similar contributions in the future. In the 2013-2014 election cycle, he again wishes to contribute at least $60,000 to various candidates and $75,000 to noncandidate political committees. Brief for Appellant McCutcheon 11-12. . . .

II

[I]n one paragraph of its 139-page opinion, the Court [in *Buckley v. Valeo*, 424 U.S. 1 (1976)] turned to the $25,000 aggregate limit under FECA. As a preliminary matter, it noted that the constitutionality of the aggregate limit "ha[d] not been separately addressed at length by the parties." *Id.*, at 38. Then, in three sentences, the Court disposed of any constitutional objections to the aggregate limit that the challengers might have had:

> The overall $25,000 ceiling does impose an ultimate restriction upon the number of candidates and committees with which an individual may associate himself by means of financial support. But this quite modest restraint upon protected political activity serves to prevent evasion of the $1,000 contribution limitation by a person who might otherwise contribute massive amounts of money to a particular candidate through the use of unearmarked contributions to political committees likely to contribute to that candidate, or huge contributions to the candidate's political party. The limited, additional restriction on associational freedom imposed by the overall ceiling is thus no more than a corollary of the basic individual contribution limitation that we have found to be constitutionally valid.

Ibid. . . .

III

. . . An aggregate limit on *how many* candidates and committees an individual may support through contributions is not a "modest restraint" at all. . . .

To put it in the simplest terms, the aggregate limits prohibit an individual from fully contributing to the primary and general election campaigns of ten or more candidates, even if all contributions fall within the base limits Congress views as adequate to protect against corruption. . . . A donor must limit the number of candidates he supports, and may have to choose which of several policy concerns he will advance — clear First Amendment harms that the dissent never acknowledges. . . .

IV

With the significant First Amendment costs for individual citizens in mind, we turn to the governmental interests asserted in this case. This Court has identified only one legitimate governmental interest for restricting campaign finances: preventing corruption or the appearance of corruption. *See Davis v. Federal Election Comm'n*, 554 U.S. 724, 741 (2008); *Federal Election Comm'n v. National Conservative Political Action Comm.*, 470 U.S. 480, 496-97 (1985). We have consistently rejected attempts to suppress campaign speech based on other legislative objectives. No matter how desirable it may seem, it is not an acceptable governmental objective to "level the playing field," or to "level electoral opportunities," or to "equaliz[e] the financial resources of candidates." *Arizona Free Enterprise Club's Freedom Club PAC v. Bennett*, 564 U.S. 721 (2011). . . .

Moreover, while preventing corruption or its appearance is a legitimate objective, Congress may target only a specific type of corruption — "*quid pro quo*" corruption. As *Buckley* explained, Congress may permissibly seek to rein in "large contributions [that] are given to secure a political *quid pro quo* from current and potential office holders." 424 U.S., at 26. In addition to "actual *quid pro quo* arrangements," Congress may permissibly limit "the appearance of corruption stemming from public awareness of the opportunities for abuse inherent in a regime of large individual financial contributions" to particular candidates. *Id.*, at 27.

Spending large sums of money in connection with elections, but not in connection with an effort to control the exercise of an officeholder's official duties, does not give rise to such *quid pro quo* corruption. Nor does the possibility that an individual who spends large sums may garner "influence over or access to" elected officials or political parties. *Citizens United v. Federal Election Comm'n*, 558 U.S. 310, 359 (2010); *see McConnell v. Federal Election Comm'n*, 540 U.S. 93, 297 (2003) (Kennedy, J., concurring in judgment in part and dissenting in part). And because the Government's interest in preventing the appearance of corruption is equally confined to the appearance of *quid pro quo* corruption, the Government may not seek to limit the appearance of mere influence or access. *See Citizens United*, 558 U.S., at 360. . . .

The difficulty is that once the aggregate limits kick in, they ban all contributions of *any* amount. But Congress's selection of a $5,200 base limit indicates its belief that contributions of that amount or less do not create a cognizable risk of corruption. If there is no corruption concern in giving nine candidates up to $5,200 each, it is difficult to understand how a tenth candidate can be regarded as corruptible if given $1,801, and all others corruptible if given a dime. And if there is no risk that additional candidates will be corrupted by donations of up to $5,200, then the Government must defend the aggregate limits by demonstrating that they prevent circumvention of the base limits. . . .

Quite apart from the foregoing, the aggregate limits violate the First Amendment because they are not "closely drawn to avoid unnecessary abridgment of associational freedoms." *Buckley*, 424 U.S., at 25. . . .

With modern technology, disclosure now offers a particularly effective means of arming the voting public with information. Today, given the Internet, disclosure offers much more robust protections against corruption [than in 1976, when *Buckley* was decided]. *See Citizens United, supra*, at 370-371. Reports and databases are available on the FEC's Web site almost immediately after they are filed, supplemented by private entities such as OpenSecrets.org and FollowTheMoney.org. Because massive quantities of information can be accessed at the click of a mouse, disclosure is effective to a degree not possible at the time *Buckley*, or even *McConnell*, was decided. . . .

Justice THOMAS, concurring in the judgment.

I adhere to the view that this Court's decision in *Buckley v. Valeo*, 424 U.S. 1 (1976) (per curiam), denigrates core First Amendment speech and should be overruled. . . .

Justice BREYER, with whom Justice GINSBURG, Justice SOTOMAYOR, and Justice KAGAN join, dissenting.

Nearly 40 years ago in *Buckley v. Valeo*, 424 U.S. 1 (1976) (*per curiam*), this Court considered the constitutionality of laws that imposed limits upon the overall amount a single person can contribute to all federal candidates, political parties, and committees taken together. The Court held that those limits did not violate the Constitution. *Id.*, at 38; *accord, McConnell v. Federal Election Comm'n*, 540 U.S. 93, 138, n.40, 152-153, n. 48 (2003) (citing with approval *Buckley*'s aggregate limits holding). . . .

Today a majority of the Court overrules this holding. It is wrong to do so. . . .

The plurality's first claim — that large aggregate contributions do not "give rise" to "corruption" — is plausible only because the plurality defines "corruption" too narrowly. [T]he anticorruption interest that drives Congress to regulate campaign contributions is a far broader, more important interest than the plurality acknowledges. It is an interest in maintaining the integrity of our public governmental institutions. And it is an interest rooted in the Constitution and in the First Amendment itself.

Speech does not exist in a vacuum. Rather, political communication seeks to secure government action. A politically oriented "marketplace of ideas" seeks to form a public opinion that can and will influence elected representatives.

[The government's anticorruption interests] are rooted in the constitutional effort to create a democracy responsive to the people — a government where laws reflect the very thoughts, views, ideas, and sentiments, the expression of which the First Amendment protects. . . .

Since the kinds of corruption that can destroy the link between public opinion and governmental action extend well beyond those the plurality describes, the plurality's notion of corruption is flatly inconsistent with the basic constitutional rationale I have just described. Thus, it should surprise no one that this Court's case law (*Citizens United* excepted) insists upon a considerably broader definition. . . .

The plurality invalidates the aggregate contribution limits for a second reason. It believes they are no longer needed to prevent contributors from circumventing federal limits on direct contributions to individuals, political parties, and political action committees. *Ante*, at 1452-1456. *Cf. Buckley*, 424 U.S., at 38. . . . The plurality is wrong. Here, as in *Buckley*, in the absence of limits on aggregate political contributions, donors can and likely will find ways to channel millions of dollars to parties and to individual candidates, producing precisely the kind of "corruption" or "appearance of corruption" that previously led the Court to hold aggregate limits constitutional. Those opportunities for circumvention will also produce the type of corruption that concerns the plurality today. . . .

In the past, when evaluating the constitutionality of campaign finance restrictions, we have typically relied upon an evidentiary record amassed below to determine whether the law served a compelling governmental objective. . . . Without further development of the record, however, I fail to see how the plurality can now find grounds for overturning *Buckley*. [This] decision . . . substitutes judges' understandings of how the political process works for the understanding of Congress. . . .

>> ***The End of the* Buckley *Settlement?***   Does *McCutcheon* represent the end of *Buckley* as the framework for addressing the constitutionality of campaign-finance-reform efforts? To the extent that *Buckley* stood for the proposition that contribution limitations are consistent with First Amendment doctrine, in contrast with expenditure limitations, *McCutcheon*, at the very least, muddies the waters. What is left of the *Buckley* settlement?

>> ***Corruption Once More.***   Chief Justice Roberts's plurality opinion reaffirms the proposition laid down in *Citizens United* that the government can only justify campaign-finance regulations to limit quid pro quo corruption. Moreover, contributing and spending money so as to influence office-holders and would-be office-holders does not constitute quid pro quo corruption. The plurality implies that spending money "in an effort to control the exercise of an officeholder's official duty" does give rise to quid pro quo corruption. What is the distinction between contributions and/or expenditures that are meant to procure influence and access and contributions and/or expenditures that are meant to control the exercise of an office-holder's official duties?

>> ***Right of Political Participation?***   In the opening paragraph of the plurality opinion, Chief Justice Roberts references a right to political participation that includes the right to vote as well as the right to contribute to a candidate's campaign. Does *McCutcheon* imply that the constitutional scrutiny that attaches to limitations on the right to contribute to a political campaign also attaches to limitations on the right to vote?

G. PUBLIC FINANCING OF ELECTIONS

One way to address the constitutionality of campaign-finance statutes, particularly where the state wants to create a holistic scheme, as Congress attempted to do in FECA 1974, is for the government to provide funding for campaigns. As you may recall, FECA 1974 contained a public finance component, which the Court addressed in *Buckley*. A 2011 decision by the Supreme Court addressing the State of Arizona's public finance scheme makes clear that the Court's deregulatory posture is clearly applicable in the public finance context. While the Court's discussion in *Buckley* seems to sanction public finance as a regulatory mechanism, the Arizona case makes clear that constitutional limits apply, which might make public finance schemes less viable options than one might think. Both cases are excerpted below.

Buckley v. Valeo

424 U.S. 1 (1976) (per curiam)

. . .

III. PUBLIC FINANCING OF PRESIDENTIAL ELECTION CAMPAIGNS

A series of statutes for the public financing of Presidential election campaigns produced the scheme now found in §6096 and Subtitle H of the Internal Revenue Code of 1954, 26 U.S.C. §§6096, 9001-9012, 9031-9042 (1970 ed., Supp. IV). Both the District Court and the Court of Appeals sustained Subtitle H against a constitutional attack. Appellants renew their challenge here, contending that the legislation violates the First and Fifth Amendments. We find no merit in their claims and affirm.

A. Summary of Subtitle H

Section 9006 establishes a Presidential Election Campaign Fund (Fund), financed from general revenues in the aggregate amount designated by individual taxpayers, under §6096, who on their income tax returns may authorize payment to the Fund of one dollar of their tax liability in the case of an individual return or two dollars in the case of a joint return. The Fund consists of three separate accounts to finance (1) party nominating conventions, §9008(a), (2) general election campaigns, §9006(a), and (3) primary campaigns, §9037(a).

Chapter 95 of Title 26, which concerns financing of party nominating conventions and general election campaigns, distinguishes among "major," "minor," and "new" parties. A major party is defined as a party whose candidate for President in the most recent election received 25% or more of the popular vote. §9002(6). A minor party is defined as a party whose candidate received at least 5% but less than 25% of the vote at the most recent election. §9002(7). All other parties are new parties, §9002(8), including both newly created parties and those receiving less than 5% of the vote in the last election.

Major parties are entitled to $2,000,000 to defray their national committee Presidential nominating convention expenses, must limit total expenditures to that amount, §9008(d), and may not use any of this money to benefit a particular candidate or delegate, §9008(c). A minor party receives a portion of the major-party entitlement determined by the ratio of the votes received by the party's candidate in the last election to the average of the votes received by the major parties' candidates. §9008(b)(2). The amounts given to the parties and the expenditure limit are adjusted for inflation, using 1974 as the base year. §9008(b)(5). No financing is provided for new parties, nor is there any express provision for financing independent candidates or parties not holding a convention.

For expenses in the general election campaign, §9004(a)(1) entitles each major-party candidate to $20,000,000. This amount is also adjusted for inflation. See §9004(a)(1). To be eligible for funds the candidate must pledge not to incur expenses in excess of the entitlement under §9004(a)(1) and not to accept private contributions except to the extent that the fund is insufficient to provide the full entitlement. §9003(b). Minor-party candidates are also entitled to funding, again based on the ratio of the vote received by the party's candidate in the preceding election to the average of the major-party candidates. §9004(a) (2)(A). Minor-party candidates must certify that they will not incur campaign expenses in excess of the major-party entitlement and that they will accept private contributions only to the extent needed to make up the difference between that amount and the public funding grant. §9003(c). New-party candidates receive no money prior to the general election, but any candidate receiving 5% or more of the popular vote in the election is entitled to post-election payments according to the formula applicable to minor-party candidates. §9004(a) (3). Similarly, minor-party candidates are entitled to post-election funds if they receive a greater percentage of the average major-party vote than their party's candidate did in the preceding election; the amount of such payments is the difference between the entitlement based on the preceding election and that based on the actual vote in the current election. §9004(a)(3). A further eligibility requirement for minor- and new-party candidates is that the candidate's name must appear on the ballot, or electors pledged to the candidate must be on the ballot, in at least 10 States. §9002(2)(B).

Chapter 96 establishes a third account in the Fund, the Presidential Primary Matching Payment Account. §9037(a). This funding is intended to aid campaigns by candidates seeking Presidential nomination "by a political party," §9033(b)(2), in "primary elections," §9032(7). The threshold eligibility requirement is that the candidate raise at least $5,000 in each of 20 States, counting only the first $250 from each person contributing to the candidate. §9033(b)(3), (4). In addition, the candidate must agree to abide by the spending limits in §9035. See §9033(b)(1). Funding is provided according to a matching formula: each qualified candidate is entitled to a sum equal to the total private contributions received, disregarding contributions from any person to the extent that total contributions to the candidate by that person exceed $250. §9034(a). Payments to any candidate under Chapter 96 may not exceed 50% of the overall expenditure ceiling accepted by the candidate. §9034(b).

B. Constitutionality of Subtitle H

Appellants argue that Subtitle H is invalid (1) as "contrary to the 'general welfare,'" Art. I, §8(2) because any scheme of public financing of election campaigns is inconsistent with the First Amendment, and (3) because Subtitle H invidiously discriminates against certain interests in violation of the Due Process Clause of the Fifth Amendment. We find no merit in these contentions.

Appellants' "general welfare" contention erroneously treats the General Welfare Clause as a limitation upon congressional power. It is rather a grant of power, the scope of which is quite expansive, particularly in view of the enlargement of power by the Necessary and Proper Clause. Congress has power to regulate Presidential elections and primaries, *United States v. Classic*, and public financing of Presidential elections as a means to reform the electoral process was clearly a choice within the granted power. It is for Congress to decide which expenditures will promote the general welfare: "(T)he power of Congress to authorize expenditure of public moneys for public purposes is not limited by the direct grants of legislative power found in the Constitution." *United States v. Butler.* Any limitations upon the exercise of that granted power must be found elsewhere in the Constitution. In this case, Congress was legislating for the "general welfare" to reduce the deleterious influence of large contributions on our political process, to facilitate communication by candidates with the electorate, and to free candidates from the rigors of fundraising. See S. Rep. No. 93-689, pp. 1-10 (1974). Whether the chosen means appear "bad," "unwise," or "unworkable" to us is irrelevant; Congress has concluded that the means are "necessary and proper" to promote the general welfare, and we thus decline to find this legislation without the grant of power in Art. I, §8.

Appellants' challenge to the dollar check-off provision (§6096) fails for the same reason.

Equal protection analysis in the Fifth Amendment area is the same as that under the Fourteenth Amendment. In several situations concerning the electoral process, the principle has been developed that restrictions on access to the electoral process must survive exacting scrutiny. The restriction can be sustained only if it furthers a "vital" governmental interest, *American Party of Texas v. White*, that is "achieved by a means that does not unfairly or unnecessarily burden either a minority party's or an individual candidate's equally important interest in the continued availability of political opportunity." *Lubin v. Panish.* These cases, however, dealt primarily with state laws requiring a candidate to satisfy certain requirements in order to have his name appear on the ballot. These were, of course, direct burdens not only on the candidate's ability to run for office but also on the voter's ability to voice preferences regarding representative government and contemporary issues. In contrast, the denial of public financing to some Presidential candidates is not restrictive of voters' rights and less restrictive of candidates'. Subtitle H does not prevent any candidate from getting on the ballot or any voter from casting a vote for the candidate of his choice; the inability, if any, of minor-party candidates to wage effective campaigns will derive not from lack of public funding but from their inability to raise private contributions. Any disadvantage suffered by operation of the eligibility formulae under Subtitle H is thus limited to the claimed denial of the enhancement of opportunity to communicate with the electorate that the formulae afford eligible candidates. But eligible candidates suffer a countervailing denial. As

we more fully develop later, acceptance of public financing entails voluntary acceptance of an expenditure ceiling. Noneligible candidates are not subject to that limitation. Accordingly, we conclude that public financing is generally less restrictive
of access to the electoral process than the ballot-access regulations dealt with in
prior cases. In any event, Congress enacted Subtitle H in furtherance of sufficiently
important governmental interests and has not unfairly or unnecessarily burdened
the political opportunity of any party or candidate.

It cannot be gainsaid that public financing as a means of eliminating the
improper influence of large private contributions furthers a significant governmental interest. S. Rep. No. 93-689, pp. 4-5 (1974). In addition, the limits on contributions necessarily increase the burden of fundraising, and Congress properly
regarded public financing as an appropriate means of relieving major-party Presidential candidates from the rigors of soliciting private contributions. See id., at
5. The States have also been held to have important interests in limiting places
on the ballot to those candidates who demonstrate substantial popular support.
Congress' interest in not funding hopeless candidacies with large sums of public
money necessarily justifies the withholding of public assistance from candidates
without significant public support. Thus, Congress may legitimately require "some
preliminary showing of a significant modicum of support," *Jenness v. Fortson*, as an
eligibility requirement for public funds. This requirement also serves the important public interest against providing artificial incentives to "splintered parties and
unrestrained factionalism." *Storer v. Brown.*

At the same time Congress recognized the constitutional restraints against
inhibition of the present opportunity of minor parties to become major political
entities if they obtain widespread support. As the Court of Appeals said, "provisions
for public funding of Presidential campaigns . . . could operate to give an unfair
advantage to established parties, thus reducing, to the nation's detriment, . . . the
'potential fluidity of American political life.'"

1. General Election Campaign Financing

Appellants insist that Chapter 95 falls short of the constitutional requirement
in that its provisions supply larger, and equal, sums to candidates of major parties, use prior vote levels as the sole criterion for pre-election funding, limit new-
party candidates to post-election funds, and deny any funds to candidates of parties
receiving less than 5% of the vote. These provisions, it is argued, are fatal to the
validity of the scheme, because they work invidious discrimination against minor
and new parties in violation of the Fifth Amendment. We disagree.

As conceded by appellants, the Constitution does not require Congress to
treat all declared candidates the same for public financing purposes. As we said
in *Jenness v. Fortson*, "there are obvious differences in kind between the needs and
potentials of a political party with historically established broad support, on the
one hand, and a new or small political organization on the other. . . . Sometimes
the grossest discrimination can lie in treating things that are different as though
they were exactly alike, a truism well illustrated in *Williams v. Rhodes*, supra." Since
the Presidential elections of 1856 and 1860, when the Whigs were replaced as a
major party by the Republicans, no third party has posed a credible threat to the
two major parties in Presidential elections. Third parties have been completely

incapable of matching the major parties' ability to raise money and win elections. Congress was, of course, aware of this fact of American life, and thus was justified in providing both major parties full funding and all other parties only a percentage of the major-party entitlement. Identical treatment of all parties, on the other hand, "would not only make it easy to raid the United States Treasury, it would also artificially foster the proliferation of splinter parties." The Constitution does not require the Government to "finance the efforts of every nascent political group," merely because Congress chose to finance the efforts of the major parties.

Furthermore, appellants have made no showing that the election funding plan disadvantages nonmajor parties by operating to reduce their strength below that attained without any public financing. First, such parties are free to raise money from private sources, and by our holding today new parties are freed from any expenditure limits, although admittedly those limits may be a largely academic matter to them. But since any major-party candidate accepting public financing of a campaign voluntarily assents to a spending ceiling, other candidates will be able to spend more in relation to the major-party candidates. The relative position of minor parties that do qualify to receive some public funds because they received 5% of the vote in the previous Presidential election is also enhanced. Public funding for candidates of major parties is intended as a substitute for private contributions; but for minor-party candidates such assistance may be viewed as a supplement to private contributions since these candidates may continue to solicit private funds up to the applicable spending limit. Thus, we conclude that the general election funding system does not work an invidious discrimination against candidates of nonmajor parties.

2. Nominating Convention Financing

The foregoing analysis and reasoning sustaining general election funding apply in large part to convention funding under Chapter 95 and suffice to support our rejection of appellants' challenge to these provisions. Funding of party conventions has increasingly been derived from large private contributions and the governmental interest in eliminating this reliance is as vital as in the case of private contributions to individual candidates. The expenditure limitations on major parties participating in public financing enhance the ability of nonmajor parties to increase their spending relative to the major parties; further, in soliciting private contributions to finance conventions, parties are not subject to the $1,000 contribution limit pertaining to candidates. We therefore conclude that appellants' constitutional challenge to the provisions for funding nominating conventions must also be rejected.

3. Primary Election Campaign Financing

Appellants' final challenge is to the constitutionality of Chapter 96, which provides funding of primary campaigns. They contend that these provisions are constitutionally invalid (1) because they do not provide funds for candidates not running in party primaries and (2) because the eligibility formula actually increases the influence of money on the electoral process. In not providing assistance to candidates who do not enter party primaries, Congress has merely chosen to limit at this time the reach of the reforms encompassed in Chapter 96. This Congress could do without constituting the reforms a constitutionally invidious discrimination. The governing principle was stated in *Katzenbach v. Morgan*:

> (I)n deciding the constitutional propriety of the limitations in such a reform measure we are guided by the familiar principles that a "statute is not invalid under the Constitution because it might have gone farther than it did," *Roschen v. Ward*, 279 U.S. 337, that a legislature need not "strike at all evils at the same time," *Semler v. Dental Examiners*, 294 U.S. 608, 610, and that "reform may take one step at a time, addressing itself to the phase of the problem which seems most acute to the legislative mind," *Williamson v. Lee Optical Co.*, 348 U.S. 483, 489.

The choice to limit matching funds to candidates running in primaries may reflect that concern about large private contributions to candidates centered on primary races and that there is no historical evidence of similar abuses involving contributions to candidates who engage in petition drives to qualify for state ballots. Moreover, assistance to candidates and nonmajor parties forced to resort to petition drives to gain ballot access implicates the policies against fostering frivolous candidacies, creating a system of splintered parties, and encouraging unrestrained factionalism.

The eligibility requirements in Chapter 96 are surely not an unreasonable way to measure popular support for a candidate, accomplishing the objective of limiting subsidization to those candidates with a substantial chance of being nominated. Counting only the first $250 of each contribution for eligibility purposes requires candidates to solicit smaller contributions from numerous people. Requiring the money to come from citizens of a minimum number of States eliminates candidates whose appeal is limited geographically; a President is elected not by popular vote, but by winning the popular vote in enough States to have a majority in the Electoral College.

We also reject as without merit appellants' argument that the matching formula favors wealthy voters and candidates. The thrust of the legislation is to reduce financial barriers and to enhance the importance of smaller contributions. Some candidates undoubtedly could raise large sums of money and thus have little need for public funds, but candidates with lesser fundraising capabilities will gain substantial benefits from matching funds. In addition, one eligibility requirement for matching funds is acceptance of an expenditure ceiling, and candidates with little fundraising ability will be able to increase their spending relative to candidates capable of raising large amounts in private funds.

For the reasons stated, we reject appellants' claims that Subtitle H is facially unconstitutional.

Arizona Free Enterprise Club's Freedom Club PAC v. Bennett

564 U.S. 721 (2011)

Chief Justice ROBERTS delivered the opinion of the Court.

Under Arizona law, candidates for state office who accept public financing can receive additional money from the State in direct response to the campaign activities of privately financed candidates and independent expenditure groups. Once a set spending limit is exceeded, a publicly financed candidate receives roughly one dollar for every dollar spent by an opposing privately financed candidate. The publicly financed candidate also receives roughly one dollar for every dollar spent by independent expenditure groups to support the privately financed candidate, or to oppose the publicly financed candidate. We hold that Arizona's matching funds scheme substantially burdens protected political speech without serving a compelling state interest and therefore violates the First Amendment.

I

A

The Arizona Citizens Clean Elections Act, passed by initiative in 1998, created a voluntary public financing system to fund the primary and general election campaigns of candidates for state office. All eligible candidates may opt to receive public funding. Eligibility is contingent on the collection of a specified number of five-dollar contributions from Arizona voters and the acceptance of certain campaign restrictions and obligations. Publicly funded candidates must agree, among other things, to limit their expenditure of personal funds to $500; participate in at least one public debate; adhere to an overall expenditure cap; and return all unspent public moneys to the State. In exchange for accepting these conditions, participating candidates are granted public funds to conduct their campaigns. In many cases, this initial allotment may be the whole of the State's financial backing of a publicly funded candidate. But when certain conditions are met, publicly funded candidates are granted additional "equalizing" or matching funds.

Matching funds are available in both primary and general elections. In a primary, matching funds are triggered when a privately financed candidate's expenditures, combined with the expenditures of independent groups made in support of the privately financed candidate or in opposition to a publicly financed candidate, exceed the primary election allotment of state funds to the publicly financed candidate. During the general election, matching funds are triggered when the amount of money a privately financed candidate receives in contributions, combined with the expenditures of independent groups made in support of the privately financed candidate or in opposition to a publicly financed candidate, exceed the general election allotment of state funds to the publicly financed candidate. A privately financed candidate's expenditures of his personal funds are counted as contributions for purposes of calculating matching funds during a general election.

In an election where a privately funded candidate faces multiple publicly financed candidates, one dollar raised or spent by the privately financed candidate results in an almost one dollar increase in public funding to each of the publicly financed candidates. Once the public financing cap is exceeded, additional expenditures by independent groups can result in dollar-for-dollar matching funds as well. . . . The matching funds provision is not activated, however, when independent expenditures are made in opposition to a privately financed candidate. Matching funds top out at two times the initial authorized grant of public funding to the publicly financed candidate. Under Arizona law, a privately financed candidate may raise and spend unlimited funds, subject to state-imposed contribution limits and disclosure requirements.

An example may help clarify how the Arizona matching funds provision operates. Arizona is divided into 30 districts for purposes of electing members to the State's House of Representatives. Each district elects two representatives to the House biannually. Arizona's Fourth District had three candidates for its two available House seats. Two of those candidates opted to accept public funding; one candidate chose to operate his campaign with private funds.

In that election, if the total funds contributed to the privately funded candidate, added to that candidate's expenditure of personal funds and the expenditures of supportive independent groups, exceeded $21,479 — the allocation of public funds for the general election in a contested State House race — the matching funds provision would be triggered. A publicly financed candidate would continue to receive additional state money in response to fundraising and spending by the privately financed candidate and independent expenditure groups until that publicly financed candidate received a total of $64,437 in state funds.

B

Petitioners in this case, plaintiffs below, are five past and future candidates for Arizona state office and two independent groups that spend money to support and oppose Arizona candidates. They filed suit challenging the constitutionality of the matching funds provision. The candidates and independent expenditure groups argued that the matching funds provision unconstitutionally penalized their speech and burdened their ability to fully exercise their First Amendment rights.

The District Court entered a permanent injunction against the enforcement of the matching funds provision, but stayed implementation of that injunction to allow the State to file an appeal. The Court of Appeals for the Ninth Circuit stayed the District Court's injunction pending appeal. After hearing the case on the merits, the Court of Appeals reversed the District Court. The Court of Appeals concluded that the matching funds provision "imposes only a minimal burden on First Amendment rights" because it "does not actually prevent anyone from speaking in the first place or cap campaign expenditures." In that court's view, any burden imposed by the matching funds provision was justified because the provision "bears a substantial relation to the State's important interest in reducing *quid pro quo* political corruption." We stayed the Court of Appeals' decision, vacated the stay of the District Court's injunction, and later granted certiorari.

II

"Discussion of public issues and debate on the qualifications of candidates are integral to the operation" of our system of government. *Buckley v. Valeo.* As a result, the First Amendment " 'has its fullest and most urgent application' to speech uttered during a campaign for political office." *Eu v. San Francisco County Democratic Central Comm.* "Laws that burden political speech are" accordingly "subject to strict scrutiny, which requires the Government to prove that the restriction furthers a compelling interest and is narrowly tailored to achieve that interest." *Citizens United.*

Applying these principles, we have invalidated government-imposed restrictions on campaign expenditures, *Buckley, supra,* restraints on independent expenditures applied to express advocacy groups, *Massachusetts Citizens for Life*, limits on uncoordinated political party expenditures, and regulations barring unions, nonprofit and other associations, and corporations from making independent expenditures for electioneering communication, *Citizens United, supra*.

At the same time, we have subjected strictures on campaign-related speech that we have found less onerous to a lower level of scrutiny and upheld those restrictions. For example, after finding that the restriction at issue was "closely drawn" to serve a "sufficiently important interest," see, e.g., *McConnell v. Federal Election Comm'n*, we have upheld government-imposed limits on contributions to candidates, *Buckley, supra*, caps on coordinated party expenditures, *Colorado Republican Federal Campaign Comm.*, and requirements that political funding sources disclose their identities, *Citizens United, supra*.

Although the speech of the candidates and independent expenditure groups that brought this suit is not directly capped by Arizona's matching funds provision, those parties contend that their political speech is substantially burdened by the state law in the same way that speech was burdened by the law we recently found invalid in *Davis v. Federal Election Comm'n*. In *Davis*, we considered a First Amendment challenge to the so-called "Millionaire's Amendment." Under that Amendment, if a candidate for the United States House of Representatives spent more than $350,000 of his personal funds, "a new, asymmetrical regulatory scheme [came] into play." *Davis*. The opponent of the candidate who exceeded that limit was permitted to collect individual contributions up to $6,900 per contributor — three times the normal contribution limit of $2,300. The candidate who spent more than the personal funds limit remained subject to the original contribution cap. Davis argued that this scheme "burden[ed] his exercise of his First Amendment right to make unlimited expenditures of his personal funds because" doing so had "the effect of enabling his opponent to raise more money and to use that money to finance speech that counteract[ed] and thus diminishe[d] the effectiveness of Davis' own speech." *Id.*

In addressing the constitutionality of the Millionaire's Amendment, we acknowledged that the provision did not impose an outright cap on a candidate's personal expenditures. *Id.* We nonetheless concluded that the Amendment was unconstitutional because it forced a candidate "to choose between the First Amendment right to engage in unfettered political speech and subjection to discriminatory fundraising limitations." *Id.* Any candidate who chose to spend more than $350,000 of his own money was forced to "shoulder a special and potentially significant burden" because that choice gave fundraising advantages to the candidate's adversary. *Ibid.* We determined that this constituted an "unprecedented penalty" and "impose[d] a substantial burden on the exercise of the First Amendment right to use personal funds for campaign speech," and concluded that the Government had failed to advance any compelling interest that would justify such a burden. *Id.*

A

1

The logic of *Davis* largely controls our approach to this case. Much like the burden placed on speech in *Davis*, the matching funds provision "imposes an unprecedented penalty on any candidate who robustly exercises [his] First Amendment right[s]." *Id.* If the law at issue in *Davis* imposed a burden on candidate speech, the Arizona law unquestionably does so as well.

The penalty imposed by Arizona's matching funds provision is different in some respects from the penalty imposed by the law we struck down in *Davis*. But those differences make the Arizona law *more* constitutionally problematic, not less. First, the penalty in *Davis* consisted of raising the contribution limits for one of the candidates. The candidate who benefited from the increased limits still had to go out and raise the funds. He may or may not have been able to do so. The other candidate, therefore, faced merely the possibility that his opponent would be able to raise additional funds, through contribution limits that remained subject to a cap. Here the benefit to the publicly financed candidate is the direct and automatic release of public money. That is a far heavier burden than in *Davis*.

Second, depending on the specifics of the election at issue, the matching funds provision can create a multiplier effect. In the Arizona Fourth District House election previously discussed, if the spending cap were exceeded, each dollar spent by the privately funded candidate would result in an additional dollar of campaign funding to each of that candidate's publicly financed opponents. In such a situation, the matching funds provision forces privately funded candidates to fight a political hydra of sorts.

Third, unlike the law at issue in *Davis*, all of this is to some extent out of the privately financed candidate's hands. Even if that candidate opted to spend less than the initial public financing cap, any spending by independent expenditure groups to promote the privately financed candidate's election — regardless whether such support was welcome or helpful — could trigger matching funds. What is more, that state money would go directly to the publicly funded candidate to use as he saw fit. That disparity in control is a substantial advantage for the publicly funded candidate. That candidate can allocate the money according to his own campaign strategy, which the privately financed candidate could not do with the independent group expenditures that triggered the matching funds.

In some ways, the burden the Arizona law imposes on independent expenditure groups is worse than the burden it imposes on privately financed candidates, and thus substantially worse than the burden we found constitutionally impermissible in *Davis*. If a candidate contemplating an electoral run in Arizona surveys the campaign landscape and decides that the burdens imposed by the matching funds regime make a privately funded campaign unattractive, he at least has the option of taking public financing. Independent expenditure groups, of course, do not.

Once the spending cap is reached, an independent expenditure group that wants to support a particular candidate — because of that candidate's stand on an issue of concern to the group — can only avoid triggering matching funds in one of two ways. The group can either opt to change its message from one addressing the merits of the candidates to one addressing the merits of an issue, or refrain from speaking altogether. Presenting independent expenditure groups with such a choice makes the matching funds provision particularly burdensome to those groups. And forcing that choice — trigger matching funds, change your message, or do not speak — certainly contravenes "the fundamental rule of protection under the First Amendment, that a speaker has the autonomy to choose the content of his own message."

2

Arizona contends that the matching funds provision is distinguishable from the law we invalidated in *Davis*. The State correctly points out that our decision in *Davis* focused on the asymmetrical contribution limits imposed by the Millionaire's Amendment. But that is not because—as the State asserts—the reach of that opinion is limited to asymmetrical contribution limits. It is because that was the particular burden on candidate speech we faced in *Davis*. And whatever the significance of the distinction in general, there can be no doubt that the burden on speech is significantly greater in this case than in *Davis*: That means that the law here—like the one in *Davis*—must be justified by a compelling state interest.

The State argues that the matching funds provision actually results in more speech by "increas[ing] debate about issues of public concern" in Arizona elections and "promot[ing] the free and open debate that the First Amendment was intended to foster." Not so. Any increase in speech resulting from the Arizona law is of one kind and one kind only—that of publicly financed candidates. Thus, even if the matching funds provision did result in more speech by publicly financed candidates and more speech in general, it would do so at the expense of impermissibly burdening (and thus reducing) the speech of privately financed candidates and independent expenditure groups.

In disagreeing with our conclusion, the dissent relies on cases in which we have upheld government subsidies against First Amendment challenge. But none of those cases—not one—involved a subsidy given in direct response to the political speech of another, to allow the recipient to counter that speech. And nothing in the analysis we employed in those cases suggests that the challenged subsidies would have survived First Amendment scrutiny if they were triggered by someone else's political speech.

The State and the Clean Elections Institute assert that the candidates and independent expenditure groups have failed to "cite specific instances in which they decided not to raise or spend funds," and have "failed to present any reliable evidence that Arizona's triggered matching funds deter their speech." The record in this case, which we must review in its entirety, does not support those assertions.

In addition, some candidates may be willing to bear the burden of spending above the cap. That a candidate is willing to do so does not make the law any less burdensome. While there is evidence to support the contention of the candidates and independent expenditure groups that the matching funds provision burdens their speech, "it is never easy to prove a negative"—here, that candidates and groups did not speak or limited their speech because of the Arizona law. *Elkins v. United States*. In any event, the burden imposed by the matching funds provision is evident and inherent in the choice that confronts privately financed candidates and independent expenditure groups. Indeed even candidates who sign up for public funding recognize the burden matching funds impose on private speech, stating that they participate in the program because "matching funds . . . discourage[] opponents, special interest groups, and lobbyists from campaigning against" them.

The State correctly asserts that the candidates and independent expenditure groups "do not . . . claim that a single lump sum payment to publicly funded candidates," equivalent to the maximum amount of state financing that a candidate can obtain through matching funds, would impermissibly burden their speech. The State reasons that if providing all the money up front would not burden speech, providing it piecemeal does not do so either. And the State further argues that such incremental administration is necessary to ensure that public funding is not under- or over-distributed. These arguments miss the point. It is not the amount of funding that the State provides to publicly financed candidates that is constitutionally problematic in this case. It is the manner in which that funding is provided—in direct response to the political speech of privately financed candidates and independent expenditure groups.

B

Because the Arizona matching funds provision imposes a substantial burden on the speech of privately financed candidates and independent expenditure groups, "that provision cannot stand unless it is 'justified by a compelling state interest,'" *Davis* (quoting *Massachusetts Citizens for Life*). There is a debate between the parties in this case as to what state interest is served by the matching funds provision. The privately financed candidates and independent expenditure groups contend that the provision works to "level[] electoral opportunities" by equalizing candidate "resources and influence." The State and the Clean Elections Institute counter that the provision "furthers Arizona's interest in preventing corruption and the appearance of corruption."

1

"Leveling the playing field" can sound like a good thing. But in a democracy, campaigning for office is not a game. It is a critically important form of speech. The First Amendment embodies our choice as a Nation that, when it comes to such speech, the guiding principle is freedom—the "unfettered interchange of ideas"—not whatever the State may view as fair. *Buckley, supra* (internal quotation marks omitted).

2

[T]he State and the Clean Elections Institute disavow any interest in "leveling the playing field." They instead assert that the "Equal funding of candidates" provision, serves the State's compelling interest in combating corruption and the appearance of corruption. But even if the ultimate objective of the matching funds provision is to combat corruption—and not "level the playing field"—the burdens that the matching funds provision imposes on protected political speech are not justified.

Burdening a candidate's expenditure of his own funds on his own campaign does not further the State's anticorruption interest. Indeed, we have said that "reliance on personal funds *reduces* the threat of corruption" and that "discouraging [the] use of personal funds[] disserves the anticorruption interest." *Davis, supra,* at 740-741. That is because "the use of personal funds reduces the candidate's dependence on outside contributions and thereby counteracts the coercive pressures and attendant risks of abuse" of money in politics. *Buckley*. The matching funds provision counts a candidate's expenditures of his own money on his own campaign as contributions, and to that extent cannot be supported by any anticorruption interest.

Perhaps recognizing that the burdens the matching funds provision places on speech cannot be justified in and of themselves, either as a means of leveling the playing field or directly fighting corruption, the State and the Clean Elections Institute offer another argument: They contend that the provision indirectly serves the anticorruption interest, by ensuring that enough candidates participate in the State's public funding system, which in turn helps combat corruption.

The flaw in the State's argument is apparent in what its reasoning would allow. By the State's logic it could grant a publicly funded candidate five dollars in matching funds for every dollar his privately financed opponent spent, or force candidates who wish to run on private funds to pay a $10,000 fine in order to encourage participation in the public funding regime. Such measures might well promote participation in public financing, but would clearly suppress or unacceptably alter political speech. How the State chooses to encourage participation in its public funding system matters, and we have never held that a State may burden political speech — to the extent the matching funds provision does — to ensure adequate participation in a public funding system. Here the State's chosen method is unduly burdensome and not sufficiently justified to survive First Amendment scrutiny.

III

We do not today call into question the wisdom of public financing as a means of funding political candidacy. That is not our business. But determining whether laws governing campaign finance violate the First Amendment is very much our business. We have said that governments "may engage in public financing of election campaigns" and that doing so can further "significant governmental interest[s]," such as the state interest in preventing corruption. *Buckley*. But the goal of creating a viable public financing scheme can only be pursued in a manner consistent with the First Amendment. The dissent criticizes the Court for standing in the way of what the people of Arizona want. But the whole point of the First Amendment is to protect speakers against unjustified government restrictions on speech, even when those restrictions reflect the will of the majority. When it comes to protected speech, the speaker is sovereign.

Laws like Arizona's matching funds provision that inhibit robust and wide-open political debate without sufficient justification cannot stand.

The judgment of the Court of Appeals for the Ninth Circuit is reversed.

It is so ordered.

Justice KAGAN, with whom Justice GINSBURG, Justice BREYER, and Justice SOTOMAYOR join, dissenting.

Imagine two States, each plagued by a corrupt political system. In both States, candidates for public office accept large campaign contributions in exchange for the promise that, after assuming office, they will rank the donors' interests ahead of all others. As a result of these bargains, politicians ignore the public interest, sound public policy languishes, and the citizens lose confidence in their government.

Recognizing the cancerous effect of this corruption, voters of the first State, acting through referendum, enact several campaign finance measures previously approved by this Court. They cap campaign contributions; require disclosure of substantial donations; and create an optional public financing program that gives candidates a fixed public subsidy if they refrain from private fundraising. But these measures do not work. Individuals who "bundle" campaign contributions become indispensable to candidates in need of money. Simple disclosure fails to prevent shady dealing. And candidates choose not to participate in the public financing system because the sums provided do not make them competitive with their privately financed opponents. So the State remains afflicted with corruption.

Voters of the second State, having witnessed this failure, take an ever-so-slightly different tack to cleaning up their political system. They too enact contribution limits and disclosure requirements. But they believe that the greatest hope of eliminating corruption lies in creating an effective public financing program, which will break candidates' dependence on large donors and bundlers. These voters realize, based on the first State's experience, that such a program will not work unless candidates agree to participate in it. And candidates will participate only if they know that they will receive sufficient funding to run competitive races. So the voters enact a program that carefully adjusts the money given to would-be officeholders, through the use of a matching funds mechanism, in order to provide this assurance. The program does not discriminate against any candidate or point of view, and it does not restrict any person's ability to speak. In fact, by providing resources to many candidates, the program creates more speech and thereby broadens public debate. And just as the voters had hoped, the program accomplishes its mission of restoring integrity to the political system. The second State rids itself of corruption.

[T]oday, the majority holds that the second State's system—the system that produces honest government, working on behalf of all the people—clashes with our Constitution. The First Amendment, the majority insists, requires us all to rely on the measures employed in the first State, even when they have failed to break the stranglehold of special interests on elected officials.

I

A

Campaign finance reform over the last century has focused on one key question: how to prevent massive pools of private money from corrupting our political system. If an officeholder owes his election to wealthy contributors, he may act for their benefit alone, rather than on behalf of all the people. And even if these contributions are not converted into corrupt bargains, they still may weaken confidence in our political system because the public perceives "the opportunities for abuse[s]." *Buckley*. To prevent both corruption and the appearance of corruption—and so to protect our democratic system of governance—citizens have implemented reforms designed to curb the power of special interests.

For this reason, public financing systems today dot the national landscape. Almost one-third of the States have adopted some form of public financing, and so too has the Federal Government for presidential elections. We declared the presidential public financing system constitutional in *Buckley v. Valeo*. Congress, we stated, had created the program "for the 'general welfare' — to reduce the deleterious influence of large contributions on our political process," as well as to "facilitate communication by candidates with the electorate, and to free candidates from the rigors of fundraising." *Buckley*. We reiterated "that public financing as a means of eliminating the improper influence of large private contributions furthers a significant governmental interest." *Id.* And finally, in rejecting a challenge based on the First Amendment, we held that the program did not "restrict[] or censor speech, but rather . . . use[d] public money to facilitate and enlarge public discussion and participation in the electoral process." *Id.* We declared this result "vital to a self-governing people," and so concluded that the program "further[ed], not abridge[d], pertinent First Amendment values." *Id.* We thus gave state and municipal governments the green light to adopt public financing systems along the presidential model.

But this model, which distributes a lump-sum grant at the beginning of an election cycle, has a significant weakness: It lacks a mechanism for setting the subsidy at a level that will give candidates sufficient incentive to participate, while also conserving public resources. Public financing can achieve its goals only if a meaningful number of candidates receive the state subsidy, rather than raise private funds. If the grant is pegged too low, it puts the participating candidate at a disadvantage: Because he has agreed to spend no more than the amount of the subsidy, he will lack the means to respond if his privately funded opponent spends over that threshold. So when lump-sum grants do not keep up with campaign expenditures, more and more candidates will choose not to participate. But if the subsidy is set too high, it may impose an unsustainable burden on the public fisc.

B

As the Court explains, Arizona's matching funds arrangement responds to the shortcoming of the lump-sum model by adjusting the public subsidy in each race to reflect the expenditures of a privately financed candidate and the independent groups that support him.

This arrangement, like the lump-sum model, makes use of a pre-set amount to provide financial support to participants. But the Arizona system improves on the lump-sum model in a crucial respect. By tying public funding to private spending, the State can afford to set a more generous upper limit — because it knows that in each campaign it will only have to disburse what is necessary to keep a participating candidate reasonably competitive. Arizona can therefore assure candidates that, if they accept public funds, they will have the resources to run a viable race against those who rely on private money. And at the same time, Arizona avoids wasting taxpayers' dollars. The question here is whether this modest adjustment to the public financing program that we approved in *Buckley* makes the Arizona law unconstitutional.

II

Arizona's statute does not impose a "restriction," or "substantia[l] burde[n]," on expression. The law has quite the opposite effect: It subsidizes and so produces *more* political speech. Except in a world gone topsy-turvy, additional campaign speech and electoral competition is not a First Amendment injury.

A

At every turn, the majority tries to convey the impression that Arizona's matching fund statute is of a piece with laws prohibiting electoral speech.

There is just one problem. Arizona's matching funds provision does not restrict, but instead subsidizes, speech. The law "impose[s] no ceiling on [speech] and do[es] not prevent anyone from speaking." *Citizens United.* The statute does not tell candidates or their supporters how much money they can spend to convey their message, when they can spend it, or what they can spend it on. Rather, the Arizona law, like the public financing statute in *Buckley,* provides funding for political speech, thus "facilitat[ing] communication by candidates with the electorate." *Id.* What the law does—all the law does—is fund more speech.

No one can claim that Arizona's law discriminates against particular ideas, and so violates the First Amendment's sole limitation on speech subsidies. The State throws open the doors of its public financing program to all candidates who meet minimal eligibility requirements and agree not to raise private funds. Arizona disburses funds based not on a candidate's (or supporter's) ideas, but on the candidate's decision to sign up for public funding. So under our precedent, Arizona's subsidy statute should easily survive First Amendment scrutiny.

IV

This case arose because Arizonans wanted their government to work on behalf of all the State's people. On the heels of a political scandal involving the near-routine purchase of legislators' votes, Arizonans passed a law designed to sever political candidates' dependence on large contributors. They wished, as many of their fellow Americans wish, to stop corrupt dealing—to ensure that their representatives serve the public, and not just the wealthy donors who helped put them in office. The legislation that Arizona's voters enacted was the product of deep thought and care. It put into effect a public financing system that attracted large numbers of candidates at a sustainable cost to the State's taxpayers. Indeed, by increasing electoral competition and enabling a wide range of candidates to express their views, the system "further[ed] . . . First Amendment values." *Buckley* (citing *New York Times*). Less corruption, more speech. Robust campaigns leading to the election of representatives not beholden to the few, but accountable to the many. The people of Arizona might have expected a decent respect for those objectives.

Today, they do not get it. The Court invalidates Arizonans' efforts to ensure that in their State, "'[t]he people . . . possess the absolute sovereignty.'" *Id.* No precedent compels the Court to take this step; to the contrary, today's decision is in tension with broad swaths of our First Amendment doctrine. No fundamental principle of our Constitution backs the Court's ruling; to the contrary, it is the law struck down today that fostered both the vigorous competition of ideas and its ultimate object—a government responsive to the will of the people. Arizonans deserve better. Like citizens across this country, Arizonans deserve a government that represents and serves them all. And no less, Arizonans deserve the chance to reform their electoral system so as to attain that most American of goals.

Truly, democracy is not a game. I respectfully dissent.

▶▶ *The Chilling Effect of Public Financing.* In *Arizona Free Enterprise*, the Court argued that Arizona's program of matching funds could chill the speech of wealthier candidates by inducing them to refrain from spending for fear that such spending would trigger the release of public funds to their opponents. The net result, the Court speculated, would be less speech rather than more. In a 2012 study designed to test the Court's hypothesis, researchers found no evidence of such a chilling effect. Conor M. Dowling et al., *Does Public Financing Chill Political Speech? Exploiting a Court Injunction as a Natural Experiment*, 11 ELECTION L.J. 302 (2012).

▶▶ *Justifications for Public Financing.* Why should the public subsidize the costs of running for office? In a sense, the question might as easily be turned around: why *shouldn't* the public do so? The offices in question are public offices, exercising public power, and bearing a public trust. If the beneficiary of representative democracy is the public, why shouldn't the public pay for the benefits it receives? Nevertheless, the prevailing model for financing campaigns for office in the United States has always contemplated the use of private funds, and public financing is thus understood as a deviation from the norm requiring justification.

Ironically, the most commonly offered justification for *adding* political money to the system through public financing is the same as a justification frequently invoked to justify *reducing* money in the system by restricting contributions and expenditures: equality. Public financing is often said to mitigate the impact of differential access to wealth by leveling up instead of leveling down. In so doing, it is said to accomplish roughly the same objectives as restrictions on contributions and spending, but without suppressing speech. Public funding also may relieve candidates of some of the burdens of fundraising, allowing them to focus on campaigning and public responsiveness. And to the extent that it facilitates the emergence of challengers to incumbents, it has the potential to make elections more competitive. *See, e.g.,* JACOB ROWBOTTOM, DEMOCRACY DISTORTED: WEALTH, INFLUENCE AND DEMOCRATIC POLITICS 70-73 (2010); Richard Briffault, *Public Funding and Democratic Elections*, 148 U. PA. L. REV. 563 (1999). Public financing is also said to have the capacity to enhance political participation. Matching fund programs, in particular, by making it possible for small donors to take actions that are politically meaningful, might bring more small donors into the process. Spencer Overton, *Matching Political Contributions*, 96 MINN. L. REV. 1694 (2012).

▶▶ *Public Financing of Elections in the United States.* At present, public financing is offered for federal elections only in presidential races. Congress came very close to creating public financing for congressional and senatorial races in 1974 when such a proposal passed in the Senate, but the House did not agree, and the program remains limited to presidential elections.

At present, thirty states offer some form of public financing for at least some elections. As of 2015, thirty states offered lump-sum payments or matching grants to candidates; six states offered rebates or tax incentives to donors; and eleven states offered financial assistance to political parties. In addition, at least seventeen municipalities offer publicly financed payments or matching grants. Michael J. Malbin, *Citizen Funding for Elections* (Campaign Finance Institute 2015).

>> *Utilization of Public Funds.*   Public financing cannot succeed unless candidates for office opt into the program. Participation typically requires agreeing to limitations on fundraising and expenditures, and occasionally other rules, such as participation in public debates or adherence to a code of fair campaigning. How extensively do candidates participate in public financing programs?

On the federal level, participation by presidential candidates has been declining, to the point where many doubt the continued viability of the program. For more than 20 years, major party presidential candidates reliably took public funds in both the primaries and general elections. In 2000, George W. Bush opted out of public funding during the primaries, and by 2004 most of the major candidates of both parties did so, thereby allowing them to spend considerably more than if they had accepted public funds. In 2008, Barack Obama opted out of public financing for the general election, and in 2012 and 2016, none of the candidates took public funds for the general election, throwing the utility of the program into considerable doubt.

In 2015, in an effort to salvage the presidential election financing system, Senator Tom Udall and Representative David Price introduced legislation, the Empower Act, that would have increased the tax checkoff to twenty dollars and given candidates six dollars in public money for every one dollar they raised in small donations. Recipients would have to agree not to accept individual donations greater than $1,000 (federal law currently permits donations up to $2,700), and would have to show substantial support in at least twenty states to qualify. Would this revive incentives to accept public money in presidential elections?

On the state level, however, participation has frequently been strong. For example, in Minnesota in 2010, 81 percent of major party candidates for the House and 85 percent of major party candidates for Senate took public funding in the general election. Michael J. Malbin et al., *Public Financing of Elections After* Citizens United *and* Arizona Free Republic (Campaign Finance Institute 2011). In 2008, 96 percent of eligible races in Maine featured at least one candidate who had opted into public funding, and in Arizona the figure was 82 percent. United States Government Accountability Office, *Experiences of Two States That Offered Full Public Funding for Political Candidates* (May 2010).

>> *Effects on Electoral Competitiveness.*   One of the most commonly invoked justifications for public financing is that it makes elections more competitive. It is said to have the potential to do so in at least two ways. First, by making campaign money more widely available, public financing can facilitate runs by challengers for seats held by incumbents, thereby reducing the number of uncontested elections. Second, to the extent that public financing schemes cause financial resources to be distributed more equally among candidates, they have the potential to produce more evenly and robustly contested elections. Does public financing in fact make elections more competitive?

The evidence is conflicting. A 1998 study concluded: "there is no evidence to support the claim that programs combining public funding with spending limits have leveled the playing field, countered the effects of incumbency, and made elections more competitive." MICHAEL J. MALBIN AND THOMAS L. GAIS, THE DAY AFTER REFORM: SOBERING CAMPAIGN FINANCE LESSONS FROM THE AMERICAN STATES 137 (1998). A 2010 study of the effect of campaign financing in Arizona and Maine concluded that changes in the percentage of contested races in those states did not differ appreciably from changes in control states lacking public financing programs. U.S. Government Accountability Office, *supra*, at 41-42. On the other hand, a 2006 study of the same two states found "compelling evidence that Arizona and Maine have become much more competitive states" after the introduction of public funding. Kenneth Mayer et al., *Do Public Funding Programs Enhance Electoral Competition, in* THE MARKETPLACE OF DEMOCRACY: ELECTORAL COMPETITION AND AMERICAN POLITICS 263 (Michael McDonald and John Samples eds., 2006).

Overall, evidence of the impact of public financing is mixed. Public financing does not appear to be associated with closer, more competitive election results, though it is associated with a decline in the number of uncontested races. Candidates who receive public funding, rather than spending time raising private funds, do not necessarily spend more of their freed-up time communicating with voters, which might enhance their responsiveness to public opinion. Public financing also does not seem to produce a greatly diversified pool of candidates, though it does have a tendency to bring a more diverse group of donors — especially small donors — into the system. Michael J. Malbin, *Citizen Funding for Elections* (Campaign Finance Institute 2015). Often, small donors are enticed to participate through matching fund programs in which small donations to candidates are matched several times over with public funds.

Although enticing more ordinary people to participate more actively in politics through financial contributions is certainly more egalitarian, recent evidence suggests it may not be entirely without unintended consequences. For decades, the conventional wisdom has been that political polarization is driven to a considerable extent by wealthy elites, who tend to hold more extreme views than most voters. Bringing more voters of modest means into the financing equation, and leveraging their contributions with matching public funds, was thus thought likely to direct more funds to the kind of moderate, centrist candidates the general electorate is thought to prefer. *See, e.g.,* Jordan Kujala, *Donors, Primary Elections, and Polarization in the United States,* 64 AM. J. POL. SCI. 587 (2020). New evidence, however, suggests that small donors who are willing to contribute to political campaigns — even in very small amounts — may not hold the same, centrist views as ordinary voters who are *not* willing to contribute even small amounts to any candidate; indeed, that group may be just as extreme as the large donors whose influence public matching fund programs are meant to counteract. *See* Richard H. Pildes, *Participation and Polarization,* 22 J. CONST. L. 341 (2020). If this is the case, then inviting more small donors into the system could enhance rather than diminish the degree of extremism of party nominees.

≫ *Other Forms of Public Financing.* Public financing typically takes the form of cash payouts to candidates for office, but that is not the only way that the public can subsidize the cost of competing for office. Another common form of public subsidy is to use the tax system by permitting deductions for expenses the legislature wishes to subsidize. At present, only charitable donations are deductible for purposes of computing federal tax; donations for political purposes are not. Would the goals of public financing be advanced by allowing a deduction or tax credit for contributions to candidates and political parties? *See* John M. de Figueiredo and Elizabeth Garrett, *Paying for Politics*, 78 S. Cal. L. Rev. 591 (2005).

FINAL THOUGHTS: IS CAMPAIGN FINANCE REFORM EFFECTIVE?

An enormous amount of energy has been spent on the subject of campaign finance. The press and the public complain about it. Reformers push legislation. Others oppose it. Politicians debate it. Courts adjudicate it. Is any of this worth the candle? Is there, at the end of the day, any reason to think that campaign finance reform is effective, and thus worth pursuing?

This is an enormously difficult question to answer. Part of the difficulty arises from the lack of a clear consensus about what would count as evidence of success. Increased competitiveness of elections? More frequent defeats of incumbents? Greater socioeconomic diversity among members of Congress? Better-quality campaign discourse? The enactment of legislation that addresses the problems of the poor or the working class? Even if a standard of effectiveness could be agreed on, difficulties of measurement complicate any attempt to evaluate the success of reform empirically. What counts as a "competitive" election? What is the optimal frequency with which challengers should defeat incumbents? How do we know when legislation or government policy is "improperly" or "unduly" skewed in favor of the rich?

The political process, moreover, has many moving parts, and not all of them move in tandem. Elected officials and candidates are subject to all kinds of influences: lobbying, their own independent judgment, pressure from the political parties to which they belong, independent spending by interest groups, and so forth. Many of these influences are justifiable features of democratic practice, and any conception of the effectiveness of campaign finance reform may involve tacitly trading off some democratic values against others. Indeed, the Supreme Court's campaign-finance jurisprudence since *Buckley* takes the position that reform measures force a tradeoff of equality against free speech, and that the trade is rarely justified.

Setting aside these difficulties, one of the main areas of inquiry has been whether restrictions on campaign contributions and spending increase electoral competitiveness, as they are typically meant to do, or whether they have the perverse effect of insulating incumbents from effective challenge. The skeptical hypothesis here is simple: because incumbents by definition are better recognized and known by their constituents, they have an inherent advantage that challengers can overcome only by spending their way into the same territory. If restrictions on raising and spending money apply equally to challengers and incumbents, then such laws give incumbents an advantage. From this point of view, campaign-finance restrictions are "incumbent protection laws."

Studies attempting to assess this hypothesis have reached equivocal results. As recently as 2006, two students of the subject were able to write: "To date, scant evidence exists regarding the effects of campaign finance restrictions on election outcomes. Whether stricter regulations amount to incumbency protection laws, or whether they help challengers to compete remains an unanswered empirical question." Thomas Stratmann and Francisco J. Aparicio-Castillo, *Competition Policy for Elections: Do Campaign Contribution Limits Matter?*, 127 PUBLIC CHOICE 177 (2006). According to one study, electoral competitiveness was associated generally with more spending by both incumbents and challengers; i.e., contribution or spending restrictions might be expected to suppress rather than enhance competitiveness. MICHAEL J. MALBIN AND THOMAS L. GAIS, THE DAY AFTER REFORM: SOBERING CAMPAIGN FINANCE LESSONS FROM THE AMERICAN STATES (1998). A more recent study finds that contribution limits make elections more competitive, not less, but the impact is trivial: in states with contribution limits, incumbents won 94.3 percent of the time, compared to an incumbent reelection rate of 95.4 percent in states without such limits. Thomas Stratmann, *Do Low Contribution Limits Insulate Incumbents from Competition?*, 9 ELECTION L.J. 125 (2010). The study does, however, suggest that lowering contribution limits to a much smaller amount than is typical might increase the impact of such limits on electoral outcomes. Another study examined the effect of contribution limits on gubernatorial elections and found that they do not have a significant effect on overall spending or on outcomes, although the effects are magnified where public financing is offered. Donald A. Gross et al., *State Campaign Finance Regulations and Electoral Competition*, 30 AM. POL. RES. 143 (2002). For an argument that any effects of campaign-finance regulation are generally swamped by other considerations, see JOHN SAMPLES, THE FALLACY OF CAMPAIGN FINANCE REFORM (2006).

Do these results suggest that campaign finance reform is hopeless? Might political money be too difficult to regulate because it is too difficult to isolate and confine? Is it true that "political money, like water, has to go somewhere. It never really disappears into thin air"? Samuel Issacharoff and Pamela S. Karlan, *The Hydraulics of Campaign Finance Reform*, 77 TEX. L. REV. 1705, 1708 (1999). If campaign finance reform cannot demonstrate concrete results, does that mean it should not be undertaken at all? Is there value in trying to achieve a desirable goal even if the attempts are unsuccessful? Is campaign finance reform really about concrete results, or is it about a political symbolism of equality? If so, is a loss of free speech too high a price to pay for a merely symbolic demonstration of commitment to political equality?

CHAPTER 10

ELECTION ADMINISTRATION AND REMEDIES

A. INTRODUCTION: THE CONSEQUENCES OF ELECTORAL PROCEDURES

Gould v. Grubb
_____

536 P.2d 1337 (Cal. 1975)

TOBRINER, Justice.

In this case we must determine the constitutionality of an election procedure which automatically affords an incumbent, seeking reelection, a top position on the election ballot. . . . The present action was commenced in the Los Angeles Superior Court by . . . nonincumbent candidates in the then upcoming Santa Monica City Council election. . . . Following a four-day trial at which both parties introduced considerable expert testimony on the question of whether or not a candidate gained any significant advantage by virtue of a top ballot position, the trial court rendered a formal finding that such "ballot positional" advantage did in fact exist, [and] the court held that the ballot procedure at issue violated the equal protection clauses of both the state and federal Constitutions. . . . [We affirm.]

[The court reviewed the expert evidence offered at trial and found it showed persuasively that an advantage accrues to the candidate listed first on a ballot.] Although most of the witnesses did testify that the advantage to a top ballot position was most pronounced in so-called "low visibility" races, in which voters are more likely to be unfamiliar with many of the candidates, several of the experts testified that a significant advantage as to ballot placement accrued to the beneficiaries in virtually all elections, with the possible exception of elections for the President of the United States or perhaps a state governor.

The city contends, however, that even if a significant advantage does accrue to a candidate by virtue of a top ballot position, such ballot position may nonetheless be reserved for incumbents seeking reelection. The city emphasizes that the state and charter cities have traditionally exercised broad authority in regulating the mechanics of election procedures and contends that the question of the placement of candidates' names on a ballot is a matter which should be left largely

933

to the judgment of legislators and election officials. We recognize, of course, that legislative bodies retain considerable discretion in formulating election procedures and devising regulations for the form and content of ballots. As in all other areas of governmental action, however, the exercise of such discretion remains subject to constitutional limitations.

The "incumbent first" ballot provision at issue here establishes two classifications of candidates for public office: incumbents seeking reelection and nonincumbent candidates. The salient constitutional issue, of course, is whether by according disparate treatment to these two classes of candidates, the city has denied nonincumbent candidates, or their supporters, the equal protection of the law. U.S. Const., 14th Amend.; Cal.Const., art. 1, §7(a). As our numerous recent decisions establish, a court must determine at the threshold of any "equal protection" analysis the "level of scrutiny" or "standard of review" which is appropriate to the case at hand. The classification scheme at issue here [relates] directly to the electoral process, and in recent years both this court and the United States Supreme Court have had frequent occasion to reiterate that the "fundamental" nature of the right to vote and the importance of preserving the integrity of the franchise require that the judiciary give close scrutiny to laws imposing unequal burdens or granting unequal advantages in this realm. *Knoll v. Davidson*, 525 P.2d 1273 (Cal. 1974); *Dunn v. Blumstein*, 405 U.S. 330 (1972); *Reynolds v. Sims*, 377 U.S. 533 (1964). . . .

In light of the trial court's finding that candidates in the top ballot position receive a substantial number of votes simply by virtue of their ballot position, a statute, ordinance or election practice which reserves such an advantage for a particular class of candidates inevitably dilutes the weight of the vote of all those electors who cast their ballots for a candidate who is not included within the favored class. Indeed, in a close race it is quite possible that a candidate with fewer "conscious" supporters than an opponent will actually win an election simply because his high position on the ballot affords him the advantage of receiving the vote of unconcerned or uninformed voters. In such an instance, the challenged provision effectively undermines the fundamental democratic electoral tenet of majority rule. . . .

The only justification which the city has proffered in support of the "incumbent first" ballot procedure falls far short of the mark. The city contends that in placing all incumbents on the top of the ballot, the election provision facilitates efficient, unconfused voting; in this regard, the city asserts that in most elections the principal decision for most voters is deciding whether to vote for or against the incumbent and the placement of the incumbent's name at the head of the ballot permits the voters to isolate this candidate quickly and without confusion.

Even if the city's view of the general voting process is an accurate one, however, there surely are alternative means of identifying incumbent candidates on the ballot which avoid the considerable discrimination against voters for nonincumbents inherent in the present positional priority procedure. The most obvious alternative is the simple expedient of permitting a candidate to designate himself as the incumbent on the ballot; such designation, of course, is presently authorized by state law and by many local ordinances throughout California. In our view, whatever legitimate interest the state might have in informing voters of the identity of incumbents is fully satisfied by such ballot designation.

An amicus brief filed on behalf of the city argues that since "someone" must get the benefit of the top ballot position, the city may reasonably choose to give such benefit to incumbents. In the first place, the factual premise of this argument is inaccurate, since a rotational ballot procedure can largely eliminate the distorting effects of ballot placement. Moreover, and more fundamentally, we emphatically reject the notion that the government may consciously choose to favor the election of incumbents over nonincumbents in a manner which distorts the preferences of participating voters. . . . We thus conclude that an election procedure which grants positional preference to incumbents violates the equal protection clause of both our state and federal Constitutions. . . .

In addition to the question of the validity of the "incumbent first" ballot procedure, the instant case also presents the issue of the constitutional permissibility of an "alphabetical order" ballot listing procedure. . . . We have concluded that a procedure which invariably reserves advantageous ballot positions for candidates whose names begin with letters occurring early in the alphabet is unconstitutional. We recognize, of course, that the listing of candidates in alphabetical order is not entirely irrational, for such a system does promote efficiency in voting by making it easier for voters to locate the name of the candidate of their choice on the ballot, especially in races involving a large number of candidates. As discussed above, however, because the substantial advantage which accrues to a candidate in a top ballot position may significantly distort the equality and integrity of the electoral process, the simple rationality of an alphabetical order procedure is not sufficient to sustain such a provision in this context. Instead, the disparate treatment resulting from such a classification scheme must be shown to be necessary to achieve a compelling governmental interest.

Under this standard of "close scrutiny," we believe that the alphabetical ordering of candidates' names on the ballot is impermissible. . . . [T]he alphabetical ordering of the ballot is by no means "necessary" to further the state interest in promoting voting efficiency, for the state has alternative means, such as affording voters sample ballots in advance of the election, by which the state can largely fulfill its legitimate desire to speed the electoral process. Indeed, the City of Santa Monica, as virtually all jurisdictions in California, already utilizes the sample ballot procedure to further just such a goal. In light of this and comparable alternatives, the city cannot properly justify a ballot procedure which invariably imposes a substantial disadvantage on a distinct, fixed class of candidates' proponents. . . .

>> *The Ballot Order Effect.* Numerous social science studies have examined the impact on election outcomes of the order in which candidates are listed on the ballot. These studies generally show that ballot order does have an effect on outcomes, but the effect is usually small — generally somewhere between one and five percent — and does not appear in every race or in every jurisdiction. For example, one early study found an effect, but it was statistically significant in fewer than half the races studied, and the magnitude of the effect varied widely from county to county. Another study found a vote advantage of 2.3 percent for top-listed candidates in a gubernatorial primary, but that advantage rose to 4.5 percent for down-ballot races such as state committeeman. Some studies have found no systematic effect. *See* F. Michael Alvarez, et al., *How Much Is Enough? The "Ballot Order Effect" and the Use of Social Science Research in Election Law Disputes*, 5 Elec. L.J. 40 (2006) (summarizing numerous studies). A more recent study focusing on Texas found that "the ballot order effect is indeed small in high-profile races, such as those for U.S. Senator," but "it is larger elsewhere; in down-ballot judicial elections it can be ten percentage points or more." Darren Grant, *The Ballot Order Effect is Huge: Evidence from Texas*, 172 Pub. Choice 421 (2017).

Why would ballot order have an effect? The most common theories stress either fatigue — voters get tired of concentrating as they work down a ballot, and this leads them to take lazy shortcuts — or "primacy effects, which predispose individuals toward 'selecting the first object considered in a set.'" But surely these influences would affect only certain kinds of voters: those who have not bothered to inform themselves and to make voting decisions in advance, and thus go into the voting booth unprepared. This inference is supported by results showing that ballot order effects are greater in down-ballot races in years when a presidential race appears on the ballot. *Id.* at 438-439. Apparently some segment of the electorate shows up to vote for president without having given much, or even any, thought to the other races appearing on the ballot, and rather than abstaining in those contests, votes haphazardly.

The standard remedies for the problems raised by ballot order effect involve either randomization or rotation of candidate placement. In a randomization jurisdiction, election officials will randomly select in advance an order in which candidates will be listed — by, for example, randomizing the alphabet and listing candidates by name, or randomizing the order in which parties appear on the ballot. All ballots in all races for that year will then follow that pattern, but the pattern will differ every year, preventing systematic bias over time. In a rotation jurisdiction, election officials print numerous different versions of the same ballot, each listing the candidates in a different order, thereby distributing widely, and thus presumably neutralizing, any ballot order effect in the listed races. The latter solution is more costly; according to one estimate, printing multiple ballots in a rotational format can increase printing costs by roughly 14 percent. Mary Beth Beazley, *Ballot Design as Fail-Safe: An Ounce of Rotation Is Worth a Pound of Litigation*, 12 Elec. L.J. 18, 47 (2013). Moreover, because of the complexity of the printing instructions, rotational ballots generate additional risks of error at the ballot printing and distribution phases.

⟫ *Substantive Consequences of Procedural Choices.*   The task of holding democratic elections requires lawmakers and administrators to make innumerable choices. When should elections be held, and over what period? By what method should voters cast votes? How should ballots be designed? Where should votes be cast? How many polling places should be created and staffed, open for what duration?

Under any conception of democracy, the outcome of elections should be determined by the votes of the electorate rather than by procedural decisions made by legislatures, incumbent officials, or county clerks. Yet, as every law student knows from studying civil procedure, procedural choices often have substantive consequences; in some circumstances, such choices may even be "outcome-determinative."

The potential linkage between outcomes and procedures poses many difficulties for election administrators. Virtually every procedural choice can have consequences not only for voter turnout, but for the accuracy with which voters cast their votes. Moreover, the impact of these choices may not fall equally on all populations of voters, and different populations may in turn exhibit different general voting tendencies. As a result, administrative choices may affect the final tallies, and in very close races, the ultimate outcome itself. Consider some examples:

- *Method of voter registration.* The use of an online voter registration procedure, as opposed to a paper system, appears to increase voter turnout by about 3 percent, especially for younger voters. Jinhai Yu, *Does State Online Voter Registration Increase Voter Turnout?*, 100 Soc. Sci. Q. 620 (2019). Considerable evidence suggests that younger voters today take more liberal positions on social issues than older voters.

- *Timing of voter registration.* Preregistration of young people before they turn 18 increases their turnout once they become eligible by between 2 and 13 percent. John B. Holbein and Sunshine Hillygus, *Making Young Voters: The Impact of Preregistration on Youth Turnout*, 60 Am. J. Pol. Sci. 364 (2015).

- *Method of voting.* A recent study finds that conducting elections by mail produces an increase in turnout of about 2.5 percent. However, "despite the fact that nonvoters tend to lean more [D]emocratic as a whole," the authors found no significant partisan skewing of the results. Michael Barber and John B. Holbein, *The Participatory and Partisan Impacts of Mandatory Vote-by-Mail*, 6 Sci. Advances 35 (Aug. 2020). Another study found that black and Latino voters were somewhat less likely to vote by mail than in person. Mindy Romero, *et al.*, *Voter Choice Act: How Did Voters Experience the New Reform in 2018?* (U. Cal. New Electorate Project 2019).

- *Timing of voting.* A recent study finds that voter turnout increases by 0.22 percent for each day of early voting, meaning that a one-week period of early voting would increase turnout by about 1.5 percent, and a three-week period would increase it by nearly 5 percent. The results are not partisan-neutral: the authors estimate that a nationwide early voting period of 23 days (as used in Ohio) would have given Democrats control of the Senate in 2012, and that a 46-day early voting period (used in Missouri and Wisconsin) would have flipped the Senate for Democrats in 2016. Ethan Kaplan and Haishan Yuan, *Early Voting Laws, Voter Turnout, and Partisan Vote Composition: Evidence from Ohio*, 12 Am. Econ. J.: App. Econ. 32 (2020).

- *Location of polling places.* Turnout is significantly higher among car owners than non-owners. Among whites, voters with access to a car turn out at an average rate of 68 percent, while those without a car turn out at a rate of 39 percent. Among blacks the figures are 53 percent and 29 percent, and among Hispanics, 50 percent versus 25 percent. Thus, "car access has an effect that widens existing participatory gaps." Justin de Benedictis-Kessner and Maxwell Palmer, *Driving Turnout: The Effect of Car Ownership on Electoral Participation*, __ Pol. Sci. & Res. __ (Dec. 2021).

- *Ballot design.* "Poor ballot design and instructions have led to the disenfranchisement of hundreds of thousands of voters in the last several federal elections. . . . There is compelling evidence that when basic usability principles are ignored in the design of ballots and drafting of instructions, a significant percentage of voters will be disenfranchised, and the affected voters will disproportionately be poor, minority, elderly and disabled voters." Lawrence Norden, et al., *Better Ballots* (Brennan Ctr. for Justice 2008).

≫ *Procedural Neutrality?* If it is agreed that the outcome of elections should be determined by the will of the people rather than the procedural choices of administrators, how can administrators identify procedures that would be truly "neutral" in the sense of having no effect on the result? Recall the quotation from Benn and Peters that concluded Chapter 4:

> The will of the people cannot be determined independently of the particular procedure employed, for it is not a natural will, nor is it a sum of similar wills of persons sharing common interests, but the result of going through a procedure which weighs some wills against others. . . . Until the count is made, there may be no way of telling which . . . majority . . . will "rule."

S.I. Benn and R.S. Peters, Principles of Political Thought 397-399 (1959).

Suppose that this statement is correct, and there is no way to identify the winner of an election other than by working through a set of pre-established electoral procedures. There is, in other words, no set of electoral procedures that is "neutral" in the sense that it reproduces without distortion some antecedently existing popular will the content of which can be known in some way other than by holding an actual election; or to put it yet another way, the popular will that counts is, to some degree, constructed by the very procedures used to measure it. That means, in turn, that there exists no set of procedural choices that will not to some degree influence the results of elections, especially where public opinion is closely divided.

To acknowledge this fact, however, is not the same thing as saying that procedural choices are by definition arbitrary, or that there is no way to distinguish better from worse procedural choices. The question instead becomes: by what criteria might we distinguish better from worse procedural choices? What criteria might be candidates for making such a distinction? What principles would you name? Do all your criteria point in the same direction in every set of circumstances? If they do not, how should an appropriate balance be struck among competing considerations?

Bush v. Gore

531 U.S. 98 (2000) (per curiam)

[This case arose out of the recount of votes in Florida in connection with the 2000 presidential election between Governor George W. Bush of Texas, the Republican candidate, and Vice President Al Gore, the Democratic candidate. Following the vote and an initial round of litigation, the Florida Election Canvassing

Commission certified Bush the winner of Florida's electoral votes by a margin of 537 votes. Gore then filed a statutory contest proceeding, arguing that votes had been illegally counted in numbers sufficient to change the outcome of the election. In conducting an appellate review of various aspects of the counting of presidential votes, the Florida Supreme Court interpreted the state election code to require that certain disputed ballots be counted in Gore's total. In addition, the court ruled that approximately 9,000 additional ballots (the so-called undercounts or undervotes) in Miami-Dade County had to be recounted manually and the totals included in the final count. Finally, the court held that similarly undercounted ballots throughout the state might also need to be manually counted, and remanded the case for such a determination. In conducting any recounts, the court held, canvassers should be guided by the statutory standard of attempting to effectuate the "clear intent of the voter."

[Bush then appealed to the U.S. Supreme Court, which took the case on an extraordinarily expedited basis.]

The closeness of this election, and the multitude of legal challenges which have followed in its wake, have brought into sharp focus a common, if heretofore unnoticed, phenomenon. Nationwide statistics reveal that an estimated 2% of ballots cast do not register a vote for President for whatever reason, including deliberately choosing no candidate at all or some voter error, such as voting for two candidates or insufficiently marking a ballot. . . . This case has shown that punch card balloting machines can produce an unfortunate number of ballots which are not punched in a clean, complete way by the voter. . . .

The right to vote is protected in more than the initial allocation of the franchise. Equal protection applies as well to the manner of its exercise. Having once granted the right to vote on equal terms, the State may not, by later arbitrary and disparate treatment, value one person's vote over that of another. See, *e.g., Harper v. Virginia Bd. of Elections,* 383 U.S. 663, 665 (1966). ("[O]nce the franchise is granted to the electorate, lines may not be drawn which are inconsistent with the Equal Protection Clause of the Fourteenth Amendment"). It must be remembered that "the right of suffrage can be denied by a debasement or dilution of the weight of a citizen's vote just as effectively as by wholly prohibiting the free exercise of the franchise." *Reynolds v. Sims,* 377 U.S. 533, 555 (1964).

There is no difference between the two sides of the present controversy on these basic propositions. Respondents say that the very purpose of vindicating the right to vote justifies the recount procedures now at issue. The question before us, however, is whether the recount procedures the Florida Supreme Court has adopted are consistent with its obligation to avoid arbitrary and disparate treatment of the members of its electorate.

Much of the controversy seems to revolve around ballot cards designed to be perforated by a stylus but which, either through error or deliberate omission, have not been perforated with sufficient precision for a machine to count them. In some cases a piece of the card—a chad—is hanging, say by two corners. In other cases there is no separation at all, just an indentation.

The Florida Supreme Court has ordered that the intent of the voter be discerned from such ballots. . . . The recount mechanisms implemented in response to the decisions of the Florida Supreme Court do not satisfy the minimum requirement for non-arbitrary treatment of voters necessary to secure the fundamental right. Florida's basic command for the count of legally cast votes is to consider the "intent of the voter." *Gore v. Harris,* 772 So. 2d, at 270. This is unobjectionable as an abstract proposition and a starting principle. The problem inheres in the absence of specific standards to ensure its equal application. The formulation of uniform rules to determine intent based on these recurring circumstances is practicable and, we conclude, necessary.

The law does not refrain from searching for the intent of the actor in a multitude of circumstances; and in some cases the general command to ascertain intent is not susceptible to much further refinement. In this instance, however, the question is not whether to believe a witness but how to interpret the marks or holes or scratches on an inanimate object, a piece of cardboard or paper which, it is said, might not have registered as a vote during the machine count. The factfinder confronts a thing, not a person. The search for intent can be confined by specific rules designed to ensure uniform treatment.

The want of those rules here has led to unequal evaluation of ballots in various respects. . . . As seems to have been acknowledged at oral argument, the standards for accepting or rejecting contested ballots might vary not only from county to county but indeed within a single county from one recount team to another.

The record provides some examples. A monitor in Miami-Dade County testified at trial that he observed that three members of the county canvassing board applied different standards in defining a legal vote. 3 Tr. 497, 499 (Dec. 3, 2000). And testimony at trial also revealed that at least one county changed its evaluative standards during the counting process. Palm Beach County, for example, began the process with a 1990 guideline which precluded counting completely attached chads, switched to a rule that considered a vote to be legal if any light could be seen through a chad, changed back to the 1990 rule, and then abandoned any pretense of a *per se* rule, only to have a court order that the county consider dimpled chads legal. This is not a process with sufficient guarantees of equal treatment. . . .

The State Supreme Court ratified this uneven treatment. It mandated that the recount totals from two counties, Miami-Dade and Palm Beach, be included in the certified total. The court also appeared to hold *sub silentio* that the recount totals from Broward County, which were not completed until after the original November 14 certification by the Secretary of State, were to be considered part of the new certified vote totals even though the county certification was not contested by Vice President Gore. Yet each of the counties used varying standards to determine what was a legal vote. Broward County used a more forgiving standard than Palm Beach County, and uncovered almost three times as many new votes, a result markedly disproportionate to the difference in population between the counties.

In addition, the recounts in these three counties were not limited to so-called undervotes but extended to all of the ballots. The distinction has real consequences. A manual recount of all ballots identifies not only those ballots which show no vote but also those which contain more than one, the so-called overvotes. Neither category will be counted by the machine. This is not a trivial concern. At oral argument, respondents estimated there are as many as 110,000 overvotes statewide. As a result, the citizen whose ballot was not read by a machine because he failed to vote for a candidate in a way readable by a machine may still have his vote counted in a manual recount; on the other hand, the citizen who marks two candidates in a way discernable by the machine will not have the same opportunity to have his vote count, even if a manual examination of the ballot would reveal the requisite indicia of intent. Furthermore, the citizen who marks two candidates, only one of which is discernable by the machine, will have his vote counted even though it should have been read as an invalid ballot. The State Supreme Court's inclusion of vote counts based on these variant standards exemplifies concerns with the remedial processes that were under way. . . .

In addition to these difficulties the actual process by which the votes were to be counted under the Florida Supreme Court's decision raises further concerns. That order did not specify who would recount the ballots. The county canvassing boards were forced to pull together ad hoc teams comprised of judges from various Circuits who had no previous training in handling and interpreting ballots. Furthermore, while others were permitted to observe, they were prohibited from objecting during the recount.

The recount process, in its features here described, is inconsistent with the minimum procedures necessary to protect the fundamental right of each voter in the special instance of a statewide recount under the authority of a single state judicial officer. Our consideration is limited to the present circumstances, for the problem of equal protection in election processes generally presents many complexities.

The question before the Court is not whether local entities, in the exercise of their expertise, may develop different systems for implementing elections. Instead, we are presented with a situation where a state court with the power to assure uniformity has ordered a statewide recount with minimal procedural safeguards. When a court orders a statewide remedy, there must be at least some assurance that the rudimentary requirements of equal treatment and fundamental fairness are satisfied. . . .

Upon due consideration of the difficulties identified to this point, it is obvious that the recount cannot be conducted in compliance with the requirements of equal protection and due process without substantial additional work. It would require not only the adoption (after opportunity for argument) of adequate statewide standards for determining what is a legal vote, and practicable procedures to implement them, but also orderly judicial review of any disputed matters that might arise. . . .

The judgment of the Supreme Court of Florida is reversed, and the case is remanded for further proceedings not inconsistent with this opinion. . . .

Justice STEVENS, with whom Justice GINSBURG and Justice BREYER join, dissenting.

[This Court has] never before called into question the substantive standard by which a State determines that a vote has been legally cast. And there is no reason to think that the guidance provided to the factfinders, specifically the various canvassing boards, by the "intent of the voter" standard is any less sufficient—or will lead to results any less uniform—than, for example, the "beyond a reasonable doubt" standard employed everyday by ordinary citizens in courtrooms across this country.

Admittedly, the use of differing substandards for determining voter intent in different counties employing similar voting systems may raise serious concerns.

Those concerns are alleviated—if not eliminated—by the fact that a single impartial magistrate will ultimately adjudicate all objections arising from the recount process. . . .

Even assuming that aspects of the remedial scheme might ultimately be found to violate the Equal Protection Clause, I could not subscribe to the majority's disposition of the case. As the majority explicitly holds, once a state legislature determines to select electors through a popular vote, the right to have one's vote counted is of constitutional stature. As the majority further acknowledges, Florida law holds that all ballots that reveal the intent of the voter constitute valid votes. Recognizing these principles, the majority nonetheless orders the termination of the contest proceeding before all such votes have been tabulated. Under their own reasoning, the appropriate course of action would be to remand to allow more specific procedures for implementing the legislature's uniform general standard to be established.

In the interest of finality, however, the majority effectively orders the disenfranchisement of an unknown number of voters whose ballots reveal their intent—and are therefore legal votes under state law—but were for some reason rejected by ballot-counting machines. . . .

Justice GINSBURG, with whom Justice STEVENS joins, and with whom Justice SOUTER and Justice BREYER join as to Part I, dissenting.

I agree with Justice Stevens that petitioners have not presented a substantial equal protection claim. Ideally, perfection would be the appropriate standard for judging the recount. But we live in an imperfect world, one in which thousands of votes have not been counted. I cannot agree that the recount adopted by the Florida court, flawed as it may be, would yield a result any less fair or precise than the certification that preceded that recount. . . .

Even if there were an equal protection violation, I would agree with Justice Stevens, Justice Souter, and Justice Breyer that the Court's concern about [the lack of time] is misplaced. Time is short in part because of the Court's entry of a stay on December 9, several hours after an able circuit judge in Leon County had begun to superintend the recount process. More fundamentally, the Court's reluctance to let the recount go forward—despite its suggestion that "[t]he search for intent can be confined by specific rules designed to ensure uniform treatment,"—ultimately turns on its own judgment about the practical realities of implementing a recount, not the judgment of those much closer to the process. . . .

Justice BREYER, with whom Justice STEVENS and Justice GINSBURG join except as to Part I-A-1, and with whom Justice SOUTER joins as to Part I, dissenting.

The Court was wrong to take this case. It was wrong to grant a stay. It should now vacate that stay and permit the Florida Supreme Court to decide whether the recount should resume.

The political implications of this case for the country are momentous. But the federal legal questions presented, with one exception, are insubstantial. . . .

[Moreover], there is no justification for the majority's remedy, which is simply to reverse the lower court and halt the recount entirely. An appropriate remedy would be, instead, to remand this case with instructions that, even at this late date, would permit the Florida Supreme Court to require recounting *all* undercounted votes in Florida, including those from Broward, Volusia, Palm Beach, and Miami-Dade Counties, whether or not previously recounted prior to the end of the protest period, and to do so in accordance with a single-uniform substandard. . . .

By halting the manual recount, and thus ensuring that the uncounted legal votes will not be counted under any standard, this Court crafts a remedy out of proportion to the asserted harm. And that remedy harms the very fairness interests the Court is attempting to protect. The manual recount would itself redress a problem of unequal treatment of ballots. . . .

I fear that in order to bring this agonizingly long election process to a definitive conclusion, we have not adequately attended to that necessary "check upon our own exercise of power," "our own sense of self-restraint." *United States v. Butler*, 297 U.S. 1, 79 (1936) (Stone, J., dissenting). Justice Brandeis once said of the Court, "The most important thing we do is not doing." What it does today, the Court should have left undone. I would repair the damage done as best we now can, by permitting the Florida recount to continue under uniform standards.

I respectfully dissent.

Early in its analysis, the Court says: "Our consideration is limited to the present circumstances, for the problem of equal protection in election processes generally presents many complexities." This language appears to confine the decision to its facts. More than two decades after deciding it, the Supreme Court has not once relied upon or cited *Bush v. Gore* in any subsequent opinion, even though it has issued many rulings in the field of election law. Despite what appears to be the Court's warning to litigants and lower courts not to rely on the opinion, lower courts may slowly be developing a body of equal protection jurisprudence relying on the Court's analysis. According to one recent review of the decisional law, lower courts now apply *Bush v. Gore* "in three main sets of circumstances: (1) laws and other legal directives that expressly or intentionally afford substantially different opportunities to vote to different groups of voters; (2) laws that delegate authority to local officials to determine important election-related policies; and (3) vague laws that implicitly leave room for potentially inconsistent interpretations or applications by local officials." Michael T. Morley, Bush v. Gore*'s Uniformity Principle and the Equal Protection Right to Vote*, 28 Geo. Mason L. Rev. 229 (2020).

Courts sometimes confine judicial opinions to their facts, but they usually do so long afterwards, when the disutility of the opinion in other settings has slowly become apparent. Can a court confine a decision to its facts prospectively?

≫ *Reaction to* **Bush v. Gore.** The Court's decision in *Bush v. Gore* released a torrent of criticism and commentary. The immediate reaction was harsh, especially from liberals. Professor and celebrity lawyer Alan Dershowitz called the decision "lawless," and described it as one in which a majority of the Justices "substitute[d] their political judgment for that of the people." Alan M. Dershowitz, Supreme Injustice: How the High Court Hijacked Election 2000 (2001). Lawyer and legal writer Vincent Bugliosi wrote that in its decision in *Bush v. Gore*, "the Court committed the unpardonable sin of being a knowing surrogate for the Republican Party instead of being an impartial arbiter of the law." Vincent Bugliosi,

THE BETRAYAL OF AMERICA: HOW THE SUPREME COURT UNDERMINED THE CONSTI-
TUTION AND CHOSE OUR PRESIDENT 41 (2001). Legal philosopher Ronald Dworkin called the decision "one of the least persuasive Supreme Court opinions that
I have ever read." Ronald Dworkin, *A Badly Flawed Election*, N.Y. REV. BOOKS (Jan.
11, 2001).

Among conservatives, opinion was divided. Some defended the Court's reasoning on the merits but disputed its judgment in stopping the recount. *See, e.g.,*
Michael W. McConnell, *Two-and-a-Half Cheers for* Bush v. Gore, 68 U. CHI. L. REV.
657 (2001). Others defended the Court's decision to halt the recount but conceded
the weakness of its legal reasoning. *See, e.g.,* Richard A. Epstein, *"In Such Manner as
the Legislature Thereof May Direct": The Outcome in* Bush v. Gore *Defended*, 68 U. CHI.
L. REV. 613 (2001). A small number thought the decision very fine in all respects.
See, e.g., Nelson Lund, *The Unbearable Rightness of* Bush v. Gore, 23 CARDOZO L. REV.
1219 (2002).

As the dust settled and the opinion received more serious and sustained
analysis, criticism tended generally to fall into a few recurring categories. The
sheer volume and breadth of analysis defies condensation; for a more complete
overview of the immediate reaction from all sides of the political spectrum, see
HOWARD GILLMAN, THE VOTES THAT COUNTED: HOW THE COURT DECIDED THE
2000 PRESIDENTIAL ELECTION 151-162 (2001). For an overview of the academic
literature generated during the first few years after the decision, see Richard
L. Hasen, *A Critical Guide to* Bush v. Gore *Scholarship*, 7 ANN. REV. POL. SCI. 297
(2004).

⟫ *The Politicization of Election Procedure.* Unfortunately, precisely because
of its impact on electoral outcomes, election procedure has in recent years
become a principal arena of intense, bitter, and now seemingly continual political struggle. Here are some examples of state legislation enacted since the 2020
election:

- California made voting by mail available in all elections without excuse.
  The state will automatically mail ballots to all registered voters.
- Texas made it a felony for an election official to mail a ballot to a voter who
  did not formally request one.
- New Jersey expanded its early voting period by nine days.
- Iowa reduced its early voting period by nine days.
- Georgia expanded the availability of early voting for rural counties but pro-
  hibited the further expansion of early voting for urban areas in which it
  had been previously expanded.
- Illinois and Virginia expanded the availability of ballot drop boxes, which
  permit voters drive-up access to voting facilities.
- Georgia banned the use of outdoor drop boxes, but permits their use at
  indoor locations during periods when such locations are fully staffed by
  election officials.
- Alabama banned curbside voting altogether.
- Georgia criminalized the provision of food or drink to voters waiting in line
  to vote.

- Texas required voters to provide a driver's license number or social security number both when applying for and when casting absentee ballots.
- Iowa now requires voters who fail to produce photo ID when they vote to return with ID by 5 p.m. the same day for their ballots to count.
- A new Arizona law strips eligibility to vote by absentee ballot from voters who have not voted in two consecutive election cycles and fail to respond to a mailed notification.
- In Arizona, Florida, Georgia, Idaho, Tennessee, and Texas, private individuals may no longer donate funds to local election offices for the purpose of supporting election operations; such offices may expend only funds appropriated by the relevant legislature.
- Arizona has stripped the authority of the Secretary of State, a Democrat, to represent the state in litigation challenging provisions of its election code, and transferred that authority to the Attorney General, a Republican, but only until the term of the incumbent Secretary of State concludes in 2023.
- Arkansas transferred authority to investigate election complaints from local election boards to the state board, presently composed of five Republicans and one Democrat. Georgia transferred authority to investigate election irregularities from the Secretary of State to the state election board. The incumbent Georgia Secretary of State, Brad Raffensperger, gained brief fame for resisting President Trump's insistent requests to change Georgia's vote totals during the 2020 election.

The cleavage that divides the combatants in the battle over election administration might be described in different ways. In one sense, it is clearly partisan in that Democrats and Republicans take very different positions about how elections should be administered. For the most part, states controlled by Democrats have enacted measures to make voting easier and more widely available, whereas states controlled by Republicans have enacted measures that make voting more onerous. But to the extent that the two major parties now align themselves along cleavages of a more profoundly ideological nature—in the degree to which they to adhere to liberal versus populist forms of democracy, for example, or in the extent to which they continue to adhere to liberalism at all—then might their approaches to election administration be described as conforming to basic, underlying assumptions about the conditions of legitimate governance? A third view, more cynical, might be that both parties are trying equally, as best they can, to rig elections, in one case by making it easier for their own likely supporters to vote, and in the other by making it harder for those most likely to oppose them to do so, with collateral damage to the participation of supporters deemed an acceptable cost. Is there a meaningful difference between trying to secure a partisan advantage by making voting easier and more inclusive, and by trying to make it harder and less inclusive?

Was the Supreme Court's decision in *Bush v. Gore* a principled application of prior equal protection jurisprudence? Or was it the opening volley in an era of nakedly partisan contestation over the procedures by which elections are to be decided?

B.   *ELECTORAL INTEGRITY*

1.   *What Counts as a "Good" Election?*

⟫   *The Concept of "Electoral Integrity."*   Any examination of the ground-level practice of electoral democracy is met at the outset with a significant problem: How should we judge elections? By what standard ought they to be evaluated? Around the globe, election observers, regulators, candidates, voters, and scholars seem to agree that elections should be conducted with "integrity," but what exactly does that concept mean? Generally speaking, electoral integrity involves measuring an election against two distinct benchmarks. First, electoral integrity requires at a minimum that an election be conducted substantially in accordance with applicable law. Thus, an election in which legally ineligible voters are permitted to vote, legally eligible voters are turned away, election districts are unconstitutionally gerrymandered, ballot boxes are stuffed, or votes are bought and sold, may lack integrity. Second, electoral integrity can refer to the fundamental consistency with democratic norms of the electoral laws themselves. If a jurisdiction's electoral laws significantly tilt the playing field in favor of incumbents, for example, then even strict compliance with those laws may not result in electoral outcomes characterized by "integrity." *See* SARAH BIRCH, ELECTORAL MALPRACTICE 30-31 (2011).

A final consideration concerns the inevitable problem of slippage: how closely must an election be conducted in accordance with controlling law and aspirational democratic norms to satisfy the condition of electoral integrity? Presumably, integrity is not an all-or-nothing proposition, but rather designates a spectrum of possible results. Assuming perfection is unattainable, how far from the ideal may an election deviate? It has been suggested, for example, that "as long as the rules of the game remain more or less intact, it may not matter that they are suboptimal as long as all parties suffer or benefit equally from them." Svitlana Chernykh *et al.*, *Constitutions and Election Management, in* ADVANCING ELECTORAL INTEGRITY 99 (Pippa Norris *et al.* eds., 2014). Do you agree?

⟫   *Democratic "Best Practices."*   A common way in which election observers judge the integrity of elections is to identify a set of best practices in election administration and to evaluate electoral systems according to how closely they adhere to such practices. Analysts who take this approach often use as a starting point international agreements such as the Universal Declaration of Human Rights and the International Covenant on Civil and Political Rights. These documents guarantee political rights such as self-determination and political participation. For example, the Universal Declaration of Human Rights provides specifically that "[t]he will of the people shall be the basis of the authority of government; this will shall be expressed in periodic and genuine elections which shall be by universal and equal suffrage and shall be by secret vote or by equivalent free voting procedures."

From these broad statements of democratic principles, organizations and scholars have derived more specific principles and best practices that allow them to measure and evaluate the soundness of elections around the globe. For instance, the International Institute for Democracy and Electoral Assistance, an intergovernmental organization whose members are states and whose mission is to furnish electoral expertise and advice to democracies around the world, has derived a list of 20 principles that it contends define a good election. These include periodic elections; universal and equal suffrage; freedoms of association, assembly, movement, and expression; transparency of information; the rule of law; and so forth. PIPPA NORRIS, WHY ELECTIONS FAIL 6-7 (2015). The Venice Commission of the European Union has promulgated a Code of Good Practice in Electoral Matters that addresses conditions and frequency of suffrage, respect for fundamental rights, and procedural protections.

Domestically, Heather Gerken, a legal scholar, has argued for the creation in the United States of a "democracy index" that would evaluate each state's electoral processes along three dimensions: thoroughness of voter registration, inclusiveness of ballot casting, and accuracy in vote counting. HEATHER GERKEN, THE DEMOCRACY INDEX (2009). In a 2014 report, the U.S. Presidential Commission on Election Administration developed a set of best electoral practices including online voter registration, interstate exchange of registration information, convenient location of polling places, use of large-scale voting centers, dissemination of information about line length at polling stations, and many others. U.S. Presidential Commission on Election Administration, *The American Voting Experience: Report and Recommendations* (2014).

How would the United States fare under a best practices approach? Most comparative studies conclude that election administration in the United States is mediocre by global standards. One study, for example, places the United States fiftieth worldwide, well behind high-scoring countries such as Denmark, Finland, Norway, Sweden, the Netherlands, Switzerland, and Austria. Pippa Norris, *Why American Elections Are Flawed (and How to Fix Them)*, Harvard Kennedy School Working Paper 16-038 (Sept. 2016).

The "best practices" approach to election administration seems to presuppose a single set of practices and arrangements that is best for all democracies, at all times, regardless of their history, resources, or local circumstances and preferences. Is there really one universally "best" way to practice democracy? Consider an alternative account of "democratic particularism":

> In this account, each *demos* is distinct — in its history, in its inheritances, in its characteristics, and in its experiences — and its commitment to and implementation through law of democracy is consequently the product of a context that is local and particular. In this story, all democracies arise by definition from a long course of decisions made in unique and sometimes difficult circumstances, and on their path to democratic self-governance often institutionalize distinctive local customs and understandings. . . . On this account, the content of election law is necessarily differentiated from state to state, and quite properly tailored to suit the society that will live under it. The particularistic account, moreover, takes a considerably broader view of what institutions and practices count as "democratic." The relevant point of comparison is not some ideal, ideologically prescribed set of best practices, but the actual, historical condition of the populace under prior regimes. On this view, not every society's *telos* is to achieve some kind of platonic ideal of democracy; it is more than sufficient, and no less consistent with liberal ideals, for a society to adopt practices that

simply make it better off than it was before—more egalitarian, more responsive to the needs of a larger portion of its citizenry, more attentive, perhaps, to human rights and human dignity.

James A. Gardner, *Introduction—Election Law: Universal or Particular?, in* COMPARATIVE ELECTION LAW (James A. Gardner, ed., 2022). If differences in the way democracy is practiced are valid among different nations, are similar deviations valid subnationally, within a single, federal nation like the United States?

» ***Administrative Challenges of U.S. Elections.***   In a democracy the size of the United States, administering elections poses obvious challenges. There are well over a half million popularly elected officials in the United States at the national, state, and local levels. U.S. Census Bureau, *Census of Governments*, Vol. 1, No. 2 (1992). If most officials have terms of roughly two years, then about a quarter million elections are held every year, one for every 1,200 Americans. This means that in large states like New York, Texas, and Florida, state election officials must run somewhere on the order of 15,000 elections every year. That means certifying candidates for the ballot by processing nominating papers and signature petitions, designing and printing ballots with the correct candidates listed in the correct places, moving voting equipment into and out of thousands of polling places, hiring and training temporary poll workers to administer the elections on site, collecting each and every ballot cast, and accurately counting them. This is a monumental administrative task.

How well do state and local governments perform these tasks? On one hand, the public now hears a good deal every election cycle about elections that have gone badly; media coverage of long lines, turned away voters, and malfunctions of voting equipment have become commonplace. On the other hand, even with reporters apparently on the prowl for embarrassing stories about electoral glitches, only a handful of elections in any given year seem to have troubles that rise to the level of newsworthiness. This seems to suggest strongly that the overwhelming majority of elections in the United States are competently and professionally administered, and conducted without serious problem. (How can this observation be squared with the mediocre U.S. record as measured by adherence to best practices?)

Public fascination with problem elections also obscures the fact that in a great many electoral races no problem of a tainted or questionable outcome can possibly arise because the race for the office in question is uncontested. For example, between 1988 and 1996, about 35 percent of all state legislative seats were uncontested, i.e., were sought by a single candidate running without an opponent. Pervill Squire, *Uncontested Seats in Legislative Elections*, 25 LEGIS. STUD. Q. 131, 133 (2000). Even among contested races, lopsided victories seem to be the rule. In the 2000 congressional elections, more than 80 percent of all races were decided by margins exceeding 20 percent. Samuel Issacharoff, *Gerrymandering and Political Cartels*, 116 HARV. L. REV. 593, 623 (2002). Under these circumstances, even if errors occur during the administration of the election, it is all but impossible for them to have any impact on the ultimate outcome of the election. (Of course, the fact that so many races are uncontested might itself reflect a different kind of problem, if not one of ground-level election administration.)

To say all this is by no means to dismiss the problem of tainted elections as either nonexistent or, when it occurs, trivial. Some elections do go badly, and the results will be questionable to the extent that there is genuine uncertainty about who is entitled to the seat.

≫ *Considerations of Cost.*   Election integrity is undoubtedly a deeply important public goal, but it is not the only important public goal, and presumably even voters dissatisfied with present practices would not support pursuing absolute electoral integrity at any cost. This suggests that there is some optimal level of spending on elections that would achieve a desirable degree of electoral integrity at an acceptable price. Are we anywhere near that level of spending?

The decentralization of American election administration makes the collection and comparison of data difficult, but two recent studies have attempted to quantify current spending levels. Both studies find that elections are financed mainly by local governments, using funds raised through general tax revenues, such as local property and sales taxes. States do not contribute a large proportion of funds, but they often provide general support services, such as a statewide voter registration list and central oversight and supervision through a state board of elections. Federal funds account for less than 4 percent of all funds expended on elections. In recent years, local governments nationwide spent between $4 and $6 billion on elections — about 0.25 percent of all local spending. In a typical year, election spending in most jurisdictions appears to run from about $4.50 to $8.50 per capita. A few jurisdictions spend $10 or more per capita, and only a handful spend as much as $20 per capita. Scholars, as well as election officials, generally characterize these amounts as far lower than required. Joshua S. Sellers and Roger Michalski, *Democracy on a Shoestring*, 74 VAND. L. REV. 1079 (2021); Charles Stewart III, *The Cost of Conducting Elections* (MIT Election Data and Science Lab 2022).

2. *Fraud*

The single most frequent charge made today against the integrity of American elections is that they are routinely distorted by voting fraud occurring on a massive scale. The frequency and magnitude of these charges can at times be difficult to process. For example, it is not uncommon elsewhere in the world for losing candidates to claim that elections have been stolen through fraud and other devices, yet in 2016 the *winning* candidate for president, Donald Trump, made the astonishing claim that his own election was tainted by "millions of people who voted illegally," all apparently for his opponent, Hillary Clinton. Following his defeat in the 2020 election, Trump notoriously asserted, and continues to repeat, that the election had been stolen from him.

In this section, we examine the phenomenon of vote fraud in its historical and contemporary contexts.

≫ *What Does It Take to Steal an Election?*   Standard nineteenth-century electioneering practices included widespread bribery, physical intimidation, and social pressure, applied effectively in an era before the advent of the secret ballot. Yet even by the low standards of the nineteenth century, one series of elections stands out for the scale of fraud and violence: elections held in Kansas during the mid-1850s, which were riven by tensions over the spread of slavery into territories and new states.

Under the Missouri Compromise of 1820, new states admitted north of the southern border of Missouri were to be free, and those south of that line were to be slave states. In 1854, Congress enacted the Kansas-Nebraska Act, which undid the earlier compromise. Under the terms of the Act, new states applying for admission to the union, wherever located, were free to decide for themselves whether to be slave or free. This change in federal law unleashed a mighty struggle in Kansas among free soil and pro-slavery interests for political control of the territory, a struggle that played itself out in a series of territorial elections between 1855 and 1857 for governor, local and territorial legislative offices, and non-voting territorial delegates to Congress. Below is an account of the Kansas electoral landscape near the Missouri border in 1855.

Nicole Etcheson

Bleeding Kansas: Contested Liberty in the Civil War Era (2005)

The day of the election proved tumultuous. Frederick Starr reported that Missouri River ferries carried eight hundred men a day, for three days prior to the election, across the river. Organized in companies, some of these men went as far inland as Pawnee, some 120 miles into the territory. At the Leavenworth election, there appeared five times the number of voters recorded in the census. When the free-soil judge of election resigned, he was replaced by one sympathetic to slavery. Some judges refused to take the governor's oath, while others decided that voters did not have to take their oath. Intimidated, most free-soil supporters simply did not vote. A Missourian who had lived in Kansas since the fall of 1854 saw no violence at the Leavenworth election, although he reported an open display of bowie knives and guns. He himself did not vote, he explained, "because [he] considered squatters directly insulted by Missouri, by taking our rights in voting away from us."

Similar irregularities occurred at other polling places: voters from outside the territory cast ballots, judges of election refused to follow procedures set by the governor, and free-soil candidates, judges, and voters withdrew from the polling places. A report from Lawrence estimated that from seven hundred to three thousand Missourians had come to vote, forcing the judge of election to hand over the poll book. Free soilers were so intimidated that they did not even try to vote. With banners flying, the Missourians had marched in to a drumbeat. Provisioned with two fieldpieces, wagons, tents, and food, they wore pieces of white or blue ribbon — or hemp — in their buttonholes, from which arose their password, "all right on the hemp." So many Missourians turned out that, according to one Lawrence resident, having a surplus for the Lawrence polls, a camp on the Wakarusa was able to spare extra voters for another polling place.

Although reports from Lawrence indicated no violence, free soilers blamed their loss on the threat of violence. Election judge N.B. Blanton failed to appear at the Lawrence polls, he said, after Missourians threatened to hang him if he insisted on enforcing the governor's oath. One of Blanton's fellow judges, James B. Abbott, did show up but quickly became frustrated when the other two judges outvoted him each time on the acceptability of ballots. Seeing himself outnumbered, he too resigned and was replaced.

More flagrant intimidation occurred at Bloomington. Missourians broke in the windows of the log house that served as a polling place and picked it up by one corner, letting it fall. Samuel J. Jones entered the house with a half-dozen Missourians. One of the election judges ran out of the house carrying the ballot box and hurrahing for Missouri. Pointedly looking at his watch, Jones gave the remaining judges five minutes to resign or be killed. They resigned.

Free-soil sources provided other dramatic accounts of organized nonresident voting and intimidation. Missourians verified them. Moore recorded that a "great crowd," presumably including himself, went over to Kansas on election day and that "all voted that pleased, no objections, no swearing in voters." A Doniphan man was unnerved by the Missourians' behavior. He noted that armed men, who were "cutting up," were "pretty well corned [drunk], and were noisy and boisterous." A Missourian later recalled that he had voted at the March 1855 election while still residing in Missouri. He intended to move to Kansas and, in fact, did so not long after the election. Because he was "naturally anxious to have a voice in moulding the institutions" where he intended to reside, he did not regard his vote as ethically wrong.

That view was widely accepted among the proslavery party. In an editorial three days before the election, the Atchison *Squatter Sovereign* insisted that residency was unnecessary for voting. "By the Kansas act, every man in the Territory on the day of the election is a legal voter, if he have not fixed a day for his return to some other home." On election day, many Missourians told a Lawrence man that they had a legal right to vote because residents could vote and "they were residents while they were here." One Missourian explained, "By the Nebraska Bill every man who happened to inhabit the territory at the time of the election was a qualified voter. No man was ever sworn *that he would not go away.*"

Missourians also rationalized their actions by asserting that the threat to Missouri was so severe that it justified measures that seemingly violated democratic processes. A Missouri Lawyer wrote in his diary of the proslavery victory in Kansas, "It is certain th[a]t the Missourians regard this as a simple question whether they shall leave here — or those abolitionists shall leave Kansas." Fearing that free Kansas would harbor fugitive slaves and endanger the safety of slave property in their state, Missourians asked, "If Kansas be settled by Abolitionists, can Missouri remain a slave state?" Many Missourians thought not. In fact, if abolition should spread to Missouri, one southern state after another would be endangered, until slavery everywhere was under siege. . . .

In a memorial presented to Congress, the free-soil settlers protested that the disruption of the March 30 election was "a well matured and settled plan" to "enslave" them. The memorial rehearsed complaints about the massive invasion of the polls, intimidation of judges and voters, and Atchison's role in encouraging Missouri voting. "Foreign oppression" threatened to destroy popular sovereignty's promise of majority rule. Unless the provisions of the Kansas-Nebraska Act were enforced, Kansas was destined to become "a vassal province" of Missouri.

Massive election fraud, on a scale sufficient to alter the results of elections, may have occurred in the nineteenth century, but does it still occur today? For the most part, the answer is clearly that it does not, suggesting that modernizing election reforms such as voter registration and the secret ballot, along with parallel changes in democratic culture, may have been generally successful in reducing outright voter fraud. Still, consider the account below, describing vote fraud in Chicago during the 1982 election.

Hearing Before a Subcommittee of the Senate Committee on the Judiciary

Statement of Dan K. Webb, U.S. Attorney for the Northern District of Illinois (1983)

The Office of the United States Attorney for the Northern District of Illinois has had a long history of active investigation of vote fraud. Since the early 1970s, our office has been one of the few, if not the only, United States Attorney's Office in the country to actively monitor voting practices on election days. . . . There are several federal statutes which condemn vote fraud and which we rely on in our prosecutions. When a federal candidate is on the ballot, specific federal statutes become applicable. These statutes prohibit voting more than once, supplying false information to vote, voting in the name of another person, and paying people to vote. 42 U.S.C. §§1973i(c),(e). Further, the civil rights statutes (18 U.S.C. §§241,242) prohibit conspiracies and substantive conduct directed at depriving the public-at-large of their constitutional right to the fair and impartial administration of federal elections. Also, voter intimidation directed at influencing the results of a federal contest is outlawed by statute. 18 U.S.C. §594. When a federal candidate is not on the ballot, the federal civil rights statutes prohibit the deprivation of voters' federal constitutional right to vote in a local election in accordance with the one-person-one-vote principle. Serious vote fraud committed with the assistance of election judges violates these civil rights statutes. Finally, the mail fraud statute (18 U.S.C. §1341) has been used to prosecute vote fraud that is perpetrated through the use of the mails. This statute has been applied most often to fraudulent schemes involving absentee ballots.

Our office, together with the Federal Bureau of Investigation and the Immigration and Naturalization Service, have undertaken an intensive and wide-ranging investigation of alleged vote fraud in the November 1982 general election. Offices at stake in this election in Illinois included representatives in Congress and Governor. Because this investigation is quite active right now and is subject to grand jury scrutiny, I am unable to discuss the investigation in detail. I will, however, describe it in broad outline. . . . Based on indictments and convictions that we have obtained concerning the November 1982 general election, we have uncovered certain species of vote fraud. All of these crimes occurred in Chicago in areas that were dominated by one political party. In each instance of fraud there was one prerequisite, and that was that the leader of the dominant political party at the precinct level (the precinct captain) controlled the actions of the officials administering the election at the polling place (the election judges).

With the election judges in his control, the precinct captain perpetrated the most common type of vote fraud, which consisted of forging on ballot applications the names of persons who did not come in to vote and then voting ballots in their names. Either the precinct captain himself, one of his workers, or an election judge would do the forging. For example, in an extreme case a large number of ballot applications were forged and then an equal number of ballots were taken to a back room, voted, and then placed in the ballot box.

Another type of fraud consisted of a precinct worker getting into line and posing as a legitimate voter and then voting in the name of this person.

Another type of vote fraud consisted of false registration. Here, a precinct captain caused another person who did not live in his precinct to register to vote in his precinct in order to increase the number of votes that the precinct captain controlled.

Another instance of fraud that we uncovered concerned elderly and disabled voters. Such voters will need assistance to vote. We found examples of election judges who voted ballots on behalf of these people without the authorization or understanding of the elderly voters.

We also uncovered instances of precinct captains and precinct workers paying people to vote.

Another instance of fraud that we found involved absentee ballots. Under this scheme, false information was submitted in order to obtain blank absentee ballots, which were then voted by the precinct captain.

Perhaps the most flagrant example of vote fraud that we have prosecuted occurred in the 30th Precinct of the 27th Ward. In this precinct, in November, a precinct captain and his son in effect ran their own election at the end of the day. Instead of properly tabulating the vote, the election judges stood aside and watched the precinct captain's son take one straight Democratic ballot and run it though the tabulating machine 203 times.

The principal vote fraud problem that we have uncovered is the forging of ballot applications and the fraudulent voting of ballots in the forged names by precinct captains and persons working for the precinct captains. To accomplish this illicit process, the precinct captain needs a pool of registered voters whose names he can forge. Persons who have died or who have moved are prime candidates for this pool. It is therefore imperative to assure an honest election that these names be removed from the voting rolls prior to each election.

In Chicago, these names are supposed to be removed in periodic canvasses. We have found that all too often these canvasses have not been performed. Again, the canvasses are supposed to be conducted by the election judges. The judges, however, are often controlled by the local precinct captains, who do not want good canvasses and who prevent the canvasses from being properly performed. These faulty canvasses contribute significantly to vote fraud.

Another serious problem that we uncovered involves illegal aliens and other non-citizens who illegally register to vote and vote in various elections.

We have found that many illegal aliens register to vote for the purpose of acquiring voter registration cards, which they then use to commit additional crimes. We have found instances of illegal aliens using an illegally obtained voter registration card to fraudulently obtain passports, public aid, and food stamps. We

also found that on one occasion a non-citizen used an illegally obtained voter registration card in order to get security clearance to work for a contractor selling weapons parts to the United States Department of Defense.

Furthermore, our investigation shows that some of these aliens actually cast
illegal votes in various elections. We have found instances in which some persons
have actively sought the registration of illegal aliens for the very purpose of influencing the outcome of an election. If these people do not vote, their illegal registrations can still lead to a dishonest election because they constitute additional
names added to the pool that can be fraudulently voted.

We have obtained the convictions of seven aliens charged with offenses
related to their illegal registration and voting, including passport fraud and
fraud against the government. Also, our office and INS have referred to the
State's Attorney's Office twenty-nine cases resulting in indictments. The illegal alien registration problem stems in part from the ease with which persons
may register to vote in Illinois. Persons who want to register to vote should be
required to furnish identification. I understand that legislation has recently
been passed that would alleviate this problem by requiring identification when a
person registers to vote.

In analyzing the results of our investigation, we can point to certain circumstances that are conducive to vote fraud. The first prerequisite is that one party
dominate the precinct, and that there not be any hotly-contested local races in that
precinct. If there is a hotly-contested local race, or if both major political parties
are viable in that particular precinct, there will be enough persons watching the
activity in the polling place to prevent most kinds of vote fraud. If the people in the
polling place—judges and watchers—observe each other and have an adversary
relationship, an honest election is the likely result. Vote fraud cannot occur if election judges do their job. Therefore, a precondition to a dishonest election is that
the judges, either because of their economic situation or personality, must be of a
type to be dominated by a precinct captain.

We have also found that a significant amount of fraud occurs in those areas
where it is hard for a precinct captain to make his quota by legitimate means. For
example, if the voter pool consists of a substantial number of transients or otherwise unreliable people. A precinct captain will have a hard time getting out the vote
legitimately, and he may have to resort to illegal methods.

Our investigation of the November 1982 election has resulted so far in the
indictment, conviction, and penitentiary sentence for a precinct captain, the indictment of three other precinct captains, and the indictment and conviction of other
precinct workers and election judges. In addition to the seven convictions of aliens,
we have obtained vote fraud convictions of five persons, and vote fraud indictments
against fourteen others. Our investigation is continuing, and we expect additional
results in the near future.

———————

The U.S. Attorney estimated that 10 percent of the votes cast in Chicago in
1982 were fraudulent. But did the fraud change the outcome? According to the
U.S. Attorney, large-scale vote fraud is possible only where an election is not closely

contested. But if the election is not closely contested, why would the dominant party bother to engage in fraud?

>> *The Modern Revival of Charges of Vote Fraud.* Recent years have seen a marked growth in the number and frequency of charges of election fraud, much of it occurring on the heels of the disputed 2000 presidential election and the Supreme Court's decision in *Bush v. Gore.* For example, according to one well-known conservative political commentator, "Election fraud, whether it's phony voter registrations, illegal absentee ballots, shady recounts or old-fashioned ballot-box stuffing, can be found in every part of the United States." JOHN FUND, STEALING ELECTIONS: HOW VOTER FRAUD THREATENS OUR DEMOCRACY 7 (2004). Accounts like this have been instrumental in heightening popular and legislative demand for measures that reduce the possibility of voting by the ineligible such as citizenship verification measures, requirements that voters produce photo identification, and regular purges of ineligible voters from voter registration lists.

Since 2016, however, the landscape has changed dramatically, largely at the instigation of Donald Trump, and then by his supporters in the Republican Party. As indicated earlier, Trump claimed repeatedly following his 2016 victory that millions of illegal votes were cast, a claim that exceeds any other claim of voter fraud, credible or otherwise, by orders of magnitude. He then claimed, and continues to claim, that he lost the 2020 election to Joe Biden only because the election was "stolen" due to massive, widespread fraud.

Some of the specific claims made by Republicans verge on the bizarre. For example, Arizona Republican Party workers charged that election officials in Maricopa County, which contains Phoenix and accounts for about 62 percent of the state's population, were deliberately handing out indelible Sharpie pens to voters in an effort to induce them to spoil their ballots. Everything about this claim was false: no election workers handed out such pens, the use of Sharpies was incapable of spoiling a ballot, and any ballots marked with a Sharpie were duly counted. A lawsuit brought by voters who claimed their Sharpie-marked ballots had not been counted was voluntarily withdrawn by the plaintiffs, presumably once they bothered to learn the facts. David T. Canon and Owen Sherman, *Debunking the "Big Lie": Election Administration in the 2020 Presidential Election,* 51 PRES. STUD. 541 (2021). Indeed, the Trump Campaign brought more than 50 lawsuits around the country alleging various kinds of fraud and irregularities in vote tabulation, with only a single success, which resulted in the invalidation of about 200 ballots in Westmoreland County, Pennsylvania, *id.,* a county Trump won by a 2-to-1 margin. Indeed, a federal district judge in Michigan took the unusual step of imposing sanctions on Trump's legal team for filing a frivolous lawsuit, and Trump's personal lawyer, Rudy Giuliani, was suspended from the practice of law by the New York Court of Appeals for making false statements to courts and to the public about the election.

Subsequent investigations of Republican claims of vote fraud have produced no credible support. *See, e.g.,* Andrew C. Eggers, et al., *No Evidence for Systematic Voter Fraud: A Guide to Statistical Claims About the 2020 Election,* 118 PNAS __(2021). To the contrary, all available evidence points to the same conclusion: claims of widespread, result-altering election fraud concerning the 2016 and 2020 elections are simply fabrications. Indeed, the same may in general be said about such claims regarding earlier elections: Upon investigation, virtually all claims of suspected double voting and other forms of voter fraud turn out to be the result either of erroneous record keeping by the state or innocent mistake on the part of the voter. *See* Justin Levitt, *The Truth about Voter Fraud* (Brennan Center for Justice 2007). According to one careful study, "Voter fraud is a politically constructed myth. [Charges of fraud] fall apart when we interrogate them. Voter fraud politics are robust in part because they capitalize on general and widely held folk beliefs that are rooted in facts and real historical experience, notions such as corruption in party politics and government but also stereotypes and class- and racially biased preconceptions of corruption among groups long stigmatized by their marginal or minority status in U.S. society." LORRAINE C. MINNITE, THE MYTH OF VOTER FRAUD 6 (2010).

The author argues, among many other things, that voter fraud on the "retail," or individual level, makes no sense:

> [F]or the vast majority of Americans committing an act of voter fraud — forging a voter registration card, stealing an identity to vote more than once, or knowingly voting illegally — is even more irrational than the individual act of voting. What would an individual voter on their own get out of committing an election crime? The incentives to cast an illegal ballot need to be pretty high to risk a felony conviction and five years in jail. . . . Why would an undocumented immigrant who may have obtained a fake Social Security number in order to be paid for the low-wage labor he or she provides a U.S. employer come out from the shadows to cast a ballot that could deport that individual forever? . . . The best facts we can gather to assess the magnitude of the alleged problem of voter fraud show that, although millions of people cast ballots every year, almost no one knowingly and willfully casts an illegal vote in the United States today.

Id. at 5-6. A corollary of this argument is that election fraud makes "sense" only when it is executed at the wholesale level — when enough votes can reliably be manipulated to swing the result. Who is in a position to swing an election through wholesale vote stealing? Individuals who show up at the polls impersonating eligible voters? Or public officials who have actual access to the election machinery? Should we be more worried about illegal voting by individuals or by legislative or administrative rules that manipulate the behavioral incentives for large classes of people? If election fraud is a threat, who is threatened, and by what means?

⨠ *Vote Fraud and Race.*   One recent development appears to be the emergence of a new generation of vote suppression techniques aimed at racial minorities. In earlier times, vote suppression might have been undertaken through violence or intimidation. The new generation of vote suppression, in contrast, works through the deliberate provision of false information to voters in minority neighborhoods. For example, broadsheets, sometimes designed to look as though officially issued, have been circulated providing incorrect information about the date or place of voting, misrepresenting conditions of voter eligibility, or wildly exaggerating the penalties for attempting to vote when ineligible (e.g., deportation or losing one's children). *See* Gilda R. Daniels, *Voter Deception*, 43 IND. L. REV. 343 (2010). Another technique appears to be "vote caging" — the aggressive challenging at the polls of the eligibility of voters who present themselves, undertaken for the purpose of so delaying the progress of voting at the polling place as to discourage voters from waiting around to cast their votes. *See* Chandler Davidson et al., *Vote Caging as a Republican Ballot Security Technique*, 34 WM. MITCHELL L. REV. 533 (2008). *See generally* FRANCES FOX PIVEN ET AL., KEEPING DOWN THE BLACK VOTE: RACE AND THE DEMOBILIZATION OF AMERICAN VOTERS (2009).

These examples involve action by private individuals acting outside the administrative apparatus, but there is evidence that even official actions sometimes have suppressive effects in minority neighborhoods. For example, one study found that lines at polling places were on average more than twice as long in minority neighborhoods than in white ones: the average wait to vote in majority-minority precincts was 24 minutes compared to 11 minutes in majority white precincts. Charles Stewart III, *Waiting to Vote in 2012*, 28 J.L. & POL. 439 (2013). The most common explanation for long wait times is provision of an insufficient number of voting machines or polling locations in affected neighborhoods. Is that kind of electoral administration evidence of intentional discrimination? Consider another study finding that email inquiries to election officials regarding voter ID requirements were on average about 5 percent less likely to receive a reply when the inquirer had an obviously Latino name. Ariel R. White et al., *What Do I Need to Vote? Bureaucratic Discretion and Discrimination by Local Election Officials*, 109 AM. POL. SCI. REV. 129 (2015). Is this an example of conscious or unconscious bias? Is the degree of intentionality relevant to how the law ought to treat racial disparities in election administration?

▶▶ *Challenges of Detection.* On a typical Election Day, millions of people vote. Each vote involves numerous transactions: prior registration, spending time at or in the vicinity of a polling place, checking in with poll workers, filling out a ballot, submitting it for counting, and so forth. Given the great many ways in which a voting transaction may go wrong, how is it possible successfully to monitor the behavior of all voters and catch all instances of misbehavior, much less detect and prevent any inadvertent errors from creeping into the process? How thorough can election oversight be? If it cannot be comprehensive, how much is enough? Is comprehensive oversight simply unnecessary because elections are generally well run? Because we trust the government to run clean and accurate elections under ordinary conditions? Because private actors have a sufficient interest in democratic processes to report irregularities to authorities? Is election fraud underreported? Or might it be overreported?

3. Securing Electoral Integrity: Institutional Options

If a democratic society's goal is to hold free and fair elections characterized by electoral integrity, how is that goal best achieved? The ground rules of democracy are in a sense the most important rules a democratic society adopts because they determine, or at least strongly influence, how every other decision will be made. Enforcement of such rules is, moreover, a large and complex task, and partisan pressure is an open and integral part of routine democratic contestation. The ultimate prize — possession of power — is highly attractive. In these circumstances, what kind of body can be trusted to implement and enforce duly enacted democratic ground rules fairly and impartially?

a. The Administrative Model

In modern democracies, the front line of election administration is occupied by public officials employed by a government agency that has by law been charged with conducting elections — a so-called "Election Management Body" (EMB). Around the world, three major models have emerged: "(1) the independent model; (2) the executive/governmental model; [and] (3) the mixed model."

> Most countries (63%) fall in the first category. This model is common among countries that were part of the "third wave" of democratization, a response to authoritarian regimes incapable of conducting free and fair elections. The idea is that independent commissions might function as an "island of integrity" in a country without established democratic institutions. This model successfully aided the consolidation of constitutional democracy in countries like India and Mexico. It has also found favor in some established democracies, like Australia and Canada.
>
> The next most common model (23%) is for a component of the executive branch to run elections. This model is common among Western European countries, including countries that are commonly regarded as having well-functioning systems like Belgium, Denmark, Finland, Germany, Ireland, Norway, and the U.K. At first glance, it might seem problematic to vest election administration in a government ministry that is appointed by the ruling party or coalition. That entity might be tempted to rig the game in favor of those holding power. Yet in practice, this system often functions well. This can be attributed to the professional civil service of many countries which employ this model. The competency of these ministries may allow them to resist political pressure and to run credible elections.
>
> The remainder of countries (12%) have mixed systems, in which authority is divided among different public entities. A classic example of this model is France, where national authority is divided between the Ministry of the Interior and Constitutional Council, a quasi-judicial institution that oversees elections. Another is Japan, which divides election management responsibilities between a government agency (the Ministry of Internal Affairs and Communications) and a five-person independent commission (the Central Election Management Council). In general, this category is used to describe countries in which authority is divided horizontally among different branches of government – most often, executive and judicial authorities. . . .

Daniel P. Tokaji, *Comparative Election Administration: A Legal Perspective on Electoral Institutions, in* COMPARATIVE ELECTION LAW (James A. Gardner, ed., 2022).

In the domain of election administration, the United States is a significant outlier in two ways: first, in the degree to which the U.S. system is decentralized; and second, in the degree to which chief election administrators are themselves elected, often in partisan elections.

» *Decentralization of U.S. Election Administration.*   One of the unusual features of American democracy is that the administration of elections is highly decentralized.

Although Article I, §4 of the U.S. Constitution authorizes Congress to regulate the "Times, Places and Manner of holding Elections for Senators and Representatives," it has rarely invoked that power, preferring to leave the regulation of federal elections to the states. In any case, the overwhelming majority of elections in the United States are for state and local offices, administered under the exclusive authority of the states. Moreover, most states redelegate much of their authority over elections to the county level, meaning that American elections, even for federal offices, are administered by a patchwork of state and county authorities operating with limited central coordination.

This system is sometimes criticized as unusually and unnecessarily vulnerable to problems. Local governments typically have few resources to devote to election administration. Polling places tend to be staffed by thousands of volunteer workers, and training of those workers is frequently spotty and unsystematic. Most other democracies staff their polling places with civil service professionals, thoroughly trained and supervised by a central election administration authority. *See* Daniel P. Tokaji, *The Future of Election Reform: From Rules to Institutions*, 28 YALE L. & POL'Y REV. 125, 137-143 (2009).

Is there any justification, other than historical accident, for the extreme decentralization of American election administration? Consider the following account:

> [T]he decentralized American way of voting enhances and facilitates our exercise of meaningful popular sovereignty. . . . [D]ecentralization may well "interfere" with a certain vision of uniform, direct, plebiscitary national self-rule—but . . . in fact, almost everything about our electoral structure does so too. . . . [L]ocal administration can improve citizens' sense of efficacy and ownership in the democratic process, provide opportunities for experimentation and innovation, place obstacles in the way of corrupting influence, and increase turnout. The local dimension of American voting becomes much more intelligible and defensible, and much less a scandalous accident of history, when incorporated into the family of ideas built around popular sovereignty and the state.

ALEC C. EWALD, THE WAY WE VOTE: THE LOCAL DIMENSION OF AMERICAN SUFFRAGE (2009). This account suggests that the problem, if there is one, is not decentralization itself so much as decentralization on the cheap. Do you agree? Would a fully funded and well-trained cadre of election administrators under the direction of a multitude of state and local authorities be as good as a fully centralized, professional, national election bureaucracy? See HEATHER K. GERKEN, THE DEMOCRACY INDEX: WHY OUR ELECTION SYSTEM IS FAILING AND HOW TO FIX IT (2009), which proposes a state-by-state index of effectiveness in electoral administration as a way to provide states with proper incentives in a decentralized system.

More instrumentally, "decentralization helps prevent national elections from being captured by one party or the other. Further, it provides a check against catastrophic incompetence, insofar as a mistake in one state or county—for example, the failure to supply polling places with the access cards needed for electronic voting—will not bleed over into others." Tokaji, *supra*, at 142. Are these better reasons to prefer decentralized election administration? If so, why haven't other countries embraced decentralization? Is decentralization a peculiarly American phenomenon?

Even if decentralization of election administration offers certain advantages, in most states the state legislature retains considerable discretion concerning what powers will be made available to local governments. In recent decades, certain local legislation, often of a progressive character—minimum wage laws, for example, or "sanctuary city" immigration policies, or local mask mandates in response to the Covid pandemic—have prompted state legislatures to revoke local lawmaking powers. These battles have now spilled over into the domain of election administration, typically with Republican-controlled state legislatures withdrawing powers that have been exercised by Democratic-controlled local governments, often located in densely populated urban areas. In many cases, state legislation revoking local authority was prompted by local efforts to expand voting access during the pandemic election of 2020, efforts that were opposed by officials at the state level. Richard Briffault, *Election Law Localism and Democracy*, 100 N.C. L. REV. __ (2022). *See also* Joshua S. Sellers and Erin A. Scharff, *Preempting Politics: State Power and Local Democracy*, 72 STAN. L. REV. 1361 (2020).

b. Partisanship in Election Administration

Richard L. Hasen

Beyond the Margin of Litigation: Reforming U.S. Election Administration to Avoid Electoral Meltdown

62 Wash. & Lee L. Rev. 937 (2005)

In thirty-three states, the secretary of state (or other statewide official charged with responsibilities as the Chief Elections Officer of the state (CELO)) is elected through a partisan election process. No state currently elects the CELO through a nonpartisan election. The remaining states use an appointments process. Many states let the governor appoint the CELO, sometimes subject to confirmation of a house or both houses of the state legislature. Some states use various appointments measures for boards or commissions to run elections. Most of these commissions use a bipartisan model that either splits representation on the board evenly between the two major parties, or gives an advantage to the majority party in the state.

On the county and other local levels, there is an even greater variation, and the state-based method of selection does not necessarily match the county level. In California, for example, the secretary of state runs in a partisan election, but on the county level the local elections official may either be a county clerk elected in a nonpartisan election or a registrar of voters appointed by and serving at the pleasure of the county board of supervisors. In Florida, the secretary of state used to be a partisan elected position; the secretary now is appointed and serves at the pleasure of the Governor. But the county supervisor of elections still runs in a partisan election. Generally speaking, there is no distinct pattern in the U.S. for the selection of county and local election officials. . . .

The case for nonpartisan election administration begins with the 2000 Florida debacle. . . . The Florida example shows that discretionary decisions in the context of a recount can affect the outcome of a close election, and that there may be at least the appearance, if not the fact, of some discretionary decisions being made to benefit the decisionmaker's party and candidates. Indeed, even if an election administrator chosen through partisan election or appointment makes a principled decision regarding recount rules that coincides with the interests of his or her party's candidates, opponents in today's highly charged partisan atmosphere will naturally accuse the official of bias. Even worse, an election administrator who makes a principled decision that contradicts the interests of his or her party will be accused of not being sufficiently loyal to the party. . . .

A recent study . . . found potential partisan bias on the local level in the purging of felons. During the Florida 2000 felon purge, "67 percent of people on the felons list were kept on the voter rolls in counties with Democratic supervisors, while 41 percent of people on the felons list in Republican counties were kept on the voter rolls." . . . Until states can in fact produce accurate lists of ex-felons, there is at least the potential for bias in the way that election administrators use felon lists. In the meantime, the potential for partisan bias perhaps best explains Republican attempts in Florida to shift the power for managing voter rolls from county canvassing boards—many of which are dominated by Democrats—to the Republican-appointed secretary of state. . . .

It is, of course, impossible to know in most instances the extent to which a discretionary decision made by a partisan elections official can best be explained by partisan bias rather than a reasoned decision on an issue on the merits. What is possible to measure is growing mistrust in the elections process, which must no doubt be driven in part by concerns over the partisan decisions of elected officials. Concerns about partisan manipulation of the process appear the most likely explanation for the large gap between Democratic and Republican faith in our system of election administration following President Bush's re-election. The fact is, however, that significant numbers of non-Democratic voters, including Republicans, have expressed concern about the integrity of the electoral process. . . .

What can be done? Removing the opportunity for partisan election officials to make discretionary decisions is a good first step. . . . But it will be impossible to remove all ambiguities, and therefore the possibility of exercising discretion, from the hands of election administrators. For this reason, I advocate that states move toward a model of nonpartisan election administration so as to further minimize the chances of election meltdown and, along the way, restore some public trust in the process of election administration.

I propose we create a cadre of individuals, much as exists today in Australia and Canada, where the allegiance of the CELO is to the integrity of the process itself, and not to any particular electoral outcome. The difficult question is how to create a truly nonpartisan, professional administrator and lower staff to do the job on the state and local level. . . .

Appointment, rather than election (even a nominally nonpartisan election), does seem the best way to choose a neutral CELO, but the danger is that the appointee could be just as partisan as the formerly elected candidate. For this rea-son, it makes sense to require that the CELO be nominated by the governor and approved by a large supermajority of the state legislature (say a 75% vote), insur-ing that only a consensus candidate who is seen as above politics will gain enough bipartisan support to be awarded the position. . . .

Once the CELO position is created, it will be necessary to insulate him or her from political pressure. This should be done in two ways: First, the CELO should receive a long term without the possibility of reappointment. A CELO could be removed by the legislature only under the rules for impeaching a state executive. This model best assures the independence of the administrator. Second, the state's constitution should guarantee a certain budget level for the office, so that the CELO is not dependent on legislators for favorable treatment. . . .

The Australian and Canadian systems differ in many particulars from each other, but both apparently command widespread support among their citizenry. The Australian system relies upon a three-member commission, the Australian Electoral Commission (AEC), consisting of a judge or retired judge as chair, the electoral commissioner, and one other nonjudicial member, which so far has always been Australia's statistician. The members are appointed by the Governor General acting on the advice of the Prime Minister, without formal consultation with the opposition.

The Canadians rely on a single officer "appointed by a resolution of the House of Commons (the elected chamber of the Canadian Parliament) that requires a simple majority." "Although the appointment procedure would theoretically empower a majority government to impose its nominee on opposition parties, in practice all appointments have been agreed to by other parties and have not occa-sioned a vote in the House of Commons." "The Governor General may dismiss the CEO, but only for cause and at the request of both Houses of Parliament, including the unelected Senate."

In neither case have the country's election administrators been caught in much controversy. The AEC's actions have not attracted any serious objections from the opposition. The Canadian chief elections officer also has been above reproach. The United States itself has endorsed independent election administra-tion in other countries as a means of promoting democracy.

Is partisanship combined with decentralization the worst of both worlds? If partisanship causes election officials to act in their own self-interest, does decentral-ization give them easier access to the means of doing so successfully? For such an argument, see Heather K. Gerken, The Democracy Index: Why Our Election System Is Failing and How to Fix It (2009).

▶▶ *Elected Election Officials.* Roughly 63 percent of local election officials are elected rather than appointed. David C. Kimball and Martha Kropf, *The Street-Level Bureaucrats of Elections: Selection Methods for Local Election Officials*, 23 Rev. Pol. Res. 1257 (2006). Survey data suggest that election officials of different partisan affilia-tion hold different views about election administration. For example, "Democratic local election officials are significantly more likely to support provisional voting," a practice that allows people to cast a ballot when their eligibility to vote is in doubt (see below regarding the Help America Vote Act). Martha Kropf et al., *Representative Bureaucracy and Partisanship: The Implementation of Election Law*, 73 PUB. ADMIN. REV. 242 (2013). Is that surprising? Is it disturbing? Should we assume that elected administrators will be unable to set aside their personal or partisan preferences in administering the law?

Public sentiment in favor of electing as many officials as possible dates back to the democratizing movement of the Jacksonian period. During this period in the early nineteenth century, the method for selecting many kinds of public officials was changed from executive appointment to popular election because of an often widespread suspicion that appointments were made as a form of patronage, leading to the installation of partisan officials indebted to their patrons. Elected officials were thus seen as more rather than less independent than their appointed counterparts.

Do functionally independent EMBs in fact perform better than other models? The evidence is mixed. Not all formally independent EMBs are truly independent in practice, and the critical factor in successful election administration may not be formal independence so much as impartiality. Impartiality, in turn, may be best secured not through institutional arrangements that promote independence, but by arrangements that deter factional capture: "[A] bipartisan (or multipartisan) structure of election management may work as effectively as a nonpartisan structure in achieving the goal of impartiality." Tokaji, *Comparative Election Administration, supra.*

A notable domestic example of a bipartisan EMB structure is the Federal Election Commission, created by Congress in 1974 to administer federal campaign finance laws. By law, the FEC consists of six commissioners, of whom no more than three may be from the same political party. Because commission action requires the vote of a majority of commissioners, the agency can act only in a roughly bipartisan fashion. Has this made it impartial? Consider a scathing report written by an outgoing chair of the FEC in 2017:

> Over the past ten years . . . the effectiveness of the FEC has deteriorated. . . . While the FEC's employees strive to fulfill its mission, the Commission itself—made up of six Commissioners—is not performing its duty. A bloc of three Commissioners routinely thwarts, obstructs, and delays action on the very campaign finance laws its members were appointed to administer. This bloc [has] voted in lockstep 98% of the time [since] 2015. Due to the bloc's ideological opposition to campaign finance law, major violations are swept under the rug and the resulting dark money has left Americans uninformed about the sources of campaign spending. The Commission's work is essential to the integrity and fairness of the political process and to ensure public trust in government. As the FEC explains on its website, campaign finance law seeks to "limit the disproportionate influence of wealthy individuals and special interest groups in the outcome of federal elections; regulate spending in campaigns for federal office; and deter abuses by mandating public disclosure of campaign finances." This incredibly significant Commission is not performing the job that Congress intended, and violators of the law are given

a free pass. Because of this, candidates and committees are aware that
they can ignore the laws enacted to protect the integrity of our elections.

Ann M. Ravel, *Dysfunction and Deadlock: The Enforcement Crisis at the Federal Election
Commission Reveals the Unlikelihood of Draining the Swamp* (FEC, Feb. 2017). The FEC
has routinely been characterized as suffering from paralysis because its bipartisan
composition has resulted in continual deadlock on even the most basic actions.

Could a system of independently elected election administrators perform
worse? If elections of CELOs were retained, would nonpartisan elections be preferable to partisan ones? Would a cadre of professional civil servants administering
elections ease public fears or exacerbate them? At the end of the day, is it possible
for any element of society to stand outside society to enforce its rules? Is the problem intractable?

c.   The Judicial Oversight Model

In most constitutional democracies, the actions of government agencies are
subject ultimately to judicial oversight to ensure compliance with binding law,
and that is generally as true of agencies administering elections as it is of agencies
administering other kinds of programs. Does judicial oversight solve, or at least mitigate, the problems inherent in administrative oversight of democratic processes?

»   *Elected Judges.*   The Framers of the U.S. Constitution opted decisively for
judicial independence. Having experienced a form of colonial justice in which the
king "made Judges dependent on his Will alone for the tenure of their offices, and
the amount and payment of their salaries," *Declaration of Independence*, the Framers created a system in which federal judges enjoy lifetime appointment. During
the nation's first three decades, most states also established appointive judiciaries.
Things began to change on the state level, however, during the Jacksonian period,
when a strong impulse toward greater democracy swept the nation. In 1832, Mississippi became the first state to create an entirely elective judiciary. After 1846, every
single new state admitted to the union elected most or all of its judges, and many
of the older states amended their constitutions to switch from appointment to election. Not all of this movement, however, was driven entirely by Jacksonian ideology.
In New York, for example, the switch to an elective judiciary also responded to a
widespread belief that the state's governors had been distributing judgeships as a
kind of patronage. *See* Peter J. Galie, The New York State Constitution: A Reference Guide 128-129 (1991). In addition, those favoring judicial election often
did so out of the belief that the appointment process had been "thoroughly corrupted by partisanship," with party leaders heavily influencing the actual selections
for partisan purposes. G. Alan Tarr, Without Fear or Favor: Judicial Independence and Judicial Accountability in the States 47 (2012). The election
of judges thus rests historically at least in part on the belief that elected judges
will actually be more independent, more fair, and more impartial than appointed
judges.

A system of judicial elections, however, poses obvious problems to the maintenance of judicial independence and impartiality. First, it is possible that the public will be unable meaningfully to evaluate the qualifications of judicial candidates
and the performance of sitting incumbents. Second, an elective judiciary raises

the possibility that judges will pander to public opinion in their decisions rather than impartially apply the law. Third, requiring judges to run for election requires them to mount campaigns, and campaigning is both costly and requires significant technical expertise. The need to rely on others for campaign funds and organizational assistance opens judicial candidates to the possibility of undue influence by whoever supplies them with the necessary help. Often this will be a political party, though in many cases it may be large individual or corporate donors.

Today 38 states subject all or nearly all of their judges to some kind of electoral accountability, but they have taken varied approaches to walking the fine line between electoral accountability and judicial independence and impartiality. The most common method of election for the highest court of a state, used by 16 states, is the so-called Missouri Plan, a hybrid system in which judges are appointed initially by the governor, often from a list of candidates recommended by a bipartisan or nonpartisan screening commission, and then stand periodically for democratic review in uncontested, nonpartisan retention elections. Sixteen states favor contested elections, but require that elections be nonpartisan in an attempt to eliminate the lowest kind of partisan politics from judicial elections. Six states, in contrast, have full-blown partisan judicial elections, in which judicial candidates, like candidates for any other office, stand for election as nominees of political parties. Judicial Elections in the 21st Century (Chris W. Bonneau and Melinda Gann Hall, eds., 2017). Some states use a mix of methods for courts of different levels; New York, for example, uses gubernatorial appointment for the highest court but partisan election for lower courts.

All states, however, whatever their formal system for electing judges, have tried to push such elections into a particular mold, one in which judicial candidates campaign for office solely or mainly on the basis of their character, formal qualifications for office, experience, knowledge, and work habits, rather than on the basis of their partisan affiliation, political ideology, or promises about how they will rule in particular categories of cases. In this respect, the prevailing model for judicial elections draws heavily on republican and Progressive beliefs about how politics ought to be conducted, how campaigns ought to be run, and what kinds of people are best suited to hold elective office. On this model, the people are not asked to decide among different strategies for achieving competing policy goals; instead, they are asked only to evaluate the fundamental character, integrity, and likely impartiality of candidates for judicial office. The Utah Constitution, for example, states expressly that "[s]election of judges shall be based solely upon consideration of fitness for office without regard to any partisan political considerations." Utah Const. art. VIII, §8(4).

States have encouraged campaigns of this type mainly by pursuing a regulatory strategy of limiting what judicial candidates can say during campaigns for office through a code of judicial conduct. These codes, similar to ethical codes that regulate the behavior of lawyers, generally prohibit candidates from campaigning on the basis of how they will rule in particular cases, or from touting their partisan or ideological qualifications.

The desirability, much less the constitutionality of these canons of judicial conduct was never seriously questioned until recently. Where once an election for judge might be conducted much like an election for officers of a gentlemen's club, judicial elections today, like elections for other public offices, have become more competitive and more ideologically charged. Parties and individual candidates have contested judgeships vigorously, often backed by large sums of money. Each new election cycle brings fresh records for judicial campaign spending. Whereas incumbent judges in the past routinely won reelection, now well-heeled interest groups view sitting judges as potential targets, even in uncontested retention elections.

In these circumstances, it was inevitable that some candidate for judicial office would want to be freed to campaign by speaking out on politically charged issues — abortion, criminal procedure, privacy, taxes, high jury verdicts — upon which he or she might as judge be called upon to rule. In the case below, the Supreme Court considered a challenge brought by such a candidate.

Republican Party of Minnesota v. White

536 U.S. 765 (2002)

Justice SCALIA delivered the opinion of the Court.

The question presented in this case is whether the First Amendment permits the Minnesota Supreme Court to prohibit candidates for judicial election in that State from announcing their views on disputed legal and political issues.

I

Since Minnesota's admission to the Union in 1858, the State's Constitution has provided for the selection of all state judges by popular election. Minn. Const., Art. VI, §7. Since 1912, those elections have been nonpartisan. Act of June 19, ch. 2, 1912 Minn. Laws Special Sess., pp. 4-6. Since 1974, they have been subject to a legal restriction which states that a "candidate for a judicial office, including an incumbent judge," shall not "announce his or her views on disputed legal or political issues." Minn. Code of Judicial Conduct, Canon 5(A)(3)(d)(i) (2000). This prohibition, promulgated by the Minnesota Supreme Court and based on Canon 7(B) of the 1972 American Bar Association (ABA) Model Code of Judicial Conduct, is known as the "announce clause." Incumbent judges who violate it are subject to discipline, including removal, censure, civil penalties, and suspension without pay. Minn. Rules of Board on Judicial Standards 4(a)(6), 11(d) (2002). Lawyers who run for judicial office also must comply with the announce clause. Those who violate it are subject to, *inter alia*, disbarment, suspension, and probation. Rule 8.4(a); Minn. Rules on Lawyers Professional Responsibility 8-14, 15(a) (2002).

In [1998], Gregory Wersal ran for associate justice of the Minnesota Supreme Court. . . . Wersal filed this lawsuit in Federal District Court seeking a declaration that the announce clause violates the First Amendment and an injunction against its enforcement. Wersal alleged that he was forced to refrain from announcing his views on disputed issues during the 1998 campaign, to the point where he declined response to questions put to him by the press and public, out of concern that he might run afoul of the announce clause. Other plaintiffs in the suit, including the Minnesota Republican Party, alleged that, because the clause kept Wersal from announcing his views, they were unable to learn those views and support or oppose his candidacy accordingly. . . .

II

Before considering the constitutionality of the announce clause, we must be clear about its meaning. Its text says that a candidate for judicial office shall not "announce his or her views on disputed legal or political issues." Minn. Code of Judicial Conduct, Canon 5(A)(3)(d)(i) (2002).

We know that "announc[ing] . . . views" on an issue covers much more than *promising* to decide an issue a particular way. The prohibition extends to the candidate's mere statement of his current position, even if he does not bind himself to maintain that position after election. All the parties agree this is the case, because the Minnesota Code contains a so-called "pledges or promises" clause, which *separately* prohibits judicial candidates from making "pledges or promises of conduct in office other than the faithful and impartial performance of the duties of the office" *ibid.* — a prohibition that is not challenged here and on which we express no view. . . .

It is clear that the announce clause prohibits a judicial candidate from stating his views on any specific nonfanciful legal question within the province of the court for which he is running, except in the context of discussing past decisions—and in the latter context as well, if he expresses the view that he is not bound by *stare decisis.* Respondents contend that this still leaves plenty of topics for discussion on the campaign trail. These include a candidate's "character," "education," "work habits," and "how [he] would handle administrative duties if elected." Indeed, the Judicial Board has printed a list of preapproved questions which judicial candidates are allowed to answer. These include how the candidate feels about cameras in the courtroom, how he would go about reducing the caseload, how the costs of judicial administration can be reduced, and how he proposes to ensure that minorities and women are treated more fairly by the court system. Minnesota State Bar Association Judicial Elections Task Force Report & Recommendations, App. C (June 19, 1997), reprinted at App. 97-103. Whether this list of preapproved subjects, and other topics not prohibited by the announce clause, adequately fulfill the First Amendment's guarantee of freedom of speech is the question to which we now turn.

III

As the Court of Appeals recognized, the announce clause both prohibits speech on the basis of its content and burdens a category of speech that is "at the core of our First Amendment freedoms"—speech about the qualifications of candidates for public office. The Court of Appeals concluded that the proper test to be applied to determine the constitutionality of such a restriction is what our cases have called strict scrutiny. Under the strict-scrutiny test, respondents have the burden to prove that the announce clause is (1) narrowly tailored, to serve (2) a compelling state interest. *E.g., Eu v. San Francisco County Democratic Central Comm.,* 489 U.S. 214, 222 (1989). In order for respondents to show that the announce clause is narrowly tailored, they must demonstrate that it does not "unnecessarily circumscrib[e] protected expression." *Brown v. Hartlage,* 456 U.S. 45, 54 (1982). The Court of Appeals concluded that respondents had established two interests as sufficiently compelling to justify the announce clause: preserving the impartiality of the state judiciary and preserving the appearance of the impartiality of the state judiciary. 247 F.3d, at 867. Respondents reassert these two interests before us, arguing that the first is compelling because it protects the due process rights of litigants, and that the second is compelling because it preserves public confidence in the judiciary. Respondents are rather vague, however, about what they mean by "impartiality." . . . Clarity on this point is essential before we can decide whether impartiality is indeed a compelling state interest, and, if so, whether the announce clause is narrowly tailored to achieve it.

A

One meaning of "impartiality" in the judicial context—and of course its root meaning—is the lack of bias for or against either *party* to the proceeding. Impartiality in this sense assures equal application of the law. That is, it guarantees a party that the judge who hears his case will apply the law to him in the same way he applies it to any other party. This is the traditional sense in which the term is used. See Webster's New International Dictionary 1247 (2d ed. 1950) (defining "impartial" as "[n]ot partial; esp., not favoring one more than another; treating all alike; unbiased; equitable; fair; just"). It is also the sense in which it is used in the cases cited by respondents and *amici* for the proposition that an impartial judge is essential to due process. . . .

We think it plain that the announce clause is not narrowly tailored to serve impartiality (or the appearance of impartiality) in this sense. Indeed, the clause is barely tailored to serve that interest *at all*, inasmuch as it does not restrict speech for or against particular *parties*, but rather speech for or against particular *issues*. To be sure, when a case arises that turns on a legal issue on which the judge (as a candidate) had taken a particular stand, the party taking the opposite stand is likely to lose. But not because of any bias against that party, or favoritism toward the other party. *Any* party taking that position is just as likely to lose. The judge is applying the law (as he sees it) evenhandedly.

B

It is perhaps possible to use the term "impartiality" in the judicial context (though this is certainly not a common usage) to mean lack of preconception in favor of or against a particular *legal view*. This sort of impartiality would be concerned, not with guaranteeing litigants equal application of the law, but rather with guaranteeing them an equal chance to persuade the court on the legal points in their case. Impartiality in this sense may well be an interest served by the announce clause, but it is not a *compelling* state interest, as strict scrutiny requires. A judge's lack of predisposition regarding the relevant legal issues in a case has never been thought a necessary component of equal justice, and with good reason. For one thing, it is virtually impossible to find a judge who does not have preconceptions about the law. As then-Justice Rehnquist observed of our own Court: "Since most Justices come to this bench no earlier than their middle years, it would be unusual if they had not by that time formulated at least some tentative notions that would influence them in their interpretation of the sweeping clauses of the Constitution and their interaction with one another. It would be not merely unusual, but extraordinary, if they had not at least given opinions as to constitutional issues in their previous legal careers." *Laird v. Tatum*, 409 U.S. 824, 835 (1972) (memorandum opinion). Indeed, even if it were possible to select judges who did not have preconceived views on legal issues, it would hardly be desirable to do so. "Proof that a Justice's mind at the time he joined the Court was a complete *tabula rasa* in the area of constitutional adjudication would be evidence of lack of qualification, not lack of bias." *Ibid.* The Minnesota Constitution positively forbids the selection to courts of general jurisdiction of judges who are impartial in the sense of having no views on the law. Minn. Const., Art. VI, §5 ("Judges of the supreme court, the court of appeals and the district court shall be learned in the law"). And since avoiding judicial preconceptions on legal issues is neither possible nor desirable, pretending otherwise by attempting to preserve the "appearance" of that type of impartiality can hardly be a compelling state interest either.

C

A third possible meaning of "impartiality" (again not a common one) might be described as openmindedness. This quality in a judge demands, not that he have no preconceptions on legal issues, but that he be willing to consider views that oppose his preconceptions, and remain open to persuasion, when the issues arise in a pending case. This sort of impartiality seeks to guarantee each litigant, not an *equal* chance to win the legal points in the case, but at least *some* chance of doing so. It may well be that impartiality in this sense, and the appearance of it, are desirable in the judiciary, but we need not pursue that inquiry, since we do not believe the Minnesota Supreme Court adopted the announce clause for that purpose. Respondents argue that the announce clause serves the interest in openmindedness, or at least in the appearance of openmindedness, because it relieves a judge from pressure to rule a certain way in order to maintain consistency with statements the judge has previously made. The problem is, however, that statements in election campaigns are such an infinitesimal portion of the public commitments to legal positions that judges (or judges-to-be) undertake, that this object of the prohibition is implausible. Before they arrive on the bench (whether by election or otherwise) judges have often committed themselves on legal issues that they must later rule upon. . . .

More common still is a judge's confronting a legal issue on which he has expressed an opinion while on the bench. Most frequently, of course, that prior expression will have occurred in ruling on an earlier case. But judges often state their views on disputed legal issues outside the context of adjudication — in classes that they conduct, and in books and speeches. Like the ABA Codes of Judicial Conduct, the Minnesota Code not only permits but encourages this. . . .

The short of the matter is this: In Minnesota, a candidate for judicial office may not say "I think it is constitutional for the legislature to prohibit same-sex marriages." He may say the very same thing, however, up until the very day before he declares himself a candidate, and may say it repeatedly (until litigation is pending) after he is elected. As a means of pursuing the objective of openmindedness that respondents now articulate, the announce clause is so woefully underinclusive as to render belief in that purpose a challenge to the credulous. . . .

IV

. . . There is an obvious tension between the article of Minnesota's popularly approved Constitution which provides that judges shall be elected, and the Minnesota Supreme Court's announce clause which places most subjects of interest to the voters off limits. But the First Amendment does not permit Minnesota to achieve its goal by leaving the principle of elections in place while preventing candidates from discussing what the elections are about. The Minnesota Supreme Court's canon of judicial conduct prohibiting candidates for judicial election from announcing their views on disputed legal and political issues violates the First Amendment.

Justice O'CONNOR, concurring.

I join the opinion of the Court but write separately to express my concerns about judicial elections generally. Respondents claim that "[t]he Announce Clause is necessary . . . to protect the State's compelling governmental interes[t] in an actual and perceived . . . impartial judiciary." Brief for Respondents 8. I am concerned that, even aside from what judicial candidates may say while campaigning, the very practice of electing judges undermines this interest. . . .

We of course want judges to be impartial, in the sense of being free from any personal stake in the outcome of the cases to which they are assigned. But if judges are subject to regular elections they are likely to feel that they have at least some personal stake in the outcome of every publicized case. . . .

Moreover, contested elections generally entail campaigning. And campaigning for a judicial post today can require substantial funds. . . . Unless the pool of judicial candidates is limited to those wealthy enough to independently fund their campaigns, a limitation unrelated to judicial skill, the cost of campaigning requires judicial candidates to engage in fundraising. Yet relying on campaign donations may leave judges feeling indebted to certain parties or interest groups. . . . Minnesota has chosen to select its judges through contested popular elections instead of through an appointment system or a combined appointment and retention election system along the lines of the Missouri Plan. In doing so the State has voluntarily taken on the risks to judicial bias described above. As a result, the State's claim that it needs to significantly restrict judges' speech in order to protect judicial impartiality is particularly troubling. If the State has a problem with judicial impartiality, it is largely one the State brought upon itself by continuing the practice of popularly electing judges.

Justice STEVENS, with whom Justice SOUTER, Justice GINSBURG, and Justice BREYER join, dissenting.

. . . The Court's disposition rests on two seriously flawed premises — an inaccurate appraisal of the importance of judicial independence and impartiality, and an assumption that judicial candidates should have the same freedom "'to express themselves on matters of current public importance'" as do all other elected officials. *Ante*, at 781-782. Elected judges, no less than appointed judges, occupy an office of trust that is fundamentally different from that occupied by policymaking officials. Although the fact that they must stand for election makes their job more difficult than that of the tenured judge, that fact does not lessen their duty to respect essential attributes of the judicial office that have been embedded in Anglo-American law for centuries. . . .

Consistent with that fundamental attribute of the office, countless judges in countless cases routinely make rulings that are unpopular and surely disliked by at least 50 percent of the litigants who appear before them. It is equally common for them to enforce rules that they think unwise, or that are contrary to their personal predilections. For this reason, opinions that a lawyer may have expressed before becoming a judge, or a judicial candidate, do not disqualify anyone for judicial service because every good judge is fully aware of the distinction between the law and a personal point of view. It is equally clear, however, that such expressions after a lawyer has been nominated to judicial office shed little, if any, light on his capacity for judicial service. Indeed, to the extent that such statements seek to enhance the popularity of the candidate by indicating how he would rule in specific cases if elected, they evidence a lack of fitness for the office.

By recognizing a conflict between the demands of electoral politics and the distinct characteristics of the judiciary, we do not have to put States to an all or nothing choice of abandoning judicial elections or having elections in which anything goes. . . . A candidate for judicial office who goes beyond the expression of "general observation about the law . . . in order to obtain favorable consideration" of his candidacy, *Laird v. Tatum*, 409 U.S. 824, 836, n.5 (1972) (memorandum of Rehnquist, J., on motion for recusal), demonstrates either a lack of impartiality or a lack of understanding of the importance of maintaining public confidence in the impartiality of the judiciary. . . . The judicial reputation for impartiality and open-mindedness is compromised by electioneering that emphasizes the candidate's personal predilections rather than his qualifications for judicial office. . . .

Justice GINSBURG, with whom Justice STEVENS, Justice SOUTER, and Justice BREYER join, dissenting.

Whether state or federal, elected or appointed, judges perform a function fundamentally different from that of the people's elected representatives. Legislative and executive officials act on behalf of the voters who placed them in office; "judge[s] represen[t] the Law." *Chisom v. Roemer*, 501 U.S. 380, 411 (1991) (Scalia, J., dissenting). Unlike their counterparts in the political branches, judges are expected to refrain from catering to particular constituencies or committing themselves on controversial issues in advance of adversarial presentation. Their mission is to decide "individual cases and controversies" on individual records, *Plaut v. Spendthrift Farm, Inc.*, 514 U.S. 211, 266 (1995) (Stevens, J., dissenting), neutrally applying legal principles, and, when necessary, "stand[ing] up to what is generally supreme in a democracy: the popular will," Scalia, *The Rule of Law as a Law of Rules*, 56 U. Chi. L. Rev. 1175, 1180 (1989). . . .

The ability of the judiciary to discharge its unique role rests to a large degree on the manner in which judges are selected. The Framers of the Federal Constitution sought to advance the judicial function through the structural protections of Article III, which provide for the selection of judges by the President on the advice and consent of the Senate, generally for lifetime terms. Through its own Constitution, Minnesota, in common with most other States, has decided to allow its citizens to choose judges directly in periodic elections. But Minnesota has not thereby opted to install a corps of political actors on the bench; rather, it has endeavored to preserve the integrity of its judiciary by other means. Recognizing that the influence of political parties is incompatible with the judge's role, for example, Minnesota has designated all judicial elections nonpartisan. See *Peterson v. Stafford*, 490 N.W.2d 418, 425 (Minn. 1992). And it has adopted a provision, here called the Announce Clause, designed to prevent candidates for judicial office from "publicly making known how they would decide issues likely to come before them as judges." *Republican Party of Minnesota v. Kelly*, 247 F.3d 854, 881-882 (CA8 2001). . . .

The rationale underlying unconstrained speech in elections for political office — that representative government depends on the public's ability to choose agents who will act at its behest — does not carry over to campaigns for the bench. As to persons aiming to occupy the seat of judgment, the Court's unrelenting reliance on decisions involving contests for legislative and executive posts is manifestly out of place. . . .

The Court sees in this conclusion, and in the Announce Clause that embraces it, "an obvious tension," *ante*, at 787: The Minnesota electorate is permitted to select its judges by popular vote, but is not provided information on "subjects of interest to the voters," ibid. — in particular, the voters are not told how the candidate would decide controversial cases or issues if elected. This supposed tension, however, rests on the false premise that by departing from the federal model with respect to who *chooses* judges, Minnesota necessarily departed from the federal position on the *criteria* relevant to the exercise of that choice. . . . Judges are not politicians, and the First Amendment does not require that they be treated as politicians simply because they are chosen by popular vote. Nor does the First Amendment command States who wish to promote the integrity of their judges in fact and appearance to abandon systems of judicial selection that the people, in the exercise of their sovereign prerogatives, have devised.

›› *Nonpartisan Elections After* **White**   *White* held that candidates for judicial office — and by implication, any office — cannot be prohibited from campaigning on the merits of substantive issues. In so doing, the decision seems to undermine the chief rationale for nonpartisan elections: steering voters toward focusing on the competence, experience, and character of the candidates rather than on their substantive positions, which are deemed unimportant compared to their personal characteristics. Does this mean that *White* effectively invalidates nonpartisan elections as an electoral procedure — not just in judicial races, but in all elections? If candidates can't be prohibited from campaigning on substantive grounds, can they be prohibited from announcing their partisan affiliation? Can they be prohibited merely from displaying their partisan affiliation on the ballot?

These questions have begun to percolate up through the lower courts. In *Sanders County Republican Central Committee v. Bullock*, 698 F.3d 741 (9th Cir. 2012), the court invalidated a Montana law making it a criminal offense for any political party to endorse, contribute to, or spend in support of or in opposition to a judicial candidate. On the other hand, in *Ohio Council 8, AFSCME v. Husted*, 814 F.3d 329 (6th Cir. 2016), the court rejected a challenge to Ohio's nonpartisan election law prohibiting candidates from displaying their partisan affiliation on the ballot. The court sustained the law as a minimal burden on speech rights because candidates have a multitude of other forums in which to communicate with voters, and because they are "entirely free to associate themselves with the parties of their choice and express their party affiliation in forums other than the general election ballot." It also held that the law advanced Ohio's interest in "minimizing partisanship in judicial elections." Under *White*, is such a state interest legitimate?

Shortly thereafter, the Sixth Circuit ruled expressly that "candidates have a constitutional right to portray themselves as a member of a political party," *Winter v. Blau*, 834 F.3d 681 (6th Cir. 2016), while simultaneously affirming that the state (Kentucky, in this case) had a legitimate interest in prohibiting such self-identification on the ballot itself. Is this position coherent—is there any point in a state requiring nonpartisan elections when candidates are free to maintain partisan ties and to broadcast them without limitation during the campaign? Conversely, the Third Circuit recently invalidated a Delaware law that required candidates for judicial office to declare a party affiliation, and blocked them from appearing on the ballot without such a designation. *Adams v. Governor of Delaware*, 922 F.3d 166 (3d Cir. 2019).

Williams-Yulee v. Florida Bar

135 S. Ct. 1656 (2015)

ROBERTS, C.J., delivered the opinion of the Court, except as to Part II. BREYER, SOTOMAYOR, and KAGAN, JJ., joined that opinion in full, and GINSBURG, J., joined except as to Part II.

Our Founders vested authority to appoint federal judges in the President, with the advice and consent of the Senate, and entrusted those judges to hold their offices during good behavior. The Constitution permits States to make a different choice, and most of them have done so. In 39 States, voters elect trial or appellate judges at the polls. In an effort to preserve public confidence in the integrity of their judiciaries, many of those States prohibit judges and judicial candidates from personally soliciting funds for their campaigns. We must decide whether the First Amendment permits such restrictions on speech.

We hold that it does. Judges are not politicians, even when they come to the bench by way of the ballot. And a State's decision to elect its judiciary does not compel it to treat judicial candidates like campaigners for political office. A State may assure its people that judges will apply the law without fear or favor—and without having personally asked anyone for money. . . .

I

A

When Florida entered the Union in 1845, its Constitution provided for trial and appellate judges to be elected by the General Assembly. [Florida changed its system of judicial selection several times over the ensuing 130 years.] Under the system now in place, appellate judges are appointed by the Governor from a list of candidates proposed by a nominating committee—a process known as "merit selection." Then, every six years, voters decide whether to retain incumbent appellate judges for another term. Trial judges are still elected by popular vote, unless the local jurisdiction opts instead for merit selection.

[Canon 7C(1) of the Florida Judicial Code of Conduct] provides:

> A candidate, including an incumbent judge, for a judicial office that is filled by public election between competing candidates shall not personally solicit campaign funds, or solicit attorneys for publicly stated support, but may establish committees of responsible persons to secure and manage the expenditure of funds for the candidate's campaign and to obtain public statements of support for his or her candidacy. Such committees are not prohibited from soliciting campaign contributions and public support from any person or corporation authorized by law.

Florida statutes impose additional restrictions on campaign fundraising in judicial elections. Contributors may not donate more than $1,000 per election to a trial court candidate or more than $3,000 per retention election to a Supreme Court justice. Campaign committee treasurers must file periodic reports disclosing the names of contributors and the amount of each contribution.

Judicial candidates can seek guidance about campaign ethics rules from the Florida Judicial Ethics Advisory Committee. The Committee has interpreted Canon 7 to allow a judicial candidate to serve as treasurer of his own campaign committee, learn the identity of campaign contributors, and send thank you notes to donors.

Like Florida, most other States prohibit judicial candidates from soliciting campaign funds personally, but allow them to raise money through committees. According to the American Bar Association, 30 of the 39 States that elect trial or appellate judges have adopted restrictions similar to Canon 7C(1). Brief for American Bar Association as *Amicus Curiae* 4.

B

Lanell Williams-Yulee, who refers to herself as Yulee, has practiced law in Florida since 1991. In September 2009, she decided to run for a seat on the county court for Hillsborough County, a jurisdiction of about 1.3 million people that includes the city of Tampa. Shortly after filing paperwork to enter the race, Yulee drafted a letter announcing her candidacy. The letter described her experience and desire to "bring fresh ideas and positive solutions to the Judicial bench." The letter then stated:

> An early contribution of $25, $50, $100, $250, or $500, made payable to "Lanell Williams-Yulee Campaign for County Judge," will help raise the initial funds needed to launch the campaign and get our message out to the public. I ask for your support [i]n meeting the primary election fund raiser goals. Thank you in advance for your support.

Yulee signed the letter and mailed it to local voters. She also posted the letter on her campaign Web site.

Yulee . . . lost the primary to the incumbent judge. Then the Florida Bar filed a complaint against her. As relevant here, the Bar charged her with violating Rule 4-8.2(b) of the Rules Regulating the Florida Bar. That Rule requires judicial candidates to comply with applicable provisions of Florida's Code of Judicial Conduct, including the ban on personal solicitation of campaign funds in Canon 7C(1).

Yulee admitted that she had signed and sent the fundraising letter. But she argued that the Bar could not discipline her for that conduct because the First Amendment protects a judicial candidate's right to solicit campaign funds in an election. . . .

II

. . . The parties agree that Canon 7C(1) restricts Yulee's speech on the basis of its content by prohibiting her from soliciting contributions to her election campaign. The parties disagree, however, about the level of scrutiny that should govern our review.

We have applied exacting scrutiny to laws restricting the solicitation of contributions to charity, upholding the speech limitations only if they are narrowly tailored to serve a compelling interest. . . . [W]e hold today what we assumed in *White*: A State may restrict the speech of a judicial candidate only if the restriction is narrowly tailored to serve a compelling interest.

III

. . . Canon 7C(1) advances the State's compelling interest in preserving public confidence in the integrity of the judiciary, and it does so through means narrowly tailored to avoid unnecessarily abridging speech. This is therefore one of the rare cases in which a speech restriction withstands strict scrutiny.

A

The Florida Supreme Court adopted Canon 7C(1) to promote the State's interests in "protecting the integrity of the judiciary" and "maintaining the public's confidence in an impartial judiciary." The way the Canon advances those interests is intuitive: Judges, charged with exercising strict neutrality and independence, cannot supplicate campaign donors without diminishing public confidence in judicial integrity. This principle dates back at least eight centuries to Magna Carta, which proclaimed, "To no one will we sell, to no one will we refuse or delay, right or justice." The same concept underlies the common law judicial oath, which binds a judge to "do right to all manner of people . . . without fear or favour, affection or ill-will," 10 Encyclopaedia of the Laws of England 105 (2d ed. 1908), and the oath that each of us took to "administer justice without respect to persons, and do equal right to the poor and to the rich," 28 U.S.C. §453. Simply put, Florida and most other States have concluded that the public may lack confidence in a judge's ability to administer justice without fear or favor if he comes to office by asking for favors.

The interest served by Canon 7C(1) has firm support in our precedents. We have recognized the "vital state interest" in safeguarding "public confidence in the fairness and integrity of the nation's elected judges." *Caperton v. A.T. Massey Coal Co.*, 556 U.S. 868, 889 (2009). The importance of public confidence in the integrity of judges stems from the place of the judiciary in the government. Unlike the executive or the legislature, the judiciary "has no influence over either the sword or the purse; . . . neither force nor will but merely judgment." The Federalist No. 78, p. 465 (C. Rossiter ed. 1961) (A. Hamilton). The judiciary's authority therefore depends in large measure on the public's willingness to respect and follow its decisions. It follows that public perception of judicial integrity is "a state interest of the highest order." *Caperton*, 556 U.S. at 889.

The parties devote considerable attention to our cases analyzing campaign finance restrictions in political elections. But a State's interest in preserving public confidence in the integrity of its judiciary extends beyond its interest in preventing the appearance of corruption in legislative and executive elections. As we explained in *White*, States may regulate judicial elections differently than they regulate political elections, because the role of judges differs from the role of politicians. Politicians are expected to be appropriately responsive to the preferences of their supporters. Indeed, such "responsiveness is key to the very concept of self-governance through elected officials." The same is not true of judges. In deciding cases, a judge is not to follow the preferences of his supporters, or provide any special consideration to his campaign donors. A judge instead must "observe the utmost fairness," striving to be "perfectly and completely independent, with nothing to influence or controul him but God and his conscience." As in *White*, therefore, our precedents applying the First Amendment to political elections have little bearing on the issues here.

The concept of public confidence in judicial integrity does not easily reduce to precise definition, nor does it lend itself to proof by documentary record. But no one denies that it is genuine and compelling. In short, it is the regrettable but unavoidable appearance that judges who personally ask for money may diminish their integrity that prompted the Supreme Court of Florida and most other States to sever the direct link between judicial candidates and campaign contributors. Moreover, personal solicitation by a judicial candidate "inevitably places the solicited individuals in a position to fear retaliation if they fail to financially support that candidate." Potential litigants then fear that "the integrity of the judicial system has been compromised, forcing them to search for an attorney in part based upon the criteria of which attorneys have made the obligatory contributions." A State's decision to elect its judges does not require it to tolerate these risks. The Florida Bar's interest is compelling.

B

Yulee acknowledges the State's compelling interest in judicial integrity. She argues, however, that the Canon's failure to restrict other speech equally damaging to judicial integrity and its appearance undercuts the Bar's position. In particular, she notes that Canon 7C(1) allows a judge's campaign committee to solicit money, which arguably reduces public confidence in the integrity of the judiciary just as much as a judge's personal solicitation. Yulee also points out that Florida permits judicial candidates to write thank you notes to campaign donors, which ensures that candidates know who contributes and who does not.

It is always somewhat counterintuitive to argue that a law violates the First Amendment by abridging *too little* speech. We have recognized, however, that underinclusiveness can raise "doubts about whether the government is in fact pursuing the interest it invokes, rather than disfavoring a particular speaker or viewpoint." Underinclusiveness can also reveal that a law does not actually advance a compelling interest.

Although a law's underinclusivity raises a red flag, [a] State need not address all aspects of a problem in one fell swoop; policymakers may focus on their most pressing concerns. . . .

Viewed in light of these principles, Canon 7C(1) raises no fatal underinclusivity concerns. The solicitation ban aims squarely at the conduct most likely to undermine public confidence in the integrity of the judiciary: personal requests for money by judges and judicial candidates. The Canon applies evenhandedly to all judges and judicial candidates, regardless of their viewpoint or chosen means of solicitation.

Yulee relies heavily on the provision of Canon 7C(1) that allows solicitation by a candidate's campaign committee. But Florida, along with most other States, has reasonably concluded that solicitation by the candidate personally creates a categorically different and more severe risk of undermining public confidence than does solicitation by a campaign committee. The identity of the solicitor matters, as anyone who has encountered a Girl Scout selling cookies outside a grocery store can attest. When the judicial candidate himself asks for money, the stakes are higher for all involved. The candidate has personally invested his time and effort in the fundraising appeal; he has placed his name and reputation behind the request. The solicited individual knows that, and also knows that the solicitor might be in a position to singlehandedly make decisions of great weight: The same person who signed the fundraising letter might one day sign the judgment. This dynamic inevitably creates pressure for the recipient to comply, and it does so in a way that solicitation by a third party does not. Just as inevitably, the personal involvement of the candidate in the solicitation creates the public appearance that the candidate will remember who says yes, and who says no.

In short, personal solicitation by judicial candidates implicates a different problem than solicitation by campaign committees. . . .

Likewise, allowing judicial candidates to write thank you notes to campaign donors does not detract from the State's interest in preserving public confidence in the integrity of the judiciary. Yulee argues that permitting thank you notes heightens the likelihood of actual bias by ensuring that judicial candidates know who supported their campaigns, and ensuring that the supporter knows that the candidate knows. Maybe so. But the State's compelling interest is implicated most directly by the candidate's personal solicitation itself. A failure to ban thank you notes for contributions not solicited by the candidate does not undercut the Bar's rationale. . . .

Taken to its logical conclusion, the position advanced by Yulee and the principal dissent is that Florida may ban the solicitation of funds by judicial candidates only if the State bans *all* solicitation of funds in judicial elections. The First Amendment does not put a State to that all-or-nothing choice. We will not punish Florida for leaving open more, rather than fewer, avenues of expression, especially when there is no indication that the selective restriction of speech reflects a pretextual motive.

C

After arguing that Canon 7C(1) violates the First Amendment because it restricts too little speech, Yulee argues that the Canon violates the First Amendment because it restricts too much. In her view, the Canon is not narrowly tailored to advance the State's compelling interest through the least restrictive means.

Indeed, Yulee concedes — and the principal dissent seems to agree — that Canon 7C(1) is valid in numerous applications. Yulee acknowledges that Florida can prohibit judges from soliciting money from lawyers and litigants appearing before them. In addition, she says the State "might" be able to ban "direct one-to-one solicitation of lawyers and individuals or businesses that could reasonably appear in the court for which the individual is a candidate." She also suggests that the Bar could forbid "in person" solicitation by judicial candidates. But Yulee argues that the Canon cannot constitutionally be applied to her chosen form of solicitation: a letter posted online and distributed via mass mailing. No one, she contends, will lose confidence in the integrity of the judiciary based on personal solicitation to such a broad audience.

This argument misperceives the breadth of the compelling interest that underlies Canon 7C(1). Florida has reasonably determined that personal appeals for money by a judicial candidate inherently create an appearance of impropriety that may cause the public to lose confidence in the integrity of the judiciary. That interest may be implicated to varying degrees in particular contexts, but the interest remains whenever the public perceives the judge personally asking for money.

Moreover, the lines Yulee asks us to draw are unworkable. Even under her theory of the case, a mass mailing would create an appearance of impropriety if addressed to a list of all lawyers and litigants with pending cases. So would a speech soliciting contributions from the 100 most frequently appearing attorneys in the jurisdiction. . . . We decline to wade into this swamp. The First Amendment requires that Canon 7C(1) be narrowly tailored, not that it be "perfectly tailored." . . .

Finally, Yulee contends that Florida can accomplish its compelling interest through the less restrictive means of recusal rules and campaign contribution limits. We disagree. A rule requiring judges to recuse themselves from every case in which a lawyer or litigant made a campaign contribution would disable many jurisdictions. And a flood of postelection recusal motions could "erode public confidence in judicial impartiality" and thereby exacerbate the very appearance problem the State is trying to solve. Moreover, the rule that Yulee envisions could create a perverse incentive for litigants to make campaign contributions to judges solely as a means to trigger their later recusal — a form of peremptory strike against a judge that would enable transparent forum shopping. . . .

In sum, because Canon 7C(1) is narrowly tailored to serve a compelling government interest, the First Amendment poses no obstacle to its enforcement in this case. . . .

The desirability of judicial elections is a question that has sparked disagreement for more than 200 years. Hamilton believed that appointing judges to positions with life tenure constituted "the best expedient which can be devised in any government to secure a steady, upright, and impartial administration of the laws." The Federalist No. 78, at 465. Jefferson thought that making judges "dependent on none but themselves" ran counter to the principle of "a government founded on the public will." 12 The Works of Thomas Jefferson 5 (P. Ford ed. 1905). The federal courts reflect the view of Hamilton; most States have sided with Jefferson. Both methods have given our Nation jurists of wisdom and rectitude who have devoted themselves to maintaining "the public's respect . . . and a reserve of public goodwill, without becoming subservient to public opinion." Rehnquist, Judicial Independence, 38 U. Rich. L. Rev. 579, 596 (2004).

It is not our place to resolve this enduring debate. Our limited task is to apply the Constitution to the question presented in this case. Judicial candidates have a First Amendment right to speak in support of their campaigns. States have a compelling interest in preserving public confidence in their judiciaries. When the State adopts a narrowly tailored restriction like the one at issue here, those principles do not conflict. A State's decision to elect judges does not compel it to compromise public confidence in their integrity.

The judgment of the Florida Supreme Court is

Affirmed.

Justice GINSBURG, with whom Justice BREYER joins as to Part II, concurring in part and concurring in the judgment.

I join the Court's opinion save for Part II. As explained in my dissenting opinion in *Republican Party of Minnesota v. White*, 536 U.S. 765, 803 (2002), I would not apply exacting scrutiny to a State's endeavor sensibly to "differentiate elections for political offices . . . , from elections designed to select those whose office it is to administer justice without respect to persons," *id.* at 805.

I write separately to reiterate the substantial latitude, in my view, States should possess to enact campaign-finance rules geared to judicial elections. . . . The Court's recent campaign-finance decisions, trained on political actors, should not hold sway for judicial elections. . . . When the political campaign-finance apparatus is applied to judicial elections, the distinction of judges from politicians dims. Donors, who gain audience and influence through contributions to political campaigns, anticipate that investment in campaigns for judicial office will yield similar returns. Elected judges understand this dynamic. . . .

Disproportionate spending to influence court judgments threatens both the appearance and actuality of judicial independence. Numerous studies report that the money pressure groups spend on judicial elections "can affect judicial decisionmaking across a broad range of cases." . . . Multiple surveys over the past 13 years indicate that voters overwhelmingly believe direct contributions to judges' campaigns have at least "some influence" on judicial decisionmaking. . . . States should not be put to the polar choices of either equating judicial elections to political elections, or else abandoning public participation in the selection of judges altogether. Instead, States should have leeway to "balance the constitutional interests in judicial integrity and free expression within the unique setting of an elected judiciary." *White*, 536 U.S., at 821 (Ginsburg, J., dissenting).

Justice SCALIA, with whom Justice THOMAS joins, dissenting.

I

The first axiom of the First Amendment is this: As a general rule, the state has no power to ban speech on the basis of its content. One need not equate judges with politicians to see that this principle does not grow weaker merely because the censored speech is a judicial candidate's request for a campaign contribution. . . .

One likewise need not equate judges with politicians to see that the electoral setting calls for all the more vigilance in ensuring observance of the First Amendment. When a candidate asks someone for a campaign contribution, he tends (as the principal opinion acknowledges) also to talk about his qualifications for office and his views on public issues. This expression lies at the heart of what the First Amendment is meant to protect. In addition, banning candidates from asking for money personally "favors some candidates over others—incumbent judges (who benefit from their current status) over non-judicial candidates, the well-to-do (who may not need to raise any money at all) over lower-income candidates, and the well-connected (who have an army of potential fundraisers) over outsiders." *Carey v. Wolnitzek*, 614 F.3d 189, 204 (6th Cir. 2010). This danger of legislated (or judicially imposed) favoritism is the very reason the First Amendment exists.

Because Canon 7C(1) restricts fully protected speech on the basis of content, it presumptively violates the First Amendment. We may uphold it only if the State meets its burden of showing that the Canon survives strict scrutiny—that is to say, only if it shows that the Canon is narrowly tailored to serve a compelling interest. I do not for a moment question the Court's conclusion that States have different compelling interests when regulating judicial elections than when regulating political ones. Unlike a legislator, a judge must be impartial—without bias for or against any party or attorney who comes before him. I accept for the sake of argument that States have a compelling interest in ensuring that its judges are *seen* to be impartial. I will likewise assume that a judicial candidate's request to a litigant or attorney presents a danger of coercion that a political candidate's request to a constituent does not. But Canon 7C(1) does not narrowly target concerns about impartiality or its appearance; it applies even when the person asked for a financial contribution has no chance of ever appearing in the candidate's court. And Florida does not invoke concerns about coercion, presumably because the Canon bans solicitations regardless of whether their object is a lawyer, litigant, or other person vulnerable to judicial pressure. So Canon 7C(1) fails exacting scrutiny and infringes the First Amendment. This case should have been just that straightforward.

II

The Court concludes that Florida may prohibit personal solicitations by judicial candidates as a means of preserving "public confidence in the integrity of the judiciary." It purports to reach this destination by applying strict scrutiny, but it would be more accurate to say that it does so by applying the appearance of strict scrutiny. . . .

Neither the Court nor the State identifies the slightest evidence that banning requests for contributions will substantially improve public trust in judges. Nor does common sense make this happy forecast obvious. The concept of judicial integrity "dates back at least eight centuries," and judicial elections in America date back more than two centuries—but rules against personal solicitations date back only to 1972. The peaceful coexistence of judicial elections and personal solicitations for most of our history calls into doubt any claim that allowing personal solicitations would imperil public faith in judges. Many States allow judicial candidates to ask for contributions even today, but nobody suggests that public confidence in judges fares worse in these jurisdictions than elsewhere. And in any event, if candidates' appeals for money are "'characteristically intertwined'" with discussion of qualifications and views on public issues, how can the Court be so sure that the public will regard them as improprieties rather than as legitimate instances of campaigning? In the final analysis, Florida comes nowhere near making the convincing demonstration required by our cases that the speech restriction in this case substantially advances its objective.

But suppose we play along with the premise that prohibiting solicitations will significantly improve the public reputation of judges. Even then, Florida must show that the ban restricts no more speech than necessary to achieve the objective.

Canon 7C(1) falls miles short of satisfying this requirement. The Court seems to accept Florida's claim that solicitations erode public confidence by creating the perception that judges are selling justice to lawyers and litigants. Yet the Canon prohibits candidates from asking for money from *anybody*—even from someone who is neither lawyer nor litigant, even from someone who (because of recusal rules) cannot possibly appear before the candidate as lawyer or litigant. Yulee thus may not call up an old friend, a cousin, or even her parents to ask for a donation to her campaign. The State has not come up with a plausible explanation of how soliciting someone who has no chance of appearing in the candidate's court will diminish public confidence in judges.

No less important, Canon 7C(1) bans candidates from asking for contributions even in messages that do not target any listener in particular—mass-mailed letters, flyers posted on telephone poles, speeches to large gatherings, and Web sites addressed to the general public. . . .

Even on the Court's own terms, Canon 7C(1) cannot stand. The Court concedes that "underinclusiveness can raise 'doubts about whether the government is in fact pursuing the interest it invokes.'" Canon 7C(1)'s scope suggests that it has nothing to do with the appearances created by judges' asking for money, and everything to do with hostility toward judicial campaigning. How else to explain the Florida Supreme Court's decision to ban *all* personal appeals for campaign funds (even when the solicitee could never appear before the candidate), but to tolerate appeals for other kinds of funds (even when the solicitee will surely appear before the candidate)? It should come as no surprise that the ABA, whose model rules the Florida Supreme Court followed when framing Canon 7C(1), opposes judicial elections—preferring instead a system in which (surprise!) a committee of lawyers proposes candidates from among whom the Governor must make his selection. See *White*, 536 U.S., at 787.

The Court tries to strike a pose of neutrality between appointment and election of judges, but no one should be deceived. A Court that sees impropriety in a candidate's request for *any* contributions to his election campaign does not much like judicial selection by the people. . . . When a society decides that its judges should be elected, it necessarily decides that selection by the people is more important than the oracular sanctity of judges, their immunity from the (shudder!) indignity of begging for funds, and their exemption from those shadows of impropriety that fall over the proletarian public officials who must run for office. . . .

Justice KENNEDY, dissenting.

With all due respect for the Court, it seems fair and necessary to say its decision rests on two premises, neither one correct. One premise is that in certain elections—here an election to choose the best qualified judge—the public lacks the necessary judgment to make an informed choice. Instead, the State must protect voters by altering the usual dynamics of free speech. The other premise is that since judges should be accorded special respect and dignity, their election can be subject to certain content-based rules that would be unacceptable in other elections. In my respectful view neither premise can justify the speech restriction at issue here. . . .

While any number of troubling consequences will follow from the Court's ruling, a simple example can suffice to illustrate the dead weight its decision now ties to public debate. Assume a judge retires, and two honest lawyers, Doe and Roe, seek the vacant position. Doe is a respected, prominent lawyer who has been active in the community and is well known to business and civic leaders. Roe, a lawyer of extraordinary ability and high ethical standards, keeps a low profile. As soon as Doe announces his or her candidacy, a campaign committee organizes of its own accord and begins raising funds. But few know or hear about Roe's potential candidacy, and no one with resources or connections is available to assist in raising the funds necessary for even a modest plan to speak to the electorate. Today the Court says the State can censor Roe's speech, imposing a gag on his or her request for funds, no matter how close Roe is to the potential benefactor or donor. The result is that Roe's personal freedom, the right of speech, is cut off by the State.

The First Amendment consequences of the Court's ruling do not end with its denial of the individual's right to speak. For the very purpose of the candidate's fundraising was to facilitate a larger speech process: an election campaign. By cutting off one candidate's personal freedom to speak, the broader campaign debate that might have followed—a debate that might have been informed by new ideas and insights from both candidates—now is silenced.

Elections are a paradigmatic forum for speech. Though present day campaign rhetoric all too often might thwart or obscure deliberative discourse, the idea of elections is that voters can engage in, or at least consider, a principled debate. That debate can be a means to find consensus for a civic course that is prudent and wise. This pertains both to issues and to the choice of elected officials. The First Amendment seeks to make the idea of discussion, open debate, and consensus-building a reality. But the Court decides otherwise. . . .

Is *Williams-Yulee* reconcilable with *White*? The essence of the Court's decision in *White* is that once a state decides to elect its judges it cannot shield the election from the consequences of that decision without violating the First Amendment. Fundamentally, for First Amendment purposes, elected judges are very much like politicians. *William-Yulee* seems to depart from a contrary premise. Chief Justice

Roberts declares authoritatively that elected judges are not politicians. Consequently, the First Amendment applies differently in the context of judicial campaigns than it does in the context of electoral campaigns. How much of *White* remains after *Williams-Yulee*?

>> *Should Judicial Elections Be Eliminated?* The most serious challenge to elective judiciaries may not be legal so much as political. The "unseemly spectacle of expensive, bitterly contested, partisan elections for seats on the highest court in the state," PETER J. GALIE, ORDERED LIBERTY: A CONSTITUTIONAL HISTORY OF NEW YORK 105 (1996), has long made many observers queasy, and things seem only to have gotten worse. Judicial elections today are increasingly coming to resemble elections to other kinds of office, including a dramatic rise in the amount of money spent by candidates and outside groups, and the use of sometimes sharp mass media advertising, including attack ads. *See, e.g.*, Brennan Center for Justice, *The New Politics of Judicial Elections, 2000-2009* (2010); HERBERT M. KRITZER, JUSTICE ON THE BALLOT: CONTINUITY AND CHANGE IN STATE SUPREME COURT ELECTIONS (2016); HALL, *supra*.

Spending on judicial races more than doubled between the 1990s and 2000s, and previously unheard-of amounts were poured into state supreme court races by outside interest groups. James Sample, et al., *The New Politics of Judicial Elections, 2000-2009* (Brennan Center for Justice 2010); Douglas Keith, et al., *The Politics of Judicial Elections, 2017-2018* (Brennan Center for Justice (2019). Efforts to gain control of the state judiciary have not, however, been limited to attempts to win judicial seats in ordinary elections; they have also included attempts to inflict electoral punishment on judges who make rulings that on the merits might be characterized as philosophically liberal. For example, in 2010 three justices of the Iowa Supreme Court were ousted in retention elections—the first time any Iowa justice had not been retained—in retaliation for a 2009 decision striking down on state constitutional grounds a state law restricting abortion. The outcome of this election was heavily influenced by a surge of spending by out-of-state groups that routinely support Republican causes. David Pozen, *What Happened in Iowa?*, 111 COLUM. L. REV. SIDEBAR 90, 98 (2011).

Similar, though unsuccessful efforts were mounted in Alaska, Colorado, Kansas, Illinois and Florida targeting supreme court justices based on rulings they joined concerning abortion, taxes, tort reform, and health care. In Pennsylvania, following a historic 2018 ruling by the state supreme court invalidating on state constitutional grounds a grotesque partisan gerrymander favoring Republicans (Chapter 4), Republican leaders in the state legislature introduced a motion to impeach the four Democrats on the court who had ruled to invalidate the gerrymander. Although most of these efforts have been unsuccessful, even the unsuccessful ones subject theoretically independent courts to discipline imposed by the other branches because of their sheer *in terrorem* effect.

A U.S. Supreme Court decision, *Caperton v. A.T. Massey Coal Co.*, 556 U.S. 868 (2009), highlights the seamier side of judicial elections. There the Court invalidated on due process grounds a judgment of the West Virginia Supreme Court where the winning litigant had spent nearly $3 million in support of the election campaign of one of the judges who heard the case—and who had declined to recuse himself. No less a legal celebrity than retired U.S. Supreme Court Justice

Sandra Day O'Connor has dedicated herself to leading a nationwide movement to abolish judicial elections.

Under public pressure, Arkansas (2002) and North Carolina (2004) abandoned partisan judicial elections, although North Carolina reinstated them in 2016 in what was widely viewed as a nakedly partisan attempt by Republicans to maintain control of the state bench. In total, 13 states have at one time or another moved away from conventional, across-the-board partisan judicial elections in favor of nonpartisan elections (Arkansas, Georgia, Kentucky, Mississippi, North Carolina), the Missouri Plan (Colorado, Florida, Indiana, Iowa, Oklahoma, Tennessee, Utah), or outright gubernatorial appointment (New York Court of Appeals judges). *See* CHRIS W. BONNEAU AND MELINDA GANN HALL, IN DEFENSE OF JUDICIAL ELECTIONS 3 (2009). Although to Americans of the Jacksonian era the merits of an elective judiciary seemed self-evident, judicial elections have few defenders today. Nevertheless, a small number of contrarians are still willing to make the case for an elective judiciary:

> [W]e argue that, contrary to the claims of judges, professional legal organizations, interest groups, and legal scholars, judicial elections are democracy-enhancing institutions that operate efficaciously and serve to create a valuable nexus between citizens and the bench. We argue that, rather than being eradicated, judicial elections should be retained if not restored to their original form of partisan, competitive races, the situation that existed before modern reform advocates convinced the states to remove partisan labels and challengers from these contests.

Id. at 2. The authors go on to argue that levels of voter interest and participation in judicial elections are generally high, voter interest is suppressed by the nonpartisan rather than partisan election format, "highly spirited and expensive campaigns" increase voter interest and participation in judicial elections, partisanship in judicial elections decreases their cost and therefore relieves fundraising pressure on judicial candidates, and that voters have the capacity to distinguish strong from weak judicial candidates.

But is a lively campaign and high levels of voter engagement an unalloyed good when it comes to selecting judges? Might close attention from voters alter the behavior of judges in undesirable ways? The evidence suggests that elected judges deciding how to rule are cognizant of public opinion, and that this awareness, and the desire to be reelected, can alter their decision making. Elected judges also are aware of the likely sources of financial support for their reelection campaigns, and this too can influence their decision making. *See, e.g.,* Michael S. Kang and Joanna Shepherd, *Partisanship in State Supreme Courts: The Empirical Relationship Between Party Contributions and Judicial Decision Making,* 44 J. LEG. STUD. S161 (2015); KRITZER, *supra*; Michael S. Kang and Joanna Shepherd, *The Partisan Foundations of Judicial Campaign Finance,* 86 S. CAL. L. REV. 1239 (2013); CHARLES GARDNER GEYH, WHO IS TO JUDGE? THE PERENNIAL DEBATE OVER WHETHER TO ELECT OR APPOINT AMERICA'S JUDGES (2019).

⟫ *Appointed Judges and Partisan Capture.*   Even if the case for judicial elections is weak, mustn't any mode of judicial selection be compared to its alternatives before it may reasonably be condemned? Is gubernatorial appointment of judges self-evidently a better method? Does anything guarantee that governors will appoint the best quality candidates instead of using such appointments to elevate party hacks, loyal supporters, or political dependents? *See* James A. Gardner, *New York's Inbred Judiciary: Pathologies of Nomination and Appointment of Court of Appeals Judges*, 58 BUFF. L. REV.: THE DOCKET 15 (2010).

In Chapter 2 we saw that authoritarian chief executives who possess the power of judicial appointment routinely attempt to deploy it to capture the judiciary for the purpose of neutralizing it as an institutional check on the exercise of executive power. Is judicial selection in the United States immune from such developments? Clearly the answer is no.

Control over the ideological commitments of judges has long been a strategic objective of the Republican Party. That goal has been pursued single-mindedly on the federal level since the Reagan Administration through careful, highly selective ideological vetting of judicial appointees. According to one leading account of the conservative movement, "in no other area was the process of strategic investment as prolonged, ambitious, complicated, and successful as in the law." STEPHEN M. TELES, THE RISE OF THE CONSERVATIVE LEGAL MOVEMENT: THE BATTLE FOR CONTROL OF THE LAW 3 (2008).

This careful strategizing produced notable success in many areas, including, for example, slow but steady erosion of the right to abortion, the invalidation of affirmative action programs in employment and education, and the startling discovery of a robust but previously unacknowledged right of private gun ownership. In the domain of election law, many view *Bush v. Gore* as a tipping point. A new, comprehensive study of Supreme Court voting patterns in election law cases finds "remarkably little evidence of partisan influence in Supreme Court election law cases in the 20th century." That is to say, majority coalitions of justices prior to 2000 regularly included a mix of justices nominated by Democratic and Republican presidents. That changed after 2000: beginning with *Bush v. Gore* and continuing through *Citizens United* in 2010, the majority coalition in election law cases consisted exclusively of appointees of one party in 35 percent of election law cases. Over the next decade, 2011 through 2021, that number increased to 41 percent. The author concludes:

> The lesson is clear. In an era of razor-thin presidential [vote] margins, the Supreme Court's election law rulings can mean the difference between victory and defeat. When 44,000 votes out of 158 million decide who wins the presidency, court decisions on campaign finance, Voter ID requirements, early voting periods, and precinct locations have immense importance. They can tip the election outcome in one direction or another.

Anthony J. Gaughan, *The Influence of Partisanship on Supreme Court Election Law Rulings*, 36 NOTRE DAME J. LAW, ETHICS & PUB. POLICY ___ (2022). Another recent study finds: "there was no meaningful change in the [Supreme Court's] position relative to that of the general public . . . between 2010 and 2020. . . . There was, however, a sharp shift when Kavanaugh replaced Roberts as the court's median voter in 2021, with the court moving away from the general public to correspond almost exactly to the ideological position of the average Republican voter." Stephen

Jessee, Neil Malhotra, and Maya Sen, *A Decade-Long Longitudinal Survey Shows That the Supreme Court is Now Much More Conservative Than the Public*, 119 PNAS __ (2022).

The pace of these changes may well soon accelerate. In February, 2016, Justice Antonin Scalia, the Court's leading conservative voice, died unexpectedly. One month later, President Obama nominated Merrick Garland, a judge of the District of Columbia Court of Appeals, and by all accounts a judicial moderate, to replace him. In a sharp break with tradition and inter-branch and inter-party comity, the Senate Majority Leader, Mitch McConnell, refused to bring the nomination to the Senate for confirmation, claiming falsely that Senate practice precluded taking up Supreme Court nominations during the final year of a presidential administration. In January, 2017, ten days after taking office, President Trump nominated Neil Gorsuch to fill the vacancy, and the Senate confirmed the nomination. In September 2020, just two months before the conclusion of President Trump's term, Justice Ruth Bader Ginsburg, a member of the Court's shrinking liberal wing, died. Eight days later, Trump nominated Amy Coney Barrett to fill the vacancy. Senator McConnell, apparently forgetting the rule he applied to a Democratic president, quickly brought the nomination to the Senate floor, and the Senate confirmed on October 27, 2020, one week before Election Day. Those two appointments altered the balance on the Court to six Republican appointees and three Democratic ones.

The behavior of Senate Republicans has led many on the political left to call for political retaliation by expanding the size of the Court to allow a Democratic president enough new appointments to alter (or as proponents assert, to restore) its ideological balance. *See, e.g.,* STEPHEN M. FELDMAN, PACK THE COURT! A DEFENSE OF SUPREME COURT EXPANSION (2021). Others, pointing to President Roosevelt's failed Court-packing plan of 1937, have warned that doing so would irreparably damage the Court's institutional legitimacy.

In fact, court-packing has already become a tool of judicial capture by Republicans at the state level. In 2016, the Arizona legislature expanded the size of the Arizona Supreme Court from five to seven to permit the Republican governor to appoint two new justices. That same year, the Georgia legislature enacted legislation to expand the Georgia Supreme Court from seven to nine. At the time of the enactment, four of the justices were Democratic appointees and three were Republican appointees, so the new positions allowed the Republican governor to alter the partisan balance on the court. Unsuccessful attempts at court-packing were made in Florida (2007) and in Iowa (2009), the latter following a decision by the Iowa Supreme Court striking down a state law prohibiting same-sex marriage. Other unsuccessful attempts were made in South Carolina (initially by Democrats but then, in 2013, by Republicans) and Louisiana (2017). Conversely, but to the same end, attempts have been made by Republican-controlled legislatures to shrink the size of the state supreme court to deny Democratic governors new appointments, most notably in Montana. Marin K. Levy, *Packing and Unpacking State Courts*, 61 WM. & MARY L. REV. 1121 (2020). Would a move by Democrats to pack the federal courts, or the Supreme Court in particular, be significantly different in kind? How much political capital and goodwill does the Supreme Court at this point actually retain? And is any method of judicial selection free from the possibility of abuse?

C. THE ADMINISTRATIVE MODEL IN ACTION: FRONT-END ENFORCEMENT OF ELIGIBILITY REQUIREMENTS

Notwithstanding an extensive array of criminal prohibitions of election misconduct, *see* U.S. Election Assistance Comm'n, *Election Crimes* (Dec. 2006), the principal legal approach to promoting the accuracy, integrity, and legitimacy of elections, and the one that most often touches the lives of ordinary voters, is administrative. Regimes of administrative regulation seek to accomplish public goals by creating a structure that will make violations of the law much more difficult to accomplish, and in consequence the main form of regulation of conduct is civil, rather than criminal. Administrative methods of control have several advantages over traditional criminal law enforcement. In an administrative regime, potential violations of the law usually come to official attention directly and routinely, instead of via third-party reporting or other forms of field investigation and detection. Violations can often be headed off before they occur through direct administrative correction of problems, and without the complications, expense, and delay of judicial proceedings. For example, in an administrative regime, officials can turn away ineligible voters before they vote rather than attempting to punish illegal voting after it occurs, with all the attendant burden and uncertainty.

1. Voter Registration

Every state except North Dakota requires voters to register as a condition of eligibility to vote in elections administered within the state. This includes voting not only in state and local elections, but in federal elections as well. Here, for example, is New York's registration requirement:

> A person shall not be entitled to vote in any election held pursuant to this chapter unless he shall be registered. . . .

N.Y. Elec. Law §5-100. Voter registration, typically administered by a statewide election official such as the Secretary of State or a statewide Board of Elections, is a procedure in which the registrant's eligibility to vote can be confirmed. Registration creates an opportunity before the voter shows up at the polls to determine his or her eligibility, thereby avoiding awkward controversies arising at the polling place on Election Day that can be difficult or impossible to resolve on the spot. State registration laws therefore generally make registration conditional upon a demonstration of eligibility by the voter. Here again is New York's provision:

> No person shall be qualified to register for and vote at any election unless he is a citizen of the United States and is or will be, on the day of such election, eighteen years of age or over, and a resident of this state and of the county, city or village for a minimum of thirty days next preceding such election.

N.Y. Elec. Law §5-102(1). In the New York system, then, registration is permitted only upon a showing that the registrant satisfies the state's eligibility requirements relating to citizenship, age, residency, and duration of residency. At the same time, successful registration by eligible voters creates an administrative record of their eligibility, which they can then invoke at the polling place as evidence of their legal entitlement to vote.

Voter registration requirements seem entirely benign. What could be wrong with a procedure that verifies a voter's eligibility, especially well before the election? Yet it has often been remarked that turnout in American elections is substantially lower than turnout in advanced democracies elsewhere in the world, and blame is frequently placed on the difficulty and burden of registration under American election laws. In most of the world's democracies the burden of registering voters rests on the government; here, that burden falls on the voter. Moreover, voter registration requirements in the United States have an ugly history. Consider the following account.

Alexander Keyssar

The Right to Vote (2000)

Before the 1870s in most states, there were no official prepared lists of eligible voters, and men who sought to vote were not obliged to take any steps to establish their eligibility prior to election day. They simply showed up at the polls with whatever documentary proofs (or witnesses) that might be necessary. . . . [M]ost antebellum proposals for registration systems were rejected as unnecessary and partisan.

Between the 1870s and World War I, however, the majority of states adopted formal registration procedures, particularly for their larger cities. The rationale for requiring voters to register and have their eligibility certified in advance of elections was straightforward: it would help eliminated fraud and also bring an end to disruptive election-day conflicts at the polls. Especially in urban areas, where corruption was believed to be concentrated and voters were less likely to be known personally to election officials, advance registration would give the state time to develop lists of eligible voters, check papers, interrogate witnesses, and verify the qualifications of those who wished to vote. . . .

In New Jersey, a state with a long and colorful history of electoral disputes, Republicans instituted registration requirements in 1866 and 1867. All prospective voters had to register in person on the Thursday before each general election . . . , and no one was permitted to vote if his name was not on the register. In 1868, the Democrats gained control of the state government and repealed the registration laws, stating that they penalized poor men who could not afford to take time off from their jobs to register. In 1870, the Republicans returned to power and reintroduced registration. . . . During these years, and for decades thereafter, the two parties also feuded over the hours that polls would be open. . . .

In Illinois, a durable registration system was hammered into place in the 1880s. It was crafted by the business and social elites of Chicago, who were dismayed by their loss of political control of the city to allegedly corrupt Democratic politicians. Their primary vehicle of reform was the Union League Club, founded in 1879 to . . . "preserve the purity of the ballot box." In the early 1880s, the club . . . engaged in a kind of political vigilantism, hiring investigators to check polling places and offering a $300 reward to those who helped in the apprehension and conviction of anyone who voted illegally in Chicago in 1883. . . .

To register, a prospective voter had to appear in person before the election judges, on the Tuesday of either the third or fourth week prior to an election. . . . Following the two days of registration, the clerks, assisted by the police, conducted a house-to-house canvass of the precinct to verify the names of all adult male residents and compile a "suspected list" of improperly registered voters. Anyone whose name appeared on the so-called suspected list would be removed from the election rosters unless he appeared before the judges again, . . . and made a convincing and verifiable case for his eligibility. . . . [T]he small size of the precincts . . . meant that anyone who moved even a few blocks was likely to have to register again [and] there were only two days on which a person could register. . . .

The impact of these laws was highly variable . . . , [but] it can be said with certainty that registration laws reduced fraudulent voting and that they kept large numbers (probably millions) of eligible voters from the polls. In cities such as Philadelphia, Chicago, and Boston, only 60 to 70 percent of eligible voters were registered between 1910 and 1920; in wards inhabited by the poor, the figures were significantly lower. . . . [S]cholars have estimated that one third or more of [the national drop in voter turnout] can be attributed to the implementation of the registration schemes.

>> *False Positives and False Negatives.*   Voter eligibility screening mechanisms can have two different kinds of flaws: they can be too lax, thus permitting ineligible voters to vote (false negatives), or they can be too sensitive, thus barring eligible voters from voting (false positives). Both kinds of errors impair the accuracy of the final tally, but are they equivalent? Is there any basis for preferring one kind of error to the other, or for evaluating their relative demerits?

One possibility is to consider both kinds of errors equally bad and seek simply to keep their overall magnitude to a minimum. If, for example, imposing a voter registration requirement in a particular jurisdiction will exclude incorrectly some number of eligible voters but will also prevent improper voting by some other number of noncitizens, nonresidents, or ineligible felons, we might simply tally up the score and impose the restriction if it excludes more ineligible than eligible voters. Is this a satisfactory approach? Can we predict the likely effects of voter screening mechanisms on specific populations with sufficient accuracy to adopt it?

Even if we can predict accurately the likely impact of eligibility enforcement measures, is it really the case that all deviations from electoral accuracy are equivalently bad? During the nineteenth and early twentieth centuries, it was not uncommon for courts and legislators to think about the electoral process in terms of its "purity." As we saw in Chapter 3, both voter residency requirements and felon disfranchisement have sometimes been justified as measures to protect "the purity of the ballot box" against the introduction of votes that are in some sense "tainted." If the wrongful casting of ineligible votes is properly viewed as an "infection" of an otherwise healthy political process, we might prefer false positives to false negatives because the exclusion of eligible voters, though lamentable, at least does not cause a comparable taint to the process. This could lead to a very strict view about excluding improper votes, *see, e.g., Carter v. Lambert*, 155 S.W.2d 38, 40 (Ky. 1941) ("[T]he bribery of one vote is sufficient to void the nomination of a successful candidate"), accompanied by a correspondingly more forgiving approach to the mistaken exclusion of eligible voters. Is the electoral process "tainted" in some way by the inclusion of ineligible votes? How, and in respect of what considerations?

Conversely, a tally of harms rather than errors might yield a different conclusion. Who precisely is harmed by errors of inclusion and exclusion? No doubt the public is harmed by both kinds of errors when it is deprived of an accurate electoral tally. But might it not be said that eligible voters wrongfully excluded from voting suffer an individual harm through deprivation of their vested right to participate in the process of democratic self-governance through voting? In contrast, ineligible voters who are mistakenly permitted to vote receive only an erroneous windfall benefit. Evaluated in terms of their impact on individuals, then, errors in vote canvassing resulting from false positives might on these grounds be deemed worse than errors resulting from false negatives.

≫ *The Motor Voter Law.*   In 1993, in an effort to improve voter registration rates nationwide, Congress enacted the National Voter Registration Act (NVRA, or "motor voter" law), 52 U.S.C. §§20501, et seq. Finding that "discriminatory and unfair registration laws and procedures can have a direct and damaging effect on voter participation in elections for Federal office and disproportionately harm voter participation by various groups, including racial minorities," *id.* §20501 (3), Congress decreed that for purposes of voting in federal elections, "each State shall establish procedures to register to vote in elections for Federal office (1) by application made simultaneously with an application for a motor vehicle driver's license. . . ." *Id.* §20503-2. Thus, states were prohibited from forcing voters to make a separate effort to register to vote; every state's bureau of motor vehicles became in essence a satellite office of its board of elections. The law also required states to permit voter registration by mail. *Id.* §20505.

The NVRA also lengthened to 30 days the amount of time in which voters are permitted to register before an election, and limited the circumstances in which a voter may be removed from the registration rolls to those specifically provided by state law. It also provided that states must make systematic efforts to keep voter registration rolls accurate: "Each state shall . . . conduct a general program that makes a reasonable effort to remove the names of ineligible voters from the official lists of eligible voters by reason of (A) the death of the registrant; or (B) a change in the residence of the registrant." 52 U.S.C. §20507.

Although the motor voter law made voter registration much easier for many, it did not in the end increase voter turnout. Turnout in the 1996 presidential election, the first after enactment of the NVRA, was the lowest in modern history, at a mere 51 percent. Was Congress addressing the right problem?

≫ *Time Lags and Purges.*   Did the NVRA make voter registration rolls more accurate? It is difficult to say, as there is little systematic data on the accuracy of registration rolls either before or after passage of the Act. However, it is clear that many state and local registration rolls still contain many inaccuracies, if for no other reason than the unavoidable administrative lag between the time a voter's eligibility in a district changes through death, relocation, or the onset of mental illness, and the reflection of that change in a corrected voter registration record. The great mobility of the population poses special problems in the United States:

> One force drives many of the problems encountered in maintaining registration lists: residential mobility. Registration lists are usually thought of as static. . . . The American population, however, is on the move. Every year, 12 percent of people in the United States move from one residence to another. Every four years, almost half of all Americans move. [States] with more mobile populations are more likely to report registration issues. . . .
>
> A related challenge for the registration system is recording errors. The most troublesome errors are (1) incorrect information in records, such as typographical errors, (2) obsolete information, such as changes in names or signatures, (3) duplicate or obsolete records, such as when a person moves but does not notify the election office, and (4) improperly dropped records, such as when a person has not moved but is dropped from the rolls.

Daron Shaw et al., *A Brief Yet Practical Guide to Reforming U.S. Voter Registration Systems*, 14 ELECTION L.J. 26, 29-30 (2015).

In some jurisdictions, the number of voters on the registration rolls exceeds the number that could possibly be eligible to vote in the jurisdiction, mainly because ineligible voters are not regularly purged from the list. Is there any harm to having the names of ineligible voters remain on a registration list? If a voter is registered but dead, or has moved away, he or she is unlikely to show up at the polls to vote. Does the presence of such names on the rolls create a risk of fraud through voter impersonation? How great a risk? Is the risk of fraud sufficient to justify aggressive purges of voter registration lists in an effort to root out every ineligible name?

Note that administrative attempts to correct inaccurate or outdated voter rolls are themselves processes capable of introducing error. In particular, the sources of information that administrators rely on to correct voter registration rolls must be more accurate than the rolls themselves. This has not always been the case. One notorious example is the "Crosscheck" system, which purported to compare voter databases across states for the purpose of identifying double voting. This system, first developed in Kansas by then-Kansas Attorney General Kris Kobach, a vocal believer in widespread voter fraud, was subsequently adopted by 28 states. The system, which relied on rudimentary data such as names and birthdates, proved wildly inaccurate. Evidently, there are far more people with the same name and birthdate than one might initially imagine. According to one academic study, Crosscheck would invalidate 300 legitimate voter registrations for every double-voter it identified. Sharad Goel, et al., *One Person, One Vote: Estimating the Prevalence of Double Voting in U.S. Presidential Elections* (Stanford U. Working Paper 2017).

Moreover, the incidence of registration list purges does not appear to be neutral. Following *Shelby County*, "formerly covered jurisdictions increased their purge rates . . . more than noncovered jurisdictions," purging more than nine million names between 2012 and 2016. Jonathan Brater, et al., *Purges: A Growing Threat to the Right to Vote* (Brennan Center for Justice 2018). Such purges are not, however, limited to the U.S. South. In one five-year period, Ohio purged two million names from the state's voter rolls by using a method that purported to identify obsolete listings through a combination of non-response to mailed inquiries and subsequent non-voting for a period of four years. Under this system, voters in neighborhoods that supported Barack Obama for president in 2012 saw more than twice as many registration purges as neighborhoods where Obama earned less than forty percent of the vote. CAROL ANDERSON, ONE PERSON, NO VOTE: HOW VOTER SUPPRESSION IS DESTROYING OUR DEMOCRACY 77 (2019).

Ohio's method of purging voter registration lists was challenged as incompatible with the requirements of the NVRA in *Husted v. A. Philip Randolph Institute*, 584 U.S. __ (2018). In a 5-4 decision, the Supreme Court upheld the state's methodology. The dissenters argued that in the United States, non-voting, even for long periods of time, is not a reliable indicator that a person has changed residences. In 2014, for example, more than 40 percent of Ohio's registered voters did not vote. Moreover, in 2012, Ohio sent address change inquiries to 1.5 million non-voters — about 20 percent of its registered voter population — and received only 60,000 return cards, a response rate of about 4 percent. The dissenters thus would have read the NVRA to permit only more reliable methods of address-change verification.

2.   *Voter Identification Requirements*

Crawford v. Marion County Election Board

553 U.S. 181 (2008)

Justice STEVENS announced the judgment of the Court and delivered an opinion in which THE CHIEF JUSTICE and Justice KENNEDY join.

At issue in these cases is the constitutionality of an Indiana statute requiring citizens voting in person on election day, or casting a ballot in person at the office of the circuit court clerk prior to election day, to present photo identification issued by the government.

Referred to as either the "Voter ID Law" or "SEA 483," the statute applies to in-person voting at both primary and general elections. The requirement does not apply to absentee ballots submitted by mail, and the statute contains an exception for persons living and voting in a state-licensed facility such as a nursing home. Ind. Code Ann. §3-11-8-25.1(e). A voter who is indigent or has a religious objection to being photographed may cast a provisional ballot that will be counted only if she executes an appropriate affidavit before the circuit court clerk within 10 days following the election. §§3-11.7-5-1, 3-11.7-5-2.5(c). A voter who has photo identification but is unable to present that identification on election day may file a provisional ballot that will be counted if she brings her photo identification to the circuit county clerk's office within 10 days. §3-11.7-5-2.5(b). No photo identification is required in order to register to vote, and the State offers free photo identification to qualified voters able to establish their residence and identity. §9-24-16-10(b). . . .

I

In *Harper v. Virginia Bd. of Elections,* 383 U.S. 663 (1966), the Court held that Virginia could not condition the right to vote in a state election on the payment of a poll tax of $1.50. We rejected the dissenters' argument that the interest in promoting civic responsibility by weeding out those voters who did not care enough about public affairs to pay a small sum for the privilege of voting provided a rational basis for the tax. *See id.* at 685 (opinion of Harlan, J.). Applying a stricter standard, we concluded that a State "violates the Equal Protection Clause of the Fourteenth Amendment whenever it makes the affluence of the voter or payment of any fee an electoral standard." *Id.* at 666 (opinion of the Court). We used the term "invidiously discriminate" to describe conduct prohibited under that standard, noting that we had previously held that while a State may obviously impose "reasonable residence restrictions on the availability of the ballot," it "may not deny the opportunity to vote to a bona fide resident merely because he is a member of the armed services." *Id.* at 666-667. Although the State's justification for the tax was rational, it was invidious because it was irrelevant to the voter's qualifications.

Thus, under the standard applied in *Harper,* even rational restrictions on the right to vote are invidious if they are unrelated to voter qualifications. In *Anderson v. Celebrezze,* 460 U.S. 780 (1983), however, we confirmed the general rule that "evenhanded restrictions that protect the integrity and reliability of the electoral process itself" are not invidious and satisfy the standard set forth in *Harper.* 460 U.S. at 788, n.9. Rather than applying any "litmus test" that would neatly separate valid from invalid restrictions, we concluded that a court must identify and evaluate the interests put forward by the State as justifications for the burden imposed by its rule, and then make the "hard judgment" that our adversary system demands.

In later election cases we have followed *Anderson*'s balancing approach. . . .

II

The State has identified several state interests that arguably justify the burdens that SEA 483 imposes on voters and potential voters. While petitioners argue that the statute was actually motivated by partisan concerns and dispute both the significance of the State's interests and the magnitude of any real threat to those interests, they do not question the legitimacy of the interests the State has identified. Each is unquestionably relevant to the State's interest in protecting the integrity and reliability of the electoral process. . . .

Election Modernization. Two recently enacted federal statutes have made it necessary for States to reexamine their election procedures. Both contain provisions consistent with a State's choice to use government-issued photo identification as a relevant source of information concerning a citizen's eligibility to vote.

In the National Voter Registration Act of 1993 (NVRA), 107 Stat. 77, 42 U.S.C. §1973gg *et seq.,* Congress established procedures that would both increase the number of registered voters and protect the integrity of the electoral process. §1973gg. The statute requires state motor vehicle driver's license applications to serve as voter registration applications. §1973gg-3. While that requirement has increased the number of registered voters, the statute also contains a provision restricting States' ability to remove names from the lists of registered voters. §1973gg-6(a)(3).

These protections have been partly responsible for inflated lists of registered voters. For example, evidence credited by Judge Barker [at trial] estimated that as of 2004 Indiana's voter rolls were inflated by as much as 41.4%, and data collected by the Election Assistance Committee in 2004 indicated that 19 of 92 Indiana counties had registration totals exceeding 100% of the 2004 voting-age population, Dept. of Justice Complaint in *United States v. Indiana,* No. 1:06-cv-1000-RLY-TAB (S.D. Ind., June 27, 2006), p. 4, App. 313.

In HAVA, Congress required every State to create and maintain a computerized statewide list of all registered voters. 42 U.S.C. §15483(a) (2000 ed., Supp. V). HAVA also requires the States to verify voter information contained in a voter registration application and specifies either an "applicant's driver's license number" or "the last 4 digits of the applicant's social security number" as acceptable verifications. §5483(a)(5)(A)(i). If an individual has neither number, the State is required to assign the applicant a voter identification number. §15483(a)(5)(A)(ii).

HAVA also imposes new identification requirements for individuals registering to vote for the first time who submit their applications by mail. If the voter is casting his ballot in person, he must present local election officials with written identification, which may be either "a current and valid photo identification" or another form of documentation such as a bank statement or paycheck. §5483(b)(2)(A). If the voter is voting by mail, he must include a copy of the identification with his ballot. A voter may also include a copy of the documentation with his application or provide his driver's license number or Social Security number for verification. §15483(b)(3). Finally, in a provision entitled "Fail-safe voting," HAVA authorizes the casting of provisional ballots by challenged voters. §15483(b)(2)(B).

Of course, neither HAVA nor NVRA required Indiana to enact SEA 483, but they do indicate that Congress believes that photo identification is one effective method of establishing a voter's qualification to vote and that the integrity of elections is enhanced through improved technology. . . .

Voter Fraud. The only kind of voter fraud that SEA 483 addresses is in-person voter impersonation at polling places. The record contains no evidence of any such fraud actually occurring in Indiana at any time in its history. Moreover, petitioners argue that provisions of the Indiana Criminal Code punishing such conduct as a felony provide adequate protection against the risk that such conduct will occur in the future. It remains true, however, that flagrant examples of such fraud in other parts of the country have been documented throughout this Nation's history by respected historians and journalists,[11] that occasional examples have surfaced in

---

11. Infamous examples abound in the New York City elections of the late nineteenth century, conducted under the influence of the Tammany Hall political machine. "Big Tim" Sullivan, a New York state senator, and — briefly — a United States Congressman, insisted that his "repeaters" (individuals paid to vote multiple times) have whiskers:

"'When you've voted 'em with their whiskers on, you take 'em to a barber and scrape off the chin fringe. Then you vote 'em again with the side lilacs and a mustache. Then to a barber again, off comes the sides and you vote 'em a third time with the mustache. If that ain't enough and the box can stand a few more ballots, clean off the mustache and vote 'em plain face. That makes every one of 'em good for four votes.'"

A. Callow, *The Tweed Ring* 210 (1966) (quoting M. Werner, Tammany Hall 439 (1928)).

recent years, and that Indiana's own experience with fraudulent voting in the 2003 Democratic primary for East Chicago Mayor[13]—though perpetrated using absentee ballots and not in-person fraud—demonstrate that not only is the risk of voter fraud real but that it could affect the outcome of a close election.

There is no question about the legitimacy or importance of the State's interest in counting only the votes of eligible voters. Moreover, the interest in orderly administration and accurate recordkeeping provides a sufficient justification for carefully identifying all voters participating in the election process. While the most effective method of preventing election fraud may well be debatable, the propriety of doing so is perfectly clear.

In its brief, the State argues that the inflation of its voter rolls provides further support for its enactment of SEA 483. The record contains a November 5, 2000, newspaper article asserting that as a result of NVRA and "sloppy record keeping," Indiana's lists of registered voters included the names of thousands of persons who had either moved, died, or were not eligible to vote because they had been convicted of felonies. The conclusion that Indiana has an unusually inflated list of registered voters is supported by the entry of a consent decree in litigation brought by the Federal Government alleging violations of NVRA. Consent Decree and Order in *United States v. Indiana*, No. 1:06-cv-1000-RLY-TAB (S.D. Ind., June 27, 2006). Even though Indiana's own negligence may have contributed to the serious inflation of its registration lists when SEA 483 was enacted, the fact of inflated voter rolls does provide a neutral and nondiscriminatory reason supporting the State's decision to require photo identification.

Safeguarding Voter Confidence. Finally, the State contends that it has an interest in protecting public confidence "in the integrity and legitimacy of representative government." Brief for State Respondents, No. 07-25, p. 53. While that interest is closely related to the State's interest in preventing voter fraud, public confidence in the integrity of the electoral process has independent significance, because it encourages citizen participation in the democratic process. As the Carter-Baker* Report observed, the "electoral system cannot inspire public confidence if no safeguards exist to deter or detect fraud or to confirm the identity of voters."

III

States employ different methods of identifying eligible voters at the polls. Some merely check off the names of registered voters who identify themselves; others require voters to present registration cards or other documentation before they can vote; some require voters to sign their names so their signatures can be

---

13. According to the uncontested factual findings of the trial court, one of the candidates paid supporters to stand near polling places and encourage voters—especially those who were poor, infirm, or spoke little English—to vote absentee. The supporters asked the voters to contact them when they received their ballots; the supporters then "assisted" the voter in filling out the ballot. . . .

* [The Carter-Baker Commission was a bipartisan, blue-ribbon panel, chaired by former President Jimmy Carter and former Secretary of State James Baker, that studied the election process and recommended reforms.—EDS.]

compared with those on file; and in recent years an increasing number of States have relied primarily on photo identification. A photo identification requirement imposes some burdens on voters that other methods of identification do not share. For example, a voter may lose his photo identification, may have his wallet stolen on the way to the polls, or may not resemble the photo in the identification because he recently grew a beard. Burdens of that sort arising from life's vagaries, however, are neither so serious nor so frequent as to raise any question about the constitutionality of SEA 483; the availability of the right to cast a provisional ballot provides an adequate remedy for problems of that character.

The burdens that are relevant to the issue before us are those imposed on persons who are eligible to vote but do not possess a current photo identification that complies with the requirements of SEA 483. The fact that most voters already possess a valid driver's license, or some other form of acceptable identification, would not save the statute under our reasoning in *Harper*, if the State required voters to pay a tax or a fee to obtain a new photo identification. But just as other States provide free voter registration cards, the photo identification cards issued by Indiana's BMV are also free. For most voters who need them, the inconvenience of making a trip to the BMV, gathering the required documents, and posing for a photograph surely does not qualify as a substantial burden on the right to vote, or even represent a significant increase over the usual burdens of voting.[17]

Both evidence in the record and facts of which we may take judicial notice, however, indicate that a somewhat heavier burden may be placed on a limited number of persons. They include elderly persons born out-of-state, who may have difficulty obtaining a birth certificate;[18] persons who because of economic or other personal limitations may find it difficult either to secure a copy of their birth certificate or to assemble the other required documentation to obtain a state-issued identification; homeless persons; and persons with a religious objection to being photographed. If we assume, as the evidence suggests, that some members of these classes were registered voters when SEA 483 was enacted, the new identification requirement may have imposed a special burden on their right to vote.

The severity of that burden is, of course, mitigated by the fact that, if eligible, voters without photo identification may cast provisional ballots that will ultimately

---

17. To obtain a photo identification card a person must present at least one "primary" document, which can be a birth certificate, certificate of naturalization, U.S. veterans photo identification, U.S. military photo identification, or a a U.S. passport. Ind. Admin. Code, tit. 140, §7-4-3 (2008). Indiana, like most States, charges a fee for obtaining a copy of one's birth certificate. This fee varies by county and is currently between $3 and $12. *See* Indiana State Department of Health Web page. Some States charge substantially more. Affidavit of Robert Andrew Ford, App. 12.

18. As petitioners note, Brief for Petitioners in No. 07-21, p. 17, n.7, and the State's "Frequently Asked Questions" Web page states, it appears that elderly persons who can attest that they were never issued a birth certificate may present other forms of identification as their primary document to the Indiana BMV, including Medicaid/Medicare cards and Social Security benefits statements; *see also* Ind. Admin. Code, tit. 140, §7-4-3 ("The commissioner or the commissioner's designee may accept reasonable alternate documents to satisfy the requirements of this rule").

C. The Administrative Model in Action: Front-End Enforcement of Eligibility Requirements   997

be counted. To do so, however, they must travel to the circuit court clerk's office within 10 days to execute the required affidavit. It is unlikely that such a requirement would pose a constitutional problem unless it is wholly unjustified. And even assuming that the burden may not be justified as to a few voters, that conclusion is by no means sufficient to establish petitioners' right to the relief they seek in this litigation.

IV

Given the fact that petitioners have advanced a broad attack on the constitutionality of SEA 483, seeking relief that would invalidate the statute in all its applications, they bear a heavy burden of persuasion. . . .

The record says virtually nothing about the difficulties faced by either indigent voters or voters with religious objections to being photographed. While one elderly man stated that he did not have the money to pay for a birth certificate, when asked if he did not have the money or did not wish to spend it, he replied, "both." App. 211-212. From this limited evidence we do not know the magnitude of the impact SEA 483 will have on indigent voters in Indiana. The record does contain the affidavit of one homeless woman who has a copy of her birth certificate, but was denied a photo identification card because she did not have an address. *Id.* at 67. But that single affidavit gives no indication of how common the problem is.

In sum, on the basis of the record that has been made in this litigation, we cannot conclude that the statute imposes "excessively burdensome requirements" on any class of voters. *See Storer v. Brown*, 415 U.S. 724, 738. A facial challenge must fail where the statute has a "'plainly legitimate sweep.'" *Washington State Grange*, 552 U.S. at 449 (quoting *Washington v. Glucksberg*, 521 U.S. 702, 739-740, and n.7 (1997) (Stevens, J., concurring in judgments)). When we consider only the statute's broad application to all Indiana voters we conclude that it "imposes only a limited burden on voters' rights." *Burdick*, 504 U.S. at 439. The "'precise interests'" advanced by the State are therefore sufficient to defeat petitioners' facial challenge to SEA 483. *Id.* at 434. . . .

Justice SCALIA, with whom Justice THOMAS and Justice ALITO join, concurring in the judgment.

. . . [Under *Burdick*,] the first step is to decide whether a challenged law severely burdens the right to vote. Ordinary and widespread burdens, such as those requiring "nominal effort" of everyone, are not severe. Burdens are severe if they go beyond the merely inconvenient. . . .

Of course, we have to identify a burden before we can weigh it. The Indiana law affects different voters differently, but what petitioners view as the law's several light and heavy burdens are no more than the different *impacts* of the single burden that the law uniformly imposes on all voters. To vote in person in Indiana, *everyone* must have and present a photo identification that can be obtained for free. The State draws no classifications, let alone discriminatory ones, except to establish *optional* absentee and provisional balloting for certain poor, elderly, and institutionalized voters and for religious objectors. Nor are voters who already have photo identifications exempted from the burden, since those voters must maintain the accuracy of the information displayed on the identifications, renew them before they expire, and replace them if they are lost.

The Indiana photo-identification law is a generally applicable, nondiscriminatory voting regulation, and our precedents refute the view that individual impacts are relevant to determining the severity of the burden it imposes. . . .

Insofar as our election-regulation cases rest upon the requirements of the Fourteenth Amendment, weighing the burden of a nondiscriminatory voting law upon each voter and concomitantly requiring exceptions for vulnerable voters would effectively turn back decades of equal-protection jurisprudence. A voter complaining about such a law's effect on him has no valid equal-protection claim because, without proof of discriminatory intent, a generally applicable law with disparate impact is not unconstitutional. *See, e.g., Washington v. Davis,* 426 U.S. 229, 248 (1976). The Fourteenth Amendment does not regard neutral laws as invidious ones, *even when their burdens purportedly fall disproportionately on a protected class. A fortiori* it does not do so when, as here, the classes complaining of disparate impact are not even protected.* *See Harris v. McRae,* 448 U.S. 297, 323, and n.26 (1980) (poverty); *Cleburne v. Cleburne Living Center, Inc.,* 473 U.S. 432, 442 (1985) (disability). . . .

Even if I thought that *stare decisis* did not foreclose adopting an individual-focused approach, I would reject it as an original matter. This is an area where the dos and don'ts need to be known in advance of the election, and voter-by-voter examination of the burdens of voting regulations would prove especially disruptive. A case-by-case approach naturally encourages constant litigation. Very few new election regulations improve everyone's lot, so the potential allegations of severe burden are endless. A State reducing the number of polling places would be open to the complaint it has violated the rights of disabled voters who live near the closed stations. Indeed, it may even be the case that some laws already on the books are especially burdensome for some voters, and one can predict lawsuits demanding that a State adopt voting over the Internet or expand absentee balloting.

That sort of detailed judicial supervision of the election process would flout the Constitution's express commitment of the task to the States. *See* Art. I, §4. It is for state legislatures to weigh the costs and benefits of possible changes to their election codes, and their judgment must prevail unless it imposes a severe and unjustified overall burden upon the right to vote, or is intended to disadvantage a particular class. Judicial review of their handiwork must apply an objective, uniform standard that will enable them to determine, *ex ante,* whether the burden they impose is too severe.

---

    * A number of our early right-to-vote decisions, purporting to rely upon the Equal Protection Clause, strictly scrutinized nondiscriminatory voting laws requiring the payment of fees. *See, e.g., Harper v. Virginia Bd. of Elections,* 383 U.S. 663, 670 (1966) (poll tax); *Bullock v. Carter,* 405 U.S. 134, 145 (1972) (ballot-access fee); *Lubin v. Panish,* 415 U.S. 709, 716-719 (1974) (ballot-access fee). To the extent those decisions continue to stand for a principle that *Burdick v. Takushi,* 504 U.S. 428 (1992), does not already encompass, it suffices to note that we have never held that legislatures must calibrate *all* election laws, even those totally unrelated to money, for their impacts on poor voters or must otherwise accommodate wealth disparities.

The lead opinion's record-based resolution of these cases, which neither rejects nor embraces the rule of our precedents, provides no certainty, and will embolden litigants who surmise that our precedents have been abandoned. There is no good reason to prefer that course. . . .

Justice SOUTER, with whom Justice GINSBURG joins, dissenting.

Indiana's "Voter ID Law" threatens to impose nontrivial burdens on the voting right of tens of thousands of the State's citizens, and a significant percentage of those individuals are likely to be deterred from voting. The statute is unconstitutional under the balancing standard of *Burdick v. Takushi,* 504 U.S. 428 (1992): a State may not burden the right to vote merely by invoking abstract interests, be they legitimate, or even compelling, but must make a particular, factual showing that threats to its interests outweigh the particular impediments it has imposed. The State has made no such justification here, and as to some aspects of its law, it has hardly even tried. . . .

II

Under *Burdick,* "the rigorousness of our inquiry into the propriety of a state election law depends upon the extent to which a challenged regulation burdens First and Fourteenth Amendment rights," 504 U.S. at 434, upon an assessment of the "character and magnitude of the asserted [threatened] injury," *ibid.* (quoting *Anderson, supra,* at 789), and an estimate of the number of voters likely to be affected.

A

The first set of burdens shown in these cases is the travel costs and fees necessary to get one of the limited variety of federal or state photo identifications needed to cast a regular ballot under the Voter ID Law. The travel is required for the personal visit to a license branch of the Indiana Bureau of Motor Vehicles (BMV), which is demanded of anyone applying for a driver's license or nondriver photo identification. The need to travel to a BMV branch will affect voters according to their circumstances, with the average person probably viewing it as nothing more than an inconvenience. Poor, old, and disabled voters who do not drive a car, however, may find the trip prohibitive, witness the fact that the BMV has far fewer license branches in each county than there are voting precincts. Marion County, for example, has over 900 active voting precincts, yet only 12 BMV license branches; in Lake County, there are 565 active voting precincts, to match up with only 8 BMV locations; and Allen County, with 309 active voting precincts, has only 3 BMV license branches. The same pattern holds in counties with smaller populations. Brown County has 12 active voter precincts, and only one BMV office; while there were 18 polling places available in Fayette County's 2007 municipal primary, there was only 1 BMV license branch; and Henry County, with 42 polling places approved for 2008 elections, has only 1 BMV office.

The burden of traveling to a more distant BMV office rather than a conveniently located polling place is probably serious for many of the individuals who lack photo identification. They almost certainly will not own cars, and public transportation in Indiana is fairly limited. According to a report published by Indiana's Department of Transportation in August 2007, 21 of Indiana's 92 counties have no public transportation system at all, and as of 2000, nearly 1 in every 10 voters lived within 1 of these 21 counties. Among the counties with some public system, 21 provide service only within certain cities, and 32 others restrict public transportation to regional county service, leaving only 18 that offer countywide public transportation. . . .

Although making voters travel farther than what is convenient for most and possible for some does not amount to a "severe" burden under *Burdick,* that is no reason to ignore the burden altogether. It translates into an obvious economic cost (whether in work time lost, or getting and paying for transportation) that an Indiana voter must bear to obtain an ID.

For those voters who can afford the roundtrip, a second financial hurdle appears; in order to get photo identification for the first time, they need to present " 'a birth certificate, a certificate of naturalization, U.S. veterans photo identification, U.S. military photo identification, or a U.S. passport.' " As the lead opinion says, the two most common of these documents come at a price: Indiana counties charge anywhere from $3 to $12 for a birth certificate (and in some other States the fee is significantly higher), and that same price must usually be paid for a first-time passport, since a birth certificate is required to prove U.S. citizenship by birth. The total fees for a passport, moreover, are up to about $100. So most voters must pay at least one fee to get the ID necessary to cast a regular ballot. As with the travel costs, these fees are far from shocking on their face, but in the *Burdick* analysis it matters that both the travel costs and the fees are disproportionately heavy for, and thus disproportionately likely to deter, the poor, the old, and the immobile.

B

To be sure, Indiana has a provisional-ballot exception to the ID requirement for individuals the State considers "indigent" as well as those with religious objections to being photographed, and this sort of exception could in theory provide a way around the costs of procuring an ID. But Indiana's chosen exception does not amount to much relief.

The law allows these voters who lack the necessary ID to sign the poll book and cast a provisional ballot. Ind. Code Ann. §3-11-8-25.1. As the lead opinion recognizes, though, that is only the first step; to have the provisional ballot counted, a voter must then appear in person before the circuit court clerk or county election board within 10 days of the election, to sign an affidavit attesting to indigency or religious objection to being photographed (or to present an ID at that point). Unlike the trip to the BMV (which, assuming things go smoothly, needs to be made only once every four years for renewal of nondriver photo identification, this one must be taken every time a poor person or religious objector wishes to vote, because the State does not allow an affidavit to count in successive elections. And unlike the trip to the BMV (which at least has a handful of license branches in the more populous counties), a county has only one county seat. Forcing these people to travel to the county seat every time they try to vote is particularly onerous for the reason noted already, that most counties in Indiana either lack public transportation or offer only limited coverage.

That the need to travel to the county seat each election amounts to a high hurdle is shown in the results of the 2007 municipal elections in Marion County, to which Indiana's Voter ID Law applied. Thirty-four provisional ballots were cast, but only two provisional voters made it to the County Clerk's Office within the 10 days. All 34 of these aspiring voters appeared at the appropriate precinct; 33 of them provided a signature, and every signature matched the one on file; and 26 of the 32 voters whose ballots were not counted had a history of voting in Marion County elections.

All of this suggests that provisional ballots do not obviate the burdens of getting photo identification. And even if that were not so, the provisional-ballot option would be inadequate for a further reason: the indigency exception by definition offers no relief to those voters who do not consider themselves (or would not be considered) indigent but as a practical matter would find it hard, for nonfinancial reasons, to get the required ID (most obviously the disabled).

C

Indiana's Voter ID Law thus threatens to impose serious burdens on the voting right, even if not "severe" ones, and the next question under *Burdick* is whether the number of individuals likely to be affected is significant as well. Record evidence and facts open to judicial notice answer yes.

Although the District Court found that petitioners failed to offer any reliable empirical study of numbers of voters affected, we may accept that court's rough calculation that 43,000 voting-age residents lack the kind of identification card required by Indiana's law. The District Court made that estimate by comparing BMV records reproduced in petitioners' statistician's report with U.S. Census Bureau figures for Indiana's voting-age population in 2004, and the State does not argue that these raw data are unreliable.

The State, in fact, shows no discomfort with the District Court's finding that an "estimated 43,000 individuals" (about 1% of the State's voting-age population) lack a qualifying ID. Brief for Respondents in No. 07-25, p. 25. If the State's willingness to take that number is surprising, it may be less so in light of the District Court's observation that "several factors . . . suggest the percentage of Indiana's voting age population with photo identification is actually lower than 99%," 458 F. Supp. 2d at 807, n.43, a suggestion in line with national surveys showing roughly 6-10% of voting-age Americans without a state-issued photo-identification card.

So a fair reading of the data supports the District Court's finding that around 43,000 Indiana residents lack the needed identification, and will bear the burdens the law imposes. . . .

The upshot is this. Tens of thousands of voting-age residents lack the necessary photo identification. A large proportion of them are likely to be in bad shape economically. The Voter ID Law places hurdles in the way of either getting an ID or of voting provisionally, and they translate into nontrivial economic costs. There is accordingly no reason to doubt that a significant number of state residents will be discouraged or disabled from voting. . . .

Thus, petitioners' case is clearly strong enough to prompt more than a cursory examination of the State's asserted interests. And the fact that Indiana's photo identification requirement is one of the most restrictive in the country makes a critical examination of the State's claims all the more in order.

III

Because the lead opinion finds only "limited" burdens on the right to vote, it avoids a hard look at the State's claimed interests. But having found the Voter ID Law burdens far from trivial, I have to make a rigorous assessment of " 'the precise interests put forward by the State as justifications for the burden imposed by its rule,' [and] 'the extent to which those interests make it necessary to burden the plaintiff's rights.' " *Burdick*, 504 U.S. at 434 (quoting *Anderson*, 460 U.S. at 789).

A

. . . There is no denying the abstract importance, the compelling nature, of combating voter fraud. But it takes several steps to get beyond the level of abstraction here.

To begin with, requiring a voter to show photo identification before casting a regular ballot addresses only one form of voter fraud: in-person voter impersonation. The photo ID requirement leaves untouched the problems of absentee-ballot fraud, which (unlike in-person voter impersonation) is a documented problem in Indiana; of registered voters voting more than once (but maintaining their own identities) in different counties or in different States; of felons and other disqualified individuals voting in their own names; of vote buying; or, for that matter, of ballot-stuffing, ballot miscounting, voter intimidation, or any other type of corruption on the part of officials administering elections.

And even the State's interest in deterring a voter from showing up at the polls and claiming to be someone he is not must, in turn, be discounted for the fact that the State has not come across a single instance of in-person voter impersonation fraud in all of Indiana's history. Neither the District Court nor the Indiana General Assembly that passed the Voter ID Law was given any evidence whatsoever of in-person voter impersonation fraud in the State. This absence of support is consistent with the experience of several veteran poll watchers in Indiana, each of whom submitted testimony in the District Court that he had never witnessed an instance of attempted voter impersonation fraud at the polls. It is also consistent with the dearth of evidence of in-person voter impersonation in any other part of the country.

The State responds to the want of evidence with the assertion that in-person voter impersonation fraud is hard to detect. But this is like saying the "man who wasn't there" is hard to spot, and to know whether difficulty in detection accounts for the lack of evidence one at least has to ask whether in-person voter impersonation is (or would be) relatively harder to ferret out than other kinds of fraud (*e.g.*, by absentee ballot) which the State has had no trouble documenting. The answer seems to be no; there is reason to think that "impersonation of voters is . . . the most likely type of fraud to be discovered." U.S. Election Assistance Commission, *Election Crimes: An Initial Review and Recommendations for Future Study* 9 (Dec. 2006). . . .

In sum, fraud by individuals acting alone, however difficult to detect, is unlikely. And while there may be greater incentives for organized groups to engage in broad-gauged in-person voter impersonation fraud, it is also far more difficult to conceal larger enterprises of this sort. The State's argument about the difficulty of detecting the fraud lacks real force.

Nothing else the State has to say does much to bolster its case. The State argues, for example, that even without evidence of in-person voter impersonation in Indiana, it is enough for the State to show that "opportunities [for such fraud] are transparently obvious in elections without identification checks," Brief for Respondents in No. 07-25, p. 54. Of course they are, but Indiana elections before the Voter ID Law were not run "without identification checks"; on the contrary, as the Marion County Election Board informs us, "[t]ime-tested systems were in place to detect in-person voter impersonation fraud before the challenged statute was enacted," Brief for Respondents in No. 07-21, p. 6. These included hiring poll workers who were precinct residents familiar with the neighborhood, and making signature comparisons, each effort being supported by the criminal provisions mentioned before. *Id.*, at 6-8.

For that matter, the deterrence argument can do only so much work, since photo identification is itself hardly a failsafe against impersonation. Indiana knows this, and that is why in 2007 the State began to issue redesigned driver's licenses with digital watermarking.

Despite all this, I will readily stipulate that a State has an interest in responding to the risk (however small) of in-person voter impersonation. . . .

The State's asserted interests in modernizing elections and combating fraud are decidedly modest; at best, they fail to offset the clear inference that thousands of Indiana citizens will be discouraged from voting. The two remaining justifications, meanwhile, actually weaken the State's case. . . .

The State is simply trying to take advantage of its own wrong: if it is true that the State's fear of in-person voter impersonation fraud arises from its bloated voter checklist, the answer to the problem is in the State's own hands. The claim that the State has an interest in addressing a symptom of the problem (alleged impersonation) rather than the problem itself (the negligently maintained bloated rolls) is thus self-defeating; it shows that the State has no justifiable need to burden the right to vote as it does, and it suggests that the State is not as serious about combating fraud as it claims to be.

The State's final justification, its interest in safeguarding voter confidence, similarly collapses. The problem with claiming this interest lies in its connection to the bloated voter rolls; the State has come up with nothing to suggest that its citizens doubt the integrity of the State's electoral process, except its own failure to maintain its rolls. The answer to this problem is not to burden the right to vote, but to end the official negligence. . . . .

Without a shred of evidence that in-person voter impersonation is a problem in the State, much less a crisis, Indiana has adopted one of the most restrictive photo identification requirements in the country. . . .

If more were needed to condemn this law, our own precedent would provide it, for the calculation revealed in the Indiana statute crosses a line when it targets the poor and the weak. If the Court's decision in *Harper v. Virginia Bd. of Elections*, 383 U.S. 663 (1966), stands for anything, it is that being poor has nothing to do with being qualified to vote. . . . The State's requirements here, that people without cars travel to a motor vehicle registry and that the poor who fail to do that get to their county seats within 10 days of every election, likewise translate into unjustified economic burdens uncomfortably close to the outright $1.50 fee we struck down 42 years ago. Like that fee, the onus of the Indiana law is illegitimate just because it correlates with no state interest so well as it does with the object of deterring poorer residents from exercising the franchise. . . .

———————

» *Voter ID Requirements Following* **Crawford.**   Following the decision in *Craw-ford*, several states enacted new photo ID requirements, and the pace of adoption rose following the Supreme Court's decision in *Shelby County* halting Justice Department preclearance of voting regulations in states previously covered under Section 4 of the Voting Rights Act. At present, 19 states require voters to produce photographic identification at the polling place. Fifteen states require no presentation of ID at all, while the rest require identification, but accept non-photographic forms. The stringency of ID requirements closely tracks partisan control of state government.

Empirical studies of the actual impact of photo ID requirements have produced equivocal results. On one hand, such studies consistently show that the overwhelming majority of voters possess compliant ID, even in states with strict requirements. On the other hand, although the number of voters disqualified for lack of compliant ID is generally small, the impact is not distributed evenly across populations: black, Hispanic, and elderly voters are less likely to possess compliant photo ID. One recent study estimates that "minority voters are 2.5 to 6 times more likely to lack photo identification than white voters." Phoebe Henninger, *et al.*, *Who Votes without Identification? Using Individual-Level Administrative Data to Measure the Burden of Strict Voter Identification Laws*, 18 J. EMP. LEG. STUD. 256 (2021). Often, the disparate impact of voter ID laws seems intentional, and indeed quite deliberately crafted. For example, in Texas and Tennessee, acceptable forms of voter identification include gun licenses but not student ID cards. In invalidating a North Carolina law imposing strict photo ID requirements, the U.S. Court of Appeals for the Fourth Circuit noted that the law "retained only those types of photo ID disproportionately held by whites and excluded those disproportionately held by African Americans." *N.C. State Conference NAACP v. McCrory*, 831 F.3d 204, 216 (4th Cir. 2016).

On the other hand, although some studies have reported a slight drop in voter turnout after the introduction of photo ID requirements, in at least some cases turnout actually *increased* following adoption of such laws. *See* Eugene D. Mazo, *Finding Common Ground on Voter ID Laws*, 49 U. MEMPHIS L. REV. 1233 (2019); Daniel J. Hopkins, *et al.*, *Voting but for the Law: Evidence from Virginia on Photo Identification Requirements*, 14 J. EMP. LEG. STUD. 79 (2017).

At the same time, there is evidence that the introduction of strict voter ID requirements increases public perceptions of the integrity of the election, even if such laws actually contribute little or nothing to electoral integrity. Increased trust in elections can itself increase voter turnout. *See* Kyle Endres and Costas Panagopoulos, *Photo Identification Laws and Perceptions of Electoral Fraud*, 8 RES. & POLS. __

(2021). Nevertheless, the effect may be otherwise among the most directly affected populations. Consider the following analysis:

> [Vote] suppression occurs via complexity and chaos. Potential voters will find no Bull Connors or Klansmen either at polling places or in local election boards. Instead, when they seek to vote, they will encounter confusion and ambiguity, or often not encounter the appropriate information at all. It is not Jim Crow but Kafka. Voter ID turns the exercise of a constitutional right into a supplication for a government benefit. The voting booth becomes the welfare office. . . .
>
> Voter ID, by its very nature, generates inconvenience, annoyance, and difficulty for low-income citizens. [These] seem like minor barriers, but they can form formidable barriers to participation, in any government or private program. . . . [I]nconvenience, annoyance, and difficulty are *costs*: they demand resources of time, energy, and money that are scarce for everyone, and especially for low-income people. . . . Like recycling or any "large-number small-payoff" problem, people lack strong incentives to perform a particular act. But if that is the case, then raising the costs of voting, particularly for those who lack resources to begin with, can achieve a significant reduction in voting.

Jonathan Zasloff, *Jim Crow as Kafka: Voter Suppression on the Ground*, UCLA Public Law & Legal Theory Research Paper No. 19-46 (Dec. 4, 2019).

≫ *Voter ID in the Courts.* New, strict voter ID requirements continue to generate litigation in the lower courts. In the federal courts, most ID requirements have been upheld against facial challenge, often because more recently enacted statutes have for the most part made compliance easier than the Indiana statute upheld in *Crawford. See, e.g., Frank v. Walker*, 768 F.3d 744 (7th Cir. 2014) (upholding Wisconsin photo ID requirement); *Lee v. Virginia State Board of Elections*, 843 F.3d 592 (4th Cir. 2016) (upholding Virginia's statute). However, where photo ID requirements are unusually harsh in operation, or can be shown to have a racially discriminatory impact or to have been motivated by racial animus, federal courts have been willing to strike them down. *See Veasey v. Abbott*, 796 F.3d 487 (5th Cir. 2015) (invalidating Texas voter ID requirement as a violation of Section 2 of the Voting Rights Act); *N.C. State Conference NAACP v. McCrory*, 831 F.3d 204, 227 (4th Cir. 2016) (invalidating North Carolina voter ID law on the ground that it "retained only those types of photo ID disproportionately held by whites and excluded those disproportionately held by African Americans"). Moreover, although *Crawford* has been understood to counsel skepticism toward facial attacks on voter ID statutes, federal courts have been willing to entertain as-applied claims when particular individuals can show undue hardship to themselves and others similarly situated. *See Frank v. Walker*, 819 F.3d 384 (7th Cir. 2016).

Another route to challenging voter ID requirements lies in state court under state constitutional law. State constitutions frequently contain provisions protecting or regulating voting and democratic processes in ways that have no counterpart under the federal Constitution, and *Crawford* has no binding effect on how state courts interpret these or any other provisions of state constitutions. Immediately following *Crawford*, a challenge to Indiana's voter identification law was brought in state court under the Indiana Constitution. The plaintiffs argued that the photo identification requirement established a new and unauthorized substantive qualification for voting, a contention the Indiana Supreme Court rejected on the ground that voter identification requirements are administrative in nature and thus do not establish substantive qualifications for eligibility to vote. The plaintiffs also raised a facial challenge under Indiana's Equal Privileges and Immunities Clause, the state constitutional equivalent of the federal Equal Protection Clause. The court rejected this claim, but held that future as-applied challenges might be brought by particular classes of voters actually affected unequally by the law. *League of Women Voters of Indiana v. Rokita*, 929 N.E.2d 758 (Ind. 2010).

In another case brought under a state constitution, the Missouri Supreme Court invalidated a photo ID requirement on the ground that it unconstitutionally burdened the right to vote. *Weinschenk v. State*, 203 S.W.3d 201 (Mo. 2006). The court relied on a provision of the Missouri Constitution expressly granting the right to vote, holding that "the more expansive and concrete protection of the right to vote under the Missouri Constitution [confers] greater protection than its federal counterpart." *Id.* at 212. This ruling was overturned by voters in 2016, who approved an amendment to the Missouri Constitution specifically overruling the result in *Weinschenk*. Results in subsequent state constitutional challenges to voter ID laws in state courts have been mixed. For example, in a ruling sustaining Oklahoma's voter ID requirement, the Oklahoma Supreme Court held that "the lack of evidence of in-person voter fraud in the state is not a barrier to reasonable preventative legislation." *Gentges v. Oklahoma State Election Board*, 419 P.3d 224, 231 (2018). For an overview, see Joshua A. Douglas, *State Judges and the Right to Vote*, 77 Ohio St. L.J. 1, 14-21 (2016).

>> *Analogies to ID Requirements in Other Contexts.*　It is sometimes argued that the requirement of photographic identification is so routine and uncontroversial in so many other contexts—boarding a plane, cashing a check, buying alcohol, and so forth—that the objection to requiring it in voting is therefore puzzling. Consider the following response:

> While a photo-identification requirement in voting and other contexts aims to ensure that a person is who she represents herself to be and/or meets particular qualifications, the costs of erroneous exclusion differ with voting. John Fund, for example, asserts that the Clinton administration hypocritically pushed for photo-identification requirements for cigarette purchases but opposed such requirements for voting. But for those who consider widespread participation a critical democratic value, erroneously preventing a legitimate voter from casting a ballot poses more harm than erroneously preventing a twenty-two-year-old adult from buying cigarettes.
>
> Erroneous exclusion of air travelers or legitimate credit-card users who lack photo identification may inconvenience individuals and slow the economy, but these harms are different not only with respect to the type of harm they prevent, but also in their motivations. In the airline and commercial contexts, participants do not have "votes" that are weighed relative to one another to assess the will of the entire citizenry and determine who will govern society. Liquor stores, airlines, and

department stores generally lack incentives to exclude legitimate consumers, whereas some politicians benefit by reducing turnout among particular demographic populations likely to vote against them. While the benefits of deterring one terrorist outweigh the costs of excluding ten thousand "safe" air travelers who lack photo identification, the benefits of excluding one fraudulent voter do not outweigh the costs of excluding ten thousand legitimate voters. This paradox is all the more disconcerting because so many of those performing the calculus of voting regulation stand to gain from erring on the side of implementing rules that reduce turnout.

A similar cost-benefit analysis explains the lack of photo-identification requirements in many financial contexts. Merchants lose millions of dollars a year through credit card fraud, but they generally do not require photo identification or even a signature when individuals use a credit card at a gas pump or use credit card numbers online. Empirical data about the extent of fraudulent transactions and the true costs of a photo-identification requirement help individual merchants determine whether the requirement would increase or decrease expected profits.

Spencer Overton, *Voter Identification*, 105 MICH. L. REV. 631, 651 (2007).

3. HAVA and Election Technology

The discord and confusion surrounding the 2000 presidential election in Florida brought suddenly and dramatically to public attention a situation that few Americans had been aware of: elections in the United States are administered primarily on the local level, frequently by undertrained and under-resourced election administrators, using vote-counting technology that is often old, unreliable, and prone to error. The ensuing public outcry got Congress's attention, and in response it enacted the Help America Vote Act of 2002 (HAVA).

HAVA has three principal parts. The first part provides federal grants to states to improve and update their vote-counting technology. The second part creates a new federal agency, the Election Assistance Commission (EAC), to serve as a national clearinghouse for information on voting and election standards, practices, and technologies. The third piece of the legislation establishes standards to which states are required to adhere when administering federal elections, standards designed to prevent a repeat of the problems that appeared in Florida in 2000.

Under Section 102 of HAVA, federal grants are to be used mainly for the purpose of assisting states to replace punch card and lever voting machines with other, more reliable systems. Congress initially allocated $650 million for this purpose, creating an instantaneous market for voting technology that relied on optical scanning or touch-screen technology.

Title III of HAVA established uniform election technology requirements for federal elections. Under Section 301,

(a) Requirements. — Each voting system used in an election for Federal office shall meet the following requirements:

(1) In general.—

(A) [T]he voting system (including any lever voting system, optical scanning voting system, or direct recording electronic system) shall—

    (i) permit the voter to verify (in a private and independent manner) the votes selected by the voter on the ballot before the ballot is cast and counted;

    (ii) provide the voter with the opportunity (in a private and independent manner) to change the ballot or correct any error before the ballot is cast and counted (including the opportunity to correct the error through the issuance of a replacement ballot if the voter was otherwise unable to change the ballot or correct any error); and

    (iii) if the voter selects votes for more than one candidate for a single office—

        (I) notify the voter that the voter has selected more than one candidate for a single office on the ballot;

        (II) notify the voter before the ballot is cast and counted of the effect of casting multiple votes for the office; and

        (III) provide the voter with the opportunity to correct the ballot before the ballot is cast and counted.

Section 301(a)(2)(A) also requires that "[t]he voting system shall produce a permanent paper record with a manual audit capacity for such system."

Finally, in an effort to address the problem of differential hand recount standards identified in *Bush v. Gore*, Section 301(a)(6) provides: "Each State shall adopt uniform and nondiscriminatory standards that define what constitutes a vote and what will be counted as a vote for each category of voting system used in the State."

Perhaps the most important innovation of HAVA, however, is its establishment of a uniform procedure for casting "provisional" votes. Under Section 302(a), a state administering a federal election may not prohibit anyone who arrives at the polls from casting a ballot on the ground that he or she is ineligible to vote, or to vote at that particular polling place. Instead, each voter is permitted to vote a provisional ballot, which is maintained separately and then referred to state election officials for an investigation to determine whether the voter is in fact eligible and whether therefore the vote ought to be counted:

> If an individual declares that such individual is a registered voter in the jurisdiction in which the individual desires to vote and that the individual is eligible to vote in an election for Federal office, but the name of the individual does not appear on the official list of eligible voters for the polling place or an election official asserts that the individual is not eligible to vote, such individual shall be permitted to cast a provisional ballot as follows: . . .
>
> (2) The individual shall be permitted to cast a provisional ballot at that polling place upon the execution of a written affirmation by the individual before an election official at the polling place stating that the individual is—

(A) a registered voter in the jurisdiction in which the individual desires to vote; and

(B) eligible to vote in that election.

(3) An election official at the polling place shall transmit the ballot cast by the individual or the voter information contained in the written affirmation executed by the individual under paragraph (2) to an appropriate State or local election official for prompt verification under paragraph (4).

(4) If the appropriate State or local election official to whom the ballot or voter information is transmitted under paragraph (3) determines that the individual is eligible under State law to vote, the individual's provisional ballot shall be counted as a vote in that election in accordance with State law.

This system is obviously designed to prevent the loss of eligible votes as the result of administrative error, and to replace systems in which voters erroneously deemed to be ineligible are turned away with a system of "vote now, verify later" in order to preserve potentially eligible votes.

How well has HAVA worked? According to one commentator, "As sensible as HAVA's requirements might appear on paper, they have proven an enormous challenge to implement in practice." Daniel P. Tokaji, *Early Returns on Election Reform: Discretion, Disenfranchisement, and the Help America Vote Act*, 73 GEO. WASH. L. REV. 1206 (2005). Congress has not provided adequate financing. States have lagged in replacing obsolete voting equipment. Poorly trained poll workers have often failed correctly to implement the provisional voting requirement, causing the loss of many thousands of probably eligible votes. Elections have been plagued by litigation, often involving last-minute challenges to administrative decisions that invite judicial disruption of carefully laid plans. Moreover, some improvements facilitated by HAVA, such as updating of voting technology, may have had unintended consequences. For example, some of the new technology is costlier than the old technology to support and maintain, and as federal funding for HAVA mandates is phased out, states and localities have had to pick up the bill, sometimes causing them to skimp on other aspects of election administration that contribute as much or more to the accuracy and legitimacy of outcomes as superior voting technology. *See* MARTHA KROPF AND DAVID C. KIMBALL, HELPING AMERICA VOTE: THE LIMITS OF ELECTION REFORM (2012).

Stewart v. Blackwell

444 F.3d 843 (6th Cir. 2006)

The plaintiffs are African-American and Caucasian voters residing in Hamilton, Montgomery, Sandusky, and Summit Counties in Ohio. They filed their complaint on October 11, 2002 alleging that: (1) the use of unreliable, deficient voting equipment, including the punch card ballot, in some Ohio counties but not other counties violates the Equal Protection Clause of the Fourteenth Amendment; (2) the use of error prone voting equipment deprives voters of their due process right to have their votes counted accurately; and (3) the use of punch card voting systems in Hamilton, Montgomery, and Summit Counties has a disparate impact on African-American voters in violation of Section 2 of the Voting Rights Act of 1965. The plaintiffs sought declaratory and injunctive relief prohibiting the defendants from: (1) continuing to allow the use of "non-notice" and deficient punch card and optical scan voting equipment in some Ohio counties while using more reliable voting equipment in other counties; (2) using non-notice punch card voting equipment in Hamilton, Montgomery, and Summit Counties; and (3) using non-notice optical scan voting systems in Sandusky County. . . .

I

A. Background Information on Voting Technology

Ohio law empowers the Secretary of State to certify voting equipment. Ohio Rev. Code §3506.15. The Secretary has certified two general types of equipment: (1) "Notice" equipment such as Digital Recording Electronic (DRE) and precinct-count optical scan equipment that prevent overvotes (when a voter votes for more than the permissible number of candidates for a given office) and warn voters when they are casting undervotes (when a voter does not vote in a particular race or votes for fewer candidates than is permissible for a given office) — together, overvotes and undervotes are referred to as "residual votes"; and (2) "Non-notice" equipment such as punch card and central-count optical scan equipment that do not provide notice of and the opportunity to correct residual votes. In the 2000 general election, approximately 72.5% of Ohio voters used non-notice equipment and 27.5% used notice equipment.

In the 2000 general election, the most frequently used equipment in Ohio was the Votomatic punch card, a non-notice system that relies on a ballot card with pre-scored, square perforations or "chad" that correspond to the names of the candidates listed in an accompanying booklet. Names of candidates or other identifying information for ballot measures do not appear on the actual ballot. The punch card system does not provide independent notice of an overvote or undervote. A vote is recorded by the machine when light passes through the detached holes. Problems with the machines can cause "hanging chad" that remain attached to the ballot by one, two, or three corners; "pierced chad" that are penetrated by the stylus but not dislodged from the ballot; and "dimpled chad" that are dented but not penetrated or dislodged. Because of these inherent chad problems, light often cannot pass through the holes and a vote is not recorded. Problems inherent in the punch card machines are sometimes caused by the build up of chads which may make it difficult or impossible to cleanly punch the card and record a vote.

Optical scan systems resemble answer sheets used in standardized testing. The voter is given a ballot listing the names of all candidates and ballot initiatives and either uses a pencil to darken the circle next to the preferred candidate or draws a straight line connecting two parts of an arrow. Optical scan systems can be either precinct-count systems, which enable voters to scan the ballot at the polling place thereby providing independent notice of and an opportunity to correct residual votes, or central-count systems, which do not provide independent notice or the opportunity to correct mistakes.

Electronic DRE machines come in several varieties, but most often resemble automated teller machines or ATMs used at banks. Voters either touch the name of the preferred candidate on the screen or press a button that corresponds to the preferred candidate. All forms of DRE technology currently used in Ohio make it impossible to overvote for the same office or ballot initiative. DRE systems can also be programmed to warn voters if their ballots contain undervotes. DRE systems (like precinct-count optical scan systems), therefore, provide independent notice of residual votes.

In the 2000 general election, sixty-nine of eighty-eight Ohio counties used punch card ballots. Eleven counties used optical scan equipment, six used electronic equipment, and two used automatic or "lever" voting machines. These systems utilize different methods of reading and counting votes. Some of the systems allow voters to check their ballots for residual votes. For example, one county and part of another county utilized precinct-count optical scan equipment, and six others use electronic voting equipment that allows a voter to verify their ballot on a screen before the final ballot is cast. Most systems, however, including the ones operated by the four county defendants, scan and count ballots at a central location after the polls have closed. Thus, in total, eighty-one of eighty-eight Ohio counties used non-independent-notice equipment—voting technology that does not provide a voter with notice from the voting device that a problem might exist before the ballot is finally cast—in the 2000 general election.

Only three counties collected statistics on overvotes—Hamilton County, which had 2,916 overvotes, Summit County, which had 1,470 overvotes, and Montgomery County, which had 2,469 overvotes. This is a total of 6,855 overvotes in those three counties, which represents approximately 34% of the total residual votes cast in those counties. Franklin County used notice technology and there were zero overvotes.

B. The Statistical Evidence

The plaintiffs' expert, Dr. Martha Kropf, testified regarding estimates of intentional and unintentional undervoting based on data collected by National Elections Studies and the Voters News Survey in exit polls and surveys in presidential elections between 1980 and 1996. Kropf testified that intentional undervoting in presidential elections is a relatively rare event that is estimated to involve between .23% and .75% of all residual votes. Dr. Kropf concluded that when levels of undervoting exceed this threshold and vary by equipment it is probable that they resulted from unintentional undervoting that is associated with problems of the punch card ballot. She also found no difference between African-American and non African-American voters in levels of intentional undervotes. Kropf measured the performance of voting equipment by examining presidential and U.S. Senate races at the top of the ballot because these are statewide elections where all voters face the same candidates, and media coverage, levels of candidate competition, and voter mobilization are relatively uniform. Kropf reported an overall statewide residual vote rate of 2.29% for punch card systems and 2.14% for central-count optical scans. That is, voters in punch card counties are approximately four times as likely not to have their votes counted as a voter using reliable electronic voting equipment. In some counties specific precincts encountered more severe problems with residual voting. In Akron City Precinct 3-F the residual vote rate was 15% and in Dayton City's 14th Ward Precinct C the residual vote rate was 17%.* In addition, the counties in Ohio experiencing the highest percentage of residual votes in the 2000 presidential election were those in which voters used punch card technology while the counties experiencing the lowest percentage of residual votes used other technology. The twenty-nine counties in Ohio with the highest residual vote percentages were all counties that used punch card machines; the seven counties with the lowest residual vote percentages were all counties that did not use punch card machines as their primary voting system.

Roy Saltman, formerly of the National Bureau of Standards and the author of two federal studies on the use of computers in vote tallying testified that his studies "demonstrate that punch cards are inherently fragile, and they become less stable when ballots are handled or manipulated or sent through a reader, resulting in overvotes, undervotes, and inconsistent vote tabulations." Saltman explained that lost votes are not attributable solely to voters' failure to follow instructions. According to Saltman, "[w]hen the ballot is then handled or manipulated or sent through a reader, it is more likely that additional chads will be dislodged and fall out. And if that happens, the votes indicated on the ballot are changed because the presence of holes indicates votes." Dana Walch, Director of Election Reform for the Ohio Secretary of State's Office, confirmed the plaintiffs' evidence that there is "a higher residual vote rate in punch card counties than in . . . counties with other types of voting technology." Walch further testified that problems with the punch card ballots "were the result of some physical failure of the ballot or voter error. . . ." In response to this evidence, the district court acknowledged that "running the punch card ballots repeated times through the counting machinery will result in different results."

The Caltech MIT Voting Technology Project report—a joint venture between the two institutions to study, in part, the reliability of existing voting equipment—which is referenced throughout the record, is also informative. As the report notes, that "[i]f voting equipment has no effect on the ability of voters to express their preferences, then the residual vote should be unrelated to machine types." *See* Caltech-MIT Voting Technology Project, *Residual Votes Attributable to Technology: An Assessment of the Reliability of Existing Voting Equipment* (Version 2: March 30, 2001), available at http://www.vote.caltech.edu (last accessed April 1, 2006). The report concluded that the error rate from punch cards is 50 percent higher than other technologies and that the pattern holds up when "holding constant turnout, income, racial composition of counties, age distribution of counties, literacy rates, the year of a shift in technology, the number of offices and candidates on the ballot, and other factors that operate in a county or in a particular year." Report at 22. In conclusion, the report stated that "[t]he incidence of such residual votes with punch card methods . . . is forty to seventy percent higher than the incidence of residual votes with the other technologies," Report at 17, and cautioned that "[i]f election administrators wish to avoid catastrophic failures, they may heed th[is] warning . . . Stop using punch cards," Report at 11. . . .

_____

* The 2000 presidential election in Ohio was decided by a margin of 3.51%.

Finally, in response to the legislature's slow response to the electoral problems, the Secretary of State wrote a letter stating that "the possibility of a close election with punch cards as the state's primary voting device invites a Florida-like calamity."

C. The Plaintiffs' Voting Rights Act Claim

On their Voting Rights Act claim, the plaintiffs alleged that the punch card system used in Hamilton, Montgomery, and Summit Counties produces a higher residual vote rate for African-American voters than for white voters. The plaintiffs presented regression analysis that the correlation between overvoting and the percentage of African-American voters in a given precinct in Hamilton County was .517 and in Summit County it was .682. The plaintiffs' experts characterized these correlations as "strong." In Montgomery County, where only data of overvotes mixed with undervotes was available at the precinct level, there was a smaller, but nevertheless "strong" .440 correlation.

The plaintiffs' expert, Dr. Richard Engstrom, analyzed the data based on methods of statistical analysis approved by the Supreme Court and other federal courts in voting rights cases. . . . Dr. Engstrom concluded that: (1) African-Americans in Hamilton County overvoted at a rate seven times higher than non African-Americans; (2) in Summit County, African-Americans overvoted at a rate nine times higher than non African-Americans; and (3) in Montgomery County (where only combined over and undervote statistics are available on a precinct basis), African-Americans had a residual voting rate 2.5 times that of non African-Americans. In contrast to the three punch card counties, Franklin County had no overvotes because it used DRE machines that prevent overvoting.

Based on this information, Dr. Engstrom testified that punch card equipment interacts with socioeconomic conditions, resulting in statistically significant disparities between the levels of residual voting among African-American and non African-American voters. . . .

III

A. The Right to Vote

Voting is a fundamental right. For more than a century the Supreme Court has acknowledged the fundamental nature of the right to vote. *See Yick Wo v. Hopkins*, 118 U.S. 356, 371 (1886). "Especially since the right to exercise the franchise in a free and unimpaired manner is preservative of other basic civil and political rights, any alleged infringement of the right of citizens to vote must be carefully and meticulously scrutinized." *Reynolds*, 377 U.S. at 562.

In *Bush v. Gore*, 531 U.S. 98 (2000), the Court emphasized that states, after granting the right to vote on equal terms, "may not, by later arbitrary and disparate treatment, value one person's vote over that of another." *Id.* at 104-05. That is, the right to vote encompasses "more than the initial allocation of the franchise. Equal protection applies as well to the manner of its exercise." *Id.* . . .

IV

Supreme Court precedent and our own *Mixon* framework instructs that if the Ohio statute permitting localities to use deficient voting technology "infringe[s] on the right to vote," then strict scrutiny applies; if the statute does not "infringe on the right to vote," and merely regulates some tangential aspect of the franchise, then rational basis review applies. *Mixon,* 193 F.3d at 402. This begs the question of what the "right to vote" encompasses. We easily conclude that the right to have one's vote counted on equal terms is part of the right to vote. No other conclusion is possible from the case law and thus, strict scrutiny applies.

All of the precedent indicates that having one's vote properly counted is fundamental to the franchise. *See e.g., Bush,* 531 U.S. at 104-05 (indicating that having one's vote counted on equal terms with others in the relevant jurisdiction is the quintessential "right to vote" case); *Reynolds,* 377 U.S. at 555 ("[T]he right of suffrage can be denied by a debasement or dilution of the weight of a citizen's vote just as effectively as by wholly prohibiting the free exercise of the franchise."); *Classic,* 313 U.S. at 315 ("Obviously included within the right to choose, secured by the Constitution, is the right of qualified voters within a state to cast their ballots and have them counted."); 42 U.S.C. 1973l(c)(1) (defining the right to vote to include "having such ballot counted properly and included in the appropriate total of votes cast"). Case law, statutory definitions, and common sense indicate that the "right to vote" is infringed in this case by the use of the two deficient technologies challenged by the plaintiffs. . . .

Strict scrutiny requires us to determine whether the use of the two challenged technologies in some jurisdictions but not others is a practice "narrowly tailored to further compelling governmental interests." *Grutter v. Bollinger,* 539 U.S. 306, 326 (2003). Under this standard, the State's proffered justifications of cost and training are wholly insufficient to sustain its continued certification of the technologies. Administrative convenience is simply not a compelling justification in light of the fundamental nature of the right. Moreover, Ohio's reliance on the cost of upgrading the technology fails in light of the monies already devoted to the process. Additionally, Ohio has used cost as if it were a silver bullet. Any change from the status quo necessarily involves some cost. The State has failed to put forth any evidence indicating that it cannot manage the costs and instead, the evidence indicates that the State has either budgeted for the transition from its own funds or through funds provided by the federal government. The mere fact that there is some cost involved does not make that factor compelling. Further, the State's alleged concern with voter fraud, likewise, in this case, is not compelling in light of the Secretary of State's report concluding that the technology can securely be implemented. *See also* HB 262, 125 Gen. Assem., Reg. Sess. (Ohio 2004). Finding no compelling reason supporting the State's continued certification of the deficient non-notice technology, *i.e.,* punch-card system and central-count optical scan systems, and in light of the fundamental nature of the right to vote, the State's actions violate the Equal Protection Clause. The continued certification of this technology by the Secretary of State does not provide the minimal adequate procedural safeguards to prevent the unconstitutional dilution of votes based on where a voter resides. *See Bush,* 531 U.S. at 109. Unequal treatment and unfairness are perpetrated by allowing this technology to remain certified and the State's reasons for maintaining this disparate system are far from compelling.

Our decision is consistent with binding Supreme Court precedent. In *Harper,* the Supreme Court held that using wealth or ability to pay as a factor in the power of the franchise "is to introduce a capricious or irrelevant factor." *Harper*, 383 U.S. at 668. Likewise, the maintenance of disparate technologies—that the State itself has recognized is inherently flawed and that "[t]he evidence is overwhelming that thousands of Ohio voters have been disenfranchised by antiquated voting equipment"—debases and devalues citizens' votes and is arbitrary and capricious. The technology provided to a voter by the State, like that voter's wealth, has no relation to voting qualifications or the value of that vote. "[T]he right to vote is too precious, too fundamental to be so burdened or conditioned." *Harper*, 383 U.S. at 670.

Furthermore, as in *Reynolds:*

> Overweighing and overvaluation of the votes of those living [in a county with adequate technology] has the certain effect of dilution and under-valuation of the voters of those living [in a county with deficient technology]. The resulting discrimination against those individual voters living in disfavored areas is easily demonstrable mathematically. Their right to vote is simply not the same right to vote as that of those living in a favored part of the State. . . . Weighting the votes of citizens differently, *by any method or means,* merely because of where they happen to reside, hardly seems justifiable.

377 U.S. at 563 (emphasis added). By maintaining a system in which these two technologies are utilized, voters in Ohio vote under two separate standards. Although voters approach the polls with the opportunity to vote in the same elections for the same candidates, once they step into the voting booth, they have an unequal chance of their vote being counted, *not* as a result of any action on the part of the voter, but because of the different technology utilized. Voters able to utilize notice technology choose candidates and before their vote is turned in and counted, the technology notifies them of any errors that would result in the vote being disregarded. Those voters forced to use non-notice technology are not notified of any errors in their ballot and, should errors exist, their votes are disregarded; moreover, voters using the two challenged technologies have an additional likelihood of disenfranchisement due to the inherent deficiencies of the punch-card and central-count optical scan. . . .

Although we apply strict scrutiny, we note that the use of this technology would also fail under rational basis review. . . . An individual's vote is the lifeblood of a democracy. To that extent, we find it difficult to conjure up what the State's legitimate interest is by the use of technology that dilutes the right to vote. The State says that its interests in failing to decertify non-notice and substandard technology is based on the cost of replacement and training workers on the new machines. We fail to see how the interest is justified or rational at the expense of tens of thousands of votes.

V

The Plaintiff's Voting Rights Act Claim

Section 2(a) of the Act prohibits the use of any electoral practice or procedure that "results in a denial or abridgement of the right of any citizen of the United

States to vote on account of race or color. . . ." The right to vote is defined in 42 U.S.C. §1973l(c)(1) to include "all action necessary to make a vote effective" including "casting a ballot and having such ballot counted properly." The language of the Act clearly encompasses within the "right of any citizen of the United States to vote" the right to "hav[e] such ballot counted properly." Because the African-American plaintiffs claim that they are disproportionately denied the right to have their ballots counted properly, the district court erred in concluding that the plaintiffs did not state a claim for a violation of the right to vote under the Voting Rights Act.

Finding that the plaintiffs' evidence supports a denial of the right to vote, the next inquiry is under section 2(b) of the Act to determine whether the evidence establishes a violation of the Act. . . . The plaintiffs here alleged that punch cards in these three counties have a discriminatory effect and presented evidence to support their claim. The plaintiffs presented evidence demonstrating that "minority voters disproportionately reside in punch-card counties and that, even within those counties, punch-card machines discard minority votes at a higher rate." 344 F.3d at 918. . . . Because the plaintiffs properly stated a claim under the Act, the question then for the district court under Section 2(b), is whether under the totality of circumstances, the evidence demonstrates a discriminatory result. On remand, the district court will consider the voluminous amount of the plaintiffs' evidence. . . .

Before *Stewart* could be remanded, Ohio voluntarily abandoned the voting machines attacked by the plaintiffs. Consequently, in an appeal of the panel's decision to the en banc Sixth Circuit, the court sitting en banc vacated the panel's decision as moot. 473 F.3d 692 (6th Cir. 2007).

≫ *Race and Accurate Voting.* The plaintiffs in *Stewart* introduced evidence showing that the ability successfully to use various forms of voting technology is not randomly distributed in the voting population. Other studies have reached similar results. For example, one analysis of the 2000 presidential election voting patterns in south Florida counties with "large numbers of blacks, Hispanics, and registered Democrats" showed that "presidential overvotes were cast disproportionately by Democratically-inclined voters." Michael C. Herron and Jasjeet S. Sekhon, *Overvoting and Representation: An Examination of Overvoted Presidential Ballots in Broward and Miami-Dade Counties*, 22 ELECTORAL STUD. 21 (2003). *See also* Paul Moke and Richard B. Saphire, *The Voting Rights Act and the Racial Gap in Lost Votes*, 58 HASTINGS L.J. 1 (2006).

How would a Section 2 Voting Rights Act claim fare on the merits in these circumstances? What other kinds of evidence might a plaintiff need to produce to strengthen the claim?

≫ *Voting Technology and Security Risks.* An important consideration in the introduction of new technology to make voting easier and the tabulation of votes more reliable is its vulnerability to hacking. Experts have long warned against an overly hasty adoption of electronic voting methods because of the potential risks to the secrecy of the ballot and to the reliability of election results. *See, e.g.,* Caltech/MIT Voting Technology Project, *What Has Changed, What Hasn't, and What*

Needs Improvement (2013). During the 2016 election, the nature of these concerns changed dramatically. What had previously often been viewed as gloomy and speculative warnings from expert technicians suddenly took on great urgency when evidence emerged that hackers in Russia, possibly backed by the Russian government, had broken into the servers of the Democratic National Committee. As more evidence emerged, charges were made that the Russians had deliberately tried to interfere with the election to tilt the result in favor of Donald Trump. (There was no evidence, however, that the hacking actually changed any results.) *See, e.g.*, Eric Lipton et al., *The Perfect Weapon: How Russian Cyberpower Invaded the U.S.*, N.Y. Times, Dec. 13, 2016. Just before leaving office, President Obama directed that retaliatory measures be taken against Russia. What lessons should be drawn from this episode? Is there any effective way to preclude the risk of outside interference with American democracy?

Ironically, one of the most frequently criticized characteristics of the U.S. electoral system—its decentralization—emerged as one of the most important defenses against successful electronic tampering with presidential elections. The fact that election administration is conducted by thousands of localities, using different technologies, each with its own system for storing and maintaining records, provides substantial protection against catastrophic manipulation of the entire electoral system. Is this a sufficient form of security? Are the goals of security and efficiency in tension?

In February, 2018, Special Counsel Robert S. Mueller, III, who was appointed to investigate Russian meddling in the 2016 election, filed an indictment against several Russian-controlled organizations and numerous Russian nationals. The indictment charged that the defendants "knowingly and intentionally conspired with each other (and with persons known and unknown to the Grand Jury) to defraud the United States by impairing, obstructing, and defeating the lawful functions of the government through fraud and deceit for the purpose of interfering with the U.S. political and electoral processes, including the presidential election of 2016." It continued:

> 4. Defendants, posing as U.S. persons and creating false U.S. personas, operated social media pages and groups designed to attract U.S. audiences. These groups and pages, which addressed divisive U.S. political and social issues, falsely claimed to be controlled by U.S. activists when, in fact, they were controlled by Defendants. Defendants also used the stolen identities of real U.S. persons to post on ORGANIZATION-controlled social media accounts. Over time, these social media accounts became Defendants' means to reach significant numbers of Americans for purposes of interfering with the U.S. political system, including the presidential election of 2016.

> 5. Certain Defendants traveled to the United States under false pretenses for the purpose of collecting intelligence to inform Defendants' operations. Defendants also procured and used computer infrastructure, based partly in the United States, to hide the Russian origin of their activities and to avoid detection by U.S. regulators and law enforcement.

> 6. Defendant ORGANIZATION had a strategic goal to sow discord in the U.S. political system, including the 2016 U.S. presidential election.

Defendants posted derogatory information about a number of candidates, and by early to mid-2016, Defendants' operations included supporting the presidential campaign of then-candidate Donald J. Trump ("Trump Campaign") and disparaging Hillary Clinton. Defendants made various expenditures to carry out those activities, including buying political advertisements on social media in the names of U.S. persons and entities. Defendants also staged political rallies inside the United States, and while posing as U.S. grassroots entities and U.S. persons, and without revealing their Russian identities and ORGANIZATION affiliation, solicited and compensated real U.S. persons to promote or disparage candidates. Some Defendants, posing as U.S. persons and without revealing their Russian association, communicated with unwitting individuals associated with the Trump Campaign and with other political activists to seek to coordinate political activities.

7. In order to carry out their activities to interfere in U.S. political and electoral processes without detection of their Russian affiliation, Defendants conspired to obstruct the lawful functions of the United States government through fraud and deceit, including by making expenditures in connection with the 2016 U.S. presidential election without proper regulatory disclosure; failing to register as foreign agents carrying out political activities within the United States; and obtaining visas through false and fraudulent statements.

In his final report, released in March, 2019, Mr. Mueller went into considerably greater detail regarding the nature of the Russian interference. Below is an excerpt from the Executive Summary of the report.

Report on the Investigation into Russian Interference in the 2016 Presidential Election

Office of the Special Counsel, March 2019

Russian Social Media Campaign

The Internet Research Agency (IRA) carried out the earliest Russian interference operations identified by the investigation—a social media campaign designed to provoke and amplify political and social discord in the United States. The IRA was based in St. Petersburg, Russia, and received funding from Russian oligarch Yevgeniy Prigozhin and companies he controlled. Priozhin is widely reported to have ties to Russian President Vladimir Putin. . . .

The IRA later used social media accounts and interest groups to sow discord in the U.S. political system through what it termed "information warfare." The campaign evolved from a generalized program designed in 2014 and 2015 to undermine the U.S. electoral system, to a targeted operation that by early 2016 favored candidate Trump and disparaged candidate Clinton. The IRA's operation also included the purchase of political advertisements on social media in the names of U.S. persons and entities, as well as the staging of political rallies inside the United States. To organize those rallies, IRA employees posed as U.S. grassroots entities and persons and made contact with Trump supporters and Trump Campaign officials in the United States. The investigation did not identify evidence that any U.S. persons conspired or coordinated with the IRA. . . .

Russian Hacking Operations

At the same time that the IRA operation began to focus on supporting candidate Trump in early 2016, the Russian government employed a second form of interference: cyber intrusions (hacking) and releases of hacked materials damaging to the Clinton Campaign. The Russian intelligence service known as the Main Intelligence Directorate of the General Staff of the Russian Army (GRU) carried out these operations.

In March 2016, the GRU began hacking the email accounts of Clinton Campaign volunteers and employees, including campaign chairman John Podesta. In April 2016, the GRU hacked into the computer networks of the Democratic Congressional Campaign Committee (DCCC) and the Democratic National Committee (DNC). The GRU stole hundreds of thousands of documents from the compromised email accounts and networks. Around the time that the DNC announced in mid-June 2016 the Russian government's role in hacking its network, the GRU began disseminating stolen materials through the fictitious online personas "DCLeaks" and "Guccifer 2.0." The GRU later released additional materials through the organization WikiLeaks. . . .

The presidential campaign of Donald J. Trump ("Trump Campaign" or "Campaign") showed interest in WikiLeaks's releases of documents and welcomed their potential to damage candidate Clinton. Beginning in June 2016, [identity deleted] forecast to senior Campaign officials that WikiLeaks would release information damaging to candidate Clinton. WikiLeaks's first release came in July 2016. Around the same time, candidate Trump announced that he hoped Russia would recover emails described as missing from a private server used by Clinton when she was Secretary of State (he later said that he was speaking sarcastically). . . . WikiLeaks began releasing Podesta's stolen emails on October 7, 2016, less than one hour after a U.S. media outlet released video considered damaging to candidate Trump. . . .

Russian Contacts with the Campaign

The social media campaign and the GRU hacking operations coincided with a series of contacts between Trump Campaign officials and individuals with ties to the Russian government. The Office investigated whether those contacts reflected or resulted in the Campaign conspiring or coordinating with Russia in its election-interference activities. Although the investigation established that the Russian government perceived it would benefit from a Trump presidency and worked to secure that outcome, and that the Campaign expected it would benefit electorally from information stolen and released through Russian efforts, the investigation did not establish that members of the Trump Campaign conspired or coordinated with the Russian government in its election interference activities.

The Russian contacts consisted of business connections, offers of assistance to the Campaign, invitations for candidate Trump and Putin to meet in person, invitations for Campaign officials and representatives of the Russian government to meet, and policy positions seeking improved U.S.-Russian relations. . . .

2015.   Some of the earliest contacts were made in connection with a Trump Organization real-estate project in Russia known as Trump Tower Moscow. Candidate Trump signed a Letter of Intent for Trump Tower Moscow by November 2015, and in January 2016 Trump Organization executive Michael Cohen emailed and spoke about the project with the office of Russian government press secretary Dmitry Peskov. The Trump Organization pursued the project through at least June 2016, including by considering travel to Russia by Cohen and candidate Trump.

Spring 2016.   Campaign foreign policy advisor George Papadopoulos made early contact with Joseph Mifsud, a London-based professor who had connections to Russia and traveled to Moscow in April 2016. Immediately upon his return to London from that trip, Mifsud told Papadopoulos that the Russian government had "dirt" on Hillary Clinton in the form of thousands of emails. One week later, in the first week of May 2016, Papadopoulos suggested to a representative of a foreign government that the Trump Campaign had received indications from the Russian government that it could assist the Campaign through the anonymous release of information damaging to candidate Clinton. Throughout that period of time and for several months thereafter, Papadopoulos worked with Mifsud and two Russian nationals to arrange a meeting between the Campaign and the Russian government. No meeting took place.

Summer 2016.   Russian outreach to the Trump Campaign continued into the summer of 2016, as candidate Trump was becoming the presumptive Republican nominee for President. On June 9, 2016, for example, a Russian lawyer met with senior Trump Campaign officials Donald Trump Jr., Jared Kushner, and campaign chairman Paul Manafort to deliver what the email proposing the meeting had described as "official documents and information that would incriminate Hillary." The materials were offered to Trump Jr. as "part of Russia and its government's support for Mr. Trump." The written communications setting up the meeting showed that the Campaign anticipated receiving information from Russia that could assist candidate Trump's electoral prospects, but the Russian lawyer's presentation did not provide such information.

Days after the June 9 meeting, on June 14, 2016, a cybersecurity firm and the DNC announced that Russian government hackers had infiltrated the DNC and obtained access to opposition research on candidate Trump, among other documents.

In July 2016, Campaign foreign policy advisor Carter Page traveled in his personal capacity to Moscow and gave the keynote address at the New Economic School. Page had lived and worked in Russia between 2003 and 2007. After returning to the United States, Page became acquainted with at least two Russian intelligence officers, one of whom was later charged in 2015 with conspiracy to act as an unregistered agent of Russia. Page' s July 2016 trip to Moscow and his advocacy for pro-Russian foreign policy drew media attention. The Campaign then distanced itself from Page and, by late September 2016, removed him from the Campaign.

July 2016 was also the month WikiLeaks first released emails stolen by the GRU from the DNC. On July 22, 2016, WikiLeaks posted thousands of internal

DNC documents revealing information about the Clinton Campaign. Within days, there was public reporting that U.S. intelligence agencies had " high confidence" that the Russian government was behind the theft of emails and documents from the DNC. And within a week of the release, a foreign government informed the FBI about its May 2016 interaction with Papadopoulos and his statement that the Russian government could assist the Trump Campaign. On July 31, 2016, based on the foreign government reporting, the FBI opened an investigation into potential coordination between the Russian government and individuals associated with the Trump Campaign.

Separately, on August 2, 2016, Trump campaign chairman Paul Manafort met in New York City with his long-time business associate Konstantin Kilimnik, who the FBI assesses to have ties to Russian intelligence. Kilimnik requested the meeting to deliver in person a peace plan for Ukraine that Manafort acknowledged to the Special Counsel' s Office was a "backdoor" way for Russia to control part of eastern Ukraine; both men believed the plan would require candidate Trump' s assent to succeed (were he to be elected President). They also discussed the status of the Trump Campaign and Manafort' s strategy for winning Democratic votes in Midwestern states. Months before that meeting, Manafort had caused internal polling data to be shared with Kilimnik, and the sharing continued for some period of time after their August meeting.

Fall 2016.   On October 7, 2016, the media released video of candidate Trump speaking in graphic terms about women years earlier, which was considered damaging to his candidacy. Less than an hour later, WikiLeaks made its second release: thousands of John Podesta' s emails that had been stolen by the GRU in late March 2016. The FBI and other U.S. government institutions were at the time continuing their investigation of suspected Russian government efforts to interfere in the presidential election. That same day, October 7, the Department of Homeland Security and the Office of the Director of National Intelligence issued a joint public statement "that the Russian Government directed the recent compromises of e-mails from US persons and institutions, including from US political organizations." Those "thefts" and the "disclosures" of the hacked materials through online platforms such as WikiLeaks, the statement continued, "are intended to interfere with the US election process."

Post-2016 Election.   Immediately after the November 8 election, Russian government officials and prominent Russian businessmen began trying to make inroads into the new administration. The most senior levels of the Russian government encouraged these efforts. The Russian Embassy made contact hours after the election to congratulate the President-Elect and to arrange a call with President Putin. Several Russian businessmen picked up the effort from there.

Kirill Dmitriev, the chief executive officer of Russia's sovereign wealth fund, was among the Russians who tried to make contact with the incoming administration. In early December, a business associate steered Dmitriev to Erik Prince, a supporter of the Trump Campaign and an associate of senior Trump advisor Steve Bannon. Dmitriev and Prince later met face-to-face in January 2017 in the Seychelles and discussed U.S.-Russia relations. During the same period, another business associate introduced Dmitriev to a friend of Jared Kushner who had not served on the Campaign or the Transition Team. Dmitriev and Kushner's friend collaborated on a short written reconciliation plan for the United States and Russia, which Dmitriev implied had been cleared through Putin. The friend gave that proposal to Kushner before the inauguration, and Kushner later gave copies to Bannon and incoming Secretary of State Rex Tillerson.

On December 29, 2016, then-President Obama imposed sanctions on Russia for having interfered in the election. Incoming National Security Advisor Michael Flynn called Russian Ambassador Sergey Kislyak and asked Russia not to escalate the situation in response to the sanctions. The following day, Putin announced that Russia would not take retaliatory measures in response to the sanctions at that time. Hours later, President-Elect Trump tweeted, "Great move on delay (by V. Putin)." The next day, on December 31, 2016, Kislyak called Flynn and told him the request had been received at the highest levels and Russia had chosen not to retaliate as a result of Flynn's request.

On January 6, 2017, members of the intelligence community briefed President-Elect Trump on a joint assessment-drafted and coordinated among the Central Intelligence Agency, FBI, and National Security Agency—that concluded with high confidence that Russia had intervened in the election through a variety of means to assist Trump' s candidacy and harm Clinton's. A declassified version of the assessment was publicly released that same day. . . .

Following the 2020 election, the National Intelligence Council found no evidence "that any foreign actor attempted to alter any technical aspect of the voting process in the 2020 US elections, including voter registration, casting ballots, vote tabulation, or reporting results." However, the Council concluded that Russia attempted surreptitiously to influence public opinion through American media and through contacts with American officials and opinion leaders. Its goal was not to support either candidates Trump or Biden, but rather "undermining public confidence in the electoral process, and exacerbating sociopolitical divisions in the US." The Council also concluded that Iran attempted to influence public opinion "to undercut former President Trump's reelection prospects"; that the Iran-backed organization Hizballah, along with Cuba and Venezuela, made smaller-scale efforts to influence the election results; and that China sat this one out. National Intelligence Council, *Foreign Threats to the 2020 US Federal Elections* (Mar. 10, 2021).

≫   ***Legal Consequences of Foreign Interference in Elections.***   It appears that interference with elections, either through cyberattacks on election infrastructure or through propagation of false or divisive information, is on the rise around the world. The UN Charter guarantees each signatory nation the right of "self-determination," which in a democracy presumably means the right of a people to choose its leaders free from foreign manipulation. Interference with another nation's democratic processes through the projection of force into that nation's territory thus would clearly be a serious breach of international law, justifying armed retaliation by the attacked nation or its allies. But what about when one nation interferes with another's democratic processes through cyberattacks or misinformation? Principles of international law are murky in this area. Although actual manipulation of election results through cyber interference would likely violate international principles of non-interference in the affairs of other nations, no consensus has emerged concerning other forms of electoral meddling that fall short of this threshold. As a result, it is unclear whether a legally justifiable response to non-coercive forms of electoral interference could include armed retaliation. Chimène I. Keitner, *Foreign Election Interference and International Law, in* Jens David Ohlin and Duncan B. Hollis, Defending Democracies: Combating Foreign Election Interference in a Digital Age (2021).

D. POST-CANVASS REMEDIES AND JUDICIAL OVERSIGHT

Despite the best efforts of election administrators to carry off elections of exemplary accuracy and integrity, mistakes do from time to time occur. What happens when the results of an election are put in doubt by credible charges of error or fraud in the voting or counting? This section deals with corrections at the back end, after the initial canvass of the votes, to elections the quality of which have been called into question. Following the typical sequence of post-election scrutiny provided by law, this section examines recounts, election contests, and judicial remedies.

1. Recounts

In every American jurisdiction, the first response to a charge that election results are inaccurate is some kind of recount. The purpose of a recount is not to make judgments about the legality of ballots cast, but simply to ensure that all ballots cast have been correctly counted.

In what circumstances is a recount available? In some states, recounts are conducted automatically. In Kentucky, for example, some recounting is performed in every election as a form of random spot-checking. *See* Ky. Rev. Stat. Ann. §117.383(8) (requiring "a manual recount of randomly selected precincts representing three percent (3%) to five percent (5%) of the total ballots cast in each election"). More typically, recounts are undertaken automatically only when an election is very close. In South Carolina, for example, an automatic recount is triggered whenever a candidate wins by less than 1 percent of the vote. S.C. Code Ann. §7-17-280. In Florida, a more populous state, an automatic recount is triggered when a candidate wins by one-quarter of 1 percent or less. Fla. Stat. §102.166. (Florida's automatic recount provisions figure prominently in *Bush v. Gore*, above.)

In other states, recounts are available only upon request. In Maine, any losing candidate may request a recount. Me. Rev. Stat. Ann. tit. 21-A, §737-A. In Texas, a candidate may request a recount only if the margin of victory was 10 percent or less. Tex. Elec. Code Ann. §212.022.

What is the point of conducting a recount that continues to count ballots that may have been illegally cast? Recent recounts in Minnesota and Washington have cost approximately 16 cents and 31 cents per ballot, respectively. Conny

B. McCormack, *Re-Counting the Vote: What Does It Cost?* (Pew Charitable Trust, Oct. 2010). Why isn't this a waste of time and money?

» ***The Frequency and Result of Recounts.***   How common are recounts, and how often do they change election results? According to a study of all statewide elections conducted in the United States between 1980 and 2007 — a total of 7,645 elections — recounts were conducted in only 23 instances. Only two of these recounts resulted in a reversal of the initial result of the election. Moreover, recounts generally resulted in trivial changes in the final vote margin — the average change in the margin of victory of the winning candidate was less than one vote out of every 2,500 counted. This data suggests that vote counting has historically been remarkably accurate, even in very close elections, which are the only kind likely to trigger a recount. Finally, the study noted, the accuracy of an initial count, and correspondingly the unlikelihood of a change in result following a recount, increases with the number of ballots cast — apparently a kind of law of large numbers that applies to the repeated act of casting ballots. FairVote, *Survey and Analysis of Statewide Election Recounts,* 1980–2007 (2009).

Presumably, recounts occur more frequently at the district and local levels, and since the number of ballots cast is smaller we might expect the results to change more frequently — though perhaps still generally infrequently — at the local level.

2. *Election Contests*

The purpose of a recount is to ensure an accurate count of ballots actually cast; recounts do not address the legality or validity of the votes cast. Obviously, however, an accurate count of votes may not be the end of the story. An election result, accurately tallied, may be wrong for other reasons — the election may have been sufficiently tainted by fraud or error to put the officially reported outcome in doubt. In these cases, states supply a different procedure to test the validity of final ballot counts. The most common is a system of election "contests" in which the candidate who loses after the official count, or in many cases any eligible voter, challenges the results.

Below is an example of a typical state contest statute.

Georgia Code §§21-2-521 et seq.

§21-2-521. The nomination of any person who is declared nominated at a primary as a candidate for any federal, state, county, or municipal office; the election of any person who is declared elected to any such office . . . ; the eligibility of any person declared eligible to seek any such nomination or office in a run-off primary or election; or the approval or disapproval of any question submitted to electors at an election may be contested by any person who was a candidate at such primary or election for such nomination or office, or by any aggrieved elector who was entitled to vote for such person or for or against such question.

§21-2-522. A result of a primary or election may be contested on one or more of the following grounds:

(1) Misconduct, fraud, or irregularity by any primary or election official or officials sufficient to change or place in doubt the result;

(2) When the defendant is ineligible for the nomination or office in dispute;

(3) When illegal votes have been received or legal votes rejected at the polls sufficient to change or place in doubt the result;

(4) For any error in counting the votes or declaring the result of the primary or election, if such error would change the result; or

(5) For any other cause which shows that another was the person legally nominated, elected, or eligible to compete in a run-off primary or election.

§21-2-524. (a) A petition to contest the result of a primary or election shall be filed in the office of the clerk of the superior court having jurisdiction within five days after the official consolidation of the returns of that particular office or question and certification thereof . . . and shall allege: (1) The contestant's qualification to institute the contest; (2) The contestant's desire to contest the result of such primary or election and the name of the nomination, office, or question involved in the contest; (3) The name of the defendant; . . .(5) Each ground of contest; . . .(7) The relief sought; and (8) Such other facts as are necessary to provide a full, particular, and explicit statement of the cause of contest.

§21-2-527.

(a) After hearing the allegations and evidence in the contest, the court shall declare as nominated, elected, or as eligible to compete in a run-off primary or election that qualified candidate who received the requisite number of votes and shall pronounce judgment accordingly. . . . In the case of a contest involving a question submitted to electors at an election, the court shall pronounce judgment as to whether the same was approved or disapproved. . . .

(b) When a defendant who has received the requisite number of votes for nomination, election, or to compete in a run-off primary or election is determined to be ineligible for the nomination or office sought, the court shall pronounce judgment declaring the primary or election invalid with regard to such nomination or office and shall call a second primary or election to fill such nomination or office and shall set the date for such second primary or election.

(c) If misconduct is complained of on the part of the poll officers of any precinct, it shall not be held sufficient to set aside the contested result unless the rejection of the vote of such precinct would change such result.

(d) Whenever the court trying a contest shall determine that the primary, election, or runoff is so defective as to the nomination, office, or eligibility in contest as to place in doubt the result of the entire primary, election, or runoff for such nomination, office, or eligibility, such court shall declare the primary, election, or runoff to be invalid with regard to such nomination, office, or eligibility and shall call for a second primary, election, or runoff to be conducted among all of the same candidates who participated in the primary, election, or runoff to fill such nomination or office which was declared invalid and shall set the date for such second primary, election, or runoff.

⟫   *Taint of Process vs. Substantive Change in Outcome.*   Note that many of the provisions of the Georgia statute limit the availability of contests to situations in which electoral irregularities are alleged to have changed the result of the election, or at least to have put the result in doubt. Why should it not be sufficient for a contest that the election was tainted by any irregularity, or at least by extreme irregularities such as fraud or violence? Should a candidate who employs fraud or violence be immune from an election contest if he wins by a sufficient margin of uncoerced votes? What does a statute such as this protect—the integrity of the process or the accuracy of the outcome? Did the legislature make the right choice?

Procedures for election contests vary widely from state to state. For an overview, see Joshua A. Douglas, *Procedural Fairness in Election Contests*, 88 IND. L.J. 1 (2013).

3.   The Availability of Judicial Oversight

Before turning to the kinds of remedies courts can provide in electoral litigation, a preliminary question must first be addressed: should judicial review be available at all, and if so, in what circumstances? As we have seen, judicial intrusion into the electoral process, especially before it has been completed, can change outcomes. Judicialization of elections can also create unpredictability, delay, and uncertainty—all enemies of successful democratic self-government. Ultimately, such difficulties seem to have the capacity, if frequent and intrusive enough, to threaten the legitimacy of democratic processes.

Then there is the additional problem posed by federal judicial intrusion into state processes, a situation in which issues of federalism and interjurisdictional comity are never far from the surface. Should federal judicial intrusions be minimized for these reasons? Or is a healthy degree of federal intrusion into state political processes inevitable given the Constitution's commitment of primary responsibility for administering federal elections to the states?

When courts do intervene, how should they do so? Should they adopt a posture of deference toward state legislatures and state election administrators on the ground that legislatures and administrators possess greater competence than courts? Or are courts better suited than actors embedded within the political process to navigate and administer that process?

Colegrove v. Green

328 U.S. 549 (1946)

Mr. Justice FRANKFURTER announced the judgment of the Court and an opinion in which Mr. Justice REED and Mr. Justice BURTON concur.

[The case presented a challenge to the malapportionment of Illinois congressional districts, which had not been redrawn in several decades, and which had become unequal in population due to non-uniform population growth. The state moved to dismiss on the ground that the complaint did not present a justiciable controversy.]

We are of opinion that the petitioners ask of this Court what is beyond its competence to grant. This is one of those demands on judicial power which cannot be met by verbal fencing about "jurisdiction." It must be resolved by considerations on the basis of which this Court, from time to time, has refused to intervene in controversies. It has refused to do so because due regard for the effective working of our Government revealed this issue to be of a peculiarly political nature and therefore not meet for judicial determination.

. . . Nothing is clearer than that this controversy concerns matters that bring courts into immediate and active relations with party contests. From the determination of such issues this Court has traditionally held aloof. It is hostile to a democratic system to involve the judiciary in the politics of the people. And it is not less pernicious if such judicial intervention in an essentially political contest be dressed up in the abstract phrases of the law.

The petitioners urge with great zeal that the conditions of which they complain are grave evils and offend public morality. The Constitution of the United States gives ample power to provide against these evils. But due regard for the Constitution as a viable system precludes judicial correction. Authority for dealing with such problems resides elsewhere. Article I, section 4 of the Constitution provides that "The Times, Places and Manner of holding Elections for . . . Representative, shall be prescribed in each State by the Legislature thereof; but the Congress may at any time by Law make or alter such Regulations. . . ." The short of it is that the Constitution has conferred upon Congress exclusive authority to secure fair representation by the States in the popular House and left to that House determination whether States have fulfilled their responsibility. If Congress failed in exercising its powers, whereby standards of fairness are offended, the remedy ultimately lies with the people. Whether Congress faithfully discharges its duty or not, the subject has been committed to the exclusive control of Congress. An aspect of government from which the judiciary, in view of what is involved, has been excluded by the clear intention of the Constitution cannot be entered by the federal courts because Congress may have been in default in exacting from States obedience to its mandate. . . .

To sustain this action would cut very deep into the very being of Congress. Courts ought not to enter this political thicket. The remedy for unfairness in districting is to secure State legislatures that will apportion properly, or to invoke the ample powers of Congress. The Constitution has many commands that are not enforceable by courts because they clearly fall outside the conditions and purposes that circumscribe judicial action. The Constitution has left the performance of many duties in our governmental scheme to depend on the fidelity of the executive and legislative action and, ultimately, on the vigilance of the people in exercising their political rights.

Dismissal of the complaint is affirmed.

Baker v. Carr

369 U.S. 186 (1962)

Mr. Justice BRENNAN delivered the opinion of the Court.

This civil action was brought to redress the alleged deprivation of federal constitutional rights. The complaint, alleging that by means of a 1901 statute of Tennessee apportioning the members of the General Assembly among the State's 95 counties, "these plaintiffs and others similarly situated, are denied the equal protection of the laws accorded them by the Fourteenth Amendment to the Constitution of the United States by virtue of the debasement of their votes," was dismissed by a three-judge court. The court held that it lacked jurisdiction of the subject matter and also that no claim was stated upon which relief could be granted. . . . We hold that the dismissal was error, and remand the cause to the District Court for trial and further proceedings consistent with this opinion. . . .

Tennessee's standard for allocating legislative representation among her counties is the total number of qualified voters resident in the respective counties, subject only to minor qualifications. Decennial reapportionment in compliance with the constitutional scheme was effected by the General Assembly each decade from 1871 to 1901. [But for the last 60 years] all proposals in both Houses of the General Assembly for reapportionment have failed to pass.

Between 1901 and 1961, Tennessee has experienced substantial growth and redistribution of her population. In 1901 the population was 2,020,616, of whom 487,380 were eligible to vote. The 1960 Federal Census reports the State's population at 3,567,089, of whom 2,092,891 are eligible to vote. The relative standings of the counties in terms of qualified voters have changed significantly. It is primarily the continued application of the 1901 Apportionment Act to this shifted and enlarged voting population which gives rise to the present controversy. . . .

[W]e hold today only (a) that the [lower] court possessed jurisdiction of the subject matter; (b) that a justiciable cause of action is stated upon which appellants would be entitled to appropriate relief; and (c) because appellees raise the issue before this Court, that the appellants have standing to challenge the Tennessee apportionment statutes. Beyond noting that we have no cause at this stage to doubt the District Court will be able to fashion relief if violations of constitutional rights are found, it is improper now to consider what remedy would be most appropriate if appellants prevail at the trial.

Justiciability

In holding that the subject matter of this suit was not justiciable, the District Court relied on *Colegrove v. Green,* and subsequent per curiam cases. We understand the District Court to have read the cited cases as compelling the conclusion that since the appellants sought to have a legislative apportionment held unconstitutional, their suit presented a "political question" and was therefore nonjusticiable. We hold that this challenge to an apportionment presents no nonjusticiable "political question." . . .

Of course the mere fact that the suit seeks protection of a political right does not mean it presents a political question. Such an objection "is little more than a play upon words." *Nixon v. Herndon.* Rather, it is argued that apportionment cases, whatever the actual wording of the complaint, can involve no federal constitutional right except one resting on the guaranty of a republican form of government, and that complaints based on that clause have been held to present political questions which are nonjusticiable.

We hold that the claim pleaded here neither rests upon nor implicates the Guaranty Clause and that its justiciability is therefore not foreclosed by our decisions of cases involving that clause. The District Court misinterpreted *Colegrove v. Green* and other decisions of this Court on which it relied. Appellants' claim that they are being denied equal protection is justiciable, and if "discrimination is sufficiently shown, the right to relief under the equal protection clause is not diminished by the fact that the discrimination relates to political rights." . . .

We have said that "In determining whether a question falls within (the political question) category, the appropriateness under our system of government of attributing finality to the action of the political departments and also the lack of satisfactory criteria for a judicial determination are dominant considerations." *Coleman v. Miller.* The nonjusticiability of a political question is primarily a function of the separation of powers. Much confusion results from the capacity of the "political question" label to obscure the need for case-by-case inquiry. Deciding whether a matter has in any measure been committed by the Constitution to another branch of government, or whether the action of that branch exceeds whatever authority has been committed, is itself a delicate exercise in constitutional interpretation, and is a responsibility of this Court as ultimate interpreter of the Constitution. . . .

[The Court undertook a detailed examination of all prior cases in which it had found a nonjusticiable political question, including cases from the areas of foreign relations, armed conflict, federal recognition of Indian tribes, and the Guaranty Clause.]

The doctrine of which we treat is one of "political questions," not one of "political cases." The courts cannot reject as "no law suit" a bona fide controversy as to whether some action denominated "political" exceeds constitutional authority. The cases we have reviewed show the necessity for discriminating inquiry into the precise facts and posture of the particular case, and the impossibility of resolution by any semantic cataloguing. . . .

[Regarding *Luther v. Borden*,] several factors were thought by the Court in *Luther* to make the question there "political": the commitment to the other branches of the decision as to which is the lawful state government; the unambiguous action by the President, in recognizing the charter government as the lawful authority; the need for finality in the executive's decision; and the lack of criteria by which a court could determine which form of government was republican. But the only significance that *Luther* could have for our immediate purposes is in its holding that the Guaranty Clause is not a repository of judicially manageable standards which a court could utilize independently in order to identify a State's lawful government. The Court has since refused to resort to the Guaranty Clause — which alone had been invoked for the purpose — as the source of a constitutional standard for invalidating state action. . . .

We come, finally, to the ultimate inquiry whether our precedents as to what constitutes a nonjusticiable "political question" bring the case before us under the umbrella of that doctrine. A natural beginning is to note whether any of the common characteristics which we have been able to identify and label descriptively are present. We find none: The question here is the consistency of state action with the Federal Constitution. We have no question decided, or to be decided, by a political branch of government coequal with this Court. Nor do we risk embarrassment of our government abroad, or grave disturbance at home if we take issue with Tennessee as to the constitutionality of her action here challenged. Nor need the appellants, in order to succeed in this action, ask the Court to enter upon policy determinations for which judicially manageable standards are lacking. Judicial standards under the Equal Protection Clause are well developed and familiar, and it has been open to courts since the enactment of the Fourteenth Amendment to determine, if on the particular facts they must, that a discrimination reflects no policy, but simply arbitrary and capricious action.

This case does, in one sense, involve the allocation of political power within a State, and the appellants might conceivably have added a claim under the Guaranty Clause. Of course, as we have seen, any reliance on that clause would be futile. But because any reliance on the Guaranty Clause could not have succeeded it does not follow that appellants may not be heard on the equal protection claim which in fact they tender. True, it must be clear that the Fourteenth Amendment claim is not so enmeshed with those political question elements which render Guaranty Clause claims nonjusticiable as actually to present a political question itself. But we have found that not to be the case here. . . .

We conclude that the complaint's allegations of a denial of equal protection present a justiciable constitutional cause of action upon which appellants are entitled to a trial and a decision. The right asserted is within the reach of judicial protection under the Fourteenth Amendment.

The judgment of the District Court is reversed and the cause is remanded for further proceedings consistent with this opinion. Reversed and remanded.

≫ *Election Litigation.*   Unlike federal courts, which are courts of limited jurisdiction, state courts were always free to adjudicate questions of political process and procedure arising under state law. Nevertheless, even though it applied by its terms solely to federal courts, *Baker* seems to have had the effect of sensitizing the bar generally to the availability of judicial review of democratic processes, whether at the state or federal levels. In that sense, *Baker* has come to represent the constitutionalization of democratic politics and is the case that opened the way for the federal courts to police the structure of democratic politics. Following *Baker*, there appears to be no area of democratic politics that is not subject to some form of federal judicial review on constitutional grounds.

The result has been a steady increase in litigation seeking judicial review of electoral laws or administrative decisions, with a sudden and substantial increase in litigation following *Bush v. Gore.* According to one count, slightly more than 100 cases were filed arising out of the 1996 election, which leaped to 360 in 2004, and topped out at 424 in 2020. Richard L. Hasen, *Research Note: Record Litigation Rates in the 2020 Election: An Aberration or a Sign of Things to Come?*, 21 ELECTION L.J. 150 (2022). Another count determined that the Trump Campaign alone filed 80 Election Day and post-Election Day lawsuits in 2020 in the eleven most closely contested jurisdictions. Jacob Kovacs-Goodman, *Post-Election Litigation in Battleground States: A*

Summary, HealthyElections.org (Feb. 1, 2021). Yet another recent study finds that the legal expenses of the major political parties were about level between 2003 and 2015, at about $5 million per year, but shot up to around $15 million in 2016, $28 million in 2019, and more than $35 million in 2020, with some litigation still not concluded at the time the data was collected. Derek T. Muller, *Reducing Election Litigation,* 90 FORDHAM L. REV. 561 (2021).

Judicial oversight of election legislation and administration may produce good results in some or even many cases, but is this amount of litigation simply too much? Are there countervailing costs when courts are involved so heavily and so ubiquitously in the resolution of electoral disputes?

» *Doctrines of Judicial Restraint.* As we have seen, the Supreme Court revived the political question doctrine as a limitation on its powers of judicial oversight in *Rucho v. Common Cause* (Chapter 4), effectively leaving control over redistricting to state legislatures and state courts, and to Congress to the extent it might wish to invoke its own powers to oversee congressional elections conducted by the states.

Since *Baker,* the Court has developed several other tools of self-restraint in the electoral arena. One such doctrine concerns the timing of judicial intervention. In *Purcell v. Gonzalez,* 549 U.S. 1 (2006) (per curiam), the Court vacated a lower court order, issued less than three weeks before an upcoming general election, enjoining Arizona's implementation of a new voter ID requirement. The court below had ruled that the ID requirement would likely have a suppressive effect on voting. On appeal, the Supreme Court did not disagree, but found that the Court of Appeals had neglected to consider other relevant factors. "Court orders affecting elections," the Court observed, "especially conflicting orders, can themselves result in voter confusion and consequent incentive to remain away from the polls. As an election draws closer, that risk will increase." The combination of a rapidly impending election and "the need for clear guidance to the State of Arizona," the Court ruled, made the last-minute issuance of the injunction reversible error.

The impact of *Purcell* remained relatively limited until the pandemic election of November, 2020. To cope with public health restrictions imposed by many states and local jurisdictions, which imposed a variety of limits on the conditions under which groups of people could gather indoors, election administrators around the country introduced a flurry of new procedures aimed at protecting public health, including expanded absentee voting, mail balloting, drive-up ballot drops, and extended deadlines for submission and counting of mail ballots. A large number of these changes were challenged in court, often shortly before Election Day. Widespread invocation of *Purcell* by federal courts in general had the effect of precluding challenges to last-minute changes in voting procedures of any and all kinds. This was true whether the measure was designed to make voting easier—for example, by permitting administrators to mail absentee ballots pre-emptively to all voters— or to make voting more challenging, such as by shrinking the availability of voting options other than by personal appearance during a time when many feared venturing into potentially crowded public polling places. *See* Wilfred U. Codrington III, Purcell *in Pandemic,* 96 N.Y.U. L. Rev. 941 (2021). As Justice Sotomayor complained in dissenting from the Court's refusal to intervene in ongoing lower court litigation, "This Court's inaction continues a trend of condoning disenfranchisement. Ironically, this Court has wielded *Purcell* as a reason to forbid courts to make voting safer during a pandemic, overriding two federal courts because any safety-related changes supposedly came too close to election day." *Raysor v. DeSantis*, 591 U.S. __ (2020).

In addition, the Court appears to have become more aggressive in deploying Article III standing as a barrier to successful election law challenges. One of the earliest such cases was *United States v. Hays*, 515 U.S. 737 (1995), where it held that only people residing physically within a racially gerrymandered district have standing to challenge it, notwithstanding the impact of racial gerrymandering in one district on voters residing within other districts. In another redistricting case, the Court held that voters lacked standing to challenge a state legislature's mid-decade redrawing of district lines for partisan advantage. *Lance v. Coffman*, 549 U.S. 437 (2007). In another, the Court held that a chamber of a state legislature lacked standing to defend its own districting plan against charges of racial gerrymandering, *Virginia House of Delegates v. Bethune-Hill*, 139 S.Ct. 1945 (2019).

Outside the redistricting area, the Court has been equally aggressive in dismissing cases for lack of standing. Thus, for example, the sponsors of a state ballot initiative lacked standing to defend its constitutionality even when state officials refused to do so. *Hollingsworth v. Perry*, 570 U.S. 693 (2013). A candidate for elective judicial office lacked standing to challenge a state law requiring him to be a member of a political party. *Carney v. Adams*, 141 S.Ct. 493 (2020). And most recently, no one had standing to challenge a policy decision by the Trump Administration to exclude from the decennial census count unlawful immigrants residing in the United States, a practice very plausibly alleged to be blatantly unconstitutional. *Trump v. New York*, 141 S.Ct. 530 (2020) (per curiam). For a discussion of the earlier cases in this line, s*ee* Saul Zipkin, *Democratic Standing*, J. L. & Pols. 179 (2011).

4. *Judicial Remedies*

When an election is contested, what standards are applied by courts adjudicating the contests? What remedies are available to cure voting irregularities, and in what circumstances? This section takes up the question of how courts enforce provisions of election codes governing the processes of voting and vote-counting.

Whitley v. Cranford

119 S.W.3d 28 (Ark. 2003)

Ronald Whitley appeals an order of the Hot Spring County Circuit Court voiding the May 21, 2002, Hot Spring County Democratic Preferential Primary for the office of Justice of the Peace, District 4. Whitley alleges that the trial court erred in voiding the election where 183 voters were presented with ballots omitting the Justice of the Peace race, where there was no fraud, and in finding that the incomplete ballots deprived the 183 voters from their right to participate in the election. . . . We hold that providing 183 voters with ballots omitting the Justice of the Peace race rendered the outcome of this election uncertain, and required that the election be voided. . . .

Facts

Ronald Whitley and James Cranford opposed each other as candidates in the Democratic Preferential Primary for the position of Justice of the Peace, District 4, Hot Spring County. On election day, for reasons that are not stated by the parties, nor apparent from the record, some ballots included the District 4 Justice of the Peace race, and some did not. The parties have not argued and the record does not show that the error in the ballots was discoverable and correctable at any time prior to the election. Rather, the problem with the ballots was only apparent after the election began. Ballots used at the Fenter–B polling site in the election on May 21, 2002, did not include the Justice of the Peace race. The record shows that seventy-six voters cast ballots at the Fenter–B polling site.

Ballots used at the Ward 4 polling site in the election on May 21, 2002, did not include the Justice of the Peace race[;] however, voters brought the omission to the attention of polling officials, and the correct ballots were then used. Nonetheless, 107 voters had already cast ballots before the correction was made. The total number of voters who voted using ballots omitting the Justice of the Peace races is 183. Of votes cast using ballots including the Justice of the Peace race, 299 were cast for Whitley, and 244 ballots were cast for Cranford. Out of the votes cast in the Justice of the Peace race, Whitley received fifty-five more votes than Cranford.

There were 1172 ballots cast that contained no vote in the Justice of the Peace race, which includes the 183 voters who were presented with ballots that did not include the race. When the 1172 under-votes are added to the 299 votes cast for Whitley and the 244 votes cast for Cranford, the total ballots presented to voters in the Justice of the Peace race is 1715. Five hundred forty-three people cast votes in the Justice of the Peace election.

Cranford filed [an election contest]. The circuit court held a hearing, and then voided the election, finding that the unintentional failure to include the Justice of the Peace race on the ballots presented to 183 voters deprived those voters of the right to participate in the election, rendered the result of the election uncertain, and defeated the requirement of a free election.

Election Contests

. . . [T]he case before us . . . is a suit to void the election because the result is uncertain. Cranford alleged that it was not possible to determine the outcome of the election. Under that assertion, leaving the election certification as it stood would mean that the possessor of the office would not occupy that position based on a free and equal election as guaranteed by the Constitution. The 183 voters who received the incomplete ballots could not vote. Thus, those 183 voters did not cast a ballot in the justice of the peace race, and there are therefore no legal votes to be added or illegal votes that could be excluded. There are no votes by the 183 voters to consider, and no way to determine how they would have voted short of calling the 183 voters in to court to declare how they would have voted. Such an endeavor would be fraught with intimidation and contrary to the well-founded principle of secret ballots. On this subject in *Rubens v. Hodges*, 837 S.W.2d 465 (1992), this court stated: "the elector may not testify that he intended to vote for a particular candidate. 29 Elections, C.J.S. 281 (1965)." Votes that were never cast may not be counted.

Voiding Elections

Article 3, section 2, of the Arkansas Constitution, provides that "[e]lections shall be free and equal.". . . This guarantee must exist because "[i]t is of the utmost importance that the public should have confidence in the administration of the election laws, and to know that the will of the majority, when fairly expressed, will be respected." *Wheat v. Smith,* 7 S.W. 161 (1888). Where an election is not free and equal as required under the Constitution, this court has voided elections. The first instance in the cases is where the result was rendered uncertain by fraud and intimidation. The oft-cited case of *Patton v. Coates,* 41 Ark. 111 (1883), interprets article 3, section 2, of the Constitution in voiding an election because fraud and intimidation rendered the result uncertain. In other cases where the voters have received insufficient notice, elections have also been voided. *Phillips v. Mathews,* 155 S.W.2d 716 (1941); *see also Phillips v. Rothrock,* 110 S.W.2d 26 (1937). It must also be noted that although the election in the case was not voided, in *Swanberg v. Tart,* 778 S.W.2d 931 (1989), this court discussed the alleged failure to comply with absentee voting laws, but declined to void the election, noting that elections will not be voided where the wrong does not render the result uncertain. . . .

In the case before us, of the 1715 voters that received ballots, 543 people cast votes in the Justice of the Peace race. Eleven hundred seventy-two voters received ballots, but did not cast a vote in the Justice of the Peace race. Of these 1172 voters, 183 received ballots that did not include the Justice of the Peace race.

In voiding the election, the 543 votes of those who cast a vote in the Justice of the Peace race were held for naught. The wrong or error that caused the trial court to conclude that the 543 votes were void was a failure by election officials to provide accurate and correct ballots to all polling sites. This court has a long history of plainly expressing its reluctance to void an election. In *Alexander v. Davis,* 58 S.W.3d 330 (2001), this court recently noted that there are narrow limits that must be followed in exercising the power to void an election. *Id.* In *Jones v. Glidewell,* 13 S.W. 723 (1890), this court stated:

> It is a serious thing to cast out the votes of innocent electors for acts done by others, and it is the province of the courts to see that every legal vote cast is counted when the possibility exists.

Jones, 13 S.W. 723. . . . More recently in *Womack v. Foster,* 8 S.W.3d 854 (2000), this court similarly stated, "It is also well settled that the courts do not favor disenfranchising a legal voter because of the misconduct of another person, such as an election official." In *Womack,* the invalid absentee ballots did not render the result doubtful, and the court quoted *Spires v. Compton,* 837 S.W.2d 459 (1992), where we stated:

> This court has held many times that elections will not be invalidated for alleged wrongs committed unless those wrongs were such to render the result doubtful. *Swanberg,* 778 S.W.2d 931. Put in other terms, we have said that the failure to comply with the letter of the law by election officers,

especially in matters over which the voter has no control, and in which no fraud is perpetrated, will not as a general rule render an election void, unless the statute expressly makes it so.

Spires, 837 S.W.2d 459. In *Womack*, the petitioner failed because he could not show a doubtful outcome, not because no fraud was alleged with regard to the 5000 other votes.

From these cases it is clear that where it is possible to purge the illegal or improper votes and leave the election valid, this court will do so. It is also clear that even a failure to comply with the law by election officials does not result in automatic invalidation of the election. In *Patton, supra*, this court first interpreted article 3, section 2, and expressed a concern in discussing the power to void an election:

> Upon the other hand, it devolves upon the courts not to press this principle too far, nor apply it lightly to slight indications of fraud, violence or intimidation. Its application, indeed, is a matter of the greatest and most anxious responsibility inasmuch as it involves, necessarily, the disenfranchisement, in the particular election, of all the honest voters of the township.

Patton, 41 Ark. at 126. "Where an election has been legally held and fairly conducted, nothing will justify the exclusion of the vote of an entire precinct except the impossibility of ascertaining for whom the majority of votes were given." *City of Newport*, 367 S.W.2d 742.

In *Patton* this court cited article 3, section 2, of the Arkansas Constitution, which provides in part: "Elections shall be free and equal. . . ." *Patton*, 41 Ark. at 126. The oft quoted test of when an election may be voided was set out in *Patton*:

> The wrong should appear to have been clear and flagrant, and in its nature diffusive in its influences, calculated to effect more than can be traced, and sufficiently potent to render the result really uncertain. If it be such, it defeats a free election, and every honest voter and intimidated or deceived voter is aggrieved thereby. It is his interest to sacrifice his own vote to right the evil. If it be not so general and serious, the court cannot safely proceed beyond the exclusion of particular illegal votes, or the supply of particular legal votes rejected.

Patton, 41 Ark. at 126. . . .

The facts of *Patton* involve grievous and pervasive fraud and intimidation[:] "[i]t can never be precisely estimated how far the latter (fraud) extends. Fraud is secret, and timidity shrinks from observation . . . yet it cannot be said that elections are 'free and equal' where fraudulent combinations for illegal voting override honest votes. . . ." *Patton*, 41 Ark. at 124. Although fraud rendered the election result uncertain in *Patton*, this court did not limit its holding to fraud. Article 3, section 2, contains no mention of fraud or intimidation. . . .

In *Patton*, this court did not limit the test to showing fraud and intimidation. Rather than use the words "fraud and intimidation" in the test, this court in *Patton* used the word "wrong." *Patton*, 41 Ark. at 126. The wrong must render the result of the election uncertain. If the wrong can be purged then the election could be valid because it would no longer be uncertain.

> [E]lections will not be invalidated for alleged wrongs committed unless said wrongs were such to render the result doubtful. In order to destroy the result of an election it must be shown that wrongs against the freedom of election have prevailed, not slightly and in individual cases, but generally and to the extent to rendering the result doubtful.

Lewelling, 398 S.W.2d 665.

Later cases reinforce the conclusion that elections may be voided in the absence of fraud. In *Files, supra,* this court found that there was no showing that even if the disputed votes had been counted, the outcome would have been different. The discussion in *Files* shows that the issue of whether an election is to be voided is based on whether the result of the election is uncertain:

> . . . There is no allegation, however, in Arnold's complaint that anyone acted fraudulently. Arnold relies entirely on the assertion that an unknown number of people were deprived of their right to vote for Files as a ground for voiding the election. Nowhere in Arnold's complaint does he allege that the irregularities enumerated were sufficient to render the outcome of the election really uncertain and such an inference drawn from those allegations would be strained indeed. . . . It is desirable that election returns have a high degree of stability and finality. *Reed v. Baker,* 495 S.W.2d 849. An Election should not be voided for any wrong less grave than that described in *Patton.* The purpose of any contest of an election is to determine which candidate received the greatest number of votes, and we have held that exclusion of votes, even if erroneous, is not prejudicial unless there is a showing that, if counted, those would materially affect the result in an election contest. *Horne v. Fish,* 127 S.W.2d 623. Appellant's allegations do not establish that the result was really uncertain or name any particular votes, except his own, which could have been supplied in the proceeding. This would not be sufficient to justify the court in setting aside the election. See *Wilson v. Ellis,* 324 S.W.2d 513.

Files, 594 S.W.2d 836. As is apparent from the above quote in *Files,* and a careful reading of *Patton,* an election may be voided when the outcome is uncertain. Fraud is not an essential element. The Constitution does not even mention fraud. . . .

In the case before us, 183 people were presented ballots that simply omitted the Justice of the Peace race. After the election, Whitley was certified by the Hot Spring County Board of Election Commissioners as receiving 299 votes, or fifty-five votes more than Cranford. Had the 183 ballots included the Justice of the Peace race, the outcome might have been different. It is impossible to determine how many of the 183 voters would have voted in the race and of that number how many would have voted for which candidate. Where the result is uncertain, the entire vote must be held for naught. *Patton, supra.* There is no other possible outcome because it is impossible to determine who would have won had the 183 voters cast their ballots in the Justice of the Peace race. Although the 183 voters can be identified, the mere ability to identify the voters does not mean the errors in this election can be negated. The election was held on May 21, 2002. To call voters into court to declare their vote on a later date would be to hold the election for those voters anew. The 183 voters cast no ballots in the Justice of the Peace race, and thus, there are no legal votes to be added or illegal votes to be excluded. It is not possible to trace what does not exist. Votes that were never cast obviously cannot be discovered and determined at a later time. In this case, the errors rendered the result uncertain, and a free election was defeated under article 3, section 2, of the Constitution and under our holding in *Patton* and the cases that followed *Patton.*

Slight Deviation and Lack of Fraud

Whitley admits there was an error or a "wrong" in failing to include the Justice of the Peace race on all ballots, however, he argues that the proper analysis in this case is to determine whether that failure constitutes a slight deviation from the legal requirements, and if so, then the election should be declared valid. . . .

In arguing a slight deviation, Whitley points out that 1715 ballots were cast, and that only 183, or slightly more than ten percent, did not include the Justice of the Peace race. Whitley argues that close to ninety percent of voters had a chance to vote in the Justice of the Peace race, and that of those presented with a chance to vote in the race the majority voted for Whitley. Whitley thus concludes that he received a majority vote, and that any deviation was slight and should be ignored. Whitley cites *Womack, supra* for the proposition that where the deviation is slight, and the error is caused by an election official, legal voters should not be disenfranchised by the misconduct of another, in this case election officials who failed to provide the correct ballot. . . . However, the wrong cannot be ignored in this case because the outcome is uncertain. We cannot know how the 183 people who received the defective ballots would have voted. Are we to assume that as in the votes cast by ballots including the Justice of the Peace race, roughly a third would choose to vote in the race? If we make that assumption, then there would be sixty-one voters who would have cast votes in the Justice of the Peace election. Fifty-six votes for Cranford would be sufficient to tip the balance in his favor. How do we know how those fifty-six or more votes would have been cast?

It is true that mere failure of an election official to comply with the letter of the law will not void an election unless the statute expressly requires that outcome. There is no statute dictating that this omission by election officials requires that the election be voided in this case[;] however, the fact remains that it is impossible to determine who won this election.

Denial of the Right to Participate in the Election

Whitley also argues that the trial court erred in finding that the omission of the Justice of the Peace race denied the voters receiving the defective ballots the right to participate in the election. Whitley argues:

> This Court should recognize and declare that voters have an obligation in the election process. Voters have a duty to go to the polls with the knowledge and understanding of the contests for which they will be presented. They have a duty to read carefully and review the ballot to determine if it properly represents all of the candidates. Such error or omission on the part of voters should not be an opportunity for this court to disregard or disenfranchise those voters who did carefully read and review the ballot.

Whitley further argues that those who received the defective ballots "carelessly chose to ignore the omission or in the alternative, intentionally chose to disregard their opportunity to vote in the contest." . . . [Our] cases do not place an affirmative duty on a voter to examine the ballot for accuracy before voting. . . .

Affirmed.

ANNABELLE CLINTON IMBER, Justice, dissenting.

Today the majority does that which in its entire recorded history this court has never done — it upholds the voiding of an election where there has been no allegation of fraud, intimidation, violence, or coercion. This holding thus disenfranchises those voters who freely and legally cast their votes in this election and I must strongly dissent. . . .

Only twice in this court's history have the circumstances surrounding an election been egregious enough for us to hold the election should be voided. The first took place over a hundred years ago during the reconstruction period following the Civil War and the passage of the Thirteenth and Fourteenth Amendments. This was the case of *Patton v. Coates*, 41 Ark. 111 (1883). In *Patton*, elections were held in which voters were being threatened and intimidated if they attempted to vote for the candidates of their choice. In some cases, violence ensued and some voters were compelled to vote for a particular candidate or were kept from voting at all. *Id.* In addition to the allegations of threats, violence, and intimidation, allegations of fraud were rife in several townships and one ward. *Id.* A trial was held and the circuit court refused to void the election or suppress the votes from the precincts in question. *Id.* This court, after reviewing the evidence of the violence and fraud, reversed the circuit court:

> There is a distinction, in the nature of things, between particular illegal votes which may be proven and exactly computed, and which certainly ought to be excluded, wherever cast, and the effects of fraudulent combinations, coercion, and intimidation. *It can never be precisely estimated how far the latter extend.* Fraud is secret, and timidity shrinks from observation. Their effects depend on moral perversions, nervous organizations and constitutional idiosyncracies. They cannot be arithmetically computed. Awe is silent and undemonstrative. Peace may be abject as well as the result of satisfaction. Yet it cannot be said that elections are "free and equal" where fraudulent combinations for illegal voting override honest votes, or where fear deters from the exercise of free will, although there may be no turbulence. . . .
>
> [W]herever such practices or influences are shown to have prevailed, not slightly and in individual cases, but generally, and to the extent of rendering the result uncertain, the whole poll must be held for naught.

Id. at 124-25 (emphasis added).

This passage is important because it sets the threshold for courts as to when an election should be voided. The majority focuses on the words "to the extent of rendering the result uncertain" and, because it is uncertain in the instant case whether Whitley or Cranford would have won had those 183 votes been cast, the majority holds for naught the 1532 voters who expressed their will in either choosing a candidate or choosing not to vote at all in the District 4 race. This is contrary to the letter and spirit of *Patton*. *Patton* tells us that when (1) practices such as fraud, violence, and intimidation have prevented voters from exercising their free will *and* (2) due to those practices the result has been rendered uncertain, only then should an election be voided.

The majority would have us void any election in which, through mistake or accident, an election result is uncertain. We have consistently refused to do so in the past. In the case of *Files v. Hill*, 594 S.W.2d 836 (1980), there were numerous irregularities in an election, including voting machines that did not operate properly to the extent that some voters were not even allowed to vote, write-in votes that were not properly counted, and unclear or erroneous instructions by election officials. When Files challenged the election, he presented evidence of 1522 persons who had tried to vote for him but were prevented from doing so because of faulty voting machines or an inability to write-in a candidate. *Id.* Because Files had lost by more than 1522 votes, and because he could produce no evidence as to how many other voters would have voted for him had they been given the opportunity, the trial court refused to void the election and dismissed the claim. *Id.* On appeal, we affirmed the trial court, holding that even these numerous irregularities were not the "wrongs" spoken of in *Patton* serious enough to void an election:

> As stated in [*Patton v. Coates*], if the wrong be not so general and serious, the court cannot safely proceed beyond the exclusion of particular illegal votes or the supply of particular legal votes rejected. So far as the allegations in this complaint go, they would justify at most only the addition of the particular votes of the 1522 persons listed. Furthermore, the results reached in *Patton would not have been reached had it not been for the elements of threats and acts of violence. Jones v. Glidewell*, 13 S.W. 723. Neither is there any allegation of coercion, *which was essential in* Jones.

594 S.W.2d at 840 (emphasis added).

Contrary to the majority's assertion, the *Files* court does require some extreme "wrong," such as fraud, violence, intimidation, or coercion, before it will render an election void. If no such circumstances exist, the only remedy is to add any legal votes that were rejected or subtract any illegal votes that were cast, if those votes can be traced. Here, Cranford presented only one person, his brother Russell Cranford, to say that he would have voted for Cranford had he been given the opportunity. Under the *Files* analysis, the most these allegations justify is adding that one vote to the total, which would not change the result of the election. The majority's holding renders our precedent in *Files* questionable at best.

The case of *Jones v. Glidewell*, cited in *Files, supra*, was an 1890 case in which Glidewell was certified as the winner of an election for Pulaski County treasurer. Jones contested the election, and the trial court found that, while Jones did indeed win the majority of votes, those votes were obtained through illegal practices "of such character, and so wide spread, as to avoid the election." *Jones v. Glidewell*, 13 S.W. 723, 724 (1890). During the voting, many voters were required to open their ballots to show whether they had voted for the Democratic or Republican candidate. *Id.* This had followed a period of widespread threats of "social ostracism, of expulsion from the community, of personal violence, and of persecutions from Republican candidates for township offices [if the Democrats won]." 13 S.W. at 724.

We affirmed the trial court's voiding of the election—notably, the only time we have done so—because the coercive act of requiring voters to open their ballots was of such a nature as to render the election one that was not free and equal. *Id.* In discussing the coercion that was perpetrated on the voters, we said, "No course *which in itself* violates the law and tends to prevent a free election, can be justified." 13 S.W. at 727 (emphasis added). Obviously, the act of requiring a voter to disclose his secret ballot is one which in itself violates the law, and because it is such a coercive act, it prevents a free election.

In a very recent case in which constitutional violations were present, we refused to void an election even though fraud and misconduct were alleged regarding approximately 1,000 votes of the total 6,000 votes cast, because no fraud or misconduct was alleged in regard to the other 5,000 votes. *See Womack v. Foster,* 8 S.W.3d 854 (2000). We stated in *Womack* that "the courts do not favor disenfranchising a legal voter because of the misconduct of another person, such as an election official." *Id.* at 149, 8 S.W.3d at 869. In the instant case, the majority is willing to disenfranchise the legal votes of 543 voters who cast ballots in the District 4 race, and another 989 voters who cast legal ballots and chose not to vote in the election at all. To disenfranchise these 1532 voters in favor of 183 who were not allowed to vote flies in the face of our precedent, both recent and ancient.

None of the elements spoken of in *Patton* or *Jones,* and reiterated in *Files,* are present in this case. There has been no allegation of fraud, no threats, no violence, and no coercion. A mistake resulted in the District 4 race being left off of 183 ballots that were cast—certainly a much less egregious wrong than those present in *Files v. Hill, supra,* where well over a thousand voters wanted to vote in an election and attempted to do so, but were prevented by faulty voting machines. Yet we did not void the election in *Files* and we should not affirm the trial court's voiding of the District 4 race in this case.

We have consistently held, for over a century, that the voiding of an election is an extreme measure to which we have resorted only in cases where fraud, threats of intimidation, violence, or coercion cause an election result to be uncertain. Because the majority breaks from our long line of precedent, I must respectfully dissent.

⯈ *The Role of State Constitutions.* Note that this case turns decisively on the "free and equal" elections clause of the Arkansas Constitution. Virtually all law controlling basic election procedures is state law, and state constitutions are of course the highest form of state law. Unlike the U.S. Constitution, state constitutions frequently contain provisions specifically addressing electoral practices and procedures. Many states have constitutionalized rules protecting elections from violence or physical interference with voting, providing for secrecy of the ballot, establishing specific election crimes, and directing the legislature to enact various kinds of protective legislation. For an overview, see James A. Gardner, *Voting and Elections, in* STATE CONSTITUTIONS FOR THE 21ST CENTURY: THE AGENDA OF STATE

CONSTITUTIONAL REFORM (G. Alan Tarr and Robert F. Williams eds., SUNY Press 2006); Joshua A. Douglas, *The Right to Vote Under State Constitutions*, 67 VAND. L. REV. 89 (2014).

>> *Reluctance to Invalidate.* The court proceeds here from a baseline presumption — although plainly a rebuttable one — that elections should not be invalidated just because they have been conducted subject to irregularities. Indeed, the court goes further and maintains that elections presumptively should not be invalidated even if they are conducted by election officials in plain contravention of controlling procedural law. This is overwhelmingly the majority rule in the United States. In the words of the California Supreme Court, "It is a primary principle of law as applied to election contests that it is the duty of the court to validate the election if possible; that is to say, the election must be held valid unless plainly illegal." *Rideout v. City of Los Angeles*, 185 Cal. 426, 430 (1921).

What accounts for this rule? Why is it so urgent for a court to avoid invalidating an election? Elections are extremely important proceedings in a democratic society; surely it is highly important that they be held according to the rules. If an election is run improperly, why not simply invalidate it and run it again properly?

Disenfranchising the Innocent. Consistent with authority in other jurisdictions, the Arkansas Supreme Court suggests in *Whitley* that a contested election should not be invalidated due to the mistakes of officials because doing so disenfranchises innocent voters who cast their votes properly. But if the election is simply invalidated and rerun, those same voters will be eligible to vote again. If they have the same opportunity to vote in a properly run second election as they had in the improperly run first pass, to what extent have they been disenfranchised?

Respecting Expressions of the Popular Will. Judicial reluctance to invalidate elections is sometimes also expressed in terms of an obligation to observe and respect the expressed will of the voters. According to the Texas Supreme Court, for example,

> [s]ince the will of the legal voters as expressed at the polls is the matter of paramount concern, and, in the absence of any showing of fraud, or reasonable indication that such will has not been fairly expressed and the evidence thereof properly preserved, the courts have been liberal in construing and enforcing . . . only the provisions of the election laws which are not upon their face clearly mandatory.

Honts v. Shaw, 975 S.W.2d 816, 822 (Tex. 1998). This emphasis on respecting the will of the electorate gives this justification a pragmatic cast: the voters have spoken and courts, the people's servants, must heed their will. But can't the expression of the voters' will be influenced by the procedures that are used to determine it? If the election is run under procedures different from those that have been determined, through democratically enacted legislation, to be the appropriate ones, what reason is there to think that the election expresses the voters' will in the required way? Why doesn't this justification equally support the proposition that elections should be invalidated whenever there is any significant departure from governing procedures on the ground that the resulting calculation of the voters' will relies on information that is irrelevant because it has been collected under inappropriate circumstances?

Regarding these questions, consider this account given by the New Mexico Supreme Court in *Gunaji v. Macias*, 31 P.3d 1008, 1016 (N.M. 2001):

> Recognizing that the call for a new election does have some appeal, we instead adopt a more realistic and pragmatic approach, in that holding a new election takes time and is cumbersome. We are drawn to the case of *Huggins v. Super. Ct.*, 788 P.2d 81, 84 (Ariz. 1990), where the contestant in an election contest demanded the election be nullified and a new election held because the margin of victory was exceeded by the number of invalid votes. The court said:
>
>> A second election, however, is not immune from illegal ballots and may prove no better than the first. Moreover, a second election is costly, and the costs are not limited to the heavy fiscal expense of running an election another time. Some votes will be lost in a second election that were properly recorded in the first; these include voters who have died, voters who have moved, and voters whose interest in the office or electoral issue is too attenuated to pull them to the polls a second time.
>
> The *Huggins* court went on to quote from Note, *Developments in the Law: Elections*, 88 Harvard L. Rev. 1111, 1315 (1975):
>
>> There may . . . be identifiable biases in second elections. Candidates with ready access to financing and with strong and continuing party organizations will be able to mobilize a second campaign in the short time available much more effectively than opponents who lack such advantages. Candidates with support concentrated among less active voters may be disadvantaged in a second election if such supporters do not turn out to cast ballots when only one office is at stake.
>
> We find that these last factors of election economy, relative certitude of result, and fairness to the candidates to be compelling. To hold a new election would not be to capture the will of the electorate as it existed at the time of the contested election, but would rather reflect an entirely different set of circumstances in terms of the composition of the electorate and the attractiveness of the candidates, making it an exercise in futility to try to replicate the election.

Are these really better explanations? As to the first, it is true that elections are time-consuming and costly, but is not the price of electoral *in*accuracy also significant? Even if democracy is not to be pursued at any price, is it so clear that the price of a second election is clearly excessive?

The other reason we might call the Heraclitus Justification — just as one may never step twice into the same river because it constantly changes, so too the will of the voters is constantly evolving, and its measurement on one day cannot substitute for its measurement on a different day. Yet by the same token, the law's decision to measure the will of the voters on the first Tuesday after the first Monday in

November is just as arbitrary as measuring their will a few weeks later. Why is the first will more significant or more legitimate than the second?

▶▶   *Adjustment of Vote Totals.*   Outright invalidation of an election is, of course, an extreme remedy reserved for extreme cases. As the court indicates in *Whitley*, the preferred remedy is to identify specific irregular votes or ballots and deal with them separately, thereby preserving and counting all votes properly cast. Where this is possible, the most common approach is to invalidate illegally cast ballots — those cast by ineligible voters, for example, or cast under conditions contrary to those required by law — and adjust final totals by excluding only the disqualified votes. *See* Steven F. Huefner, *Remedying Election Wrongs*, 44 Harv. J. on Legis. 265, 279-283 (2007).

The more difficult cases arise where some irregularity is known to have occurred, but cannot be associated reliably with specific ballots. In some cases, it may not even be possible to know the precise number of ballots affected by some irregularity. In these situations, courts sometimes attempt to gain purchase on the problem by converting it into one of evidentiary burden. Thus, the party contesting an election may be charged with the burden of proving that the number of tainted ballots is sufficiently large to alter the results, or at least to cast upon the official tally some significant degree of doubt. *See Developments in the Law: Voting and Democracy*, 119 Harv. L. Rev. 1127, 1155-1165 (2006).

▶▶   *Breach of Ballot Secrecy.*   Suppose that all ballots have been counted and the winner declared in a very close race. Shortly thereafter, we learn that several people who cast ballots — enough to change the outcome of the election — were ineligible to vote. We know who was ineligible and where each of them voted, but because of the secrecy of the ballot we don't know for whom they voted. Were we to learn their votes, we could determine with certainty who actually won the election. Can these voters be compelled to reveal how they voted? In general, "good faith voters cannot be compelled to disclose how they voted." *Mahaffey v. Barnhill*, 855 P.2d 847, 850 (Colo. 1993). However, voters who engage in fraud or misconduct sometimes are held to have waived the secrecy of their ballot: "If the elector disregards the terms upon which he is allowed to vote, and thereby secures the counting of an illegal ballot, he forfeits the privilege of secrecy in favor of the superior right of a party injured by his act to have the truth disclosed." *Patterson v. Hanley*, 68 P. 821, 825 (Cal. 1902).

If people who engaged in vote fraud are ordered to disclose their votes, can we trust their evidence? If not, can we impute a particular vote to them? Suppose a candidate for office is found to have participated in or solicited fraudulent voting. Can we safely assume that a vote known to be fraudulent was cast for that candidate? Or should we assume instead that voters venal enough to defraud the public are also venal enough to defraud their political patrons? If so, should we presume instead that fraudulent or irregular votes are likely to have been cast in roughly the same distribution as valid votes cast by all voters? By other voters in that precinct? *Compare Qualkinbush v. Skubisz*, 826 N.E.2d 1181 (Ill. App. 2004), *Borders v. Kings County*, No. 05-2-00027-3 (Wash. Super. Ct. June 6, 2005), and *Bradley v. Perrodin*, 106 Cal. App. 4th 1153 (Cal. App. 2003).

E. CONGRESS AS ELECTION ADMINISTRATOR: SPECIAL PROBLEMS OF PRESIDENTIAL ELECTIONS

As we have seen repeatedly, contentious problems of administration can arise in any election. However, as the 2020 presidential election painfully revealed, the unusual complexity and decentralization of the constitutionally prescribed process for electing presidents makes it vulnerable to a unique set of additional potential problems. The impact of any such problems—even problems of a kind that arise and are resolved routinely in elections to other offices—is magnified tremendously by both the high visibility of the presidency, and the degree to which presidential politics tend to dominate the American political imagination. Furthermore, unlike other areas of law, in which the standard constitutional separation of powers provides that legislatures make laws, courts interpret them, and executives enforce them, in the realm of presidential elections, Congress performs all three functions.

This section provides an overview of the somewhat arcane procedures governing presidential elections, a brief history of some important conflicts that have emerged and their resolution, and some of the unresolved legal issues surrounding the election of U.S. presidents.

▶▶ *The Constitutional Framework.*   Unlike Senators, Representatives, or state chief executives or legislators, the President of the United States (along with the Vice President) is not elected by the voters. Article II, §1, provides: "Each State shall appoint, in such Manner as the Legislature thereof may direct, a Number of Electors, equal to the whole Number of Senators and Representatives to which the State may be entitled in the Congress. . . ." This provision creates the Electoral College, and it is the votes of these electors, rather than the people, that decide who will become President.

Two features of Article II, §1, are noteworthy. First, because the provision calls for the "appoint[ment]" of electors, it does not impose any requirement of popular election, or even popular involvement. Early in the nation's history, state legislatures often chose presidential electors directly (as they chose Senators before the Seventeenth Amendment). In the presidential election of 1800, for example, electors in ten states were chosen directly by the legislature, whereas only six states relied to any degree on popular election. This changed dramatically during the democratizing Jacksonian period, and by 1836 all states but one chose electors by popular election (South Carolina was the lone holdout).

Second, because Article II vests the appointment of electors in the state legislatures, state law controls how electors are appointed in each state. This means that if a state chooses to select electors by popular election (as all now do), procedures for those elections are specified by the state's election laws. It is thus state law that determines for presidential candidates, as for candidates for all other offices, how a candidate qualifies for the ballot, how presidential votes are cast and counted, and how post-canvassing electoral disputes are resolved. Unlike candidates for any other office, however, candidates for the presidency run in all fifty states, and their campaigns therefore operate simultaneously under fifty different legal regimes.

Additionally, state law must decide how to resolve certain questions that are specific to presidential contests. For example, a state may decide to award electors on a winner-take-all basis to the candidate who places first in statewide presidential voting, or it might decide to hold elections for electors on a districted basis so as to split its electoral vote roughly proportionately. Virginia, for instance, awarded electoral votes by district in the first three elections, but switched to winner-take-all for the election of 1800. Kentucky used a district system from its admission in 1792 through 1824, but switched to winner-take-all for the election of 1828. ALEXANDER KEYSSAR, WHY DO WE STILL HAVE THE ELECTORAL COLLEGE? 32-33 (2020). Today, only Maine and Nebraska choose electors by district.

Once the members of the Electoral College are chosen, they must get down to business, and the basic procedures are spelled out in Amendment XII (1804):

> The Electors shall meet in their respective states and vote by ballot for President and Vice-President . . . and they shall make distinct lists of all persons voted for as President, and of all persons voted for as Vice-President, and of the number of votes for each, which lists they shall sign and certify, and transmit sealed to the seat of the government of the United States, directed to the President of the Senate;-The President of the Senate shall, in the presence of the Senate and House of Representatives, open all the certificates and the votes shall then be counted;-The person having the greatest Number of votes for President, shall be the President, if such number be a majority of the whole number of Electors appointed; and if no person have such majority, then from the persons having the highest numbers not exceeding three on the list of those voted for as President, the House of Representatives shall choose immediately, by ballot, the President. But in choosing the President, the votes shall be taken by states, the representation from each state having one vote. . . .

The constitutional back-up procedure—election of the president by the House of Representatives—has been used only twice. The first instance was in the election of 1800, when backroom deal-making broke a deadlock in the House, which selected Thomas Jefferson over Aaron Burr on the thirty-sixth ballot. The second time was in the election of 1824, in which the House chose Federalist John Quincy Adams over Democrat Andrew Jackson. Angry charges were circulated that the House decision resulted from a "corrupt bargain" between the third-place candidate, Speaker of the House Henry Clay, and the Federalists, under which Clay agreed to throw his support to Adams in exchange for appointment as Secretary of State, at the time a common stepping-stone to the presidency. KEYSSAR, *supra*, at 98. As Keyssar explains in regard to the election of 1800,

> Once the election landed in the House of Representatives, . . . the nation faced the prospect of a risky, prolonged deadlock, with the political party that had lost the election wielding the power to decide which Republican would become president. The electoral system designed by the framers had, in sum, proven to be a poor fit with the partisan political realities that obtained at the turn of the century.

Id. at 41.

⟫   *The Electoral Count Act.*   Although the Twelfth Amendment is one of the more detailed regulatory provisions of the U.S. Constitution, it is nevertheless silent concerning many procedural matters. For about seventy years, these gaps in constitutional specification did not cause any serious difficulties, and Congress tended to resolve ambiguities informally and consensually. That changed during the election of 1876, when bitter disputes in Florida, Louisiana, and South Carolina over which officials had the authority to certify the state's electoral vote totals resulted in the transmission to Congress of conflicting vote counts, cast by competing slates of electors, each purporting to be the state's legally binding set of presidential electors. Lacking any constitutional guidance about how to resolve disputes concerning the validity of electoral votes, and having failed to provide for itself any standing procedures by which to do so, Congress became deadlocked along partisan lines. The deadlock was broken only when Congress appointed a commission consisting of five Senators, five Representatives, and five Justices of the Supreme Court, to determine the validity of the competing electoral vote slates. The commission, which ultimately broke along partisan lines, voted 8-7 to recommend counting electoral votes cast in favor of the Republican, Rutherford B. Hayes. Intense negotiations in Congress resulted in a compromise in which Democrats agreed to accept Hayes as president in exchange for the withdrawal of federal troops from occupied southern states—that is, the termination of Reconstruction.

Recognizing that the ambiguities in the constitutional framework required resolution, Congress set out to draft clarifying legislation. It took a decade, and the result, the Electoral Count Act of 1887 (ECA), 3 U.S.C. §1, *et seq.*, is today widely thought to be so complex and poorly drafted that it raises as many problems as it solves.

Roughly speaking, the baseline procedure contemplated by the ECA works like this. States choose their presidential electors on Election Day in November. Any post-canvassing disputes are resolved by the state pursuant to its own laws of recount and electoral contest. On the second Wednesday in December, the presidential electors, assumed by now to have been determined under state law to be entitled to their office, meet in a place specified by state law and cast their votes. After they vote, the electors prepare a certificate recording their votes and transmit it to various state and federal officials, including the President of the U.S. Senate. In addition, the state's "executive"—a term the ECA does not define—issues a Certificate of Ascertainment for the winning candidate's slate of electors. That certificate is transmitted ultimately to Congress. Congress then meets in joint session on January 6 following the election. The envelopes containing the electoral votes are opened one by one by the President of the Senate (normally the Vice President of the United States), the results are announced and tallied, and the winner, if there is one, determined and announced.

⟫   *Resolution of Disputes under the ECA.*   The ECA also attempts to anticipate and resolve various problems that might arise if things go wrong under the normal procedure for counting electoral votes. Section 5 of the ECA purports to establish a conclusive presumption of validity for electoral votes identified as valid by the standing laws of the state transmitting them:

> If any State shall have provided, by laws enacted prior to the day fixed for the appointment of the electors, for its final determination of any controversy or contest concerning the appointment of all or any of the electors of such State, by judicial or other methods or procedures, and such determination shall have been made at least six days before the time fixed for the meeting of the electors, such determination made pursuant to such law so existing on said day, and made at least six days prior to said time of meeting of the electors, shall be conclusive, and shall govern in the counting of the electoral votes as provided in the Constitution, and as hereinafter regulated, so far as the ascertainment of the electors appointed by such State is concerned.

Nevertheless, recognizing that various kinds of questions on the validity of electoral votes may arise, the ECA creates a procedure by which members of Congress may object to electoral votes during the counting in joint session. Such objections must be presented in writing, must clearly state the ground, and must be signed by at least one Representative and one Senator. If a properly framed objection is made, counting is suspended, and the House and Senate immediately go separately into session to debate and vote on the objection.

Where a state has forwarded only a single set of electoral votes, Section 15 of the ECA provides for resolution of objections as follows:

> [N]o electoral vote or votes from any State which shall have been regularly given by electors whose appointment has been lawfully certified to according to section 6 of this title from which but one return has been received shall be rejected, but the two Houses concurrently may reject the vote or votes when they agree that such vote or votes have not been so regularly given by electors whose appointment has been so certified.

Section 6, referred to in the preceding passage, requires certification of a state's electoral votes by the state's "executive." Thus, the electoral votes of a state, upon certification by the state's executive, must be accepted by Congress for purposes of tallying electoral votes, unless the two houses agree that the votes have not been "regularly given." The meaning of that term is undefined.

In cases where a state has transmitted to Congress more than one set of electoral votes, Section 15 of the ECA provides:

> If more than one return or paper purporting to be a return from a State shall have been received by the President of the Senate, those votes, and those only, shall be counted which shall have been regularly given by the electors who are shown by the determination mentioned in section 5 of this title to have been appointed, if the determination in said section provided for shall have been made, . . . but in case there shall arise the question which of two or more of such State authorities determining what electors have been appointed, as mentioned in section 5 of this title, is the lawful tribunal of such State, the votes regularly given of those electors, and those only, of such State shall be counted whose title as electors the two Houses, acting separately, shall concurrently decide is supported

by the decision of such State so authorized by its law; and in such case of more than one return or paper purporting to be a return from a State, if there shall have been no such determination of the question in the State aforesaid, then those votes, and those only, shall be counted which the two Houses shall concurrently decide were cast by lawful electors appointed in accordance with the laws of the State, unless the two Houses, acting separately, shall concurrently decide such votes not to be the lawful votes of the legally appointed electors of such State. But if the two Houses shall disagree in respect of the counting of such votes, then, and in that case, the votes of the electors whose appointment shall have been certified by the executive of the State, under the seal thereof, shall be counted.

Section 15 thus appears to resolve some forms of uncertainty only by creating new ones. The provision removes congressional discretion to choose arbitrarily among competing slates of presidential electors, but apparently gives it the discretion to decide whether certain electoral votes were "regularly given," which "executive" authority of the state is the proper certifying authority, and whether electoral votes were given "in accordance with the laws of the State." It is unclear, moreover, whether the ECA gives Congress the authority to settle these issues according to its own discretion, or whether it is obliged to follow authoritative rulings of state courts concerning the application of state law. However, if members of Congress have independent discretion to decide for themselves whether a state has followed its own laws, then it is unclear what the ECA actually accomplishes.

A final type of problem anticipated by the ECA is handled in Section 2: "Whenever any State has held an election for the purpose of choosing electors, and has failed to make a choice on the day prescribed by law [Election Day], the electors may be appointed on a subsequent day in such a manner as the legislature of such State may direct." This section appears to concern the possibility that a state may be unable to hold a presidential election on Election Day, requiring it to choose electors subsequently, in which case the provision authorizes the legislature to set aside state law and to appoint electors itself. However, the reach of the provision is uncertain, as it is unclear what counts as "making a choice" *on* Election Day. Vote counting, for example, often drags into subsequent days, and if there is a recount or contest under state law, final results may be delayed for weeks. Yet, given other references in the ECA to the lawful processes of state vote counting, it would be odd to read Section 2 to authorize a state legislature to ignore election results and appoint its own slate of electors every time someone files an election contest authorized by state law.

Given the ECA's many ambiguities, is there any chance that the Supreme Court might issue authoritative clarifications? Probably not. It seems quite reasonable to consider such questions to be "political" ones, the resolution of which the Constitution commits expressly to Congress. This appears to have been the dominant assumption of the members of the Congress that adopted the ECA. Stephen A. Siegel, *The Conscientious Congressman's Guide to the Electoral Count Act of 1887*, 56 Fla. L. Rev. 541, 565 (2004).

>> *Congressional Counting Prior to 2021.* Although commentators had from time to time noticed and warned about the ambiguities of the Electoral Count Act, those issues long remained latent. Since 1876, only one incident arose in which a state transmitted two different slates of presidential electors. In the 1960 election pitting Vice President Richard M. Nixon against Senator John F. Kennedy, an initial count of the vote in Hawaii had Nixon ahead, but was extremely close, and contested. The matter wound up in the state courts, but moved slowly through the system. Fearing that Congress might discard Hawaii's electoral votes altogether if he did not certify them by the date in December specified by the ECA, the governor of Hawaii certified Nixon as the winner of the state's electoral votes. After the state's electors had already met and cast their votes for Nixon, the Hawaii Supreme Court ruled that the popular vote totals required an adjustment that made Kennedy the winner. The governor, lacking guidance from the ECA about how to handle this issue, issued a new, corrected certification showing Kennedy as the winner, and transmitted it to Congress.

The President of the Senate at the time was Vice President Richard Nixon himself, one of the candidates for office. In an act of statesmanship, Nixon used his discretion as presiding officer to propose a solution to the dual slate problem against his own interests: he used a parliamentary maneuver to bypass formal procedures by asking unanimous consent to recognize the votes of the later-certified, Democratic slate of electors on the ground that it represented the final and most accurate electoral determination by the state courts. The members of the joint session agreed, obviating the need to go any further under the ECA.

>> *The 2021 Electoral Vote Count.* The era of statesmanlike agreement came abruptly to an end on January 6, 2021. Details of what happened that day are, at this writing, still emerging, and a congressional investigatory committee has not yet published its findings. Preliminary news reports, however, seem to suggest the following. At the urging of President Trump, who had claimed continually since Election Day that the election had been "stolen" from him by vote fraud perpetrated by Democrats, numerous Republican members of Congress agreed to object to the counting of electoral votes for Joe Biden cast in Arizona, Georgia, Michigan, Nevada, Pennsylvania, and Wisconsin. All were swing states that went narrowly for Biden; that President Trump had claimed to have actually won but for fraud by Democrats; and in which litigation by the Trump campaign to overturn the results under state law had been unsuccessful.

As Congress proceeded alphabetically through the states, an objection was filed to the electoral votes of Arizona by Representative Paul Gosar (R-AZ) and Senator Ted Cruz (R-TX) on the grounds that Arizona's electoral votes had not been "regularly given." The objection was founded on allegations of election irregularities, many of which had been rejected by courts in litigation. *See* Derek Muller, *Electoral Votes Regularly Given*, 55 GA. L. REV. 1529, 1544 (2021). The two chambers voted separately on the objection, which failed in the Senate by a vote of 6-93, and in the House by 121-303. Ballotpedia, *Counting of electoral votes (January 6-7, 2021)*. Before Congress reached Georgia in the count, the process was interrupted by a violent occupation of the U.S. Capitol by supporters of President Trump who were unwilling to accept the results of the presidential election. When the counting resumed, some Republicans who had planned to file objections to the electoral votes of other states were apparently too shaken to proceed with their plan. Nevertheless, by the time Congress reached Pennsylvania, an objection was filed, this time by Representative Scott Perry (R-PA) and Senator Josh Hawley (R-MO), on similar grounds. The objection was rejected in the Senate by 7-92 and in the House by 138-282. *Id.*

Other evidence suggests that Trump supporters had developed a legal theory according to which Vice President Pence had discretion as presiding officer to reject electoral votes even if the joint session was unwilling to do so, and that attempts had been made to pressure Pence into exercising his discretion in Trump's favor. Pence resisted these efforts and declared Biden the winner. Jerry H. Goldfeder, *Excessive Judicialization, Extralegal Interventions, and Violent Insurrection: A Snapshot of Our 59th Presidential Election*, 90 FORDHAM L. REV. 335 (2021).

The 2021 electoral vote count exposed dramatically the ambiguities and other inadequacies of the Electoral Count Act, and many have called for its amendment or replacement. Is it possible to draft a statute that would be so free from ambiguity that no member of Congress could draft a qualifying objection? Is the principal problem one of statutory craftsmanship, or of partisan polarization so extreme as to render impossible the exercise of compromise, much less statesmanship, or even self-restraint? Or, worse, is the problem one of an illiberal unwillingness to accept liberal democratic outcomes? If the latter, can Congress be trusted to perform even the seemingly ministerial task of counting votes? And if not, where else should that discretion be lodged? During the 2000 election, after rulings by the Florida Supreme Court initiated a recount of votes from certain disputed counties, the Republican-controlled Florida Legislature threatened to invalidate the results of the election by using what it deemed to be its inherent Article II power to appoint its own slate of electors, who would have favored Bush. This would likely have produced the transmission to Congress of competing slates of electors, a dispute that Congress would then have had to resolve under the ECA. The Supreme Court's decision in *Bush v. Gore*, by stopping the recount, resulted in the certification by Florida of a Republican slate of electors for Bush, mooting the legislature's threat. Some have argued that the Supreme Court was motivated to intervene as it did precisely to prevent the dispute from landing in the lap of Congress. *See, e.g.,* Elizabeth Garrett, *Leaving the Decision to Congress, in* THE VOTE: BUSH, GORE, AND THE SUPREME COURT (Cass R. Sunstein and Richard A. Epstein, eds., 2001); CHARLES L. ZELDEN, *BUSH V. GORE*: EXPOSING THE HIDDEN CRISIS IN AMERICAN DEMOCRACY (2008). Was the Court correct—judicial resolution of disputed presidential elections is better than congressional resolution?

» ***The "Independent State Legislature Doctrine."*** One potentially significant constitutional issue now brewing among Republican campaign lawyers and, to a lesser extent, in the courts, is the so-called "independent state legislature doctrine" (ISLD), a novel reading of Article II that, if accepted, would radically alter the election law landscape. Article II, §1, you will recall, provides: "Each State shall appoint, in such Manner as the *Legislature* thereof may direct, a Number of Electors, equal to the whole Number of Senators and Representatives to which the State may be entitled in the Congress. . . ." The provision expressly delegates the power to appoint electors to the state "legislature" rather than to the "state," and the question is whether this choice of words has any legal significance.

Proponents of the ISLD claim that it does; the constitutional language, they assert, delegates the power to decide how presidential electors are chosen to the state legislature *exclusively*. Consequently, proponents claim, no other organ or instrument of state government may participate at all in the relevant decision-making process. Thus, if the legislature enacts a law establishing a procedure for selecting presidential electors, the governor may not veto it, nor may the state judiciary invalidate or alter it as a matter of state law. Indeed, the ISLD postulates that when a state legislature exercises its power to regulate presidential elections, it cannot lawfully be subjected to any constraints on its power that appear in the state constitution. The doctrine holds, in other words, that in the context of regulating presidential elections, the state legislature is completely unconstrained by the checks and balances and constitutional constraints on its authority that apply to every other decision it makes. The legislature, in these circumstances, is said to exercise a power granted directly by the federal Constitution, a power structured in a way that essentially creates a new, single-purpose body—a presidential election regulator unconstrained by the very constitution that created it in the first place.

One might, quite rightly, be skeptical of such a doctrine. The Constitution is filled with provisions that express nothing but reverence for the sovereignty of the states, and in particular for their sovereign authority to establish and control their own internal processes of democratic self-governance. Yet, three justices of the U.S. Supreme Court have expressed, in passing and in contexts where the issue was not presented squarely for decision, some enthusiasm for the ISLD. For instance, in an opinion dissenting from a denial of certiorari in a case seeking review of a Pennsylvania Supreme Court decision that modified the terms of a Pennsylvania election statute on state constitutional grounds, Justice Alito, joined by Justices Gorsuch and Thomas, wrote:

> It would be highly desirable to issue a ruling on the constitutionality of the State Supreme Court's decision before the election. That question has national importance, and there is a strong likelihood that the State Supreme Court decision violates the Federal Constitution. The provisions of the Federal Constitution conferring on state legislatures, not state courts, the authority to make rules governing federal elections would be meaningless if a state court could override the rules adopted by the legislature simply by claiming that a state constitutional provision gave the courts the authority to make whatever rules it thought appropriate for the conduct of a fair election.

Republican Party of Pennsylvania v. Boockvar, 592 U.S. __ (2020) (order denying certiorari).

Academic commentary has been overwhelmingly negative. For example, as two commentators have recently argued, proponents of the ISLD "stand lawful federalism on its head. They theory invokes constitutional provisions designed to protect states against federal interference . . . and instead uses these provisions to disrespect both the wishes of the state peoples who create, empower, and limit their legislatures, and the wishes of the elected legislatures themselves." Vikram David Amar and Akhil Reed Amar, *Eradicating* Bush-*League Arguments Root and Branch: The*

Article II Independent-State-Legislature Notion and Related Rubbish, 2021 SUP. CT. REV. __ (2021). *See also* Mark S. Kraus, *Debunking the Non-Delegation Doctrine for State Regulation of Federal Elections,* 108 VA. L. REV. __ (2022); Hayward H. Smith, *Revisiting the History of the Independent State Legislature Doctrine,* 53 ST. MARY'S L.J. __ (2022). For a nuanced but generally supportive treatment of the ISLD, see Michael T. Morley, *The Independent State Legislature Doctrine,* 90 FORDHAM L. REV. 501 (2021).

U.S. Constitution

We the People of the United States, in Order to form a more perfect Union, establish Justice, insure domestic Tranquility, provide for the common defence, promote the general Welfare, and secure the Blessings of Liberty to ourselves and our Posterity, do ordain and establish this Constitution for the United States of America.

Article I

Section 1. All legislative Powers herein granted shall be vested in a Congress of the United States, which shall consist of a Senate and House of Representatives.

Section 2. The House of Representatives shall be composed of Members chosen every second Year by the People of the several States, and the Electors in each State shall have the Qualifications requisite for Electors of the most numerous Branch of the State Legislature.

No Person shall be a Representative who shall not have attained to the Age of twenty-five Years, and been seven Years a Citizen of the United States, and who shall not, when elected, be an Inhabitant of that State in which he shall be chosen.

[Representatives and direct Taxes shall be apportioned among the several States which may be included within this Union, according to their respective Numbers, which shall be determined by adding to the whole Number of free Persons, including those bound to Service for a Term of Years, and excluding Indians not taxed, three fifths of all other Persons.][1] The actual Enumeration shall be made within three Years after the first Meeting of the Congress of the United States, and within every subsequent Term of ten Years, in such Manner as they shall by Law direct. The Number of Representatives shall not exceed one for every thirty Thousand, but each State shall have at Least one Representative; and until such enumeration shall be made, the State of New Hampshire shall be entitled to chuse three, Massachusetts eight, Rhode Island and Providence Plantations one, Connecticut five, New York six, New Jersey four, Pennsylvania eight, Delaware one, Maryland six, Virginia ten, North Carolina five, South Carolina five, and Georgia three.

When vacancies happen in the Representation from any State, the Executive Authority thereof shall issue Writs of Election to fill such Vacancies.

The House of Representatives shall chuse their Speaker and other Officers; and shall have the sole Power of Impeachment.

---

1. Changed by section 2 of the fourteenth amendment.

Section 3. The Senate of the United States shall be composed of two Senators from each State, [chosen by the Legislature thereof,][2] for six Years; and each Senator shall have one Vote.

Immediately after they shall be assembled in Consequence of the first Election, they shall be divided as equally as may be into three Classes. The Seats of the Senators of the first Class shall be vacated at the Expiration of the second Year, of the second Class at the Expiration of the fourth Year, and of the third Class at the Expiration of the sixth Year, so that one-third may be chosen every second Year; [and if Vacancies happen by Resignation, or otherwise, during the Recess of the Legislature of any State, the Executive thereof may make temporary Appointments until the next Meeting of the Legislature, which shall then fill such Vacancies.][3]

No Person shall be a Senator who shall not have attained to the Age of thirty Years, and been nine Years a Citizen of the United States, and who shall not, when elected, be an Inhabitant of that State for which he shall be chosen.

The Vice President of the United States shall be President of the Senate, but shall have no Vote, unless they be equally divided.

The Senate shall chuse their other Officers, and also a President pro tempore, in the absence of the Vice President, or when he shall exercise the Office of President of the United States.

The Senate shall have the sole Power to try all Impeachments. When sitting for that Purpose, they shall be on Oath or Affirmation. When the President of the United States is tried, the Chief Justice shall preside: And no Person shall be convicted without the Concurrence of two thirds of the Members present.

Judgment in Cases of Impeachment shall not extend further than to removal from Office, and disqualification to hold and enjoy and Office of honor, Trust or Profit under the United States: but the Party convicted shall nevertheless be liable and subject to Indictment, Trial, Judgment and Punishment, according to Law.

Section 4. The Times, Places and Manner of holding Elections for Senators and Representatives, shall be prescribed in each State by the Legislature thereof; but the Congress may at any time by Law make or alter such Regulations, except as to the Place of Chusing Senators.

The Congress shall assemble at least once in every Year, and such Meeting shall [be on the first Monday in December,][4] unless they shall by Law appoint a different Day.

Section 5. Each House shall be the Judge of the Elections, Returns and Qualifications of its own Members, and a majority of each shall constitute a Quorum to do Business; but a smaller number may adjourn from day to day, and may be authorized to compel the Attendance of absent Members, in such Manner, and under such Penalties as each House may provide.

---

2. Changed by section 1 of the seventeenth amendment.
3. Changed by clause 2 of the seventeenth amendment.
4. Changed by section 2 of the twentieth amendment.

Each House may determine the Rules of its Proceedings, punish its Members for disorderly Behavior, and, with the Concurrence of two thirds, expel a Member.

Each House shall keep a Journal of its Proceedings, and from time to time publish the same, excepting such Parts as may in their Judgement require Secrecy; and the Yeas and Nays of the Members of either House on any question shall, at the Desire of one fifth of those Present, be entered on the Journal.

Neither House, during the Session of Congress, shall, without the Consent of the other, adjourn for more than three days, nor to any other Place than that in which the two Houses shall be sitting.

Section 6. The Senators and Representatives shall receive a Compensation for their Services, to be ascertained by Law, and paid out of the Treasury of the United States. They shall in all Cases, except Treason, Felony and Breach of the Peace, be privileged from Arrest during their Attendance at the Session of their respective Houses, and in going to and returning from the same; and for any Speech or Debate in either House, they shall not be questioned in any other Place.

No Senator or Representative shall, during the Time for which he was elected, be appointed to any civil Office under the Authority of the United States, which shall have been created, or the Emoluments whereof shall have been encreased during such time; and no Person holding any Office under the United States, shall be a Member of either House during his Continuance in Office.

Section 7. All Bills for raising Revenue shall originate in the House of Representatives; but the Senate may propose or concur with Amendments as on other Bills.

Every Bill which shall have passed the House of Representatives and the Senate, shall, before it become a Law, be presented to the President of the United States; If he approve he shall sign it, but if not he shall return it, with his Objections to that House in which it shall have originated, who shall enter the Objections at large on their Journal, and proceed to reconsider it. If after such Reconsideration two thirds of that House shall agree to pass the Bill, it shall be sent, together with the Objections, to the other House, by which it shall likewise be reconsidered, and if approved by two thirds of that House, it shall become a Law. But in all such Cases the Votes of both Houses shall be determined by Yeas and Nays, and the Names of the Persons voting for and against the Bill shall be entered on the Journal of each House respectively. If any Bill shall not be returned by the President within ten days (Sundays excepted) after it shall have been presented to him, the Same shall be a Law, in like Manner as if he had signed it, unless the Congress by their Adjournment prevent its Return, in which Case it shall not be a Law.

Every Order, Resolution, or Vote to which the Concurrence of the Senate and House of Representatives may be necessary (except on a question of Adjournment) shall be presented to the President of the United States; and before the Same shall take Effect, shall be approved by him, or being disapproved by him, shall be repassed by two thirds of the Senate and House of Representatives, according to the Rules and Limitations prescribed in the Case of a Bill.

Section 8. The Congress shall have Power To lay and collect Taxes, Duties, Imposts and Excises, to pay the Debts and provide for the common Defense and general Welfare of the United States; but all Duties, Imposts and Excises shall be uniform throughout the United States;

To borrow money on the credit of the United States;

To regulate Commerce with foreign Nations, and among the several States, and with the Indian Tribes;

To establish an uniform Rule of Naturalization, and uniform Laws on the subject of Bankruptcies throughout the United States;

To coin Money, regulate the Value thereof, and of foreign Coin, and fix the Standard of Weights and Measures;

To provide for the Punishment of counterfeiting the Securities and current Coin of the United States;

To establish Post Offices and post Roads;

To promote the Progress of Science and useful Arts, by securing for limited Times to Authors and Inventors the exclusive Right to their respective Writings and Discoveries;

To constitute Tribunals inferior to the Supreme Court;

To define and punish Piracies and Felonies committed on the high Seas, and Offenses against the Law of Nations;

To declare War, grant Letters of Marque and Reprisal, and make Rules concerning Captures on Land and Water;

To raise and support Armies, but no Appropriation of Money to that Use shall be for a longer Term than two Years;

To provide and maintain a Navy;

To make Rules for the Government and Regulation of the land and naval Forces;

To provide for calling forth the Militia to execute the Laws of the Union, suppress Insurrections and repel Invasions;

To provide for organizing, arming, and disciplining the Militia and for governing such Part of them as may be employed in the Service of the United States, reserving to the States respectively, the Appointment of the Officers, and the Authority of training the Militia according to the discipline prescribed by Congress;

To exercise exclusive Legislation in all Cases whatsoever, over such District (not exceeding ten Miles square) as may, by Cession of particular States, and the acceptance of Congress, become the Seat of the government of the United States, and to exercise like Authority over all Places purchased by the Consent of the Legislature of the State in which the Same shall be, for the Erection of Forts, Magazines, Arsenals, dock-Yards, and other needful Buildings; — And

To make all Laws which shall be necessary and proper for carrying into Execution the foregoing Powers, and all other Powers vested by this Constitution in the Government of the United States, or in any Department or Officer thereof.

Section 9. The Migration or Importation of such Persons as any of the States now existing shall think proper to admit, shall not be prohibited by the Congress prior to the Year one thousand eight hundred and eight, but a tax or duty may be imposed on such Importation, not exceeding ten dollars for each Person.

The privilege of the Writ of Habeas Corpus shall not be suspended, unless when in Cases of Rebellion or Invasion the public Safety may require it.

No Bill of Attainder or ex post facto Law shall be passed.

No capitation, or other direct, Tax shall be laid, unless in Proportion to the Census or Enumeration herein before directed to be taken.[5]

No Tax or Duty shall be laid on Articles exported from any State.

No Preference shall be given by any Regulation of Commerce or Revenue to the Ports of one State over those of another: nor shall Vessels bound to, or from, one State, be obliged to enter, clear, or pay Duties in another.

No Money shall be drawn from the Treasury, but in Consequence of Appropriations made by Law; and a regular Statement and Account of the Receipts and Expenditures of all public Money shall be published from time to time.

No Title of Nobility shall be granted by the United States: And no Person holding any Office of Profit or Trust under them, shall, without the consent of the Congress, accept of any present, Emolument, Office, or Title of any kind whatever, from any King, Prince, or foreign State.

Section 10. No State shall enter into any Treaty, Alliance, or Confederation; grant Letters of Marque and Reprisal; coin Money; emit Bills of Credit; make any Thing but gold and silver Coin a Tender in Payment of Debts; pass any Bill of Attainder, ex post facto Law, or Law impairing the Obligation of Contracts, or grant any Title of Nobility.

No State shall, without the Consent of the Congress, lay any Imposts or Duties on Imports or Exports, except what may be absolutely necessary for executing its inspection Laws: and the net Produce of all Duties and Imposts, laid by any State on Imports or Exports, shall be for the Use of the Treasury of the United States; and all such Laws shall be subject to the Revision and Controul of the Congress.

No State shall, without the Consent of Congress, lay any duty of Tonnage, keep Troops, or Ships of War in time of Peace, enter into any Agreement or Compact with another State, or with a foreign Power, or engage in War, unless actually invaded, or in such imminent Danger as will not admit of delay.

Article II

Section 1. The executive Power shall be vested in a President of the United States of America. He shall hold his Office during the Term of four Years, and, together with the Vice-President, chosen for the same Term, be elected, as follows.

Each State shall appoint, in such Manner as the Legislature thereof may direct, a Number of Electors, equal to the whole Number of Senators and Representatives to which the State may be entitled in the Congress; but no Senator or Representative, or Person holding an Office of Trust or Profit under the United States, shall be appointed an Elector.

[The Electors shall meet in their respective States, and vote by Ballot for two persons, of whom one at least shall not be an Inhabitant of the same State with themselves. And they shall make a List of all the Persons voted for, and of the Number of Votes for each; which List they shall sign and certify, and transmit

---

5. But see the sixteenth amendment.

sealed to the Seat of the Government of the United States, directed to the President of the Senate. The President of the Senate shall, in the Presence of the Senate and House of Representatives, open all the Certificates, and the Votes shall then be counted. The Person having the greatest Number of Votes shall be the President, if such Number be a Majority of the whole Number of Electors appointed; and if there be more than one who have such Majority, and have an equal Number of Votes, then the House of Representatives shall immediately chuse by Ballot one of them for President; and if no Person have a Majority, then from the five highest on the List the said House shall in like Manner chuse the President. But in chusing the President, the Votes shall be taken by States, the Representation from each State having one Vote; a quorum for this Purpose shall consist of a Member or Members from two thirds of the States, and a Majority of all the States shall be necessary to a Choice. In every Case, after the Choice of the President, the Person having the greatest Number of Votes of the Electors shall be the Vice President. But if there should remain two or more who have equal Votes, the Senate shall chuse from them by Ballot the Vice-President.][6]

The Congress may determine the Time of chusing the Electors, and the Day on which they shall give their Votes; which Day shall be the same throughout the United States.

No Person except a natural born Citizen, or a Citizen of the United States, at the time of the Adoption of this Constitution, shall be eligible to the Office of President; neither shall any Person be eligible to that Office who shall not have attained to the Age of thirty-five Years, and been fourteen Years a Resident within the United States.

[In Case of the Removal of the President from Office, or of his Death, Resignation, or Inability to discharge the Powers and Duties of the said Office, the same shall devolve on the Vice President, and the Congress may by Law, provide for the Case of Removal, Death, Resignation or Inability, both of the President and Vice President, declaring what Officer shall then act as President, and such Officer shall act accordingly, until the Disability be removed, or a President shall be elected.][7]

The President shall, at stated Times, receive for his Services, a Compensation, which shall neither be encreased nor diminished during the Period for which he shall have been elected, and he shall not receive within that Period any other Emolument from the United States, or any of them.

Before he enter on the Execution of his Office, he shall take the following Oath or Affirmation:—"I do solemnly swear (or affirm) that I will faithfully execute the Office of President of the United States, and will to the best of my Ability, preserve, protect and defend the Constitution of the United States."

Section 2. The President shall be Commander in Chief of the Army and Navy of the United States, and of the Militia of the several States, when called into the actual Service of the United States; he may require the Opinion in writing, of the principal Officer in each of the executive Departments, upon any subject relating to the Duties of their respective Offices, and he shall have Power to

---

6. Superseded by the twelfth amendment.
7. This clause has been affected by the twenty-fifth amendment.

Grant Reprieves and Pardons for Offenses against the United States, except in Cases of Impeachment.

He shall have Power, by and with the Advice and Consent of the Senate, to make Treaties, provided two-thirds of the Senators present concur; and he shall nominate, and by and with the Advice and Consent of the Senate, shall appoint Ambassadors, other public Ministers and Consuls, Judges of the supreme Court, and all other Officers of the united States, whose Appointments are not herein otherwise provided for, and which shall be established by Law: but the Congress may by Law vest the Appointment of such inferior Officers, as they think proper, in the President alone, in the Courts of Law, or in the Heads of Departments.

The President shall have Power to fill up all Vacancies that may happen during the Recess of the Senate, by granting Commissions which shall expire at the End of their next Session.

Section 3. He shall from time to time give to the Congress Information of the State of the Union, and recommend to their Consideration such Measures as he shall judge necessary and expedient; he may, on extraordinary Occasions, convene both Houses, or either of them, and in Case of Disagreement between them, with Respect to the Time of Adjournment, he may adjourn them to such Time as he shall think proper; he shall receive Ambassadors and other public Ministers; he shall take Care that the Laws be faithfully executed, and shall Commission all the Officers of the United States.

Section 4. The President, Vice President and all civil Officers of the Unites States, shall be removed from Office on Impeachment for, and Conviction of, Treason, Bribery, or other high Crimes and Misdemeanors.

Article III

Section 1. The judicial Power of the United States, shall be vested in one supreme Court, and in such inferior Courts as the Congress may from time to time ordain and establish. The Judges, both of the Supreme and inferior Courts, shall hold their Offices during good Behavior, and shall, at stated Times, receive for their Services, a Compensation, which shall not be diminished during their Continuance in Office.

Section 2. The judicial Power shall extend to all Cases, in Law and Equity, arising under this Constitution, the Laws of the United States, and Treaties made, or which shall be made, under their Authority; — to all Cases affecting Ambassadors, other public Ministers and Consuls; — to all Cases of admiralty and maritime Jurisdiction; — to Controversies to which the United States shall be a party; — to Controversies between two or more States; — between a State and Citizens of another State; — between Citizens of different States; — between Citizens of the same State claiming Lands under Grants of different States, and between a State, or the Citizens thereof, and foreign States, Citizens or Subjects.

In all Cases affecting Ambassadors, other public Ministers and Consuls, and those in which a State shall be Party, the supreme Court shall have original

Jurisdiction. In all the other cases before mentioned, the supreme Court shall have appellate Jurisdiction, both as to Law and Fact, with such Exceptions, and under such Regulations as the Congress shall make.

The trial of all Crimes, except in Cases of Impeachment, shall be by Jury; and such Trial shall be held in the State where the said Crimes shall have been committed; but when not committed within any State, the Trial shall be at such Place or Places as the Congress may by Law have directed.

Section 3. Treason against the United States, shall consist only in levying War against them, or in adhering to their Enemies, giving them Aid and Comfort. No Person shall be convicted of Treason unless on the Testimony of two Witnesses to the same overt Act, or on Confession in open Court.

The Congress shall have Power to declare the Punishment of Treason, but no Attainder of Treason shall work Corruption of Blood, or Forfeiture except during the Life of the Person attainted.

Article IV

Section 1. Full Faith and Credit shall be given in each State to the public Acts, Records, and judicial Proceedings of every other State. And the Congress may by general Laws prescribe the Manner in which such Acts, Records and Proceedings shall be proved, and the Effect thereof.

Section 2. The Citizens of each State shall be entitled to all Privileges and Immunities of Citizens in the several States.

A Person charged in any State with Treason, Felony, or other Crime, who shall flee from Justice, and be found in another State, shall on demand of the executive Authority of the State from which he fled, be delivered up, to be removed to the State having Jurisdiction of the Crime.

[No Person held to Service or Labour in one State, under the Laws thereof, escaping into another, shall, in Consequence of any Law or Regulation therein, be discharged from such Service or Labour, but shall be delivered up on Claim of the Party to whom such Service or Labour may be due.][8]

Section 3. New States may be admitted by the Congress into this Union; but no new State shall be formed or erected within the Jurisdiction of any other State; nor any State be formed by the Junction of two or more States, or parts of States, without the Consent of the Legislatures of the States concerned as well as of the Congress.

The Congress shall have Power to dispose of and make all needful Rules and Regulations respecting the Territory or other Property belonging to the United States; and nothing in this Constitution shall be so construed as to Prejudice any Claims of the United States, or of any particular State.

---

8. Superseded by the thirteenth amendment.

Section 4. The United States shall guarantee to every State in this Union a Republican Form of Government, and shall protect each of them against Invasion; and on Application of the Legislature, or of the Executive (when the Legislature cannot be convened) against domestic Violence.

Article V

The congress, whenever two-thirds of both Houses shall deem it necessary, shall propose Amendments to this Constitution, or, on the Application of the Legislatures of two-thirds of the several States, shall call a Convention for proposing Amendments, which, in either Case, shall be valid to all Intents and Purposes, as part of this Constitution, when ratified by the Legislatures of three-fourths of the several States, or by Conventions in three-fourths thereof, as the one or the other Mode of Ratification may be proposed by the Congress: Provided that no Amendment which may be made prior to the Year One thousand eight hundred and eight shall in any Manner affect the first and fourth Clauses in the Ninth Section of the first Article; and that no State, without its Consent, shall be deprived of its equal Suffrage in the Senate.

Article VI

All Debts contracted and Engagements entered into, before the Adoption of this Constitution, shall be as valid against the United States under this Constitution, as under the Confederation.

This Constitution, and the Laws of the United States which shall be made in Pursuance thereof; and all Treaties made, or which shall be made, under the Authority of the United States, shall be the supreme Law of the Land; and the Judges in every State shall be bound thereby, any thing in the Constitution or Laws of any State to the contrary notwithstanding.

The Senators and Representatives before mentioned, and the Members of the several State Legislatures, and all executive and judicial Officers, both of the United States and of the several States, shall be bound by Oath or Affirmation, to support this Constitution; but no religious Test shall ever be required as a Qualification to any Office or public Trust under the United States.

Article VII

The Ratification of the Conventions of nine States shall be sufficient for the Establishment of this Constitution between the States so ratifying the Same.

(The first 10 Amendments were ratified December 15, 1791.)

Amendment I

Congress shall make no law respecting an establishment of religion, or prohibiting the free exercise thereof; or abridging the freedom of speech, or of the press; or the right of the people peaceably to assemble, and to petition the Government for a redress of grievances.

Amendment II

A well regulated Militia, being necessary to the security of a free State, the right of the people to keep and bear Arms, shall not be infringed.

Amendment III

No Soldier shall, in time of peace be quartered in any house, without the consent of the Owner, nor in time of war, but in a manner to be prescribed by law.

Amendment IV

The right of the people to be secure in their persons, houses, papers, and effects, against unreasonable searches and seizures, shall not be violated, and no Warrants shall issue, but upon probable cause, supported by Oath or affirmation, and particularly describing the place to be searched, and the persons or things to be seized.

Amendment V

No person shall be held to answer for a capital, or otherwise infamous crime, unless on a presentment or indictment of a Grand Jury, except in cases arising in the land or naval forces, or in the Militia, when in actual service in time of War or public danger; nor shall any person be subject for the same offence to be twice put in jeopardy of life or limb; nor shall be compelled in any criminal case to be a witness against himself, nor be deprived of life, liberty, or property, without due process of law; nor shall private property be taken for public use, without just compensation.

Amendment VI

In all criminal prosecutions, the accused shall enjoy the right to a speedy and public trial, by an impartial jury of the State and district wherein the crime shall have been committed, which district shall have been previously ascertained by law, and to be informed of the nature and cause of the accusation; to be confronted with the witnesses against him; to have compulsory process for obtaining witnesses in his favor, and to have the Assistance of Counsel for his defence.

Amendment VII

In suits at common law, where the value in controversy shall exceed twenty dollars, the right of trial by jury shall be preserved, and no fact tried by a jury, shall be otherwise reexamined in any Court of the United States, than according to the rules of the common law.

Amendment VIII

Excessive bail shall not be required, nor excessive fines imposed, nor cruel and unusual punishments inflicted.

Amendment IX

The enumeration in the Constitution, of certain rights, shall not be construed to deny or disparage others retained by the people.

Amendment X

The powers not delegated to the United States by the Constitution, nor prohibited by it to the States, are reserved to the States respectively, or to the people.

Amendment XI

(Ratified February 7, 1795)

The Judicial power of the United States shall not be construed to extend to any suit in law or equity, commenced or prosecuted against one of the United States by Citizens of another State, or by Citizens or Subjects of any Foreign State.

Amendment XII

(Ratified June 15, 1804)

The Electors shall meet in their respective states and vote by ballot for President and Vice-President, one of whom, at least, shall not be an inhabitant of the same state with themselves; they shall name in their ballots the person voted for as President, and in distinct ballots the person voted for as Vice-President, and they shall make distinct lists of all persons voted for as President, and of all persons voted for as Vice-President, and of the number of votes for each, which lists they shall sign and certify, and transmit sealed to the seat of the government of the United States, directed to the President of the Senate; — The President of the Senate shall, in presence of the Senate and House of Representatives, open all the certificates and the votes shall then be counted; — The person having the greatest number of votes for President, shall be the President, if such number be a majority of the whole number of Electors appointed; and if no person have such majority, then from the persons having the highest numbers not exceeding three on the list of those voted for as President, the House of Representatives shall choose immediately, by ballot, the President. But in choosing the President, the votes shall be taken by states, the representation from each state having one vote; a quorum for this purpose shall consist of a member or members from two-thirds of the states, and a majority of all the states shall be necessary to a choice. [And if the House of Representatives shall not choose a President whenever the right of choice shall devolve upon them, before the fourth day of March next following, then the Vice-President shall act as President, as in the case of the death or other constitutional disability of the President. —][9] The person having the greatest number of votes as Vice-President, shall be the Vice-President, if such number be a majority of the whole number of Electors appointed, and if no person have a majority, then from the two highest numbers on the list, the Senate shall choose the Vice-President; a quorum for the purpose shall consist of

---

9. Superseded by section 3 of the twentieth amendment.

two-thirds of the whole number of Senators, and a majority of the whole number shall be necessary to a choice. But no person constitutionally ineligible to the office of President shall be eligible to that of Vice-President of the United States.

Amendment XIII

(Ratified December 6, 1865)

Section 1. Neither slavery nor involuntary servitude, except as a punishment for crime whereof the party shall have been duly convicted, shall exist within the United States, or any place subject to their jurisdiction.

Section 2. Congress shall have power to enforce this article by appropriate legislation.

Amendment XIV

(Ratified July 9, 1868)

Section 1. All persons born or naturalized in the United States, and subject to the jurisdiction thereof, are citizens of the United States and of the State wherein they reside. No State shall make or enforce any law which shall abridge the privileges or immunities of citizens of the United States; nor shall any State deprive any person of life, liberty, or property, without due process of law; nor deny to any person within its jurisdiction the equal protection of the laws.

Section 2. Representatives shall be apportioned among the several States according to their respective numbers, counting the whole number of persons in each State, excluding Indians not taxed. But when the right to vote at any election for the choice of electors for President and Vice-President of the United States, representatives in Congress, the Executive and Judicial officers of a State, or the members of the Legislature thereof, is denied to any of the male inhabitants of such State, being twenty-one years of age,[10] and citizens of the United States, or in any way abridged, except for participation in rebellion, or other crime, the basis of representation therein shall be reduced in the proportion which the number of such male citizens shall bear to the whole number of male citizens twenty-one years of age in such State.

Section 3. No person shall be a Senator or Representative in Congress, or elector of President and Vice-President, or hold any office, civil or military, under the United States, or under any State, who, having previously taken an oath, as a member of Congress, or as an officer of the United States, or as a member of any State legislature, or as an executive or judicial officer of any State, to support the Constitution of the United States, shall have engaged in insurrection or rebellion against the same, or given aid or comfort to the enemies thereof. But Congress may by a vote of two-thirds of each House, remove such disability.

---

10. Changed by section 1 of the twenty-sixth amendment.

Section 4. The validity of the public debt of the United States, authorized by law, including debts incurred for payment of pensions and bounties for services in suppressing insurrection or rebellion, shall not be questioned. But neither the United States nor any State shall assume or pay any debt or obligation incurred in aid of insurrection or rebellion against the United States, or any claim for the loss or emancipation of any slave; but all such debts, obligations and claims shall be held illegal and void.

Section 5. The Congress shall have power to enforce, by appropriate legislation, the provisions of this article.

Amendment XV

(Ratified February 3, 1870)

Section 1. The right of citizens of the United States to vote shall not be denied or abridged by the United States or by any State on account of race, color, or previous condition of servitude —

Section 2. The Congress shall have power to enforce this article by appropriate legislation.

Amendment XVI

(Ratified February 3, 1913)

The Congress shall have power to lay and collect taxes on incomes, from whatever source derived, without apportionment among the several States, and without regard to any census or enumeration.

Amendment XVII

(Ratified April 8, 1913)

The Senate of the United States shall be composed of two Senators from each State, elected by the people thereof, for six years; and each Senator shall have one vote. The electors in each State shall have the qualifications requisite for electors of the most numerous branch of the State legislatures.

When vacancies happen in the representation of any State in the Senate, the executive authority of such State shall issue writs of election to fill such vacancies: *Provided,* That the legislature of any State may empower the executive thereof to make temporary appointments until the people fill the vacancies by election as the legislature may direct.

This amendment shall not be so construed as to affect the election or term of any Senator chosen before it becomes valid as part of the Constitution.

Amendment XVIII

(Ratified January 16, 1919)

[**Section 1.** After one year from the ratification of this article the manufacture, sale, or transportation of intoxicating liquors within, the importation thereof into, or the exportation thereof from the United States and all territory subject to the jurisdiction thereof for beverage purposes is hereby prohibited.

[**Section 2.** The Congress and the several States shall have concurrent power to enforce this article by appropriate legislation.

[**Section 3.** This article shall be inoperative unless it shall have been ratified as an amendment to the Constitution by the legislatures of the several states as provided in the Constitution within seven years from the date of the submission hereof to the States by the Congress.][11]

Amendment XIX

(Ratified August 18, 1920)

The right of citizens of the United States to vote shall not be denied or abridged by the United States or by any State on account of sex.

Congress shall have power to enforce this article by appropriate legislation.

Amendment XX

(Ratified January 23, 1933)

Section 1. The terms of the President and Vice President shall end at noon on the 20th day of January, and the terms of Senators and Representatives at noon on the 3d day of January, of the years in which such terms would have ended if this article had not been ratified; and the terms of their successors shall then begin.

Section 2. The Congress shall assemble at least once in every year, and such meeting shall begin at noon on the 3d day of January, unless they shall by law appoint a different day.

Section 3. If, at the time fixed for the beginning of the term of the President, the President elect shall have died, the Vice President elect shall become President. If a President shall not have been chosen before the time fixed for the beginning of his term, or if the President elect shall have failed to qualify, then the Vice President elect shall act as President until a President shall have qualified; and the Congress may by law provide for the case wherein neither a President elect nor a Vice President elect shall have qualified, declaring who shall then act as President, or the manner in which one who is to act shall be selected, and such person shall act accordingly until a President or Vice President shall have qualified.

Section 4. The congress may by law provide for the case of the death of any of the persons from whom the House of Representatives may choose a President whenever the right of choice shall have devolved upon them, and for the case of

---

11. Repealed by section 1 of the twenty-first amendment.

the death of any of the persons from whom the Senate may choose a Vice President whenever the right of choice shall have devolved upon them.

Section 5. Sections 1 and 2 shall take effect on the 15th day of October following the ratification of this article.

Section 6. This article shall be inoperative unless it shall have been ratified as an amendment to the Constitution by the legislatures of three-fourths of the several States within seven years from the date of its submission.

Amendment XXI

(Ratified December 5, 1933)

Section 1. The eighteenth article of amendment to the Constitution of the United States is hereby repealed.

Section 2. The transportation or importation into any State, Territory, or possession of the United States for delivery or use therein of intoxicating liquors, in violation of the laws thereof, is hereby prohibited.

Section 3. This article shall be inoperative unless it shall have been ratified as an amendment to the Constitution by conventions in the several States, as provided in the Constitution, within seven years from the date of the submission hereof to the States by the Congress.

Amendment XXII

(Ratified February 27, 1951)

Section 1. No person shall be elected to the office of the President more than twice, and no person who has held the office of President, or acted as President, for more than two years of a term to which some other person was elected President shall be elected to the office of the President more than once. But this Article shall not apply to any person holding the office of President when this Article was proposed by the Congress, and shall not prevent any person who may be holding the office of President, or acting as President, during the term within which this Article becomes operative from holding the office of President or acting as President during the remainder of such term.

Section 2. This article shall be inoperative unless it shall have been ratified as an amendment to the Constitution by the legislatures of three-fourths of the several States within seven years from the date of its submission to the States by the Congress.

Amendment XXIII

(Ratified March 29, 1961)

Section 1. The District constituting the seat of Government of the United States shall appoint in such manner as the Congress may direct:

A number of electors of President and Vice President equal to the whole number of Senators and Representatives in Congress to which the District would be entitled if it were a State, but in no event more than the least populous State; they shall be in addition to those appointed by the States, but they shall be considered, for the purposes of the election of President and Vice President, to be electors appointed by a State; and they shall meet in the District and perform such duties as provided by the twelfth article of amendment.

Section 2. The Congress shall have power to enforce this article by appropriate legislation.

Amendment XXIV

(Ratified January 23, 1964)

SECTION 1. The right of citizens of the United States to vote in any primary or other election for President or Vice President, for electors for President or Vice President, or for Senator or Representative in Congress, shall not be denied or abridged by the United States or by any State by reason of failure to pay any poll tax or other tax.

Section 2. The Congress shall have power to enforce this article by appropriate legislation.

Amendment XXV

(Ratified February 10, 1967)

Section 1. In case of the removal of the President from office or of his death or resignation, the Vice President shall become President.

Section 2. Whenever there is a vacancy in the office of the Vice President, the President shall nominate a Vice President who shall take office upon confirmation by a majority vote of both Houses of Congress.

Section 3. Whenever the President transmits to the President pro tempore of the Senate and the Speaker of the House of Representatives his written declaration that he is unable to discharge the powers and duties of his office, and until he transmits to them a written declaration to the contrary, such powers and duties shall be discharged by the Vice President as Acting President.

Section 4. Whenever the Vice President and a majority of either the principal officers of the executive departments or of such other body as congress may by law provide, transmit to the President pro tempore of the Senate and the Speaker of the House of Representatives their written declaration that the President is unable to discharge the powers and duties of his office, the Vice President shall immediately assume the powers and duties of the office as Acting President.

Thereafter, when the President transmits to the President pro tempore of the Senate and the Speaker of the House of Representatives his written declaration that no inability exists, he shall resume the powers and duties of his office unless the Vice President and a majority of either the principal officers of the executive department or of such other body as Congress may by law provide, transmit within four days to the President pro tempore of the Senate and the Speaker of the House of Representatives their written declaration that the President is unable to discharge the powers and duties of his office. Thereupon, Congress shall decide the issue, assembling within forty-eight hours for that purpose if not in session. If the Congress, within twenty-one days after receipt of the latter written declaration, or, if Congress is not in session, within twenty-one days after Congress is required to assemble, determines by two-thirds vote of both Houses that the President is unable to discharge the powers and duties of his office, the Vice President shall continue to discharge the same as Acting President; otherwise, the President shall resume the powers and duties of his office.

Amendment XXVI

(Ratified July 1, 1971)

Section 1. The right of citizens of the United States, who are eighteen years of age or older, to vote shall not be denied or abridged by the United States or by any State on account of age.

Section 2. The Congress shall have power to enforce this article by appropriate legislation.

Amendment XXVII

(Ratified May 7, 1992)
No law varying the compensation for the services of the Senators and Representatives shall take effect, until an election of Representatives shall have intervened.

Italics indicate principal cases.

A

Abbott v. Perez, 357, 459
Abrams v. Johnson, 334, 381, 432
Abrams v. United States, 600, 644, 844
Adams v. Clinton, 120
Adams v. Governor of Del., 973
Adarand Constructors, Inc. v. Pena, 390, 391, 433
Adderley v. Florida, 675
Akins v. Texas, 248
Akron v. Bell, 501
Alabama Legislative Black Caucus v. Alabama, 446, 447, 448
Alexander v. Davis, 1034
Allen v. State Bd. of Elections, 331, 396
American Party of Tex. v. White, 510, 548, 598, 913
Americans for Prosperity Found. v. Bonta, 715
Anderson v. Bessemer City, 436
Anderson v. Celebrezze, 543, *548*, 556, 559, 560, 563, 564, 567, 570, 571, 572, 592, 603, 604, 605, 668, 671, 681, 701, 724, 993, 1002
Anderson v. Dunn, 196
Anderson v. Martin, 680
Animal Defenders Int'l v. United Kingdom, 698
Arizona v. Inter Tribal Council of Ariz., Inc., 160, 314, 352
Arizona Free Enter. Club's Freedom Club PAC v. Bennett, 908, *916*, 927
Arizona State Legislature v. Arizona Indep. Redistricting Comm'n, 279, 280, 284, 286, 290, *310*, 318
Arkansas Educ. Television Comm'n v. Forbes, 887
Arkansas State Conference NAACP v. Board of Apportionment, 478
Arlington Heights, Village of v. Metropolitan Hous. Dev. Corp., 176, 248, 249, 254, 396, 410, 436, 461, 470
Ashcroft v. Free Speech Coalition, 810
Associated Enters., Inc. v. Toltec Watershed Improvement Dist., 237

Associated Press v. United States, 696
Attorney Gen. of Territory of Guam v. United States, 121
Austin v. Michigan Chamber of Commerce, 812, *863*, 870, 871, 874, 877, 878, 879, 881, 882, 885, 886, 889
Avery v. Midland Cnty., 218, 229, 230, 231, 233, 236, 238

B

Baker v. Carr, 202, 203, 251, 257, 270, 271, *1028*, 1030, 1031
Baker v. Pataki, 178
Ball v. James, 237
Ballentine v. United States, 121
Barry v. City of N.Y., 519
Bartlett v. Strickland, 386
Bartnicki v. Vopper, 810
Bates v. City of Little Rock, 603, 698, 714, 859
Beaumont; FEC v., 887
Beer v. United States, 332, 333, 338, 396, 397, 416, 448
Bethel Sch. Dist. No. 403 v. Fraser, 886
Bethune-Hill v. Virginia State Bd. of Elections, 421, 422, 448
Bland v. Fessler, 685
Bluman v. Federal Election Comm'n, 902
Board of Dirs. of Rotary Int'l v. Rotary Club of Duarte, 543
Board of Educ. v. Barnette, 627
Board of Trs. v. Garrett, 339
Boerne, City of v. Flores, 152, 339, 340
Bond v. United States, 343
Borders v. Kings Cnty., 1043
Bradley v. Perrodin, 1043
Branti v. Finkel, 631
Branzburg v. Hayes, 686
Brnovich v. Democratic Nat'l Comm., 461, 476-477
Broadrick v. Oklahoma, 508
Brown v. Board of Educ. (347 U.S. 483), 135
Brown v. Board of Educ. (349 U.S. 294), 135

Brown v. Hartlage, 660, 967
Brown v. Socialist Workers '74 Comm.,
    714
Brown v. Thomson, 217
Buckley v. American Constitutional Law
    Found., 721, 724
Buckley v. Valeo, 592, 627, 631, 662, 702,
    707, 713-714, 716, 718, 721, 722, 733,
    736, 747, 754, *755,* 768, 769, 772,
    783, 785-790, 793, 794, 797, 798, 799,
    802-804, 808, 809, 811, 812, 813, 814,
    815, 819, 821, 822, 829, 830, 832, 834,
    836, 841, 842, 848, 849, 859, 864, 870,
    871, 874-875, 876, 877, 880, 881, 882,
    884, 890, 891, 903, 907-910, *911,* 918,
    919, 922-926, 930
Bullock v. Carter, 170, 506, 510, 546,
    548, 549, 550, 556, 559, 561, 568,
    998
Burdick v. Takushi, 558, 563, 564, 566, 567,
    569, 571, 608, 615, 701, 997, 998, 999,
    1000, 1002
Burns v. Fortson, 128
Burns v. Richardson, 219, 244
Burroughs v. United States, 707, 809
Burson v. Freeman, 666, 673, 676, 682, 887
Bush v. Gore, 938, 943, 945, 955, 985, 1008,
    1013, 1014, 1023, 1030, 1050
Bush v. Vera, 408, 426, 427, 429, 432, 433,
    436, 437
Butler; United States v., 913, 943
Byers v. Sun Sav. Bank, 172

C

Cahaly v. LaRosa, 685
California Democratic Party v. Jones, 598,
    607, 615, 616, 617, 618, 619, 620, 622
California Or. Power Co. v. Beaver
    Portland Cement Co., 231
Calvin v. Jefferson Cnty. Bd. of Comm'rs,
    222
Campbell v. Davidson, 501
Canon v. Justice Court, 704
Cantwell v. Connecticut, 713
Caperton v. A.T. Massey Coal Co., 976,
    983
Carey v. Wolnitzek, 980
Carney v. Adams, 1032
Carrington v. Rash, 123, 126, 139, 195
Carter v. Lambert, 990
Castañon v. United States, 121
Cawthorne v. Amalfi, 529
Chandler v. Miller, 502
Chapman, In re, 527

Chappelle v. Greater Baton Rouge Airport
    Dist., 503
Chavez, State ex rel. v. Evans, 501
Chen v. City of Houston, 427
Chiafalo v. Washington, 78
Chisom v. Roemer, 387, 971
CIO; United States v., 876, 877
Cipriano v. City of Houma, 170, 229, 233,
    235, 238, 555
Citizens Against Rent Control v. Berkeley,
    848
Citizens for Legislative Choice v.
    Miller, 500
Citizens United v. Federal Election Comm'n,
    713, 721, 724, 747, 752, *871,* 890, 891,
    893-905, 908, 909, 910, 918, 919, 926,
    985
City of. *See name of city*
Classic; United States v., 125, 144, 164,
    582, 588, 913, 1014
Cleburne v. Cleburne Living Ctr., Inc.,
    998
Clements v. Fashing, 504, 552
Clingman v. Beaver, 616
Cogswell v. City of Seattle, 682
Colegrove v. Green, 202, 271, 431, *1026,*
    1028, 1029
Coleman v. Miller, 1029
Colorado Gen. Assembly v. Salazar, 306
*Colorado Republican Fed. Campaign Comm.
    v. Federal Election Comm'n (518 U.S.
    604),* 566, 571, *828,* 834, 835, 836, 848,
    919
Colorado Republican Fed. Campaign
    Comm. v. Federal Election Comm'n
    (533 U.S. 431), 804, 835, 848
Communications Workers v. Beck, 867
Communist Party v. Subversive Activities
    Control Bd., 709
Cook v. Gralike, 183, 499, 681
Cooper v. Harris, 447, 459
Cornelius v. NAACP Legal Def. & Educ.
    Fund, Inc., 675, 676
Cort v. Ash, 860
Cotton v. Fordice, 176
Cousins v. Wigoda, 567, 589, 590, 759
Cox v. Larios, 218
Cox Broad. Corp. v. Cohn, 724
Crane; State v., 504
Crawford v. Marion Cnty. Election Bd., 466,
    992, 1004, 1005
Cromartie I. *See* Hunt v. Cromartie
Cromartie II. *See* Easley v. Cromartie
Crookston v. Johnson, 685

Cruikshank; United States v., 247

CSC v. Letter Carriers. *See* U.S. Civil Serv.
   Comm'n v. National Ass'n of Letter
   Carriers, AFL-CIO

Curtis Publ'g Co. v. Butts, 647-648, 651

D

Daily Herald Co. v. Munro, 684

Danielson v. Fitzsimmons, 502

Davidson v. City of Cranston, 222

Davis v. Bandemer, 264, 265, 266, 267,
   272, 273, 274, 276, 277, 303, 379, 419,
   423, 424

Davis v. Commonwealth Election
   Comm'n, 143

Davis v. Federal Election Comm'n, 722,
   724, 818, 908, 919-921, 922

Davis v. Hildebrant. *See* Ohio ex rel. Davis
   v. Hildebrant

Davis v. Schnell, 145

Democratic Party of U.S. v. Wisconsin ex
   rel. La Follette, 598, 603, 608, 609

Democratic Party of Wash. v. Reed, 616

Democratic Party of Wis. v. La Follette,
   589

Department of Commerce v. *See name of
   opposing party*

Dillon v. Fiorina, 501

Doe #1 v. Reed, 719

Duke v. Cleland, 543

Dunn v. Blumstein, 126, 129, 170, 195,
   198, 250, 251, 254, 255, 556, 591,
   934

Duplantier v. United States, 519

E

Easley v. Cromartie (Cromartie II), 433, 442,
   446, 447, 449, 456, 457-458

Economic Freedom Fund; State v., 684

Edmonson v. Leesville Concrete Co., 416,
   727

Elkins v. United States, 921

Ellis v. Mayor & City Council
   of Balt., 220

Elrod v. Burns, 510, *624,* 631, 859

Employment Div. v. Smith, 152

Escamilla v. Cuello, 502

*Eu v. San Francisco Cnty. Democratic Cent.
   Comm.,* 566, 567, 568, 569, 570, 571,
   572, *590,* 595, 608, 668, 918, 967

Evans v. Cornman, 126, 555

Evenwel v. Abbott, 221

Exon v. Tiemann, 501

Ex parte. *See name of party*

F

Family PAC v. McKenna, 718

Farrakhan v. Gregoire, 389

Farrakhan v. Washington, 178

Federal Election Comm'n v. *See name of
   opposing party*

Ferguson, Application of, 502

Files v. Hill, 1036, 1039, 1040

First Nat'l Bank of Boston v. Bellotti, 724,
   856, 863, 869, 870, 871, 875, 877, 878,
   880, 881, 882, 886, 889, 893

Flast v. Cohen, 270

Forsyth Cnty. v. Nationalist Movement,
   678

Fortson v. Dorsey, 244, 255, 376, 396

Frank v. Canada (Att'y Gen.), 129

Frank v. Walker, 768 F. 3d 744 (7th Cir.
   2014), 1005

Frank v. Walker, 819 F. 3d 384 (7th Cir.
   2016), 1005

Franklin v. Massachusetts, 228

Frisby v. Schultz, 684

Frost & Frost Trucking Co. v. Railroad
   Comm'n of Cal., 263

Fuller v. Haines, 183

Fullilove v. Klutznick, 390

G

Gaffney v. Cummings, 217, 264, 272, 273,
   277, 394

Garrison v. Louisiana, 650, 654, 655

Gentges v. Oklahoma State Election Bd.,
   1006

Georgia v. Ashcroft, 384, 385

Georgia v. United States, 395

Gertz v. Robert Welch, Inc., 646

Gibbons v. Ogden, 338

Gibson v. Florida Legislative
   Investigation Comm., 704-705

Giles v. Harris, 350

Gill v. Whitford, 268, 273, 289

Gomez v. Campbell-Ewald Co., 685

Gomillion v. Lightfoot, 247, 251, 254, *262,*
   272, 337, 394, 395, 396, 397, 406, 446

Gore v. Harris, 940

Gould v. Grubb, 933

Grace; United States v., 667

Gratz v. Bollinger, 390, 391

Gray v. Sanders, 125, 235

Green v. Board of Elections, 172

Greene v. Raffensberger, 529

Gregory v. Ashcroft, 343, 498, 502

Griffin v. Padilla, 503

Grovey v. Townsend, 583

Growe v. Emison, 226
Grutter v. Bollinger, 390, 391, 1014
Guernsey v. Allen, 681
Guinn v. United States, 80, 83, 583
Gunaji v. Macias, 1042

H

Hadley v. Junior Coll. Dist., 198, 230, 231,
    233, 234, 236
Hague v. CIO, 667
Hansen v. Finchem, 529
Harper v. Canada, 790
Harper v. Hall, 302
Harper v. Virginia Bd. of Elections, 139, *164,*
    171, 198, 235, 255, 547, 939, 993, 996,
    998, 1003, 1014-1015
Harris v. Arizona Indep. Redistricting
    Comm'n, 217, 218
Harris v. McRae, 998
Harrison v. Chesshir, 125
Hawke v. Smith (253 U.S. 221), 312, 317
Hayden v. Pataki, 178, 389
Hays; United States v., 408, 1032
Heiner v. Donnan, 126
Hellmann v. Collier, 501
Hill v. Stone, 230
Hirst v. United Kingdom, 173
Holder v. Hall, 457, 472
Hollingsworth v. Perry, 1032
Holt Civic Club v. City of Tuscaloosa, 195
Honts v. Shaw, 1041
Hopfmann v. Connolly, 504
Horne v. Fish, 1036
Houston Lawyers' Ass'n v. Attorney Gen.,
    387
Hudson Water Co. v. McCarter, 196
Huggins v. Superior Court, 1042
Hunt v. Cromartie (Cromartie I), 432,
    434, 435, 436, 437, 449
Hunter v. City of Pittsburgh, 132, 136-137,
    197, 210
Hunter v. Underwood, 174, 176, 388
Husted v. A. Philip Randolph Inst., 992

I

Igartua de la Rosa v. United States, 121
Illinois ex rel. Madigan v. Telemarketing
    Assocs., 646
Illinois State Bd. of Elections v. Socialist
    Workers Party, 255, 510
Indiana; United States v., 994, 995
Initiative Petition No. 426, In re, 222
In re. *See name of party*

International Soc'y for Krishna
    Consciousness, Inc. v. Lee, 675

J

Jenness v. Fortson, 556, 592, 598, 600, 914
Johnson v. Breseden, 179
Johnson v. DeGrandy, 382, 383
Johnson v. Governor of State of Fla., 178,
    389
Johnson v. United States, 289
Jones v. Glidewell, 1034, 1039, 1040
Jones v. Governor, 179
Judicial Campaign Complaint Against
    O'Toole, In re, 657

K

Karcher v. Daggett, 215, 429
Katzenbach v. Morgan, 148, 152, 153, 353,
    916
Kessler v. Grand Cent. Dist. Mgmt. Ass'n,
    239
Keyes v. School Dist. No. 1, Denver, Colo.,
    248
Kingsley Int'l Pictures Corp. v. Regents,
    860
Kirkpatrick v. Preisler, 215, 217
Knight First Amendment Inst. v. Trump,
    731
Knoll v. Davidson, 934
Korematsu v. United States, 165
Kotch v. River Port Pilot Comm'rs, 234
Kovacs v. Cooper, 684
Kramer v. Union Free Sch. Dist. No. 15, 139,
    170, 195, 197, 198, 230, 233, 234, 235,
    255, 555
Kusper v. Pontikes, 255, 591, 603, 605,
    606, 611, 627, 756, 759

L

Laird v. Tatum, 969, 971
Lamone v. Benisek, 269, 286
Lance v. Coffman, 1032
Lane v. Wilson, 82, 257, 262, 583
*Lassiter v. Northampton Cnty. Bd. of
    Elections, 124,* 141, *144,* 151, 164, 166,
    250
Lawyer v. Department of Justice, 433
League of United Latin Am. Citizens v.
    Perry, 268, 273, 304, 421, 428, 429
*League of Women Voters v. Commonwealth,
    299*
League of Women Voters of Ind. v.
    Rokita, 1006

League of Women Voters of Ohio v. Ohio Redistricting Comm'n, 302
Lee v. Daniels, 505
Lee v. Virginia State Bd. of Elections, 1005
Legislature of State of Cal. v. Eu, 499, 502
Lochner v. New York, 165, 167
Lockport v. Citizens for Cmty. Action, 136, 137
Lorillard Tobacco Co. v. Reilly, 810
Los Angeles Police Dep't v. United Reporting Publ'g Corp., 887
Louisiana v. United States, 396
Louisiana; United States v., 146
Lubin v. Panish, 255, 510, 548, 550, 556, 913, 998
Lugar v. Edmondson Oil Co., 728
LULAC v. Perry. *See* League of United Latin Am. Citizens v. Perry
Luther v. Borden, 614, 1029

M

Mahaffey v. Barnhill, 1043
Mahan v. Howell, 217, 426
Marbury v. Madison, 16, 153, 270, 281
Marston v. Lewis, 128
Massachusetts Citizens for Life; Federal Election Comm'n v., 809, *839*, 848, 849, 864, 865, 866, 867, 878, 884, 885, 886, 919, 922
May v. Town of Mountain Vill., 131
McConnell v. Federal Election Comm'n, 713-714, *797*, 814, 815, 871, 873, 879, 880, 882, 885, 886, 889, 890, 908, 909, 919
McCulloch v. Maryland, 150, 338, 348, 353, 493, 495
McCutcheon v. Federal Election Comm'n, *906*, 910
McDonald v. Board of Election Comm'rs, 507
McGinty v. Western Australia, 240
McIntyre v. Ohio Elections Comm'n, *699*, 704, 716, 725, 726
McLaughlin v. Florida, 124
McPherson v. Blacker, 62, 144, 555
Meredith v. Jefferson Cnty., 391
Merrill v. Caster, 478
Merrill v. Milligan, 478
Metro Broad., Inc. v. FCC, 390, 413
Meyer v. Grant, 702, 720
Miami Herald Publ'g Co. v. Tornillo, *694*, 697, 764
Miller v. Johnson, 152, 276, *409*, 421, 423, 424, 427, 428, 429, 432, 436, 440, 447, 448

Miller v. Treadwell, 564
Milliken v. Bradley, *134*, 137
Mills v. State of Alabama, 666, 671, 680, 682, *687*, 764, 858
Minnesota v. Clover Leaf Creamery Co., 508
Minnesota Majority v. Mansky, 675
Minnesota Voters Alliance v. Mansky, *672*
Minor v. Happersett, *114*, 250
Mississippi Republican Exec. Comm. v. Brooks, 376, 463
Mobile, City of v. Bolden, *246*, 359, 360, 361, 365, 372, 379, 412, 463, 465, 470
Monitor Patriot Co. v. Roy, 645, *648*, 651, 654, 656, 662
Montana; Department of Commerce v., 228
Montejo v. Louisiana, 881
Morrison; United States v., 339
Morse v. Frederick, 886
Munro v. Socialist Workers Party, 469, 600, 670
Myers v. Anderson, 83

N

NAACP v. Button, 543, 603, 844
NAACP v. State of Alabama ex rel. Patterson, 603, 698, 708, 709, 711, 714, 756, 759
National Conservative Political Action Comm.; Federal Election Comm'n v., *820*, 830, 833, 848, 865, 908
National Org. for Marriage, Inc. v. McKee, 718
National Right to Work Comm.; FEC v., 798, 844, 845, 848, 887
Neal v. Delaware, 82, 247
Near v. Minnesota ex rel. Olson, 888
Neil v. Biggers, 437
NetChoice, LLC v. Moody, 730
Nevada v. Hibbs, 339
Newberry v. United States, 587, 588, 737, 738
New York; Department of Commerce v., 225
New York City Bd. of Estimate v. Morris, 237
New York State Bd. of Elections v. Lopez Torres, *596*, 879
New York Times Co. v. Sullivan, 552, 627, 646, 647, 649, 650, 651, 653, 654, 655, 926
Nixon v. Herndon, 350, 580, 1029

Nixon v. Shrink Mo. Government PAC, 803, 806, 808, 880
Nixon; United States v. (418 U.S. 683), 16
Nixon v. United States (506 U.S. 224), 522
Norman v. Reed, 543, 544, 566, 567, 568, 598
North Carolina v. Covington, 357
North Carolina State Conference of NAACP v. McCrory, 459, 1004, 1005
Northwest Austin Mun. Util. Dist. No. One v. Holder, 351
Northwest Austin Mun. Util. Dist. No. One v. Mukasey, 340, 341, 342, 343, 344, 345, 346, 348, 353, 354
Novosel v. Nationwide Ins. Co., 517

O

O'Brien; United States v., 644, 756, 785
O'Callaghan v. State (914 P.2d 1250), 616
O'Callaghan v. State (6 P.3d 728), 616
O'Connor, In re, 502
Oettle v. Guthrie, 686
Ohio v. American Express Co., 289
Ohio ex rel. Davis v. Hildebrant, 312
Ohio Council 8, AFSCME v. Husted, 973
One Wis. Inst. Inc. v. Nichol, 460
Oregon v. Mitchell, 128, 152, 153, 159, 160, 161

P

Palko v. Connecticut, 847
Parents Involved in Cmty. Sch. v. Seattle Sch. Dist., 391
Patriotic Veterans v. Zoeller, 685
Patterson v. Hanley, 1043
Patterson v. Padilla, 503
Patton v. Coates, 1034, 1035, 1036, 1037, 1038, 1039, 1040
Pearson v. Callahan, 881
Pell v. Procunier, 686
Perry v. Perez, 460
Perry Educ. Ass'n v. Perry Local Educators' Ass'n, 667, 668, 675
Personnel Adm'r of Mass. v. Feeney, 248, 254, 413
Peterson v. Stafford, 972
Phillips v. Mathews, 1034
Phillips v. Rothrock, 1034
Phoenix v. Kolodziejski, 233, 235, 555
Pickering v. Board of Educ., 510, 514
Pierce v. Society of Sisters, 857
Pipefitters Local Union No. 562 v. United States, 841, 844, 845, *849*, 855, 876, 877

Plante v. Gonzalez, 519
Plaut v. Spendthrift Farm, Inc., 971
Playboy Entmt. Group, Inc.; United States v., 810
Pleasant Grove City v. Summum, 675
Plyler v. Doe, 120
Pocket Veto Case, 77
Police Dep't of Chi. v. Mosley, 859
Pope v. Williams, 124
Powell v. McCormack, 487-488, 489, 490, 491, 493
Presley v. Etowah Cnty. Comm'n, 331, 332, 344, 349
Prosser v. Elections Bd., 425
Provincial Electoral Boundaries, In re (Sask.), 240
Purcell v. Gonzalez, 469, 721, 1031

Q

Qualkinbush v. Skubisz, 1043
Quinn v. Milsap, 503

R

Ramey v. Rockefeller, 129
Ray v. Blair, 74, 76, 77
Raysor v. DeSantis, 1032
Red Lion Broad. Co. v. Federal Commc'ns Comm'n, 688, 693, 697, 858
Reed v. Baker, 1036
Reese; United States v., 247
Regents of Univ. of Cal. v. Bakke, 389, 409, 413
Reno v. American Civil Liberties Union, 873
Reno v. Bossier Parish, 333, 339, 346, 473
Republican Party of Minn. v. Kelly, 972
Republican Party of Minn. v. White, 665, *966*, 972, 973, 976, 979, 981, 982-983
Republican Party of Pa. v. Boockvar, 1051
Reyes Mata v. Lynch, 470
Reynolds v. Sims, 126, 137, 139, 164, 165, *206*, 217, 218, 219, 227, 230, 231, 233, 234, 236, 244, 248, 250, 251, 255, 285, 406, 417, 668, 934, 939, 1013, 1014, 1015
Rice v. Cayetano, 143
Richardson v. Ramirez, 167, 175, 176, 388
Richmond v. J.A. Croson Co., 390, 391, 409, 415
Richmond, City of v. United States, 395, 396
Rideout v. City of L.A., 1041
Rideout v. Gardner, 685

Ripon Soc'y, Inc. v. National Republican Party, 591
Roach v. Electoral Comm'r, 174
Roberts v. United States Jaycees, 543, 609, 812
Robertson v. Bartels, 501
Rome, City of v. United States, 340, 353, 354, 363
Roschen v. Ward, 916
Roth v. United States, 649, 756
Rubens v. Hodges, 1033
Rucho v. Common Cause, 264, *268*, 276, 278, 286, 287, 290, 299, 302, 303, 1031
Rutan v. Republican Party of Ill., 631

S

Salyer Land Co. v. Tulare Lake Basin Water Storage Dist., *230*, 237, 238, 239
San Antonio Indep. Sch. Dist. v. Rodriguez, 135, 506
Sanders Cnty. Republican Cent. Comm. v. Bullock, 973
Sauve v. Canada, 173
Saxbe v. Washington Post Co., 686
Schaefer v. Townsend, 501
Schaumburg v. Citizens for Better Env't, 802
Schneider v. State, 125
Semler v. Dental Exam'rs, 916
Session v. Perry, 306
Shaw v. Hunt (Shaw II), 432, 433, 434, 440, 448, 449
Shaw v. Reno (Shaw I), 152, 275, 351, 405, 407, 408, 409, 412, 413, 415, 417, 419, 421, 424, 432, 433, 434, 436, 441, 442, 446, 447, 449, 458
Shelby Cnty. v. Holder, 327, 335, *341*, 354, 355, 356, 357, 358, 359, 388, 446, 448, 460, 471-472, 476, 991, 1004
Shelton v. Tucker, 759, 860
Shub v. Simpson, 502
Silberberg v. Board of Elections, 686
Simmons v. Galvin, 178, 389
Smiley v. Holm, 312
Smith v. Allwright, 144, 350, *581*, 583, 587, 592, 608, 609, 613
South Carolina v. Katzenbach, 327, *335*, 339, 340, 341, 344, 346, 350, 353, 356, 360, 396
Southern Cal. Rapid Transit Dist. v. Bolen, 238
Sparks v. Boggs, 661

Speechnow.org v. Federal Election Comm'n, 752, 903
Spires v. Compton, 1034-1035
State v. *See name of opposing party*
State ex rel. *See name of party*
Stewart v. Blackwell, 1009, 1016
Stewart v. Foster, 119
Stone v. Smith, 145
Storer v. Brown, 506, 548, 550, 556, 559, 560, 561, 567, 569, 572, 573, 591, 603, 701, 914, 997
Stratton v. Hall, 125
Strauder v. West Virginia, 151
Sugarman v. Dougall, 119, 559
Susan B. Anthony List v. Driehaus, 657
Swanberg v. Tart, 1034
Sweezy v. New Hampshire, 758

T

Talley v. California, 700, 701, 711
Tashjian v. Republican Party of Conn., 559, 566, 567, 568, 570, 571, 572, 591, 592, 593, *602*, 608, 609, 611, 613, 614, 617, 618
Taylor v. Attorney-Gen., 174
Tennant v. Jefferson Cnty. Comm'n, 216, 218
Terry v. Adams, 254, 350, *583*, 608, 613
Thomas v. Collins, 711, 860
Thornburg v. Gingles, *360*, 380, 381, 382, 383, 384, 386, 389, 405, 428, 448, 451, 464, 465
Thornhill v. Alabama, 667
Timmons v. Twin Cities Area New Party, *565*, 575, 609, 611, 615, 616
Trump v. Hawaii, 660
Trump v. Mazars USA, LLP, 729
Trump v. New York, 1032
Trump v. Twitter, 726
Trump v. Vance, 16
Turner v. Fouche, 503
Twin Cities Area New Party v. McKenna, 565, 568, 571

U

United Auto. Workers; United States v., 798, 841, 844, 859, 876, 877, 881
United Jewish Orgs. of Williamsburgh, Inc. v. Carey, 389, *392*, 398, 399, 403, 405, 407
United Public Workers v. Mitchell, 508, 511, 512, 515, 516, 628
United States v. *See name of opposing party*

United States Gypsum Co.; United States
  v., 437
United States House of Representatives;
  Department of Commerce v., 223
U.S. v. *See name of opposing party*
*U.S. Civil Serv. Comm'n v. National Ass'n of
  Letter Carriers, AFL-CIO,* 508, 510, 511,
  512, 624, 626, 628, 759, 887
U.S. Term Limits, Inc. v. Thornton, 488, 498,
  499, 501, 614, 680, 681
Utah v. Evans, 224

V

Vanasco v. Schwartz, 652, 656
Van Bergen v. Minnesota, 685
Veasey v. Abbott, 460, 461, 1005
Victory Processing v. Fox, 685
Vieth v. Jubilirer, 267, 270, 272, 273, 277,
  278, 279, 284, 285, 287, 303, 423
Village of. *See name of village*
Virginia, Ex parte, 149, 150, 151,
  338, 354
Virginia v. Reno, 224
Virginia House of Delegates v.
  Bethune-Hill, 1032
Virginia State Bd. of Pharmacy v. Virginia
  Citizens Consumer Council, Inc., 553,
  591, 858

W

Walters v. National Ass'n of Radiation
  Survivors, 356
Waples v. Marrast, 586
Ward v. Rock Against Racism, 679
Washington v. Davis, 246, 248, 249, 252,
  254, 256, 396, 463, 998
Washington v. Finlay, 470
Washington v. Glucksberg, 997
Washington v. State, 172, 178
Washington State Grange v. Washington
  State Republican Party, 620, 997
Washington State Republican Party v.
  Washington State Grange, 621

Weinschenk v. State, 1006
Wells v. Edwards, 219
Wesberry v. Sanders, 203, 207, 218, 223,
  668
Western Tradition P'ship v. Attorney Gen.,
  890
Wheat v. Smith, 1034
Whitcomb v. Chavis, 242, 243, 244, 245,
  246, 248, 249, 251, 369, 379, 394, 395
White v. Regester, 243, 248, 249, 252, 254,
  255, 361, 365, 369, 376, 379, 380, 394,
  396, 417, 462-463
Whitley v. Cranford, 1032, 1041, 1043
Whitney v. California, 659
Williams v. Rhodes, 139, 506, 510, 543,
  545, 548, 550, 551, 554, 556, 570, 573,
  577, 591, 604, 627, 842, 844, 864, 914
Williams v. Salerno, 129
Williamson v. Lee Optical Co., 124, 507,
  508, 916
Williams-Yulee v. Florida Bar, 973, 982-983
Williby v. Zuckerberg, 727
Wilson v. Ellis, 1036
Winter v. Blau, 973
Winters v. New York, 858
Wisconsin v. City of N.Y., 223
Wisconsin Right to Life, Inc.; Federal
  Election Comm'n v., 871, 873, 875,
  881, 884, 886
Wit v. Berman, 130
Womack v. Foster, 1034, 1035, 1037, 1040
Wright v. Rockefeller, 395, 396
Wygant v. Jackson Bd. of Educ., 390

Y

Yarbrough, Ex parte, 82, 144, 149, 247,
  582
Yick Wo v. Hopkins, 150, 164, 208, 352,
  1013

Z

Zeilenga v. Nelson, 501
Zimmer v. McKeithen, 365, 379

Abramowitz, The Disappearing Center: Engaged Citizens, Polarization, and American Democracy (2010), 297, 541, 542

Abramowitz, Incumbency, Campaign Spending, and the Decline of Competition in U.S. House Elections, 53 J. Pol. 34 (1991), 779

Abramowitz and McCoy, United States: Racial Resentment, Negative Partisanship, and Polarization in Trump's America, 681 Ann. Am. Acad. 137 (2019), 479

Abramowitz et al., Incumbency, Redistricting, and the Decline of Competition in U.S. House Elections, 68 J. Pol. 75 (2006), 292, 293, 309

Abrams, "Raising Politics Up": Minority Political Participation and Section 2 of the Voting Rights Act, 63 N.Y.U. L. Rev. 449 (1988), 382

Acharya et al., Deep Roots: How Slavery Still Shapes Southern Politics (2018), 93

Akkerman, Populist Parties under Scrutiny — One Common Vision or a Scattered Agenda?, in Populism and Democracy (Hardt et al. eds. 2020), 41

Aldrich, Why Parties? The Origin and Transformation of Political Parties in America (1995), 534

Aldrich and Rohde, The Logic of Conditional Party Government, in Congress Reconsidered (Dodd and Oppenheimer eds. 7th ed. 2001), 296

Aleinikoff and Issacharoff, Race and Redistricting: Drawing Constitutional Lines After Shaw v. Reno, 92 Mich. L. Rev. 588 (1993), 399, 430

Allcott and Gentzkow, Social Media and Fake News in the 2016 Election, 31 J. Econ. Persp. 211 (2017), 638

Allen, Documentary Disenfranchisement, 86 Tul. L. Rev. 389 (2011), 178

Altman, Democratic Self-Determination and the Disenfranchisement of Felons, 22 J. Applied Phil. 263 (2005), 173

Altman, Expressive Meaning, Race and the Law: The Racial Gerrymandering Cases, 5 Legal Theory 75 (1999), 408

Altman and McDonald, Public Participation GIS: The Case of Redistricting, in Proceedings of the 47th Annual Hawaii International Conference on System Sciences (2014), 319

Altman and McDonald, Redistricting and Polarization, in American Gridlock: The Sources, Character, and Impact of Political Polarization (Thurber and Yoshinaka eds. 2015), 291, 298

Alvarez, et al., How Much Is Enough? The "Ballot Order Effect" and the Use of Social Science Research in Election Law Disputes, 5 Elec. L.J. 40 (2006), 936

Amar and Amar, Eradicating Bush-League Arguments Root and Branch: The Article II Independent-State-Legislature Notion and Related Rubbish, 2021 Sup. Ct. Rev., Article 2, 1051–1052

Anderson, One Person, No Vote: How Voter Suppression Is Destroying Our Democracy (2019), 111, 992

Ansolabehere, de Figueiredo, and Snyder, Why Is There So Little Money in U.S. Politics?, 17 J. Econ. Persp. 105 (2003), 824

Ansolabehere and Iyengar, Going Negative: How Attack Ads Shrink and Polarize the Electorate (1995), 782, 783

Ansolabehere and Persily, Vote Fraud in the Eye of the Beholder: The Role of Public Opinion in the Challenge to Voter Identification Requirements, 121 Harv. L. Rev. 1737 (2008), 478

Ansolabehere and Snyder, The Effects of Redistricting on Incumbents, 11 Election L.J. 490 (2012), 293

Ansolabehere and Snyder, The End of Inequality: One Person, One Vote and the Transformation of American Politics (2009), 215, 293

Ansolabehere and Snyder, The Incumbency Advantage in U.S. Elections: An Analysis of State and Federal Offices, 1942-2000, 1 Election L.J. 315 (2002), 293

Ansolabehere and Snyder, Party Control of State Government and the Distribution of Public Expenditures, 108 Scand. J. Econ. 547 (2006), 291

Ansolabehere and Snyder, Reapportionment and Party Realignment in the American States, 153 U. Pa. L. Rev. 433 (2004), 214

Ansolabehere and Snyder, Soft Money, Hard Money, Strong Parties, 100 Colum. L. Rev. 598 (2000), 791

Argersinger, "A Place on the Ballot": Fusion Politics and Antifusion Laws, 85 Am. Hist. Rev. 287 (1980), 565, 566

Aristotle, Politics, 28

Arrow, Social Choice and Individual Values (2d ed. 1963), 33

Article 19 Global Campaign for Free Expression, Comparatve Study of Laws and Regulations Restricting the Publication of Electoral Opinion Polls (Jan. 2003), 684

Ashdown, Distorting Democracy: Campaign Lies in the 21st Century, 20 Wm. & Mary Bill Rts. J. 1085 (2012), 651

Austen-Smith, Campaign Contributions and Access, 89 Am. Pol. Sci. Rev. 566 (1995), 826

Bailey, The Idea of Presidential Representation (2019), 187

Bailey, An Universal Etymological English Dictionary (1793), 313

Bailey and Katz eds., Ethnic Group Politics (1969), 418

Bailyn, The Ideological Origin of the American Revolution (1967), 192

Bainbridge et al., Letter to Elizabeth M. Murphy, Sec'y, U.S. Sec. & Exch. Comm'n (Mar. 23, 2012), 901

Bakshy et al., Exposure to Ideologically Diverse News and Opinion on Facebook, 348 Science 1130 (2015), 639

Ballotpedia, Counting of electoral votes (Jan. 6-7, 2021), 1049

Banduci, Donovan, and Karp, Minority Representation, Empowerment, and Participation, 66 J. Pol. 534 (2004), 404

Barber and Holbein, The Participatory and Partisan Impacts of Mandatory Vote-by-Mail, 6 Sci. Advances 35 (Aug. 2020), 937

Bartels, Ethnic Antagonism Erodes Republicans' Commitment to Democracy, PNAS (Jan. 2020), 46

Bartels, Unequal Democracy: The Political Economy of the New Gilded Age (2008), 191

Bauer, When "The Pols Make the Calls": McConnell's Theory of Judicial Deference in the Twilight of Buckley, 153 U. Pa. L. Rev. 5 (2004), 815

Baum et al., Estimating the Effect of Asking about Citizenship on the U.S. Census: Results from a Randomized Control Trial (HKS Research Working Paper Series, April 2019), 225

Baumgartner and Leech, Basic Interest: The Importance of Interest Groups in Politics and in Political Science (1998), 823

Bawn et al., A Theory of Political Parties: Groups, Policy Demands and Nominations in American Politics, 10 Persp. on Pol. 571 (2012), 540–541

Bayerlein et al., Populism and COVID-19: How Populist Governments (Mis) Handle the Pandemic (V-Dem Inst., Working Paper 121, 2021), 45

Beazley, Ballot Design as Fail-Safe: An Ounce of Rotation Is Worth a Pound of Litigation, 12 Elec. L.J. 18 (2013), 936

Bebchuk and Jackson, Corporate Political Speech: Who Decides?, 124 Harv. L. Rev. 83 (2010), 899

Bebchuk and Jackson, Shining Light on Corporate Political Spending, 101 Geo. L.J. 923 (2013), 901

Beckel, Outsized Influence (IssueOne 2021), 735

Becker, The Declaration of Independence (1922), 15

Beeman, Deference, Republicanism, and the Emergence of Popular Politics in Eighteenth-Century America, 49 Wm. & Mary Q. 401 (1992), 58

Behrens, Uggen, and Manza, Ballot Manipulation and the "Menace of Negro Domination": Racial Threat and Felon Disenfranchisement in the United States, 1850-2000, 109 Am. J. Soc. 559 (2003), 176

Behrman, Equal or Effective Representation: Redistricting Jurisprudence in Canada and the United States, 51 Am. J. Leg. Hist. 277 (2011), 240

Beitz, Political Equality: An Essay in Democratic Theory (1989), 28, 431

Bender, Community and Social Change in America (1978), 138

Benn and Peters, Principles of Political Thought (1959), 320, 938

Bennett, Should Parents Be Given Extra Votes on Account of Their Children?: Toward a Conversational Understanding of American Democracy, 94 Nw. L. Rev. 503 (2000), 123

Bensel, The American Ballot Box in the Mid-Nineteenth Century (2004), 673

Berelson, Lazarsfeld, and McPhee, Voting: A Study of Opinion Formation in a Presidential Campaign (1954), 780

Berman, Democracy and Dictatorship in Europe (2019), 71

Bermeo, On Democratic Backsliding, 27 J. Democ. 5 (2016), 5

Bernstein and Staszewski, Judicial Populism, 106 Minn. L. Rev. 283 (2021), 106

BeVier, Money and Politics: A Perspective on the First Amendment and Campaign Finance Reform, 73 Cal. L. Rev. 1045 (1985), 789

Bickel, Reform and Continuity (1971), 551

Birch, Electoral Malpractice (2011), 946

Bishop and Cushing, The Big Sort: Why the Clustering of Like-Minded America Is Tearing Us Apart (2009), 298

Blasi, Free Speech and the Widening Gyre of Fund-Raising: Why Campaign Spending Limits May Not Violate the First Amendment After All, 94 Colum. L. Rev. 1281 (1994), 776

Bloomberg, Contracting Around *Citizens United:* A Systemic Solution, 66 Syracuse L. Rev. 301 (2016), 906

Blum and Campbell, Assessment of Voting Rights Progress in Jurisdictions Covered Under Section Five of the Voting Rights Act (2006), 341

Bohman and Rehg, Deliberative Democracy: Essays on Reason and Politics (1997), 25

Bolingbroke, The Idea of a Patriot King (1738), 481

Bonneau and Hall, In Defense of Judicial Elections (2009), 984

Bonneau and Hall eds. Judicial Elections in the 21st Century (2017), 965

Bowman, High Crimes and Misdemeanors: A History of Impeachment for the Age of Trump (2019), 522

Braden, The Constitution of the State of Texas: An Annotated and Comparative Analysis (1977), 507

Branch, At Canaan's Edge: America in the King Years, 1965-68 (2006), 324

Branch, Parting the Waters: America in the King Years, 1954-63 (1988), 85

Brater et al., Purges: A Growing Threat to the Right to Vote (Brennan Ctr. for Justice 2018), 991–992

Bratton and Ray, Descriptive Representation, Policy Outcomes, and Municipal Day-Care Coverage in Norway, 46 Am. J. Pol. Sci. 428 (2002), 404

Brennan, The Ethics of Voting (2011), 32

Brennan and Hill, Compulsory Voting: For and Against (2014), 32

Brennan Center for Justice, The New Politics of Judicial Elections, 2000-2009 (2010), 983

Briffault, Campaign Finance Disclosure 2.0, 9 Election L.J. 273 (2010), 717

Briffault, Election Law Localism and Democracy, 100 N.C. L. Rev. ___ (2022), 960

Briffault, A Government for Our Time? Business Improvement Districts and Urban Governance, 99 Colum. L. Rev. 365 (1999), 239

Briffault, Issue Advocacy: Redrawing the Elections/Politics Line, 77 Tex. L. Rev. 1751 (1998-1999), 793

Briffault, On Dejudicializing American Campaign Finance Law, 27 Ga. St. U. L. Rev. 887 (2011), 775, 816

Briffault, The Political Parties and Campaign Finance Reform, 100 Colum. L. Rev. 620 (2000), 834

Briffault, Public Funding and Democratic Elections, 148 U. Pa. L. Rev. 563 (1999), 927

Briffault, Super PACs, 96 Minn. L. Rev. 1624 (2012), 752

Briffault, Two Challenges for Campaign Finance Disclosure After *Citizens United* and *Doe v. Reed*, 19 Wm. & Mary Bill Rts. J. 983 (2011), 901

Bronars and Lott, Do Campaign Donations Alter How a Politician Votes? Or, Do Donors Support Candidates Who Value the Same Things That They Do?, 40 J.L. & Econ. 317 (1997), 823

Broockman, Black Politicians Are More Intrinsically Motivated to Advance Blacks' Interests: A Field Experiment Manipulating Political Incentives, 57 Am. J. Pol. Sci. 521 (2013), 403

Broockman, Distorted Communication, Unequal Representation: Constituents Communicate Less to Representatives Not of Their Race, 58 Am. J. Pol. Sci. 307 (2013), 403

Brookings Institution, Lift Every Voice: The Urgency of Universal Civic Duty Voting (July 20, 2020), 32

Brunell, Redistricting and Representation: Why Competitive Elections Are Bad for America (2008), 295

Brunell, The Relationship Between Political Parties and Interest Groups: Explaining Patterns of PAC Contributions to Candidates for Congress, 58 Pol. Res. Q. 681 (2005), 826

Bugliosi, The Betrayal of America: How the Supreme Court Undermined the Constitution and Chose Our President (2001), 943–944

Bullock and Dunn, The Demise of Racial Redistricting and the Future of Black Representation, 48 Emory L.J. 1209 (1999), 398

Bulman-Pozen, Partisan Federalism, 127 Harv. L. Rev. 1077 (2014), 65

Burke, Speech to the Electors of Bristol (1774), 181

Burkhardt, History of Fake News, 53 Lib. Tech. Rep. 5 (2017), 638

Burstein and Hirsh, Interest Organizations, Information, and Policy Innovation in the U.S. Congress, 22 Soc. F. 174 (2007), 826

Cain, Democracy More or Less: America's Political Reform Quandary (2015), 21

Cain, Party Autonomy and Two-Party Electoral Competition, 149 U. Pa. L. Rev. 793 (2001), 619

Cain, The Reapportionment Puzzle (1984), 265, 267

Cain and Zhang, Blurred Lines: Conjoined Polarization and Voting Rights, 77 Ohio St. L.J. 867 (2016), 443

Calabresi, A Common Law for the Age of Statutes (1982), 356

Callow, The Tweed Ring (1966), 994

Caltech-MIT Voting Technology Project, Residual Votes Attributable to Technology: An Assessment of the Reliability of Existing Voting Equipment (Version 2: Mar. 30, 2001), 1012

Caltech/MIT Voting Technology Project, What Has Changed, What Hasn't, and What Needs Improvement (2013), 1016–1017

Cammack, Aristotle on the Virtue of the Multitude, 41 Pol. Theory 175 (2013), 28

Campbell, Polarized: The Reality of American Politics (2016), 297

Campbell et al., The American Voter (1960), 154, 155, 156

Canon and Sherman, Debunking the "Big Lie": Election Administration in the 2020 Presidential Election, 51 Pres. Stud. 541 (2021), 955

Caplan, The Myth of the Rational Voter: Why Democracies Choose Bad Policies (2007), 29, 158

Caren, Big City, Big Turnout? Participation in American Cities, 29 J. Urban Aff. 31 (2007), 536–537

Carey, The Effects of Term Limits on State Legislatures: A New Survey of the 50 States, 31 Legis. Q. 105 (2006), 500

Carpini and Keeter, What Americans Know About Politics and Why It Matters (1996), 156

Center for Responsive Politics, Swift Vets & POWs for Truth: Expenditures 2004, 754

Chandler, The Plurality Vote: A Reappraisal, 30 Pol. Stud. 87 (1982), 577

Chappell, Campaign Contributions and Congressional Voting: A Simultaneous Probit-Tobit Model, 62 Rev. Econ. & Stat. 77 (1982), 823

Charles, Corruption Temptation, 102 Cal. L. Rev. 25 (2014), 770

Charles, Understanding *Citizens United* (2012) (working paper), 893

Charles and Fuentes-Rohwer, The Court's Voting Rights Decision Was Worse Than People Think (2021), 477

Charles and Fuentes-Rohwer, Race and Representation Revisited: The New Racial Gerrymandering Cases and Section 2 of the VRA, 59 Wm. & Mary L. Rev. 1559 (2018), 442, 458

Charles and Fuentes-Rohwer, Voting Rights Law and Policy in Transition, 127 Harv. L. Rev. F. 243 (2014), 359

Chen and Cottrell, Evaluating Partisan Gains from Congressional Gerrymandering, 44 Electoral Stud. 329 (2016), 298, 299

Chernykh et al., Constitutions and Election Management, in Advancing Electoral Integrity (Norris et al. eds. 2014), 946

Chin, Rehabilitating Unconstitutional Statutes: An Analysis of *Cotton v. Fordice*, 71 U. Cin. L. Rev. 421 (2002), 176

Chong and Druckman, Framing Theory, 10 Ann. Rev. Pol. Sci. 103 (2007), 683, 781

Cinelli et al., The Echo Chamber Effect on Social Media, 118 PNAS 1 (2017), 639

Citrin et al., What If Everyone Voted? Simulating the Impact of Increased Turnout in Senate Elections, 47 Am. J. Pol. Sci. 75 (2003), 32

Clayton, How Do Electoral Gender Quotas Affect Policy?, 24 Ann. Rev. Pol. Sci. 235 (2021), 404

Codrington, *Purcell* in Pandemic, 96 N.Y.U. L. Rev. 941 (2021), 1031

Cohen, *Citizens United* v. Democracy? (2011) (unpublished paper), 895

Cohen, Deliberation and Democratic Legitimacy, in The Good Polity: Normative Analysis of the State (Hamlin and Pettit eds. 1989), 24

Colby, In Defense of the Equal Sovereignty Principle, 65 Duke L.J. 1087 (2016), 356

Colgan, Wealth-Based Penal Disenfranchisement, 72 Vand. L. Rev. 55 (2019), 178

Commission on Political Activity of Government Personnel, Findings and Recommendations (1968), 513

Common Cause, Taking Elections off the Auction Block (May 2010), 778

Common Cause et al., Deceptive Practices 2.0: Legal and Policy Responses (N.D.), 659

Conroy, The Voting Rights Act of 1965: A Selected Annotated Bibliography, 98 Law. Libr. J. 663 (2006), 324

Corporate Support for Party Convention, FEC Advisory Opinion 1978-46, 792

Corrado, Campaign Finance Reform: A Sourcebook (1997), 792

Cottrill and Peretti, Gerrymandering from the Bench? The Electoral Consequences of Judicial Redistricting, 12 Election L.J. 261 (2013), 309

Cox, Partisan Fairness and Redistricting Politics, 79 N.Y.U. L. Rev. 751 (2004), 307

Cox and Miles, Documenting Discrimination?, 108 Colum. L. Rev. Sidebar 31 (2008), 358

Cox et al., What It Means to Be an American: Attitudes in an Increasingly Diverse America Ten Years after 9/11 (Brookings, Sept. 6, 2011), 107

Craig, Rucker, and Richeson, The Pitfalls and Promise of Increasing Racial Diversity; Threat, Contact, and Race Relations in the 21st Century, 27 Cur. Dir. Psy. Sci. 188 (2017), 479

Craig, Rucker, and Richeson, Racial and Political Dynamics of an Approaching "Majority-Minority" United States, 677 An. Am. Acad. 204 (2018), 479

Crotty, American Parties in Decline (2d ed. 1984), 574

Crum, The Voting Rights Act's Secret Weapon: Pocket Trigger Litigation and Dynamic Preclearance, 119 Yale L.J. 1993 (2010), 335

Cunningham, The Jeffersonian Republican Party, in History of U.S. Political Parties (Schlesinger ed. 1973), 609

Cutler, Party Government Under the American Constitution, 134 U. Penn. L. Rev. 25 (1987), 574

Dahl, Democracy and Its Critics (1989), 113

Dahl, A Preface to Democratic Theory (1956), 20

Dalton et al., Political Parties and Democratic Linkage: How Parties Organize Democracy (2011), 531

Daly, Idealists, Pragmatists, and Textualists: Judging Electoral Districts in America, Canada and Australia, 21 B.C. Int'l & Comp. L. Rev. 261 (1998), 240

Daniels, Voter Deception, 43 Ind. L. Rev. 343 (2010), 659, 956

Davidson and Grofman eds., Quiet Revolution in the South: The Impact of the Voting Rights Act, 1965-1990 (1994), 324, 338, 443

Davidson et al., Vote Caging as a Republican Ballot Security Technique, 34 Wm. Mitchell L. Rev. 533 (2008), 957

Debates in the Federal Convention of 1787 (1902), 317

de Benedictis-Kessner and Palmer, Driving Turnout: The Effect of Car Ownership on Electoral Participation, Pol. Sci. & Res., First View (Dec. 2021), 937

de Figueiredo and Garrett, Paying for Politics, 78 S. Cal. L. Rev. 591 (2005), 930

Degler, Place Over Time: The Continuity of Southern Distinctiveness (1977), 66

de Maistre, Considerations on France (1796), 37

Democracy Index, The Economist (2016), 3

Dershowitz, Supreme Injustice: How the High Court Hijacked Election 2000 (2001), 943

Deusen, The Jacksonian Era, 1828-1848 (1959), 72

Developments in the Law: Elections, 88 Harv. L. Rev. 1111 (1975), 1043

Developments in the Law: Voting and Democracy, 119 Harv. L. Rev. 1127 (2006), 1043

Devins and Baum, The Company They Keep: How Partisan Divisions Came to the Supreme Court (2019), 105

De Witt, The Progressive Movement (1915), 73

Dharia et al., What Should Presidential Candidates Tell Us About Themselves? Proposals for Improving Transparency in Presidential Campaigns (Fordham Univ. Sch. of Law, Democracy and the Constitution Clinic, Jan. 2020), 521

Diamond, Ill Winds: Saving Democracy from Russian Rage, Chinese Ambition, and American Complacency (2019), 3, 6, 108

Dinkin, Campaigning in America: A History of Election Practices (1989), 777

Disch, The Tyranny of the Two-Party System (2002), 577

Dixon, Democratic Representation: Reapportionment in Law and Politics (1968), 430

Dornbusch and Edwards, The Macroeconomics of Populism, in The Macroeconomics of Populism in Latin America (Dornbusch and Edwards eds. 1991), 45

Dothan, Comparative Views on the Right to Vote in International Law: The Case of Prisoners' Disenfranchisement, in Comparative International Law (Roberts et al. eds. 2016), 173

Douglas, Procedural Fairness in Election Contests, 88 Ind. L.J. 1 (2013), 1026

Douglas, The Right to Vote under Local Law, 85 Geo. Wash. L. Rev. 1039 (2017), 132, 1041

Douglas, State Judges and the Right to Vote, 77 Ohio St. L.J. 1 (2016), 1006

Dowling et al., Does Public Financing Chill Political Speech? Exploiting a Court Injunction as a Natural Experiment, 11 Election L.J. 302 (2012), 927

Downs, An Economic Theory of Democracy (1957), 18, 31, 157

Druckman and Nelson, Framing and Deliberation: How Citizens' Conversations Limit Elite Influence, 47 Am. J. Pol. Sci. 729 (2003), 781

Duverger, Political Parties: Their Origins and Activity in the Modern State (1954), 575

Dworkin, A Badly Flawed Election, New York Review of Books (Jan. 11, 2001), 944

Dworkin, The Decision That Threatens Democracy, New York Review of Books (May 13, 2010), 897

Dworkin, Sovereign Virtue: The Theory and Practice of Equality (2000), 733, 784–785

Earnest, Old Nations, New Voters: Nationalism, Transnationalism, and Democracy in the Era of Global Migration (2008), 120

Eatwell and Goodwin, National Populism: The Revolt against Liberal Democracy (2018), 42, 44, 46

Eggers et al., No Evidence for Systematic Voter Fraud: A Guide to Statistical Claims About the 2020 Election, 118 PNAS 45 (2021), 955

Eichhorn and Bergh eds. Lowering the Voting Age to 16: Learning from Real Experiences Worldwide (2020), 161

Eismeier and Pollock, Strategy and Choice in Congressional Elections: The Role of Political Action Committees, 30 Am. J. Pol. Sci. 197 (1986), 824, 825

Ekins, The State of Free Speech and Tolerance in America (Cato Inst., Oct. 31, 2017), 107

Elkin and Soltan eds. Citizen Competence and Democratic Institutions (1999), 158–159

Elliot ed., Debates on the Federal Constitution (1836), 318

Elmendorf and Schleicher, Informing Consent: Voter Ignorance, Political Parties, and Election Law, 2013 U. Ill. L. Rev. 363, 682

Elmendorf and Spencer, The Geography of Racial Stereotyping: Evidence and Implications for VRA Preclearance After Shelby County, 102 Cal. L. Rev. 1123 (2014), 358

Emery, Watergate: The Corruption of American Politics and the Fall of Richard Nixon (1995), 740

Encyclopaedia of the Laws of England (2d ed. 1908), 975

Endres and Panagopoulos, Photo Identification Laws and Perceptions of Electoral Fraud, 8 Res. & Pols. 3 (2021), 1004–1005

Engstrom, Partisan Gerrymandering and the Construction of American Democracy (2013), 274, 306

Engstrom, Race and Southern Politics: The Special Case of Congressional Redistricting, in Writing Southern Politics (Steed and Moreland eds. 2006), 445

Enten, It's Much Harder to Protect Southern Black Voters' Influence Than It Was 10 Years Ago, www.fivethirtyeight .com (Dec. 5, 2016), 387

Epstein, "In Such Manner as the Legislature Thereof May Direct": The Outcome in Bush v. Gore Defended, 68 U. Chi. L. Rev. 613 (2001), 944

Epstein et al., Estimating the Effect of Redistricting on Minority Substantive Representation, 23 J.L. Econ. & Org. 499 (2007), 445

Erickson, Wright, and McIver, Statehouse Democracy: Public Opinion and Policy in the American States (1993), 25

Erie, Rainbow's End: Irish-Americans and the Dilemmas of Urban Machine Politics, 1840-1985 (1988), 418

Etcheson, Bleeding Kansas: Contested Liberty in the Civil War Era (2005), 950

Eubank and Rodden, Who Is My Neighbor? The Spatial Efficiency of Partisanship, 7 Stats. & Pub. Pol'y 87 (2020), 299

Ewald, "Civil Death": The Ideological Paradox of Criminal Disenfranchisement Law in the United States, 2002 Wis. L. Rev. 1045, 172, 173

Ewald, The Way We Vote: The Local Dimension of American Suffrage (2009), 959

FairVote, Survey and Analysis of Statewide Election Recounts, 1980-2007 (2009), 1024

Farrand ed., Records of the Federal Convention of 1787 (1911), 490, 496, 497

FEC Advisory Opinion 1978-10, Allocation of Costs for Voter Registration, 792

FEC Advisory Opinion 1978-50, 792

Federal Communications Commission: Report on Editorializing by Broadcast Licensees (1949), 690

Federal Electoral Boundaries Commission for New Brunswick, Federal Representation 2004, 425

The Federalist No. 10 (Madison), 54

The Federalist No. 15 (Hamilton), 493

The Federalist No. 37 (Madison), 77

The Federalist No. 39 (Madison), 53, 317

The Federalist No. 56 (Madison), 497

The Federalist No. 63 (Madison), 51

The Federalist No. 68 (Hamilton), 58, 77

The Federalist No. 78 (Jefferson), 979

Feingold, Representative Democracy versus Corporate Democracy: How Soft Money Erodes the Principle of "One Person, One Vote," 35 Harv. J. on Legis. 377 (1998), 792

Feldman, Pack the Court! A Defense of Supreme Court Expansion (2021), 986

Fiorina, Retrospective Voting in American National Elections (1981), 156

Fish, The Civil Service and the Patronage (1905), 629–630

Fishkin, The Dignity of the South, 123 Yale L.J. Online 175 (2013), 356

Fishkin and Gerken, The Party's Over: *McCutcheon*, Shadow Parties, and the Future of the Party System, 2014 Sup. Ct. Rev. 175, 542

Fiss, Why the State?, 100 Harv. L. Rev. 781 (1987), 784

Flanders, How Do You Spell M-U-R-K-O-W-S-K-I? Part I: The Question of Assistance to the Voter, 28 Alaska L. Rev. 1 (2011), 564

Folke et al., Patronage and Elections in U.S. States, 105 Am. Pol. Sci. Rev. 567 (2011), 632

Ford ed., The Works of Thomas Jefferson (1905), 979

Fowler, Electoral and Policy Consequences of Voter Turnout: Evidence from Compulsory Voting in Australia, 8 Q.J. Pol. Sci. 159 (2013), 32

Frendeis and Waterman, PAC Contributions and Legislative Behavior: Senate Voting on Trucking Deregulation, 66 Soc. Sci. Q. 401 (1985), 823

Frug, City Making: Building Communities Without Building Walls (1999), 131

Frum, Trumpocracy: The Corruption of the American Republic (2018), 110

Fund, Stealing Elections: How Voter Fraud Threatens Our Democracy (2004), 955

Funke et al., The Cost of Populism: Evidence from History, VOX EU (Feb. 16, 2021), 45

Funke et al., Populist Leaders and the Economy (Kiel Working Paper No. 2169, Oct. 2020), 45

Galie, The New York State Constitution: A Reference Guide (1991), 964

Galie, Ordered Liberty: A Constitutional History of New York (1996), 983

Galston, Emerging Constitutional Paradigms and Justifications for Campaign Finance Regulation: The Case of 527 Groups, 95 Geo. L.J. 1181 (2007), 753

Gans, Voter Turnout in the United States, 1788-2009 (2011), 30

Gardner, Anonymity and Democratic Citizenship, 19 Wm. & Mary Bill Rts. J. 927 (2011), 706

Gardner, Illiberalism and Authoritarianism in the American States, 70 Am. U. L. Rev. 829 (2021), 7

Gardner, The Incompatible Treatment of Majorities in Election Law and Deliberative Democracy, 12 Election L.J. 468 (2013), 26

Gardner, Introduction — Election Law: Universal or Particular?, in Comparative Election Law (Gardner ed. 2022), 948

Gardner, Neutralizing the Incompetent Voter: A Comment on *Cook v. Gralike*, 1 Election L.J. 49 (2002), 683

Gardner, New York's Inbred Judiciary: Pathologies of Nomination and Appointment of Court of Appeals Judges, 58 Buff. L. Rev.: The Docket 15 (2010), 985

Gardner, One-Person, One-Vote and the Possibility of Political Community, 80 N.C. L. Rev. 1237 (2002), 227

Gardner, Representation without Party: Lessons from State Constitutional Attempts to Control Gerrymandering, 37 Rutgers L. J. 881 (2006), 302

Gardner, Southern Character, Confederate Nationalism, and the Interpretation of State Constitutions: A Case Study in Constitutional Argument, 76 Tex. L. Rev. 1219 (1998), 486

Gardner, Voting and Elections, in State Constitutions for the 21st Century: The Agenda of State Constitutional Reform (Tarr and Williams eds. 2006), 1040–1041

Gardner, What Are Campaigns For?: The Role of Persuasion in Electoral Law and Politics (2009), 640–643, 780

Garrett, Is the Party Over? Courts and the Political Process, 2002 Sup. Ct. Rev. 95, 623

Garrett, The Law and Economics of "Informed Voter" Ballot Notations, 85 Va. L. Rev. 1533 (1999), 682

Garrett, Leaving the Decision to Congress, in The Vote: Bush, Gore, and the Supreme Court (Sunstein and Epstein eds. 2001), 1050

Garrow, Protest at Selma: Martin Luther King, Jr. and the Voting Rights Act of 1965 (1978), 324

Gaughan, The Influence of Partisanship on Supreme Court Election Law Rulings, 36 Notre Dame J. Law, Ethics & Pub. Policy ___ (2022), 985

Gauja, Political Parties: Private Associations or Public Utilities in Comparative Election Law (Gardner ed. 2022), 593

Gay, Spirals of Trust?: The Effect of Descriptive Representation on the Relationship between Citizens and Their Government, 46 Am. J. Pol. Sci. 717 (2002), 404

Gelman and King, Enhancing Democracy Through Legislative Redistricting, 88 Am. Pol. Sci. Rev. 541 (1994), 214

Gelman and King, A Unified Method of Evaluating Electoral Systems and Redistricting Plans, 38 Am. J. Pol. Sci. 514 (1992), 303

Gerber, Does Campaign Spending Work?, 47 Am. Behav. Scientist 541 (2004), 779

Gerber and Green, The Effect of a Nonpartisan Get-Out-The-Vote Drive: An Experimental Study of Leafletting, 62 J. Pol. 846 (2000), 782

Gerhardt, Impeachment: What Everyone Needs to Know (2018), 522, 523

Gerken, The Democracy Index: Why Our Election System Is Failing and How to Fix It (2009), 947, 959, 962

Gerken, Mexico's 2007 Election Reforms: A Comparative View, Series II, No. 1 Mex. L. Rev. 163 (2009), 790

Geyh, Who is to Judge? The Perennial Debate over Whether to Elect or Appoint America's Judges (2019), 984

Gibson, Boundary Control: Subnational Authoritarianism in Federal Democracies (2012), 85, 326

Gidron and Hall, The Politics of Social Status: Economic and Cultural Roots of the Populist Right, 68 Brit. J. Soc. 57 (2017), 44

Gilens, Affluence and Influence: Economic Inequality and Political Power in America (2012), 21, 191

Gilens and Page, Testing Theories of American Politics: Elites, Interest Groups, and Average Citizens, 12 Persp. on Pol. 564 (2014), 21

Gilligan and Matsusaka, Public Choice Principles of Redistricting, 129 Public Choice 381 (2006), 291

Gillman, The Votes That Counted: How the Court Decided the 2000 Presidential Election (2001), 944

Ginsburg, et al., The Law of Democratic Disqualification, 111 Cal. L. Rev. ___ (forthcoming 2023), 527

Glazer and Moynihan, Beyond the Melting Pot (1963), 418

Goel et al., One Person, One Vote: Estimating the Prevalence of Double Voting in U.S. Presidential Elections (Stanford U. Working Paper 2017), 991

Goldfeder, Excessive Judicialization, Extralegal Interventions, and Violent Insurrection: A Snapshot of Our 59th Presidential Election, 90 Fordham L. Rev. 335 (2021), 1050

Gopoian, What Makes PACs Tick? An Analysis of the Allocation Patterns of Economic Interest Groups, 28 Am. J. Pol. Sci. 259 (1984), 826

Gormley ed., The Pennsylvania Constitution A Treatise on Rights and Liberties (2004), 300

Grant, The Ballot Order Effect is Huge: Evidence from Texas, 172 Pub. Choice 421 (2017), 936

Green et al., Getting Out the Vote in Local Elections: Results from Six Door-to-Door Canvassing Experiments, 65 J. Pol. 1083 (2003), 782

Grenzke, Shopping in the Congressional Supermarket: The Currency Is Complex, 33 Am. J. Pol. Sci. 1 (1989), 823

Griffin, Electoral Competition and Democratic Responsiveness: A Defense of the Marginality Hypothesis, 68 J. Pol. 911 (2006), 294

Griffin and Keane, Descriptive Representation and the Composition of African American Turnout, 50 Am. J. Pol. Sci. 998 (2006), 445

Grofman and Brunell, The Art of Dummymander: The Impact of Recent Redistricting on the Partisan Makeup of Southern House Seats, in Redistricting in the New Millennium (Galderisi ed., 2005), 267

Grofman and Feld, Rousseau's General Will: A Condorcetian Perspective, 82 Am. Pol. Sci. Rev. 567 (1988), 29

Grofman and King, The Future of Partisan Gerrymandering After *LULAC v. Perry,* 6 Election L.J. 2 (2007), 303

Gross et al., State Campaign Finance Regulations and Electoral Competition, 30 Am. Pol. Res. 143 (2002), 931

Grumback, Laboratories of Democratic Backsliding (Apr. 20, 2022), 7

Guinier, [E]racing Democracy: The Voting Rights Cases, 108 Harv. L. Rev. 109 (1994), 431

Guinier, The Tyranny of the Majority (1994), 35, 431, 444

Gulati, Revisiting the Link Between Electoral Competition and Policy Extremism in the U.S. Congress, 32 Am. Pol. Res. 495 (2004), 294

Gulati and Farrar-Myers, The Impact of Outside Group Expenditures in U.S. House Elections, 2010-2014 (unpublished paper 2017), 904, 905

Haber, Efficiency and Uplift: Scientific Management in the Progressive Era, 1890-1920 (1964), 486, 536

Habermas, Between Facts and Norms: Contributions to a Discourse Theory of Law and Democracy (Rehg, trans., 1996), 25

Habrajano and Hajnal, White Backlash: Immigration, Race & American Politics (2015), 325

Hacker and Pierson, Let Them Eat Tweets: How the Right Rule in an Age of Extreme Inequality (2020), 735

Hacker and Pierson, Restoring Healthy Party Competition, in Democracy Unchained: How to Rebuild Government for the People (Orr et al. eds. 2020), 93

Hacker and Pierson, Winner-Take-All Politics: How Washington Made the Rich Richer – and Turned Its Back on the Middle Class (2010), 191

Hall and Wayman, Buying Time: Moneyed Interests and the Mobilization of Bias in Congressional Committees, 84 Am. Pol. Sci. Rev. 797 (1990), 827

Halmai, Illiberalism in East-Central Europe (European Univ. Inst. Working Paper Law 2019/05), 43

Hamm et al., The Impact of *Citizens United* in the States: Independent Spending in State Elections, 2006-2010, 77 J. Pol. 535 (2015), 904–905

Hamm et al., Independent Spending in State Elections, 2006-2010: Vertically Networked Political Parties Were the Real Story, Not Business, 12 The Forum 305 (2014), 904

Hansen et al., The Effects of *Citizens United* on Corporate Contributions in the 2012 Presidential Election, 77 J. Pol. 535 (2015), 904

Hart, Why Do Some Firms Give? Why Do Some Give a Lot?: High-Tech PACs, 1977-1996, 63 J. Pol. 1230 (2001), 825

Hartz, The Liberal Tradition in America (1955), 48

Haselswerdt, Con Job: An Estimate of Ex-Felon Voter Turnout Using Document-Based Data, 90 Soc. Sci. Q. 262 (2009), 177

Hasen, Beyond the Margin of Litigation: Reforming U.S. Election Administration to Avoid Electoral Meltdown, 62 Wash & Lee L. Rev. 937 (2005), 960

Hasen, Chill Out: A Qualified Defense of Campaign Finance Disclosure in the Internet Age, 27 J.L. & Pol. 557 (2012), 715

Hasen, *Citizens United* and the Illusion of Coherence, 109 Mich. L. Rev. 581 (2011), 902

Hasen, A Critical Guide to *Bush v. Gore* Scholarship, 7 Ann. Rev. Pol. Sci. 297 (2004), 944

Hasen, Entrenching the Duopoly: Why the Supreme Court Should Not Allow the States to Protect the Democrats and Republicans from Political Competition, 1997 Sup. Ct. Rev. 331, 577

Hasen, Fixing Washington, 126 Harv. L. Rev. 550 (2012), 770

Hasen, Lobbying, Rent Seeking, and the Constitution, 64 Stan. L. Rev. 191 (2012), 902

Hasen, The Nine Lives of *Buckley v. Valeo*, in First Amendment Stories (Garnett and Koppelman eds. 2011), 783–784

Hasen, Race or Party?: How Should Courts Think about Republican Efforts to Make it Harder to Vote in North Carolina and Elsewhere, 127 Harv. L. Rev. 58 (2014), 443

Hasen, Research Note: Record Litigation Rates in the 2020 Election: An Aberration or a Sign of Things to Come?, 21 Election L.J. 150 (2022), 1030

Hasen et al., The Effects of *Citizens United* on Corporate Contributions in the 2012 Presidential Election, 77 J. Pol. 535 (2015), 904

Hayduk, Democracy for All (2006), 120

Hebert, An Assessment of the Bailout Provisions of the Voting Rights Act, in Voting Rights Act Reauthorization of 2006: Perspectives on Democracy, Participation, and Power (Henderson ed., 2007), 355

Heerwig and Shaw, Through a Glass Darkly: The Rhetoric and Reality of Campaign Finance Disclosure, 102 Geo. L.J. 1443 (2014), 717

Heighten and Wolfinger, The Political Implications of Higher Turnout, 31 Brit. J. Pol. Sci. 179 (2001), 32

Hellman, Defining Corruption and Constitutionalizing Democracy, 111 Mich. L. Rev. 1385 (2013), 770, 891

Hellman, Money Talks But It Isn't Speech, 95 Minn. L. Rev. 953 (2011), 786

Henninger, et al., Who Votes without Identification? Using Individual-Level Administrative Data to Measure the Burden of Strict Voter Identification Laws, 18 J. Emp. Leg. Stud. 256 (2021), 1004

Herron and Sekhon, Overvoting and Representation: An Examination of Overvoted Presidential Ballots in Broward and Miami-Dade Counties, 22 Electoral Stud. 21 (2003), 1016

Hibbing and Theiss-Morse, Stealth Democracy: Americans' Beliefs About How Government Should Work (2002), 295

Hill et al., How Quickly We Forget: The Duration of Persuasion Effects from Mass Communication, 30 Pol. Comm. 521 (2013), 683

Hillygus and Shields, The Persuadable Voter: Wedge Issues in Presidential Campaigns (2008), 782

Hirschl, City, State: Constitutionalism and the Megacity (2020), 240

Hjalmarsson et al., The Voting Behavior of Young Disenfranchised Felons: Would They Vote If They Could?, 12 Am. L. & Econ. Rev. 356 (2010), 177

Ho, Captive Constituents: Prison-Based Gerrymandering and the Current Redistricting Cycle, 22 Stan. L. & Pol. Rev. 355 (2011), 222

Ho, Something Old, Something New, or Something Really Old? Second Generation Racial Gerrymandering Litigation as Intentional Racial Discrimination Cases, 59 Wm. & Mary L. Rev. 1887 (2018), 459

Hoebeke, The Road to Mass Democracy: Original Intent and the Seventeenth Amendment (1995), 79

Hoffer and Hull, Impeachment in America, 1635-1805 (1984), 522

Hofstadter, The Age of Reform: From Bryan to F.D.R. (1955), 486

Hofstadter, The Idea of a Party System: The Rise of Legitimate Opposition in the United States, 1780-1840 (1790), 532, 535, 536

Holbein and Hillygus, Making Young Voters: The Impact of Preregistration on Youth Turnout, 60 Am. J. Pol. Sci. 364 (2015), 937

Holbrook, Do Campaigns Matter? (1996), 779

Holbrook and McClurg, The Mobilization of Core Supporters: Campaigns, Turnout, and Electoral Composition in United States Presidential Elections, 49 Am. J. Pol. Sci. 689 (2005), 782

Hopkins et al., Voting but for the Law: Evidence from Virginia on Photo Identification Requirements, 14 J. Emp. Leg. Stud. 79 (2017), 1004

Horowitz, Electoral Systems: A Primer for Decision Makers, 14 J. Democracy 115 (2003), 264, 258

Huckfeldt and Sprague, Citizens, Politics, and Social Communication: Information and Influence in an Election Campaign (1995), 780

Huefner, Remedying Election Wrongs, 44 Harv. J. on Legis. 265 (2007), 1043

Hurd, Promoting Private Enforcement of the Voting Rights Act and the Materiality Provision: Contrasting *Northeast Ohio Coalition for the Homeless v. Husted* and *Schweir v. Cox,* 87 U. Cin. L. Rev. 1379 (2018), 478

Huyse, Justice after Transition: On the Choices Successor Elites Make in Dealing with the Past, 20 Law & Soc. Inq. 51 (1995), 527

Issacharoff, Campaign Finance Regulation in the Modern Age: The Constitutional Logic of Campaign Finance Regulation, 36 Pepp. L. Rev. 373 (2009), 790

Issacharoff, Fragile Democracies (2015), 103, 529

Issacharoff, Gerrymandering and Political Cartels, 116 Harv. L. Rev. 593 (2002), 948

Issacharoff, On Political Corruption, 124 Harv. L. Rev. 118 (2010), 771, 870, 891

Issacharoff, Private Parties with Public Purposes: Political Parties, Associational Freedoms, and Partisan Competition, 101 Colum. L. Rev. 274 (2001), 594, 617

Issacharoff and Karlan, The Hydraulics of Campaign Finance Reform, 77 Tex. L. Rev. 1705 (1999), 931

Issacharoff and Karlan, Standing and Misunderstanding in Voting Rights Law, 111 Harv. L. Rev. 2276 (1998), 409

Iyengar and Kinder, News That Matters: Television and American Opinion (1987), 682, 781

Iyengar et al., The Origins and Consequences of Affective Polarization in the United States, 22 Ann. Rev. Pol. Sci.7.1 (2019), 479

Jacobs and Page, Who Influences U.S. Foreign Policy?, 99 Am. Pol. Sci. Rev. 107 (2005), 191

Jacobson, The Effects of Campaign Spending in Congressional Elections, 72 Am. Pol. Sci. Rev. 469 (1978), 779

Jacobson, How Do Campaigns Matter?, 18 Ann. Rev. Pol. 31 (2015), 782

Jardina, White Identity Politics (2019), 325

Jennings and Niemi, Generations and Politics: A Panel Study of Young Adults and Their Parents (1981), 780

Jensen, The Last Party System: Decay of Consensus, 1932-1980, in The Evolution of American Electoral Systems (P. Kleppner et al. eds. 1981), 574

Jensen, The Winning of the Midwest: Social and Political Conflict, 1888-1896 (1971), 777

Jessee, Malhotra, and Sen, A Decade-Long Longitudinal Survey Shows That the Supreme Court is Now Much More Conservative Than the Public, 119 PNAS ___ (2022), 985–986

Johnson, A Dictionary of the English Language (1755, 1785, 1792, 1802), 313

Johnson and Kelling, Placing Facebook: "Trending," Napalm Girl, and Journalistic Boundary Work, 12 Journalism Prac. 817 (2018), 638, 639

Johnstone, The State of the Republican Form of Government in Montana, 74 Mont. L. Rev. 1 (2013), 64

Kagan, The Jungle Grows Back: America and Our Imperiled World (2018), 46

Kalla and Broockman, The Minimal Persuasive Effects of Campaign Contact in General Elections: Evidence from 49 Field Experiments, 112 Am. Pol. Sci. Rev. 148 (2018), 780–781

Kamarck, Returning Peer Review to the American Presidential Nomination Process, 93 N.Y.U. L. Rev. 709 (2018), 99, 107

Kang, The End of Campaign Finance Law, 98 Va. L. Rev. 1 (2012), 901, 902

Kang, Sore Loser Laws and Democratic Contestation, 99 Geo. L.J. 1013 (2011), 576

Kang, The Year of the Super PAC, 81 Geo. Wash. L. Rev. 1902 (2013), 752

Kang and Shepherd, The Partisan Foundations of Judicial Campaign Finance, 86 Cal. L. Rev. 1239 (2013), 984

Kang and Shepherd, The Partisan Price of Justice: An Empirical Analysis of Campaign Contributions and Judicial Decisions, 86 N.Y.U. L. Rev. 69 (2011), 791

Kang and Shepherd, Partisanship in State Supreme Courts: The Empirical Relationship Between Party Contributions and Judicial Decision Making, 44 J. Leg. Stud. S161 (2015), 984

Kaplan, The Law of Civil Service (1958), 513

Kaplan and Yuan, Early Voting Laws, Voter Turnout, and Partisan Vote Composition: Evidence from Ohio, 12 Am. Econ. J.: App. Econ. 32 (2020), 937

Karlan, *Georgia v. Ashcroft* and the Retrogression of Retrogression, 3 Election L.J. 21 (2004), 385

Karlan, Maps and Misreadings: The Role of Geographic Compactness in Racial Vote Dilution Litigation, 24 Harv. C.R.-C.L. L. Rev. 173 (1989), 383

Katz, The Problem of Candidate Selection and Models of Party Democracy, 7 Party Pols. 277 (2001), 580

Katz et al., Documenting Discrimination in Voting: Judicial Findings Under Section 2 of the Voting Rights Act Since 1982, 39 U. Mich. J.L. Reform 643 (2007), 365, 357

Kau and Rubin, Congressmen, Constituents, and Contributors: Determinants of Roll Call Voting in the House of Representatives (1982), 823

Keith et al., The Politics of Judicial Elections, 2017-2018 (2019), 983

Keitner, Foreign Election Interference and International Law, in Defending Democracies: Combating Foreign Election Interference in a Digital Age (Ohlen and Hollis eds. 2021), 1023

Ketcham, Presidents Above Party: The First American Presidency, 1789-1829 (1984), 483

Key, Politics, Parties, and Pressure Groups (1958), 541

Key, Southern Politics (1950), 579

Keyssar, The Right to Vote: The Contested History of Democracy in the United States (2000), 110, 160, 641, 988

Keyssar, Why Do We Still Have the Electoral College? (2020), 1045

Kimball and Kropf, The Street-Level Bureaucrats of Elections: Selection Methods for Local Election Officials, 23 Rev. Pol. Res. 1257 (2006), 962

Klar and Krupnikov, Independent Politics: How American Disdain for Parties Leads to Political Inaction (2016), 536

Klarman, The Framers' Coup: The Making of the United States Constitution (2016), 51

Klumpp et al., The Business of American Democracy: *Citizens United*, Independent Spending, and Elections, 59 J.L. & Econ. 1 (2016), 905

Klumpp et al., The Voting Rights of Ex-Felons and Election Outcomes in the United States, 59 Int'l Rev. L & Econ. 40 (2019), 177

Kousser, Gutting the Landmark Civil Rights Legislation (2013), 357

Kousser, The Shaping of Southern Politics: Suffrage Restriction and the Establishment of the One-Party South, 1880-1910 (1974), 84, 324

Kousser, Term Limits and the Dismantling of State Legislative Professionalism (2005), 501

Kovacs-Goodman, Post-Election Litigation in Battleground States: A Summary, HealthyElections.org (Feb. 1, 2021), 1030–1031

Krasno and Green, Preempting Quality Challengers in House Elections, 50 J. Pol. 920 (1988), 779

Kraus, Debunking the Non-Delegation Doctrine for State Regulation of Federal Elections, 108 Va. L. Rev. __ (2022), 1052

Kritzer, Justice on the Ballot: Continuity and Change in State Supreme Court Elections (2016), 983, 984

Kropf and Kimball, Helping America Vote: The Limits of Election Reform (2012), 1009

Kropf et al., Representative Bureaucracy and Partisanship: The Implementation of Election Law, 73 Pub. Admin. Rev. 242 (2013), 963

Kruschke, Encyclopedia of Third Parties in the United States (1991), 609

Kujala, Donors, Primary Elections, and Polarization in the United States, 64 Am. J. Pol. Sci. 587 (2020), 929

Kurland and Lerner eds., The Founder's Constitution (1987), 62

Landau and Dixon, Abusive Judicial Review: Courts against Democracy, 53 U.C. Davis L. Rev. 1313 (2020), 104

Lappin, The Right to Vote for Non-Resident Citizens in Europe, 65 Int'l & Comp. L.Q. 859 (2016), 129

La Raja, Political Participation and Civic Courage: The Negative Effect of Transparency on Making Small Campaign Contributions, 36 Pol. Behavior 753 (2013), 718

La Raja and Rauch, Voters Need Help: How Party Insiders Can Make Presidential Primaries Safer, Fairer, and More Democratic (Brookings Inst., Jan. 31, 2020), 624

La Raja and Schaffner, The Effects of Campaign Finance Spending Bans on Electoral Outcomes: Evidence from the States About the Potential Impact of *Citizens United v. FEC*, 33 Electoral Stud. 102 (2014), 905

Lardeyret, The Problem with PR, 2 J. Democracy 30 (Summer 1991), 577

Lau and Redlawsk, How Voters Decide: Information Processing During Election Campaigns (2006), 157

Lawson, Black Ballots: Voting Rights in the South, 1944-1969 (1976), 324

Lax and Phillips, The Democratic Deficit in the States, 56 Am. J. Pol. Sci. 148 (2012), 190

Lee, The Global Rise of "Fake News" and the Threat to Democratic Elections in the USA, 22 Pub. Admin. & Pol'y 16 (2019), 638, 639

Leighley and Nagler, Who Votes Now? Demographics, Issues, Inequality, and Turnout in the United States (2014), 31

Leonard, The Invention of Party Politics (2002), 533, 535

Lessig, Republic, Lost: How Money Corrupts Congress – and a Plan to Stop It (2011), 769

Lessig, What an Originalist Would Understand "Corruption" to Mean, 102 Cal. L. Rev. 1 (2014), 768

Lever, Must We Vote for the Common Good?, in Political Ethics (Crookston et al. eds. 2016), 33

Levitsky and Way, Competitive Authoritarianism: Hybrid Regimes after the Cold War (2010), 5

Levitsky and Ziblatt, How Democracies Die (2018), 99

Levitt, All About Redistricting, http://redistricting.lls.edu/, 226

Levitt, Citizenship and the Census, 119 Colum. L. Rev. 1355 (2019), 225

Levitt, The Truth about Voter Fraud (Brennan Ctr. for Justice 2007), 956

Levitt, Weighing the Potential of Citizen Redistricting, 43 Loy. L.A. L. Rev. 513 (2011), 319

Levy, Not so *Novus* an *Ordo:* Constitutions without Social Contracts, 37 Pol. Theory 191 (2009), 50

Levy, Packing and Unpacking State Courts, 61 Wm. & Mary L. Rev. 1121 (2020), 986

Levy and Orr, The Law of Deliberative Democracy (2016), 25

Lincoln, Gettysburg Address (1863), 493

Litt, Beyond Pluralism: Ethnic Politics in America (1970), 418

Locke, Second Treatise of Government (1690), 12, 15, 26

Long, Shouting Down the Voice of the People: Political Parties, Powerful PACs, and Concerns About Corruption, 46 Stan. L. Rev. 1161 (1994), 838

López-Guerra, Democracy and Disenfranchisement: The Morality of Electoral Exclusions (2014), 200

Lowenstein, Associational Rights of Major Parties: A Skeptical Inquiry, 71 Tex. L. Rev. 1741 (1993), 596

Lowenstein, Militant Democracy and Fundamental Rights, I, 31 Am. Pol. Sci. Rev. 417 (1937), 529

Lowenstein, Political Bribery and the Intermediate Theory of Politics, 32 UCLA L. Rev. 784 (1985), 664

Lublin, The Paradox of Representation: Racial Gerrymandering and Minority Interests in Congress (1997), 443

Lublin and McDonald, Is It Time to Draw the Line? The Impact of Redistricting on Competition in State House Elections, 5 Election L.J. 144 (2006), 309

Lund, The Unbearable Rightness of *Bush v. Gore*, 23 Cardozo L. Rev. 1219 (2002), 944

MacDonald, Adventures in Redistricting: A Look at the California Redistricting Commission, 11 Election L.J. 472 (2012), 307

MacDonald and Cain, Community of Interest Methodology and Public Testimony, 3 U.C. Irvine L. Rev. 609 (2013), 428

Madison, Letter to S. Roane (Sept. 2, 1819), in Writings of James Madison (Hunt ed. 1908), 77

Madison, Notes of Debates in the Federal Convention of 1787 (Norton 1987), 34

Maerz et al., State of the World 2019: Autocratization Surges — Resistance Grows, 27 Democratization 909 (2020), 3

Maglicocca, Amnesty and Section Three of the Fourteenth Amendment, 36 Const. Comm. 87 (2021), 528

Malbin, Citizen Funding for Elections (Campaign Finance Inst. 2015), 906, 928, 929

Malbin and Gais, The Day After Reform: Sobering Campaign Finance Lessons from the American States (1998), 929, 931

Malbin et al., Public Financing of Elections After *Citizens United* and *Arizona Free Republic* (Campaign Finance Inst. 2011), 928

Manin, The Principles of Representative Government (1997), 199

Mansbridge, Rethinking Representation, 97 Am. Pol. Sci. Rev. 515 (2003), 185

Mansbridge, Should Blacks Represent Blacks and Women Represent Women? A Contingent "Yes," 61 J. Pol. 628 (1999), 401

Manza and Uggen, Locked Out: Felon Disenfranchisement and American Democracy (2006), 177

Markus, The Impact of Personal and National Economic Conditions on the Presidential Vote: A Pooled Cross-Sectional Analysis, 32 Am. J. Pol. Sci. 137 (1988), 779

Marschall and Ruhil, Substantive Symbols: The Attitudinal Dimension of Black Political Incorporation in Local Government, 51 Am. J. Pol. Sci. 17 (2007), 445

Marshall, False Campaign Speech and the First Amendment, 153 U. Pa. L. Rev. 285 (2004), 656, 658

Martineau, Society in America (1837), 65

Masket, No Middle Ground: How Informal Party Organizations Control Nominations and Polarize Legislatures (2009), 542

Masket et al., The Gerrymanders Are Coming! Legislative Redistricting Won't Affect Competition or Polarization Much, No Matter Who Does It, 45 PS: Pol. Sci. & Pol. 39 (2012), 297

Mason, A Cross-Cutting Calm: How Social Sorting Drives Affective Polarization, 80 Pub. Op. Q. 351 (2016), 479

Massaro, Foreign Nationals, Electoral Spending, and the First Amendment, 34 Harv. J.L. & Pub. Pol'y 663 (2011), 902

Massingham, Political Activity Reporter (1959), 516

May, Bending Toward Justice: The Voting Rights Act and the Transformation of American Democracy (2013), 324

Mayer, Disclosures on Disclosure, 44 Ind. L. Rev. 255 (2010), 717

Mayer et al., Do Public Funding Programs Enhance Electoral Competition, in The Marketplace of Democracy: Electoral Competition and American Politics (McDonald and Samples eds. 2006), 929

Mazo, Finding Common Ground on Voter ID Laws, 49 U. Memphis L. Rev. 1233 (2019), 1004

Mazo, Residency and Democracy, 42 Fla. St. U. L. Rev. 611 (2016), 128, 501

Mazo and Dimino eds. The Best Candidate (2020), 624

McCarty, Poole, and Rosenthal, Does Gerrymandering Cause Polarization?, 53 Am. J. Pol. Sci. 666 (2009), 298

McCarty and Schickler, On the Theory of Parties, 21 Ann. Rev. Pol. Sci. 175 (2018), 541

McCloskey and Zaller, The American Ethos: Public Attitudes toward Capitalism and Democracy (1984), 106

McConnell, Reconsidering *Citizens United* as a Press Clause Case, 123 Yale L.J. 412 (2013), 897–898

McConnell, Two-and-a-Half Cheers for *Bush v. Gore*, 68 U. Chi. L. Rev. 657 (2001), 944

McCormack, Re-Counting the Vote: What Does It Cost? (Pew Charitable Trust Oct. 2010), 1023–1024

McCrary et al., Alabama, in Quiet Revolution in the South: The Impact of the Voting Rights Act 1965-1990 (Davidson and Grofman eds. 1994), 387

McDonald and Budge, Elections, Parties, Democracy: Conferring the Median Mandate (2005), 189

McDonald and Popkin, The Myth of the Vanishing Voter, 95 Am. Pol. Sci. Rev. 963 (2001), 177

McGann et al., Gerrymandering in America (2016), 298, 299

McGeveran, Mrs. McIntyre's Persona: Bringing Privacy Theory to Election Law, 19 Wm. & Mary Bill Rts. J. 859 (2011), 718

McGhee and Shor, Has the Top Two Primary Elected More Moderates?, 15 Persp. on Pol. 1053 (2017), 622

McMillan, Constitutional Development in Alabama, 1798-1901 (1955), 175

Meiklejohn, Free Speech and Its Relation to Self-Government (1948), 645

Mencken, A Carnival of Buncombe (Moos ed. 1956), 214

Mickey, Paths Out of Dixie: The Democratization of Authoritarian Enclaves in America's Deep South, 1944-1972 (2015), 71, 85, 326

Mill, Considerations on Representative Government (1861), 123, 188

Mill, Considerations on Republican Government (1869), 705

Miller and Grofman, Redistricting Commissions in the Western United States, 3 U.C. Irvine L. Rev. 637 (2013), 309

Minnesota State Bar Association, Judicial Elections Task Force Report & Recommendations (June 19, 1997), 967

Minnite, The Myth of Voter Fraud (2010), 956

Moke and Saphire, The Voting Rights Act and the Racial Gap in Lost Votes, 58 Hastings L.J. 1 (2006), 1016

Montanaro, The Democratic Legitimacy of Self-Appointed Representatives, 74 J. Pols. 1094 (2012), 201

Montesquieu, The Spirit of the Laws (1748), 58

Morley, *Bush v. Gore*'s Uniformity Principle and the Equal Protection Right to Vote, 28 Geo. Mason L. Rev. 229 (2020), 943

Morley, The Independent State Legislature Doctrine, 90 Fordham L. Rev. 501 (2021), 1052

Morley, The Intratextual Independent "Legislature" and the Elections Clause, 109 Nw. U. L. Rev. Online 131 (2015), 317

Morse, The Future of Felon Disenfranchisement Reform: Evidence from the Campaign to Restore Voting Rights in Florida, 109 Cal. L. Rev. 1141 (2021), 179

Mounk, The People vs. Democracy: Why Our Freedom Is in Danger and How to Save It (2018), 43, 107

Muirhead, The Promise of Party in a Polarized Age (2014), 635

Muller, The Compact Clause and the National Popular Vote Interstate Compact, 6 Election L.J. 372 (2007), 79

Muller, Electoral Votes Regularly Given, 55 Ga. L. Rev. 1529 (2021), 1049

Muller, Reducing Election Litigation, 90 Fordham L. Rev. 561 (2021), 1031

Müller, The Problem with Illiberal Democracy, Social Europe (Jan. 27, 2016), 43

Müller, What Is Populism? (2016), 39

Muntean, Corporate Independent Spending in the Post-BCRA to Pre-*Citizens United* Era, 13 Bus. & Pol. 1 (2011), 899

Mutch, Campaigns, Congresses, and Courts: The Making of Federal Campaign Finance Law (1988), 739

Myers and Levy, Racial Population Projections and Reactions to Alternative News Accounts of Growing Diversity, 677 Ann. Am. Acad. 215 (2018), 479

NAACP Legal Defense Fund, Democracy Diminished: State and Local Threats to Voting Post-*Shelby County, Alabama v. Holder* (2016), 357

National Intelligence Council, Foreign Threats to the 2020 US Federal Elections (Mar. 10, 2021), 1022

Nelson, The First Amendment, Equal Protection, and Felon Disenfranchisement: A New Viewpoint, 65 Fla. L. Rev. 111 (2013), 177

Neuborne, Is Money Different?, 77 Tex. L. Rev. 1609 (1999), 787

Neuborne, One Dollar-One Vote: A Preface to Debating Campaign Finance Reform, 37 Washburn L.J. 1 (1997), 790

Nickerson et al., Partisan Mobilization Campaigns in the Field: Results from a Statewide Turnout Experiment in

Michigan, 59 Pol. Res. Q. 85 (2006), 782

Norden et al., Better Ballots (Brennan Ctr. for Justice 2008), 938

Norris, Why American Elections Are Flawed (and How to Fix Them), Harvard Kennedy School Working Paper 16-038 (Sept. 2016), 947

Norris, Why Elections Fail (2015), 947

Norris and Inglehart, Cultural Backlash: Trump, Brexit, and Authoritarian Populism (2019), 4, 44

Norton, Campaign Speech Law with a Twist: When the Government Is the Speaker, Not the Regulator, 61 Emory L.J. 209 (2011), 682

Note, Developments in the Law: Elections, 88 Harv. L. Rev. 1111 (1975), 1042

Note, Fusion and the Associational Rights of Minor Political Parties, 95 Colum. L. Rev. 683 (1995), 572

Nye, Rainer, and Stratmann, Do Black Mayors Improve Black Employment Outcomes? Evidence from Large U.S. Cities, J.L. Econ. & Org. (2014), 403

Obama, State of the Union Address (Jan. 27, 2010), 890

Office of the Special Counsel, Report on the Investigation into Russian Interference in the 2016 Presidential Election (March 2019), 1018

Official Proceedings of the Constitutional Convention of the State of Alabama, May 21st, 1901 to September 3rd, 1901 (1940), 175

Online Civic Culture Center, News Sharing on UK Social Media: Misinformation, Disinformation & Correction (2019), 638

O'Rourke, The Impact of Reapportionment on Congress and State Legislatures, in Voting Rights and Redistricting in the United States (Rush ed. 1998), 257

Orr and Levy, Regulating Opinion Polling: A Deliberative Democracy Perspective, 39 UNSW L.J. 318 (2016), 684

Ortiz, The Democratic Paradox of Campaign Finance Reform, 50 Stan. L. Rev. 893 (1998), 783

Ortiz, Got Theory?, 153 U. Pa. L. Rev. 459 (2004), 297

Osnos, The Fearful and the Frustrated: Donald Trump's Nationalist Coalition Takes Shape — For Now, The New Yorker (Aug. 24, 2015), 325

Outten, Schmitt, Miller, and Garcia, Feeling Threatened about the Future: Whites' Emotional Reaction to Anticipated Ethnic Demographic Changes, 38 Personality & Soc. Psychol. Bul. 14 (2012), 479

Overton, Matching Political Contributions, 96 Minn. L. Rev. 1694 (2012), 927

Overton, Voter Identification, 105 Mich. L. Rev. 631 (2007), 1007

Owens, Black Substantive Representation in State Legislatures from 1971-1994, 86 Soc. Sci. Q. 779 (2005), 402

Page and Shapiro, The Rational Public: Fifty Years of Trends in Americans' Policy Preferences (1992), 156

Paine, Common Sense (Penguin 1986) (1776), 821

Parliamentary History of England (1782), 490, 491

Persily, In Defense of Foxes Guarding Henhouses: The Case for Judicial Acquiescence to Incumbent-Protecting Gerrymanders, 116 Harv. L. Rev. 649 (2002), 308

Persily and Cain, The Legal Status of Political Parties: A Reassessment of Competing Paradigms, 100 Colum. L. Rev. 775 (2000), 595

Persily and Lammie, Perceptions of Corruption and Campaign Finance: When Public Opinion Determines Constitutional Law, 153 U. Pa. L. Rev. 119 (2004), 771–772

Pew Research Center, Political Polarization in the American Public (2014), 298

Phillips, The Politics of Presence (1995), 401

Pierson, American Hybrid: Donald Trump and the Strange Merger of Populism and Plutocracy, 68 Brit. J. Soc. 106 (2017), 735

Pildes, Foreword: The Constitutionalization of Democratic Politics, 118 Harv. L. Rev. 28 (2004), 292, 558

Pildes, Is Voting Rights Law Now at War with Itself? Social Science and Voting

Rights in the 2000s, 80 N.C. L. Rev. 1517 (2002), 383

Pildes, Participation and Polarization, 22 J. Const. L. 341 (2020), 929

Pildes, Principled Limitations on Racial and Partisan Redistricting, 106 Yale L.J. 2505 (1997), 422

Pildes and Anderson, Slinging Arrows at Democracy: Social Choice Theory, Value Pluralism, and Democratic Politics, 90 Colum. L. Rev. 2121 (1990), 34

Pildes and Niemi, Expressive Harms, "Bizarre Districts," and Voting Rights: Evaluation Election-District Appearances After *Shaw v. Reno*, 92 Mich. L. Rev. 483 (1993), 408, 424, 425

Pinto-Duschinsky, Send the Rascals Packing: Defects of Proportional Representation and the Virtues of the Westminster Model, 25 Times Literary Supp. 10 (Sept. 25, 1998), 577

Pitkin, The Concept of Representation (1967), 184, 400

Piven et al., Keeping Down the Black Vote: Race and the Demobilization of American Voters (2009), 957

Polsky and Charles, Regulating Section 527 Organizations, 73 Geo. Wash. L. Rev. 1000 (2005), 754

Popelier, A Constitutional Perspective on Electoral Gender Quotas, in Comparative Election Law (Gardner ed. 2022), 404

Popkin, The Reasoning Voter: Communication and Persuasion in Presidential Campaigns (1991), 156

Post, Citizens Divided: Campaign Finance Reform and the Constitution (2014), 788

Powell, Elections as Instruments of Democracy (2000), 189

Pozen, What Happened in Iowa?, 111 Colum. L. Rev. Sidebar 90 (2011), 983

Prakash and Yoo, People ≠ Legislature, 39 Harv. J.L. & Pub. Pol'y 351 (2016), 319

Preuhs, The Conditional Effect of Minority Descriptive Representation: Black Legislators and Policy Influence in the American States, 68 J. Pol. 585 (2006), 402

Przeworski, Why Bother With Elections? (2018), 521

Public Citizen, The Last Major Soft Money Loophole: Section 527 Groups in the 2004 Election, 754

Quade, PR and Democratic Statecraft, 2 J. Democracy 36 (Summer 1991), 577

Quist, The Role of Money and Incumbency in 2007-2008 State Elections (National Inst. on Money in State Politics May 6, 2010), 778

Ranney, The Doctrine of Responsible Party Government (1954), 537

Raskin, Legal Aliens, Local Citizens: The Historical, Constitutional and Theoretical Meanings of Alien Suffrage, 141 U. Pa. L. Rev. 1391 (1993), 120

Rave, Fiduciary Voters?, 66 Duke L.J. 331 (2016), 32

Ravel, Dysfunction and Deadlock: The Enforcement Crisis at the Federal Election Commission Reveals the Unlikelihood of Draining the Swamp (Feb. 2017), 964

Rawls, Political Liberalism (1993), 22, 823

Reed, Sense and Nonsense: Standing in the Racial Districting Cases as a Window on the Supreme Court's View of the Right to Vote, 4 Mich. J. Race & L. 389 (1999), 409

Reeves, President Nixon: Alone in the White House (2001), 740

Rehfeld, The Concept of Constituency: Political Representation, Democratic Legitimacy, and Institutional Design (2005), 432

Rehfeld, Representation Rethought: On Trustees, Delegates, and Gyroscopes in the Study of Political Representation and Democracy, 103 Am. Pol. Sci. Rev. 214 (2009), 185, 188

Rehnquist, Judicial Independence, 38 U. Rich. L. Rev. 579 (2004), 979

Renan, Presidential Norms and Article II, 131 Harv. L. Rev. 2187 (2018), 101

Reynolds, Representation and Rights: The Impact of LGBT Legislators in Comparative Perspective, 107 Am. Pol. Sci. Rev. 259 (2013), 403–404

Ribstein, The First Amendment and Corporate Governance, 27 Ga. St. U. L. Rev. 1019 (2011), 899

Richardson, Messages and Papers of the Presidents 98 (1899), 513

Riker, Duverger's Law Revisited, in Electoral Laws and Their Political Consequences (Grofman and Lijphart eds. 1986), 575

Riker, Liberalism Against Populism: A Confrontation Between the Theory of Democracy and the Theory of Social Choice (1982), 34

Robison and Moskowitz, The Group Basis of Partisan Affective Polarization, 81 J. Pol. 1075 (2019), 479

Rodan, Participation without Democracy (2018), 201

Roig, A Quantum Congress, 90 Chi.-Kent L. Rev. 431 (2015), 200

Romero et al., Voter Choice Act: How Did Voters Experience the New Reform in 2018? (U. Cal. New Electorate Project 2019), 937

Root, Addresses on Government and Citizenship (Bacon and Scott eds. 1916), 798

Rosberg, Aliens and the Right to Vote, 75 Mich. L. Rev. 1092 (1977), 120

Rose, A World after Liberalism: Philosophers of the Radical Right (2021), 108

Rose-Ackerman, Corruption and Democracy, 90 Proc. Ann. Meeting Am. Soc'y Int'l L. 83 (1996), 769

Rosenblum, Political Parties as Membership Groups, 100 Colum. L. Rev. 813 (2000), 595

Rosenbluth and Shapiro, Responsible Parties: Saving Democracy from Itself (2018), 624

Rosenstone, Behr, and Lazarus, Third Parties in America: Citizen Response to Major Party Failure (rev. 2d ed. 1984), 576, 577

Ross, Enlightened Democracy: The Case for the Electoral College (2d ed. 2012), 62

Rousseau, The Social Contract (1762), 27

Rowbottom, Democracy Distorted: Wealth, Influence and Democratic Politics (2010), 775, 927

Royden and Li, Extreme Maps (Brennan Ctr. for Justice 2017), 298

Rusk, The Effect of the Australian Ballot Reform on Split Ticket Voting: 1876-1908, Am. Pol. Sci. Rev. 1221 (1970), 673

Rustin-Paschal, Online Behavioral Advertising and Deceptive Campaign Tactics: Policy Issues, 19 Wm. & Mary Bill Rts. J. 907 (2011), 659

Ryan et al., Voting with an "Unsound Mind"? A Comparative Study of the Voting Rights of Persons with Mental Disabilities, 39 UNSW L. J. 1038 (2016), 162

Sabl, The Two Cultures of Democratic Theory: Responsiveness, Democratic Quality, and the Empirical-Normative Divide, 13 Persp. on Pol. 345 (2015), 190

Sajó ed., Militant Democracy (2004), 529

Sample, Democracy at the Corner of First and Fourteenth: Judicial Campaign Spending and Equality, 66 N.Y.U. Ann. Surv. Am. L. 727 (2011), 791

Sample et al., The New Politics of Judicial Elections, 2000-2009 (Brennan Ctr. for Justice 2010), 791, 983

Samples, The Fallacy of Campaign Finance Reform (2006), 931

Sances, Is Money in Politics Harming Trust in Government? Evidence from Two Survey Experiments, 12 Election L.J. 53 (2013), 717

Sanders, Against Deliberation, 25 Pol. Theory 347 (1997), 25

Saward, The Representative Claim, 5 Contemp. Pol. Theory 297 (2006), 186

Scalia, The Rule of Law as a Law of Rules, 56 U. Chi. L. Rev. 1175 (1989), 971

Schaffner et al, Teams without Uniforms: The Nonpartisan Ballot in State and Local Elections, 54 Pol. Res. Q. 7 (2001), 537

Schantz ed., American Presidential Elections: Process, Policy, and Political Change (1996), 599

Schattschneider, Party Government (1942), 633

Schattschneider, The Semisovereign People: A Realist View of Democracy in America (1960), 822–823

Schauer and Pildes, Electoral Exceptionalism and the First Amendment, 77 Tex. L. Rev. 1803 (1999), 787

Scheppele, Autocratic Legalism, 85 U. Chi. L. Rev. 545 (2018), 7

Scheppele, The Party's Over, in Constitutional Democracy in Crisis? (Graber et al. eds. 2018), 96

Schlozman, Verba, and Brady, The Unheavenly Chorus: Unequal Political Voice and the Broken Promise of American Democracy (2012), 191

Schumpeter, Capitalism, Socialism and Democracy (1950), 17

Sellers, Election Law and White Identity Politics, 87 Fordham L. Rev. 1515 (2019), 325

Sellers and Michalski, Democracy on a Shoestring, 74 Vand. L. Rev. 1079 (2021), 949

Sellers and Scharff, Preempting Politics: State Power and Local Democracy, 72 Stan. L. Rev. 1361 (2020), 960

Senate Committee on Commerce, Promoting Fair Practices in the Conduct of Election Campaigns for Federal Elective Offices, and for Other Purposes, S. Rep. 92-96, 92d Cong., 1st Sess. (May 6, 1971), 773

Shaw et al., A Brief Yet Practical Guide to Reforming U.S. Voter Registration Systems, 14 Election L.J. 26 (2015), 991

Sheff, The Myth of the Level Playing Field: Knowledge, Affect, and Repetition in Public Debate, 75 Mo. L. Rev. 143 (2010), 783

Sheridan, A Complete Dictionary of the English Language (1797), 313

Shiffrin, Government Speech, 27 UCLA L. Rev. 565 (1980), 682

Shugerman, Hardball vs. Beanball: Identifying Fundamentally Antidemocratic Tactics, 119 Colum. L. Rev. Online 85 (2019), 111

Sides, Vavrek, and Tesler, Identity Crisis (2018), 325

Siegel, The Conscientious Congressman's Guide to the Electoral Count Act of 1887, 56 Fla. L. Rev. 541 (2004), 1048

Siegel, The Trump Presidency, Racial Realignment, and the Future of Constitutional Norms, in Amending America's Unwritten Constitution (Albert, Roznai, and Williams eds. 2021), 103

Sigler, Defensible Disenfranchisement, 99 Iowa L. Rev. 1725 (2014), 173

Silberman and Durden, Determining Legislative Preferences on the Minimum Wage: An Economic Approach, 84 J. Pol. Econ. 317 (1976), 823

Simon, Beyond Post-Watergate Reform: Putting an End to the Soft Money System, 24 J. Legis. 167 (1998), 792–793

Sitaramin, Contracting Around Citizens United, 114 Colum. L. Rev. 755 (2014), 906

Smith, Civic Ideals (1997), 70

Smith, A Moderate, Modern Campaign Finance Reform Agenda, 12 Nexus 23 (2007), 739

Smith, Revisiting the History of the Independent State Legislature Doctrine, 53 St. Mary's L.J. ___ (2022), 1052

Smith, The Unchanging American Voter (1989), 155

Smith, Unfree Speech: The Folly of Campaign Finance Reform (2001), 789

Solimine, The Three-Judge District Court in Voting Rights Litigation, 30 Mich. J.L. Reform 79 (1996), 334

Sorauf, Party Politics in America (2d ed. 1972), 594

Sorauf, Patronage and Party, 3 Midwest J. Pol. Sci. 115 (1959), 629–630

Spencer and Wood, Citizens United, States Divided: An Empirical Analysis of Independent Political Spending, 89 Ind. L.J. 315 (2014), 905

Spitz, Majority Rule (1984), 72

Squire, Uncontested Seats in Legislative Elections, 25 Legis. Stud. Q. 131 (2000), 948

Stark, Beyond Quid Pro Quo: What's Wrong with Private Gain from Public Office?, 91 Am. Pol. Sci. Rev. 108 (1997), 769

Steen, Self-Financed Candidates in Congressional Elections (2006), 778

Steenbergen and Lodge, Process Matters: Cognitive Models of Candidate Evaluation, in Electoral Democracy (MacKuen and Rabinowitz eds. 2003), 156

Stein ed., Random House Dictionary of the English Language (1966), 465

Steinfeld, Property and Suffrage in the Early sAmerican Republic, 41 Stan. L. Rev. 335 (1989), 163

Stephanopoulos, Aligning Campaign Finance Law, 101 Va. L. Rev. 1425 (2015), 190

Stephanopoulos, The Causes and Consequences of Gerrymandering, 59 Wm. & Mary L. Rev. 2115 (2018), 291

Stephanopoulos, Elections and Alignment, 114 Colum. L. Rev. 283 (2014), 26, 190

Stephanopoulos, The South After *Shelby County*, 2013 Sup. Ct. Rev. 55, 388

Stephanopoulos and McGhee, Partisan Gerrymandering and the Efficiency Gap, 82 U. Chi. L. Rev. 831 (2015), 304

Stewart, The Cost of Conducting Elections (MIT Election Data and Science Lab 2022), 949

Stewart, Waiting to Vote in 2012, 28 J.L. & Pol. 439 (2013), 957

Stewart, Ansolabehere, and Persily, Revisiting Public Opinion on Voter Identification and Voter Fraud in an Era of Increasing Partisan Polarization, 68 Stan. L. Rev. 1455 (2016), 478

Stone, Goode: Bad and Indifferent, Washington Monthly (July-Aug. 1986), 418

Stouffer, Communism, Conformity, and Civil Liberties: A Cross-section of the Nation Speaks Its Mind (1955), 106

Stratmann, Can Special Interests Buy Congressional Votes? Evidence from Financial Services Legislation, 45 J.L. & Econ. 345 (2002), 823, 824

Stratmann, Do Low Contribution Limits Insulate Incumbents from Competition?, 9 Election L.J. 125 (2010), 931

Stratmann, The Market for Congressional Votes: Is Timing of Contributions Everything?, 41 J.L. & Econ. 85 (1998), 823

Stratmann and Aparicio-Castillo, Competition Policy for Elections: Do Campaign Contribution Limits Matter?, 127 Pub. Choice 177 (2006), 931

Strauss, What Is the Goal of Campaign Finance Reform?, 1995 U. Chi. Legal F. 141 (1995), 770, 772, 774, 776

Sukhatme et al., Felony Financial Disenfranchisement, 75 Vand. L. Rev. __ (2023), 179

Sullivan, Against Campaign Finance Reform, 1998 Utah L. Rev. 311, 790

Sullivan, Political Money and Freedom of Speech, 30 U.C. Davis L. Rev. 663 (1997), 784

Sullivan, Two Concepts of Freedom of Speech, 124 Harv. L. Rev. 143 (2010), 894

Sundquist, Party Decay and the Capacity to Govern, in The Future of American Political Parties: The Challenge of Governance (J. Fleishman ed. 1982), 574

Sunstein, Infotopia (2006), 29

Sunstein, The Partial Constitution (1993), 789

Sunstein, Republic.com (2011), 639

Surowiecki, The Wisdom of Crowds (2004), 29

Swain, Black Faces, Black Interests: The Representation of African Americans in Congress (1993), 402, 445

Swindler ed., Sources and Documents of the U.S. Constitutions (1978), 596

Tarr, Without Fear or Favor: Judicial Independence and Judicial Accountability in the States (2012), 964

Teachout, The Anti-Corruption Principle, 94 Cornell L. Rev. 341 (2009), 768, 891

Teachout, Corruption in America: From Benjamin Franklin's Snuff Box to *Citizens United* (2014), 768

Teles, The Rise of the Conservative Legal Movement: The Battle for Control of the Law (2008), 985

Thernstrom, Whose Votes Count? (1987), 383

Thompson, Election Time: Normative Implications of Temporal Properties of the Electoral Process in the United States, 98 Am. Pol. Sci. Rev. 51 (2004), 788

Thompson, Just Elections: Creating a Fair Electoral Process in the United States (2002), 788

Thompson, Two Concepts of Corruption: Making Campaigns Safe for Democracy, 73 Geo. Wash. L. Rev. 1036 (2005), 777, 815

Tillman, The Original Public Meaning of the Emoluments Clause: A Reply to Professor Zephyr Teachout, 107 Nw. U. L. Rev. Colloquy 180 (2013), 768–769

Tocqueville, Democracy in America (1835), 110

Tokaji, Comparative Election Administration: A Legal Perspective on Electoral Institutions, in Comparative Election Law (Gardner ed. 2022), 958, 963

Tokaji, Early Returns on Election Reform: Discretion, Disenfranchisement, and the Help America Vote Act, 73 Geo. Wash. L. Rev. 1206 (2005), 1009

Tokaji, The Future of Election Reform: From Rules to Institutions, 28 Yale L. & Pol'y Rev. 125 (2009), 959

Tokaji, The Obliteration of Equality in American Campaign Finance Law: A Transborder Comparison, 5 J. Parliamentary & Pol. L. 381 (2011), 790

Tokaji, Public Rights and Private Rights of Action: The Enforcement of Federal Election Laws, 44 Ind. L. Rev. 113 (2010), 478

Torchinsky and Reese, State Legislative "Responses" to *Citizens United:* Five Years Later, 66 Syracuse L. Rev. 273 (2016), 905

Toward a More Responsible Two-Party System, 44 Am. Pol. Sci. Rev. Supp. (1950), 540, 541

Tribe, American Constitutional Law (1978), 609

Udani, Campbell, and Fogarty, How Local Media Coverage of Voter Fraud Influences Partisan Perceptions in the United States, 18 State Pol. & Pol. Q. 193 (2013), 478

Uggen and Manza, The Political Consequences of Felon Disenfranchisement Laws in the United States, 67 Am. Soc. Rev. 777 (2002), 177

United States Census Bureau, Census of Governments (1992), 948

United States Census Bureau, Census of Governments (2002), 238

United States Government Accountability Office, Experiences of Two States That Offered Full Public Funding for Political Candidates (May 2010), 928, 929

Urbinati, Me the People: How Populism Transforms Democracy (2019), 43

U.S. Commission on Civil Rights, Voting: 1961 Commission on Civil Rights Report (1961), 324

U.S. Commission on Civil Rights, The Voting Rights Act: Ten Years After (1975), 363

U.S. Election Assistance Commission, Election Crimes: An Initial Review and Recommendations for Future Study (Dec. 2006), 987, 1002

U.S. Presidential Commission on Election Administration, The American Voting Experience: Report and Recommendations (2014), 947

Vandamme and Verret-Hamelin, A Randomly Selected Chamber: Promises and Challenges, 13 J. Pub. Delib. 1 (2017), 200

Van Deusen, The Jacksonian Era, 1828-1848 (1959), 72

V-Dem Institute, New Global Data on Political Parties (Oct. 26, 2020), 530

Vile, Constitutionalism and the Separation of Powers (2d ed. 1998), 60

Virginia Constitutional Convention, Proceedings (1901-1902), 84

Volokh, Private Employees' Speech and Political Activity: Statutory Protection Against Employer Retaliation, 16 Tex. Rev. L. & Pol. 297 (2012), 517

Wagner, Importing Constituents: Prisoners and Political Clout in New York (Prison Policy Initiative Report 2002), www.prisonpolicy.org, 178

Waldron, The Wisdom of the Multitude, 23 Pol. Theory 563 (1995), 28

Warren, Democracy and Deceit: Regulating Appearances of Corruption, 50 Am. J. Pol. Sci. 160 (2006), 771

Washington, Farewell Address (Sept. 19, 1796), 531

Weaver, Nonpartisan Elections in Local Government: Some Key Issues and Suggested Guide Lines for Decision-Making (Citizens Research Council of Mich. 1971), 536

Webster, Compendious Dictionary of the English Language (1806), 313

Webster's New International Dictionary (1950), 968

Webster's Third New International Dictionary (1976, 2002), 465, 677

Weissberg, Collective vs. Dyadic Representation in Congress, 72 Am. Pol. Sci. Rev. 535 (1978), 200

Welch, Campaign Contributions and Legislative Voting: Milk Money and Dairy Price Supports, 35 W. Pol. Q. 267 (1982), 823

Werner, Tammany Hall (1928), 994

West, Descriptive Representation and Political Efficacy: Evidence from Obama and Clinton, 79 J. Pol. 351 (2017), 404

White, Free Speech and Valuable Speech: Silence, Dante, and the "Marketplace of Ideas," 51 UCLA L. Rev. 799 (2004), 697

White, Misdemeanor Disenfranchisement? The Demobilizing Effects of Brief Jail Spells on Potential Voters, 133 Am. Pol. Sci. Rev. 311 (2019), 177

White et al., What Do I Need to Vote? Bureaucratic Discretion and Discrimination by Local Election Officials, 109 Am. Pol. Sci. Rev. 129 (2015), 957

Wiebe, The Search for Order 1877-1920 (1967), 73, 484

Wilcox, Organizational Variables and Contribution Behavior of Large PACs: A Longitudinal Analysis, 11 Pol. Bev. 157 (1989), 825

Williams, Reforming the Electoral College: Federalism, Majoritarianism, and the Perils of Subconstitutional Change, 100 Geo. L.J. 173 (2011), 79

Wills, The Negro President (2003), 67

Wilson, Constitutional Government in the United States (1918), 187

Wilson and Brewer, The Foundations of Public Opinion on Voter ID Laws: Political Predispositions, Racial Resentment, and Information Effects, 77 Pub. Op. Q. 962 (2013), 478

Winkler, "Other People's Money": Corporations, Agency Costs, and Campaign Finance Law, 92 Geo. L.J. 871 (2004), 899

Wolbrecht and Campbell, Leading by Example: Female Members of Parliament as Political Role Models, 51 Am. J. Pol. Sci. 921 (2007), 404

Wolf and Cea, A Critical History of the United States Census and Citizenship Questions, 108 Geo. L.J. Online 1 (2019), 225

Wood, The Creation of the American Republic, 1776-1787 (1969), 194

Wood, Note, Truth, Lies, and Stolen Valor: A Case for Protecting False Statements of Fact Under the First Amendment, 61 Duke L.J. 469 (2011), 646

Wood, The Radicalism of the American Revolution (1992), 49, 72, 163

Wright, Contributions, Lobbying, and Committee Voting in the U.S. House of Representatives (1989), 823

Wright, PACs, Contributions, and Roll Calls: An Organizational Perspective, 79 Am. Pol. Sci. Rev. 400 (1985), 823

Wright, Politics and the Constitution: Is Money Speech?, 85 Yale L.J. 1001 (1976), 786

Yankah, Compulsory Voting and Black Citizenship, 90 Fordham L. Rev. 639 (2021), 32

Youn, First Amendment Fault Lines and the *Citizens United* Decision, 5 Harv. L. & Pol'y Rev. 135 (2011), 786

Young, Justice and the Politics of Difference (1990), 25

Yu, Does State Online Voter Registration Increase Voter Turnout?, 100 Soc. Sci. Q. 620 (2019), 937

Zakaria, The Rise of Illiberal Democracy, 76 For. Aff. 22 (1997), 43

Zaller, The Nature and Origins of Mass Opinion (1992), 156

Zasloff, Jim Crow as Kafka: Voter Suppression on the Ground, UCLA Public Law & Legal Theory Research Paper No. 19-46 (Dec. 4, 2019), 1005

Zelden, *Bush v. Gore:* Exposing the Hidden Crisis in American Democracy (2008), 1050

Zipkin, Democratic Standing, J. L. & Pols. 179 (2011), 1032

Zipkin, The Election Period and Regulation of the Democratic Process, 18 Wm. & Mary Bill Rts. J. 533 (2010), 788

A

Absentee voting, 944-945

Access. *See* Ballot access

Accountability, 16, 21, 46, 194, 201, 292-293

Adams, John, 67, 69, 182, 534

Adams, John Quincy, 74, 1045

Adjustment of vote totals, 1043

Administration of elections, 933-1052
  absentee voting, 944-945
  administrative model, 987-1023
    decentralization of administration
      and, 958-960
    overview, 958-960
    registration of voters, 987-992.
      See also Registration of voters
    technology and elections, 1007-1023.
      See also Technology and elections
    voter identification requirements,
      992-1007. *See also* Voter
      identification requirements
  consequences of electoral procedures,
    933-945
  design of ballots, 938
  drop boxes, 944
  early voting, 944
  election contests, 1024-1026
  Electoral College, 1044-1052. *See also*
    Electoral College
  enforcement of eligibility requirements,
    987-1023. *See also* Enforcement of
    eligibility requirements
  executive/governmental model, 958
  funding restrictions, 945
  incumbents, ballot order of, 933-936
  independent model, 958
  integrity of elections, 946-986. *See also*
    Integrity of elections
  judicial oversight model, 964-986. *See also*
    Judicial oversight of elections
  mail-in voting, 944
  mixed model, 958
  partisanship in, 960-964
  politicization of election procedures,
    944-945
  polling places, location of, 937
  procedural neutrality, 938
  recounts, 1023-1024
    frequency of, 1024

  in presidential elections, 938-944
  results of, 1024
  registration of voters, 987-992. *See also*
    Registration of voters
  voting. *See* Voting

Administrative Procedure Act
  of 1946, 225

Advisory party primaries, 79

Affirmative action, 389-391

Age
  mandatory retirement ages, 502
  qualifications for voting, 159-162
    manner versus qualifications,
      160-161
    sixteen-year-olds, 161
    Twenty-Sixth Amendment and,
      118, 160

Age Discrimination in Employment Act of
  1967, 502

Agency representation, 184

Aggregation problem, 319-320

Aggregative theories of democracy, 18-20

Alabama
  African American voter registration
    in, 323
  at-large elections in, 246-257
  Corrupt Practices Act, unconstitutionality
    of restrictions on campaign speech
    in mass media, 687-688
  curbside voting ban in, 944
  disclosure requirements in, 698
  felony convictions, qualifications for
    voting in, 167
  majority-black districts in, 446-447
  mandatory retirement ages in, 502
  reapportionment in, 206-214
  redistricting in, 478-479
  voter identification requirements in,
    356-357
  Voting Rights Act and covered
    jurisdictions, 328-329, 331-332

Alaska
  fair campaign codes in, 656-657
  primary elections in, 615-616
  redistricting in, 427
  retention elections in, 983
  Voting Rights Act and, 328
  write-in votes in, 564

Albania, felony convictions and
   qualifications for voting in, 173
Alienage, qualifications for voting, 119-120
Alienation, 45-46
American Declaration of the Rights and
   Duties of Man, 121
Anderson, John B., Jr., 548-556, 578
Angle, Sharron, 794
Anonymity
   effects on behavior, 706
   statements about candidate's character,
      704-705
Anticipatory representation, 185-186
Apportionment, 201-240
   abroad, 239-240
   Census and, 224-225
   citizenship and, 224-225
   Congress
      construing "equal," 215-216
      malapportionment of districts,
         203-206
      nationwide apportionment, 227-229
   construing "equal," 215-218
   Equal Protection Clause and, 215,
      217-218, 220, 222, 230
   Fourteenth Amendment and, 218, 227
   general districts, 203-240
   harm from malapportionment, 214-215
   incarcerated non-voters and, 221-222
   judicial elections, 218-219
   justifications for deviation, 218
   local governments, 218
   minority undercounts and, 222-224
   overview, 201-202
   political question doctrine and, 202-203,
      1026-1030
   "political thicket" and, 202-203
   redistricting. See Redistricting
   relevant population base, 219-221
   special districts, 229-239
      business improvement districts
         (BIDs), 238-239
      variety of, 237-239
      water storage districts, 230-237
   state legislatures
      construing "equal," 217-218
      malapportionment of districts,
         206-214
   Voting Rights Act and, 218, 224
Argentina
   age qualification for voting in, 161
   populism in, 41, 45
Aristotle, 28
Arizona
   2021 electoral vote count and, 1049
   absentee voting restrictions in, 945
   "court packing" in, 986

election code challenges, designation of
   public official to bring, 945
independent districting commission in,
   310-318
minority undercounts in, 223
non-English speakers as elected officials
   in, 502
precinct requirements in, 461-476
public financing of elections in,
   916-927, 945
special districts in, 237
third person assistance in voting,
   prohibition on, 461-476
voter identification requirements
   in, 1031
Voting Rights Act and, 328
Arkansas
   African American voter registration
      in, 323
   ballot measures in, 680-681
   disclosure requirements in, 698
   election complaints, authority to
      investigate in, 945
   judicial elections in, 984
   misbehavior, automatic removal of
      elected officials for, 524
   qualifications for office in, 486-487
   term limits in, 488-498
   voiding of elections in, 1032-1041
Armed forces, qualifications for voting,
   123-126
Arrow's Theorem, 33-34
Articles of Confederation, 61
Association, right of, 63, 542-543, 594-600
At-large elections, 241-246
   alternatives to, 258-261
   reapportionment and, 243-246
   Voting Rights Act and, 387
Australia
   administration of elections in, 958,
      961-962
   apportionment in, 240
   blank ballots in, 565
   compulsory voting in, 32
   party bans in, 529
   proportional representation in, 432
   residency requirements in, 129
   vote of no confidence in, 521
Austria
   age qualification for voting in, 161
   integrity of elections in, 947
"Authentic" representation, 399-404
Authoritarianism
   autocratic legalism, 7
   competitive authoritarianism, 5
   "playbook" of, 5-7
   populism and, 43-47

South as "authoritarian enclave," 84-85, 325-326
Autocratic legalism, 7
Azerbaijan, felony convictions and qualifications for voting in, 173

B
Bachmann, Michele, 776
Bailout from VRA coverage. *See* Voting Rights Act of 1965
Ballot access, 544-565
    Anderson-Burdick framework, 563-564
    Equal Protection Clause and, 548-556, 563-564
    Fifteenth Amendment and, 564
    filing fees, 546-548
    First Amendment and, 563-564
    Fourteenth Amendment and, 563-564
    individual rights model, 556-558
    minor parties, 545-546
    "none of the above," 564-565
    official ballot, access to, 545-546
    overview, 544-545
    write-in votes, 558-564
Ballot measures
    disclosure of contributions for, 718
    issue advocacy, 793-794, 799-800
    nonprofit issue advocacy corporations, limitations on campaign expenditures, 838-849
    speech on ballot, 680
    substantive issues, designation of positions of candidates, 680-682
    suggestive wording of, 681-682
Ballots
    design of, 938
    order of incumbents on, 933-936
    punch card ballots, 1009-1016
    secrecy, 1043
"Ballot selfies," 685-686
Banks, campaign expenditures by
    independent expenditures, limitations on, 855-863
    prohibition on, 747
Barrett, Amy Coney, 459, 986
Barry, Marion, 89
BCRA. *See* Bipartisan Campaign Reform Act of 2002
Belgium
    administration of elections in, 958
    campaign speech in, 697
    compulsory voting in, 32
Bell, John, 578
Bentham, Jeremy, 18
Berlusconi, Silvio, 41
Bernstein, Carl, 740
Biden, Joe, 477-478, 528, 955, 1049

BIDs (Business improvement districts), 238-239
Bipartisan Campaign Reform Act of 2002 (BCRA), 791-819
    corruption and, 814-815
    deference and, 815-819
    disclosure requirements under, 713-714
    electioneering communications and, 795-797, 808-810
    enactment of, 794-797
    federal candidates and, 795
    issue advocacy and, 799-800
    national parties and, 795, 802-805
    overview, 736
    soft money and, 789-799
    state, district, and local parties and, 795, 805-808
Blair, Edmund, 74
Blanket primaries, 601, 607-616
Bonilla, Henry, 428
Brazil
    age qualification for voting in, 161
    authoritarianism in, 3
    impeachment in, 523
Breckenridge, John C., 578
Brennan Center for Justice, 298, 904
Bribery
    campaign promises vs., 664-665
    regulation of campaign finance and, 770
Brown, Scott, 905-906
Bryan, William Jennings, 72
Buchanan, Pat, 42
Buckley case (1976)
    balancing of liberties, 788-789
    campaign period, significance of, 787-788
    contributions vs. expenditures, 789-790
    equating spending and speech, 785-786
    First Amendment and, 784-785
    opinion, 755-767
    public financing of elections and, 911-916
    reaction to, 783-791
    "tank of gas" metaphor, 786-787
Bulgaria, exit polling prohibited in, 684
Burke, Edmund, 181-182, 187
Burr, Aaron, 1045
Bush, George W., 30, 110, 794-795, 928, 1050
Business improvement districts (BIDs), 238-239

C
California
    administration of elections in, 960
    Citizens Redistricting Commission, 427-428

California (*Continued*)
   disclosure requirements in, 715
   felony convictions, qualifications for
      voting in, 167-172
   incarcerated non-voters and, 222
   independent districting commission in,
      307, 309, 427-428
   mail-in voting in, 479, 944
   minority undercounts in, 223
   Presidential Tax and Transparency
      Act, 503
   primary elections in, 590-593,
      607-615, 622
   recall elections in, 526
   redistricting in, 427-428
   right to instruct representatives in, 183
   robocalls in, 685
   special districts in, 230-238
   tax returns, candidates releasing in, 503
   term limits in, 499-500, 502
   Voting Rights Act and, 328-329
Campaign contributions
   banks, prohibition on contributions, 747
   Buckley case. *See Buckley* case
   corporations, prohibition on
      contributions, 747
   disclosure requirements
      as compelled speech, 706-718. *See also*
         Compelled speech
      FECA, 739, 745-746
   judges, solicitation by, 973-983
   limitations on
      aggregate limits, 906-910
      BCRA, 795
      FECA, 739, 743-744
   speech vs. money, 657-658
   Super PACs, 752, 903-905
   unions, prohibition on
      contributions, 747
Campaign expenditures
   banks
      independent expenditures,
         limitations on, 855-863
      prohibition on expenditures, 747
   Buckley case. *See Buckley* case
   Citizens United case, 871-910. *See also*
      Citizens United case
   corporations. *See* Corporations
   disclosure requirements
      corporations and, 899-901
      FECA, 739, 745-746
   First Amendment and, 819
   by foreign nationals, 902
   limitations on, 819-871
      banks, 855-863
      BCRA, 795
      corporations, 863-869

FECA, 739, 744-745
   ideological but nonpartisan PACs,
      820-827
   nonprofit issue advocacy
      corporations, 838-849
   political parties, 828-838
   Super PACs, 903-905
   unions, 849-855
lobbying and, 901-902
PACs. *See* Political action committees
political parties and
   distinctiveness of, 837-838
   limitations on expenditures,
      828-838
   treatment of, 833-834
unions
   independent expenditures,
      limitations on, 849-855
   prohibition on expenditures, 747
Campaign finance, 733-931. *See also*
      Bipartisan Campaign Reform Act
      of 2002
   abroad, 790
   anti-corruption justifications for
      regulation of, 768-772
      appearance of corruption, 771-772
      bribery and, 770
      conceptions of corruption, 770
      constitutional considerations,
         768-769
      corruption of politics, 771
      defining corruption, 769
      dependence corruption, 769-770
      extortion and, 772
   Buckley case. *See Buckley* case
   citizenship and, 783
   Citizens United case, 871-910. *See also*
      Citizens United case
   contributions. *See* Campaign
      contributions
   effectiveness of reforms, 930-931
   effect of money, 777-783
      agenda-setting, 781-782
      framing, 781-782
      minimal effects thesis and, 778-779
      on mobilization, 782
      on persuasion, 780-781
      priming, 781-782
      on vote share, 779-780
      winners outspending losers, 778
   electioneering communications, 795-797,
      808-810
   equality justifications for regulation of,
      772-776
      "buying" of office, 772-773
      influencing politics, equalizing
         opportunity, 774-776

institutional entities, disproportionate
influence of, 774
rich, overrepresentation of, 773-774
expenditures. *See* Campaign
expenditures
FECA, 736-749. *See also* Federal Election
Campaign Act of 1974
historical background, 736-747
issue advocacy, 793-794, 799-800
in judicial elections, 790-791
negative advertising and, 782-783
overview, 733-736
PACs. *See* Political action committees
populism and, 733-735
public financing, 911-931. *See also* Public
financing of elections
soft money, 791-793, 798-799
unintended harm as justification for
regulation of, 776-777
campaign discourse, coarsening
of, 777
fundraising, excessive time spent
in, 776
Campaign-free election days, 680
Campaign promises, 660-665
Campaign speech, 637-731
abroad, 697-698
disclosure requirements as compelled
speech, 698-731. *See also*
Compelled speech
"fake news," 638-639
false statements, 646-660. *See also* False
statements
First Amendment doctrine, 643-646
Hatch Act and, 511-517
historical background, 640-643
Eighteenth Century, 640-641
Nineteenth Century, 641-642
Twentieth Century, 642-643
individualism and, 645
institutional understanding of politics
and, 645-646
in mass media, 686-698
abroad, 697-698
editorials, 687
fairness doctrine, 688-697
Progressives on, 642-643
restrictions on, 643-686
bribery vs. promises, 664-665
campaign promises, 660-665
constraints of office, 665-666
content-neutral restrictions, 644
false statements, 646-660
time, place, and manner restrictions,
666-686
social media, blocking speech on,
726-731

speech vs. money, 657-658
structural understanding of politics and,
645-646
time, place, and manner restrictions,
666-686
agenda-setting and, 682-683
"ballot selfies," 685-686
campaign-free election days, 680
electioneering, prohibiting, 666-680
exit polling, prohibiting, 683-684
framing and, 682-683
racial designation of
candidates, 680
robocalls, 684-685
speech on ballot, 680
substantive issues, designation of
positions of candidates, 680-682
suggestive wording of ballot measures,
681-682
underlying theories, 644-646
Canada
administration of elections in, 958,
961-962
apportionment in, 239-240
campaign finance in, 790
Charter of Rights and Freedoms,
129, 173
Elections Act 2000, 684
exit polling, prohibiting, 684
felony convictions, qualifications for
voting in, 173
First Nations, 425
party bans in, 529
redistricting in, 425
residency requirements in, 129-130
unwritten constitutional norms in,
100-101
Candidates, 504-521
candidate "branding," 619-621
coercion by private employers, 517
drug testing of, 502
fusion candidacies, 565-574
government employment, forgoing,
511-517
health information, disclosure of,
519, 521
personal financial information,
disclosure of, 517-521
primary elections, 579-624. *See also*
Primary elections
racial designation of, 680
resign-to-run requirements, 504-511
substantive issues, designation of
positions of candidates, 680-682
tax returns, releasing, 502-503
Capitol insurrection (2021). *See* January 6
Capitol insurrection

Carter, Jimmy, 683
Census Act of 1790, 223-224
Census Bureau, 221-223, 948
Census Clause, apportionment and, 223
Central Intelligence Agency (CIA), 516-517
Chávez, Hugo, 41, 45, 103
Chile, alienage and qualifications for voting
    in, 120
Citizenship
    apportionment and, 224-225
    campaign finance and, 783
    Fourteenth Amendment and, 322
    qualifications for voting, 112-123
        alienage and, 119-120
        in District of Columbia, 120-121
        equality, ramifications for, 121-123
        historical background, 112-114
        residency, relation to, 129-130
        in territories, 120-121
        women, 114-118
Citizens United case (2010), 871-910
    analysis of, 893-897
    corporations vs. PACs, 891-893
    corruption and, 891, 910
    counteracting effects of, 905-910
    freedom of press and, 897-898
    identity of speaker, 891-893
    impact of, 903-905
    opinion, 871-890
    political participation and, 910
    reaction to, 890-891
Civil Rights Act of 1957, 88, 323
Civil Rights Act of 1960, 88, 323
Civil Rights Act of 1964, 92
Civil Rights Movement, 85-92
Civil War, 85
Clay, Henry, 1045
Clinton, Bill, 523, 793-794
Clinton, Hillary, 30, 46, 74, 76, 101, 659,
    734, 776, 949
Closed primaries, 601, 619
Colombia, threats to independent judiciary
    in, 103
Colorado
    campaign expenditures in, 828-833,
        835-837
    fair campaign codes in, 657
    gerrymandering in, 306
    judicial elections in, 984
    redistricting in, 425, 427
    residency requirements in, 131-132
    retention elections in, 983
    Voting Rights Act and, 329
Communications Decency Act of 1996
    Section 230, 726-731
    social media, blocking speech on,
        726-731

Compact Clause, 78-79
Compelled speech, 698-731
    anonymous statements about candidate's
        character, 704-705
    campaign contributions, 706-718
        for ballot measures, 718
        BCRA, 713-714
        collateral consequences of, 717-718
        effectiveness of disclosure, 716-717
        FECA, 706-713
        harassment, likelihood of, 714-715
        identity of speaker compared, 716
        retaliation, likelihood of, 714-715
    deterrence and, 705
    effects of anonymity on behavior, 706
    identity of speaker, 699-706
    overview, 698
    petition signers, 718-726
Compelling interests, racial discrimination
    and gerrymandering and, 421
Competitive authoritarianism, 5
Compulsory voting, 32-33
Conditional districts, 383-385
Condorcet, Marquis de, 29, 258
Congress
    apportionment
        construing "equal," 215-216
        malapportionment of districts,
            203-206
        nationwide apportionment, 227-229
    constitutional qualifications, exclusivity
        of, 487-498
    expulsion, 487-488, 527
    residency requirements, 501
    term limits
        efforts to establish, 498-499
        state constitutions attempting to
            establish, 488-498
Connecticut
    disabilities, voters with, 479
    incarcerated non-voters and, 222
    mail-in voting in, 479
    primary elections in, 602-607
    registration of voters in, 479
    Voting Rights Act and, 329
Constitution. *See also specific Clause or*
        Amendment
    federalism and, 61-62
    lack of examples to draw from, 3
    liberalism and, 16
    republicanism, influence of, 54-58
    text of, 1053-1069
Contributions. *See* Campaign contributions
Cooper, Roy, 95
Corporations
    campaign expenditures
        Citizens United case, 871-890

corporate democracy and, 898-901
disclosure requirements and, 899-901
"distorting effects" of, 870
independent expenditures,
    limitations on, 863-869
    PACs vs., 891-893
    prohibition on, 747
freedom of speech and, 870-871, 893
Correa, Rafael, 104
Corruption, 768-772
    appearance of corruption, 771-772
    BCRA and, 814-815
    bribery and, 770
    Citizens United case and, 891, 910
    conceptions of corruption, 770
    constitutional considerations, 768-769
    corruption of politics, 771
    defining corruption, 769
    dependence corruption, 769-770
    extortion and, 772
"Court packing," 986
Covered jurisdictions of VRA, 328-329,
    331-332
Cranston, Alan, 741, 746
Crosscheck system, 991
Cruz, Ted, 1049
Cuba, age and qualifications for voting
    in, 161
Cumulative voting, 259-260
Cycling and indeterminacy problem, 33-34
Czech Republic
    campaign speech in, 697
    exit polling, prohibition in, 684

D

Davis, Gray, 526
Davis, Jack, 818-819
Declaration of Independence, 15, 61
Delaware
    incarcerated non-voters and, 222
    judicial elections in, 973
    registration of voters in, 479
Delegate representation, 184
Deliberative democracy, 24-25
Democracy and democratization,
    1-35, 71-93
    adherence to democratic and
        constitutional norms, 99-100
    aggregative theories of democracy, 18-20
    American Revolution, 49-50
    backsliding of, 4-5
    baseline of analysis, 47-68
    basic tenets of, 10-17
    Civil Rights Movement and, 85-92
    commitment of American public to,
        106-108
    competitive authoritarianism versus, 5

decline of, 3-9
election law inheriting from, 9-35
elector defections and, 74-78
enduring political impact of slavery
    and, 92-93
equality and, 16
fair party competition, 93-99
fall of slavery and, 79-84
fear of failure of, 479
federalism, 61-65. *See also* Federalism
free civil society and, 16
freedom of speech and, 637-640
global perspective, 3-9
historical narrative, 48-49
human rights and, 16
independent judiciary, 103-106
    judicial populism and, 105
    political polarization and, 104-105
liberal conceptions of democracy, 17-26
    deliberative democracy, 24-25
    democratic minimalism, 17-18
    economic theory of democracy, 18-20
    thicker theories of democracy, 21-23
majoritarianism in, 26-35. *See also*
    Majoritarianism
modern liberalism, 15-17
National Popular Vote (NVP) plan, 78-79
normalization of political opposition
    and, 16
pluralism, 20-21
    modern theories of, 20
    pitfalls of, 21
popular sovereignty and, 16
presidential elections, institutional
    evolution of, 73-74
prospects for, 93-108
republicanism, 50-60. *See also*
    Republicanism
    decline of, 72-73
rule of law and, 16
Senate, transformation of, 79
South as "authoritarian enclave," 84-85,
    325-326
in United States, 47-50
unwritten constitutional norms, 100-103
Democratic minimalism, 17-18
Democratic particularism, 947-948
Demos, 109-112
Denmark
    administration of elections
        in, 958
    campaign speech in, 697
    felony convictions, qualifications for
        voting in, 173
    integrity of elections in, 947
Dent, Harry, 740
Descriptive representation, 184, 445

Dickinson, John, 51
Disabilities, voters with, 479
Disclosure
  BCRA, 713-714
  campaign contributions
    as compelled speech, 706-718. *See also*
      Compelled speech
    FECA, 739, 745-746
  campaign expenditures
    corporations and, 899-901
    FECA, 739, 745-746
  as compelled speech, 698-731.
      See also Compelled speech
  petition signers, 719-726
Disenfranchisement
  Civil Rights Movement and, 85-92
  felony convictions and, 172-173, 176-178
  voiding of elections, risk of
    disenfranchisement of
    innocent, 1041
Disinformation, 639
District of Columbia
  qualifications for
    voting in, 120-121
  Twenty-Third Amendment and,
    120-121
  virtual representation and, 194-195
District of Columbia Voting Rights
    Amendment (proposed), 194-195
Do Not Call Registry, 684
Droop, Henry, 260-261
Drop boxes, 944
Due Process Clause, poll taxes and, 167
Duke, David, 543-544
Duverger's Law, 575

E
Early voting, 479, 944
ECA. *See* Electoral Count Act of 1887
ECHR (European Court of Human Rights),
    697-698
Economic inequality, 735-736
Economic theory of democracy, 18-20
Ecuador
  age qualification for voting in, 161
  independent judiciary, threats to, 104
  populism in, 41
Efficiency gap, 304-305
Elected officials, 481-530
  candidates. *See* Candidates
  characteristics of, 481-486
  Congressional term limits
    efforts to establish, 498-499
    state constitutions attempting to
      establish, 488-498
  disqualification and removal, 521-530
    expulsion, 487-488, 527

    impeachment, 522-524. *See also*
      Impeachment
    incompetence, removal for, 524-526
    individual disqualification, 529-530
    lustration, 527-529
    militant democracy and, 529-530
    misbehavior, automatic removal
      for, 524
    party bans, 529-530
    recall elections, 526
    vote of no confidence, 521-522
  effect of term limits, 500-501
  mandatory retirement ages, 502
  non-English speakers, 502
  "patriot king" model, 481-483
  Progressives on, 484-486
  qualifications for office, 486-503
    constitutional qualifications,
      exclusivity of, 487-498
    district residency requirements,
      501-502
    nonelective offices, 503
    other qualifications, 502
    in presidential elections, 502-503
    Scarlet Letter provisions, 498-499
  term limits. *See* Term limits
Election Assistance Commission
    (EAC), 1007
Election contests, 1024-1026
Electioneering
  communications, 795-797, 808-810.
    See also Campaign speech
  time, place, and manner, 666-680
Elections Clause
  age qualification for voting, 160
  independent districting commissions
    and, 310-318
Electoral College, 1044-1052
  2021 electoral vote count, 1049-1050
  candidates, silence as to
    selection of, 623
  constitutional framework, 1044-1045
  elector defections, 74-78
  failure to select electors, 1048
  federalism and, 62
  independent state legislature doctrine
    and, 1050-1052
  multiple slates of electors, 1047-1049
  National Popular Vote (NVP) plan
    and, 78-79
  objections, 1047
  popular vote vs., 30
  problems with, 73
  resolution of disputes, 1046-1048
  selection of electors, 1044-1045
  Twelfth Amendment and, 74-76, 1045
  validity of electoral votes, 1046-1047

voting by, 1045
Electoral Count Act of 1887 (ECA)
  2021 electoral vote count and, 1049-1050
  failure to select electors, 1048
  historical background, 1046
  multiple slates of electors, 1047-1049
  objections, 1047
  problems with, 1049-1050
  procedures under, 1046
  resolution of disputes, 1046-1048
  validity of electoral votes, 1046-1047
Electoral integrity. *See* Integrity
      of elections
Electronic voting, 959, 1011
Enforcement Act of 1870, 322
Enforcement Act of 1871, 322
Enforcement of eligibility requirements,
      987-1023
  registration of voters, 987-992.
      See also Registration of voters
  technology and elections, 1007-1023.
      See also Technology and elections
  voter identification requirements,
      992-1007. *See also* Voter
      identification requirements
Equal Protection Clause
  affirmative action and, 389-391
  apportionment and, 215, 217-218, 220,
      222, 230
  ballot access and, 548-556, 563-564
  discriminatory manipulation of
      representation and, 246
  federal rights protection, 63
  felony convictions, qualifications for
      voting, 175-176, 179
  gerrymandering and, 264-265, 268
  liberalism and, 16
  literacy tests and, 148
  nonelective offices and, 503
  poll taxes and, 167
  predominant factor test and, 433-442
  quotas and, 389-391
  racial discrimination and
      gerrymandering and, 409-420
  redistricting and, 433-442
  voter identification requirements
      and, 1006
Erdoğan, Recep, 39
Ethics in Government Act of 1978, 517-519
European Convention for the Protection of
      Human Rights and Fundamental
      Freedoms (ECHR)
  campaign speech, 697-698
  felony convictions, qualifications for
      voting, 173-174
European Court of Human Rights (ECHR),
      697-698

European Union
  Code of Good Practice in Electoral
      Matters, 947
  Venice Commission, 947
Executive/governmental model, 958
Exit polling, 683-684
Expatriate voting, 129
Expenditures. *See* Campaign expenditures
Expulsion, 487-488, 527
Extortion, regulation of campaign finance
      and, 770

F
Factions, 540-541
Fair campaign codes, 652-657
Fairness doctrine, 688-697
"Fake news," 638-639, 659
Fall, Albert B., 737
False statements, 646-660
  evidence, treating speech as, 659-660
  fair campaign codes, 652-657
  "fake news," 638-639, 659
  libel and
      efficacy of, 651
      as mechanism for policing false
          statements, 646-651
  rationale for regulating, 656
  speech by words or money, 657-658
  voter deception, 658-659
Fannie Lou Hamer, Rosa Parks, and Coretta
      Scott King Voting Rights Act
      Reauthorization and Amendments
      Act of 2006, 338-340
FCPA (Federal Corrupt Practices Act of
      1910), 737-738
FEC. *See* Federal Election Commission
FECA. *See* Federal Election Campaign Act
      of 1974
Federal Bureau of Investigation (FBI),
      516-517
Federal Communications
      Commission (FCC)
  affirmative action and, 390
  fairness doctrine and, 688-693
Federal Corrupt Practices Act of 1910
      (FCPA), 737-738
Federal Election Campaign Act of 1974
      (FECA), 736-749
  amendments to, 740-743
  campaign contributions and. *See also*
      Campaign contributions
  banks, corporations, and unions,
      prohibition on, 747
  compelled speech, disclosure
      requirements as, 706-713
  disclosure requirements, 739, 745-746
  limitations, 739, 743-744

Federal Election Campaign Act of 1974
    (FECA) (*Continued*)
    campaign expenditures and. *See also*
        Campaign expenditures
    banks, corporations, and unions,
        prohibition on, 747
    disclosure requirements, 739, 745-746
    limitations, 739, 744-745
    FEC, establishment of, 746-747
    First Amendment and, 742
    historical background, 738-739
    overview, 736
    PACs and, 739, 745, 750
    public financing of elections and, 746
    schematic representation of, 748-749
Federal Election Commission (FEC)
    establishment of, 746-747
    Hatch Act, applicability of, 516-517
    partisanship and, 963-964
    soft money and, 792
Federalism, 61-65
    Constitution and, 61-62
    Electoral College and, 62
    federal rights protection, 63
    indirect federal power, 63-64
    local governments, role of, 62-63
    regulation of elections and, 61-62
    uniformity versus diversity, 64-65
The Federalist Papers, 51, 53-60
Feingold, Russ, 792, 794
Felony convictions
    qualifications for voting, 167-179
        abroad, 173-174
        election crimes, 178
        Equal Protection Clause and, 167-172
        justifications for disenfranchisement,
            172-173
        moral turpitude, crimes of, 174-176
        partisan politics and, 176-177
        racial discrimination and, 176-177
        restoration of voting rights, 178-179
        voter referenda regarding, 96, 179
    Voting Rights Act and, 178, 388-389
Fifteenth Amendment
    attempts to repudiate, 80-82, 84, 322-323
    ballot access and, 564
    demos and, 110
    discriminatory manipulation of
        representation and, 246
    enforcement of, 85
    gerrymandering and, 264
    "grandfather clauses" and, 82-84
    lineage, qualifications for voting, 142
    literacy tests and, 145, 152
    qualifications for voting, 118, 322
    slavery and, 80

Voting Rights Act and, 1, 325-326,
    358-359
"White Primary" cases and, 583-587
"Filler people," 398-399
Fillmore, Millard, 578
Financing of elections. *See* Campaign
    finance
Finland
    administration of elections in, 958
    economic inequality in, 735
    felony convictions, qualifications for
        voting in, 173
    integrity of elections in, 947
First Amendment
    ballot access and, 563-564
    campaign expenditures and, 819
    campaign speech and, 643-646. *See also*
        Campaign speech
    "fake news" and, 638-639, 659
    FECA and, 742
    federal rights protection, 63
    freedom of association, 63, 542-543,
        594-600
    freedom of press and Press Clause,
        686-698
        abroad, 697-698
        campaign speech and, 686. *See also*
            Campaign speech
        Citizens United case and, 897-898
        editorials, 687
        fairness doctrine, 688-697
    freedom of speech. *See* Freedom
        of speech
    Free Exercise Clause, 152
    judges, solicitation of campaign
        contributions by, 973-982
    liberalism and, 16
    militant democracy and, 530
    patronage and, 624-632
    political parties and, 542-543, 594
    primary elections and, 596-600
    public employees, constitutional claims
        by, 624-632
    term limits and, 499
First-past-the-post system, 188, 241, 305, 575
501(c)(4) organizations, 754
527 organizations, 753-754
Florida
    2000 presidential election in, 938-944,
        1007, 1050
    administration of elections in, 960-961
    African American voter registration
        in, 323
    Amendment 4, 179
    "court packing" in, 986
    disenfranchisement in, 176

disputed 1876 presidential election
    and, 1046
fairness doctrine in, 694-697
felony convictions, qualifications for
    voting in, 96, 179
gerrymandering in, 298
judges, solicitation of campaign
    contributions by, 973-982
judicial elections in, 984
public financing of elections in, 945
recounts in, 1023
retention elections in, 983
two-party system in, 578-579
Voting Rights Act and, 328, 382
Ford, Gerald, 74, 740
Foreign interference in elections
    legal consequences of, 1022-1023
    Russia, interference in 2016 presidential
        election by, 1017-1022
Foreign nationals, campaign expenditures
    by, 902
Fourteenth Amendment
    age qualification for voting, 159
    apportionment and, 218, 227
    ballot access and, 563-564
    citizenship and, 322
    Due Process Clause, poll
        taxes and, 167
    Equal Protection Clause. *See* Equal
        Protection Clause
    gerrymandering and, 264
    literacy tests and, 148, 152
    lustration and, 527-528
    majority-black districts and, 446
    poll taxes and, 167
    residency requirements
        and, 128-129
    slavery and, 79
    term limits and, 499
    Voting Rights Act and, 339, 433, 460
Fourth Amendment, literacy tests
    and, 147
France
    administration of elections in, 958
    campaign speech in, 697
    economic inequality in, 735
    exit polling, prohibiting, 684
    felony convictions, qualifications for
        voting in, 173
    populism in, 41
Franklin, Benjamin, 51, 163
Fraud in elections, 949-957
    2000 presidential election, claims of
        fraud in, 477-478
    conspiracy theories, 3
    detection, challenges of, 957
    investigations of, 952-954
    likelihood of, 4-5, 949-955
    modern charges of, 955-956
    race and, 956-957
    "vote caging," 956-957
    voter identification requirements and,
        994-995
Free civil society, 16
Freedom of association, political parties
    and, 542-543, 594-600
Freedom of press
    abroad, 697-698
    campaign speech and, 686-698
    Citizens United case and, 897-898
    editorials, 687
    fairness doctrine, 693-697
Freedom of speech
    campaign speech, 637-731. *See also*
        Campaign speech
    compelled speech, disclosure
        requirements as, 698-731.
        See also Compelled speech
    constitutional protection, 63
    content-neutral restrictions, 644
    of corporations, 870-871
    corporations and, 893
    disinformation and, 639
    fair campaign codes and, 657
    "fake news" and, 638-639, 659
    individualism and, 645
    institutional understanding of politics
        and, 645-646
    liberal democracy and, 637-640
    "marketplace of ideas" and, 644
    misinformation and, 639
    "post-truth" and, 638
    siloing, 639
    social media and, 638-639
    structural understanding of politics and,
        645-646
Freedom Riders, 88-91
Freedom to Vote Act (proposed), 358
Fusion candidacies, 565-574

G
Gandhi, Mahatma, 85
Garfield, James A., 736
Garland, Merrick, 95
Geographical communities, 132-138
    consolidation of cities, 132-133
    counties, reorganization
        of, 136-137
    local government boundaries,
        significance of, 137-138
    multidistrict remedies for single-district
        violations, 134-136

Georgia
   2021 electoral vote count and, 1049
   African American voter registration
      in, 323
   ballot drop boxes in, 944
   "court packing" in, 986
   drug testing of candidates in, 502
   early voting in, 944
   election complaints, authority to
      investigate in, 945
   election contests in, 1024-1026
   gerrymandering in, 409-420
   judicial elections in, 984
   misbehavior, automatic removal of
      elected officials for, 524
   public financing of elections in, 945
   qualifications for office in, 486
   redistricting in, 427, 432
   voters waiting in line, criminalization of
      providing food or drink to, 944
   Voting Rights Act and, 328-329
Germany
   administration of elections in, 958
   age qualification for voting in, 161
   campaign speech in, 697
   economic inequality in, 735
   felony convictions, qualifications for
      voting in, 173
   lustration in, 527
   party bans in, 529
   political parties in, 531, 593
Gerry, Elbridge, 51, 261
Gerrymandering, 261-320
   aggregation problem, 319-320
   Equal Protection Clause and,
      264-265, 268
   evolution of, 458-459
   Fifteenth Amendment and, 264
   Fourteenth Amendment and, 264
   harms from, 290-299
      electoral competitiveness, decline
         in, 292
      expressive harms, 407-408
      extent of harms, 298-299
      governmental accountability, lack of,
         292-293
      legislative polarization, 295-298
      legislator responsiveness, lack of,
         293-294
      policy, distortion of, 290-291
      voter alienation, 294-295
   historical background, 261-262
   independent districting commissions
      and, 307-318
   overview, 261-262
   partisan gerrymandering

      efficiency gap, 304-305
      justiciability, 268-290
      partisan bias, 303-304
      standards, 303-305
      state constitutions and, 299-303
   political question doctrine and, 264, 267
   popular sovereignty and, 318-319
   public participation as remedy, 319
   racial discrimination and
      compelling interests, 421
      Equal Protection Clause and, 409-420
      expressive harms, 407-408
      majority-black districts, 405-407,
         446-447
      overview, 262-264
      predominant factor test, 421-424,
         432-433
      standing to challenge, 408-420
      strict scrutiny, 421
   re-redistricting and, 305-307
   as "self-limiting enterprise," 266-267
   state constitutions and, 299-303
   transparency as remedy, 319
   unilateral gerrymandering, 264-266
Gingrich, Newt, 95
Ginsburg, Ruth Bader, 459, 986
Giuliani, Rudy, 955
Gleason, John, 740
Gore, Al, 30, 794
Gorsuch, Neil, 986
Gosar, Paul, 1049
Governors, powers regarding
      elections, 95-96
"Grandfather clauses," 82-84
Grant, Ulysses S., 528
Greece, felony convictions and
      qualifications for voting in, 173
Guam, qualifications for voting in, 121
Guiteau, Charles J., 736
Gyroscopic representation, 186

H
Haldeman, H.R., 740
Hamilton, Alexander, 34, 73, 532, 534
Harding, Warren G., 737
Hare, Thomas, 260-261
Hatch Act Modernization Act of 2012, 517
Hatch Act of 1939, 511-517, 624, 738
HAVA. *See* Help America Vote Act of 2002
Hawaii
   apportionment in, 219-220
   disabilities, voters with, 479
   Electoral College and, 1049
   lineage, qualifications for voting, 143
   Office of Hawaiian Affairs (OHA), 143
   redistricting in, 427

registration of voters in, 479
Voting Rights Act and, 329
write-in votes in, 558-563
Hawley, Josh, 1050
Hayes, Rutherford B., 1046
Heard, Alexander, 739
Help America Vote Act of 2002 (HAVA)
   election modernization and, 994
   federalism and, 64
   provisional votes and, 1008-1009
   technology and, 1007-1008
Hofeller, Thomas, 225
Hoyer, Steny, 752
Hughes, Howard, 740
Human rights, 16
Humphrey, Hubert, 623
Hungary, authoritarianism in, 3, 7-9, 530
Hunt, E. Howard, 739

I

Idaho
   independent districting commission
      in, 309
   public financing of elections in, 945
   right to instruct representatives in, 183
   Voting Rights Act and, 329
Identification requirements. *See* Voter
   identification requirements
Illiberalism, 37-108
   alternatives to liberalism, 38-47
   populism, 38-47. *See also* Populism
   slavery and, 66-67
   Three-Fifths Clause and, 67-71, 321
   in United States, 65-71
Illinois
   alienage, qualifications for voting, 120
   apportionment in, 219, 1026-1027
   ballot drop boxes in, 944
   "ballot selfies" in, 686
   Constitution, 219
   disabilities, voters with, 479
   incarcerated non-voters and, 222
   mail-in voting in, 479
   patronage in, 624-631
   registration of voters in, 479, 988-989
   retention elections in, 983
Impeachment, 522-524
   "high crimes and misdemeanors,"
      522-523
   impeachable offenses, 522-523
   President, 522
   procedures, 523-524
   uses of, 523
Incumbents
   ballot order of, 933-936
   redistricting and, 429

Independent campaign expenditures,
      limitations on
   banks, 855-863
   corporations, 863-869
   ideological but nonpartisan PACs,
      820-827
   nonprofit issue advocacy corporations,
      838-849
   unions, 849-855
Independent districting commissions,
      307-318, 427-428
Independent judiciary, 103-106
   judicial populism and, 105
   political polarization and, 104-105
Independent state legislature doctrine,
      1050-1052
Indeterminacy problem, 33-34, 429-431
India
   economic inequality in, 735
   "none of the above" in, 564-565
Indiana
   disabilities, voters with, 479
   early voting in, 479
   gerrymandering in, 264-266
   judicial elections in, 984
   mail-in voting in, 479
   multimember districts in, 242-243
   right to instruct representatives in, 183
   robocalls in, 684-685
   voter identification requirements in,
      992-1006
Influence districts, 383-387
Initiatives. *See* Ballot measures
Integrity of elections, 946-986
   administrative challenges, 948-949
   administrative model, 987-1023. *See also*
      Administration of elections
   decentralization of administration
      and, 958-960
   overview, 958-960
   registration of voters, 987-992. *See also*
      Registration of voters
   technology and elections, 1007-1023.
      See also Technology and elections
   voter identification requirements,
      992-1007. *See also* Voter
      identification requirements
   "best practices," 946-948
   concept of, 946
   elected election officials and, 962-964
   fiscal considerations, 949
   fraud, 949-957. *See also* Fraud in elections
   judicial oversight model, 964-986. *See also*
      Judicial oversight of elections
   partisanship in election administration
      and, 960-964

Inter-American Commission on Human
　　Rights, 121
Interest pluralism, 540-541
International Covenant on Civil and
　　Political Rights, 946
International Institute for Democracy and
　　Electoral Assistance, 946-947
Invalidation of elections. *See* Voiding of
　　elections
Iowa
　　"court packing" in, 986
　　early voting in, 944
　　independent districting commission
　　　in, 308
　　judicial elections in, 984
　　retention elections in, 983
　　voter ID requirements in, 945
Iraq, economic inequality in, 735
Ireland
　　administration of elections in, 958
　　campaign speech in, 697
　　proportional representation in, 432
Israel
　　felony convictions, qualifications for
　　　voting in, 173
　　party bans in, 529
　　proportional representation in, 432
Issue advocacy
　　BCRA and, 799-800
　　nonprofit issue advocacy corporations,
　　　limitations on campaign
　　　expenditures, 838-849
　　overview, 793-794
Italy
　　backsliding of democracy in, 3
　　populism in, 41

J
Jackson, Andrew, 68-69, 72, 187, 534, 1045
Jackson, Ketanji Brown, 459
Jacksonian democracy, 162-163, 964
January 6 Capitol insurrection (2021), 525,
　　528-529, 639, 1049-1050
Japan, administration of elections in, 958
Jefferson, Thomas, 15, 67-69, 72, 534, 1045
Jim Crow, 28, 84, 176, 326, 355
John Lewis Voting Rights Advancement Act
　　of 2021 (proposed), 358, 479
Johnson, Andrew, 523
Johnson, Boris, 41
Johnson, Lyndon B., 1-2, 323-324, 326
Judicial elections. *See* Judiciary
Judicial oversight of elections, 964-986
　　judicial restraint, 1031-1032
　　litigation, 1030-1031
　　political question doctrine and,
　　　1026-1030

standing and, 1032
voiding of elections, 1032-1043
　　adjustment of vote totals, 1043
　　as breach of ballot secrecy, 1043
　　disenfranchisement of innocent, risk
　　　of, 1041
　　popular will, respecting, 1041-1043
　　reluctance, 1041
　　state constitutions and, 1040-1041
Judicial populism, 105
Judiciary
　　appointed judges, 984-986
　　"court packing" and, 986
　　independent judiciary, 103-106
　　　judicial populism and, 105
　　　political polarization and, 104-105
　　judicial elections, 964-972
　　　campaign finance in, 790-791
　　　elimination of, 983-984
　　　nonpartisan judicial elections,
　　　　972-983
　　　Voting Rights Act and, 387
　　judicial oversight of elections, 964-986.
　　　See also Judicial oversight of
　　　elections
　　judicial populism, 105
　　partisan capture and, 984-986
　　political polarization and, 104-105
　　solicitation of campaign contributions by
　　　judges, 973-983
　　Supreme Court, U.S.
　　　"court packing" and, 986
　　　ideological shifts on, 459, 985-986
　　　politicization of, 985-986
Justice Department
　　Civil Rights Division, 330
　　redistricting and, 405, 409-420
　　Voting Rights Act and, 224-225, 330, 334,
　　　356, 444, 1004

K
Kansas
　　election fraud during pre-Civil War
　　　territorial period, 950-951
　　misbehavior, automatic removal of
　　　elected officials for, 524
　　registration of voters in, 991
　　retention elections in, 983
Kansas–Nebraska Act of 1854, 950
Kavanaugh, Brett, 459, 985
Kennedy, Anthony M., 459
Kennedy, John F., 85, 524-525, 623,
　　739, 1049
Kentucky
　　campaign promises in, 660-664
　　disabilities, voters with, 479
　　disenfranchisement in, 176

early voting in, 479
electoral votes in, 1045
judicial elections in, 973, 984
mail-in voting in, 479
recounts in, 1023
King, Martin Luther, Jr., 86
King, Rufus, 51
Kobach, Kris, 991
Ku Klux Klan Act of 1871, 528

L

LaFollette, Robert, 578
LaGuardia, Fiorello, 536
Leadership PACs, 751-752
Lee, Richard Henry, 15
Le Pen, Jean, 41
Le Pen, Marine, 41, 734
Libel
    "actual malice" standard, 646-648, 651
    false campaign statements and
        efficacy of, 651
        as mechanism for policing false
            statements, 646-651
Liberal democracy, 1-35. *See also* Democracy
    and democratization
Liddy, G. Gordon, 739
Lieberman, Joseph, 511
Limited voting, 259
Lincoln, Abraham, 70
Lineage, qualifications for voting, 143
Literacy, qualifications for voting, 144-159
    contemporary political behavior and,
        153-156
    Fifteenth Amendment and, 145, 152
    Fourteenth Amendment and, 148, 152
    Fourth Amendment and, 147
    interpretation tests, 146-148
    literacy tests, 144-146
    non-English speakers, 148-152
    racial discrimination and, 144-148
    rational ignorance and, 157-158
    rational irrationality and, 158
    rehabilitating voter competence, 156-157
Lobbying, 200, 770, 901-902
Locke, John, 12-15, 26-27, 48, 112
Long, Huey, 42
Louisiana
    candidates, racial designation of, 680
    "court packing" in, 986
    disputed 1876 presidential election
        and, 1046
    early voting in, 479
    literacy tests in, 146-147
    special districts in, 229-230
    Voting Rights Act and, 328, 332
Lowenstein, Daniel Hays, 595-596
Low voter turnout, 30-31

Lustration, 527-529
Luxembourg, prohibition on exit polling
    in, 684

M

Madison, James, 51, 53-60, 532, 736
Mail-in voting, 479, 944
Maine
    disabilities, voters with, 479
    mail-in voting in, 479
    recounts in, 1023
    registration of voters in, 479
    right to instruct representatives in, 183
Maistre, Joseph de, 37-38
Majoritarianism, 26-35
    constitutional solutions, 35
    cycling and, 33-34
    defining majority rule, 29
    duty to vote and, 32-33
    indeterminacy problem and, 33-34
    liberal justifications for limiting majority
        power, 34
    low voter turnout and, 30-31
    majority of what kinds of votes, 30
    pluralist justifications for, 28
    rational non-participation and, 31
    scope of franchise and, 29-30
    "tyranny of majority," 34-35
    "wisdom of multitude," 28-29
Majority-black districts
    effect of, 444-445
    Fourteenth Amendment and, 446
    gerrymandering and, 405-407, 446-447
    predominant factor test and, 447-458
    Voting Rights Act and, 446
Malapportionment of districts, 203-215
Malawi, alienage and qualifications for
    voting in, 120
Malta
    age qualification for voting in, 161
    campaign speech in, 697
    proportional representation in, 432
Manchin, Joe, 358
Maryland
    age qualification for voting in, 161
    early voting in, 479
    felony convictions, qualifications for
        voting in, 173
    gerrymandering in, 268-290
    incarcerated non-voters and, 222
    mail-in voting in, 479
Massachusetts
    disabilities, voters with, 479
    early voting in, 479
    fair campaign codes in, 652, 657
    mail-in voting in, 479
    right to instruct representatives in, 182

Mass media. *See also* Social media
  abroad, 697-698
  campaign speech in, 686-698
  editorials, 687
  fairness doctrine, 693-697
McCain, John, 776, 792, 794
McCain–Feingold Act. *See* Bipartisan
       Campaign Reform Act of 2002
McCarthy, Eugene, 623
McCarthy, Joseph, 42
McCarthy, Kevin, 752
McConnell, Mitch, 95, 986
McCrory, Pat, 95
McHenry, Patrick, 752
McKinley, William, 737
McMahon, Linda, 776
Meehan, Marty, 794
Mental disability, qualifications for
       voting, 162
Mercer, John, 51
Mexico, administration of
       elections in, 958
Michigan
  2021 electoral vote count and, 1049
  "ballot selfies" in, 685-686
  geographical communities in, 134-136
  gerrymandering in, 298
  right to instruct representatives in, 183
  state legislatures, powers regarding
       elections, 96
  Voting Rights Act and, 328
Militant democracy, 529-530
Mill, John Stuart, 121-123, 188, 705
Miller, Joe, 564
Minimal effects thesis, 778-779
Minnesota
  electioneering, prohibiting, 672-680
  election of judges in, 665-666
  fair campaign codes in, 657
  fusion candidacies in, 565-574
  judicial elections in, 966-972
  mail-in voting in, 479
  public financing of elections in, 928
  recounts in, 1023
  robocalls in, 685
Minority set-asides, 390
Minor parties, ballot access, 545-546
Misinformation, 639
Mississippi
  African American voter registration
       in, 323
  felony convictions, qualifications for
       voting in, 167
  judicial elections in, 964, 984
  Voting Rights Act and, 328, 331
Missouri
  mandatory retirement ages in, 502

nonelective offices in, 503
  residency requirements in, 501
  right to instruct representatives in, 183
  Scarlet Letter provisions in, 499
  special districts in, 230
  voter identification requirements
       in, 1006
Missouri Compromise of 1820, 950
Missouri Plan, 965, 984
Mitchell, John, 739
Modi, Narendra, 41
Monroe, James, 74
Montana
  campaign expenditures by corporations
       in, 890-891
  disabilities, voters with, 479
  judicial elections in, 973
  robocalls in, 685
Montesquieu, Baron de, 58
Morales, Evo, 41, 104
Moses, Bob, 85-92
"Motor Voter Law," 990. *See also* National
       Voter Registration Act of 1993
Mueller, Robert S., III, 1017-1022
Multimember districts, 241-246
  demise of, 257
  reapportionment and, 243-246
Multiple residency, qualifications for voting,
       130-131
Murkowski, Lisa, 564

N
Namibia, economic inequality in, 735
National Association for the Advancement
       of Colored People (NAACP), 88,
       543, 698-699
National Popular Vote (NVP) plan, 78-79
National Security Agency, 516-517
National Security Council, 516-517
National Voter Registration Act of
       1993 (NVRA)
  age qualification for voting, 160-161
  election modernization and, 993-994
  federal rights protection, 63
  indirect federal power and, 63
  overview, 990
  purges and, 990-992
  time lags and, 990-992
  voter identification requirements and,
       993-995
Nebraska, unicameral legislature in, 536
Negative advertising, 782-783
Netherlands, integrity of elections in, 947
Nevada
  2021 electoral vote count and, 1049
  disabilities, voters with, 479
  incarcerated non-voters and, 222

mail-in voting in, 479
"none of the above" in, 564
registration of voters in, 479
right to instruct representatives in, 183
Voting Rights Act and, 333
New Hampshire
    "ballot selfies" in, 685
    campaign speech in, 648-651
    Voting Rights Act and, 328
New Jersey
    apportionment in, 215-216
    ballot measures in, 681
    early voting in, 479, 944
    incarcerated non-voters and, 222
    independent districting commission
        in, 307
    registration of voters in, 988
New Mexico, voiding of elections in, 1042
Newsom, Gavin, 526
New York
    alienage, qualifications for voting,
        119-120
    "ballot selfies" in, 686
    campaign finance in, 780
    candidates, coercion by private
        employers in, 517
    fair campaign codes in, 652-655
    felony convictions, qualifications for
        voting in, 173
    geographical communities in, 136-137
    incarcerated non-voters and, 222
    independent districting commission
        in, 309
    judicial elections in, 984
    mail-in voting in, 479
    minority undercounts in, 223
    non-geographical sub-communities in,
        138-143
    primary elections in, 596-600
    registration of voters in, 479, 987-988
    residency requirements in, 130
    special districts in, 237
    Voting Rights Act and, 328, 391-397
New Zealand
    alienage, qualifications for voting, 120
    campaign-free election days in, 380
    party bans in, 529
    residency requirements in, 129
Nicaragua, age and qualifications for voting
    in, 161
Nineteenth Amendment
    demos and, 110
    qualifications for voting, 118
Nixon, Richard M., 74, 523, 623,
    739-740, 1049
Nonconnected political committees, 751
Nonelective offices, 503

Non-English speakers
    elected officials, 502
    literacy tests and, 148-152
"None of the above," 564-565
Non-geographical sub-communities
    lineage, 143
    school districts, 139-143
Nonpartisan primaries, 601, 622
Normalization of political opposition, 16
North Carolina
    African American voter registration
        in, 323
    gerrymandering in, 268-290, 298,
        405-407
    judicial elections in, 984
    literacy tests in, 144-145
    majority-black districts in, 447-458
    redistricting in, 432-442
    state legislatures, powers regarding
        elections, 95-96
    voter identification
        requirements in, 357, 459-460,
        1004-1005
    Voting Rights Act and, 328-329
North Dakota
    disabilities, voters with, 479
    mail-in voting in, 479
    registration of voters in, 479
Norway
    administration of elections in, 958
    campaign speech in, 697
    integrity of elections in, 947
NVRA. *See* National Voter Registration Act
    of 1993

O

Obama, Barack, 325, 776, 890, 928,
    992, 1017
O'Brien, Larry, 740
Ohio
    ballot access in, 545-546, 548-556
    campaign finance in, 780
    disclosure requirements in, 699-704
    fair campaign codes in, 657
    gerrymandering in, 298, 302
    independent districting commission
        in, 309
    judicial elections in, 973
    punch card ballots in, 1009-1016
    registration of voters in, 992
    voter deception in, 658-659
Oklahoma
    early voting in, 479
    judicial elections in, 984
    primary elections in, 616-617
    voter identification requirements
        in, 1006

Open primaries, 601, 619
Orbán, Viktor, 8-9, 39, 43
Oregon
    mail-in voting in, 479
    mental disability, qualifications for
        voting, 162
    residency requirements in, 501

P
PACs. *See* Political action committees
Park Geunhye, 523
Participation in political process, 381-382
Parties. *See* Political parties
Partisan politics
    in administration of elections, 960-964
    contemporary partisanship, nature of,
        634-635
    elected election officials and, 962-964
    felony convictions, disenfranchisement
        for, 177-178
    partisan gerrymandering
        efficiency gap, 304-305
        justiciability, 268-290
        partisan bias, 303-304
        standards, 303-305
        state constitutions and, 299-303
"Patriot king" model, 481-483
Patronage, 624-632, 736
Pell, Claiborne, 741-743
Pence, Mike, 1050
Pendleton Civil Service Act of 1883, 736-737
Pennsylvania
    2021 electoral vote count and, 1049-1050
    alienage, qualifications for voting, 119
    geographical communities in, 132-133
    gerrymandering in, 298-302
    impeachment of judges in, 983
Penrose, Boies, 737
"People's Pledge," 905-906
Perón, Juan, 41
Perot, H. Ross, 578
Perry, Scott, 1050
Peru, prohibition on exit polling in, 684
Petitions
    certification of, 948
    disclosure requirements, 719-726
Philippines, authoritarianism in, 3
Pierce, Franklin, 577
Plato, 112
Plumer, William, 68
Pluralism, 7, 20-22
    interest pluralism, 540-541
Poland, authoritarianism in, 3, 530
Polarization. *See* Political polarization
Political action committees (PACs), 750-754
    access to elected officials and, 826
    campaign expenditures

        corporations vs., 891-893
        ecosystem of, 825-826
        ideological but nonpartisan PACs,
            limitations on expenditures,
            820-827
        influence of, 826-827
        reasons for expenditures, 823-824
        role of, 822-823
        Super PACs, limitations on, 903-905
    ecosystem of, 825-826
    FECA and, 739, 745, 750
    501(c)(4) organizations, 754
    527 organizations, 753-754
    ideological but nonpartisan PACs,
        limitations on expenditures,
        820-827
    influence of, 826-827
    leadership PACs, 751-752
    nonconnected political committees, 751
    party committees, 750
    reasons for expenditures, 823-824
    role of, 822-823
    separate segregated funds (SSFs),
        750-751
    Super PACs, 752, 903-905
Political parties, 531-635
    anti-party politics, 532-534
    ballot access and, 544-565. *See also*
        Ballot access
    BCRA and
        national parties, 795, 802-805
        state, district, and local parties, 795,
            805-808
    campaign expenditures, limitations on,
        828-838
    candidate "branding," 619-621
    candidate selection, 579-624
    defining, 531
    descriptions of party system, 541-542
    different uses of term, 541
    distinctiveness of, 837-838
    factions and, 540-541
    fair party competition, 93-99
    First Amendment and, 542-543, 594
    freedom of association and, 542-543,
        594-600
    government regulation of, 595-600
    interest pluralism and, 540-541
    Jacksonian democracy and, 534-536
    membership, party control over, 543-544
    militant democracy and, 529-530
    minor parties, ballot access, 545-546
    nonpartisanship and, 536-537
    party bans, 529-530
    party government, 633-634
    patronage and, 624-632
        dangers of, 736

effectiveness of, 632
First Amendment and, 624-632
public employees, constitutional
claims by, 624-632
primary elections, 579-624.
See also Primary elections
Progressives and, 536-537
public vs. private entities, 593-594
republicanism and, 532-534
responsible party government, 537-540
rise of modern party, 534-536
third parties, 578
treatment of, 833-834
two-party system, 565-579
fusion candidacies, 565-574
multiparty systems vs., 576-577
as one-party system, 578-579
origins of, 575-576
state institutionalization of, 565-579
two specific parties vs., 577-578
Washington on, 531-532
Political polarization
gerrymandering, legislative polarization
and, 295-298
judiciary and, 104-105
racial discrimination and, 443
Voting Rights Act and, 368-373, 443
Political question doctrine
apportionment and, 202-203, 1026-1030
gerrymandering and, 264, 267
judicial oversight of elections and,
1026-1030
Polling places, location of, 937
Poll taxes
prohibition on, 118, 163-167
Twenty-Fourth Amendment and, 118,
163-164
Popular sovereignty
gerrymandering and, 318-319
in liberal democracy, 16
Populism, 2, 38-47
alienation and, 45-46
Arrow's Theorem and, 33-34
authoritarianism and, 43-47
bigotry and, 46-47
campaign finance and, 733-735
challenge of, 39-40
definition of, 39
democracy and, 6, 42-43
historical background, 41-42
independent judiciary and, 103-105
as inherently illiberal, 43
judicial populism, defined, 105-106
lack of performative success of, 44-45
Trump and, 41, 734-735
varieties of, 40-41
Portugal

campaign speech in, 697
political parties in, 593
Post-canvass remedies, 1023-1043
election contests, 1024-1026
recounts, 1023-1024
frequency of, 1024
in presidential elections, 938-944
results of, 1024
voiding of elections, 1032-1043
adjustment of vote totals, 1043
as breach of ballot secrecy, 1043
disenfranchisement of innocent, risk
of, 1041
popular will, respecting, 1041-1043
reluctance, 1041
state constitutions and, 1040-1041
"Post-truth," 638
Powell, Adam Clayton, Jr., 487-488
Powell, Colin, 74, 76
Precinct requirements, 461-477
Predominant factor test
Equal Protection Clause and, 433-442
gerrymandering and, 421-424, 432-433
majority-black districts and, 447-458
redistricting and, 432-442, 447-458
President
constitutional qualifications, exclusivity
of, 487-498
impeachment, 522
qualifications for office, 502-503
republicanism and, 58-60
Presidential elections
1876 disputed election, 1046
2000 election in Florida, 938-944,
1007, 1050
2016 election interference by Russia,
1017-1022
2020 claims of voter fraud, 477-478
durational residency requirements in,
128-129
Electoral College and, 1044-1052. *See also*
Electoral College
elector defections, 74-78
institutional evolution of, 73-74
National Popular Vote (NVP) plan, 78-79
primary elections in, 623-624
qualifications for office, 502-503
recounts, 938-944
tax returns, releasing, 502-503
Press Clause. *See also* Freedom of press
campaign speech and, 686
Citizens United case and, 897-898
Price, David, 928
Primary elections
blanket primaries, 601, 607-616
candidate "branding" and, 619-621
closed primaries, 601, 619

Primary elections (*Continued*)
  constitutional claims regarding, 622-623
  eligibility to vote in, 580-587, 601-624
  federal regulation of, 587-589
  First Amendment and, 596-600
  independent voters and, 602-607
  nonpartisan primaries, 601, 622
  open primaries, 601, 619
  overview, 579-580
  party autonomy in, 617-619
  in presidential elections, 623-624
  semiclosed primaries, 601, 616-617
  state regulation of, 589-593
  "top-two" primaries, 622
  "White Primary" cases, 580-587
Progressives, 72-73, 484-486, 536-537, 642-643
Promissory representation, 185
Proportional representation, 383, 431-432
Proportional voting, 258-259
Public employees
  candidates forgoing government employment, 511-517
  Hatch Act and, 511-517
  patronage, constitutional claims regarding, 624-632
Public financing of elections, 911-931
  Buckley case and, 911-916
  chilling effect of, 927
  current status of, 927-928
  electoral competitiveness, effect on, 928-929
  FECA and, 746
  forms of, 929-930
  justifications for, 927
  public funds, utilization of, 928
Puerto Rico, qualifications for voting in, 121
Punch card ballots, 1009-1016
Purging of voter registration rolls, 2, 323, 991-992

Q
Quotas
  Equal Protection Clause and, 389-391
  redistricting and, 404-405

R
Racial discrimination
  accurate voting and, 1016
  affirmative action, 389-391
  apportionment, minority undercounts and, 222-224
  election fraud and, 956-957
  felony convictions, disenfranchisement for, 176-177
  gerrymandering and. *See* Gerrymandering

  literacy tests and, 144-148
  majority-black districts
    effect of, 444-445
    Fourteenth Amendment and, 446
    gerrymandering and, 405-407, 446-447
    predominant factor test and, 447-458
    Voting Rights Act and, 446
  multiracial society, fear of, 479
  overview, 321-325
  political polarization and, 443
  quotas, 389-391
  redistricting and. *See* Redistricting
  token representation and, 443-444
  voter identification requirements and, 1004-1005
  Voting Rights Act. *See* Voting Rights Act of 1965 (VRA)
  white identity politics and, 325
Raffensperger, Brad, 945
Rational non-participation, 31
Reagan, Ronald, 74, 525, 683, 693, 985
Recall elections, 526
Recounts, 1023-1024
  frequency of, 1024
  in presidential elections, 938-944
  results of, 1024
Redistricting
  communities of interest, respect for, 426-429
  compactness, 424-425
  contiguity, 424-425
  elimination of districts, 431-432
  Equal Protection Clause and, 433-442
  gerrymandering. *See* Gerrymandering
  incumbents, protection of, 429
  independent districting commissions, 307-318, 427-428
  indeterminacy problem and, 429-431
  judicial role in, 226
  Justice Department and, 405, 409-420
  local community and, 226-227
  neutrality in, 424
  plans, 225-226
  political boundaries, respect for, 426-429
  predominant factor test and, 432-442, 447-458
  proportional representation and, 431-432
  strict scrutiny and, 433
  Voting Rights Act Section 2 and, 405-432. *See also* Gerrymandering
  Voting Rights Act Section 5 and, 391-405
    "authentic" representation, 399-404
    "filler people," 398-399
    quotas, 404-405
    "safe" seats, 397-398

Redistricting Transparency Act of 2010 (proposed), 319
Referenda. *See* Ballot measures
Registration of voters, 987-992
    Crosscheck system, 991
    false negatives, 989-990
    false positives, 989-990
    historical background, 988-989
    method of, 937
    "Motor Voter Law" and, 990
    overview, 987-988
    purges. *See* Purging of voter registration rolls
    recent statutory changes, 479
    time lags, 990-992
    timing of, 937
Reid, Harry, 794
Religious Freedom Restoration Act of 1993 (RFRA), 152
Representation, 181-320
    agency representation, 184
    alignment of preferences and policy, 188-191
    anticipatory representation, 185-186
    apportionment, 201-240. *See also* Apportionment
    "authentic" representation, 399-404
    cumulative voting and, 259-260
    delegate representation, 184
    descriptive representation, 184, 445
    discriminatory manipulation of, 240-320
        at-large elections, 241-246
        disparate impact vs. disparate treatment, 246-257
        Equal Protection Clause and, 246
        Fifteenth Amendment and, 246
        gerrymandering, 261-320. *See also* Gerrymandering
        methods of election, 241-261
        multimember districts, 241-246, 257
        overview, 240-241
        place system, 241-242
        racial discrimination, 246-257
        in reapportionment, 243-246
    gerrymandering. *See* Gerrymandering
    gyroscopic representation, 186
    limited voting and, 259
    majority-black districts
        effect of, 444-445
        Fourteenth Amendment and, 446
        gerrymandering and, 405-407, 446-447
        predominant factor test and, 447-458
        Voting Rights Act and, 446
    median voter and, 189
    of minorities, 188
    non-elective forms of, 191-201

        extraterritorial exercise of police powers and, 195-199
        lot, selection of representatives by, 199-200
        non-governmental individuals or organizations, 200-201
        virtual representation, 191-199
    overview, 181-182
    positive political theory and, 188-191
    principles of, 184-191
        agency representation, 184
        anticipatory representation, 185-186
        authorization, 184
        delegate representation, 184
        descriptive representation, 184
        general interests, representing, 185
        gyroscopic representation, 186
        particular interests, representing, 185
        promissory representation, 185
        surrogate representation, 186
        trustee model, 185
    promissory representation, 185
    proportional representation, 383, 431-432
    proportional voting and, 258-259
    reciprocity of representation and interests, 186
    redistricting. *See* Redistricting
    right to instruct representatives, 182-184
    single transferrable voting (STV) and, 260-261
    surrogate representation, 186
    token representation, 443-444
    trustee model, 185
    vector theory of representation, 188-189
    Voting Rights Act and
        at-large districts, 387
        conditional districts, 383-385
        influence districts, 383-387
        maximization of minority voting power, 382
        opportunity to participate and elect, 382
        participation in political process, 381-382
        proportional representation, 383
        racially polarized voting, 368-373
        safe districts, 383-385
        vote dilution, 364-368, 380-381
    of whole or of parts, 186-188
Republicanism, 50-60
    Constitution, influence on, 54-58
    decline of, 72-73
    democratic optimization, 53-54
    political parties and, 532-534
    popular self-government and, 50-53

Republicanism (*Continued*)
   President and, 58-60
   Senate and, 60
Residency
   Congress, residency
      requirements, 501
   elected officials, district residency
      requirements, 501-502
   qualifications for voting, 123-132
      armed forces, 123-126
      citizenship, relation to, 129-130
      durational residency requirements,
        126-129
      Fourteenth Amendment and, 128-129
      multiple residency, 130-131
      nonresidents, voting by, 131-132
      in presidential elections, 128-129
      students, 129
Riker, William H., 33-34, 575
Roberts, John G., 985
Robocalls, 684-685
Romania, campaign speech in, 697
Roosevelt, Franklin D., 738, 986
Roosevelt, Theodore, 578
Ross, Wilbur, 224
Rousseau, Jean-Jacques, 27-28
Rousseff, Dilma, 523
Rule of law, 4, 7, 16, 47
Russell, Richard B., 74
Russian interference in 2016 presidential
      election, 1017-1022
Ryan, Paul, 752

S
Safe districts, 383-385
Sanders, Bernie, 46
Scalia, Antonin, 986
Scalise, Steve, 752
Scarlet Letter provisions, 498-499
Schumpeter, Joseph, 17
Schwarzenegger, Arnold, 526
Scott, Rick, 60
Scott, Winfield, 577
Secret Service, 516-517
Securities and Exchange Commission
      (SEC), 900
Self-governing *demos*, 109-110
Semiclosed primaries, 601, 616-617
Senate
   as "Millionaire's Club," 60, 773
   republicanism and, 60
   Seventeenth Amendment and, 79,
      120, 1044
   transformation of, 79
Sentencing Project, 167
Separate segregated funds (SSFs), 750-751

Serbia, felony convictions and qualifications
      for voting in, 173
Seventeenth Amendment
   regulation of elections and, 62, 161
   Senate and, 79, 120, 1044
Shays, Chris, 794
Sherman, Roger, 51
Siloing, 639
Sinema, Kyrsten, 358
Singapore, virtual representation in, 201
Single transferrable voting (STV), 260-261
Slavery
   abolition of, 79-84, 322
   enduring political impact of, 92-93
   Fifteenth Amendment and, 80
   Fourteenth Amendment and, 79
   illiberalism and, 66-67
   overview, 321
   Thirteenth Amendment and, 79, 322
   Three-Fifths Clause and, 67-71
Small Business Jobs Act of 2010, 794
Smith, Adam, 18
Social contract theory, 50
Social media
   blocking speech on, 726-731
   freedom of speech and, 638-639
Socrates, 112
Soft money, 791-793, 798-799
Sore losers, 561, 572, 576
South Carolina
   African American voter registration
      in, 323
   alienage, qualifications for voting, 119
   "court packing" in, 986
   disputed 1876 presidential election
      and, 1046
   qualifications for office in, 486
   recounts in, 1023
   robocalls in, 685
   Voting Rights Act and, 328, 335-338
South Dakota, Voting Rights Act and, 328
South Korea, impeachment in, 523
Spain
   blank ballots in, 565
   campaign-free election days in, 380
   felony convictions, qualifications for
      voting in, 173
   party bans in, 529
   political parties in, 593
Special districts, 229-239
   business improvement districts (BIDs),
      238-239
   variety of, 237-239
   water storage districts, 230-237
Speech. *See* Campaign speech; Freedom
      of speech
Standing, 1032

Stans, Maurice, 740
State constitutions
    Congressional term limits, attempting to
        establish, 488-498
    partisan gerrymandering and, 299-303
    voter identification requirements and,
        1005-1006
State legislatures
    apportionment
        construing "equal," 217-218
        malapportionment of districts,
            206-214
    independent state legislature doctrine,
        1050-1052
    powers regarding elections, 95-96
States' rights, 355-356
Stevenson, Adlai, 623
Strict scrutiny
    gerrymandering, racial discrimination
        and, 421
    redistricting and, 433
Student Non-Violent Coordinating
        Committee (SNCC), 85, 88-89
Students, qualifications for voting, 129
Super PACs, 752, 903-905
Supreme Court, U.S.
    "court packing" and, 986
    ideological shifts on, 459, 985-986
    politicization of, 985-986
Surrogate representation, 186
Sweden
    campaign speech in, 697
    economic inequality in, 735
    felony convictions, qualifications for
        voting in, 173
    integrity of elections in, 947
Switzerland
    campaign speech in, 697
    felony convictions, qualifications for
        voting, 173
    integrity of elections in, 947
    political parties in, 531

T
Taft–Hartley Act of 1947, 738
Teapot Dome scandal, 737-738
Technology and elections, 1007-1023
    HAVA and, 1007-1008
    punch card ballots, 1009-1016
    race and, 1016
    security risks, 1016-1018
    Voting Rights Act and, 1009-1016
Telephone Consumer Protection Act of
        1991, 684
Tennessee
    apportionment in, 1028-1030
    electioneering, prohibiting, 666-672

felony convictions, qualifications for
        voting in, 167
    judicial elections in, 984
    public financing of elections in, 945
    residency requirements in, 126-127
    two-party system in, 579
Term limits
    Congress
        efforts to establish, 498-499
        state constitutions attempting to
            establish, 488-498
    effect of, 500-501
    First Amendment and, 499
    Fourteenth Amendment and, 499
    Scarlet Letter provisions, 498-499
    state officials, 499-500
Territories, qualifications for voting in,
        120-121
Texas
    apportionment in, 218, 221
    ballot access in, 546-548, 944
    candidates, resign-to-run requirements,
        504-511
    gerrymandering in, 306-307, 460-461
    multimember districts in, 243-246
    public financing of elections in, 945
    recounts in, 1023
    redistricting in, 426-429, 432-433,
        460-461
    residency requirements in, 123-126
    special districts in, 229
    voiding of elections in, 1041
    voter identification requirements in,
        357, 945
    Voting Rights Act and, 328-329
    "White Primary" cases, 581-587
Thailand, economic inequality in, 735
Thicker theories of democracy, 21-23
Third parties, 578
Thirteenth Amendment
    enduring political impact of slavery, 92
    slavery, abolition of, 79, 322
Three-Fifths Clause, 67-71, 321
Thurmond, J. Strom, 74
Tillman Act of 1907, 737
Tocqueville, Alexis de, 110
Token representation, 443-444
"Top-two" primaries, 622
"Town House Project," 740
Traficant, Jim, 527
Travel, right to, 126-130
Truman, Harry, 74
Trump, Donald
    2016 election, 30, 74, 325, 733-735, 949,
        955, 1017
    2020 election, 102, 477-478, 945, 955,
        1049-1050

Trump, Donald (*Continued*)
    campaign financing, 733-735
    Capitol insurrection and, 102, 639,
        1049-1050
    election fraud claims by, 949, 955
    fake news and, 639
    illiberalism and, 39, 98, 101-102
    impeachment proceedings, 523
    income of voters for, 46
    party nomination processes and, 107, 530
    populism and, 41, 734-735
    Russian election interference claims
        and, 1017
    Supreme Court nominations by, 986
    tax returns not released by, 101, 502-503
    travel ban for Muslims and, 660
    Twenty-Fifth Amendment and, 525
    Twitter and, 726-731
    on voting rights, 2
Turkey
    authoritarianism in, 3, 530
    economic inequality in, 735
Twelfth Amendment, 74-76, 1045
Twenty-Fifth Amendment, 525-526
Twenty-Fourth Amendment, 110, 118,
    163-164
Twenty-Sixth Amendment, 110, 118, 160
Twenty-Third Amendment, 120-121
Twitter, 726-731
Two-party system, 565-579
    fusion candidacies, 565-574
    multiparty systems vs., 576-577
    as one-party system, 578-579
    origins of, 575-576
    state institutionalization of, 565-579
    two specific parties vs., 577-578
"Tyranny of majority," 34-35

U
Udall, Tom, 928
Unilateral gerrymandering, 264-266
Union campaign expenditures
    independent expenditures, limitations
        on, 849-855
    prohibition on, 747
United Arab Emirates, economic inequality
    in, 735
United Kingdom
    administration of elections in, 958
    age qualification for voting in, 161
    backsliding of democracy in, 3
    Brexit, 734
    campaign speech in, 697-698
    economic inequality in, 735
    felony convictions, qualifications for
        voting in, 173-174
    party bans in, 529

    populism in, 41
    residency requirements in, 129
    unwritten constitutional norms in, 100
    vote of no confidence in, 521
United Nations
    Charter, 1022
    Convention on the Rights of Persons
        with Disabilities, 162
Universal Declaration of Human Rights, 946
Unwritten constitutional norms, 100-103
Uribe, Álvaro, 103
Uruguay
    alienage, qualifications for voting, 120
    compulsory voting in, 32
Utah
    independent districting commission
        in, 309
    judicial elections in, 965, 984
    minority undercounts and, 224

V
Van Buren, Martin, 534-535, 578
Vance, Zebulon, 528
Venezuela
    authoritarianism in, 3
    independent judiciary, threats to, 103
    populism in, 41, 45
Vermont, mail-in voting in, 479
Virginia
    African American voter registration
        in, 323
    ballot drop boxes in, 944
    disabilities, voters with, 479
    disenfranchisement in, 84, 176
    early voting in, 479
    electoral votes in, 1045
    gerrymandering in, 298, 422
    incarcerated non-voters and, 222
    independent districting commission in,
        309-310
    mail-in voting in, 479
    registration of voters in, 479
    two-party system in, 579
    voter deception in, 659
    Voting Rights Act and, 328-329, 331
Virgin Islands, qualifications for voting
    in, 121
Voiding of elections, 1032-1043
    adjustment of vote totals, 1043
    as breach of ballot secrecy, 1043
    disenfranchisement of innocent, risk
        of, 1041
    popular will, respecting, 1041-1043
    reluctance, 1041
    state constitutions and, 1040-1041
"Vote caging," 956-957
Vote dilution, 364-368, 380-381

Vote of no confidence, 521-522
Voter identification requirements, 992-1007
    election modernization and, 993-994
    Equal Protection Clause and, 1006
    fraud and, 994-995
    judicial restraint and, 1031
    litigation involving, 1005-1006
    other identification requirements
        compared, 1006-1007
    overview, 2
    politicization of election procedures
        and, 945
    racial discrimination and, 1004-1005
    as safeguarding voter confidence,
        995-1004
    state constitutions and, 1005-1006
    Voting Rights Act and, 357, 459-460,
        1004-1005
Voting, 109-179
    American *demos*, 110-112
    ballot access, 544-565. *See also*
        Ballot access
    competence, qualifications based on,
        143-179
        age, 159-161. *See also* Age
        felony convictions, 167-179. *See also*
            Felony convictions
        literacy, 144-159. *See also* Literacy,
            qualifications for voting
        mental disability, 162
        wealth, 162-167. *See also* Wealth,
            qualifications for voting
    compulsory voting, 32-33
    disabilities, voters with, 479
    early voting, 479, 944
    enforcement of eligibility requirements,
        987-1023
        registration of voters, 987-992. *See also*
            Registration of voters
        technology and elections, 1007-1023.
            See also Technology and elections
        voter identification requirements,
            992-1007. *See also* Voter
            identification requirements
    mail-in voting, 479, 944
    membership, qualifications based on,
        112-143
        citizenship, 112-123. *See also*
            Citizenship
        geographical communities, 132-138.
            See also Geographical
            communities
        non-geographical sub-communities,
            138-143. *See also* Non-geographical
            sub-communities
        residency, 123-132. *See also* Residency
    method of, 937

precinct requirements, 461-477
primary elections, 579-624. *See also*
    Primary elections
registration of voters, 987-992. *See also*
    Registration of voters
self-governing *demos*, 109-110
technology and elections, 1007-1023.
    See also Technology and elections
third person assistance in, 461-477
timing of, 937
voter deception, 658-659. *See also* Fraud
    in elections
voter identification requirements,
    992-1007. *See also* Voter
    identification requirements
write-in votes, 558-564
Voting Rights Act of 1965 (VRA)
    apportionment and, 218, 224
    bailout provision, 328, 354-355
    Congressional incentive and, 356
    enactment of, 323-324
    evolution of jurisprudence, 1-2
    expansive legislation and, 152-153
    federal rights protection, 63
    felony convictions, qualifications for
        voting, 178
    Fifteenth Amendment and, 1, 325-326,
        358-359
    Fourteenth Amendment and, 339,
        433, 460
    future prospects, 357-359, 478-479
    gerrymandering and. *See*
        Gerrymandering
    Justice Department and, 224-225, 330,
        334, 356, 444, 1004
    literacy tests, prohibition of, 146, 152
    majority-black districts and, 446
    past discrimination, effect of, 461
    political polarization and, 443
    precinct requirements and, 461-476
    punch card ballots and, 1009-1016
    redistricting and, 391-405
        "authentic" representation, 399-404
        "filler people," 398-399
        quotas, 404-405
        "safe" seats, 397-398
    representation and. *See* Representation
    residency requirements and, 128
    Section 2, 359-389
        at-large districts and, 387
        conditional districts and, 383-385
        felony convictions and, 388-389
        Fifteenth Amendment and, 358-359
        Fourteenth Amendment and, 433
        gerrymandering and. *See*
            Gerrymandering
        influence districts and, 383-387

Voting Rights Act of 1965 (VRA)
  (*Continued*)
    judicial elections and, 387
    maximization of minority voting
      power and, 382
    opportunity to participate and
      elect, 382
    participation in political process and,
      381-382
    private rights of action, 478
    proportional representation and, 383
    racially polarized voting and, 368-373
    redistricting and, 405-432. *See also*
      Gerrymandering
    results test, 359-380
    safe districts and, 383-385
    Section 5 compared, 387-388
    vote dilution, 364-368, 380-381
  Section 4
    bailout provision, 328, 354-355
    constitutionality of, 335-338
    voting tests or devices, 327-328
  Section 5, 327-359
    bail-in mechanism, 334-335
    baseline, 333-334
    constitutionality of, 335-338, 340-354
    coverage formula, 340-354
    future prospects, 357-359
    nonretrogression standard,
      332-334, 384
    preclearance requirement, 330, 460
    reauthorization of, 338-340
    redistricting and, 391-405. *See also*
      Redistricting
    scope of, 330-332
    Section 2 compared, 387-388
    standard of, 330-332
    state responses, 356-357
    three-judge courts, 334
    voter identification requirements
      and, 357
  slavery, enduring political impact of, 92
  South as "authoritarian enclave" and,
    325-326
  states' rights and, 355-356

  third person assistance in voting and,
    461-476
  token representation and, 443-444
  voter deception and, 659
  voter identification requirements and,
    357, 459-460, 1004-1005
Voting Rights Amendments of 1970, 159
VRA. *See* Voting Rights Act of 1965

W
Wallace, George, 42, 74, 578
Warren, Elizabeth, 905-906
Washington (state)
  exit polling, prohibiting, 684
  fair campaign codes in, 657
  incarcerated non-voters and, 222
  misbehavior, automatic removal of
    elected officials for, 524
  petition signers, disclosure requirements,
    719-726
  primary elections in, 622
  recounts in, 1023
Washington, George, 60, 483, 531-532, 736
Watergate scandal, 739-740
Wealth, qualifications for voting, 162-167
  Franklin on, 163
  poll taxes, 118, 163-167
  property ownership, 162-163
Weaver, James B., 578
West Virginia, apportionment in, 216
White identity politics, 325
"White Primary" cases, 580-587
Wilson, Edith, 524
Wilson, Woodrow, 187, 524
Wisconsin
  2021 electoral vote count and, 1049
  fair campaign codes in, 652
  gerrymandering in, 302-303
  state legislature, powers regarding
    elections, 96
  voter deception in, 659
"Wisdom of multitude," 28-29
Women's suffrage, 114-118
Woodward, Bob, 740
Write-in votes, 558-564